THE PRESIDENT AND THE APPRENTICE

THE

PRESIDENT

AND THE

APPRENTICE

Eisenhower and Nixon, 1952–1961

Irwin F. Gellman

Yale

UNIVERSITY

PRESS

New Haven & London

Published with assistance from the Mary Cady Tew Memorial Fund.

Yale University Press books may be purchased in quantity for educational, business, or
promotional use. For information, please e-mail sales.press@yale.edu (U.S. office) or
sales@yaleup.co.uk (U.K. office).

Set in Electra type by Westchester Publishing Services. Printed in the United States
of America.

Library of Congress Control Number: 2015935011
ISBN 978-0-300-18105-0 (cloth : alk. paper)

A catalogue record for this book is available from the British Library.

This paper meets the requirements of ANSI/NISO Z39.48-1992
(Permanence of Paper).

10 9 8 7 6 5 4 3 2

To Ruth Ann Segerstrom Moriarty
with
gratitude and love

CONTENTS

Illustrations follow page 268.

PREFACE

When Herbert Brownell Jr. told Dwight D. Eisenhower that his advisers had selected Richard M. Nixon as his running mate in 1952, the general readily concurred. Ike saw in Nixon a young, talented politician who, like himself, was a strong foe of communism and had distinguished himself as a congressman in 1948 by his pursuit of Alger Hiss, later shown to have spied for the Soviet Union. Eisenhower would also come to value Nixon's political insight and his ability to connect with his Republican constituency. Not yet forty years old at the time he was nominated, Nixon saw his place on the 1952 ticket as a priceless opportunity, and he never lost his determination to make the most of it. Yet he never completely understood Ike's military character and would be left dumbfounded by some of Ike's decisions.

The two men were never partners. Theirs was not a "strange political marriage," as Jeffrey Frank claims in *Ike and Dick*. Eisenhower, the supreme commander of the Allied Expeditionary Force in World War II, the former chief of staff of the Army, the first supreme commander of the North Atlantic Treaty Organization, did not have partners. He led a team of subordinates, who were expected to go where Ike sent them, be his eyes and ears, provide intelligent and informed advice, deliver his messages, execute his decisions, and occasionally become casualties. Whether the battlefield was military or political, Ike often had his soldiers take the heat instead of himself.

Having seen how unprepared Harry S Truman was to assume the presidency on Franklin D. Roosevelt's death, Eisenhower kept Vice President Nixon aware of most of the decisions made in the White House. Nixon attended Ike's weekly meetings, presided in Ike's absence, acted as a liaison with both houses of Congress, met with dozens of foreign heads of state, and tirelessly represented the administration on the campaign trail. He had more responsibility and more authority than any vice president before him. He shared frequent breakfasts and lunches with the president, and was one of a small circle of advisers who could walk into the Oval Office without an appointment. When Eisenhower, after a futile year of trying to get Joseph McCarthy to cooperate with his administration, decided in 1954 that the senator was doing far more harm than good, Nixon was part of the small team that ruined him. When Eisenhower wanted to advance the cause of civil rights, he turned to Nixon, first as the head of the President's Committee on Government Contracts, and then as the point man in passing the Civil Rights Act of 1957. (Some historians have given the credit for this legislation largely to then–Senate majority leader Lyndon Johnson, but Johnson actually eviscerated two major provisions that were unacceptable to the southern caucus.)

Nixon evolved into one of Ike's most valuable subordinates. When Eisenhower suffered a major heart attack in September 1955, Nixon, Secretary of State John Foster Dulles, and White House chief of staff Sherman Adams were largely in charge of the White House for several months. At the time, the public did not know the severity of Eisenhower's illness, nor did anyone know that Nixon, overstressed and overmedicated, was at the very limits of his ability to function in the first half of 1956. Nor did John Foster Dulles reveal that his cancer surgery that year had been unsuccessful; he would die in the spring of 1959.

Both Eisenhower and Dulles relied increasingly on Nixon as a foreign policy counselor. Nixon's trips to Asia, Latin America, Africa, Eastern Europe, and the Soviet Union were never ceremonial goodwill journeys; he conducted delicate business and sometimes tense negotiations with foreign leaders, and he gave Eisenhower detailed reports on what he saw, heard, and did. In the process, he became close friends with Dulles. This immersion in foreign affairs as vice president gave Nixon the background, when he became president, to conduct a foreign policy that included winding down the war in Vietnam, détente with the Soviet Union, and a historic opening of relations with China.

Little of this is known, or properly understood.

Instead, many historians, journalists, and others have advanced the proposition that Ike and Nixon disliked each other and barely spoke throughout the Eisenhower presidency. In past decades, critics described Ike's presidential leadership as inept and Nixon as hyperpartisan. While Ike's image has improved to that of a near-great or great president, Nixon remains an inconsequential vice president. This divergence in their reputations has created a paradox: given that Eisenhower is now seen as firmly in control of his administration, and that he was so wildly popular that he certainly did not need Nixon's help to win the presidency, why did he allow Nixon to stay on the ticket? Even if we concede that he might have done so once by mistake, in 1952, why did Ike run with him again four years later?

At this point, more than a half-century since Eisenhower left office, the fog of misunderstanding has become bipartisan. The conservative British historian Paul Johnson's slim volume *Eisenhower: A Life*, published in 2014 and based entirely on secondary sources, includes just a single paragraph on the president's relationship with his vice president.

> Ike's attitude toward Nixon remains a mystery to this day. He behaved toward his vice president throughout the eight years they served together as if he were a burden or an embarrassment rather than an asset. Asked if Nixon had ever made a positive contribution to his administration, Ike avoided an answer and said he'd like to think about it. Of course Ike had never chosen Nixon to run with him. And he disliked having around him a man he could not fire. (p. 107)

From the other side of the political spectrum, Elizabeth Drew concurs with Johnson. A liberal journalist and television personality, Drew has covered the capital since 1959 for distinguished magazines like *The Atlantic Monthly* and *The New Yorker*. Her book *Richard M. Nixon* (2007) describes Ike and Dick's "relationship" as "distant" (p. 16); she writes that Nixon complained of never having been invited to Ike's Gettysburg home (he was) and that "moderates and other opponents" tried to dump Nixon from the Republican ticket in 1956 (except for one man, Harold Stassen, they did not). Nixon stayed on the ticket even though the president "had doubts" about his running mate (he did not). Drew and Johnson, who might agree on little else in politics, both believe that Eisenhower had little use for Nixon.

Neither author departs from the conventional understanding; their books depend mainly on others' impressionistic accounts. Neither spent time in the archives that house the voluminous records showing how Eisenhower and Nixon interacted. In this, they are hardly alone.

I have been working on this book for twenty years. I spent seven years reviewing documents related to Nixon's vice presidency, located at the National Archives in Laguna Nigel and in the Nixon presidential library in Yorba Linda, California. Historians have usually consulted the largest part of the Nixon manuscripts, called the 320 series (approximately 845 boxes), which is organized alphabetically. Thus the boxes containing As include Sherman Adams; the B boxes, Herbert Brownell; the E boxes, Eisenhower; the S boxes, Harold Stassen; and so forth. This organization allows researchers to avoid reading systematically through the files and instead to cherry-pick the best-known names. But a thorough examination of every box yielded critical documents that otherwise would not have turned up. For instance, I found the seven pages of notes that Ike made while watching the "Checkers" speech in 1952. No previous historian has ever cited them.

Besides the massive Nixon collection, there are other archives, many of which no one else has cited. For example, Dr. Arnold Hutschnecker acted as a private physician to Nixon during Eisenhower's first term; his papers, formerly available but now closed under National Archive policies, show clearly that he was never—as Anthony Summers' *Arrogance of Power* as well as Hutschnecker's *New York Times* obituary had it—Nixon's psychotherapist. Bela Kornitzer served as a translator when Nixon went to Austria in 1956 and kept detailed and informative notes of that trip. United States ambassador to Peru Theodore Achilles left material on Nixon's trip to Lima in 1958.

I have been visiting the Eisenhower archives in Alibene, Kansas, for more than four decades. These contain many thousands of pages of documents, including Eisenhower's official files, his diaries, and minutes of his cabinet and legislative meetings; they give a detailed, day-to-day account of the president's interaction with his closest aides, including Nixon. Other crucial manuscripts at the library are Bernard Shanley's diary and the William Rogers papers.

Henry Cabot Lodge Jr. initially urged Ike to run for president in 1952 and helped to manage his campaign. After his election victory, Ike appointed Lodge United States Representative to the United Nations and depended on him as a political adviser. Lodge also served as Nikita Khrushchev's personal escort on his visit to America in 1959 and as Richard Nixon's running mate in 1960. He had extensive contact with Ike and Nixon throughout the 1950s, yet historians describing the Ike-Nixon association do not cite Lodge's papers, which are at the Massachusetts Historical Society in Boston.

There are essential microfilm collections that do not even require one to travel farther than the nearest library. These include Eisenhower's diaries, his office files, and records of his weekly meetings with cabinet and legislative leaders.

My intent in this book is to tell the story the historical record tells. I have not attempted a comprehensive account of the Eisenhower administration. Important events, such as Eisenhower's battles over the military budget, his stand on the Suez crisis in 1956, and the creation of the interstate highway system, are dealt with glancingly if at all. I have instead focused on the most widely misunderstood aspect of his time in office. We will not understand how Ike's presidency worked until we have a more accurate picture of how Eisenhower and Nixon interacted and viewed each other, how they ran their political campaigns, how they tried to mediate with Senator McCarthy and later ruined him, how they acted in the struggle over civil rights, how they shaped diplomatic affairs, and how they looked at economic issues.

Paul Johnson believes the two men's relationship is "a mystery." It need not be. We have only to look at what is in front of us.

ACKNOWLEDGMENTS

During the almost two decades that I have worked on this project, no one has helped me more than my wife Gloria Gae. She has assisted with the research, commented on the early drafts, and followed the thematic changes until I completed the manuscript. After she thought that the chapters were suitable for others to review, I sent them out to specialists. Herbert Parmet, who has written biographies of Eisenhower, Nixon, and many other presidents, read almost the entire manuscript and was generous with his comments. Melvin Small and Evan Thomas read the entire work and also made worthwhile suggestions. Daun van Ee, who worked on Eisenhower's private papers for over a quarter century, and Michael Birker, who has studied the Eisenhower years for a similar period, commented on the first two-thirds of the volume. Michael Mayer, David Nichols, and Timothy Thurber read many chapters and were particularly helpful with their comments on civil rights. Louise Stevenson provided her own viewpoints as an American studies specialist on a large portion of the volume. Dan Frick also offered his perspective on Nixon's character.

Many scholars who have studied specific aspects of the Eisenhower presidency were gracious in reviewing chapters on domestic matters. Travis Jacobs, the expert on Ike at Columbia, looked at and commented on my chapter on the general's role at the university during the 1952 presidential campaign. Richard Fried, Gunther Bischof, and Athan Theoharis assisted with comments on Senator Joseph McCarthy, as did David Nichols, who has completed a manuscript on Ike and McCarthy. Besides Mayer, Nichols, and Thurber, there were several others who assisted with the civil rights sections. Clayborne Carson provided valuable information on the papers of Martin Luther King Jr. Carol Anderson generously shared National Association for the Advancement of Colored People documents with me. Michael Klarman assisted with the judiciary's position on civil rights during this period. My friend of almost a half-century, David Levering Lewis, offered his unique insights on the civil rights contributions of Truman and Eisenhower. Clarence Lasby, who has written on Ike's heart attack, commented on my work in this area. James Worthen reviewed my chapter on the 1958 congressional elections. Former secretary of state George Shultz, Keith Olson, Iwan Morgan, and David Stebenne helped with my chapter on economics and the steel strike.

Many individuals looked at my chapters on foreign affairs. Michael Hunt and long-time friend William Brinker reviewed the diplomatic events during the first term. Kyle Longley looked at Nixon's trip to Central America and the Caribbean. David Mayers concentrated on United States–Soviet interaction. I depended on Thomas Noer, Andrew DeRoche, and James Meriwether to help with Nixon's African trip. Raymond Garthoff and Sergei Khrushchev read the chapter on Nixon's mission to the Soviet Union. Edmund Kallina Jr. inspired my chapter on Cuba, and David Barrett reviewed it, focusing on the CIA's role.

Others who have read portions of the manuscript were Donald Ritchie, who concentrated on the Senate; Rob Odle corrected several mistakes in the discussion of Nixon's journey to Austria, and Donald Critchlow provided his acumen on the GOP. Will Swift challenged me to look more closely at the personalities of my characters. Mark Stoler helped with his skill as a military/diplomatic historian. George Colburn, who has spent decades recording the Eisenhower presidency on film, gave me his sweeping perspective, and Luke Nichter helped with the Nixon tapes. Herbert Klein and General Donald Hughes worked for Nixon during his vice presidency and provided insight that could not be otherwise attainable. Susan Eisenhower added her firsthand knowledge concerning her family and her grandfather. Robert Ferrell, Richard Breitman, Allen Matusow, and Justus Doenecke constantly encouraged me to complete the project when my efforts seemed stalled. Finally, I went to graduate school with Garry Clifford. We remained friends for almost fifty years until he passed away last year. He was a brilliant scholar, who was an exhaustive researcher and an exceptional writer. His counsel to me as I was writing this volume was to follow the results of my research and not to concern myself with the shortcuts that other authors took. I hope that I have followed his advice.

Along with advice from the above scholars, I have depended upon exceptional archivists. This volume primarily relies on the millions of documents housed at the Nixon and Eisenhower libraries. I spent more than seven years examining documents at the Nixon presidential library in California. Susan Naulty went far beyond the call of duty preparing documents for me to examine; her assistant Beverly Lindy rose to the same level. Gregory Cumming later assumed command and provided additional assistance. Loie Gaunt, who had worked for Nixon since the early 1950s, was a valuable source of information. Diane Nixon and Paul Wormser, who managed the National Archive's regional office in Laguna Niguel, could not have been more gracious. Diane reviewed more than a hundred boxes of documents and declassified them for me. Without their diligence, I would not have seen thousands of Nixon documents that I needed to complete this study.

Karl Weissenbach directs the Eisenhower presidential library in Abilene, Kansas, and he has welcomed me as a serious scholar, as had his predecessor Dan Holt (his wife Marilyn has written on Mamie and shared the results of her research with me). For years until his retirement, James Leyerzapf served as my guide to the Eisenhower manuscripts as few could do. Timothy Rives followed the high standard that Jim set, and Chelsea Millner could not have been more helpful.

I had spent several decades doing research at the Eisenhower presidential library before visiting the Nixon libraries. Besides the documents stored in Abilene, Louis Galambos and Daun van Ee edited one volume on Ike's pre-presidency and eight volumes on his presidency, totaling over ten thousand pages and containing extensive explanatory footnotes. Several microfilm collections covering the Eisenhower diaries, his office files, and legislative and cabinet meetings contain many thousands of documents that are crucial to any comprehensive study of the Eisenhower presidency. Several essential manuscript collections are on microfilm: Henry Cabot Lodge Jr., Karl Mundt, and Thomas Paterson.

The Truman presidential library also provided crucial material. Sam Rushay, Ray Geselbracht, and Randy Sowell are models for archivists. Bob Clark, at the Franklin Roosevelt presidential library fits in a similar category. Claude Anderson at the Lyndon Johnson presidential library took me through the exhaustive oral history collection and other documents that were essential for this volume. Jeff Hartley at Archives II in College Park, Maryland, provided documents from CREST. Joe Dmohowski at the Whittier College library could not have been more accommodating and pleasant to work with. Carol Hegeman, the supervisory historian at the Eisenhower National Historic Site in Gettysburg, Pennsylvania, interviewed John Eisenhower and Dolores Moaney; portions of those oral histories dealt with civil rights, and their recollections were essential for this volume. Matthew Beland provided an attractive environment at Drew University to examine the Bela Kornitzer papers.

Several audio-visual archivists could not have been more accommodating. Kathy Struss has helped me for more than two decades, and she deserves praise for her thorough knowledge of the photographic collection. Jonathan Movroydis,

Jon Fletcher, and Chris Barber at the Nixon library and Nixon Foundation were outstanding. Becky Ruud graciously supplied the images from Whittier College, and Matthew Hanson found the photo of Adlai Stevenson and Eleanor Roosevelt.

I have used the Shadek-Fackenthal Library and its staff to assist me. Led by Scott Vine, with support from Jenn Buch and Louise Kulp, these three set the standard for research librarians. Mary Shelly, succeeded by Meg Massey with assistance from Diane Roda, handled countless inter-library loan requests. Since I am not well trained on computers, Courtney Cunningham and Meghan Kelly filled that void. Archivists Christopher Rabb and Michael Lear provided their professional assistance. Others who assisted me and provided a cheerful setting were Denise Chmielewski, Nicole Rearich, Rick Thompson, Carol Kornhauser, Ken Siegert, Sue Wood, Mike Horn, Andy Gulati, and Tom Karel. My student assistant Kristina Montville was more than that; she also reviewed chapter drafts for their readability.

Alexander Hoyt is more than my agent; he is a friend and a brilliant scholar in his own right. He took this project to William Frucht at Yale. In an era when fact checking and scrupulous editing are passé, Bill is a throwback. He expects his authors to be as good or better than they are, and he mirrors that theme. This is a team effort, and the result is the best of all worlds. Jaya Aninda Chatterjee relied on her computer knowledge to assist in the manuscript's production. I would also like to thank the press's director John Donatich, coordinator Mary Pasti, designers Karen Stickler and James Johnson, publicist Jennifer Doerr, and marketing director Heather D'Auria. Brian Ostrander supervised the production of the volume for Westchester Publishing Services and Jay Boggis was an outstanding copy editor.

Lastly, I would like to thank two physicians for keeping me in reasonably good health. Dicran Baron, MD, made sure that my heart functioned normally, and Nadeem Paroya, MD, managed my type-2 diabetes. Both care about their patients, and I am grateful.

All of the above have tried to help me make this the best possible volume, and I appreciate their efforts. I have thanked several other individuals in my footnotes. If I left anyone out who supported this effort, I apologize. They, as well as those whom I have mentioned, attempted to make this a better book. Even though I gained a great deal from scholars, librarians, and others, I alone am responsible for all errors in fact and interpretation.

THE PRESIDENT AND THE APPRENTICE

INTRODUCTION: CHANGING THE STORY

Ever since the 1952 presidential election, authors who opposed Dwight Eisenhower on philosophical and political grounds have dominated the discussion of his White House years. At the same time, a number of misconceptions about those years have gone unexamined. For too long, the fable that Eisenhower spent more time playing golf than governing was accepted as fact. It was said that Secretary of State John Foster Dulles, for example, shaped American diplomacy and White House chief of staff Sherman Adams took on such an outsized management role that he earned the title assistant president. In reality, foreign policy in the Eisenhower administration was formulated by Eisenhower; Secretary Dulles dutifully carried out Ike's directives. Eisenhower was a skillful, hands-on president (he had, after all, overseen the invasions of North Africa, Italy, and France during World War II) who set his own agenda. Adams managed the president's schedule and protected him from unwarranted intrusions but did not act for him or enforce his decisions.

Historical consensus has been especially unkind to Richard Nixon, who is thought to have played a minimal role as Eisenhower's vice president, in an administration that accomplished so little that there was not much for a vice president to do. In addition, it is said that the president neither depended on nor liked Nixon. The reality is that the president and his apprentice respected and trusted each other. Nixon was deeply involved in many far-reaching initiatives and emerged as one of the most important presidential advisers.

The negative portrayals of Eisenhower began before he became president and slowly changed only after his death. After World War II, both major political parties tried to draft him as their presidential nominee. He refused and in 1948 accepted the presidency of Columbia University. Many faculty members, especially those in the social sciences and the humanities, considered a military man unsuitable to lead the university, and throughout his tenure the complaints, ranging from petty to serious, grew more vocal and intense. Historian Travis Jacobs, in *Eisenhower at Columbia*, wrote: "Some faculty members criticized Eisenhower because he did not seem interested in the academic needs of the university, but their major complaint was that he never was a full-time president due to his failing health and extensive travel schedule." Neither issue posed any threat to his tenure.[1]

During the 1952 presidential campaign, the faculty and staff split into warring camps: those who supported the Democratic candidate, Adlai Stevenson, and others who backed Eisenhower. According to reports in the *New York Times*, some grew so hostile that they refused to talk to colleagues on the other side. After Ike's convincing triumph, some Stevenson loyalists refused to accept defeat and used undergraduate lectures, graduate seminars, and writings to trivialize the winner.[2]

They remained unconvinced after Eisenhower defeated Stevenson again in 1956. Columbia historian Richard Hofstadter, in *Anti-Intellectualism in American Life*, described Ike as having a "conventional" mind and "fumbling inarticulateness." William Leuchtenburg's 1993 book *In the Shadow of FDR* (written after he had decamped from Columbia for North Carolina) provided a negative assessment of Eisenhower's presidency, stating that he left the Oval Office with "an accumulation of unsolved social problems that would overwhelm his successors in the 1960s."[3]

Up at Harvard, historian Arthur Schlesinger Jr., who worked on Stevenson's staff during the 1952 and 1956 campaigns and would later be a special assistant to President John Kennedy, charged that Eisenhower had accepted McCarthyism "with evident contentment." Throughout his career, Schlesinger regularly belittled Eisenhower. As late as 1983 he described the former president as "a genial, indolent man of pied syntax and platitudinous conviction, fleeing from public policy to bridge, golf and westerns."[4]

In his prestigious *Oxford History of the American People*, published in 1965, Samuel Eliot Morison used his chapter on the Eisenhower years to highlight the president's failures: "Peace and order were not restored abroad; violence and faction were not quenched at home." The former president received a copy of the book and scribbled on the dedication page: "The author is not a good historian. . . . In those events with which I am personally familiar he is grossly inaccurate."[5]

Morison co-wrote with Leuchtenburg and Henry Steele Commager (also a Columbia professor until 1956) a widely assigned college textbook, *The Growth of the American Republic*, in which the authors downgraded the Eisenhower presidency with a backhanded compliment: "Eisenhower had made an important contribution toward unifying the nation, but not a few asked whether the price that had been paid was too high."[6]

The academic criticism was not limited to Cambridge and New York. Before Ike's first term was finished, Norman Graebner, a diplomatic historian at the University of Virginia, argued that the president was returning the United States to a "New Isolationism." Several months before Ike left office, Graebner concluded that the president's advocates had "measured his success by popularity, not achievements." Two years later, in the preface to an edited volume of chapters by well-known authors, historian Dean Albertson wrote that "informed reaction to the Eisenhower administration was unfavorable."[7]

Many journalists criticized Eisenhower for his lack of leadership. Marquis Childs, a syndicated columnist, enumerated his subject's weaknesses in his 1958 book *Eisenhower: Captive Hero. New York Times* reporter James Reston found in Ike a symbol of the times: "Optimistic, prosperous, escapist, pragmatic, friendly, attentive in moments of crisis and comparatively inattentive the rest of the time." Columnist Richard Rovere summarized Ike's lackluster achievements: "The good that Eisenhower did—largely by doing so little—was accomplished . . . in his first term."[8]

Political scientists painted their own unflattering portraits. James Barber, who analyzed presidential performance according to a four-part matrix—active/positive, active/negative, passive/positive, and passive/negative—put Ike in the last box and asserted that he left "vacant the energizing, initiating, stimulating possibilities" of his office. A counselor to John Kennedy during his congressional years, Harvard professor Richard Neustadt, used 160 pages of his 1960 book on presidential power to enumerate how poorly Eisenhower had governed.[9]

In the 1960s, Eisenhower responded to his detractors with two volumes of memoirs, *The White House Years*, in which he defended his record on such controversial subjects as Senator Joseph McCarthy of Wisconsin and his own refusal to aid Britain and France during the 1956 Suez invasion. Those recollections and later books by close associates—such as Sherman Adams's *Firsthand Report* and Ezra Taft Benson's *Cross Fire*—emphasized the administration's achievements. Attorney General Herbert Brownell, years later, commented in his memoirs: "There was never any doubt in the Eisenhower administration about who was in charge and who made the decisions. The president did."[10]

Such testimonials did little to overcome the consensus on Ike's mediocrity. The fiction that Eisenhower had governed weakly, and that he had failed to use the bully pulpit effectively, continued to be accepted without careful analysis. This impression still lingers.

Cracks in the concrete began to appear when the well-respected journalist Murray Kempton wrote in the late 1960s that pundits had underestimated Eisenhower's acumen. After the Dwight D. Eisenhower Presidential Library and Museum opened in the spring of 1962 and the National Archives started to release thousands upon thousands of administration documents, Herbert Parmet became one of the first historians to examine them and was surprised by what he uncovered. His *Eisenhower and the American Crusades*, published in 1972, represented the first time a serious scholar suggested that Eisenhower had accomplished far more than previous writers had allowed.[11]

Others followed. In the early 1980s, political scientist Fred Greenstein examined the recently opened files of Ann Whitman, the president's private secretary, and determined that Ike had employed a "hidden hand" to manage the federal bureaucracy. In *The Hidden-Hand Presidency: Eisenhower as Leader*, Greenstein elaborated on this theme: the president, he wrote, "was once assumed to have been a well-intentioned political innocent, but he emerges from the historical record as a self-consciously oblique political sophisticate with a highly distinctive leadership style."[12] Though this interpretation gained popularity, the book outraged Arthur Schlesinger Jr., who wrote in his journal on February 12, 1981, that Greenstein was "a nice fellow—but his thesis these days—Eisenhower the Activist President—is a lot of bullshit."[13]

Despite Schlesinger's objections, documentation of the efficacy of Eisenhower's management inaugurated a trend toward a more positive view of his presidency. In Stephen Ambrose's 1984 book *Eisenhower: The President*, Ike emerges as a brilliant leader. Ambrose later called him "the American of the twentieth century. Of all the men I've studied and written about he is the brightest and the best."[14]

Unfortunately, this assessment is tainted by scandal. While some Eisenhower scholars questioned Ambrose's research after the book's publication, the enormity of his falsifications was not revealed until after his death. Ambrose lied about his relationship with Eisenhower. He claimed that Ike was so impressed with his book on the Civil War general Henry Halleck that he called Ambrose out of the blue and asked him to write his biography. Two Ambrose letters contradict this account. On September 10, 1964, the historian wrote to Ike that he was thrilled to be appointed associate editor of the Eisenhower papers and thought "it only fair that you have an opportunity to see some of my writing." One sample was the Halleck book. On October 15, Ambrose informed the former president that he was editing World War II documents and wanted "to begin a full-scale, scholarly account of your military career." He was not considering "a complete biography, as I know little about politics and have even less interest in them."[15]

Ambrose also claimed that he had talked with Ike alone for "hundreds and hundreds of hours" over five years; his footnotes record nine separate interviews. But Ike's daily logs show that the historian met with the former president only three times, for a total of less than five hours. They never met privately; one of Eisenhower's aides was always present.[16]

The most damaging charge to result from these phantom sessions concerns the issue Ambrose singled out as the major failure of Eisenhower's presidency: civil rights. He quoted Ike as saying he regretted "the appointment of that dumb son of a bitch Earl Warren." He also wrote that Eisenhower "personally wished that the Court had upheld Plessy v. Ferguson, and said so on a number of occasions (but only in private)." For the remark on the chief justice, Ambrose cited an undated interview with the former president; for the opinion on *Plessy*, he did not provide a source. No one has supplied any documentation that confirms either statement. Ambrose declared, also without any documentation, that "Eisenhower had no Negro friends, not even more than one or two acquaintances. . . . He was uncomfortable with . . . Negroes, so much so that he did not want to hear their side." These assertions, which have no foundation in fact, lead to the expected conclusion: Ike "ignored the Negro community."[17]

Ambrose also manufactured events that never took place. The historian claimed that at a legislative leaders' meeting on April 17, 1956, Eisenhower told the assemblage a racist joke that the famous golfer Bobby Jones had told him while they were in Augusta, Georgia. Ambrose cited as his source the official minutes of that day's meeting. I had read the minutes from this meeting and did not remember the president using any racial slurs. I then asked the three most knowledgeable scholars who have researched Ike and civil rights, Michael Mayer, David Nichols, and Timothy Thurber, and they did not recall the president ever referring to African Americans in that manner. Finally, I examined the notes from the April 17 meeting, which are publicly available in the Eisenhower Presidential Library. Although Ike did talk about presenting a moderate civil rights bill, he did not mention Bobby Jones or use any epithet.[18]

Rather than review this allegedly explosive document for himself, Taylor Branch, in his Pulitzer Prize–winning *Parting the Waters*, not only depended on Ambrose but also invented his own version of the fable. Ike, according to Branch, "bridled at the company of Negroes." He approved only "minimal contact between whites and Negroes, even in public places." As a career Army officer, he perceived "Negroes as inherently subordinate." Ike's "private secretary winced with embarrassment when he passed along the latest 'nigger jokes' from his friends at the Bobby Jones golf course in Augusta."[19] The papers of Ann Whitman, Eisenhower's private secretary (which include, along with her daily diary, some nine thousand pages of personal letters, memos, notes, schedules, and other documents), are also publicly available. The Eisenhower Presidential Library, where the archive is housed, describes it as "unique in its revelation of the personal side of the President" and notes that it includes "Whitman's observations on Eisenhower's personality and temperament, and his relations with his staff." The papers contain no mention of racist jokes or of Whitman's embarrassment at Eisenhower's telling them.[20]

Ambrose's fabrications received widespread coverage, but little changed. *Eisenhower: The President* has not been pulled from library shelves, and its publisher, Simon and Schuster, still sells it in print and as an eBook, touting it as an outstanding reference work with "numerous interviews with Eisenhower himself." Even the Eisenhower Presidential Library bookstore sells it.[21]

By the first decade of the twenty-first century, most authors had rejected the notion of Eisenhower as ineffective. David Nichols has shown, in *A Matter of Justice*, how Eisenhower advanced the cause of civil rights and, in *Eisenhower 1956*, how he skillfully managed the Suez crisis. Journalist Jim Newton's *Eisenhower* concentrated on how well the president managed the White House, and historian Jean Edward Smith followed with *Eisenhower: In War and Peace*. In this massive, full-length biography, a quarter of which is devoted to the presidency, Smith concludes that next to Franklin D. Roosevelt, Ike "was the most successful president of the twentieth century."[22]

Although the narrative on the Eisenhower presidency has shifted dramatically, from the story of an inept leader to that of a near-great one, most accounts of the actual events during his administration have remained unchanged. (One recent exception is Evan Thomas's *Ike's Bluff*, which describes how the president thought about nuclear weapons from a strategic vantage point and analyzes how Ike combined his generalship and his civilian authority to maintain a fragile peace during the height of the Cold War.) If we no longer see Eisenhower as the golf-playing innocent happily ignoring the nation's problems, we do not yet have an unclouded picture of how the man actually governed. The mythology still obscures our vision.

President Eisenhower's organization revolved around the team concept. To Ike, a military professional who became the civilian commander-in-chief, the use of the team approach emerged logically from his West Point experience. The picture that will emerge in this book is of a military man at the top of the pyramid; his subordinates worked in layers below him and provided information. He listened well and assimilated a wide variety of material before arriving at a decision.[23]

Eisenhower took charge of the budgetary, civil rights, legal, defense, and diplomatic issues that he thought needed his personal attention. To reach the best solutions to complicated problems, he designated others inside his administration to carry out specific assignments. Secretary Dulles, for instance, provided valuable advice on foreign affairs. Secretary of Defense Charles Wilson managed his department's sprawling bureaucracy while the president shaped military policy. The president depended on Secretary of the Treasury George Humphrey and other advisers to help formulate fiscal policy. Although Ike admired and respected Attorney General Brownell, the president nevertheless played a major role in the justice department's direction. He valued these individuals but kept them in their place, emphasizing whenever necessary that he was in charge. In many important aspects of his administration, including critical areas where historians have depicted him as passive or disengaged, the initiatives and policies were Eisenhower's even when others appeared to be the prime movers.

Depictions of Eisenhower's connection to Nixon have followed a particularly dark path. The relationship between the two men is variously described as ambivalent or based on mutual loathing. In the spring of 1960, columnist and commentator Joseph Kraft wrote in an article in *Esquire* entitled "Ike vs. Nixon" that "it is remarkable that anyone could even suppose a close rapport between the President and Nixon." The two men's linkage puzzled Ambrose, who described them as at best ambivalent toward one another. More recently, in his 2010 book *American Caesars*, British author Nigel Hamilton states: "Eisenhower had never liked or trusted Nixon, nor did he feel confident about Nixon holding the reins of America's imperial power." Hamilton claimed that Ike censored Nixon's speeches, rarely allowed him to enter the Oval Office, and prevented him from participating in "Cabinet and senior government meetings, save as an observer." These statements do not deviate at all from the mainstream view among historians; none of them are accurate.[24]

A former presidential speechwriter, Emmet John Hughes, in *The Ordeal of Power*, released in 1963, claimed: "The relationship between Eisenhower and Nixon, at its warmest over the years, could never be described as confident and comradely." A prepublication excerpt that appeared in *Look* magazine in November 1962 alleges that Eisenhower told Hughes before the 1956 Republican national convention that Nixon "was not presidential timber." Reporters asked the former president to comment, and he denied ever making that statement. No one has acknowledged Ike's disclaimer, and the derogatory characterization is regularly used to describe the two men's relationship.[25]

Partisan biographers like Earl Mazo and Bela Kornitzer published sympathetic accounts about Nixon during his vice presidency, and after leaving office Nixon defended himself in *Six Crises*. Many authors cast these works aside in favor of less complimentary depictions. *The New Republic* serialized a book by William Costello, *The Facts About Nixon*, just before the 1960 presidential election. Costello declared that Nixon had failed to assist GOP candidates in the 1954 elections and that the vice president was "was widely blamed for the Republican party's reckless flirtation with the treason issue." These accusations were without merit. Most Republicans applauded Nixon for aiding the party's candidates, and they supported him in his efforts to remove subversives from the federal bureaucracy.[26]

Two decades later, Fawn Brodie released *Richard Nixon*. Written when she was dying of cancer and published posthumously, it was widely regarded as a weak book. It still made the bestseller lists. The book's jacket contained the hyperbolic thesis, "Here *for the first time* is a carefully documented record of the evolution of Nixon's lying." Brodie suggested that it had "a pathological origin." During the 1952 fund speech, according to the author, Nixon told two egregious lies. He claimed that the "slush fund had not been kept secret, which it had," and second, "he had paid his donors no special favors, which was not true." This account is erroneous: the fund was not secret, and no one showed that any contributors received "special favors."[27]

Brodie further claimed that the "baldest lie of his vice presidency" came in 1960, during the fourth presidential debate with Kennedy, over Cuban policy. The senator called for assisting anti-Castro rebels while the vice president advised patience, claiming that he had given the same advice to Eisenhower. The truth, Brodie insisted, was that inside the White House Nixon had urged a more vigorous policy. She continued: "Nixon freely admitted his part in the [Bay of Pigs] invasion." The archival documents show that Ike had approved only limited actions such as quick and sporadic amphibious raids and dropping parachutists on the island. They further show that Nixon could not have had a part in the Bay of Pigs because the Eisenhower administration never began developing any invasion plan.[28]

Anthony Summers, in his 2000 bestseller *The Arrogance of Power*, garnered headlines by claiming that Nixon went into psychotherapy sessions with Dr. Arnold Hutschnecker, who, according to Summers, gave the impression that he was a practicing psychiatrist. The *New York Times*, a decade later, blithely embraced Summers's allegations in Hutschnecker's obituary. The newspaper did not mention that the doctor was not a board-certified psychiatrist and never claimed to be one, or that he testified under oath at Senate and House hearings in November 1973 that he had never treated Nixon for psychological or psychiatric reasons. Hutschnecker's records of his appointments with Nixon reveal that the doctor met with the vice president for several annual checkups and on a few other occasions for stress-related illness.[29]

Time magazine editors Nancy Gibbs and Michael Duffy, in *The Presidents Club*, looked at the relationships among the presidents since Harry Truman. They include chapters on Eisenhower's association with Truman, Kennedy, and Lyndon Johnson, as well as Nixon's association with Johnson, Gerald Ford, Jimmy Carter, Ronald Reagan, and George H. W. Bush. Although Ike spent more time with Nixon than with Truman, Kennedy, and Johnson combined, there is no chapter on Eisenhower and Nixon. Instead, the authors repeat the misinformation that "Eisenhower . . . never felt much warmth toward his vice president." They also state that the Ike had Nixon fire cabinet members, even though he never had that authority.[30]

Jeffrey Frank's 2013 book *Ike and Dick* magnifies the factual and interpretative errors. Frank is a well-respected journalist and novelist but untrained as a historian, and his book shows evidence of insufficient research. The small number and limited range of written sources cited suggest that he may have spent a month in the Eisenhower and Nixon presidential libraries; each contains millions of documents that would take years to examine properly. In addition, Frank did not cite any of the thousands upon thousands of documents readily available on microfilm, including Eisenhower's diaries, legislative conferences, and cabinet meetings. On the basis of the tiny sample he cites, Frank advanced the proposition that the president could be cold blooded or worse and that Nixon reacted as well as he could without losing his integrity. The relationship that emerges is that of a son trying to win the affection of a distant, bullying father. Ike's opinion of Nixon, according to Frank, changed over time "from the mild disdain that he felt for most politicians to hesitant respect."[31]

John Malsberger's *The General and the Politician: Dwight Eisenhower, Richard Nixon, and American Politics*, published in 2014, concentrates on the interaction between Ike and Dick and how they formed a "political partnership." This is a mischaracterization. Eisenhower, a five-star general, governed alone from the top of the pyramid; he commanded and subordinates followed orders. There were no partners.[32]

The relationship between the president and vice president matured over eight years. At first, they did not know each other's strengths and weaknesses, but as Nixon became familiar with how Ike governed, he was better able to adapt the president's ideas to practical proposals and make himself a trusted part of the administration. This evolving relationship is almost completely absent from most accounts. Instead, incorrect information has been repeated for so long that it has been converted into fact.

Earlier authors have relied on three incidents to demonstrate Eisenhower's low regard for Nixon. The first starts with the 1952 fund crisis; the second is the unsuccessful "dump Nixon" drive spearheaded by White House disarmament adviser Harold Stassen a month before the 1956 Republican convention; the third came on August 24, 1960, when Eisenhower answered a reporter's question concerning what contribution Nixon had made to the administration by saying, "If you give me a week, I might think of one." The comment made front-page headlines.[33]

Written records of the time show clearly that the general did not try to oust Nixon from the 1952 ticket, and the stubborn fact that he was not removed should give pause to those who stress a theme of discord between the two men. This is an example of the incoherence that bits of lingering mythology give to the standard picture of Eisenhower: he is now seen as a strong leader—yet too hapless to influence the selection of his own running mate. In the second case, Ike suggested to Nixon months before the 1956 Republican convention that he take a cabinet post to gain experience managing a large bureaucracy. The president did not demand that Nixon leave the vice presidency but told him to make the decision he thought best. If Ike had wanted a different running mate for his second term, he certainly had the popularity to choose someone else. He did not approve and certainly never championed Stassen's initiative. Nixon saw a cabinet post as a demotion that would damage his political future, and he chose to run for reelection. Lastly, the accounts of the August 1960 press conference did not mention that the president was leaving the podium because that was his final question. He stated that he would respond the following week; he did not disclose that he was feeling poorly. No press conference was held the next week, and at the one that followed, no reporter asked the president to comment on the vice president's value. After Ike made his intemperate remark, he apologized to Nixon. Authors have omitted that fact.

Such regularly repeated anecdotes affirm the unsubstantiated argument that Ike and Nixon were at odds. In reality, the two men worked well together. Ike grew to have great confidence in his vice president and had Nixon express opinions during crucial meetings and summarize those of others. Nixon depended on the president to provide these opportunities, and he put forward his best effort to become a versatile utility player on Ike's team. More than anyone else in the administration, he understood the president's intentions on many different fronts and became an articulate spokesman for his policies. Because of Nixon's desire to advance the president's initiatives and because Eisenhower recognized his vice president's talents, Nixon gradually assumed a more diverse set of duties than anyone else in the administration.

The president considered Nixon knowledgeable in political matters. He provided valuable advice regarding interaction between the executive and Congress, and during the two campaigns. Nixon initially tried to curb McCarthy's excesses, and when McCarthy angered the president by attacking the Army, Nixon assisted in the White House's quiet but effective campaign against the senator. The vice president became the administration's leading spokesman on civil rights. He chaired the President's Committee on Government Contracts, advancing minority employment and education. He also regularly spoke out for equal rights and helped push the Civil Rights Act of 1957 through the Senate.

While in Congress, Nixon had been a committed internationalist. As vice president, he traveled to Asia, Latin America, Europe, and Africa; became one of Ike's most trusted forward observers; and matured into an expert on world affairs. The president briefed him before he left and debriefed him upon his return. Nixon relayed both his findings and his discussions with Ike to the National Security Council and to relevant cabinet members. He learned a great deal in his travels and met many world leaders, with whom he remained in contact. He and Dulles became intimate friends and shared ideas on the diplomatic initiatives.

The president's heart attack in 1955 has received a great deal of attention. During his recovery that fall and winter, Nixon assumed added responsibilities. Already overworked, he grew weary and suffered from insomnia; physicians prescribed barbiturates to relieve his symptoms. No one knew how incapacitated both the president and the vice president were during this period.

Even in this troubling situation, Ike and Nixon worked well together. The vice president's two military advisers were among the many who refuted the allegations of discord between the leaders. Robert Cushman, who handled national security matters for the vice president, recalled that he never heard Nixon say anything critical of the president. Nixon's appointment secretary, Donald Hughes, reported that no animosity existed between the leaders.[34]

Three months after leaving office, Nixon commented in a letter to a constituent, Mrs. Barbara Berghoefer, that while he did not know how history would view Ike, "for devotion to duty, for unshakeable dedication to high moral principle, for a determination always to serve what he regarded as the best interests of all Americans—on each of these scores, Mr. Eisenhower ranks with the greatest leaders our nation has ever had." He was privileged to have worked with Ike and to have learned "that real leadership is not a matter of florid words or action for its own sake. It is, rather, the undeviating application of the basic principles to the shifting details of day-to-day problems."[35]

Sitting in the Oval Office on July 21, 1971, more than two years after Eisenhower's death, President Nixon reflected on his own role in that earlier administration. He believed he had made a substantial contribution to solving a wide range of problems. During the second term, he recalled, the president had him substitute for him at cabinet and NSC meetings as well as participate in many critical decisions. Ike, Nixon concluded, had treated him "extremely well."[36] Due to lingering partisan bitterness and the Watergate scandal, Nixon remains an easy target. The fable that Ike limited Nixon's role in the administration and that the two were antagonistic toward each other has permitted the selective rehabilitation of Ike's reputation without requiring a similar reexamination of Nixon's, and this selectivity blocks an accurate understanding of the Eisenhower presidency. The enormous weight of the evidence points to a fundamentally different relationship. Ike entered the presidency ready to lead. Nixon was eager to follow.

Part One

1952–1957

THE NOMINEES

Vice President Harry Truman had suddenly assumed the presidency when Franklin D. Roosevelt died of a massive cerebral hemorrhage on April 12, 1945. As the 1948 presidential campaign approached, the embattled and unpopular Truman asked General Dwight Eisenhower to lead the Democratic ticket. Truman would step down to become his running mate. The general declined the invitation, and Truman ran for the presidency. That November, he surprised the pundits by beating the heavily favored Republican challenger, Governor Thomas Dewey of New York.

Even before Truman's inauguration, adversaries in both parties looked forward to replacing him in 1952. For Republicans, who had not won a presidential election since 1928, the stakes were high. They feared that if the GOP did not win the next presidential election, the party would always be in the minority and never win the White House again. Eisenhower once again seemed uninterested in running. Three months before the Normandy invasion, the general had talked in London with one of FDR's speechwriters, the Pulitzer Prize–winning playwright Robert Sherwood, about his opposition to political involvement. While members of his family were loyal Republicans, he said, he himself had never voted. As an Army officer, he owed the federal government his "full loyalty and devotion regardless of its coloration." He therefore rejected partisanship and any thought of public office.[1]

"Mr. Republican," Ohio senator Robert Taft, felt no such restriction. After Dewey's defeat, Taft, the spokesman for the GOP's conservative wing, decided to enter the next contest. He offered the nation a clear alternative to Truman's liberalism. He would end or restrict the New Deal and Fair Deal, lower federal expenditures, balance the government's budget, and bring most United States troops home from Europe and Asia to lessen the nation's vast global commitments.[2]

This political calculus changed abruptly toward the end of March 1952, when the president announced that he would not seek reelection. Several Democrats came forward to vie for their party's nomination: Senators Estes Kefauver from Tennessee and Stuart Symington from Missouri as well as Governor Adlai Stevenson from Illinois, who eventually won.

On the Republican side, Taft pushed forward. He had the support of GOP partisans and won influential enforcements because of the prestige he had gained in the Senate. He also had powerful enemies within the GOP's eastern establishment. Many party leaders believed he could not win because he appealed exclusively to the party's base and not to disgruntled Democrats and independents. He was not a dynamic spokesman, and his principles tended to be extremely conservative, representing a midwestern isolationist opinion in a time of broad international commitments.

Henry Cabot Lodge Jr. led the effort to draft Eisenhower to run for the presidency. Senator Lodge, from a wealthy aristocratic family in Massachusetts, had won election to the Senate three times. He had fought in World War II with distinction, the first in the upper house to serve on active duty since the Civil War. Lodge had met the general during the fighting and had tried unsuccessfully to draft him to run for the presidency in 1948. When Ike agreed to run four years later, Lodge managed the victorious movement for his nomination.[3]

Those who saw Eisenhower as a sure winner persuaded him to challenge Taft for the nomination by warning him that Taft would return the nation to isolationism. That threat plus the general's sense of duty changed his mind. By spring 1952, Ike had decided to run. He had taken a leave of absence a year earlier from his position as president of Columbia University to serve as NATO's supreme commander in Europe. Now he resigned his Army commission, flew back to the United States, and announced his decision to seek the presidency during a driving rainstorm in his hometown of Abilene, Kansas.[4]

The two contenders each brought strengths and weaknesses: Ike was a global hero who had led the Allied forces to victory over the Third Reich, but he had no political experience. Taft had evolved into a national GOP spokesman, but he had serious wounds from his decades of political skirmishes. Many found him offensive. The candidates' character traits aside, the nomination battle sparked a visceral philosophical struggle between moderates and conservatives in the party.

When Taft and Eisenhower traveled to Chicago at the start of July for the Republican national convention, the thermometer had reached the century mark, and inside the 13,000-seat International Amphitheatre, the temperature generated by the two nominees' partisans was even higher. The winner needed 604 delegates, and the initial balloting, on July 11, showed how closely divided the convention was. In the first ballot, Ike had 595 votes, Taft had 500, and a few favorite-son candidates took the remainder. Before that ballot officially concluded, the Minnesota delegation switched its vote to Ike, making him the party's presidential nominee.[5]

Eisenhower and his organization briefly celebrated their victory. Herbert Brownell, one of the general's campaign managers, quickly turned to the next pressing task. Whom did the general want as his running mate? The nominee had not given it much thought; he had not even realized that the choice was his. He and Brownell discussed several possibilities, and Ike wrote out a list, placing Senator Richard Nixon from California at the top.[6]

Brownell took the names back to Eisenhower's supporters, congregated in a smoke-filled room at the Conrad Hilton Hotel. He did not present the general's list; instead the group, with Governor Dewey presiding, went through their own potential candidates. Taft was brought up first and quickly discarded. Senator Everett Dirksen from Illinois came next, but his speech attacking Dewey at the convention eliminated him. The conversation gradually shifted to Nixon. He was young, charismatic, and a westerner, admired for exposing Alger Hiss as a communist spy. In less than two hours, the group agreed that he should be the vice-presidential nominee. Brownell telephoned Ike, who accepted the recommendation.[7]

Nixon had hardly dreamt about being offered a spot on the presidential ticket. Sitting in his hotel room, perspiring from the hot, humid Chicago day, he received a phone call from Brownell while still in his underwear. He quickly showered, shaved, dressed, and rushed over for a fifteen-minute audience with Eisenhower. Then he went to the convention auditorium, where he was nominated and approved by acclamation.[8]

That night, the party's nominees appeared together before the convention's delegates. Nixon and his wife Pat stood on the rostrum beside Ike and Mamie. As the assembly cheered, Nixon impulsively clutched his running mate's wrist and raised it above both of their heads, like a referee raising a boxer's glove. With his other hand, the senator pointed to the general, as if to say, here I am running for vice president with a certifiable hero.[9]

The two had met briefly twice before. Their first serious conversation had come when Nixon stopped in Paris for less than an hour in the middle of May 1951, for a meeting with the general at NATO headquarters. The day before the nomination, as the state delegations invited the prospective candidates to speak to their groups, Nixon had escorted the general to meet the California delegation.[10]

Still, the choice was not a surprise. Ike admired Nixon's handling of the Hiss inquiry in 1948 and preferred that his running mate be a younger man who would balance the ticket and attract a more youthful base. Two weeks after his nomination, he said he had picked Nixon because he was "dynamic, direct and square." Close advisers like Dewey, business executive Ellis Slater, and Los Angeles newspaper publisher Virgil Pinkley had lobbied for Nixon and applauded his selection. Paul Helms, a businessman from Southern California and one of the general's social friends, was overjoyed that Ike had chosen "a young man as a running mate that was progressive and aggressive." The national press split along party lines. Papers that championed the GOP pronounced themselves pleased with the choice. The *San Francisco News* told its readers that Nixon symbolized "the new spirit of youth that has infected the Republican Party and which has been encouraged by General Eisenhower." Those that supported the Democrats portrayed him as unsuitable for the vice presidency.[11]

With the convention adjourned, Ike and his advisers returned to their Denver headquarters to map campaign strategy. As a break from their recent around-the-clock activities, the group traveled to Ike's friend Aksel Nielsen's ranch near Fraser, Colorado, in the Rocky Mountains. The general planned to organize his forces along military lines and would begin his campaign after Labor Day. He supervised the operation while his lieutenants carried out specific assignments. Republican National Committee (RNC) chairman Arthur Summerfield directed the national campaign, while Governor Sherman Adams of New Hampshire handled the general's daily schedule.[12]

Nixon, without an initial assignment, returned to Washington, D.C., the Sunday after his nomination. Even the excessive heat of the late afternoon did not dampen his followers' exuberance. Photographers snapped pictures as the smiling nominee descended from the plane, and cars and cameras lined the street outside his home. His daughters had placed a sign on the front lawn: WELCOME HOME DADDY![13]

After a brief vacation, the Nixon family and several close advisers flew from the capital to Denver's Stapleton Airport on Saturday afternoon, July 26. The family left the plane with Dick carrying Julie and Pat holding Tricia's hand and went to their rooms at the Brown Palace Hotel, where Eisenhower had established his campaign headquarters. At his press conference, Nixon predicted that President Truman's performance would be the central issue: he said of the Stevenson campaign, "What we have is some new faces but the same old deal."[14]

Early the next morning, Nixon drove seventy-two miles west to Fraser, where Ike was still vacationing at the Nielsen ranch. The general wanted to meet his running mate in an informal setting to make a preliminary evaluation. The senator arrived in a gray summer suit that he quickly discarded for fishing attire. In this disarming setting, the general gave his guest his first and last trout-fishing lesson. The vice-presidential nominee failed to catch anything and never learned to enjoy the sport. Afterward, Nixon and GOP senator Frank Carlson of Kansas peeled a large pan of potatoes while Ike cooked dinner for a dozen guests. These activities may seem inconsequential, but they gave the general the opportunity to observe how Nixon behaved in an informal setting.[15]

Ike, Nixon, and others then returned to the Brown Palace, where RNC publicity director Robert Humphreys outlined the campaign strategy. The party strategists and the general decided that Ike would avoid partisanship and would not comment on personalities; Nixon would attack Truman and Stevenson and focus on Democratic vulnerabilities. Throughout the early stage of the campaign, Eisenhower and Nixon refined their plans by meeting with leading Republicans to discuss a wide variety of topics, including campaign organization, party unity, farm problems, and foreign policy. Together and separately, they courted Republican activists in Los Angeles, Cleveland, New York City, and Washington to invigorate party regulars. What excited the GOP more than their presence was Eisenhower's rising popularity in the Gallup Poll, which in mid-September reached 55 percent for the general and 40 percent for Stevenson, a spread of 15 points.[16]

While Ike planned and organized, Nixon campaigned, returning to Los Angeles on Monday, July 28, for the first time since the convention. Temperatures in the mid-nineties did not stop the several hundred supporters who noisily greeted him and his family as they deplaned. Governor Warren welcomed him home, endorsed his nomination, and foresaw victory in November. Nixon, of course, concurred: "We'll have a constructive program. . . . We'll not only clean house of corruption but we'll build a new house that all Americans will be proud of."[17]

The Republican theme during the campaign was (alliteratively, at least) the three Cs: communism, corruption, and Korea. The first dealt with the revelations that the Soviet Union had planted spies in the federal government, of which the most spectacular example was the exposure of Hiss, a high-ranking state department official. The corruption centered on scandals in the Truman bureaucracy. Some friends of the president and members of the White House staff had received payoffs and were labeled influence peddlers or "5 percenters" for the fee they charged. Internal Revenue officials had abused their positions and had left their jobs or been forced to resign. Finally, the Korean conflict had dragged on since 1950, and America had become weary of this unpopular war. These three points, Republicans felt, were symptoms of the more serious illness. The real campaign theme was a no-confidence vote on the Truman presidency.

In Whittier that evening, more than 40,000 spectators lined the streets while Dick and Pat sat perched on the back of a convertible on a three-quarter-mile parade route. At Whittier College's football field, 20,000 enthusiasts waved home-made banners proclaiming HELLO DICK—HELLO PAT, WELCOME FROM SANTA ANA, and WELCOME FROM LONG BEACH. The *Christian Science Monitor* reported: "Here was a spontaneous community outpouring of appreciation that said more about Americanism than anybody could pack into a July Fourth oration." Nixon, who had sat on the Whittier football team's bench cheering the first string, fed the celebratory mood by telling his listeners this was "the greatest night Pat and I will ever experience. . . . It took me 18 years to do it, but I've finally made it. I've got off the bench and onto the playing field."[18]

The candidate spent most of his address reading from a letter that Mrs. David Sanders from Oakland, California, had sent him the day after the GOP convention. She was nineteen years old, lived on $85.00 a month, and had a two-month-old son. She had been a secretary but now stayed at home with her parents, where she cared for her baby while her husband served as a Marine corpsman in Korea. She had never seen or heard of Nixon but was convinced he was "a great American." He and Ike had fought in World War II and understood the loneliness of being "separated from [their] loved ones." She hoped they would win, end the "police action," and bring the soldiers home. To do her part, she enclosed a check for $10.00 and volunteered her skills: "Since I can't vote I would feel it a great honor to have helped you in anyway small or large."[19]

While Dick was testing this theme with the audience, Pat prepared for her role. She and Dick were private people who lived in a world of constant political chatter, sometimes riveting, more often meaningless. Above all she was a mother. She spoke to reporters at Eisenhower headquarters while washing Tricia and Julie's faces and changing their dresses before sending them off to play. To prevent snobbery in her daughters, she told them that the vice president was "just the president's helper." As the candidate's wife, she proudly repeated that her husband had made no secret deals to become the running mate. She smiled and tossed her hair when asked about politics: "That's Dick's job and we've always regarded it that way."

He made the speeches; she was his companion. She shook hands, answered phones, did secretarial work, ironed his clothes, and talked to people. She had studied merchandising in college and prodded him to buy new clothes; she often shopped for him. His favorite color was blue, but his campaign suits were mainly gray. Her taste in evening dresses ran to modest necklines and short sleeves. In daytime, she stuck to well-styled inexpensive clothes and would adapt her existing wardrobe for the campaign. She had also learned to like hats while in the capital because they were "the only items of wearing apparel the senator ever notices!"

Pat did not advertise that after her parents died, she had worked her way through the University of Southern California and had graduated cum laude. She was as gifted intellectually as he was. He sometimes was rigid and dogmatic; so was she. When he was depressed, she bolstered his morale. Her greatest political gift to him was an ever-present strength.[20]

While the Nixons established their campaign routine, the senator focused on the critical task of uniting the Eisenhower and Taft factions. Taft's zealots believed that Dewey had stolen the nomination for Ike, and Nixon saw that one of his roles was to heal the breach between the two wings and reestablish party harmony. Although he never thought Taft could be elected, Nixon admired his political acumen. Taft had come to Nixon before the convention and had asked for his support. When Nixon refused, Taft handled the rejection well.[21]

The Taft loyalists had to be placated if the GOP was going to win in November. Nixon's confidant William Bullitt, who had been ambassador to the Soviet Union and France under Franklin Roosevelt, applauded Nixon's nomination but was dejected at Taft's defeat. Thomas Jenkins, a Republican congressman from Ohio, had gotten to know the nominee when he chaired a Herter mission subcommittee to Europe on which Nixon had served in 1947. Jenkins hoped that Dick would seek to heal the breach between the Ike and Taft factions. Nixon understood that his minority party had to stand united. Besides, he admired many of Taft's principles and planned to incorporate them into the campaign.[22]

Nixon and others understood that if the party did not unite they might lose the election. The general did not comprehend this political reality. He had never been a professional politician and did not realize that his popularity was only part of winning. He had to have the partisans who worked energetically for the GOP, and he had to appeal to their party loyalty.

Ike, not understanding the value of the Taft wing, had rejected an invitation to speak before the Ohio Republican convention. Nixon realized the significance of this gathering, and on the last day of July, he seized the opportunity. More than 3,300 delegates, alternates, and others filled the Palace Theatre in Columbus. The GOP also had special radio and television hookups. Those who first took the podium lavished praise on Taft. As usual, Nixon came to the microphone without a prepared text; he spoke from notes. He first reminded his audience that he had an Ohio heritage because his father was born and raised there. Then he described the state's most famous native son, Taft, as a "magnificent thoroughbred and magnificent champion." He condemned the Democrats: Stevenson for accepting the backing of Jack Kroll, chief of the Congress of Industrial Organization's Political Action Committee (CIOPAC), and Jack Avery, a Chicago boss and Democratic committeeman from Illinois. They would resort to any scheme to win, including lying about Republican candidates' credentials and stuffing ballot boxes. The mere mention of their names stimulated GOP activists to work harder. While insisting he never doubted Stevenson's "good intentions," Nixon argued that Stevenson was the president's "captive candidate" and thus could not stamp out the corruption of Truman's political cronies. The clear message was that Ike was the far better alternative. Nixon's listeners responded wildly to partisan heat and clapped politely when the senator urged them to campaign for Eisenhower.[23]

The following afternoon, Nixon flew to Denver to report on his Ohio speech. He next went to Los Angeles for talks with his advisers, and on Sunday, August 3, addressed the California Republican State Central Committee in Sacramento. From the rostrum in the Assembly chamber, he appealed to the members to unite behind Ike. The GOP, he cautioned, could not afford to repeat the overconfidence and apathy of 1948; this time the party would run its campaign aggressively from start to finish. Governor Warren, who had been Dewey's running mate in 1948, added that the "selection of Nixon was like a breath of fresh air in this country," and Senator William Knowland seconded the sentiment.[24]

Nixon held a press conference in Denver on August 12, linking Stevenson to the "Truman gang" because, at the president's invitation, the governor had attended a cabinet meeting, thus making himself "an ex-officio member of the Truman Cabinet." Then he invaded Stevenson territory, addressing the Illinois State Fair in Springfield. The next afternoon, before a cheering crowd of 7,000 in Chicago, Nixon reminded his listeners that Estes Kefauver had been the overwhelming choice in the Democratic primaries and that Truman and the party bosses had cavalierly rejected that mandate for the "hand-picked" Stevenson. In return, Nixon continued, Stevenson had acknowledged his debt to the party machine by choosing Wilson Wyatt, "the darling of the left wing of the CIO and ADA [Americans for Democratic Action]. . . . The Democratic ticket will be known as the Truman-Stevenson ticket from now on out. The voice will be that of Stevenson but the hand will be that of Harry Truman." Eisenhower was the people's choice, reflecting the popular opposition to the administration's foreign policies, to its farm program, and to federal control over tidelands. Where, Nixon asked, did Stevenson stand on these issues? Americans, the senator held, wanted an end to corruption, communist global victories, and domestic subversion. He optimistically predicted lower taxes and prices under the GOP. "A vote for Stevenson," Nixon concluded, "can mean nothing more than four more years of Trumanism. A vote for Eisenhower is a vote for change—for a better and stronger America; for prosperity built on peace rather than war." He attacked the Democrats for their deficit spending and appealed to his audience to restore the principle of a balanced budget.[25]

Toward the end of August, *U.S. News & World Report* quizzed Nixon on a variety of topics. As for Senator Joseph McCarthy, by mid-1952 he had won a national following for his advocacy of seeking out and removing communist spies from the federal payroll. Nixon explained that his colleague was the creation of the Truman administration; its refusal to confront the enemy's domestic infiltration had angered McCarthy to the point of confrontation with the White House. While the president was failing on the home front, he and his secretary of state, Dean Acheson, were responsible for the fall of China to communist domination under Mao Tse-Tung.[26]

The article examined Nixon's connection to Hiss, and the vice-presidential nominee wanted to find out more about Stevenson's association with Hiss. During Hiss's first trial, Stevenson had served as a character witness, an action that would haunt him during the campaign. On August 21, Nixon told the *Boston Post* that the governor's decision might become a major campaign issue. On September 1, on the ABC program *Washington Merry-Go-Round*, Nixon declared that the administration's effort to "cover up" the Hiss case would cause heated debate. By mid-month he had instructed his staff to prepare a memorandum on Hiss's relationship to Stevenson: how well they knew each other; what Stevenson said in his deposition for Hiss; whether the governor minimized the threat of domestic subversion; and why some asserted that Stevenson was Hiss's deputy.

Nixon also wanted to study Stevenson's speeches for vulnerable points, such as when he attacked Congress for overriding Truman's veto and giving veterans in the postal service credit for time served in the military. The senator asked for flattering remarks that Stevenson had made about Truman, Acheson, and the state department. But he limited this research to political matters. When T.C. Link, an investigative reporter for the *St. Louis Post Dispatch*, offered potentially explosive material, alleging that the governor was homosexual, Nixon declined. First, he did not believe the governor was "queer," and second, even if it were true, he would not use it. "I have always felt that a man's record as it deals with his attitude on political issues is fair game in a campaign," he wrote the reporter, but "his personal stuff (true or false) is below the belt. . . . As you know, they have spread some pretty nasty stuff about Eisenhower also."[27]

Nixon did not consider either Stevenson or John Sparkman, the Democratic vice-presidential nominee, his primary targets. This contest, like his first congressional race in 1946, had a fundamental theme: time for a change. The senator understood that the country would vote on Truman's performance, and public opinion polls showed an increasing majority rating the administration lower and lower.[28]

In addition to scrutinizing Truman's record, the Republicans used Eisenhower to magnify the Democratic administration's failures. When Truman tried to respond in early September by criticizing Eisenhower, Nixon reminded voters that Truman had showered accolades on the general until he announced he would run as a Republican. "The new Truman-Stevenson line," the vice-presidential contender predicted, "will be the biggest boomerang in the campaign. The American people love a fighter, but they hate a dirty fighter. They will be repulsed by these dirty tactics of Truman and Stevenson."[29]

Democrats were in a quandary. Eisenhower, the wartime hero, had no political record, and attacking him would most likely lose them votes. This left Nixon as the logical target. As an effective partisan spokesman who regularly skewered Democrats, after the convention the vice-presidential nominee continued his assault on the Truman administration through nationally publicized speeches and appearances. He had a six-year congressional record that the Democrats could attack.

Max Lowenthal, a White House assistant, was put in charge of focusing attention on Nixon's past. If the general were elected, he told Truman, Nixon would "be within a heartbeat of the biggest temporal office and responsibility on earth." Eisenhower and others "touted Nixon as the crusader of virtue to appeal especially to America's youth. Yet he is the beneficiary of a notorious gambler-wiretapper-fixer whom two Congressional committees have unsuccessfully hunted high and low—a fugitive from Congress." This was a reference to Henry "The Dutchman" Grunewald, a gangster who had allegedly lent $5,000 to Nixon's 1950 campaign fund; Nixon had then concealed the connection by having Senator Ralph Brewster, Republican from Maine, rush to confess that he was responsible for this loan. Lowenthal charged that Nixon had "violated his innumerable preaching to everybody that a public official has a solemn duty to tell an investigating committee everything he knows they want and that he has in his possession." In fact, Brewster had engineered the Grunewald loan. Nixon categorically denied knowing anything about the transaction, and there is no evidence to contradict him.[30]

Stevenson, meanwhile, was busily building his campaign organization and planning his strategy. During the initial stages, he spoke before the annual American Legion convention but did not impress them as a sufficiently staunch anticommunist. He also gave a speech before a Detroit union audience that left it visibly uninspired. He seemed reluctant to attack his opponents forcefully and quickly discovered that he was glued to Truman's record and required to defend it.[31]

George Ball, who aided the governor in his presidential race, wrote in his memoirs that Ike took "the high road with only occasional detours down the slope." Nixon, on the other hand, "would, by infallible instinct, operate at the level where the language of abuse would have the maximum resonance." Although Stevenson disliked these assaults, "he scornfully refused to take on Nixon. He was campaigning against Eisenhower and would not demean himself by arguing with Eisenhower's hired gun."[32]

Stevenson grew to loathe Nixon, who repeatedly demanded that he state specifically where he stood on unpopular Truman programs. When Stevenson claimed, toward the end of August, that he had a plan to end the Korean War but refused to disclose the particulars for fear it would provide vital military information to the enemy, Nixon scoffed that Stevenson was using this emotional issue as a political gimmick. If he had a solution, Nixon argued, he should disclose it.[33]

As early as August 4, Stevenson was receiving confidential information from someone who was called his "spy in the Eisenhower camp," who told him that the primary campaign issue was the administration's failures in China and Korea, and that Nixon would "push hard on the Hiss business." Stevenson reasoned that the latter tactic would be ineffective because he had said only that Hiss had a good reputation working in the state department in 1945 and 1946, and, besides, the Republican chairman of the Carnegie Endowment's board, John Foster Dulles, had lobbied for Hiss's appointment as its president. Stevenson also believed Eisenhower would do everything possible to gain Taft's active backing and would also implore farmers to return to the GOP ranks. Another source close to Ike relayed to the governor that the Republicans would "hit" the Stevenson campaign with charges of corruption during the Truman administration.[34]

To signal his independence from the White House, Stevenson selected his own campaign manager and directed his organization from Springfield, Illinois. He also stated that federal corruption had to stop, a comment that surely annoyed Truman. Even with this friction, the two reconciled their disagreements and cooperated to try to defeat their common adversary. The thought of a Republican in the White House was sufficient to mobilize millions of Democrats. The first lady of the party, Eleanor Roosevelt, had advanced Stevenson as the standard bearer since early in 1952; he was a witty, intelligent liberal whose speeches carefully delineated Democratic ideals. After the governor received the nomination, she championed his cause, believing that he could negotiate better with Joseph Stalin than Ike. Her disenchantment with the general and with anyone who shared a ballot line with McCarthy colored her perspective. The national board of Americans for Democratic Action (ADA) announced for the governor and described Eisenhower as politically naïve. His running mate was inexperienced, and his attachment to McCarthyism made him unacceptable.[35]

The *New York Post* was more influential, and more partisan. Early in the contest, Arthur Schlesinger Jr. predicted in a column that Ike would "take the high road," while his running mate would "rouse the animal emotions of the crowd" and "be the hatchet man, assuming the main burden of attack, denunciation and smear." Nixon responded by labeling the historian a "dangerous liberal."[36]

The American Weekly took the opposite approach, chronicling Pat and Dick's life from their courtship through their maturation as a close-knit family with two children. The *Saturday Evening Post* featured a story by Pat using the catchy title, "I Say He's a Wonderful Guy," tracing their relationship and her husband's career.[37]

As the war of the written word accelerated, Nixon continued campaigning. His visit to the Northeast was extended in early September with a four-day tour of Maine to test certain themes. On the fourth of September, stopping in Connecticut for a Republican state convention, he attacked Stevenson for advocating a Federal Employment Practices Commission (FEPC) while his running mate favored a filibuster against it. Stevenson, he said, had developed "his own special method of riding the Truman horse side-saddle—and like all side-saddle riders, his feet hang well out to the left." His audience applauded with delight; Nixon began calling the Democrat "Side-Saddle Adlai."[38]

This detour did not detract from Nixon's primary commitment in Maine. The Pine Tree State, traditionally Republican, held the first state elections in the nation on September 8. Predicting that the outcome in Maine would foreshadow a national trend, Nixon ridiculed Stevenson for having "pooh-poohed the Communist threat from within." Republicans, Nixon pledged, would drive the Reds from the federal bureaucracy while Truman continued to hide "Communist skeletons in its political closet." Truman was running a "Scandal-a-Day Administration," and Stevenson was "a hopeless, helpless, but far from harmless captive of Truman and company." For the ninth time in a row, Maine Republicans won every statewide contest.[39]

While Nixon was energizing the base, Eisenhower began his campaign in the South. Over the next two months, he would travel more than 50,000 miles by plane and train, interrupting his schedule to meet with Taft in New York on September 12 at 60 Morningside Heights, the presidential residence at Columbia University where the trustees still allowed Ike to reside. Democrats labeled the meeting the "Surrender at Morningside Heights" because Eisenhower supposedly had acceded to Taft's demands in exchange for the senator's pledge to support the Ike-Nixon ticket.[40]

Two days later, while the general was responding to these accusations, Nixon appeared on *Meet the Press*, where the show's moderator Lawrence Spivak questioned him on two major topics: Truman as the central issue of the campaign and Stevenson as "a reluctant captive" of the White House. Peter Edson asked the vice-presidential nominee if he could preside over the country if the general died. The candidate replied that he would not have to assume the presidency because Ike would serve one, possibly two terms. He answered a question regarding Senator McCarthy, who had won his primary. When asked if he planned to campaign in Wisconsin, he said did not know if his or the general's schedules would take either man through the state and what either would do if on the same platform with McCarthy.[41]

That afternoon, the Nixons flew to California and spent the evening at the Mission Inn in Riverside, where they had been married twelve years earlier. Proclaiming this contest "the most intensive campaign in the history of American politics," he declared himself ready "to start hitting hard." In a letter to George Creel, a prominent California Democrat who had assisted him in his 1950 senatorial race, Nixon wrote "up to this point" his activities had been "preliminary to the big show although I have felt it was necessary to tie Stevenson to those who nominated him." He expected "to do my real slugging commencing" in mid-September.[42]

Nixon had run three successful congressional campaigns in California in which he had appealed to a large majority of Republican voters and captured significant numbers of independents and disenchanted Democrats. He planned to follow the same tactics. From his nomination in July until September, he had tested various political themes, starting with attacking Truman for his failures and then linking Stevenson to the administration. Once the two men were connected, the Democratic candidate would not be able to reverse the downward spiral. Nixon then presented Eisenhower as the bright light: the general was mounting a crusade for peace and prosperity at home and would eliminate the corruption in the federal bureaucracy.

Ike vaguely recognized Nixon's political usefulness. Having spent four decades in the military and having been responsible for millions of lives during World War II, he was supremely confident and comfortable making final decisions. He did not intend to share power with Nixon, nor did they ever become intimate friends. Throughout his military service, he understood that he had to persuade skeptical congressmen to his side, and he had testified at congressional hearings to support his positions. That did not mean he enjoyed this duty. As he moved up in rank and interacted more frequently with politicians, he grew to dislike many of them. They worked, he thought, for their own ends rather than the good of the nation. Although he did not discuss his opponents' shortcomings publicly, he had no reservations about criticizing them privately and employing others to air his views. When he met with Taft, he did so to restore party unity and did not entertain any thought of surrender to the Ohio senator's principles. To his military way of thinking, victors did not surrender.

Through July, August, and early September Ike vaguely mapped out his campaign, spoke to various groups, and made lofty statements about providing an efficient government with honest and patriotic employees. He paid little attention to where his running mate went or what he said or did. Then, on September 18, Nixon suddenly became a problem.

THE FUND CRISIS

Journalists and historians overwhelmingly agree that the fund crisis, which prompted the nationally televised address that became famous as Nixon's "Checkers Speech," marked the start of the distrust between Eisenhower and Nixon. Joseph Alsop in 1960 and Jeffrey Frank in 2013 both describe the general watching the broadcast and, at a certain moment, becoming so disgusted with Nixon's performance that he angrily jabbed his pencil into his legal pad, tearing the page. Presumably the forthright general was angered by his running mate's dishonesty.[1]

Neither author—nor any of the others who recount this incident—reviewed Eisenhower's written notes taken during the telecast, which are housed in the Nixon archives. If they had, they would have found a letter from Allen Lowe to Nixon dated November 28, 1956, attached to an offset copy of seven pages in Eisenhower's handwriting. Lowe, the manager of the Hotel Carter in Cleveland, where the general was staying, watched along with about fifteen other guests as Eisenhower made notes on a legal pad during the speech. In the letter, Lowe told Nixon that he believed Ike had "made up his mind about your immediate future as he watched you deliver your telecast." He added that he accompanied the general to his train later that evening, and as Ike was about to board, Ike turned to Lowe and gave him his notes as a souvenir, praising Nixon's speech without any evidence of anger. The notes are entirely positive, with lines such as: "I've . . . seen brave men in tough situations—None ever came through better." The seven pages are undamaged, without any tear from a pencil jab.[2]

By the middle of September, the 1952 GOP presidential ticket had established the outlines of its campaign. Nixon understood that his major contribution was to mobilize the partisan troops by attacking the weaknesses in the Truman administration. While the vice-presidential nominee engaged in hand-to-hand combat, Eisenhower kept himself above the fray, surveying the battle-ground and reaching out to new converts. As he preached the fulfillment of his lofty dreams in stilted prose with distinct religious overtones to adoring audi-ences, his running mate translated these generalizations into specifics that the Republican faithful could grasp and applaud.[3]

Although Nixon had been campaigning almost from the moment he was nominated, the race's official launch was on Wednesday, September 17. Nixon had started his three previous campaigns in Pomona, California, and this one was no exception. To get to the event, over 1,100 of his friends and enthusiasts from Whittier jammed on board eighteen coaches on a Union Pacific Stream-liner, the "Nixon Special." His father Frank walked the aisles in his former rail-road uniform, denim-striped overalls, and neckerchief. By the time national television and radio coverage began, at 8:30 p.m., 15,000 people had crowded into the Los Angeles station for Nixon's address.[4]

The candidate heaped criticism on the Truman administration for scandals, domestic subversion, and inflation. Corrupt Democrats, he insisted, would not reform their illicit practices: "No administration with the greedy, gouging, grum-bling history of the Truman regime can accomplish these things." Stevenson, "the handpicked, handcuffed candidate," would only bring four years of the same.[5]

After the address, he and Pat boarded the Nixon Special. Campaign trains were then a staple of presidential races; Nixon's was air-conditioned throughout and had an intercom system in each car. Car N-1, just behind the engine cars, was for the Nixons; the next one served as a VIP lounge for the prominent people who regularly boarded and exited; the next two cars served as staff sleeping quar-ters and offices. Reporters had their own lounge with a buffet, a car to compose their columns that was equipped with speakers so they could listen to Nixon's speeches, and a car with a Western Union telegraph office so they could file stories.

Although the train was state of the art, there was almost no ability to com-municate between the presidential and vice-presidential nominees' trains. They stopped sporadically for approximately twenty minutes along their routes, pro-viding scarcely any time for the candidates or their representatives to use a telephone. The two phone lines on the train itself worked only at designated stops: one could only receive incoming calls from Nixon headquarters in the capital, and another line was "for outgoing emergency calls." There was no direct link between the two trains. They ran on separate routes, usually in different time zones, and stopped at different times. Thus neither camp could contact the other with any regularity. Fred Seaton, from Ike's staff, seldom talked to Nixon's campaign manager, Murray Chotiner, who traveled with his candidate.[6]

Nixon knew that many people were criticizing the Eisenhower/Nixon ticket for being slow to start campaigning. Some warned that without an infusion of energy, the team would lose the election. With that uneasiness at the front of his mind, he wasted little time warming to the task of sparking the Republican fires.[7]

During his first full day of campaigning, he traveled about 400 miles through the San Joaquin Valley, the central inland region of California. At a 9:00 a.m. whistle-stop in Bakersfield, he lambasted Truman for telling monumental lies: that the Democrats had produced prosperity and that Ike would destroy the economy and lead the nation into another depression. Neither the president nor Stevenson, he charged, had made "plans for a solid prosperity based on peace." He deplored the current administration's record of passing higher taxes and raising the national debt, and asserted it was causing inflation. In this agricultural heartland, the candidate also asserted that a Republican administration would be more sympathetic to farming concerns.[8]

While Nixon was honing his political pitches in California's inland empire, Peter Edson, Washington, D.C., correspondent for Newspaper Enterprise Association, was preparing to publish a story that had begun seeping in after the Republican convention regarding a nebulous fund established on Nixon's behalf. Rumors were circulating that the senator had received assistance from a hundred businessmen who had each given him up to $250 annually "to supplement" his salary. Edson had been unable to confirm these allegations. He liked Nixon personally but felt that if they were verified, he "would have serious misgivings about his ability to be President in case anything should happen to General Eisenhower."[9]

Edson had been a *Meet the Press* panelist during Nixon's interview on September 14, and after the show had asked the senator about the rumors. Nixon matter-of-factly referred him to Los Angeles attorney Dana Smith, an originator and trustee of the fund, who would explain its purpose. Edson telephoned Smith the next morning, and two days later he wrote the senator that Smith "was most co-operative, furnishing all information except the list of donors to the fund."[10]

The following day, September 18, Edson published a long, careful article explaining that unconfirmed sources alleged that the senator had been "taking a second salary on the side, contributed by certain rich Californians who might have reason to get something in return." The reporter had called Smith for an explanation of the fund, and Smith had replied that he had helped raise the money because the Nixons lived modestly and had no independent source of income. According to the attorney, fifty to a hundred "Southern California political angels" had given up to $500 each, for a total of about $17,000, to cover Nixon's "office expenses in the Senate—so he could do a good job."[11]

Leo Katcher's article in the *New York Post*, which reached the newsstands the same day, took a far different tone: SECRET RICH MEN'S TRUST FUND KEEPS NIXON IN STYLE FAR BEYOND HIS SALARY. Arthur Rowse, the author of the sole book written about the press and the fund, classified the *Post* as a blatantly partisan Democratic organ and described how the paper had "embellished" the facts with its inflammatory headline. The article itself did not present any evidence of a "millionaire's club." Indeed, if read carefully, the story, which ran almost an entire page, demonstrated that the rumors of Nixon's receiving a second salary were false. According to Dana Smith, he and other Nixon loyalists had established a fund to assist the senator in selling "the American free enterprise system" and combating the "big government" viewpoint by paying travel, secretarial service, postage, and other similar expenses.[12]

The headlines falsely claimed that Nixon revealed the existence of the "secret" fund due to imminent disclosure. In fact it had never been clandestine, and the candidate freely directed reporters to Smith for information concerning it. Katcher tried to link the donors with unethical influence in buying the senator's vote, but he could not substantiate any cause-and-effect relationship. He also stated erroneously that one contributor had given money because the Nixons needed to hire a maid and buy a larger house.[13] Talk of scandal quickly dominated the campaign news.

The story reached Ike's campaign train, "Look Ahead, Neighbor," as it sped through Nebraska. Bernard Shanley, an adviser on the train, first learned about the media explosion at 2:00 a.m. on the morning of the nineteenth, "and from then on for a time we were in a terrible turmoil, and certainly each one of us had grave concern as to what the outcome of the Nixon episode would be." Shanley immediately recognized the problem—the *Post's* allegations contradicted Eisenhower's crusade against corruption. Eisenhower's press secretary, James Hagerty, confronted by reporters, replied that the presidential nominee never commented on newspaper articles. Republican National Committee chairman and campaign coordinator Arthur Summerfield, his assistant, Robert Humphreys, and Congressman Hugh Scott from Pennsylvania immediately expressed confidence in Nixon's honesty.[14] Over the next several days, the inability to exchange information between the two campaign trains created friction among the candidates' advisers. The task of talking to each other grew into a nightmare.[15]

With Republican strategists in disarray, Democratic National Committee (DNC) chairman Stephen Mitchell insisted that the senator had supplemented his salary with private donations and therefore should resign from the GOP ticket. If he refused, Mitchell said, Ike should demand his ouster.[16]

At the White House, presidential adviser Max Lowenthal informed Truman that Nixon might "be one heart-beat from the most powerful office in the world, for the public good or for lining his own pocket." Since the senator espoused virtue, the fund "issue raised by the too limited revelations in his case go to the very foundations of our system of government. For this reason we are moved to bring them as dispassionately as we can before the American people." Truman agreed and decided to have "someone go to work on this right away."[17]

While Democrats embellished the accounts of Nixon's possible transgressions, he received a welcome testimonial from Senator Taft. RNC chairman Summerfield had telephoned Taft the day of the Katcher article, and the senator, without speaking to either candidate, dictated a telegram to RNC headquarters, asserting his confidence in his colleague. Mr. Republican ridiculed the Democrats and their newspaper allies who insisted on Nixon's removal. The vice-presidential nominee, Taft wrote, had done nothing improper.[18]

With this endorsement from the man who had almost won the nomination, Nixon stopped for an appearance in Marysville, California. As his train sounded the two-minute warning whistle that the engineer was going to pull out, a heckler shouted out: "Tell us about the $16,000, Dick." Nixon cried out: "Hold the train! Hold the train!" Replying angrily to the question, the candidate claimed that left-wingers had smeared him since he first began fighting against the communists. This money was not a slush fund; it was used only to pay expenses. Despite the false charges, Nixon promised, he would continue to fight, "and the more they smear me the more I'm going to expose the Communists and the crooks and those that defend them until they throw them all out of Washington!"[19]

While Nixon marshaled his defense, Eisenhower asked for the facts about the fund before making any decision. He was new to partisan politics but had made political judgments within his military framework. He would not express any opinion until his subordinates provided concrete answers. That afternoon, former United States senator Fred Seaton from Nebraska, an adviser on Ike's train, reached Nixon by telephone, and they talked briefly about releasing documentary evidence to absolve Nixon of wrongdoing.[20]

Eisenhower spoke in Kansas City, Missouri, that evening, where he told 14,000 spectators that, "knowing Dick Nixon as I do, I believe that when the facts are known to all of us, they will show that Dick Nixon would not compromise" his principles. The general then lashed out at Stevenson for the corruption that Democratic city bosses had encouraged and condoned. After a long day, Hagerty released a statement from Ike: "I have long admired and applauded Sen. Nixon's American faith and his determination to drive Communist sympathizers from office of public trust. There has recently been leveled against him a charge of unethical practices. I believe Dick Nixon to be an honest man. I am confident that he will place all the facts before the American public, fairly and squarely." The general would not drop his running mate from the ticket "unless there are developments." Hagerty added, "Everything is awaiting the report of the trustees."[21]

The general also drafted a letter to Nixon, which was never sent. He was "ready to consult with you on the matter whenever it is physically possible." Ike expressed confidence in his running mate's integrity and urged "immediate publication" of the facts about the use of the fund. Nixon must underline to the public that he had "never received a cent," and Ike wondered if the former chairman of the Committee on Ethics, Senator Paul Douglas, Democrat from Illinois, should be invited "to examine your complete records and to make his findings public?"[22]

That evening the Nixon and Eisenhower camps simultaneously announced that the senator was going to make a full accounting to the public. Nixon had agreed to do this because of "continued misrepresentations concerning the disbursement of a fund which was collected and expended for legitimate political purposes."[23]

James Reston of the New York Times was on the Eisenhower train and felt that Ike and his associates were worried about the repercussions of a resignation. Edward Folliard of the Washington Post interpreted the general's public statement as a Nixon endorsement. On CBS radio, Eric Sevareid concluded that Nixon was about to resign, as did Drew Pearson. Conservative radio commentators Fulton Lewis Jr., Paul Harvey, and Lowell Thomas defended the vice-presidential nominee.[24]

Nixon expected these attacks. Since the Hiss affair, many of Hiss's defenders in the media had attacked Nixon. Far more worrisome was the demand from the New York Herald Tribune for his resignation. This was a Republican newspaper whose editor, William Robinson, was a close friend of Ike. Harold Stassen further compounded the problem by wiring Nixon that he should cable the general to remove himself. Although the senator had not personally benefited from the money, Stassen wrote, the issue clouded the general's crusade to clean up the federal bureaucracy. He did not know if Ike would accept Nixon's resignation, but if he did, Governor Warren should fill the vacancy.[25]

Adding to the senator's miseries, from Des Moines, Iowa, DNC chairman Mitchell pressed the Republicans to replace Nixon: "The time has come for General Eisenhower to cast away all pretensions of requiring his supporters to have a 'sense of public morals' or to cast away his running mate." Mitchell demanded to know who had given the money and how was it spent; in addition, Nixon must release his income taxes.[26]

Stevenson, far from acting outraged, refused to condemn Nixon's fund without "all the evidence." He inquired: "Who gave the money, was it given to influence the Senator's position on public questions, and have any laws been violated?" The GOP would ascertain the facts, make them public and then act. "Condemnation without all the evidence," Stevenson proclaimed, "a practice all too familiar to us, would be wrong."[27]

This restraint, in sharp contrast to Mitchell's loud partisan cries, seemed puzzling, and George MacKinnon, who directed Nixon's research section, discovered why. The Illinois governor had maintained a far larger fund: $69,000 for food, travel and other items in 1949 and 1950, and an additional $66,000 for 1951 and 1952. In other words, Stevenson had a fund of at least $135,000 and had not publicly accounted for any of it.[28]

On Sunday, September 20, a poll of almost 100 newspapers, mostly favoring the GOP ticket, showed that two-thirds of them objected to the Nixon fund; a few called for immediate resignation; others suggested that he should go if he had violated any law; and those who supported him suggested that, given his modest income, the fund was essential. The *New York Times* reacted less righteously. Its editorial page disapproved of these funds but saw nothing illegal. Even with this concession, Republicans "must now face, and decide without loss of time, . . . whether Mr. Nixon's record in this matter has not impaired his usefulness as a candidate for the office of Vice President."[29]

When Nixon stopped that morning in Eugene, Oregon, two placards over the heads of the 2,000 in the crowd read: "Will the Veep's salary be enough, Dick?" and "No Mink Coats for Nixon—Just Cold Cash." The senator responded to the latter by boasting that Pat had and would continue to wear "a good Republican cloth coat" and did not own a mink (a reference to the corruption in the Truman administration). Charles Porter, an ADA activist who carried one of the signs, claimed it was torn to bits after the train's departure. He made a citizen's arrest of the culprit and signed a disorderly conduct complaint.[30]

That afternoon, Governor Dewey called the senator. Speaking for "the guys" close to Eisenhower—men of the eastern establishment—Dewey informed the beleaguered candidate that "a lot of his old friends" with a single exception wanted the senator to get off the ticket. From the governor's perspective, Nixon's best strategy was to appear on television and ask the American people, not the general, to decide whether he should leave the ticket. He probably would receive a million replies over the next three or four days. If the count was 60 percent to resign, he should go; if he had 90 percent favorable, he should stay. That way, Dewey reasoned, "if you stay on, it isn't blamed on Ike, and if you get off it isn't blamed on Ike."[31]

Eisenhower felt that the *Herald Tribune* and others with similar editorials had acted "on a hair-trigger." He wrote Bill Robinson: "I have had a sound regard for Dick Nixon, as a member of the United States Navy, as a strong Congressman and Senator, and as a man. I have had reason to believe in his honesty and character. As you know, I've admired him greatly." Ike refused to believe that his choice for the vice presidency was a "bad" man. But if Nixon had done "a real wrong," the general would move decisively. He realized he had to resolve this issue quickly, but "the elemental principles of fairness and justice" outweighed expediency.[32]

Some advocates were deeply disturbed over Nixon's treatment. Tom Bewley, his former law partner, wrote Nixon that the people living in Whittier were "damn mad about" the false allegations, and "the tide is turning in your favor." Many believed the senator was getting "a raw deal." Although some "heavy contributors" were anxious about their names' being released, "the small five dollar people" wanted to donate money. Bewley had talked with Nixon's parents, who wanted to issue a public statement, but the attorney advised against it. With that admonition against publicity, his mother sent a telegram to her son: "GIRLS ARE OK THIS IS TO TELL YOU WE ARE THINKING OF YOU AND KNOW EVERYTHING WILL BE FINE. LOVE ALWAYS." When he received that wire, Congressman Pat Hillings recalled, Nixon "broke down and cried."[33]

By late afternoon, hopeful signs were beginning to appear. Dana Smith released a full accounting of the $18,235 fund and listed the seventy-six California donors. One of them, J. B. Van Nuys, from a prominent pioneer family, stated that the contributors had not asked Nixon for any special favors. Republican senators Hugh Butler from Nebraska and George Aiken of Vermont acknowledged that many of their colleagues received outside assistance. Ruth Arnold, a campaign aide in the capital, cabled the train that the senator's popularity was increasing and his speeches were receiving excellent grades. She and the rest of the staff were working feverishly to arrange future stops: "EVERYONE WANTS YOU EVERYWHERE BUT WE ARE TRYING TO RESTRAIN THEIR ARDOR IN ORDER TO GIVE

YOU A FEW HOURS SLEEP EACH NIGHT." Despite this optimism, Nixon still faced reporters' endless questions about a possible resignation. He refused to respond.[34]

While the senator maintained his frantic schedule, Eisenhower continued his midwestern swing. In an off-the-record session on his train with almost a hundred reporters, he stated that Nixon had better be as "clean as a hound's tooth" in his financial dealings. If he had used the money for personal expenses, he was out. Once the questions about the money's use were answered, Ike would meet with his running mate to make a decision.[35]

Stephen Mitchell was not so circumspect. He resented Nixon's accusations that the fund charges were a "leftist smear." Stop making excuses, the DNC chair exclaimed, and resign. Watching from the White House, Truman enjoyed Nixon's travail and commented that this fund closely paralleled the 1852 presidential election, in which Franklin Pierce's running mate, Rufus King, "found himself mixed up in a lot of things." When Library of Congress researchers sought the particulars, they found no scandal attributed to King.[36]

Truman's faux pas was nowhere near as damaging as the information originating from Illinois that confirmed the existence of Stevenson's fund. Don Forsyth, a Springfield insurance executive, had been the governor's campaign manager until the presidential contest. Forsyth admitted that Stevenson had raised money by pressing state employees, but refused to divulge the amount of money in the fund or how much had been spent.[37]

As the Stevenson fund started to arouse reporters' interest, Nixon fought against those who opposed his positions, while the general waited for answers. Democrats fragmented, recognizing Stevenson's integrity was in question. The momentum toward disclosure accelerated and became a Nixon strength. Dana Smith had kept scrupulous financial records.

The Eisenhower-Nixon research staff wired Chotiner early on the morning of the twenty-first about rumors that if the general fired his running mate, Ike's supporters would desert him. Democrats welcomed this expected defection, the researchers argued, and were going to aggravate it by smearing Nixon and dragging Ike down by claiming he could not survive without Nixon's supporters. Even though some newspaper editors understood the fund's purpose and its justification, they believed the senator had exercised poor judgment, and that was grounds for disqualification. The general, moreover, had been placed in a precarious position. He could not dump Nixon and maintain his popularity. If Nixon stayed, Ike might lose; if the senator withdrew in order to further the Eisenhower crusade, Nixon could still run in the future. If he refused to leave, he would be permanently tarnished. The research staff had moved from reporting to drawing a radical conclusion: "PRESENT OMINOUS EDITORIAL SILENCE INDICATES NIXON REPEAT NIXON SHOULD MOVE FAST TO WITHDRAW PERSONALLY, UNEQUIV-OCALLY, AND IMMEDIATELY."[38]

Stassen had reached a similar conclusion, reasoning that the general could not successfully clean up the government as long as Nixon's fund hovered over him. Nixon had to proffer his resignation and let Warren replace him. If Ike consented, it would "divert any drag from here on for him and for you and above all for the essential movement for good government in Washington. In the long run it will also strengthen you and aid your career whatever may be the immediate decision or results."[39]

The Nixon camp chose George MacKinnon to contact Stassen, a fellow Minnesotan and political ally. During their conversation, they decided not to release the former governor's wire because, according to MacKinnon, Stassen was only trying to be helpful and would gladly discuss the fund issue with Nixon by telephone. He did not wish to press his views too adamantly. Even with this accommodation, MacKinnon suggested that Nixon release his income tax returns for the past decade and call on the other candidates to do the same. That might settle the fund issue. MacKinnon added optimistically that almost every prominent GOP spokesman had come out for Nixon, including John Foster Dulles, Congressman Charles Halleck of Indiana, and Senator Karl Mundt from South Dakota. Joe McCarthy encouraged voters to support his colleague and attacked Stevenson for having portrayed Hiss as a loyal American while Nixon not only saw through the charade but was responsible for this traitor's conviction.[40]

Leading Democrats sent mixed signals. The DNC chairman still aggressively pursued Nixon's removal and issued a challenge: "Here's a Holy Joe that's been talking pretty big—now let him put up some facts." From a rally in New York, James Farley, Roosevelt's postmaster general, told a partisan audience that the Stevenson-Sparkman ticket was the "strongest ticket" in his memory and that the fund fiasco guaranteed a Democratic victory. Governor Eugene Talmadge of Georgia deflated some Democratic bombast when he went on *Meet the Press* and took the position that if Nixon had spent the money for his personal use, "it was wrong, but if he took the money to pay his office and political expenses, everyone does that."[41]

Drew Pearson used his column and radio show to sow dissension within Republican ranks. He had been on the presidential nominee's train when the fund story broke and watched Eisenhower's advisers disagree over how to respond. The general, according to Pearson, recognized this discord; he looked grim and was uncertain how to proceed. Adding to the general's dilemma, Pearson asked on his radio program for Ike to investigate how Nixon could afford a home in Whittier and another one in Washington on a salary of $15,000.[42]

In this charged environment, such questions posed serious problems for the Republican campaign, and that afternoon the Eisenhower-Nixon research service suggested several options. Ike might drive the Democratic allegations off the front pages by dramatically reconvening the Republican national convention "TO PUT NIXON ON TRIAL FOR HIS POLITICAL LIFE." Vindication could be turned into a campaign asset. Alternatively, Nixon could be replaced, and Ike would win: "IN ANY EVENT, EISENHOWER MUST NOT BE THE JUDGE IN THIS CASE, BUT MUST EMERGE IN THE PRESS AS THE MAN WHO INSURES THAT THE PROCEDURES OF JUSTICE ARE SET UP AND FOLLOWED."[43]

Roscoe Drummond, writing for the *Christian Science Monitor,* did not describe desperation; instead, he portrayed a general who was still evaluating the elements of a subordinate's case to determine its merits before moving toward a court-martial. Ike would not act precipitously. He realized that the Republican hierarchy supported his running mate, and if he forced Nixon's removal, "he would run into a very formidable revolt among the top GOP organization leaders throughout the country." He needed facts to exonerate Nixon from moral and ethical violations. Until he had conclusive evidence, he would withhold judgment.[44]

While the presidential nominee waited for clarification, the Nixon train headed toward Portland, Oregon. From the moment the fund crisis broke, Pat Nixon had behaved calmly while concealing her growing frustration with the false accusations hurled against her husband; according to her husband, she never lost "her fighting spirit." During this ride, Nixon talked with Pat about resigning to ensure a Republican victory. Seven years later, he recalled that she "insisted that I should not give any weight to this type of advice on the ground that I had more political judgment and experience than those who were attempting to advise me and her intuition would be that my running from the fight would be disastrous to the success of the ticket—apart from what it would do to me personally."[45]

Shortly after 10:00 p.m. on the West Coast, at midnight in Auburn, Nebraska, Eisenhower was finally able to place a telephone call to his running mate. It was the first time the two had spoken since the scandal broke. "Hello, Dick," Ike began. "You've been taking a lot of heat the last couple of days." Nixon agreed, and the general asked if it had been "pretty rough." Nixon did not mince words: "General, sometimes you have to shit or get off the pot." The general did not want to condemn "an innocent man." At a dinner with friends, Ike said, all had agreed that Nixon should present his side on national television, where he would divulge his family's finances. Three or four days after the program, after the response to the broadcast had been digested, they could determine how best to proceed.

Nixon responded that Eisenhower needed the fund issue resolved and should not consider "personal feelings." If his remaining on the ticket "would be harmful," the senator would "get off" and "take the heat." Ike appreciated the offer, declined it, and after fifteen minutes, ended the conversation: "Well, Dick, go on the television show, and good luck."[46]

Nixon, staying on the eleventh floor at the Benson Hotel in Portland, discussed this conversation with his advisers, and came down to the second-floor press-room at 1:15 a.m. As he, Chotiner and Bill Rogers entered the room, silence fell over the assembled reporters. Looking relaxed and confident, the senator informed the audience that he and Ike had conferred, and after their talk, Nixon alone had decided to interrupt his tour and return to Los Angeles. From there, he would speak to the American public about his "entire personal financial history from the time I entered political life" in a half-hour nationwide television and radio broadcast on Tuesday or Wednesday. Then he would resume his campaign schedule. When asked to comment on the calls for his resignation, he left the room.[47]

For the Nixon staff, it was the worst of times. William Arnold, the senator's public-relations specialist in his D.C. office, recalled that the trip "was extremely rugged. Those were really dark hours." The Nixons left Portland on a chartered United Air Lines plane, arriving in Los Angeles at 2:38 p.m. A large Republican crowd stood on the airport tarmac while a loudspeaker repeated: "Fight, Dick, fight, Dick, fight." He responded by pledging "never to let you down." Press secretary James Bassett added that the senator had been under "terrific pressure and he must have complete seclusion for this, the most important speech of his life."[48]

Nixon drove to the downtown Ambassador Hotel and secluded himself in his suite to prepare for his upcoming address. In the evening, he and Bill Rogers took a break and tried to sneak out of their rooms for a swim. With a squad of reporters following his every movement, Nixon, at the pool, removed his robe and proceeded to belly flop into the water. He swam a little and then returned to his room, "incommunicado, working on his biggest speech."[49]

After releasing a statement that his running mate was going to speak to the country, Eisenhower crossed into Kentucky, ignoring the fund controversy and instead resuming his attacks on the Democrats. Despite this partisan emphasis, Republican dignitaries who boarded the train were clearly worried about the future. No consensus had crystallized.[50]

Bert Andrews, the capital bureau chief for the *New York Herald Tribune* and a principal defender of Nixon's role in the Hiss affair, was traveling with the general. Unlike many Nixon staffers, who now distrusted the general's motives, Andrews felt that Ike was sympathetic to his running mate's plight. This feeling grew stronger when he listened to another off-the-record conference conducted by the general, in which he characterized Nixon as "a model public servant" and someone whom the general liked "personally very much." Ike's campaign was rooted in his crusade for clean government, and in that spirit he wanted his running mate to give the public "the whole works."[51]

The general's train happened to be heading for Ohio, where the House Republican whip, Leslie Arends from Illinois, boarded and cautioned the nominee that having Nixon resign would be "disastrous" for four reasons: Democrats had manufactured the smear to serve their purposes; the fund was neither unethical nor illegal; the damage to the ticket had been done; and the process of choosing a replacement would reopen the political wounds inflicted at the convention.[52]

As the train raced toward Cincinnati, Eisenhower became angry when he learned that the RNC's executive committee had come out for Nixon's retention. Summerfield had acted without his permission, he said, and the RNC did not speak for him. When Senator Taft met the train late that evening, he repeated his earlier endorsement of the Californian and announced to the press: "We can only achieve progress . . . through the election of Eisenhower—and Nixon." The senator was upset. He felt that Ike should immediately have supported his running mate.[53]

Although communications for and against Nixon were inconclusive, the *New York Herald Tribune* provided a major boost by reversing its call for resignation. The accounting records, it said, demonstrated that Nixon's actions were above reproach. In the same newspaper, Democratic senator Hubert Humphrey from Minnesota wrote that while "the costs of public service are big," still his colleague was morally wrong to accept the money. From within Republican ranks, Representative Glenn Davis from Wisconsin applied a far different standard; he was "disgusted but not too surprised, at the way in which Dick Nixon had been crucified by the scandalmongers" and was chagrined by Republicans "of faint heart and little faith" who called for Nixon's removal.[54]

Stephen Mitchell, who had been the loudest in his attacks, abruptly halted his insistence on Nixon's resignation. "Nixon is now Eisenhower's and the Republican party's problem." When reminded that he had claimed to know more about the Nixon fund than what had been released to the public, Mitchell replied: "I will have no more to say about that at this time."[55]

Mitchell's silence had to do with Stevenson. Questions about the Illinois governor's fund were accelerating and becoming an embarrassment. Kent Chandler, a former Republican mayor from Lake Forest, Illinois, and an Eisenhower advocate, charged Stevenson with using a fund to raise certain state employees' salaries. A former state-purchasing agent, William McKinney, admitted that he regularly compiled lists of potential contributors for the governor and estimated that he had raised over $100,000. That evening, Stevenson refused to supply the specific amount, confirming that he had augmented some salaries but without any "question of improper influence" from the contributors.[56]

Eisenhower ignored Stevenson's response. The general had chosen his line of march regarding the Nixon fund and redirected his energies to campaign issues. He happened to be traveling through Ohio, where Taft counseled him to keep Nixon on the ticket.

Nixon understood that he was preparing for the most significant speech of his political career. The front-page banner of the Los Angeles Times editorial must have helped his morale: "WE STAND BY NIXON." While the paper's editors did not know where the Republican leadership stood on the fund issue, they were amused that the Truman administration, previously silent on its own scandals, could righteously condemn Nixon. The newspaper had reported on the senator's character, his sense of duty to the public welfare, his honorable military service, and his congressional record. He had acted unwisely, the editorial said, by accepting financial assistance that had placed a cloud over his achievements, and his adversaries were attempting to smear him. The hypocrisy was evident: "From the high mountaintop of their own accumulated record of official scandals, dishonesty, malfeasance and public betrayals, Nixon's detractors are attempting to raise the molehill of his possible political shortsightedness into a veritable Himalaya of misdoing." Some within the GOP believed these hysterics, and their public uncertainty helped the Democratic tactics. The newspaper would not sacrifice Nixon because his enemies caused havoc. It had supported his candidacy as well as his congressional objectives, "and backs him now—without any qualification or condition."[57]

Paul Hoffman, a close Eisenhower adviser, had endorsed Nixon as the general's running mate; he also happened to live in Los Angeles and agreed to supervise the fund investigation by hiring the accounting firm of Price Waterhouse & Co. to audit the trust account. He then hired the prestigious West Coast legal firm of Gibson, Dunn & Crutcher to render a legal opinion. Its conclusion: "Nixon did not obtain any financial gain" from the fund, nor did he violate any state or federal statute. An intimate adviser on Eisenhower's train, Herbert Brownell, had attended law school with Herbert Sturdy, who worked at Gibson,

Dunn & Crutcher and kept Brownell apprised concerning Nixon's case. Brownell was convinced Nixon had acted properly.[58]

More damaging to Nixonphobes were the admissions from many other senators that needed money from outside sources to pay for expenses. Democratic senator from Tennessee Estes Kefauver, who considered himself a "neighbor and friend" of the Nixon family, had just returned from Europe and docked in New York aboard the *Independence*. The winner of most Democratic primaries in 1952 and chairman of a renowned criminal investigating committee, he had known Nixon from the start of his congressional tenure and would "be very much surprised if he did anything wrong."[59]

While Nixon opponents retrenched, Edward "Ted" Rogers, the candidate's television consultant, was preparing him for the broadcast. Rogers and Chotiner had begun discussing that eventuality on Friday, and from the moment the candidate suspended his tour to fly back to Los Angeles, Rogers had worked on the program. He had managed to get NBC to accept $75,000, paid by the RNC as well as the Republican House and Senate election committees, to free up a half hour at 6:30 p.m., Pacific Time, on Tuesday.[60]

The GOP had paid for sixty-four television station hook-ups, plus several hundred radio stations, to carry the speech. The program's rating, according to Nielsen Media Research, was 48.9 percent of the television viewers, which translated into 9,100,000 homes—by far the largest audience that had ever seen or heard this type of political address up to that time.[61]

Early Tuesday morning, while the senator was working on his speech and was unavailable for a television rehearsal, Ted Rogers had found a "dead ringer" for the senator so that the camera director, John Claar, who had never seen his subject, could gauge camera settings. That afternoon, Rogers conferred with Nixon to finalize the details. He would speak from a closed studio in an empty 750-seat theater; only Pat would be with him on the set. One camera would be employed.[62]

As Nixon was leaving for the studio, Dewey phoned and insisted on talking to him. The governor recommended that Nixon use the broadcast to resign from the ticket as well as his Senate seat, and then run in a special election. Would he? Dewey demanded. Nixon, dumbfounded, replied that Dewey would have to listen to the address for an answer and slammed down the receiver.[63]

At 5:45 p.m., he left the hotel, "nervous but also fighting mad," as one journalist described him. A police escort took him to NBC's El Capitan Theatre on Vine Street, where forty or fifty well-wishers waited on the sidewalk to shout encouragement.[64]

The Nixons arrived about fifteen minutes before airtime, had their make-up applied, and walked onto the set. Until that moment, none of the television crew had seen the Nixons, and once they appeared, the technicians worked feverishly to adjust the lighting and check sound levels. Rogers and Nixon chose a library set because they wanted "the more informal visual approach." Beside him on the wall was a bookshelf. He sat on a wooden chair with a simple wooden desk on which he placed five pages of notes. Pat sat several feet away in an overstuffed chair looking directly at him; she maintained that pose throughout the telecast because she had no idea when the camera would focus on her.[65]

Five minutes before the broadcast, Nixon remembered that he "didn't think I could do it. Then I sat down put my head in my hands & prayed 'God—Thy will be done *not mine.*'" He later recalled that one of Pat's best friends, Helene Drown, a devout Catholic, contacted the superior of a convent for the sisters of the Carmelite Order in Long Beach, California, to pray for Nixon. These nuns spent their lives "in prayer and reparation," and Nixon later said "they came through for me."[66]

Knox Manning, a famous television voice, introduced Nixon, and the next shot focused on the candidate sitting at a desk looking directly at the camera. Millions of viewers watched this drama on a relatively small screen in black and white. Nixon appeared comfortable in this setting. He had given most of his speeches from notes, and he had practiced until he was satisfied. Under these melodramatic circumstances, he depended on much of what he had already said regarding the fund.[67]

First, he repeated to viewers that he never personally took "one cent" of the fund. There was nothing secret about it, and no contributor ever received preferential treatment. With those declarations, Nixon explained that he employed thirteen individuals for official business, and while Senator Sparkman had paid his wife for secretarial work for over a decade, Pat Nixon had never been on his payroll. He did not have any outside income: he had closed down his law practice and stopped accepting fees for speaking engagements. As a consequence, his family lived modestly, and to cover expenses that were not provided for in his senatorial budget, he had accepted Dana Smith's offer to establish a trust.

The *Post* article had impugned his honesty, and Nixon had suggested to Sherman Adams, who worked closely with Eisenhower, that a reputable accounting firm audit his fund and a prominent law firm render a legal opinion. Their findings bore out his contentions that he had done nothing wrong. With the accusations of wrongdoing successfully answered, the senator presented a detailed financial picture of his net worth that illustrated how "very little" material comforts the Nixons had: a house in Washington and another in Whittier; mortgages; minimal life insurance that he had borrowed against; some savings and cash. His wife did not have a mink coat.

During an interview at the convention, Pat had mentioned that she intended to buy a dog for her children. A Texas breeder listening to that broadcast had offered the Nixons a cocker spaniel and sent the puppy free of charge. Tricia had named her Checkers, and this was one gift that the Nixons were keeping.

Turning to Mitchell's opinion that if Nixon could not afford to run for office, he should not have done so, the senator adamantly disagreed. Great political leaders such as Abraham Lincoln often came from humble surroundings. Nixon emphasized that he had not inherited great wealth like Stevenson. Yet even with that fortune, the governor had kept his fund secret, and his running mate still employed his wife. Both men, Nixon urged, should disclose their financial status.

Since the Hiss case, Nixon said, opponents had continually smeared him. At that point, he rose without notes and stood by the desk. He had regularly told audiences that he and Ike were running to replace Truman and Acheson, while Stevenson was defending the administration and would not ferret out communists from the federal bureaucracy. Washington was in an abysmal state, and only Eisenhower had the resolve to clean it up. Nixon next recounted the emotional letter he had quoted at his Whittier homecoming in July, in which a nineteen-year-old mother said she was depending on the GOP ticket to bring her husband home from Korea.

Finally, the senator addressed the possibility of his resignation, telling his listeners that he was no quitter; neither was Pat. He left the decision about whether he should stay or go in the hands of the RNC and asked his audience to contact the committee to express its wishes. He reiterated: "Eisenhower . . . is a great man, and a vote for Eisenhower is a vote for what is good for America." The senator stretched his hands out at the camera in a gesture of appeal, but ended the broadcast without supplying the RNC's address.[68]

Thirty reporters watched the performance from a conference room above the theater lobby; Bassett and Chotiner had watched from the sponsor's booth, while Rogers remained in the control booth for the first part of the speech; then he went on stage, squatting down next to the camera pedestal. Toward the end, he gave Nixon his ten and five minute cues, then thirty seconds, and CUT.[69]

Nine years later, Ted Rogers reflected on those last several minutes of the telecast. Nixon, he observed, was overwhelmed with emotions that filled the studio, even affecting the workers. An "emotionally charged silence" engulfed the studio throughout the broadcast. In the last three minutes, "the tension and emotion was almost stifling—it was difficult to breathe!" At the close, the senator "was in a complete emotional daze, and the number one cameraman, tears streaming down his own face, jumped around and steadied RN. Every technician was weeping." Nixon turned, went to the back drapes, and buried his face.

When he came back to the desk, Chotiner and Bassett charged out of the booth to prevent him from collapsing.

The Nixons left the studio at about 7:20. A hundred or so people were gathered at the stage door and more were out front, chanting, "We want Dick; we want Dick." As the Nixon contingent drove away toward the hotel, a voice called from the cheering crowd: "Let me know if your children ever want another cocker spaniel." Rogers walked them to their car and hailed a cab to go home, where he "collapsed on the front yard of my house, and a couple of my wife's friends carried me into the house." He had worked without rest since Saturday morning.[70]

On the way back to the hotel, while the Nixons were stopped at a light, a large Great Dane came alongside the car. Nixon, who was riding in the front passenger seat, broke the tension by commenting: "Well, at least we got the dog vote tonight." Arriving at the hotel, he walked by the cigar counter clerk in the lobby and thought "that guy's almost as poor as I am . . . I feel sorry for him."

The public's reaction to the address did not justify his despondency. Messages and wires of support started coming into the hotel, and the two secretaries stationed in his suite answered telephones without a break until almost midnight. Messages of praise started pouring into Nixon's capital campaign office halfway through the broadcast.[71]

Eisenhower was on his train that day heading toward Cleveland. Bert Andrews, who was traveling on the train, considered Ike fair minded and did not detect any negativity toward Nixon. In addition, the general had already passed through Senator Taft's hometown of Cincinnati, and Senator Knowland, who had been in Hawaii, had returned to the United States and boarded Ike's train to serve as a liaison between the two candidates. Although this caused some to speculate that Knowland might replace Nixon as the general's running mate, Knowland quickly surmised that Ike had become sympathetic toward Nixon once the fund had become clearly explained to him. Another Republican senator on board, Frank Carlson from Kansas, backed Nixon and believed that Eisenhower had decided to retain him even before his address.[72]

Eisenhower kept his own counsel and paid more attention to keeping his schedule: he was to address 15,000 Republicans at a rally in Cleveland's Public Hall at 9:30 p.m. He decided to delay that appearance; and he, Mamie, and a dozen advisers went to watch the broadcast from the manager's office. The general and wife sat alone on a couch in front of the television set, where Ike intently concentrated on the address and took seven pages of notes on a lined legal pad; he wrote with a pencil in large, bold strokes, sometimes underlining for emphasis. When the speech ended, the general turned to Summerfield and said, "You certainly got your money's worth." Mamie was in tears.[73]

Lucius Clay initially believed "it was so corny that it would be an immediate flop. I went downstairs to get a newspaper. I found the elevator man was crying and the doorman was crying, and I knew then that I was wrong."[74]

Downstairs in the auditorium, the GOP faithful had been arriving since the doors were opened at 6:30. Band and organ music filled the hall, and Congressman George Bender from Cleveland officially called the meeting to order at 7:30. Over the next two hours a parade of political hopefuls went to the rostrum, and after Senator Taft gave a ringing appeal for a November victory, the large crowd sat silent, listening to Nixon's radio broadcast piped over the loudspeaker. A reporter from the *Minneapolis Star* captured the mood: "This city's huge public hall was an eerie scene Tuesday night when thousands sat in almost hypnotic silence under the spell of a voice that was pleading political honesty."[75]

The general went to the rostrum a half hour after Nixon's defense, his face grim and hard, gripping the reading stand so tightly with both hands that his knuckles turned white. Instead of using his prepared text on inflation, he spoke from his handwritten notes: "I have been a warrior and I like courage," he said. "Do I myself believe this man is the kind of man America would like to have for its Vice President?" The audience provided a resounding affirmation. Eisenhower reminded his listeners that during World War II, an intimate friend, General George Patton, had made a mistake by slapping a soldier, and after a reprimand went forward. Ike recalled making his own difficult decisions: "I have seen many men in tough situations. I have never seen any come through in better fashion than Sen. Nixon did tonight. . . . I happen to be one of those people who, when I get in a fight, would rather have a courageous and honest man by my side than a whole boxcar full of pussy-footers."

Eisenhower, who had raised the issue of corruption throughout the campaign, recalled a case where an internal revenue collector had "sold his birthright for a dirty mess of dollars. Between that and whatever error of judgment may have been committed by Sen. Nixon, there is a gulf as wide as the Pacific." The general promised to clean up the government and to decide on the matter of Nixon's retention in the best interests of the United States. As he finished, Senator Taft flashed a broad smile.[76]

As he was going to the platform, Ike handwrote a telegram for Hagerty to rewrite while the general was speaking. The press secretary scribbled his changes while seated on the stage, and at the conclusion of the performance, Eisenhower shared the draft with his audience: "YOUR PRESENTATION WAS MAGNIFICENT.

WHILE TECHNICALLY NO DECISION RESTS WITH ME, YET YOU AND I KNOW THAT THE REALITIES OF THE SITUATION WILL REQUIRE A PERSONAL PRONOUNCEMENT WHICH SO FAR AS THE PUBLIC IS CONCERNED WILL BE CONSIDERED DECISIVE." Calling upon Nixon to fly to meet him the next day in Wheeling, West Virginia, Eisenhower highlighted his own reaction to the speech: "I CANNOT CLOSE THIS TELEGRAM WITHOUT SAYING THAT WHATEVER PERSONAL ADMIRATION AND AFFEC-TION I HAVE FOR YOU—AND THEY ARE VERY GREAT—ARE UNDIMINISHED." The response from the audience, according to one correspondent observing that elec-trically charged scene, "was deafening."[77]

Besides sending this telegram, Eisenhower further clarified his thoughts that evening in a letter to General Benjamin Caffey, concluding that once "all the facts were presented, the decision was relatively easy. There is nothing like ad-versity to bring out the best in a real man—and Nixon came through with flying colors." Ike and his brother Edgar spoke late that night, and the next day, Edgar telegraphed him: "IF YOU DON'T UNQUALIFIEDLY ENDORSE NIXON AFTER THAT TALK LAST NIGHT, YOU MIGHT AS WELL FOLD YOUR TENT AND FADE AWAY."[78]

Out West, Nixon was receiving kudos for his effort. Western Union's lines to Los Angeles were so jammed that Eisenhower's telegram did not get through. Nixon learned about it via press reports, and without the full context of the gen-eral's remarks, he applied the most pessimistic interpretation. He and his party had hoped for Eisenhower's unconditional endorsement. When it did not come, they were confounded and depressed. What did Nixon need to do to win Ike's trust, and why should he travel across the United States without assurances that the general would embrace him when he arrived?

Don Mozley, a columnist traveling with Nixon, noted the candidate's and his staff's feelings: "the mood changed to bewilderment and anger, as a result of what was considered a rather poorly-timed suggestion that the tour be interrupted again, for a top level meeting." Ike's request for a meeting took "the edge off the senator's dramatic appeal for public understanding of his expense fund." Nixon could meet with Eisenhower any time. He told Eisenhower's team that until firm arrangements were detailed, he was resuming his schedule. The next day Nixon would head for Missoula, Montana, and would complete his tour on Septem-ber 27. Then he would be "delighted" to confer with his running mate.[79]

While the nation was riveted on the Nixon saga, details about Stevenson's fund were emerging haltingly because the governor refused to divulge the names of the state officials whose salaries he had augmented. In fact, during Nixon's broad-cast, Stevenson was speaking in Baltimore about his own fund. His reticence in the face of increasing pressure for disclosure was causing heightened anxiety within the Democratic Party.[80]

Stevenson's refusal to provide information brought forth more accusations from Illinois Republicans. C. Wayland Brooks, an attorney and Illinois RNC committeeman, called on the governor to resign and demanded a congressional inquiry regarding the contributors, the size of their donations, and how the money was allocated. As a result of Brooks' pressure, reporters asked Mitchell, given his insistence on Nixon's ouster, if would he be consistent and call for Stevenson's removal. The DNC chairman replied, "I think that's ridiculous."[81]

While Democrats rejected any comparison between the Stevenson and Nixon funds, the audience for Nixon's speech was so moved that viewers began the largest outpouring of written responses to a speech in American political history. That evening, however, neither Nixon nor his staff comprehended the full impact of his speech; they were far more concerned with its effect on one man.

While Mitchell was trying to extricate himself from a predicament of his own making, millions of letters, cards, wires, phone calls and petitions swamped RNC headquarters in the capital. By 9:00 the next morning, Summerfield had learned that 25,000 telegrams had reached his office. Within a week, two to three million Americans had communicated with RNC headquarters. The ratio ran approximately 350 to 1 in Nixon's favor, and the staff was still sorting the letters at the end of February 1953.[82]

While the overwhelming majority expressed approval, a few of those who wrote in called for Nixon's removal because the fund had tarnished him. Some opposed his linkage to ultraconservative GOP senators like McCarthy and William Jenner of Ohio; a correspondent named Kathryn Weis simply distrusted him. If he remained on the ticket, she would vote Democratic.[83]

These negative sentiments were minuscule compared to the sheer mass of the positive responses. Dana Smith was receiving telegrams that were running fifty to one in favor of the senator and had received over $2,000 for the campaign. Norris Poulson, a friend and House colleague from Los Angeles, wired the RNC: "I AM FOR NIXON ONE THOUSAND PERCENT. LET'S NOT TURN YELLOW." Stassen, who had twice urged him to resign, sent his congratulations "ON A SUPERB PRESENTATION." Congressman Gerald Ford from Michigan and his wife Betty, old friends, "were thrilled" with the speech and felt that the senator had drawn a tremendous outpouring of approval in their district.[84]

Over 27,000 letters and at least as many postcards and telegrams came from California. John "Jack" Irwin, who had worked on Nixon's senatorial staff and was currently practicing law, could not reach the telegraph company on Tuesday night but cabled the RNC the next morning to say that the speech was "one of the most moving that I have ever witnessed." Within minutes after Nixon closed, several clients telephoned Irwin in tears asking where they should send telegrams. In Beverly Hills, doctors had confined Harry Warner, president of Warner Bros Pictures, to his bed for an illness and warned him not to read or listen to anything. He disobeyed and watched the speech. He wrote the next morning that he had been in the film industry for half a century and had never "seen in any motion picture the drama that even approached that which I witnessed last night. Here was a man who bared his soul for the American public to see!" Warner told the RNC that he would gladly place his family's lives in the hands of the GOP ticket, adding, "the Lord took my only son from me—and last night I wished that Richard Nixon were my son."[85]

Beverly Lindy, assistant archivist at the Richard Nixon Library & Birthplace from 1995 to 2003, spent more than two years sorting the fund communications and, at this writing, two years cataloguing a portion of the responses. She reported that the largest number of responses came from California and the East, especially New York and New Jersey, and the Midwest; fewer came from the farming states. Businessmen typed, while most families handwrote; and a large military segment expressed their sentiments. In describing the speech, the vast majority used words like "honesty," "integrity," "courage," and "humility." Others wrote that they were praying for the senator; many were disappointed with Ike and hoped that he would remove liberal advisers like Dewey and Sherman Adams; many opposed Hiss and domestic subversion, while they supported Taft, General Douglas MacArthur, and Joe McCarthy. Some suggested that the ticket be reversed, with Nixon heading it and Eisenhower in the second spot.[86]

Stevenson received approximately a hundred letters and telegrams. Steven Cottege, from Upper Darby, Pennsylvania, thought Ike and Nixon were "putting on [an act] or, crying on others shoulder is revolting." Gloria Shelton in Brooklyn, New York, viewed the speech as a "brazen performance" and called Nixon "a menace as deadly as Hitler or the Communism he professes to fight." Peggy Schwartz, a "good Democrat" from Miami, Florida, wept sarcastically for Checkers, while others wondered: "Well, just what did he do with the money and is he going to keep it up, he did not even admit he made an error in accepting it." Not all the correspondence came from Democrats. The Dopps, living in Oakland, California, wired chairman Mitchell to demand "THE MORAL STRENGTH TO APOLOGIZE FOR WHAT YOU PERSONALLY HAVE DONE TO NIXON."[87]

Ike and his advisers were exhausted from the previous night's events in Cleveland. They left the hall and hailed a cab to take them to their train, which would leave at 3:00 a.m. As they stood outside the taxi, the driver proclaimed: "I'm for Nixon; get in."[88]

As for the senator, he flew from Los Angeles near midnight with 800 well-wishers seeing him off. He initially thought that he had cleared the fund obstacle, but as unconfirmed reports filtered back to him, his enthusiasm faded. The general did not seem to have definitively resolved the issue. Nixon considered submitting his resignation. Eisenhower's failure to endorse Nixon so enraged Chotiner that he refused to accept a call from Fred Seaton, who was traveling with the general: "Let the bastards wait for us this time." Nixon wearily boarded the plane and remarked from his seat "It was kind of tough, today." The Nixon party did not touch down in Missoula, Montana, until 3:00 a.m. Once again, he and his staff, with minimal sleep, tried to relax on the flight before resuming the campaign schedule. They were upset that Ike had made a public announcement for a rendezvous in Wheeling; a private telephone call to discuss the matter would have been preferable.[89]

Leading Republicans championed Nixon. At Eau Claire, Wisconsin, Joe McCarthy said: "It was a great speech and I believe it clearly vindicates Dick Nixon in the eyes of the nation." Bill Knowland added: "I have full confidence in the integrity of my colleague, Dick Nixon." Senator Mundt joined in the chorus. Dewey, who had twice urged Nixon to resign, called the address "a superb statement by a man of shining integrity and great purpose in the service of his country."[90]

Former president Herbert Hoover, who had been vacationing in the western mountains, supplied his own public accolade: "From intimate acquaintance with Senator Nixon since before he entered public life, I can say that if everyone in the city of Washington possessed the high level of courage, probity and patriotism of Senator Nixon this would be a far better nation." Hoover argued that the Democratic attacks had backfired: "The Republican party will be firmer in the heart and confidence of the American people." The senator gratefully replied through Western Union: "DEAR CHIEF NONE OF THE THOUSANDS OF MESSAGES I RECEIVED MEANT AS MUCH TO ME AS YOURS."[91]

More than 5,000 people flooded the streets of Missoula to hear Nixon speak from the top of a decorated truck in front of the Florence Hotel. He directed his remarks to young people: "Some of you—especially the kids—may wonder if it's worth going into politics after what I've been through in the last few days. Don't hesitate. Go into politics and help to clean it up." The crowd cheered, and one woman shouted that she wished she had $25,000 to donate to his campaign. Dick and Pat shook hands and then interrupted the tour for an unscheduled flight to meet with the general, to determine Nixon's fate.[92]

The flight to Wheeling had not been confirmed until Eisenhower spoke to Summerfield from a phone booth at a 9:00 a.m. whistle stop in Portsmouth, Ohio, where the general was swamped with "I like Dick" telegrams. After their conversation, the RNC chairman was "certain" that the senator would remain on the ticket. By the time Ike reached Kenova, West Virginia, an hour and a half later, a large crowd expressed its support for his running mate, and the general responded: "Matter of fact, I like him, too."[93]

As for Nixon, he left Montana in his chartered DC-6 at 11:00 a.m. The plane stopped in Denver to refuel and get a new crew. Upon landing, without any public notice, he found several hundred supporters awaiting him; in addition, his secretaries took a large amount of correspondence relating to his fund speech onto the plane. Nixon walked out to a loading ramp to thank his followers and declared: "We have not begun to fight."[94]

That bold proclamation was for public consumption. In fact, Nixon's entourage was living in a state of limbo. *San Francisco Examiner* reporter Clint Mosher, who accompanied the candidate, remarked: "Nixon was emotionally taut as a violin string." He did not know what to expect when he landed. Was he as clean as a hound's tooth?[95]

Their DC-6 was the largest plane ever to land at Stifel Field, Wheeling's mountaintop airport. Making the approach even more difficult was the cold weather. The pilot, as reporter Don Mozley described it, "braked exceptionally hard and pulled up near the small terminal," touching down forty-five minutes behind schedule on a chilly, starlit night at 9:57 p.m.[96]

Outside, 2,500 chanted: "We want Nixon." The senator looked out his window and was astonished to see Eisenhower, who had come directly from his train to the plane. Nixon, Mosher wrote, "stood pale and ramrod straight in the plane aisle." The door suddenly opened, and Ike bounced in with his piercing blue eyes and famous smile. Nixon said that Ike did not have to come to the plane. The general rushed forward and exclaimed: "Why Dick—you're my boy!" Nixon never uttered a word, and with his free hand, he sat down, turned to the window and cried. The general, too, had tears in his eyes and broke the tension by asking Nixon to ride with him. Pat and Mamie left the airport in another car. Pat barely was able to utter: "Certainly." Her husband took out a clean handkerchief, dried his eyes, regained his composure, and stepped out of the plane with Ike.[97]

Ike and Nixon sat in the back seat of a large Chrysler sedan on the way to Wheeling Island Stadium, with Sherman Adams in the front passenger seat. Adams heard the general concede, "You've had a hard time, young fellow. It was a hard thing for you to go through and I want you to know I understood that." Nixon's place on the ticket was secure.[98]

When the two principals arrived, the 13,000-seat high school football stadium was about half filled with shivering people who had waited nearly four hours for them to appear. Mamie and Pat sat next to each other on the platform, sharing Mamie's white fur coat for warmth while they watched their husbands. Eisenhower spoke first, just after 11:00 p.m. He pronounced his junior partner vindicated and then read Summerfield's telegram saying that he had reached 107 of the 138 RNC members and all had voted to keep Nixon on the ticket. Then Ike told the crowd that he had received a telegram from Hannah Nixon, and read it aloud: she trusted that "THE ABSOLUTE TRUTH MAY COME OUT CONCERNING THIS ATTACK ON RICHARD, AND WHEN IT DOES I AM SURE YOU WILL BE GUIDED RIGHT IN YOUR DECISION TO PLACE IMPLICIT FAITH IN HIS INTEGRITY AND HONESTY."[99]

Eisenhower turned the microphone over to Nixon, who told the audience that Ike had advised: "Take my case to the people, tell the truth, and then we will decide what will be done." He had followed that advice, he said, and had demonstrated that he was "as clean as a hound's tooth." Nixon now demanded that Stevenson at last disclose the nature of his own fund. If the governor continued to equivocate, it would be an admission that he had something to hide, and the voters would reject him in November. Exhausted and drained, Nixon turned to his friend and Senate colleague Bill Knowland, who was standing nearby, buried his face on Knowland's shoulder and wept.[100]

Don Mozley had witnessed the Ike-Nixon exchange on the plane. When he arrived at the stadium, CBS reporter Howard K. Smith asked if he had "a *hint* of what will happen tonight." Mozley replied that Nixon would stay. Eric Sevareid, the CBS national commentator, listened to the conversation as he was writing up his report of Nixon's resignation from the ticket. According to Mozley, "The sound of a script being torn to shreds could be heard for miles." While the local CBS affiliate was waiting for Ike's remarks, Mozley took the microphone and started telling the story of the dramatic airport meeting. CBS headquarters in New York was monitoring the local station, and when they heard Mozley relate Ike's assurance: "You're my boy!" CBS New York put him on its national network. His commentary set the tone for the evening news.[101]

Chairman Summerfield telegraphed Nixon that Ike and the RNC officially wanted him to remain on the ticket. He told the press, "The matter is a closed book and Sen. Nixon has been completely vindicated."[102]

But it was not a closed book for Nixon. In his memoir *Six Crises*, he recalled the events in minute detail over fifty-six pages. He never forgot that the general had not immediately come to his defense, and never understood why Ike had not proclaimed his absolution after the broadcast. "It left a deep scar," he wrote, "which was never to heal completely."[103]

To Nixon, this episode would be the fund crisis, where he survived false accusations to remain on the national ticket. To his adversaries, this event would become the Checkers Speech, where the candidate gave a maudlin account that illustrated his phoniness.

Eisenhower had a far different perspective. He routinely stated that he was in no hurry to make the wrong decision. As he told one reporter, "nobody in war or anywhere else ever made a good decision if he was frightened to death. You have to look facts in the face, but you have to have the stamina to do it without just looking hysterical."[104] His own memoirs deal with the episode in just five pages: "The underdog had come off the floor to win a fight; his popularity was more firmly based than ever." Eisenhower viewed the fund crisis not as a test of character or loyalty but as an obstacle on the political battlefield. As the events unfolded, he constantly reiterated his confidence in Nixon and added that he would not make any decision until he had assembled the necessary facts. That had been his approach in the military, and he followed it in this instance. When he declared that Nixon was his boy, that resolved any doubt, and he went on with his campaign.[105]

3

To Victory

The fund episode ended without damaging Eisenhower's campaign. During a whistle-stop at Frederick, Maryland, on September 25, he told a cheering crowd that the attack on Nixon was un-American; as far as Ike was concerned, Nixon was "my partner right down to the end and on thru." Traveling on to Silver Springs, Eisenhower mentioned that telegrams praising Dick were still flooding into the RNC's headquarters. By the end of the month, Ike's staff had composed a form letter praising his running mate and sharing his "deep faith" in the senator. From the general's perspective, Nixon was "a courageous, four-square, young American, with years of service ahead for his country. My personal confidence in him was never shaken; and his manly and full statement to the American people, answering the unfair attacks on his integrity, more than justified that confidence."[1]

In a lengthy letter to Nixon on October 1, the general passionately outlined his feelings. He confided that he "did not enter this contest from any impulse of personal ambition," and during the exhausting campaign, he was trying "to make clear to the American people what is on my mind and heart." Under no circumstances, Ike stated, would he "violate my own basic convictions and my own conscience."

He was running because he believed the Democrats would continue, "perhaps beyond redemption, on the path toward Socialism." According to the general, "No person, not even the President, has the right to try to place himself above the Constitution." He expected to act forcefully on the domestic front by cleaning up the mess in the nation's capital and also promised the "decentralization and diffusion of powers." He rejected the idea of "inherent powers" like federal control of state tidelands, opposed unnecessary expenditures, and would halt them by reducing the deficit and reducing inflationary pressure. After those had been eliminated, he wished to lower taxes and keep social security viable by having the United States "restore the sound dollar."

On the subject of foreign affairs, he had been a military officer for more than four decades, and no one, during his time in uniform, had ever asked him for diplomatic advice. The one time he volunteered it, his counsel had been ignored. Despite that dismissal, the general held strong internationalist views. He intended to develop the Atlantic coalition and would economically aid Western Europe to prevent a communist takeover. The United Nations, in his view, represented "possibly the only hope—for peace." He violently disapproved of many controversial decisions at the Teheran, Yalta, and Potsdam conferences because the United States had no "right to barter away the lives and liberties of other people into the hands of ruthless Communist tyranny." Even with those positions, he would not consider severing diplomatic relations with the Soviet Union until he had carefully studied that proposal. As for the Korean conflict, he had no magical cure to end the fighting; however, if he were directing the military operations, his first priority would be to "organize manpower." The Soviets, he reasoned, had supplied the weapons and the Red Chinese the troops for the North Koreans; from United Nations forces, supporting South Korea, the United States provided most of the weapons and 90 percent of the soldiers. This was unacceptable. The United States had to help the South Koreans and other Asiatic non-Communist nations to defend themselves, and thereby minimize or end "the drain on Western manpower."

Eisenhower also recognized his role as the national GOP leader and some of the party's Byzantine intricacies. "I have labored hard and earnestly to eliminate divisions in the Republican party and to state and to re-state a firm middle of the road policy at home, and an intelligent, forward-looking program in the foreign field." Under current conditions, he could not do much more; his energy was directed at winning the presidency.

Sometimes political linkage, Eisenhower continued, spilled over from his military career. He highlighted his relationship to General George Marshall and acknowledged that many conservative Republicans had sharply criticized Marshall for his supposed diplomatic blunders in the Far East. Ike had worked closely with Marshall during the Second World War and "always defended General Marshall's patriotism and sense of duty." That glowing endorsement had a caveat because Ike, too, had serious questions about errors of judgment that Marshall had made during the early stages of the Cold War.[2]

Just after writing of his concerns about Marshall's postwar decisions, Ike journeyed to Wisconsin, where Senator McCarthy was running for reelection. The general found the senator repugnant but agreed with much of his anticommunist stance. As for General Marshall, in the early summer of 1951, McCarthy had accused him of participating in "a conspiracy so immense and an infamy so black as to dwarf any previous such venture in the history of man." Ike was in a quandary: he deplored McCarthy's wild statements, even though he questioned some of Marshall's actions.

As Ike prepared to speak in Wisconsin, one of the general's speechwriters, John Emmet Hughes, inserted a paragraph that affirmed his belief in Marshall's loyalty and implicitly rejected McCarthy's accusations against Marshall. Others on Ike's staff, and the Wisconsin Republican party officials, vehemently objected to this paragraph. Nothing positive could result from embarrassing McCarthy and damaging GOP prospects in the state. Arriving in Milwaukee on the evening of October 3, the general presented a highly partisan attack on the Democratic administration's laxness in regard to domestic subversion, while excluding any reference to Marshall. McCarthy practically forced Ike to shake hands after the address, leaving the impression that the general and senator had reconciled.

Reporters had read the original Marshall passage and noted its exclusion. In their columns, many wrote that Ike had succumbed to McCarthy's demands by striking the reference to Marshall. As soon as that story appeared, Democrats pounced on the Republican nominee for surrendering to the GOP's right wing. Some journalists were deeply troubled and wondered if the general had moved to the right, thereby damaging his appeal to moderates.[3]

Ike explained his actions in a handwritten letter to Stassen two days after the speech. The general had stricken the Marshall reference because his staff opposed it, as did Wisconsin governor Walter Kohler Jr., who, according to Ike, "was so determined in his argument for revision—that I felt it difficult to campaign through his state if I completely disregarded his advice." Besides, the general argued, the search for communist infiltrators and their methods had been preserved; McCarthy, Ike believed, had "never made the flat allegation that General Marshall was traitorous by design."[4]

At the end of September, Truman boarded a train to campaign for Democrats, angry that Eisenhower was attacking his administration's policies. Truman held Marshall in the highest esteem and loyally defended him while criticizing the Republican presidential candidate for abandoning his mentor. He acted independently and staged his appearances in front of his loyalists, who urged him to give the Republican hell.

Stevenson spoke eloquently in terms of lofty goals and a brighter tomorrow. He was stuck with the president's partisan statements as well as his defense of his record. The governor knew that voters were tired of the Korean conflict and angry over the corruption in the federal bureaucracy, yet Stevenson had to defer to the president even though many Americans no longer saw him as a credible leader.[5]

The resolution of the fund crisis instantly changed Nixon from the politician who exposed Hiss to a candidate with his own constituency. He resumed his campaign schedule by boarding his plane on the evening of September 25, for Salt Lake City. Don Mozley noted that the senator showed "obvious relief" after his discussions with the general. Eagerly resuming his battle against the Democrats, Nixon described Stevenson as "the Chlorophyll candidate" who was "trying to cover up the odor from Washington."[6] From Utah, he flew to Amarillo, Texas, and spoke to an enthusiastic audience about the wide gulf separating current federal policies from those of the Lone Star State. Promising to support Texas's states' rights advocacy, especially its tidelands claim to offshore oil, he drew loud applause from his audience. As for the Illinois governor, Nixon continued to call him "Sidesaddle Adlai," whose "feet hang well to the left."[7]

Nixon instinctively recognized the discord between the president and his party's nominee. As the GOP vice-presidential candidate, he answered Truman's assaults while Stevenson had to defend the White House, respond to Nixon, and somehow draw Ike into a national debate. The governor never could accomplish the latter. Nixon made Stevenson's task even more challenging by focusing on Truman as the issue. In Virginia on October 1, for example, he denounced the president's failure in Asia. If the administration had prevented the communists from conquering Mainland China, the Korean War would not have broken out. Rather than accept responsibility for the massive failure, Truman, Nixon argued, was trying to blame Ike for the Soviet domination of Eastern Europe due to errors that the general had allegedly made at the end of the Second World War. For this slur on Ike, the vice-presidential nominee demanded a retraction from the president that never came; so Nixon called upon Stevenson, who dismissed any thought of repudiating Truman's assertions.[8]

Truman responded with the same level of partisanship during a speech in San Francisco. Ike, he charged, had betrayed his liberal backers by refusing to defend Marshall against McCarthy. Speaking of how the Republican convention had accepted Nixon instead of Warren, Truman said that the delegates had "turned away from your liberal Governor, and chose another Californian who is not worthy to lace his shoes."[9]

Nixon boarded his train for a whistle-stop tour that traveled to the Northeast and crossed into the Midwest. At this stage of the campaign, former secretary of state Acheson gave a speech staunchly defending the administration's foreign policies, providing ammunition for a new Nixon salvo. Acheson, by Nixon's logic, had lost much of the Far East by allowing the communists to conquer China and by failing to anticipate the Korean conflict. Nixon preferred to have a "khaki-clad President than one clothed in State Department pinks." Greeting his mother in Harrisburg, Pennsylvania, he went further: "Stevenson himself hasn't even backbone training, for he is a graduate of Dean Acheson's spineless school of diplomacy which cost the free world 600,000,000 former allies in the past seven years of Trumanism."[10]

To Nixon, Truman represented the epitome of crass partisanship. On a swing through Vermont, Nixon pronounced: "no one stooped as low as Truman in his attack on Eisenhower." Nixon's emphasis on Truman and Acheson led him to declare that Stevenson had "been dropped from second to third place on the national ticket." When the senator spoke in Wilkes-Barre, Pennsylvania, he referred to "Truman-Acheson-Stevenson and Company." Even more cutting, he labeled the Illinois governor "the body-and-soul captive of the Truman-Acheson clique." The Democratic presidential nominee was the "waltzing-mouse candidate" for "the Truman-Acheson stumblebum program" that caused the Korean conflict.[11]

At a major address in Pittsburgh on October 8, Nixon spoke at the Syria Mosque, where he assured his listeners that Ike was already a world leader while Stevenson had no international experience. "Nothing," Nixon stressed, "would please the Kremlin more than to have the people of this country choose a second-rate President." He called upon voters to disappoint the Soviet tyrants.[12]

Large enthusiastic audiences that came out to hear the senator did not persuade the *New York Post* to moderate its anti-Nixon coverage. To try to convince readers how ineffectual Nixon was, reporter Paul Sann accompanied Eisenhower on his swing through California, providing commentary on the discord within the GOP. Sann stated that the general was trying to win the state's "precious but doubtful 32 electoral votes." In Sacramento, Ike described his running mate as "a man who has shown himself to be of great courage and well equipped for the high office for which the Republican Party has named him as their candidate." During the next six stops, the general did not refer to Nixon, but in San Francisco, he called the senator "a young man whose courage and forthrightness . . . have stirred admiration and approbation all over our country." The reporter speculated that Ike had not discussed Nixon in greater detail because Warren was still miffed that Nixon had thwarted his favorite-son candidacy at the 1952 convention.[13]

The RNC ignored this criticism, recognizing Nixon's value as a public speaker. It purchased a half hour on CBS for approximately $75,000 on the evening of October 13 for him to address a national audience. As in the fund speech, he refused any rehearsal time and spoke from notes; Bill Rogers assisted in the preparation of the presentation, and Ted Rogers handled the lighting and makeup. Unlike the fund address, the senator sat alone, without Pat, in an empty studio, with a stenographer who supplied a transcription while reporters and photographers watched on a television monitor in a building a mile away.[14]

For the first time during the campaign, Nixon carried the threat of domestic subversion to Stevenson, charging that the governor had not taken communist infiltration in the United States seriously, while Eisenhower comprehended the peril and would respond with the necessary measures to prevent any further spread. "The failure to deal effectively with the Communist threat at home and abroad," Nixon claimed, "is the greatest issue of this campaign." The governor had minimized or even dismissed the Red menace, and this disqualified him from the presidency. He had demonstrated this insensitivity by not recognizing the significance of communist domestic penetration; his deposition as a good-character reference for Hiss at Hiss's first perjury trial proved that pivotal point. Nixon pointed out, just as he had done in his 1950 senatorial campaign against Helen Gahagan Douglas, that he did not question Stevenson's loyalty but had grave doubts about his judgment. The governor had voluntarily testified to Hiss's good character, reaffirming Hiss's assertions that he was not a communist, or far worse, a Soviet spy. Stevenson had placed the prestige of his gubernatorial office behind his deposition, and even after Hiss was found guilty, he never retracted his testimony.[15]

Eisenhower and his running mate discussed Hiss when they met in New York City on October 19. By this time, some of Truman's most caustic barbs had deeply wounded the general. While Ike refused to respond in kind, he and his advisers encouraged Nixon's attacks on the president. One example came from Abbott Washburn, who worked for the Ike campaign in New York City; he wrote Chotiner, informing him that a task force of attorneys had been assembled over the last several weeks to focus on Fair Deal corruption: "This material is all drawn from Congressional hearings and is libel free." Truman had also described John Williams, Republican from Delaware, as a "good-for-nothing Senator." Washburn hoped that "H.S.T. should be nailed on this one, and Dick is the logical one to do it."[16]

Truman, meanwhile remained on the offensive, on October 15 calling Eisenhower a proponent of a "master race theory" because he had endorsed Senator Pat McCarran for reelection. McCarran was an author of legislation passed in 1952 that imposed restrictions on immigration. More than two-thirds of Congress, Nixon included, had overridden Truman's veto. The senator admitted that the law had flaws but argued that it had codified various immigration measures and removed discrimination against Asian applicants.[17]

That evening, the vice-presidential nominee spoke at Muskegon, where he charged Truman with permitting dozens of United States citizens of dubious loyalty to hold key United Nations posts. During a grand jury investigation of eleven of these individuals, Nixon proclaimed, many had refused to state whether they belonged to any communist organizations. Nine of the eleven, former federal employees, had appeared before the Senate internal security committee, where three of them refused to say if they were or were not guilty of espionage. All except one received salaries in the $10,000 range—significant compensation, Nixon emphasized, for potentially disloyal Americans. He understood that dedicated Reds worked at the UN, but American communists made "a mockery" of that body, whose stated goal was to seek international peace.[18]

Continuing through the Midwest, Nixon spent a day in Indiana where he supported GOP candidates, including incumbent conservative Senator William Jenner. As liberal Democrats condemned him for endorsing one of their enemies, Nixon fought back by describing "Adlai the Appeaser—the man whose slavish devotion to the dubious foreign policy of Truman and Acheson could bring on World War III." These two administration principals had failed, but an Eisenhower government would triumph. Nixon's evaluation of Stevenson was stinging: "A second-rate Presidential candidate, loaded down with a political grab bag of failures, cannot succeed." If this was insufficient to spark hatred from Democrats, the senator finished his exhausting tour by describing the Democratic presidential nominee as carrying "a Ph.D. from Dean Acheson's cowardly college of Communist containment."[19]

Stevenson believed that Nixon's utterances did not originate with him. Eisenhower and his staff supplied the impetus. If this was true, it was also true that Stevenson himself was largely echoing and amplifying Truman's charges. In Milwaukee in early October, for instance, the governor declared that his opponent lacked "backbone" for accepting endorsements from Jenner and McCarthy while refusing to defend General Marshall in front of them.[20]

By the middle of the month, the Democratic nominee had commenced his second trip to the West, where he decided not only to answer Nixon and McCarthy's assertions that he had been "soft" on communism but also to belittle them. In San Francisco, he adapted the mocking chant FDR had used in 1940 against three Republican congressmen who opposed his policies "[Joseph] Martin, [Bruce] Bartin and [Hamilton] Fish," changing it to "Nixon and Dirksen and Taft." He also noted that Ike was trying to ride two political horses: Nixon and Warren. Stevenson praised the latter, but when he mentioned the former, the audience booed. Several days later, he discovered that Nixon had proposed an inquiry of General Marshall: "As for Nixon, we would take his enthusiasm for investigation and disclosure more seriously if he would do a more complete job on himself."[21]

Stevenson was just getting started. Beginning his last campaign sweep two weeks before the voting, he seemed invigorated, and his advisers thought that their candidate was closing on Ike. At this propitious moment, on October 23, Stevenson addressed an audience at Cleveland Arena to answer the charges brought against him in the Hiss matter. First, he accused Eisenhower of directing this ignoble attack, for without his explicit consent, the GOP would not slander him or General Marshall, the man most responsible for Ike's ascendancy in the military. Next, Stevenson provided a detailed description of his association with Hiss, asserting that lawyers had a duty "to give testimony in a court of law and to give it honestly and willingly," and he had followed those principles. Even though John Foster Dulles and Eisenhower had served with Hiss on the board of trustees for the Carnegie Endowment, Stevenson said, he had never charged them with being "soft" on communism. He bitterly resented "the sly and ugly campaign that is being waged in behalf of the General, and I am deeply shocked that he would lead a so-called 'crusade' which accepts calumny and the big doubt as its instruments."

Stevenson singled out two Republicans who employed these tactics: McCarthy stood first in line, but the governor dismissed him as an isolated demagogue. Nixon, on the other hand, "set the pace" for the smears against Democrats. This "brash and patronizing young man" had asked voters "to place him a heartbeat from the Presidency." Although Nixon had not identified Stevenson as a communist, he had implied as much. Stevenson had performed ethically and objected to innuendoes that he was a communist sympathizer.[22]

While the Nixon contingent evaluated his effectiveness in putting Stevenson on the defensive, Eisenhower addressed a Detroit audience on October 24, pledging that if elected he would travel to Korea to evaluate how best to proceed in the conflict. Although he did not promise victory, this momentous declaration drew banner headlines in newspapers across the country and added to his political momentum in the final weeks of the race. This international military hero had promised a bold step toward ending the war.[23]

Nixon, in Texas for the second time in the campaign, at Texarkana on October 27, in an attempt to appeal to disenchanted southern Democrats to vote for the GOP, he declared that the president, his secretary of state, and their presidential nominee were "traitors to the high principles in which many of the nation's Democrats believe. Real Democrats are outraged by the Truman-Acheson-Stevenson gang's toleration and defense of communism in high places."[24]

Nixon's rhetoric had reached the highest level of extreme partisanship, and Truman reacted bitterly. The president had already, on October 23, labeled Nixon "one of the most anti-labor men in the Congress," who continually fought against union objectives. Several days later, he called the senator a "reactionary." At the beginning of November, he would describe him as a tool of a "millionaires' club" who voted for the rich, not the people. If Ike won and died in office, this tool of the rich would move into the White House.[25]

These descriptions were flattering compared to the president's reaction to Nixon's Texarkana remarks. Four years later, Truman insisted that Nixon had personally accused him of treason. When RNC chairman Leonard Hall offered to donate $1,000 to any charity in exchange for proof that Nixon had uttered any declaration that Truman or Stevenson was a "traitor," or that Nixon had called the Democratic organization a "party of treason," Truman replied that Nixon had said this "all over the West," and it also was published in newspapers. When no reference was found, a Truman spokesman repeated the allegation but added that Nixon "had been careful to make it between formal engagements and to keep it off the record." That response, too, was fallacious. The senator's declaration during the height of 1952 race was tasteless. Truman compounded the controversy by his exaggerations. After the fact, he framed the matter as a choice over which man was truthful: he was, and therefore Nixon was dishonest.[26]

During the last few days of the contest, Nixon highlighted the importance of the "forgotten man" who faced high prices, taxes, and insecurity. He had developed this theme on the evening of October 29 in his last national television broadcast, declaring that there were "only six days to save America." He addressed his listeners as "the forgotten man and the forgotten woman," the taxpayers and the troops in Korea, and those who lived on fixed incomes, victimized by inflation.[27]

Stevenson ended his campaign at Chicago Stadium by thanking his loyalists and predicting victory. Eisenhower, the governor proposed, did not deserve the trust and confidence of the American people because he had endorsed Taft, McCarthy, and Jenner, who would direct the politically naïve general in their warped path of thinking. The governor reminded voters that the GOP was the party of the Great Depression without a sound economic program. Before Americans cast their lot with the GOP, they should remember the economic blight associated with the last Republican president. He then turned from this dismal vision to a positive one. He had traveled across the country and had seen its majesty. Now the voters had a choice to decide their future based on the widely diverging ideas of the candidates.[28]

On the afternoon of November 3, the Eisenhowers and Nixons met in Boston. At 5:30 p.m. Nixon addressed a crowd at Boston Garden from a third-floor window, with Pat making a brief appearance. The two then proceeded to the auditorium, where Congressman Christian Herter introduced the senator for a fifteen-minute address covered live on radio and television. After Eisenhower publicly greeted the Nixons at the station, they left for the airport and took off just after midnight on November 4 to fly to California to cast their ballots. While they were preparing to leave, the general, just about midnight, appeared on television for his second time, urging voters to go to the polls.[29]

After Nixon cast his vote, he went to the Ambassador Hotel in downtown Los Angeles, where he listened to the returns over the radio in his suite and watched television commentary. A few minutes before 8:00 p.m., the people in the ballroom exploded in celebration, singing "Dixie" when Virginia Democrats conceded their state to the Republicans; this concession signaled the fragmentation of the Solid South. Next Florida, New York, Illinois, and California swung into the GOP column, and after those triumphs, Ike proclaimed victory.[30]

Once the president-elect spoke, Nixon went to the Gold Room to make a statement, but in the pandemonium, he needed fifteen minutes to struggle through the packed room. He called on Americans to "Join together behind the leadership of Gen. Dwight Eisenhower to advance the cause of freedom and to bring about peace throughout the world." Just before midnight, he went to Republican headquarters in the Alexandria Ballroom, pushed through the audience of a thousand to the stand beneath a 120-foot election-return blackboard that confirmed a Republican triumph. Responding to an exuberant throng, he said: "We have won the election, but we must make sure that our administration is one for all the people."[31]

Stevenson graciously conceded early on the morning of November 5. He had emerged in defeat as a national personality and the chief Democratic spokesman.[32]

The GOP had won the White House for the first time in twenty-four years. Ike had run 16 percent ahead of the other GOP candidates, and equally important, the Republicans captured both houses of Congress: 221 to 213 in the House and 48 to 47 in the Senate, with one independent who caucused with the Democrats. Vice President Nixon would be the tie-breaking vote who gave the Republicans control. When Gallup sent out a special survey, it found six factors contributed to the lopsided triumph: the general's personal popularity, the political ferment in the South, the Korean issue, and overwhelming support from independents, women, and young voters.[33]

The final election tally showed that 62.7 percent of registered voters cast their ballots, for a total vote of 66,550,918: 13,000,000 more than in 1948. The GOP ticket carried thirty-nine states with 442 electoral votes, while the Democrats captured nine states with eighty-nine electoral votes. The Republican national percentage was 53.1 percent compared with 44.4 percent for the Democrats. Even in defeat, Stevenson had gotten 27,314,992 votes, a total that FDR exceeded only in his 1936 trouncing of Alfred Landon.[34]

For the first time since 1928, Republicans had cracked the rim of the Democratic Solid South, winning Florida, Tennessee, Texas, and Virginia; Eisenhower did particularly well in urban and suburban areas. As for the Deep South, the Democrats held on to those states, in some cases, like South Carolina, just barely. The GOP won 48.1 percent of the southern vote compared to 57 percent of the North. This victory extended only to the presidential level. Republicans did not capture any Senate seat, and out of 99 Democratically held House seats in the South, the GOP took only 6.[35]

Eisenhower probably was the only candidate who could have captured the White House and brought Republican control of both houses of the Congress on his coattails. He had not run a spectacular campaign, had refused to comment on personalities, and had concentrated on the issues. He was a military hero who promised to go to Korea and restore integrity to the White House. Voters took him at his word. As he prepared to enter his presidency, he was a confident leader.[36]

Shortly after midnight on November 5, 1952, Ike called Nixon in Los Angeles to exchange mutual congratulations regarding their triumph, and later that morning the vice president–elect spoke briefly to the general. Early the next day, anxious to be reunited with their children, Pat and Dick boarded a commercial airliner in Los Angeles with staff members and returned to Washington National Airport. In response to a question concerning Ike's pledge to go to Korea, Nixon said that he did not intend to accompany the general, but after both had returned from their vacations, they would confer about expanding his vice-presidential duties.[37]

The next day, the vice president–elect held a press conference, announcing that he had submitted his resignation from the Senate, effective January 1, 1953. He also stated that he did not know when the general would leave for Korea. Finally, he was interested in building the two-party system in the South and thought that television would play major role in future national campaigns. He predicted that future presidential races might be transformed; whistle-stops might cease, and "we may have back porch campaigns, with television, press and radio bringing the candidates right to the people."[38]

While Nixon was presenting these views, the Eisenhowers were in Georgia, resting. The president-elect had appointed Brownell and Clay, two of his closest political advisers, to select his cabinet. After he returned to New York City, he summoned Nixon on November 24 for a two-hour meeting, their first face-to-face discussion since their joint appearance in Boston at the end of the race. Afterward, Nixon held an impromptu news conference in which he discussed how Ike wanted him to prepare for the transition to the new administration.[39]

Nixon was a member of the Chowder and Marching Club, a group of Republican congressmen who convened on January 7, 1953, to discuss their new responsibilities as the majority party in both houses. That same day, Ike wired Dick a happy birthday greeting and added "the responsibility of leading the new Administration toward the goals of our Crusade." Two days later Nixon turned forty years old.[40]

The president-elect again welcomed Nixon to New York City on January 11, and the next day Ike assembled the cabinet appointees for lunch to comment on his upcoming inaugural address. He knew what he intended to say but asked his listeners for their input. Soliciting advice from others was a method he had long used to prepare for unforeseen contingencies.[41]

Shortly after Nixon returned to Washington from this conference, he spoke before the RNC on January 17 at the Mayflower Hotel, praising the pre-inaugural cabinet meeting and the capabilities of the members. He gave a preview of what the president was planning. The new administration, he noted, had "a big job ahead, a job which is made more difficult by the fact that we are inheriting from the outgoing administration a whole host of problems which we must clear up before we can begin building anew." If Ike was going to succeed, he needed backing from the Republican congressional leadership.[42]

Nixon was starting to act as a Republican cheerleader, urging the faithful to prepare for the responsibilities of the new administration. The GOP was completing its arrangements for the three days of inaugural celebrations from January 18 through 20. A Republican had last entered the White House in 1929; it had been almost a quarter century since the GOP had had cause to celebrate an inauguration. More than a half million people were expected to descend on the nation's capital for a concert at Constitution Hall, tours of the capital, the inauguration, and several balls that evening. Over 10,000 volunteers served on scores of committees to oversee every detail of the multifaceted programs, while underwriters contributed $700,000 to cover the expenses.[43]

On a clear, brisk morning on January 20, 1953, the Eisenhowers and Nixons left for the National Presbyterian Church for the services scheduled for 9:30 a.m. Once these were over, the group quickly preceded to the motorcade rendezvous at the White House where the automobiles lined up for their passengers. Eisenhower and Truman led the procession, barely speaking to one another. Each blamed the other for personal attacks made during the passion of the campaign, and neither was willing to take the first step toward reconciliation.[44]

At noon on January 20, Truman, Eisenhower, and Nixon were escorted to the three seats in the middle of the center aisle of the platform erected in front of the Capitol building. The day was sunny, and the temperature climbed to fifty degrees. Ike sat in the middle, with Truman on his right and Nixon on his left. The wives were close by, with Pat between Mamie and Bess. The incoming president and vice president took their oath of office in front of 125,000 spectators.[45]

Chief Justice of the United States Fred Vincent swore in Eisenhower, who offered a prayer before commencing his inaugural address. Then the new president and his vice president led their family and friends to a luncheon in the Vandenberg room at the Senate. Nixon briefly slipped away, mounted the rostrum in the Senate, and convened that venerable body into session as its presiding officer. This was supposed to be a routine session to confirm eight cabinet selections, but it ended on a sore note. Wayne Morse, independent from Oregon, objected to the unanimous consent request for immediate consideration, and Nixon's first decision was to rule that the senator had the right to block the confirmations.[46]

From the Capitol, the new leaders drove to the north portico of the White House and went to their reviewing seats for the afternoon parade that was delayed because the Supreme Court justices arrived late. That evening the Eisenhowers and Nixons attended the inaugural balls. The business of governance would begin in the morning.[47]

Eisenhower, sixty-two when he assumed the presidency, was the oldest man who had yet been elected to that post and the only general elected president in the twentieth century. Trained as a military leader who commanded millions, he was prepared for the task ahead.

Nixon, at just past forty, was the second-youngest vice president in American history after John Breckinridge, who was elected in 1856 at thirty-six years old. Nixon also was the first vice president elected from the far West. By the end of the 1952 campaign, he came to personify the voice of GOP partisanship, and he emerged for many Republicans as the good Dr. Jekyll and to passionate Democrats as the evil Mr. Hyde. On March 7, 1953, he seemed resigned: "it was a very rough campaign as far as I, personally, was concerned but we seem to have survived it and we can take some comfort in the fact that if they hadn't been attacking me they would have been going after Eisenhower or somebody else." That might have been consolation for the others, but throughout Nixon's political life it gave him little solace.[48]

Nixon acutely understood that his image had been tarnished, and he needed help "to combat the apparently successful attempt to injure my reputation which was launched by Drew Pearson and some of the left-wingers during the last two weeks of the campaign." He did not believe that this assault had cost the ticket votes, but there were doubts about his integrity "among some of the relative intelligent people, even on our side." He would not reply to the negativity hurled in his direction, "but apparently some type of rehabilitation program is necessary and in order."[49]

Nixon's worries did not trouble the new president, who deplored extreme partisanship because it placed party above the nation. His focus was to govern the vast machinery of the federal government. Nixon's single constitutional duty was to preside over the Senate. As vice president, he depended upon Eisenhower for anything else.[50]

4

THE GENERAL AS A MANAGER

Eisenhower was the eighth general to become president, and the only one in the twentieth century. His hero and model was the first president, George Washington. Both men viewed duty as paramount; both displayed a clear sense of patriotism and an innate decency; both had a dignified presence and great self-confidence; and both understood the need for flexibility and organization.

Henry Cabot Lodge had run his own reelection campaign for a third term in the Senate and also served as the chairman of the Eisenhower's campaign advisory committee, a job he thought would take "about one day a week." He lost his race to John Kennedy on November 4, and five days later the president-elect appointed Lodge as his "personal liaison between the Truman administration and the new one." From his offices at the Statler Hotel in the capital, Lodge managed the transition until January 22, 1953. While he was attending to those duties, on December 1, 1952, Eisenhower announced his appointment as United States Representative to the United Nations.[1]

Ike believed in a team concept where everyone pulled for the betterment of the whole. He listened carefully and mulled over what, if any, action to take. More than any other postwar president, he valued a well-developed line of authority as the best mechanism to avoid errors. In the end, however, he and he alone made the final decisions.[2]

He relied on his staff to keep the White House functioning smoothly and expected his subordinates to obey his directives. New Hampshire governor Sherman Adams, who had energetically worked on the presidential campaign, resigned his elected position and was selected as the first White House chief of staff, with the responsibility of guarding the White House gate. His curt and occasionally offensive manner caused hurt feelings; he made many enemies who felt slighted when he refused them access to the president.[3]

The deputy chief of staff, General Wilton "Jerry" Persons, was one door from Adams' office. He had known Ike since 1931, when they served together in the Army. During the 1930s, Persons had been stationed in the capital, where he lobbied Congress for the Army; after World War II he served in Paris, under Eisenhower's command, as a special assistant. As the president's deputy in charge of congressional relations, he and his staff worked to create a spirit of bipartisanship, respect for Congress, and cooperation with the legislative branch to get the administration's bills approved.[4]

Unlike many of his predecessors, Ike used his cabinet as a major policymaking body. The cabinet was a creation of the president. It had no statutory authority and was not mentioned in the Constitution. Department heads and other officials whom the president designated attended as regular members. Cabinet secretaries were expected to take an active role in managing their departments. During cabinet meetings, the president had two major objectives: first, to inform his listeners about his proposals, and second, to hear their views. Cabinet officers and their subordinates as well as their staffs had to comprehend the direction the White House was taking. These gatherings helped to avoid uncertainty and to give the president input that he might not have anticipated. Those who needed to know were included; those who did not play an integral role were excluded. When it came time for a decision, the president did not ask for votes.[5]

He held three regular gatherings when Congress was in session. On Mondays, he met with legislative leaders; Wednesdays he saw the National Security Council (NSC) that had been created by statute; and Fridays were reserved for the cabinet. During each, he encouraged frank debate and deplored those who pontificated. If you did not have a significant contribution, you had better remain silent. At the same time, every person could expect to be called upon— so you had better have something cogent to say.[6]

Ike held weekly press conferences, usually on Wednesdays, to get his message directly to the American public. He appointed James Hagerty, a well-respected journalist and loyal counselor, as his press secretary. Although the president could be extremely sensitive to attacks from reporters, he never looked at them as the enemy. He counted many publishers and broadcast executives as friends. Criticism from the media sometimes upset him, but it had little effect on his popularity.[7]

During his first year in office, the Gallup Poll's approval ratings for Eisenhower ranged from a low of 65 percent to a high of 75 percent. Ike had successfully transferred his popularity as a five-star general over to his presidency.[8]

As president, Ike partially stepped out of his military role. He had acquired his management skills over forty years in the Army and understood how a massive bureaucracy functioned. He had learned to deal with world leaders like

FDR, Winston Churchill, and Charles de Gaulle, and had become a superb bureaucratic politician. But partisanship was different. He used the word "politician" as a pejorative, often preceded by "repugnant." He never comprehended the intricacies of partisan politics and instead tried to position himself as above the fray.[9]

Before announcing for the presidency, he did not know any national committee persons from either party. Such relationships were irrelevant, he said, because he was still reluctant to enter the political arena, although he had not "irrevocably" rejected the option of running for the White House. Even the decision to run for president did not change his negative opinion of professional politicians.[10]

With a popular war hero at the top of the ticket, Republicans in 1953 won slim congressional majorities after two decades in the minority. To devise positive programs, the administration now had to work with a congressional leadership that had been out of power for two decades. Although Ike had commanded vast armies, Nixon later remarked, the president-general "was least at ease with those leaders of his political party."[11]

The new president did not analyze voting patterns or fully comprehend grass-roots politics. He had little appreciation of how his supporters had built a victorious coalition. Even though he hoped to expand his party's base, he never translated this intent into action. Americans did not strongly associate Ike with the Republican Party, and he did not encourage the association. He seemed to govern above politics and made no secret of his distaste for elected officials, and he never reconciled this attitude with his position as leader of the GOP. Nor did he seem to grasp the contradiction.

Ike had beaten Senator Taft for the presidential nomination and, with Nixon's help and encouragement, had wooed him ever since. Now Taft was the Senate majority leader. Despite some minor disagreements and a few major explosions, the two men grew to respect one another and worked well together. The president went so far as to give Taft open access to the Oval Office, one of a handful to receive such deferential treatment.[12]

But as their cooperation increased, Taft's health declined. He complained of an undiagnosed illness in the spring of 1953, and the mystery was solved by early summer. Taft had incurable cancer; he succumbed on the last day of July. Early in the next month, he was one of the few senators given a memorial service in the Capitol Rotunda. Ike had lost an influential ally in the Senate. The vacuum would never be filled to his satisfaction.[13]

Even before sitting the Oval Office, Ike had certain domestic concerns. When campaigning in 1952, he recognized that the American electorate associated the Great Depression with Republicans and the presidency of Herbert Hoover.

Voters, especially Democratic ones, vividly remembered that during the nation's most severe economic disaster, Hoover and Andrew Mellon, his treasury secretary, pursued a laissez-faire economic policy. Ike repeatedly promised voters that if the threat of a depression arose, he would marshal the full powers of the federal government to prevent it.

Once in the White House, Ike appointed advisers who expressed varied economic views. Gabriel Hauge, who held a doctorate in economics from Harvard University, had written Ike's campaign speeches on economic subjects. After the election, he continued to counsel the president, paying particular emphasis to the political consequences of economic actions. Treasury secretary George Humphrey shared some of the president's firm positions, such as the benefit of balanced budget and the detrimental effects of massive public works spending. Arthur Burns, the chairman of the Council of Economic Advisers (CEA) under Eisenhower, supported tax cuts and spending on public works projects to halt economic downturns.[14]

Ike wanted to reduce spending, balance the budget, and eliminate some New Deal and Fair Deal programs that he considered too expensive. Although he understood that some programs, like Social Security, were beneficial and not subject to elimination, his overriding objective was to put the nation on a sound financial footing. He fervently believed in the power of the individual and free enterprise, and opposed what he saw as a constant drift toward big government and deficit spending. He also advocated policies to keep inflation low, to maintain the strength of the dollar, and to pay off the ten billion dollar national debt that he had inherited. If he could accomplish these objectives, he believed, the United States economy would not confront any severe economic downturns and would grow at an acceptable rate.[15]

By appointing Hauge, Humphrey, and Burns, Ike not only formulated the administration's principles but also defined the range of differing opinion he would consider. Although some Republicans, such as Senator Taft, wanted to slash Truman's 1953 budget and replace it with a balanced budget, Ike refused to take such a drastic step. He moved initially to limit that year's deficit by reducing military spending and slowing increases in social services.[16]

His plans changed when the fighting in Korea ended. The federal government reduced military expenditures, and after the July armistice, the administration decreased its purchases. Production fell as a consequence, and the nation experienced a mild recession that lasted almost a year. Unemployment rose from 2.6 percent in the summer of 1953 to 6.1 percent in September 1954. The CEA chairman, Arthur Burns, spoke for those in the administration who called for reducing taxes and increasing public work programs in response to the downturn. Secretary Humphrey led those who objected to these measures. The president accepted Burns's argument and initiated a massive tax cut of $7 billion in the spring of 1954. The administration also passed legislation that extended unemployment benefits to an additional four million workers. The bipartisan agreement over using deficit spending to end the recession made this cooperation significant.[17]

Besides the stark reality of economic concerns, the president was deeply troubled that the nation had become too secular. To counteract that swing, he promoted the religious revival of the 1950s. In a nation of some 150 million people, over 95 million claimed some affiliation: almost 70 percent were Protestants; 23 percent were Catholics; 4 percent were Jews. Fundamentalist and evangelical sects were rising rapidly. As the suburbs blossomed, church construction and new congregations mushroomed. Newspapers enlarged their coverage of religion. Billy Graham had emerged as a dominant figure in this movement, and his crusades, first televised in 1951, reached enormous audiences. Norman Vincent Peale, of the Marble Collegiate Church in New York City, sold over 2,000,000 copies of *The Power of Positive Thinking* during the early 1950s. Movies with biblical themes, such as *Quo Vadis* in 1952, *The Ten Commandments* in 1956, and *Ben Hur* three years later, were box office hits.[18]

Ike fervently believed that religion was an integral part in the American way of life. As historian Craig Keller has noted, he was "not a sophisticated theologian," but his "beliefs were heart-felt expressions." His mother, Ida, belonged to the River Brethren, a Mennonite offshoot, and she converted to the Bible Student movement, which took the name Jehovah's Witnesses in 1931. Ike had read the Bible by the age of nine, an achievement for which his mother rewarded him with a gold watch. Although he did not belong to any church during his childhood or his military career, he was strongly affected by his religious upbringing. When preparing for a major battle, Ike wrote, he "prayed long and hard."[19]

During his presidential campaign, he spent about 10 percent of his time focusing on spiritual values. He "felt strongly that the nation was becoming far too secular, that God was no longer a part of our daily life." Just before moving into the White House, he gave a Christmas address to the Freedoms Foundation at the Waldorf Astoria Hotel, saying, "our form of Government has no sense unless it is founded in a deeply felt religious faith, and I don't care what it is." Throughout his presidency, Ike brought people of diverse faiths into his administration and intentionally tried to reflect the religious preferences of the church-going public.[20]

Even though he had not belonged to an organized church for decades, he began his inaugural address with a prayer. Once in the White House, he decided that his new mission demanded that he join a congregation. Mamie had been a Presbyterian since childhood, and early on the morning of February 1, 1953, in a ceremony that received wide press coverage, Reverend Edward Elson of the National Presbyterian Church baptized him. Eisenhower thus became the second president, after Calvin Coolidge, to join a church after reaching the White House.[21]

Ike followed this symbolic gesture with other actions to demonstrate his commitment. Cabinet meetings commenced with a moment of silent prayer. The president also initiated the National Prayer Breakfast as well as the National Day of Prayer. He developed a cordial relationship with evangelist Billy Graham and invited him to participate at some of these events. These actions were well advertised and welcomed in the Christian community.[22]

One summer day in early July, the president preached to his private secretary, Ann Whitman. He affirmed that all mankind was equal before God. While many relied on religion as a crutch, others sincerely believed. Atheists, he asserted, were stupid because they did not think. Materialism left a spiritual void; he craved some form of religious "affection." Ike "could accept the theory that the earth was created by a fiery volcano," but because "intense heat destroyed life," he reasoned, "the first protoplasm must have come from somewhere." The answer was a divine being.[23]

Early in 1954, the phrase "under God" was added to the Pledge of Allegiance, and on Flag Day that summer, Ike signed the law that placed "In God We Trust" on United States currency. In February 1955, he supported a "Back to God" drive where Americans could express their faith in a supreme being. In the last year of the first term, he hired Frederic Fox, a Congregational minister, to serve on the White House staff to coordinate religious issues. Dubbed the "White House Pastor," Reverend Fox was the first clergyman to work in the executive offices since the Lincoln administration.[24]

In part, the emphasis on religion was a reaction to the threat of communism. The Republican ticket had run largely on a platform of fighting domestic subversion and international communism. Espionage remained on the front pages throughout 1953. At the beginning of the summer, Attorney General Brownell and his deputy William Rogers attended a meeting with the president concerning the guilt of the convicted spies Ethel and Julius Rosenberg. Two justice officials presented evidence that these two had funneled information on the development of the atomic bomb to Soviet agents; Eisenhower then made the decision to carry out the death sentence. They were executed on June 19.[25]

Also that year, J. Robert Oppenheimer, the father of the atom bomb, was accused of being a security risk. The Atomic Energy Commission suspended his security clearance, and a special panel denied Oppenheimer reinstatement.[26]

At the end of November 1953, a Gallup Poll asked whether it was a good or bad idea that the Republicans were planning to bring up cases of communist infiltration during the FDR and Truman presidencies. Forty-six percent approved this action, and 36 percent disapproved. In February 1954, another Gallup survey asked if communists were working for the federal government. Seventy-four percent answered yes and just 10 percent said no. That July, Gallup asked whether Congress was abusing its powers in investigating communism: 40 percent said yes while 42 percent said no.[27]

These results showed that although Americans believed Soviet agents had penetrated the federal bureaucracy, they were unsure how to address the problem. Ike passionately opposed the Soviet threat, yet he too wondered how to defeat it. At the start of March 1954, he asked Nixon if he was acquainted with communists outside the Iron Curtain. The vice president replied that he had interrogated many in the Communist Party of the United States of America (CPUSA) during his four years on the House Committee on Un-American Activities. The president admitted that the only communists he had known had been Soviet citizens. "I would like for somebody to show me a Communist," he added.[28]

Despite the complexity of rooting out subversion, the president adopted policies based on the premise that government employment and security status were a privilege, not a right. Disloyal workers needed to be removed from the federal payroll, yet the administration had to protect individual rights. Ike addressed the nation: "We cannot defeat Communism by destroying Americanism. We must observe every requirement of law and ethics." He was obligated to protect the innocent, and throughout that summer, he pushed for communist control legislation by pressing senators unsuccessfully to expedite a bill in their committee that would cripple the CPUSA. He declared that wherever he went, in every speech, his pledges to fight communism always drew "the biggest 'whoops and hollers'" from the audience.[29]

The president formulated a loyalty program, Executive Order 10450, dealing with the removal of security risks, which went into force on April 27, 1954, and by the following October 1,456 federal employees had resigned for a variety of reasons. Under a Truman administration executive order, over 400 state department officials had been fired or forced to resign due to alleged homosexual behavior and for other reasons; the Eisenhower government used similar grounds to terminate even more foreign service officers.[30]

Ike had promised to involve his vice president in the administration's decisions, and his reliance on the staff system required him to have an active vice president. As commander of the Allied Forces in 1945, he had been dismayed by the mass confusion that resulted when an uninformed Vice President Truman succeeded Franklin Roosevelt. Nixon had to be kept fully apprised, so as to make a smooth transition if the worst happened.

He and Nixon had talked briefly about an expanded vice-presidential role. Although this left Nixon encouraged, details were missing. Henry Wallace as vice president had been chairman of the Board of Economic Warfare (BEW) during World War II, and by statute Alben Barkley sat on the National Security Council (NSC). The BEW no longer existed, and Barkley had never had much influence on national security. Political scientist Jack Peltason has written that until the 1950s, the vice president was chosen to "balance the ticket" and was a "fifth wheel" in the administration. "The office was often dismissed as a joke." Another political scientist, Joel Goldstein, labeled the position "a political graveyard."[31]

Nixon was the thirty-sixth vice president and the second youngest. John Breckinridge, who ran with James Buchanan, took office in 1857 at the age of thirty-six. Like Nixon, he was trained as a lawyer and had served in both houses of Congress. Three vice presidents, John Adams, Thomas Jefferson, and Martin Van Buren, had succeeded the outgoing president by running and winning the office. After Van Buren did it, in 1841, no sitting vice president had been elected president. (None would manage it again until George H. W. Bush, in 1988.)[32]

The United States Constitution said only that the vice president must be at least thirty-five years old and would serve as president of the Senate, without any vote except to break a tie. During his tenure, Nixon exercised that duty eight times. More critically, in case of the president's removal, death, resignation, or disability, the vice president would assume the presidency. John Tyler was the first vice president to become president under that clause, after William Henry Harrison died in 1841. Almost 20 percent of all presidents came from the vice presidency after the deaths of their predecessors. When Eisenhower entered the White House as the thirty-third president, seven predecessors had died in office, four from natural causes and three from assassins' bullets.[33]

Nixon, though well aware of this statistic, was more focused on the fact the GOP was the minority party. He also understood that Ike was not a passionate partisan. The Republican Party, from Nixon's standpoint, had to maintain its base, win new converts, appeal to independents, and encourage Democrats to switch their allegiance. After the 1952 election, he predicted, campaigns would change due to television. Whistle-stop contests might end, and "television, press and radio" might bring the candidates directly "to the people."[34]

He also understood that during the contest he had become a lightning rod for Democratic harangues. That needed to stop, and the best way to accomplish it was through moderation. Ike initially encouraged his cabinet to avoid making inflammatory speeches. His government rested on a foundation of deeds, not bombast. Nixon concurred, and by end of February he was "devoting practically all of my time now to some hard, unpublicized work as a participant in the meetings of the Cabinet and the National Security Council. In the long run I believe that this type of activity will produce some good public relations nationally."[35]

This purposeful silence frustrated many Nixon zealots. They were livid about the attacks on their standard bearer and the GOP, and they struck back when the opportunity arose. Nixon, in the second week of March, advised restraint. The left wingers, he said, would never lower their decibel level, but his loyalists must brush the opposition aside: "There will be a time," he assured them, "when we will go on the offensive again but in the meantime I think we are making some real progress in consolidating our position."[36]

Nixon, full of energy and enthusiasm, was eager to find opportunities to demonstrate his value. Ike's management style provided many. On June 16, 1953, Nixon wrote a memorandum to his file concerning how Ike believed "in giving the people around him who are on his team as much opportunity as possible to assume responsibility—to take the ball and run with it." Eisenhower wanted Nixon to know what was happening at the White House, so he was invited to the meetings chaired by the president. As vice president, he built up close relations with Lyndon Johnson and several others. When Senate Republican William Langer, who chaired the judiciary committee, held up Earl Warren's confirmation to the Supreme Court, Nixon persuaded Langer to permit the appointment to go through on schedule. He further worked as a troubleshooter between the White House, cabinet, and the Congress, and promoted administration proposals throughout the nation.[37]

Eisenhower did not include his vice president among his chief economic advisers, but Nixon routinely offered his advice on the political impact of economic programs. On March 19, 1954, at a morning cabinet meeting, for example, after Dr. Burns stated that he was closely watching several danger signs in the recession, Nixon recorded in his diary that he had called for additional spending no matter what Big Business and Wall Street lobbied for because "great numbers of ordinary people . . . felt that a recession was in progress and . . . we had to take this into account or otherwise psychological factors would be set up which would result in real trouble."[38]

Toward the end of 1955, the vice president, at a cabinet meeting, argued that the administration was coming under unfair criticism that its policies had not benefited wage earners. The administration's policies, he said, had "been in the best interests of the great majority of Americans, regardless of their occupations."

The following spring, he admitted that Democrats had effectively targeted the GOP as the party of big business. The current prosperity, however, benefited Republicans: "This certainly ought to be proof positive that the main hope for our economy is going to have to come from individual initiative and private investment rather than from government."[39]

The president also encouraged his vice president to promote religion. Nixon saw in Ike a "deeply religious man who earnestly seeks Divine guidance on the grave problems which involve the peace of the world and the future of our country." Yet Nixon felt uncomfortable speaking publicly about his religious upbringing. His parents, he later wrote, never wore religion "on the sleeve, and consequently I just always felt embarrassed, frankly, uneasy." Whenever he referred to God in a speech, "it was too familiar. I didn't consider God to be familiar."[40]

Nixon's Quaker spiritual values did not come from the Friends' East Coast tradition. This framework provides a simple building, a "meeting house," where members congregate on Sundays, dress modestly, say "thee" and "thou," pray quietly, look for their "inner light," and adhere to a pacifist tradition. But the Nixon family belonged to the West Coast "steeple house" branch, whose traditions more closely resembled evangelical Protestantism. These values, not so quietly personal, created the fabric of the family's social life. Members frequently participated in evangelical rallies. One year Frank Nixon took his teenage son Richard to Los Angeles to hear the Chicago radio revivalist Paul Rader, and at that gathering the son accepted Christ as his savior. The family regularly attended the East Whittier Friends Church, where a minister preached at four different services. There were spoken prayers, hymn singing, and music. Richard taught a Bible class, sang in the choir, played piano, attended Sunday school, went to Christian Endeavor youth meetings, and attended Wednesday evening prayer gatherings.[41]

He attended a Quaker institution, Whittier College, while continuing to go to the local church. After college, he entered Duke Law School and attended a variety of religious services nearby. During World War II, he rejected the option of conscientious objection that his faith provided and enlisted in the Navy. His first congressional campaign had the active support of radio fundamentalist Robert Shuler from the Trinity Methodist Church in Los Angeles. After his family moved to the capital, the Nixons decided against joining Herbert Hoover's meeting house assembly and chose a Congregational church. At the conclusion of the fund speech in 1952, much of the correspondence that flooded into Republican campaign headquarters referred to Nixon's being in the writers' prayers and asking for God's blessings.[42]

Several members of the Nixon family had met Billy Graham. Frank and Hannah shook his hand at his 1949 Los Angeles crusade. Approximately two years later, while Graham and Senator Clyde Hoey, from his home state of North Carolina, were having lunch in the Senate cafeteria, Hoey introduced his guest to Senator Nixon; later that afternoon Nixon and Graham played golf together. When the evangelist held a five-week crusade in Washington, D.C., early in 1952, he again saw Nixon. Their acquaintance would develop into a long, mutually beneficial friendship.[43]

As vice president, Nixon participated in several events that focused on Christianity. During a speech to promote a "Back to God" program on February 1, 1953, sponsored by the American Legion, the vice president declared that the United States was "a great moral and spiritual force for good in the world." Powerful empires, he stressed, had fallen from internal decay more often than from military conquest. A few days later, during Brotherhood Week, Nixon urged Americans to practice the Judeo-Christian tradition daily because "Americanism has come to mean Brotherhood." Later that month, at a black-tie dinner of the National Conference of Christians and Jews, where Pat served as honorary co-chairman, he preached faith and brotherhood. That summer he addressed The Washington Pilgrimage on spiritual values. Its president, David Cook III, enthusiastically wrote him that the speech "helped to give us confidence that religion will once again form the girders of our nation."[44]

Besides this religious activity, Nixon took the initiative on domestic subversion. Soon after entering office, he sent two memoranda that the president rejected, asking for $150,000 from the president's confidential fund to finance an inquiry into Hiss's espionage activities. All of the executive branches of government were to cooperate with the investigation, and the vice president could also ask Congress to play a role. The proposed committee would begin with Hiss's first employment by the federal government in 1933 and look into his entire career as a spy for Soviet military intelligence. Hiss had held sensitive positions in the state department, yet no one had determined the magnitude of his spying or the members of the ring to which he belonged. Nixon wanted to "assess the damage."[45]

Nixon was motivated to confirm that Soviet spies were active in the federal bureaucracy. Liberals rejected that accusation, pronounced Hiss innocent of espionage, and blamed Nixon for persecuting him. Many politicians and correspondents, including Nixon, earnestly believed that liberals never forgave him for his role in the Hiss perjury conviction. The highest-ranking confirmation of this came from former president Truman, who maintained that no one had ever proven Hiss was a spy.[46]

The vice president had no doubt about Hiss's guilt. On February 5, 1954, he said, "Under the old loyalty program our friend, Hiss, would have been loyal. Under our program we could get rid of him." Whittaker Chambers, Hiss's accuser, complained two years later that people still believed Hiss was wrongly convicted. Father John Cronin warned Nixon that some members of both parties "have never forgiven you for exposing Alger Hiss." This came as no surprise. At the end of March, Nixon speculated that revenge might have motivated some of the antipathy directed against him during the campaign: "During the Hiss-Chambers trial I was told in no uncertain terms that I had better be right concerning Hiss, or I would be a dead duck! I am convinced that I was right, but I am even more convinced that some sources still hope to make me a dead duck."[47]

The public question of Hiss's guilt, kept alive for years, was finally closed in the late 1990s with the release of the Venona documents. Historians John Haynes and Harvey Klehr, who have specialized in Soviet espionage in the United States, along with Alexander Vassiliev, a Soviet researcher who gained special access to classified material, published the main Soviet security agency Komitet gosodarst-vennoy bezppasnosti (KGB) documents that confirm Hiss spied for the Soviet Union. In their book *Spies*, the authors write: "Any reasonable person will conclude that the new documentation of Hiss's assistance to Soviet espionage, along with the massive weight of prior accumulated evidence, closes the case."[48]

Nixon searched for methods to prevent spying. As the new administration started, he cooperated with both houses of Congress on proposals to investigate educational institutions dealing with loyalty issues. That summer he explored security risks at independent federal agencies, especially the government printing office. At the end of 1953, he raised the question of outlawing the CPUSA.[49]

The infiltration of Soviet spies had forced both the Truman and Eisenhower governments to institute security clearances. A quarter-century after Ike left office, Nixon conceded that some of the investigations "were not, perhaps, conducted in a way that would meet all the standards that we would have liked, but something had to be done. You just couldn't leave these people in those positions."[50]

As a former member of HUAC, Nixon followed the committee's deliberations. Harold Velde of Illinois chaired the body and almost immediately started a controversy when he publicly proclaimed that HUAC would investigate the role of some clergy in domestic subversion. Nixon moved to block this inquiry and advised the administration to keep close watch on the congressional committees for areas of possible friction. Such diligence would prevent the embarrassing probes that had followed earlier investigations. Despite outlandish behavior by some committee members, Nixon felt strongly that HUAC had useful purposes and continued to support its funding throughout his vice presidency.[51]

Excluded from the debate over domestic subversion, Nixon nonetheless contributed to the president's comprehension of national politics, eventually becoming the one person familiar with the full breadth of the president's policies. He was the only member of the administration, other than the president, who attended all three major weekly meetings. Ike added to the vice president's stature at these meetings by frequently asking, "Dick, what do you think?" He quickly came to rely on Nixon's sense of how Congress might react to administration proposals. Nixon began to anticipate Eisenhower's objectives and compiled a list of presidential imperatives—priorities for bringing legislative proposals forward. As he got to know the president, Nixon grew convinced that Ike believed "in giving the people around him who are on his team as much opportunity as possible to assume responsibility—to take the ball and run with it." He welcomed those broad guidelines.[52]

As a regular attendee at cabinet meetings, Nixon melded neatly into the president's scheme, becoming part of the team idea that Ike promoted and serving as a sort of high-ranking officer at the general-president's side. He spoke infrequently, but when he did, the others listened attentively because Nixon filled a conspicuous vacuum: no other cabinet member had his political skills. At the end of January 1953, the president informed the secretaries that Nixon and Jerry Persons would be the liaisons between the executive and legislative branches. At a February gathering, the vice president encouraged cabinet secretaries to meet with congressional committee chairmen regarding subjects related to congressional investigations. Ike concurred. Nixon additionally counseled that the administration pressure private contractors to hire local workers in areas of high unemployment, because this made for good politics. Watching him, presidential speech writer John Emmet Hughes commented on "the judicious interventions of Nixon, crisp and practical and logical: never proposing major objectives, but . . . shrewd in suggesting or refining methods—rather like an effective trial lawyer."[53]

In April 1953, Ike announced that he was going to Augusta, Georgia, for a short vacation, and Nixon would preside over the next week's cabinet meeting. Ever since the first cabinet meetings under John Adams, no vice president had ever been the chair: Nixon would be the first. On April 17, he opened with the usual prayer and focused the group's attention on winning the 1954 congressional elections. He encouraged his audience to develop positive programs and speak in districts where they could assist Republican aspirants. The upcoming campaign, he said, would not be decided on local issues but would be a referendum on Ike's leadership and on the Republican congressional majority. Nothing concrete came out of this gathering; that was unimportant. The president had shown his confidence in Nixon by having him preside.[54]

Those who commented felt that Nixon had done well; the meeting had held to the president's priorities. Eisenhower was pleased enough that over the remainder of the administration, Nixon chaired approximately 10 percent of the meetings. This acknowledgment enhanced the vice president's prestige. If the president became impaired, the cabinet secretaries would not find it unusual to see Nixon in charge.[55]

Nixon understood, better than most of his former congressional brethren, that the majority held power through deciding the agenda and controlling chairmanships. With the exception of UN ambassador Lodge, who was stationed in New York, Nixon had the most legislative experience in the executive branch—four years in the House and two in the Senate. Republicans had barely secured their majority at the start of the Eisenhower presidency, and the vice president knew they could easily lose it in the next election. That was a dominant reason he fought persistently for party harmony.

The razor-thin Republican majority in the Senate meant that Nixon could not leave the capital while Congress was in session. If he did, he "would really catch it from all sides if I should happen to be absent in case of a tie vote!"[56]

Nixon and congressional liaison Jerry Persons shared congressional responsibilities and went to the same meetings in the Oval Office. Persons came to respect the vice president's political acumen. In the summer of 1954, he told Nixon that during a conversation with Ike, he had recommended that the vice president "ought to sit down with the President more often on political problems." Ike concurred. He "always assumed that anybody who had anything to discuss with him would take the initiative and not wait to be called in."[57]

Ike met with Republican congressional spokesmen weekly at his legislative leaders meeting. He usually invited eight GOP leaders, four from each chamber, who would discuss upcoming legislative issues. Ike would sit at the center of the oval table with Senate majority leader Taft on his right and the Speaker of the House, Joseph Martin Jr., on his left. Directly across from the president sat Nixon with Massachusetts senator Leverett Saltonstall, Republican whip, on his left and Senator Styles Bridges from New Hampshire, chairman of the committee on appropriations, on his right. The White House congressional relations staff prepared the agenda. As he did with his cabinet, Ike used these gatherings to educate politicians on his motives and to encourage spirited debate. In turn, they provided the White House with a variety of opinions, some of which the president had not considered.[58]

Nixon provided input within his comfort zone. During the group's first meeting, for instance, on January 26, 1953, he commented that while the Democrats' attack on the McCarran Act was "largely false," the immigration issue had been hotly contested during the campaign, would continue to be discussed, and needed resolution. Ike sought to resolve the issue by establishing a study group that would offer revisions. At the May 12 gathering, the vice president cautioned his audience about reductions in the Air Force budget: Democratic senators Lyndon Johnson of Texas and Stuart Symington from Missouri, he said, would object to any reductions as weakening national defense. Nixon wanted Republicans to challenge that claim; they were not weakening the military but streamlining it.[59]

On the morning of June 21, Nixon observed the president at a legislative gathering where he "seemed to be in a relaxed mood and it seemed to me leading all through the meeting with considerable decisiveness." Then someone brought up a Drew Pearson article claiming that the president refused to support some Republican senators, including Styles Bridges. "The President," Nixon wrote in his diary, "blew his top and said that he wished that everybody in his whole organization would quit reading the columnists and quit reporting such incidents to him." With Bridges sitting across from him, the president asserted that he would be the first to tell the senator if he withheld his backing. Another incident occurred after Roscoe Drummond wrote in a column that Eisenhower would call a special session of Congress if the White House did not get its legislative agenda passed. Ike repeated the message: before any reporter learned of his decisions, he would communicate them to the legislative leaders. As Nixon recorded it, Eisenhower emphatically concluded that "we simply couldn't have the columnists running the government and affecting every decision that we made."[60]

Nixon knew Speaker Martin and majority whip Charles Halleck of Indiana, but not well. He relied on the members of the Chowder & Marching Club, a group founded in 1949 that included himself and Gerald Ford as charter members, to give him a sense of the Republican mood in the House. Four years after its founding, several members had reached the Senate, and Nixon gave the group greater prominence when he won the vice presidency. The group met on Wednesday morning for breakfast sessions to discuss pending legislation, had briefings with cabinet members, and held social gatherings. Pat and Dick still attended some of these events; he listened to members, informally sold them on the president's ideas, and reported their comments back to the White House.[61] Press secretary Hagerty recalled later that Nixon did this "to perfection. . . . One of his greatest jobs is the shoulder for the members of the Congress to cry on." He "was the direct link between the executive branch and the . . . legislative branch of the government."[62] Ike told Nixon on June 19 that he "was the most detached political observer in his organization and that he wanted [him] to have complete consultation at all times."[63]

By the end of the first year in office, with the president's active encouragement, Nixon had expanded the traditional duties of his predecessors. In the coming years, he would gain even greater responsibilities. Working quietly, he provided Ike with crucial data on how Republican and Democratic senators were moving forward on his domestic agenda and what they opposed. He added a degree of sophistication, explaining to cabinet members how to deal with congressional committees. By the nature of Eisenhower's organization, the vice president had to play an integral role. Nixon embraced that model.

In addition to these duties, Nixon spoke across the nation promoting the president's proposals. Toward the end of January 1953, Eisenhower cautioned cabinet members against making speeches. "What we want to do," Nixon said, reinforcing Eisenhower's point, "is to convince the people right at the outset that this is a working Administration." From the start of the New Year until the end of March, he had turned down 1,000 invitations for speeches.[64]

The hiatus lasted only until April 23, when Nixon addressed 1,700 guests of the American Newspaper Publishers Association at the Waldorf Astoria Hotel in New York City, marking the administration's first hundred days. He set the stage by claiming Eisenhower had faced staggering domestic crises upon entering office. Inflation had risen; the federal bureaucracy was bloated; corruption was endemic. The free enterprise philosophy was at the core of Republican values, and the new leadership expected to maximize individual initiative. The president immediately moved to change the political climate. He brought the best people into government. He promised to balance the budget and reduce taxes while maintaining essential services. The president was building a cooperative relationship with Congress and treated its representatives as equals rather than as whipping boys, as the FDR and Truman administrations had done. As for domestic subversion, the government was enforcing an effective loyalty program where spies were being exposed and the rights of the innocent were guaranteed.

The vice president's performance and avoidance of partisan rhetoric had the desired results. When Gallup polled its sample in September 1953, 82 percent knew who Nixon was. Only 45 percent of voters had been able to identify him after the Republican national convention. Registered Republicans had a 73 percent favorable opinion of him and only 3 percent unfavorable, while Democrats were 32 percent favorable and 22 percent unfavorable, and independents were 46 percent favorable and 14 percent unfavorable. Those who expressed positive feelings approved of the fund speech and felt that Nixon was "a good, honest and capable man who has kept his place and that, as a young, hard-working man, he has supplied a fresh and vigorous viewpoint to the National Government." Those who disapproved felt he lacked the qualifications for the vice presidency and had failed to clear his name of the fund charges.[65]

Pat Nixon had already become a popular figure in the GOP. She had a distinct style and was a complex woman in an era when political wives were expected to blandly tend to house and family. As second lady, she presided over the Ladies of the Senate, a group originated during World War I to assist the Red Cross sewing and rolling bandages. Pat was pleased with her reception: "the women are very sweet to me and are complimentary." Even the Democrats' wives got along with her. "They can be just the opposite so I'm glad they seem to like me."[66]

That was only one duty. Sometimes she attended as many as twenty gatherings a day. She granted newspaper, television, radio, and magazine interviews. Reporters constantly inquired why she did not wear a mink coat, and the reply was always the same: she was happy with her Republican cloth coat. When the mink growers of America offered her a fur coat without publicity, she declined the offer. She appeared at a wide variety of functions. She awarded trophies at the National Capital Flower and Garden Show, received the Outstanding Homemaker of the Year given by the capital chapter of the Home Fashion League, and was named Woman of the Year by the *Los Angeles Times*.[67]

Pat had a powerful ally at the White House. Ike liked her, and Mamie went further. The two wives had first met at the nominating convention and saw each other occasionally during the campaign; the most poignant photograph was Mamie sharing her mink coat with Pat on a cold, damp evening as their spouses addressed the stadium crowd in Wheeling, West Virginia, after the fund speech. Two days after the inauguration, the first lady invited Pat to receive with her at a White House function for about 800 female guests. Pat wrote: "She was most friendly—took me up to her living quarters afterwards and showed me all the rooms. Then [the Eisenhowers] invited Dick & I to receive with them at the reception for the diplomats. The usual procedure is to entertain separately. So they have been extremely friendly."[68]

On April 24, Mrs. Eisenhower had Pat plus six cabinet members' wives assist at an afternoon White House reception for members of the Daughters of the

American Revolution. At the end of the month, Pat, wearing her Red Cross out-fit, hosted a luncheon in Mamie's honor given by the Ladies of the Senate.[69]

Just before the family returned from vacation, Pat learned that Dick would shortly fly to Denver where the Eisenhowers were relaxing. Ike invited both Nixons to come to Colorado for a rest. Pat was grateful: "the President has been *extremely* friendly. Even invited me—but I had too much to do here."[70]

Mamie was forming a warm friendship with Pat. At the beginning of 1954, the first lady told a social friend, Ellis "Slats" Slater, that the Nixons were "two of their [the Eisenhowers] best friends." When Mamie was too ill with the flu in March 1955 to leave the White House, Pat opened the fifth annual National Cap-itol Garden Club League ceremonies. The following month, the Congressional Club held an affair to honor Mamie, and she was pleased that Pat sat at her table. The first lady asked Pat to join her for lunch in the third week of May. Mamie suggested that they might play cards, but in a postscript added: "I would love to have you come to lunch—even if you don't play games!" Pat and Mamie also exchanged gifts. For Christmas 1955, Mamie sent Pat a "lovely picture" of herself. Pat wrote a handwritten letter thanking her because she had "wanted one ever since I have known you and at last my wish is realized."

When Ike gave his wife a birthday party on November 14, 1954, Pat gave her a triple strand of pearls and earrings. Mamie was delighted that "all of our good friends" had come, and she "loved every minute of it!" A year later, Pat supplied Mamie with her favorite chocolates, Russell Stover, and sent a nosegay of pink roses (Mamie's favorite color), violets, and white carnations. At another lun-cheon on May 31, 1956, the second lady presented her with a "lovely Brazilian jade amulet," and Mamie said that she would "long cherish it as a token of our friendship."[71]

The president, meanwhile, was developing a cordial friendship with Dick. On January 7, 1953, he wired Dick a birthday greeting: "The responsibility of leading the new Administration toward the goals of our Crusade." Two days later Nixon turned forty years old. The following January, the Eisenhowers hosted a White House white-tie dinner for the Nixons, with eighty guests watching as the president and the first lady entered the formal dining area at 8:00 p.m.[72]

Pat wrote to her confidante Helene Drown: "It was truly a brilliant party as only White House ones can be." She was thrilled with "all the splendor—the beauty of the rooms, the striking gowns of the guests, the music by the Red-coated marines, the beautifully decorated tables, the chance to visit with the President, the after-dinner entertainment in the ball-room." Arriving at the White

House for a similar party in 1955, the Nixons were immediately escorted upstairs to the residence where they spent a quarter hour with the Eisenhowers.[73]

The president included other personal touches. On July 12, 1953, the anniversary of their nomination, Ike gave his running mate a black onyx inkstand, with a plate inscribed: "With high esteem." During Ike's September vacation in Denver, he invited Nixon to visit for business and to play golf. When the president chose Nixon for his partner, this brought the vice president into a very small, select circle. Nixon was a novice and Ike coached him. Ike privately suggested to some friends, including Nixon, that they read Eric Hoffer's *The True Believer*, a best seller analyzing totalitarian mass movements. In the summer of 1956, he sent Nixon an autographed photograph of them together at the airport, because the president thought that it was a good picture of him.[74]

Besides seeing each other at weekly meetings, they met regularly for breakfast or lunch throughout 1954. On January 7, the president wrote that "it has been much too long since we have had a chance for a quiet talk." He saw Nixon five days later and suggested that they meet once a month or every three weeks. They did.[75]

The president also told his vice president that he "wanted me to feel free to come into the office at any time that I had an issue that I wished to discuss with him." During his Army service, Ike had managed his bureaucracy so "that anybody who had something that he considered important should have the right to walk in." Nixon did not need an appointment, and "regardless of who was in there he would clear them out so that I could take up the matter with him." To make certain that the vice president was comfortable with this arrangement, Ike reiterated the point on several occasions.[76]

At the end of 1954, the president praised Nixon and others for helping "on problems of the gravest import to our country and to our world." Each member of his cabinet, the president declared, should feel "great satisfaction in your accomplishments, just as I feel a profound pride that this is so. In large measure the cooperation that was achieved was due to your personal efforts." On January 20, 1956, Eisenhower once more thanked his vice president for his "loyal and dedicated assistance" since taking office.[77]

Ike invited Nixon to the small stag dinners he gave at the White House—a much sought-after invitation. The vice president attended several and occasionally lobbied for supporters to be included. Robert DiGiorgio, who co-owned a large fruit corporation in California and had raised a large amount of money for the 1952 presidential campaign, attended one. In recommending him to Ike, Nixon noted that DiGiorgio was "a leading member of the Italo-American community in the country, in addition, is a fine, decent fellow." He believed Ike would enjoy his company. Nixon even arranged for Mrs. Norman "Buff" Chandler, the wife of the *Los Angeles Times* publisher, to have breakfast with the president, for which she thanked "Vice President Dick."[78]

The president spoke to friends about Nixon. In February 1953, Slats Slater wrote that Ike's "impression of Nixon is good and growing. He said Nixon sits very quietly at cabinet meetings, but when he says something it is to the point, well considered, and that others listen." At the end of July, after the two spoke again, Slater again recorded Ike's impressions: "Nixon is good, attends all cabinet and security meetings. And when Ike went to Augusta in the spring, a cabinet meeting was held just the same and Nixon conducted it well."[79]

At the end of 1954, when Paul Helms in California seemed to imply that Nixon was just "another politician," Ike responded: "I find him a most useful, capable and very loyal supporter." Helms promptly replied that he did not rate Nixon as just another politician: "I have almost a father and son attitude toward Dick."[80]

Eisenhower also recorded his thoughts about his vice president in his diary. On May 14, 1953, he included Nixon in a group of younger men who were important contributors to the administration's success. At the start of June, Ike wrote that Nixon was "not only bright, quick and energetic—but loyal and cooperative." A couple of weeks later Nixon hesitantly asked for an autograph from Ike, who seldom granted any. The president autographed a picture that hung in Nixon's office. Shortly before Christmas, Ike wrote his close friend "Swede" Hazlett that he was "trying to keep" certain individuals "in the public eye" so that the American people would learn more about them. Each was "a good executive and would certainly have my support." Of those in the executive department, he mentioned Ambassador Lodge, Attorney General Brownell, his deputy William Rogers, Nixon, and several others. At the end of January 1954, in a confidential letter to his brother Edgar, Ike identified Brownell, Nixon, Senators Knowland and Dirksen, and five others as his "trusted political advisers."

Sometime that spring or summer, the president made a handwritten list for Project X, possibly the time capsule located at his Gettysburg farm. Item #1 was Nixon: "Energetic—physically strong—politically astute—ambitious—good personality. Only weakness that I can detect (or think I can) is that he is very fond of nightlife in Washington. Sometimes has a bedraggled morning appearance."[81]

Nixon understood that he and the president worked well together. He also knew that behind Ike's broad grin and grandfatherly façade was a complicated personality. In *Six Crises*, he presented the president as "a far more complex and devious man than most people realized, and in the best sense of those words." Ike had many attributes. He knew how to break tension; he was a superb listener; and he was knowledgeable over a wide range of subjects. Once he arrived at a decision, they were generally good ones, and he stood by them.[82]

Nixon never called Eisenhower "Ike" during his White House tenure; it was always "Mr. President." When the occasion arose, Nixon discussed the political aspects of legislative or administrative determinations. Under some circumstances, he counseled the president to use patronage as a lever to win votes for his programs; the cabinet should highlight the positive nature of the White House programs; the State of the Union Message needed to be simple, brief, and limited to a few major items.[83]

As for their personal relationship, Nixon described it as "somewhat arms-length." They were "friends, but not cronies." The Nixons and Eisenhowers moved in different social circles. Ike was old enough to be Nixon's father and was evolving into a mentor. Nixon shared the president's "views as to the fundamental principles that should guide our foreign and domestic policies." When the occasion demanded candor, they spoke bluntly to one another.[84]

Nixon recorded some of his conversations with the president on dictabelts during the first term. On January 14, 1954, he commented that the president had an "amazing ability to hear briefing & cut through facts & figures—go to heart of problem—ask question." On the first of March, while discussing the Bricker amendment, an effort to take treaty power from the president, Ike urged his listeners "to keep our sense of humor." The cabinet could not "solve these problems with our mouths turned down rather than turned up." Ike often said to members of his administration: "Long faces never solve difficult problems." According to the vice president, Eisenhower thought in terms of five or ten years for what would benefit the nation. For Nixon, "Ike breaks tension", "Always listens", "Cuts through facts—wide knowledge."[85]

Sometimes Nixon and Eisenhower mixed politics with other items on the president's agenda. When they rode back and forth to the Marine base at Quantico, Virginia, that summer for a conference, the president told Nixon about his schedule for the next few months. It was not heavy for two reasons: he would not have "a brainstorming political trip," and while his doctor said that he was in "fine health" for his age, "he just needed more rest that he had previously required." They also chatted about politics and how pleased the president was that *Time* magazine said that "one of his greatest strengths was that he was able to present a partisan issue in a non-partisan way."[86]

Ike turned to childhood reflections. As a youth, he had boxed, but did not enjoy watching matches. He also complained about long cocktail hours because an extended period of drinking made guests hungrier. He felt uneasy when people flattered him to his face.

Then the president spoke about his experiences in World War II. Even though some thought he and his boss in World War II, General George Marshall, were close friends, they were not. Marshall's policy was to let his subordinates make "their own decisions," and they were not to discuss them with him unless "absolutely necessary." Ike, for instance, had sent the *Queen Mary* with 14,000 soldiers on board to Australia. Two enemy submarines were lurking in nearby waters. He did not sleep for two nights and only told Marshall about the situation after the danger had passed. With that mission completed, Marshall made Ike the supreme commander in Europe. Nixon inferred from the story that the president preferred "his subordinates carry the ball and do not take things up with him unless they feel it is necessary to do so."[87]

Ike called General George Patton "one of his closest friends," whom he protected from adversaries. As a general, Ike claimed that Patton "was great at chasing the enemy and mopping them rather than in conducting a drawn out evenly fought battle." Patton's rival, General Bernard "Monty" Montgomery, was "a very difficult man." Ike had to call him in twice and "let him know who was boss." After those encounters, Monty "played the game extremely well."

The vice president also remembered Ike said that once he made the decision to go forward with the Normandy landings on the French coast in June 1944, he relaxed and slept well. Nixon followed that practice after he entered the White House.[88]

Eisenhower told Nixon that "one of the most heart-rendering decisions" he ever made was the firebombing of Dresden, Germany. The city was not an ideal military target, but the objective was to demoralize the German population and force the collapse of the Third Reich. That single night of bombing cost thousands of German lives. The military action was immoral according to Ike, but so was Hitler's devastation of Europe. It would have been worse to allow the Fuhrer to continue his regime.[89]

The close association between Ike and Nixon led to an innovation in the politics of the executive branch: never before had a vice president emerged as a major presidential adviser. Ike provided the team structure for this to happen; Nixon seized the opportunity.

5

The Worst Kind of Politician

Upon entering the Oval Office, Dwight Eisenhower had identified his priorities. Developing a warm relationship with Senator Joseph McCarthy of Wisconsin was not one of them. In 1952 McCarthy had embarrassed Ike by viciously attacking General George Marshall as a traitor, and when Ike journeyed to Wisconsin during the campaign, he was further embarrassed when the press learned that Ike had deleted a powerful endorsement of Marshall from a speech in order to avoid making an implicit criticism of McCarthy.[1]

Two months after the election, the new president was still annoyed at McCarthy's claim that Ike "practically had to waltz with him all through Wisconsin if I was going to carry the state." Ike rejected the senator's boast; he had never deviated from his campaign plan and had received 200,000 more votes than McCarthy. He told speechwriter Emmet Hughes that McCarthy had "better get a little smart and realize that he isn't going to become—a Tsar—just yet!"[2] To Ike, the senator represented the worst kind of politician, and as president he planned to avoid him. He steadfastly refused to criticize him in public. To do so would only give McCarthy the press coverage he craved.

McCarthy was thus left for Nixon and others to deal with. Nixon and McCarthy had known each other since 1947, when Nixon entered Congress and began serving on the House Un-American Activities Committee, and after McCarthy launched his anticommunist crusade in 1950 he had asked Nixon for advice. Before the 1952 campaign began in earnest, during an interview on August 22, Nixon announced that in order to win control of Congress the ticket would back all GOP congressional candidates, including McCarthy. This did not mean that he or Ike endorsed "the views or the methods of Republican candidates which happen to be different from their own." As for "so-called McCarthyism," said Nixon, the Republican administration would investigate charges

91

of subversion against government employees, but these probes would be conducted fairly and would protect individual rights.[3]

A few days later, in an interview with *U.S. News & World Report*, Nixon asserted that the term *McCarthyism* was Truman's creation. Some, he said, viewed McCarthyism positively, as an effective program to confront domestic subversion; to others it meant "smear, unfair charges, charges not based on fact." He declared himself opposed to the latter.[4]

Even engulfed in controversy, McCarthy easily won his primary on September 9, and Nixon told *Look* magazine that the new administration would "give full hearing to the McCarthy charges, letting the chips fall where they may." Journalist Ralph de Toledano wrote Whittaker Chambers that GOP regulars were shocked at the junior senator's "overwhelming victory" and Ike and Nixon would "have to eat crow." The vice-presidential nominee had behaved badly toward McCarthy by not enthusiastically backing him and would have to change his posture if the Republicans expected to win in November. If not, many supporters, particularly anticommunists in California, would be "furious" and would desert Nixon.[5]

When the fund crisis reached its apex and Nixon needed his support the most, McCarthy remarked that Americans should examine Adlai Stevenson's "dismal" record. Stevenson, McCarthy said, thought Hiss was "a great American, Nixon brought about his conviction . . . and Hiss once recommended Stevenson for a top political job." After the fund speech, McCarthy publicly declared that "It was a great speech and I believe it clearly vindicates Dick Nixon in the eyes of the nation."[6]

Stevenson accused Eisenhower on October 22 of encouraging Nixon and McCarthy to make slanderous statements distorting his association with Hiss. In the closing weeks of the race, the Democratic nominee charged that McCarthy was orchestrating the Republicans' campaign. When Nixon appeared before 15,000 spectators in Superior, Wisconsin, two days later, he endorsed the statewide Republican ticket, called McCarthy "my good friend" and called for his reelection.[7]

McCarthy won, and the GOP gained control of the Senate, making him something more than a minority gadfly. New majority leader Robert Taft selected him to preside over the committee on government operations, the Senate's most powerful investigative body. As chairman, McCarthy appointed himself to the chair of the permanent subcommittee on investigations, a post that gave him a substantial budget to conduct wide-ranging inquiries.[8]

McCarthy respected Taft's opinion; he considered Taft a mentor and usually followed his advice. Ever since McCarthy burst onto the national scene, Taft had effectively deployed him to embarrass the Truman administration, a mission McCarthy relished. Now that Republicans controlled both Congress and the White House, Eisenhower thought McCarthy should continue his anticommunist efforts but stop trying to embarrass the administration. He expected Taft to bring him to heel.

Nixon, having served for two years in the Senate with both Taft and McCarthy, held a more nuanced opinion. Even though he understood that Ike would win any fight with the senator, he thought the cost of creating a split in the party might be too high. They had a single vote majority in the Senate, and McCarthy was only one of forty-eight Republican prima donnas who, together with the independent Wayne Morse, made up their caucus. The vice president saw maintaining party harmony as the main priority.[9]

During the second cabinet meeting, on January 30, Nixon volunteered to act as an intermediary between the administration and McCarthy, an offer the president welcomed. Sometimes he would treat the senator bluntly. One day, Nixon's receptionist, Dorothy Donnelly, overheard the vice president lecture the senator: "You're right about some things, Joe, but you can't go shooting off your mouth."[10]

As the Senate's presiding officer, Nixon regularly saw McCarthy on the Senate floor; they telephoned one another; and they began holding private meetings, often for dinner on Sundays, with others who favored keeping McCarthy on the Eisenhower team. Deputy attorney general Bill Rogers hosted the first gathering, in January, at his home in Bethesda, Maryland; deputy chief of staff Jerry Persons hosted supper at his apartment on California Avenue; the vice president sponsored lunches in his private retreat in the Capitol building; sometimes the group met in the evening at the Carlton Hotel.[11]

The meetings did not ensure McCarthy's loyalty. In April, after Eisenhower chose Charles "Chip" Bohlen as ambassador to the Soviet Union, McCarthy used the confirmation hearings to argue strenuously against the appointment. With the support of New Hampshire Republican Styles Bridges and a few others, the Wisconsin senator insisted that the selection be withdrawn due to Bohlen's links to the eastern establishment, the "Yalta sell-out" (in 1945, Bohlen had served as FDR's translator at the Yalta Conference), and the Truman administration. Eisenhower admired Bohlen, whom he had worked with during World War II, and refused to withdraw the nomination. Reports leaked that the FBI had uncovered damaging personal material on Bohlen. To prevent their becoming available to public scrutiny, Taft and Alabama senator John Sparkman reviewed the FBI material and cleared the nominee of any loyalty issues. This did not satisfy McCarthy, who denounced Bohlen on the Senate floor: "We find that his entire history is one of complete, wholehearted, 100 percent cooperation with the Acheson-Hiss-Truman regime." Two days later, on March 27, the Senate confirmed Bohlen by a vote of seventy-four to thirteen. Taft, who along with Nixon had led the confirmation effort, pleaded with the president: "No more Bohlens."[12]

Taft was inclined to excuse McCarthy's behavior. Although Bohlen's appointment was not worth a divisive intraparty battle and "perhaps McCarthy joined the opposition a little too vociferously," he said to Donald Rowley, publisher of Ohio's Star-Bacon Newspapers, "that was principally because the newspapers insist on playing up everything he does or says."[13] Ike, aware that America's allies were paying close attention, remarked that Taft gave "McCarthy ideas and McCarthy, with his readiness to go to extremes in calling names and making false accusations, simply terrifies the ordinary European statesman."[14]

At a cabinet meeting the same day as the confirmation, the president asked what action should be taken regarding McCarthy. He refused the obvious option of openly denouncing him. The White House had significantly improved its congressional relations in the past two months, and that positive step should be encouraged and strengthened. Congressional allies, Ike added, needed to assist in their opposition to "extreme minorities." Nixon concurred; the executive branch had to have "the very best possible relationships with the Congress."[15]

Starting in April, when Taft's health began to deteriorate, the job of managing McCarthy—and of trying to convince him that his grandstanding often harmed party interests—fell increasingly to Nixon. By June, although it was clear that Ike opposed some of McCarthy's activities, Nixon still hoped to avoid "a head-on fight." The president knew that his slim congressional majority must be preserved. Nixon, who counted votes better than anyone else in his party, recognized every vote as vital.

In midsummer, Slats Slater, one of Ike's golf and bridge buddies, recorded a conversation in which Ike opined that "the newspapers made McCarthy and that he would fade out of the picture quickly if they would ignore most of the furor he creates which is certainly not entitled to front page play any more than is the work of other congressional committees."[16] When Taft controlled the majority, McCarthy could not summon anywhere near enough votes to defeat a nominee. He could make wild charges, but after he finished speaking they had no substantial impact. But after Taft died on July 31, his successor, William Knowland of California, had less influence on the Wisconsin senator.

And McCarthy had his chairmanship of the permanent subcommittee on investigations, a post that gave him the legislative authority to inquire in a multitude of directions. In the last week of March, he went on television to announce that he had negotiated an agreement with Greek shipowners located in New York that they would stop trading with Mainland China and other Russian satellite ports. On learning of this, Harold Stassen, the president's Mutual Security director, branded the settlement "phony" and charged that McCarthy was undermining American foreign policy. Stassen went further in congressional testimony and later asked McCarthy if the agreement included a pledge that his subcommittee would not look into the practices of the ship owners. McCarthy was outraged by the accusation.[17]

To resolve the squabble, Nixon, with Ike's consent, arranged a luncheon between the senator and Secretary of State Dulles at which he conceded that the agreement was in the national interest. When questioned about the episode, the president told a press conference that while McCarthy did not have the authority to negotiate treaties, the senator had not, as Stassen charged, "undermined" diplomacy. "Infringed," he suggested, would be a more suitable description. Stassen altered his posture and followed the White House's lead. Taft took a middle course: he said McCarthy "did a real service scaring" the ship owners but had exceeded his authority by trying to act as secretary of state in negotiating a formal agreement.[18]

Several months later, Democratic senators Symington and McClellan persuaded McCarthy to send a letter to the president asking him to provide a policy statement in regard to Allied trade with the People's Republic of China. Nixon recognized this request as a partisan ploy to embarrass the administration. No matter how the president replied, some group would take exception. He explained to McCarthy the uncomfortable position in which the Democrats had placed the president. The senator withdrew the letter.[19]

McCarthy continued his shotgun blasts at vulnerable federal agencies. The weakest was probably the International Information Agency (IIA), especially its Voice of America (VOA) division. Even though Ike championed winning the hearts and minds of people in foreign countries, he did not initially interfere with McCarthy's assault on that agency.

Almost as soon as he was installed as a committee chairman and the 1953 inaugural ceremonies were completed, the senator commenced his investigation. The IIA, which had had its budget severely cut for 1953, resulting in the departure of 600 employees, was suspect on several grounds. The new director, Robert Johnson, had no experience in the federal bureaucracy and little inkling of the ferocious assault that McCarthy and other Republican conservatives would mount. The agency had no major stalwarts to protect it from the charge of being "soft on communism"—no Foster Dulles at its helm nor congressional champions promoting its accomplishments. Shortly after McCarthy began his campaign to rid the IIA and VOA of communist sympathizers, Reed

Harris, a well-respected administrator, resigned as a protest against further weakening of morale.[20]

To ameliorate some of the worst of the senator's attacks, Nixon met with Johnson and his executive assistant, Martin Merson, on April 14. He urged them to cooperate with McCarthy and arranged for the three men to meet the next day. McCarthy then canceled the meeting and never rescheduled. After McCarthy's staffers David Schine and Roy Cohn went on their infamous European tour to root out subversive books at the IIA's stations, Johnson and Merson again saw Nixon during the first week of May in an effort to defend their agency.[21]

Johnson spoke with Nixon about his troubled agency in the middle of the month. Its relations with the state department were awful; low salaries made it impossible to attract well-qualified applicants; the demoralized staff made frequent blunders. As a result, Johnson admitted, "the program has been infiltrated with Communist sympathizers, left-wingers, and incompetents." He later added that some unnamed individuals had sabotaged IIA operations.[22]

In the midst of McCarthy's attack toward the end of April, presidential speechwriter Emmet Hughes wrote a diary entry about his lunch with deputy chief of staff Jerry Persons, who conceded that the senator might be "an SOB" but maintained he was a complicated character. Hughes disagreed. McCarthy was more than "a little more difficult than others [senators]." He was self-absorbed. Persons handled congressional relations and wanted to keep McCarthy an administration supporter. Persons, who realized that the Republicans had been in the minority for two decades and needed to advance constructive proposals, replied that "this damn party really doesnt have any sense of responsibility yet—some of the guys are getting it—others may never get it—but its gonna take time and a lot of work—or theyll wreck the whole goddam show." [All spellings are as written.]

Persons then described a conversation he had had with the president: "the boss was all for letting McCarthy have it once or twice and has gotten pretty mad at me for restraining him." Persons urged a conciliatory attitude, recalling General Marshall's admonishment: "Never let your personal feelings get in the way of official business or youre sunk." Ike should work with the senator, Persons argued, maintaining that "some of the boys liked him." The president replied: "Goddam it, Jerry, doesnt it make you feel a little UNCLEAN." Persons shot back: "Not a bit, sir—if I was doing it for myself, sure Id feel unclean, but when its not for me, when its for what I thinks best in the long run for the government, no sir, I don't feel dirty one bit."[23]

Even though Ike did not come to the IIA's assistance, he addressed the issue of Schine and Cohn's destroying books on June 14, when he spoke at the Dart-

mouth College commencement. Departing from his text, he cautioned his listeners: "Don't join the book burners. Don't think you are going to conceal faults
by concealing evidence that they ever existed." Some thought the president was
about to repudiate McCarthy and his two staffers, but three days later, he back-
tracked and told a press conference that the state department had the obligation
to burn books that led unsuspecting readers to accept communist doctrine.[24]

Nixon talked to McCarthy after the Dartmouth speech, exacting a pledge
from the senator that he would shortly finish his IIA inquiry. The vice president
warned: "You should not be known as a one-shot senator." To Johnson and
Merson, this promise came too late: they submitted their resignations at the beginning of July. On August 1, IIA was replaced by the United States Information
Agency (USIA). McCarthy, meanwhile, had moved on to other pursuits; he
never issued a report on his investigation of IIA. Around USIA's first anniversary,
in 1954, the vice president spoke to nearly 1,000 employees, telling them, "We
all know that we are in a death struggle with the forces of slavery represented by
the international communist conspiracy." The agency, he conceded, had become a whipping boy for those who wanted to slash federal spending, and yet it
had to explain America's actions to the rest of the world: "I believe that the job
that this Agency has, in the long-run, is certainly as important and in the long-
run maybe more important than the job of the military, the FOA and even the
State Department in these fields." Winning hearts, souls, and minds was an
essential task, and he pledged to fight for USIA appropriations.[25]

On one occasion, a McCarthy employee surprised his boss. In late June, the
senator hired J. B. Matthews as the subcommittee on investigations' chief investi-
gator. At the beginning of July, the *American Mercury* published an article that
Matthews had written entitled "Reds and Our Churches." The first sentence
read: "The largest single group supporting the Communist apparatus in the
United States today is composed of Protestant clergymen."[26]

When the three Democrats on the McCarthy subcommittee learned about
this article, they and one Republican member, Charles Potter of Michigan, voted
in a July 9 committee meeting for Matthews to be fired. Despite the majority
vote, McCarthy refused, asserting that only he as the chairman had the right to
hire and fire. Protestant clergy from across the United States expressed their outrage to the White House. Those who already despised McCarthy saw this incident as another example of the senator's uncontrollable excesses, and they joined
the chorus demanding a correction.

Two days later, Nixon suggested to Senator Potter that he reverse his vote and
give Matthews the option of resigning. This satisfied neither the clergy and their
supporters, who demanded Matthews's removal, nor the White House advisers,

who fervently wished the president would denounce both the author and the man who had hired him. That afternoon the staff hastily drafted a statement for Ike's approval. Meanwhile, McCarthy decided to accept Matthews' resignation and to announce it that evening on conservative radio host Fulton Lewis Jr.'s broadcast.

At 5:24 p.m., the White House released Eisenhower's statement deploring Matthews' commentary as "alien to America" and as showing "contempt for the principles of freedom and decency." Nixon and Bill Rogers waylaid McCarthy and kept him from reaching Lewis's studio until after the president's message had gone out. The senator appeared a half hour later, leaving the distinct impression that Ike's statement had prompted him to fire Matthews.[27]

Emmet Hughes saw the president "spry and in fine humor" at 10:45 a.m. on July 15. The speechwriter said that the reaction to Matthews's resignation ran ten to fifteen to one in favor. The president "grinned wrily [wryly]": "it all worked out pretty well. God, though, I certainly thought it was something to hear *that guy* talk about not censoring anybody, when all he's been doing is trying to act like a goddam censor himself."[28]

Embarrassment did not cause McCarthy to rethink his tactics. Rather than proceed cautiously after this humiliation, he decided to attack the CIA. He had been dropping hints of his intention to investigate the agency since before the inauguration, and both Nixon and Central Intelligence Director Allen Dulles had met with him to try to talk him out of it.[29] The futility of these attempts became apparent on July 9, when the permanent subcommittee on investigations issued a subpoena to William Bundy, the CIA liaison to the NSC, ordering him to appear before the subcommittee. McCarthy had discovered that Bundy was Dean Acheson's son-in-law and that he had given $400 to Hiss's defense fund. He wanted to interrogate Bundy about that contribution under oath.[30]

After the subpoena was delivered, Nixon and deputy attorney general Rogers met with three members of the subcommittee—Senators McCarthy, Mundt, and Potter—to discuss the implications of forcing a CIA employee to testify. The vice president, joined by Mundt and Potter, insisted that the agency's covert operations must remain secret and could not become a vehicle for any Senate inquiry. Besides interceding with McCarthy's colleagues, Nixon also vouched for Bundy's loyalty. He had observed Bundy at NSC meetings and found his actions beyond reproach. Nixon also pledged to have Dulles check Bundy's clearance. With these assurances and the pressure from the other senators, McCarthy agreed to withdraw the subpoena.[31]

According to Hughes, Nixon and Rogers "had it out with" McCarthy in a private conversation, insisting he conclude his CIA inquiry. They told him: "Joe you just haven't got the votes in committee." The vice president even had Dirksen to vote against his colleague. Rogers added: "He fought and griped like hell, he didn't like it, but he knew he had to play ball—and I think he will."[32]

Even with that accord, McCarthy postured for the press. On July 10 he asserted that "we have the right to subpoena the people of any Government bureau. If we did not, it would be impossible to uncover corruption, communism, and other wrong action. . . . [CIA employees] are not sacrosanct." Allen Dulles publicly conceded that no CIA directive prohibited its members from testifying before congressional committees. Four days later, he and McCarthy agreed to a nebulous formula where his subcommittee might call CIA employees without imperiling national security.[33]

Nixon and Rogers had dinner with Emmet Hughes on the evening of July 16 at the Silver Fox restaurant, where they chatted for four hours. Hughes had a favorable impression of the vice president at cabinet meetings, and the dinner confirmed his opinion: Nixon was "realistic, politically astute, and on the 'liberal' side of whatever issues emerged; he is candid, clear and unpretentious." After Nixon evaluated Taft's possible successors, the conversation turned to McCarthy. Both Nixon and Rogers called him "a brash, lusty, unscrupulous . . . type—utterly devoid of coherent scheming or long-range planning."

Rogers believed that McCarthy did not know what he was planning from one minute to the next. He desperately wanted to be liked and could be charming. The deputy attorney general labeled him "a counterpuncher—when he thinks he's getting pushed around, he snarls back—he knows damn well he isn't liked by the Administration, he's never asked anywhere, he's cussed in private—and he does all he understands how to do—hit back." Nixon added that the gossip that McCarthy was planning to run for the presidency "and his big conspiracy and all that—[are] crap—pure crap."[34]

Early in October, the Nixons left on a goodwill mission across the Pacific. During his travels, he informed his staff: "I do not want anyone in the party to be on the defensive re McCarthy—we do not want to be in position of defending him either but we do not want to give the impression that we have to defend our attitude on Communists in Government."[35]

With Taft having died in July and Nixon abroad, Eisenhower decided to take luster from the senator by pushing his own anticommunist crusade. He approved Attorney General Brownell's request to expose the espionage activities of Harry Dexter White, who had worked in sensitive treasury posts under FDR. Truman appointed White director of the International Monetary Fund at the end of 1946; several months later, he abruptly resigned and left government service. In 1948 he was called before a federal grand jury on suspicion of spying, and late that summer, he defended himself before HUAC. Three days after his HUAC testimony, he died suddenly of a heart attack.

On November 6, 1953, speaking before the Executive Club of Chicago, Brownell charged that the previous administration had appointed White to the IMF while knowing that he was suspected of espionage. A livid Truman quickly responded during an evening television-radio address, claiming that Brownell was lying about Truman's actions and that he fired White instantly upon learning of his spying. "I have been accused," he said, "of knowingly betraying the security of the United States." He accused the attorney general of pandering to McCarthyites for political advantage. By reacting aggressively when his loyalty was questioned, Truman initially helped to mute Brownell's charges.

Brownell had not anticipated such an explosive reaction. He toned down his allegations of the former president's complicity, claiming that his speech had been misrepresented, and said he had only accused the previous administration of laxity. Truman helped the attorney general by admitting that he had read an FBI report concerning White's spying, but on the advice of FBI director Hoover had decided not to fire White because that would alert his ring that it was under surveillance. Hoover immediately denied that this ever took place, and former secretary of state James Byrnes sided with Hoover. Truman then contradicted himself by proclaiming White's innocence and describing Brownell's investigation as an attempt by Republicans to besmirch a dead man's reputation.

During a nineteen-minute press conference in December, Ike defended his attorney general. He said he approved Brownell's decision to reveal the facts surrounding White's spying, but he did not think Truman knowingly appointed a Russian spy. He was not, he insisted, attempting to spotlight the previous administration's failures but merely pointing out that White should never have reached such a high post and that it should not happen again.[36]

Although Truman's attempt to portray Brownell as throwing a bone to the Republican right for political advantage was partially successful within the Democratic Party, his counterattack did not persuade many media observers. Despite those mixed results, Truman kept himself on a consistent course throughout the Eisenhower presidency. He would not have his character questioned under any circumstances. Any Republican attack, real or imagined, upon his loyalty would be met with full-throated outrage.

Eisenhower learned a lesson. Brownell was an ineffective choice to promote the administration's anticommunist cause. Nixon had won his credentials by exposing Hiss and by campaigning against the communist menace. From this point on, Nixon would be the administration's main spokesman on the issue.

When Nixon returned to the capital, the staff that had traveled with him reported on the "very bad" morale of the career foreign service officers wherever the vice president stopped. The staff identified three factors: attacks on the diplomatic corps had "cast a public odium on the foreign service"; the state department had not announced an end to the firing of possible communists, causing anxiety within the bureaucracy; and employees viewed the assistant secretary for personnel and security, Robert McLeod, with "almost a pathological hatred." A McCarthy ally, McLeod was seen as his state department stooge. He knew nothing about the Foreign Service and had never visited an overseas diplomatic post.[37]

At the end of the year, while vacationing with their families at the Key Biscayne Hotel, Nixon and Rogers met with McCarthy. They did not try to get any commitments from him, nor did the senator make any promises. The vice president nonetheless thought that while McCarthy would continue his investigations of domestic subversion and other government issues in the New Year, he would devote some of his energies to legislation and would support the president's agenda. McCarthy, Nixon believed, would "spread his activities during the next year because of his own self interest that he needs to have a broadened field of activity."[38]

After leaving these talks, McCarthy held a press conference in Miami on December 30 to announce that his subcommittee would investigate tax settlements under the Truman administration "which had been compromised at ridiculously low figures," as little as twenty cents on the dollar. He questioned the terms of other settlements for a variety of reasons[39] and added a new threat: he was considering reviewing the cases of former assistant attorney general James McInerney, where he failed to prosecute subversives. The senator claimed he had discussed this plan with Nixon, who "thought it was a good idea." He was going to have Bill Rogers turn over pertinent documents to the Senate committee on government operations. McCarthy never conducted this investigation.[40]

Just about every American who had heard of McCarthy had an opinion. Gallup had conducted polls throughout 1953, and in mid-December half of respondents had a favorable view of McCarthy while 29 percent disapproved. The pollsters asked a second question as well: if the congressional candidate in your district had the senator's support, how would you vote? On this question, 21 percent said they would be more likely to vote for the candidate, 26 percent less likely, and 45 percent saw no difference.[41]

The individual inside the administration who worked the hardest to prevent an Eisenhower-McCarthy confrontation was Nixon, whom Sherman Adams described as the "principal protagonist in this behind-the-scenes drama." This assignment was no mystery: the goal was to keep the senator on the team. Reporters frequently described the vice president as the White House liaison to McCarthy.[42]

How well did Nixon do? He was responsible for McCarthy's sending a letter to the White House opposing James Conant's appointment as United States high commissioner for West Germany rather than staging a floor fight. On the Chip Bohlen appointment, the senator could have been far more vicious, but the vice president had urged restraint. During the controversy over the Greek shipowners, Nixon arranged the luncheon at which Foster Dulles and McCarthy came to an agreement. In the debilitating attacks on IIA and VOA, Nixon could not get McCarthy to meet with the agency director, but he did persuade him to conclude his inquires and pursue other subjects. The effort to subpoena Bill Bundy ended with CIA director Allen Dulles and McCarthy trying to display a cooperative spirit. Nixon's efforts in these matters, though conducted quietly, were reported in the press. Each case required a deft touch.

The president followed McCarthy's activities but allowed Taft, Nixon, and others to try to moderate the senator's extremes. He was not, for Eisenhower, one of the priorities on which he focused his attention. The next year, McCarthy would become the enemy.

6

THE COLLISION

For two decades or so after Eisenhower left office, most journalists and historians thought he had been far too passive in dealing with Joseph McCarthy. This
view began to change in the early 1980s, and today the overwhelming consensus is that the president used a "hidden-hand" approach to bring the senator
down. He did not overtly conspire to cause the senator's collapse and never publicly attacked him. He believed that giving McCarthy more press only played
into his hands. Yet the details of this "hidden hand" have never been fully
laid out. Once the president decided to make McCarthy's downfall a priority,
he developed the strategy and coordinated his staff, select cabinet members,
and Nixon to bring it about. Thirty years afterward, Nixon explained why Ike
went after McCarthy. First and foremost, the senator had attacked his beloved
Army; second, Ike disliked McCarthy personally; third, McCarthy had defamed
General Marshall; fourth, McCarthy drew attention from the administration's
accomplishments; finally, Eisenhower thought that the senator "was swinging
wildly, and . . . therefore doing more harm to the [anticommunist] cause than
good."[1]

During most of Ike's first year in office, the priority was keeping McCarthy a
firm supporter of the Republican majority in the Senate. In the second week of
September, deputy attorney general Rogers, who fondly called McCarthy "Jumping Joe," said to Secretary of the Army Robert Stevens, "half of the battle is to
have [a] good relationship with him." Stevens answered, "We are getting along
well with Joe." Then McCarthy drew headlines by making accusations about
subversion within the Army Signal Corps.

The cooperative spirit had already started to evaporate when Army attorney
John Adams wrote Stevens on December 10 that McCarthy wanted one of his
chief assistants, G. David Schine, who had been drafted in early November, to

receive special treatment after basic training. Adams argued that Schine should not work with classified documents because he "would have no compunction about compromising such material, and then starting a Congressional investigation."[2]

Feeling that a break was inevitable, McCarthy foes within the administration, such as Henry Cabot Lodge, Sherman Adams, and Herbert Brownell, began to meet privately. For this group of presidential counselors, compromise was no longer an option. Advisers sympathetic to keeping the senator on the team, such as Nixon, Bill Rogers, and Jerry Persons, were excluded from these meetings.[3]

Nixon continued to try to manage the senator while following the president's dictates concerning him. As the vice president left his office on the evening of January 4, 1954, a reporter asked him how he was dealing with McCarthy; he replied that he was still acting as a peacemaker and hoping to get the senator to concentrate on waste and corruption rather than anticommunism. When McCarthy was told of Nixon's remarks, he called the story "a lie." Nixon, he insisted, would never have said such a thing.[4]

While McCarthy continued to capture headlines as the leader of the anticommunist crusade, by the beginning of 1954 he was increasingly seen as not only ruthless but reckless as well. He doggedly went after the enemy, or the alleged enemy, but he employed dubious methods. Still, even given the wide diversity of opinion on McCarthyism, at the start of the year his favorable ratings stood at 50 percent, and throughout the year they never slipped below 30 percent.[5]

The senator was unaware that the president had begun to assemble his lieutenants to move against him. Many years later, Henry Cabot Lodge recalled that Ike had scheduled a meeting in the attorney general's office on January 21. According to Lodge, this was "Eisenhower's first move against McCarthy and led to McCarthy's ultimate downfall."[6]

At the start of 1954, McCarthy found a new subject. Irving Peress, a reserve Army captain, was a dentist from Queens, New York, who was drafted in October 1952 and assigned to Camp Kilmer, New Jersey. When asked to sign a loyalty oath, he refused. The Army did not notice this embarrassing oversight until the end of 1953. In the meantime, Peress completed his service and was honorably discharged shortly before McCarthy could interview him.[7]

Acting as a one-man subcommittee, McCarthy called the dentist to testify at the Manhattan federal courthouse on January 30, 1954, where Peress invoked the Fifth Amendment. The senator was furious, and several weeks later he called the camp commander, Brigadier General Ralph Zwicker, to testify. Zwicker was a West Point graduate and a highly decorated soldier under Eisenhower's command during World War II. In a bitter exchange in the Federal Building in Manhattan, the senator humiliated the general by declaring that he was "not fit to wear that uniform" and should "be removed from any command." Even more demeaning was his flippant remark that Zwicker did not have "the brains of a five-year-old-child."[8]

Private Schine, meanwhile, had been assigned to basic training at Fort Dix, New Jersey. Almost from the moment of his induction, Roy Cohn, an intimate of Schine's and chief counsel to McCarthy, pressured the Army to grant Schine weekend passes, excessive telephone calls, relief from kitchen duties, and other privileges.[9]

The differences between McCarthy and the administration were sharply drawn at the GOP's traditional Lincoln Day events. Nixon in previous years had told the party faithful about the Truman administration's poor judgment, but McCarthy stirred up partisan hatred, calling the New and Fair Deal era "twenty years of treason." Ike disapproved of this language, and of the senator's description of Democrats as "political sadists." The president, according to Nixon, never liked "to indulge in name calling; prefers subtle approach—constructive talk." The GOP, Ike knew, needed Democratic voters to win elections.[10]

With these ritual celebrations of party unity behind them, the Army and McCarthy resumed their collision course. On February 19, Secretary Stevens forbade his service's officers from testifying before McCarthy's subcommittee, and telephoned the senator about the order. If anyone from the Army must appear, Stevens would go himself.[11]

The following Tuesday, February 23, Jerry Persons called Stevens to a strategy meeting in the vice president's office. Nixon, Persons, Stevens, Stevens's legal counsel John Adams, and Senators Knowland and Dirksen attended. Stevens asked the group for advice on his "show-down" with McCarthy, but first offered his opinion that the Army would admit its errors in the Peress case and then protest the senator's humiliation of General Zwicker.

The politicians replied that the senator would "tear [Stevens] to pieces." Nixon later explained to *New York Times* columnist Arthur Krock that the Army representatives did not "seem to understand the American system of government at all." McCarthy, by chairing the session, would control the scope of the inquiry. Although Stevens could not "be salvaged," the vice president thought McCarthy could "be tamed" since he had accepted compromise throughout the previous year. McCarthy was a loyal Republican, Nixon observed, but he had "a power complex and any impressive argument that an action by him endangers his possession of power wins him over." The group finally concluded that Stevens should have lunch the next day with the four Republican subcommittee members in Dirksen's private office, right next to Nixon's. Dirksen believed he could

get his Wisconsin colleague to attend since he was one of the few friends Mc-
Carthy had left in the Senate.[12]

On February 24, Stevens left the Pentagon under the illusion that he was
headed for a secret luncheon. He arrived to find Dirksen's door surrounded by
scores of newspapermen; someone had leaked the meeting to the press. One
capital insider quipped that Stevens was "like a goldfish in a tank of barracuda."
The main course was fried chicken, which gave the gathering its name: it became notorious as "the chicken lunch." By the end of the meal, Senator Karl
Mundt of South Dakota had drafted a memo of understanding in which Stevens
pledged to allow General Zwicker to continue testifying, while McCarthy
avoided making any written commitment. Stevens returned to the Pentagon, apparently satisfied with the outcome, and telephoned Nixon that "he had done
what he had done for the team." McCarthy, always ready with a pithy quote,
told reporters that "Stevens couldn't have surrendered more abjectly if he had
gotten down on his knees." Stevens's good feeling about the lunch vanished when
the stories in that afternoon's newspapers were all about how he had given in to
McCarthy.[13]

With McCarthy's accounts of the meeting circulating throughout Washington, Stevens received a telephone call at 6:38 p.m. from Fred Seaton, who said
he would talk to reporters about McCarthy's misinterpretation of the results.
Stevens was angry: "But if it turns out I am a yellow-belly and McCarthy is a
hero," the secretary would strenuously object and supply his own account of his
agreement with McCarthy.[14]

Later that evening Stevens telephoned Hagerty to tender his resignation. An
hour and a half later, he called Nixon "in a terrible emotional state." He had
decided to resign the next day, even though no one had called for such a drastic
measure. Nixon tried to dissuade him; they would meet the next morning to
work up a press statement outlining how the Army would resolve the Peress
matter and defend General Zwicker.[15]

On Thursday morning, Nixon saw Ike at an NSC meeting. The president had
been kept apprised of the Stevens fiasco and said as he looked around the table,
"Well, Dick, I see you are still smiling." Nixon noted that when the president
was "under great stress he usually has a tendency to show a very calm exterior."
Eisenhower had already seen Senator Dirksen about a statement backing Stevens
on the positive results of the chicken lunch. Persons, Lodge, and Lucius Clay
commented that McCarthy was considering a run for the presidency, to which
Ike responded that he and his team had "better quit being nice to this guy—he's
a bad friend."[16] At that point, he began to assemble a team to bring the senator
down.

Ike first met with Nixon, Sherman Adams, and Persons. The latter three worked for the remainder of the day in Persons' office on a White House statement. The final version stressed that the Army had never retreated from its original policy of defending against abuse of Army personnel at congressional hearings. McCarthy, Stevens said, had given those assurances at the chicken lunch, but Mundt had not included them in his memorandum of understanding. While they drafted the declaration, Ike "practiced chip shots on the South Lawn," his usual way of relieving tension. The group took the finished copy to the White House's second-floor study, where the president reviewed it and "made it stronger." Then Hagerty released it to the press.[17]

The presidential statement included three items that McCarthy would never admit: that he had been abusive toward Zwicker, that he had made a promise to Stevens about future good conduct, and that calling more officers in the Peress case might be unnecessary. When the statement was released, McCarthy labeled its account of the chicken lunch understanding "completely false."[18]

Ike kept to his policy of not publicly rebuking McCarthy, but this did not prevent him from venting privately. According to Hagerty's diary, the president was "very mad and getting fed up—it's his Army and he doesn't like McCarthy's tactics at all." Ike vowed he was "not going to take this one lying down—my friends tell me it won't be long in this Army stuff before McCarthy starts using my name instead of Stevens. He's ambitious. He wants to be President. He's the last guy in the world who'll ever get there, if I have anything to say."[19]

Nixon, in an interview with Arthur Krock, described Hagerty as advocating a public assault on McCarthy while others warned "against this as certain, whatever it does to McCarthy, to split the Republican party wide open with loss of Congress the first electoral consequence."[20]

At the end of February, McCarthy told the press that Eisenhower was not trying "to curb" his "powers." Both of them had pledged during the 1952 campaign to rid the nation of the communist menace, and McCarthy was adhering to that commitment. He was "going to write Bob Stevens a friendly letter" pointing out the issues surrounding the bungling of Peress's honorable discharge.[21]

At the White House for the weekly legislative conference, House majority leader Charles Halleck criticized his Senate colleagues for their inept handling of the Army-McCarthy matter. Halleck, an Eisenhower supporter, thought Secretary Stevens was "a good, honest man" and affirmed that House GOP members regarded the "present controversy as a bad fight among Republicans." He thought the Republican senators should have defended Stevens more effectively and shuddered at the thought "of a televised fight between Republicans" pitting McCarthy against Stevens. Ike assured those present that Stevens was cooperating with GOP senators. The president conceded that Congress had the right to investigate within certain limits and instructed Stevens to admit that the Army had blundered. He did not excuse McCarthy's treatment of Zwicker, saying, "You can't keep Communism out of the United States by destroying Americans."[22] Nixon chimed in, holding that security risks needed to be driven from the federal government: "There will be no cover-up in this administration." Congressional committees regularly asserted their right to investigate, and the administration had to cooperate. But it must insist on "fair play." Both Stevens and Zwicker were patriots. "To abuse them is indefensible."[23]

After adjournment, according to Nixon, Ike "swore considerably about his exasperation at being unable to get the Republicans and the country to see what he was trying to do and to get the united support he thought the program was entitled to." Shaking his head, Ike concluded that "the [GOP] elephant is losing a lot of hide these days."[24]

That afternoon, Nixon, Bill Rogers, Dirksen, Persons, Len Hall, and Arthur Summerfield gathered in a room at the Carlton Hotel. Hall demanded that Dirksen direct McCarthy to cancel the hearing set for Thursday, where Stevens was scheduled to testify. Persons had privately informed the vice president before the conference that the Army secretary "was in no condition to attend such a meeting." According to Dirksen, McCarthy was irate that Stevens had contacted Democratic members of the subcommittee and had called Colonel Robert McCormick, owner of the *Chicago Tribune*, who then wrote an editorial about the chicken luncheon that was critical of McCarthy. Dirksen, the others insisted, had to have McCarthy take the initiative in canceling the hearing. He must give no hint that Stevens was involved in the decision.[25]

That evening, the Nixons attended an informal dinner party at the Knowlands, where Jean and Joe McCarthy were also present. After supper, Knowland, McCarthy, and Nixon discussed the Stevens case. The Wisconsin senator was upset by the adverse national reaction to his Army investigation and did not understand "why a dinky little fifth amendment Communist [Peress] should get so much attention." He had made plans to travel to Arizona for ten days and would postpone the hearing. He seemed concerned about his image and thought he might "remain relatively quiet for a few months." The Republican Party, he said, was failing to implement an effective program against domestic subversion, but he conceded that his confrontation with the Army had created a serious breach within the GOP.[26]

On March 2, Nixon entered the White House through the East Wing side door. He, Sherman Adams, Persons, and Hagerty had lunch with the president in anticipation of Eisenhower's press conference the next day. The president seemed in excellent spirits and asked Nixon to sit beside him instead of directly across from him, where the vice president usually sat. Ike declared his staff was "actually afraid of McCarthy" and recounted a story about his West Point boxing coach who "used to hit him clear across the ring." If Ike did not rise smiling, the instructor "would turn his back and walk out of the room."[27]

Ike, Nixon believed, now seemed "more reasonable" about how the Army had bungled the Peress matter. Hagerty submitted a draft for the press conference that, as Nixon saw it, contained "a very dangerous paragraph which took pretty much the complete left wing line that those who investigated Communism were as great a danger as the Communists themselves and that the methods of the investigators of Communism were the same as Communists methods." Nixon also objected to a paragraph that implied Congress had many more-pressing issues than domestic subversion. The statement also specifically referred to General Zwicker. Ike struck this line "because that would be considered to be direct criticism of McCarthy and he did not want to elevate him to that position." In its place, the president substituted the phrase: "You can't defeat Communism by destroying Americanism."[28]

The lunch ended at 2:30. Nixon decided to send Hagerty more suggestions for the press conference. His principal point was that whatever Ike said "would make news and would do the job," and they should therefore "make the statement as tight as possible." The vice president composed an alternative passage that was more temperate than Hagerty's combative comparison of McCarthy's methods with those of the communists. Nixon saw no advantage in inflaming the situation further.[29]

The presidential press conference on the morning of March 3, lasting only 26 minutes, attracted 256 reporters, the most ever to attend such an event under Eisenhower. The president read a prepared statement admitting the Army's mistakes dealing with the Peress case. He never mentioned McCarthy or Stevens; he praised General Zwicker and stressed the "disregard for fair play" that some congressional committees had exhibited.[30]

Two hours later, McCarthy answered the presidential declaration, pledging to continue his quest to root out "Fifth Amendment Communists" such as Peress; no one would deter his crusade. Where the president's remarks had been measured and moderate, McCarthy's response was combative. He did not recognize that he was being given an opportunity to extend an olive branch.[31]

While Republicans quarreled, Adlai Stevenson was in Miami delivering the keynote address to the Southeastern Democratic Conference. On the eve of the event, DNC chairman Stephen Mitchell launched the congressional campaign: "It is now time to make President Eisenhower our target and charge him with full responsibility for the actions of all Republicans."[32] NBC and CBS radio and television carried Stevenson's speech on the evening of Saturday, March 6. He opened: "I do not propose to respond in kind to the calculated campaign of deceit to which we have been exposed, nor to the insensate attacks on all Democrats as traitors, Communists, and murderers of our sons." With this disclaimer out of the way, he responded to some extreme GOP allegations and made some of his own. His appeal went directly to the partisans in his audience. Republicans had tarred the Democrats and the New Deal with the label "Twenty Years of Treason," and now "a group of political plungers has persuaded the President that McCarthyism is the best Republican formula for political success." But McCarthy had made his assaults on Secretary Stevens and General Zwicker, and thus split the Republicans. As a consequence, "A political party divided against itself, half McCarthy and half Eisenhower, cannot produce national unity—cannot govern with confidence and purpose."[33]

Asked about Stevenson's speech during his press conference the following morning, March 7, Eisenhower called it the opening salvo in the 1954 Democratic congressional campaign. As for the charge that the GOP was split "half Eisenhower and half McCarthy," the president answered: "At the risk of appearing egotistical—and you can so interpret it if you choose—I say nonsense."[34] McCarthy demanded equal time to answer Stevenson, who the senator claimed had personally attacked him. Since the two networks had carried the address as a public service, the senator had precedent on his side to make a response.[35]

At the White House on Monday, March 8, the president arrived late at the Republican legislative conference, something that seldom occurred. He had read the Sunday newspapers' accounts of Stevenson's theme: the GOP was divided into Eisenhower and McCarthy factions. The president urged the party to unite behind him; Representative Halleck announced that his House colleagues were closing ranks, but Nixon, who had served in both houses, reminded the group that the Senate was much harder to manage. Majority leader Knowland, he stressed, "had a particularly difficult job because each Senator had to be treated as an individual and it was not possible to get them in line as a body as was often the case in the House."[36]

Ike declared that the administration could no longer ignore the friction that McCarthy was fomenting. Rather than continuing the infighting, the GOP had to battle the Democrats to retain a congressional majority. No individual, he insisted, could set himself above principles. Elections were based on principles and not personalities. He would not "tolerate disloyalty for political purposes. . . . Joe [McCarthy] is not [the] only one who fights communism."[37]

That afternoon, Ike tapped Nixon to answer Stevenson. Realizing that any response critical of McCarthy would cause division within the GOP and probably damage his support among conservatives, the vice president was reluctant to take on the assignment. Ike envisioned an address that would concentrate on the administration's positive aspects and look forward to future accomplishments. He predicted the speech "would be [a] knock-out!"[38]

Ike called Nixon into his private office late that afternoon. Nixon now reversed himself and said he would give the speech, but not as an answer to Stevenson's; instead it would be an appeal to enact the administration's legislative proposals. The president was agreeable and even suggested that the vice president treat Stevenson and McCarthy "with an easy backhand so to speak and he referred to the fact that after all we were the leaders and they were just flies."[39]

According to Nixon's account, Eisenhower had selected Nixon because he occupied "the unique position in the party in that he has been elected by the people at large, he has had political experience in both the House and the Senate and he can sometimes take positions which are more political than it would be expected that I take." He also had served on the House Committee on Un-American Activities, where he exposed Alger Hiss as a Russian agent. With that pedigree, Nixon could speak with authority on domestic subversion.[40]

C.D. Jackson, the president's adviser on psychological warfare, wrote Nixon the following day to warn that McCarthy was undermining Eisenhower's programs. He did not suggest the president openly attack the senator but that "McCarthy's aggression be recognized as a *fact*, both inside the White House and on the Hill, and that the Republicans in the Senate be told to make up their minds as to whether they wish to join McCarthy's guerrillas or rally to the President and his program, both foreign and domestic." The senators aligned with McCarthy had "a deliberate, calculated campaign to brand the entire opposition party as traitors to the country, there is a tremendous jump—a jump which millions of Americans will not make—a jump which the President cannot afford to condone either by silence or by such carefully balanced rebuke that it is only understood to be a rebuke by the professionals." The unwholesome standard that some GOP senators were preaching would undermine the president's prestige as well as sabotage his legislative proposals.

Jackson wrote that he had carefully watched Nixon since the 1953 inauguration and admired "the extraordinary way in which you blended political sagacity with political courage. This has not only earned you a position of great esteem and respect in the minds of the President and his important advisers, but I am sure has earned you a position of great respect and leverage on Capitol Hill."[41]

McCarthy's activities and the resultant headlines frustrated the president. Instead of concentrating on the positive, Ike believed, newspapers spotlighted McCarthy's outrageous declarations "in broadcasting his completely unwarranted and despicable insinuations." As a military commander, Ike had learned to speak only positively about his subordinates in public. He made an exception by openly expressing his disapproval of McCarthy. Although some White House advisers counseled that he should condemn the senator, they were not charged with enacting a legislative agenda. "It is a sad commentary on our government," he wrote Roland Redmond, a New York attorney, "when such a manifestly useless and spurious thing can divert our attention from all the constructive work in which we could and should be engaged."[42]

The president held his weekly press conference on Wednesday morning, March 10. Edward Folliard of the *Washington Post* cited McCarthy's demand for equal time to answer Stevenson and asked if the networks had discharged their public service duty by giving the RNC the privilege of selecting who should respond. Ike replied that the networks had acted responsibly. Merriman Smith of United Press wondered if Nixon was the proper person to answer the Democrats. The president responded that the reporters knew "how greatly I admire the Vice President, how much I trust him." He was confident that his vice president would accomplish his mission. Martin Agronsky of ABC inquired if Ike had personally selected Nixon and had relayed that choice to RNC chairman Hall. The president disingenuously answered that he had attended the gathering where the choice was made but did not "remember that I was the one that suggested it. I most certainly concurred heartily."[43]

That evening Nixon saw Ike at the Sulgrave Club at a stag dinner for Senators Knowland and Homer Ferguson of Michigan. The president grinned as he shook Nixon's hand, remarking: "I hope you are taking plenty of vitamins for that speech you are going to make Saturday night." He talked to a group that included Senators Dirksen and McCarthy. They appeared "quite cordial," although Nixon sensed "that there was considerably more coolness in his [Ike's] attitude toward McCarthy than he previously had evidenced at social functions."[44]

Nixon's instincts were right. The president had concluded that the Republican Party had within it "a reactionary and recalcitrant splinter group." McCarthy was not necessarily motivated by "political conviction," and the dissident faction supported him "since his actions, methods and statements have created embarrassment for the Administration." It was possible, Ike thought, that the opposition employed him for just that purpose.[45]

But Nixon was also attuned to electoral consequences. Congressman Patrick Hillings, who had succeeded Nixon in his California House seat, claimed that most congressmen hoped the vice president would not attack McCarthy because they wanted to use the "Reds in Government" issue during the upcoming races. Donald Jackson, another Southern California congressman and a Nixon supporter, cautioned: "Don't mention McCarthy by name. Don't take him on." He was only a senator; Ike led the party.[46]

On Friday morning, March 12, the president held his regular cabinet meeting. Before it convened, the members discussed the day's headlines: a sensational thirty-four page report issued by the Army concerning how McCarthy's staff, particularly his lead attorney, Roy Cohn, had threatened "to wreck the Army" if it did not give preferential treatment to Private Schine.[47]

Nixon had skipped the meeting and was secluded at the Statler Hotel, composing his address. At 10:30 a.m., he took an urgent telephone call from Senator Knowland, who "was very much upset" and so distraught that he asked Senator Eugene Milliken, chairman of the GOP policy committee, to call a meeting so that Knowland could submit his resignation as majority leader. He had found out about the Army report through the newspapers; no one in the administration had given him any inkling. He felt that he could not cooperate with a White House that "fed materials to columnists who were opposed to us and to Democratic members without letting the leadership know what was happening."[48]

Shortly after this exchange, Eisenhower sent a message to Nixon to come immediately to the cabinet meeting. As Nixon arrived during the closing item, the president remarked that the Senate leadership had protested the Army's releasing the Schine investigation without first consulting with the GOP senators. Ike, Nixon, and Persons emphasized that the senators should have been notified.[49]

Once the meeting adjourned, Ike sought Nixon's advice regarding Knowland's threat of resignation. The president wanted Nixon's opinion of the Army-McCarthy conflict and the majority leader's role in it. Ike understood that Knowland was angry that the report had been released without his knowledge, but he seemed angrier over Knowland's opposition to the White House. Knowland had gone to Secretary Dulles's home and attacked him on his handling of the Berlin conference. Now he "was blaming the Administration every time something happened." Nixon defended Knowland, saying he appeared stressed from "the tough votes he had" on various pieces of legislation. Nixon followed the president into the Oval Office and added: "The trouble with Knowland was that he always wanted to be a Knight on Horseback and he had to recognize that sometimes it was necessary to get out of the Armor so that it could be shined up."[50]

They next turned to the pending address. If Nixon wished to talk over any aspect of the speech, he just needed to give "a ring and come down" to the Oval Office. Ike had "complete confidence" in his abilities and suggested that he assure Americans that the administration "had a progressive, dynamic program which benefited all the people" and wanted the audience to understand that "a little snapping at our heels isn't going to deter us." The president appreciated Nixon's style of seeming to address one or two watching rather than all the viewers, and wished that he would "work a smile or two into the program," especially when referring to Stevenson. Nixon agreed that he had difficulty with that technique, while the president used it "extremely well." He added that he "planned to stick a few barbs into" the speech. Ike approved: "It was best to laugh at [Stevenson] rather than to hit him meanly."

Ike suggested that Nixon might include the concept of leadership in his rebuttal. The president had commanded millions of soldiers during World War II. Parenthetically, he thought that Secretary Dulles was doing an excellent job and some mention should be made of his diplomatic acumen.

Eisenhower also mentioned domestic subversion; that was the primary reason behind Ike's decision that Nixon should give the broadcast. Nixon had played a major role in exposing Alger Hiss, but many mistakenly believed "that McCarthy got Hiss." One reason the president placed Nixon at the top of the 1952 vice president list was "because you had gotten Hiss and you had done it decently."

A half hour before airtime the next evening, Nixon arrived at Studio 13 at Broadcast House, the new facility for the CBS capital affiliate. A staff member and a secret service agent accompanied him. His set was an empty desk, covered by a leather blotter pad. Behind him was textured wallpaper. He sat alone without a prepared script and spoke from nine pages of notes written on a yellow legal pad. As he explained to his viewers, he wanted to talk to them as if they were sitting across from him.[51]

Promptly at 10:30, he opened by promising not to attack either McCarthy or Stevenson. Instead he would concentrate on the three false charges that the Democratic leader had made, concerning defense policy, domestic subversion, and presidential leadership. He would answer them with facts. Explaining the New Look—the administration's new policy of strategic deterrence, announced the previous month by Secretary Dulles—he emphasized that it succeeded in halting aggression whereas the Truman administration had been responsible for communist gains, including the fall of Mainland China and the Korean War. Almost as an aside, he appeared to ad lib: "Isn't it wonderful that finally we have a Secretary of State who isn't taken in by the Communists, who stands up to them." Nixon then returned to the theme by saying that if Stevenson had a more productive defense policy than the president, he should offer it. Rather than propose an effective alternative, he merely complained.

On the matter of communist subversion, Nixon compared traitors to rats. Some argued, he said, that what "'we ought to do is to go out and shoot 'em.' Well, I'll agree they're a bunch of rats, but just remember this. When you go out to shoot rats, you have to shoot straight, because when you shoot wildly it not only means that the rat may get away more easily, you make it easier on the rat.

"But you might hit someone else who's trying to shoot rats too. And so we've got to be fair. For two very good reasons: One, because it's right, and two, because it's the most effective way of doing the job."

Nixon pointed out that he had served on HUAC and brought Hiss to justice through accepted legal procedures. The administration was following a prudent plan of action, and over 2,400 federal employees had left government service under the Eisenhower loyalty program. Without mentioning McCarthy, the vice president cautioned against irresponsible measures: "Men who have in the past done effective work exposing Communists in this country have, by reckless talk and questionable method, made themselves the issue rather than the cause they believe in so deeply."

Lastly, Nixon praised the president's leadership style. As vice president he saw Ike daily and felt that he acted as the leader of the free world should behave. He made momentous decisions and afterwards, "I have never seen him mean, I have never seen him rash, I have never seen him impulsive, I have never seen him panicked." His sole objective was to do "what is good for America." Instead of arguing over inconsequential disputes that made headlines, the nation needed to enact the administration's proposals. "Let's join together and get behind our President in making the American dream come true."[52]

After Nixon finished, Ike phoned, commending the effort as "a magnificent job and the very best possible that could have been done under the circumstances." He was pleased that Nixon had smiled several times. The speech, according to the president, would satisfy 85 percent of the estimated ten million in the audience, but "the people who were violently anti-McCarthy or violently pro-McCarthy could never be satisfied by anything except all-out war."[53]

Ike had other reasons to be satisfied. Nixon had done virtually everything he had recommended. He had not assaulted McCarthy or Stevenson for partisan advantage. He projected a calm, moderate demeanor and relied on sound reasoning rather than emotional appeals. Even the apparently offhand mention of Secretary Dulles came from Ike's coaching.

When reached for comment, Stevenson sarcastically thanked the vice president for agreeing that McCarthy was a disruptive force, even though he was not mentioned by name, and objected to what he considered Nixon's misleading use of government figures regarding subversives on the federal payroll. The vice president had exaggerated the number of employees who had left government service as a result of questionable loyalty.[54]

McCarthy clearly was miffed. The address placed him on notice that the administration saw him as a liability. He told reporters he expected to remain in office for many years and did not "intend to treat traitors like gentlemen." He would push forward with his crusade independently, even if the administration objected.[55]

On Monday, March 15, returning to Washington after spending the weekend at his Gettysburg farm and Camp David, Ike was "in excellent spirits" at that morning's Republican legislative gathering. Later that day, Nixon, Hall, Tom Stephens, and others held one of their strategy sessions; they noted that the Gallup Poll still showed McCarthy with an overall favorable rating.[56] Despite these positives, Len Hall told Nixon that he had visited McCarthy at his apartment and seen the extent of his emotional distress. The senator had opened the door with a gun in his hand—which he always carried, according to Hall, "because of the threats that had been made against him." A few days later, Senator Mundt added to the unstable profile. He told the others he had gone over to McCarthy's apartment and stayed until 2:00 a.m. on March 20; his wife was "almost in tears and him having very little influence due to the fact that Joe said that he knew that his political life was at stake and that he was not going to agree to anything that would make it difficult for him to defend himself." If those were not enough troubles, one of the worst kept secrets in the Senate was growing less and less secret. McCarthy's alcoholism had gotten out of control.[57]

While McCarthy was sinking into despair, Jerry Persons considered resigning because Ike seemed to be losing confidence in his judgment regarding the McCarthy affair. Nixon and Persons had met privately on March 22 over rumors that the president "was under considerable pressure to dump" Persons. Some new White House staffers did not understand that when Ike was angry he would say things that he did not mean to carry out. Ike could have been expressing his frustration that Persons was sympathetic to McCarthy.[58]

Two days later, Nixon had lunch with several Republican leaders about the upcoming Army hearings. The vice president opposed McCarthy's participation. The president was considering speaking as the party leader, he told them, "urging that [the GOP subcommittee members] not allow Joe to sit in these hearings." Hall and Mundt felt that McCarthy "was in no condition whatever to attend a hearing and to participate in it." Dirksen and others dissented, and the option was rejected; the junior senator from Wisconsin would be an interrogator.[59]

Ike and Nixon chatted several times in the last week of March. After the morning legislative meeting on March 24, the president asked what was wrong with McCarthy. Did he "want to be a dictator?" Nixon dismissed that thought, noting that some McCarthy allies in the Senate, like Herman Welker of Idaho, believed he "was seeking publicity."[60]

Nixon gained more insight from two afternoon gatherings at the Carlton Hotel with Hall, Stephens, and others. By this time the RNC chairman had "gone completely sour on McCarthy" and intended to write him off. The president proposed on March 25 that he give a televised address listing McCarthy among the challenges facing the country: "The fear of Russia, the fear of Communism, the fear of depression and the fear of McCarthyism."[61]

When Nixon saw the president at the Friday morning cabinet meeting, Ike was "in a very relaxed mood." He told those assembled that the major difference between a military commander and a president was this: "In the case of the military, you had a pretty good idea about what course a battle was going to take. In the case of politics, he said, you never knew what was going to happen."[62]

The vice president was as fatalistic as the president. He explained to John McDowell, a former House colleague and fellow HUAC member, that the administration needed to focus on communists and not the Army. Sometimes, Nixon lamented, he had trouble selling "an idea to all the members of the committee. You can be sure I will continue to do what I can to get things on the track." Some in Congress refused to relinquish their investigatory prerogatives. He wished that "Possibly out of this latest hullabaloo over McCarthy, Cohn and Schine some progress will be made toward bringing order out of the confusion which exists."[63]

The president commented on April 8, in a private letter to Milton Katz, the Ford Foundation's associate director, that there were "quite a number who are afraid of him [McCarthy]—afraid to challenge him in any way." Ike's priority was to get his moderate program through Congress, and he needed every possible vote. Even given that political reality, the president would not appease or make any attempt to woo "McCarthy or . . . others who constitute what I suppose you call the 'fringe.'"[64]

The televised hearings convened on April 22 and lasted almost two months, adjourning on June 17. Shifts in public opinion started to develop. At the start of the hearings, almost half of those polled supported McCarthy. When they ended, over half registered unfavorable opinions, while only a third still viewed him favorably. The *Des Moines Sunday Register* reported a local poll that illustrated how much the senator had slipped: from March to June, his negative ratings went from 20 to 35 percent; his positive numbers slipped from 15 to 12 percent.[65]

Despite the damage McCarthy was doing to the GOP, the president still refused to confront him in public. Private antagonism was another matter. Ike told Nixon on April 2 that the senator was "probably [Kremlin leader George] Malinkov's [sic] best helper in the United States." The vice president recognized that the president felt "very emotional on the McCarthy subject at this point" because he blamed McCarthy "for diverting attention from his program and for diverting his followers in the Republican Party."[66]

Twenty days later, just after the first day's televised hearings, Ike wrote Swede Hazlett, saying, "It saddens me that I must feel ashamed for the United States Senate." After a breakfast at the end of the month, Nixon asked the president if the hearings should be halted. Ike called them "a damn shameful spectacle" but did not want to be seen as having stopped them; the president "was particularly vindictive in his mention of McCarthy." Despite that animosity, Nixon optimistically hoped to "expedite some settlement which would put McCarthy on the stand and then bring the hearings to a close."[67]

Throughout May and June, the president remained consistent. He called the spectacle "this shameful inquiry." Secretary of Army Stevens had been one of his administration's brightest prospects, "but . . . somehow he just didn't have the toughness in his makeup which was necessary to do the job." Ike tried to bolster the secretary's resolve and encouraged the Army to provide as much information as possible to the senators without compromising national security. He was clear that there could be no hint of a "cover-up." But when McCarthy called upon the president to allow some members of his White House staff, such as Sherman Adams, to testify about their internal discussions, the president asserted executive privilege, maintaining that executive branch employees needed to be completely candid, and therefore their conversations would not be disclosed.[68]

Reports about some of the president's actions reached FBI headquarters. Louis Nichols, an assistant director, wrote J. Edgar Hoover's closest aide, Clyde Tolson, on May 21 that *Chicago Tribune* columnist Walter Trohan had heard that Ike refused to consent to the hearings' adjournment. Various members of the White House staff who handled congressional relations, including Persons, Jack Martin, and Jerry Morgan, lamented that the president would not discuss the McCarthy situation with the press. His handling of the matter, Ike declared, was "none of the press' business" and he was "not going to talk about it." Majority leader Halleck was "gone," and Senator Dirksen, who was sympathetic to McCarthy, had "now broken with the White House."[69]

Nixon, probably more than anyone, saw the president's chagrin but still worked to end the hearings, which became increasingly harmful to the party the longer they dragged on. He continued to hold strategy sessions, usually in the late afternoon at the Statler or Carlton hotels. Occasionally, he chaired luncheons in his private Capitol hideaway. He continued to talk to McCarthy by telephone and in person. In the second week in June, for instance, Senator Dirksen held a cocktail party for Senator Bridges. McCarthy was there talking to Secretary of Defense Wilson, and Nixon joined in the discussion.[70]

The press reported that Nixon remained in the background during the hearings. He broke his silence on May 24, claiming that he had not watched any of them, and insisted the administration was "smashing the Communist conspiracy to bits" without violating anyone's rights. Because the Democrats were not supporting the president in these efforts, voters had to elect more Republicans. When director of the CIA (DCI) Allen Dulles, in the second week of June, visited the vice president to discuss McCarthy's threats to investigate the CIA, Nixon let him know that he had reached an agreement with the three other Republicans on the subcommittee that if McCarthy proposed such an inquiry, they would vote against their chairman.[71]

By the time the hearings adjourned, on June 17, the ugliness the senator had generated had mesmerized the American viewing audience. His misuse of the parliamentary tactic, point of order, became an everyday mocking admonishment. His scurrilous attack on a young lawyer, Frederick Fisher Jr., for having joined a communist-front organization as a youth, resulted in the lead attorney, Joseph Welch, denouncing McCarthy on June 9: "Until this moment, I think I never really gauged your cruelty or your recklessness. . . . Let us not assassinate this lad further, Senator. You have done enough. Have you no sense of decency, sir, at long last? Have you left no sense of decency?" For a moment the hearing room was silent; then applause erupted. The senator looked around as if to ask, what did I do? The next evening, Eric Sevareid said on his radio broadcast: "The personal tragedy of McCarthy is that the nerve or chord or cluster of cells that produce what men call conscience was not granted to him."[72]

The anticommunism crusade found itself deeply divided. Taking the Senate floor on March 9, Senator Ralph Flanders, Republican from Vermont, denounced McCarthy for fracturing a once unified party. When the president was asked at his press conference the next day to address Flanders' remarks, he answered that "the danger of us [Republicans] engaging in internecine warfare" was retarding legislative proposals. Ike did not read the senator's entire speech, but he regarded dividing the party as a serious offense.[73]

On June 1, Flanders again spoke on the Senate floor, comparing McCarthy to Hitler, and ten days later, the Vermont senator introduced a resolution to strip his Wisconsin colleague of his chairmanship. That effort failed, but Flanders was not dissuaded. At the end of July, Flanders submitted Senate Resolution 301 to censure McCarthy for conduct unbecoming a United States senator.[74]

On the first of August, Nixon told reporters that he doubted the Senate would pass a censure resolution in its present or possibly any form. The very next day the Senate proved him wrong, passing a resolution to appoint a special committee to examine the charges. On the fifth, Nixon waited for the bell in the upper chamber to sound a quorum call, and at 12:28 p.m., he announced the appointment of a panel of three Republicans and three Democrats, including Arthur Watkins, Republican of Utah, as chairman. The senators met informally in the vice president's ceremonial Capitol office that afternoon, where Nixon complimented them by predicting the Senate would approve their majority report. He jokingly offered to serve as the body's counsel.[75]

In the middle of the month, McCarthy provided *Newsweek* with the answers he planned to present to the Watkins committee: he proclaimed his innocence on all charges. He hired Edward Bennett Williams, one of the nation's most prominent defense attorneys, to represent him.[76]

On September 27, the same day Congress adjourned to prepare for the midterm campaigns, the Watkins committee unanimously approved a report to censure McCarthy on two grounds: not appearing before a Senate committee investigating his 1952 finances and his abuse of General Zwicker. Nixon promptly praised the committee for conducting its hearings "in very admirable fashion." The members had been selected because five were not seeking reelection and the sixth had only token opposition. The vice president also predicted that their recommendations would "have great weight with the Senate." Debate on the issue was delayed until after the election.[77]

The Senate came back into session on November 8 specifically to consider the McCarthy censure resolution; the floor debate opened two days later. Only three members of the upper house had ever been censured. Never before had the Senate convened in special session to debate this single item. Nixon presided, and the senators had no time limit on their speeches. The vice president told a California supporter, John Dinkelspiel, that he had "taken a completely neutral stand on the whole McCarthy problem in the past and will continue to do so." He also heard the opinions of his California associates. Columnist Kyle Palmer of the *Los Angeles Times* wrote: "Somebody should think up a gimmick to stop this McCarthy business; it is doing no good for the party or the country."[78]

In this charged atmosphere, the Senate prepared to vote on December 2: some to censure a vile buffoon and others to acquit a champion of the anticommunist cause. Moments before the roll call, the senator from Wisconsin entered the chamber. He had been hospitalized for a bursitis attack, and his arm was in a sling; he had clearly been drinking heavily. When the vote was tallied, all Democrats said aye, while the Republicans split twenty-two for and twenty-two against. Bridges, Dirksen, Knowland, Goldwater, and others held firm; Saltonstall and Flanders voted to censure. The total was sixty-seven to twenty-two; only the senior senator from Wisconsin, Alexander Wiley, and John Kennedy from Massachusetts, who was hospitalized, did not vote.[79]

Ike, on the thirteenth anniversary of Pearl Harbor, wrote his social friend and fellow golfer, Clifford Roberts, that "the so-called splinter group," twenty-two of the Republican senators, had voted against censure. Some of them, the president thought, believed they were voting "on the right of the Senate to conduct legitimate investigations of the Executive Branch." Ike did not think that this " 'Rightest' thinking" in the GOP nationally was "as prevalent as this Senate ratio." McCarthy had publicly apologized for supporting Ike in 1952, saying Ike had not been tough enough on communists, and the president's response should be that he apologized for accepting McCarthy's 1952 endorsement. The senator would continue to hunt headlines, while Ike would try to convert Democrats, win independents, and get out the Republican vote. Even if McCarthy and his loyalists broke "off a fairly good hunk of Republican strength," the party could flourish. "If we could get every Republican committed as a Moderate Progressive, the Party would grow so rapidly that within a few years it would dominate American politics."[80] Hagerty, on the same day, noted the Wisconsin senator had attacked the president for "weakness and supineness." The president expected these attacks and dismissed them. No longer, the press secretary thought, would the president work with right-wing Republicans.[81]

Six days later, the president informed Slats Slater that "McCarthy would hang himself, and why get into any kind of a contest with a skunk." Ike granted that the senator had "contributed a great deal to the elimination of Communists—or at least scaring others away," but added: "but his smear tactics are frightening."[82]

Shortly after the censure resolution passed, the vice president noted the mounting animosity between liberals and conservatives. He was "at a loss as to just what action can be taken to create some unity where a considerable amount of bad feeling now exists." He would work within the GOP to "do everything I can to explore every possible method to accomplish this objective." Despite that lofty goal, the vice president understood that the philosophical gulf among Republican senators had intensified.[83]

Nixon believed that the best analysis of McCarthy's collapse came from a *Los Angeles Times* editorial on the morning of December 9. The *Times* editors, who had supported McCarthy's crusade to rid the federal bureaucracy of communists, wrote that he "did the necessary dirty work which his squeamish colleagues declined to do." He won the backing of millions and deluded himself into believing that he had emerged as the spokesman for the GOP's conservative wing. He did not have leadership talent and never seriously challenged Eisenhower's supremacy. The president would not publicly mention McCarthy by name but left that to others in the administration. Even then McCarthy might have survived politically "if he hadn't succumbed to delusions of grandeur." When he openly assaulted the president, he was finished. "Perhaps," the editorial concluded, "his usefulness to his country will be remembered along with the evils he did to himself."[84]

Nixon wrote on the same day that Ike deserved support from the public for doing "a fair sane and effective job of dealing with Communism in the United States." Members of both parties opposed McCarthy, and he had extremists both attacking and defending him. Nixon thought the nation had far more pressing concerns and hoped the McCarthy episode would fade away over the next few months and that the nation would turn to issues "which will serve to unite us rather than to divide us."[85]

Nixon held a press conference on September 5, 1955. Referring to "the McCarthy issue—leaving out the man," Nixon stated that it "is no longer a serious divisive force in the Republican Party." McCarthy had taken on "the top man" and failed. The GOP rank-and-file, he said, backed the president and his administration's efforts to eliminate the communist menace in the United States.[86]

Even after the senator's humiliation, Nixon maintained contact with McCarthy and tried to bring him back into the Republican fold. As the 1956 presidential campaign approached, McCarthy announced his opposition to Ike's reelection and promoted Nixon, J. Edgar Hoover, Knowland, and other "good candidates." When the national convention neared at the start of August and rumors surfaced that Nixon might be replaced on the Republican ticket, McCarthy appeared on television to support his renomination: "I think he has an extremely good record—I can see no reason for dumping him at all." The vice president thanked the senator "that during this latest political storm you have spoken out in my behalf."[87]

After the ticket was renominated, the vice president noted that during the contest, "re: McCarthy—if people request him, he ought to be used—he's got to be rehabilitated." He still had a magnetic appeal among the Irish-Catholics in Boston and elsewhere; he should do some television programs because many believed "that the administration dumped on him."

When Nixon campaigned in Wisconsin that fall, two reporters offered differing perceptions of his contact with McCarthy. The *Minneapolis Star* held that McCarthy was snubbed on several occasions. At a Milwaukee press conference and on a television panel, the vice president refused to comment on the senator's campaign efforts or his senatorial duties. After Nixon spoke to a Marquette University audience, McCarthy entered the hall to rousing applause, but was not officially acknowledged or invited to sit on the platform. He sat in the front row instead. At another political rally he was barred from entering.[88]

Neither reporter knew that Nixon's press secretary, Herbert Klein, was specifically assigned to keep McCarthy away from the vice president. Klein was to ensure that the senator would not cause Nixon any embarrassment while he campaigned in Wisconsin.[89]

These precautions to minimize McCarthy's access to Nixon marked the last public events at which both men were seen together. After the senator's censure, his ability to function quickly declined. Reporters abandoned him; he could no longer create headlines, and the majority of Americans seemed to have lost interest in him. After the 1954 elections, he lost his committee chairmanship. His drinking continued, out of control. Although liver disease was not listed as the cause of his death, booze and melancholy greatly contributed to it. He passed away on May 2, 1957.[90]

That evening the vice president issued a statement. The senator was "one of the most controversial figures of his generation.

"Years will pass before the results of his work can be objectively evaluated, but his friends and many of his critics will not question his devotion to what he considered to be the best interests of his country."[91]

Four days later, Nixon attended a mass for McCarthy at St. Matthews Cathedral in the capital and then went to a memorial service in the Senate. The Nixons sent a contribution to the New York Foundling Hospital in McCarthy's name.[92]

Almost a quarter century after McCarthy had been censured, Nixon summarized the era in an oral history. McCarthy "was very attractive in many ways— he was a genial Irishman, a nice guy, interesting guy at a party." He could conduct a reasonable two-way conversation and "then could go out and say the most outlandish things. . . . Although he was right on many issues, unfortunately being wrong on some issues and by overstating a good case, he made a good case totally a bad case; that was his undoing. He became the issue rather than the cause he was fighting."[93]

Eisenhower, Nixon, and McCarthy came at the communist issue from vastly different backgrounds. Although the president followed a consistent anticommunist position, he refused to condone McCarthy's reckless behavior. As president, he concentrated on his legislative objectives in 1953 and waited until the following year to focus on McCarthy. Ike quietly deployed his White House loyalists as foot soldiers. Brownell, for example, handled legal issues, and Nixon spoke as the principal anticommunist spokesman for the administration, blunting McCarthy's claim to be the primary anticommunist crusader. While they each carried out their mission, the president acted as the commander who surveyed the entire battlefield. After mobilizing his forces, he placed the full weight of his office behind the expectation that he would destroy his adversary. Although he never openly attacked McCarthy, he made this position abundantly clear inside the White House. His subordinates understood this and energetically tried to ruin the senator.

Many authors, focusing on the shared goals, political bond, and undoubted friendship between Joe McCarthy and Richard Nixon, have failed or refused to see any daylight between them. Drew Pearson, in a column on November 6, 1954, predicted that while the senator's political life was over, "Nixon is not finished as a McCarthyite campaigner. He used exactly McCarthy's tactics, but he's smoother and handsomer." Four years later, Dorothy Schiff, publisher of the *New York Post*, editorialized that "Nixonism has replaced McCarthyism as the greatest threat to the prestige of our Nation today. In fact, we have considered the former far more dangerous than the latter because of its greater subtlety." Historian Gary Donaldson asserted that Nixon "had made a political name for himself as a communist hunter in the McCarthy mold."[94]

But it is precisely because he was not in the McCarthy mold—because the two men differed in their political styles, personal characteristics, and ultimately their concern for the nation's values—that the McCarthy matter was crucial to Nixon's fortunes under Eisenhower. He emerged from the episode as one of Ike's principal political advisers. By placing himself at the center of the administration's efforts, first to accommodate McCarthy and then to ruin him, he earned Eisenhower's lasting trust and also added to his public stature. He defined himself as staunchly anticommunist but not recklessly so. He had not, in the end, sided with those who, in an effort to remove subversives from important government institutions, were willing to damage those institutions. Through his dealings with McCarthy, the vice president grew into more than a single-issue politician; he matured into a sophisticated member of the team.

·

7

TRUMAN, EISENHOWER, NIXON, AND CIVIL RIGHTS

While the media concentrated on domestic spying and the threat of a nuclear holocaust, the movement for African American equality was inching forward. Almost every author who has written on President Harry Truman's civil rights record has held him up as a hero in this struggle. Attorney Michael Gardner made that case in *Harry Truman and Civil Rights* (2002) and, four years later, added that this president's most significant contribution might have been "his crusade to make civil rights equality a reality in America." Ken Hechler, who served on Truman's White House staff, reinforced Gardner: "Harry Truman emerged as a champion of civil rights who during his presidency accomplished much and foreshadowed much more." Journalist Robert Shogan published an op-ed piece in the winter of 2013 proclaiming Truman "Lincoln's heir." His book *Harry Truman and the Struggle for Racial Justice* expanded on that theme by grossly exaggerating Truman's role in desegregating the armed forces and influencing Supreme Court decisions on civil rights.[1]

In fact, Truman did take several dramatic steps to protect black veterans returning home from World War II. In the winter of 1946, when chief of police Lynwood Shull in Batesburg, South Carolina, blinded Isaac Woodward, a discharged black soldier still wearing his uniform, Truman angrily demanded that Shull be prosecuted. He was, and after thirty minutes of deliberation, an all-white jury found him not guilty. Other violent acts against black service men, including several murders, further enraged the president. As a World War I veteran who had fought in France, Truman honored those who defended their country as a matter of patriotism.[2]

Besides coming to the aid of black soldiers, Truman created a civil rights commission that produced the groundbreaking presidential report on the state of civil rights, "To Secure These Rights." He was the first president to address the NAACP, and he highlighted his appearance by delivering his speech in front of the Lincoln Memorial. After the Democratic Party convention in 1948, he issued executive orders desegregating the federal bureaucracy and the armed forces. Four years later, he became the first president to address a predominately black audience at Howard University. He also appointed an African American judge, William Hastie, to the Third Circuit Court of Appeals.[3]

Although many have held that Truman integrated the military on principle, others argued that he threw in his lot for desegregation, as an electoral ploy to win African American votes, only after southerners bolted the Democratic Party at its July 1948 national convention. Few steps were taken toward integrating the military until the Korean War, when Mao Tse-tung arguably had a more profound influence on desegregation than the president. The Chinese soldiers he sent into the battle killed and wounded enough frontline (white) United States troops that the Army had to bring up its only reserves, who happened to be African Americans. Military necessity, not presidential directive, is what forced integration.[4]

During his presidency, Truman routinely called upon Congress to pass civil rights legislation but did not lobby energetically for any bill. Knowing that many of the upper chamber's southern committee chairmen would vehemently oppose any civil rights law, he may have felt there was no point in fighting a losing legislative battle.[5]

Even within this context, not everyone considers Truman's civil rights policies an unqualified success. African American historian Carol Anderson argues that Truman's record was "impressive" only when compared to the lackluster performances of Franklin Roosevelt and Dwight Eisenhower. "Is it any wonder that Truman has emerged in a pantheon occupied by only Abraham Lincoln and maybe Lyndon Johnson?" Despite this faint praise, Anderson questioned Truman's commitment, commenting that while there "may have been some level of consciousness-raising, the actual attainment of civil rights, given the persistence of disfranchisement, lynching, and housing discrimination left those facing the onslaught of Jim Crow . . . wondering when the vaunted 'progress' would finally catch up to them."[6]

Some historians have emphasized that Truman grew up in the Confederate climate of Missouri and that his relatives had owned slaves. His mother hated Abraham Lincoln so much that she refused to sleep in the Lincoln Bedroom when her son invited her to the White House. Truman, to his credit, overcame his background and championed the civil rights cause. These advocates have failed to note Truman's derogatory references to black people. While in the White

House, he often used "nigger" during staff meetings to describe African Americans. At one gathering, shortly after World War II, he referred to New York Congressman Adam Clayton Powell Jr. as "that damned nigger preacher."[7]

Truman did not use such language in public. The power of the vote had been denied to African Americans within decades after the Civil War, particularly in the Democratic-dominated South. Blacks who were able to cast ballots remained overwhelmingly in the party of Lincoln through the 1932 presidential election, but four years later, Franklin D. Roosevelt's landslide brought a cataclysmic shift. From 1936 through 1960, approximately seven out of ten black people voted Democratic in presidential elections. Even though FDR did not actively solicit these voters, they believed his efforts to revive the nation from the Great Depression benefited them. Through the 1950s, white America generally avoided facing the racism that permeated the nation. When Truman ran for president in 1948, publicly singling out African Americans by emphasizing civil rights, he received about the same percentage of their votes as his predecessor.[8]

While the national mainstream media largely ignored racial issues, the black press had little impact outside its targeted audience. Out of approximately 225 African-American newspapers, most were weeklies, and only a handful came out daily. Their civil rights coverage after World War II began a slow but perceptible change. Southern journalists Gene Roberts and Hank Klibanoff reported that "the Negro press . . . had the front-row seat during the early dramas, while the white press sat in the balcony, if it came to the performance at all."[9]

The 1950 United States census graphically illustrated how poorly represented black citizens had become. Of the approximately 150,000,000 citizens, about 10 percent were classified as nonwhite. An estimated 8.5 million were African Americans over twenty-one and therefore eligible to vote; 68 percent of these lived in the Old Confederacy and comprised 22 percent of its population, and of that group, 62 percent were urban dwellers who lived primarily in poor, segregated neighborhoods. The postwar explosion of the suburbs had largely passed them by.

At that point the Great Migration was largely completed. Black citizens, hoping for better education and more money, had been leaving the South in large numbers, about 150,000 per year, since the start of the Depression. The largest exodus was to northern and midwestern urban areas where southern blacks assimilated into already overcrowded segregated ghettos.[10]

Relatively few African Americans voted. Many black southerners were prevented, intimidated, discouraged, and murdered. In the North, possibly 20 percent of blacks cast ballots. None of the ninety-six senators were black. Of the

435 congressmen, 2 were black: William Dawson, a machine politician from the south side of Chicago first elected in 1942, and Adam Clayton Powell Jr., pastor of the 15,000-member Abyssinian Baptist Church in Harlem, New York, who joined Dawson two years later.[11]

Nor did black people have effective lobbyists promoting their cause. Despite its limited political power, insufficient funding, and inadequate staffing, the National Association for the Advancement of Colored People (NAACP) was the most influential organization, with many chapters spread across the country. The NAACP jealously guarded its prominent position and fought with other groups over turf rather than unite into a solid front.[12]

Henry Lee Moon, director of public relations for the NAACP, complained in 1948 that Truman lacked significant civil rights accomplishments. Moon was frustrated with white peoples' argument for patience: "The doctrine of gradualism finds scant acceptance among the Negro people today." Although racism would not be eradicated instantly, he wrote, Americans had "to take a clear, consistent, and unequivocal line against racial discrimination and segregation."[13]

As the presidential election of 1952 approached, Earl and Merle Black estimated that one out of five southern blacks were enfranchised. Their voice in Old Confederacy state contests was negligible; white southerners had absolute control of the local, state, and national outcomes. Haunted by the Civil War, the historians continued, these southerners "despised and loathed the Republican party." As Democrats whose numbers were crucial to the party's congressional majorities, they fought hard to make sure that the New Deal's benefits went primarily to whites. The first break over civil rights within the Democratic Party came in 1948, when southern politicians bolted their party, called themselves Dixiecrats, and ran Strom Thurmond as their presidential candidate. After that election, the Democratic Party was severely divided over civil rights. Outside the South, prejudice was less open and obvious, but still practiced on a grand scale. Restrictive covenants in many neighborhoods throughout the country, for instance, prevented the sale of homes to African Americans. Clubs, unions, jobs, and schools were closed to them.[14]

When the national parties' convention delegates were selected in 1952, even while the national ticket's nominees were undecided, the black delegates had already been chosen. Approximately 33 to 40 black delegates from 17 states, or 2.4 percent of the total of 1,200, went to the Republican gathering. The major civil rights issue on the agenda that year was the NAACP's call for a federal employment practice commission (FEPC) to protect African American economic employment opportunities. Of the two leading candidates, neither Senator Taft nor General Eisenhower favored this measure. Despite this lack of support, civil rights proponents pushed for a platform plank calling for an FEPC. Before a floor fight could be launched, the committee reached a compromise: "the Federal government should take supplemental action within its constitutional jurisdiction to oppose discrimination against race, religion or national origin." With this resolution, the black delegates voted 36 for Eisenhower as the presidential nominee, 6 for Taft and 2 for Governor Warren.[15]

Before the Democratic convention opened on July 21, Truman called for a forceful civil rights plank, while the segregationist and presidential contender Senator Richard Russell from Georgia vigorously opposed an FEPC. Walter White, the NAACP's executive secretary, went before the platform committee, warning that if the platform did not call for a substantial FEPC, Democrats would forfeit their large black turnout at the polls and seriously jeopardize the presidential ticket as well as congressional races. The platform committee passed a strong civil rights statement. The black delegates enthusiastically endorsed Adlai Stevenson for the president but sharply split on the selection of Senator John Sparkman of Alabama as his running mate. Adam Clayton Powell called Sparkman a "definite roadblock to victory" and declared that he would not campaign for him. He returned to Harlem threatening to urge his constituents to boycott the polls in November if Democrats did not act aggressively on civil rights. William Dawson, on the other hand, applauded Sparkman's place on the ticket and denounced Powell's action.[16]

None of the candidates looked especially promising on civil rights. Stevenson did not have a strong record, Sparkman was an avowed segregationist, and Eisenhower had spent his career in the military without taking any political position on the subject. Speaking for the Army on the readiness of black soldiers before the Senate armed services committee on April 3, 1948, he had presented the Army's position that black soldiers were "less well educated than" their white counterparts. If the Army integrated, he said, African Americans would be relegated to minor posts. In their own companies, black troops competed on an equal footing. As they became better educated, the disparity with whites would disappear. Although segregation had moderated since he entered the Army in 1910, he stated: "If we attempt merely by passing a lot of laws to force someone to like someone else, we are just going to get into trouble." During the 1952 campaign, Democrats berated him for having supported segregation in this testimony.[17]

Eisenhower, who seldom referred to anyone by race, never mentioned the one black soldier he was intimately associated with for over a quarter century. Corporal John Moaney was assigned to the general in England during late August 1942 as one of the African American soldiers on the general's staff. From that start, the two men became fast friends.[18]

After the fighting ended, Ike returned to the United States, and John Moaney remained with him as his valet. John married Dolores Butler, who then worked for Mamie as her cook and housekeeper. When Ike accepted the presidency at Columbia University in New York City, the Moaneys went with the Eisenhowers. Once Ike declared for the presidency, he was required to resign his commission and lost his military staff. Ike warned Sergeant Moaney that if he lost, Moaney would be without a job. The sergeant grinned: "Don't worry, General, . . . I think you and I can always make a living."[19]

The former sergeant accompanied his boss during the 1952 campaign. After the Eisenhowers moved into their White House residence, John and Dolores settled into quarters on the third floor. As the president's aide, the reenlisted sergeant laid out Ike's clothes by 7:00 a.m. and saw him to bed at night. After the president's heart attack in September 1955, Moaney massaged him with warm rubbing alcohol. While Ike was healing from ileitis surgery in June 1956, the sergeant made certain that the president traveled with Mountain Valley bottled water to normalize his digestive system. Early in 1958, the president told press secretary James Hagerty to give Moaney the message if the launch of *Explorer I* was canceled. When the president visited the Royal Family's vacation home at Balmoral Castle in Scotland in the summer of 1959, Ike was accompanied only by his son, his physician, and Moaney.[20]

Having a faithful servant does not by itself tell us anything significant; but the Moaneys were more than servants. In *At Ease*, published in 1967, Ike described them as "regular members of our household." John was "my companion" from whom "I have been inseparable for almost a quarter of a century; in my daily life, he is just about the irreplaceable man." Ill health prevented John from attending Ike's funeral in 1969, but he was named an honorary pallbearer. Dolores was included with the mourners as part of the Eisenhower family.[21]

While Ike seldom referred to the color of the Moaneys' skin, Dolores angrily resented the Eisenhowers being called racists, saying that Ike and Mamie unfailingly treated them with dignity. When the president greeted her, he always took off his hat and "treated me like a lady." If anyone used a racial slur in his and the Moaneys' presence, Ike exclaimed: "You will not talk that way in my house again!"[22]

The strong bond between the Eisenhowers and the Moaneys has been overlooked as well as the recent scholarship that points to Ike's strong civil rights commitment. Michael Beschloss typifies the continual use of the discredited themes in a *New York Times* article on November 16, 2014. First, Beschloss maintains, Ike expressed doubts about integration, and second, he praised southerners, according to Earl Warren's memoirs, as "not bad people" who desired to make certain that "their sweet girls" did not sit in public schools with "some big overgrown Negroes." The first statement is false, and the second cannot be accepted as fact because Warren had difficulties with Ike and Warren's book was published posthumously; therefore, no one could challenge his accusations. These two charges, based on erroneous interpretations and hearsay, are constantly reiterated as the evidence of Ike's bias toward blacks.[23]

While Nixon's civil rights background has also received little attention, many portray him as a racist. During my twenty years of Nixon research, I have not found him uttering any racial slurs. I have listened to hundreds of hours of Nixon's White House tapes, but not as many as the principal expert on these tapes, Luke Nichter, who has listened to most of them. Nichter states, "I cannot recall a single instance in which Richard Nixon used the word 'nigger'; instead, he used terms like 'negro' and 'black,' which was commonly used then by those who were educated and came of age in mixed-race communities."[24]

Nixon's parents were devout Quakers, and he was raised with "a strong family tradition against discrimination." To the Nixons, civil rights stood as "a great moral issue." While attending Yorba Linda public schools, he interacted with Asian classmates from Korea and Japan as well as Mexican twins whom he played with after school. Although few African Americans settled in this rural part of Southern California, some Whittier residents recalled black people working in the town: a shoeshine boy and an employee of a boys' school. Several remembered that African Americans could not live in the town.[25]

Dean Kotlowski, in *Nixon's Civil Rights*, writes that as a youth, Nixon did not know any black people. This is incorrect. When he was enrolled at Whittier College, three African Americans also attended and became friends of his. George Venable from Los Angeles majored in biology and was graduated in 1932. Nixon had a cordial relationship with him.[26] Nathaniel George, a track star, was a physical education major from the District of Columbia who was graduated in 1931, Nixon's sophomore year, and then settled in Los Angeles. According to several friends, George "was a great colored athlete" at the college. While there, he joined a social club, the Orthogonians that Nixon helped to organize. Fellow members reminisced that Nate was "a real piece of ebony" and "a real nice guy."[27]

Nixon's closest black friend was William "Bill" Brock, starting fullback on the football team. He came from Pasadena, California, and transferred from Pasadena Junior College to Whittier. He was the only black player on the squad and became an Orthogonian with Nixon's sponsorship. Bill was a "big guy," "light skinner," and "well liked," according to teammates. He majored in mathematics and physics and received an engineering degree the year after Nixon started law school.[28]

Nixon watched from the bench as Brock played first string. After graduation, Brock had difficulty finding a job in the midst of the depression, and in 1936, disheartened by the racism around him, he joined the Young Communist League. Four years later, he left and ended any association with the League's members. He found work at the defense contractor Hughes Aircraft Company in 1950 but was fired when he revealed his past communist membership. Brock cooperated with the FBI and testified to have his clearance restored. Even with this support, he was suspended and disallowed from any job in the defense industry. He believed that he had experienced "a definite miscarriage of justice."[29]

In desperation, on August 12, 1952, Bill wrote to Nixon, then the vice-presidential nominee, explaining his predicament. The candidate replied three days later that the campaign prevented him from examining the case. In December, Bill wrote again, pleading: "Frankly, you are my last hope, and I humbly beg your consideration." Throughout his vice presidency, Nixon quietly and forcefully lobbied to get Brock's security clearance reinstated. Although Brock was not reinstated by the time Nixon left office, Bill never forgot this assistance.[30]

Clearly, neither Eisenhower nor Nixon distinguished himself as a civil rights activist before running for national office. Except for Eisenhower's Senate testimony, neither appears to have advocated segregationist policies. There is no sign that either harbored any personal racial animus, and much to say that they did not.

Both men addressed civil rights issues during the campaign. Replying to critics, Ike proclaimed on September 4: "Discrimination is criminally stupid." He opposed the poll tax, lynching, and filibusters that stymied votes on civil rights bills, and pledged to end "every vestige" of segregation in the capital and the armed forces. He remained staunchly opposed to a compulsory FEPC, a stand that hurt him with black voters. Democratic governors Robert Kennon of Louisiana, Allan Shivers of Texas, and James Byrnes from South Carolina had the opposite reaction and endorsed the general.[31]

Despite Ike's pledges, African American leaders overwhelmingly came out for Stevenson after he called for the enactment of a compulsory FEPC. His running mate, Senator Sparkman, reinforced this by supporting that stance. Adam Clayton Powell enthusiastically endorsed Stevenson after meeting with him, and William Dawson predicted the largest African American turnout ever. Shortly before the balloting, 100,000 cheered Stevenson in Harlem. Roy Wilkins, assistant executive secretary of the NAACP, met with Ike for seventy minutes in early September, and after the interview, announced that the candidate "gives the impression that he is ill informed" on civil rights. Truman agreed; the general, he said, still favored segregation. Democrats effectively portrayed the general as evasive and unresponsive to African American aspirations. Before Election Day, blacks felt comfortable inside the Democratic Party and with its nominee.[32]

Nixon barely touched on civil rights during the contest. Prominent Republicans such as Paul Hoffman, Arthur Sulzberger of the *New York Times,* and Bill Robinson of the *New York Herald Tribune* suggested that the vice-presidential candidate make "civil liberties and the rights of minorities" a major theme in his public statements, but this never became a major subject during the race. Still, during his August interview with *U.S News & World Report,* when asked about his civil rights position he replied that he twice voted for anti–poll tax bills in the House and backed antilynching measures. Although he disapproved of FEPC federal legislation, he favored voluntary commissions for each state, of the kind that had operated successfully during World War II. He further announced his opposition to filibusters and would vote for cloture by a Senate majority. Mirroring his running mate, he opposed segregation in the armed forces. As for the District of Columbia, the federal government had the authority to end segregation there. Integration, he cautioned, was not "going to be done overnight."[33]

Neither Nixon's nor Sparkman's views satisfied the NAACP board of directors, who termed both men "unsatisfactory" due to their voting records. The black press throughout the campaign also attacked Nixon for signing a restrictive covenant against African Americans, Jews, and other minorities on the home he had purchased in 1951. The articles failed to mention that Democrats, including Senator Kefauver, lived in the same subdivision and signed the same document, as well as that the Supreme Court in *Shelley v. Kraemer* (1948) had struck down such covenants as unenforceable. Nixon later stated he "never considered that the covenant was binding on me or my neighbors. The whole idea of segregation and restrictive covenants is repugnant to the American concept of equality."[34]

When voters went to the polls on November 4, Eisenhower easily won both the popular and electoral vote. He broke the "Solid South" with victories in Tennessee, Virginia, Texas, and Florida; the GOP also claimed control of both houses of Congress. Even with those victories, Republicans held just six congressional seats in the Old Confederacy: one in North Carolina, two in Tennessee, and three in Virginia. From 1954 through 1960, the party gained just one additional seat, from Texas, for a total of seven.[35]

Within days after Eisenhower's triumph, many African American newspapers predicted doom. The *Cleveland Call and Post* editorialized: "nothing in the pre-election campaign gives the Negro any hope that he can relax his crusade for full citizenship and turn it over to either General Eisenhower or Governor

Stevenson for solution." The *Chicago Defender* worried that "while the Republi-can party revels in what it considers a resounding victory, from where we sit, the nation suffered an incalculable defeat." The *Washington Afro-American* repeated the standard refrain: "We've heard plenty of words, we now await action."[36]

The *Detroit Tribune,* one of a handful of African-American newspapers that had endorsed the Republican ticket, was not so glum. H. A. Howard, a black real estate broker who owned the *Los Angeles Star Review* in Watts, came out for the GOP a few weeks before the election to attempt to win black votes for the party. Many customers, he wrote in a letter to Nixon, "cancelled their ads" and patronized other papers. He wanted Nixon to know "the difficulties I had during the campaign just because I being a Negro and supporting the Republi-can ticket."[37]

From the election until the inauguration, African Americans lobbied the president-elect about his pledge to end segregation in the District of Columbia. Ike met with a four-man NAACP delegation early in December, and Walter White came away encouraged. The general declared that he would use his "ut-most influence" to change the Senate rule that allowed filibusters to frustrate civil rights legislation; he would eliminate segregation in the capital; and he would consider blacks for high government offices. Later in the month, the vic-tor promised a group of African American clergymen that he would form a com-mission to study discrimination against minority groups at hotels, restaurants, and employment.

African Americans actively participated at Ike's inaugural. Soprano Dorothy Maynor was the first of her race to sing at an inaugural ceremony; hundreds of black people went to the two inaugural balls; black band leaders and singers en-tertained during the celebrations. The Booker T. Washington high school band from Norfolk, Virginia, performed in the inaugural parade.[38]

These steps did not translate into civil rights legislation. Before the Senate convened, the new majority leader, Robert Taft, with the president's concur-rence, opposed a compulsory FEPC. That was expected; however, when a possi-ble vote to change the cloture rule was brought up, the senator refused to take action. Southerners could still use the filibuster to block civil rights bills.[39]

Taft had no need to worry about African American pressure. Eisenhower had drawn under a quarter of the black vote: the American National Election Studies from the University of Michigan found 20 percent, Gallup, 21 percent, and Samuel Lubell, 25 percent. The black media estimated that three to four million African Americans had voted, the largest outpouring of black voting in American presidential history—but they had voted overwhelmingly for Democrats.[40]

A more reliable count came from the NAACP, which sent out letters to its chapters in order "to get a complete and accurate picture of the role of the Negro vote." The organization directed its representatives to assemble election statistics from the daily papers and local boards of elections.[41] It ultimately produced a survey of 47 cities in 21 states, recording a total of 1,304,135 votes. Using that number and other figures assembled from black newspapers and scholarly studies, it estimated that approximately two million black people had cast ballots nationally in 1952, or less than 25 percent of eligible black voters. The NAACP chose not to disclose its totals but instead, for public consumption, used the higher number that pollsters and the black media had established. The total number of African Americans who went for Ike came up to 27 percent, or slightly less than the three out of ten who had voted Republican since Roosevelt's 1936 landslide.[42]

If the general had not received a single black vote, he would have still won easily. From a purely partisan perspective, he did not owe black people any political debt.[43]

8

EISENHOWER AND CIVIL RIGHTS:
THE FIRST TERM

In 1986, when the Public Broadcasting Service (PBS) ran *Eyes on the Prize: America's Civil Rights Years*, covering 1954 through 1962, it described a nation in turmoil. The struggle to enforce the *Brown v. Board of Education* decision, the brutality of the White Citizens' Councils and the Ku Klux Klan, the horrific murder of Emmet Till in Mississippi, the arrest of Rosa Parks for refusing to give up her bus seat in Montgomery, Alabama, the rise of Martin Luther King Jr., and other well-known events were presented as the era's defining features. The Eisenhower administration's proactive civil rights measures are simply not part of the story.[1]

The overstatement of Truman's civil rights accomplishments and the emphasis on Lyndon Johnson's very real ones seem to have created the unnecessary corollary that Eisenhower did little in this area. Two scholarly books, James Duram's *A Moderate Among Extremists* (1981) and Robert Burk's *The Eisenhower Administration and Black Civil Rights* (1984), severely criticize the president for ignoring civil rights issues. Stephen Ambrose's popular and otherwise laudatory biography identifies civil rights as Ike's worst failure. As we have seen, Ambrose made up events and claimed that the president told him he regretted "the appointment of that dumb son of bitch Earl Warren" and that he "personally wished that the Court had upheld *Plessy v. Ferguson*, and said so on a number of occasions (but only in private)." On the same page, Ambrose writes that while planning a dinner party for Earl Warren, Ike told Warren that white southerners did not want their daughters sitting next to "black bucks." These claims cannot be verified.[2]

Robert Shogan's 2013 book *Harry Truman and the Struggle for Racial Justice* builds on these efforts. A former *Los Angeles Times* reporter and the author of fourteen previous books, Shogan exaggerated Truman's humanitarian efforts in the civil rights arena and minimized the president's partisan political considerations.[3]

A careful reading of Shogan's bibliography shows that he based his book primarily on secondary sources. He never conducted research at the Eisenhower presidential library, nor does he cite the twenty-one published volumes of the president's papers (which are also available online) or any of the thousands of Eisenhower documents that have been microfilmed and are readily available at libraries across the nation. Rather than consult any of this material, Shogan repeated the erroneous allegations of those who preceded him. He described Ike as having a "passive approach to civil rights" and added: "Eisenhower's most evident deficiency in civil rights was his failure to speak out for the cause of racial justice."[4]

Although Truman did employ his bully pulpit, he did not get any civil rights legislation passed. Ike, acting with little fanfare, moved forcefully to desegregate the capital in his selection of the city's commissioners; Truman did not. Eisenhower brought more blacks into the government bureaucracy than ever before. He demanded the integration of the armed forces, including those in the South; Truman, despite having signed the executive order requiring integration, did not insist that it be carried out. Eisenhower chose Brownell and Rogers, passionate promoters of civil rights, to lead the justice department, and in his court appointments almost always selected jurists who supported racial justice. Truman appointed attorneys general who were not known for their civil rights efforts, and during the 1952 presidential election, Attorney General James McGranery ordered the justice department not to initiate any civil rights case that could embarrass Adlai Stevenson. Truman's four Supreme Court appointments were undistinguished—three were close friends and political associates—and he did not identify those favorable to racial justice for the lower courts.[5]

Historian Michael Mayer swam against the powerful undertow of Truman enthusiasm by producing well-researched scholarly articles on the civil rights policies of both Truman and Eisenhower. Instead of agreeing with the consensus, Mayer presents Ike as an epochal figure in the civil rights struggle. David Nichols, in *A Matter of Justice* (2007), shows that Ike proposed and enacted a strong civil rights program, and Timothy Thurber, in *Republicans and Race* (2013), shows how actively Republican politicians, including the president, worked on civil rights, and how little credit they have received.[6]

When Eisenhower began his presidency, the nation seemed uninterested in race relations. On February 2, 1953, the Gallup Poll published its findings regarding the issues Americans would most like to discuss with the president. Fifty-four percent would have talked about the Korean War; smaller percentages focused on domestic subversion, the economy, and other issues; and 6 percent had no idea. Only 1 percent mentioned civil rights. Five days later, Gallup asked its sample if they favored a federal law "requiring employers to hire people without regard to color or race," or whether each state should enforce its own laws. Thirty-one percent supported national legislation, while 47 percent chose states' rights.[7]

Despite that lack of concern, the president actively sought to include African Americans in his administration. The highest-ranking black appointee during the Eisenhower presidency was J. Ernest Wilkins, a prominent Republican from Chicago with an impressive resume. Born in 1894 at Farmington, Missouri, Wilkins had fought in France during World War I, earned a degree in 1921 from the University of Chicago Law School, and served as president of the Bar Association of Cook County.[8] As Eisenhower's assistant secretary of labor for international affairs, he became the first African American to be seated at a White House cabinet meeting when he took the role of acting secretary of labor during James Mitchell's absence. The *Chicago Defender* featured the event on its front page. When asked to describe the session, Wilkins praised Ike's leadership and called it a "challenging experience."[9]

Wilkins was appointed vice chair on the President's Committee on Government Contracts (PCGC) in 1953 and was selected to the President's Committee on Government Employment Policy two years later. He became an original member, and the only African American, on the civil rights commission in 1958 and played a leading role in its first hearings on the denial of voting rights to black citizens in Montgomery, Alabama. He died of a heart attack on January 19, 1959.[10]

Another black Republican from Chicago, Archibald Carey Jr., was tapped for a post on the President's Committee on Government Employment Policy in 1955. The objective of this body was to increase the number of blacks in white-collar jobs; their numbers rose from 4,979 in 1956 to 9,295 in 1960.[11]

African Americans also worked in the Eisenhower White House. Lois Lippman was the first black White House secretary, a role she described as "the biggest and most-interesting job I ever had." Boston born and having taken courses at Harvard, she had worked at the Eisenhower campaign headquarters in New York City before being hired by the chief of staff, Sherman Adams, as a stenographer and telephone receptionist. Her primary duties, as she saw them, were to be efficient and tight-lipped.[12]

The appointment that drew the most comment came when E. Frederic Morrow took his position as the first black White House aide in an executive post.

He joined CBS as a writer in 1951 and traveled on Eisenhower's 1952 campaign train as a consultant. Initially, he worked for Commerce Secretary Sinclair Weeks; in the summer of 1955, Sherman Adams offered him a job on the White House staff charged with "special projects," where his primary function was to defend the administration before black audiences. Morrow served for the remainder of Eisenhower's tenure but later grew disenchanted with the president's racial attitudes.[13]

Eisenhower did not select Valores "Val" Washington as the director of the RNC's minority division. He already held that position from the mid 1940s and was labeled the "black Mr. Republican." Once Ike announced his candidacy, however, Washington enthusiastically supported the general's campaign. After the GOP won the White House, he was responsible for relations with the black press, a duty he performed well since he was a former newspaperman and had great rapport with his fellow reporters. He also invited African Americans to White House functions, lobbied for black appointees, and published articles favorable to the administration's civil rights initiatives.[14]

Besides these prominent black appointees, other high-ranking members of the administration were outspoken civil rights advocates. Along with Brownell and Rogers, chief of staff Adams favored civil rights initiatives. Adams's deputy, Jerry Persons, was a committed segregationist, but the president recognized Persons' bias and excluded him from discussions regarding racial issues.

Eisenhower charged Secretary of the Cabinet Maxwell "Max" Rabb to coordinate racial issues for the Oval Office and serve as an intermediary between the president and African Americans. Among his other duties, Rabb served as the direct link to Congressman Powell, whose demands on civil rights were seen as impeding the White House's legislative objectives. When delicate civil rights topics arose at the White House, Ike's resolution was simple: "Give it to Max."[15]

Once his staff was in place, Ike quickly moved on his campaign pledges. He told his cabinet on January 26, 1953, that he opposed a federal employment practices commission and understood that Senator Taft planned to avoid a confrontation over the desegregation of the capital by refusing to let the matter come to a vote. This reluctance did not prevent presidential action. By the end of the year, the federal government had moved energetically to end discrimination in theaters, hotels, and restaurants in Washington. Historian Constance Green placed this transformation in perspective: "Measured by the distance still to be traversed to reach the goal of a truly interracial society, the advances . . . were small. Gauged by the obstacles overcome, they were tremendous."[16]

The president also acted aggressively on his campaign promise to complete the integration of the military. Although this met with resistance, especially in the

South, the armed forces integrated military schools, Veteran Administration hospitals, and naval bases. Richard Dalfiume, in *Desegregation of the U.S. Armed Forces*, asserts that by the end of 1953, integration was almost complete: "A quiet racial revolution had occurred with practically no violence, bloodshed, or conflict."[17]

Ike took another civil rights initiative even before entering the White House. The president-elect had appointed Henry Cabot Lodge, who had vigorously supported civil rights for African Americans as his liaison officer during the transition from the Truman administration. Lodge had spoken with the chief NAACP lobbyist and its capital director, Clarence Mitchell Jr., on December 4, 1952, regarding civil rights issues. Lodge had known Mitchell during his years in the Senate and wrote the general on that day that Mitchell handled "himself better 'on the Hill'" than anyone. Lodge added the following summer to the president that Mitchell was "an outstanding colored man" for whom Lodge had "developed great regard."[18]

Mitchell was concerned that the new administration might disband the Truman Contract Compliance Committee, which was ordered to enforce the nondiscrimination clause in government contracts. That meant that employers who received federal contracts had to extend fair treatment to minority groups in hiring practices. Lodge told Mitchell that Eisenhower would give his request careful study and then reminded Ike, when they met in Augusta, Georgia, "that there are no colored postal inspectors and no one in the policy-making levels of the Post Office Department who is colored. This, too, provides an opportunity for drastic and effective action."[19]

At a White House press conference on April 23, 1953, Alice Dunnigan of the Associated Negro Press asked the president what he was going to do about the vacant chairmanship of the Truman committee. Ike responded evasively but promised a definite reply "very soon." On August 13 he signed Executive Order 10479, creating an interdepartmental body called the President's Committee on Government Contracts. He designed it to fight racial discrimination in employment opportunities and wanted his countrymen to understand that the federal government meant "business" in pursuing this objective.[20]

After consulting with Max Rabb, the president chose Nixon to chair this body to illustrate its importance. Rabb considered himself a "good friend" of the vice president and thought him a wise selection. The vice president, who applauded the president's directive, told White House aide Bernard Shanley that eliminating segregation in the capital would confirm the administration's commitment to halt bigotry. Speaking before an Independence Day celebration at Gettysburg in early July, the vice president said: "There is no more appropriate place than

Gettysburg for us to say that there is no prejudice against race or color." In mid August, the president wrote Nixon that he was appointing him to focus on ways to foster civil rights and act against discrimination. His administration, he wrote, intended to fight bigotry; inside the federal bureaucracy, "tolerance of inequality would be odious."[21]

The president selected prominent leaders for the executive board. In addition to vice-chair J. Ernest Wilkins, they included John Roosevelt, FDR's youngest son; Fred Lazarus Jr., president of the American Retail Federation; John Mc-Caffrey, president of International Harvester; George Meany, president of the American Federation of Labor; Walter Reuther, United Automobile Workers president; and Helen Reid, publisher of the *New York Herald Tribune*. Six government agencies had representatives on the committee; the most significant were deputy attorney general Rogers, who served as counsel, and Secretary of Labor James Mitchell.[22]

Members of the committee were sworn in at New York's Waldorf Astoria Hotel on August 19, and the first formal meeting took place on the afternoon of September 14. Their first orders of business were requesting an increase in their $125,000 budget, enforcing the nondiscrimination clause in government contracts, and including a strong educational component in the committee's operations. George Meany "stressed that the desirable way to achieve compliance was by persuasion, mediation and conciliation rather than by invoking sanctions."[23]

Although Eisenhower thought in the same terms, many, especially in the South, feared otherwise. Governor James Byrnes of South Carolina, an avowed segregationist who had broken with the Democratic Party to endorse Ike for president, worried that the new committee would act against his state's interests. Eisenhower had written the governor that as president, he had an obligation to enforce nondiscrimination laws in federal contracts. Byrnes objected, anxious that civil rights activists would create dissension and some government officials would use the committee to force integration. In a long telephone conversation on the morning of September 3, the president told Byrnes that Nixon would examine federal guidelines to determine if the government was carrying out its obligations. The president later talked with Nixon about the South Carolinian's objections, and the following day, Ike sent his vice president a letter outlining his views: (1) the federal government had a responsibility "to insure equality" where it had jurisdiction; (2) he opposed FEPC legislation as "ineffective"; and (3) "all public officials . . . should attempt to promote justice and equality through leadership and persuasion."[24]

Nixon recognized the southern opposition and also knew that the PCGC had no enforcement powers. The committee's main benefit was the opportunities it gave him to meet with business, union, and black leaders on civil rights. At one point, for instance, he asked how many African Americans owned car dealerships. The reply was that millions bought cars, but only three or four were business owners. Armed with this information, Nixon lobbied companies to get more African Americans into ownership. He also lobbied businesses to employ more blacks in executive positions. Although labor talked sympathetically about civil rights, job training, and promotions for blacks, the unions resisted change.[25]

NAACP executive secretary Walter White lauded the president's measures "to reduce job discrimination" but wondered if the GOP's business advocates would seriously promote job equality and how the South would react if they did.[26]

While segregationists portrayed Nixon as a villain, Val Washington continually spotlighted the administration's positive civil rights record and advised the vice president how he could best enhance the president's proposals. Trying to popularize Nixon inside the black community, he had a photograph taken with the vice president and Evermont Robinson, the first African American doorkeeper appointed to the upper chamber, and also counseled Nixon to speak before select black audiences.[27] Rabb agreed and had the vice president appear at the national convention of the National Association of Colored Women. Many black audiences wanted to hear Nixon. Both Washington and Rabb were eager to accommodate them.[28]

At the end of January 1954, Nixon addressed a youth legislative conference at the Metropolitan Baptist Church in the capital. The United States, he pronounced, had to prove to the world that it was "working toward the principles which will guarantee to all peoples regardless of their national origin, background, color, creed, and equal opportunity—equal recognition under the law as American citizens." This would not happen overnight; it would take time.[29]

Eisenhower's first year in office ended with bold measures against segregation in the capital and in the armed forces. Through the PCGC, his vice president worked to reinforce the administration's efforts in civil rights. Decades later, one of the president's longtime aides, Andrew Goodpaster, reflected on Ike's position on race relations. The president had been raised in the nineteenth century in rural Kansas, Goodpaster noted, without intimate knowledge of black people, and later many of his white military acquaintances were southerners who uniformly deprecated the black race. To Ike, although every American was equal before the law, civil rights had to be approached cautiously.[30]

The president and vice president never comprehended how blacks resented the call for patience. Martin Luther King Jr.'s 1963 letter to clergymen from the jail in Birmingham, Alabama, describing the aberration that gradualism had come to signify, could just as easily have been written in the 1950s: "We know through painful experience that freedom is never voluntarily given by the oppressor; it must be demanded by the oppressed. . . . We have waited for more than 340 years for our constitutional and God-given rights."[31]

Despite the administration commitment to gradualism, at the end of February 1954, Adam Clayton Powell publicly applauded the president's initiatives during his first year: "The Honorable Dwight D. Eisenhower has done more to eliminate discrimination and to restore the Negro to the status of first class citizenship than any President since Abraham Lincoln."[32]

Two and a half months later, on May 17, 1954, the Supreme Court shocked Americans with its decision in *Brown v. Board of Education*, which reversed the "separate but equal" ruling in the 1896 case of *Plessy v. Ferguson*. The Court held that "separate but equal" was inherently *un*equal and ordered schools to integrate. In principle, the court made school segregation illegal; in practice, it gave no time frame to remedy the injustice. With *Brown II* a year later, the Court ordered that desegregation commence "with all deliberate speed," a vague standard that allowed southern states to delay integration for years.[33]

The herculean task of reversing laws and attitudes was evident at a party nine days after the first *Brown* decision. Mrs. Thomas Clark, whose husband was an associate justice on the Court, spoke out against the unanimous decision at a social gathering. "The colored people themselves," she argued, "would not feel happy in mixing with whites, except those of the North."[34]

Throughout his presidency, Eisenhower never publicly commented on *Brown*. He was the government's chief executive and felt his obligation was to enforce Supreme Court decisions, not to agree or disagree with them. Richard Kluger, in *Simple Justice*, eloquently condemns the president for never using his moral authority to advance school desegregation. "If Dwight Eisenhower and Richard Nixon had used the power of the White House to insist that the nation meet its moral obligations to black Americans," he wrote, "racism in the nation might long since have become a fugitive."[35]

The implication is that the violent civil rights struggles of the 1950s and 1960s might have been avoided if only Eisenhower—an uninspiring orator who seldom engaged in public moral suasion—had used his bully pulpit to promote *Brown*. What's forgotten in this argument is that he did support integration. On January 25, 1956, he wrote in his diary: "I favor the elimination of segregation, because I believe that equality of opportunity for every individual in America is one of the foundation stones of our system of Government."[36] Eisenhower also made vital Supreme Court appointments: Chief Justice Warren, who orchestrated the *Brown* ruling; Associate Justice John Harlan, whose father had been the single dissenter in *Plessy*; and William Brennan Jr., a fifty-year-old northern liberal who, at the time of his appointment, could reasonably be expected to support civil rights for many years after Eisenhower left office. And he did.[37]

The president did not limit his attention to the Supreme Court. The Court of Appeals for the Fifth Circuit encompassed six states from the Old Confederacy, Alabama, Florida, Georgia, Louisiana, Mississippi, and Texas, and quickly emerged as a main battleground in the challenges to *Brown*. Eisenhower knew Elbert Tuttle from Georgia and Louisiana's John Minor Wisdom, who had been part of Ike's inner circle during the 1952 campaign. Both were prominent attorneys, and the president appointed them to the Court of Appeals in 1954 and 1957 respectively because they would enforce the *Brown* decision. As the president had anticipated, both would emerge as staunch defenders of *Brown*.[38]

Nixon read the *Brown* decision the day after its release and was not surprised. He and deputy attorney general Rogers agreed that the decision was constitutionally sound but that enforcement would be another matter. After *Brown*, Nixon increased his advocacy for civil rights. In September 1954, he gave a speech in Wilmington, Delaware, where white parents had forced suspension of desegregation efforts by refusing to send their children to integrated schools. Appealing to his listeners to accept the *Brown* decision, Nixon pointed out that he and Pat sent their daughters to an integrated school. "There is no reason," he said, "why Americans, regardless of race, creed or color, cannot be educated together"[39]

In January 1955 Nixon returned to the Metropolitan Baptist Church, speaking to the same youth group he had addressed a year earlier. Val Washington warned him that the attendees, "many left-wingers," would demand "all out integration with no holds barred" and urged him to stress "that this Administration is doing everything possible on desegregation in every field." With this caution, Nixon emphasized as school integration was completed, prejudice would also disappear: "All of us," he contended, "as Americans, want our country to be one which opportunity for ourselves and our children will be equal."[40]

Six months later, on June 25, Nixon visited Harlem for the first time. With two Secret Service agents and ten city detectives guarding him, the hatless vice president shook hands with astonished passersby and talked to small boys, who rushed up to meet him, about the Brooklyn Dodgers' winning streak. He stopped at two insurance companies, a weekly newspaper, the *New York Age Defender*, and the Harlem YMCA. That evening he attended an awards dinner in Harlem for about 200 guests, where he told his audience that Ike had given his "unqualified moral support" to the administration's civil rights program. The program was based on achievable goals and "the realization of the American dream of providing equal opportunity for all of our citizens, regardless of race, creed, or color." Relying on "persuasion rather than compulsion," the effort deserved the cooperation of African American leaders: "The most eloquent proof of how things have changed is that it is no longer news when Negroes are invited to lunch or dinner at the White House with the President."[41]

The next day, Nixon went before the forty-sixth annual NAACP convention at Atlantic City, New Jersey. His audience was ready to be antagonistic: The *New York Times* had reported that while in Harlem, Nixon had urged "patience" and "go slow on integration." He extolled Ike's civil rights measures and declared "the greatest progress since 1865 has been made toward the objective to which this organization is dedicated." He then listed the government's actions and that added the president was working on the completion of school integration that would wipe out bigotry.[42]

Roy Wilkins, who succeeded Walter White as the NAACP executive secretary, closed the gathering, alleging that a "conspiracy to deny equality to Negroes" was gaining momentum. Since the *Brown* decision, he said, southern groups had prevented black people from registering to vote and from enrolling their children in nonsegregated schools. Northern Democratic congressmen were playing "poker politics, with the civil rights of Negroes as the joker card," and their Republican counterparts were behaving "like Dixiecrats." In his memoirs, Wilkins recalled that when Nixon spoke, the delegates "gave him the coldest shoulder I have ever seen. The delegates just sat there like stone men and women as he talked—looking at him hard."[43]

Black newspapers had a wide range of reactions. The *New York Amsterdam News* objected to Nixon's emphasis on gradualism. The *St. Louis American* gave him a "B" on his performance, holding that FDR and Truman had done more than Eisenhower. James Hicks wrote two articles for the *Afro-American*, calling the vice president "one of the most charming men in American politics today." Nixon, he wrote, had walked in smiling, pitched his message to the professionals sitting before him, and opened his remarks on advancing integration. He "could charm a ring-tailed baboon if he could get the baboon to look him in the eye." As a consequence, the reporter concluded, "the sum and substance of the whole thing was that many of the people who came to jeer settled back in their seats and remained to cheer Nixon."[44]

The Ku Klux Klan offered its condemnation. Its journal, the *White Sentinel*, labeled the vice president "a politician of the lowest rank" for appearing before the convention. "The NAACP is dedicated to the mongrelization of the people of America and the destruction of the American Way of Life. Nixon should be impeached." An editorial in the *Richmond News Leader* stated that by advocating public school integration, the president and vice president had betrayed their commitment to states' rights.[45]

While the vice president faced attacks from many directions, he worked to make the PCGC meaningful. With a small staff, meager budget, and opposition from southern congressmen, he had minimal flexibility. Despite these limitations, the committee took action that no governmental agency had previously taken on civil rights. Even though the PCGC had no enforcement power, it focused a national spotlight on federal job discrimination.

In November 1953, Ike signed an executive order requiring nondiscrimination clauses in federal contracts. After December, contractors doing business with the federal government were forced to post notices in their buildings explaining antidiscrimination clauses. After some delay, PCGC began providing the notices; in June 1955, the committee distributed 55,000 posters in more than 359 cities that read: "There are no closed doors when you apply for a job with a Government Contractor. Jobs must be filled on the basis of qualifications, not race, religion or national origin." In October, PCGC announced that job discrimination would end on interstate airlines, steamships, and railroads. Nixon's year-end statement noted that the committee had "made some significant progress." It had avoided publicity, he wrote, because the president wanted action not words, but now it should appeal to the public to make it "aware of what we have done."[46]

In March 1955, Nixon initiated a special meeting of the PCGC to open new channels of communications with labor leaders. Unions had resisted training and advancement for black workers. The vice president told a group of union officials that the PCGC would cooperate with them to end job discrimination. George Meany and others pledged their support, but this was cosmetic. Surrendering white slots for new hires and hiring African Americans instead had little chance of approval from the rank and file.[47]

At the end of May, Nixon went before the Capital Press Club, where he praised the administration's civil rights initiatives but reserved the highest praise for "Negro leaders who have" recommended "a course of moderation in this field" and mobilized black opinion without calling for violence. Nixon optimistically assured these reporters: "While the fight to remove discrimination in employment has been a long uphill climb, we are over the top and our progress in the days ahead will be increasingly fast. If we continue to support a program of moderation, patience, and hard work and resist the demagogues whose primary interest is in using the cause of prejudice rather than removing it, our efforts will be crowned with complete success."[48]

Nixon next presided over a conference on equal job opportunity for sixty-five businesses, industrial organizations, and voluntary groups. Prominent leaders like Henry Ford II and RCA's David Sarnoff attended. Thinking this would be a "big occasion and we must play it big," Nixon encouraged the participants to halt job discrimination and to hire and to promote minorities through training programs. If big businesses with nationwide reach put these measures in place, antidiscrimination would be extended to the South. He predicted that "what industry has done, what selective industries and plants have done in the deep south, their experience in successful integration and employment . . . is a fair indication of what we may expect as the school integration program goes into effect in the same southern states."[49]

Due to inadequate funding and a tiny staff, the PCGC could rarely act upon complaints of discrimination. In late 1955, it investigated charges against the District of Columbia and Baltimore phone companies for their refusal to hire "colored operators." John Roosevelt, acting for PCGC, negotiated with The Chesapeake & Potomac Telephone Company in the capital to have African Americans put "into job classifications which previously were not open." George McKibben went to the company's Baltimore division, and for the first time in its history, two black women were hired as switchboard operators.[50]

Clarence Mitchell handled the complaints going to the PCGC. As the only registered black lobbyist in the capital, he was sometimes called "the most powerful Negro on Capitol Hill." Mitchell not only filed complaints before Nixon's committee but also lobbied the vice president on federal aid to education. He and Nixon grew to have a cordial relationship.[51]

Eisenhower devised other approaches to encourage "both tolerance and progress in our race relations problems." In March 1956, he wrote evangelist Billy Graham, who had refused to speak before segregated audiences since 1953, to ask him to lobby clergymen on civil rights. Ministers, Ike suggested, should advocate the election of "a few qualified Negroes to school boards" and to city councils. He also proposed allowing black students to enter graduate programs "strictly on the basis of merit."[52]

The president may have been considering these options in response to the Southern Manifesto, released in March 1956. This document, circulated by Senators Strom Thurmond of South Carolina, Richard Russell of Georgia, and Henry Byrd of Virginia, argued that the Supreme Court had acted unconstitutionally in making its ruling in *Brown*, and the signers pledged to do everything legal to reestablish *Plessy's* "separate but equal." Only Senators Gore, Kefauver, and Lyndon Johnson refused to sign; 101 of the 128 congressmen from the eleven former Confederate states also signed.[53]

Eisenhower was concerned that these extremists would disrupt orderly school integration. His initial suggestion was that Graham reason with religious groups that feared racial confrontation and violence. The evangelist replied that he did not engage in partisan politics, but he invited the vice president to address religious groups in his home state of North Carolina. The trip was billed as strictly nonpolitical. When Eisenhower and Nixon agreed, the preacher was pleased because he believed that "Dick," who had become a friend, was "in need of a boost in Protestant religious circles" and had to demonstrate in person his "sincerity and ability." Graham arranged the entire affair and accompanied the vice president everywhere he went.[54]

By this time, Graham had gained international recognition. With heavy press and photographic coverage, Nixon began his one-day tour—August 5, 1956—by addressing the Southern Baptist Home Mission Program, Ridgecrest Assembly. He talked about religion's separation from the state and warned that communism challenged the Christian faith. Believers had to fight atheism. He then turned to *Brown*, proclaiming the decision by itself would not prevent demagoguery: "The churches can help create the climate of understanding and good will which is essential in the implementation of the law of the land." He then moved on to the Presbyterian Men's Council Synod of Appalachia and, in the evening, spoke at the Montreat Methodist Summer Assembly. All together, he addressed almost 15,000 Christians, many who saw and heard him in person for the first time.[55]

Lela Breard, a realtor from Monroe, Louisiana, regretted these appearances. The South would never accept integration. "Birds and beasts do not mix. God segrated [sic] the races when he made black and white. We do not believe in slavery and have a warm friendly feeling for the negroes. They need better living conditions and should have equal rights in voting and education but by all means segregated. There is a physical difference between the two races which will forever forbid social and political equality and inter-marriage."[56]

While Nixon was promoting integration, Stevenson was damaging his own civil rights credentials. He went before a black audience in Los Angeles on February 6, 1956, and advocated only gradual enforcement of *Brown*. Within three days, NAACP executive secretary Roy Wilkins wrote him: "To Negro Americans 'gradual' means either no progress at all, or progress so slow as to be barely perceptible." Stevenson and Eisenhower, to Wilkins, seemed to be advancing similar themes. The once and future Democratic presidential nominee was, in fact, even more circumspect than the president. Because he could not afford to alienate southern voters, Stevenson said nothing against the Southern Manifesto. Arthur Schlesinger Jr. confided in his journal that Stevenson had no strong feelings regarding civil rights; he saw his candidate's gradualism as counterproductive and felt that desegregation would only come through government coercion.[57]

A month and a half before Democrats gathered for their convention in Chicago, Roy Wilkins addressed the NAACP's forty-seventh annual gathering, pronouncing that both parties had left black people "out in the cold" by refusing to move aggressively on school integration. Toward the end of July, the House passed a civil rights bill by 277 to 126. Democratic congressmen split 111 for and 102 against, a number that demonstrated the division within the party: northern Democrats pushed for *Brown's* enforcement while southerners adamantly opposed it. The bill died in the Senate judiciary committee.[58]

In spite of this stalemate, when asked at the beginning of August which party had done the most for them during the last decade, 67 percent of northern blacks chose Democrats while a scant 16 percent preferred the GOP. If they had to cast their presidential ballots at that moment, 62 percent would select Stevenson versus 32 percent for Ike. Congressional races were more lopsided. Blacks would vote 74 percent Democratic to 21 percent Republican.[59]

When the Democratic national convention opened in the middle of the month, twenty-four delegates, 1.7 percent of the total, were African Americans. The GOP conclave was not much better: thirty-six or 2.7 percent were black. Eleanor Roosevelt chaired her party's platform committee on civil rights. The NAACP and liberals pressed for a strong plank, while southerners opposed it. The committee accepted a compromise to promote party unity.[60]

Republicans had a huge advantage. They were overjoyed that Ike was running for reelection. As for civil rights, the president had a record. At a press conference at the beginning of August, he deplored "anyone that stirs up racial hatred" and urged that "people of good will and real sensibilities" must cooperate. Extremism was counterproductive.[61]

In his memoirs, Arthur Larson, undersecretary of labor and a presidential speechwriter, did not count Ike as a civil rights advocate. He described a meeting he had with Ike shortly before the Republican convention, in which Larson suggested that the president give a powerful civil rights message. From Larson's viewpoint, Ike "was neither emotionally nor intellectually in favor of combating segregation." He saw the president as a nineteenth-century figure born in the South who did not intend to challenge that region's customs. Ike objected to racial mingling, reflecting the views of the vast majority concerning miscegenation. Even though he only had a son, he did not think "that a Negro should court my daughter." According to Larson, Eisenhower disliked such words as "discrimination" and "racial." His duty as president on civil rights only extended to integrating federal institutions.[62]

Before leaving for the GOP convention, the president called Attorney General Brownell in San Francisco. The platform committee's civil rights plank said: "The Eisenhower Administration . . . and the Republican Party" supported "the *Brown* decision"; Ike insisted that the words "Eisenhower Administration" be removed. He reminded the attorney general that his administration had not endorsed the ruling and held that "the whole issue had been set back badly." If the committee did not consent, he threatened not to attend the convention. The GOP followed the president's instructions. The platform still went "a little further toward the liberal position than the Democrats," according to Charles Thomson and Frances Shattuck, who studied both parties' platforms. The GOP recited the administration's achievements, and the party accepted *Brown* more than the Democrats did.[63]

At the Republican convention, Dr. Helen Edmonds, a professor of history at North Carolina College, became the first black woman to second a presidential nomination at a Republican convention; J. Ernest Wilson seconded Nixon's nomination. Patricia Spaulding served as the first black page at the national gathering.[64]

In his acceptance speech, Eisenhower alluded to the party's "social justice" accomplishments. His administration had eliminated discrimination in the military, in the capital, and in government contracts. He said of Nixon's contribution that "no one has been more effective and more energetic than our Vice President who has headed one of the great Committees [PCGC] in this direction."[65]

Black newspapers carried the portion of Nixon's acceptance speech that discussed civil rights. Pledging that African Americans would "receive first class citizenship," he declared that America was "proud" of its black citizens and the administration "should not and we will not rest until every Negro has an opportunity to obtain proper housing, proper medical care and the unlimited ability to live as every American should live."[66]

At the start of the campaign, Stevenson emphasized the civil rights issue, declaring that he supported the *Brown* decision and that the Democratic platform rejected any "use of force to interfere with the orderly determination of these matters by the courts." He deplored Eisenhower's comment that "it makes no difference whether or not I endorse it" and attacked the president for his refusal to come out forcefully for *Brown,* implying that he himself had done so. Ike, he said, ignored "human needs." In fact, Stevenson had resisted liberal pressure to act boldly on civil rights and was just as much a gradualist as the president—as well as skeptical regarding the federal government's role in desegregation. On September 25, he told an audience that he backed public school integration. Nine days later he informed Harlem listeners that the president had not used his bully pulpit to champion *Brown*. He rejected any GOP claims that Republicans had pushed for civil rights; the Democrats, in reality, had started the momentum.[67]

Vice-presidential nominee Estes Kefauver, speaking in Orlando, Florida, in mid-September, reversed his earlier unequivocal support for school desegregation. He went on a radio program stating southern conditions required "patience" on integration. He accepted the Supreme Court ruling but, like his running mate, objected to armed force or federal intervention in the South. He later gave a speech in which he mentioned "outside agitators who made the trouble" over school integration in his home state of Tennessee.[68]

The president was less equivocal. At his press conference on September 11, he deplored racial violence and said he hoped the South would abide by court orders. If they refused to integrate, he warned, the court could find them in contempt and ask the justice department for assistance. United States marshals could possibly jail offenders. He also congratulated the public schools of Louisville, Kentucky, where 12,500 of the 50,000 students were black, and how they had planned for integration over the past two years, with the result that desegregation began without "the slightest trouble."[69]

Nixon's mission during the campaign was to appeal to black voters. He declared that he would not attend "meetings in Southern States where the audience is segregated. If [they] insist on segregation, meeting[s] must be held outside—no exceptions."[70] Toward the end of the month, Bryce Harlow, a White House staffer and political adviser, provided further guidance from the president. In a memorandum following a meeting with Ike, Harlow told Nixon that the president believed that "the real answer lies . . . in the hearts of man" and that the administration should push for "moderate, steady advance in keeping with the Supreme Court decision, avoiding extremes on both sides." Law and order were local responsibilities, and unless the local authorities asked for assistance, the federal government had no jurisdiction. If a locality refused to follow a federal court order, then the attorney general would "assist the Court to whatever degree is necessary."[71]

Nixon gave his first major speech devoted to civil rights in Louisville, Kentucky, on September 27. Before his presentation, he demanded: "No segregation." He had already been briefed on the city's achievement with its public schools and shared the president's view that most Louisville families had accepted the end of segregation. He cautioned his audience against extremists who would interfere with the reform and advised that "in the long run education and persuasion rather than compulsion are the most effective weapons in dealing with this problem at the national level." Integrated facilities dramatically improved the American image abroad, and most critically: "If we deprive the Negro of his dignity, we stifle him. If we allow him to develop in a society untainted by discrimination, the entire country profits by his genius in art and music and literature." The next day the vice president was asked whether the Senate would confirm the appointment of an African American to the Supreme Court; he said it would.[72]

Ike responded at a White House press conference to Stevenson's charge that the Republicans were running on the Democratic civil rights record by claiming credit for Truman's desegregation of the armed forces. Ike's retort was that Truman had hardly been the first military leader to advocate integrating the armed forces—or to do it. He himself was the first combat commander to integrate black troops into white battlefield units where black soldiers volunteered "for front line service" during World War II. General George Patton initially opposed the concept but later "became the most rabid supporter of the idea." At the beginning of his presidency, Ike said, even before *Brown*, he had directed the departments of defense and health, education and welfare to eliminate segregation at Army post schools. Some southern units had trouble with social issues such as dances, but "gradually, it was ironed out, and the progress went ahead."[73]

Democratic Congressman Adam Clayton Powell met with Eisenhower on October 11 and afterward broke with the Democratic Party by publicly endorsing his reelection. Democrats denounced Powell's decision; Eleanor Roosevelt withdrew her backing of his ministry. Despite this opposition, Powell continued to support Ike's cause.[74]

Some African Americans seemed receptive to the congressman's arguments. The *Chicago Daily News* reported that black Republicans were working energetically for Eisenhower, distributing a newsletter that listed the administration's major African American appointments. Reverend Archibald Carey in Chicago said that volunteers knocking on doors were receiving "enthusiastic responses." These were "the same doors which were formerly slammed in their faces when they went to campaign for Republicans." A *New York News* straw poll showed that the president was attracting a significant number of black Democrats.[75]

Eisenhower welcomed African Americans into the party. When queried on television on October 12 concerning Stevenson's complaint that he had been "virtually silent" on civil rights, the president responded that while the Supreme Court ruled on *Brown*, it had not provided guidelines on integrating public schools. This was an emotional subject "that really comes down finally into the heart—as much as it does into the head." Moderation was the solution, and violence had to be rejected. He had eliminated segregation where the federal government had jurisdiction, and had done so "quietly, not tub-thumping, and we have not tried to claim political credit. . . . This is a matter of justice, not of anything else."[76]

A week later, addressing an audience at the Hollywood Bowl in California, he charged that Democrats had developed a formula of "much oratory and little performance" on civil rights. His administration had "acted with patience, human understanding and with concern for the equal standing of all before the law" and had fought for civil rights without trying to claim "partisan credit." "The final battle against intolerance is to be fought—not in the chambers of any legislature—but in the hearts of men."[77]

Nixon did not make extravagant projections of how Congressman Powell's endorsement would benefit the ticket. The popular minister might entice blacks to vote Republican, but even without his backing, the party had "made some gains" among African Americans. Speaking at a rally in Rochester, New York, on October 16, Nixon paid tribute to Republican Congressman Kenneth Keating, who had co-sponsored civil rights legislation that had failed before Congress adjourned. He called for a Republican congressional majority, predicting that without it, "civil rights will get nothing but a deep freeze for the next few years, and we can't let that happen."[78]

These declarations were the prelude to the vice president's address to the Alfred E. Smith Memorial Foundation Dinner, in New York City on October 18. Smith, a Democrat, had been governor of New York and in 1928 became the first Catholic to run for president. Nixon limited his remarks primarily to civil rights. "Most of us here," he said, "will live to see the day when American boys and girls shall sit, side by side, at any school—public or private—with no regard paid to the color of their skin."[79]

He then traveled by train to Chicago. On October 25, he rode through the Chicago Loop to the cheers of a lunchtime crowd of between 150,000 and 200,000. After the motorcade, he appeared on the south side of the city, where the African American community was concentrated. Approximately 3,500 jammed into the Trianon ballroom while another 1,500 listened over a loudspeaker outside. He highlighted the president's dedication to civil rights and anticipated that if Stevenson won, he would follow Truman's example: "a lot of talk, a lot of promises, but no action." Southern Democrats controlled many congressional chairmanships, and if that continued, "civil rights legislation will never see the light of day." To get to Ike's desk, that legislation needed a Republican congressional majority.[80]

At the end of the month, Nixon returned to New York City, landing at LaGuardia Field in a driving rain. That evening he headed for Harlem, the first time in years that a Republican had campaigned there. This district, the heart of the largest African American community in the United States, comprised about 400,000 voters, or 6 percent of the Empire State's total. The GOP had planned an elaborate outdoor rally with Duke Ellington providing the entertainment at the corner of Seventh Avenue and 125th Street.[81]

When the storm prevented the outside activities, the organizers moved inside to the Hotel Theresa's ballroom, which accommodated about 350. Actress Helen Hayes and Franklin Roosevelt's youngest son, John, were present. White House assistant Frederic Morrow had abandoned his earlier projection that the GOP would lose African American voters and now saw them shifting to Ike. Morrow introduced Jacob Javits, who was running for the United States Senate. Javits had initially looked for someone to replace Nixon on the ticket, but now claimed full confidence in the vice president. If he became president, Javits said, Nixon would govern "in the image of Eisenhower."[82]

Morrow then introduced Nixon. He later reported that the vice president received "a thunderous ovation" and was "at his best," giving "one of the most dynamic speeches" of the campaign. Nixon told his audience that Ike would move forward on civil rights legislation. The president had not achieved everything black people wished for, but he had made progress. Accomplishing more would require "action, not words: deeds not speeches" in civil rights. Conceding that Stevenson favored civil rights, he reminded his audience that southern congressmen controlled the legislative process: the president needed a Republican Congress. Otherwise, with the Democratic Party divided almost equally on the issue, no civil rights bill would pass. Nixon highlighted the administration's commitment: "better education for all of our people, newer jobs at better pay in better positions, better and cheaper housing, the end of Jim Crow in interstate transportation and, most important of all, a recognition of the dignity of man." Such lofty objectives did not satisfy everyone. As Nixon left the hotel, a small crowd outside booed him.[83]

Leading up to the election, the black press anticipated a strong voter turnout. A Gallup Poll analysis indicated that the president's support among African Americans had jumped from 21 percent in 1952 to 42 percent in 1956. Before the election, thirty-nine weeklies or semiweeklies in the African American press supported Ike, versus twenty-nine for Stevenson. On the day of the balloting, the *Atlanta Daily World* predicted that although Ike would win, he would not receive as large a majority as in his first campaign. In its next edition, newspaper reversed itself and reported on the Eisenhower landslide. Black newspapers, in their analysis, proclaimed that black voters had become a key factor in many local and state elections. Some in the media speculated that they were shifting to the GOP; others saw the switch as a protest vote against southern Democrats.

A few pointed out that many black voters split their tickets, voting for Ike because Stevenson had lost his appeal in African American communities.[84]

Roy Wilkins, the NAACP executive secretary, declared that blacks had helped elect many liberals to Congress. In the South, the black vote "was strictly a protest vote against the ruthless and unyielding attitude of the Southern Democrats." Wilkins saw the increased black vote for Republicans as a plus. As long as they voted overwhelmingly Democratic, blacks had no bargaining power because Democrats took them for granted, while Republicans thought they belonged to the opposition. The shift toward the GOP meant both parties had to court black votes.[85]

Henry Lee Moon, the NAACP public relations director, had compiled precinct counts from his organization's chapters across the nation. He knew that the newspapers' claim of four and a half million black votes was incorrect, but he concealed the real figures. Later, he admitted that black voting had increased only slightly over 1952, without revealing that this translated to just over 2 million black voters.[86]

African Americans had not shifted their allegiance to the GOP. They had simply not come out for Stevenson. Overall, three in ten blacks remained Republicans.[87]

In the summer of 1957, the research division of the RNC provided its analysis of black voting. The researchers assumed incorrectly that 3.5 million African Americans had voted, and that in Louisiana and Tennessee their vote might have made the difference in the presidential race. The GOP had made its greatest gains in the South, where Democrats heavily outnumbered Republicans, but not enough to alter the outcomes. Gains outside the South were far less impressive: approximately 5 percent of black voters had moved from the Democratic column to the Republican.[88]

The groups that reported on elections had not closely followed the African American exodus from the South and its effects on voting patterns. Blacks demographically were emerging as the largest minority in the United States living in urban areas. By 1960, 75 percent lived in cities. African American voters gravitated toward the Democratic Party because it was responsible for the New Deal legislation that offered much-needed economic assistance. The Eisenhower/Nixon ticket's support for civil rights was not enough to overcome the effects of urban concentration and Democratic policies aimed at helping the poor.[89]

By maximizing Truman's achievements and minimizing Eisenhower's, most authors have created a distorted account. In his first term, Ike took more concrete measures toward civil rights than his predecessor had done. Realizing that white southerners would not accept *Brown* instantly, he counseled a gradual approach to integration, not realizing that many blacks and white liberals heard "patience" as "never." He did not understand why African Americans were dissatisfied, not recognizing the political significance of the moral leadership he might have provided had he been more outspoken.

Still Ike's use of Nixon as the administration's civil rights spokesman is ignored. As PCGC chairman, the vice president learned at first hand of painful consequences of job discrimination, and he tried, with minimal success, to ameliorate some of them. More than anyone else in the administration, he regularly used his bully pulpit to proclaim the administration's civil rights achievements. Prominent African American reporter Simeon Booker recalled: "Nixon was the civil rights workhorse having put together the GOP's civil-rights program."[90]

Despite these tangible efforts, in the mid 1950s, blacks confronted a Republican Party that had moved forward on civil rights but was philosophically opposed to big government and outspokenly for free enterprise. Within these parameters, blacks heard exclusion and a withdrawal of help. Republicans did not comprehend that African Americans were casting their lot with the liberal wing of the Democratic Party because it championed large social welfare programs in a society where discrimination and the denial of opportunity were a daily reality.

Black leaders in the mid-1950s faced another quandary. Southern Democratic congressmen, who were committed racists, controlled many congressional committees and vigorously fought integration. African Americans in the Old Confederacy who opposed the white Democratic-elected officials, and who were able to cast ballots, had one option: the GOP. Outside the South, African Americans, who were primarily urban dwellers, moved into the liberal wing of the Democratic Party. Until the liberals took clear control of that party, blacks would speak from two separate perspectives.

9

IKE, NIXON, AND DULLES

Long before Eisenhower assumed the presidency, he had evolved into a committed internationalist. He commanded the Allied armies that marched from North Africa through Sicily, Italy, France, and Germany. Before receiving his stars, he had served in Latin America and Asia and participated in his own capital's bureaucratic intrigues. After he accepted the presidency of Columbia University in 1948, he interrupted his tenure to assume command of NATO in Paris in order to strengthen Western European forces against Soviet expansion.

While in Paris, Eisenhower decided to run for the presidency primarily because he was worried that Robert Taft would turn the nation toward isolationism. As the general who understood the might of the Soviet armed forces, he was not naïve about the role of the military in the postwar world. America, he believed, could not return to a stance of noninvolvement while Moscow was pursuing an aggressively expansionist policy. He walked into the Oval Office as a staunch cold warrior.

He was also uniquely equipped to acknowledge the awesome destructiveness of nuclear weaponry and to understand that another world war could bring global annihilation. To avoid that horror, he promoted collective security and approved of the United Nations' sending troops to Korea. Although he wished for peace through negotiations, he accepted the strategy of containment as the best way to halt the Kremlin's advances.[1]

In June 1952, as the Republican national convention approached, he wrote that his party should advocate a foreign policy of "positive, forward looking action and leadership in the promotion of collective security." He opposed any thought of isolationism: "America cannot live alone, and . . . her form of life is threatened by the Communistic dictatorship." The response had to be more than military: the United States had to reach out and trade with other nations as well as cooperate with and lead the rest of the free world. "Exclusive reliance upon a mere power of retaliation," he warned, "is not a complete answer to the broad Soviet threat."[2]

Late in the presidential campaign, Ike pledged to go to Korea if elected, and within a month of his triumph, he did. Although it fulfilled a campaign promise, the visit did not stop the violence. Neither the South nor the North was ready to sue for peace. Their objectives remained mystifying.[3]

Just as Eisenhower's internationalism was unquestioned, so was his running mate's. As a congressman in the fall of 1947, Nixon traveled to Europe on the Herter mission, a House effort to examine European postwar economic conditions, and later vigorously supported the Marshall Plan and aid to Greece and Turkey. He endorsed Truman's decision to send American soldiers to Korea. When Taft approached him to back his presidential bid, Nixon refused because the Ohioan thought in nationalist, isolationist terms, a concept that Nixon had rejected: "it implied abandoning the rest of the world to Communism."[4]

Eisenhower's appointment of John Foster Dulles as secretary of state strengthened his administration's commitment to internationalism and to the role of spiritual values in foreign affairs. Born in 1888, two years before Eisenhower, Dulles came from a prominent family. A grandfather, John W. Foster, had been Benjamin Harrison's secretary of state and an uncle, Robert Lansing, had held the same post under Woodrow Wilson.[5]

Dulles had entered Princeton University at the age of sixteen, the youngest member of his class; after completing his degree, he studied law at George Washington University and graduated in 1911. The following year, he married Janet Avery and also began his career at the powerful Wall Street firm of Sullivan & Cromwell. Specializing in corporate law and international business, he emerged in the decade after the First World War as one of the wealthiest and best-known members of his profession. He became deeply involved in lay Presbyterian activities and served as an adviser at various international conferences, including the drafting of the United Nations charter in San Francisco. By the end of the Second World War, Dulles was the acknowledged Republican leader of his party's international wing. He advised Thomas Dewey on foreign affairs during his two unsuccessful runs for the White House in 1944 and 1948. Even in defeat, Dulles's stature rose. He saw the struggle between America and Russia as a fight of the faithful versus nonbelievers, and himself as a leader on the side of the righteous. Journalist William Miller wrote of the reaction among Protestant leaders to his appointment to Eisenhower's cabinet: "When in 1953 Dulles became Secretary of State there was considerable gratification among many Protestants that their man had made it."[6]

There was one incident in Dulles's past that might have endangered his appointment. He had become chairman of the board of the Carnegie Endowment for International Peace at the end of 1946. Before accepting the post, he had vigorously pushed for the appointment of Alger Hiss as its president. Hiss won confirmation and, as president of the Endowment, saw Dulles regularly. When Eisenhower joined the board in 1948, he too communicated periodically with Hiss. Nixon became part of the equation in the summer of 1948, when a *Time* magazine editor, Whittaker Chambers, testified in front of Richard Nixon and the House Committee on Un-American Activities that Hiss had been a communist spy. Hiss, who had denied the charge under oath, was convicted of perjury, served time in prison, and spent the rest of his life trying to clear his name (following his death, archives released after the fall of the Soviet Union showed that he was a spy). Chambers had been a Soviet spy, left the Communist Party in the 1930s, and emerged as the former agent who identified Hiss as a communist in the summer of 1948. Nixon, relying on Chambers's testimony, was credited with exposing Hiss. For the Endowment and its trustees, the incident was a temporary embarrassment. Before the Hiss inquiry, Dulles had had minimal contact with Nixon. The Californian consulted him early in 1948 about proposed legislation to restrict the activities of the Communist Party of the United States, later referred to as the Mundt-Nixon bill. He wanted Dulles's advice on drafting a bill that would not impinge on the constitutional protection of free speech. Several months later, Nixon wrote Dulles about proposed legislation that would outlaw the CPUSA.[7]

By the time Dewey won the presidential nomination, Nixon's role in Dulles's life had changed markedly. After the congressman questioned Hiss about his involvement in espionage, he arranged a meeting in New York with Foster Dulles and his brother Allen on August 12. Nixon brought a transcript of Hiss's testimony. The brothers read it, paced the floor, and concluded that Hiss quite possibly could have been a Soviet spy. They told Nixon he had a strong case and should pursue his quarry. Later that month, Foster Dulles asked for and received Hiss's resignation. He testified at each of the two perjury trials that followed (the first ended in a hung jury), appearing in the second as the final witness for the prosecution.[8]

In letters written during the 1948 presidential race, Foster addressed Nixon as "My dear Congressman Nixon." A year later, the letters began "Dear Dick." In 1951, Dulles spoke at Whittier College on peace in Asia. After he had served as the chief United States negotiator for a peace treaty with Japan, Nixon voted to confirm it. They were not yet close friends, but they had established a cordial relationship.[9]

With Eisenhower's nomination in 1952, the interaction between Nixon and Dulles increased. In August they traveled to the general's Colorado headquarters to discuss campaign tactics. When those sessions concluded, Dulles wrote Nixon about the Hiss case as a potential campaign issue. He was especially concerned about his role in Hiss's appointment as president of the Carnegie Endowment. He concluded that it was unlikely to "cause any embarrassment" because at Hiss's trial, he had testified for the prosecution while Adlai Stevenson had been a defense witness. Still, it was important to confirm the details. First, Dulles wrote, he had not been on the three-man committee that had selected Hiss. He conceded that he had been a trustee and had suggested several names including Hiss. The committee approached a few candidates, who declined the post, and then offered the job to Hiss, who accepted and was formally appointed at the December 1946 board meeting, the same one at which Dulles became chairman. On the last day of the year, Alfred Kohlberg, a fervent anticommunist, wrote Dulles that Hiss had Soviet affiliations. Dulles replied that he could not remove Hiss without evidence and asked Kohlberg to substantiate his allegations. Kohlberg could not, and Dulles did not pursue the charge because it "was not conclusive."[10]

Nixon had his staff check Dulles's recollections for accuracy. James Gleason, an executive assistant, telephoned Kohlberg, who vividly recalled the incident. He had seen Dulles on January 2, 1947, and Dulles had admitted that he had recommended Hiss to the board of directors. Kohlberg warned him that several individuals described Hiss as "a sort of a fellow-traveler," but these sources had "no firsthand evidence." (Fellow travelers had sympathized with the Soviet Union's communist experiment, but were not necessarily looked upon as spies.) Without credible proof, Dulles refused to condemn Hiss. The two men never discussed the matter again. Gleason read Dulles's statement to Kohlberg over the phone, and Kohlberg confirmed its accuracy.[11]

Nixon ignored or missed the discrepancy between the Dulles statement and Gleason's interview with Kohlberg. If the candidate had listened carefully, he would have noticed that Dulles's account of his role in Hiss's selection, which he described as minimal, differed from Kohlberg's claim that Dulles chose him. In fact, Dulles had strongly urged Hiss's appointment and now denied having done so. Nixon had good reason to investigate Dulles's association with Hiss. As Eisenhower's running mate, he had already answered a question in Springfield, Illinois, about Dulles, Stevenson, and Hiss. The nominee replied that Stevenson had testified in Hiss's favor while Dulles had been "one of the most effective witnesses for the prosecution." Nixon later wrote that he was examining the linkage between Hiss and Stevenson for a speech later in the campaign.[12]

Dulles again contacted "Dear Dick" on August 18 about some speeches he would give on the West Coast in September. While none of them were partisan, Dulles solicited suggestions and asked if he should inform Senator Knowland, who lived in Northern California, about his trip. Nixon felt that "it would be a nice courtesy" and extended "his very best wishes."[13]

During the rest of the campaign, Nixon and Dulles did not write one another, nor did they spend time together after Eisenhower's victory. While the vice president–elect waited for some sign of his new responsibilities, Dulles worked directly with Eisenhower on foreign affairs, especially the Korean conflict.

When Dulles took control of the state department, he personally acted in the areas he saw as priorities. He did not delegate well and was not an effective manager. He focused on Soviet relations, liberation of Eastern Europe, cooperation with America's Western European allies, and protection of American interests in Asia. He defended South Korea, promised to protect Taiwan from a Mainland Chinese invasion, and constructed multilateral alliances to maintain the status quo in Indochina.

Few doubted his brilliance. He argued logically, believed in tough bargaining, and usually opposed summitry. He defended his department from attack and inspired his staff's loyalty, even though he did not make the best use of it. He wrote his own speeches, reasoning that it sharpened his ideas. Supporters thought he was an exceptional leader with an attractive sense of humor. Opponents found him stiff and boring. He certainly was not charismatic and often gave dull, uninspiring addresses.[14]

Eisenhower seldom interfered with Dulles's bureaucracy, but he oversaw diplomatic strategy, elevating the National Security Council into a policymaking body. The National Security Act of 1947, which specified its membership, had established the NSC. A second piece of legislation in 1949 added the vice president to the council. Truman had used his NSC sporadically. When he was unable to preside, Secretary of State Dean Acheson, not the vice president, chaired the meetings. Throughout Truman's administration, the NSC considered certain topics, such as estimating and responding to Soviet aggression, but national security policy was not addressed with coherent, long-range plans.[15]

Eisenhower set more ambitious goals. He declared at his first NSC gathering, in January 1953, that he "was staffing it with men of very high caliber." Nixon was tasked with reporting on the military budget and its political implications. Robert Cutler, administrative assistant to the president, was named special assistant to the president for national security affairs—in effect, the nation's first National Security Advisor. As the NSC's executive officer he oversaw the staff, organized the agenda, and carried out policy. Cutler had met Ike socially in 1948, when the general was the president at Columbia University, and Cutler became part of the inner circle of advisers during Eisenhower's presidential run. He vigorously assisted in fundraising and acted as the general's personal secretary on his campaign train.[16]

That such a close adviser was put in charge of the NSC shows its importance in Ike's eyes. The group usually assembled on Thursday mornings; no votes were ever recorded, only plans of action. In addition to the regular membership, the president had the secretaries of state, defense, and treasury, and the directors of mutual security and defense mobilization as frequent guests. The director of Central Intelligence and the chairman of the Joint Chiefs of Staff would periodically send representatives.[17]

When Ike was unavailable or left the room, he handed the gavel over to Nixon. In August 1953, the night before the first time Nixon was scheduled to stand in for the president, who was on vacation, he had dinner with Ike's special assistant, Bernard Shanley. Nixon, Shanley recalled, was tired after several "wearing receptions and by the time he had his second old fashion, the lid was off." Nixon did not handle liquor well, and Shanley wondered how well he would recover from any hangover for the next day's gathering. But it turned out there was nothing to worry about: Nixon did an outstanding job as chair, and his performance was duly reported to Eisenhower. Of the roughly 366 NSC meetings over his two terms, Ike presided over 90 percent, and Nixon handled the remainder.[18]

Eisenhower used these sessions to expand the participants' horizons in viewing international affairs. He urged council members to be adventurous in exploring options. From his experience in World War II, for instance, Ike had become convinced of the importance of psychological warfare and wanted to apply it as a weapon in the postwar battle against communism. The foreign policy arsenal had to include such unconventional tactics. Ike reauthorized the collection of information that had begun under Truman and broadened the activities of intelligence agencies, electronic surveillance, and mail intercepts.[19]

C. D. Jackson, who served in the Office of Strategic Services (OSS) during World War II and afterwards became publisher of *Fortune* magazine, joined the administration to direct psychological warfare, but despite the president's confidence he stayed only briefly and had minimal impact. The effectiveness of propaganda turned out to be difficult, if not impossible, to measure.[20]

The president, who had used the OSS for covert actions throughout the war, had no doubts about the benefits of the CIA. Allen Dulles, Foster's brother, had been involved in those wartime operations, and early in his term the president made Allen the director of Central Intelligence (DCI). He considered the familial relationship a "good thing" and valued Allen's "unique knowledge," "great honesty," and "integrity." Allen was totally immersed in his job, and his staff showed absolute loyalty to its director. As for weaknesses, Ike knew that the CIA had expanded haphazardly and that some employees were incompetent or undisciplined. He was troubled by "a complete lack of security consciousness throughout" the agency and the fact that "too much information" was being "leaked at cocktail" parties.[21]

Allen Dulles enjoyed Nixon's confidence as well. They had met aboard the *Queen Mary* in September 1947, when Nixon was a member of the Herter mission and Dulles was serving as an adviser to the congressional committee on conditions in postwar Europe. They saw each other again less than a year later when Nixon met with the brothers to review their testimony in the Hiss case.[22]

As DCI, Allen thought highly enough of the new vice president that he invited Nixon to present the CIA orientation address on February 10, 1953, during which Nixon said he thought America's greatest mistake was that "we misjudged the character of the world Communist conspiracy." The Kremlin's mission, he said, was to overthrow democracies, and to defeat it the United States needed strong allies who would guarantee efforts to forestall communist aggression. The administration therefore had to extend foreign aid and provide military equipment. Containment meant a draw and was unacceptable. UN forces had to defeat the communist enemy on Korea, and the Eastern European states had to be freed from Soviet domination. To make informed decisions on such complex problems, the American government had to have superior intelligence. After all, the main worldwide struggle was the battle "for the minds and hearts and the souls of men."[23]

Nixon's anticommunist message echoed Ike's. When Ike assumed command of American diplomacy, he had stored up decades of knowledge from his military experience. His most pressing matter was the stalemate on the Korean peninsula. Red China had entered the conflict using "volunteers" who were killing and maiming American soldiers. He had pledged to end that conflict and bring American troops home.[24]

Ike had negotiated with the Soviets during World War II over the deployment of troops in Germany and had taken charge of the main military defense against them when Truman asked him to head the NATO forces in Europe. As president, he quickly concluded that no nation could win a nuclear war. The primary obligation of his leadership, as he saw it, was to maintain an uneasy peace, to maneuver diplomatically to reduce tensions that could precipitate an atomic catastrophe, and to strengthen the Western European alliance.[25]

Other regions posed lesser concerns. The colonies of the old European empires were rapidly moving toward independence; Israeli-Arab hatred created continual anxiety; unrest in Latin America was challenging the rule of (often American-supported) dictators. The United States feared that the new prime minister of Iran, with its enormous oil reserves, might be moving the country toward the Soviet sphere of influence. Besides these multilateral and bilateral concerns, the president pushed for freer trade and economic assistance to stabilize allies. "Trade not aid" became the administration slogan, but this theme oversimplified the reality. International commerce and foreign economic aid had complex foundations of which Ike was well aware. The constant question was how to combine aid, trade, military action, and promotion of democracy in a way that strengthened America's allies and weakened its enemies.[26]

The vice president regularly listened to the president's views on foreign policy and absorbed his ideas. In high-level meetings, Ike was not a secretive leader: he routinely explained his reasoning and asked for weaknesses in his arguments. Nixon, a team player, supported his boss and often echoed his sentiments. On July 21, 1953, Ike wrote Foster Dulles that Western Europeans were expressing "a sorry picture of American prestige and America's position in the world." America had to explain "better our policies, purposes, and our determination." At an NSC meeting nine days later, Nixon reiterated the president's concern that Americans returning from abroad were noting a decline in United States prestige, with the implication that the current administration was somehow responsible.[27]

The first priority of Ike's diplomacy was to deal with the Soviet leadership. Having directed the Allied forces through France, he recognized the massive size of the Soviet military presence in Eastern Europe and knew that Josef Stalin alone made military decisions. With his death in early March, weeks after Eisenhower took office, the Kremlin's bureaucracy appeared to signal a spirit of cooperation. Eisenhower was skeptical; he would respond cautiously and wait for a new Soviet leader to emerge.

The vice president echoed the president's skepticism of Soviet intentions. In February, he suggested that the government propose "some kind of sensational offer on the disarmament side" that the Soviets would reject, so as to "put them on the spot." After Stalin's death, he warned that the new leadership might generate greater hostility rather than a relaxation of tensions. At the end of summer, he sought to reassure the public that American military policy remained constant: the armed forces were "standing up to the USSR and not knuckling down to it." The government, he argued, had to defend "all vital parts of the free world by applying the principle of concentration of forces." As he reassured the American public of the administration's hardline posture toward the Kremlin, he privately recognized the United States–Soviet relations were complex and needed flexibility.[28]

Foreign aid required funding, and that meant congressional approval. But foreign aid was a favorite target among some representatives. Many congressmen from both major parties viewed it as a wasteful expenditure. Congressman Otto Passman, Democrat from Louisiana, told a state department official: "Son, I don't smoke and I don't drink. My only pleasure in life is kicking the shit out of the foreign aid program of the United States of America."[29] Under such circumstances, the administration had to mount an impressive sales job. At a legislative meeting toward the end of April, the vice president stressed that even though reducing the budget was a national priority, the country had to maintain military preparedness. Chairing an NSC meeting in the second week of September, Nixon wondered if the United States was giving enough support to the French effort to defeat the communists in Indochina.[30]

Early in the Eighty-Third Congress, John Bricker, a Republican senator from Ohio, introduced a constitutional amendment that would limit the president's authority to make treaties by requiring Congress to pass separate enabling legislation The president, not surprisingly, opposed any limitations on his prerogatives. Nixon and Bricker had established a cordial relationship during their time in the upper chamber, and Nixon tried to build on that trust to persuade Bricker to withdraw the amendment. The Ohioan refused, and by the end of May, Nixon concluded that the president would oppose the amendment even if it meant "breaking up the party."[31]

To prevent such a damaging consequence, the vice president tried to negotiate a compromise. Neither side would budge. Nixon cautioned the cabinet that many senators favored the legislation. Even Lyndon Johnson would vote for it because powerful Texas interests backed the idea. By fall, the vice president had enlisted enough votes against the amendment that he was convinced it would not pass, but he noted in a personal letter that this "took quite a bit of doing." "Sitting in the chair I have an opportunity to get a much needed brushing up on my constitutional law during the course of a debate!"[32]

When the Senate voted on the amendment, in February 1954, it failed to gain the necessary two-thirds of the upper house by just one vote, sixty to thirty-one. Nixon had correctly gauged the popularity of the measure, but he also saw the president's resolve. During the final stages leading up the vote, when Nixon remarked, "As in any battle, you need a second line of retreat," Ike responded that you had one way to retreat and several ways to go forward.[33]

Many Republican stalwarts viewed the United Nations as communistic or socialistic. From his internationalist perspective, Ike intended to use the United Nations to advance and legitimize American policies. He appointed Henry Cabot Lodge, his campaign manager and a distinguished former senator, as United

Nations representative and also relied upon Secretary Dulles. As usual, the president established the plans, and his associates hammered out the details.[34]

As the Senate's presiding officer, Nixon had several roles concerning the United Nations. On June 1, Ike asked him to lobby against a Senate bill that would strip funds to the United Nations if Communist China gained admission to the organization. (At the time, the United Nations recognized the government in Taiwan as representing all of China.) The president believed "a hostile, punitive measure such as this, unworthy of our responsibilities of leadership and our great traditions, would be a priceless gift to those who would see us weak and alone."[35]

Nixon had heard, and even been somewhat sympathetic to, Republican opposition to the United Nations since he entered Congress, but once again, his loyalty to the president dictated his actions. On September 21, 1953, he visited the UN for the first time. Afterward, he told reporters that he, the president, and the vast majority of Americans had "faith and hope" in the world body.[36]

While Ike relied on Nixon for specific actions and for congressional liaison, the president's chief diplomatic counselor was his secretary of state. Dulles had experience, great knowledge, and a strong character, and he did not intimidate easily. These attributes quickly made him the most influential member of Ike's cabinet; he had instant access to the Oval Office. Like Eisenhower, Dulles was a firm internationalist who promoted collective security and was unswerving in his anticommunist commitment. The president and his secretary sometimes disagreed, but they respected each other's viewpoints. Dulles knew that Ike made the ultimate decisions. Ike later reminisced that Dulles "knew more about international affairs than anyone else." They worked harmoniously, but while Dulles "helped formulate policy, the final decisions were always mine to make, and I made them."[37]

Although Eisenhower's declaration might be considered self-serving, many years later Virgil Pinkley, a Los Angeles newspaper publisher who was working on a book concerning Eisenhower's diplomacy, wrote Henry Cabot Lodge on May 7, 1971, about Secretary Dulles deciding foreign policy issues. Lodge rejected that assumption and "vividly" remembered Dulles telling him that such allegations were untrue. Dulles told Lodge "that in every sense of the word he [Dulles] was carrying out Eisenhower policies and that he never wrote or said anything having to do with public affairs without the authority of the President." Lodge added that one of the traits that made Eisenhower "a great executive . . . was his ability to delegate and his generosity in seeing to it that subordinates got credit. This led the superficially minded to say that he had abdicated to Foster

Dulles" and others. "The truth was that President Eisenhower was always running the show."[38]

The bond between Dulles and Nixon evolved far differently. Nixon had saved Foster from possible embarrassment by alerting him to Alger Hiss's communist connections. The two did not publicize their close association—sometimes, for privacy, they met in the basement of the state department—but they saw each other often and generally backed each other's arguments. One measure of cooperation dealt with senators and their contact with the secretary's senior staff. By early summer the state department's legal adviser, Herman Phleger, who was leading the state department's opposition to the Bricker amendment, had developed a profound dislike for its sponsor; the feeling was wholeheartedly returned. Nixon and Senator Knowland defended Phleger, and Dulles appreciated their support. In the middle of August, he recommended one of his Wall Street partners, Arthur Dean, for appointment as his political deputy, while knowing that the choice would be attacked in the press. Nixon dismissed the secretary's doubts and encouraged him to hire Dean.[39]

The vice president and secretary also knew they needed congressional support. Dulles had briefly served in the Senate and understood the necessity of good relations; Nixon promoted Dulles's leadership. In mid-June, he scheduled a breakfast talk for the secretary to meet new members of Congress. Dulles would speak for an hour about the administration's foreign policy and urge his listeners to support it. Nixon felt that such an appearance offered an opportunity for the secretary to sell controversial programs like foreign economic assistance before the novice congressmen lined up with the isolationist faction.[40]

Nixon also assisted Dulles with Governor Dewey, who wielded great influence nationally in the Republican Party. The three met several times for dinner, sometimes with their wives present; the governor brought up sensitive problems, such as the charge that Dulles was anti-Semitic and advised him on how to counter such accusations. The president and Dulles approached Dewey to tour Central America, attend Panama's fiftieth independence celebration, go to the inauguration of the Costa Rican president, and also stop in Mexico City. Nixon was given the task of briefing Dewey about the growing communist presence in Guatemala, a matter of concern to the administration.[41]

Besides phone calls and congressional cooperation, the two saw each other at cabinet and NSC meetings. The Nixons often substituted for the Eisenhowers at diplomatic events where Dulles and his wife were also guests.[42]

Both men also had the ceremonial duty of greeting foreign dignitaries at the Military Air Transport Service (MATS) at National Airport. Before those welcomes and departures, they often had time to discuss diplomatic questions. One of the most memorable landings came when Konrad Adenauer, chancellor of the Federal Republic of Germany, flew into MATS in the midst of a morning drizzle on April 7 for a twelve-day state visit. Dulles had already gone to see Adenauer in Europe, where they formed a personal bond and even prayed together. For the vice president, this was his first meeting with the German. He welcomed his guest and called for United States–West German friendship. Adenauer needed that reassurance and was grateful; that was why he had come to America.[43]

The combination of Dulles and Nixon worked so smoothly that in September, Ike decided he no longer needed to meet incoming or outgoing heads of state at the airport. Dulles would establish a protocol with the vice president and others to escort guests to the White House. With this directive, Nixon and Dulles interacted even more. The secretary offered his vast knowledge, and the vice president eagerly absorbed it; they eventually came to consult each other on a wide range of issues. Sometimes they agreed to present differing points of view to the president. Occasionally, Dulles used Nixon as an additional voice for diplomatic priorities. This was one of the key ways Nixon gained insight into the intricacies of foreign policy and the process by which decisions were made.[44]

By the end of June, the secretary considered the vice president the best person ever to hold that post. At the July 11 cabinet meeting commemorating the first anniversary of Eisenhower's and Nixon's nomination, Dulles presented Nixon with a desk set and added that the administration "had a two-man, not a one-man, team."[45]

Foster meant what he said, and throughout his tenure, Dulles and Nixon bonded professionally and socially. They saw each other frequently and often phoned one another. Both came from rural settings, held deep Christian beliefs, had graduated from law school, and had practiced law. They had joined the Republican Party for different reasons, but both advocated the East Coast brand of internationalism and considered communism the greatest threat facing the country. Benjamin Goldberg, who studied their relationship, concluded: "While Nixon served as Dulles' alter-ego, Dulles served as Nixon's informant."[46] This was only partly correct. They interacted and came to rely on each other as like-minded equals.

Out of the limelight, the duo saw each other regularly for dinner and often included their wives. Each man was fascinated with sports, especially baseball. Nixon described Dulles as a "vigorously athletic type" who swam in the cold water at his private retreat, Duck Lake. Nixon himself had played a variety of sports in his youth, none of them well.[47]

Although Secretary Dulles used some phrases, including "brinkmanship" and "massive retaliation," that still spark an emotional response, many of his diplomatic contributions within the Eisenhower administration remain unappreciated. The president employed Foster Dulles as his premier foreign policy adviser and used his brother Allen and others in lesser capacities. Nixon was a separate voice, and he matured into an extra set of eyes and ears that provided the president with another perspective. The vice president also served as a counselor to Foster Dulles, and they bounced ideas off of each other. The result of the interaction between the president, vice president, the secretary of state, and the other members of the diplomatic team provided Ike with a wide range of options to consider before he reached his eventual decision. This was a complicated process with many subtleties, but usually the system functioned well and maintained a fragile peace for the United States.

NIXON IN ASIA

While Eisenhower was shaping his diplomatic priorities in 1953, Adlai Stevenson, the de facto head of the Democratic Party, had set out on a world tour at the beginning of March to establish his own diplomatic credentials. He described his impressions of Asia, the Middle East, and Europe in several articles published in *Look* magazine, where he warned that Red Chinese aggression could be deterred only if America appealed to the masses with something better than communism. From his stop in Saigon, he predicted that "If Viet-Nam falls, all of Indochina is doomed." He also recognized that the wars in Southeast Asia were more than a struggle against European colonialism. "This revolution," he argued, "is not just anti-Western, it is pro-Asian." He continued on to India, where he expressed the hope that democracy would triumph.[1]

In May, Ike had dispatched Secretary Dulles and Harold Stassen, director of the Mutual Security Administration, to Europe and the Middle East. The secretary of state returned with the sobering assessment that many foreign leaders misperceived American motives. These impressions, he told Eisenhower, would have to be corrected through personal diplomacy. That summer, the president sent his brother Milton on a fact-finding tour to South America to make recommendations on how to improve hemispheric relations.[2]

At the start of his vice presidency, Nixon had no diplomatic responsibilities at all. In December 1952, the president-elect had him represent the incoming administration at the inauguration of the Mexican president. After the inauguration, he had a seat on the National Security Council but no specific assignment. He watched the president and studied his diplomatic initiatives but did not contribute a great deal to the discussions.

That spring, the Nixons thought about taking a European vacation in late summer or early fall. Those plans vanished at the start of June, when Eisenhower asked Nixon about his summer schedule; the vice president replied that he had no definite plans. Ike said, "I want you to go on a good will trip and take Pat with you." The following day, the president told the cabinet that "the Far East was the sore spot," and he was sending the Nixons there.[3]

A press release on July 7 announced that the Nixons would travel to the Far East and South Asia in order "to become acquainted with the leaders of the countries visited, to hear their views, to gain firsthand impressions, to convey the sincere greetings of the people of the United States to the peoples of the areas visited and to carry the personal greetings of the President."[4]

Although some columnists saw Nixon's journey as a response to Stevenson's, the administration decided to emphasize a significant difference between itself and its predecessor. The Truman government had sent Secretary of State Acheson to Europe seventeen times, but he had never visited Asia. Ike wanted to demonstrate that his administration would recognize Asia's importance.[5]

It would be a mistake, however, to read Eisenhower's decision to send Nixon to Asia as a public-relations ploy for either domestic or international consumption. By the mid-fifties, the Cold War had become the permeating reality of American international relations, and George Kennan's concept of "containment" was its dominant strategy. Many Republican conservatives viewed the strategy as inadequate, since it aimed only to halt the advance of communism and was not focused on reversing its progress (by, for instance, supporting a Nationalist Chinese invasion of Mainland China). Nixon's trip, however, is best seen not as a battle of ideologies but as a mission with multiple purposes.

The vice president decided that he needed to be fully briefed to prepare for his journey. On many of his stops, he would be the highest-ranking American official ever to visit. He discussed his agenda with Secretary Dulles; office directors in the state department or their deputies conducted in-depth country briefings; the CIA went over various topics for three and a half hours. This was how he prepared for all of his foreign assignments.

Just before he left the capital, Ike conferred with him at the White House for an hour to discuss the trip. No journalist noted the significance of Nixon's interviews with Eisenhower and the other officials. Andrew Goodpaster, a close presidential adviser on foreign affairs, later called the vice president a "senior emissary." Ike had Nixon travel for special reasons and had him perform specific duties.[6]

Other than the nations to be visited, no details were announced. At the end of September, Nixon told an NBC radio audience that he and Pat were traveling "to listen and learn." He expected to limit ceremonial occasions so that "we can spend the maximum amount of time talking to people in all walks of life, seeing factories and farms and educational institutions, getting a real feel of these countries rather than just spending our time talking to the top officials of these countries because, after all, if that was all we were going to do we could sit here in Washington and read the reports of our diplomats." He also emphasized the strategic significance of Asia, tariff barriers impeding trade, and the French fight against communist insurgents in Indochina.[7]

Pat Nixon was excited to be taking her first major trip abroad. Attending the Mexican president's inauguration in December 1952, the Nixons had talked with taxi drivers, doormen, and bellhops, and were cheered on their departure from Mexico City. She recalled: "Local officials said they had never seen such enthusiasm."[8] In Asia, she planned to play an independent role by going to schools, hospitals, orphanages, elder care facilities, refugee camps, welfare centers, and marketplaces. She would serve as a separate set of eyes and ears for her husband. Like him, she expected to carry out her duties in an exemplary fashion.[9]

The entourage traveled for almost ten weeks and flew over 38,000 miles. Their plane was a sister ship to the president's *Columbine*, a four-engine Lockheed Constellation with a gleaming galley for meals, a comfortable lounge, working space for the vice president and his secretary, ten sleeping berths, and closet space for hanging bags.[10]

The Constellation touched down in New Zealand on the afternoon of October 12. The weather was chilly, but this did not prevent Prime Minister Sidney Holland and others from welcoming the vice president, the highest-ranking American official ever to visit there. Nixon had been stationed in the Pacific during World War II and had served with New Zealand's Third Division.[11]

The United States, Australia, and New Zealand had signed the ANZUS defense treaty in 1952, and the Eisenhower administration wanted to reaffirm its ties to these two nations. New Zealand was aligned with the British Commonwealth, and Great Britain had already granted diplomatic recognition to the People's Republic of China, a measure the United States rejected. Ike hoped to nudge the New Zealanders closer to the American position, and Nixon's stay was intended to highlight their countries' similar heritage.[12]

The vice president spoke candidly to the cabinet, telling its members that he distrusted the Soviets' declarations of peaceful intentions. If Moscow sent troops to Indochina, he asserted, the United States would respond with force: Indochina was central to Western interests. If it fell to the communists, all of Southeast Asia would follow, altering the balance of power in the Pacific. He also addressed financial issues that were critical to his listeners. He pledged to advance New Zealand's application for a loan from the Export-Import Bank and to ease American tariffs on lumber, dairy products, and wool—all significant New Zealand exports.[13]

In the trip's first major speech to the public, on October 13, Nixon said that the United States would retain its military superiority and remain allied with the British Commonwealth. Most Americans, he stressed, believed they had "no better allies in the world" and "under no circumstances are we going to allow our enemies to drive us apart." Until the Kremlin proved its peaceful intentions, he would remain a skeptic.[14]

His audiences gave him prolonged applause. The newspapers commented on his sense of humor and echoed his views on preventing communist expansion. The American embassy was pleased that the vice president and his wife had "made a remarkably fine impression in so short a time." Prime Minister Holland wrote Eisenhower that Nixon's visit was "an indication of the growing bond of friendship between our two countries."[15]

While Dick was reaching out to the Kiwis, Pat began a diary. Upon arrival, the party had suffered through a "very stiff" lunch; "protocol and British reserve was hard to overcome." The newspapers had ads on the front pages. They also carried news, but "one had to thumb through to discover it!" On the second day, she attended a luncheon that was really a full-course meal "with wines and champagne even if it was in the middle of the day!" Before a formal dinner, she asked if she should wear white gloves and was told they were unnecessary; the hosts, unbeknownst to her, changed their instructions, and she arrived to find the other women in white gloves.[16]

On the last full day, she went to a Maori native village: "I felt faint when some of the disheveled oldsters lined up for a session of nose rubbing but attempting to be good sports 'we took it.'" Native women prepared their lunch at the king's palace "in filthy clothes in a kitchen so unsanitary that I had difficulty in keeping from vomiting when I went to the kitchen to greet the women. I just couldn't eat a bite." Dinner was held at the seventy-six-year-old Auckland Club, where women had never been admitted; they were delighted that the tradition was broken for this event.[17]

On the way from Auckland to Sydney, Australia, Nixon was briefed by Avery Peterson, counselor to the United States embassy in Canberra. A member of the diplomatic corps would brief him before every stop on his journey to bring him up to date on the most pressing topics for discussion.[18]

Australia was the third member of ANZUS, and like the Kiwis it actively participated in the alliance. Prime Minister Robert Menzies was especially worried about the growing power of Mainland China and shared his people's prejudice against the Chinese and fear of the Japanese.[19] In his radio address, Nixon repeated the message he had conveyed in Auckland: the ANZUS nations must prevent communist expansion in Asia and had to be vigilant in confronting it. The Aussies had appreciated the American presence during World War II, and Nixon struck a warm note by recalling his own wartime service: "My remembrance of their fighting qualities and of the comradeship which grew up between us remains for me an inspiration to this day."[20]

From Sydney the Nixons traveled to Melbourne, where the vice president visited the site of the 1956 summer Olympics. This was an ideal photographic event, and he had told his staff to spotlight these occasions. He wanted favorable reports sent to the United States and insisted that reporters ride directly behind him and take photographs: "Push the local officials into the picture," he ordered. "Even if they don't print the pictures it will please the officials." He wanted a cross-section of people. "Whenever you are with me," he wrote in a memo to his staff, "look for opportunities for me to break away from the protocol people and greet ordinary people who may be standing along the side. For example, children, cripples, old people, etc. Such opportunities must be looked for and you must not be bashful about getting the photographers interested in that type of shot." The security agents balked, but Nixon insisted that his routes be publicized. There was just one taboo: "Secret Service men and anyone else who is with us at receptions should assume the responsibility of being sure that no photographers are snapping shots when I have a drink in my hand."[21]

Prime Minister Menzies impressed Nixon as "British to his boot heels" but an adamant supporter of ANZUS. Menzies was deeply concerned about the independence movement in Western New Guinea (annexed by Indonesia in 1969) and hoped that the Dutch would retain control. If Indonesia fell to the communists, he feared, the rest of Southeast Asia would be vulnerable, and Australia might find itself isolated in a hostile region of the world. Such logic demonstrated why the Australians vigorously backed the American policy toward Indochina.[22]

Pat served a different role. At one Sydney luncheon she shook hands with 400 people. She was surprised that "huge crowds gathered to see me." According to the *Melbourne Sun*, she "stole the show at every function she attended in Sydney . . . looked smart and happy every second." She met as many people as possible and had an extra smile for children.[23]

Men and women seldom mingled in public. At the Caulfield Race Course in Melbourne, women watched the horses from separate stands, bet at separate windows, and used women's lounges and refreshment facilities—common practice at the time at racetracks throughout Australia. Pat was not allowed to sit with her husband during the races, and she drew attention by objecting to the social segregation.²⁴ Rules were bent as a result. Melbourne women scored a minor victory when they were allowed to attend a luncheon in the state parliamentary building in honor of the vice president. In Sydney, in a rare departure, luncheons and dinners accommodated both sexes.²⁵

From Australia, the Nixons preceded to what the American ambassador to Indonesia Hugh Cumming Jr. described as "your first Asian stopping point." For the next two weeks, they would journey through Southeast Asia, and Nixon would see at first hand the complexities the United States confronted there.²⁶

Nixon insisted that he have only a translator with him when conferring with foreigners. "I want to talk to as many controversial people as possible. The natural tendency is usually to discourage them but I want to see them all if possible. I want to hear what they have to say and let them feel they can get in." He asked to limit American personnel at dinners so that more Asians could attend.²⁷

The Nixons landed in Jakarta on October 21. Their host, Achmed Sukarno, ruled Indonesia single-handedly and promoted diplomatic neutrality. During his talks with Sukarno, Nixon came to believe that his host was not a communist but was naïve about the harmlessness of his country's communist party. Sukarno had no significant opposition and spoke as the leader of his nation's independence movement; but he made no effort to groom any successor, and Nixon feared a void once Sukarno left power. At that moment, the communists might have an opportunity to gain power.²⁸

Nixon was not pessimistic about Indonesia's immediate future. He was concerned about Sukarno's absolute authority but not particularly troubled by the measures the government employed to sustain it. Stability was more important. Indonesia's economic condition did worry him. The economy rested on rubber exports and to a lesser extent on tin, and thus was vulnerable to price fluctuations; Nixon felt the United States should intervene more forcefully in commodities markets to keep prices stable. Communists were active in the labor movement, but no one had risen as a leader to challenge Sukarno. Finally, of the significant number of Chinese living in Indonesia, thousands were studying in Mainland China while the United States allowed only "a planeload" to be educated in America. That imbalance should be corrected.²⁹

After two days in Indonesia, the Nixons flew to Singapore, then a British Crown Colony that had recently emerged from a state of emergency. After the plane landed, the vice president walked to the wire fence, reached over, and took the hand of a tiny Malay boy. The crowd surged forward with broad grins and virtually pulled the vice president off his feet.³⁰

The vice president especially wanted to talk with Malcolm MacDonald, the British commissioner general for Southeast Asia, who commanded the troops that had recently pushed the communists from the countryside. After a three-hour private luncheon, the vice president complimented his British host on how he defeated communist guerrillas by using overwhelming force against them and winning support from the nationals in the region. After their meeting, Nixon held a press conference, declaring that the communist rebels were losing and their defeat would be "a victory of the free world."[31]

MacDonald was so ebullient about his meeting with the vice president that he sent a letter to Eisenhower calling Nixon's visit "an unqualified success." The vice president, he wrote, had demonstrated that the United States was sincerely interested in Asian affairs, and he and his wife "mixed freely with citizens of every race, class and creed, and left upon them all a fine impression of the American democratic spirit."[32]

The Nixons arrived in Kuala Lumpur, Malaya, on October 26. Guerrillas operating out of the nation's rural areas, which consisted mostly of tropical forest, had caused sporadic havoc with their efforts to drive the British out. Although the recent military action had brought a pause, fighting might resume at any time. More important, from the British point of view, was that rubber and tin prices were declining. Malaya produced a third of these commodities worldwide and exported a quarter of its rubber and a third of its tin to the United States. Falling prices were depressing the economy, creating favorable conditions for the communists.[33]

Nixon met for some ninety minutes with the high commissioner, Sir Gerald Templer, who planned "to win the hearts and minds" of the Malayans. They would not fight to preserve British rule against the insurgents, but they would fight for independence. Templer believed that realization made victory possible: a quarter of the effort was military and the rest economic. Approximately 75,000 British soldiers effectively contained 5,000 or 6,000 terrorists; each army company also adopted a Malayan village. Templer had outlawed the Communist Party and driven its members from the labor unions. Nixon felt that this decision was the only way to prevent Red Chinese penetration. Even with these measures, the British leader warned, if Indochina fell to the communists, Malaya could be next.[34]

General Templer then drove the vice president to a rural British police station. The immediate danger worried Rose Mary Woods: "The Boss is out now visiting an outpost—that is really risky business in this place and I will be awfully glad when we hear that they are back—when we rode around town and the outskirts yesterday to see a tin mill, rubber mill, etc. they used two little jeeps with machine guns on them to guard the V.P. rough country!"[35] A communist organizer, Liew Fong, carrying a pistol and wearing dungarees, a cotton shirt, a fairly expensive wrist watch, and two fountain pens, had surrendered at 6:30 that morning. He had been without food for six days. Standing stiffly at attention, he advised his comrades to follow his example. Templer was overjoyed: "The Vice President was rather naturally, tickled to death, and so was I for that matter."[36]

The general characterized Nixon as "an extremely nice man in every way," who wanted to learn and help. He had "charming manners" and "was the very reverse of everything that one had expected after reading press reports of the American elections." The vice president felt Templer had done "a magnificent job" and pledged to work with United States officials to devise some method of long-term price stabilization for tin and rubber. Prosperity would bring tranquility: communists, he believed, could not thrive in peaceful times.[37]

MacDonald and Templer spoke with one voice. The British had defeated the communists by pledging Malayan independence and also by deploying overwhelming numbers of troops to drive the guerillas into the jungle. Nixon readily accepted this model as the best method of eliminating colonialism and defeating the enemy in Southeast Asia.

He continued on to Bangkok, arriving October 28 to meet with Premier Pibul Songgram. Several thousand Chinese Nationalist troops were still living in the northern section of Thailand after Mao's takeover of China in 1949. They were not at all welcomed by the local population and were gradually being airlifted to Taiwan, but they remained an irritant. No firm date was set for the last of them to leave. The Thai population had a historical fear of domination by the Chinese and would likely oppose communist political or military advances. Even though the country was relatively prosperous and had a homogeneous population, Nixon worried that the government was not moving toward democratic values; he told the premier his government should be moving faster. The Thais echoed the warning that he heard throughout Southeast Asia. If Indochina fell to the communist insurgency, Thailand would be vulnerable.[38]

Donald Health, the United States ambassador to the Associated Nations (Cambodia, Laos, and Vietnam), met the vice president in Phnom Penh and accompanied him through his travels in those three nations. Each had been part of the French colonial empire, and the United States continued to support efforts to maintain France's political and military influence. Eisenhower, like Truman before him, felt that the French were preventing the spread of communism.[39]

Nixon spent October 30 in Cambodia. To avoid a civil revolt, the French had granted Cambodia limited independence earlier that year. King Norodom Sihanouk was resigned to the presence of French troops but asserted that his subjects "were now bitterly suspicious of the French." He added that Mao had overthrown the Nationalist government because he appealed "to the poor against the great landowners." In his country, the communist slogan "was not economic but nationalist." The king convinced Nixon that, as he would tell the NSC in May 1954, "the native peoples were unwilling to fight Communism in order to perpetuate French colonialism."[40]

Even though Sihanouk followed a neutralist policy, he lobbied for American military and economic assistance. Funds should come directly from the United States, he argued, and France should be eliminated as the middleman. When the king asked for direct American aid to build up Cambodian military forces without the need for French troops, Nixon did not make any commitment.[41]

On the last day of October, Nixon arrived in Saigon having been made keenly aware of three major issues concerning the Indochina war. First, it affected the entire region: if Vietnam fell to the communists, so would the rest of the area. Second, the United States, France, and Vietnam had similar objectives, and the French could ensure greater involvement of the Vietnamese population by granting them full independence. Finally, the French, Cambodians, Laotians, and Vietnamese had to cooperate to defeat what he saw as their common enemy; disunity would only benefit the communist forces.[42]

Nixon had dinner with Emperor Bao Dai on November 1. After a ceremonial toast, he warned against the removal of French soldiers: if they left, he said, the Vietminh would fill the vacuum. The Vietnamese leader replied that Soviet imperialism slowed the momentum toward independence, but his country was growing stronger with the help of the United States. The next morning Nixon and Bao Dai met privately for an hour, and then continued their conversation after a midday dinner. Nixon noted that the ruler had never appeared in uniform in front of his troops and was not participating actively as commander-in-chief of the Vietnamese forces. But when he pressed Bao Dai on why this was so, the ruler would not answer. Bao Dai conceded that French troops could not be ousted at present because if they departed, his country would be immediate prey for the communists. He refused to entertain direct negotiations with Ho Chi Minh, a position Nixon vehemently supported.[43]

The French commissioner-general, Maurice Dejean, told Nixon that neither the French nor the Associated States would surrender Indochina to the communists. Nixon replied: "If Southeast Asia goes, the groundwork will be laid for the world conquest which Communist leaders want." That afternoon the vice president stood in the steaming heat watching military exercises during which Vietnamese troops accidentally fired mortar shells and machine gun bullets dangerously close to him. Henri Navarre, the commander-in-chief of the armed forces in Saigon, impressed the vice president with the high morale of his troops, but Navarre added that training of the Vietnamese army needed to be accelerated. The general told Nixon that the French needed C-47 transport aircraft; Nixon promised to relay that request to the president.[44]

Nixon interrupted his tour of Vietnam for a four-hour journey to Vientiane, Laos, early in the morning of November 4. He met with the prime minister, Prince Souvanna Phouma, who acknowledged his country hoped for financial assistance from the United States and France. The vice president told his host that Americans admired the Laotian stand against communist aggression and their cooperative attitude toward the French.[45]

After lunch with the prince, the Nixon party flew to Hanoi and motored through the heart of the city while hundreds of police patrolled the streets to prevent trouble from Vietminh sympathizers. Fifty miles south, French Union forces were engaged in fierce combat with communist insurgents. At a black tie dinner for the governor of North Vietnam, Nguyen Huu Tri, the vice president acknowledged the delicate conditions and declared that the communists had taken Mainland China, retreated after North Korea invaded its southern neighbor, and were deadlocked in Indochina. The French and Vietnamese troops' role "in the world resistance to the Communist evil," he declared, "is similar to that played by the United Nations forces in Korea."[46]

Nixon and General Navarre visited troops near the area of intense combat, in Tonkin. Nixon spoke with French and Vietnamese personnel from various battalions and rode in their vehicles. He heard a barrage against the Vietminh at Lai Cac and ate rations for lunch, a French "soldier's meal washed down by 'Algerian red.'"[47]

That evening Nixon spoke to a French audience. "The tide of aggression," he said, "has reached its peak and has finally begun to recede. . . . I am convinced that the die is now cast, that inevitable victory can be won, and it will be won." The United States, he declared, would oppose any negotiations to end the war if these resulted in the Indochinese people losing their freedom. The fighting would not be concluded until victory was guaranteed. Congratulating the French government for its efforts to make Indochina independent, he added "victory will be possible only if Frenchmen and Vietnamese fight together and remain united." Dejean added that the French would "never abandon the Indo-Chinese peninsula to a foreign power."[48]

The third leg of the Nixon's trip started on November 5 in the British Crown Colony of Hong Kong, the last British outpost in China. Hong Kong was a city of traders, ships, and spectacular scenery. It also was the cleanest city, with the best water supply and police force that Nixon would visit. He was the second American vice president, after Henry Wallace in 1944, to visit the city; crowds

lined the streets to see him.[49] A convoy of eleven vehicles with security personnel drove him to the police stations at Sha Tau Kok and Lok Ma Chau in the
New Territories, where he could peer across a concrete fence to the Chinese
border just 200 yards away. He saw Chinese guards patrolling and peasants on
both sides of the barrier farming. In the distance flew the red flag of the People's
Republic of China.[50]

Before departing on November 8, he praised the city for its efficient handling
of Chinese refugees. Hong Kong was a "shining example of what life could be
like on the mainland if the Government there changed its ways or the present
Government were changed." The People's Republic of China (PRC) could not
indefinitely erase the friendship that had existed between China and the Western world.[51]

Nixon's next stop was Taiwan, to visit its leader, Chiang Kai-shek. From the
moment communist forces had driven Chiang from power and taken control of
the mainland in 1949, Republicans had accused Truman and the Democrats of
having "lost" China. The GOP reasoned that Truman had "allowed" the communists to take control of the world's most populous nation. Nixon accepted that
premise and joined those who hoped to remove the communist leaders and replace them with a pro-Western, democratic government.[52]

When Eisenhower assumed the presidency, he mentioned in his State of the
Union address that the American policy that prohibited Chiang from launching military operations across the Taiwan Straits would be revised. Shortly afterwards, he gave a White House dinner for Madame Chiang. The administration
seemed to be moving aggressively toward the "Asia Firsters" in the Republican Party, but Eisenhower still proceeded cautiously in the war of words between Mao's PRC and Chiang's Nationalist regime.[53]

After his Asian trip was announced, Nixon told Wellington Koo, the Taiwanese
ambassador to the United States, that he had "no official mission except to convey the goodwill of the American people and to study, on the spot, the facts and
problems for the President's information." Later, at a Blair House event,
Nixon asked Koo to tell his superiors that he did not want parties but rather
wanted to spend as much time as possible with the Taiwanese people. Koo relayed the preference and added that Nixon was "very sympathetic toward our
cause." Taiwanese leaders could "tell him frankly anything we wanted," he
added, "but we should not press him for any reply on any concrete question."
Nixon's mission was to listen and learn.[54]

The Nixon party landed on November 8 at Pinchill Air Force base in Taipei.
President and Madame Chiang Kai-shek, along with high Taiwanese and American officials, welcomed the party. Dick and Pat were taken to the presidential

residence as houseguests.[55] Throughout the five-day stay, Nixon routinely discarded the speeches the embassy prepared for him, preferring to speak without notes. He addressed the National Assembly, reviewed troops with Chiang, and spoke at a groundbreaking at the first Christian center of higher education on the island, Tunghai University in Taichung.[56]

The generalissimo had prospered from his relationship with the United States. It defended his island from invasion and provided economic aid. America refrained from interfering in the island's internal politics, but the Nationalists did not return the favor: they vigorously lobbied Congress. Their representatives, known as "the China lobby," were one of the most effective such groups in Washington. Historian Nancy Tucker captured the essence: "Chiang Kai-shek kept a tight rein on political developments in Taiwan and insisted that the United States be a supporter, a banker, and a shield, but keep its advice and opinions to itself."[57]

The vice president held five private conversations lasting almost nine hours with Chiang, who was immaculately dressed and equally disciplined in his thinking. Nixon described him as a conservative revolutionary. By the end of their discussions, the two had begun a long-standing friendship.[58]

During October and November, two United States senators, fourteen congressmen, and two admirals also had interviews with the generalissimo. To all of them, he made four major points: the United States had no Asia policy; America was spending its resources in Korea and Indochina to no effective purpose; the Soviets were benefiting from America's muddled activities in Asia; and the only solution was to drive the communists from Mainland China.[59]

Chiang expanded on these themes during his talks with Nixon. The United States, he said, was needlessly bogged down by allocating assets to Korea and Indochina. The only way to end the stalemate was to support an amphibious force of 600,000 to invade south China. Chiang emphasized to Nixon: "If it is the desire of the United States to avoid a Third World War and at the same time to defeat Communism, the only thing to do is to help us launch a counter-attack on the Mainland." Once the invaders consolidated a beachhead, the Chinese people would abandon Mao and rally to the Nationalist cause. The Soviets would not intervene.

This effort would take three to six years. Chiang would supply the troops, and the United States had to furnish the war materiel and training, specifically to his Navy and Air Force. American assistance had not, in the past, come to the island in a timely fashion. The Eisenhower administration also had to persuade the British, who had recognized Mao, to alter their policy of cooperating with the PRC in Hong Kong and to stop interfering with the generalissimo's anticommunist crusade. Chiang liked Senator Knowland's idea of developing a broad

Pacific pact that would include Taiwan, the Philippines, Thailand, and Pakistan. Chiang also wanted to reconcile with the Japanese, and he needed American cooperation to heal the centuries-old antipathy between the two cultures.[60]

Nixon answered that Moscow and Peking directed Ho Chi Minh's activities and that at some point, American assistance to Vietnam would end. He also promised to talk to Admiral Arthur Radford, chairman of the Joint Chiefs of Staff, about Nationalist military requirements when he returned to Washington. Nixon and the admiral sat on the NSC and, he said, knew each other "quite well." Radford had significant military influence. Nixon thanked Chiang for his counsel: "Whatever policy the Government of the United States may decide upon, it must be clear-cut and positive and should be decided immediately. It would be wrong to dilly-dally and wink at realities." The generalissimo's views, he said, "helped to develop my own thinking" and would allow him to speak with greater knowledge. Two months in Asia did not "make me an expert. But at least I am now better informed about Asia than before I made this trip."[61]

One incident in Washington marred this stopover. During the Nixon party's first day in Taipei, Secretary Dulles held a press conference in which he speculated that the United States might recognize Communist China. No such possibility existed, he insisted, as long as China remained the aggressor in Korea and Indochina. As for admission to the United Nations, the PRC might be represented in the General Assembly while Taiwan retained its seat on the Security Council. The Taiwanese press reacted angrily, fearing Dulles was moving toward a two-China policy.[62]

Nixon, without consulting the state department, released a statement that the United States was not considering diplomatic recognition or United Nations admission and would not contemplate those questions "unless Red China quits following Communist policy and quits taking orders from Moscow." Dulles's remarks, Nixon claimed, had not embarrassed him, and the Nationalist leaders had not been disturbed.[63]

Ambassador Koo felt Nixon's statement was "designed to discourage any interpretation of Dulles' words as signaling a new and softer United States policy toward Peiping." The generalissimo, however, was unconvinced. Shortly after Nixon made his statement, Koo spoke with Dulles. The ambassador reminded his listener that the British government had lost most of its investment on the mainland. When Chiang recaptured it, he would protect Britain's legitimate interests and not try to annex Hong Kong. Koo also had warned Nixon that the United States should not identify too closely with the English and the French "because such an association would lead the Asiatic people to think that the United States was supporting colonialism."[64] Dulles's comments briefly upset

Chiang, but Nixon reassured him that the Eisenhower administration firmly supported the generalissimo and his legitimacy; however, Eisenhower discouraged any grandiose dream of an invasion of the mainland.

During Nixon's next stop, in South Korea, the president and secretary of state demonstrated graphically how much they had come to rely on him. In the 1952 campaign, Ike had pledged to go to Korea to end the conflict there. He fulfilled his commitment that December but then entered office with no solution. A partial solution came spontaneously in March, when Stalin died and Mao decided that the fighting was too costly in men and material. In this altered environment, the warring factions edged toward an armistice, and on July 27, United Nations forces and their opposition signed an agreement ending the hostilities. Neither side had won; yet after three years, carnage had given way to a shaky stalemate.

To South Korea's president, the seventy-eight-year-old Syngman Rhee, the armistice was unacceptable. He felt his nation's troops, along with American air power and material, could drive the enemy across the Yalu River into China. Only by uniting the Korean peninsula under his leadership could the threat of another invasion from the north be permanently defused.[65]

Eisenhower vehemently rejected Rhee's argument. Secretary Dulles concurred, adding however that any unification based on bringing Mainland China into the United Nations or, worse, onto the Security Council was impossible. Both men decided to use Nixon's visit to reinforce their positions. Dulles warned that the South Korean leader might want to move boldly against the North. If Nixon blinked, Rhee might believe that the United States was "secretly disposed to support him."[66] Nixon arrived in Seoul knowing what was expected of him and the complexities of dealing with America's truculent ally. A month after his bilateral discussions, he wrote that "Rhee was a good trader and had to be dealt with firmly."[67]

Before the armistice was finalized, in early July, Nixon asserted that the administration was "doing everything possible to end the war in an honorable and expeditious fashion." After landing in Seoul on November 12, he followed the outline he had been given: Asians had to cooperate and solve the problems that divided them. The South Koreans had another view. Nixon found the route in to the capital plastered with signs: "North Korea must be liberated under the Republic of Korea."[68]

General Templer, who during Nixon's visit to Kuala Lumpur had strongly influenced his thinking on colonialism in Southeast Asia, had paid Syngman Rhee the ultimate compliment. While complaining vehemently about the lack of strong Malayan leaders, he said, "I hate to say this because I don't like the son-of-a-bitch, but what the Malayans need is a Rhee!" Nixon entered the meeting prepared to respect Rhee and knowing he needed Rhee's support—which would not be easy to earn, given his assignment.

Nixon and Rhee met for two hours for talks that the vice president later characterized as "extremely frank, cordial and friendly." He handed Rhee a letter, dated November 4, from Eisenhower to the Korean president. This explosive communication reminded Rhee that the White House was presently planning a strategy to pass a bilateral mutual defense treaty through the Senate early in 1955. If Ike felt the South Koreans were unilaterally going to resume the war, the administration would renounce the pact. The United Nations armistice demanded that both warring sides keep the peace. If Rhee violated it, the United States and the other United Nations forces would have to decide how to react to protect their own security interests. Ike was also going before Congress to ask it for economic assistance for the Republic of Korea. Those funds would be designated for economic rehabilitation and not for a new military offensive.

As for the vice president's authority, Ike wrote that Nixon had his "complete confidence and you can talk to him as you would to me." He was more than the vice president; he was the Senate president and was a former member of both houses of Congress. Many senators would consult him when the treaty came up for approval, and congressmen would ask for his advice when the economic assistance bill was brought before both houses. Rhee had two options: he could hand his reply to Nixon or send it to the American embassy.[69]

Rhee accepted the communication with "considerable emotional shock," but never became "angry or emotional." He replied that he feared that three million of his countrymen would remain enslaved in the North, and he had an obligation to unify his nation "by peaceful means if possible but by force if necessary." Although he recognized that the United States deplored a renewal of hostilities, he was convinced a divided Korea would eventually lead to war. Leaning close to Nixon, he said: "I pledge to you that before I take any unilateral action at any time I shall inform President Eisenhower first." American representatives in South Korea considered Rhee's promise a major step forward that prevented him from acting unilaterally. It would remain secret because neither the United States nor South Korea wished the communists to know about it. If they did, America would lose a powerful bargaining chip. Even though Rhee pledged to advise the United States before acting, the North did not know that Eisenhower had threatened to withdraw American support.[70]

Even as he assured Secretary Dulles of Rhee's sincerity, Nixon saw an issue of confidence. Rhee dealt in personalities, and he distrusted the American ambassador Ellis Briggs and other high-ranking American officials on the peninsula. He did not confide in anyone representing the Eisenhower administration.[71]

It was therefore a victory that before replying to Ike's letter, Rhee sent a draft to Nixon, asking for suggestions. None were needed. Nixon informed Secretary Dulles that Rhee pledged "that he would never take any unilateral action without first informing the President."[72]

Nixon continued on to Tokyo. During his travels, he repeatedly heard expressions of bitterness and hatred toward Japan from nations it had occupied during World War II. Nixon's party landed at Haneda Airport on Sunday afternoon, November 15. He was the first major state guest since the surrender. The vice president had asked that the fifteen-mile route to the embassy be lined with school children wearing American and Japanese flags. He also wanted to meet "common people," and during the drive, he had the car stop several times so he could shake hands with onlookers. Once at the embassy, Ambassador John Allison watched the vice president pat the shoulder of the chief butler, "who turned as red as if he had just finished a quart of saki."[73]

The next morning Nixon met with Prime Minister Shigeru Yoshida for two hours, coming away with an impression of the prime minister as an anticommunist who did not believe the Soviets posed an immediate threat to his regime. He later described Yoshida in *Leaders* as "hard-as-nails," a reserved individual who had worked successfully with General Douglas MacArthur during the American occupation.[74]

From that meeting, Nixon drove to the imperial palace with Pat in a "black-horse drawn carriage" reserved for important guests. Emperor Hirohito welcomed the Nixons Western style: he wore shoes. The vice president was dressed "in striped trousers and cutaway coat." He and the emperor had a half-hour private conversation and then attended a small luncheon.[75]

Nixon hinted that he was going to make a significant address in Tokyo on November 19, at a luncheon of some 700 influential people given by the American Chamber of Commerce in Japan and the American-Japan Society. Two days earlier, he had called the current level of Japanese troops "the nucleus, the beginning, of a force which eventually will be adequate to provide the defense of Japan." Secretary Dulles had called for rearmament that summer. Gallup polled Americans in mid-September about strengthening the Japanese army to repel a communist attack, and 63 percent felt it should be done. When Senator Knowland stopped in Japan at that time, he bluntly told government officials to rearm. What Nixon kept hidden was that Secretary Dulles had asked him to use his speech of November 19 to take Japan's temperature on the issue.[76]

The vice president spoke from notes for fifty-five minutes. The *New York Times* article reporting on the speech was headlined: "JAPAN'S DISARMING WRONG." Nixon said that the United States had made a mistake in 1946 in having Japan include in its Constitution an article forbidding rearmament. In the wake of victory, Americans had misjudged the Soviet Union's intentions; their former allies were not peaceful but menacing. Japan therefore needed to take on more of the burden of defending itself against communist aggression. Nixon could have added that Eisenhower wanted to reduce the military budget and the Joints Chiefs proposed that one way to accomplish this was through increased military spending by Japan. The speech left many Japanese, including Yoshida, unpersuaded.[77]

During a press conference on November 24, Secretary Dulles endorsed Nixon's stance. The United States had indeed erred in 1946, and the error needed to be rectified. Later he permitted newsreel cameras to memorialize his answer on film. He included himself among those who had made wrong assumptions about the Kremlin's intentions.[78]

One issue that Nixon did not publicly mention was the communist influence at the universities, in labor unions, and among the intelligentsia. Hundreds of Japanese were studying in China. The island's leadership was not concerned because communists had never played a significant role on the island. Nixon, however, was still disturbed by the threat of subversion, and he felt that the Malayan model of outlawing the Communist party should extend to Japan, even though he vigorously opposed such legislation in the United States.[79]

The debate over rearmament intensified as, en route to the Philippines, the vice president landed at the United States air base on Okinawa for a two-hour refueling. The stop was for more than topping the tanks: Nixon hoped to evaluate the American soldiers' position. Communists were hurting the United States in Asia by asserting that the Eisenhower administration favored its own brand of colonialism. After reviewing the delicate situation, Nixon told the NSC just before Christmas that the United States had to devise a "face-saving-legalistic device" that permitted the continuation of American troops on Japanese soil on terms the government could readily accept.[80]

When the party landed in Manila on November 20, the Philippines had just completed an election won by the challenger, Ramón Magsaysay, with two-thirds of the vote. The vice president's itinerary had been deliberately arranged so that he did not arrive until ten days after the voting, so as not to give the impression of American interference. In fact, the United States had flagrantly intervened in favor of Magsaysay.[81]

The vice president quickly decided that the president-elect was an exceptional personality and told reporters that he could "become a great Asian leader" if he could first solve his country's economic problems. Magsaysay had gained prominence fighting the communist-led Huk guerrillas and had, Nixon thought, "the keenest understanding of the Communist threat abroad and at home of any man I have talked to." Nixon confidentially informed the state department that the president-elect combined "two qualities needed for leadership in Asia: (a) magnetic appeal to all classes of people, (b) genuine regard for the people's welfare." He was pro-American but could not be viewed as a "stooge." All things considered, the United States "must not allow Magsaysay to fail." Much later, Nixon described Magsaysay as a revolutionary and a nation builder.[82]

The last scheduled stops began on November 25, when the party flew from Manila to Rangoon, Burma. Upon touching down, Nixon deplaned, attended various receptions, and spoke over national radio, telling his listeners that the United States was not seeking any military bases in their country.[83] The most controversial issue on his agenda was the question of the Kuomintang (Chinese Nationalist) troops stationed just inside Burma's northern border. The government wanted Chiang Kai-shek to withdraw them, or else the Burmese military was going to drive them out of the country. Nixon supported that demand and promised to find a solution that would avoid bloodshed. The Burmese were gratified by Nixon's assurances and agreed to let him solve the problem. The government agreed to wait several months, after which it expected the Kuomintang to start leaving.[84]

On Thanksgiving Day, the Nixons traveled to the ancient city of Pegu, some forty miles north of Rangoon, to see the shrine of the famous reclining Buddha. Due to "a rash of anti-American slogans" and the threat posed by roaming communist bands, the Nixons were escorted into town by two truckloads of troops. They arrived to find hostile signs reading, BURMA NOT A PLACE FOR YANKEE WARMONGERS. A voice over a loudspeaker in a passing bus called for United States imperialists to leave Asia. While the security detail discussed how to proceed, the vice president and his wife abandoned their guards and walked alone for thirteen blocks to confront the demonstrators. The Nixons wanted to show that they "were not afraid of them." They walked through the crowd. Nixon smiled, shook hands, and asked the agitators questions. His demeanor stunned many of them; they seemed uncomfortable and backed away. He greeted a protester with a sign: "I'm Mr. Nixon. How are you?" The man was flabbergasted and too frightened to speak. The vice president asked for their leader to step forward, and a part-time schoolteacher, who spoke English, did. The Nixons then went in to the temple for a half hour to inspect the Pagoda. When they emerged, the opposition had vanished.[85]

Pat described the encounter to a *Washington Star* reporter: "That was the most exciting thing of the whole trip. It was the only time I was a little frightened." She admitted her heart was "pounding pretty fast."[86]

The Nixons then landed in Columbo, Ceylon, on November 27 for a three-day visit. Police had removed the anti-American graffiti from the walls. The vice president spoke over Radio Ceylon the next evening, assuring his audience that the United States supported "the orderly progress towards self-government throughout the world." He said, "The United States has no imperialistic ambitions whatsoever in Asia or in any other part of the globe." Bilateral discussions concentrated on trade, especially rice and rubber. The government also wanted developmental loans but looked to the United Nations as the most desirable source. Nixon commented afterward that the Ceylonese were anticommunist and "were very shrewd and sophisticated traders."[87]

At the end of November, Nixon reached India, a country—and region—to which American policy assigned only secondary importance. Prime Minister Jawaharlal Nehru preached neutralism and had won widespread popularity for it. Secretary Dulles, in an effort to ameliorate Nehru's anxiety that the United States might provide military assistance to Pakistan, had visited New Delhi in the spring and attempted to persuade the prime minister that American aid protected Karachi from communism. Nehru countered that his people feared Pakistan far more than the Soviets and that American arms in Pakistani hands would be directed against India. Such antithetical positions left no room for compromise. In the middle of November, Eisenhower reminded Dulles: "That is one area of the world where, even more than most cases, emotion rather than reason seems to dictate policy." Although Nehru espoused impartiality, he appeared to favor the Kremlin and the Chinese.[88]

Nixon would later describe Nehru as a revolutionary and a nation builder who held himself out as a major Asian leader. Their first meeting, a brief courtesy call, was cordial. The next day Nixon presented Eisenhower's letter to the prime minister, calling for both nations to seek greater understanding of the other's policies. Nehru responded that the Indians wished to cooperate with the president and were "passionately devoted to the cause of peace."[89]

The following day, Nehru and Nixon talked for two hours. The prime minister, according to his guest, spent two-thirds of that time talking about United States military assistance to Pakistan. Nehru was unalterably opposed: the equipment, he insisted, would be used against his people. The United States ambassador to India, George Allen, commented that sending arms to Pakistan could move India closer to the communist bloc. Nehru had just signed a trade treaty with the Soviet Union, and United States–Indian relations would "be seriously strained." After the meeting, Nixon spoke with reporters but refused to discuss American intentions regarding Pakistan.[90]

The next day, Nixon addressed the Indian parliament, promising that the United States had no ambitions in Asia. America hoped that the Indian subcontinent would develop independently of outside interference. Translated, this was a warning to the communists to stay away. People throughout the region, Nixon said, yearned for peace, a relaxation of tensions between the competing ideologies, and an end to outside domination. "Languages differ, religions differ, skin colors differ," the vice president said, but the "hunger for security from aggression is universal."[91]

Nixon flew from New Delhi into Kabul civil airport on the afternoon of December 4. He recalled a pleasant visit with Afghanistan officials. During his drive into town, in the Middle East for the first time, he saw camels. He discussed bilateral issues with government officials and had a state black-tie dinner with King Mohammed Zahir Shah. Before his departure, he spoke on the importance of educating Afghanistan's youth at Habibia College, established fifteen years earlier and run by Americans.[92]

The party landed in Karachi on December 6. Rather than locating that country in the Indian subcontinent, the United States classified Pakistan as part of the Middle East. Eisenhower needed allies in that region, and Pakistan seemed to fit the mold. When Great Britain granted independence to India, the majority religion was Hinduism; Pakistan was separated as an Islamic enclave. Secretary Dulles had visited Karachi in the spring, and General Mohammed Ayuh Khan came to Washington at the end of September to discuss military assistance. In early November, the Pakistanis leaked these negotiations to the *New York Times*.[93]

Even before Nixon reached Karachi, the American embassy lobbied him to support the Pakistani position favoring military assistance. The state department, however, urged him to avoid the subject. Despite that careful tone, reporter Selig Harrison attended an off-the-record conference with Nixon in New Delhi at the United States embassy. Nixon already had a negative impression of Nehru and reasoned that military assistance to Pakistan would "help to keep [him] in line."[94]

Rumors about aid circulated throughout Karachi long before the vice president landed. Upon arrival, the Nixons went to the governor-general's residence, where they were quartered. Their agenda was full: they met hundreds of people, attended state banquets, and toured the countryside. The vice president quickly provided encouragement. The United States had assisted nations in economic need, and Pakistan's independent policies encouraged him.[95]

Pakistani officials made light of Indian anxiety about an invasion from the north. The governor-general of Pakistan, Ghulam Mohammed, told Nixon that given the millions of Muslims in India, he would personally fly to New Delhi and assure Nehru that he had nothing to fear. He conceded that although Nehru would be angry if the United States granted the aid, that would not drive India into the Chinese or Soviet orbits. Ghulam Mohammed worried far more about the publicity given to military assistance. If the United States did not provide it, that would be "disastrous." Prime Minister Mohammed Ali added that his nation needed to defend the Islamic state from communism. In addition, Nehru used his neutrality as a diplomatic lever to intimidate the United States.[96]

Nixon sided with the Pakistanis. In a nationwide radio broadcast, he pledged American friendship: "A strong, independent Pakistan is an asset to the free world." The vice president represented a consensus forming within the administration that aid to Karachi and a "tough line" with India would prevent Nehru from extending his influence to Southeast Asia and provide the United States some diplomatic leverage.[97]

The Nixons had completed their published schedule, but the state department added Iran and Libya.

In Iran, the former prime minister, Muhammad Musaddiq, a suspected communist sympathizer who had expropriated British oil holdings, had been removed in a coup d'état in August 1953. The American ambassador to Tehran, Loy Henderson, did not hide his opposition to the Musaddiq regime, and Eisenhower, with Great Britain's participation, approved a covert CIA operation that assisted in the coup d'état. Shah Mohammed Reza Pahlavi had replaced Musaddiq with Fazolallah Zahedi.[98]

Just before Nixon left the United States, early in October, the president had decided that the vice president should avoid Iran "because of its unsettled conditions." On the eighth, Ike wrote in his diary that the United States "helped bring about . . . the restoration of the Shah to power in Iran and the elimination of Mossadegh. The things we did were 'covert.' If knowledge of them became public, we would not only be embarrassed in that region, but our chances to do anything of like nature in the future [would] almost totally disappear." But by the second week of November, the state department had concluded that the Iranian political situation had stabilized. Nixon announced on November 16 that he would go to Tehran to meet with the shah and the new prime minister.[99]

The Nixons touched down in the afternoon on December 9; the vice president stated that the United States had recently given $45,000,000 in emergency financial assistance "to help this Government and this people to be strong, independent and free." This guaranteed peace: "We believe it is essential to maintain independence from foreign control or domination of any type." After leaving the airport, he ordered his car stopped so that he could shake hands with astonished spectators. He was there to show Eisenhower's support for the shah's regime.[100]

During the short stay, Nixon had several conversations with the shah, starting a cordial relationship that lasted until the shah's death. The shah wanted first to stabilize his nation's economy and then move into foreign affairs. Nixon perceived that as a ruler, Pahlavi was proceeding tentatively, but the vice president thought he was "beginning to have more guts." He admired Prime Minister Zahedi and referred to him a decade later as "one of the free world's most courageous and able statesman [*sic*]."[101]

Ambassador Henderson believed that Nixon's visit had increased "American prestige and popularity in Iran." If the British moved forward on an oil settlement with a friendly Iranian regime, that settlement would bring political stability and economic prosperity. Nixon agreed. Domestic peace meant that communists could not create chaos. The Iranians had made concessions to Britain for an oil agreement; now the United States cabinet, in what was still, in 1954, the world's largest exporter of oil, had to stabilize its price.[102]

Two days before the Nixons were scheduled to leave Tehran and come home, a final destination was added. Their Constellation landed at Wheelus Air Force Base, near Tripoli, Libya, on December 12 for a meeting with King Idris I, who was miffed that no major American official had come to see him since the two countries had failed to negotiate a new air-base agreement after two years of bargaining. The vice president met privately with Prime Minister Mahmud Muntasser. The latter was flattered that Nixon was there to discuss the impasse over the agreement, and they pledged to conclude it.[103]

The next morning, Nixon flew to meet with the king at his desert palace near Bengazi, a round trip of some 700 miles. The vice president assured his host that the United States would provide financial aid, but first both nations had to sign a base arrangement. Under those terms, Idris I successfully expedited the negotiations.[104]

Nixon's journey had been far more than a goodwill mission. In terms of his personal development as a statesman, he met foreign leaders with whom he would interact for years and learned about complicated issues throughout Asia and the subcontinent, which strengthened his understanding of international affairs. He went to New Zealand and Australia to affirm the viability of ANZUS, traveled to Indochina to observe how the French military was leading the campaign against local communist forces, and listened to British experts who had successfully dealt with communist insurgents. More immediately, he returned home convinced of three things: the French colonial empire was crumbling; if Indochina fell, the rest of Southeast Asia would be in jeopardy; and if Mao moved toward conquest, the United States had to be prepared to react.

Nixon had also acted as the president's confidential emissary, warning Syngman Rhee not to invade North Korea and Chiang Kai-shek not to consider an amphibious invasion of the Chinese Mainland. Without mentioning Ike's approval, he had informed the Japanese that they had to rearm. He had tried unsuccessfully to persuade the prime minister of India to live with American military aid to Pakistan, and then actively pressed for that aid. Almost as an afterthought, he had traveled to Iran to prop up the shah and on to Libya to placate the king and persuade him to sign an agreement for an American military base.

The trip and its aftermath also demonstrated how skillfully Eisenhower managed his subordinates. After Nixon returned, the president gave him new responsibilities. He was now a firsthand observer of conditions abroad; the president used him at cabinet and NSC meetings to present his findings and listen to how others responded. Nixon also became an important public spokesman for the administration's diplomacy and foreign policy decisions. No president had ever regularly employed his vice president as eyes and ears to help formulate policy; no vice president had ever received this kind of opportunity or benefited to such an extent.

THE BATTLES OVER ASIA

By the time the Nixons landed at National Airport on December 14, the morning drizzle had lifted, and brilliant sunshine had broken through the cloud ceiling to shine on the distant Capitol dome. They came down the airport ramp just before 2:00 p.m. and were greeted by diplomats from the countries they had visited as well as American officials. Although Congress was in recess, several senators were also at the terminal.[1] A police motorcade escorted the couple to the White House, where Eisenhower, wearing only a gray suit despite the chill, welcomed them on the north portico as they emerged from their limousine. The president grasped Nixon's hand "with a twinkle in his eye" and said, "It looks like we have a little interest in you, Dick!" Ike then turned to Mrs. Nixon: "but, Pat, the reports on you have been wonderful!" He then invited them upstairs to the second-floor residence to have coffee and see Mamie, who was nursing a cold. After a half-hour of conversation, the Nixons returned to their automobile and headed home.[2]

Ike then did something he rarely did. He wrote a longhand letter on green White House stationery to Dick. He noted that he was proud of the Nixons' accomplishments abroad, "yet I must say I'm glad to have you home. . . . All the principal figures in the Administration, have missed your wise counsel, your energetic support and your exemplary dedication to the service of the country." He was pleased that the couple appeared well after such a taxing journey and looked forward to a quiet time when Dick could relay his "adventures and accomplishments."[3]

Two weeks earlier, during a press conference on December 2, Eisenhower mentioned that he had been following the Nixons' travels and had received encouraging reports of the vice president's successes in creating an atmosphere of American-Asian cooperation. At a later press conference, the president repeated that he had received glowing reports everywhere the vice president visited and that the Nixons were representing their nation "in an admirable fashion." Ike said he had not asked Nixon whether he was going to prepare a report like the one Milton Eisenhower had done on South America, but if Nixon did, the president would make it public.[4]

What the president did not mention was that the trip marked the beginning of the vice president's increased involvement in international relations. Nixon would become a sounding board at cabinet and NSC meetings for many of the diplomatic issues in Asia and would serve as a public spokesman for the administration's perspective on Asian matters. His extended tour of the region greatly enhanced his foreign policy credentials.

The morning after his return, Nixon addressed the White House Conference of Mayors, emphasizing the necessity for peace in Asia and describing the struggle against Soviet expansion. If the region achieved economic stability, he said, the communists would fail to attract converts, and Asian nations would not become prey to totalitarian regimes.[5]

That afternoon, the vice president gave a presentation to the NSC, setting a precedent for future missions, describing his visits with various officials, and concluding with some recommendations: the administration should look to Asia as a priority and spend on economic and military assistance programs. Bernard Shanley termed the report "fabulous" and wrote in his diary that the audience "cheered and clapped when he finished. The President said later that it was one of the outstanding presentations he had ever heard." Nixon also spoke to the cabinet, briefed legislative leaders and spent two days at the state department discussing his travels. Director of Central Intelligence (DCI) Dulles asked to meet with him about his journey.[6]

Nixon spoke on nationwide television and radio on the evening of December 23. He had gone on the mission, he said, for two reasons: to examine Korean conditions since the armistice and to explore the complexities confronting Asian countries. He had met thousands of "ordinary people" and had shaken hands with over 100,000, including some communists, and had both seen and been told that communist penetration was mounting a dangerous assault on democratic institutions in the area. At the same time, he warned, communist propagandists were using racial discrimination in the United States to damage America's image abroad.[7]

Korea presented itself as the most urgent issue. Eisenhower had told his closest advisers that if the People's Republic of China violated the armistice there, he might consider using nuclear weapons to defend Syngman Rhee's government. The South Korean president had even offered to send troops to Indochina. Ike rejected the offer, preferring to leave the defense of Indochina to the French. American and Korean troops were stationed at the 38th parallel to defend the South, not to fight elsewhere.[8]

Rhee initiated potentially monumental problems when he wrote Ike on March 11, 1954, requesting permission to attack the North. During Nixon's visit in 1953, Rhee had promised to notify the United States before taking any unilateral military action. Here was his notification. Since the armistice was signed, Koreans had been dying by the thousands in the war with the North, and Rhee believed the only solution was to drive the communists from the peninsula. The South Koreans would do the fighting while the Americans provided the logistical support. Once the attack commenced, Chiang Kai-shek pledged to invade the mainland.[9]

Eisenhower responded nine days later that he would not agree to any invasion proposal. The United States and its allies had signed the armistice in order to end the bloodshed. In addition, Ike wrote, the Republic of Korea could not "alone achieve the unification of Korea by a military decision, and unilateral action by your Government would expose your armed forces to disastrous defeat and possible destruction."[10]

Throughout the remainder of the Eisenhower presidency, a mutual defense treaty between the two nations guaranteed South Korea's security. Even though Nixon had learned that the North had violated the armistice by reinforcing its positions with men and materiel, American and UN troops kept to its terms. The United States protested to the UN, and the only option was to restore a balance by increasing the South's strength. Despite these infractions, no hostilities broke out, and Nixon wrote privately on June 10, 1957, that "no serious incidents have occurred jeopardizing the status of the Armistice."[11]

Besides the uneasy truce on the Korean peninsula, the president had to consider how to deal with Mao. The British had already recognized the PRC and were pressuring the president in late 1953 to allow expanded trade with Mainland China. Ike and Treasury Secretary George Humphrey were sympathetic, and they unsuccessfully lobbied Congress for increased trade with the Soviet bloc. After the NSC meeting of March 11, 1954, the vice president wrote: "the President was extremely eloquent in his discussion of the trade problem. He feels deeply that this is one area in which our policy must be re-examined."[12]

The president and some of his advisers believed the United States needed to trade with communist nations because this would make them less dangerous. Their leaders, as well as their populations, would be less likely to wage all-out war against trading partners on whom they depended for food and industrial products. Some pundits and Republican hard-line congressmen vehemently disagreed—they felt cooperation with communists was morally repugnant—and Nixon set out to modify their stance. At the same time, he maintained that communists did "not react normally," and he "was skeptical of the possibility of inducing evolutionary change in the Soviet Union or in the satellites."

With the armistice in Korea, the conflict in Indochina took center stage in Asia. The French government hoped to maintain its colonial empire, but the Vietminh led by Ho Chi Minh had started a military campaign to force the French to leave. As the fighting grew more intense, the French seemed to lose their resolve, and even large amounts of U.S. economic and military assistance to the French could not prevent the insurgents from gaining ground.

During an NSC meeting on January 18, 1956, Nixon predicted that one or more of the great powers would develop "the backward nations of Asia." If the United States did not fill this vacuum, the Kremlin would. Each emerging state would first become economically dependent and then would evolve into "a political and military satellite." He and the president concurred that the administration could accept something less than Western-style capitalism or democracy in the Asian nations if this would keep their governments out of the Soviet orbit.[13]

Nixon vociferously lobbied for assistance to the Asian nations, especially those that depended on one or two products for export. He conceded in 1954 that many of those nations, particularly former colonies of European empires, distrusted America. Still, he felt that the "average man" whom he had met in his travels was a "friendly, sympathetic individual who was profoundly pleased to be treated as an equal by a Westerner." A year later, he reiterated that the administration could not surrender any more territory because doing so encouraged enemy aggression. Losses to advancing communism in Vietnam would damage American strategic interests in Taiwan and South Korea. If either were threatened, Japan and the Philippines could be next.[14]

As the administration tried to formulate a coherent Indochina policy in the first months of 1954, the NSC looked at many different options in Asia. Council members offered a widely divergent set of strategies. The vice president, on the basis of his 1953 mission, saw French colonialism collapsing in the face of rising nationalist movements. The French and British governments were paralyzed abroad and befuddled at home. Admiral Arthur Radford, chairman of the Joint Chiefs of Staff, argued forcefully to strengthen French forces in Indochina, but he cautioned against putting American soldiers on the battlefield. Secretary Dulles wanted to form regional Southeast Asian defensive organizations to halt communist gains. Whatever action the NSC recommended, the administration had to act forcefully so that Congress would follow its lead.[15]

In early April 1954, Ike told a press conference about his fear of the "domino effect," but he offered no substantial countermeasures. Without support from the British and the French, the United States would not intervene militarily in Indochina; and without support from Congress he believed he could not. As the debate continued, conditions in Vietnam deteriorated.[16]

On April 16, with French troops in the midst of a two-month battle at Dienbienphu that would turn out to be their last major engagement in Vietnam, Nixon spoke extemporaneously and off the record before the American Society of Newspaper Editors, warning that the war in Asia was expanding and the French were losing. The current predicament was caused by communist infiltration from Mainland China alongside the indigenous Vietminh. The communist forces were succeeding by presenting themselves as fighting for independence against French colonialism. While the United States opposed foreign domination, the French were enabling the communists by refusing to accept the inevitable end of colonial rule.[17]

A question and answer session followed. One editor, Talbot Patrick, posed a hypothetical question. Having recently returned from a four-month journey to Asia and North Africa, did Nixon believe the United States should commit troops to prevent a communist takeover in the event the French abandoned Indochina?

Nixon did not envision that happening. But since the United States was the leader of the Free World, the administration could not retreat from its opposition to communist expansion. To halt it in Indochina, and thus throughout Asia, "we must take the risk now by putting American boys in. . . . I believe that the Executive Branch of the Government has to take the politically unpopular position of facing up to it and doing it, and I personally would support such a decision." The audience cheered.[18]

Ignoring the confidential nature of the vice president's remarks, the *Times* of London named him as the official advocating sending American soldiers to Indochina. On Sunday, after the London newspaper had identified him, the *New York Times* named Nixon on its front page.[19]

Democratic and Republican leaders reacted angrily, reflecting their constituents' opposition to sending United States troops to Indochina. Senator Albert Gore Sr. of Tennessee commented that the vice president had "no constitutional responsibility in this matter." Several months later, a Gallup Poll found that 72 percent of respondents opposed committing soldiers. In his 1956 book *The New Isolationism*, the diplomatic historian Norman Graebner described the national reaction as "violent," which was an overstatement.[20]

Secretary of State Dulles was not disturbed; he thought dispatching troops to Indochina was unlikely. He and Nixon had discussed the matter late in the afternoon on April 19. The vice president said he was not seeking headlines but only endorsing state department policy. Dulles hoped that the controversy might have had a positive effect in French newspapers. Nixon repeated that his point was that "if the only way to hold Indochina was to go in, we might have to."[21]

That evening, the secretary told Alexander Smith, Republican senator from New Jersey, that the vice president was only highlighting Asia's importance. Dulles himself, he assured the senator, was "strongly opposed to getting our soldiers bogged down in Asia." Nixon's comment "was unfortunate, but it will blow over."[22]

The uproar quickly reached the president, who was vacationing in Augusta, Georgia. He telephoned Nixon on the morning of April 19 to tell him not to be disturbed by the press assault over his "perfectly innocent" comments. Ike would have answered the question the same way. As for Senator Gore, he was only looking for an opportunity to embarrass the vice president. Some columnists, Ike knew, claimed that the comment was floated as a trial balloon, but that was "ridiculous." Nixon responded that such erroneous speculation had an upside: "at least it might prepare the people to support measures short of actual intervention in Indo-China by our troops more readily." Ike seemed unconcerned by the incident. It might bring home the crucial significance of Indochina to the American public.[23]

In May, *Collier's* magazine printed a story that as leader of the free world, America could not afford a "further retreat to the Communists" in Asia, particularly in Indochina. Even though sending American soldiers there would be politically unpopular, Nixon would back such an effort. The United States needed to confront its problems directly: "The speech before the editors did stir up a lot of controversy," Nixon granted, "but if I had it to do over again I would give the same answer to the question—even knowing in advance that there was the possibility of its being made public."[24]

By mid-July, the initial brouhaha had faded, and the motives that the media assigned to the vice president amused him. He wrote the questioner that as for the comments being planted or a trial balloon, "At least the two of us know the truth even if we can get very few others to believe it!"[25]

While Nixon was defending his position on sending troops to the Far East, events in Vietnam continued their downhill course. The French forces, who thought they would have an advantage if the Vietminh attacked their supposedly impregnable defenses at Dienbienphu, instead found themselves at a disadvantage.[26]

The vice president had seen firsthand how the French military interacted with its Vietnam allies when he visited there in November. After returning to Washington, he warned his countrymen that the situation was cause for deep anxiety. In private, he cautioned the NSC that the French refusal to give up their colonial empire in Indochina was increasingly untenable. Their own troops were suffering declining morale, yet they would not train and arm local soldiers for fear that these might eventually turn on their occupier.[27]

At a meeting on March 24, United States naval intelligence painted a "very dark picture." When the question of American intervention came up, Eisenhower pointed out that only one of the Joint Chiefs, Admiral Radford, backed it. Secretary Dulles agreed with the admiral: the administration had to be prepared for skepticism from the public, from Congress, and from factions within the British and French governments. Nixon confided to the secretary that "if our policies were limited to what our allies and what misinformed American opinion would support . . . we would all go to hell." Dulles agreed.[28]

While the administration struggled with this question throughout April, Vietminh attacks on Dienbienphu increased. The French still expected to hold on to their empire. Colonialism in the Far East was collapsing, yet the imperial powers would not accept the inevitable.[29] Talks in Geneva among the United States, France, Britain, the Soviet Union, and the People's Republic of China to resolve the fate of the French possessions in Indochina began on April 26 and continued for two months. Foster Dulles was in Geneva for most of the talks and tried to limit the communist gains to their battlefield victories.

Toward the end of April, Nixon and some in the military argued at an NSC meeting that the United States should consider air strikes to defend Dienbienphu. The United States, Nixon said, was "going to resist further expansion in that area and also it would have the effect of bolstering the morale of the French and the Vietnamese troops." Ike rejected that option. He demanded collective responsibility, and without public backing and congressional approval as well as British and French concurrence, he would not consider any military option.[30]

On the last day of the month, Nixon walked into the Oval Office after breakfast to meet with Robert Cutler, the president's national security advisor. Cutler wanted to inform the allies that if the United States sent troops into Indochina, it might also use atomic weapons. Eisenhower repeated that he would not move unilaterally, and, in any case, he doubted that the bomb could be used effectively in Vietnam. Atomic weapons would not even be mentioned until the allies agreed on some collective action. The president, with the vice president concurring, emphasized that air strikes would raise the French and Vietnamese morale; he considered proceeding even if the British objected.[31]

The Vietminh launched their final assault on Dienbienphu on May 1. Two days later, at a legislative meeting, Ike talked about the Indochina predicament and the need to eliminate British colonialism from the region. In Nixon's view, the United States had "to be positive rather than be placed in a position of doing nothing to avert the collapse of the Free World position in Indo-China."[32]

The French surrendered Dienbienphu on May 7, and the NSC met the next day. Despite their loss, the French still refused to budge on ending their colonial empire. If they decided to negotiate with the Vietminh, a wide range of commitments that they had already rejected in Geneva would have to be reconsidered. Their performance so far, and the American domestic environment, made an intervention highly unlikely.[33] With France's colonial empire in Indochina in its final stage of disintegration, the president wrote his secretary of state that he "had to steer a course between the unattainable and the unacceptable." Nixon saw several complications: France might give its Indochinese colonies some kind of self-rule. The communists were worried that, if no decision was reached, the United States might enter the war. Despite this, the Gallup Poll found that 58 percent of Americans approved of Soviet and Chinese attendance at the Geneva gathering while 28 percent opposed it.[34]

The French government fell on June 12, and the new one, led by Premier Pierre Mendès-France, announced that it would promptly decide the fate of France's Indochinese possessions. Toward the end of the month, at a state department briefing for influential congressmen, Senate majority leader Knowland, speaking for the Republican hard-liners, referred to the recent Geneva gathering as "the Far Eastern Munich." While the press featured the inflammatory comment, Ike refused to get embroiled directly in the fragmentation of the French empire.[35]

On July 9, Secretary Dulles, who had come back to Washington from the Geneva conference, telephoned Nixon regarding the fruitless negotiations. The vice president urged the secretary not to return to Switzerland. The administration had accused both of Eisenhower's Democratic predecessors, Truman and Roosevelt, of surrendering to the communists, and if the United States agreed to the Geneva accords, many Republicans would see it as "a failure of diplomacy." Nixon was also convinced that the Vietnamese would continue to fight against French colonialism. Dulles held that he should return to defend the administration's position, to which Nixon relented.[36]

The conference reconvened on July 14, and a cease-fire was signed in Switzerland seven days later; the United States did not sign the agreement. Vietnam was divided along the seventeenth parallel, and national elections were scheduled for the summer of 1956. A month later, Nixon speculated that "any soft policy toward Communist China" would not be effective over the next twenty-five to fifty years. If the United States were indecisive, the Chinese would completely dominate Asia.[37]

The president was adamant about protecting Japan both politically and economically. He saw that nation as "the key to the future political complexion of large areas in that part of the world." If the United States did not support increased Japanese trade, Tokyo might "fall within the Communist orbit," in which case "the consequences for the United States would be dire." Both the president and his secretary of state were well acquainted with conditions in Japan. At a cabinet meeting on August 6, 1954, the secretary stressed the necessity of encouraging Japanese exports. Even if there was not a large market for them in the United States, there might be one in Southeast Asia. Ike added that Japanese economic conditions were complicated and a variety of measures were necessary. With some qualifications, he argued against the position, popular among conservatives, that demanded "*no* East-West trade." The Japanese, he thought, might trade with their communist neighbors and "set up influences behind the iron curtain detrimental to Communism."[38]

Adding Japan to the equation intensified the American movement toward a policy of collective security in Asia. On September 8, 1954, the United States, Great Britain, France, Australia, New Zealand, the Philippines, Thailand, and Pakistan signed the Southeast Asia Treaty Organization (SEATO). Secretary Dulles approved of this structure, as Nixon recalled, believing it gave "an aura of an interest bigger than just the selfish United States going in there and knocking over the little Vietnamese." That goal never materialized; SEATO never became a unified mutual-defense coalition in the mold of NATO.[39]

Mao's China loomed large in just about every Asian discussion. During Nixon's 1953 visit, he had listened to a variety of recommendations concerning American treatment of Red China, from recognition to absolute isolation. The vice president considered the administration's position prudent. The United States tried to create friction between China and the Soviet Union; it tried to inhibit Mao's aggressive tenancies; it continued its assistance to Japan; and it would sign a defensive treaty with Taiwan. Throughout the first term, Nixon painted the PRC as America's principal adversary in the Far East. He affirmed that Secretary Dulles's massive retaliation policy had significantly reduced China's resolve to send troops into Indochina.[40]

Much of the vice president's assault on Mao stemmed from the Quemoy-Matsu affair. Just before SEATO was organized, the United States received intelligence warnings of an offensive directed against those islands. Chinese

Nationalist troops had garrisoned the islands near the mainland as a possible launching point for an invasion. As anticipated, the PRC began bombarding the islands. This decision and the American reaction illustrated how each nation perceived the other's motives. The PRC saw the United States as the principal impediment to its diplomatic objectives, such as reuniting Taiwan with the mainland, and the Eisenhower administration believed that the Chinese were ready to place Asia under a communist umbrella.[41]

In a meeting on April 13, 1954, the NSC discussed conditions in the Far East. Nixon understood that the president rejected the Chinese Nationalists' plans to attack the mainland. Ike not only opposed Chiang Kai-shek's dreams of military conquest, he also advocated American trade with the mainland because it would benefit bilateral relations and move the People's Republic of China away from total reliance on the Soviet Union. In addition, Allen Dulles admitted that the CIA had "meager information" concerning events inside Red China. Bilateral trade would provide some firsthand intelligence. This opportunity notwithstanding, Nixon saw no chance of United Nations admission or United States recognition until Mao gave some convincing demonstration of peaceful intentions.[42]

After the bombs started to fall on Quemoy and Matsu, on September 12, the president chaired a NSC meeting. He thought Mao's action had a positive psychological value for his countrymen while also damaging United States credibility. Nixon concurred: if the administration did not make a satisfactory response, the government's image would suffer throughout the world. The United States had to find a way to halt the attacks.[43]

The president acted forcefully by urging Congress to pass the Formosa Resolution, which authorized the United States to use armed forces to defend Taiwan. Once the measure cleared the House, the vice president thought the Senate would quickly pass it and grant Eisenhower the authority he had requested—which it did, in January 1955.[44]

The PRC shelled the islands through February. Early in March, Secretary of State Dulles told Nixon that he opposed any deal with Mainland China on the islands because Mao would only be emboldened to accelerate his efforts to destroy Chiang. At the cabinet meeting on the morning of the eleventh, Dulles reported "in gloomy terms" about communist plans to invade the islands. The president later called a meeting on Taiwan with the Dulles brothers and several military advisers. The discussions centered on the generalissimo's ability to defend his nation without United States intervention, which Eisenhower considered doubtful. If America had to send troops, he asked, how many men and materials would be required "without the use of the atomic bomb?"[45]

Painstakingly evaluating his options, Ike tested both the public and the Communist Chinese reactions to the prospect of the administration's defending Taiwan with nuclear weapons. Nixon fired the first salvo during a Los Angeles speech before 2,500 Republicans, proclaiming the administration's foreign policy to be "peace without surrender." He did not mention the offshore islands, but warned that giving up any more Asian islands "would be almost catastrophic."[46]

Dulles struck the next day by announcing that the United States would employ "a doctrine of less-than-massive retaliation" worldwide. The American military would use "small nuclear weapons against military targets" but would avoid using hydrogen bombs on urban centers. When a reporter asked if this applied to Quemoy and Matsu, the secretary answered that that was Mao's decision. On the afternoon on March 16, Nixon called Foster Dulles to say that he was speaking in Chicago the following day and wanted to describe the atomic bomb as a tactical weapon in the American arsenal, ready for use if necessary. Dulles supported the message and hoped the vice president would "strike a solemn note about the situation in Asia."[47]

In two major speeches the next day, Nixon warned Americans to be prepared for the worst. In the event of a war, the Chinese could expect atomic retaliation: "We must have the courage and willingness to meet the threat of freedom." Many weapons had become obsolete, and the United States had replaced them with nuclear ones. "Tactical atomic explosives are now conventional and will be used against military targets of any aggressive force." The vice president wanted peace, but he did not want the communists to misconstrue American expectations: "We must be firm and prepared to resist further aggression if we want to keep a substantial part of Asia on our side."[48]

If Mao doubted the president's position, a question from Charles von Fremd of CBS at the White House press conference on March 16 resolved any ambiguity. Von Fremd asked Ike to comment on Secretary Dulles's statements. At first the president was evasive: he did not envision a circumstance in which nuclear weapons would be used. But then he allowed that they could "be used on strictly military targets and for strictly military purposes." As commander-in-chief, he saw "no reason why they shouldn't be used just exactly as you would use a bullet or anything else."[49]

The vice president followed this line during his midwestern trip in early April. He made his stance slightly less bellicose. No one, he told the American Association of School Administrators, wished for war. Some Democrats charged that a "war party" within the GOP craved combat over the offshore islands. These critics were succumbing to Soviet propaganda. The administration, Nixon insisted, did not have a war faction: "The nation can be sure that there will be no 'trigger happy' decisions as . . . [Eisenhower and Dulles] lead the nation during this period of world tension."[50]

By mid-April, the PRC signaled that Mao was ready to cease bombing Quemoy and Matsu. In a series of telephone calls on April 27, Foster Dulles looked for a resolution to stop the shelling, yet he was having political difficulties with several crucial senators. Senator Bourke Hickenlooper of Iowa objected to any negotiations that would "recognize these bandits." Dulles assured him that the state department would not act without "definite evidence of good faith."[51]

To assist with congressional doggedness, Dulles asked Nixon for a meeting with recalcitrant Republican senators like Hickenlooper, Bridges, and Knowland. The vice president quietly set up a "private conversation" for the secretary to explain his case. Nixon approved of the diplomatic measures and reasoned that if Mao rejected a cease-fire, he would lose "world opinion."[52]

Knowland reacted negatively. A staunch backer of Chiang Kai-shek who vigorously opposed American recognition of the PRC or its admission to the United Nations, he led the Senate forces promoting the United States–Taiwanese defense treaty as well as the Formosa Resolution. He believed the communists were intent on world conquest and would stop at nothing to achieve it. As Republican Senate minority leader, he became extremely negative at White House briefing sessions, declaring at one point: "the fat is in the fire now." "Once we get into this kind of a pow-wow," he said of Dulles's proposed negotiations, Mao would "be surprised if we are not prepared to give not only our shirts but someone else's, and we will be accused of running out."[53]

By the first week of June, a de facto cease-fire was in place. Nixon credited Secretary Dulles for ending the Chinese bombing. It was, Nixon later averred, his greatest achievement as secretary. Six months later, the vice president compared Dean Acheson's policy in Korea, which he called a failure, with the Eisenhower-Dulles success in the offshore islands conflict. The latter team had guided the United States through the Korean armistice, the Geneva talks over Indochina, and the bombing on Quemoy and Matsu, and had found solutions without resorting to war.[54]

While the United States and the PRC were backing away from their dangerous confrontation, twenty-nine nations from Africa, the Middle East, and Asia were gathering at Bandung, Indonesia, from April 15 to 24 to discuss nationalism and anticolonialism. Secretary Dulles foresaw anti-Western diatribes and hoped he could rely on pro-Western participants to defend the United States. The state department did not send a delegation.

When the meeting convened, the anticipated large-scale propaganda against the West did not materialize. Prime Minister Nehru's advocacy of neutralism won few converts, and the PRC foreign minister, Chou En-lai, displayed a surprising degree of moderation, sending signals that Mao wanted to negotiate an end to the Quemoy-Matsu confrontation. Dulles found these measures unexpected and pleasing. The United States supported the end of colonialism, Nehru's pressure for a solid neutral bloc failed, and the subject of American racism barely came up.[55]

At the end of the first term, few would have claimed that the policy in Asia had been a robust success. Hard-liners at home and abroad were frustrated by Eisenhower's restraint, and the truce in Korea was counterbalanced by a deteriorating situation in Indochina and by threats to Taiwan. Yet the boundaries of containment established under Eisenhower would endure for another twenty years.

TROUBLE WITH GOOD NEIGHBORS

Early in 1955, the president began making preparations for Nixon's second major trip: Central America and the Caribbean. Since before the turn of the twentieth century this region had had a complicated relationship with the United States. These nations generally survived on cash crops grown for export, and American businesses supplied the capital and technical skills to harvest those crops, controlling vast tracts of land, transportation networks, and government leaders in order to maintain their monopolies. One American firm, the United Fruit Company, achieved such a dominant position that it gave rise to the phrase "banana republic." The United States stationed troops in these countries in the first third of the twentieth century and interfered unabashedly in their politics. Perhaps the most famous example occurred when President Theodore Roosevelt encouraged a group of separatists to create the new nation of Panama out of what was then part of Colombia—sending naval ships to support the revolt—for which the rebels rewarded him by ceding the land to create the Panama Canal. As a result of such actions, the American ambassadors emerged as the second most influential individuals in these nations' capitals, with the possible exception of the *caudillo*, the military strongman.[1]

The trips by Nixon and others were generally presented as goodwill missions: the press reported the public functions and published photographs of handshakes and smiling faces. Far more important, however, were the private conversations where the travelers gleaned valuable information for the president. Ike deftly briefed his surrogates before they left and debriefed them upon their return; their analyses added nuance and insight to the discussions in the National Security Council and elsewhere. He was not insecure, and he wasted no time worrying over who took credit for perceptive contributions, but only one individual was responsible for the ultimate decision. Many in the public arena did not understand this aspect of his administration.

Ike's interest in hemispheric affairs dated back to his youth. Before going to West Point he had considered a business venture in Argentina. His first overseas posting with the Army was in Panama, at the start of 1922, when he was assigned to the 20th Infantry Brigade as executive officer at Camp Gaillard on the Pacific side of the isthmus. There he served under Major General Fox Conner, who became a mentor and was influential in advancing Ike's career. In his two-plus years at this post, he learned about the region and the strategic value of the Panama Canal and the Caribbean.[2]

As the recently installed president, he understood some of the complexities of hemispheric relations. Holding a cabinet meeting on the morning of July 3, 1953, the president turned to South American problems since he had sent his brother Milton there to make recommendations on how to improve inter-American solidarity. Ike spoke of the "leftist dangers" in Mexico and in Bolivia, where the price of tin was critical to that nation's economic stability. Many other Latin American nations also depended on agricultural or mineral monocultures. He ended the discussion by what Emmet Hughes described as "one of his remarkable moments of wide vision." The United States, according to Ike, worked diligently for "UNITY, UNITY, UNITY" in Western Europe. His administration had "to take a broader look at Latin America and see it as a whole, as we do Europe." The single-commodity reliance in the Western Hemisphere made "no sense at all. Don't we have to think in terms of unity here?"[3]

Secretary of State Dulles was not well grounded in hemispheric affairs. In February 1954, while preparing for the Tenth Inter-American Conference in Caracas, Venezuela, he asked Nixon for advice on which senators should accompany him to the meeting. At a National Security Council (NSC) meeting on March 18, after he returned, the secretary described his difficulty getting an anticommunist resolution passed but said he had left the meeting in a positive atmosphere. Nixon supported Dulles's account, telling the group that Congress had been "generally very favorable" about the conference and even outspoken critics "had made flattering comments on Secretary Dulles' performance."[4]

Privately, however, Nixon was less satisfied. Dulles had lobbied the conference for a strong anticommunist declaration as a tactic against the Soviet Union, and once it was accepted, he returned home. This caused the vice president to think that the secretary did not "have time for Latin America." Dulles saw the region in terms of the struggle against communist expansion, but beyond that it held little interest for him.[5] The division of Inter-American Affairs was the weakest in the state department,[6] and the assistant secretary of state in 1953, John Cabot, believed that while the president was interested in Western Hemisphere issues, he was not "making the nitty-gritty decisions and making sure that they stuck." In 1954, Henry Holland replaced Cabot. Ike, Dulles, and Nixon all gave him high grades. He had been raised in Texas and earned a law degree from the University of Texas in 1936. During World War II, he served as a special assistant at the United States embassy in Mexico, where he learned to speak Spanish fluently. After the war he joined a prestigious Houston law firm where Dillon Anderson, a prominent Republican, was a partner. Anderson vouched for Holland's abilities and confirmed that he was bilingual and was well versed in Latin America matters. The Senate unanimously confirmed him on March 1.[7]

Besides Holland, the president made his brother Milton his "principal confident" and "special ambassador to Latin America." Milton often made weekend visits to the residential quarters of the White House, where he and Ike discussed hemispheric affairs. One of the first diplomatic assignments that the president handed out was to Milton. From June 23 to July 29, 1953, he visited ten South American nations and returned with specific recommendations for improving inter-American relations. Milton later claimed that the Eisenhower administration was responsible for the Alliance for Progress, for which John F. Kennedy took the credit. Dean Rusk, JFK's secretary of state, agreed. JFK had invented the phrase, but Ike originated the concept, and Milton's efforts had given "birth to the ideas."[8]

As for Milton's opinion of Nixon, he later wrote that Ike "was aggrieved that I did not share his high opinion of the Vice-President." During Ike's tenure, however, the two men maintained a cordial relationship; both championed improving hemispheric bonds. After a state dinner for Prime Minister Menzies early in 1955, Milton wrote Nixon to say how much he enjoyed their conversation. He invited the Nixons to visit him at Pennsylvania State University, where he was president, saying he would "love" to compare notes on Latin American issues, and the two men subsequently spent an hour at the White House talking about Brazil.[9]

In August 1954, when Secretary Dulles requested that Nixon and his wife "take a swing through Central America," the vice president should not have been surprised. At the end of the year, the White House announced that the Nixons would tour the Caribbean and Central America the following February.[10] This too was described as a "goodwill mission."

Murray Chotiner, one of Nixon's closest political counselors, saw the trip in domestic political terms. He had long thought that Americans concentrated on Europe and Asia at the expense of Latin America; changing this emphasis would help the Republicans win Hispanic voters in California, Arizona, and New Mexico. Just after the 1954 midterm elections, Chotiner had advised the vice president: "We cannot win . . . [Hispanics] by appointing a Chairman of a Latin-American Committee four weeks before each election." If Nixon could repeat the success of his Asian sojourn, a Latin American trip "would be most effective."[11]

Nixon received detailed briefings from the state department starting three weeks before his mission. The CIA had recently carried out a coup d'état that ousted the existing left-wing government in Guatemala and replaced it with a regime favorable to American interests; now the country needed to be stabilized. The state department also wanted the vice president to push for the elimination of communist infiltration throughout the Western Hemisphere and for the completion of the inter-American highway.[12]

Although these preparations were essential, nothing was more critical than Eisenhower's confidential briefing at the White House on February 2. The president's public statement three days later was typically vague: he stressed that the mission would "reaffirm and strengthen the good partnership between the United States and other peoples of the hemisphere in which he has particular interest." Nixon, too, spoke in generalities. He would try to foster understanding and meet with a wide variety of people from divergent walks of life. The Western Hemisphere had a common heritage of freedom "and a tradition of working together to solve the problems of the Americas."[13]

Nixon especially wanted photographers to take pictures of him in contact with "common people" wherever he stopped. Similar pictures taken during his Asian trip had played well with both American and foreign audiences. Pat's visits to schools, orphanages, and other social service institutions had also been "useful," and the vice president wanted them fully covered.[14]

In each country, Nixon attended a reception for the American colony; in his remarks at each reception, he reiterated the same theme: every United States citizen was an ambassador of goodwill, and when an American behaved poorly and acted arrogantly, it damaged the United States's image. He even suggested to the state department that all passport recipients receive a letter from the United States president reminding them that when traveling abroad, they were goodwill ambassadors.[15]

On Sunday morning, February 6, the Nixons hugged their daughters goodbye at the airport for the month-long journey. Amid snow and ice, they left Washington for Havana aboard an Air Force Constellation.[16] Having been well briefed, Nixon knew that Cuba was one of the most sports-minded nations in the world, and upon his arrival he referred to native-born athletes like Orestes

"Minnie" Minoso of baseball's Chicago White Sox and world welterweight boxing champion, "Kid" Gavilan. The vice president later paid tribute to Cuba's
national hero, José Marti, by placing a floral wreath at his monument in the
capital's central park while police with machine guns kept away demonstrators.[17]

Late that afternoon, visiting president-elect Fulgencio Batista at his country
estate near the capital, Nixon presented his host with an autographed photograph
of Eisenhower. Batista was inaugurated a few weeks after the vice president's
departure. The visit left the impression that the United States supported Batista
and that he had a close relationship with United States ambassador Arthur
Gardner.[18]

In his speeches, Nixon reminded audiences that Cuba was the sixth-best customer for American exports. In that spirit of cooperation, the United States
would not lower its quota on imports of Cuban sugar. On February 8, he spoke
before the Cuban Senate to warm applause, reiterating the close bonds between
the two nations: "as partners and friends there is no problem that Cuba and
the United States cannot solve, and no enemy we cannot withstand."[19]

Nixon then spent three days in Mexico. He had grown up around Mexicans
in Southern California; he and Pat had driven through Mexico on their honey-
moon in 1940; and he had represented the president at the inauguration of
Adolfo Ruiz Cortines in 1952.[20]

Ike knew that Mexico was the biggest customer for American exports, and he
strove to improve bilateral relations. Early in his administration, he had met with
Ruiz Cortines at the joint dedication of the Falcon Dam spanning the Rio
Grande. Eisenhower was worried that the weak Mexican economy would foster
political turmoil and lead to communist infiltration.[21]

Nixon arrived on February 9, had a talk with Ruiz Cortines, shook hands with
everyone he could, and laid a wreath at the Column of Independence.[22] On their
second day, their largest crowd engulfed the couple as they visited the Basilica
of Guadalupe, the nation's most sacred shrine. As they entered the church where
The Shrine of Our Lady of Guadalupe was housed, the crowd showered them
with ticker tape.[23]

Ambassador Francis White believed that Nixon had improved bilateral relations. He had paid his respects to the Independence Movement, gone to the most
sacred Catholic shrine, addressed the Congress, called for expanded student
exchange, and called Mexico an economically awakening giant. By stressing
these issues, the vice president reflected his boss's viewpoints. America's immediate southern neighbor needed to develop by peaceful means, and it needed
assistance from the Eisenhower government. This message, and Nixon's emphasis
on bilateral ties, clearly reinforced Ruiz Cortines's plans.[24]

The next stop, in Guatemala, was both delicate and crucial. The government of Jaboco Arbenz Guzmán had been democratically elected in 1951 on a platform of moderate land reform. The United Fruit Company, which owned vast tracts of land in the country, opposed any discussion of land expropriation. Charging that the Arbenz regime was infiltrated with communists, the company refused to bargain with the government. The Truman administration accepted the allegations that the Guatemalan government was turning radically to the left. When Ike assumed power, he ordered the CIA to plan the regime's overthrow. Although the operation did not proceed smoothly, Arbenz was ousted, and a military junta led by Carlos Enrique Castillo Armas assumed control.[25]

Few people at the time guessed that the CIA was involved, and even fewer understood Ike's deep interest. His posting in the Canal Zone had taught him the strategic importance of the region and the Caribbean's role in guarding the entrance to the canal. He had traveled on the Great White Fleet from New Orleans to his post via Havana. He also was acquainted with the United Fruit Company's far-flung enterprises in the area and considered it crucial to Central American economies.

In January 1953, shortly before his inauguration, Eisenhower held a private luncheon for five guests on the sixth floor of the Commodore Hotel in New York City. Among the participants were his private secretary, Ann Whitman, and her husband, Edmund, who worked for United Fruit. Ike asked Edmund what the company "was going to do about Guatemala." The communists, Ike went on, were penetrating labor unions, the government, the press, and agriculture. He wanted to know if the country had enough land to distribute to farmers without expropriating United Fruit's holdings, and if the company had tried to resolve its differences "with the bad boys." Edmund responded that the regime refused to entertain any compromise, and the company would not negotiate with communists. How much of the population, the president-elect responded, supported Arbenz? Edmund believed the overwhelming majority of the citizenry opposed the communists but that despite their small numbers, the communists had the political acumen to take over the government.[26]

Shortly after Ike entered office, he instructed the state department and CIA to coordinate efforts to oust the Arbenz regime under the code name PBSUCCESS. The agency recruited and helped train soldiers for Castillo Armas; it also hired pilots to fly planes over the capital to give the illusion of the rebels' superior military power. The CIA sent out radio broadcasts to convince listeners that the invaders were triumphing and jammed the government-run radio stations. In June 1953, Arbenz resigned and left the country; early the following month, Castillo assumed command of a military junta, and that winter he won a staged presidential election. The Eisenhower administration propped up the regime with military and economic assistance.[27]

Nixon was informed about the administration's activities in Guatemala as early as June 30, 1953, when CIA managers came to the White House and briefed Nixon, the cabinet and others about the operation.[28]

Years later, as president, Nixon said that he "totally approved" of the coup. Besides supporting it (without mentioning the CIA's involvement) within government circles during the Eisenhower years, he publicly applauded Arbenz's downfall. Just after the ouster, White House press secretary Hagerty discussed the Guatemala situation with Secretary Dulles. Nixon was getting ready to give a speech where he would highlight a Senate resolution in favor of the coup that passed with only one dissenting vote. Appearing on television on July 2, he commended the administration's foreign policies, especially the removal of Arbenz. The Guatemalan president, he said, had been moving his nation toward communism, and if it gained a foothold in the Americas, the Soviets might expand their subversion throughout the Western Hemisphere.[29]

A month later, Nixon spoke before the Veterans of Foreign Wars, telling the assemblage that Guatemala's communist army was "ten times as strong as the army of liberation" but that 90 percent of the population opposed the government. Just hours after the revolt erupted, "the Communist leaders had to run for their lives." Even this triumph did not guarantee success. American aid alone would not drive out the communists; the people had to support democracy. The United States had "to offer a positive alternative" to the leftists; people in "the uncommitted areas of the world" had to recognize that freedom was the best form of government.[30]

In his remarks upon landing in Guatemala on Saturday, February 12, Nixon said: "You have won the admiration of the people of the world for the way your heroic people overthrew Communism. You also gave hope to enslaved peoples all over the world for your bravery." That night he met with President Castillo Armas to get his input on the state of the country. Despite the afternoon's accolades, he quickly realized how unstable the local conditions were. Arbenz loyalists were bitter at their leader's overthrow; Castillo Armas's followers were disappointed that only six million dollars in American assistance had filtered into the treasury to help stabilize the economy.[31]

Nixon saw the toppling of Guatemala's allegedly communist regime as a major defeat for the Soviets, and he thought Arbenz's "puppet" administration would be remembered for "terror, atrocities and hatred." Without a positive alternative, the Kremlin would use the region's social and economic problems to create unrest. Although Castillo Armas had suspended 300 labor unions, Nixon met with several labor representatives and urged that they build stronger organizations with no foreign ideology. Communist unions did not protect workers, he said, but only served the interests of the Soviet Union.[32]

Although the vice president's public utterances drew headlines, his work behind the scenes was more significant. He cabled Secretary Dulles that the United States had to support the regime vigorously "to preserve in power the first government in history resulting from overthrow of a Communist regime." Dissidents threatened the stability of the government. Arbenz and his associates had robbed the treasury, and to make matters worse, coffee prices were falling. The United States needed to make loans to counteract rising unemployment; a $10,000,000 grant was necessary to balance the currency; the United States had to provide $27,000,000 to complete the inter-American highway in order to attract tourism. If the administration did not move promptly, it might endanger the struggle against international communism.[33]

Even with the influx of American money, the state department characterized the new regime as "inept." Castillo was assassinated in 1957 by a palace guard who then committed suicide; in a eulogy, Nixon said he had "the highest regard and admiration for him." The fallen leader had fought communist infiltration in his country, and his loss "was a real tragedy for the people of his country as well as the nations of the Free World." The administration, he warned, was closely watching developments in Guatemala to see if the communists were trying to capitalize on the murder.[34]

After his stay in Guatemala, Nixon briefly stopped in El Salvador. Robert Hill, who had recently been installed as ambassador, was deeply impressed with the outcome of the Nixons' visit.[35] Hill took an unusual step that pleased the vice president by publishing letters in the *New York Times* and the *Los Angeles Times* in which he declared that Nixon's trip had had "a tremendous influence toward achieving the hemispheric solidarity which is vital to the future of the United States and Latin America."[36]

Ten months before the vice-presidential party arrived in Tegucigalpa, Honduras, Eisenhower had expressed his concern about labor unrest in the northern section of that nation, where 14,000 laborers were on strike against the United Fruit Company. The president worried that communist agitators from neighboring Guatemala were causing dissension. He instructed Nixon that as soon as he landed at the airport, on February 17, he should inform President Julio Lozano Diaz that the local communist threat must be eliminated. Lozano greeted the vice-presidential party, and large crowds on bicycles followed the procession to the presidential palace. Nixon said later that the United States government as well as private investors expected to provide additional monies to develop the economies of Central American nations.[37]

In Nicaragua, where he arrived on February 19, he confronted a far more complex situation. That nation and its neighbor, Costa Rica, were fighting a series of long-simmering border skirmishes. Recognizing the explosiveness of this dispute, the state department advised Nixon not to get involved. Nicaragua had been ruled—brutally—by the Somoza family since 1936. President Anastasio "Tacho" Somoza Garcia was currently the caudillo, and the fervently anticommunist American ambassador Thomas Whelan had formed a close association with the family. The United States approved of Nicaragua's anticommunist commitment and its avid backing of American policies in Central America.[38]

Tacho, in his olive-green military uniform covered with decorations, greeted the vice-presidential party at the airport and immediately took them to the presidential palace in the capital city of Managua, where he displayed a miniature arsenal and claimed the Costa Rican leaders had gathered to assassinate him. He posed as the wounded party and described Costa Rican president José "Don Pepe" Figueres as "crazy." Nicaragua had tried to foment a revolt against Figueres the previous January. The United States hoped that the Organization of American States would mediate the dispute.[39]

Nixon refrained from voicing any opinion regarding Somoza's rule or the border conflict. Before leaving Managua, he received assurances from Somoza that he was willing to suspend the fighting. Arriving in Costa Rica with that pledge, the vice president met with Figueres, who had earlier said that he "would not sit at the table" with Somoza. But after a long conversation with Nixon and Assistant Secretary Holland, he agreed to meet Somoza "more than halfway" in ending the fighting. Before leaving Costa Rica, the vice president had all but signed a peace agreement between the two states.[40]

Besides this political settlement, Figueres addressed a business luncheon with Nixon present. The Costa Rican president applauded the efforts of United Fruit to stabilize the prices of bananas and coffee; he was pleased to announce that the company and his administration were cooperating to improve economic conditions. Nixon, in his wholly approving response, noted that while governments could be accommodating, "in general real progress comes through initiative of private enterprise and this leads to better wages, better working conditions and better way of life throughout the hemisphere."[41]

Panama was Nixon's last stop in Central America. José Antonio Remón had won the presidency in 1952 with a pledge for a new canal treaty, which was negotiated in 1954 and ratified the following year. Remón never witnessed the benefits; he was assassinated in January 1955.[42]

The vice president called for the completion of the inter-American highway within four years instead of the projected ten. Since the United States paid two-thirds of the cost and only 125 miles remained, it was up to the Americans to accelerate the schedule. Nixon declared that "dribbling out the funds as we are presently doing is penny-wise and pound foolish." Finishing the road would increase tourism and other economic activity.[43]

While Nixon was carrying out these official functions, his wife made headlines by visiting the Pale Seco Leprosarium, which served 116 patients in Panama Bay. She was deeply moved as she shook hands with some of the almost cured. Other patients, some without feet or toes, a few without hands, sang and danced with a carnival band while she tapped her feet. She spoke to many, while others hid behind newspapers or placed their hands over their faces.[44]

Ann Whitman, Eisenhower's private secretary, wrote her counterpart in the vice president's office, Rose Mary Woods, that the president read "with the greatest of interest, the editorial from the Panama newspaper. It's wonderfully enthusiastic isn't it—and I know rightly so." Eisenhower had fond memories of his posting there, appreciated being updated on current conditions, and was pleased that the Nixon mission was proceeding so well.[45]

Over the weekend, Nixon journeyed to United States possessions in the West Indies. Starting on Saturday, February 26, he stopped in the Virgin Islands. On Sunday, the party landed in Puerto Rico, where they were welcomed by Governor Luis Muñoz Marin and other officials. That evening Nixon attended a state dinner, and on Monday he toured the island and addressed a joint session of the Legislative Assembly, where he complimented the commonwealth's economic progress and pledged economic assistance.[46]

On March first, the Nixon party visited the Dominican Republic, where General Rafael Trujillo Molina had governed brutally since shortly after the end of World War II. During his stay, Nixon held a private meeting with Trujillo, who used the event as propaganda to showcase his cordial relationship with the United States.[47]

When Nixon landed in Haiti on March 3, the cabinet greeted him at the airport, and a caravan of cars escorted him to the presidential palace in Port au Prince. Again, people lined the route and gave him a rousing welcome. As had become his custom, he got out of his car and talked to people at roadside. President Paul Magloire was disappointed at the amount of United States aid his country was receiving, and Nixon, while making no promises, agreed to talk to the agencies providing assistance.[48]

Walter White, executive secretary of the NAACP, happened to be in Haiti on vacation. He and the vice president had a cordial relationship, and they talked at a private luncheon. White also wrote in his syndicated column that he worried about the vice president's health after such a hectic mission: Nixon looked "so drugged with fatigue after a month of dawn-to-midnight engagements . . . that he appeared to be walking in his sleep."[49]

At the White House Correspondents' Dinner on March 5, Eisenhower welcomed Nixon back and commended him for a job well done. Ike privately told Secretary Dulles that he and Nixon both felt the trip had valuable results and that these tours "were a fine thing."[50]

The press offered nearly unanimous praise. Drew Pearson, who regularly attacked the vice president, editorialized that he was "doing a terrific job on his good-will tour of the Caribbean. Everywhere Nixon has gone he has handled himself like a veteran diplomat, Mrs. Nixon is also doing a bang-up job." Marquis Childs seconded Pearson's praise. Nixon had accomplished many goals, such as mediating between Nicaragua and Costa Rica, and securing economic assistance to Guatemala.[51]

Not everyone was elated. Some Protestants disapproved of Nixon's support for the Catholic Church in Latin America. John Mackey, president of the World Presbyterian Alliance, called the Catholic Church a "breeding ground for communism." A month later, he criticized the church for siding with the region's dictators. Evangelists in Mexico claimed that Catholics had interfered with their conversion efforts. Nixon responded that Catholic leaders in Guatemala had helped to drive communists from their country, and those communists were "the great enemy of all religions, all freedom, all humanity."[52]

The vice president answered such religious complaints, but he was more concerned with economics. Even before the completion of his mission, he started to signal the administration's support for sweeping reforms by calling on the Central American and Caribbean countries to form a strong regional coalition to thwart communist aggression. Fourteen of the region's nations grew coffee, and for eight any fall in prices had critical economic effects. Nixon thought the problem was overproduction and that growers needed to discipline themselves through some kind of quota system—a move that many nations in the Western Hemisphere opposed. Even though the United States was a major coffee importer, he pledged American assistance.[53] On his homeward flight, he told reporters that United States trade with Latin America exceeded its trade with Europe. The Eisenhower administration had to provide market access to Latin American goods that deserved "primary consideration." Although this might damage American producers in some industries, it was crucial to the stability of the Western Hemisphere.[54]

After returning to the United States, Nixon reported to the NSC on March 10 and to the cabinet the following morning. Ike had sent him, he told his listeners, to keep the United States informed about Latin American activities. Latin America was strategically significant; it was one of the best customers for United States exports; the countries voted with the administration at the United Nations and the Organization of American States (OAS); and the region's population was growing at twice the world rate. For the first time since the colonial era, its population exceeded that of the United States.

The communist threat in the Americas was constant, Nixon reported. Cuba had the largest Communist Party, but it appeared to be losing influence; Mexico was working against its internal communist menace. As for Guatemala, Nixon judged that its communists had failed. The Guatemalan people wanted the party eliminated, and Castillo Armas had "overwhelming popular support."

Many Latin American countries suffered from their reliance on an agricultural monoculture and were vulnerable to the whims of the commodity markets. El Salvador depended on cotton, Honduras on bananas, and Cuba on sugar. Despite this lack of diversity, the United States carried out an enormous volume of trade within the Western Hemisphere. This, Nixon said, needed to be increased through lower American tariffs and more economic assistance. Mexico was seeking private capital to build its domestic industries. Puerto Rico had the "highest per capita income" in Latin America, but it was still lower than Mississippi's. Haiti, the poorest nation in the Western Hemisphere, was "a picture of poverty and pregnancy."

Nixon presented portraits of the leaders that he met. Ruiz Cortines "was honest and capable" and hoped to raise his people's living standards. Castillo Armas, a "middle-of-the-road type," was "a good man with good intentions," but he needed United States support to maintain stability. The vice president found Figueres "cocky and extroverish [sic] but popular with his people." Batista was "a remarkable man," "strong, vigorous," and Trujillo "an absolute dictator."

Nixon noted the paradox that most of Latin America was under one-man rule. He said that in his private conversations, he had unsuccessfully urged Batista and Trujillo "to adopt democratic processes." Years later, after leaving the vice-presidency, Nixon noted the dilemma such leaders created for the United States. Tyrants like Trujillo and Somoza had allied themselves with the United States against international communism while simultaneously butchering their own citizenry. The United States, Nixon argued, needed to enact new policies that favored democracies over totalitarian regimes. Latin American governments, having evolved mostly from the Spanish colonial model, did not inherit democracy as an institution, and the United States had to recognize those differences. It should recognize the authoritarian heritage but must encourage democratic reforms.

Even with these contradictions, Nixon was somewhat optimistic. From his perspective, he had gained a deeper insight into the region and had established essential contacts with the leaders and citizens through his goodwill efforts. Summing up for Ike, the vice president was "very proud of my country's prestige and accomplishment as a good partner, and very sure that our partnership with the other Republics of this hemisphere should be even further strengthened and extended."[55]

Along with the vice president's major recommendations, he included the completion of the inter-American highway. Throughout his journey in Central America, he occasionally mentioned speeding up the construction from fifteen or twenty years more to a target date of three years. Construction had started in 1934, and the United States had spent about $54,000,000, which was approximately two-thirds of the total cost to date. Throughout the remainder of March, Nixon lobbied vigorously to accelerate the schedule. He argued that the highway would increase tourism, add to economic intercourse, possibly add to rapid military deployment, and especially assist Guatemala because it had the longest sections that needed to be finished.

In principle, Ike concurred, but wanted additional information before recommending the new construction. Nixon convinced Republican senators Saltonstall and Bridges regarding the value of opening transportation of goods and tourists to the region. Besides these advantages, the initiative would demonstrate to the Central Americans that the United States was working to strengthen hemispheric cooperation. The senators were concerned about graft and corruption in Central American regimes, but Nixon and Ike assured them that American engineers would carefully supervise the building. By the end of the summer, the administration had followed Nixon's lead for an early completion of the inter-American highway in order to increase hemisphere commerce and intercourse. As of this writing it had not been completed.[56]

The vice president also expanded his suggestions to United States programs that reached out globally and had special significance for the Americas. Nixon had supported international exchange legislation since coming to Congress in 1947. From his perspective, Americans traveling abroad had an obligation to create a positive impression of the United States. The United States had to convince developing nations that the United States supported their aspirations, and the exchange program, according to Nixon, provided the greatest return on investment by counteracting communist propaganda.

Under this umbrella, he took the unusual step as a vice president to testify before the April 26, 1955, session of the Senate subcommittee of the committee on appropriations to restore earlier budget cuts and to lobby for $15,000,000 for educational exchange. Milton Eisenhower, who read these congressional proceedings, wrote Nixon that their views coincided in "one of our best foreign programs."[57]

Other legislation that Nixon and Eisenhower favored was the Reciprocal Trade Agreements. Both advocated unencumbered commerce, and the president particularly abhorred protectionism. Ike passionately fought for freer trade as a means to stimulate private enterprise. Nixon believed that the president was ideologically committed, while Secretary Dulles primarily searched for a good deal. Initially, the administration preached "trade, not aid," but the administration quickly saw that this slogan did not work in practice. The preferred option for developing nations was trade venues, but the administration also had to consider vehicles to keep these nations from succumbing to communist inducements. Nixon's trip gave him a forum for increased commerce. He highlighted trade and encouraged private investment as well as economic assistance.[58]

Nixon not only pushed for more attention to Latin America within the administration, but he used a public forum to direct the spotlight to gain greater awareness. After making his confidential reports inside government counsels, he flew to Los Angeles in mid March to give a major speech at the Biltmore Bowl before 1,200 guests of the World Affairs Council. He called on the United States to treat Latin America on an equal footing with other regions of the world. To prop up the Guatemalan government, he proclaimed: "the Castillo Armas Government can do more good for the people of Guatemala in two years than the Communists did in ten years."[59]

Nixon spent January 1956 heavily involved with Brazil. Eisenhower had become involved with what was labeled a special relationship between the two nations at the start of his presidency. The United States, under the previous administration, had pledged a $300,000,000 loan to settle Brazilian debts. That summer, Milton Eisenhower visited the South American giant, and after returning to the United States, he told his brother that the friendly relations between the two countries were disintegrating. During the following two years, the United States offered a minimal amount of financial aid.[60]

By late 1955, bilateral friction had worsened. That October, Juscelino Kubitschek had been elected and announced that as president-elect he would fly to the United States to reestablish cordial bonds. On the morning of January 5,

1956, he and Eisenhower met for breakfast in Key West, Florida. They spoke about Ike's friends in the oil industry, and the Brazilian said that he would confer with one of these individuals on legislation "that would attract American capital on a fair basis." The Brazilian president-elect proceeded to Washington, received a warm welcome, and was the guest of honor at a dinner that the vice president hosted.[61]

Kubitschek did little to satisfy the Brazilian demands for economic assistance or guarantees to prevent communist penetration in its government. To help improve conditions, Assistant Secretary Holland took the initiative in the middle of December 1955 to have Nixon represent the United States at Kubitschek's inauguration, and Secretary Dulles asked Nixon to go.[62]

This was the vice president's first trip to South America and to the only Portuguese-speaking nation in the Western Hemisphere. Nixon attended the inauguration on January 31, 1956. The following day, Nixon, at his specific request, met with labor leaders and called for free unions, not those based on a communist model. On February 2, he held talks with the president and administration officials. The hosts desired economic aid, while their guests offered some aid based on a strong anticommunist stance.[63]

On the third, Nixon journeyed to the Volta Redonda, a giant steel mill started in 1941 with the first major Export Import Bank loan totaling $105,000,000; this project for the Brazilians had emerged as a symbol of the nation's progress and industrialization. Nixon announced that the Eximbank had authorized another $35,000,000 to expand the steel mill's capacity and predicted that the nation was "on the threshold of an era of progress unequalled in the history of any nation in this hemisphere."[64]

Despite the grant and Nixon's public relations efforts, the special relationship between the two states did not materially improve. Kubitschek's government pressed for more money. Ike and Nixon recognized that Brazil needed more capital, but it was not made a priority. The president questioned the need. As a result of this impasse, the amount of support that the Brazilian asked for was not forthcoming. As for the anticommunist theme that the United States hoped for, Kubitschek announced that although he would not recognize the Soviet Union, he would trade with it.[65]

That summer Eisenhower attended a meeting of the American Presidents in Panama to promote hemispheric solidarity. Although nothing major immediately emerged from the conference, the United States, through its president, tried to demonstrate its concern for advancement in the Americas.[66]

Toward the end of the summer, Assistant Secretary Holland decided to resign from his post. He wrote the president: "The period of your administration has been one of great progress in the hemisphere." In economic matters, trade and private investment had increased; the Eximbank had expanded loans and other agencies had provided a greater amount of technical assistance. As for political affairs, the OAS had assumed a larger role in keeping the peace; more Latin American presidents had come to the United States; and the Panama Treaty had been modified to the advantage of that tiny country's nationalistic feelings. Even cultural associations such as educational exchange had accelerated.[67]

Milton Eisenhower later recalled that his brother's role in hemispheric affairs had been underestimated. While at the Panama gathering in 1956, when Ike was unavailable, Milton represented him. The meeting resulted in the appointment of an inter-American organization of presidential representatives; Milton chaired this body, which led to concrete actions later in the Eisenhower presidency. The president's brother realized that the United States had not acceded to everything that the Latin American states desired. He wanted to move toward economic growth and social change that included discarding "the anachronistic social policies . . . inherited from Spain and Portugal." The United States was not responsible for Latin American unwillingness to act boldly; those countries had their own obligations. "Only they can make the social changes," he highlighted, "and their failure to do so must be levied right at them and not the United States."[68]

Nixon concurred with many of Milton's assessments. After his Latin American missions, the vice president not only was more knowledgeable about the region, but the president also used the vice president's firsthand observations in NSC and cabinet meetings. Nixon expanded his influence as the president and the secretary of state gave him more duties that he successfully carried out. Each time he traveled abroad, he enhanced his knowledge through detailed briefings, and at each destination, these were reinforced, modified, refined, and altered. The totality of these activities was having a cumulative effect. Nixon's global perspective was becoming more sophisticated, and he was gaining influence as one of the administration's most knowledgeable foreign policy spokesmen.

13

THE U.S. RESPONSE TO NEUTRALISM

In looking for the origins of President Nixon's restoration of United States relations with China in the early 1970s, many historians search no farther than his October 1967 article in *Foreign Affairs*, "Asia After Viet Nam." But the roots of Nixon's thinking about East Asia go back to his vice presidency. Following his ambitious tour in 1953, Nixon went back to the region in 1956, visiting the Philippines, Taiwan, Indochina, and Pakistan and getting into a disagreement with Jawaharlal Nehru. His coolness toward India and relative warmth toward Pakistan, as well as his China policy, all appear in nascent form on this journey.

During his first term, Eisenhower had grown deeply disturbed that some developing nations were moving toward neutralism. At an informal press conference on June 6, 1956, he declared that while nothing guaranteed peace, "waging peace" was costing the United States $40 billion annually. As for neutrality, the United States had practiced that policy in its early nationhood, but today the term *neutral*, rather than addressing right and wrong, referred only to military alliances.

The next day, through the state department, the president modified his position. The United States championed collective security as embodied by the United Nations and agreed that nations could justifiably be neutral and not intervene in the fate of others. The administration's mutual security program encouraged the independence of emerging nations rather than endangering it as the Soviets did.[1]

That day, June 7, Nixon gave a commencement address at Lafayette College entitled "A Peaceful Crusade for Freedom." The United States, he said, had to meet the challenge of the Soviet Union's "New Look" by mounting a counterattack in the "war for men's minds." The battle was between antagonistic ideologies: a "titanic struggle" of the communists against the democracies. The former had already gained 600 million subjects in Mainland China. Whereas

Stalin had fought wars, his successors preached "peaceful coexistence," and some neutrals found that slogan appealing. As a result, the United States no longer could rely solely on military power but had to expand its exchange programs, increase contact within the Iron Curtain, and engage the newly independent nations. College educators needed to promote travel so that young people would be encouraged to spread the truth about the American way of life around the globe.[2]

In supporting the foreign aid package to developing nations, Secretary Dulles had privately acknowledged that many Asians were hostile to the United States and even saw it as more of a menace than the Soviet Union. He perceived neutrality in black-and-white terms: if it meant opposition to the United States, then neutral states, by definition, sided with the enemy. In a commencement address at Iowa State College on June 9, Dulles called foreign assistance a "peace insurance policy." The United States had budgeted $40 billion a year for security: $36 billion went to military aid and $4 billion to a group of programs, including economic assistance, that went under the heading of "mutual security." Of this, the largest amount, $1.5 billion, went to South Korea, Taiwan, and South Vietnam. The United States allocated $700 million for economic assistance to counteract Soviet propaganda and Soviet economic commitments to developing countries.[3]

Late on the evening before the secretary's speech, Ike was rushed to the hospital for emergency ileitis surgery, and the ground rules for shaping American diplomacy were altered to accommodate the president's recovery. Despite that medical crisis, the president's remarks concerning neutral nations, Nixon's comments dealing with winning the hearts and minds of the uncommitted nations, and Dulles's declaration on the importance of the mutual security program were not accidental. Their messages were directed, in large part, toward the Far East. Early in the summer of 1955, the president had written his brother Milton about undertaking a goodwill mission "to the newly organized democracies" in that region, especially Japan, the Philippines, and South Korea. He also included as possibilities Burma, Indonesia, Ceylon, India, and Pakistan, the nations that had sponsored the Bandung conference.

At the end of March 1956, USIA deputy director Abbott Washburn wrote a memorandum exploring the possibility that the president might attend the tenth anniversary of Philippines Independence in Manila on July 4. Ike had been stationed there for four years, serving on General Douglas MacArthur's staff, before the outbreak of World War II. Washburn held out an added enticement. President Ramón Magsaysay would invite Asian leaders to hear the president give a major foreign policy speech.[4]

Ike's surgery prevented any trip to the Philippines, giving Foster Dulles the opportunity to approach Nixon about attending the celebration. Sherman Adams told the secretary that Ike thought the trip was undesirable and anyone whom the state department was considering representing him at the anniversary celebration had to consult the White House.[5]

The president began to consider sending a delegation with "someone who would be particularly *persona grata* to Magsaysay." He and Nixon had developed a cordial relationship during his 1953 visit, so the vice president appeared the ideal choice. The mission remained in limbo until a week after the president's surgery. Ike briefly met with Nixon and Dulles at Walter Reed Hospital and approved of the trip on the condition that the Philippine government wanted "to put on a good show, making it worthwhile."[6]

Nixon and his wife left for the airport, where they boarded the presidential Super Constellation and arrived in Southern California on the last day of June.[7] From the West Coast, the vice president went to Hawaii. Upon arrival, he stated that he regretted Hawaii had not achieved statehood. As for his speech in Manila, he would touch upon "the whole subject of Asia, the new nations there and the outlook for that part of the world."[8]

After reaching Manila on July 3, Nixon and President Magsaysay discussed American military bases in the Philippines. Attorney General Brownell, two years earlier, had issued a legal opinion that the United States had title to its bases, and Filipino nationalists resented that declaration. After six hours of talks, the Filipino president and American vice president issued a joint statement. The United States would transfer title papers and title claims held by the United States to its military bases. The two nations would negotiate a new agreement founded on Philippine sovereignty that would also apply to their bilateral defensive pact as well as additional land and more personnel. As was the international protocol, sovereignty over diplomatic and consular establishments was exempt.[9]

Magsaysay and his advisers were "immensely pleased" by the agreement. The Filipino president assured the vice president that the land required for base expansion would be allocated. Government officials, according to Nixon, were consumed with local, not international issues. He realized that the titles were a "phony" issue: "The main thing was to assure support for President Magsaysay and to keep his enemies on the run."[10]

With this settlement in hand, Nixon, on July 4, gave his major address in the afternoon at Luneta Park during a summer downpour over a loudspeaker that barely worked. "As I stood looking over the sea of faces of those million and more people that memorable day," he recalled, "I too was proud to be an American and proud to have the privilege of representing my fellow Americans on this never-to-be forgotten occasion."[11]

The core of his message was that the United States and its allies, including the partnership with the Philippines, were combating the Soviet Union, its Eastern European allies, and other communist states. The neutral nations had emerged in the midst of this momentous struggle. Some looked at the American model during its infancy; others practiced neutrality to avoid military conflict; still others used neutrality to gain economic concessions from both democratic and communist governments. Nixon warned those countries that bargained with both blocs took "a fearful risk" in not differentiating the free from the communist orbit. He invoked the old proverb: "He who sups with the devil must have a long spoon." Without pointing directly at Prime Minister Nehru of India, Nixon announced: "The so-called neutralist nations cannot continue to work both sides of the street by accepting American dollars and resources and at the same time cozing [sic] up to the Communists."[12]

Well-regarded columnist David Lawrence called the address the "greatest speech of [Nixon's] career." Others applauded Nixon's efforts. USIA deputy director Washburn proclaimed the address "was the best statement of foreign policy for the area which we have had in many a day." Nixon's Manila journey would provide material for his agency for weeks.[13]

The Sino-Soviet bloc's media generally ignored the speech. The state department recorded: "The general reaction was caustic with a layer of sarcasm but was not acrimonious or abusive, when judged by past Soviet bloc performance." *Izvestia* described the vice president's journey as propaganda for the upcoming American presidential election. The PRC demanded that the United States halt its colonial practices and prevent Chiang Kai-shek from interfering with domestic affairs on Mainland China.[14]

On the last day of his stay, Nixon held a press conference, asserting that United States assistance had "stopped the tide of Communist aggression threatening not only Europe but Asia." A reporter inquired why the American government had not been more conciliatory since the Soviets had taken a more moderate stance. The vice president answered that when Khrushchev and other Kremlin officials stopped "acting like Stalin, we'll have hope for peace in the world."[15]

Nixon's declaration that no nation should be neutral irritated Prime Minister Nehru, who learned about the vice president's address in London at the British Commonwealth prime ministers' conference. When Nehru faced a crowded room of correspondents at India House on July 6, one reporter asked him to comment on what the vice president had said. Nehru responded that the vice president and the secretary of state were "not wise and they do little good." He said he disliked "neutralism" as a term because it was "normally used in wartime." Besides, the world could not "be divided up into good and evil." Nixon and Foster Dulles wished that every nation should behave under their guidelines.[16]

As a result, Nixon's scheduled stop in India was canceled. At a press conference at Karachi airport, the vice president discovered Nehru had inferred that Soviet assistance was "not inconsistent with freedom." Nixon pointed out that the prime minister did not read "history correctly." Aid from Moscow might result in the recipient's becoming a Red satellite: "Soviet aid is given not with strings but with a rope. . . . Any country taking assistance from the Soviet runs almost certain risk of having that rope tied around its neck." That he answered Nehru's complaints from Pakistan, India's arch enemy, only added to the insult.[17]

Not only did Nehru take offense, but a potential Democratic candidate for president, Senator Estes Kefauver, also denounced the vice president for feuding with the prime minister. Kefauver worried that Nixon and Dulles's anti-Indian policies might drive Nehru and other leaders "into more open friendship with the Soviet system."[18]

Early in August, the powerful industrialist Paul Hoffman wrote the Indian ambassador to the United States, G. L. Mehta, that as an American concerned with United States–Indian relations, he was "quite distressed over the misunderstanding which has developed between . . . [Nixon] and Prime Minister Nehru." Hoffman knew that the vice president had championed economic assistance to India and recognized its growing role in international affairs. Despite his "strong views" concerning Nehru's acceptance of Soviet aid, the businessman believed, the vice president was still sympathetic toward India. Hoffman helped resolve the dispute, and Nixon appreciated his efforts to clear up "any misunderstanding which Mr. Nehru might still have."[19]

When Nixon left Manila on the morning of July 8, the friction arising from United States–Indian relations did not affect the next stage of his journey to Saigon. He had stopped in Vietnam during his 1953 mission and had received continual updates on conditions there, including the administration's action to send several hundred troops to consult and train South Vietnamese soldiers. These advisers were barred from participating in combat.[20]

On August 23, 1954, American ambassador in Saigon Donald Heath wrote Nixon that the United States had to halt the spread of communism in Vietnam. The objective would be difficult and would require financial aid and "some very effective, intelligent diplomacy." Ngo Dinh Diem had been elected president and headed "the first truly nationalist government this country has seen since

1949." Heath hoped the French would lend support. Whether or not that happened, the United States would need to act: "In these days to come Asia will be more and more of a problem for us and for the free world." Nixon had observed firsthand what was needed, and the ambassador was pleased that the vice president "had a thorough look-see at Asia and [was] back there back-stopping sound policy toward this rather tormented area."[21]

After landing in inclement weather on July 8, 1956, Nixon met with local officials. Diem had completed his second year as president. At the 1954 Geneva conference, the signers of the accords agreed that national elections would be held in the summer of 1956. Diem balked at that date because Ho Chi Minh would rig elections in the North. Nixon affirmed his government's support for Diem as well as his position against holding elections.[22]

Under these circumstances, Nixon promptly met with Diem who explained his plans for agrarian reform and that he was attempting to transfer acreage from landowners to peasants to accelerate this goal. The result would give land to the poor and weaken communist complaints appealing to dispossessed peasants. Diem pressed for American economic assistance to buy some of the land to implement these changes. United States agencies, however, decided against funding.[23]

The vice president evaluated the South Vietnamese president soon after they met as "a capable leader who has support of the people and who understands communism." Several weeks later, he wrote to Diem that he was "confident that under your courageous leadership your country will continue to go forward in a healthy and prosperous way." The two met again in 1957, when Nixon warmly welcomed Diem to the United States. Two decades later, Nixon reminisced that the United States should have backed Diem rather than permit his assassination.[24]

On the seventh, Nixon visited Chiang Kai-shek and presented a personal letter from Ike in which he pledged steadfast backing. The president understood that communists occasionally changed tactics, but their objective of world domination remained constant.[25]

Chiang met with Nixon again for several hours the next day; he cautioned against any modification of American diplomacy in Asia. Robert Donovan, reporter for the *New York Herald Tribune*, had recently published *Eisenhower: The Inside Story*, which gave the impression that the administration was moving toward a "Two Chinas" concept. Chiang urged the United States against taking this step, and further to isolate Mao: no bilateral trade or cultural exchange. United Nations admission and American recognition were out of the question, Chiang insisted, because "the entire anti-Communist front in Asia will collapse."

If that happened, it might trigger the "domino effect." Nixon agreed with many of these suppositions and, upon his return, lobbied the state department to encourage expanding Taiwanese trade in Southeast Asia.[26]

Next, Nixon briefly stopped in Bangkok[27] and then landed in Karachi, Pakistan. The expected ninety-minute stay lasted for four hours. For half of the time, President Iskander Mirza and Nixon discussed military and economic aid as well as a treaty with the United States. The Pakistanis were anxious about Indian atomic bomb capabilities and infiltration from Afghans using Soviet weapons. Mirza did not anticipate war with his two neighbors; still he wanted the military hardware to protect his borders.[28]

From Karachi, the Nixons flew to Ankara, Turkey. The vice president considered this stop an imperative. In his opinion, the "Turks were certainly among our best allies and could not be permitted to become disenchanted." United States prestige in the Middle East had deteriorated, so the administration had to keep good faith with its friends.[29]

When Nixon deplaned at Ankara airport in the evening on July 9, 1956, his party was met by President Celal Bayer. The Turkish government discussed the Soviet threat to the north and the need for economic assistance. The regime was particularly anxious over the fate of Cyprus, close to its coastline, with a significant Turkish minority. As far as Bayer was concerned, maintaining the status quo under British rule was far preferable to Greek control. Nixon later commented: "the Turks had a positively pathological attitude on the Cyprus problem."[30]

Concluding his seven-nation tour, the Nixons left Turkey on the morning of the tenth and flew to Palma, Majorca. United States ambassador to Spain, John Lodge, welcomed the couple along with the Spanish minister of foreign affairs, Don Alberto Martin Artago, who had played a prominent part in the 1953 United States–Spanish agreements, especially those dealing with American military bases on Spanish soil. Nixon only stayed for several hours; during that interim, he helped to complete the Navy-to-Navy ammunition annex that was signed within the week.[31]

Secretary Dulles and other officials welcomed the party upon its return. The vice president and the secretary drove off to discuss the journey. While they probably discussed the frequent appeals for economic assistance, the House that summer was hotly debating the foreign aid appropriation.[32]

One missing ingredient was the president's active participation. In Nixon's previous trips, Ike briefed the vice president before his departure and debriefed him upon his return. Recovery from stomach surgery, however, limited the president's activity for at least a month. To highlight the extent of Ike's impairment, when Nixon went to see the president on July 12, he only asked for three minutes.[33]

During that Thursday morning at the National Security Council (NSC) meeting, the vice president summarized the results of his trip. Each nation that he had visited had received American military and economic assistance. Some were confused over the United States stance concerning neutralism. The vice president underscored the necessity to be unequivocal in the American stand against communism. "Any doubts about this," he underlined, "particularly doubts in Asia, could have a catastrophic effect on the entire U.S. position." He also commented on the International Cooperation Administration (ICA), a United States agency that handled technological and economic affairs. Nixon reflected the judgment of American ambassadors who supervised ICA personnel and the programs they implemented overseas. Some employees handled their jobs with skill, and others "were altogether useless." The vice president evaluated Nehru's neutralism. The United States, Nixon conceded, had to court the prime minister and concurrently must emphasize "firmly and courteously the difference between accepting assistance from the Communist countries and accepting aid from the United States. If we do not make this clear, our friends will gradually have been nibbled away."[34]

The mission's significance went far beyond press reports of goodwill. Nixon reinforced the American-Filipino and the American-Taiwanese alliances, openly endorsed the direction of Diem's presidency in South Vietnam; and in Thailand, Pakistan, and Turkey, Nixon strengthened their pro-Western bonds. Lastly, when United States–Spanish bargaining over military bases was floundering, the vice president resolved the impasse.

The president, vice president, and secretary of state had made public declarations on the Soviet Union, Asia, and neutralism. In private, their thinking was far more complex, but they did not publicly articulate the more nuanced considerations. If Ike wanted to confuse the media about his positions on these topics, he did. His stilted language was reported verbatim, and many commentators took this presidential charade literally, concluding that this lack of clarity illustrated a failure of presidential leadership. They were fooled. Foster Dulles made headlines with declarations like massive retaliation and brinkmanship, for which critics lambasted him. He, they pronounced, was a dogmatist who did not comprehend the nuances of his diplomatic craft. Adversaries were correct that he embellished some state department declarations bordering on the edge of nuclear holocaust, but they were wrong about his being one-dimensional.[35]

While Ike, Nixon, and Dulles were attacked for their alleged glaring weaknesses, what they said in private, especially at the regular NSC gatherings and in personal correspondence demonstrated that they were far more sophisticated than they were given credit. The president realized that the communist bloc was not a monolith; he pressed for avenues, particularly through trade, to open the Kremlin and its allies to Western influence. Red China, for example, was cloaked in secrecy, and the president hoped to find ways such as opening bilateral trade to determine Mao's real motivations. Dulles, although he sometimes took outrageous positions, was cautious and careful in analyzing diplomatic alternatives. He talked, for example, of massive retaliation, but he and the president recognized the horrors of another world war.

Finally, Nixon, the inflexible anticommunist in public, was far more flexible in private. He had traveled to Asia twice, had talked to a variety of experts, and had witnessed firsthand the vastness of the region. He had absorbed the counsel of the president and his secretary of state, and by the end of the first term, the trio generally agreed upon policy. Although the vice president spoke out against the PRC, he made room for a minute opening for what Mao had to do to join the international community if he stopped his aggression such as the bombardment of Quemoy and Matsu. Inside the NSC, he was less bombastic and realized that the United States needed to establish intercourse with the PRC. Ike's arguments for bilateral trade and Allen Dulles's reminder that the United States had to find some method for the CIA to gain information on Mainland China were convincing to him. Nixon was willing to explore alternatives, but he would not move radically from his public statements until he saw Moscow take positive measures.

Scholars point to Nixon's 1967 *Foreign Affairs* article as the prelude of his presidential diplomacy toward China; they should go further back to the secret discussions on the Far East during Eisenhower's first term. They need to search beyond the obvious and sensational, and examine the private, mountainous NSC records. Ike trained Nixon as an energetic pupil who had begun his education by absorbing the standard policies.

During the first term, Ike had served well as one of Nixon's principal mentors. As president, he viewed his vice president's missions to the Americas and Asia from a military perspective. As Nixon successfully completed each task, the president selected him for another one. From Eisenhower's years in the Army, Nixon had passed the test for usefulness, behaving exemplarily during his foreign missions and contributing what he had learned as a firsthand observer traveling abroad at cabinet and NSC meetings as well as promoting the administration's diplomatic objectives in public.

After Ike's heart attack in September 1955, the vice president and secretary of state forged an intimate friendship. Dulles believed that Nixon had acted above reproach during the president's recovery. The secretary of state, like the president, confided in Nixon and served as a mentor.

These years provided Nixon his start as a hands-on participant in the arena of international diplomacy. Without taking account of his service under Eisenhower and Dulles, the administration's diplomatic maneuvering has not been adequately portrayed, and Nixon's activities in foreign affairs have been minimized. The genesis of his diplomatic training during his vice-presidential tenure, in reality, provided the experience that would later serve him as a foreign policy expert.

14

INCUMBENT POLITICS

For almost seventy years after the Civil War, all but two elected presidents, Cleveland and Wilson, had been Republicans. Then the Great Depression upset the GOP's dominance and relegated it to a distant second place. Republicans had no political strength in the Deep South, and even where they were competitive in the Border States, they sometimes had trouble finding attractive candidates. From the moment Eisenhower became president, he enjoyed a popularity unmatched by any national Republican figure since Herbert Hoover in 1928. Yet he functioned as the party's leader without quite understanding that role.

Congressman Charles Halleck of Indiana, the House majority leader and an avid Eisenhower supporter, called his association with Ike "one of the happiest, greatest experiences of my life." But he noted that "Eisenhower wasn't worth a damn as a politician. He was a great President, but he wasn't a politician."[1]

As president, Ike refused to engage in partisan battles or make personal attacks on his opponents, and he limited his appearances before partisan audiences. He envisioned managing the GOP as he had managed the Army, but he did not understand that many partisans would not simply follow orders. His supporters from Citizens for Eisenhower were precisely that; they adored their military hero but were not especially committed to the Republican Party. Most Republican activists, on the other hand, were followers of Senator Taft and his Fortress America, small-government principles. They viewed Ike with suspicion; he was not one of them.

Ike, for his part, realized that the GOP needed to increase its base if it were to regain majority status, and he hoped to encourage the Citizens for Eisenhower-Nixon, some supportive Democrats, and independents to take an active role in promoting Republican candidates. Party regulars, who composed the overwhelming majority of Republican volunteers manning offices and answering telephones during off-year elections, were suspicious of these outsiders. The Citizens groups jelled to support Ike, but their allegiance did not necessarily transfer to other Republican candidates.[2]

Ike did not know how to bring the Citizen groups inside the GOP. It would take a time-consuming effort, and as president he had other priorities. In the spring of 1953, he and Republican National Committee (RNC) chairman Len Hall decided that Ike would not campaign nationwide the following year. He would be sixty-four years old, he had a full schedule as chief executive, and he did not wish to endanger his health with an exhausting series of campaign appearances. He would give several television addresses, but they would not necessarily be partisan.

Ike's approval ratings averaged just over 69 percent during his first year in office. During the first nine months of 1954, they ranged from 61 to 71 percent. Despite his overwhelming and sustained approval, the image of the GOP slowly fell in 1954 as the Army-McCarthy hearings came to their notorious end. Omitting the South, in February, Republicans were favored 53 to 47 percent over Democrats; by August, the national poll gave the Democrats a 52 to 48 percent edge over the GOP.[3]

By the end of the first year, Eisenhower was successfully addressing both his domestic and foreign policy priorities. In foreign affairs, he ended the Korean War with an armistice and announced his support for America's global commitments by maintaining United States troops in Western Europe and pledging to defend American interests in Asia. On the domestic front, he moved to stop deficient spending and toward a balanced budget. By expanding Social Security, he also calmed New Dealers' anxieties that he would reverse FDR's social programs.

But the president's coattails did not transfer to the Republican candidates in the 1953 special elections. Democrats won congressional seats in Wisconsin's ninth and New Jersey's eighth districts, while Republican Glenard Lipscomb won the twenty-forth district in California. The GOP also lost the governor races in Virginia and New Jersey.[4]

Nixon's background and outlook differed from the president's. When he left the Navy at the end of World War II, he was uncertain how to use his legal training until the Committee of 100, a group of Republican volunteers in his congressional district, asked him if he would be interested in running for the House of Representatives. He jumped at the chance, interviewed, and was endorsed by the group. He won his district in 1946 and was overwhelmingly reelected two years later. He then ran for the United States Senate in 1950, and once more won an impressive victory. By then, he had become a confident professional politician. He had started at the district level and progressed to the national stage. Unlike Ike, who was begged to run, Nixon energetically campaigned to sell himself.[5]

Nixon realized that turning the GOP into the majority would take a concerted year-round effort. Just after the inauguration, he affirmed that one of his primary tasks was getting more Republicans elected to Congress the following year, to preserve and, if possible, expand the GOP's thin majority. By late summer, he planned on having a major role in the election. On September 14, 1953, he asked California party activists to supply more information, especially from grassroots feedback, to help him prepare for the state contests.[6]

Many Republicans, aware of the 1953 losses, rushed to have Nixon speak in their states to generate enthusiasm for the next election cycle. At the end of November, Undersecretary of Commerce Walter Williams urged the vice president to come to Seattle that following February. In December, Iowa state chairman and national GOP committeeman Jim Schramm wrote to Len Hall, "Everyone out here wants to hear Nixon." Peter Howard, a Republican activist in Northern California, hoped Nixon would address the Alameda County Republican fundraising dinner to send Senator Thomas Kuchel and Congressman John Allen back to Capitol Hill: "Your presence at this affair," he wrote Nixon, "would be of enormous value in keeping this second largest population center in California, registered predominantly Democratic, in the Republican ranks."[7]

When the Gallup Poll took the first "enthusiasm quotient" of the vice president (meaning the number of people who held him in high regard) in January 1954, the quotient stood at 30.8 percent. Part of the positive response came because the vice president regularly interacted with the public. Individuals who had not seen him for years were flattered when the vice president, who had a phenomenal memory for names, addressed them by theirs. He regularly had photographs taken with supporters.[8]

Speaking before the RNC on February 5, 1954, Nixon began to test themes for the fall elections. If the GOP divided along liberal and conservative lines, he said, Republicans would be defeated. Eisenhower had dismantled "Trumanism" (the term used by the GOP and others to deride the previous administration's failures) and made appointments on the basis of honesty, efficiency, and loyalty. His commitment to free enterprise had ended the drift toward socialism. Abroad, the United States had established "peace with honor"; Secretary Dulles was doing a "splendid job."[9]

Six days later, the vice president spoke at a Lincoln Day Dinner in Connecticut before 4,000 Republican partisans. On the cold, clear night on the hundredth anniversary of the founding of the Republican Party, Nixon rallied his audience: first, if the party lost in the upcoming campaign, that would be "a slap at President Eisenhower and his program"; and second, Democrats would build on that defeat to oppose the president's reelection campaign in 1956. The GOP had to come together and embrace independent and Democratic voters under the Republican banner.[10]

Throughout the spring, Nixon continued to speak and raise money for Republican hopefuls. He constantly stressed the need to reelect a Republican Congress to back Eisenhower. Democrats claimed they supported the president, the vice president said, but many Democratic senators and congressmen had opposed the president's legislative initiatives—for instance, on moving toward a balanced budget and limiting the expansion of social welfare programs.[11]

On June 10, 1954, Nixon wrote in his diary that Ike was not "as free and easy" as he had been in his first year. He sensed that the president "was almost resigned to do the best he could and . . . had determined in his mind that he was not going to be interested in keeping the job anyway."[12] Just days later, his opinion changed. He and the president left the White House Sunday morning to play a round of golf. Ike, "in a very good humor," declared that he would not campaign vigorously in the fall because he did not believe "it was wise to go on a barnstorming political trip." He was sixty-three years old, and even though his physician said that he was in "fine health" for his age, "he just needed more rest than he previously had required."[13]

Several days later, they discussed Ike's political skills. *Time* magazine had noted that one of Eisenhower's greatest strengths was his ability to present his proposals in a nonpartisan manner. Ike hoped that both he and Nixon "would continue not to speak in a purely partisan way" on issues important to the campaign. The vice president had successfully used that technique in his California races and planned to do so again.[14]

At this time, according to Nixon's diary, Ike told the vice president that he did not need a scheduled appointment and should feel free to come into the Oval Office any time if he had an issue to discuss. The president had a "standing rule that anybody who had something that he considered important should have the right to walk in." He said that Nixon "was the most detached political observer in his organization and that he wanted to have complete consultation at all times." That was the reason that he kept Nixon thoroughly briefed and had him attend all White House meetings: "so that [Nixon] could make as great a contribution as possible on the political side in both selling the program and advising the Administration on political problems."[15]

Nixon then sparked a political firestorm. On the evening of June 26 at a Republican fundraiser in Milwaukee, Wisconsin, that had been widely advertised and assured approximately $300,000 in revenue, he first preached unity to a cheering partisan audience: "If the Republican Party is to continue to be a great party, its members must be united on fundamental principles which transcend the differences we have." Then he launched into an assault on the Truman administration's failures in Asia. Truman had not recognized the communist threat in that region, and as a consequence "the Acheson policy was directly responsible for the loss of China." Without that "loss," the United States would not have had to fight the Korean War and would not face a crisis in Indochina. The Eisenhower-Dulles diplomacy of strength was correcting the previous administration's mistakes.

Nixon turned to domestic concerns, praising the current administration for adopting a free enterprise approach that had stopped the two previous Democratic presidents' momentum toward socialism. Under Truman, taxes and inflation were high, and price controls remained in place. Ike had lowered taxes, stopped inflation, and removed price controls. Whereas the Democrats did not recognize the domestic communist conspiracy, the Republican government was actively working with FBI director Hoover to halt subversion. Finally, said Nixon, the president had instituted "a new moral climate" in the federal bureaucracy. For these reasons, the GOP had to unite to continue to give the president a Republican congressional majority.[16]

Wisconsin Republicans were overjoyed. Governor Walter Kohler commended Nixon "for a job well done." Congressman John Byrnes, from the eighth district, declared that he had done "a magnificent job." The audience was energized, Byrnes declared, and the vice president had "provided the stimulant needed to secure the unity of purpose among Wisconsin Republicans which is so badly needed." He predicted that the speech might become the keynote for the upcoming races. Daniel Gainey, a strong backer of Citizens for Eisenhower-Nixon and a member of the RNC leadership, wrote Secretary of Commerce Sinclair Weeks that he thought Nixon had delivered "one of the most resounding, coherent, aggressive, political speeches I have ever listened to." To underline his sentiment, he sent Weeks a copy: "Every man and woman in the audience left the meeting filled with a new point of view, fight, and determination for G.O.P. victory in November."[17]

New York Times columnist James Reston was less impressed. The vice president, he wrote, had squandered the prestige he had acquired on his 1953 foreign mission by taking such an aggressively partisan tone. Secretary Dulles was trying to formulate a bipartisan foreign policy, despite loaded phrases like "the loss of China" that undercut that effort, and he still sought backing from Democrats. The secretary, Reston suggested, was "not eager to see his future problems complicated by a partisan argument."[18]

Dulles expressed his own concerns. Two days after the speech, he told Eisenhower that Senator Lyndon Johnson was "sore" about it. Dulles recommended that either he or the president explain to the vice president "speeches of this sort do not help bipartisanship." Ike replied that he did not think Nixon meant to dampen the cooperative spirit. Whatever the intent, the secretary answered, the president should have a word with Nixon.[19]

Later that day, Ike dictated a letter to Nixon. He said he understood "the impulse—particularly before a partisan audience—to lash out at our political opponents," especially when there was good cause. Yet in foreign relations, where he was "constantly working to produce a truly bipartisan approach, . . . keeping up attacks against Acheson and the others will . . . hamper our efforts." Then he decided not to send the letter. Instead, the president sent a note asking the vice president to come to see him when he had "a little time."[20]

After a late afternoon meeting the next day, Ike asked the vice president to remain in the Oval Office, and afterwards wrote a memorandum of their discussion. The president said that he was concerned about Nixon's "castigation" of Acheson's diplomacy. Secretary Dulles, he said, was trying to strike a bipartisan tone, and one Democrat had stated that members of his party were "smarting" at Nixon's address. The vice president replied that he had not attacked Democrats, only Acheson, but that he would omit any reference to him in the future. His remarks had been intended to distance the current administration from the previous one. The president replied that while some Democrats had disagreed with Acheson during his tenure, "today they feel that any criticism of him reflects in some degree upon them."

Nixon stressed that Acheson's own bipartisanship applied only to Europe and the Marshall Plan, not to Asia, a region that he had generally ignored. Eisenhower, Dulles, and the late Arthur Vandenberg, Republican senator from Michigan, championed the bipartisan spirit, and had criticized Truman's diplomacy in Asia. Ike agreed that the United States had indeed "lost China" through the state department's insistence that Chiang Kai-shek include communists in his regime. But he specifically objected to McCarthy's phrase, "20 years of treason."

That accusation flung at Democrats was "indefensible," and Nixon should never imply anything similar during his speeches.[21]

Nixon, in his diary, recorded his own interpretation of the conversation. He and Ike had had an "extremely friendly" talk in which he said that his address had laid out the facts from political and judicial standpoints. When the president asked whether the attack on Acheson would continue, Nixon replied: "We direct our fire against the opposition so as to heal the wounds in our Party."[22]

The next morning, at a staff session to prepare for a press conference several hours later Ike and his advisers agreed that he "must vigorously defend Nixon from Democratic attack." Several members of the "left-wing press," staffers warned, would try to trip him up. At the conference, Edward Folliard of the *Washington Post* asked Eisenhower whether Nixon was blaming Acheson "for the loss of China," the Korean conflict, and the Indochina crisis. The president answered that everyone was entitled to his own opinion. Although he had not read the speech, he admired and respected Nixon. As president, he was pushing for cooperation in foreign affairs and might have said something different himself, but he was not disturbed "too much" and remained in close contact with the vice president. They usually agreed, and "I wouldn't try to excommunicate him from the party if I were you. [Laughter]." Afterward, press secretary Hagerty called Nixon with a full report; Ike wanted to be certain that the reporters did not "distort anything he said." Nixon "was very pleased."[23]

Democrats were not. One reporter at the press conference noted that House minority leader Sam Rayburn, in a speech on the floor, had said that Nixon's address threatened the spirit of cooperation and warned if anyone else made that type of speech, bipartisanship would cease. Nixon's address, Rayburn said, made "the blood of some of us boil." Democratic senator J. William Fulbright from Arkansas agreed that Nixon's assault would end cooperation in foreign affairs. Adlai Stevenson, speaking in Denver on the evening of July 3, claimed the vice president "seemed to have achieved an all-time high of irresponsibility."[24]

The vice president, no stranger to partisan warfare, wrote privately to Governor Kohler on July 9 that the speech had "kicked up a little storm! I feel, however, that our Republicans needed a shot in the arm and that in the long run controversy over whether the Acheson policy was good or bad will be more helpful to our cause than harmful." A week later, he wrote George Nagle, Republican finance committee chairman in Iowa: "The speech stirred up a lot of reaction from our Left Wing friends, but I think that indicates that they were hurt by it!"[25]

Merriman Smith, dean of the White House press corps and a reporter for United Press, corrected the impression that Ike and Nixon were at odds. Smith wrote in August that Ike's staff was "amused and a little astonished at the effort of someone in New York to spread a story that the President and Vice-President Richard M. Nixon are miffed at each other." An unidentified reporter alleged that the president refused to see his vice president except at cabinet meetings. Smith supplied a corrective. The two men saw each other at cabinet, NSC, and legislative meetings. Ike met with Nixon possibly more than anyone in the cabinet, with the exception of Secretary Dulles. Recently the president and Nixon had had lunch, and they had played golf on several occasions.[26]

Still, the clash between Ike and Nixon over his Milwaukee address graphically illustrated their fundamental differences. The president listened to everyone, including Democrats who were angry at the attack on Truman-Acheson diplomacy. For John Foster Dulles, Nixon's remarks created an impediment. But the president also heard from Republicans who were at the event and relayed to Ike how well it was received. Then there was Nixon's own perception: he had not questioned bipartisanship itself but only criticized Acheson's failed initiatives in Asia, a critique with which many Republicans concurred, and he appreciated, possibly more than Eisenhower did, that appealing to the party's base before the midterm elections would help Ike advance his agenda with the new Congress. Nixon was far more sensitive to the Republican base and understood its hot-button issues. Eisenhower felt that he did not owe the Republican Party; it owed him.

Nixon owed the party his political success. He had been elected four times to three different offices because Republican leaders had helped him attract Republican voters. Ike and Nixon would view the 1954 campaign from very different perspectives. The president watched the contests and then decided how to react. The vice president plunged into the fight, righteously campaigning for his party.

THE ILL-WILL TOUR VERSUS THE BIG LIE

Even though Nixon had not completed his campaign arrangements when Congress adjourned on September 10, 1954, he held a precampaign kickoff breakfast five days later.[1] His campaign stops followed a fixed routine. After the itinerary was mimeographed, no changes were possible. Anyone who wanted alterations before that had to discuss them with Murray Chotiner, the vice president's campaign manager, or the appropriate advance man. Upon landing, the vice president left the plane first, followed by candidates on board, reporters, VIP guests, and finally the staff. After local dignitaries greeted him, he held press interviews, usually at the air terminal and occasionally at a hotel. He then did newspaper, radio, and television interviews. When those were completed, the police escorted him to his venue. Since he was not the one running for office, there were no parades or convertibles with tops down. Only one person rode with him in his car. Before his address, he would have analyzed each candidate's resume and spent at least a half hour reviewing it so that he could sound extemporaneous when he mentioned details on the platform with him. He spoke for twenty or thirty minutes; handshaking and personal greetings were discouraged because of his tight schedule. This procedure was repeated five or six times daily, with the largest gatherings in the evening. Between campaign swings, he returned to the capital and spent a day in his office.[2]

The pace was hectic. Late in the evening, after the vice president finished his public appearances, he dictated his addresses to his secretary Rose Mary Woods since he had no speechwriters. She shared her frantic schedule with Ann Whitman, the president's private secretary: "We have been typing and assembling speech excerpts on the plane and have a great time!" Woods averaged four or five hours of sleep a night and seemed "to leave the hotel every morning at dawn!" The pace, she believed, "was even more rugged than the one in '52." One break was mandatory. Since the vice president was a devout baseball fan, no afternoon meetings were permitted during World Series telecasts.[3]

Nixon gave his first major speech before the Republican state convention in Columbus, Ohio, a critical state for the GOP. Besides providing local candidates such as Congressman Frank Bow with media exposure and an endorsement, Nixon told the party faithful attending the convention to press for a large turnout. If the Democrats won control of Congress, they would try to torpedo Ike's programs and prepare to defeat his reelection bid in 1956.[4] Nixon would return to Ohio in early October, appearing in Toledo, Cleveland, and Akron.[5]

He traveled on to Topeka, Kansas, where he met GOP 1936 presidential nominee Alfred Landon and addressed an afternoon rally on an extremely hot day. That evening, he appeared at the Wichita Forum, where 3,500 listened to his call for reelecting a Republican congressional majority. Ike and his Eighty-Third Congress had established a good record, and if control of Congress changed, "Trumanism" would resurface, returning the United States to the path of socialism.[6]

The heat followed his entourage to Missouri where Nixon plugged the reelection of Congressman Jeffrey Hillelson. Roscoe Hobbs, chairman of the GOP's state finance committee, was overjoyed. Nixon's presence helped raise money. The event, in Hobbs's view, "was a howling success."[7] Nixon then stopped in Huron, South Dakota, where he endorsed the reelection of Senator Karl Mundt and Congressman Harold Lovre while dodging the sensitive farm recession. Local headlines focused on how the administration was kicking out communists and their fellow travelers from the federal payrolls by the thousands.[8]

From September 20 until September 25, he continued his whirlwind pace. On Monday, he took a DC-3 from Grand Island to Bellevue and on to Omaha, Nebraska, where he filmed a television spot for the Community Chest and attended an evening rally.[9] He returned to Minneapolis and Duluth the following day and then headed for Michigan. That evening, in front of 4,000 people in East Lansing, Nixon rejected Adlai Stevenson's allegations that the administration had been responsible for an "alarming deterioration of our world position." Stevenson criticized United States foreign policy, Nixon said, but offered no constructive alternatives; he had not even taken positions on the conflicts in Korea and Indochina. Stevenson and the Americans for Democratic Action, the vice president charged, "set class against class, farmer against city dweller, worker against employer." As for civil rights, Ike had done more in his two years in office than Democratic presidents had accomplished in two decades.[10]

Rose Mary Woods admitted that the address was "a pretty slashing attack on Stevenson," with controversial statements included in an effort "to get rid of the apathy in the campaign." Nixon wrote presidential adviser Harold Stassen that the speech "was necessary to call Stevenson on some of his rather reckless innuendoes." Dave Kendall, a local Republican National Committee (RNC) committeeman, thought the party could win the state: "Our only real enemies are time and apathy. The first can be overcome by hard work and the second by an intelligent approach."[11]

Late in the afternoon on Friday, Nixon telephoned presidential aide Bernard Shanley. The GOP, he insisted, needed a spark "to fire up the organization and get them off their doffs, which they weren't doing." He had decided to concentrate in Republican strongholds, to get out their vote, and "not to work in the strong Democrat areas to stir them up." In this off-year election, the question was which major party could get out the largest percentage of its "hard core."[12]

The vice president moved on to Boston, where he told a press conference that "the McCarthy issue was beaten to death before the censure action was taken," and then ended his trip in New Hampshire, where he rallied party loyalists at the Republican state convention.[13]

Eisenhower closely monitored Nixon's movements from his summer residence in Denver and wrote a "Dear Dick" letter on September 22, saying that four influential Oklahomans had come to see him about having the vice president visit their state and campaign for Republican Fred Mock for senator. Despite the vice president's heavy commitments, Ike suggested that he consider the request. Ike himself would make just four speeches, two formal presidential addresses and two campaign events. He dreaded "the motorcades. I fear that I am getting a little old for this sort of thing."[14]

Despite those complaints, the following evening the president flew to Los Angeles, where he addressed a sympathetic audience at the Hollywood Bowl. His administration had stopped corrupt practices and now the American people had "clean government." He had reduced the budget and ended the war in Korea; the United States now enjoyed prosperity without war. Many international trouble spots like Iran, Suez, and Guatemala had been defused. As for domestic subversion, "security risks have been removed from sensitive positions." For these and many other reasons, the electorate should return a Republican Congress.[15]

A few days after the speech, United Nations representative Lodge wrote the president about a possible Democratic attack on the GOP's "isolationist and reactionary wing." The party had to abandon that faction, he said, and instead publicize the administration's accomplishments. Campaign speeches needed to contain "just enough cleverly contrived thrusts at the Democrats to give the speech a little mustard. But these thrusts . . . must be so shrewdly worded that they will be believable to *rank and file Democrats and independents*." Without divulging the author, Eisenhower forwarded these suggestions to Nixon because he was "speaking in more states than almost any other person."[16]

Before the end of September, Ike wrote the vice president: "Good reports have been reaching me from all parts of the country as a result of your intensive—and I am sure exhaustive—speaking tour." Having read excerpts from Nixon's attack on Stevenson, the president understood why many people were so enthusiastic about the vice president's appearances. Ike admitted that he not only had not reduced Nixon's official obligations but also was "constantly suggesting other places for you to visit. . . . These burdens I impose upon you [are] the penalty for being such an excellent and persuasive speaker."[17]

At a Democratic fundraising dinner in Indianapolis in mid September, Stevenson described how Republicans like Governor Dewey, Attorney General Brownell, and Nixon had defamed Democrats, including Harry Truman and Dean Acheson. While mocking Nixon for allegedly advising GOP candidates to avoid issues and debates, Stevenson expressed confidence that voters would exercise sound judgment. America, he said, had "already made its decision on those demagogues who rely on defamation, deceit, and double-talk." He prayed that his party would "recognize and respect the difference between cynical politics and principles, between ruthless partisanship and patriotism" and called for an honest debate between the parties. Democrats would "not be guilty of sowing discord, mistrust, and hate in this lovely land." Under those wholesome circumstances, voters would decide "on the merits."[18]

Eleanor Roosevelt labeled Nixon "a clever campaigner" who attacked Truman as if he were the issue. Instead of swallowing this ploy, she said, Americans should carefully analyze and examine the vice president's statements and the administration's record. Stephen Mitchell, chairman of the Democratic National Committee (DNC) was far less circumspect, accusing Nixon of an "outright lie" regarding the number of communists the administration had removed from the federal government. Senator Olin Johnson, Democrat from South Carolina, demanded the vice president prove his allegations that thousands of subversives employed by the Truman administration had employed had since been fired.[19]

As the political rhetoric grew hotter, Nixon set out on the second swing of his travels. He endorsed local candidates in Troy, New York, on September 29 and Wilmington, Delaware, on the thirtieth.[20] Then he flew to New Jersey to campaign with the party's senatorial nominee, Congressman Clifford Case, who was in a tight race. In late summer, Case had discussed his contest with Nixon at the White House and asked the vice president to campaign for him. The president and others enthusiastically backed Case. Douglas Dillon, the American ambassador to France, wrote Ike on September 1, urging him to visit New Jersey. If that was impossible, Dillon hoped that Secretary of the Treasury Humphrey would go. A week later, the president wrote that he had "tried to help Clifford Case in a number of ways; I am, of course, most anxious to see him in the Senate." While Ike did not travel to New Jersey, Humphrey did visit on October 20. Case would eventually win the election by the closest margin in the state's history.[21]

Nixon campaigned with Case for eight hours. They landed at Caldwell-Wright Airport and appeared at a garden party in Montclair on a terribly hot afternoon before a crowd of 2,000. Aware that the state GOP had split over the congressman's "liberal" record, the vice president called for unity, emphasizing that Case had helped in the fight against communists while Stevenson provided the "quips and criticisms" and DNC chairman Mitchell used "smear and fear."[22]

The vice president moved on to Norwalk, Connecticut, for another round of endorsements and speeches, and then flew to Lexington, Kentucky, where John Sherman Cooper was battling former vice president Alben Barkley for the Senate. Nixon called for a Cooper triumph and claimed he was "confident we are on the way to victory on November." Cooper lost.[23]

In the midst of campaigning, Nixon wrote RNC publicity director James Bassett that he should look at the attacks on Ike and himself by prominent Democrats like Stevenson and Truman: "it might be to our advantage to answer." The GOP should make note of sparse attendance at Democratic rallies and the opposition's limited financial resources, and Bassett should inform "friendly newspaper men who will use it." Republicans had to do a better job of feeding these stories to favorable columnists so that they could hammer the ADA and promote a Republican Congress: "The fault lies directly on us for failing to pay attention to them and give them material that they can use." Nixon especially wanted the party to release figures on the security risks who had been removed from federal posts.[24]

Nixon went to Iowa on October 5. Robert Goodwin, RNC committeeman from Des Moines, considered the vice president's appearance critical because GOP apathy was the worst he had ever encountered: "There's getting to be a lot of chiefs out here and the number of indians are dwindling." Nixon had received great press, television and radio coverage, and the party faithful hoped that would stimulate the state ticket, particularly Congressman Thomas Martin, who was challenging two-term senator Guy Gillette; Martin upset the incumbent.[25]

The next day, Nixon dictated a memorandum on the state of the campaign. "If we lose," he forecast, "it will be only because of division and apathy in our own organization and by failing to adopt the correct strategy for the campaign." Voter turnout was crucial. Republicans should emphasize the administration's achievements, minimize its failures, concentrate on their strongholds, and avoid stirring up Democrats. The party should not send him to speak in heavily Democratic districts where the chance of winning was remote.[26]

He conferred with the president in Denver. They played golf in the afternoon, and later the vice president told the press that he regretted Stephen Mitchell's characterization of him as a liar. He did not want to return to Trumanism where "the Communist danger was ignored and underestimated." The vice president introduced Ike to a national television audience on October 7. The president endorsed Nixon's role in the campaign and told his listeners that if they did not vote Republican, the nation would get a "cold war of partisan politics." Rather than campaign on the stump, the president said he would make three television speeches before the election.[27]

Governor Dewey had urged the president to take a more active part in the various contests. Ike replied after his broadcast that he did not think that any president could "pass that popularity on to a Party or to an individual." Intelligent candidates would attract their own loyalists. Besides, he was sixty-four years old and could not both carry out his executive duties and participate in an extended speaking regime. He notified RNC chairman Hall that the upcoming races were not a vote of confidence for him but were about local candidates and their issues. Ike's brother Edgar reinforced these convictions. Presidential oratory, Edgar reasoned, would not win the election. Republicans had to "get out and see that their supporters are actually taken to the polls to vote."[28]

One presidential appointee embarrassed the administration in the midst of the campaign. During a press conference in Detroit on October 11, Charles Wilson, who led General Motors during the Truman presidency, defended his practices as secretary of defense. Some Democrats suggested that new defense contracts be earmarked for the regions of high unemployment. Wilson balked, saying that jobs went where the appropriate technology existed and that he "had a lot of sympathy for the jobless in labor surplus areas but he always respected bird dogs more than Kennel dogs, . . . one who'll go out and hunt for food, rather than sit on his fanny and yelp."

Democrats demanded his resignation. To calm the outrage, the White House released a statement that the secretary's remarks had been exaggerated and that the president had never found Wilson "in the slightest degree indifferent to human misfortune." This testimonial did not prevent Democrats from seizing upon Wilson's tasteless analogy. Nixon later acknowledged that the "bird dog" quote followed the GOP for the rest of the campaign.[29]

While Ike was bemoaning Wilson's miscue, Nixon headed for New Mexico to support Governor Edwin Mecham, who had written to the vice president in mid August, extolling his "great popularity throughout" the state. During Nixon's visit, he praised the governor's clean record. Mecham appreciated this endorsement, saying Nixon had "provided convincing, clinching voting reasons for those of our citizens who had been sitting on the fence." But he did not get enough voters off the fence. Mecham lost his reelection bid.[30]

From there, the vice president moved on to his native state, where, of course, he endorsed the Republican slate. He immediately confronted apathy and insufficient fundraising, but the party temporarily halted its internal bickering to present a united front. Between October 10 and 13, Nixon attended the Fisherman's Fiesta in San Pedro, urged Congressman Oakley Hunter's reelection in Fresno, stopped in Santa Barbara and Salinas, called Earl Warren, "a great Chief Justice," and finished his tour with a new barb for the opposition. He christened Stevenson and Mitchell "Doom-o-crats" because they had predicted a Republican recession, whereas the year was ending with prosperity. They pushed the nation to the left, but Eisenhower had halted that trend: "two more years of the Truman policies would have taken us straight down the road that leads to Socialism."[31]

He traveled to Richmond, California, for a fundraiser for Martinez attorney John Baldwin, who was challenging the incumbent Congressman Robert Condon in the heavily Democratic sixth district. Truman's softness on communism, he said, had led to the fall of Mainland China and caused the Korean conflict. Under Eisenhower, according to the Civil Service Commission, 6,926 security risks had left the government.[32]

Nixon returned to California on October 24, announcing that Condon had actively associated with communists and that the Atomic Energy Commission had banned him from witnessing secret atomic tests—the only congressman thus designated. He must either clear his name, the vice president insisted, or resign from the ticket. Three days later, Nixon added based on FBI reports that the Navy had denied Condon access to "classified naval installations," in a district with many military bases. He was the only congressman in American history "whose participation in Communist activities has been so extensive that he in effect has been designated a security risk." The Democratic Party should repudiate him, Nixon said, and its failure to do so represented "the same blindness and ignorance we saw in the old Truman red herring days."[33]

The vice president released a statement that none of the state's Democratic contenders had repudiated Condon while the Republicans had. Baldwin defeated Condon by around 2,000 votes, and the victor praised the vice president's actions: "Your work in the District on that day stimulated many of our Republicans to get out and go to work, and this helped tremendously in the final outcome."[34]

Nixon finished his California tour with radio and television coverage at San Mateo High School on October 29 before 1,200, with the former child movie star Shirley Temple at his side. About half way through the address, James Heavey yelled out from the balcony: "Tell us a dog story, Dick." Before local police could escort Heavey to the exit, the vice president asked that he not be removed. After Nixon completed his address, Heavy left his seat and walked briskly toward the stage, where the police and Secret Service agents blocked his way. With the microphones and cameras off, Nixon berated Heavey for his heckling and reminded him of the Democratic goon squads that hounded him during the 1950 senatorial race. After the vice president finished his tongue lashing, he told the police: "Now, throw him out."[35]

Seventy percent of California's registered voters went to the polls on Election Day. Even though registered Democrats outnumbered Republicans by about 750,000, Governor Goodwin Knight and Senator Thomas Kuchel won easily. The congressional distribution did not change: nineteen Republicans and eleven Democrats returned to the House.[36]

The vice president's last stop on his second swing was a speech before the Retail Druggists Association in Houston on October 14. During this talk he did not mention any statewide candidate, possibly in consideration of Texas's Democratic governor Allan Shivers, who was seeking reelection. He and Nixon had become friends since the governor came out for Ike in the 1952. To show his appreciation, Nixon gave the Republican governor of Colorado, Dan Thorton, a $100 check to send quietly to the Shivers reelection fund so the Texan would not be embarrassed "in a Democratic primary if any publicity were given to the fact that he was receiving contributions from Republicans."[37]

Stevenson's opinion of Nixon did not mirror Shivers's. On October 2, the Democratic spokesman called the vice president "the most eloquent gloom and doom prophet in America today." Eight days later, when asked to comment on the vice president's allegation that the Democrats had no constructive alternative to the administration's decisions, Stevenson flashed a smile and said he was reminded of a juror who told a neighbor: "I don't want to listen to the evidence. I like to make up my own mind."[38]

At a rally in San Francisco on October 16, Stevenson peppered his speech with jabs against the vice president: "Mr. Nixon expresses his views on foreign policy and everything else, freely and frequently, and changes them in the same manner." As the administration spokesman in foreign affairs, he prevented bipartisanship: "This I understand is known as the smile and smear technique of campaigning. The President smiles while the Vice President smears." Electing a Democratic Congress would end right-wing domination in favor of moderation and cooperation from Democrats, who would work for national unity.[39]

Democrats had reason for concern. The October 4 Gallup Poll found 48 percent of voters favoring the GOP while 52 percent approved of the Democrats. That was too close. DNC chairman Mitchell stood firm in his accusation that Nixon lied about the number of federal employees fired from their posts due to subversive activities; Mitchell took the charge personally because the vice president's message was that Democrats were soft on communists, or worse. He pronounced that the Republican Party had switched from McCarthy to Nixon as the "chief slanderer" of Democrats.[40]

Fletcher Knebel, in his column "Potomac Fever," sarcastically observed: "Democrats accused Vice President Nixon of using the 'big lie' method. Nobody is sure which hurts your opponent more in politics, lying about them—or telling the truth about them."[41]

Before Nixon started his final campaign swing, he altered his schedule to add stops in the West, where there was a chance to elect a senator in Nevada. He also considered trips to Montana, New Mexico, Wyoming, Colorado, or Iowa, wherever the races were "closest and a last minute pitch might be helpful."[42] A day before the trip began, he met with Ike at the White House for fifty minutes and later told reporters that the campaign would be won or lost in the last two weeks: "To put it bluntly, this is a campaign which cannot be won by the Left-Wing Democratic opposition. But it can be lost by Republicans and those moderate Democrats who supported President Eisenhower just two years ago, if they fail to organize and get the voters to the polls."[43]

On Tuesday, October 19, Nixon toured Pennsylvania with his wife. In Philadelphia they attended a $50 a plate luncheon that raised $50,000. That night, in Pittsburgh, they went to a $100 a plate dinner and raised $300,000. Pat commented: "not bad for a day's work!!" Six-term Congressman James Corbett thanked the husband and wife team. He won even though Pennsylvania went for the Democratic governor by a majority of 279,000.[44]

The vice president spent two days in Illinois stumping for conservative Joseph Meeks, who was trying unsuccessfully to oust incumbent Democratic senator Paul Douglas. Douglas stated that he had supported Ike, but Nixon rejected that claim; Douglas had backed Truman and the ADA. Nixon also angrily denounced the Democrats for a "vicious whispering campaign" against the president and his secretary of state that they favored the Arabs over the Israelis in the Middle East. The administration, he said, was searching for a just peace for both sides.[45]

After the Illinois stop, Nixon awoke early on October 22 and took a Convair to Montana to promote five-term Congressman Wesley D'Ewart's race against incumbent senator James Murray. The president was upset that the senator had posed for a personal photograph with Ike and used it in a campaign advertisement. During his address, Nixon reflected Ike's feelings by chiding Murray for having the worst voting record on the administration's proposals.[46]

In Montana, Nixon proclaimed that he had decided to take "the gloves off" on left-wing Democrats who had "been sniping at J. Edgar Hoover and the President's security program." He charged that the Communist Party had infiltrated the Democratic Party, and they were cooperating to defeat Republican candidates. He did not imply that all Democrats were communists and even praised some as great Americans, "but," as Montana's Democratic senator Mike Mansfield recalled, "it's the implication in speeches like that which convey the impression." Mansfield also held that Nixon played "the number racket" to attack Democrats as soft on communism. To demonstrate his own anticommunist credentials and sounding very much like McCarthy, the senator said that "if there is one Communist in the service of the government of the United States, it is one Communist too many."[47]

During the last full week of campaigning, Nixon raced nonstop. He spent the morning of October 24 moving from Phoenix to Salt Lake City, where he responded to Stevenson's quip that the vice president had emerged as "McCarthy with a white collar." Nixon countered: "Mr. Stevenson not only testified for Alger Hiss but he has never made a forthright statement deploring the terrible damage that Hiss and others like him did to America because of the protection and comfort they received from the Truman administration and its predecessor." Republicans, Nixon thought, were peaking just at the right moment, and if they increased their momentum, they would retain control of Congress.[48]

The vice president went on to Las Vegas to endorse Ernest Brown for the Senate. The next day he moved onto Pocatello and Boise, Idaho, where Ike had received almost a two-to-one majority in 1952. There Nixon called for the reelection of Senator Henry Dworshak and reminded his audience that every Democrat running for the Senate in the West had ADA backing. In Corvallis, Oregon, he called for an end to discrimination. At Beth Israel Congregation in Portland, he was the guest of honor at a dinner celebrating the 300th anniversary of Jews in America. He then went to a Masonic temple gathering where he compared the two parties' diplomatic records: "The Eisenhower-Dulles policy has been as good for America as the Truman-Acheson policy was bad."[49]

After three days in California, he moved to Spokane and Seattle, Washington, on October 30. Between two speaking appearances he sent a message to try to embarrass Stevenson about his accusations that the vice president had smeared, slandered, and slurred Democrats. Noting with a smile that the governor's "principal target seems to be me," he challenged Stevenson to answer him about the loss of China and the Korean War, the failure to keep communists out of the federal government, and a Democratic economy based on "high taxes, high spending, inflation and controls" that had not produced prosperity.[50]

Acceding to GOP requests for presidential appearances, Ike staged a last-minute campaign tour of his own, which apparently gave him a new appreciation of the yeoman work his vice president had done. In a letter that he released to the media toward the end of October, Ike wrote that he admired "the tremendous job you have done since the opening of the present campaign. You have personally carried a back-breaking load of hard, tedious, day by day and state by state campaigning." Pat, he added, had "aroused my admiration as an able campaigner; there is no question but that she is the most charming of the lot."[51]

Retired brigadier general William Gruber confirmed what Ike had written to Nixon. The week before the 1954 election, Gruber spent "a pleasant two hours with" his friend the president and later wrote the vice president that Ike was "very attached to you." He encouraged Nixon to assert himself "more positively regarding some of the White House staff that give him [Ike] such poor advice."[52]

DNC chairman Mitchell rejected any positive assessment of the GOP, accusing Nixon and RNC chairman Hall of staging a "gutter campaign" by raising the soft-on-communism issue against the Democrats. ADA co-chairman Arthur Schlesinger Jr. wrote the vice president, asserting that his organization had been established to fight communist influence in the liberal community. The historian had promoted that objective; he also spoke out against McCarthy in 1952 and opposed Nixon's campaign tactics in 1954. The vice president's attack on the ADA, Schlesinger wrote, was the lowest point of the campaign. Drew Pearson continued to produce anti-Nixon columns, reporting on the last day of October that at a stop in Charleston, West Virginia, the vice president had drawn a disappointingly small crowd. Chotiner sent Pearson a telegram pointing out that Nixon had not stopped there during the campaign.[53]

Most Democrats relied upon Stevenson to answer Nixon's salvos. Four days after describing Nixon as "McCarthy in a white collar," Stevenson objected to Nixon's "character assassination" of Democrats and called his campaign swings an "ill-will tour." At a Democratic gathering in Brooklyn, he said that Nixon "peddles his herrings, perversion and subversion as the witches' brew of Republican victory." On October 29, in Trenton, New Jersey, the once and future presidential nominee attacked Ike for sanctioning Nixon's communist-in-the-government tactics. The president had approved, and his "favorite campaigner, the heir apparent, the chief staff—the Vice President of the United States, Mr. Nixon—is the leader of it all." Historian Walter Johnson, who edited the Stevenson papers, wrote that his subject perceived the vice president as "without principles or conscience."[54]

Stevenson launched his sharpest attack on the president and vice president in a seventy-five minute speech on the evening of October 30, at a Democratic gathering at Cooper Union in New York City. He declared that the president's domestic and foreign policies were both failures, and the administration's proposals now could not pass without Democratic majorities in both houses of Congress. GOP conservatives had stymied any positive movement toward military preparedness and free world alliances. The nation had "been systematically imperiled by compromises, contradictions, and appeasement." Stevenson's sharpest assault on Nixon was the accusation that he called for "sending American boys to fight in Indochina" and pronounced "peace in the world is an achievement of the Eisenhower Administration."

As for the accusations that Democrats were soft on communism, Stevenson proclaimed: "To say that one or another American or party lacks patriotism or favors Communism or wants to subvert our society—when his only crime is disagreement—is to shake our system to the foundations." The administration's farm program "was erected on a foundation of false pledges and broken promises." The tax law benefited corporations and stockholders. Voters had to cast their ballots for moderation, and the way to accomplish that goal was a Democratic Congress.[55]

Eisenhower did not take Democratic criticisms well, and he disliked Stevenson. In an October 23 letter to his friend Swede Hazlett, he wrote that the former governor was not "a very dangerous opponent. However, if he should slip into a position of real responsibility, he would represent a great risk for the country."[56]

The president instructed Nixon to reply to Stevenson's speech. The vice president had read it and asked NBC to grant equal time for a rebuttal, but his request was denied. So he sent the *New York Times* and other major newspapers a condensation of what he would have said. Stevenson, Nixon exclaimed, had made "one of the most vicious, scurrilous attacks ever made by a major political figure on" an American president. When Republicans tried to engage their opposition concerning its record, Democrats screamed: "smear! . . . to put it bluntly, they smeared themselves."[57]

Nixon charged Stevenson five instances of the "big lie" method. First, Stevenson claimed the administration's foreign policy was a failure when, in reality, it was a great success; second, Democrats declared the GOP would lead the nation into recession, or worse, a depression, yet 1954 was the "best peace time year in American history"; third, the Democrats hysterically attacked Ike's security risk program as unsuccessful when it had removed thousands of subversives from the federal payroll; fourth, opponents outrageously referred to corruption in the administration when there was none; and lastly, Stevenson disingenuously argued that a Democratic Congress would assist the president more than a Republican one, yet in 1954 Democrats had voted with the White House only 40 percent of the time.[58]

After Nixon's statement circulated, he and the president went on television the evening of November 1. Nixon spoke first, carrying out the president's instruction to answer Stevenson without mentioning names. The vice president then lauded his boss: "No man could be more dedicated, no man could work harder, no man could believe more deeply in America than he does." Ike came on and appealed for a large turnout to elect a Republican majority.[59]

By the end of the campaign, Nixon was exhausted. Fearing the possibility of a Democratic minilandslide, he and Ike both rushed out in the last week to prevent a disaster. Nixon realized that he "was out carrying the load." Ike refused to fire partisan salvos; yet, he encouraged the vice president to hit their opponents hard.[60]

Shortly before Election Day, the Gallup Poll gave the president a 57 percent approval rating; concurrently, American voters supported the Democratic Party by 51.5 percent to 48.5 percent for the GOP. In Newsweek's survey of fifty well-respected journalists, forty-seven predicted that the Democrats would gain control of the House with 240 or more seats; thirty-nine saw the Senate with forty-nine Democrats and forty-six Republicans.[61]

The survey was correct: Democrats won control of Congress. But the final tabulation was closer than anticipated: forty-eight Democrats, forty-seven Republicans and one Independent occupied Senate seats, a net Democratic gain of two. If one half of a percent in each precinct in Oregon, Montana, and Wyoming had swung to the GOP, the Senate would have gone Republican by fifty to forty-six. The balance in the House was 232 Democrats to 203 Republicans, a shift of seventeen seats. Democrats would not surrender their Senate majority until 1980 and the House not until 1994. Just as significant, Republicans had twenty-nine governors going into the election and ended up with twenty after the balloting; Democrats raised their share from nineteen to twenty-seven, a net gain of eight.[62]

Eisenhower had avoided intense partisanship throughout his campaign appearances. As the campaign progressed, he realized that a Republican Congress was crucial to the passage of his proposals, but he did not fully recognize the linkage between party and partisanship. He admitted he was "a totally inexperienced 'politician.' "[63]

That admission was misleading. Eisenhower closely followed the campaign and regularly spoke with Nixon and other Republicans about their appearances. He did not object to his vice president's attacks on Stevenson and the Democrats, and he openly complimented Nixon and encouraged voters to cast their ballots for the Republican Party. But he would not accept the partisan label. Nixon would.

After the election was over, Nixon received accolades from his side. The president thanked him several times throughout the contest; John Foster Dulles told Nixon he had done "a wonderful job." Len Hall wrote: "No one in history ever stumped the country in an off-year election as you did this year." The *New York Journal American* declared: "virtually single-handed, he averted a GOP debacle." The newspaper publisher Gardner Cowles Jr. wrote, "all of us in the Republican Party owe you a debt of gratitude."[64]

Nixon allowed that "it was a tough campaign." In forty-eight days, he had traveled 26,000 miles—an average of over 500 miles a day—to ninety-five cities in thirty-one states, and averaged four hours of sleep a night. He had given one hundred press, radio, and television interviews. On a typical day, he had held three press conferences, given six speeches, shaken 532 hands, and dictated forty to fifty letters. To him, the election hinged on local conditions and turnout, since no overriding issues were being debated.[65]

That America had gone through a mild recession from September 1953 until July 1954 was, from his perspective, a "spotty factor." In the coalfields where unemployment had risen, Democrats generally won; in more prosperous areas, Republicans did better. Declining farm incomes in some regions had cut into Republican majorities, but the GOP did not lose a large number of seats. In Iowa, for example, Thomas Martin, despite experts' predictions, beat incumbent senator Guy Gillette. In Ohio, Nebraska, Kansas, and Colorado, Republicans gained three senators and two congressmen. Sixteen of the nineteen congressional seats lost by the GOP had belonged to members who voted for the flexible price supports pushed by Secretary of Agriculture Ezra Taft Benson. Democrats had tried to target the economic downturn as heralding another Republican depression, but it never became a national issue.[66]

McCarthy had also divided Republicans. During the election, his name both attracted and repelled voters. Nixon rarely mentioned him, and he framed the communist issue as a contrast between the Democrats, whom he saw as soft on communism, versus Republicans, who were preventing the spread of domestic subversion. Several days before the election, McCarthy publicly called on his loyalists to vote Republican. Nixon speculated that the division within the GOP over McCarthy's value had caused pro-McCarthy voters to stay home in Illinois, Michigan, and Wisconsin. In Connecticut, Nixon felt the Republican senatorial candidate, John Lodge, "ran a tremendously good race" and barely lost to Abraham Ribicoff. The McCarthy upheaval, Nixon thought, might have made the difference.[67]

Some Republicans were angry about how the president abandoned McCarthy. William Randolph Hearst Jr. believed Ike had "made a mistake" and should have brought the senator into the party as a sign of unity. "Had he done so," the publisher reasoned, "he well might have avoided the loss of the Senate." A Nixon advocate thought it had been "utterly asinine" of the administration "to wreck McCarthy." Joseph Meek's loss to incumbent Paul Douglas in Illinois was at least partially due to Meek's association with McCarthy.[68]

To Nixon, the campaign was "like pulling teeth." He had barnstormed in New Jersey for Clifford Case, who just eked out a victory. He had worked energetically for Senator Guy Condon in Oregon, but his challenger, Richard Neuberger, proved more attractive. Iowa was organized well, and the GOP swept the state. Pennsylvania faced internal bickering and had a weak gubernatorial candidate, who lost. Illinois was likewise fragmented between the party's conservative and liberal wings.[69]

Despite these complicated reasons for success and failure, Nixon thought the outcome was "a dead heat." No party that held the White House had won an off-year election since the Democrats accomplished it at the height of the Depression, in 1934. The Democrats were the technical winners, Nixon reasoned, but many had predicted much larger GOP losses. The administration as "the party in power gained a virtual stand-off."[70]

When the cabinet met on November 5 for a post-mortem, Nixon summed up the results by pulling a mechanical toy drummer from his pocket. He started it and released it on the table. The president and the others stared in surprise and amusement as the drummer marched across the table beating the drum. The moral, Nixon told them, was that "We've got to keep beating the drum about our achievements."[71]

Nixon had spent six days in California, made six to eight speeches daily and visited every district where the contests were close, and greatly increased his own popularity in his home state. Many followers, including Senator Knowland, thanked him for his efforts. Kyle Palmer, influential *Los Angeles Times* columnist, editorialized that Nixon had "carried the GOP fight through the nation this year in magnificent fashion, contributing more than any other than the President to the party's fight, both by personal effort and by advice. The GOP losses in the off-year were not greater is due in large part to Nixon's fighting heart and his fighting speeches."[72] Yet the tough campaign left him deeply disturbed. Sitting at home in front of the fireplace one cold day after the results had been tallied, both of them tired and depressed, he told Pat he was considering making it his last campaign.[73]

DNC chairman Mitchell issued a press release on November 8 in which he pointed to "the smear as a campaign weapon." He believed the GOP had used "the insinuation of treason against Democratic candidates as a political device." Ike had said he opposed McCarthyism as a campaign weapon, but when Nixon and others slandered Democrats' patriotism, the president did not object and even lauded the vice president for the battle he had waged. Mitchell asked Ike to disassociate himself "from such character assassination by public disavowal" and added, "I hope that Mr. Nixon will see fit to retract and apologize for his campaign excesses, and that we will hear no more of the same from him."[74]

After this opening salvo, newspapers circulated articles that Mitchell and Stevenson were "head hunting" for Nixon, as the price Democrats would exact in exchange for their cooperation with the administration in the new congressional session. The vice president had to apologize for his attacks or else the Democrats would not pass any of Eisenhower's legislation. Senate majority leader Johnson allegedly called Nixon a "fascist." Senator John Sparkman of Alabama said he would always remember Nixon's accusations that the Democrats were "a party of treason." This statement did not affect Nixon's popularity in the South, but a "certain degree of bitterness . . . will linger." Congressman Chester Holifield of California told the fifth annual California convention of the CIO that a new threat faced America: "McNixonism. . . . McCarthyism can be practiced without McCarthy." The vice president had become "McCarthy in spats."[75]

The incoming speaker of the House, Sam Rayburn, wrote that Nixon had "made one of the greatest spectacles of himself in the campaign that any man of prominence has made in my memory. . . . He stooped mighty low, . . . he is hurt now and will remain crippled throughout his life." In January 1955, Rayburn added that Nixon had "violated all the rules of the political game, and we are going to try to hold his feet to the fire for a long time."[76]

That same month, the new DNC chairman, Paul Butler, opened a "Chamber of Smears" in his office to illustrate how Nixon and others had "maligned and slandered the Democratic party and its candidates in the 1954 campaign." Butler made the vice president his party's "Public Enemy No. 1." In July 1956, ADA chairman Joseph Raub Jr. protested that the vice president's charge during the campaign that (as Raub described it) "the Democrats had put 8,000 communists in the government, and that the Democrats had tried to cover that up, was about the shadiest piece of campaigning that I had ever seen." This was a mischaracterization.[77]

RNC chairman Hall immediately answered some of Mitchell's accusations, writing in a press release that "our country would face the unhappy prospect of partisan strife brought on by short-sighted, ill-advised, loud-talking men like Mr. Mitchell." When Nixon discussed the Truman record, Hall contended, the Democrats cried smear. The vice president had asked for specific examples where he had vilified any senator but received no answer from Mitchell. He simply labeled the vice president a "liar" for exposing the facts and also tried to impugn Ike's integrity.[78]

Ike too, of course, heard the Democratic protests about Nixon's campaigning. According to pollster Samuel Lubell, the president responded that "Nixon must have done a good job if the Democrats complain so much." In a brief meeting on November 4, the president mentioned that the *New York Times* was attacking the vice president for "smears." Both men agreed that the newspaper had been embarrassed that its projections that Democrats would gain eight Senate and fifty House seats had fallen short.[79]

During a Republican legislative conference on January 11, 1955, the president asked the GOP leadership "about the sudden rash of attacks" on Nixon. Ike had read the vice president's addresses; they were carefully worded. Some of those present answered that "the ultra-new dealers—the ADA and the CIO" were sensitive to charges that their groups were soft on communism. Others believed the "best defense is a good offense." A few suggested the communism allegation drove "a wedge: between Democratic moderates and radicals."[80]

At a press conference the following day, United Press reporter Merriman Smith, asked the president about the criticisms leveled against Nixon. Ike prefaced his reply by stressing that the sole party of treason was the Communist Party of the U.S.A., and both major political parties had loyal Americans. But "in the heat of campaign, words, particularly if they are taken out of context, can be made the subject of possibly legitimate criticism." Even so, the president did not believe the vice president "was guilty of indiscretions." Nixon was a loyal and patriotic American whom he admired; he had never heard the vice president make "any sweeping condemnation of any party."[81]

Eisenhower, the military hero, never bore the brunt of abuse from Democrats; Americans saw him as above either making or receiving partisan attacks. Nixon was a partisan—wholeheartedly and effectively—and thus an appropriate and more reachable target. Republican senator Homer Ferguson from Michigan, who lost his bid for reelection in 1954, later suggested that the Democrats "were afraid to say anything about Ike so they took Nixon on and tried to discredit him."[82]

The vice president repeatedly maintained that he stuck to the record and never smeared any member of the opposition. The historian Edward Curtis commented at the time that the vice president never referred to Democrats as a "bunch of fellow-travelers." Nixon felt that some of his opponents deliberately exaggerated what he said and "tried to pin McCarthy's 'Twenty years of treason' line on me." As late as January 1958, Nixon denied that he had called Senators O'Mahoney, Murray, or John Carroll of Colorado "friendly to communism" during the campaign.[83]

Although the vice president conceded that the last two weeks were frantic, he insisted he never uttered a false declaration. He constantly reiterated that "what was wrong with our predecessors in the Administration in handling the Communist threat at home and abroad was their failure to recognize the danger rather than any deliberate disloyalty on their part." He did not challenge their patriotism; he did question their judgment. The campaign was "pretty rough," and Democrats distorted his statements to charge that he had called their party treasonous and smeared individual senatorial nominees. "I would not have been so stupid," Nixon wrote, "to have followed such a line."[84]

In his speech in Pocatello, Idaho, Nixon criticized five Democratic senatorial candidates: Neuberger, Carroll, O'Mahoney, Glen Taylor of Idaho, and Sam Yorty of California. Three of them lost. He drew attention to the denial of incumbent Democratic Congressman Robert Condon's security clearance when he campaigned for his GOP California challenger, and also attacked "the extreme left-wing A.D.A. group which apparently now controls the Democratic National Committee."[85]

Nixon expected Democrats to try to discredit him. In the second week of November, he wrote the author Victor Lasky that "ADA left-wingers in the Democratic Party . . . are trying to throw the cloak of injured innocence around a larger number than themselves." He told the *New York Journal American* reporter Frank Coniff that "the left wingers now are out after me in full cry. Frankly, they don't bother me however because I know we are on the right side."

Subtle distinctions seldom withstand the heat of an election campaign. The vice president did not accuse all Democrats of being soft on communism, but they thought he had. He claimed that some of the decisions made during the Truman administration allowed Soviet spies to work in the federal bureaucracy, and many on both sides heard this as a charge of deliberate subversion. When Nixon announced that a large number of federal employees hired during the

Roosevelt and Truman years had been fired for domestic subversion since Eisenhower entered the White House, Democrats demanded names. The vice president did not provide them, and without concrete evidence Democrats correctly objected to the accusations.

Secret American and Soviet documents released in the 1990s and early 2000s have now identified some of the espionage agents employed by Moscow in the 1930s and 1940s. Nixon's allegations were shown not to be spurious as Democrats claimed; many United States citizens had in fact supplied the Kremlin with classified material. (Three of the most controversial figures, Julius and Ethel Rosenberg and Alger Hiss, were confirmed to have passed secrets on to Soviet agents.) Nixon's charges, unsubstantiated in 1954, were correct; Democratic denials proved to be untrue.

Almost thirty years after the event, Milton Eisenhower, Ike's younger brother, reminisced that Nixon had disappointed Ike "because of the harsh, ultra-conservative, anti-communist speeches he made in the mid-term election of 1954." He contended: "Nixon's hatchet tactics in politics irritated the President. Certainly he never condoned them."[86] These recollections represent a consensus reached long after the fact. At the time, Ike and Republican loyalists openly praised Nixon's efforts. Democrats viciously attacked them. Most authors who describe these elections present Nixon's conduct from the latter perspective. Eisenhower approved of his vice president's campaigning style—directed, embraced, and encouraged it—even as he knew that the role was turning Nixon into a lightning rod for partisan opposition.

While Ike blurred political lines with his nonpartisan oratory, Nixon was a combative figure who waged unending political warfare, and false accounts piled up until they were accepted as fact. Yet Nixon and his Democratic counterparts were equally zealous in their pursuit of victory and their efforts to stoke the passions of their respective bases. In that off-cycle election, each side feared that its supporters were too apathetic. Just as Nixon allowed partisan audiences to interpret his words as more inflammatory than they appeared in print, so the Democrats' "smear" charges should be perceived for what they were: overheated campaign rhetoric. Like Nixon, they too desperately wanted to win an election.

16

THE INCAPACITATED PRESIDENT

Two-plus years into his administration, the questions about Eisenhower's vitality that were raised during the 1952 campaign had long since vanished. On January 20, 1955, Major General Howard Snyder, Ike's personal physician, gave him a physical examination and found the president in "good shape." Despite this welcome news, secretary to the president Bernard Shanley was concerned with Ike's health and had an extended conversation with Nixon about "lightening the President's burden." The vice president even "offered to speak to the Cabinet without the President being present."

In the middle of August, Congress adjourned after acting on the administration's legislative proposals. Ike and Mamie left Washington's humid, hot summer weather and flew to Denver to stay with Mamie's mother. Shanley reported to Nixon a week later that "although we have been pretty busy, the change of locale and atmosphere helps. The President looks fine and this seems just what he needs."[1]

Nixon remained in the capital. He flew to Denver on September 4 for a conference with Ike on the latest international developments: the potentially explosive Middle Eastern situation created by the Arab-Israeli friction, Gamal Abdel Nasser's assumption to power in Egypt, and United Nations disarmament talks and their effects on national security. In a letter to former National Security Advisor Robert Cutler, the vice president reported that Ike was "in exceedingly good spirits and I am sure that the change from the sometimes 'hot air' of Washington to the cool and invigorating atmosphere in Denver is proving beneficial to him."[2]

Eisenhower left Denver for Fraser, Colorado, on September 19, where his banker friend Aksel Nielson had an 8,600-acre ranch. Four days later, the president woke up at 5:00 a.m. having "had my best night's sleep in years." He made bacon and eggs for his guests and then briefly returned to his mother-in-law's before heading to his office at Lowry Air Force Base. Ann Whitman wrote that she had *"never seen him look or act better. . . .* He was delightful, patient with the pile of work."[3]

That Friday he went to Cherry Hills Country Club, where he played eighteen holes of golf, ate a hamburger with large slices of raw onion for lunch, and played another nine holes. He later complained of heartburn and indigestion. This was not unusual; he often had some kind of stomach upset. Upon leaving the club, he went to his mother-in-law's home, painted for three hours, had dinner, and retired at 10:00 p.m. with Mamie asleep in the adjoining bedroom.

With a driving rainstorm outside, Ike woke up at 2:30 a.m. on Saturday, September 24, with pain in his chest and stomach. Mamie heard her husband stir, went in to check on him, and gave him some milk of magnesia. Fifteen minutes later, Ike started to perspire and felt a sharp pain in his chest. Mamie, who was hypervigilant about her husband's health, called Dr. Snyder. He rushed over, diagnosed his patient with "acute coronary thrombosis," and gave him a morphine injection so that he could get back to sleep.[4]

Dr. Snyder telephoned Ann Whitman to say that the president would not be coming to the office that morning due to "digestive upset." He gave acting presidential press secretary Murray Snyder, stationed in Denver, the same story, and he in turn told the press corps.[5]

Ike rose around noon and was given an electrocardiogram. Dr. Snyder confirmed his diagnosis of a heart attack and ordered an ambulance to drive Eisenhower to nearby Fitzsimons Army Hospital. While he was being transported, the doctor located Murray Snyder and told him that the president had had "a mild coronary thrombosis." Before the acting press secretary released this medical alert to the reporters, he first phoned his boss James Hagerty, back in Washington. With Hagerty's approval, Snyder issued the statement at approximately 5:30 p.m. Eastern Standard Time. Bulletins concerning Ike's heart attack flashed around the nation and the world. At 7:50, Hagerty and Dr. Thomas Mattingly, Ike's cardiologist at Walter Reed Hospital, took off from the capital; they landed in Denver, still under pelting rain, four hours later. Hagerty's task was to disseminate information about Ike's condition to the press, and Mattingly was there to consult with the local military doctors about the president's condition.[6]

Pat and Dick Nixon had spent the hot fall afternoon in the Washington suburbs at the wedding of Drusilla Nelson, one of the vice president's secretaries. A reception followed, but the Nixons decided to skip it and return home. In his living room, the vice president picked up the *Washington Evening Star* and read a short item concerning the president's indigestion. Like others close to Ike, he knew it was a recurring problem and thought nothing more about it.[7]

While the vice president rested, Hagerty confidentially told the White House operator what had occurred and that he would be calling many people. His first call was to the vice president. The operator could not initially reach him and left a message concerning "an urgent matter." Nixon promptly returned the call; Hagerty suggested that the vice president "sit down." Ike had had a heart attack, he said, and was in the hospital. The press secretary knew nothing more except that Murray Snyder was going to tell the press in a half-hour.

Nixon, clearly shocked, responded "My God! That's awful. Is there anything I can do?" Hagerty promised to provide an update before he left for Denver that evening. Nixon answered that he could be called at any hour.[8]

Hagerty's next call went to deputy chief of staff, Jerry Persons, whose boss, Sherman Adams, was in Scotland. Persons, like the vice president, was stunned, but recovered enough to say that he would try to reach as many cabinet members as possible. John Foster Dulles was next on Hagerty's list. He too was upset from a personal as well as from a foreign policy viewpoint. If the president's future were uncertain, American diplomatic leadership might be jeopardized.[9]

In the midst of these notifications, Murray Snyder telephoned Hagerty to say that Dr. Snyder had removed the word "mild" from his diagnosis; the president had suffered an "anterior coronary thrombosis." He had been placed under an oxygen tent and was "doing as well as could be expected." Ike's physicians had agreed to have the internationally renowned cardiologist Paul Dudley White fly to Denver as a consultant.

This was an alarming turn, but Dr. White's appointment at least relieved Nixon and would reassure the public that every possible measure was being taken. Hagerty and Nixon concurred that after the press secretary arrived at the hospital, he would inform the vice president of any developments no matter what time it was.[10]

Ann Whitman called Hagerty concerning any legal matters that would arise over the president's illness. She had talked to acting attorney general William Rogers (Brownell was vacationing at a Spanish resort), asking him to look into those issues. Hagerty then talked to Jerry Persons about the implications of long-term presidential disability. How would they handle the signing of official documents and the delegation of powers? Hagerty had no answers. They agreed that they should ask Rogers to examine the issues. Ten years later, in the wake of President Kennedy's assassination, the nation would pass the Twenty-fifth Amendment to the Constitution to address the problem of presidential incapacity; but in 1955 there was only a vague provision in Article II that in the past had provided little guidance.[11]

As the press secretary prepared to leave for Denver, Nixon was reacting to the news. He called Rose Mary Woods, informed her of the president's condition, and told her to return to her apartment, where she had a special telephone that would ring if the vice president did not answer his home line. She relayed messages throughout that eventful evening.[12]

Within minutes after Ann Whitman telephoned Rogers, he received a call from the vice president, asking him to come over to his house. Arriving by taxi, Rogers saw reporters already congregating in front of Nixon's residence. He went inside where they talked for an hour. Nixon had forgotten to tell Pat what was happening; he told her and then telephoned Mamie in Denver to express his sympathies. With the commotion outside and the housekeeper inside supervising his daughters, Nixon and Rogers tried to eat dinner but had difficulty finishing it due to the constant distractions. Nixon had his daughters ride their bicycles in front of the house while he and Rogers snuck out the back door. Adele Rogers had meanwhile driven over and was parked on the next street. She drove them to the Rogers house in nearby Bethesda, Maryland.[13]

Once Nixon and Rogers arrived at his home, they invited Jerry Persons to join them. Adele Rogers made hamburgers at 10:00 p.m. while telephone calls went back and forth from Bethesda to Denver. Shortly after midnight, Persons left, and by 1:30 a.m., Rogers retired. Nixon borrowed pajamas and stayed over. Besides the strain of the moment, he had a severe case of hay fever. At 4:00 Sunday morning, he called Hagerty for an update. The press secretary reported that Ike was sedated and sleeping soundly. Nixon could not.[14]

While Nixon tried to sort out how to proceed, Murray Chotiner, his principal political adviser, phoned from Seattle offering to help. Herb Klein, who assisted with press relations, was disappointed that the vice president had been unavailable to speak with reporters, but Louis Guylay, the RNC public relations director, thought otherwise: "The VP was smart to stay incognito last night."[15]

By Sunday morning, the president's heart attack was on the front page of every major newspaper. The media ran continual updates on Ike's condition and published articles on the seriousness of heart problems. Nixon understood that he would have to meet the press, and after leaving the Rogers house he stopped by his own home, where he assembled his family for the 11:00 service at the Westmoreland Congregational Church. Reporters had accompanied him there, and afterward he invited a few back to his living room for an informal chat. He provided the correspondents the few details he knew about the president's condition. Until it became clearer, he said, the government would function as usual.[16]

After the reporters left, Secretary Dulles telephoned the vice president, recalling his uncle Robert Lansing, who had been secretary of state when President

Woodrow Wilson suffered his debilitating stroke in September 1919. Wilson's wife, Edith, and his physician, Dr. Cary Grayson, controlled access to the president. They distrusted Lansing and largely kept him away from the president, causing damage to American foreign policy. Dulles would fight against any recurrence. He proposed that chief of staff Sherman Adams, who would be back in the capital by Monday, fly to Colorado to act as a liaison between Denver and Washington. As for Nixon's scheduled trip to the Middle East, the secretary suggested it be postponed because "it would not be wise to risk himself there."[17]

Hagerty, true to his word, relayed constant updates to the vice president. When the press secretary learned from medical experts that Ike "had had a slightly more than moderate attack," Nixon received immediate word. Hagerty told the press that the vice president would not travel to Denver but would instead preside over the regular cabinet and NSC meetings in the capital. These measures would show that the administration was functioning normally. Hagerty also informed the press that he had asked acting Attorney General Rogers for a legal opinion on what presidential prerogatives might be delegated to others, presumably the vice president.[18]

Ann Whitman called her counterpart in the vice president's office, Rose Mary Woods, on the morning of Monday, September 26. She was greatly relieved because Ike was awake "and asking for his breakfast—we are keeping our fingers crossed—the sun came out today."[19]

That morning, Nixon left his home for the Senate Office Building and then went to the executive mansion for a two-hour luncheon with Sherman Adams, Bill Rogers, and Jerry Persons. As he departed, he refused to answer most of the reporters' questions, but did acknowledge that he would remain in the capital for the entire week. By the end of the business day, Wall Street had reacted with one of the worst falls in stock market history.

Shortly before 6:00, Nixon spoke with *New York Times* columnist Arthur Krock, telling him he had received "remarkably encouraging" reports from Denver. As vice president, he told Krock, he sought national stability and wanted Americans to comprehend that Ike was in charge and the government was operating normally. He did not expect any political capital from the president's adversity.[20]

At 8:10, Secretary Dulles telephoned Nixon from the Waldorf Towers in New York City. Raising again the "awful" situation that had arisen after Wilson's stroke, Dulles insisted that nothing should be done to suggest that Ike's illness was serious. Sherman Adams had already flown back to Washington, and Attorney General Brownell would arrive the following day. The return of such high-ranking officials to the capital would increase confidence in the administration and reassure the public.[21]

Twenty minutes after that conversation, Nixon joined Sherman Adams, Republican National Committee (RNC) chairman Len Hall, his aide Lou Guylay, and Jerry Persons at Bill Rogers' home to discuss the political consequences of Ike's heart attack. Adams, who saw himself as the president's alter ego, would take direction from the president after they conferred at the hospital. No one thought that the president would run for reelection, and Nixon wanted to limit any scramble for the 1956 nomination. His concern was the president's convalescence and the routine running of government operations.[22]

Encouraging letters and telephone calls came to the vice president's office from across the nation. Murray Chotiner, peering into the future, told Rose Mary Woods that this was "really going to be a wonderful opportunity for Dick to show the country what he is made of—to help put down some of the sniping that has been going on against him." Norman Cousins, editor of *The Saturday Review*, wrote to offer the vice president his best wishes as he took on "additional burdens such as have seldom been known in history. Regardless of political affiliations, Americans have an obligation to give you the fullest possible support in helping you carry out the policies of the President."[23]

On the morning of Tuesday, September 27, Nixon met with the director of the budget, Rowland Hughes, for an hour to discuss budget issues before Thursday's cabinet meeting. Two policemen stood outside the vice president's outer door, with one or two Secret Service agents nearby for added security. Surrounding them were ten to fifty people from the media. RNC chairman Hall visited the vice president at 11:00 a.m. When the tall, confident chairman emerged, he smiled but refused to comment on whether the president would run for reelection.

After Hughes's departure, Nixon emerged from his office for a luncheon at the treasury building. As he moved toward the elevator, he answered some queries while a staffer tried to impede the crush of reporters moving toward Nixon. He walked from the building and got into his limousine to the clatter of feverishly snapping cameras.

Secretary Humphrey hosted the luncheon for the vice president, Sherman Adams, Attorney General Brownell, who had just returned to the capital, and Bill Rogers. The gathering lasted an hour and forty minutes. Afterward, as they posed for the cameras, Brownell made the most newsworthy announcement, assuring the country that the president's recuperation was going well enough that he saw no reason for a legal opinion regarding any delegation of powers.

After returning briefly to his office, Nixon next drove to the Pentagon, where he met with Secretary of Defense Charles Wilson and other high-ranking members of the department to plan the agenda for that Friday's NSC gathering. Leaving that meeting, Nixon reiterated to the press that the administration was following its regular routine and the president's team was functioning well.

The next day the vice president had breakfast with Senator Knowland, who had just flown in from the West Coast. Upon leaving, Nixon told reporters that the two of them did not discuss politics and would not comment on the 1956 presidential nomination. Knowland was the Senate minority leader: they went over pending legislation. Knowland saw no national emergency; the government was operating efficiently.

Nixon later met with special assistant to the president on the NSC, Dillon Anderson, for an hour on the next day's meeting. Assistant press secretary Snyder, who had flown back from Denver, announced that Nixon had signed some official papers that had no legal ramifications, and thus, no delegation of powers was required. He was also assuming several additional ceremonial duties for the president. Hagerty in Denver explicitly stressed that he saw no necessity to transfer any presidential prerogatives to the vice president.[24]

The NSC meeting that convened at 10:00 a.m. on September 29 was the first one since the president's heart attack. Nixon asked for a silent prayer to speed Ike's recovery. As was customary, he sat across from the president's empty chair.[25]

The following day, he followed a similar procedure during the cabinet meeting; the agenda was comprehensive, and the conference lasted until noon. Secretary Dulles outlined international developments, particularly the unstable conditions in the Middle East. Arthur Burns presented a report on the economy and predicted that growth would continue without any new government policies. Regarding the president's progress, Nixon noted that Ike was steadily improving and had had an "excellent night." To aid him when he returned to the capital, the cabinet secretaries needed to resolve as many routine issues as they could without involving the president. Still, he emphasized, there must be "no end-runs to the Vice President." The channels of communication were well defined and must be followed. If any legal issues arose, they should go through the attorney general's office.[26]

Cabinet business would flow through the White House staff. Sherman Adams would leave for Denver after the meeting to coordinate those efforts; Jerry Persons would remain in the capital to act as a conduit to Colorado. This arrangement pleased Persons because, as he later commented, he and Adams had a mutually respectful relationship "that made things at this particular time a good deal easier than they might have been otherwise."[27]

Nixon recognized Adams's special connection to the president and understood that the chief of staff objected to any hint that Nixon was the acting president.

Instead, many perceived Adams performing that role. Nixon later recollected that Adams "did this not because he was *against* me but because he was *for* the President."[28]

Secretary Dulles recognized the potential for friction between Adams and Nixon; the secretary sometimes manipulated rumors of a feud between them to fend off their interference when he sought direct access to the president. Even so, he had come to rely on Nixon. To demonstrate his affinity with the vice president, at the conclusion of the meeting Dulles addressed the group: "I realize that you [Nixon] have been under a heavy burden during these past few days and I know I express the opinion of everybody here that you have conducted yourself superbly and I want you to know we are proud to be on this team and proud to be serving in this Cabinet under your leadership." Later that afternoon, Nixon telephoned the secretary, thanking him for that "generous thing." Dulles replied, "It was little and much deserved."[29]

Before the long gathering ended, the participants agreed that no one should speak to the press. Despite this understanding, Nixon addressed the media, stating that no changes were contemplated and that Sherman Adams would fly to Denver the next day to supervise the management of the summer White House. The chief of staff was the "logical choice" and the "ideal man for the position."[30]

Dulles was displeased. He had requested silence so that the rumors and indecision that followed President Wilson's stroke would not be repeated, and he wanted Adams to be the liaison between the capital and Denver. Hagerty, harried and overworked, was "delighted" that Adams was coming. Dulles insisted that no one must have the impression that the president would communicate only with Nixon. Once Adams was in Colorado, Dulles thought, "he can police it." Later that afternoon, he spoke with Secretary Wilson; they concurred that the cabinet must present a picture of unity. Wilson speculated that "Nixon may be pressured to talk too much," but little could be done to stop him.[31]

Nixon telephoned Dulles that evening to apologize for talking to reporters. The vice president understood that the secretary had cautioned him that the press would pressure him to respond. The admonishment seemed simple to carry out, but in fact it was not. The vice president explained that as he was leaving, some wondered if the NSC and the cabinet could make decisions without the president. When he saw that speculation on the wires, he said, he had to correct it. Dulles conceded that it was a "good excuse."[32]

That evening, seeing significant improvement, the doctors removed Ike's oxygen tent. The center of political power had shifted to Denver.[33]

Nixon continually rejected the idea of any delegation of powers and carefully watched Ike's convalescence. He wrote C. D. Jackson, a close friend of the president and an adviser on psychological issues, "this Administration is still an Eisenhower Administration and not a substitute." He was attempting to resolve routine matters so that Ike did not face "an overflowing desk when he returns."[34]

With the emergency over, Nixon took time to answer the letters from many comrades who pledged their allegiance. To his friend and former House colleague Charles Kersten, he wrote, "There are times in our life when we are even more grateful than ever for expressions of friendship from those we have known over the years."[35]

The letters written to Nixon's office typically said: "You and Ike are in our prayers." Ep Hoyt, publisher of the *Denver Post*, editorialized that the vice president's performance since the heart attack "has won converts to his integrity and sincerity. And we think that many Americans, however cool they were to the vice president two years ago, think better of him today." General Bedell Smith, Ike's chief of staff in World War II, applauded Nixon's efforts and offered, if called upon, to reduce the vice president's workload. From a partisan perspective, Senator Barry Goldwater believed that Nixon had gained stature across America; the vice president's deliberations, he wrote, were "bringing full credit to your already crowned head."[36]

Pat Nixon wrote her close friend Helene Drown at the beginning of October that she had to cancel her planned trip to San Francisco. "It was a madhouse around here that day. . . . In fact the wire services and security are with Dick constantly—consequently there is no peace. They visit and prowl at night which is a little hard on light-sleeper me." But Ike was rapidly recovering, and "the chances for an early return look good."[37]

One week after Ike was rushed to the hospital, he showed rapid improvement. That Saturday, October 1, newspapers published a letter from the president to his vice president, instructing him to continue to chair NSC and cabinet meetings as long as Eisenhower remained in Colorado. Hagerty regularly called Nixon with medical updates.[38]

In addition to maintaining his regular hours at the Senate Office Building, Nixon went daily to the White House, where Jerry Persons was responsible for supervising the staff with Sherman Adams in Denver. The deputy and the vice president were friends. Nixon came in to see Persons each day to review current conditions. Later, recalling those difficult days, Persons said that Nixon "was very meticulous in all of his relationships. . . . To my knowledge, he never went in the President's office."[39]

At the start of the month, Nixon had a long chat with Harold Stassen, special assistant to the president on disarmament, who was engaged in United Nations talks devoted to that subject. Stassen predicted that the president would not run for reelection and offered Nixon his support. That evening the vice president had dinner with Dulles, who told him he resented Stassen's interference in diplomatic matters.[40]

Nixon continued to preside over cabinet meetings, with Adams either relaying information and instructions from Denver or flying back to attend the gathering. He also gave weekly reports on his boss's steady improvement. Nixon relayed a message from Ike thanking the cabinet secretaries for carrying out the routine business of government so diligently. The members sent their tape-recorded greetings and a gift for the president's sixty-fifth birthday.[41]

Although Dulles and others summarized some foreign policy issues during cabinet meetings, the NSC remained the main forum for discussing foreign policy. Secretary Dulles dominated while the vice president presided; most of these discussions went into some depth. The president's staff secretary and defense liaison, Colonel Andrew Goodpaster, briefed Nixon every two or three days outside the meetings to keep him current. As usual, the administration did not publicly mention any subjects under consideration. Dillon Anderson, special assistant to the president for National Security Affairs, recalled the vice president's leadership at the NSC gatherings. He chaired the body "with consummate grace and taste" and usually did not talk much except to address the "domestic political feasibility of this policy or that." Anderson thought that with an "incapacitated" president far from the capital, Nixon could "have looked like an usurper" and could "have come on too strong." But the vice president acted superbly: "This was perhaps his finest hour, up till then."[42]

Dulles visited the president on October 11 and reviewed a wide range of topics, especially the approaching Geneva foreign ministers conference and United States–Soviet relations. After returning to the capital, Dulles met with Nixon and several cabinet members. Four days later, he telephoned the vice president, asking him to obtain bipartisan support regarding Arab-Egyptian problems; if cooperation was not forthcoming and the United States were not perceived as impartial, America could forfeit friendly associations within the Arab world. Nixon pledged his support but wondered whether the Democrats would follow. He backed the Eisenhower-Dulles commitment to "peaceful change" and promised to advance the spirit of Geneva, which had generated a thaw in the Cold War climate.[43]

The president reinforced the Nixon-Dulles bond even further. On October 19, he wrote his vice president and asked him to discuss Dulles's upcoming trip to Geneva during a cabinet session because the secretary carried "a heavy load of responsibility" in his mission. The cabinet had to unite behind him and affirm that he spoke for the administration. To emphasize this message, the White

Nixon campaigning, August 6, 1952. *Courtesy of Whittier College Special Collections & Archives.*

Harry Truman, Mamie, and Ike at the White House on June 2, 1952. *Dwight D. Eisenhower Presidential Library.*

Nixon meeting with Haile Selassie, May 17, 1957, in Washington, D.C. *Richard Nixon Presidential Library and Museum.*

Nixon with Carlos Castillo Armas, president of Guatemala, February 12, 1955. *Richard Nixon Presidential Library and Museum.*

Nixon and President Ramón Magsaysay in the Philippines on November 24, 1953. *Richard Nixon Presidential Library and Museum.*

Nixon in South Korea on November 18, 1953. *Richard Nixon Presidential Library and Museum.*

Nixon and Chiang Kai-shek, July 7, 1956. *Richard Nixon Presidential Library and Museum.*

Nixon's parents and daughters; left to right: Tricia, Hannah, Frank, and Julie Nixon in 1954. *Courtesy of Whittier College Special Collections & Archives.*

Nixon with Checkers, 1954. *Richard Nixon Presidential Library and Museum.*

Mamie Eisenhower and Pat Nixon on March 27, 1958, at a luncheon in Washington, D.C. *Dwight D. Eisenhower Presidential Library.*

Eisenhower and Sergeant John Moaney at the Gettysburg farm in Pennsylvania. *Eisenhower National Historic Site, post-presidency 1961–1967.*

Pat Nixon with, from left, secretaries Loie Gaunt, Dorothy Cox, and P. J. Everts; Richard Nixon's personal secretary Rose Mary Woods; and personal friend Margaret Brock in April 1956. *Richard Nixon Presidential Library and Museum.*

WILLIAM BROCK

Pasadena,   California
Major in Math. - Physics
Track   3-4
Football   3-4

William Brock (1935 yearbook), who played football with Nixon at Whittier College. *Courtesy of Whittier College Special Collections & Archives.*

Meeting in the Oval Office, June 23, 1958. From left: Lester Granger, Martin Luther King Jr., E. Frederic Morrow, Ike, A. Philip Randolph, William Rogers, Rocco Siciliano, and Roy Wilkins. *Dwight D. Eisenhower Presidential Library.*

Martin Luther King Jr. and his wife Coretta at the United States embassy in Mexico City, with Ambassador Robert Hill (far left) and another unidentified man, July 21, 1958. *Richard Nixon Presidential Library and Museum.*

Ike and Nixon with Ghana's finance minister, K. A. Gbedemah, on October 10, 1957, at the White House. *Dwight D. Eisenhower Presidential Library.*

From left: Sherman Adams, Nixon, Dr. Paul White, and John Eisenhower arriving in Denver, Colorado, on October 8, 1955. *Dwight D. Eisenhower Presidential Library.*

Cabinet meeting chaired by Nixon, July 22, 1955. *Dwight D. Eisenhower Presidential Library.*

Republican Lincoln Day rally on February 5, 1954, at the Uline Arena (now Washington Coliseum), Washington, D.C. *Dwight D. Eisenhower Presidential Library.*

Republican National Convention in San Francisco, August 22–23, 1956. *Dwight D. Eisenhower Presidential Library.*

Eleanor Roosevelt and Adlai Stevenson at the Democratic National Convention, August 13, 1956. *Franklin Delano Roosevelt Presidential Library.*

Nixon coming out of a voting booth in the 1950s. *Courtesy of Whittier College Special Collections & Archives.*

The Nixons with train porters, 1956 presidential campaign. *Richard Nixon Presidential Library and Museum.*

Nixon speaking from the back of the "Dick Nixon Campaign Special," 1956. *Courtesy of Whittier College Special Collections & Archives.*

From left: Adlai Stevenson, Ike, and Thomas Dewey on February 25, 1958, at a dinner in Washington, D.C. *Dwight D. Eisenhower Presidential Library.*

Ike and William Knowland at a congressional breakfast meeting on July 29, 1955, in Washington, D.C. *Dwight D. Eisenhower Presidential Library.*

Ike and Harold Stassen at the White House, March 29, 1955. *Dwight D. Eisenhower Presidential Library*.

Ike, John Foster Dulles, and Adlai Stevenson at the White House, October 1, 1953. *Dwight D. Eisenhower Presidential Library*.

Nixon, Ike, and Senator Everett Dirksen on August 24, 1960, at a dinner in Washington, D.C. *Dwight D. Eisenhower Presidential Library.*

Henry Cabot Lodge Jr., Ike, and Nixon on September 12, 1960, at the start of the presidential campaign. *Dwight D. Eisenhower Presidential Library.*

From left: Nixon, Ike, Earl Warren, and Alexander Wiley at a prayer breakfast in Washington, D.C., on February 4, 1954. *Dwight D. Eisenhower Presidential Library.*

From left: Janet Dulles, Christian Herter, Nixon, John Foster Dulles, and Ike on April 23, 1959, at Walter Reed Hospital. *Dwight D. Eisenhower Presidential Library.*

The Eisenhowers, the Nixons, and Doris and Herbert Brownell at a dinner in Washington, D.C., on November 21, 1957. *Dwight D. Eisenhower Presidential Library.*

Ike welcomes the Nixons, returning from South America, at the airport, on May 15, 1958. *Dwight D. Eisenhower Presidential Library.*

Nixon at Schwechat Airport in Vienna, Austria, on December 19, 1956. *Richard Nixon Presidential Library and Museum.*

Ferenc Daday, *Nixon at Andau*, 1970. *Richard Nixon Presidential Library and Museum.*

House released the letter to the press. Then on October 26, the president issued a statement that he and Dulles had agreed on the substance of the matters under consideration at Geneva; Ike hoped that the bargaining would "actually be productive of the peaceful progress for which the whole world longs."[44]

The president's hospital confinement forced Nixon to reduce many regular activities. On October 10, he announced that he would resume a limited speaking schedule but would remain close to Washington.[45] Until the president's heart attack, he had written most of his own speeches. He would highlight critical sentences and ad-lib depending upon the audience. Now, others assisted him or actually provided complete speeches that he modified. Father John Cronin, a Catholic priest whom Nixon had met in 1947, worked for free. He finished one speech on October 14 to be delivered five days later, and immediately began drafting another address for Monday, October 17.[46]

Nixon gave the first address, using some of Cronin's prose, on Monday at the Waldorf Astoria Hotel in New York City before the International Air Transport Association. His call for ease of movement between nations received warm and spontaneous applause.[47] Two days later, in the hotel's grand ballroom, he addressed the closing session of the twenty-forth annual *New York Herald Tribune* Forum.[48] This time, speaking before a large audience with a national television hook-up, Nixon used much of Cronin's text, a well-prepared address that praised the Eisenhower-Dulles diplomacy as leading toward a new "spirit of Geneva." The vice president proclaimed that the Big Four foreign ministers' gathering, coming in ten days, might be momentous: "the chances for peace today are better than at any time since World War II." There was hope for calming the arms race in the Middle East and Asia, an effort in which the United Nations, imperfect but promising, might play a useful role. To ensure disarmament, the United States insisted on adequate inspection safeguards. The administration would advance its policy of peace through strength.[49]

Eric Sevareid told listeners on CBS Radio News that Nixon's address "was perhaps the best written speech he has ever given." It had no isolationist tone; he advocated liberal foreign trade, international aid, and firmness toward Moscow, and paid tribute to the Democratic Congress as well as the UN. The vice president acted as the administration spokesman, but Sevareid warned that Nixon would probably lose the backing of the GOP's right wing.[50]

In early October, the president's physicians permitted him to take on a severely limited workload. On the tenth of the month, they allowed him out of his hospital room to breathe the Rocky Mountain air and sit in the sunshine. Hagerty warned against excessive optimism even though the president had passed the critical two-week recovery period. A week later, Ann Whitman reported how much better Ike appeared. By the end of the month, he was walking. The doctor had advised him that it would be four months before they could tell him what level of activity he could take on permanently without straining his heart.[51]

Outside of family, White House staff, and medical care, Nixon had been the first official visitor to fly to Denver to meet with the president. The vice president, Eisenhower's son John, Sherman Adams, and Dr. White left the capital on the morning of October 8 and went to Fitzsimons Army Hospital. Nixon and Ike had a fifteen-minute chat and another talk the following day. He recalled Ike telling him about the initial pain from the heart attack. "It hurt like hell, Dick. . . . I never let Mamie know how much it hurt."[52]

On October 10, after the vice president's departure, the president commented to Sherman Adams that his heart attack had focused attention on Nixon. He was "a darn good young man" but "[I] still consider him a bit immature." His "judgments are given accurately and thoughtfully." Adams responded that the vice president lacked experience and seasoning: "He has not quite reached a maturity of intellect."[53]

When Nixon telephoned Eisenhower's brother Milton later in October, Milton said to him, "I have every confidence that . . . [Ike] will have a complete recovery."[54] This was a huge relief that reduced Nixon's fear of long-term paralysis at the head of the government. For nearly a month, Nixon wrote in his diary, Eisenhower had been unable to make "a great decision. He had advanced to the point that he can be consulted and not make great decisions." By the end of the month, Nixon anticipated Ike's return to work in the near future.[55]

In the middle of the month, Pat Nixon, who had been reluctant to burden Mamie with correspondence, sent her a handwritten note. Pat knew that the first lady had received a tremendous amount of mail, all of which she personally answered, and that those who wrote were "filled with admiration and appreciation." She wanted Mamie "to know that our thoughts and prayers have been with you constantly." Dick "was grateful for the opportunity of seeing the President and you whom he admires and loves."[56] The first lady replied on the eighteenth, thanking Pat for her lovely letter and "kind sentiments." The Eisenhowers appreciated how the Nixons "brightened our spirits during this time of anxiety." She and Ike loved sitting on the hospital terrace and enjoying the "heavenly view of the mountains." He was "more himself every day," and she hoped that they would soon see the rolling hills of Gettysburg from their farmhouse's sun porch.[57]

In early November, Sherman Adams informed the cabinet that Ike would shortly leave Denver and return to the White House. Nixon would orchestrate the welcome and anticipate a "full turnout" of the cabinet, the diplomatic corps, the White House staff, Congress, and the public. The vice president would offer "official greetings," and then the president would take his bubble limousine in a motorcade to 1600 Pennsylvania Avenue.[58]

On the morning of the eleventh, Ike said his good-byes to those who had cared for him at the army hospital and drove to Lowry Air Force Base, where he boarded the presidential airplane *Columbine* for his flight to the capital. He landed at 4:00 p.m., greeted by a cheering crowd of 5,000, and spoke from the steps of the airplane: "The doctors . . . have given me a reprieve, if not a pardon." Ike then walked down a ramp from the plane unaided; he thanked his countrymen for their prayers and good wishes, and the vice president welcomed him with "Godspeed in the days ahead."[59]

Ike and Mamie spent a quiet weekend in the capital and then drove to their Gettysburg farm. On his doctors' advice, he would "try to keep official business to a minimum." Mamie was "delighted to be home," according to her husband, but missed the snow-covered Rocky Mountains and the warm sun of his hospital's porch. The Pennsylvania hills were inviting, but the weather was "murky, damp and cold."[60]

Nixon and his wife were exhausted. Rose Mary Woods noted in a memo that "for the last several weeks we [Nixon and his staff] have been working until midnight each night." The Nixons left the capital on the evening of November fifteenth for a long weekend.

The president's health had sufficiently improved by November 21 that he called his first NSC gathering since his heart attack at the presidential retreat at Camp David, Maryland; the drive from Gettysburg was only twenty-five miles. At noon, a Sikorsky H-19 helicopter picked up Nixon and Dillon Anderson; an hour later three Piasecki H-21 Bs took off from the Pentagon with eighteen other top advisers. The Secret Service vetoed having all the participants fly in one aircraft. With Ike in the chair, the group discussed recent developments with the Russians; that evening the president met with Secretaries Dulles, Wilson, and Humphrey and the vice president. The following morning Ike presided over a cabinet meeting at which Dulles summarized the current state of United States–Soviet relations. Just before the meeting finished, the president thanked the group for working harmoniously while he was incapacitated.[61]

Throughout December, Ike showed steady physical improvement. He presided over his regular meetings of the cabinet and NSC, and groups of legislative leaders. When he grew tired, he left early and returned if he felt well enough. He also started to think deeply about Soviet matters, particularly communist economic expansion in developing countries. As a consequence, he began to highlight the United States Information Agency's propaganda role and to make economic assistance more flexible and give it a higher priority.[62]

As was the custom, when Ike left meetings, Nixon assumed the chair. At two cabinet meetings in December, Nixon stressed the importance of reducing the demands on the president's daily schedule. Sherman Adams heartily concurred, telling cabinet officials to consult with him before presenting any questions to the president for resolution.[63]

On the Saturday before Christmas, Nixon presented gold candlesticks and gold place settings for eight, a gift from the cabinet to the president and first lady. Upon his arrival, Nixon thought that Ike was "somewhat depressed," but "he brightened considerably however when we [Hagerty, Persons, and Whitman] came in." The reason for Ike's despondency, apparently, was that his blood pressure was too high. Nixon recorded in his diary that the president's "fate was much more uncertain than the case of others who . . . could live differently in order to avoid another attack." A few days later, Jerry Persons commented that Ike "seemed to be greatly concerned over his health." When they rode together in the car to a cabinet meeting at Camp David, Ike took his pulse, and Persons noted "several instances of that type which concerned him greatly."[64]

Feeling that the Gettysburg weather did not permit him to exercise sufficiently, Ike left for Key West, Florida, on December 29 and stayed at the United States Naval Base until January 8, 1956. Before leaving, he wrote a letter thanking the cabinet for its solidarity during his absence. To Nixon, he added: "In large measure the cooperation that was achieved was due to your personal effort."[65]

The president's heart attack tested how well his administration responded to such an unexpected and devastating event. In the week that he was incapacitated, Nixon and the other members of his cabinet helped to preserve calm by recognizing that the president expected them to continue with their normal duties. That was a measure of how well Ike had governed. It also was fortunate that no pressing domestic or international crises erupted.

Eisenhower was still convalescing in January, four months after his heart attack. He rested a minimum of half an hour before lunch, and afterwards, relaxed an hour in an easy chair. Every hour during an extended gathering, he needed to leave the room for ten minutes and be alone to rest.[66] He would soon have to decide what to do over the "next five years."[67]

THE HUTSCHNECKER FICTION

On January 3, 2001, the *New York Times* ran an obituary with the headline "ARNOLD HUTSCHNECKER, 102, THERAPIST TO NIXON." This description came from a bestselling book published in 2000, *The Arrogance of Power* by Anthony Summers, which had made the sensational allegation that Hutschnecker had been Richard Nixon's "trusted psychotherapist." Summers had interviewed the then ninety-seven-year-old Hutschnecker at a time when he was showing signs of mental deterioration.[1]

Summers's book did not mention Hutschnecker's testimony at the vice-presidential confirmation hearings for Gerald Ford. Senator Howard Cannon, Democrat from Nevada, swore in the doctor as a witness on the morning of November 7, 1973, and asked him in what capacity he had treated Nixon. Only as an internist, Hutschnecker replied. Mark Hatfield, Republican from Oregon, followed up bluntly: had Hutschnecker ever acted as Nixon's psychiatrist? The reply was "Never." Hutschnecker gave identical testimony before the House committee on the judiciary on November 20.[2]

Summers ignored Hutschnecker's other denials as well. In his book *The Drive for Power*, published the year after his congressional testimonies, the doctor insisted that he had acted solely as an internist and never treated Nixon as a psychiatric patient. The vice president had come to him "for occasional checkups and to discuss how to deal with the stresses of his office, including the many official dinners he had to attend—in short, how to stay fit. There was no evidence of any illness."[3]

When I conducted my research, Hutschnecker's handwritten notes on his treatment of Nixon were preserved at the National Archives in Laguna Niguel, California, where I had access to them; other records existed at the Richard

Nixon Library & Birthplace in Yorba Linda, California. Summers could not see these files because they are closed. He could, however, have examined the vice president's calendars, which confirm how infrequently the physician saw Nixon. The schedule of visits is much more consistent with periodic physical treatment and checkups than with ongoing therapeutic sessions. Although Summers's notes and bibliography do not cite any of Hutschnecker's letters or medical files, he claimed that they contained notations that Nixon was an "emotionally deprived child," his mother was a negative influence, and his parents brutalized him; and that he discussed problems regarding his wife and other women. I examined Hutschnecker's files thoroughly before they were given to the National Archives and, under its rules, closed to researchers. I found nothing in his medical records, letters, or memoranda to substantiate Summers's claims.

The Arrogance of Power was correct on one point. Hutschnecker did treat Nixon. Most of the book's other statements regarding the Hutschnecker-Nixon relationship are incorrect. Summers erroneously claimed that Nixon saw Hutschnecker in 1951. Neither Nixon's calendars nor Hutschnecker's medical files confirm this date. Summers wrote that Hutschnecker prescribed vacations for Nixon, and it was on one of these vacations that Nixon met Charles "Bebe" Rebozo. Nixon met Rebozo in 1950, a year and a half before he ever saw Hutschnecker; Senator George Smathers introduced them.[4]

Nixon became aware of Hutschnecker when former California senator Sheridan Downey sent a copy of the doctor's book *The Will to Live* in the winter of 1951. The book advanced the idea that health was a struggle between creative and destructive forces, and it built its recommendations around sound mental health, physical fitness, and a carefully designed diet.[5]

Nixon liked what he read, and needing a family physician to supervise his annual physical, he made an appointment with the doctor in the middle of January 1952. During his first examination, the senator complained that while conducting an intensive speaking schedule in 1951 he had developed a sensation of pressure in the back of his head and "once during speech felt like black out." To treat this, Hutschnecker prescribed a sedative. Nixon returned two months later feeling better, but he had continued his exhaustive speaking engagements and now described his symptoms as an "oppressive feeling" from "pain over heart" and a "slight flicker over r.[ight] eye."[6]

A week after the 1952 Republican national convention, Hutschnecker flew to the capital to examine his patient. Initially, Nixon's blood pressure was 150 systolic; after a few minutes of rest, it dropped to 125/80. The two men discussed how to cope with the stress of the campaign. As a reminder, several days later Hutschnecker wrote him a memo enumerating the measures Nixon should take to manage stress. He first needed to take short rest periods and do only minimal work at night so not to interfere with sleep. As for his eating habits, he recommended: "Avoid fat, fried and spicy food, gravy, mayonnaise, and pastry." He should have a substantial breakfast, a light lunch, and a midafternoon snack. He should drink liquor in moderation unless tension rose, and he then could have a highball or a glass of champagne before dinner to relax. Before retiring, he might have a small snack, such as a glass of warm milk.

To avoid anxiety, Hutschnecker prescribed several common medications. He recommended Decholin as a laxative, and belladonna for stomach cramps and pain: one-half tablet after lunch and dinner, perhaps a tablet at bedtime. To prevent colds and throat irritation during the campaign, Nixon should take Chlor-Trimeton at bedtime. If anxiety became "very great" and threatened sleep, the doctor prescribed a "sleeping capsule."[7]

Hutschnecker thought the 1952 presidential campaign might be affecting Nixon's physical as well as mental health. (Although Summers claims that Nixon wanted to see the doctor after the fund crisis, the doctor was the one who asked for an appointment. It did not take place.) He recommended that the candidate ingest Seconal for "a few nights" and the "little red sleeping capsules" that he prescribed for "Miss R. Woods." He also prescribed a half or a full tablet of Decholin for bile; "after breakfast [it] might help you to carry through the day with greater ease." Nixon's frenzied schedule made it impossible to meet before the end of the campaign.[8]

Earlier that summer, Rose Mary Woods had asked Hutschnecker if he knew of a doctor in Washington who could treat Nixon because he did not want to "bother" Hutschnecker. The physician dismissed the suggestion; treating Nixon was no bother. New York was an hour away from the capital by plane, and he would fly to see his patient whenever necessary. On September 20, the doctor wrote that he was honored to be the vice president's physician: "In that way I could be of service to my country, and this would be enough compensation for me." Nixon retained him as his physician.[9]

The newly elected vice president did not take his next physical examination until the first day of February 1953, when he visited Hutschnecker's Park Avenue office in New York. The physician noted that the vice president had done "well through campaign" with a "slight let down." He "once woke up pain sharp in prostat[e]." Throughout his vice presidency, Nixon never again visited Hutschnecker at his office. They met instead at the Waldorf Astoria Hotel, in the presidential suite 35A, or at one of Nixon's offices in the Capitol building. Hutschnecker saw his patient at the Waldorf, for instance, late in the afternoon on February 1, 1954, shortly after Nixon returned from his eighty-day journey in Asia and North

Africa. His notes indicate that Nixon felt tired and was concerned about that condition continuing with the congressional campaigns commencing in September.[10]

Before that heavy schedule began, the physician traveled to the capital, conferring with the vice president on the morning of August 19. He noted that his patient again complained of a "tired feeling" and tension. After the November elections, he wrote that he hoped Nixon "managed to remain well under pressure of the intense and strainuous [sic] campaign."[11]

Hutschnecker did not maintain strict confidentiality regarding his famous patient. In the summer of 1954, reporter Helene Erksine wrote an article on the vice president for Collier's. She told Nixon that she understood he saw Dr. Hutschnecker, and the vice president readily confirmed it: "My heart is strong, lungs in fine condition, blood pressure 120 over 80." The columnist later interviewed the doctor. He did not confine his remarks solely to his role as Nixon's internist but launched into a lecture on the "age of ambivalence," which he defined as "simultaneous existence within us of opposite emotions toward the same object or person. We may be outwardly, consciously friendly, and inwardly, unconsciously hostile at the same time." Ambivalence, he added, explained man's darkest experiences, and he "could follow his drive toward cruelty and destruction unpunished. . . . Today he has no excuse."[12]

After the article was published, Hutschnecker wrote to Nixon, apologizing for granting the interview and regretting the reporter's "apparent indiscretion." He had told her, he said, of his "great respect for your winning personality and your unusual alertness of mind." He had spoken to her off the record and she had used the conversation without his permission.

The vice president did not consult Hutschnecker for more than a year. They met on January 16 and February 13, 1956, at the Waldorf Astoria. On March 21 the vice president flew to Florida for what was advertised as a sixteen-day vacation. According to Nixon, he was merely "looking forward to some sunshine and warm weather" and "a chance to have some fun and relax before the grind begins once again." His children joined him on March 30, and on April 1 the family attended sunrise Easter worship services with 75,000 people at Biscayne Bay. He completed his holiday on April 8.[13]

While in Florida, the vice president relayed to Hutschnecker through Rose Mary Woods that he was regularly swimming and walking on the beach and sometimes went out on a boat. He was getting a good deal "of rest and relaxation" without any "particular problems on his mind." He decided to become more active by playing golf but was experiencing a "residue of tension." He could not write a speech and was unable to spend more than half an hour looking at his mail. When he finished, he "felt edgy." Before going to bed, he swam or walked; that relaxed him.

Hutschnecker had prescribed several medications to relieve the vice president's tension and insomnia. Nixon was taking three Equanil, a tranquilizer, during the day and considering reducing that amount. He also took Dexamyl, a stimulant that could elevate mood and lead to psychic dependence: half a pill when he planned to talk a great deal, but in Florida more often a third of a pill every other day. During the evening, he had two or three drinks, which made him "feel good." Before going to sleep, he had half a Doriden, a potentially addictive drug for those who had trouble sleeping, and if he awoke during the night, he took another half. He wanted to know if he should reduce the amount of liquor or medication.[14]

The doctor thought Nixon's Equanil dosage was "fairly good." If Nixon was having a "bad day," he should take the "small pills" several hours before he planned to retire and another one just before he went to bed. Hutschnecker did not want this medication to make Nixon "a little dull and disinterested." Equanil might cause "something like a mental depression"; he could "become completely listless. We want a state of relaxation but not this other listlessness." The vice president could take half, a third, or even a quarter pill of Dexamyl. He could "take quite a bit of that a day." As for drinking, Nixon should be careful not to "lose control—lose sharpness." At the end of the day, he should consume a Seconal, before dinner but might not need another at bedtime. This barbiturate was a sleeping aid that relieved anxiety and insomnia.[15]

During the 1950s, this was the standard of care. All of these drugs were popular and regularly prescribed. Doriden, in higher dosages, was a hypnotic; Equanil was possibly habit forming and discontinued in the 1960s; Seconal was discouraged except for short periods. These drugs were often called "downers." Dexamyl was a potentially addicting "upper." Sleeping pills did not yet have time-release components and usually lasted for four hours; if you awoke, it was customary to take another one to get you back to sleep. Doctors usually did not discuss the drugs' pharmacology with patients; pharmacies did not supply caution labels; and when a patient went to multiple doctors, overlapping prescriptions usually went completely unmonitored. Neither doctors nor pharmacists were required to take continuing education courses to keep up on medical developments.[16]

According to Dr. Nikitas Zervanos, who practiced medicine during the 1950s, Nixon was one of many patients who, at least temporarily, "probably abused mood altering medications and needed them for purposes of keeping him stimulated (uppers) or at other times to sedate (downers) him."[17]

Hutschnecker and Nixon occasionally consulted by telephone after the vice president started to develop stomach trouble in early May. Until the afternoons he got "along fairly well." Before and during the evening meal, he felt "a little sickishness—no vomiting but sometimes with gas is a little dizziness that comes from it." He worked a full day, but by evening he was "fairly worn out." The illness had become chronic and had settled in his stomach and lower abdominal tract. He was "not particularly worried about it but I just want to get rid of it."

Doctors treated his gastritis with Pathilon, an antimuscarinic (a treatment for patients with overactive bladders), before each meal and before retiring; he also chewed antacid tablets. He followed a bland diet: a cup of coffee in the morning and a little skim milk between meals. In the evening, he usually had two one-ounce drinks in a tall glass of water. He stopped taking Equanil and instead took Doriden or Seconal every night due to trouble sleeping. Before he went to bed, he took a short walk and had some warm chocolate.[18]

Hutschnecker and Nixon communicated again on June 4. The physician believed the report from Nixon's doctors in the capital looked "pretty good," but his globulin was higher than Hutschnecker would have liked. The vice president wanted Hutschnecker to come to see him and discuss general problems. He resumed taking three Equanil pills daily, Doriden to sleep, and a Pathilon before each meal and two at bedtime.[19]

They set a lunch date for the middle of the month. Hutschnecker flew to the capital, where he and his patient discussed the results of his checkup from Walter Reed Hospital. The vice president treated his guest to lunch in room P-53, where Nixon presented the doctor with a Schaeffer pen set with a black base and a clock purchased from the Senate stationery store, as well as a small ivory carving of marching elephants that he had brought from home. These were clearly meant as a thank you, since Hutschnecker did not charge him a fee. The doctor wrote Nixon on June 21, declaring he looked better; there was "apparently a healthy lessening of stress judging from the greater ease with which you seemed to handle affairs."[20]

That was the last time Nixon saw Hutschnecker during the first term.[21] Fourteen years later, Hutschnecker speculated that Nixon stopped seeing him because gossip columnists wrote that he "was seeing a Park Avenue psychiatrist."[22]

Hutschnecker not only treated the vice president but also ingratiated himself with Nixon's private secretary Rose Mary Woods. On one occasion after he saw the vice president, he wrote a handwritten note to her: "It was good seeing you." On another occasion he signed, "Best wishes and regards, and a lot of Adrenalin." In the spring of 1954, she wrote the vice president's former law partner Thomas Bewley, who was not feeling well, that Nixon believed Hutschnecker was "particularly good in finding out just exactly what makes people tense, nervous, tired, etc. The Boss swears by him and would like him to have a chance to look you over." After the congressional elections, the doctor sent her galleys of his forthcoming book. Later he sent her a paper he had discussed with her, with a note saying he was "following the dazzling zig-zag rout and the speeches of the 'Boss' (as you call the Vice President)."[23]

Woods kept Hutschnecker current about Nixon's health. Toward the end of November 1954, she was looking forward to taking a vacation while the Nixons rested in Nassau. The vice president seemed "to be feeling very well considering the rugged campaign schedule which kept him going almost twenty-four hours a day during the campaign period." On April 28, 1955, she explained that her Boss's schedule remained "completely 'mad,'" but he would contact Hutschnecker shortly. That winter, she wrote that Nixon hoped to see him in New York City for an exam, but felt fine; he had "been extremely busy, but shows no particular sign of wear and tear!"[24]

Hutschnecker used his connection with Woods and "The Boss" to help promote his book. Late in 1954, he sent galleys of *Love and Hate in Human Nature* to the vice president. President Eisenhower, he remarked in an accompanying letter, had talked about "coexistance" [sic] and "its psychological aspect"; this might interest Nixon for "its broadened psychosomatic concept." When the book was released early in 1955, the physician sent Nixon an autographed copy. The vice president thanked him and said he had recommended it and the doctor's first book to some friends.[25]

Hutschnecker continued to promote the book to the vice president after its release. Writing on April 12, 1955, the physician acknowledged that he worried about the "total destruction" of "the whole human race," mentioned his "blueprint for peace," and said he hoped Nixon "would perceive its deeper message." He called upon Nixon's "strength and ability" as well as his "imagination and idealism" that would make him "a man of destiny." The physician claimed that he had summoned "a great deal of courage to write this letter" for two reasons: first, "it would strike you as a piece of fantasy"; and second, he was "overstepping a cordial doctor-patient relationship." Hutschnecker was more than willing to discuss his ideas at a later date, but if Nixon saw the letter "as an intrusion, please do not hesitate to immediately say so."[26]

Nixon never replied, but he invited the doctor to a state dinner for Italian president Giovanni Gronchi and his wife at the capital on the last day of February 1956. Hutschnecker complimented the vice president for the manner in which he discharged his "official duties with apparent ease and consideration, still finding time to be kind, thoughtful and interested." He hoped to see Nixon soon.

Once again, he asked a favor, if it did "not violate any ethics." The request did, of course, impinge on the doctor-patient privilege. Would Nixon give a copy of *The Will to Live* to Ike?[27]

Nixon kept his meetings with Hutschnecker and other doctors as secret as possible. Rose Mary Woods referred to the physician as "H" when making entries in Nixon's schedule. Several of the other doctors went unnoticed, and the only way they were identified was that the vice president sent them thank-you letters.

Behind Nixon's facade of physical energy lay serious health concerns. In his first memoir, *Six Crises*, he writes how, before being nominated for reelection, he "was thrown into another period of agonizing indecision, which more than any overt crisis takes a heavy toll mentally, physically, and emotionally." While that description might sound exaggerated, it was in fact an understatement.[28]

Few commented on Nixon's health during the 1952 presidential race. Aylett Cotton, a San Francisco attorney and one of the candidate's advance men, saw Nixon at the end of July and observed that he needed to "get some rest. He seemed more tired last night than I had ever seen him before." Toward the end of August, Cotton to his relief found Nixon "as relaxed as I have ever seen him, and having a wonderful time—we all figured that his relaxing, a thing that he rarely has time for." At the end of the month, Congressman Patrick Hillings, who had succeeded Nixon in the House, felt that his mentor was "holding up very well and continues to maintain his good health."[29]

Many physicians examined him for various complaints during the first term. On the Sunday morning after the 1952 convention, for example, Nixon awoke with "a heavy chest cold," and Dr. Hugh McKenna, chief of staff at St. Joseph's Hospital in Chicago, treated him at the hotel so quietly that none of the reporters lurking outside discovered the house call. Throughout his vice presidency, Nixon, like the vast majority of politicians, tried to keep health concerns hidden from media scrutiny.[30]

The vice president seldom mentioned his health issues publicly. When he did, he gave the impression that he was in excellent shape. Rex Scouten, a Secret Service agent who guarded the vice president for over five years, called him "a human dynamo." Even so, Scouten recalled that his charge had colds, sore throats, and the flu. Rarely did Nixon's physical condition appear in the press, and when it did, the coverage was minimal. In the winter of 1955, for example, the *New York Times* ran a tiny piece saying he had "a slight case of influenza" but still came into his office and planned to preside over the NSC and cabinet meetings that week. By the middle of February in the next year, Walter Reed

Hospital released its general findings of a five-day examination that concluded that the vice president was "fit."[31]

Nixon consulted a number of physicians during his first term. In December 1952, vacationing in Florida, he slipped on a piece of metal jetty while swimming in the Atlantic Ocean and suffered a "bad gash." Pat insisted that he go to the emergency room at St. Francis Hospital where Dr. Herman Boughton put several stitches on the underside of his right foot. Nixon hobbled "around on crutches" for four days, and when Ike learned about the accident, he wrote: "Stay out of the water, I need you."[32]

The vice president claimed that he was too busy in 1955 to see a doctor. After the president's heart attack, during November and December, Nixon complained of several bouts of flu but did not see a physician. His only positive health news came from Dr. William Chase whom Nixon considered "one of the finest dentists in the country" and who had served the family since the Nixons came to the capital just before Christmas: "you would be glad to hear that your teeth appear to be in excellent shape."[33]

In the middle of January 1956, he spent three days in bed with the "virus bug." He felt well enough to fly to Chicago for a Salute to Eisenhower dinner. After his arrival at his hotel, a prominent physician in the city, Dr. Morris Fishbein, treated him. After the visit, Nixon recalled that he had been "feeling a bit rocky for the past two weeks . . . and the Bellergal [used to quiet stomach distress] was very helpful in getting me through a rather long and tiring evening." Robert Spindell, who attended the event, thought the vice president looked "well, in spite of the virus infection."[34]

One doctor suggested that Nixon take a week's vacation to Florida to recuperate. The vice president followed that recommendation and, without any disclosure, consulted Dr. Donald Marion about his ill health. Even though he had not recovered, he flew to Rio de Janeiro for Juscelino Kubitschek's presidential inauguration in the first week of February. During this period, the virus lingered, and he also developed a heavy head cold. Once in Rio, he had a local physician, Dr. Genival Londres, pay a "house call" at the United States embassy. Only American ambassador James Dunn and a few others knew of the doctor's visit.[35]

After returning from Brazil, Nixon spoke with Len Hall on February 8 about not "feeling well," and for the next two days he underwent a series of tests at Walter Reed Hospital, supervised by Colonel Francis Pruitt. The vice president told him that his responsibilities over the past six months had "increased manyfold" due to Ike's heart attack and that he "sought relief of mental tension accompanied by some degree of insomnia." In the past, when he experienced fatigue, he recovered with rest. Now his fatigue persisted; he was irritable, and he could not get "an uninterrupted sleep." Dr. Walter Tkach, who assisted Dr. Howard Snyder, the president's personal physician, had prescribed sedatives for the vice president, but Nixon wanted to stop taking them as soon as possible.

Nixon also had "some transitory bouts of chest discomfort" that were not serious. After a hard day of work, he did not want to read or watch television due to eye fatigue and headaches. He also had some passing anxiety with "an upper respiratory infection." Despite these symptoms, the test results indicated that his health was "within normal limits." Several months later, he had additional tests because of "mid-epigastric discomfort." It was not painful, rather "a dull discomfort." Adding to his troubles, he had a twenty-four hour "bout of watery diarrhea, some nausea accompanied by fever." The doctors also discovered a hiatal hernia and placed him on a bland diet.[36]

He traveled to Key Biscayne from February 19 to 26, for rest. Two Secret Service agents accompanied him as well as deputy attorney general Bill Rogers. The vice president spent a great deal of time with Bebe Rebozo, who took him for an elegant dinner at Maxim's in Miami. He returned to Florida for sixteen days in March and early April under Hutschnecker's guidance.[37]

This respite did not keep his problems from worsening. While swinging a golf club in Florida, he gave his back "a good wrenching" and felt a sharp pain. Dr. John Handwerker Jr. saw the vice president and referred him to Dr. Robert Keiser, a highly regarded orthopedist from Coral Gables. This specialist paid a "house call" on the afternoon of April 3. His patient described acute pain in his lower back, and the physician ordered bed rest. Keiser diagnosed "a muscle and ligamentous strain, very likely with an associated intervertebral disc injury." When Nixon returned to Washington, he sent Keiser's findings to his local doctor. X-rays confirmed that nothing was "radically wrong," and his back seemed normal.[38]

On the weekend of May 4 to 7, the Nixons traveled to the Greenbrier resort in White Sulphur Springs, West Virginia. They stayed at one of the cottages, named "Top Notch." Nixon again felt ill and called Dr. Eugene Morhous, who served as the house doctor. Morhous prescribed medication to get rid of the "bug" quickly so that it would not spoil the Nixons' vacation.[39]

In the summer of 1957, because of the president's three widely reported health scares, the vice president kept the public partially apprised of his physical condition. He developed a mild case of farsightedness and started to wear reading glasses, especially for speeches. The White House physician, Dr. Walter Tkach, in the spring of 1960 completed a physical examination and announced that his patient's heart, lungs, and blood pressure were normal; Nixon was in "excellent health."[40]

He also contracted several bouts of flu during the second term but quickly resumed his duties. At the end of 1958, a badly infected wisdom tooth was extracted. On February 3, 1959, he returned home from his office, put his car in the garage, went to the back door of his house, slipped on icy steps, and fell on his back. He got up, went inside, took some pain medication left over from dental surgery and fell asleep. The next day an X-ray revealed two cracked ribs. The vice president suffered throughout the next month from some discomfort (laughing and sneezing were painful), but by the beginning of April he had fully recovered.[41]

These facts were made public. The vice president kept his contacts with Dr. Hutschnecker secret during the second term. The two exchanged two letters in the summer of 1958, and Nixon saw him twice for lunch in room P-53 of the Capitol, on May 1 and December 9, 1959. Nixon reported that in spite of his frantic pace, he felt "extremely well" and even with his cracked ribs, he was in "excellent health."[42]

The doctor appeared more motivated to pursue other matters. He sent a copy of his book *The Will to Live* so that Nixon could present it to the president. Nixon had Rose Mary Woods send it to Ann Whitman with the comments that it was a best seller and Ike might enjoy it. Hutschnecker also enclosed a revised edition of the volume for Nixon, and in early 1960 he sent another book, *The Meaning of Death*.[43]

Besides providing this material, the doctor offered advice. In 1959, this included a memorandum on leadership that was divided into three sections: hostility, fear, and hope; the status quo versus energy; and how leaders behaved. Before Nixon visited the Soviet Union that summer, Hutschnecker volunteered his services and said he would be "delighted" to be included. The vice president was "entering the world arena with all its promises as well as the manifold involvements of stress." Toward the end of the year, the doctor gave Nixon an outline for the administration to establish a Department of Peace. Before wishing the vice president the "warmest Christmas," Hutschnecker asked: "Does all this sound absurd?"[44]

Although Nixon saw Hutschnecker only twice during the second term, he secretly saw at least ten different doctors in the first half of 1956. He also kept his flu, tension, insomnia, and other health problems secret, along with the drugs he was taking to relieve his symptoms. He was able to conceal these problems because he was not required to report them to the public. The combination of

Ike's well-known illnesses and Nixon's unreported ones means that at the height of the Cold War, both the president and the vice president could easily have been simultaneously incapacitated, leaving no one responsible for governing. Those health conditions were never known at the time and, fortunately for the nation, their potential consequences were never tested.

IKE'S DECISION TO RUN

From the beginning of his presidency until August 1955, Ike's approval rating from the Gallup Poll was never worse than 57 percent favorable and 25 percent unfavorable. During the same period, when pollsters conducted presidential trial heats for 1956, Ike always beat Stevenson. When Gallup at the end of 1954 asked what man respondents admired most, Eisenhower was the most frequently mentioned, with Stevenson third.[1]

The president avoided speculation about his political future. On March 2, 1955, at a White House press conference, he refused to reply to a question about his reelection plans. Fifteen days later, Merriman Smith of United Press inquired whether the GOP was "strong enough to win re-election in 1956 without you." Once again, the president would not answer. At a Republican fundraiser on May 23, Eisenhower's arrival prompted chants of "We Want Ike." He would give no hint of his reelection plans, and at the end of the month told reporters that he enjoyed his job and disliked politics.[2]

Speaking to an Ohio Republican delegation at the start of August, the president, for the first time publicly, noted his age as a factor against his running again and encouraged younger men to vie for the presidency. Unless something "catastrophic" intervened, he said, he had decided to be a one-term president, but he would not announce this in public until the last moment so that he would maintain his power.[3]

Ike evaluated possible replacements in 1956. Over Christmas in 1953, his first choice seemed to be his younger brother Milton. Other Republicans included Nixon, Attorney General Brownell, his deputy William Rogers, disarmament adviser Harold Stassen, and Secretary of the Army Robert Stevens. From the legislature, the president identified Congressman Halleck and Senators Potter, Goldwater, and Knowland. A year later, Ike still considered Nixon and

Brownell candidates, along with Secretary of the Navy Robert Anderson and Under Secretary of State Herbert Hoover Jr. In early December, he picked Anderson, Hoover, Nixon, Lodge, Brownell, Halleck and, reluctantly, Stassen.[4]

As summer approached in 1955, many people pressured him to run again. When Lucius Clay, one of his strongest supporters in 1952, made his case, Ike seemed reluctant. No one had ever reached the age of seventy in the White House. In the middle of August, however, he admitted to his boyhood friend Swede Hazlett that he might run. He had tried to groom two or three able younger men, but none were ready. Still, his failure to find an acceptable substitute provided "no valid reason for my considering a second term."[5]

Ike continued to believe that he needed to maintain flexibility before making any decision and cautioned that he would be persuaded to run only by "extraordinary circumstances." On September 12, 1955, he asked his brother Milton about his reelection. The president claimed that he had tried to convince Republican leaders of his unavailability. They insisted that if he did not run, the party would lose the election.[6]

Milton typed his reply and placed it in two envelopes marked "confidential" that were then given to the president's private secretary, Ann Whitman. She opened the outside one, and only Ike saw the inside letter. It implored Ike not to take any precipitous action. He could wait until March or April 1956. Milton realized that Nixon, RNC chairman Len Hall, and various state chairmen had pressed his brother to seek another term and recommended that Ike secretly write some friends that he would not accept a second nomination. They would then leak the letter's contents to the media.

The president quickly approved of the scheme. He asked Milton to emphasize that the GOP had to develop other leaders and should not expect "a single individual to carry the burdens of political leadership." Although he had never felt healthier, he recognized that this could change instantly, and he resented being pushed into another race. He had explained his commitment to a single term before accepting the nomination in 1952 and was deeply concerned that many Republican spokesmen were now saying that unless he served a second term, everything for which he had "slaved so hard, will be lost in an upsurge of socialistic developments." Milton drafted a letter on September 20 to Undersecretary of Commerce Walter Williams, who had been prominent in Citizens for Eisenhower-Nixon in 1952, and to several others, asserting that his brother would "*not* run again." Republicans had to end their dependence on "the indispensable man" and find an alternative.[7]

While Milton tried to dampen the enthusiasm for another campaign, the president routinely praised his vice president. In March 1955, Ike sent a telegram to a Republican fundraiser in Los Angeles applauding Nixon's contributions in foreign affairs and declaring that he was proud to call the vice president his friend. On the last day of May, Ike said that Nixon had been "very useful" and had "worked as hard as any man I have known in this whole Executive Department." During the third week of June, Ike told a group of GOP leaders in San Francisco that Nixon was "growing day by day." Prominently placed in the vice president's Capitol office was an autographed photograph of the president, inscribed "with lasting appreciation of his outstanding services to the nation, and with affectionate regards from his good friend."[8]

Nixon appreciated the compliments but urged Ike to run. After the 1954 elections, Nixon told *U.S. News & World Report* that Ike was "the best leader that the United States has had in my lifetime" and that he hoped the president would seek another term. Traveling in Central America and the Caribbean, the vice president told reporters in Nicaragua on February 21, 1955: "I am with Eisenhower." In the Dominican Republic on March 1, he again urged the president to run.[9]

Two weeks later, Nixon addressed a GOP luncheon fundraiser in Los Angeles, calling for the party to rebuild its majority so that it would not have to rely on a single candidate's popularity. Ike had won due to his strength among independents, and as president he proved his worth. A more powerful party would be able to elect candidates based on Republican principles, not personalities. At present it could not. Nixon cautioned: "The Republican party is not strong enough to elect a President. We have to have a Presidential candidate strong enough to get the Republican party elected." The GOP needed Ike to run again.[10]

At a Republican luncheon in Chicago two days later, Nixon held that the Democrats could not unite their divided factions, while Republicans were united by the president. Animosities within the party had to end so that the party could gain majority status and "elect its candidate rather than having to depend upon finding a candidate who has an appeal greater than the party itself."[11]

Through the spring and summer, the vice president reiterated that the GOP needed to enlarge its base and urged Ike to seek a second term. On June 13, he told Houston reporters that Ike's staff was "very optimistic" that he would enter the race. Shortly afterward in Detroit, he asked the Young Republican biennial national convention to adopt the slogan "Let's build a Party to match our President." In mid-August, he conceded that the president had not made a decision on running again, but two days later he enthusiastically declared that "Eisenhower is the man for the job." After an hour-long conversation with the president on September 5, Nixon held a press conference in which he claimed that those closest to Ike and Republican leaders believed he would run again: "The people who know the President and desire very much that he run again are more optimistic than at any time since he was inaugurated."[12]

Nixon's own political future depended upon the president's, and the two men met throughout 1955 to discuss politics. Over breakfast on February 3, the president told Nixon that if he decided to run, he wanted Nixon as his running mate. On March 10, the two men had lunch where the president confided that he did not want to run because of his age and because he disapproved of being the "indispensable man." Nixon replied that the GOP was not strong enough to elect a candidate from its own ranks; Ike had to run.[13]

Throughout his term the vice president had given mixed signals about his own renomination. On January 21, 1953, he told the Los Angeles Times that he was unconcerned about his position in 1956. In the spring of the following year, he informed the Washington Post: "In 1956 I will complete 10 years [in Washington], and I think that will be long enough." In February 1955 he forecast that he might not be vice president in 1957. On September 5, he declined to discuss his future: "no one runs for the nomination for Vice Presidency."[14]

Until the party had a presidential nominee, it was pointless to speculate about who would take the second spot, but Nixon seemed to be preparing for another race. On July 1, 1955, he remarked that Democrats and their newspaper allies had "resorted to some pretty low blows but I frankly don't feel that they have hurt anyone but themselves by doing so." Later that month, he admitted that his speeches sparked antagonistic responses: "This procedure seems to be part of the game!" Shortly before Ike's heart attack, Nixon had said that as long as the country experienced prosperity, Democrats would face difficulty regaining the White House. Their main assault would be directed at him; he was "going to be Target Number One."[15]

Republican National Committee (RNC) chairman Hall behaved as if the Ike-Nixon ticket were a foregone conclusion. As early as July 1954, he insisted that Ike would run again and that he was "very, very fond of Mr. Nixon." The president, Hall continued, kept his vice president fully apprised so that he would be prepared for any eventuality. Nixon was "the administration's strong right arm."[16]

Hall proclaimed in the summer of 1955 that Ike would seek reelection with Nixon at his side. When asked in early September about the president's reelection plans, the chairman declined to speculate about when Ike would declare. After the president's heart attack, Hall's push for the ticket only gained force. One of Hall's assistants, Bertha Adkins, as well as state chairmen Thomas Caldecott from California and Ray Bliss from Ohio praised the two men. Senator Clifford Case of New Jersey called it a "swell ticket."[17]

Even as pressure mounted for Ike to run again, some suggested replacing Nixon as vice president. Connecticut senator Prescott Bush knew that GOP liberals disapproved of Nixon's supposed backing of Joe McCarthy. In August 1955, a Connecticut newspaper, the *Deep River News*, opined: "Eisenhower is fine, but if he dies, God help us." Bush would be an acceptable alternative. A rumor that spring had Nixon assuming Secretary Dulles's post while Congressman Halleck would run for vice president. The *New York Post*, one of the most anti-Nixon newspapers, printed an article stating that some presidential boosters opposed Nixon and wanted to replace him with the president of the Ford Foundation, Paul Hoffman. Gossip also circulated that Governor Dewey and an eastern bloc wanted to remove Nixon from the ticket.[18]

Although Nixon referred to Dewey in his unpublished memoirs as "lackluster," the two men had a cordial relationship. Dewey and the president, however, were not comfortable with one another. Still, the idea that Dewey objected to Ike's reelection ran contrary to what the governor said. When Dewey and Nixon met for lunch in April 1953, the governor confided: "Ike will have to run in '56— even if it kills him." He later asserted that the president had "done his duty for forty years to his country and I hope his sense of duty will lead him to run again." At the beginning of 1955, Dewey predicted the same national pairing. When he spoke to Billy Graham that fall, he told the preacher how much he admired Nixon's contribution to the GOP. Dewey worried that "some of the extreme right-wingers" might have too much influence, but despite this concern, Nixon was "the most able man in the Republican Party."[19]

The vice president routinely traveled to California. His visit from August 9 to 18, 1955, further cemented his ties with his Southern California supporters. A stream of politicians and influential leaders welcomed him. He had dinner with *Los Angeles Times* political editor Kyle Palmer and others in Beverly Hills. He met with John Krehbiel, chairman of the Republican committee of Los Angeles County, and 120 GOP partisans. Congressman Glen Lipscomb, an avid Nixon backer, and other elected officials conferred with him. He attended a concert at the Hollywood Bowl for the Festival of the Americas Week, chaired by Mrs. Norman "Buff" Chandler, wife of the *Los Angeles Times* publisher. She introduced the vice president to the audience, and afterward he went to a black tie banquet with 500 guests in his honor.[20]

While Nixon was being touted for future occupancy of the White House, Senator Knowland nourished a similar dream by appealing to conservatives. On January 9, 1955, he appeared on *Meet the Press*, where he informed reporters that he would not join a "draft Eisenhower" effort. He disagreed with Republican spokesmen that only Eisenhower could beat a Democratic candidate. The president, already disappointed with Knowland's past performance, read his remarks in the next morning newspapers and responded angrily in his diary: "How stupid can you get?" He could not understand why Knowland would say such things unless he planned "to destroy the Rep.[ublican] Party." Ike would make his own decision without anyone having "the slightest effect."[21]

The vice president tried to squelch negative articles. On December 8, 1954, writing to Raymond Moley, a former Franklin D. Roosevelt Brain Truster turned *Newsweek* columnist, Nixon argued that Knowland's differences with the administration had been exaggerated and "the disagreement is more apparent than real." He saw these rumors as a way to divide the Republican Party by driving a wedge between Knowland and Ike. Occasionally, he added, "they have tried to set me against Knowland or against the President."[22]

The vice president tried to reinforce a positive image by emphasizing areas of cooperation. He admired and worked well with Knowland, he said, and the White House kept lines of communication concerning the senator's demands for a tougher policy toward Mainland China. Knowland had provided direction for Senate Republicans, and the vice president backed him in his leadership post. Others accepted Nixon's lead. Congressman Edgar Hiestand from California, a Nixon ally, proclaimed that talk about antagonism between Knowland and Nixon was nonsense. Conservative commentator Fulton Lewis Jr. complimented both men; they stuck to their principles, he said, while liberals disapproved.[23]

While Knowland and Nixon fought gossip of a rivalry, California governor Goodwin "Goodie" Knight caused considerable friction. Knight had replaced Earl Warren in the fall of 1953, when Warren resigned his governorship to become chief justice of the United States. The following spring, the *Los Angeles Times* reported that Knowland, Knight, and Nixon had friendly bonds and the state GOP was united. When Knight ran for the governor's office in 1954, he won handily.[24]

Once the new governor began his own term, however, his relations with Knowland started to deteriorate. Clint Mosher, a reporter for the *San Francisco Chronicle* who kept Nixon apprised about state politics, described Knight as "sound" and "nobody's fool." Mosher encouraged the governor to back the vice president and not align with the Warren-Knowland faction because it opposed his agenda in the state legislature. Mosher commented in a telephone call to Nixon's office that "Knight is satisfied that Knowland would do anything to eliminate Dick."[25]

Yet while Knowland and Knight drifted apart, so did the governor and the vice president. During the 1952 campaign, Knight appeared miffed when Nixon arrived at the Los Angeles airport and he was pushed out of camera range. At the Republican Governors' Conference in 1954, Knight told people the vice president had snubbed him. As a consequence, when Nixon came to Los Angeles to speak in March 1955, Knight deliberately stayed away.[26]

Another political battle surfaced at the end of 1954 when Knight demanded that he be named leader of the California delegation to the next Republican national convention. He wanted Ike to run and stated that he would support any candidate that the president chose. On January 22, 1955, he held an hour-long press conference in which he endorsed Ike but refused to include Nixon as the running mate. That summer, he not only reaffirmed his demand that he lead the California delegation, but also added that he opposed any delegation that forced him to include Nixon and Knowland's delegates.[27]

The Republican Governors' Conference was scheduled for early May 1955 and would take place in Washington. Assuming that Knight would try to see Eisenhower, Nixon met with the president's appointment secretary, Bernard Shanley, on March 25 to warn him that any such meeting had to be prevented. The vice president, who thought that Knowland and Knight might have reached some accord, was now having doubts because the two "had been shooting at each other for a great many years." Shanley described the Nixon-Knowland rivalry as "a very deep-seated one."[28]

To promote the appearance of solidarity, the vice president held a luncheon for Knight in the Capitol on May 3. Before they sat down to eat, Nixon and Knight conferred for twenty minutes, and when they met the press, they pledged to work together for party harmony. Ike was scheduled to meet with the governor after lunch. Before that gathering, the president spoke with Nixon about the composition of the California delegation to the convention. Nixon suggested that the president tell Knight that it should represent the entire party. Even though the governor would try to exclude Nixon's friends, he did not wish "to get involved in State fights!!" Ike was unconcerned. Knight would do whatever the president instructed.[29]

At 3:30, the governor saw the president at the White House for a few minutes. Shanley, who sat in the meeting, felt that Knight "handled himself exceedingly well." The governor had not tried to pressure the president and merely presented a resolution requesting that Ike seek reelection. After the meeting, Ike telephoned Nixon to say "we should win him [Knight] over." The vice president concurred, emphasizing that the governor craved attention.[30]

A month later, Nixon wrote Knight: "the political dope stories have been coming out by the reams since you were here!" He emphasized that their relationship had "been extremely cordial and I was confident we would have a united delegation in 1956," and promised to "do everything I possibly can to knock down any stories or rumors to the effect that there is a Knight-Nixon feud."[31]

While Republicans maneuvered toward the 1956 election, the Democrats were conducting their own intrigues. Stevenson had campaigned energetically for his party's candidates during the 1954 elections and received plaudits for his efforts. After the votes had been counted, the Democratic Party regained control of both houses of Congress, and Stevenson emerged as the leading contender in 1956.[32] Throughout 1955, the former Illinois governor deflected talk about his political ambitions. He occasionally spoke out against the administration's policies; in April, he complained about Eisenhower's Asian diplomacy and attacked Nixon for advocating sending American troops to Indochina.[33]

A quarter century after the 1956 election, Nixon offered his opinion of Eisenhower's two-time opponent. First, he said, Ike "couldn't stand Stevenson." The president never invited him to the White House, and after his heart attack, his physicians warned Sherman Adams: "Don't raise Stevenson's name with him. It raises his blood pressure." Nixon understood that Stevenson despised him and amply returned the sentiment. He described the governor as having "a superficial, fatuous air about him that just turned me off." Although he respected Stevenson for winning his party's presidential nomination, he believed Stevenson would have been a "disaster as president." He was indecisive, and what decisions he made were the wrong ones.[34]

The political calculus changed radically with Ike's heart attack. Initially, the bulletins described it as mild, then moderate. It was probably much worse. The president later described it as a "case of extensive heart damage." At first he concentrated on surviving, and even after he improved, his doctors kept him resting and away from the tensions of his job.[35]

After seeing the president in the second week of October, Nixon concluded that for two weeks afterwards, Ike could not make "a great decision." He added on October 10: "The President in condition has advanced to the point that he can be consulted and not make great decisions."[36]

The president, at the same time, was discussing possible GOP candidates to run for the presidency. He briefly mentioned to Sherman Adams the pros and cons of Nixon's running for that spot. The president also considered others, starting with Treasury Secretary Humphrey. Adams replied that, much to his surprise, the secretary had supported the interstate highway initiative, but he was slightly older than the president and could not "liberalize himself." Henry Cabot

Lodge, according to Ike, had "the greatest amount of personal charm and persuasiveness." But he had been defeated for reelection to the Senate in 1952 and also needed "a steadying influence" like Nixon, Adams, or Robert Anderson.[37]

Toward the end of the month, the president wrote Swede Hazlett about possible successors. After Swede counseled his friend to take a "hands off" approach, Ike replied, "I am vitally concerned in seeing someone nominated who not only believes in the program I have been so earnestly laboring to have enacted into law, but who also has the best chance of election." He threw out the name of his younger brother Milton as the best candidate, without having broached the subject with Milton. Ike added that his doctors had given him permission to start exercising. If he improved, they would know in about four months how much activity he could sustain without further damaging his heart muscle. By that time, his future plans "should definitely crystallize."[38]

While flying from the capital to Gettysburg on December 13, the president spoke with press secretary Hagerty about the 1956 election. Ike vehemently opposed Senator Knowland's nomination. If Knowland emerged as a contender, the president said, "I don't want to [run], but I may have to." He asked Hagerty about former New York governor Dewey. Although the two had been friends, Hagerty saw Dewey as too closely linked to the eastern wing of the party. Ike switched to Nixon. Hagerty responded that although he "was a very excellent" vice president, he could not win the nomination even with the president's blessings. The next day Ike proposed Secretary Humphrey, "one of the ablest men I know," for president and Milton for vice president. Hagerty tried to discourage any change, favoring the reelection of Eisenhower-Nixon.[39]

Several days before Christmas, Henry Cabot Lodge visited Ike in the Oval Office. Lodge hoped the president would decide if he were going to run for reelection on what "was beneficial for him." Ike rose and walked across the room and then stated: "No, let's decide it on the basis of what's best for the country. Never mind me." He had recently been to a reception for the White House staff and their families and got tired "and wondered whether he could do a job as President if he got tired so easily." Lodge later spoke with Dr. Levine in Boston who said anyone who had been in bed would naturally have been fatigued. This had nothing to do with heart disease. Ike had to be concerned with his breathing and chest pains.[40]

Nixon described Christmas Day 1955 as "very pleasant and mild, although a little windy." Deputy chief of staff Jerry Persons called him the next morning, asking him to come to the White House to urge the president to take an extended vacation in Florida so he could relax and discuss the future with Milton.[41] When Nixon arrived, the president informed him that he was going to discuss the political landscape with others without Nixon present since he would be one of the topics under consideration. The president had not yet made a decision about running for reelection because his doctors had not determined if he was well enough to serve a second term. Nixon, according to his diary, assured the president that he could safely delegate some of his duties to others. The president was disappointed that Nixon's "popularity had not moved up as high as he had hoped it would." Nixon might take a cabinet post, Ike suggested, preferably secretary of defense. The president said that recent polls showed Chief Justice Warren leading the vice president, to which Nixon responded others polls had him ahead. Ike cut him off: Stevenson was leading Nixon in polls. Nixon replied that a more recent poll had him gaining. Ike asked Nixon to meet "from time to time to discuss the situation with regard to yourself," adding "we might have to initiate a 'crash program' for building you up." Although the vice president volunteered that he might not run again, the president would "not hear of it because he felt that it would hurt the ticket if he jettisoned me at this point." Nixon left the meeting with the impression that Ike would not run "if he thought that anybody else has a reasonable chance to win." Lucius Clay, a close presidential confidante, believed that Ike listened to everyone, "but then he goes ahead and does what he believes is right."[42]

With the chief executive still recovering from his heart attack, Nixon concentrated on reassuring the GOP and the public that the administration was smoothly carrying out the president's policies. The vice president wrote former Kansas governor Alf Landon, the Republican losing presidential candidate in 1936 "that the members of the President's official family should scrupulously avoid participation in political speculation to the time he makes his decision with regard to the future." He did not want anyone to think he was pressuring Ike to run again, even though many Americans wanted him to do just that.[43]

Nixon found much support for a presidential bid of his own if Ike did not run. Wisconsin Congressman Laurence Smith wanted to "make sure that your enemies do not steal the nomination from you." Nixon, he said, had earned the right to run for the presidency. Senator John Williams of Delaware called the vice president the most likely GOP nominee if Ike retired. Alf Landon reported that Nixon had the support of the majority of Republicans in Kansas. If Nixon ran, that state's governor, Fred Hall, was "very strongly pro-Nixon" and hoped to be his running mate.[44]

Clare Booth Luce, United States ambassador to Italy, wrote from Rome in the second week of October that she was pleased Ike was recovering and wished that he would not run for reelection because of health concerns. She and her husband Henry proposed that Nixon replace Ike in 1956. She cautioned him:

"Don't let yourself get too tired, and be prepared, with a serene spirit, if you can manage it, for much bitterness and unkindness not only from enemies but even from those you have counted as friends. The cruelest storms rage around the highest mountains."[45]

The vice president faced growing obstacles in his home state. California was a prize, with thirty-two electoral votes, tied with Pennsylvania for the second-most behind New York. Chief Justice Warren had been regularly mentioned as a possible presidential contender if Ike retired, and without Ike in the race, Warren polled as the first choice of 25 percent of voters to Nixon's 19 percent. The chief justice tried to squelch any possibility of his candidacy on April 15, 1955, saying that when he took his Supreme Court post, he had permanently left politics and would not run "under any circumstances."[46]

Yet Warren retained a large following among liberals. In early October, the Gallup Poll of voters' preferences for the first time had Nixon leading the chief justice 28 percent to 24; in November, the vice president rose to 34 percent and Warren slipped to 23 percent. Still, pundits continued to speculate what Nixon would do if Warren were drafted.[47] They did not consider Warren's "irrevocable" declaration in April to mean that he had rejected any political career. That winter, he invited the television reporter Martin Agronsky into his limousine as he left the Supreme Court building at 6:30 p.m. Warren greeted him affably as an "old friend." Agronsky asked if he enjoyed his job, and the chief justice replied, "I can't begin to tell you how satisfying is." He had had enough of "traveling on trains and planes, of sleeping in hotel rooms, of making speeches," and was happy to go home each night and sleep in his own bed. He thought that he was learning the intricacies of writing a well-reasoned opinion.[48]

Many speculated that he might reverse his course once liberals who opposed the party's conservative wing rallied around the chief justice. A Warren candidacy came up at a White House press conference on January 25, 1956. When Ike was asked to comment, he replied that if the chief justice expected to run, he should resign from the bench. Several days later, Warren saw Hagerty at a party and expressed his annoyance at Ike's remarks, further straining relations between the president and the chief justice.[49]

Unlike Warren, Senator Knowland wanted to occupy the White House, but he said in the fall that he would not announce until Ike left the hospital. At that time, Knowland believed that the president would make an early decision. He feared a delay because it would inhibit his candidacy and allow Ike to "designate" his own successor. To avoid this scenario, the senator announced in the winter of 1955 that if Ike had not decided by February 1956, he would enter the race. A week later, he extended the time frame to the middle of that month. That deadline gave Ike time to file in the primaries but prevented him from anointing Nixon as his heir apparent.[50]

Governor Knight moved less cautiously. Just after the heart attack, Clint Mosher learned that the governor suspected that some insiders had known of the president's ill health. The reporter told Nixon that the governor "was as mad as hell." Palmer and Nixon knew Ike's health "was bad and that he wouldnit [sic] be able to run." Mosher felt that Ike should make his intentions clear as soon as possible. The governor also suspected that the Los Angeles Times political columnist Kyle Palmer had traveled to the capital "to knock Knight" and that his newspaper had "been blasting hell out of him."[51]

At the beginning of October, Nixon's advocates believed that Knight expected to run for the presidency and would use his control of the California delegation at the Republican national convention to help him gain the nomination. Knight and other Nixon adversaries would block the vice president's nomination. When reporters asked Knight to discuss possible GOP presidential candidates—if Ike was excluded—he included Knowland, Secretary Dulles, Lodge, and others; the governor left Nixon off the list but added his name in a later interview.[52]

Knowland saw the struggle between the governor and the vice president as an opening for himself. In a memo to Nixon, Knowland remarked "a good primary fight out here for delegates would be a good thing for the Party because it would clarify the air if it were conducted cleanly."[53]

Thomas Kuchel, the state's junior senator, told the press that Knight's comments about his presidential possibilities were disrespectful during Ike's convalescence. The governor would have ample time to deal with presidential politics later. Nixon applauded Kuchel's statement. He should have, for he had given Kuchel the idea and was pleasantly surprised when he used it. The vice president also encouraged others to criticize Knight. Richard Bergholz, the political editor for the Los Angeles Mirror News, wrote that "Knight, by his conduct in injecting partisan politics while the President is confined to a hospital bed, forfeits any right he might have had to enter the national picture."[54]

Clint Mosher said that the governor had made "an ass of himself." Nixon replied that Knight had received bad advice. No matter how inappropriately the governor behaved, the Republican Party was tied to the president's leadership: "we have to stick together or we will all hang separately."[55]

The governor ignored suggestions that he keep quiet. During a trip to Chicago, he proclaimed that Nixon could not win in 1956 but denied having said the same about Knowland. Los Angeles mayor Norris Poulson wrote the vice president that "the best way to take care of Goodie is to show that since he cannot handle his problems at home he should think a long time before trying to get into the national picture." John Knezevick, editor and publisher of the *Palos Verde News*, bluntly described the situation to Nixon: Knight "'committed political suicide' with his idiotic outbursts."[56]

Ike returned to his duties at the White House in January 1956. When Gallup asked if he should run for another term at the end of the month, 56 percent said yes; in the second week of February, the number rose to 60 percent and toward the end of the month to 72 percent.[57]

On Friday evening, January 13, at 7:00 p.m. Ike took "elaborate secret precautions" for a dinner meeting and even brought his place cards in his pocket. His closest advisers were assembled: Brownell, Foster Dulles, George Humphrey, Lodge, and Summerfield came from the cabinet; Tom Stephens, Jerry Persons, Sherman Adams, and Jim Hagerty served on the White House staff. Howard Pyle was Arizona's governor; Len Hall was RNC chairman, and Milton Eisenhower was his brother and close adviser. After dinner, they went to the upstairs study with the president sitting with his back to the fireplace.[58]

He asked each one for their opinions if he should seek another term. Secretary Dulles argued that Ike "had a unique ability to avert this disaster [a nuclear holocaust] and that God had given him this ability and that when God gave a man this ability he should use it." Stephens said that Ike ran better than any other Republican and implied that he had to make the decision promptly. Lodge added that the president had to make the decision on "what was good for him." Lodge dismissed the health issue with the comment that anyone could die at any moment and then added that the president had united the nation behind his domestic and foreign policies. The rest of the group favored his running with one exception. His brother Milton argued against it, and several days later, Ike's son John agreed. Both his brother and his son focused on Ike's health; they had little interest in political motives and the GOP's future. As the president's health steadily improved throughout the winter, he remained uncertain. He realized that he had to come to a decision shortly because his name was being entered in the primaries. The first one, in New Hampshire, was scheduled for mid-March.[59]

In early February he met with Len Hall about his reelection. If he did run, because of health concerns he would not campaign vigorously but instead would depend upon television appearances. He tossed out potential Democratic running mates like former Texas governor Allan Shivers, Governor Frank Lausche from Ohio, and Robert Anderson. He even considered switching parties and becoming a Democrat. Hall dismissed that idea—it would have been a nightmare for him—and added Lausche's selection would be a "shocker." While he had been elected governor five times, he was a Catholic. Ike had met him early in 1955 and was impressed. Almost a year later, Lausche said on *Meet the Press* that he hoped the president would seek reelection.[60]

The president, however, was merely speculating. Lausche was a longtime partisan Democrat. Two well-respected Democrats, Senator Richard Russell of Georgia and Governor Shivers, had suggested him for their party's presidential nomination on December 9, 1955; twelve days later, he announced that would challenge the GOP incumbent George Bender for the Senate seat from Ohio. During that closely contested race, which the governor won, the president campaigned for Bender.[61]

Ike also believed that Nixon, to further his own career, should leave the vice presidency. In January 1956, the president stated that no vice president, since Martin Van Buren in 1836, who had served eight years as vice president had won the presidency. Even though he had developed diplomatic and domestic skills, Nixon needed management experience. The president seemed conflicted: "people think of him as an immature boy. It would be difficult to find a better Vice President." Sherman Adams agreed, adding that Nixon had contributed outstanding service to the administration.

When the president held his morning press conference on January 25, he refused to talk about his future but offered effusive praise for Nixon: he had "admiration, respect" and "deep affection" for him. The vice president had visited many countries and had attended "every important meeting" in the White House. Such comments boosted Nixon's prestige; the president still felt that Nixon's best option was to take a cabinet post. On February 9, Ike told RNC chairman Hall to discuss this with Nixon, but to be "very, very gentle."[62]

Most probably the president did not view Nixon's taking a cabinet job as a demotion. After serving satisfactorily in one position, military officers were often assigned to other posts to broaden their skills. The vice president had no experience directing a large bureaucracy, and Ike may have thought that this was the best way for Nixon to learn how to manage large numbers of people. From the president's training, Nixon had served well, but he still needed to manage a complex organization. The Army jargon for such training was "command experience."

While the president was making the argument for Nixon to join the cabinet, Nixon was actively pushing for Ike's reelection announcement. On January 20, the vice president spoke for twenty-five minutes at the Salute for Eisenhower dinner in Chicago, which was telecast at forty-nine of fifty-three similar dinners around the country that evening and carried over television and radio. The vice president called for four more years and explained why the Republican administration had governed better than the previous Democratic ones. He then introduced the president, who remained noncommittal.[63]

Three days later, Nixon told reporters that Ike's friends were optimistic that he would seek another term. He had recovered from his heart attack and had returned to full-time duties, excepting only some ceremonial events. During his Lincoln Day address on February 13, the vice president focused on the contributions the administration had made and the hope that Ike would run again: "Our Republican Administration is now proving, for the first time in nearly thirty years, that we can have prosperity without war, full employment outside of uniform and security without regimentation and controls." Certainly the president was better than any Democratic alternative: Stevenson, Kefauver, or Harriman, "three candidates in search of a crisis."[64]

While he refused to discuss presidential politics until Ike acted, Nixon conceded that he had no money and no organization, and had never had a press agent. He kept to his theme: Ike should run for a second term. But if Nixon would not advocate his own cause, others did. RNC chairman Hall repeatedly championed an Ike-Nixon ticket. The Chowder & Marching Club demonstrated its backing for Nixon by holding a forty-third birthday party for him on the evening of January 9, 1956. Despite the brutal winter weather, 500 guests attended the event. C & M members like Wisconsin Congressmen Melvin Laird and Glen Davis provided Nixon with an apron and chef's hat along with a cake and candles. Ike sent a congratulatory telegram; some of the White House staff was there, as well as cabinet secretaries Dulles and Humphrey. Nixon appreciated this effort, since many C & M members were friends, and he had hosted events for them throughout his tenure.[65]

In the media, no outlet did more to promote Nixon in 1956 than the *Los Angeles Times.* In mid-January, Kyle Palmer endorsed him for vice president. The newspaper published a California poll toward the end of the month showing Nixon favored for president over Knowland by 35 percent to 21.5 percent if Ike retired. On February 18, the paper endorsed Ike-Nixon for reelection. The following week, publisher Norman Chandler urged Nixon to take the offensive and fight for renomination.[66]

While Nixon's supporters were pushing for his renomination, Ike still had not decided to run again. Lodge told the president on the morning of February 7 that he could run for reelection or select his successor, but he had to make the decision quickly. Although Lodge hoped that Ike would chose the former, if the answer was "no," Ike had to prepare the nation for his nominee. The president replied that he never did anything to suggest that he would run for reelection, and he could name ten individuals who were acceptable to him, "but there is something against every one of them." When he mentioned Lodge, the reply was that he lost his Senate seat in 1952; Ike retorted that Lincoln was defeated for the Illinois Senate seat in 1858. The president continued that his physicians did not understand that he was not interested in "longevity, but whether he would be able to do the work." Although Eisenhower was concerned that he would have to campaign vigorously, Lodge stated that this was unnecessary. Besides, Long added, "it would be undignified for him to go out all over the country and try to shake hands with every Tom, Dick and Harry."[67]

Twenty days later, after the president and Secretary Dulles had finished their diplomatic business in the late afternoon on Saturday, February 27, Ike talked to him "about personal and political matters." He was inclined to seek reelection with the understanding that he would not campaign vigorously. Dulles applauded this decision. The nation required the president's leadership in foreign affairs. Ike said that he had considered others to replace him. He admired Secretary Humphrey and appreciated Attorney General Brownell's "political acumen." He also wondered about his listener, who interjected that he "was too old." The two men then turned to Nixon as a possibility. Ike believed the polls showed he was not popular enough to win. Dulles disagreed about the accuracy of the polls. If Ike did not run, the secretary would choose Nixon. As for another term as vice president, Ike argued that a cabinet post would enhance Nixon's credentials. Dulles did not realize how significant this conversation was. Press secretary Hagerty telephoned Dulles on the morning of the last day of February and said that his interchange with Ike finalized the president's decision. He had "made him decide to go ahead."[68]

On the previous afternoon, before Hagerty made that call, Eisenhower summoned Nixon, Hall, Adams, and Hagerty into the Oval Office and told them of his decision to seek another term. On the morning of February 29, he began his press conference by talking about the fundraising drive for the Red Cross and several other items; then he said that he would appear on radio and television at 10:00 p.m. to announce that he would seek reelection. He based his decision primarily on his doctors' positive prognosis. Two days later, he wrote Swede Hazlett that one of his major concerns was that he had failed to groom a successor. After he left the White House, Ike recalled that while he had planned to serve only one term, he sought a second because Republican leaders told him that Nixon was unprepared to succeed him.[69]

The GOP was ecstatic. Ike's announcement invigorated the party campaign apparatus, but Nixon's status was left in limbo. At the pre–press conference, Ike stated that the press was "giving that subject [the vice presidency] too much attention." The convention decided its presidential nominee first, and he "couldn't be sure that the Republican Party wanted him." The audience laughed at this remark. Ike continued he would not recommend anyone for the second spot until after his nomination.[70]

NIXON'S AGONY

During the White House press conference at which he announced he would seek reelection, Eisenhower noted that until he was renominated at the 1956 Republican national convention, he would not recommend anyone as his running mate. He then reiterated his "admiration" and "respect" for Nixon, who had "been for me a loyal and dedicated associate, and a successful one. I am very fond of him." During his televised speech to the nation, he did not mention anyone for vice president. The following day, a headline on *New York Times* front page read: "2D SPOT IN DOUBT."[1]

Nixon responded with a laudatory statement predicting Ike would be renominated by acclamation and would be reelected by an overwhelming majority. The president had "prayerfully weighed" his decision, which would affect "the cause of peace and freedom" for everyone. "With millions of his fellow-citizens everywhere, we rejoice that his wise, devoted, and tolerant leadership remains available during a period in which it is so urgently needed." After reading these remarks, Ike wrote his vice president that he was "deeply" touched.[2]

Nixon loyalists were upset. On the same day as the press conference, Elford "Al" Cederberg, a Michigan congressman, wrote Nixon to express his pleasure and called him the "running mate." Tom Coleman from Madison, Wisconsin, "was bitterly disappointed . . . that the President did not mention that he wanted the V.P. again." Father Cronin, a trusted Nixon adviser, hoped that the vice president was "not disappointed by the 'dump Nixon' movement. There are some people in both parties who have never forgiven you for exposing Alger Hiss."[3]

Along with the Hiss matter, many Democratic leaders had a variety of reasons for disparaging the vice president. Eleanor Roosevelt, at the end of 1955, called Nixon "the least attractive" GOP presidential candidate. Her son John, a Republican who had a cordial relationship with the vice president, told her that

Nixon was "an admirable man." That testimonial did not shake her conviction. Having never forgiven Nixon for his senatorial campaign against Helen Gahagan Douglas, Mrs. Roosevelt responded: "I know that given great responsibility men sometimes change, but Mr. Nixon's presidency would worry me." Early in 1956, she called on Stevenson to run against the Ike-Nixon ticket. Democrats would "have to work harder than ever" because she doubted that the president would survive a second term "and I doubt if the country can stand Nixon as President."[4]

Truman attacked Nixon routinely and with increasing venom. In November 1955, he told a Seattle audience that he hated Nixon and would not discuss him: "He called me a traitor and if I am traitor, then the country is in a hell of a fix." Continuing his West Coast tour, he commented to reporters: "Don't even mention his name to me!" At the Burbank airport in Los Angeles, he said, "I don't want to discuss that son of a bitch"[5] During a morning walk with reporters in New York City on February 3, 1956, the cheerful former president turned grim when a reporter inquired about a statement he had made at a Democratic dinner, where he declared that Nixon had called him and General George Marshall traitors. Truman responded that Nixon had made that allegation during the 1954 campaign. There is no evidence of this.[6]

Nixon was less worried about the Democrats than about the composition of the California delegation to the Republican national convention. In early February 1956, Nixon lobbied for himself, Knowland, and Knight to select a harmonious delegation. In the middle of the month, the governor wrote Ike that he would lead a delegation pledged to the president. If Ike had not declared by March 7, Knight would become a favorite son. He and Knowland had spoken on the morning of February 22 about the delegation, and Kyle Palmer reported that there was "developing a definite coolness between these gentlemen."[7]

Murray Chotiner argued that the White House had to intervene and force Nixon, Knowland, and Knight to cooperate. By February 27 the trio agreed. If Ike ran, they would work toward a "unity slate." Once Ike announced, Knight sent a telegram to the White House pledging the three GOP leaders' cooperation. On the first of March, the president named them to select the delegation, and six days later it was done.[8]

With Ike having decided to run, the Republican Party solidified its divergent factions. Gallup Polls throughout the winter and spring of 1956 showed that Ike would easily defeat Stevenson. The president continued to enjoy overwhelming job approval.[9]

Stevenson moved toward renomination despite these numbers. Immediately after Ike's heart attack, the former governor had made no comment, but he quietly received information that the president would retire at the end of his term. No longer a reluctant candidate, Stevenson announced for the Democratic nomination in November 1955. In February 1956, he spoke before 1,500 Democrats at Salt Lake City, predicting that in the upcoming election, the vice president would campaign on "the lowest level."[10]

At the White House pre–press conference briefing on the morning of March 7, the staff referred to a *Newsweek* article that claimed the president had asked Nixon "to withdraw." Ike said that he would refute the story and characterize the vice president as a "comer." The president had urged him "to study his own career with a desire to be in the best possible shape to serve his country in the years to come."[11] When Marvin Arrowsmith of AP inquired about a story that the president was about to dump Nixon as vice president and offer him a cabinet post, Ike replied: "if anyone ever has the effrontery to come in and urge me to dump somebody that I respect as I do Vice President Nixon, there will more commotion around my office than you have noticed yet." He said he had asked Nixon "to chart out his own course, and tell me what he would like to do." Additionally, Ike designated him one of the "comers in the Republican Party. He is young, vigorous, healthy, and certainly deeply informed on the processes of our Government." He accepted "the same principles of government" to which Ike himself was dedicated.[12]

Reporters turned to the president's health. He hinted that if he were incapacitated, he would resign. He was not referring to the occasional flu, but to his "organic fitness in the job." That possibility had nothing to do with a vigorous campaign. He had already told GOP leaders that he would not conduct the 1956 race as energetically as he had done four years earlier.[13]

The next day the Republican governor from Colorado, Dan Thornton, visited the White House, where he and the president discussed a variety of subjects including the vice-presidential nomination. The president anticipated that Thornton's name would be brought up among several others, possibly someone from the South like Robert Anderson. The president was uncertain about Nixon's future. He had served in the House, the Senate, and the vice presidency. Ike had told him that no vice-presidential candidate would be identified until after the presidential nomination: "Never in our history have we had a man announce his candidacy for Vice President."[14]

On March 11, answering a letter from C. D. Jackson, Ike indicated his irritation with the media stories about his ditching Nixon. The president could not comprehend how reporters refused to "believe the plain unvarnished truth." Ike had always spoken favorably about his vice president and emphasized that no one, not even the incumbent, "'runs' for the Vice Presidency." No previous vice president had been "kept so well informed, so busy, so usefully employed—and . . . has in the broadest sense developed such a splendid understanding of contemporary government and the possibilities in it—as Dick Nixon."[15]

The next day, Ike wrote George Whitney that Nixon was reviewing his political options. Nixon had stated that he would do whatever the president wanted, and Ike wished to groom "young men for leadership" in the GOP, like Sherman Adams, Lodge, Clifford Case, Halleck, and others.[16]

Eisenhower met with Nixon for an hour on the morning of March 13 and called any rumors of an Ike-Nixon feud nonsense. He emphasized that he saw the vice presidency leading nowhere and pushed the cabinet post: "Anything you want to do, I would go along with it." Nixon could not be "the understudy to the star of the team, rather than being a halfback in his own right." Nixon responded that whatever the president decided, he would "accept it gracefully." Although he would take a cabinet post, the media and others would view it as a demotion. They would declare that Nixon was "afraid to run again, or [the] President [was] afraid to have him." This political spin was a secondary concern. His most "serious problem" was that Pat wanted to leave the capital. If she still felt that way when the convention convened, "he would have difficulty in saying he would do *anything*."[17]

As the two men discussed Nixon's future, Nixon knew that Ike's reelection statement assured his victory in November. This action, the vice president reasoned, meant "a continuation of the Eisenhower principles of government." He optimistically predicted that the coming triumph would generate enough voters to return Republican majorities to both houses of Congress. Even with those bright prospects, the vice president would not comment on his plans.[18]

Congressional allies encouraged Nixon to make a public statement that he wished to run again. Congressman Robert Wilson from San Diego informed him that he had more backing in the House than he thought. Thomas Jenkins from Ohio, who had gone with Nixon to Europe in 1947, wrote: "If there is anything I can do to help you, I will be very glad to do it." Marguerite Church from Illinois warned if Nixon were removed as vice president, it "would do incalculable damage to the Republican cause in our great Midwest." Finally, Paul Dague from Pennsylvania, who came to the House with Nixon in 1947, saw him as someone who had helped stem "the socialistic tide." He was angry that anyone would force Nixon off the ticket. The vice president had "become the symbol of the fighting spirit that must be displayed if we are to effectively carry this battle to the precincts where it must be won." Nixon could not quit. "Stay in the fight, Dick, and be sure we're with you all the way."[19]

Far more influential than these testimonials were the first primary results. The heavily Republican state of New Hampshire scheduled its voting on March 13; its ballots showed Dwight D. Eisenhower for president and left the vice president preference blank. Eleven days before the voting, William Treat, chairman of the Republican state committee, and Lane Dwinell, the Granite State's popular governor, called on voters to write in Nixon's name for vice president because he deserved a second term. No candidate had run advertisements or visited the state. When the votes were tallied, Ike had a total of 56,464. The vice president received a ringing endorsement with 22,936 write-in ballots, or 40 percent of what the president drew.[20]

The evening of that primary Nixon had dinner with Alice Roosevelt Longworth and heard the results. His office was soon swamped "with a tremendous amount of mail." Nixon had not campaigned in New Hampshire or encouraged anyone to act in his behalf, and the result came as "a mighty pleasant surprise." He also realized that the primary and other happenings had "considerably" changed the political landscape.[21]

William Loeb, controversial ultraconservative publisher of the *Manchester Union-Leader* in New Hampshire, wrote Nixon that the result "was an absolutely spontaneous, unrehearsed, unorganized, unplanned action on the part of New Hampshire voters," and "a sheer indication of their warm feeling for you." Loeb thought the write-in demonstrated that "the left wing Republicans ain't as popular as they think they are!"[22]

To prove that these were not isolated results, William Healy, GOP candidate for secretary of state in Oregon, organized a write-in campaign for Nixon as vice president on May 18. Eisenhower won on the printed ballot and the vice president got approximately 34,000 write-in votes, the most in any Oregon election. He again demonstrated that he had a significant following.[23]

Although primary voters were proving the vice president's popularity, the president was struggling in his relationship toward Nixon. The day before the March 13 press conference, he informed the White House staff that he intended to answer one more question regarding the vice president. Ike was growing impatient that Nixon had not decided on his future. Although he was not the sole vice-presidential possibility, the president saw no advantage "politically by ditching him."[24]

The next morning, before the press conference, the president asked his staff to find some answer to Nixon's renomination in light of the New Hampshire write-in vote. He might reaffirm his esteem for the vice president and the need for him to determine his political course. When UP reporter Merriman Smith asked about Nixon's primary showing, the president stated that he would make one last comment about the vice president and then would say nothing further until after the GOP national convention convened. He agreed, he said, with the Granite State's voters: "Anyone who attempts to drive a wedge of any kind between Dick and me has just as much chance as if they tried to drive it between my brother and me."[25]

On the same day, the president asserted that he had "never heard of anyone in a position of influence suggested dumping" Nixon. He had often repeated his "extreme satisfaction in having Nixon as a friend and as an associate in government." Ike also told the press conference that Nixon "was highly acceptable to me as a running mate on a political ticket."[26]

Ike's refusal to answer more questions regarding Nixon's status did not inhibit press comment. Raymond Moley in *Newsweek* wrote about how the "Reign of Rumor" distorted the vice president's service. Arthur Krock in the *New York Times* titled his piece "Nixon Gets Big Lift for Place on Ticket"; *Life* magazine editorialized with a "Salute to Dick Nixon." *Newsweek* asked a hundred editors for their opinions: fifty-eight thought that Nixon would help the ticket, twenty-five thought he would hurt it, and seventeen said he would make no difference.[27]

The vice president regularly met with the president to discuss many different items. In the second week of April, they met to consider the vice president's political options. If Nixon wanted to run again, Ike was "happy to have you on the ticket." He later spoke with Len Hall expressing a personal "like" and "admiration for Dick." But he still thought Nixon should take a cabinet post.[28]

When 800 GOP leaders assembled in the capital on April 17, Hall opened: "We have a great team, we have an outstanding record of accomplishment under Eisenhower and Nixon." Nixon then introduced Ike by saying that the president had "restored honesty, dignity, and integrity to government." The president outlined the continuation of his crusade and hoped that Republicans, independents, and some Democrats would embrace it.[29]

Eight days later, at a White House press conference, William Lawrence of the *New York Times* asked if Nixon had reported back to the president on his political future, and Ike answered no. Roscoe Drummond of the *New York Herald Tribune* later asked for a clarification. Did the president know if the vice president wished to be renominated? Ike replied that Nixon had not given him permission to say anything.[30]

That answer presented the vice president with his opening. The next afternoon at 3:00, Nixon came to the White House and spoke to the president for approximately a half hour, telling the president that he was available for renomination, and if the press asked, Ike could say that he would be honored to run. Ike reacted enthusiastically and called Hagerty into the Oval Office. The president thought that Nixon should meet with the White House reporters and make the announcement himself. Hagerty called them into his office at 3:45 declaring that the president was "delighted" with Nixon's decision.[31]

At the Friday cabinet meeting, John Foster Dulles expressed his fellow secretaries' "gratification" that the Ike-Nixon "team" would run for reelection. Dulles later telephoned Pat to say how "delighted" he was at her husband's decision. She appreciated his "wonderful support." He always called first and was "a good friend."[32]

After that announcement, the May primaries appeared uneventful as the GOP prepared for the national convention that summer. But the political climate soon changed. On Thursday, June 7, Ike looked fine, but on Friday morning he had a slight headache and stomach discomfort. That afternoon his pain grew worse, and an ambulance was dispatched to take him to Walter Reed Army Hospital, where he was diagnosed with ileitis—inflammation of the ileum, where the small intestine meets the large intestine. Hagerty announced that the president had an "acute intestinal obstruction" but his heart functions were normal.[33]

Around midnight, the doctors decided to operate and asked Mamie to sign consent papers. She refused, so her son John did. The last order that Ike signed before he went into surgery was to alert United States forces to stand by to repel a sneak atomic attack by the Kremlin. Before the operation, Wall Street reacted with steep stock losses on Friday, June 8.[34]

A minute before 3:00 a.m. on Saturday, the president underwent anesthesia. The operation concluded successfully at 5:11 a.m. with no heart complications. The bulletin stated the "obstruction was relieved." For at least four hours, the nation had no functioning commander-in-chief.[35]

Earlier on Friday evening, Nixon told a Young Republican gathering at the Mayflower Hotel that he was disturbed over the president's condition and offered a silent prayer for his well being. He then switched to politics, speaking extemporaneously, urging the participants to work at the grassroots level to win GOP converts to return a Republican Congress in the next national elections. During his presentation, the vice president blew his nose several times. Grinning at reporters, he remarked: "I know you're not interested in the health of the Vice President, but it is hay fever, not a cold."[36]

On Monday, Sherman Adams announced that the president was recovering well. His son John knew better, describing his father as looking bad, unable to absorb food, and losing weight. He "walked slowly and hunched over." Despite this initial gloomy picture, Ike resumed his daily schedule at the end of July and appeared fully recovered.[37]

Nixon continually commented on the president's rapid convalescence. On Monday, June 11, Wall Street regained most of its earlier losses, and the next day, Nixon told his friend Jack Drown that Ike was "snapping back in excellent shape." Later, he stated that Ike was "soon going to be out of the hospital, and is going to be fit to carry the burdens of the hardest job in the world."[38] Unlike the president's heart attack, where his cardiologists took almost a half a year to release a positive prognosis, the surgeons for Ike's ileitis operation quickly assured the public that the president would recover quickly and completely. While the president improved, Nixon, Secretaries Dulles and Humphrey, Attorney General Brownell, and others kept the government agencies running smoothly, just as they had after the heart attack. When asked during a radio broadcast on June 17 if the GOP convention would renominate the president, Hagerty replied affirmatively and added that Nixon would be in the second spot.[39]

With the vice president scheduled to see the president at Walter Reed Hospital the next day, Colonel Francis Pruitt, his physician at the hospital, informed Rose Mary Woods that Ike "was looking forward to see[ing]" Nixon because he was "a tremendous fellow, I am delighted to have him with me. I have the utmost admiration for Dick Nixon."[40] Nixon and Secretary Dulles visited Ike at the hospital for about half an hour; they discussed some government business. When the vice president met with reporters, he told them that the president did not mention his political future, but others assumed that the ticket would remain intact. Toward the end of the month, the Gallup Poll asked respondents to guess whether Ike would still run for another term, and 73 percent said yes.[41]

Even though Nixon's approval ratings were mixed, within the GOP his numbers steadily rose. Dan Gainey, a key member of Citizens for Eisenhower, declared that he was Nixon's "biggest booster" in Minnesota. Governor Langlie, from Washington, enthusiastically endorsed the vice president. Senator Bridges from New Hampshire proclaimed that the vice president would "strengthen the ticket." He was an asset, not a liability, even though "a great many people, particularly extreme left wingers" opposed him. Senator Goldwater from Arizona reinforced his colleagues' positions on July 7: "The Vice President is mighty popular with the workers of the Republican party. I think his popularity with them is almost as great as that of President Eisenhower himself." Congressman Robert Corbett received more than 10,000 replies to his polls, in which 84 percent said they were satisfied with Nixon as Ike's running mate. The Minnesota and New York Republican delegations to the convention endorsed him for reelection.[42]

Not everyone applauded Nixon's contributions. Drew Pearson, in his regular column *The Washington Merry-Go-Round*, continually printed "dump Nixon" articles. At the end of June he reported that John McCloy, vice chairman of Chase National Bank, and Paul Hoffman, chairman of the Studebaker-Packard Corporation, were attempting to replace Nixon with Secretary Humphrey. Hoffman, who had been identified earlier as part of an anti-Nixon faction, had written the vice president that "Nothing could . . . be further from the truth." McCloy denied the column; he had never spoken to the president or anyone else in the administration about Nixon and thought that the vice president was "very impressive. Certainly if the President should feel Nixon was the proper candidate for Vice President, this would be conclusive and fine with me." Humphrey corresponded with Nixon shortly after the Pearson column, denying its veracity and adding that he was "for you one hundred percent and always have been." *U.S. News & World Report* declared on July 20: "Speculation of recent days that Nixon might be deleted was without foundation."[43]

Nixon's place on the ticket depended on the president. Almost a month after his ileitis surgery, the overwhelming impression was that Ike would stay in the race. Hagerty, sporting a wide grin, refused to confirm or deny this at a news conference. On Friday, July 6, one White House reporter polled a dozen of his colleagues, and the results were eleven to one that the president would run.[44]

Any lingering suspicion ended on Tuesday, July 10, when Senator Knowland left a meeting with the president at his Gettysburg farm and announced that Ike expected to run. After RNC chairman Hall conferred with the president, he told reporters: "It's Eisenhower and Nixon—that's it!"[45]

Nixon, who had just returned from abroad after these statements were released, headed for the Eisenhower farm on July 14, where he and Ike met for seventy-five minutes. Afterward, Nixon spoke to the press and pledged to do "whatever the President and the National Convention decides." If that did not end any doubt, the next day, Nixon's nemesis Governor Knight predicted an Ike-Nixon ticket on the first ballot.[46]

Ike returned to the White House in the latter part of the month looking fit. His vital signs were normal, and he had increased his workload. Although his convalescence was not completed, he seemed eager to start the campaign. Nixon was his running mate.[47]

The Democrats, meanwhile, struggled to decide their ticket. Although Stevenson commanded widespread support in his party, Senator Kefauver had upset him in the New Hampshire primary and gone on to beat him in Minnesota and Wisconsin. Stevenson won in Oregon, Florida, and California, assuring himself the nomination, especially since many Democratic bosses disapproved of Kefauver.[48]

Joseph Kennedy, patriarch of his Massachusetts clan, repeated on July 18 what he had told Stevenson two years earlier. Ike was "the most popular man that we have seen in our time and to make attacks on him in this coming campaign is to me a sure way to commit suicide." With the country experiencing prosperity and peace, the public would not grasp complicated issues. Stevenson, Kennedy advised, should concentrate the "campaign on the possibility that Mr. Nixon would become President if anything happened to Eisenhower." Democrats did not have to enumerate the vice president's weaknesses, just raise the specter. Independent voters thought "badly enough of him."[49]

What Kennedy recommended, many Democrats would follow. Eisenhower's attitude toward Nixon in the second spot from Christmas 1955 until the end of April 1956 seemed baffling. The president never uttered an unkind or unpleasant word about his vice president, constantly called him a friend, and expressed his admiration. Yet he also doggedly held to the belief that Nixon should take a cabinet post and futilely encouraged people like Robert Anderson, who had no desire for the job, to seek the vice presidency.

The president did not seem to understand that if Nixon did not run for reelection, opponents would perceive this as a demotion, damaging his future political prospects. It is possible that that the president had no better grasp of partisan politics than he had of politics within the faculty when he served as Columbia University president. Ike was a brilliant bureaucratic manager, a skill that he had learned in the Army and brought to the federal bureaucracy. The Army's way of grooming a promising young officer was to give him a succession of assignments, so that if and when he reached the high levels of command, he could call upon a wide range of experience. Nixon had done extremely well as vice president; now he could best burnish his credentials by accepting a new assignment.

Nixon, acutely conscious of political actions, knew that a move from second in line to the presidency to a cabinet post, no matter how carefully or often it was explained, would look like a demotion. If such a move were even thought to be under consideration, his position would look tenuous. A relentless striver from high school onward, he felt strongly that if he were removed from the 1956 ticket, the public would conclude that he had been dumped. Partly out of vanity and, partly out of political savvy, he knew that it was not enough that he somehow maneuver his way onto the ticket. Leaders were drafted for their posts.

Eisenhower had to pronounce him acceptable or even welcome, and possibly Nixon wanted to be asked.

The president's physical problems may have contributed to the clumsy manner in which he dealt with the situation. The media reported, in minute and glowing detail, on his heart and his ileum, but not on the president's discomfort, the medications he was taking, or the extent of his inability to function during his recovery.

In a meeting with *New York Times* columnist Arthur Krock on the afternoon on April 6, 1960, the president explained why he thought Nixon should have joined the cabinet. Ike "had no thought of trying to side-track Vice President Richard M. Nixon in 1956 when he suggested that Nixon might think a cabinet or equivalent post would better serve his aspirations to be nominated for President in 1960." He reminded Nixon that no vice president since Martin Van Buren had been elected president. Nixon considered the president's argument and rejected it. He thought that "an appointive post would be taken as a demotion" and also believed that because of the opportunities that the president had given him, his public approval would rise. While Ike considered six other Republicans who could fill the presidency, he concluded that "none had qualifications superior to Nixon's."[50]

In the spring of 1970, Robert Anderson sat down for an oral history. He recalled that Ike had approached him on several occasions throughout 1955 for the second spot because he felt "that Anderson was the best qualified to run" and that the GOP would accept him. Ike never discussed Nixon, but he was not the president's "first choice." Even with Ike's flattery, Anderson refused to budge; he was not enticed to enter elective politics and remained a Texas Democrat until after the 1956 presidential election.[51]

In a conversation with Dillon Anderson, an Eisenhower National Security Council (NSC) adviser, on February 9, 1968, the former president reiterated that "he was honestly trying to give Dick some good advice." When White House counselor Bernard Shanley recalled the drama over the 1956 vice-presidential ticket almost two decades after the fact, he said that the president sincerely felt that Nixon was "at a dead end with this job of Vice President." If he "were smart," he would take an equally significant cabinet post, "and then you'll have a real launching pad for the future." During two reminiscences, Attorney General Brownell held that Ike thought if Nixon wanted to run for the president, he needed "some administrative experience" like a cabinet position.[52]

If these opinions left any doubt as to the president's motivation, Milton Eisenhower, in the summer of 1983, recalled staying at the White House over the weekend when his brother talked to Nixon. Ike's admiration for him had increased with time. Ike offered Nixon a cabinet post because he did not see the vice presidency as "a good political springboard" for the top spot. According to his brother, the president never seriously considered another running mate in 1956. Milton stressed that while his brother might have preferred Robert Anderson, "he did not feel strongly enough about this to bring the matter to a climax."[53]

STASSEN'S FOLLY

Before Eisenhower reached the presidency, only two men had served two full vice-presidential terms: Daniel Tompkins under James Monroe and Thomas Marshall under Woodrow Wilson. Other vice presidents who almost completed both terms were John Adams under George Washington; George Clinton under Thomas Jefferson and James Madison; John C. Calhoun under John Quincy Adams and Andrew Jackson; and John Nance Garner under FDR. Just two vice presidents in the first half of the twentieth century ran for consecutive terms: Marshall and Garner.

Thus, it was hardly a foregone conclusion that Eisenhower would retain Nixon as his running mate in 1956. And there was, in fact, an effort to get him off the ticket—a largely one-man crusade that has been inflated over the years into the myth of a "Dump Nixon" movement within the Republican Party. Elizabeth Drew, for instance, in her 2007 book *Richard M. Nixon*, writes that "moderates and other opponents" tried to remove Nixon from the ticket but does not identify them. The president, she affirms, "had doubts" about keeping him, but he nonetheless survived. How he did so, in the face of Eisenhower's disdain and an apparently well-supported "Dump Nixon" movement, is left a mystery. A reader could not learn from Drew's book that no one seriously challenged Nixon for the nomination or that he had an overwhelming majority of delegates pledged to support him before the convention.[1]

On July 6, 1956, H. Brooks Baker, chairman of the one-week-old "Young Americans for Eisenhower First—Stassen Second" advised Republican National Committee (RNC) chairman Len Hall by telegram that the organization had formed and was composed of Republicans and independents in sixteen states. Supporters in Connecticut, Baker complained, had been threatened with expulsion from the local Republican Party if they backed Stassen for vice president. Even though Hall had come out for the Eisenhower-Nixon ticket, Baker felt that the chairman should not interfere with a Stassen for vice president movement. He called upon the RNC to remain neutral in the choice for the vice-presidential nominee.[2]

Stassen had reached the pinnacle of his influence. He had achieved national recognition at the age of thirty-two by being elected the youngest governor in Minnesota's history, earning himself the nickname "the boy governor." He resigned in 1943 to enlist in the Navy, where he served as an assistant to Admiral William "Bull" Halsey. While on an inspection tour of Bougainville in the South Pacific, Stassen spoke briefly with Lieutenant Nixon. The two met again in 1948 after Nixon was elected to the House, and when Stassen decided to run for the presidency that year, Nixon secretly contributed to his campaign. When Eisenhower entered office, Stassen was made director of the Mutual Security Agency until the summer of 1953, then director of the Foreign Operations Administration, handling economic aid programs. In 1955, he left that post to become the special assistant to the president for disarmament, a position that held cabinet rank, causing some to dub him the "Secretary for Peace."[3]

Throughout 1955, Stassen had called upon the president to seek reelection and predicted that Nixon would be Ike's running mate. After the president's heart attack, Stassen announced his availability to run for the presidency. By the end of the year he had abandoned that position, believing the president would seek another term.[4]

Early in 1956, Stassen claimed that he had begun advising Nixon that he had to improve his relations with independents, liberal Republicans, labor, and minorities if he were going to alter his negative image among these groups. With Ike on the ballot, the party had won the White House after two decades and also captured both houses of Congress. Two years later, with Ike usually staying above the fray while Nixon campaigned energetically, the GOP lost control of Congress and suffered a net loss of governorships and state legislatures.

Once the president announced for a second term, Stassen encouraged politicians in his home state to set aside his favorite son candidacy and instead support the president. From March until the start of May, Stassen was abroad, but shortly after he returned, he began expressing misgivings about Nixon's renomination. A Republican who was also a union official warned him that organized labor would vote against the president if Nixon were on the ticket. When Stassen visited Washington state later that month, some people told him the vice president would damage the president's reelection prospects.

Several Gallup Polls confirmed his fears. The president was far more popular than his vice president; both Stevenson and Kefauver, the leading frontrunners for the Democratic presidential nomination, defeated Nixon handily in presidential polls. Stassen commissioned his own survey in the first part of July, which verified Gallup's findings.[5] So he sent a memorandum to the president on July 19, informing him that if the same ticket were renominated, Nixon would cost it six percentage points. He had to be replaced, and Stassen suggested Governor Christian Herter of Massachusetts as the alternative.[6]

The former Minnesota governor met with Eisenhower the next morning to discuss his concerns. He later informed the press that Ike had stated that Stassen could support whomever he wished but could not say that he was speaking on the president's behalf. The president "gave neither approval nor disapproval, he neither encouraged me nor discouraged me." The only directive was that Stassen must make clear he was not acting "as a personal representative of the President."[7]

With Eisenhower at an inter-American gathering in Panama, Stassen called an afternoon press conference on July 23 to declare that, acting independently, he called on Herter to run for vice president. An Eisenhower-Herter combination, he said, would do better than Eisenhower-Nixon because Herter attracted a wide variety of Republicans, independents, minorities, and unions. Stassen called on his own supporters to switch their allegiance to Herter and said he hoped that Nixon would join the movement to nominate the governor for vice president.[8]

Stassen had already privately given his reasons to the president: Herter had diplomatic experience; he had served in the Massachusetts house of representatives from 1930 to 1943, for the last four of those years as speaker; he then went to the United States House of Representatives for a decade; and in 1952, he had upset the incumbent governor with a large popular vote, was reelected two years later, and now had decided not to run again.[9] Stassen did not mention that in the spring, when the Gallup Poll asked its sample to identify Herter, only 10 percent could do so. He also failed to mention a point that, while it would probably have discouraged Eisenhower, was crucially important to Stassen: the sixty-year-old Herter had crippling arthritis, had to walk with crutches, and had difficulty standing for long periods.[10]

Herter was not among the people the president named as possible running mates. Ike met with Nixon on March 13 after watching Herter on *Meet the Press* and remarked that the reporters had "tied him in knots—it was a pretty stupid performance." The questions centered on the vice presidency for eight or nine minutes and then shifted to his job in the state house. But after Herter interjected that he enjoyed diplomatic affairs, reporters asked him about foreign policy. Ike was disappointed: Herter "just didn't know—could simply say that he 'just has a feeling we are all right.'"[11]

Nixon and Herter had known each other since the fall of 1947, when they were both congressmen on an inspection trip to Europe as a prelude to the Marshall Plan. Herter referred to his friend as "Nick." The vice president had made Herter's son his first administrative assistant.[12] When commentators advanced him as a potential vice-presidential nominee, Herter wrote Nixon not to take these rumors seriously: "Because of my deep personal friendship for you, the last thing in the world I want to see would be any semblance of what some outsiders might consider conflicting ambitions."[13]

On the same day that Stassen appeared before the press, Nixon issued a statement saying he would abide by whatever decision the convention made concerning the vice-presidential candidate. Herter was "one of the ablest public officials it has been my privilege to know." If the delegates selected Herter, Nixon would fully support him. The vice president could afford to be gracious. He did not mention that of the 1,323 convention delegates, 900 had already pledged to support him, and he was actively pursuing more.[14]

Twenty of Nixon's former comrades in the House immediately reacted to Stassen's announcement by demanding his resignation. Representative Robert Wilson from San Diego sent Stassen a telegram: "Amazed and shocked at your divisive action today regarding replacement of Vice-President Nixon on the Republican ticket." The vice president acknowledged their support: "Your prompt and unequivocal response as one of the 'House 20' to the latest barrage sent my way has my deepest appreciation."[15]

A day after Stassen's press appearance, White House press secretary Hagerty predicted an Eisenhower-Nixon ticket. RNC chairman Hall had telephoned Herter to ask him to nominate Nixon for vice president. On the morning of July 24, Herter said that he would do whatever the president asked of him and would be honored to make the formal nomination. Seemingly unperturbed, Stassen continued his Herter drive.[16]

The president returned from the inter-American conference in Panama that morning to find his staff incensed that Stassen's actions, not Ike's diplomacy, had dominated the headlines. After exiting his airplane, the president warmly greeted Nixon and curtly acknowledged Stassen. The press took these signals as further proof that the disarmament adviser had little influence at the White House.[17]

Stassen blamed Hall and Hagerty for impeding his effort to replace Nixon and claimed that his mail and telegrams favored Herter. The Minnesotan also sent letters to the twenty congressmen who asked for his resignation, holding that he had acted to "save your seats from a serious danger posed by an avoidable weakness and to win a Republican majority in Congress instead of the minority position in which you now find yourselves."[18]

Stassen identified five contributors who had financed his polls but did not reveal who had conducted the sampling or what methodology was employed. In one question, respondents were asked which of eight potential GOP vice-presidential candidates, including Stassen and Herter, they preferred; Nixon ran last. Whatever damage the uncertainty over his nomination did to the vice president, a Roper Poll found that more people liked him than disliked him. More significantly, a Gallup survey of Republican governors, state chairmen, and national committee persons overwhelmingly favored the vice president for renomination.[19]

The president expressed his frustration over the conflict between Stassen and his adversaries and blasted Hall for attacking the disarmament adviser and backing Nixon. Three weeks earlier, Ike had asked Hall to remain neutral; he had ignored that directive. The president agreed that both the RNC chairman and Stassen had "made mistakes," but the convention delegates would choose the vice-presidential nominee. Reporters did not comprehend that Ike sincerely believed "he had no right to impose his will on the Convention."[20]

Stassen had sent a letter to every GOP House member asking him or her to replace Nixon with Herter. While the president refrained from making any public comment, Republican congressmen did not hesitate. Congressmen Patrick Hillings, from Nixon's former district, and Elford Cederberg from Minnesota passed around a petition called the "Nixon Manifesto." They then issued a joint statement saying that 180 out of 202 Republican congressmen urged Eisenhower to retain the vice president for renomination.[21]

When Stassen appeared on the Sunday television program *Face the Nation*, he said that the president had not decided whom he would back for vice president, but he conceded that no one on the White House staff had offered him any assistance. He was convinced that Herter would benefit the national ticket. Most delegates, he stated incorrectly, were not pledged to Nixon and could "reevaluate" their choice before the convention opened.[22]

Stassen flew to Gettysburg on Monday, July 30, to lobby the president. He emerged after a twenty-minute conversation to tell reporters that the president had granted him a four-week unpaid leave of absence starting on August 1. As for his Herter initiative, he told reporters that his mail was running seven to one in his favor because his choice, a less controversial figure, appealed to labor, minorities, and independents.[23]

He did not mention that he had given the president his analysis of how adversely Nixon would affect the ticket. The vice president, he now said, would cost the president more than the 6 percent he had predicted earlier. The Eisenhower-Nixon team would be weakest on the East and West Coasts and might fail to carry California, New York, and Massachusetts. A wage-earner-panel poll had confirmed his 6 percent figure, and many individuals whom Stassen had spoken with would not vote for the president if Nixon were his running mate.

The attacks on him, Stassen said, had passed through three phases: a "very heavy attack for opening the question," criticism of his "timing" for being too late, and finally "examining the facts." To assist in the evaluation, Stassen suggested that at the next White House press conference, Ike affirm that Stassen had acted appropriately by calling for an open convention where Nixon, Herter, and others would be considered for the vice presidency. Stassen hoped that Nixon would take himself out of the running and back a "non-controversial figure." He described this option as best for the nation, the Republican Party, and "the cause of peace."[24]

While Stassen captured headlines, Governor Knight, on July 23, endorsed the president for renomination but refused to include the vice president. Knight harbored thoughts of his own bid for the vice-presidential nomination and saw Nixon as unworthy.[25] The day after Knight spoke, Senator Knowland announced for the Eisenhower-Nixon team. Early in August, the California Republican central committee met and decided that a majority vote translated into a bloc vote. Knowland led that fight, for Knight would never command a majority of the delegates. Nixon's allies on the committee told him his nomination was receiving "mounting support," and *Call-Bulletin* reported on August 7 that at least half of the state's delegation backed the vice president. Shortly after that article appeared, Knowland met with Ike and asserted that the California delegation was "overwhelmingly" for Eisenhower-Nixon.[26]

On August 1, a week before that meeting, the president prepared for his weekly press conference. His staff suggested that he tell reporters he favored an open convention and that Stassen had acted within those guidelines. The delegates alone, he should emphasize, would choose the ticket, and the president added that reporters were making "a mountain out of a mole's hill." If asked, Ike would say he disagreed with the Stassen's claim that Nixon would cost the ticket "millions of votes."[27]

Later that morning, the president answered reporters' questions for about a half-hour; they primarily dealt with Stassen. The president had spoken with him, praised the "very splendid job" he had done on disarmament, and confirmed that Stassen had taken a leave of absence. He now acted as "an individual, not as any member of any official family." Nixon was "perfectly acceptable" as a running mate. He had performed well on his missions abroad and had "made a splendid record as Vice President in these past four years." When the president remarked that he had not yet been nominated, the audience laughed. He emphasized that the convention delegates could nominate whomever they desired; he and Nixon had concurred that the vice-presidential position was open for consideration.[28]

The day after the president's press conference, Governor Herter announced that he would not permit his name to be placed in nomination. On August 4, he emphasized his support for Nixon and for "the continuity of the Eisenhower administration." Nine days later, he spoke before 400 Republican women activists in Massachusetts. Having run in seventeen elections over four decades, he was pleased "not to be running for any office."[29]

Stassen's polls showing that Nixon would weaken the GOP's national ticket were placed in question. Claude Robinson, the president of the Opinion Research Corporation in Princeton, New Jersey, urged Republican Party leaders to dismiss Stassen's allegations. Polls, Robinson advised, could be manipulated to prove whatever one wished. "The G.O.P.," he wrote in a letter to Nixon, "can have no part of the Stassen movement. You have been out on the front lines and have drawn certain fire; but if any Party strategist gets chicken-hearted over that fact, he had better take a good, long look at it, for all hell is likely to break loose in the Party if your nomination does not go through on schedule." He accurately forecast that the Eisenhower-Nixon team would win between 58 to 59 percent of the vote in the general election.[30]

To counteract Stassen's findings, the Los Angeles Times released its own poll, based on a sample of 3,000 interviews, which demonstrated Nixon's strength. Voters in California preferred Nixon to Knowland and Knight by substantial margins. Norman Chandler, the newspaper's publisher, sent a telegram to Stassen saying that he had purposefully misrepresented his results and that the vice president was heavily favored over his opponents. On August 10, Nixon met with the president to present Chandler's findings.[31]

Stassen remained undeterred. On August 3, he opened an Eisenhower-Herter headquarters in the capital, staffed by several young volunteers. His mail was positive, he said, and supporters were sending contributions. The thirty reporters at the opening ceremony heard the disarmament adviser predict that Nixon would cost the president 3.6 million votes. At the beginning of his drive, Stassen said, Herter had been a long shot, but now he was even money. The Massachusetts governor had behaved appropriately by consenting to nominate Nixon; now it was up to the convention to draft Herter.[32]

Nixon's defenders were equally determined. Len Hall, defying the president's insistence that he remain neutral, predicted an Eisenhower-Nixon ticket in a *Face the Nation* interview on August 5. The president never made it a certainty, Hall admitted, but the Republican Party supported Nixon, and Stassen had not offered a credible option. "His campaign to dump Mr. Nixon is dead."[33]

As the debate over Nixon's nomination grew hotter, the Democratic national convention opened on Monday, August 13. Nominations and balloting for the president came on Thursday, and Stevenson easily won on the first ballot. The next day, the presidential nominee called for an open convention in which the delegates would chose the vice-presidential candidate. The race came down to Stevenson's chief primary opponent, Senators Estes Kefauver and John Kennedy. On the third ballot, the Tennessean captured the nomination, and that evening JFK gave the principal presidential nominating address, pointing out that the Democratic ticket faced opposition from "two tough candidates, one who takes the high road and one who takes the low road."[34]

The following week, Republicans descended on San Francisco. Several days before the convention convened, Governor Knight announced that he would lead the California delegation. He staunchly backed Ike for president but refused to endorse Nixon, insisting on an open convention. He would not yield, he said, "to steamroller pressure in violation of the President's expressed desire for an open convention, free to every Republican to speak his mind."[35]

On August 18, Nixon, Knowland, and Knight met for an hour. They emerged from the session "grim faced." Knowland and Nixon controlled forty-six delegates, Knight had twenty-three, and Senator Thomas Kuchel was the seventieth. Knight refused to announce for Nixon, a stance that created heated arguments within the delegation, and the Knowland and Nixon forces retaliated by using their control of the majority to make Knowland the delegation's chairman, a slap at the governor.[36]

Nixon had asked Los Angeles mayor Norris Poulson to alert him to "any monkey business" when the California delegation caucused. The mayor reported back that he thought Knight and Knowland had behaved "like little boys." In the midst of an unpleasant interchange between the two men, Poulson called for a recess to stop the governor from walking out. After two hours of haggling, the delegation reached a compromise: Knight would chair the delegation, and Knowland would present Nixon's name for the vice-presidential nomination.[37]

The struggle within the California delegations left irreparable scars. Pundits showcased the Nixon-Knight feud, but the real hatred was between Knight and

Knowland. The exchanges between the two men became so heated that they might have contributed to Knowland's decision to leave the Senate in 1958 and return to Oakland to run against Knight in the Republican gubernatorial primary.[38]

While the California GOP leadership was tearing itself apart, Stassen wrote Nixon on August 16 urging the vice president to let Herter replace him on the ticket and take the lead in securing his nomination. This action would be best for the president, the nation and "best, in the long run, for your future career." Nixon never replied.[39]

Stassen compiled another list of Nixon's shortcomings for the president. The vice president lacked maturity; he was linked to McCarthyism; he made indiscreet remarks about Asians; he was associated with Murray Chotiner's influence peddling; and minorities, including blacks and Jews, disliked him. If Nixon received the nomination, Stassen surmised, he would have to address these concerns through "a general statement that covered a number of subjects," such as legislation pertaining to peace, farming, and labor.[40]

Before leaving the capital on August 17 for San Francisco, Stassen spent about five minutes with the president, in which Ike reminded his listener "not to involve him in any way." The former governor said he would continue his draft Herter effort because his upcoming poll would confirm his earlier results. He was for an open convention, he said, but if he determined that his campaign had failed, he would come out for Nixon.[41]

Youthful supporters waving Ike-Herter banners greeted Stassen on his arrival in San Francisco that evening. In a press conference at the airport, he said that he knew Herter had directed the convention chairman to withdraw any attempt to place his name into nomination. That did not bother Stassen; he expected to draft the Massachusetts governor and did not require his permission.[42] On several radio and television programs the next day, he said that he had conferred with Governor Knight about an open convention. He also provided the results of a private poll's results, without saying who conducted it or how, confirming that Herter would benefit the ticket and Nixon would cost it—not 6 percent, as before, but 8 percent.[43]

Shortly before Ike flew to San Francisco, Stassen sent off a desperate plea to the president. Hall, Dewey, and Knowland, he said, strongly backed the vice president, who seemed to have the "overwhelming majority" of the delegates behind him. Stassen hoped that the president would confer with governors Johnson from Vermont, McKeldin from Maryland, Stratton from Illinois, and Knight from California. He should also talk with New York's attorney general, Jacob Javits, and Senator James Duff from Pennsylvania. In addition, Stassen recommended that Eisenhower ask the *Los Angeles Times* and the *New York Herald Tribune* to conduct "quick professional" polls to gain "valuable information" on how an Eisenhower-Nixon ticket would do against Stevenson-Kefauver.[44]

Len Hall, already at the convention, told the press that he had received some 5,000 letters regarding Stassen's action, and 80 to 85 percent favored the vice president. Once Nixon received the nomination, the RNC chairman said, he would wage a vigorous campaign. If Hall's statements were not sufficiently damaging to Stassen, the results of a Gallup Poll in the middle of the month had to be more discouraging. Republicans favored Nixon for vice president over Herter, 74 percent to 14 percent; independents ran 54 percent for Nixon to 22 for Herter.[45]

The Nixon family flew into Los Angeles on Friday, August 17, so that they could visit with Dick's parents, especially his father, who was critically ill. The vice president planned to land in San Francisco on Saturday morning so that the Sunday newspapers would provide extensive coverage. Nixon's friends did their job in publicizing his arrival. A cheering crowd mobbed him at the airport, where he called for an open convention.[46]

Stassen's campaign irritated Nixon. He wrote Milton Eisenhower that the greatest negative was the impression "being created to the effect that I am a reactionary wing of the Party and not in sympathy with the President's program." Once the race started, he would correct that erroneous idea with his speeches.[47]

The day before the convention opened, he followed a full schedule, holding interviews with the major television channels and using the opportunity to reiterate that he supported an open convention and that he would back whomever the delegates selected as their vice-presidential nominee. He emphasized the administration's record and the optimistic expectations for another Eisenhower term, and proudly summarized the last three and a half years as "the best . . . in American history and we want four more years that are even better."[48]

The GOP opened its convention in the cavernous Cow Palace, which seated 14,800 plus media. The 1,323 delegates and an equal number of alternates did not even half-fill it, but spectators filled the rest. The thirty-five million television sets in the country, tuned almost exclusively to the three major networks, reached some two-thirds of all voters. Every day's theme was the same: solidarity behind Dwight Eisenhower's reelection. The dissension of 1952 between Ike's advocates and the Taft wing had been erased. A week earlier, the Democrats had failed to keep to their schedule, so that Stevenson's acceptance speech fell out of prime time. Republicans made sure that this did not happen, and their main speakers would address the largest possible audience.[49]

Before sunset on August 21, *Columbine III*, the president's airplane, touched down at San Francisco International Airport. He had predicted that his two-day stay would be "hectic and tumultuous." Nixon was the first to shake the president's hand, and later the president gave Stassen a perfunctory handshake. A crowd of 50,000 at the airport greeted Ike with what the *New York Times* described as a "hero's welcome."[50]

This spectacle reflected not only Republican feeling but also that of the country in general. From February until August, the Gallup Polls showed Eisenhower preferred by 61 percent to 63 percent of respondents, versus Stevenson's 33 percent to 37 percent. The day the president landed, his approval rating, according to Gallup, stood at 67 percent.[51]

One bystander called out: "You look just fine, sir!"[52] Ike did then and throughout the general election contest. The Democratic strategy of making the president's health an issue evaporated more with every one of Ike's famous smiles. The president's motorcade proceeded to the St. Francis Hotel as onlookers cheered. Rumors leaked out that the president wanted to see those who wished to be put forward as vice-presidential candidates. By nightfall, no one had asked for an appointment. When the president's calendar for the following morning was released, none of Nixon's opposition was included. Stassen, who had said he expected to meet with the president, was not on the schedule.[53]

Early on Wednesday morning, six hours before the president's press conference, Nixon received an urgent message that his seventy-seven year old father Frank had suffered a ruptured artery in his stomach at 4:00 a.m. and was not expected to live. A month earlier, already severely crippled with arthritis, Frank had been admitted to Cottage Hospital in Fullerton, California, with hemorrhaging stomach ulcers and was receiving fluids and blood transfusions. Despite the pain from these ulcers, he improved sufficiently to return to his La Habra home, where he was confined to a second-floor bedroom. The Nixons had visited his parents there just days earlier. The family had watched the GOP's preliminary events in San Francisco on television, and then Dick and Pat left for the convention on Saturday. Nixon came back to La Habra on Wednesday to find his father improving, and for the rest of the day, the family congregated around Frank's television set to watch the convention proceedings.[54]

He did not need to be there: any momentum to remove him from the ticket had vanished. As that day's editorial in the *Chicago American* put it, "The renomination of Richard M. Nixon for the vice president at the Republican Convention is as certain as death and taxes today, not only because President Eisenhower sincerely wants him, but because the GOP delegates overwhelmingly favor it."[55]

Before leaving the White House, Ike had spoken with Attorney General Brownell, who doubled as a political counselor. Brownell later remembered that the president had discussed Stassen's actions with him, and the attorney general suggested that Ike tell Stassen to abandon his draft-Herter drive and second Nixon's renomination. After the president arrived in San Francisco, Hall talked to Stassen and informed him that his initiative had failed.[56]

Stassen requested an interview with the president at 9:00 a.m. and arrived at his hotel room twelve minutes later. Hall, in an oral history, recalled that he warned Stassen that unless he halted his Herter campaign and pledged to second Nixon's nomination, Ike would not see him. Stassen waited until 10:53 before Sherman Adams escorted him in to speak with Ike. The two men talked for eleven minutes, and the "dump Nixon" drive stopped.[57]

Starting his press conference at noon, the president said he felt fine. He then stated Stassen had become convinced that the convention delegates wanted Nixon for the second spot on the ticket, and as a "team player" Stassen had accepted that decision. As for the president's opinion of his vice president, "He has done everything I asked him, beautifully. So that from my viewpoint, as far as efficiency, dedication to his job, loyalty to his country is concerned, I think he is as good a man as you can get."[58]

Throughout that long afternoon, the main suspense was seeing which delegation could use the most superlatives to praise Eisenhower. Finally, a unanimous vote confirmed the obvious: Ike was the presidential nominee. Then the process was repeated for the vice-presidential nominee until the convention's permanent chairman, Congressman Joseph Martin of Massachusetts, called on the Nebraska delegation. The sole female state delegation chairman, Hazel Abel, gritted her teeth and answered "Seventeen for Nixon." A single delegate, Terry Carpenter, who enjoyed the nickname "Terrible Terry," nominated "Joe Smith." Martin banged his gavel: "You take your Joe Smith and get out of here." Carpenter later admitted: "There is no Joe Smith. Joe Smith is a symbol I was out to prove whether this was an open or closed convention."[59]

Attorney Charles Reed, another Nebraska delegate, told a slightly different story seventeen years later. According to the lawyer, he said that Carpenter was "red-hot" for Ike in '52 but was "teed off" in '56 and wanted to nominate Fred Seaton, who was an Eisenhower supporter, and he declined. Reed sat next to Carpenter when he nominated Joe Smith from Scotts Bluff. Since the convention had been "very dull," the press mobbed Carpenter. When reporters called Scotts Bluff, they discovered that one of the residences was named Joe Smith. According to many accounts, Joe Martin threw Carpenter out of the convention. That was false. He left to meet with the media.[60]

In prime time, Charles Halleck placed Ike's name into nomination for a second term as the audience cheered. The congressman praised the president for restoring prosperity and providing a mighty defense. Ike, said Halleck, was "the most universally respected, the most proudly dedicated man of our times," comparable to Abraham Lincoln. "Divine Providence has again given us a man equal to the times." As Halleck finished his speech, the delegates paraded through the Cow Palace.[61] After that outburst subsided, Governor Herter went to the podium and placed Nixon's name into nomination, calling the vice president Ike's "loyal deputy." Nixon was "a great Vice President," who had turned his position into a major force within the administration. Concluding his address, Herter urged his audience: "Let's not break up the winning team! Let's renominate the man whom Ike himself has called its most valuable member!"[62]

A succession of GOP leaders, limited to two or three minutes, seconded each man's nomination. Stassen went on for eleven minutes, emphasizing his loyalty to the president and using tepid adjectives like "able" and "experienced" to characterize Nixon. He promised to campaign for the Eisenhower-Nixon ticket but said he could not prevent others from objecting to the vice president. He urged dissident Democrats, independents, and minorities to vote Republican even though he repeatedly stressed that Nixon hurt the party's chances with those constituencies. Ending his remarks, he proclaimed that he had always been a "team player."[63]

The vice president watched the day's events with his family in his father's bedroom. The following morning, with Frank seeming to be out of immediate danger, his son asked if he should stay by Frank's side or return to give his acceptance speech. According to the vice president, his father "nearly blew his top." He insisted "of course, you've got to go."[64]

Between Stassen's challenge, his father's critical illness, and his own duties at the convention, Nixon had not found time to write his acceptance speech. Father Cronin, who had flown out from Washington about a week before the convention for that specific purpose, wrote the first draft. Thirty years later, Nixon recalled: "Father John . . . became one of our most intimate friends during the Vice Presidential years. He was often a guest in our home, and I particularly am in his debt for flying to San Francisco to assist me in preparing my acceptance speech."[65]

Dr. I. N. Kraushaar, Frank Nixon's physician, thought it would help his patient to watch his son on television delivering his acceptance speech. After the nominations for president and vice president were completed, Nixon appeared at the podium, He first greeted his audience, including the mythical Joe Smith, the symbol of an open convention. Nixon praised the president for his leadership and followed with an outline for the upcoming campaign that his partisan listeners relished. The GOP was fighting for freedom and independence; the party preached free enterprise, not socialism. Within certain guidelines, the federal government had a duty to provide economic incentives leading to prosperity and programs to eliminate poverty. As for international affairs, the free world, led by the United States, fought for democracy and battled communism. America, he said, had to fight for the hearts and minds of peoples around the world. He concluded his address on a personal note, thanking everyone who had sent his family good wishes for his father's health.

Herbert Klein, who had been a reporter for more than a decade and had cordial relations with Nixon, praised the address. Klein was not a yes man; he sincerely felt the presentation was one of the best he had ever heard and that it demonstrated how much the vice president had matured.[66]

President Eisenhower began his acceptance speech at 6:18. Near the beginning, he said of his vice president: "whatever dedication to the country, loyalty and patriotism and great ability can do for America, he will do." Later in the address, he praised Nixon's civil rights commitment and his accomplishments as chairman of the President's Committee on Government Contracts. The speech focused on the Republican Party's values: firm principle, attention on the future, cooperation and not partisanship, and dedication to global peace. The agenda for his second term would consist of measures that drew citizens together and prevented polarization. In foreign affairs, he stressed military strength and collective security. He believed that the Iron Curtain was beginning to loosen, and bilateral relations were moving toward friendlier relations. At his conclusion, he expressed his faith in God.[67]

At the close of the convention, the vice president celebrated with friends in his hotel room. His father, according to his doctor's periodic reports, was doing "very well" that day, and the next evening, he had "a very good night." The updates stopped early in September. Rather than go to the hospital, Frank remained at home so that he could die in his own bed. On the fourth of the month, at 8:25 p.m., he passed away.[68]

Frank's passing was a sad note in what otherwise was a Nixon triumph. Klein "knew that one of Nixon's innermost hurts was the thought that he might not have had the opportunity to run for reelection with Eisenhower in 1956." In the spring of 1976, Nixon confided in his unpublished memoirs, not included in *RN*, that he needed to stay on the ticket because some liberals and a majority of conservatives backed him. Even though Ike disapproved of what he called "conservative party hacks," some of them would be outraged if Nixon were dumped. He remained on the ticket for two reasons: first, he improved Ike's chances, and second, "deep down Eisenhower felt a personal loyalty to me for my services during the first four years."[69]

Stassen came back to the capital without allies. White House adviser Bernard Shanley commented in mid October when Stassen saw the president that "an awful lot of people were hoping that this was going to be his last appearance." Early in December, during a meeting with Secretary of State Dulles, Ike declared "he was very reluctant to dismiss Stassen out-of-hand." The president would try to find Stassen a position where he would not regularly attend cabinet and NSC meetings and would report directly to the state department.[70]

When asked about the Ike-Nixon landslide victory on January 27, 1957, on ABC's Sunday talk show, Stassen ignored his earlier prediction that Nixon would seriously damage Eisenhower's reelection prospects but said that if Herter had been on the ticket, Republicans would have done better in the congressional races. The next month an article appeared in *U.S. News & World Report* that contradicted this assessment. The magazine interviewed eighty-two Republicans who had lost their congressional contests; seventy-seven praised Nixon's efforts on their behalf, two thought they would have done better with Herter, and three were noncommittal. The vast majority who approved of the vice president's role thought he had done more than anyone else in their party to campaign and raise funds for GOP candidates.[71]

The unsubstantiated "Dump Nixon" gossip originated before the convention began. Drew Pearson, in late July 1956, wrote in his column that the president's brother Milton was behind the effort. *U.S. News & World Report* confirmed Pearson's accusations. Angered by these stories, Milton wrote Nixon early in August that "My support is of little consequence but I am for you 100 percent." Milton called Stassen's attack "unforgivable, harmful and childish." He was also upset that Stassen's announcement promoting Herter had upstaged Ike's more important efforts at the Panama gathering. Twenty-seven years after the Stassen episode, Milton described the "Dump Nixon" effort as "fiction."[72]

Sherman Adams was also said to be part of the conspiracy, but he unequivocally denied it. In his 1961 memoir *Firsthand Report*, he wrote that he was "never opposed to Nixon." In an oral history, Senator Prescott Bush, who had seriously considered Herter as a replacement for Nixon, recalled meeting with Adams two or three weeks before the convention as the rumors over the Massachusetts governor accelerated. When Bush raised the idea with Adams, the chief of staff snapped, "Listen, just forget about Herter or anyone else. Nixon is going to be the president's choice." At the beginning of the campaign, Adams wrote in a letter to Eisenhower, with a copy to Nixon, that Nixon had carried out his duties in an "efficient manner." Ike had "on many occasions, paid growing tribute to Mr. Nixon for his personal qualities and his official conduct, particularly emphasizing his patriotism and his dedication to the principles of the American system."[73]

In his memoir *Waging Peace*, Eisenhower writes that until he read Nixon's *Six Crises*, published in 1962, he never understood that the vice president "regarded that period as one of agonizing uncertainty, apparently believing that I might be thinking of dropping him and hoping that I would personally make the final decision." That course of action never occurred to Ike. He had told Nixon, "If you want the post it's yours . . . so far as it is in my power to make it so." Once Nixon declared in April, in Ike's mind, it resolved any doubt.[74]

But Nixon reached a different conclusion. A year after his nomination, Nixon said "that all the flurry created by the Stassen incident is almost completely forgotten." But he never forgot. In *RN*, published almost a decade after Ike's death, Nixon wrote that he thought the president had listened to advisers and friends who held Nixon would weaken the ticket. His sympathetic biographer Jonathan Aitken named Adams as the instigator.[75]

While conspiracies and villains are often intriguing, the "Dump Nixon" fiction came from Stassen's desire to run for the presidency. He realized that if he were to be a viable presidential candidate in 1960, he had to dislodge Nixon from the vice presidency. To accomplish that, he conjured up a scheme to remove Nixon and replace him with Herter, who because of his health could not be a presidential candidate after Ike completed his second term. The gigantic hurdle that he could not overcome was that Nixon had forged alliances with so many Republican partisans that he had locked up the nomination before Stassen dreamed up his plan. Adams had no interest in a conspiracy to get rid of Nixon; his overriding mission was to defend the president.

The choice of Nixon as Ike's second-term running mate changed expectations. In the years after, Nixon ran for president alongside Spiro Agnew in both 1968 and 1972; Jimmy Carter ran with Walter Mondale in 1976 and 1980; Ronald Reagan ran with George H. W. Bush in 1980 and 1984; Bush ran with Dan Quayle in 1988 and 1992; Bill Clinton ran with Al Gore in 1992 and 1996; George W. Bush ran with Dick Cheney in 2000 and 2004; and Barack Obama ran with Joe Biden in 2008 and 2012. Only one sitting president during that period dropped a sitting vice president from the ticket: in 1976, Gerald Ford exchanged Nelson Rockefeller for Robert Dole. But these precedents did not exist in 1956.

Leading up to the convention, neither Eisenhower nor Nixon understood the other's motives. Eisenhower believed that the choice of vice-presidential candidate lay, first, with Nixon himself, and second with the convention delegates. Ike could keep the door open, but Nixon had to decide for himself if he wished to run for reelection and had to articulate it to the president. He insisted that he had no right to express his own preference until he had secured his nomination, and no right to challenge the convention delegates' selection of the vice-presidential nominee. He thus felt obligated to remain open to other candidates— and he also thought Nixon's best career path lay as a cabinet member.

Nixon, rather than accept those principles at face value, continued to worry that Ike might prefer someone else as his vice president. Neither man communicated his intentions well. If they had, Nixon's angst, and all uncertainty, would have disappeared.

THE LAND OF SMEAR AND GRAB

So it was decided: Dwight Eisenhower and Adlai Stevenson would head the major parties' 1956 presidential tickets, with Richard Nixon and Estes Kefauver as their running mates. The difference from four years earlier was that Eisenhower now had a record. He had ended the Korean conflict, had presided over general prosperity with the exception of a brief, mild recession, and had worked to end corruption and subversion in the federal government. He was determined that these accomplishments would be the primary focus of the campaign.

Stevenson, paying little attention to the administration's domestic vulnerabilities during the race, did not vigorously advance New Deal domestic programs. His campaign themes included suspending H-bomb tests, ending the military draft, and Eisenhower's chances of dying in office during his second term, which would make Nixon the president. Partisan Democrats were horrified at that thought.

The president designated Republican National Committee (RNC) chairman Len Hall to manage both his and Nixon's campaigns. Over breakfast on September 3, Ike emphasized that he would not barnstorm or make whistle-stops, as he had done four years earlier, but he might travel to key areas for occasional events. He instructed Hall to revive the GOP "truth squads" that had followed Stevenson in 1952, correcting any misleading statements the Democratic candidate made.[1]

Stevenson had already started his campaign. On September 5, he went before the American Legion, calling for multilateral suspension of thermonuclear weapon testing and an end to the draft. Several months earlier, he had proposed a unilateral test ban but received scant attention for it. He did not know that the president had been moving secretly on disarmament talks. When Stevenson publicly broached the idea, the Kremlin, whose leaders did not understand that an "opposing" candidate could speak independently, ended the negotiations. Republicans scolded Stevenson for mentioning the subject.[2]

Nixon spoke at the same convention the day after Stevenson. He told the Legionaries that the Soviet Union was spreading international communism through its economic assistance programs to developing countries and that the United States had to meet that challenge with a strong national defense and salesmanship to win the hearts and minds of third-world peoples. He also replied to Stevenson on halting H-bomb testing and dispensing with the draft. Some sincerely advocated disarmament. Nixon argued that "to have followed this advice would have been not only naive but dangerous to our national security." As for ending the draft, that idea appealed to voters, but "in international affairs, particularly, the easy way is seldom the right way." The United States could not afford any action that would weaken its defenses.[3]

At first, Stevenson ignored Nixon. Democrats, he believed, had to reinvigorate the New Deal coalition by concentrating on domestic concerns and by appealing to the unions, Jews, and blacks. They had to bring the South's electoral votes into their column and identify other states where they had the best chance to win. Stevenson did win the majority of southern states (many of whose citizens voted Democratic more from lifelong habit than from fervor for the candidate), but he failed to extend his liberal base sufficiently to win anywhere else except Missouri.[4]

On the evening of September 10, the candidate spoke before the New York Democratic state convention, describing the Eisenhower administration as "Government with a false front." The president employed "ingenuous and ruthless" measures to gut New and Fair Deal programs. To weaken labor's collective bargaining power, for instance, the president had "packed" the National Labor Relations Board with antiunion appointments. The following evening in New York City, Stevenson accepted the state's Liberal Party endorsement. He would not comment, he said, on the vice president's "new personality" but wished Nixon would repudiate "the irresponsible, the vindictive and the malicious words so often spoken by the imposer who has been using his name all of these years."[5]

The president was angered by Stevenson's assaults and telephoned Nixon to say that when his opponent called "the Administration racketeers and rascals, when they say we are heartless in dealing with the problems of the people and the problems of the farmers, while they say we have no peace and no prosperity, I want them to be called on it." Nixon replied that Stevenson "was swinging very wildly." Ike suggested that the vice president should not "attack him personally but we should point out that he is wrong." Nixon then talked to Attorney General

Brownell, who disagreed with the president. He would not win with a high moral tone: "it has to be fair but you have to take the opposition on. It has to be hard-hitting."[6] Presidential speechwriter Emmet Hughes later telephoned Rose Mary Woods. Having discussed Stevenson's latest speech with the president that morning, Hughes suggested that Nixon go after Stevenson for his "pretentious and false idealism."[7]

The president welcomed 500 Republican leaders from every state to his Gettysburg farm for a picnic. Nixon spoke first. He would work to reelect the president and recapture a majority in Congress. Personal attacks would be avoided, but he would correct distortions. Democrats, for example, charged the GOP with solely representing business but the administration had created prosperity for the vast majority. Foreign policy would be a major issue, and it should be addressed in a bipartisan spirit. Democrats had accused the administration of refusing to support public school integration, but this charge was without merit and would be answered.[8]

Then the president addressed his guests. He started by assuring them, "I feel fine!" He then spent the next few minutes praising his running mate: "there is no man in the history of America who has had such a careful preparation as has Vice President Nixon for carrying out the duties of the Presidency, if that duty should ever fall upon him." He stressed that "to the Republican Party from its very beginning, one man is equal in his dignity and in his rights to all other men." The party would concentrate its campaign on the peace and prosperity the administration had brought to the nation. Besides depending on its partisan base, the GOP also had to convert voters to its principles and make sure they registered to vote.[9]

The campaigns opened with an enormous innovation. Over 95 percent of households had radios, and 67 percent, or 37 million, had television sets. Forty-nine percent of the voters switched from radio and depended on the new medium for information. The media routinely covered the candidates' speeches, press conferences, and other appearances. Both national parties accepted this reality and began advertising over television. Five-minute spots were common, and to avoid viewer resentment, they came at the ends of entertainment programs.[10]

Stevenson opened his campaign on September 13 in Harrisburg, Pennsylvania, with a nationally televised speech charging that the administration lacked leadership and urging Americans to vote Democratic. With the president performing ineffectively, Republicans would turn to their "heir apparent, Mr. Nixon. And the Vice-President seems to sail down wind no matter which way the wind blows."[11]

Democratic vice-presidential candidate Kefauver did not play a major role in the contest. He was limited to smaller venues that did not generate much news coverage. But he embraced his party's position on the vice president and regularly attacked him, demanding that he apologize to Democratic leaders for implying that they were traitors. Describing Nixon as "the real power" in the administration, the senator called him "the darling of the reactionaries" and the future "heir apparent" of the GOP. The president might not survive two terms, Kefauver hinted, and Nixon was "trying to get into the White House on false promises, a false front, and a false face." If the Republicans won, the vice president "would inevitably become the center of power."[12]

Early in the race, former first lady Eleanor Roosevelt went on *Meet the Press*, where she emphasized that a vote for Ike might be a vote for Nixon. She accused him of calling Helen Gahagan Douglas a communist during the 1950 senatorial campaign. A week after the program, she admitted that Nixon "was clever enough not to say that Mrs. Douglas was a communist because it is against the law. However, he left no doubt in anyone's mind that she was a communist." When a reporter asked the vice president about Mrs. Roosevelt's accusations, he replied that she was misinformed and denied ever suggesting that Douglas was a communist: "I questioned her judgment not her loyalty."[13]

Truman also criticized the vice president. During a September 3 interview, when questioned about his statement that Nixon had previously accused Democrats of "treason," Truman replied that Nixon had done so and had "a hell of a right to be talking about principles." At a Detroit rally, Truman described the vice president's congressional record as "one of the most reactionary" and warned: "You cannot elect Ike without electing 'Tricky Dicky.'" He expressed his "personal disgust" when someone suggested that Nixon was "better qualified" to be vice president than Alben Barkley. Barkley was a great American; Nixon was not.[14]

These attacks probably invigorated Nixon. He announced that he would travel 15,000 miles, visit thirty-two states, and employ a "running scared" theme to re-elect the president. He would caution Republican voters against complacency: "I don't think we can win with a wishy-washy Milquetoast campaign." He met with the president before leaving the capital and maintained frequent telephone contact with him throughout his journey. On his return Washington, he was debriefed at the White House.[15]

Eisenhower kicked off Nixon's trip on September 18 at Washington National Airport. In a pep talk before the vice president, 200 party leaders, and the truth squad, whose purpose was to correct Democratic misrepresentations, Ike advised Republicans to concentrate on what the administration had accomplished: "The record is there. And it is good." Nixon followed by stressing the theme that Ike had given the majority of Americans "the best four years of their lives" based on peace and prosperity. He went further: "We believe that we are on the winning side and also we believe we are on the right side."[16]

Pat went along on the trip: voters wanted to see her. The vice president knew she was excellent with crowds: "Nobody can surpass her as a campaigner. Physically she outlasts me." She enjoyed meeting and talking to people but would not discuss politics. She did not want her views confused with his. He talked politics.[17]

They traveled by airplane, the "Dick Nixon Special," mostly in a chartered DC-5. In California, Nixon called for a revival of the "great crusade" that Ike had pledged four years earlier. Once again he insisted that "meetings be arranged with people rather than with Party bosses." When Governor Knight welcomed him on September 18, Nixon was so impressed with the warm reception that he encouraged Len Hall to send the governor out to campaign; Hall "agreed 100%."[18]

At each stop, Nixon concentrated on persuading voters to cast their ballots for Republicans at every level. During each rally, he had GOP candidates for lesser offices on the platform, introduced them to the assemblage and tried to have the media cover their participation. Electing a Republican Congress was essential, he said, to give the president a working majority.[19] Throughout his travels, he regularly contrasted the president to his challenger, in Houston describing Stevenson as "the same old Truman jalopy with a 1956 paint job." In Stevenson's home state of Illinois, the choice was whether "we go forward with Eisenhower or back to the policies of the Truman regime." In Cincinnati, he told an audience that the Democratic challenger was not "even in the same league" as Eisenhower.[20]

Meanwhile, the Democratic candidate was criticizing the administration for its failures in Middle East diplomacy—the Suez Canal crisis would explode into warfare toward the end of October—and in Eastern Europe. He complained about falling farm prices and the government's antilabor initiatives. Ike's illnesses had made him a part-time president, and the real authority in the Republican Party was Nixon. During an address on September 20, Stevenson said the president had cavalierly dismissed disarmament and draft issues. With new military technology, he insisted, these were legitimate topics for debate.[21]

Nixon was still prone to incessant low-grade illnesses—he traveled with a personal physician, Dr. Malcolm Todd of Long Beach, California—but did not allow these setbacks to interrupt his schedule. Only once, in Oklahoma City on September 25, did Pat have to speak in his place—her first and last campaign speech. He took over for her after a few minutes.

Sometimes Nixon brought up labor issues, appealing to union members benefiting from the general prosperity to vote for the president. He defended the Taft-Hartley Act in Senator Taft's home state of Ohio. He also predicted that technological advances and industrial progress would soon create a four-day workweek. Walter Reuther, president of the United Auto Workers, demanded that Nixon commit his party to that proposition, but Nixon refused. Although he thought the idea was "inevitable," he believed the government should not intervene.[22]

As for agricultural policy, the vice president was optimistic about an upward trend in farm prices. When the agriculture department released statistics showing that prices had in fact dropped in August, he was upset. The GOP had spent $100,000 pitching the current program, and the announcement damaged its efforts. He recommended that all government agencies be required to clear economic releases with the White House and the RNC. "I, frankly, am so discouraged by this terrible blooper," he wrote to RNC chair Hall that "if it happens one more time I am going to cancel the balance of my schedule in the farm belt." To Secretary of Agriculture Benson, he wrote: "We have no obligation whatever to put out statistics which are harmful to us."[23]

At the end of September, the *New York Times* reported, Stevenson's "campaign was rolling in high gear." The candidate had been in ten states, speaking to large audiences. He could win. Arthur Schlesinger Jr. thought that Stevenson had done so well as to put the campaign "in a state of euphoria." John Kenneth Galbraith, a Harvard economist and speechwriter for the nominee, later recalled, "at least in the early days of the campaign, we had much hope."[24]

Others on Stevenson's staff were less pleased. John Bartlow Martin remembered that the "most maddening thing about the 1956 campaign was Eisenhower's apparently indestructible popularity." His approval ratings were in the 60 percent range, while his disapprovals barely reached 20 percent. Presidential trial heats from early September until before the balloting had the Eisenhower-Nixon ticket defeating Stevenson-Kefauver by margins ranging from eight to eighteen points. If that was not sufficiently discouraging, the incumbent was running in the midst of general prosperity, a fact that dramatically damaged the challenger's chances.[25]

Gabriel Hauge, a presidential counselor, called Nixon on October 2 to tell him that the RNC wanted him "to take on" Stevenson with regard to the "nuclear bomb thing." Stevenson had said: "If we had leadership on getting these H-bomb tests halted the other nations would go along." Hauge stressed that the president hoped to disarm but would not do it unilaterally.[26]

The next day, speaking in Western Massachusetts, Nixon stressed that the Soviets had broken many agreements, and without a firm one in place, the United States would continue its testing program. That evening, he vehemently attacked Stevenson for his naïveté in suggesting halting the H-bomb tests. He accused the Democrat of spouting "catastrophic nonsense." The *New York Herald Tribune*, a Republican newspaper, editorialized on October 5 that Nixon had "earned hearty congratulations for showing that the high road is his road—and the best road."[27]

Nixon arrived home on the evening of October 3. In an informal news conference the next morning, he commended Ike for keeping the nation out of war, attacked Stevenson for his disarmament and draft proposals, and criticized the Democratic Congress for blocking the administration's initiatives. He also dealt with regional issues. Southerners wanted to know about desegregation; Nixon hoped that moderates on civil rights would win over rigid segregationists and those who insisted on instant integration. Midwesterners were concerned about lower farm prices as well as the drought in Texas and Kansas; the vice president expressed sympathy and pledged his support. A reporter from the Northwest asked about the development of power resources, and Nixon responded that federal, state, and local agencies should cooperate with private enterprise.[28]

That afternoon and again two days later, Nixon met with the president to compare notes on the progress of the campaign. Neither man commented publicly on their conversations. During the briefing session with the White House staff for his press conference the following day, the president remarked that Nixon had encouraged him not "to extend his schedule." During the reporters' questioning, John Stacle of *Time* magazine asked what the two men had discussed. Ike replied that Nixon thought his "trip was most encouraging" and he had experienced the largest, most enthusiastic crowds of his political career. Except for depressed regions and lower farm prices, he "found people quite happy."[29]

Ike also answered inquiries about halting H-bomb testing by pointing out that the United States publicly announced when it planned an explosion, which took months of preparation. The Soviets did not inform anyone about their tests. Thus without a bilateral agreement between the superpowers, "it would be foolish for us to make any such unilateral announcement." He did not reveal that he had failed in his diplomatic push for nonproliferation, but said he realized that other nations had begun to develop nuclear weapons, and he intended to move forward on a test ban treaty. Former president Truman undercut Stevenson by declaring: "We can't possibly quit [nuclear testing] till this Russian business is under control."[30]

The president also addressed Stevenson's "loose talk" about ending the draft, a suggestion that he said could damage American security. The same day as the press conference, the Gallup Poll released its findings on the subject: 74 percent of respondents said the nation should not abandon the draft, 13 percent said it should, and an equal number had no opinion. Stevenson was advocating an unpopular idea that would weaken his electability.[31]

The Democratic candidate, in a speech at Yale University the same day, condemned Nixon and other Republicans for equating Democrats with socialists: "I do not think the American people are going to be much more impressed in 1956 by the Vice-President's threadbare shouts about socialism than they were two years ago by his loud shouts about Communism." He welcomed vigorous debate, he said, not slander.[32]

The president reassessed his participation in the race. Early in October, he announced that he would travel to Washington and California and thereafter might take "one short trip a week." He liked "to go out and see people." He planned to be in Pittsburgh on October 9 and had other stops under consideration.[33] Nixon, meanwhile, announced that on his second swing he would revisit pivotal states like Texas and California and would also concentrate on the Midwest and Northeast. Before leaving the capital, Nixon issued a statement excoriating Stevenson for leaving the impression, despite the current prosperity, that depression loomed just over the horizon. It was a time of peace, but the nominee said that the world was not peaceful, and while Americans strove for equal opportunity, the nominee claimed this was not happening. Stevenson's "ill-judged, ill-timed, ill-phrased remarks must not go unanswered."[34]

Before leaving for Pittsburgh, Ike circulated a memo to each cabinet secretary asking them to "give Dick Nixon a boost in his speeches." He circulated a two-and-a-half-page statement describing how Nixon had raised the prestige of his office to new heights. He was "a dynamic personality. A man of great personal courage, a man of extraordinary patience and resilience, and a man of boundless energy in the execution of an agreed plan." He had come from a humble background, gone to college and law school on scholarships, fought in World War II, held congressional seats, and traveled overseas on three separate occasions for the president.[35]

Ike further increased his participation after the Pittsburgh trip by going on a national television broadcast, "The People Ask the President." In his opening statement, he asked Americans to "please vote" and optimistically predicted that the UN was close to a settlement in the festering Suez Canal crisis. He answered questions concerning labor, farming, and other topics.[36]

Throughout October, the president presented his vision of America and refuted Stevenson on the H-bomb and the draft, while the Democratic nominee hammered away on these themes. He went on national television and called for disarmament. Buoyed by what he considered favorable responses from the public and the scientific community, he became bolder in seeking the end of testing. The draft was ineffective and wasteful. The United States needed a volunteer military that would be streamlined and more efficient.[37] In a speech on October 12, he declared that Nixon, not Ike, was the leader of the GOP. At the mention of the vice president's name, his audience booed and hissed. Stevenson linked the "aging President" to his "young, ambitious, anointed heir."[38]

On October 17, Stevenson frontally assaulted Nixon, describing him as "shifty," "rash," and "inexperienced." He reminded his listeners that seven presidents had died in office and been replaced by their vice presidents. Nixon, who could become chief executive at any moment, was unqualified to sit in the Oval Office because his "trade-mark is slander." Stevenson asked: "Who can safely say he knows where the Vice President stands? This is a man of many masks."[39]

The vice president took off from the capital for his second campaign swing on the morning of October 9, headed for the Lone Star State. He knew how to count electoral votes, and Texas, to him, was "insurance." He pledged to his audiences that the administration would defend states' rights in an offshore drilling controversy then roiling the region and would send assistance to help cope with the drought. As for the opposition, he warned that Stevenson was too inexperienced in foreign affairs. If he became president, the nation would suffer from a "wobbly, indecisive defense policy, tied to a blow-hot, blow-cold diplomatic policy."[40]

He arrived in Minneapolis on October 13, where he emphasized that only the president could be entrusted with "the staggering responsibilities" of the Oval Office. Dan Gainey, a prominent Republican fundraiser in Minnesota, thought the vice president's appearance was "a titanic success." The GOP had given Gainey four and a half weeks to raise $120,000, and he was confident that he would reach that goal.[41]

In Buffalo, New York, Nixon warned his audience that Stevenson's proposals on disarmament and the draft were too risky. The United States had the technology, while the Soviet Union had the manpower. Under those circumstances, the H-bomb was a necessary deterrent to war. Nixon decried "the stupidity of Mr. Stevenson's H bomb proposals. What a sucker he would be for the schemers in the Kremlin!"[42]

As the election drew nearer, the president stepped up his campaign appearances. He traveled to New York City on October 26, where he spoke for half an hour against Stevenson's proposals in Madison Square Garden before 20,000 onlookers and a national television audience.[43] Back at the White House the next day, he fulfilled a campaign pledge to undergo a complete physical examination at Walter Reed Army Hospital. The eight doctors who examined him reported a day later that Ike was in "excellent health."[44] After breakfast on October 29, he left the capital for the Sunshine State. During his stay in Florida, he gave airport speeches in Miami and Jacksonville; on his return flight, he stopped in Richmond, Virginia, for his last one. At his first stop, he talked about civil rights, promising that enforcement of federal desegregation orders like the *Brown* decision would be decided on a "state and local basis." Legislation was not the solution; "the heart of men" would be the final arbiter. He tried to bring "reason, good sense and good judgment to the performance of clear duty."[45]

As Eisenhower increased his personal appearances during the final two weeks of the race, Stevenson attacked the president more aggressively. He went before partisans at Madison Square Garden on October 23 to challenge the administration's claims that it had a successful foreign policy. Mounting crises throughout the world, Stevenson argued, proved otherwise. One of the biggest ovations he ever received came when he said that disarmament was the key to world peace. When he mentioned the president or the vice president, the audience booed and hissed—even more angrily when Stevenson projected that Nixon, as the future of the Republican Party, could not be trusted to prevent a nuclear holocaust. For the remainder of the campaign, he routinely warned about the devastation that a nuclear war would inflict and the potential for such a tragedy if Nixon were in command.[46]

Large majorities opposed Stevenson's disarmament stand. When pollsters asked respondents if they favored a continuation of H-bomb testing, 56 percent said yes and 24 percent no. That spread greatly favored the GOP. The polling on ending the draft polling was even worse for Democrats. Seventy-two percent did not want to end it, and only 10 percent did.[47]

Stevenson flew to San Francisco on October 27, where he mounted a vicious attack on the president and vice president. He worried that this speech was "far too tough" and might cost him votes, but he decided to go forward, presenting a baleful scenario in which Nixon, not Ike, would govern if Eisenhower won a second term. "In one direction," he warned, "lies a land of slander and scare, the land of sly innuendo, the poison pen, the anonymous phone call and hustling, pushing, shoving, the land of smear and grab and anything to win.

"This is Nixonland. America is something different."[48]

In Los Angeles that evening Stevenson gave an address fashioned by John Kenneth Galbraith and Clayton Fritchey, two of his speechwriters. Unions packed Gilmore Stadium, and movie stars sat in the front row. If he won a second term, Eisenhower would be a "part-time" president who would relinquish authority "to the heir apparent, hand-picked by President Eisenhower, Richard Nixon." Ike would "not lead because he won't. Richard Nixon cannot lead because the American people will not follow." Americans "just can't picture Richard Nixon as the leader of the greatest of the world's nations. They can't imagine putting Richard Nixon's hand on the trigger of the H-bomb. They just can't trust him." The crowd cheered.[49]

Pleased by such responses, Stevenson optimistically telephoned Democratic state chairmen about his chance of victory. Americans would reject "a part-time President" and most significantly, "they do not want Nixon and the Republican Party to run the destiny of America the next four years."[50]

Nixon left the capital to begin his third swing on the morning of Monday, October 22, stopping first in Flint, Michigan, to make a pitch for the labor vote. The president had given sixty-seven million wage earners prosperity; they "never had it so good." He then compared the president to his challenger: "Don't settle for second best in leadership when you already have the best in Dwight D. Eisenhower."[51] He then went on to Indiana, where he stopped at the University of Notre Dame. Since it was the football season, he referred to the president as the "all-American quarterback." Stevenson had raised the H-bomb and draft issues to frighten American voters. If America followed his recommendations, he said, it would be a prelude to another Munich.[52]

In Illinois the next day, Nixon called Stevenson's disarmament idea "a cruel hoax." He would stop testing without inspections, an idea that Premier Nikolai Bulganin welcomed. The president, however, demanded verification. Nixon followed his argument to its logical conclusion. Ike was a professional military leader, and Stevenson an "untried amateur."[53]

It was a year of unrest in Eastern Europe. The Iron Curtain seemed to be lifting ever so slightly. On October 19, the ousted leader in Poland, Wladyslaw Gomulka, returned to power and succeeded in negotiating trade concessions and troop reductions with the post-Stalinist leadership in the Soviet Union. This uprising had little effect on the presidential election. Neither the Democrats nor the Republicans used the Polish revolt as an issue. The reverse occurred in Hungary. As Moscow and Warsaw were arriving at an accommodation, protests began in Budapest, and several days later, the revolt spread to the countryside, toppling the existing regime. Kremlin leaders searched for a peaceful settlement in Hungary until the end of October.[54]

Ominous events were also occurring in Egypt over the Suez Canal. Gamal Abdel Nasser, who had led a coup d'état that overthrew the monarchy in 1953, became president under a new constitution in June 1956. His first important move in that position, on July 26, was to nationalize the canal. After this seizure, the British, French, and Israelis secretly plotted to regain it.[55]

On Sunday, October 28, Israel invaded the Sinai Peninsula. The shocked president learned of Israeli mobilization shortly after 5:00 p.m. He considered releasing a statement about the dangerous situation, saying that the United States would do "all we can to allay the situation," but held off. He confessed to Emmet Hughes that he could not understand the Israelis; they needed peaceful relations with the Arab world. "Maybe their idea is they CAN'T survive without more land." As for the French involvement, Paris was "egging" the Israelis on to take attention away from the rebellions within its North African colonies. Maybe, the president speculated, the French were "just finished as a people." That evening, he called an emergency meeting at the White House and went on national television to describe the events and his indignation at the surprise attack.[56]

The CIA had briefed Stevenson on global conditions in general and the Middle East in detail. The day after the Israeli assault, he charged that the president had shown "little inclination for the 'round-the-clock responsibilities'" that his office required. The next evening, the candidate sent a telegram to the White House asking for a pledge of "no United States involvement." At a speech in Buffalo on November 1, he described the administration's Middle Eastern policy as a failure and added: "Either the President and his Vice-President did not know how serious the situation was in the Middle East or they did not want the American people to know—at least, not till after the election."[57]

While the president planned to reply to Stevenson's attack, he and Secretary Dulles were working closely to use the United Nations to have British, French, and Israeli forces leave Egyptian territory. Ike understood and even sympathized with the problem that the British had with Nasser, but he did not want a war with the Muslim world. He summarized the situation to Emmet Hughes on October 30: "I've just never seen great powers make [such] a complete mess and botch of things. . . . Of course, in a war, there's just nobody I'd rather have fighting with me than British, but—this thing!—my God!" Ike wanted to be on the British "side in case of trouble. . . . But—we just cant go along with them on this one."[58]

On November 1, Eisenhower was scheduled to give an evening speech in Philadelphia. That afternoon, he learned that the Soviet Union had deployed troops in Hungary. Crowds using umbrellas went to the hall in a "humid rain" to hear the president accuse Stevenson, without specifically naming him, of trying to use the Suez and Hungarian crises for electoral gain. Then he returned to the capital and canceled all further campaign appearances. His primary focus as American president was to extinguish their explosive international firestorms.[59]

From the White House, Ike wrote two of his closest friends that he realized this decision could lose votes, but he needed to make these international upheavals his priorities. Besides, he believed the Democratic ticket, "about the sorriest and weakest we have ever had run for the two top offices in the land," stood little chance of defeating him. He hoped for a large popular mandate to force both Republicans and Democrats to cooperate with his agenda. If the politicians were intransigent, a substantial triumph would allow him to appeal directly to the people.[60]

Even before Ike stopped campaigning, Nixon remained in constant contact with the White House and the state department on Middle Eastern conditions. He spoke with Secretary Dulles on October 29 about the Israeli military action. Dulles wanted to know how it would affect domestic politics, and the vice president replied that it should not be allowed to interfere with the secretary and the president's decisions. No matter what the political consequences in the upcoming election, they should stand firm against the invasion.[61]

At the end of the month, Dulles advised Nixon not to emphasize the Israeli assault and to condemn the British and French involvement, but with moderation. The two allies would not drag the United States into the conflict. Nixon asked Dulles for his political analysis, and the secretary said that was the vice president's specialty. Nixon thought the ticket would suffer some insignificant losses among Jewish voters, but more critically, United States policy "has kept American boys out and at such a time you don't want a pipsqueak for Pres[ident]." Dulles considered that the president was handling the crises wonderfully and that he was going to do what was "right regardless of the election—he will not sacrifice foreign policy for political expediency." The situation grew more complex at the start of November when Dulles was rushed to the hospital for emergency surgery. The public was not informed that he had cancer.[62]

While Dulles was working closely with the president on the Middle Eastern complications, Nixon was completing his last trip to the West Coast. In San Diego a week before the balloting, he complimented Ike's leadership and contrasted it to what the nation could expect from Stevenson: "an indecisive, how-not-to-do-it man, a pathetic Hamlet on the American stage." The Democrat had injected partisan politics into Suez; voters should recognize this ploy and not "replace the greatest commander-in-chief America has ever had—in war or peace—with a jittery, inexperienced novice." Turning to the slaughter the

Soviets had inflicted on Hungary, Nixon warned that if Stevenson won, "the butchers of Budapest would make mincemeat out of a man who has the weakness and confusion and the indecision Mr. Stevenson has evidenced during this campaign."[63]

At the end of October, Nixon flew to Detroit and posed a question for the Democratic candidate: should the United States send American soldiers to Suez? The president had rejected that option and was negotiating through the UN to stop the fighting. Under such complex circumstances, the nation could not afford to elect an untested politician. It needed the man who had led the triumphant Allied forces against the Third Reich.[64]

Stevenson went on television accusing the president of damaging the Western alliance, and the president declared that Nixon would speak for the administration in response. Entering Pennsylvania by train on a bright autumn day, Nixon talked to Dulles during his stop in Harrisburg, and that evening in Hershey he addressed a national television audience. The United States, he stressed, was for the first time acting independently of the colonialism practiced by the British and the French in Asia and Africa. The nation cherished its alliance with the British, French, and the Israelis, but it had a moral imperative: "We say force is wrong when it is used by our enemies, and it is just as wrong when it is used by our friends."[65]

The vice president spent the last day of his campaign in Ohio, plugging the reelection of Senator George Bender. Nixon and his wife took time to wave their absentee ballots at the reporters before mailing them: "Here are two sure votes for Eisenhower and Nixon and all the rest." Even as Stevenson predicted a Middle East catastrophe, the vice president reminded the media that the Arab-Israeli conflict had broken out during the Truman presidency. Eisenhower was supplying the corrective to stop the current fighting.[66]

The Monday before the balloting, Gallup released its final poll results: 59.5 percent of respondents were for Ike-Nixon and 40.5 percent for Stevenson-Kefauver.[67]

The president, the vice president, and their wives appeared on election eve on a national television show carried by the three major networks. The prominent journalist John Cameron Swayze hosted a carefully orchestrated presentation in which actors playing reporters detailed the president's support as if the election returns were being tabulated. Nixon asked his audience to vote Republican to give the president another four years to finish the job that he had initiated in 1953. Ike closed the program by speaking in lofty terms of the continuation of peace and prosperity. He did not ask for votes but called upon Americans to cast their ballots for the candidates they favored.[68]

While the Republicans closed the campaign on this get-out-the vote theme, Stevenson was racing from state to state. Arthur Schlesinger's September optimism had dramatically faded. Historian Eric Goldman captured the atmosphere: "Adlai Stevenson, the lilt gone from his voice, ran with all the zest and decisiveness of a man taking the final steps to the gas chamber."[69]

On November 5, Stevenson spoke in Minneapolis at a breakfast rally, focusing on GOP deceitfulness in confronting farmers' financial woes. He added Ike's "negligence on questions of peace" and warned that "he may plunge the whole world into the horror of hydrogen war." Republicans were waging "an especially dirty smear campaign" in which Nixon had recently "put away his switchblade and now assumes the aspect of an Eagle Scout." If the GOP won control of the Senate, he warned, Joe McCarthy would regain influence.[70]

On the day before the balloting, Stevenson landed in Boston to prepare for a forty-five-minute national television speech. Senator Kefauver spoke from the capital about the two parties' different political philosophies on social legislation; the Democrats he said, were "the party with a heart." Stevenson then began his address. At the start of the campaign, he had foresworn any discussion of the president's health, but as the race drew to a close, he continually referred to "an aging President." In this speech, the Democratic nominee repeated his assault on Ike's foreign policy disasters in Hungary and the Middle East; the president had not functioned well, and as a consequence was relinquishing more responsibilities to Nixon, a development Stevenson described as frightening: "I must say bluntly that every piece of scientific evidence we have, every lesson of history and experience indicates that a Republican victory tomorrow would mean Richard M. Nixon would probably be President of this country within the next four years." No one ever revealed who wrote this sentence. Staff members as well as others gasped at Stevenson's prediction that the president would die in office.[71]

Learning of these remarks, White House press secretary Hagerty remarked that "it was just about as bad a statement as I have ever heard in politics."[72]

Election Day was clear and cool at the White House. Anticipating victory, the GOP took several floors at the Sheraton-Park Hotel. Early returns from the East and Midwest clearly indicated a landslide. RNC chairman Hall claimed victory by 10:00 p.m. Stevenson, at the Chicago Sheraton-Blackstone, quickly realized that he had been crushed but was not content with the concession statement his staff prepared and sat down to rewrite it. Eisenhower waited at the Sheraton-Park for Stevenson to speak, but as the hours passed with no word from his opponent, he prepared to return to the White House. Finally, at 1:30 on Wednesday morning, just as Ike was about to leave, the Democratic nominee appeared before television cameras. Ike did not bother to watch: "I haven't watched that fellow during the campaign. I don't see why I should start now."[73]

Instead, the president wrote his own victory statement. He saw Nixon, who thought the president was elated over his plurality but disappointed to be the first president in 108 years to fail to win either house of Congress. Democrats gained two House seats, for a total of 234, and one seat in the Senate for a total of forty-nine. Ike was angry: "Those goddamn mossback Republicans! That's the problem! We've got to have a modern Republican Party!"[74]

At 1:50 a.m., Ike went before the cameras, praising the voters who returned him to office as looking "to the future: I think that modern Republicanism has now proved itself. And America has approved of modern Republicanism." To Ike, the GOP was a party that appealed to its members, Democrats, and independents. He pledged to continue to work for the nation in domestic matters and to pursue world peace.[75]

Nixon recorded in his memoirs that conservative Republicans disapproved of the phrase "modern Republicanism." Taft's followers saw Ike's distinction diminishing their status. The vice president thought "the second term [started] off on a slightly sour note in some Republican circles." Sherman Adams agreed. Although he did not believe the president intended to split the party between liberal and conservative factions, the reference to a new brand of Republicanism did just that.[76]

Despite these intraparty tensions, Ike won by a landslide. He had received almost 35,600,000 votes, 57.7 percent of the total, while his opponent garnered slightly over 26,000,000 or 42 percent. Ike won forty-one states with 457 electoral votes, and Stevenson carried seven—six in the Old Confederacy plus Missouri—with seventy-three electoral votes.[77]

Before the new year, Ike wrote Nixon that he had "brought to the office of the Vice President a real stature that formerly it had not known; you have proved yourself an able and popular 'Ambassador' to our friends in many other parts of the world and you have worked tirelessly and effectively to interpret to the people of America—and to forward—the policies of the Administration."[78] Nixon appreciated this sentiment but understood that it came at a high price. Throughout the campaign, Democrats had tried to make voters fear his possible succession to the presidency. The optimism and confidence in Eisenhower overwhelmed the opposition. During the race, he had refused to reply to opponents' attacks because "the worst thing I could do to my detractors was to help defeat their candidates. Since we were able to accomplish that result, I suppose no other retaliation is needed!" He hoped to correct the false impressions that had circulated about him, but never succeeded in doing so. The mistrust between himself and the Democrats would grow and harden.[79]

Late in December, Adlai Stevenson analyzed why he thought he lost. The Suez invasion, he reasoned, had cost him three to five million votes. If the fighting had not broken out, he would have done better than in 1952 but still would have lost. He could not resist writing about his nemesis: "Nixon will emerge more and more as the real influence, and of course he is capable of any gymnastics that local politics seem to require."[80]

George Ball, who handled Stevenson's public relations during the campaign, offered a different analysis. Eisenhower was vulnerable on domestic issues because he did not aggressively expand New Deal programs, but Stevenson did not press him on these, choosing instead to focus on disarmament and the draft—issues that played to the president's military strengths. The crises in Suez and Hungary gave his candidate "an excuse for losing—though I never doubted we would have lost anyway."[81]

Few of those offering post-mortems mentioned Stevenson's last speech: how science, history, and experience proved that Ike would "probably" die before the end of his term, with the unthinkable consequence of Nixon becoming president. Eisenhower completed his presidency and did not die until 1969, at the age of seventy-eight. Stevenson suffered a fatal heart attack on a London street in 1965; he died at sixty-five—so much for prophesy.

THE HUNGARIAN REVOLUTION
AND THE FREEDOM FIGHTERS

Under Truman, Republicans had vehemently demanded that the administration liberate the Eastern European satellites. But when the Eisenhower administration did not threaten military intervention after disgruntled construction workers in East Berlin went on strike on June 16, 1953, over longer working hours and higher prices, the GOP showed considerably more restraint. The next day, soldiers and tanks violently suppressed the revolt, by some estimates killing more than 500, wounding over 2,000, and arresting as many as 5,100. This brutal response quickly snuffed out the rebellion.[1]

In the summer of 1955, Nixon illustrated the party's ambivalence by publicly emphasizing American determination "not to acquiesce in the enslavement of the satellite peoples." A year later, at an NSC meeting, the vice president followed Ike's direction by citing two objectives regarding the satellites: restoring democratic and popular governments, and encouraging communist states like Yugoslavia to be free of Kremlin domination. He did not advocate promoting uprisings, but neither did he wish to discourage them; he hoped to cause friction between the Soviet Union and its satellites.[2]

Even with these mixed signals, United States strategy during Eisenhower's first term was to abandon any military option toward the satellites in favor of improved bilateral relations with the Soviet Union. As the historian Chris Tudda wrote: "The Eisenhower administration never intended to risk fighting a war against the Soviet Union in order to free the captive people." Despite this decision, talk of liberation and rollback created confusion over whether American troops would come to the aid of insurgents trying to force the Soviets out of their countries.[3]

Unlike the brief riots in East Germany, those that periodically erupted in Poland under Soviet rule had far-reaching consequences. The largest worker rebellion occurred in Poznán in June 1956. Between fifty-seven and seventy-eight individuals, mostly protesters, were killed; hundreds were wounded, and thousands were arrested. The Kremlin decided to rehabilitate Wladyslaw Gomulka and brought him back to lead the Polish government, but not before Polish nationalists destroyed monuments with the Red Star and other widely hated Soviet symbols.

Reacting to the events in Poland, Hungarian students staged a spontaneous demonstration against their government on October 23 in Budapest. At first, the Kremlin did not know how to react. Soviet troops sporadically tried to quell the rebellion using force; then Moscow opted to withdraw soldiers and negotiate with the provisional government. By the end of the month, Khrushchev and most of his colleagues had reversed their position and decided to crush the rebellion. On the morning of November 4, Soviet troops and tanks, already deployed in Hungary, entered Budapest and overwhelmed the rebels. Although some continued to fight in the countryside for several weeks after resistance ended in the capital, the opposition was effectively defeated. The Kremlin purged the provisional regime and later executed its leaders. Communists who accepted Soviet dictates were put in charge.[4]

More than 2,500 Hungarians and 700 Soviet troops were killed; thousands were imprisoned. This carnage started an exodus of approximately 200,000 Hungarian refugees, many of whom walked for miles through the bitterly cold winter to seek asylum at the Austrian border. Peter Kenez, who as a teenager was one of the refugees, remembered that border guards on the Hungarian side would detain people overnight but then allow them to go free the next day. "They only made a show of controlling the borders," he wrote, "but in fact did not want to prevent people from leaving. The communist rulers reasoned that it was good to get rid of troublemakers, for that made the task of consolidation easier."[5]

Some scholars have argued that Voice of America and Radio Free Europe broadcasts encouraged the Hungarian uprisings; other authors vehemently disagree. Llewellyn Thompson, United States ambassador to Austria during the rebellion, acknowledged that some refugees were sure that the United States would intervene. He claimed that very few of the broadcasts were provocative and that the American "role had been minimal." He tried to assure the Kremlin, which did not believe him, that the United States had acted with restraint.[6]

On November 9, the president held a bipartisan legislative meeting during which the director of Central Intelligence (DCI), Allen Dulles, briefed the audience on the conditions in Hungary. As background, he noted that Moscow had been cautiously stepping back from some Stalinist policies, moderating its dictatorial practices at home and in its satellites. Unrest in Poland resulted in

Gomulka's resuming control of the Communist Party apparatus on October 20, and with his ascension the major dissatisfaction with communist rule subsided. Hungary did not follow the same path. Moscow had been willing to discuss some accommodation, Dulles explained, but when the new Hungarian leadership decided to leave the Warsaw Pact, the Kremlin felt they went too far, and Soviet troops ruthlessly crushed the rebellion.[7]

The president wrote Soviet chairman Nikolai Bulganin, urging him to withdraw his soldiers and permit the UN to determine what humanitarian supplies the Hungarian people needed. On November 11, he called upon Indian prime minister Nehru to support the UN resolution "to relieve the suffering of the people there." In a letter addressed to Yugoslavian president Josip Tito but meant to reassure the Soviet rulers, Ike emphasized that his administration's intentions had "never been to encourage or induce such revolt by any people." He went further, asserting that the United States was not seeking "any special benefit" or imposing "its concepts on these lands." If this was not sufficiently clear, he also publicly assured the Kremlin that the United States "would not look upon any government in the Eastern Europe countries as potential military allies."[8]

During a White House press conference in mid-November, the president complicated the issue when he answered a question regarding the administration's position on liberation by saying that the "free world" could never "accept the enslavement of the Eastern European tier of nations." Ike stressed that his administration had "never asked . . . for a people to rise up against a ruthless military force," but added "that the employment of such force is the negation of all justice and right in the world." He insisted "upon the right of all people to be free to live under governments of their own choosing."[9]

Throughout November, as the appalling Soviet onslaught continued, Ike rejected any suggestion of dispatching American forces. Such a measure, he thought, could threaten Hungary with annihilation and might even lead to another world war. Recalling the incident in 1967, the former president confided to Nixon that another reason he did not consider military intervention was that America's European allies would not support it.[10]

Once Nixon returned from campaigning, he attended many meetings the president conducted concerning Hungary. During a National Security Council (NSC) meeting on November 8, the vice president argued that the United States should impress upon developing nations "that no state could afford to play with the Soviet Union unless it wished to be taken over." Eisenhower added that the United States should send Nehru a film of Soviet tanks killing the Hungarian rebels, and the vice president thought another one should go to Indonesian president Sukarno. He thought the United States also should publicize the pictures of tanks killing civilians on the streets of Budapest, to illustrate graphically the brutal nature of the Kremlin regime.[11]

From mid-November almost until the end of the month, the vice president vacationed in Florida. While there, he talked by telephone to Secretary Dulles, who was in Key West recuperating from surgery. They had lunch together on November 28, the day Nixon flew back to the capital. Dulles ended his recuperation and returned to Washington in the first week of December, where one of his first actions was to talk with the president about sending Nixon to Austria to examine the refugee camps. They agreed that the vice president should go if the Austrian government consented. When Dulles raised the question with Nixon, he agreed that he would go if the journey would be useful and if it would not be viewed as a "grandstand play."[12]

Neither Eisenhower nor Nixon lived to see the fiftieth anniversary celebration of the 1956 Hungarian revolution. Scores of authors have written articles and books commemorating the event. No writer links Eisenhower's Hungarian declarations to his effort to revamp America's immigration laws. He is roundly criticized for his failure to change them, and his successful effort to bring thousands of Hungarian refugees to America is overlooked.

Nor do authors mention that Eisenhower had had firsthand experience with refugee resettlement. After World War II, as Allied Supreme Commander, he worked energetically to find homes, clothing, and food for Jewish displaced persons (DPs) in postwar Europe. He visited many DP camps and wrote a letter to Truman on October 17, 1945, expressing his support for holocaust survivors. Truman was unable to pass a law admitting DPs to the United States at the end of the year, but he directed unfilled immigration quotas to be designated for them.[13]

Hiding in plain sight was Ike's desire to change American immigration laws. During the summer of 1952, Congress overrode President Truman's veto and passed the McCarran-Walter Immigration and Nationality Act, which reasserted earlier restrictionist quota provisions that overwhelmingly favored Caucasian aliens.[14] Candidate Eisenhower condemned the law in the 1952 campaign because it implied "the blasphemy against democracy that only certain groups of Europeans are welcome on American shores." In his first State of the Union address, he called for changes in the immigration law because it "contains injustices" and "does, in fact, discriminate." A bill that did become law that summer, the Refugee Relief Act, admitted more applicants, but it did little to alter quota preferences.[15]

The Hungarian crisis became, for Eisenhower, a vehicle to attack America's immigration policy. In November 1956 he granted 6,500 visas to the freedom fighters under the 1953 legislation.[16] At a White House ceremony on November 26, he greeted the first Hungarian refugees to arrive in the United States and posed for photographs with several of them. He then committed his administration on December 1 to admit another 15,000, for a total of 21,500, and to reduce the economic burden on the Austrian government for sheltering and feeding them while many of them searched for new homes. While vacationing in Georgia, on Human Rights Day, he proclaimed that "the recent outbreak of brutality in Hungary has moved free peoples everywhere to reactions of horror and revulsion. Our hearts are filled with sorrow. Our deepest sympathy goes out to the courageous liberty-loving people of Hungary."[17]

During a speech before the Automobile Manufacturers Association on December 6, Nixon characterized the Hungarian revolution as a major turning point for Moscow. The UN, he asserted, had no armies to rescue the freedom fighters: "Our only weapon here was moral condemnation, since the alternative was action on our part which might initiate the third and ultimate world war." The Kremlin's actions in suppressing the rebellion illustrated the brute force of its dictatorship. He cautioned neutral nations: "those who invite the Communists in, run the risk of the savage slaughter which has been the lot of the freedom fighters of Hungary."[18]

For several days after that address, rumors circulated that the Nixons would go to Austria on an inspection trip. On the afternoon of December 12, White House press secretary Hagerty confirmed the rumors, releasing a statement that the Nixons would travel to Austria to report on conditions among the Hungarian refugees. The vice president would serve as the president's representative and would report to him and Congress; he would also make recommendations about what further measures the United States should undertake to assist the escapees.[19]

Eisenhower returned to the White House on December 13 and called Nixon back to the capital the next morning. That afternoon the vice president traveled to New York City to visit the UN, where he talked to members of the Austrian delegation. One of the principal reasons for his mission was that the magnitude of the refugee exodus had exceeded all expectations. He wanted to improve coordination between the United States and other agencies assisting the escapees. When asked if he planned to go to Hungary, he answered no.[20]

While Nixon was preparing for his mission, reports from Budapest described the bleak atmosphere. Workers struck to show their dissatisfaction and then returned to their jobs from 8:00 a.m. until 2:00 p.m. A curfew went into effect at dark. Guerrillas still staged sporadic resistance in the countryside. Christmas cheer had disappeared.[21]

Many of those who fled crossed into Austria, the only noncommunist nation bordering on Hungary. Austria had signed a treaty with the four Allied Powers on May 15, 1955, to end the post–World War II occupation, and the last foreign troops left in November. The central provision of the agreement was that Austria would enforce absolute neutrality. Despite this, the Austrian people united in welcoming its neighbor's refugees, a proud moment exemplifying Austrian nationalism.[22]

The staggering number of escapees revealed the limitations of the Austrian government; it simply did not have the capacity to handle the thousands upon thousands of people fleeing from the Soviet rule. The government desperately needed financial assistance and also had to identify nations that would allow emigration. How Austria maneuvered during this crisis tested its neutrality. The Kremlin and its Hungarian supporters claimed Austria was allowing Hungarian exiles to use Austria as a safe haven to launch attacks across the common border.[23]

Nixon, meanwhile, concentrated on his mission. He was given two objectives: to confer with United States and Austrian officials handling the refugee operation and, second, to meet with Austrian officials regarding its delicate neutrality.[24] DCI Dulles and his assistant, future DCI Richard Helms, briefed him on conditions in Eastern Europe. William Colby, another future DCI then stationed in Italy, conceded that the CIA wanted to aid the freedom fighters, but Eisenhower refused to permit the agency to provoke a revolt.[25]

Nixon's schedule was announced on December 16. Ambassador Thompson in Vienna, three weeks earlier, had forbidden his staff from going to the border so as not to jeopardize Austrian neutrality. From Washington, the vice president refused to comment about how close he expected to get to the border. The *New York Times* reported that both the Austrian government and the American embassy hoped he would not make that trip.[26]

For the first time during his vice presidency, Pat Nixon did not accompany her husband on a foreign mission. Deputy attorney general Bill Rogers was included in the delegation. As the Number 2 man in the justice department, he was to analyze what changes were needed in the immigration laws if and when the government confronted similar emergencies in the future.[27]

The president saw Nixon at the White House on Tuesday morning, December 18, and made clear that he was horrified by the Hungarian situation. He assigned his vice president the responsibility of determining how to move refugees into the United States, how to accelerate the resettlement, and how to provide more economic aid to the Austrian government. Nixon also brought 1,600 pounds of insulin and contributions of $450,000 from American volunteer organizations.[28]

Before he touched down in Vienna, the Soviet state newspaper *Pravda* alleged that Nixon was going to Austria without an invitation and was using the mission as subterfuge to interfere in the domestic affairs of other nations. His objective was to create chaos in Hungary by exploiting Austrian hospitality.[29]

A single Secret Service agent, Rex Scouten, traveled with the vice president. More than a half century later, he described the journey as "exhausting." From Wednesday through Saturday, Nixon worked on minimal sleep, meeting with scores of American and European officials, greeting thousands of refugees, and listening as dozens of volunteer organizations' representatives explained their humanitarian objectives.[30]

The vice president landed at Schwechat Airport on Wednesday, December 19. In his opening statement, he declared that the United States had already committed to accepting 21,500 refugees and might increase that number. He saw a group of refugees leaving for the United States, shook hands with the adults, hugged some children, and wished them a Merry Christmas and a Happy New Year. Photographers took pictures of the vice president embracing the Hungarians. This was an integral part of his mission; he was to focus attention on the plight of the refugees and prepare for their reception in America.[31]

Nixon met with Chancellor Julius Raab on Thursday morning and handed him the letter from Eisenhower that praised his nation for its humanitarianism in accepting the Hungarian escapees. Raab responded that his nation no longer needed Marshall Plan assistance but did require help in caring for the Hungarians. He asked the United States to allocate funds for those seeking asylum.[32]

After conversing with the chancellor, the vice president toured refugee camps, escorted by a forty-car motorcade containing about thirty reporters. The journey from the capital to Andau, a frontier town two miles from the Hungarian border, took an hour and a half. That was where many refugees crossed and where Red Cross representatives started to process them.[33]

After nine hours, Nixon finished his journey at Traiskirchen, a nineteenth-century military training school, where a Quaker relief organization had converted the buildings into the largest refugee camp near Vienna. The refugees presented a Christmas play before a packed auditorium, with the vice president, his staff, and other dignitaries sitting in the front row. Several young girls dressed like angels used a Nativity scene as a backdrop. The performers sang Christmas carols, a practice that the communists had forbidden. After the performance, Nixon stood, gave a short speech praising the Austrian effort, and went to a piano, where he played "Jingle Bells" to an ovation from the crowd. After his musical number, he sat between the little angels for a photographic opportunity.[34]

After returning to the embassy that evening, the vice president had Ambassador Thompson organize a trip to the border. Nixon, deputy attorney general Rogers, Congressman Robert Wilson from San Diego, vice-presidential administrative assistant Robert King, and Secret Service agent Scouten drove back to Andau.[35] Three cars with fifteen people secretly sped to the tiny village; the party arrived on Friday, in bitter predawn cold. Ministerialrat Maximilian Pammer, chief of the state police, accompanied them to the frontier. Nixon and his entourage went to a farmer's home with a small light bulb hanging outside, a sign of a safe house for the Hungarians. The farmer climbed into a large tractor that pulled a trailer where Nixon, Rogers, and Scouten sat huddled inside covered with straw and blankets, and drove toward the muddy little Einser Canal, where the "Freedom Bridge" was located. The farmer found several refugees waiting, and by 6:30 a.m. the entire group had returned to the farmhouse. Nixon later described watching the refugees crossing into Austria as "the most thrilling experience of my life."[36]

That evening, with cold and snow dominating the landscape, he boarded a special train at Westbahnhof station and headed for Salzburg, 182 miles away in Burgenland, the nation's easternmost province. At 9:30 a.m. the party went to Camp Roeder, a large holding area for escapees and the main processing point for those coming to the United States. Nixon then inspected Camp Glasenbach, where the Hungarians initially were sent before the tremendous influx.[37]

That completed Nixon's Austrian journey. His party traveled by automobile to the German border town of Freilassing and boarded a private train for the eighty-mile trip to Munich, the capital of Bavaria and a one-time stronghold of Adolf Hitler. A half hour later, they went to Riem Airport to confer with Lieutenant General William Turner, who commanded the United States Air Force in Europe. He and the vice president inspected the quarters that were designed to transport refugees to America and a staging area for the airlift. Nixon watched one plane as it took off filled with Hungarians.[38]

During his trip, the vice president had talked with Austrian officials and leaders of volunteer agencies that cared for the escapees; he had followed the train route through Austria to Germany for air transportation to the United States through Scotland and Iceland. He had accomplished his task in a week and started to formulate his recommendations to the president on what measures were needed to assist the refugees.

Nixon landed in Washington on the morning of Christmas Eve in the middle of drizzling rain. Before leaving the airport, he told the press that he had "specific recommendations" for increasing American financial assistance to the

Hungarians. International communism in Eastern Europe had taken "a mortal blow from which it cannot recover." The Hungarian rebellion, he said, had demonstrated that communism was a "gigantic failure."[39]

Bela Kornitzer, a Hungarian writer who had been in Austria during Nixon's trip, remained in Vienna for interviews with Austrian officials. Chancellor Julius Raab remarked that when he first met Nixon "I was looking for horns." But after the two leaders talked, the chancellor said, he decided that "Nixon is one of the finest men I have met in my entire career!"[40] Kornitzer also interviewed Foreign Minister Leopold Figl, who declared: "We have actually been surprised that Vice President Nixon made his visit with so deep a sense of responsibility." He illustrated his concern for the humanitarian aspects of the tragedy, and Figl said that he "was deeply impressed with his humaneness, seriousness, and sense of responsibility." He worked tirelessly to present Eisenhower with a comprehensive evaluation.[41]

On Christmas Day 1956, the vice president spoke for ten minutes during an hour-long nationwide broadcast designed to raise money for the Hungarians, highlighted by Hollywood and Broadway personalities. Nixon called on his audience to give generously in the spirit of the season and for the government to "do more." The courageous freedom fighters, he stated, had exposed the Soviet Union's weaknesses. Thousands had fled their homes, and now they had to be transported, fed, resettled, and employed. For the sake of all free people, American had to contribute to this cause.[42]

The next day, Nixon, Bill Rogers, and others involved in the refugee resettlement program met for an hour with Ike at the White House. The vice president cautioned those assembled to refrain from mentioning publicly, and especially to members of Congress who opposed the plan, the number of Hungarians coming to America. Instead, he told them, they should emphasize the high caliber of the asylum seekers. Those who opposed the immigrants out of fear that some were communist spies had exaggerated the threat; the prospect of enemy agents was almost zero. To date, 151,000 Hungarians had fled to Austria with 70,000 still in search of homes. The daily exodus was 800, and no one knew when the Kremlin would close the border.[43]

Eisenhower realized that the United States would have to absorb most of the cost, estimated at $30 to $40 million. The nations that were participating in the resettlement needed to take more immigrants, and Nixon warned that they had to be moved quickly because delay would cause uncertainty in the food supply and housing. The president expected to meet shortly with congressional leaders to draft proposals that would allow more refugees into the United States.[44]

Two days after Christmas, the vice president went to New York City, where he consulted former president Herbert Hoover about the issue. Hoover was an expert on refugees, having directed relief efforts in the two world wars, and the Nixon-Hoover friendship dated back to the vice president's first congressional race, in 1946.[45] The vice president was allowed to call Hoover "Chief," a nickname used only by close friends, and routinely sent him birthday greetings. When Nixon traveled to New York, he met the former president at his apartment in the Waldorf-Astoria Towers.[46]

Before Nixon left for Austria, Hoover had wanted to talk with him about central coordination of relief agencies, and he sent Nixon a few pages from his memoirs about the relief effort in the Soviet Union after World War I. After returning, Nixon told Hoover that he would include several of his suggestions in his recommendations on how to house, feed, and cloth the refugees. He would urge the administration to employ policies similar to those Hoover had "used so successfully in the Russian relief program of 1922."[47]

After his visit with Hoover, the vice president welcomed refugees in his inspection of Camp Kilmer, near New Brunswick, New Jersey. That facility processed approximately 1,000 Hungarian escapees per day for resettlement in the United States. The name given to this enterprise was Operation Safe Haven.[48]

On New Year's Day, Ike stated that Hungarian refugees would continue to be allowed in the United States until Congress acted on immigration. It was, he maintained, "in the national interest" for the United States and other nations to continue to provide "a haven for those victims of oppression."[49] That afternoon, the president convened a bipartisan meeting of congressional leaders; one topic on the agenda was Nixon's report on the Hungarian immigrants. Nixon suggested that any legislative bill include some flexibility and that until Congress passed a new act, the refugees continue to be permitted in the United States under current policies. Speaker Rayburn and Senator Richard Russell expressed concern over the growing number seeking asylum but did not strenuously object. After the meeting, Eisenhower publicly announced the results of the talks. More refugees would be allowed into America, and the administration position would not change until Congress enacted new legislation.[50]

The same day, Nixon released his report describing the flight of approximately 155,000 escapees into Austria. At present, 88,000 had been resettled, and of the remainder, at least 37,000 needed to find homes. The United States had already admitted 15,000 and promised to take another 6,500, a number that now appeared inadequate. All free nations had to be prepared to accept more. In addition to calling on Congress to consider new immigration laws, the vice president also said that the administration expected to provide more aid to Austria. He praised the private volunteer organization for the large sums that they had raised, and complimented the American embassy in Vienna and the United States military, who transported the freedom fighters and assisted with the speedy resettlement program. All those associated with the massive exodus were to be commended, while Soviet brutality spotlighted the failure of communist totalitarianism.[51]

Nixon specifically alluded to the inadequacies in America's immigration system, not only for the Hungarians but also for other refugees behind the Iron Curtain. He was convinced that the present immigration laws were inadequate. Public sympathy for the freedom fighters, he wrote, demonstrated the need for extensive revision of the McCarran-Walters Act to permit the nation to deal with similar emergencies in the future. Nixon argued for quick action, since the Refugee Relief Act, which provided some flexibility in the existing quota system, would expire at the end of 1956. He called for giving the president authority during emergencies to shift quotas without congressional approval.[52]

At the end of January, Ambassador Thompson reported to the vice president's administrative assistant Robert King that "we still have the refugee problem very much with us, and there are increasing signs that the initial Austrian enthusiasm for doing everything possible for the refugees is beginning to wear a bit thin." Nixon's mission had helped improve American-Austrian relations, but Austria still had too many escapees, and the United States had to help relocate them.[53]

Throughout 1957, the administration lobbied unsuccessfully for new laws. The restrictionists in Congress, led by Democratic congressman Francis Walter of Pennsylvania, effectively blocked any major reforms. In spite of that obstruction, more than 38,000 Hungarians, or almost 20 percent of the total, came to the United States and eventually received a path to citizenship. The fundamental approach to quotas, however, did not change until 1965.[54]

Nixon occasionally spoke out about the significance of the Hungarian rebellion. On April 30, 1957, he predicted that such outbreaks marked the beginning of "an internal revolt that will sweep away the Communist empire." In the fall of 1962, he wrote that the rebellion would never be forgotten: "This was man at his finest. The challenge remains, for those of us still on the battleline, to make good the sacrifice of those grim but memorable days."[55] The Hungarian émigré artist Ferenc Daday memorialized the vice president's mission on canvas in 1971 with a large painting (88 inches high by 136 inches wide) called "Nixon at Andau." It portrayed the vice president welcoming refugees as they crossed into Austria from Hungary.[56]

In *RN*, Nixon expressed frustration that the United States could not help the Eastern European satellites free themselves from Soviet domination. Armed revolt was futile against military superiority, and yet Nixon refused to concede that the Iron Curtain would last forever. "Peaceful change," he reasoned, "is the only practicable answer." That could take a generation or even a century. His pessimistic analysis failed to take into account that the Soviet Union would crumble from its own internal weaknesses. He lived to witness the empire's collapse and Hungarian independence.[57]

Part Two

1957–1961

23

IKE AND DICK RETURN

At age sixty-six, Dwight Eisenhower had won reelection with the largest popular vote in American history to that time. He also became the oldest president to begin a second term; no man had lived to seventy while serving in the White House.[1]

Throughout his first term, Eisenhower's approval ratings had never fallen below 50 percent. He would maintain this record through his second term and sometimes ascend into the low seventies. A large minority of Democrats approved of his governance; approximately two-thirds of independents and over four-fifths of Republicans expressed their satisfaction.[2]

If these numbers were not enough cause for celebration, Gallup, at the beginning of 1958, asked respondents what man they admired most, and the name most frequently mentioned was Eisenhower's. Two years later, the pollsters asked people from eleven nations to name "The most outstanding personality in the ten years 1950–1959," and again the name most frequently mentioned was Ike's.[3]

Each year, Ike sent Nixon birthday greetings and other warm missives. At the start of the second term, Ike wished him "always the very best." A year later, as the president was recovering from his mild stroke in November 1957, he told Nixon "how grateful I am for your understanding and help over these last difficult weeks." At the end of 1959, the president acknowledged "a debt . . . that I can never repay but which I shall always remember."[4]

The president and the vice president often spoke by telephone and met over breakfast or lunch. The substance of their conversations was usually noted as "off-the-record" or "subject unknown." On occasion, some glimpse of what they discussed surfaced in separate memoranda, but the fact that Ike and Nixon conferred privately so often over such a long period of time shows how closely the two of them collaborated.[5]

On December 3, 1957, Nixon saw the president from 3:37 p.m. to 4:45 p.m. No subject is recorded in the appointment schedule.[6] It was their first private meeting following Eisenhower's stroke.

The weekend weather for November 23 and 24 was near seventy degrees; it was Indian summer in Washington. Monday brought what presidential appointment secretary Gordon Gray described as "raw wind, more miserable than cold." At noon, Ike greeted King Mohammed V of Morocco at Military Air Transport Service and escorted him to Blair House. The president returned to the White House for lunch, then went to the Oval Office and rang the buzzer for Gray at 2:22. When Gray arrived, Ike complained of dizzy spells and an inability to speak. Dr. Snyder was summoned and concluded that Ike had "an occlusion of a small branch of the middle cerebral artery on the left side." In other words, a stroke. Rather than tell the public, the White House issued a statement that the president had a "chill" and had gone to bed.[7]

Sherman Adams relayed the news to Nixon. They agreed that Nixon would substitute for the president and accompany Mamie at the banquet for the king that evening. In his autobiography, Nixon commented on the first lady's "courageous" performance; she did not show any sign that her husband was in the living quarters, incapacitated in bed.[8]

Tuesday afternoon, the White House revealed that Ike had suffered "a slight stroke" with "speech impairments" and would require "complete rest" for three or four weeks. The stock market reacted as it had during the two previous health bulletins; within twenty minutes of the news flash, it fell precipitously.[9]

Wednesday morning, press secretary Hagerty told Secretary Dulles that Ike "had a good night, shaved himself, breakfasted and showered. He is in fine spirits." The stock market rebounded. That afternoon, Adams and Nixon visited the president for fifteen minutes to determine his state of mind. Ike had a small studio on the north side of the White House where he painted. Adams and Nixon thought he appeared mentally alert and was "champing at the bit" to return to work. Nixon held a formal press conference that afternoon in the press secretary's overcrowded and noisy office, in which he said that the president had difficulty choosing the right word; this, in medical terms, was called "mild aphasia." Even with that impediment, he was functioning just fine. As in the past, Nixon chaired cabinet and NSC meetings until the president had recovered. Although rumors were already circulating that Ike might resign, Nixon emphasized that such a measure had received no consideration: "The President will recover and resume his duties." No one, according to newly confirmed Attorney General William Rogers, had recommended any delegation of presidential powers.[10]

James Reston of the *New York Times* felt the vice president had matured in office. At the press conference, he wrote, Nixon was slightly nervous at first but later answered "with skill and confidence." Since Eisenhower's heart attack and the ileitis surgery, Nixon had assumed a broader role; he was receiving more of the spotlight while chief of staff Adams was fading into the background. Nixon "even looked different. He seems to have lost a little weight. His hair is cut closer on the sides and on top. His speech is more vivid and articulate and his manner more patient and courteous."[11]

The president attended Thanksgiving services at the National Presbyterian Cathedral the next day to reassure the public that his health had improved. As he left the service, his son John recalled that his "face looked drawn, and his coloring was less ruddy than usual." He had dinner with his family at the White House. Despite Ike's drawn appearance, Hagerty claimed that the recovery was proceeding well. Ike had been scheduled to travel to Paris in mid-December for a NATO summit meeting; there were rumors that Nixon might replace him.[12]

On November 29, Hagerty announced that the president had slept well. He saw Adams and Andrew Goodpaster at 9:28 a.m. and left for Gettysburg early that afternoon, accompanied by Dr. Snyder, to join his son and family. On arriving, he had a late lunch, took a nap, and then walked around his farm.[13]

The president returned to the capital early in December, and on the third he presided over a legislative meeting to show how well his recovery was going. As it was ending, Nixon specifically asked to see the president "to give him some encouraging news with regards to general conditions." At 3:00 p.m. the White House called and granted Nixon an appointment. In a memorandum dictated that day and marked EYES ONLY the vice president described what happened during their conversation. The president, Nixon observed, was "relaxed and in excellent humor and laughed on the few occasions when he happened to mix a word up." His main difficulty was transposition; for instance, he would say "tomorrow" when he meant "yesterday." The president stated his blood pressure was 122 over 80 and his pulse was 76; readings similar to those before his stroke. He was frustrated "of being unable to express myself." If he became overly tense and excited, he "would run too great a risk of another injury which could leave the country in very bad shape."

Nixon reassured the president and counseled him against resigning. The press stories about his health would pass. If he went to the NATO meeting, "one story alone would have dramatic impact in removing doubts that people might have had because of stories indicating Presidential disability." Ike should remain in office, and if he needed assistance, Nixon would help him. The president said he was considering to moving Nixon to the East Wing of the White House, where he would be more easily available to assume added duties. Some in the press, Nixon pointed out, had tried to drive a wedge between him and Ike, but they had failed. Others attempted to create friction between him and Adams, but during the conversation, Nixon stressed: "Adams and I got along perfectly and always had during these periods."[14]

Besides these private discussions, the president routinely invited his vice president to meet with Republican Party leaders like Meade Alcorn and Len Hall; to discuss diplomatic affairs with Secretary Dulles and his associates; or to talk over pending legislation with congressmen and senators.[15] He occasionally called upon Dick to join him for golf at the Burning Tree Country Club in the Maryland suburbs and other courses.[16] Ellis Slater, one of the president's friends, recorded in his diary early in the second term that Ike "talked of Nixon's great ability, of how well he had handled every task assigned to him and of the great experience he would have."[17] At a White House press conference on November 5, 1958, the president stated that Nixon had "been party to every principal governmental committee or organization that we have and, therefore, is not only kept informed of what is going on, but is in very splendid position to contribute his thinking. . . . I don't see how his role in the Executive Branch could be greater."[18]

Nixon's main weakness in Eisenhower's eyes, according to Arthur Larson, a presidential speechwriter, was that he was "too political." On January 12, 1958, the president also told Larson that his vice president was not "the sort of person you turn to when you want a new idea, but he has an uncanny ability to draw upon others' ideas and bring out their essence in a cool-headed way."[19]

On March 17, 1958, Nixon wrote William Gleeson that unfavorable rumors were surfacing about a "rift" between him and Ike. The vice president denied that they had any basis: "our relationship is most cordial." Two weeks later, Hagerty reported to Nixon that columnists were "trying to drive a wedge." The press secretary deplored an article that James Reston had written in the New York Times about the differences between Ike and Nixon. Hagerty felt that "we would all have to pull together and try to overlook a lot of these attempts to start a fight."[20]

Such reassurances did not prevent further speculation in the press about the supposed friction. Newsweek, on October 19, 1959, incorrectly reported that Ike and Nixon had split over United States–Soviet relations and that the vice president had been excluded from White House and state department councils. The president intended to negotiate with the Kremlin, while the vice president saw talks as a sign of weakness. Such accounts persisted despite White House denials.[21]

As the rumors continued into the spring of 1960, Ike wrote his brother Edgar's wife, Lucy, expressing his disappointment that the press went to extremes to increase circulation. Newspapers had "little responsibility for the accuracy of the story," and American libel laws were inadequate. Some newspapers carried "an unusual number" of columnists such as Drew Pearson, Marquis Childs, Scotty Reston, and others whom Ike found unreliable. The president had spoken before many editors and publishers on the necessity of being responsible for what they printed. "But publishers," he lamented, "just like other heads of businesses, are plagued by the difficulties they have with personnel."[22]

The critical articles did increase Nixon's name recognition. By the beginning of December 1957, he had been on the front page of *Life*, *Time*, and *Newsweek*. At the end of the year, when the Gallup Poll asked participants whether, if Nixon assumed presidency, he would do better or worse than Ike, 8 percent said better, 26 percent worse, and 45 percent about the same. At the end of the year, interviewers questioned how people rated the vice president: 28 percent rated him very favorable, 23 percent mildly favorable, 30 percent neutral and 12 percent highly unfavorable. At the end of 1958, Gallup included Nixon in its list of ten most admired men.[23]

Some reporters and columnists, like Drew Pearson and Philip Potter (of the *Baltimore Sun*), seemed to nurse a visceral hatred of Nixon. Frank Clarvoe, *The San Francisco News* editor, informed the vice president that he was one of those "who have said they 'just don't like Nixon,' without being able to give anyone, including themselves, a satisfactory explanation." Leslie Claypool, according to Rose Mary Woods, had "been notoriously inaccurate when reporting on anything which has had to do with the Boss." Herb Caen of the *San Francisco Chronicle* routinely wrote unflattering articles. In the summer of 1959, he implied in one story that Nixon had insulted the president; in another, he claimed that the vice president had made "haughty comments about a minority group" at an Italian restaurant, causing someone at his table to stomp "off in a huff."[24]

James Reston presented a more serious challenge because of the circulation and influence of the *New York Times*. According to John Stacks's 2003 biography *Scotty*, Nixon and Reston were complete opposites: "Reston tended to be sunny and optimistic, forgiving and broadminded, easy and confident in his dealings with others. Nixon was dark, full of self-doubt even self-loathing—and afflicted with a self-fulfilling paranoia about the Eastern establishment press."[25]

The vice president held a series of meetings on foreign and domestic topics that he himself had suggested. On January 20, 1957, Reston hosted one of them at a small dinner party at his home where Nixon talked about propaganda. The reporter's impression was that the vice president did not have "in any sense an original mind" and appeared "less at ease in a small group than in addressing a political rally or a news conference." He was energetic "but shallow" and thought "in terms of Political techniques more than in the substance of policy."[26]

Another interview that backfired came on February 12, when Nixon met for a half-hour with David Astor, the editor of the *London Observer*. The resulting article included an exchange that drew no notice at the time but caused trouble the following year. On January 3, 1958, columnist Marquis Childs wrote that Astor, "one of London's noted liberal editors," had asked Nixon whether anyone had spoken to him about "your sense of responsibility and your awareness" of what he had done to Helen Gahagan Douglas in the 1950 senatorial campaign. According to Astor, Nixon replied: "All I can say is that I was very young and very ambitious and I am sorry."[27]

On the last day of January, Nixon wrote a supporter and influential journalist, Adela Rogers St. Johns: "There is no foundation in fact whatever for the comments in the Marquis Childs column." During a press conference in February, the vice president called Childs "a very able reporter" who had covered him during several campaigns, but on this occasion, the columnist had used "a bad source. . . . There is not a particle of truth in the story, the anecdote, which appeared in his column."[28] The report of Nixon's alleged apology is still occasionally quoted, while his denial is not mentioned.

Although Reston's analyses of Nixon remained generally uncomplimentary, Stewart Alsop surprised his friends. He went to work at *The Saturday Evening Post* in the spring of 1958 and decided to write an article on Nixon. The columnist wrote Nixon to say that such a piece would give millions of *Post* readers a chance "to gain an understanding of you as a human being."[29]

On March 14, in his column "Matter of Fact," Alsop claimed that the vice president was acting more independently within the administration and pushing for a massive tax reduction in order to prevent the recession from growing more serious, while the president intended to wait for the economic downturn to end without any stimulus. The article attracted a great deal of attention. According to vice-presidential aide William Key, the most interesting feature was "the bitterness of some of Stewart's old friends. The liberal liners have really tee-d off on him as a rank deserter to the point that he is actually short-tempered about it."[30]

Alsop assembled material from people who had known the vice president in Whittier and at Duke, and he also journeyed to California in April for interviews. He spoke with the vice president twice at length. Alsop believed the public's sense that Nixon "lacked a certain depth, reality, warmth . . . a human quality" was inaccurate, and that his article would correct those misperceptions.[31]

The *Post* published "Richard Nixon: The Mystery and the Man" on July 12. By that time, Alsop and Nixon had developed a warm relationship, and he described the vice president as "above all an intensely practical man." As president, he would be conservative within the limits of "the existing economic and political situation." Some newspapers rejected Alsop's portrait and personally attacked him. The *Louisville Courier-Journal,* according to journalists Nora and Ralph de Toledano, published an editorial objecting to Alsop's article: "So, they end up by trying to smear Stewart Alsop." Nixon wrote conservative columnist Raymond Moley that Doris Fleeson and Drew Pearson had "severely attacked" Alsop "for being a 'turncoat.'" The vice president believed that Alsop "was genuinely surprised that his liberal friends could be even more uncompromising and unreasonable in a case like this than some of the conservatives whom he has had occasion to criticize in times past." Nixon ignored those assaults; on July 25, he wrote that he was pleased "that the article has been generally well-received throughout the country."[32]

Outside the office, Pat Nixon remained her husband's staunchest ally. Mamie Eisenhower, on the other hand, paid scant attention to politics. That did not prevent her from playing a crucial role in the Eisenhower-Nixon relationship. The first lady had developed a cordial friendship with Pat since the 1952 presidential contest, and during the second term that relationship grew more intimate. Pat sent Mamie handwritten letters with happy birthday greetings and composed get-well notes when Mamie was ill: "Just to let you know that you are in my thoughts constantly. Here's to a speedy recovery!" She ended her correspondence "With affection, Pat."[33] Pat also remembered the birthday of Mamie's mother, Mrs. Elvira Doud, with a card and a handkerchief. Mamie wrote Pat: "Your thought meant so much to her—and to me, too!"[34] Mamie invited Pat to sit with her at luncheons, during dinners, and at the State of the Union address.

Despite her longing for privacy, Pat took her duties as second lady seriously. Late in 1956, she was named the woman of the year in politics. Before holding a press conference for women reporters at the Fort Worth airport in the winter of 1959, she reminded Nixon's press secretary Herbert Klein that she would keep to her routine procedure: "no politics—usual women interest angle." Some labeled her a phony for trying to portray herself as the perfect wife and mother; admirers hailed her as an original who represented the best qualities of American women. She was praised for "her personal friendliness" and, in a poll of 500,000 housewives was chosen as "The Nation's Ideal Wife."[35]

Her routine as the vice president's wife was far from normal. For the 1956 inauguration, the designer Elizabeth Arden assembled several dresses that she believed Pat would like. Pat ordered a gown from Arden's collection that she described as not "fabulous but satisfactory—[and] as important—painless inasmuch as I didn't have to go through the expense and effort of an especially designed job." She used a friend's name when flying to New York to visit Arden's salon so as not to draw attention.[36]

Arden wanted to create Pat's "entire wardrobe," but she preferred "to be entirely independent." Dick then took her and Arden to lunch and chose "a slinky dinner dress" for Pat. He felt the diplomatic corps "would swoon." Pat wondered: "We'll see if I ever have courage to wear it!"[37]

Pat constantly emphasized that she wanted her daughters to live normal lives. By the fall of 1956, Tricia was in the fifth grade and Julie in the third at Horace Mann School, a public grammar school near their home. Tricia was in Girl Scout Troop #309 and Julie in Brownie Troop #972.[38] Their first experience with a journalist was an article by Ms. Michael Drury in the September 1957 issue of *Good Housekeeping*, "The Nixon Children." Drury presented a sympathetic portrait: the girls cleaned their own rooms and were good students who did their homework before being allowed to watch television. Their mother wanted to be certain that her daughters were not spoiled; for the article, she commented: "They really are very nice little girls."[39]

The Nixons also moved from their modest house on Tilden Street in suburban Maryland to a twenty-one-room English Tudor mansion at 4308 Forest Lane in Wesley Heights. The new house offered much more privacy: it was at the end of a dead-end street, and the back overlooked Glover Park and was surrounded by dense woods. The vice president was twenty minutes from his office during daytime and twelve minutes at night.[40] The house, for which they paid $75,000, had a basement with a reception room and a maid's quarters; the first floor had a reception hall, drawing, dining, and breakfast rooms, along with a kitchen and a butler's pantry; there were four bedrooms with four baths on the second floor with a library over the garage; the third story had three dormers with a bath.[41]

Besides wanting more privacy, they needed the space because of all the entertaining the president had allocated to his vice president. When they lived on Tilden Street, hosting a party of any size required them to remove "most of the furniture and replace [it] with people." They often held gatherings at hotels, restaurants, or the prestigious F Street Club, where the vice president hosted the president, honored cabinet members, and put on birthday celebrations for Pat.[42]

The Forest Lane property changed the social dynamic. While they still used other venues, their home became a gathering place. Senators and congressmen played poker there. They had parties for cabinet members. Their headline event came on December 19, 1958, when the president and the first lady came to dinner party with ten guests. The next day, Ike wrote Pat a letter wishing her a Merry

Christmas and thanking her for such a pleasant evening: "Everyone seemed to be in the highest possible spirits and every minute from the time we reached there until we left was truly enjoyable."[43]

This was the vice president's private residence; there was no official one. Republican congressman Stuyvesant Wainwright, from Long Island, New York, introduced a bill to provide an official residence during the 1955 House session; the president included it in his 1957 budget. Nixon opposed the legislation during his term but argued that in January 1961, the new vice president should have one. When questioned on the subject at a press conference on June 5, 1957, Eisenhower said he was "in favor of it very much." Despite that approval, the first vice president to live in an official residence was Walter Mondale in 1977.[44]

Throughout the second term, Ike and Nixon depended on each other, and Mamie and Pat formed a cordial friendship. The president gave assignments to those he trusted, and he trusted Nixon.

24

PRELUDE TO THE STRUGGLE

By the end of the first term, Eisenhower had taken more concrete actions affecting African Americans than any president since Lincoln. Ike had moved energetically to desegregate the armed forces, and unlike his predecessors, he had used his executive authority to desegregate the capital. He believed that any citizen deserved equal treatment before the federal government. Although he is routinely accused of never using his bully pulpit on behalf of the civil rights cause, this claim lacks merit. Furthermore, critics claim that he personally was unacquainted with black people. He rarely mentioned Dolores and John Moaney, and the integral part they played in the Eisenhower family.

Nixon's civil rights record as vice president is largely ignored, and he himself is partially responsible for this oversight. In his memoirs, both *Six Crises* and *RN*, he ignores his contribution. He not only acted as the Eisenhower administration's principal civil rights spokesman, but he also lobbied through his chairmanship of the President's Committee on Government Contracts to find more employment for African Americans. He, like the president, did not bring up his personal interaction with black people and did not divulge that he was assisting William Brock in restoring his security clearance.[1]

New African American personalities emerged to participate in the civil rights struggle. Blacks welcomed former baseball star Jackie Robinson to their cause. As a national sports hero, he drew more public attention to the movement. Robinson had briefly met the president. The secretary to the cabinet, Maxwell Rabb, told him that the president was trying "to eliminate the acts of violence and prejudice." Ike was also working on issues involving "equality of opportunity." Robinson responded that he wanted the president to issue a statement "condemning violence." This sports legend also communicated with Nixon. After retiring from the major leagues, Robinson went to work as an executive for the coffee company Chock Full o'Nuts in New York City and led that city's NAACP 1957 Fight for Freedom Campaign Fund drive. Robinson observed the vice president's measures promoting civil rights, and as the vice president spoke out more forcibly, Robinson became convinced that Nixon was sincere.[2]

Another African American who had come on the national stage by the end of 1956 was Martin Luther King Jr., the twenty-eight year-old minister who led the Montgomery bus boycott. Despite that victory in Alabama, some influential black leaders resented King's meteoric rise. His followers and other groups competed for donations, and the NAACP resented King's ability to raise money.[3]

This friction did not interfere with King's growing status as a national celebrity. After the 1956 elections, the minister concluded that blacks were pleased with the civil rights progress under Eisenhower. After Nixon's return from Austria in December, King called upon the vice president and the president to visit the South where they would witness economic coercion and physical violence against African Americans. In the middle of February 1957, the minister renewed his request to have both Eisenhower and Nixon journey to the Old Confederacy on a fact-finding mission. Neither man replied.[4]

Those who covered the White House for the black press complained about the manner in which the president and his staff treated them. Simeon Booker stated that Ike did not recognize black reporters and that press secretary Hagerty thought the African American media was "unimportant." Alice Dunnigan and Ethel Payne, black women who covered the White House, added that after they posed sensitive civil rights questions, Ike grew agitated and stopped calling on them.[5]

While blacks were expressing their disappointment and were clamoring for more action, by the time Ike won reelection, he already had accomplished more for the cause of civil rights in four years than his two Democratic predecessors had done in the previous two decades. Using his executive powers, he had desegregated the capital, the armed forces, and the Veterans Administration (VA); he established the President's Committee on Government Contracts (PCGC) to lobby for greater minority hiring in the private and public sectors. Finally, he had made an unprecedented number of black appointments, including J. Ernest Wilkins, an assistant secretary of labor, and Archibald Carey Jr., a Chicago minister and alderman, the first black to preside over a White House commission.[6]

The president designated his vice president as his principal advocate for civil rights. Nixon focused the spotlight on minority hiring. As chairman of the PCGC, he held meetings to publicize nondiscrimination clauses in federal government contracts and threatened enforcement if business did not follow federal guidelines. He appeared at gatherings to promote minority hiring such as the National Equal Job Opportunity Program in January 1960 and the Youth Training-Incentives Conference the following month. The PCGC expanded its activities by opening a field office in Chicago that spring to combat job discrimination.[7]

The president appointed Brownell as attorney general and Rogers as his deputy. Both men passionately preached the civil rights cause and used the justice department as their vehicle to reverse segregationist practices. The president and these two primary counselors made appointments to the Supreme Court and the federal bench who would enforce the *Brown* case; segregationists were eliminated from consideration as jurists.[8]

The first and sole black member of the White House executive staff, E. Frederic Morrow, did not begin serving until late in the first term. He evaluated the African American mood for Rabb, Adams, Nixon, and others. Violence in the South such as church bombings and segregated buses angered blacks. Once the vice president returned from Austria to report on the Soviet slaughter during the Hungarian revolt, black leaders called on him to travel to the South and examine the terror that white racists had heaped upon African Americans. Morrow felt that the "Administration's apparent indifference to the plight of the defenseless Negroes in the South" was unconscionable and pessimistically predicted little likelihood for the passage of civil rights legislation.[9]

The attorney general did not share Morrow's bleak outlook and championed the administration's civil rights initiatives during the first term. Brownell vocally praised the administration's desegregation efforts and unequivocally backed the *Brown* decision. After the Supreme Court ruled that segregation on public buses was unconstitutional late in 1956, he pledged to enforce its ruling, stating that those who disobeyed were advocating "a crime against the United States."[10]

As for civil rights legislation, Brownell drafted the 1956 bill that Republican congressional sponsors had introduced in the House. The bill had four sections: (1) the creation of a separate civil rights division in the justice department, (2) a civil rights commission, (3) authority for the justice department to intervene on actual or threatened violations of civil rights such as attendance at integrated schools, and (4) similar powers in regard to voting. The bill easily passed the House and was sent to the Senate where Democrat James Eastland of Mississippi chaired the judiciary committee and made certain that the bill never reached the Senate floor for debate during that session.[11]

The black press had reported on the Republican administration's civil rights actions during the first term, and it closely followed the 1956 presidential race. As the campaigning drew to a close, the black press anticipated a strong voter turnout. The semifinal election analysis Gallup Poll indicated that the president's appeal to Negroes had increased dramatically from 21 percent in 1952 to 42 percent in 1956.[12]

Thirty-nine weeklies or semiweeklies in the African American press endorsed Ike, and twenty-nine favored Stevenson. The black press quickly reported on the Eisenhower landslide, and in its analysis, proclaimed that black voters had become an integral factor in various local, state, and national elections. Some in the media speculated that blacks were shifting to the GOP; others saw the switch as a protest vote against southern Democrats who had blocked civil rights legislation. A few pointed out that black voters had split their tickets, voting for Ike because Stevenson had lost his appeal.[13]

Henry Lee Moon, the NAACP public relations director, compiled precinct counts from his organization's chapters across the nation. Approximately four and a half million blacks, he implied, might have registered to vote; many who had moved from the South were voting in large numbers. Moon saw this trend as "a complete reversal of the previous voting pattern." He later made far less extravagant claims in which he stated that African American voting had increased slightly over 1952. He did not reveal that this translated to just over two million black voters.[14]

Roy Wilkins, the NAACP executive secretary, advanced this spin. Blacks helped elect many liberals to Congress. In the South, the black vote "was strictly a protest vote against the ruthless and unyielding attitude of the Southern Democrats." Even if every African American had voted for Stevenson, he would have lost. However, Wilkins saw the increased vote for Republicans as a plus. As long as blacks voted overwhelmingly for the Democratic Party, they had no bargaining power because Democrats took them for granted, and Republicans thought they belonged to the opposition. The shift in voting toward the GOP meant both parties had to court black voters.[15]

The Gallup Poll seemed to confirm Wilkins' analysis, reporting 21 percent of blacks voted for Eisenhower in 1952, and four years later, that number jumped to 39 percent. Pollster Samuel Lubell had 25 percent in the first election and 36 percent in 1956. This, on its face, seemed to represent a significant shift of African Americans to the GOP camp. It was not, but rather part of the tide to the Eisenhower landslide. Overall, three in ten blacks still remained Republican. The election outcome, in reality, demonstrated a decrease in black voting for Stevenson. Congressman Adam Clayton Powell's support in Harlem for the president, for example, increased the president's percentage there by 16 percent. Thus, the increase did not mean more blacks had voted; instead some black Democrats temporarily altered their traditional pattern to balloting for the incumbent.[16]

In the summer of 1957, the research division of the Republican National Committee (RNC) provided a far more reliable analysis. The researchers assumed incorrectly that 3.5 million blacks had voted; in Louisiana and Tennessee that vote might have been the difference in winning the presidential race. The GOP had made its greatest gains in the South where Democrats heavily outnumbered Republicans; under these circumstances, the results did not change. Gains outside of the South were far less impressive at approximately 5 percent.[17]

Pundits did not closely track the black exodus from the South and its consequences on voting patterns. Demographically, blacks were emerging as the largest minority in the United States living in urban areas. By 1960, 75 percent lived in cities, which had the highest level of residential segregation in the United States. African American voters gravitated toward the Democratic Party because it promoted an activist government that offered assistance. Not only did they embrace this philosophy, but many black politicians in urban ghettos also served as dispensers of charitable services to help their constituents. Thus, the movement to the cities, the Democratic creed, and the role of black politicians created an irreversible force pushing their constituents into the Democratic camp.[18]

Although many commentators did not comprehend the forces driving blacks away from the Republican and into the Democratic Party, one major outcome of the presidential election shouted out. If the president had not received a single black vote, he still would have won in a landslide. From a purely political perspective, Ike did not owe the African American voter any debt. Whatever he proposed in the form of civil rights came from his belief that anyone who paid taxes deserved the benefit of government services. That principle was absolute. The president unequivocally favored desegregation in the work place, but favored a gradual approach in social settings as the best way to proceed. He did not realize that African Americans were frustrated and disillusioned by years of waiting; their perception was that they had already been unjustly denied their rights for centuries.

Nixon saw the GOP increase in black voters as an opportunity. By the end of November 1956, Nixon wanted to appeal to more African American voters, and he foresaw a civil rights bill as a GOP priority in the upcoming year. Blacks, he claimed, were moving to the Republican Party, and he wanted to encourage that momentum for future congressional races. Ralph McGill, the well-respected editor of the *Atlanta Constitution*, acknowledged after the election that the vice president had emerged as "the civil rights spokesman for the administration."[19]

Black columnist George Schuyler wrote Nixon the day before the voting, praising the campaign that Nixon had waged. Ike had acted on his pledges, and "many thoughtful Negroes disillusioned by twenty years of unfulfilled New-Fair

Deal pledges are going to return to the Republican fold tomorrow." Nixon stood out as the GOP's rising star and no matter what the outcome, "you are destined to do greater honor to the nation with your forthrightness, sincerity, patriotism and ability."[20]

Before the New Year, columnists speculated over the battle for a civil rights law. Attorney General Brownell had written civil rights legislation that had passed the House in 1956 and never was reported out of the Senate committee. Before the Democratic presidential convention, Democrats had no intention of addressing this kind of legislation, which could have created a deep fissure like the one that had broken out during 1948 with the Dixiecrat revolt.[21]

After Ike's victory, commentators started to anticipate the opening session of the Eighty-Fifth Congress and how the civil rights issue would be raised in 1957. Val Washington, the RNC minority affairs director, received a host of letters from black leaders to change Senate Rule XXII in regard to cloture. Under it, the Senate needed two-thirds of its membership (sixty-four votes) to stop a fili-buster. NAACP executive secretary Roy Wilkins sent a telegram to Nixon ask-ing him to support any method to curb a Senate filibuster. Richard Strout, in the influential *Christian Science Monitor*, argued that the filibuster might be-come the most contentious fight in the upcoming Congress. To get a bill passed, the cloture rule had to be changed.[22]

The vice president spoke with prominent *New York Times* columnist Arthur Krock on December 11, 1956. Nixon, as the Senate's presiding officer, was not worried about the opposing factions in the Senate and knew that he might have to offer an opinion on the cloture rule. If a senator made a motion to make a change, he would make a decision: "Then I'll be out of it."[23]

Democratic senator Clinton Anderson of New Mexico led the charge to change the number of senators for cloture from two-thirds to a simple majority. That meant senators would need forty-nine votes, not sixty-four. Anderson and Nixon had developed a cordial relationship during their congressional years. They served together in the House and lived near each other in the suburbs. Early in 1953, Anderson tried to change the cloture rule, but his motion went down to defeat by a vote of seventy to twenty-one. Six months after Nixon became vice president, Anderson complimented him on his job performance. The senator even grew more positive toward Nixon than he had toward the president. When Nixon campaigned in New Mexico during 1954, Anderson appreciated the fact that the vice president did not attack him. Now the Eighty-Fifth Congress was about to convene, and the pressure to renew the challenge against the filibuster had grown. Anderson optimistically expected to present another motion on re-vise the cloture rule.[24]

By the start of the second term, both African Americans and the Eisenhower administration were prepared to support civil rights legislation. Black voting in the presidential election suggested that Republicans had won over converts in that minority community, and the GOP wanted more blacks to return to the party of Lincoln. Democrats were split between their liberal and southern factions. Attorney General Brownell had drafted the 1956 civil rights bill and was prepared to submit a similar one in the upcoming session of Congress. Was the momentum powerful enough to get the legislation passed?

THE CIVIL RIGHTS ACT OF 1957

When Richard Rovere wrote that Ike, "if not hostile to [the *Brown* case], was strictly neutral and never uttered a word of moral support," he was not associating the Civil Rights Act of 1957 with the man who was president when it passed. Nor have many others: most authors assign credit for its passage to Senator Lyndon Johnson. Doris Kearns Goodwin, in *Lyndon Johnson and the American Dream*, described it as Johnson's legislation. LBJ's assistant, George Reedy, called LBJ "the driving force that rammed through the Senate the Civil Rights Act of 1957." Columnists Rowland Evans and Robert Novak wrote that "to pass the bill without filibuster was a legislative tour de force." Booth Mooney, in *The Politicians*, seconded Evans and Novak: getting the bill passed without a filibuster "was the greatest political miracle yet brought to pass by the Texan."[1]

Yet even the declarations of a political miracle seem understated compared to Robert Caro's account in *The Years of Lyndon Johnson: Master of the Senate*. In 327 pages (Part V, "The Great Cause"), Caro argues that the majority leader figured out just about every solution to every potential impasse. Focusing almost exclusively on LBJ, Caro dismisses the Republican role by alleging that Ike lacked "enthusiasm for civil rights." Like many other authors both before and after, Caro bases this assessment on Stephen Ambrose's flawed Eisenhower biography, which made Ike's supposed opposition to civil rights a matter of accepted historical record. In his description of the 1957 Civil Rights Act, Ambrose repeated that the president was indifferent or worse to racial issues.[2]

A central element of Caro's account is Chapter 38, "Hells Canyon," in which he claims that LBJ engineered a secret pact among the Democratic senators from the West and South. The House had passed a civil rights bill with strong enforcement measures that the southern senators found threatening and unacceptable; Johnson persuaded the southerners to accept a weaker version of the bill with the argument that if they did not, the Senate might break their filibuster and pass the House's bill. Something was going to pass, he insisted, and the South's only option was to limit the damage. He then got the western senators, who generally favored civil rights, to support southern threats to filibuster the House bill in exchange for the southern caucus's votes for legislation to build the Hells Canyon dam. With this deal, Caro argues, Johnson prevented the South from killing the bill entirely and got a piece of civil rights legislation through the Senate for the first time since the Reconstruction era.[3]

Caro's account fights against a massive weight of evidence. When asked about a connection between Hells Canyon and the civil rights bill, Oregon senator Wayne Morse and others denied that there was any deal. Several western senators, including Oregon's Richard Neuberger and New Mexico's Clinton Anderson, were strong civil rights proponents and actively campaigned for the bill; it is unlikely they would have agreed to Johnson's deal as described by Caro. My own research did not uncover a single contemporary document— no memoranda, diary entries, or correspondence—that discusses any bargain between the western and southern senators, or even noting the existence of a Democratic bloc in the West.[4]

Caro refers to an article on June 22 in the *Winston-Salem Journal* by Tom Wicker, alleging that according to "authoritative sources" and "a source within liberal ranks," "Southern Democrats" and "Western Democrats" had negotiated a deal on the Hells Canyon vote and the jury trial amendment. Given Wicker's fame, the account seems somewhat persuasive until one considers that Wicker was not yet the powerful and well-connected *New York Times* bureau chief and op-ed columnist he would later become. In 1957, he was a young Washington correspondent for the *Journal*; he served briefly in D.C. that year, where he watched the debate over the civil rights bill, and departed for a Nieman Fellowship at Harvard at the end of the summer. He had not yet cultivated many knowledgeable sources, and wherever he got the story, he did not cite a single source by name. As Wicker himself pointed out, this was his "first experience covering national politics."[5]

The Johnson presidential library conducted 2,169 oral histories of Johnson's contemporaries and associates. As of this writing, 1,940 have been opened; of those, fourteen mention the Hells Canyon Dam and two (David Black and Ramsey Clark) have nothing to do with the Civil Rights Act of 1957. In none of the remaining twelve do the subjects raise Hells Canyon spontaneously—it is always in response to the interviewer's question. Several of the recollections are vague: Republican senators George Aiken from Vermont and Jacob Javits from New York did not remember any linkage between the dam and civil rights.

Hubert Humphrey thought LBJ might have tried to link the two, but he did not recall any details.[6]

Democratic senator Russell Long, from Louisiana, remembered "vaguely" "something about Hell's [sic] Canyon." Johnson, Long thought, persuaded southerners to back the dam and "some of our friends from the West would go along with us on some other issue." Democratic senator Henry Jackson, from Washington, believed Morse was "strong for Hell's Canyon, but it had no connection to the civil rights bill."

Then there is Frank Church of Idaho. Caro, without quoting the senator, implies Church confirmed the existence of a deal. But he does not mention the line in the Johnson Library's oral history in which Church says, "There was never any quid pro quo at all." Church goes on to insist that he and Johnson never had a deal: "That's pure fiction utterly without any basis in fact."[7]

The CIO legislative director in 1957, Robert Oliver, did not recall any deal with the liberals for Hells Canyon. "If there's any deal," he told his interviewer, "the deal was between southerners and the Republicans on some other issue unrelated to civil rights," not a trade involving western Democrats and Hells Canyon. George Siegel, who worked with Johnson on legislation, also did not remember any connection, and legislative assistant George Reedy incorrectly recalled that the majority leader lost on the Hells Canyon bill. In a separate interview with the Senate Historical Office, the secretary to the majority leader, Bobby Baker, thought that Johnson got Senators Church, Henry Jackson, and Warren Magnuson from Washington, and James Murray from Nevada to vote his way.[8]

Clarence Mitchell Jr. was the director of the NAACP's capital bureau and the organization's chief lobbyist in Congress. He carefully monitored civil rights legislation in Congress and noted how and why various congressmen voted. Mitchell had met Lyndon Johnson early in 1953 and noted that the senator believed race relations were improving. When the vote came on the 1957 civil rights legislation, the majority leader was for it. Mitchell made no reference to Hells Canyon.[9]

Caro also argues that since the bill's significant provisions were removed or weakened, LBJ's great achievement in passing the law was to provide "hope" for future legislation. He does not mention the major provisions of the law that survived Senate passage and were essential to future civil rights struggles.[10]

The indisputable fact is that the Civil Rights Act of 1957 was the first law of its kind since 1875. Eisenhower actively advanced the civil rights cause throughout his tenure and was closely involved in proposing, drafting, promoting, passing, and implementing the 1957 law. Johnson's contribution was to help his southern colleagues eliminate the bill's strongest provisions, and then to pass a watered-down bill through the Senate.

The civil rights movement in the 1950s did not match the ferment of the next decade, but by the end of Eisenhower's first term, African American protests and legal actions against racism were rising. Black troops returning from World War II and the Korean War pushed for equality, sometimes at the cost of their lives, and the racial theories of the Third Reich discredited white supremacy in the United States. African American organizations drew media attention to the persecution of black people, primarily but not exclusively in the South. The brutal murder of a black teenager, Emmet Till, in Mississippi in the summer of 1955 resulted in a trial in which an all-white jury acquitted two white men, who afterward publicly admitted their guilt. African Americans pressed for the federal government to intervene, but in the 1950s it had no legal authority to do so. When the first black student to attend the University of Alabama, Autherine Lucy, was suspended on her third day of classes and then expelled in the spring of 1956 because her lawsuit protesting her suspension was considered "slander" by the university, civil rights advocates again called for federal intervention, but again, despite the *Brown* decision, the government believed it had no power to intercede. During the Montgomery, Alabama, bus boycott that began with Rosa Parks's arrest in December 1955, federal authorities had no power to intervene until December 1956, when the Supreme Court declared segregation on city buses unconstitutional.[11]

These instances of administration inaction, although justified as a matter of law, left black civil rights advocates disappointed and clamoring for more action. Ike had already accomplished more for the cause of civil rights in four years than his two Democratic predecessors had done in the previous two decades. Using his executive powers, he had desegregated the capital, the armed forces, and the Veterans Administration, and he had made an unprecedented number of black appointments, including J. Ernest Wilkins, an assistant secretary of labor, and Archibald Carey Jr., the first African American to preside over a White House commission.[12] He had established the President's Committee on Government Contracts (PCGC) to lobby for greater minority hiring in the private and public sectors, and had designated his vice president as his principal advocate for civil rights. In his position as chairman of the PCGC, Nixon focused on minority hiring and combating job discrimination.[13]

Ike appointed Herbert Brownell and William Rogers—two men who passionately preached the civil rights cause and used the justice department to reverse segregationist practices—as his attorney general and deputy attorney general.

And he made appointments to the Supreme Court and the federal bench who would enforce the *Brown* case; segregationists were routinely eliminated from consideration as jurists.[14]

Ike's most important failing on civil rights, according to many critics, was rhetorical, but nonetheless real: he did not believe that publicly calling for an end to segregation and racial violence could be as important as the many actions he took to advance the cause. That his vice president did so was laudable but insufficient. The president's voice was one thing that could not be delegated to a subordinate.

The primary weapon for defeating civil rights legislation in the Senate was the filibuster. The senators from the former Confederacy—all Democrats—had an informal agreement that they would vote against "cloture," meaning a motion to end debate and proceed to a vote, on any legislation touching on civil rights that made it to the floor. (Since the same senators frequently chaired the important committees, most such bills never got to the floor.) Because of their combined power and because cloture required a two-thirds supermajority, the Senate could not pass even the most seemingly uncontroversial bill to ease the lives of African Americans. Even efforts to outlaw the public atrocity of lynching could not get through.

Early in 1953, Democratic senator Clinton Anderson of New Mexico had proposed a change to the cloture rule, to lower the number of votes needed to stop a filibuster from two-thirds of those present to a simple majority. That meant cloture would need forty-nine votes, not sixty-four. Anderson's motion was defeated by a vote of seventy to twenty-one. He and Nixon had served together in Congress and developed a cordial relationship; they also lived near each other in the Washington suburbs and were friends. When Nixon campaigned in New Mexico during 1954, Anderson appreciated the fact that the vice president did not attack him. As the Eighty-Fifth Congress was about to convene at the start of 1957, the pressure to renew the challenge against the filibuster had grown. Anderson expected to present another motion to revise the cloture rule, but Nixon did not say how he would rule.[15]

On January 2, 1957, the day before the Senate convened, Johnson and Nixon spoke for an hour; the majority leader argued against Anderson's rule change. If Nixon allowed the motion to go forward, the southern bloc would debate the new rules for weeks or months, and possibly even mount a filibuster. Nixon partially agreed with this argument. He disapproved of liberal senators who called for major alterations in the rules, but also of southerners who opposed all changes. Nixon knew if he supported the South, that decision would be unpopular, but if he took the opposite stand, it might cause "a big open breach." By the next day he had not come to a decision. To persuade him to rule their way, Knowland and Johnson saw him in his office and assured him they had enough votes to keep Rule XXII, the cloture rule, in place.[16] The Senate opened on January 3 with forty-nine Democrats and forty-seven Republicans. Johnson was reelected majority leader.

Anderson's proposal raised a constitutional question. Could the Senate actually change its rules at this point? Nixon knew he would be required to rule on this, but the Senate had no precedent on whether it was a continuing body, in which case its procedures were fixed, or if each Congress was in effect a new body, in which case a majority could adopt or modify its existing organization at the start of the session. The Constitution said: "Each House may determine the rules of its proceedings." He telephoned Secretary Dulles for advice, since Dulles had served in the Senate and was an attorney. The secretary thought that the Senate rules could be changed and believed that the vice president had "personal and practical considerations." He further counseled Nixon not "to go against his conscience," but beyond that he did not "feel competent" and wondered whether it was "proper for him to express views."[17]

The president refused to be drawn into this struggle, but he seemed to favor the current procedure as the orderly course of business. Nixon had to decide on his own what was best. The Gallup Poll provided little guidance: 49 percent of respondents favored closing debate with just a majority vote; 35 percent favored the current filibuster rule; and 16 percent had no opinion.[18]

On January 4, thirty-one senators moved to change Rule XXII. After six hours of heated debate, Hubert Humphrey, Democrat from Minnesota, queried the presiding officer on his opinion regarding the rules. With that opening, Anderson made a motion that Nixon answer Humphrey's parliamentary inquiry.[19]

Nixon surprised many by stating that the Constitution offered no clear direction on whether the Senate was a continuing body whose rules applied from one session to the next, and that no presiding officer had ever ruled on this question. Given the lack of precedent or guidance, he could only conclude that "the majority of the new existing membership of the Senate, under the Constitution, has the power to determine the rules under which the Senate will proceed." Any previous rules that limited the new Congress's ability to make changes were "unconstitutional." Thus the Senate could do as it saw fit: keep the present rules, adopt some new ones, or make a complete change. He added that any senator could make a motion to maintain the status quo, and if the majority voted for it, the current rules would stand.[20]

Johnson made the motion to preserve the status quo, and the votes were fifty-five for and thirty-eight against. The majority leader received support from twenty-seven Democrats, including the entire southern bloc, and Knowland obtained the votes of twenty-eight Republicans. Three senators who were not present would likely have voted for change. Anderson had done much better in 1957 than he had four years earlier: a swing of just seven votes would have effectively ended Senate filibusters. Almost two decades later, Nixon called his advisory opinion one of the "hardest decisions" he ever had to make. Anderson later remarked that Nixon's ruling should go "down in history as a moment of high courage."[21]

Val Washington wrote Nixon that, watching the debate from the Senate gallery, he "felt like breaking all Senate rules and jumping over the banister and coming down and shaking your hand." Samuel Shaffer of *Newsweek* also watched the count and described it as "the single most thrilling thing" he had witnessed as a newspaperman. He believed "that history may record this ruling as comparing to the Emancipation Proclamation."[22]

Frank Church, who had just been sworn in as a freshman senator from Idaho, recalled the vote twenty years later. The majority leader had telephoned him in Boise to congratulate him on his victory. Church and other new senators, LBJ told him, were the future of the Democratic Party, and they needed to preserve "an alliance between the West and South." When Church arrived at the Senate that January, Johnson grabbed him and said: "the first thing you ought to learn is that you get along in the Congress by going along." He then advised his new colleague to vote against Anderson's motion. Church voted in the affirmative. Johnson shunned him for several months, and Church got the painful message. When Johnson told you to vote his way, you did or suffered the consequences.[23]

This drama over the cloture rule both emboldened and worried the southern bloc. There were currently enough votes to maintain the status quo; but if the filibuster was abused, it might prod enough senators to change their vote. Southern senators also knew they were becoming a more isolated minority. Gallup Polls conducted from mid January through mid August 1957 found that approximately 60 percent approved of desegregation while a third disapproved. The regional numbers reflected a vast divide: 67 percent of voters in the East supported desegregation, 61 percent in the Midwest, 75 percent in the West, and in the South, just 20 percent. In spite of this disparity, Americans did not see civil rights as a high priority. According to two polls taken in 1957, voters ranked the threat of war and economic well-being as their primary concerns. Ten percent listed integration as the third most important problem.[24]

These crosscurrents led Eisenhower to behave cautiously. Shortly after his re-election, he commented that the Supreme Court's decision on integrating public schools would cause problems in the South. That concern did not stop him from meeting with GOP legislative leaders in the last days of 1956 to announce that he would submit a bill to Congress in the new session. On January 10, 1957, during his State of the Union Address, he called for civil rights legislation. He reiterated his commitment to a moderate bill in press conferences throughout the spring.[25]

A reporter asked White House chief of staff Sherman Adams if the president intended to speak in the South on desegregation; Adams said he saw no value to such a trip. When a newsman asked Ike the same question at a press conference, he repeated Adams's reply. Congressman Adam Clayton Powell wrote Adams in March that Ike's refusal to speak in the South had a negative impact. The president did not respond publicly to the minister, but the administration did express support for desegregation.[26]

The president also encouraged Jerry Persons, his deputy chief of staff and the brother of a recent Alabama governor, to back the bill. In an oral history, Persons said he understood that "if the Negro was given the right to vote and this right was assured, that would go a long way toward correcting the situation." Persons believed in the principle of equal voting rights—everyone who qualified should have them—and considered the administration bill "a reasonable first step." He reasoned that the reversal from segregation to integration required by the *Brown* decision would have to be enforced gradually, not instantaneously.[27]

Nixon had a different perspective. Besides promoting the administration's civil rights goals, he kept up with that winter's news: church bombings in Montgomery, Alabama, and shootings in Americus, Georgia. These criminal actions were inimical to the American tradition of equality. Writing on February 25, Nixon conceded that the federal government had limited recourse against such acts, but the administration's civil rights proposals, if they became law, could move toward creating federal powers to intervene. He further affirmed that the United States "must practice full racial justice, and that we cannot have one law for whites and another for Negroes." Even while articulating this standard, Nixon echoed the president, admitting the law was "only as good as the will of the people to obey it."[28]

Nixon heard from Dr. L. K. Jackson, a black minister from Gary, Indiana, who had recently returned from travels in the South. White Citizens' Councils, the Ku Klux Klan, and other opponents, Jackson wrote, had created "deplorable conditions" for blacks. In Georgia, the state legislature had passed a resolution urging its congressional representatives to repeal the Thirteenth, Fourteenth, and

Fifteenth Amendments to the Constitution and to impeach the Supreme Court justices. In Florida, the governor and general assembly had tried, but failed, to ban the NAACP from the state. Jackson urged Nixon to stop the spread of communism "behind the Iron Curtain," and simultaneously "make democracy work here in America."[29]

The vice president wrote back a month later, deploring the deprivation of civil rights and condemning violence. Despite these outrages, he was optimistic. The president's civil rights bill, he contended, would pass Congress during the current session. Integration was proceeding slowly but would move forward. Americans were accepting the civil rights movement, and Nixon would "continue to devote my efforts wholeheartedly toward the realization of this objective."[30]

As the NAACP spokesman, Roy Wilkins pressured the federal government to protect blacks in the South from intimidation and violence. He implored the president to take a more vocal stand against segregation. Even with this appeal, the president refused to offer any public encouragement. Wilkins also regularly turned to the vice president for support and encouraged him to speak out. When Nixon said, on March 13, that "We shall never be satisfied with the progress we have been making in recent years until the problem is solved and equal opportunity becomes a reality for all Americans," Wilkins wrote to praise him, saying he recognized that the vice president sought "an end to racial discrimination and segregation" and that the NAACP pledged its "steadfast cooperation."[31]

On the second of May, after Nixon said in a Chicago speech that racial violence embarrassed the nation and gave credence to communist charges that America practiced discrimination, Wilkins wrote again, saying that the NAACP hoped the vice president's advocacy would move the civil rights bill out of congressional committee hearings so that Congress would debate and pass the legislation. He believed the White House had been silent on the bill and on the *Brown* decision. The NAACP hoped that Nixon's declaration signaled a policy reversal.[32]

Nixon replied promptly, pledging that the administration would press for the civil rights legislation during the current session of Congress. The administration, he said, had not been quiet and inactive; rather it took a similar position to the NAACP, pushing toward "equal opportunity and equal rights for all."[33]

Martin Luther King Jr. also lobbied for civil rights protection. In early March, he and Nixon were both invited to Ghana to celebrate its independence from Great Britain. On March 5, holding an impromptu news conference at Accra University College, King remarked: "We are not sure the President actually knows what is happening in the South in all details and the desperation of the situation." He suggested that the vice president should come to the South, study the conditions there, and report to the president on the violence aimed at black people. Shortly after that, Nixon and King happened to bump into one another on the college campus. Surrounded by reporters and photographers, they had a brief, pleasant chat, which concluded with the vice president inviting King to see him at the Capitol.[34]

Later, several major African American organizations held a Prayer Pilgrimage for Freedom in front of the Lincoln Memorial on May 17, the third anniversary of the *Brown* decision. King gave his first national address before fifteen to twenty thousand spectators, urging blacks to demand the right to vote. He received thunderous applause, and from that moment forward, he was firmly established as a national figure.[35]

Enhancing his growing fame, King met with the vice president on June 13, the first major administration official that he had seen, at Nixon's office in the Capitol for over two hours. Secretary of Labor James Mitchell and Reverend Ralph Abernathy Sr. joined them. The ministers complained that the president had not vigorously condemned the violence in the South, and that 30,000 Negroes in Montgomery, Alabama, had been prevented from registering to vote. King again appealed to the vice president to visit the South to see this harassment at first hand, and to have the federal government stop the intimidation. He also predicted that a massive registration drive the following year would add three million black voters for the 1958 elections.

Nixon defended Ike's civil rights record and deplored racism. The violence toward blacks in the South damaged the image of American democracy abroad. As for the civil rights bill before Congress, Nixon described it as moderate and the only legislation that Congress would pass. He would not make a tour of the South but suggested that the next PCGC meeting might be held in a southern city.[36]

After the two ministers left, Dale Wright, a reporter from *Jet* magazine, interviewed them. They repeated that they had urged the administration to halt the violence against African Americans, that Nixon was aware of the conditions and condemned those responsible, and that the PCGC would meet in a southern city that King designated. Nixon had defended the president and predicted that Ike would speak out against southern discrimination before the end of the year. "Moderately liberal white" clergy, schoolteachers, and other influential individuals, King said, needed the president to furnish leadership and offer the "much-needed rallying point" for those who favored an end to segregation. Nixon convinced King that he was sympathetic toward that goal, but King remained uncertain how "strongly" Ike felt.[37]

The vice president privately told Ike that he had not promised to make any speech in a southern state. He said he "was very much impressed" with King and thought the president "would enjoy talking to him." King opposed violence and black retaliation and promoted "an evolutionary but progressive march forward."[38]

While African American groups were pressing the administration, the Eighty-Fifth Congress began its hearings on the civil rights bill.[39] The judiciary committee took up the bill at the end of February and defeated several attempts by southern congressmen to attach crippling amendments. Speaker Rayburn and minority leader Martin then cooperated to move the legislation through the House. On June 13, the House passed the bill by the overwhelming vote of 286 to 126. Sixty more congressmen voted for this legislation in 1957 than had done so in 1956, while sixty-two fewer House members voted against it. Of the eighty-two southern congressmen who had signed the Southern Manifesto in 1956 to overturn the *Brown* decision, eighty voted against the legislation. The other two were no longer congressmen.[40]

With southerners, according to Harry McPherson's oral history, Johnson pleaded to Speaker Rayburn, "Why don't you all let this nigger bill pass?" Robert Parker, LBJ's black chauffeur, recalled his boss's blatant pandering to southerners: "Whenever I was late, no matter what the reason, Johnson called me a lazy, good-for-nothing nigger. He especially liked to call me nigger in front of southerners and racists like Richard Russell. It was . . . LBJ's way of being one of the boys."[41]

Rayburn later commented that the law did not affect any qualified voters from Texas because none had been disenfranchised "for many years." From the speaker's perspective, the House had "passed a civil rights bill that had practically all the bad features taken out of it and [was] simply limited to the right to vote."[42]

Although the House approved the legislation with relative ease and without major changes, the Senate presented a far more difficult challenge. The president vigorously lobbied Republican senators to defend the administration's proposal, and GOP minority leader Knowland led the charge for passage. Many Republican senators, including Jacob Javits from New York, Thomas Kuchel from California, Clifford Case from New Jersey, and Everett Dirksen from Illinois, worked for the bill.[43]

Liberal Democrats like Hubert Humphrey had already organized their faction. Paul Douglas from Illinois came out vehemently for the bill and vigorously fought its adversaries. He later remembered that Johnson "opposed all methods and all attempts to liberalize the position of Negroes and other minorities." The two men clashed often on civil rights. The southerners, Douglas believed, were intent on delaying any meaningful civil rights legislation, but the rest of the nation would ultimately win and pass enforceable laws.[44] Douglas's legislative assistant, Howard Shuman, subsequently said that Johnson "was tied, lock, stock, and barrel, to the Southerners, and the Southerners controlled the Senate. They elected him Leader and they were his source of power."[45]

Clinton Anderson, who had unsuccessfully challenged the cloture rule, also lent his support. Other liberal western senators, like Richard Neuberger and Wayne Morse from Oregon, Warren Magnuson from Washington, and Frank Church vigorously endorsed the bill.[46]

While Senate Republicans and liberal Democrats lined up for the civil rights legislation, Democratic senators from Texas and Tennessee cracked southern unanimity. Both Tennessee senators, Albert Gore Sr. and Estes Kefauver, had refused to sign the Southern Manifesto, and while both favored a gradualist approach toward integration, they broke with their fellow southerners by supporting the bill. Ralph Yarborough from Texas and Johnson also voted for the bill.[47]

Eighteen of the nineteen senators who had signed the Southern Manifesto in 1956 vehemently opposed the bill. The sole exception, Price Daniels from Texas, had left the Senate to run successfully for governor. The chair of the southern caucus was Richard Russell, a staunch segregationist and one of the authors of the Manifesto's final version. Even before the bill reached the Senate, he conceded some legislation would pass and that the southerners' task was to make sure it was as weak as possible. He eliminated the filibuster as an option, thinking it would ultimately harm the southern cause. If the southerners mounted a filibuster, liberals might not only assemble the votes to stop it but, thus angered, pass a civil rights bill with real teeth.[48]

Besides unity, the South had another major advantage. Russell, the mentor, and Lyndon Johnson, his student, had formed a bond of friendship and respect, and the Georgian planned to run LBJ for the presidency in 1960. Russell had tried to win the 1952 nomination and failed due to his segregationist views. If LBJ were going to win the Democratic nomination, he had to have the civil rights credentials that Russell lacked.[49]

Many historians have examined LBJ's early political career in order to prove that he promoted minority interests. He may have privately favored assisting people of color, but to be elected statewide in Texas, he had to embrace the segregationist standard and vote with the southern bloc in opposition to any civil rights action.[50] This he did without fail.

In early 1949, Russell led the filibuster against the Truman administration's efforts to bring up civil rights legislation. Johnson, a freshman senator, participated in the filibuster in his maiden speech on the Senate floor, speaking against changing the cloture rule. When Russell later proposed strengthening the cloture rule so that instead of two-thirds of those present, ending debate required two-thirds of the entire Senate membership, Johnson co-sponsored the motion. It passed.[51]

By 1957, LBJ realized that he needed a civil rights item on his resume. He had not signed the Southern Manifesto. If he had, it would have destroyed any possibility of his becoming a presidential contender. As a potential candidate, he needed a united party that was not torn apart by a painful battle over civil rights legislation; as majority leader, he assiduously counted votes. Eighteen southern senators would oppose any bill; he had to work with the remaining thirty-one Democrats to find common ground. No matter what, he needed at least eighteen Republican votes to reach a forty-eight to forty-eight tie so that Nixon could cast his deciding vote in favor of the legislation. The master of the Senate thus absolutely depended on the GOP minority.[52]

Ronnie Dugger, a Texas reporter who watched Johnson's rise, did not view him as "a racist" but rather as "a political opportunist with domestic vision." LBJ was no longer a southerner; he had transformed himself into a westerner. That was a political advantage, and southern senators recognized that LBJ was trying to avoid the southern stigma. Many of Johnson's southern colleagues described him in their oral recollections as an ally who used his position as majority leader to give the South the best possible result from the debate.[53]

Johnson reasoned that the southern senators would readily accept some of the administration's provisions. They would not object to a new civil rights division in the justice department, a bipartisan civil rights commission or, in principle, equal voting rights. The liberals wanted the strongest possible bill, but LBJ knew they understood they had to compromise.[54]

Thus he worked to get both sides to take less than they hoped for. Neither received its ideal, but each side had something positive to take back to their constituents. With liberals, he cajoled them to see the southern viewpoint and raised the threat of a southern filibuster if they would not.

Despite such showmanship, Johnson had extraordinary qualities that suited him well in his negotiations. Bryce Harlow, one of Eisenhower's congressional liaisons, recalled the majority leader's unique style. LBJ would take his six-foot, four-inch frame and stand nose to nose with his listener. If that was insufficiently intimidating, Harlow recalled, the majority leader had a "great ability to charm, to threaten, to seduce, induce, wheedle, get somebody to do what he wanted to do. He worked at it indefatigably, day and night, and wouldn't let up."[55]

While LBJ worked his side of the aisle, the administration marshaled its forces. Throughout June, Ike met with Republican congressional leaders, urging them to push forward. Although the president often questioned Knowland's political acumen, the Californian won applause for his energetic support of the bill. In the middle of the month, Ike spoke with LBJ by telephone, emphasizing that he had lived in the South, understood its institutions, and had therefore sponsored a moderate bill that accounted for southern sensibilities. Johnson replied that he first would attend to other pressing legislation and then turn to the civil rights bill. Southern senators had already expressed their animosity, and he expected a long, arduous debate. Several days later, the president told a press conference that his bill was "conceived in the thought of moderation and conciliation, not of persecution of anybody." Throughout the entire Senate debate, Ike stressed the legislation's moderate tone.[56]

Speaking on June 5 in Asheville, North Carolina, Nixon argued that "the enactment of the moderate civil rights bill now before Congress is one effective step we can take toward living up to our democratic ideals." Civil rights was a national problem, he said, not a sectional one. Both races at the local level had to act constructively and prevent extremists from taking center stage. Laws helped, but long-held prejudices would be difficult to overcome.[57]

The vice president and Johnson cooperated when they had common goals. Despite frequently opposing each other on domestic legislation, they maintained a friendship. In February 1957, LBJ wrote Nixon that he had "a little retreat" where he rested and did some of his "best thinking." He had a place there for an autographed picture of the vice president and asked for one. Nixon signed it "with deep appreciation for the wise counsel and friendship of a fine Senator and a great American." He admired the majority leader because he kept "in mind the major objectives." Johnson would "compromise on some things, but in the end he" got "the major part of his program through."[58]

The civil rights debate in the Senate magnified the two men's political differences. Nixon concentrated on passing the administration's bill intact, and Johnson worked to protect the Democratic senators from a political tsunami that would cripple his party.

Even before H.R. 6127 reached the Senate, the Republican and Democratic senators who favored the bill planned their avenue of attack. They discussed several parliamentary maneuvers and ultimately settled on Rule XIV, infrequently raised, which allowed a bill to bypass the responsible committee—in this case the judiciary committee, chaired by the southern racist James Eastland—to be placed directly on the Senate calendar for consideration. Eastland would never have allowed the bill to reach the Senate floor.

As soon as the House bill came to the Senate, on June 19, minority leader Knowland and Paul Douglas, the outspoken liberal Democrat, co-sponsored the bypass motion. Senator Russell, an expert parliamentarian, offered a point of order under Rule XXV that all bills should be sent to the appropriate committees. Nixon, presiding over the upper chamber, ruled that all bills did not have to go to committees, and therefore, Rule XIV was applicable.

The Senate voted forty-five to thirty-nine to uphold the chair's decision, and the bill went directly to the floor. This vote temporarily shattered the southern Democratic–conservative Republican coalition that had evolved since 1938. Thirty-four Republicans and eleven Democrats triumphed, while the southern bloc, including the majority leader, voted against the ruling. Had Johnson's side prevailed, the civil rights legislation would have died right there.[59]

Placing the bill directly on the Senate calendar did not guarantee success. On July 2, Nixon predicted that the Senate would hold many night sessions and "probably a filibuster."[60] The vice president did not know that the southern caucus had already decided against it. Instead, the southerners concentrated on removing what they considered the bill's most offensive provisions. Senator Sam Ervin of North Carolina called this the "soft southern strategy." He would not attack the bill's goal of securing voting rights, but would concentrate on potentially controversial aspects to scare doubting senators from supporting it. Part III would permit the federal government to send troops to prevent violations of court-ordered desegregation; and Part IV permitted it to enforce court injunctions against violations of voting rights without a jury trial.[61] Southerners threatened a filibuster to intimidate their opposition, but they never acted on the threat. Russell confirmed as much: "At no time did any member of our group declare in any of our meetings that it was his belief that a filibuster was advisable, much less that one could be successfully waged."[62]

The same day that the vice president expressed his concerns, Russell rose on the Senate floor and asked not to be interrupted. During his address, he warned his colleagues that the president's assurances that this bill was moderate were a ruse. He repeated Ervin's warning that buried in Part III was a provision carried over from the Reconstruction era that allowed the attorney general "unprecedented power to bring to bear the whole might of the Federal Government, including the Armed Forces if necessary, to force a commingling of white and Negro children in the State-supported public schools of the South."[63]

At the White House press conference the following morning, the president acknowledged that he did not fully comprehend some provisions of the bill and would ask Brownell for an explanation. Eisenhower had advertised the moderate intent of the legislation and did not intend to use military force. He assembled Republican leaders at the White House on July 9 to determine how Part III should be modified to exclude any deployment of federal troops. The next day he met with Senator Russell in the Oval Office about his objections. After the meeting, he told the press that he had not received any clarification.

That statement was accurate as far as it went. In fact, Part III had been placed in serious jeopardy by Russell's address and Eisenhower's seemingly befuddled reaction.[64]

On July 16, after eight days of debate and sixty-six speeches, the Senate voted seventy-one to eighteen—the senators from nine southern states were unanimously opposed—to take up the civil rights bill as pending business. Johnson and Knowland, along with seventy colleagues, brought a civil rights bill to the floor of the Senate for the first time in eighty-two years. The majority leader pointedly stated on the record that his vote did not mean approval; he was only moving the bill to the floor.[65]

The president, four days later, wrote his friend Swede Hazlett that the *Brown* decision had "disturbed the domestic scene" more than any other recent event. The decision reversed the folkways that many southerners had unconditionally accepted "as not only respectable but completely legal and ethical." Yet the Supreme Court decided the law of the land, and if the Court's decisions were flouted, chaos would result. Ike believed he had presented a moderate bill. If some thought it too broad, Congress could offer limiting amendments. Integration had to proceed gradually so that southerners had time to adjust, but in the end, the Supreme Court had to be respected.[66]

During a legislative meeting of Republican leaders at the White House the next day, Knowland predicted a vote on Part III that week. He believed the southerners would not be satisfied with the elimination of that section; "they would be inspired to even greater efforts to beat or weaken the rest of the bill." On July 24, Part III was struck down by a vote of fifty-two to thirty eight. Eighteen Republicans and twenty Democrats futilely joined together to try to save it. Twenty-five Republicans and twenty-seven Democrats defeated it. Johnson and eighteen southern senators were among those who voted nay. Some liberals intended to raise a revised version of Part III, but LBJ as majority leader, before the civil rights advocates even realized his parliamentary maneuver, quietly ended any further debate. Howard Shuman, Senator Douglas's aide, commented in his oral history that Eisenhower's press conference "essentially killed us."[67]

This victory for the southern caucus emboldened it to attack Part IV, which stated that federal court injunctions against interference with the right to vote could be enforced by the justice department without jury trials. According to one of George Reedy's oral histories, southerners could not "go home with a law that carried with it criminal penalties to be assessed without a jury trial."[68]

To defeat the purpose of Part IV, the southern bloc introduced an amendment that included a jury trial provision, a principle seemingly as fundamental as the right to vote. Even though southern courts had consistently ruled against African Americans and absolved whites of guilt, the jury trial principle appealed to many senators outside of the South. Northern senators feared federal judges could unilaterally enjoin unions in their disputes with management, and many columnists championed the jury trial principle.[69]

Despite the growing opposition, the president had Knowland, Nixon, and others meet with wavering Republican senators to urge them to remain steadfast. The jury trial amendment would severely cripple the justice department's enforcement powers. On the last day of July, Nixon wrote that he had a "sworn duty . . . to support legislation which will guarantee the right of all of our citizens to vote, regardless of their race, creed or color." The administration had offered a "moderate approach" and "fears many have expressed with regard to its effect will prove to be unfounded."[70]

Knowland and Nixon worked feverishly to assemble the votes to defeat the amendment, and the minority leader was confident that he had enough solid pledges to ensure victory. Two days before the vote, Nixon taped a television program in which he predicted the amendment's defeat.[71]

On the day of the vote, August 1, the vice president and Bill Rogers headed for dinner around 7:00 p.m. and stopped to talk to some Americans for Democratic Action representatives. Nixon conceded that the jury trial amendment would pass, and the liberal-oriented ADA "ought to consider whether the best strategy wouldn't be to hold the bill in conference until next year and then make an all-out fight for a stronger bill."[72]

Johnson skillfully marshaled his forces by lobbying wavering senators to vote for the amendment. When the vote was taken, on the evening of August 1, fifty-one senators (thirty-nine Democrats and twelve Republicans, including all twenty-two senators from the Old Confederacy) voted for the jury trial amendment, and forty-two senators—thirty-three Republicans and nine Democrats—voted nay.[73]

Visibly shaken, Nixon approached Johnson after the vote in a waiting room off the Senate chamber and sarcastically complimented him for getting his "bullwhip on your boys tonight." Johnson answered that he had lined up his forces just as Nixon had, but the vice president did not have the votes. Nixon later recognized the defeat: "This was one of the saddest days in this history of the Senate because this was a vote against the right to vote."[74]

The fuming president quickly declared he was "damned unhappy about the vote." White House press secretary Hagerty said that Ike thanked those senators who stood firmly against the amendment. Those who supported it confused the issues, and as a consequence, Americans would continue to be disenfranchised.[75]

At a cabinet meeting on the morning of August 2, the president held out that he might release a statement saying how the amendment weakened the legislation. Nixon and Bill Rogers remarked that "a few individuals" had advanced arguments that were simply a "cover" for their underlying motives. Four days later, at a meeting of Republican legislative leaders at the White House, Rogers described the bill in its current state "as a monstrosity—the most irresponsible act he had seen during his time in Washington." The acceptance of the jury trial provision was "like giving a policeman a gun without bullets."[76]

The same day, columnist Marquis Childs, a frequent critic of the vice president, wrote that Nixon's future might depend on the civil rights issue. Some Republicans had protested after Nixon was photographed with Martin Luther King, but the vice president ignored them; he had no intention of allowing the Democrats' divisions over race to fragment the GOP as well. He strongly supported civil rights and worked energetically to defeat the jury trial section because it interfered with the prerogatives of the federal judiciary.[77]

Johnson strengthened the vice president's standing by accusing him on August 5 of "a concerted propaganda campaign" against the jury trial amendment. Val Washington responded the next day that Johnson had voted against every civil rights bill since entering Congress, and that he and other Democrats had "emasculated" the current legislation. LBJ was "playing politics," and having voted "against the right to vote," he had no right to impugn anyone's motives. Nixon need not apologize for expressing his disappointment when millions shared his view.[78]

These partisan differences did not halt the Senate, late on the morning on August 7, from voting on the modified bill. Twenty-nine Democrats and forty-three Republicans voted yea while eighteen Democrats voted no. Seventeen were southerners; Wayne Morse voted with them because he thought the bill had become a sham.[79]

After 121 hours and 31 minutes, the majority leader closed the debate: "I shall vote for the bill. It is effective legislation. It seeks to advance the rights of all Americans. It is national rather than sectional." Two weeks later, George Reedy declared that his boss held it was a "good and fair bill."[80]

Shortly after the Senate passage, Republican leaders met with the president at the White House. The bill was not yet on the president's desk: because of the amendments, it had to go to a conference committee to reconcile the House and Senate versions. Ike realized that the Democrats had claimed ownership of the civil rights bill, and if the Republicans did not vote to pass it, they would be painted as "Horatius at the bridge," stopping the bill's passage. He spoke for some time "in favor of fighting it out to the end to prevent the pseudo liberals from getting away with their sudden alliance with the southerners on a sham bill" and noted that a "number of very prominent Negroes," including Dr. Ralph Bunche, an influential UN official, urged a veto.

Others at the gathering held widely differing opinions. Nixon declared that the GOP would be blamed if the bill failed to pass. Knowland claimed that the Senate would not pass it if the conference committee removed the jury trial amendment. Republican senator Leverett Saltonstall from Massachusetts chimed in that something needed to be passed. Acting Attorney General Rogers thought that the bill could be toughened if the public understood the issues; unfortunately for many Americans, Rogers added, they did not.[81]

Ike hoped to remove the jury trial amendment during the House-Senate committee negotiations. Nixon concurred, wishing "that it may be strengthened before it goes to the President for final action." This optimism quickly faded as many congressmen and columnists suggested that something was better than nothing. The House insisted on some minor alterations, but the jury trial amendment remained intact. On August 27, the House voted 297 to 97 in favor of the legislation and returned it to the Senate.[82]

Many in the Senate hoped to proceed promptly because of the anticipated adjournment at the end of the month. Strom Thurmond from South Carolina was unwilling to concede defeat; he asked Senator Russell, as leader of the southern caucus, to reconsider his position on an organized filibuster. The Georgian's refusal did not prevent Thurmond from speaking against the House-Senate compromise. He started his remarks at 8:45 p.m. on August 28 and finished at 9:12 p.m. on the 29th, a record for a single senator that still stands. No southerner interfered, and no one followed him. The vote was taken. It was sixty to fifteen; thirty-seven Republicans and twenty-three Democrats for, and fifteen Democrats against.[83]

Russell offered his postscript on August 30 by attacking Brownell as "a politically-minded Attorney General" who would apply the law as the NAACP instructed him and as Nixon pressured him. If the southern senators had not spoken against Parts III and IV, the bill would have resulted in "the social intermingling of the races from kindergarten to the grave." He had restricted the legislation to voting and kept the federal government out of southern "schools and social order." That was "the sweetest victory of my twenty-five years as a Senator from Georgia."[84]

Jet saw five major factors preventing effective legislation. First, neither national party passionately fought for it. Republicans wanted to use it to appeal for black votes; Democrats struggled for a compromise between their factions. Former president Truman was silent during the debate. Second, the major black organizations did not lobby energetically for a powerful bill. Third, African American leaders did not offer coherent proposals. Fourth, those who favored a strong bill had not even reviewed it. Finally, most black leaders thought that civil rights legislation had no chance of passage.[85]

Writing at the end of month, Nixon saw the GOP as trying to appeal to African Americans. Congressional Republicans "stood united behind this legislation in a most outstanding manner. This stand will undoubtedly do much to prove the good faith of our Party on this issue." While the NAACP gave the bill lukewarm support, Roy Wilkins "paid a very high tribute to" Nixon for bringing it to the Senate floor, and NAACP capital bureau director Clarence Mitchell agreed. The bill's passage, he said, inaugurated a new era in race relations.[86]

Bobby Baker, secretary to the majority leader, watched how the vice president interacted with the NAACP. He recalled: "Nixon was 1,000 percent for it [the civil rights bill]. I would see Nixon entertaining Roy Wilkins and the chief lobbyist for the NAACP [Clarence Mitchell], and Vice President Nixon was making great headway with the Negro lobbyist."[87]

Julius Adams, born in Macon, Georgia, had moved north where he became a reporter and eventually published *The Economic Bulletin* in New York City. The only African American on the New York State Republican executive committee, he believed that the Eisenhower administration had helped race relations and black Democrats were irresponsible for not admitting this. After the jury trial provision was added to the legislation, Adams recommended a veto. Southern senators, he argued, had to lose this battle if the bill was not substantially revised. He believed that blacks responded to images and symbols: "Lincoln was once his symbol and no one could pry him away from the Republicans; then came Roosevelt . . . now it is Dick Nixon."[88]

Jackie Robinson, too, called for a veto,[89] but Martin Luther King wrote Nixon to say "that civil rights legislation is urgent now, and the present bill will go a long way to insure it." Passage would spark the registration of two million African Americans to vote in the 1960 elections. King applauded the vice president "for your assiduous labor and dauntless courage in seeking to make the Civil Rights Bill a reality." Black voters would remember the vice president's stance in the upcoming presidential election. Nixon responded that he wished he could have delivered a stronger bill, but it was better than no bill at all; the final jury trial amendment included a section that gave federal judges the power to impose fines up to $300 and jail sentences up to forty-five days without a jury trial in criminal contempt cases. As for encouraging registration, Nixon predicted: "If a substantial number of negro citizens who have not exercised their franchise before, register and vote as a result of the passage of this bill, the adoption of this legislation will have marked the greatest step forward in the cause of human rights since the Emancipation Proclamation."[90]

African Americans did not extend kudos to Johnson. Roy Wilkins did not "consider him a friend." Clarence Mitchell thought LBJ was reluctant to push for the bill because it would damage the Democratic Party. Thurgood Marshall believed that Johnson's principal objective "was a strictly political move of getting something done."[91]

During the voting on the civil rights bill, LBJ and Russell voted together against any change in the cloture rule and against bypassing the judiciary committee. Johnson and the southern caucus often spoke in unison. On his own initiative, Johnson made certain that Part III would not come up for revision toward the end of the debate. When the vote came on making the bill pending business of the Senate, LBJ voted yea with reservations.

Democrats like Douglas and Humphrey and Republicans like Javits, Case, and Kuchel vociferously demanded a stronger civil rights bill, and they may have made the southerners realize that if they did not reach a settlement on some bill, a stronger one would quickly follow. Knowland worked tirelessly for the administration in the passage of the bill. He not only cooperated with Democratic liberals but also served as a powerful force holding the Republican coalition together for the White House. Watching the "Douglas-Knowland Axis" evolve, Howard Shuman noted that the minority leader "was the key person, and was extraordinarily loyal. I give him great credit because his word was very, very good. . . . He deserves credit that he's never received. Johnson, who tried to kill it, got undeserved credit."[92]

The vice president, alongside Knowland as the administration's senatorial liaison, also pressured Republicans to stand with the president. Nixon gave the advisory opinions to change the cloture rule and to bypass the judiciary committee. Both measures pushed the bill nearer to successful passage.[93]

Nixon was disappointed with the law's limitations, but despite his discouragement, Republican senators Case and Kuchel applauded his contribution. Jessie Vann, wife of the publisher of the *Pittsburgh Courier*, a black daily, and Lillian "Poppy" White, widow of Walter, the legendary NAACP executive director, praised Nixon's courageous stand. In mid-August, an editorial in the usually Democratic *Chicago Defender* vilified Johnson for lining up with the segregationists, while noting: "By virtue of his untrammeled position on integration and civil rights, Mr. Nixon's prestige has risen considerably."[94]

Many liberal observers, particularly Howard Shuman, saw Eisenhower's support as "Tepid. The bland leading the bland." Arthur Larson, a presidential speechwriter and civil rights advocate, believed Eisenhower "had little faith in legislation as a vehicle for promoting better race relations." One exception was his pride in the 1957 law. In spite of the Democratic efforts to emasculate it, led by LBJ, the president was comfortable with the act. It "did not create any new substantive civil rights; it rather provided the President with more effective powers to discharge his duty of enforcing existing law, with the aid of the federal courts."[95]

Even though the president raised the idea of a veto, he signed the bill on September 9. Simeon Booker, an African American journalist working for *Ebony*, interviewed Ike in his retirement. With the 1957 Civil Rights Act, the former president said, the federal government had committed itself to enforcing black voting rights. And once they had political power, African Americans would use it to improve their status. Any more laws were unnecessary. Ike viewed "the passage of the first civil rights law in 80 years as his biggest success," ahead of the desegregation of the armed forces and the capital.[96]

On August 5, 1965, the day before the signing of the Civil Rights Voting Act, White House press secretary Bill Moyers telephoned Eisenhower's Gettysburg office, offering to furnish transportation to Ike for the signing ceremony at the Capitol because the 1957 civil rights legislation "was the base of the present bill." During a press interview with CBS Television's Robert Pierpont that same year, Eisenhower recalled Johnson's role in the 1957 legislation: "I can remember a certain Senator from Texas who wasn't nearly so enthusiastic about civil rights in those days." On October 12, 1966, the president wrote in his diary that Johnson "blocked every roadblock he could. He argued for jury trials and contempt cases" and even "asked for a secret appointment at the White House so that he could beg me to avoid pressing for continuation of the Civil Rights Commission!!" The following summer, during an oral history session, Ike insisted that he wanted "a much stronger Civil Rights bill in '57" than he was able to get. He held that "the biggest thing you can do for minorities is to protect their absolute right to register and vote—protect it with every means there is." He tried to accomplish that goal and could not understand why Democrats received the credit: "The worst enemies of Civil Rights" were the Democrats, including LBJ.[97]

Too much emphasis has been placed on the law's weaknesses and not enough on its benefits. The justice department had its civil rights unit raised to a separate division, with an assistant attorney general in charge. Without that new authority, the federal government would not have had the necessary infrastructure in place for the challenges of the 1960s. And the creation of the Civil Rights Commission gave the federal government an entity specifically devoted to investigating the abysmal treatment of African Americans in the South.

Eisenhower was involved with the legislation from the start to the finish. He selected his attorney general and urged him to draft the law, and had Nixon and others speak out regarding its positive aspects. As president, he pressured Republicans in the House and the Senate to vote for the bill. He signed it and started to enforce its provisions.

Southern politicians realized that some law was inevitable. The leader of the southern caucus, Richard Russell, plotted a strategy to remove what he considered the bill's most objectionable provisions using whatever parliamentary roadblocks were available. Since the House had easily approved of the 1956 civil rights bill, the Jim Crow South's last bastion of defense was the Senate—and its champion was Lyndon Johnson. Whatever credit Johnson deserves for the bill's passage, he shares the blame for eviscerating Parts III and IV of the legislation. Without powerful Republican allies, far more than the Democratic side, LBJ could not have reached a majority. It was not his bill.

What about Hells Canyon? The proposal to dam the Snake River at Hells Canyon, near the Oregon-Idaho border, had been controversial throughout the 1950s for both fiscal and environmental reasons. Eisenhower opposed federal funding of hydroelectric power projects and would likely have vetoed a bill for this one had it come to his desk, but it never did. Legislation to fund the Hells Canyon dam was taken up by the House Subcommittee on Irrigation and Reclamation, part of the Committee on Interior and Insular Affairs, in February 1957, and defeated on a sixteen-to-fourteen vote in mid-July. It never came to the floor of the House. In a front-page story about the vote on July 19, the *New York Times* quoted Jack Westland, Republican from Washington and a member of the subcommittee, saying that "the nation cannot and should not finance all water resource developments with Federal funds." The *Times* did not equivocate about the project's immediate future: it reported that the House had "killed a bill today for a Federal Hells Canyon dam."

This was fourteen days before the Senate voted on the southern bloc's amendment to the civil rights bill, and twenty days before it passed the modified bill. It is hard to believe that any senator—especially one who strongly supported civil rights, as many of the western senators did—would have traded away his vote on such a visible and highly contested moral issue for a project that the House had already rejected. The absence of any mention of such a deal in the primary documents leads overwhelmingly to one conclusion: they didn't.[98]

LITTLE ROCK AND ITS CONSEQUENCES

As the summer of 1957 drew to a close and the congressional conferees nego-tiated the final provisions of the civil rights legislation, parents were preparing their children to return to school. Many states simply ignored the mandate to desegregate. Many officials in the Deep South refused to take any measures at all toward desegregation, a defiance that mirrored the sentiments of over-whelming majorities of their white constituents.[1]

Eisenhower recognized that integrating the South would be difficult and saw acceptance as a gradual process. The *Brown* decision sought to overturn deeply entrenched beliefs and habits; segregation dominated almost every aspect of southern life. Yet the Supreme Court had ruled, and its decision had to stand. The alternative was chaos and an intolerable challenge to the authority of the federal government. The president deplored extremists' arguments and called upon moderates to take a leadership role toward integration. As he said many times, the hearts and minds of men had to change.

Arkansas did not appear to be a powder keg. The state had already integrated its university, and Orval Faubus, the Democratic governor, had not run for of-fice as a segregationist. The capital, Little Rock, was preparing to take token steps toward integration when its school board agreed to admit nine African Ameri-can teenagers to the previously all-white Central High School. When opponents challenged this step in state court, a federal judge reaffirmed the *Brown* ruling and ordered the school to integrate.

But when Faubus found himself opposed in the upcoming election by a ra-bid segregationist, he decided that even glacial progress on integration could be damaging to his reelection chances. On September 2, the day before schools opened, he ordered the Arkansas National Guard to prevent the black students from entering Central High School on the grounds that their attendance might spark racial violence. When school opened the following morning, the guard turned the black teenagers away.

The president, meanwhile, was vacationing in Newport, Rhode Island, where Attorney General Brownell called him to discuss Faubus's action. The governor's claim that he used the troops to protect public safety, Brownell said, was a ruse: they were there to halt integration. The attorney general responded to the deployment by publicly declaring that the president had the power to use state or federal troops "to enforce the court order."[2]

Governor Faubus sent a telegram to the president asking him to delay any federal intervention, but Ike refused. Still, the president did not want to dispatch troops and hoped for a peaceful resolution. Brownell saw no alternative; the governor had to obey.

A Democratic congressman from the Little Rock area, Brooks Hays, tried to mediate by suggesting a meeting in Rhode Island between the governor and the president. On September 14, Faubus flew to Newport where he and the president conferred alone for about twenty minutes. The president believed the crisis had ended and that he had persuaded Faubus to capitulate, but he misread his visitor's intentions. When he learned on September 20 that Faubus had not removed the National Guard, Ike was livid and saw the governor's continuing deployment of troops as a betrayal of their understanding. A day later, Faubus suddenly removed the soldiers from the high school. Although he wondered about Faubus' motives, the president commended this action and hoped for peaceful integration in Little Rock.

On Monday, September 23, a white mob of over 1,000 went to Central High School, screamed obscenities at the African American students trying to enter, and prevented them from attending classes. Some in the crowd severely beat L. Alex Wilson, an African American reporter from Memphis, Tennessee, who edited the *Tri-State Defender*; photographers captured the assault on film, and their pictures circulated worldwide. That evening, Little Rock mayor Woodrow Mann implored the president to intervene to stop the mob from becoming more violent. The president later spoke with evangelist Billy Graham, who advised him that Faubus had left him no choice. Military intervention was the only option.[3]

The next day, as mob violence erupted again at the school, Ike nationalized the Arkansas guard and ordered 1,000 troops from the Army's 101st Airborne, chosen for their intensive training in riot control, to fly to Little Rock to enforce the court order. That evening, the president flew from Rhode Island to the capital, where he addressed the nation on why he was mobilizing troops. Arkansas had disobeyed both the Supreme Court and a direct order from the Federal District

Court, and he would use his constitutional authority to ensure that these orders were carried out. On Wednesday, Army soldiers escorted the black students to Central High School. The mob quickly evaporated, and the violence stopped.

Presidential legal adviser Arthur Larson met with Ike on October 1. According to Larson, the president told him he was fulfilling his constitutional responsibility to uphold the Court's authority, but this action did not imply either approval or disapproval of *Brown*. Ike told Larson that the Supreme Court's decision was "wrong." The Court should have limited itself "to require *equal* opportunities and that to require integration was not necessary." He understood the Court's rationale, "that segregation in itself damaged the pride and spirit— but did not find it compelling," and he opposed using force to integrate "beyond doing his constitutional duty of seeing that lawful court orders are obeyed."[4]

Swede Hazlett wrote to the president that he "had done the right thing" by sending troops. On November 18, Eisenhower replied that his primary concern, especially for southerners, was not the civil rights issue. The *Brown* decision had "nothing to do with the case," but the Supreme Court's ruling "must be upheld." Five years later, in an interview with African American reporter Simeon Booker, the former president maintained that *Brown* "was absolute in constitutional and moral law." As long as a citizen had a liability for taxes, he had "the right to benefit fully from the services of the government."[5]

Within two weeks of writing that letter, Ike suffered his third major illness while in the White House, a mild stroke. According to Larson, Ann Whitman, the president's private secretary and ultimate loyalist, "was near breakdown." Whitman felt that Ike "had really not been himself since the pressure began building up at the time of Little Rock." Although many perceived the president as "thick-skinned," he read the newspapers and "suffered a great deal under recent criticism." The stroke "was the result."[6]

Nixon blamed Faubus for the Little Rock crisis and simultaneously praised the president. On September 24, he reminded the country that most southerners were "decent, law-abiding citizens." Faubus's deployment of his National Guard "inevitably implanted the idea of violence in the minds of many people who otherwise would not have resorted to violence"; he thus bore "the major share of responsibility" for the "disgraceful" situation in Little Rock. When reporters asked Nixon if Ike should have threatened sooner to deploy federal troops, the vice president grinned: "Monday morning quarter backing is a favorite pastime in politics and sports." He believed Ike "was correct in waiting until the last possible moment before stepping in, because it is essentially a state and local responsibility." The president had given Arkansas officials every opportunity to resolve the crisis on their own and had reluctantly intervened only when it became apparent that they could not.[7]

On October 2, the president asked Nixon to play golf that afternoon. If Nixon had other commitments, he should not change them "because mine are necessarily so uncertain because of the stupidity and duplicity of one called Faubus." Nixon's commitments were not compelling; he joined the president.[8]

Ten days after the golf game, Nixon spoke in Oklahoma City where he heaped blame on Faubus for stirring up extremists with "inflammatory statements." If the governor had not indulged in such rhetoric, the Little Rock crisis would not have happened. Several weeks later, in a letter to Donald Ewing, associate editor of the *Shreveport Times* in Louisiana, Nixon wrote that Little Rock had "produced one of the most fundamental challenges to our federal system and to the Constitution itself." The decision to deploy soldiers was "one of the most difficult [Eisenhower] has ever had to make," but Governor Faubus had given him "no choice." Nixon saw race relations as a major moral question. The Supreme Court had ordered school integration, and that ruling had to be obeyed: "The problem now is to find a meeting ground which will enable the intelligent and moral leadership in the South to find an acceptable way to help make a peaceful transition possible."[9]

In surveys before and after the Little Rock upheaval, southerners consistently opposed integration far more strongly than the rest of the nation. From the summer of 1954 through June 1961, over 70 percent of southerners disapproved of the *Brown* decision; approximately 15 percent approved. Nationwide, approval for the decision ran in the high fifties. Fifty-three percent of southern blacks in February 1953 favored integration, and 69 percent in November 1957.[10]

Recognizing that the vast majority of their constituents opposed integration, southern politicians loudly denounced the president's use of force. The Democratic senators from Arkansas, J. William Fulbright and John McClellan, were silent. Richard Russell and other southern politicians accused Eisenhower of employing storm-trooper tactics. Sam Ervin accused the president of abusing his powers. None of the major Democratic contenders for the 1960 presidential nomination, including Lyndon Johnson, John Kennedy, and Hubert Humphrey, came to Eisenhower's defense.[11]

The *Jackson Daily News*, which called itself "Mississippi's Greatest Newspaper," reflected the regional hostility. Its October 1, 1957, editorial, "They Still Hate Us," thundered: "the old hatreds engendered by the War Between the States have not died out above the Mason and Dixon line." New Englanders and New Yorkers felt themselves superior to southerners. "And, to tell the truth, we didn't like them any too damned well, either."[12]

Between November 1957 and June 1958, Bruce Herschensohn, a documentary movie producer, interviewed three southern governors, James Coleman of Mississippi, Samuel Griffin of Georgia, and Faubus. None had any plans to integrate public schools. Blacks and whites, all three asserted, generally lived in harmony. When the filmmaker visited Atlanta, he saw white and colored drinking fountains as well as Confederate flags flying everywhere. These open displays of segregation were inconsequential to Governor Griffin, who proclaimed that blacks received fair treatment, they desired separation, and they did "not consider themselves an oppressed race." Any friction, the governors believed, came from outside agitators. Coleman objected to "professional NAACP agitators" and northern liberals who fomented violence. Speaking to Herschensohn nine months after the Little Rock episode, Faubus added that Ike was a military man who did not understand "the fundamentals of the democratic process of civel [sic] governments." Education was a state, not a federal concern. In a democracy, radical change such as integration was impossible. Without the support of the people, it would collapse.[13]

The Chicago Defender's White House reporter, Ethel Payne, called the president's national address ordering troops into Little Rock "the most important act of his career and the most statesmanship like talk he had ever made." Southern politicians preferred to emphasize that that Ike had stationed Army soldiers with bayonets to subdue protestors; they complained that he should have done more to justify the rationale behind his decision.[14]

From the Little Rock incident until the end of the Eisenhower presidency, the Gallup Poll sampled Americans on the nation's most important problems. Between 29 and 51 percent rated the threat of war with the Soviet Union as most pressing; economic conditions were second at a high of 40 percent and a low of 13 percent; integration ranged from 4 to 10 percent. Even with the images of white mobs confronting armed soldiers in Little Rock, civil rights were not a central concern for most.[15]

When the crisis was over, major personnel changes in the justice department began. Attorney General Brownell resigned in October. Assistant attorney general Warren Olney III, who had managed the criminal division, which included the civil rights section, since the beginning of the first term, returned to private practice. This division had not taken great interest in the subtleties of civil rights litigation, but with the passage of the Civil Rights Act, that section would become a separate division with its own assistant attorney general in charge.[16]

The president promoted deputy attorney general William Rogers as Brownell's successor. In his first press conference on December 9, Rogers announced that the administration would not ask for any civil rights legislation in

1958 because the White House favored a "cooling off" period. The Little Rock episode had to rest "for a while." He would not propose anything that might aggravate the situation and would wait to see the Civil Rights Act and the new Civil Rights Commission in operation before calling for additional laws.[17]

Harold Greene, an attorney at the justice department, later recalled that the new attorney general recognized the southern bloc's power and knew he could not antagonize it unduly. In an early meeting, Rogers cautioned: "Let's not bring too many cases. What we want to do is bring just a few cases that we establish the law solidly from the beginning." He later told columnist Arthur Krock that if Virginia encouraged "even the slightest integration," he would support its constitutionality before the Supreme Court. Rogers had not at all lost his passion and commitment to civil rights laws; but the 1957 legislation required that violations of civil rights had to go to jury trials, and he understood the difficulty of getting a conviction from a southern jury. He would still act aggressively to bring test cases from African American complaints dealing with voting rights, but he preferred to try those that were likely to bring a conviction.[18]

Many who criticize the Civil Rights Act of 1957 fail to appreciate the significance of the new division it created within the justice department. The first civil rights unit was set up under the department's criminal division in 1939. Two years later, it was elevated to a section, with a dozen lawyers and three assistants, but by the time Eisenhower became president, it had just seven attorneys. The new division, starting out with fourteen lawyers and twenty-five clerical personnel, immediately began to develop procedures to institute suits to protect voting rights and to introduce uniform standards for individuals serving on federal juries.[19]

The 1957 act called for an assistant attorney general to direct the division. W. Wilson White, who had been the United States attorney in the Philadelphia area and then directed the justice department's office of legal counsel, was the first choice. White's nomination was sent to the Senate on December 9, 1957, but held up by Senator Eastland for eight months. After he was finally confirmed, White faced constant opposition and criticism from southern politicians. Lawrence Walsh believed he was too "gentle" and not sufficiently aggressive. After being battered for a year and a half, White resigned. By the time he resigned in 1959, the division had expanded to twenty-six attorneys and twenty-nine clerical employees. Harold Tyler Jr. took White's position. Once again, Eastland held up his confirmation until July 1960; he remained at his post until shortly before the Eisenhower presidency ended.[20]

The second crucial part of the 1957 act was the establishment of the Civil Rights Commission. It had two mandates: first, to investigate any deprivation of voting rights and, second, to study laws and policies of the federal government to ensure equal protection under the Constitution. As they did with the civil rights division, southerners delayed the appointment of the six-member board, especially those members they thought were antagonistic to segregation.[21]

Their nominations were not confirmed until March 5, 1958. Despite that delay, the commission met on January 3, and later that year it held public hearings in Montgomery, Alabama, the site of the bus boycott, to assemble data on discrimination in voting and housing. The following year, the commission conducted hearings in New York City, Atlanta, Chicago, and Washington. The commission was set to expire in 1960; to guarantee its extension, a rider was attached to the Mutual Security Appropriation Act in the fall of 1959, giving it four more years.[22]

The Civil Rights Commission published its first report in September 1959, recommending a board of registrars functioning through the president to assist black registration; public school integration in the South; and more attention to low-cost housing nationwide. The United States had to resolve not only "to end discrimination but also by creating through works of faith in freedom a clear and present vision of the City of Man, the one city of free and equal men envisioned by the Constitution."[23]

Some of those who had played significant roles in the administration's civil rights policy during the first term now left government service. Maxwell Rabb, unofficially the president's counsel on civil rights issues, resigned in the spring of 1958. In his newspaper column, William White wrote: "Rabb always declined to treat civil rights as though it were civil war."[24]

That fall, Sherman Adams, a civil rights advocate, left his post as the president's chief of staff, and Jerry Persons, Adams's deputy, replaced him. Persons, whose brother had been governor of Alabama, had known the president since their years in the Army. It did not trouble Ike that he did not hide his bias, but both agreed that Persons should not participate in any civil rights discussions. The president told Harold Tyler, the assistant attorney general for civil rights, to bypass Persons and call him directly when Tyler needed to speak to him.[25]

At a press conference on August 27, 1958, Alice Dunnigan of the Associated Negro Press asked the president about rumors that J. Ernest Wilkins, an assistant secretary of labor and the highest ranking African American in the administration, was about to resign. Ike admitted that he had spoken to Wilkins about his resignation but had not requested it. He had had "a very congenial talk with him about it." Wilkins's sudden death in January 1959 ended the matter.[26]

With Wilkins's passing, E. Frederic Morrow became the most visible African American in the administration. After the Little Rock episode, he received hostile mail and angry telephone calls from irate blacks who opposed the president's civil rights stance. Ike, according to one critic, needed "to assume the moral leadership of the country" by giving a speech "in favor of every American having the right to walk this land in dignity and peace, unfettered by any restrictive bonds." Morrow felt that the "Administration's apparent indifference to the plight of the defenseless Negroes in the South" was unforgivable. Some Republican officials demanded his resignation.

Morrow publicly defended the administration's civil rights initiatives and expressed his frustration privately. The president had made more black appointments than any of his predecessors and had sent troops to Little Rock. Yet from Morrow's perspective, "there is no strong, clarion, commanding voice from the White House, righteously indignant over the plight of 18,000,000 Negroes in the United States, who are fighting for their God-given rights of human dignity and self-determination."[27]

Morrow was delighted when Eisenhower took some dramatic measures to improve race relations. Shortly after the Little Rock conflict, K.A. Gbedemah, Ghana's finance minister, came to the United States to speak at Maryland State College. On his way back to New York City, on October 8, he stopped at a Howard Johnson's Restaurant in Dover, Delaware, and asked for some orange juice. The waitress wrapped it for takeout, but Gbedemah demanded to be seated. When she refused, he demanded to see the manager and identified himself. The manager was not impressed: "colored people are not allowed to eat in here." The incident made front-page news, and when the president read about the "racial snub," he invited the Ghanaian for breakfast at the White House the following morning. Press secretary Hagerty apologized, as did the state department. Black Democratic congressman Charles Diggs Jr. called Ike's action a "laudable gesture." Many blacks had experienced that kind of humiliation daily, and not only in the South: "if the President sits down to eat with every Negro who is refused service in an American restaurant, he may as well move his office into his dining room."[28]

Ike's afternoon address the following spring before the National Newspaper Publishers Association, the industry group of black community newspapers, did not draw a similar response. Simeon Booker described the four hundred attendees as "perhaps the most distinguished assemblage of our people ever to discuss the course of race relations." Welcomed with warm applause, Ike highlighted two major civil rights themes: minorities needed more education, and a better understanding between the races required changing hearts and minds. Then, deviating from his prepared remarks, he urged his audience to practice "patience and forbearance."

Morrow had warned the president against using phrases like "patience and forbearance" because they would offend his listeners. Morrow knew immediately that the assemblage resented Ike's choice of words, but the president saw nothing inappropriate. That evening, NAACP leader Roy Wilkins denounced Ike's choice of words, and the following day Jackie Robinson wrote the president that African American "patience" had run out; black people were entitled to equality now. The president responded several weeks later that he wanted equal treatment for all Americans and was moving forward toward that objective.[29]

The president invited four black leaders to visit him on the morning of June 23. Since early in his first term, influential African Americans as well as White House staff members had lobbied the president for such a gathering. Nixon's conference with Reverend King in the summer of 1957 may have persuaded Ike to hold one of his own. After White House staffers discussed the idea with King, the White House announced that he, Roy Wilkins, union leader A. Philip Randolph, and Lester Granger, executive director of the Nation Urban League, would attend.

This was the first time that Eisenhower had met formally with African American leaders in the Oval Office. The guests presented the president with several requests. As the senior spokesman, Randolph congratulated Ike on his civil rights accomplishments and his decisive action in Little Rock. King then called on the president to employ his bully pulpit to speak against segregation and to convene a White House gathering on civil rights. Wilkins followed, advocating that the administration reintroduce the deleted Part III of the 1957 civil rights bill to give the justice department greater power to enforce civil rights laws. Finally, Granger argued that the federal government had stalled in its fair employment efforts by providing funding to states that maintained discriminatory practices.

Attorney General Rogers declared that the justice department had acted cautiously in challenging acts of discrimination and would prosecute only those cases where the government had a reasonable chance of winning. As for the resurrection of Part III, Rogers reminded Wilkins that he had agreed to its deletion.

Ike was distressed over the four men's bitterness. His administration had taken more concrete measures than its two predecessors combined and had pushed a strong civil rights agenda, and he frankly expected more goodwill. The group, in unison, responded that their anger was not with him but with the turmoil in the South. The president replied that he doubted a White House conference or the use of the bully pulpit would be advantageous, but he agreed that the federal government should take aggressive action, especially in voting rights.

After the meeting, the four leaders held a press conference where they expressed enthusiasm regarding the president's pledges. Rocco Siciliano, a presidential assistant who had helped to arrange the meeting, called it an "unqualified success—even if success in this area is built on sand." Americans had to accept integration, and that would come by changing the hearts and minds of men.[30]

Two black participants later recalled a different experience. A. Philip Randolph, in an oral history, conceded that the president sent troops into Little Rock, but complained: "We were never able to get from him any strong definitive statement with respect to the struggle for civil rights." The president seemed agreeable but would not engage in a meaningful dialogue: "He'd sit and listen to you or make a comment; he was never antagonistic; but he didn't discuss the matter." King expressed similar frustration: "I don't think [Ike] feels like being a crusader for integration."[31]

Toward the end of the summer, Ike welcomed the Negro Elks leaders in the White House. After entering the Oval Office, the group praised the president for his sympathetic and humanitarian leadership. Ike appreciated this sentiment, made several comments, had photographs taken with his guests, and gave them small souvenirs. E. Frederic Morrow, who helped to arrange the meeting, was pleased. Ike had "warmed the hearts of his visitors."[32]

Nixon offered his political impressions. On the evening of October 22, 1957, he attended a dinner at Arthur Krock's home for twelve reporters and editors. While he sipped Scotch and nibbled roast beef, the *New York Times* columnist watched Nixon refer to himself as a "moderate" on race relations; he did not believe that northern blacks would significantly increase their vote for Republicans. Little Rock, however, had eliminated any immediate GOP hopes of capturing congressional seats in the South. He expected to build the party in the region by appealing to "young, progressive forces" while rejecting "reactionaries." Racism was losing adherents, and in the long run, the party needed to support civil rights.[33]

In later interviews, the vice president said that southerners agreed with the GOP on economic issues but differed with the party on civil rights, and that the resulting political damage to the party was only temporary. Southerners would eventually realize that their civil rights stance was untenable. Moderates had to take charge: "Demagogues who advocate impossible legal approaches to the civil rights problem do more harm than good, and invariably set the cause back." Southern voters would gradually move into the GOP.[34]

In November 1957, Nixon addressed the American Council on Education. United States citizens of all races, he said, needed "an adequate education" to meet their potential: "there are moral considerations which are terribly important in this Civil Rights field." The nation had to be consistent; it could not talk democracy abroad and permit segregation at home.[35] In mid-December he conceded that the Republican Party had failed to win many black converts in the North during the recent congressional elections: "The Republican party would lose its self-respect and right to exist if it ever compromised on this basic issue of the rights of man."[36]

In the spring of 1959, meeting in Washington with the Council of Methodist Bishops, he urged it to discourage racial extremists. Nixon's "balanced consideration of the basic issue of race in this nation" had impressed Bishop G. Bromley Oxnam. He had spoken with several black bishops who "were highly pleased by the position you [Nixon] advocated with such cogency."[37]

Nixon felt it was both important and possible to reconcile the Republican position on civil rights with the need to win white southerners to the party. Early in 1958, he referred to how integration was proceeding. In 1955, eighteen states had maintained legally separated public schools for whites and blacks; currently there were six. Despite that decline, Nixon saw school desegregation as "one of the most difficult and painful issues we face today." The administration would move forward with its civil rights agenda. While Nixon understood how adversely the GOP had been damaged in the South, he singled out southerners "with moderate and conservative inclinations" for the party's outreach because those individuals would be attracted to the Republican philosophy.[38]

On October 11, 1958, the vice president wrote privately that leaders should not follow public opinion but had to stand for their own principles. Sometimes his mail went ten to one against the Supreme Court's decisions on integration, but this would not change his "view that fighting for racial justice is for me a moral as well as a legal obligation." Five weeks later, he asserted that the African American drive to reach "full equality" was "one of the brightest chapters in our nation's history." This crusade elicited deep hostility from segregationists; still, Nixon optimistically predicted that eventually "all of our citizens regardless of race, creed or ancestry will enjoy full opportunity." He stressed that "it is morally wrong to segregate human beings on the basis of race. Praise or blame, acceptance or rejection should be personal matters based on individual achievements and not the accident of birth. I could not accept Hitler's idea of a master race; I cannot accept the false principle of an inferior race."[39]

That same day, he sent a letter to Congressman Brooks Hays that was reprinted in the *New York Herald Tribune*. Hays had spent eight terms in the House and had futilely tried to resolve the Little Rock impasse peacefully by acting as an intermediary between the president and Governor Faubus. Eight days before the 1958 congressional elections, Dr. Dale Afford, an avowed segregationist, organized a last minute write-in campaign. Out of a total of 60,222 votes, Hays lost by 1,256. In his letter, Nixon wrote that he had witnessed segregation firsthand as a law student at Duke, but racism was not limited to the South; it permeated America, and Hays's defeat was a national disgrace: "When statesmanship of the type you represent in such an exemplary way becomes the victim of demagoguery and prejudice, it is time for men of good will in both of our major parties in all sections of the country to exert more positive leadership in developing the public understanding on the issue of civil rights which is essential if America is to continue to be a nation of responsible laws rather than irresponsible men."[40]

Nixon often consulted with Bill Rogers and Lawrence Walsh in the justice department on civil rights. Harold Tyler recalled that after he became assistant attorney general for civil rights, Nixon was the only member of the executive branch who not only took an interest in civil rights legislation but also called him for updates.[41]

Nixon also followed the deliberations of the Civil Rights Commission because he expected it to promote the administration's priorities on race. After the 1957 Civil Rights bill was passed, he pushed for it to be organized promptly and urged it to begin deliberations even before its members were approved by Congress. Feeling that many southern whites and blacks were refusing to listen to moderate voices, Nixon wanted the commission to work toward a realistic dialogue. He established a close relationship with the commission's chairman, John Hannah. Father Theodore Hesburgh, a commission member, lobbied the vice president to embrace the commission's recommendations. In 1959, after the administration got Congress to approve the commission's extension, Nixon regretted that it had not been extended for a longer period.[42]

Throughout the second term, Nixon communicated frequently with the NAACP leadership, including its executive director, Roy Wilkins, and its chief lobbyist, Clarence Mitchell. Both men recognized Nixon as a strong proponent of civil rights, and they regularly pressed him to do more. Val Washington, the director of minority affairs for the Republican National Committee (RNC), held a dinner meeting in the summer of 1959 that included Wilkins and Mitchell as well as Senators Kenneth Keating from New York and Hugh Scott from Pennsylvania, and RNC chairman Thruston Morton. After the meeting, Washington informed the vice president that his guests approved of Nixon's civil rights record. They also agreed that the GOP had performed better on civil rights than the Democrats, "but did [a] poor job of public relations for exploiting this—are too afraid of being accused of playing politics with the issue."[43] Jackie Robinson, who had joined the NAACP board of directors, wrote frequently to Nixon throughout the second term. He had been impressed with the vice president's positions on civil rights and spoke of himself as a political independent that supported the individual rather than a party. In a letter on December 24, 1957, he told the vice president that while much progress had occurred, everyone knew "there is a long, long way to go." He called on Nixon to stand against the racists who defied the Supreme Court. Although he respected Nixon's achievements, he was disappointed at the lack of new legislation. If the GOP did not act aggressively, Robinson warned, it would suffer the consequences.[44]

The vice president responded that the administration planned to continue "its wholehearted efforts to achieve the goal of human dignity and equality of opportunity for all Americans." The 1957 law was weaker than what the president had proposed; still, "its passage was an important milestone in American history." Nixon suggested that Robinson wait to see how "the battle for equal rights" proceeded, and he added: "While all great movements of reform started slowly and encountered bitter opposition, they soon gathered an irresistible momentum and gained rapid acceptance."[45]

Nixon had more contact with Martin Luther King. At the end of 1957, Harris Wofford Jr., a close confident of the minister and a future United States senator from Pennsylvania, wrote Nixon to say that King was "singing your praises" and that King described the vice president to his followers as "your friend Nixon." The United States ambassador to Mexico, Robert Hill, wrote that when King and his wife Coretta visited the United States embassy in Mexico City on July 21, 1958, they had "expressed a very friendly and enthusiastic attitude toward you." After King published *Stride Toward Freedom*, his account of the Montgomery bus boycott, he sent an autographed copy to the vice president.[46]

Reporter Earl Mazo, who was preparing a biography of Nixon, asked King for his impressions of the vice president, and the minister composed a lengthy reply on September 2, 1958. Before meeting Nixon, King "strong opposed" him because he knew of Nixon mainly as a right-wing Republican who had allegedly slandered Helen Gahagan Douglas during the 1950 California senatorial race and had cynically defended himself in the Checkers speech. But after meeting the vice president, he concluded that Nixon had "grown a great deal," and King "changed many of his former opinions." Nixon was a Quaker who "sincerely favored civil rights" and had "no basic racial prejudice." King believed that Nixon would have done much more than the president during the Little Rock crisis and would have spoken out on the moral issue. His foreign travels had made him aware of how domestic segregation damaged the American image abroad, and as a result he had become "a superb diplomat."

King found the vice president "to be a very personable man" with "one of the most magnetic personalities" the minister had encountered. He predicted that

Nixon's charisma would be beneficial to his political aspirations. The danger King saw was that "it will be turned on merely for political expedience when at bottom the real man has insincere motives." Nixon had "a genius for convincing one that he is sincere. When you are close to Nixon he almost disarms you with his apparent sincerity." If Nixon were pretending, King concluded, he could be "the most dangerous man in America."[47] The vice president also followed King's activities. In the fall of 1958, while King was recovering in Harlem Hospital after a black woman in New York City stabbed him in the chest, Nixon wired him to express his sorrow. The vice president could not comprehend the indignities that King had "heaped upon" him: "the Christian spirit of tolerance which you invariably display in the face of your opponents and detractors," he wrote, "will in the end contribute immeasurably in winning the support of the great majority of Americans for the cause of equality and human dignity to which we are dedicated."[48]

Besides these influential leaders, Nixon also developed a cordial relationship with E. Frederic Morrow inside the White House. The Nixons invited Morrow and his wife to their Forest Lane house during the 1957 Christmas holidays. In his thank-you note, Morrow wrote that he and Catherine had a "delightful evening" even though there were some "raised eyebrows" when they entered, but Pat Nixon made her guests feel comfortable. That was until Morrow went upstairs to the second floor, and a "not too sober female guest" demanded he retrieve her coat. Morrow explained that he was a guest, not a servant, and did not know where her coat was.[49]

Morrow considered Nixon a personal friend, and on July 30, 1958, he sought Nixon's advice on whether he should seek a career in government at the end of Eisenhower's tenure or return to the private sector. Nixon urged him to take a business position, calling him "a rare human being" with many outstanding qualities, one of the best of which, Morrow later recalled, was that he "did not resent being a Negro; that I did not use my color as an excuse for any misfortune I might encounter." He was a pioneer and must continue to blaze new trails. Morrow was pleased with the advice and that Nixon took "such a progressive view."[50]

Nixon also tried to expand the activities of the President's Committee on Government Contracts (PCGC), but southerners in Congress who opposed the PCGC's mission kept its funding sparse. By the second term, the PCGC consisted of one small office with an executive director, a single staff member, and a secretary. Others were hired to examine federal contract compliance provisions, to do surveys, to explore educational opportunities, to develop a budget, and to provide satellite offices in Los Angeles and Chicago.[51] While *U.S. News &*

World Report at the end of 1957 applauded Nixon's effort to increase minority hiring related to federal contracts, the administration was reluctant to vigorously enforce equal job opportunity and desegregation. Unions talked about integration but did not stop exclusionary practices. At the end of the decade, blacks still lagged far behind whites in employment and living standards.[52]

Irving Ferman, who had been the director of the Washington office of the American Civil Liberties Union (ACLU), was appointed director of the PCGC at the end of June 1959. An outspoken advocate of civil rights, he maintained a cordial association with the FBI by sending names from the ACLU's files to find out if they had communist or subversive connections. J. Edgar Hoover announced his approval, and Clarence Mitchell of the NAACP called Ferman's selection "welcome news." He would prove to be the most effective director in the PCGC's history.[53]

Ferman had met Nixon in May 1959. He explained that persuasion alone had been ineffective in increasing black employment, and he wanted a fixed number of qualified African Americans hired within a given period of time in jobs from which they were traditionally excluded. He also sought better job training and educational incentives for minorities: Nixon constantly reminded him "that just as important as education of a Negro child in a desegregated school was access to equal economic opportunity for him when he left."[54]

Despite its meager funding, the PCGC opened inquiries into many sensitive topics involving minority employment. It examined how businesses obeyed the nondiscrimination clauses in federal contracts and also obtained federal funds for researchers to study various methods of training minorities. The PCGC, Nixon optimistically believed, saw overt discrimination decreasing nationally, except in the South. As part of its final recommendations before it closed operations at the end of Eisenhower's second term, the PCGC asked for a permanent statutory committee that would work on equal job opportunity. Congress rejected that recommendation, and no similar body existed until the Equal Employment Opportunity Commission was created in 1965.

Nixon actively tried to persuade government agencies to enforce their contractual nondiscrimination clauses. He called for "action, rather than talk" and emphasized that the Little Rock crisis should not discourage the movement toward compliance in the committee's operations. He also advocated greater college preparation for qualified minority applicants as a means of moving them from manual labor to skilled and white-collar positions.[55] At a PCGC-sponsored luncheon on May 11, 1959, for four hundred religious leaders, Nixon drew national attention with his opening remarks, in which he called discrimination both a moral and legal wrong that had to end: "the whole field of discrimination and prejudice is . . . basically a moral problem." Americans had to accept civil rights laws because they were "right." The next speaker, Martin Luther King Jr., talked in similar terms: discrimination in employment was both a political and "a profound moral issue," and the enormous employment gap between whites and blacks was shameful. The progress made up to that point, he declared, was woefully inadequate. Churches had to meet this challenge, and their leaders actively needed to assist in eliminating discrimination.[56]

The PCGC had minor successes. Ford Motor Company started to hire a miniscule number of blacks in white-collar jobs, and small numbers of blacks were also allowed into union apprentice programs. International Latex Corporation of Dover, Delaware, became the committee's "most dramatic breakthrough." In September 1959, none of its workers were black; by the following May, after the PCGC lobbied the corporation, it had more than two hundred black employees. Since Delaware's population was over 25 percent African American, this was significant.[57]

The PCGC had difficulties with unions. Walter Reuther, president of the United Automobile Workers, in 1960 argued to increase minority recruitment, but AFL-CIO president George Meany resisted, even though blacks filled just 1.69 percent of his organization's apprentice positions. If that percentage improved at its then-current rate, blacks would gain equal representation in skill craft training in 138 years. By the middle of 1960, Meany seemed ready to relent.[58]

Irving Ferman left the PCGC in the summer of 1960. In a memo summarizing his activities, he said, "as a nation, we can no longer afford to tolerate discrimination on grounds of race, religion, or national origin. Discrimination is actually dangerous in these troubled times, as well as morally wrong, for it tends to divide us." Two years later, Ferman said that Nixon had made a "significant contribution" by urging that federal contractors be required to comply with the nondiscrimination clause in their contracts and by promoting the integration of blacks in building trade unions through better training and education. Nixon realized, said Ferman, that the nation was moving toward a white-collar majority and had to open employment opportunities in areas previously denied to minority groups.[59]

Eisenhower followed the committee's work. When it submitted its final report to him, he endorsed its recommendations and predicted that if accepted "it will bring our people closer to the great goal of full equality of opportunity." In a private memo to Nixon, the president stated: "The case of equal job opportunity had been advanced because of your steady effort."[60]

In the summer of 1958, federal judge Harry Lemley issued a decision permitting the state of Arkansas to delay integration in Little Rock for two and a half years, on the grounds that opposition from the local population as well as state officials had created a "chaotic situation." After Lemley's opinion was reversed by the Eighth Circuit Court of Appeals, it was appealed to the Supreme Court. The case, *Cooper v. Aaron*, resulted in a landmark decision in which the Court ruled that states were required to accept the *Brown* decision and abide by federal court orders. Even before the Court handed down its decision, the governors of Arkansas and Virginia closed their public schools rather than obey court orders to desegregate.[61]

The president supported the Court's decision and was ready to use troops to enforce it. At a press conference announcing this intent on October 1, 1958, he read a statement: "We must never forget that the rights of all of us depend upon respect for the lawfully determined rights of each of us. As one nation, we must assure to all our people, whatever their color or creed, the enjoyment of their Constitutional rights and the full measure of the law's protection. We must be faithful to our Constitutional ideals and go forward in good faith with the unremitting task of translating them into reality."[62]

At the start of 1959, Ike sent a special State of the Union Message on civil rights to Congress. Before any bills were presented, the Senate once again considered revising the number of votes required to end a filibuster. Liberals pushed for a rule to end filibusters by a simple majority vote but were defeated, sixty-eight to twenty-eight. Republican Thruston Morton of Kentucky offered a compromise that called for 60 percent, and it too failed, fifty-six to thirty-six. On the evening of January 12, majority leader Lyndon Johnson took the initiative and restored the pre-1949 rule that called for two-thirds of those present and voting.[63]

This minimal change allowed only slight prospects for civil rights legislation, but the president persisted. During a meeting of Republican congressional leaders at the White House on February 3, Senate minority leader Dirksen and House minority leader Halleck were both skeptical of the chances of passing any civil rights bill. Ike ignored their warnings, and two days later made seven recommendations to Congress: (1) obstructing court orders in school desegregation cases would be a federal offense; (2) the FBI would have added powers in bombings; (3) the attorney general would gain authority to investigate voting records; (4) the Civil Rights Commission would be extended; (5) the PCGC would win statutory status; (6) the federal government could provide some economic assistance to areas with desegregation problems; and (7) when public schools were shut down, education would be given to children from military families. The only piece that passed in 1959 was the extension of the Civil Rights Commission.[64]

While Congress was arguing over civil rights proposals, the lynching of Mack Parker sparked outrage. Parker, a twenty-three year-old African American, had been arrested in Mississippi on the charge of raping a white woman. Before he could be tried, on February 24, a mob took him from jail, shot him, and threw his body into a river. No one was ever prosecuted.[65]

The president deplored the murder, and Nixon was shocked at "such barbarous behavior." Even though the vice president was appalled, he did not see more legislation as a solution. Mississippi already had an antilynching law. Nixon insisted that the nation was moving forward despite this incident, and "the battle for equal rights . . . represents a long, slow struggle." He would continue to strive for "our ideal of equal opportunity for all of our citizens."[66]

By late in Eisenhower's second term, the consensus on civil rights had changed: it had evolved from a legislative and judicial issue into a moral one. After Nixon spoke at Harvard Business School on September 6, 1958, Lon Fuller, a professor at the law school who had taught Nixon at Duke, invited his former pupil to meet with his colleagues. Some two-thirds of the faculty participated in a two-hour question-and-answer session that afternoon at the law school. One guest repeated the president's remark that racial discrimination should be treated solely as a legal issue and not a moral one, and asked for Nixon's response. The vice president defended Ike, saying he believed, as Nixon himself did, that racial discrimination was both a moral and legal problem.[67]

At a White House press conference July 8, 1959, William White of the *New York Times* asked Eisenhower to respond to Martin Luther King's statement that the president had "never made a statement morally condemning segregation." Did the president, White asked, believe "racial segregation" was "morally wrong?" Ike limited his answer to local laws, excluded personal choice, and said that any interference "with the citizen's equality of opportunity in both the economic and the political fields . . . to that extent, that is morally wrong." Upon hearing Ike's reply, King said: "The President's brief remarks are encouraging. We hope he will continue to make his position clear." Clarence Mitchell of the NAACP said that while King might be comforted, the president had not gotten any legislation through that congressional session.[68]

Segregation once again faced the national spotlight in the winter of 1960. On February 1, four black students from North Carolina Agricultural and Technical College went into F.W. Woolworth's in downtown Greensboro, purchased some items, went to the segregated lunch counter, sat down, and ordered coffee. After being refused service, they stayed in their seats until the store closed. Although sit-in demonstrations had been tried elsewhere, the Greensboro protest started a mass movement that spread to thirty-one cities across eight southern states.[69]

As the national media focused on the sit-ins, a reporter at a White House press conference asked the president to comment on these protests. He replied: "I am deeply sympathetic with the efforts of any group to enjoy the rights of equality that are guaranteed by the Constitution." In April, a reporter asked former president Truman the same question. Truman answered that communists had organized the sit-ins. While businesses should serve all customers, he opposed demonstrators "shutting up a man's place of business" (ignoring the fact that the demonstrators were not doing this) and said that if it were his store, he would "throw . . . out" any demonstrators who entered. Martin Luther King felt that Truman's remarks encouraged white supremacists and illustrated "the indignities and injustices that Negroes are facing." On June 12, a reporter asked Truman if he regretted his statement. He did not.[70]

Eisenhower pressed for another civil rights bill early in 1960, calling for the new legislation during his State of the Union Message in January. His request generated no immediate action, and in the middle of the month a large group of African Americans from across the nation threatened to descend upon the capital to lobby for a strong civil rights bill.[71]

The vice president defended the administration's position. The president, Nixon affirmed, had "made some progress without going to extremes." Though school integration was moving slowly, the Civil Rights Commission had acted positively. Nixon conceded that no law would solve the issue in one, two, or five years. Legislation was not the solution. Young people nationwide would have to find the answer, and the movement toward racial harmony would take patience and goodwill.[72]

At a White House meeting with Republican legislative leaders on February 2, Attorney General Rogers presented the administration's plan. The Civil Rights Commission had recommended that the president appoint federal registrars to enforce the voting rights of minorities. This might be unconstitutional, Rogers suggested, and if it were not, it would overburden the president. So he proposed instead that the federal courts designate referees who would see that voting privileges were protected.[73]

The referee bill easily passed the House of Representatives. The southern bloc in the Senate, however, had stiffened its opposition since the military intervention in Little Rock. Herman Talmadge from Georgia stated the obvious: "the South had gotten the message loud and clear": the president intended to enforce civil rights laws, and any new legislation had to be seen in that light. The leader of the southern bloc, Senator Russell, organized an effective filibuster. Majority leader Lyndon Johnson held round-the-clock sessions in the upper chamber, with army cots brought in so that senators could readily respond to quorum calls. When the opposition held a cloture vote on March 10, it needed sixty-seven votes to prevail. The tally was forty-two (thirty Democrats and twelve Republicans) to end the debate while fifty-three (thirty-three Democrats and twenty Republicans) voted against ending the filibuster. The debate continued.[74]

In the middle of the month, Ike called for moderation, but the South stood firm. To end the filibuster, the bill was weakened, and the Senate passed it on April 8 by a vote of seventy-one to eighteen—again, the Democratic senators from nine states of the Old Confederacy stood in unanimous opposition. Political scientist Jack Peltason was skeptical: the law assigned overworked federal district judges the duty to force southerners to enroll black voters. Since these judges lived in southern communities and did not wish to be accused of being integrationists, there was little likelihood of strict enforcement.[75]

When the president signed the bill into law on May 6, many civil rights supporters complained. Federal referees ended up enrolling minute numbers of African American voters, and the sections to prevent obstruction of court orders, bombings, threats of bombings, and mob violence were widely ignored. Federal funds were also allocated to a small number of children from military families for education when public schools in their neighborhoods were closed.[76]

That was Eisenhower's last piece of civil rights legislation. In his final State of the Union Address, on January 12, 1961, he declared: "This pioneering work in civil rights must go on. Not only because discrimination is morally wrong, but also because its impact is more than national—it is world-wide."[77]

In the spring of 1960, Nixon told Arthur Krock that "the President alone can exercise the essential moral leadership against racial discrimination and should do so." In later years, Nixon exaggerated the differences between himself and the president: "I was lonely in arguing for voting rights. Eisenhower was very conservative about that. But I said that eighty percent of the world is nonwhite, and we had to think of what we did here in terms of its impact abroad."[78]

Since the end of Eisenhower's presidency, his civil rights actions and those of his predecessor have often been compared, almost always to Truman's advantage. Journalist Robert Shogun, on his book jacket, proclaimed: "Truman became the first president to make racial injustice a political priority—and the first to denounce segregation as well as discrimination." Michael Gardner asserted that Truman's greatest contribution might have been "his crusade to make civil rights equality a reality in America." Such laudatory testimonials were not applied to Ike. Stephen Ambrose, Taylor Branch, and Robert Caro labeled him at best a bystander and, at worst, antiblack. Ambrose, more than any other author, popularized the idea that Ike's greatest failure was his civil rights policies; rigorous scholarship from Michael Mayer, David Nichols, and Timothy Thurber has corrected Ambrose's fabrications for the record, but too seldom in the public mind.[79]

Truman's post-presidency paints a mixed picture. He did not speak out in support of Eisenhower's troop deployment during the Little Rock crisis, but he did criticize Governor Faubus in the *Kansas City Times* for trying to block the enforcement of the *Brown* decision, "which extends equal educational privileges as well as civic and economic rights to every member of our population, regardless of race, creed, or color, and that has been the law since 1868. It's about time we began to enforce it." A month later, he publicly praised the nation for its civil rights gains. In 1959, he gave an interview in *Ebony* where he called for everyone to be treated equally. On September 9, 1963, while visiting his daughter, Margaret Truman Daniel, in New York City, the former president told reporters that Governor George Wallace of Alabama was "making an ass of himself" with his stand against public school integration. Wallace, Truman said, should "be enforcing the laws, rather than trying to use his office to break them."[80]

Other civil rights measures that Truman took and did not take are less well known. Eisenhower is routinely attacked for not using his bully pulpit in support of the *Brown* decision, but Truman too did not use his platform to praise the decision. As the lunch-counter sit-ins intensified during the spring of 1960, the former president opposed this civil disobedience and stated that he would throw out anyone who stopped his business: "The Negro should behave himself and show he's a good citizen." From the outtakes of the films in preparation for his television memoirs, probably in the fall of 1961 and 1963–1964, and at the height of civil rights marches and violence, according to Truman archivist Ray Geselbracht, the former president slipped into the occasional use of "niggers" in material that was excluded from the televised programs. On three separate occasions during the filming, he used derogatory terms for African Americans when talking about the Civil War, and noted at one point, without any great show of disapproval, that his ancestors had owned five or six slaves per household and regularly gave them as wedding presents. He also offered the opinion that southerners who opposed integration were not bigots. Blacks who moved north, he continued, were not treated well and wished they had never left the South. On March 23, 1965, in his hometown of Independence, Missouri, Truman said the civil rights march from Selma to Montgomery, Alabama, where the police attacked 600 marchers (the media described the event as "Bloody Sunday"), was "silly." The marchers would not "accomplish a darned thing. . . . All they want is to attract attention."[81]

Eisenhower, who did not use epithets to describe black people and was never so dismissive of the civil rights protests, is nonetheless thought to have had a more negative attitude toward African Americans. In 1964, the African American journalist Simeon Booker wrote that while Ike had taken some positive measures—desegregated the capital, brought a few blacks into high posts, and sent troops to Little Rock, these were isolated events in an administration that, because of its unconcern, had "slipped into disfavor with my people." Twenty years later, Richard Rovere complained that Ike never expressed any support for *Brown* and, because of the decision, called Earl Warren his worst appointment. "If not hostile" to civil rights, Rovere wrote, Ike "was strictly neutral and never uttered a word of moral support." (Rovere, by the way, did not give a source for the remark about Warren; he may have gotten it from Ambrose's book, or possibly from the same source as Ambrose.)[82]

Ike consistently favored equality in all federal facilities, but his social views would be controversial today. He objected to the idea of a black man courting his hypothetical daughter (Ike did not have a daughter). Like the overwhelming majority of Americans in the 1950s, he disapproved of interracial marriage. Writing to a sister-in-law, Lucy Eisenhower, on May 6, 1960, he reported that he had talked to some of his southern friends about the sit-ins, "often in a tone of amusement—at other times, resentment." Most of them, he wrote, believed that the United States "must make some progress toward achieving political and economic equality among all individuals regardless of race. The trouble is that too often the possibility of an undesirable social mingling creeps into the thinking or fears of the individuals affected, and so the matter is distorted."[83]

During his presidency and post-presidency, he was regularly accused of not using his bully pulpit to support desegregation. It is not clear how much difference this would have made. George Edwards III, a political scientist who specializes on this topic, writes that no one has presented any evidence for the president's persuasive power: "There is not a single systematic study that demonstrates that presidents can reliably move others to support them."[84]

Still, Eisenhower's critics felt he had an obligation to use the power of the White House for moral suasion. An account by James Reston of the *New York Times* is typical. Reston attended the press conference on March 17, 1960, at which the president addressed the sit-ins. According to Reston, Ike refused to comment on the *Brown* case and "dealt with legalities and not the moralities." Ike supported peaceful protest and deplored violence, implying that blacks had the right to eat in public places, but not in privately owned ones. Reston thought Eisenhower had a duty to speak out for equality but did not because he was a conservative who favored the status quo. The journalist criticized Ike that almost a hundred years after the Civil War, he would not discuss "the Negro trying to eat a hamburger next to a white man." Whoever won the next presidential election, he wrote, would need "to use all his powers to meet the problems of the Sixties."[85]

Ike remained active for six years after leaving office, and in that time he often spoke out on behalf of civil rights. Early in December 1962, he told the press that "the country's racial problems must be solved by evolutionary processes rather than by force." He also supported the civil rights measures that Lyndon Johnson passed.[86]

Dolores and John Moaney remained an integral part of the Eisenhower family. Before leaving for a vacation in Wisconsin during the summer of 1964, he informed his host, Howard Young: "For some years, Mamie and I have scarcely been separated from them." When the president died at the end of March 1969, John Moaney, though too sick to attend the funeral, was named an honorary pallbearer. John survived for another nine years and continued to work for Mamie. Dolores remained with her until Mamie passed away in 1979. According to the president's grandson, David Eisenhower, the Moaneys loved the Eisenhowers, and the Eisenhowers reciprocated. During family gatherings, Dolores sat to the right of Ike's son John, a place of honor. She died at ninety-seven in the fall of 2014.[87]

THE IMPLOSION

Dwight Eisenhower's reelection landslide was a personal victory. He was the first president since Zachary Taylor, in 1848, to win the presidency without carrying either house of Congress. The Democratic majority in the House was twenty-nine and in the Senate only two. Yet Ike, who had spent a career cajoling and convincing strong personalities, did not seem disturbed by the harsh reality that Republicans had lost control of Congress. He was confident in his bureaucratic skills and unaware of why they did not transfer well to partisan politics.

Nixon understood politics and recognized the difficulties the Republicans confronted. Winners and losers in 1956 thanked him for his efforts on their behalf. Senator James Duff from Pennsylvania lost his reelection bid by 17,000 votes out of 4,500,000 cast, but congratulated Nixon "as the standby helmsman, and meanwhile the steadfast and willing co-worker with the President in all matters pertaining to that high office." Congressman Cliff Young in Nevada was defeated because "there were arrayed against us just too many dollars, too many Democrats, and too many newspapers." Joseph Carrigg from Pennsylvania appreciated the vice president's stop in Scranton: "this was the final 'shot-in-the-arm' that carried us through to a complete victory."[1]

Harold Stassen disputed the vice president's contribution. In January 1957, appearing on the ABC television network's *College News Conference*, Stassen blamed Nixon for Republican congressional losses, thus renewing the divisive tone he had sounded the preceding summer.[2]

Early in the spring, the Gallup Poll found a liberal-conservative split within the GOP. The president had added to the factionalism on election eve when he referred to "modern Republicanism," a phrase that many traditional partisans feared signaled a fundamental change in the party's principles. Ike disagreed.

He believed he was as conservative as Knowland: both emphasized private enterprise, sound fiscal policy to fight inflation, and limited expansion of the federal government. Both were anticommunists and internationalists who supported private capital abroad and multilateral assistance when needed.[3]

The president seldom confronted those who disapproved of his political objectives. Some GOP partisans feared that he wanted to alter the party's philosophy to match his own. Others acted independently, following a wide range of personalities who, in the wake of Joe McCarthy, zealously championed a crusade against communism.[4]

The vice president, far more than the president, recognized that the Republican Party needed to expand its base. If Republicans were to recapture Congress in 1958, they had to reverse their declining membership at the local and state levels. They had to appeal to women, college students, and minorities. In addition, the vice president cautioned, "If we want to avoid a shellacking in 1958 we had better see to it that the campaign to discredit the Republican Administration does not succeed."[5]

On June 6, 1957, Nixon reviewed the political landscape in a talk before the First National Conference of the Republican Party. If the phrase "modern Republicanism" divided the party, he opposed it. If it meant that Republicans were best suited to manage the nation's problems, if it embraced a wide variety of views, and if it appealed to younger voters, minorities, independents and disenchanted Democrats, then he approved. He admitted that the administration had made mistakes; but despite this, the president had done an outstanding job, and he needed a Republican Congress to continue his leadership. Nixon urged his listeners to employ the GOP themes of peace and prosperity over the last four and a half years, to unite behind a single candidate as quickly as possible, to raise money immediately, to bring the divergent factions together, and to enlarge the party's base.[6]

The first test of these principles came in the special senatorial election to fill the seat vacated by Joe McCarthy's death. Wisconsin Republicans did not heed Nixon's advice, and on August 28, 1957, Governor Walter Kohler, whom the McCarthyites refused to back, lost by 123,054 votes to Democrat William Proxmire. The vice president hoped "that the Wisconsin results will shock some of our dissident groups in other states into getting together."[7] After that loss, the president instructed Republican National Committee (RNC) chairman Meade Alcorn to consult with Nixon, saying he had "a remarkably clear conception of what is necessary if we are to avoid future Wisconsins." Ike recognized the vice president's political acumen, but he did not understand how to take advantage of it.[8]

The events in Little Rock, for example, severely damaged Republican efforts to build the party in the South. Many Republicans, especially those in the Deep South, were appalled that the president had sent federal troops to Arkansas. E.O. Spencer, RNC committeeman for Mississippi, announced his resignation from the party on October 2, and others also quit.[9]

Republicans hoped to rebound in the New Jersey gubernatorial contest, which featured the heavily favored incumbent Robert Meyer against multimillion-aire state senator Malcolm Forbes. The president did not go to New Jersey but called upon Republicans there to unite and organize for the upcoming race. The vice president, on October 23, barnstormed through seven counties with Forbes calling for an upset. Meyer won, but his slim margin, only 203,000 votes, gave Republicans hope that they would do better in the upcoming elections.[10]

After the election, the New York Times analyzed African American voting for New Jersey governor and for New York City mayor. Blacks voted overwhelmingly for the Democrats. Incumbent mayor Robert Wagner received approximately three quarters of the black vote, as he had in 1953, while Ike won more than a third in 1956. In New Jersey, the president garnered close to 40 percent. A year later, Governor Meyer won more than two thirds of the black vote.[11]

Nixon, on November 21, expressed his exasperation. Compared to their differences with Democrats, the differences within the GOP were minor. Republican bickering in Wisconsin and New Jersey over their choices of candidates undermined voters' confidence and paved "the way for victory of out-and-out CIO–New Deal candidates." Nixon supported every Republican office seeker, liberal or conservative, because unless both parties had room for diversity, the United States would come to resemble Europe, with its chaos of multiple political parties. "We must either close ranks and support all Republican candidates, or just settle back and let the ADA-CIO crowd take over."[12]

The vice president paid special attention to his home state of California. In 1958, California Democrats had a three to two majority in voter registration, and the California Democratic Council was growing in size and organization. Democrats had gained in local and statewide contests in 1956, while Republicans had lost strength. Congressman Claire Engle was preparing to run for the Senate against the incumbent Senator Knowland, and Attorney General Edmund "Pat" Brown was considering filing for the governor's race against the popular incumbent Goodwin "Goodie" Knight.[13] The political calculus changed abruptly in late January 1957, when Knowland announced that he was leaving the Senate. By spring, rumors were circulating that he would challenge Knight in the Republican primary. The senator did not mention that Knight had angered him during the selection for delegates to the Republican national convention, and

Knowland's personal animus toward Knight influenced his decision to run against him.[14]

Knight initially did not see Knowland as a threat, and in February he urged his loyalists to nominate the best possible candidate. A month later, when reporters asked the governor if he wished to run for Knowland's Senate seat, he denied any interest. At the end of March, Knight claimed that he and the senator had "friendly" relations and that if Knowland entered the primary against him, it would severely damage party unity. To make his position clear, Knight declared his intention to run for reelection on August 19.[15]

Since the Democratic Senate had a single vote majority, the vice president's vote might be necessary to break a tie vote. He therefore could not leave the capital and watched the evolving California political situation from afar. Neither Knight nor Knowland sought Nixon's advice, but the vice president knew that the senator was "determined to run for Governor." He counseled his supporters to remain neutral, and he himself took a "'wait and see' attitude."[16]

Nixon had many followers in California who kept him apprised of the political climate. From the northern part of the state, long-time advocate Harry Hancock wrote him in early March to say that any friction between Knowland and Knight "would not only wreck the party in California, but send a Democratic governor to Sacramento where we have already nearly lost the legislature." Hancock worried that Knowland hoped to use the governor's mansion as a stepping-stone to the 1960 presidential nomination, which would hurt Nixon's prospects.[17]

Knowland selected the "right-to-work" or open shop initiative that had been placed on California's ballot as Proposition 18 as his main campaign issue. A Gallup Poll on August 9 found almost three quarters of respondents favored right-to-work, while only 18 percent opposed. Union members had a different reaction: 52 percent agreed with right-to-work and 41 percent disagreed. Most labor leaders were Democrats and vigorously encouraged their members to vote Democratic. Governor Knight, who sought support from labor, pledged to veto any bill containing a right-to-work provision, and other Republicans supported the governor because they thought the issue hurt the GOP.[18]

Nixon understood that Knowland would create a charged political atmosphere in the state. He believed the senator had underestimated his opponent and would face "a much tougher fight than he and some of his close friends had expected." Still the senator was undoubtedly committed to defeating Knight, and Nixon thought that "no amount of persuasion or pressure for him to change his course will have any effect."[19]

Knowland returned to California pledging to sign "a fair and equitable [right-to-work] law if he became governor." He put labor bosses on notice that they

would not intimidate him, and by making that unconditional statement, he rallied conservatives to his cause. At the same time, he lost the union and pro-labor
vote. After a week of speaking engagements, Knowland's supporters worried that
he was hitting too hard on the right-to-work issue. The senator seemed to be
moving toward an announcement that he would run for governor, but as *San
Francisco Examiner* reporter Clint Mosher observed: "Audiences listened attentively to a dull speech, day after day, and applauded very politely at the end."
Mosher thought that Knowland would have to mount a much better primary
campaign. No one had made press arrangements, and only twelve California
newsmen followed his appearances. No accommodations were made for the
journalists, who had to improvise "by renting Hertz U-Drive cars, making own
plane connections and hotel reservations." Mosher concluded: "All the arrangements for the tour were just terrible."[20]

Knowland and Knight became openly hostile toward each other. The senator criticized the governor's liberal record, and Knight attacked Knowland as
planning to use the governor's mansion as a bridge to the presidency. He pledged
to back Nixon for the 1960 presidential nomination. Mosher watched both men
carefully. At first, they exhibited a "jovial attitude," but a later meeting "was quite
tense and the amenities were barely civil throughout."[21]

After Knowland announced for governor on October 3, an early poll had him
favored over Knight by a two to one margin. The junior senator from California, Thomas Kuchel, endorsed Knowland, as did the *Los Angeles Times* and
many prominent GOP politicians. These early signs encouraged conservatives
to raise money for the senator, while funds for the governor were scarce. Nixon
told his supporters to make their choice independent of how those decisions
might affect his future political aspirations. By the end of the month, Knowland's
expectations were rising.[22]

To prevent a serious fracture within the California GOP, Nixon encouraged
Clint Mosher to have Knight abandon his reelection effort and instead run for
Knowland's Senate seat. The vice president also persuaded Kyle Palmer, the influential political editor of the *Los Angeles Times* and a Nixon loyalist, to join in
the lobbying. On October 29, Nixon recognized that "the California political
pot is certainly boiling." The temperature rose still further the next day, when
Democrat Edmund "Pat" Brown announced for the governor's race. On the last
day of the month, newspaper stories circulated that Nixon was pressuring Knight
to run for the Senate, and those close to the governor were confirming that
Knight would comply.[23]

Knight traveled to Phoenix on November 1 to plan his next move. Mosher
had learned that the governor had made an appointment to see the president,

and Ike telephoned Nixon about the upcoming meeting. The president said that he had to be "very cagy" with the governor because he "would go out and repeat everything." Nixon hoped that by the time of the visit, the other Republican candidates would have dropped out of the primaries and "the President could be freer" to endorse Knowland and Knight.[24]

Knight saw the president on November 5 and told him that he had decided to withdraw from the gubernatorial race and run for the Senate. Ike replied that he could not endorse Knight because San Francisco mayor George Christopher had not bowed out of the senatorial primary.[25]

After this meeting, Knight released a statement in Washington and Sacramento saying he had withdrawn from the governor's race to avoid a "bitter intraparty struggle." Nixon applauded this decision, declaring it was "in the best interests of the Republican party and the people of the state of California." The vice president endorsed Knight's senatorial candidacy, adding that the Knowland-Knight combination would be the strongest GOP ticket to defeat the Democrats. The governor praised the president and vice president but made no comment about Knowland, who was equally frigid and refused to endorse Knight for the Senate.[26]

The move was quickly labeled the "Big Switch." Nixon considered it the best possible solution to the increasingly bloody political struggle and hoped "that after the original reactions simmer down he [Knight] will get the necessary support for the nomination and should be strong enough to win in November unless there is a national swing against all Republicans." Knowland congratulated Nixon on December 6 on how well he had "handled this delicate situation." Republicans, he said, "were at a low point," but for him and Knight to triumph, the GOP had "to get off the defensive and on the offensive on this military situation."[27]

Democrats, having already won in Wisconsin and New Jersey, were encouraged by the chaos among the California Republicans. They saw these political events as well as the recession, the launch of Sputnik by the Soviet Union, and other setbacks for the Eisenhower administration as the prelude to a sweeping triumph in the 1958 elections. In addition, during off-year elections, the party holding the White House traditionally lost ground in federal, state, and local contests.

Adlai Stevenson now talked about the "Eisenhower-Nixon Administration." In a January 1958 piece in the New Republic entitled "Beware the Tender Trap," Margaret Halsey postulated: "What is actually involved, in the tender trap about a 'new' Nixon, is an attempt to debase the moral currency." She sent Stevenson a copy, which only reinforced his loathing of the vice president.[28]

Four months after its publication, vice-presidential aide Charles McWhorter had lunch with Selig Harrison, a friend from Harvard University and assistant editor at the *New Republic,* who described the piece as in "questionable taste." It was "an experiment in increasing circulation and was not intended to set off any irrational and hysterical attack on" Nixon. The magazine had a subscriber base of 33,000 and had been looking for a way to increase it in advance of elections. It had mailed out 100,000 circulars and received an "unprecedented" response of 8,000 or 9,000. The attack on the vice president brought in business.[29]

Harry Truman continued his assault: "Our Party is ready to go on the offensive in this election year and abandon a previous tendency to let our opponents talk a better game, when we have a record and program which is far superior to theirs." Truman refused to attend any events where the vice president was present: "I will not sit at the same table with Nixon. He has never refuted his statement that I was a traitor; but even if he did, my feelings about him would remain the same. . . . I cannot sit with that fellow."[30]

Eisenhower dismissed these as partisan attacks and thought the Democrats were going to make the economic downturn and foreign policy major campaign topics. Despite his vulnerabilities, he defended his policies. Consumer spending and housing construction had risen recently, indicating that the recession was ending. By the end of February, he was in "better spirits" and was growing optimistic about a Republican victory in the fall.[31]

Ike also thought the Democrats might try to make his health a campaign issue, but he told a press conference in the spring that he was "going to perform the duty [as president] as long as I think I am capable of doing it." Nationally, he believed that businessmen were not contributing enough money to GOP candidates, and they needed to stop complaining about the party's dismal prospects and had to raise funds. Republicans had to unite: solidarity was key. To avoid divisiveness, he maintained his rigid policy against endorsing anyone in the Republican primaries.[32]

By this time, Nixon had evolved into one of Ike's closest political counselors. He scrutinized trends and received letters and telephone calls from across the nation. Some described bleak Republican fundraising efforts; others talked about negativity within GOP circles. The president, however, was not always easy to counsel. Nixon's friend Charles Thomas, the secretary of the Navy, had a conference with Ike in November 1957 regarding Republican criticism of the president "for lack of leadership, too much golf, etc. The President got quite angry about this."[33]

The vice president followed California politics especially closely. In December 1957, shortly after the Big Switch, actor and future United States senator

George Murphy went to Governor Knight's sold-out birthday party. Nixon's telegram to the governor was read aloud and "was a tremendous hit," according to the actor. Other leading politicians, including Knowland, did not have "the good grace (or good judgment) to send messages." Junior senator Kuchel also failed to congratulate Knight. Nixon commented: "what an ungrateful dummy!"[34]

Knowland said that the California situation was "fine." He remained in the capital as the Senate minority leader and spent only fourteen days in California during the primary campaign. He continued to highlight the right-to-work cause while labor galvanized its forces against him. Knight, by opposing the right-to-work campaign, lent respectability to Knowland's adversaries. San Francisco political reporter Earl "Squire" Behrens recalled telling Knowland that the open shop was doomed, but he refused to listen. Behrens felt that the senator "got very stodgy and pontificated too much all the time, and he had one speech that he used all the time, and he didn't have the enthusiasm of the people."[35]

Nixon was aware of corruption in labor unions as a campaign issue, but he could not "accept the view that the union movement as a whole should be condemned." He favored legislation that corrected "the abuses, but not to weaken and destroy the institution itself." In a letter to Walter Reuther, president of the United Automobile Workers, the vice president wrote that unions needed to eliminate corruption in their organizations and to provide congressional committees with answers on how they would accomplish this result. If their suggestions were inadequate, the federal government would "have to consider legislation to protect the democratic rights of union members."[36]

To avoid exacerbating the frictions within the party, Nixon intended to "steer clear of California as much as possible." But he wanted to see firsthand how the right-to-work initiative was proceeding and how Knowland and Knight were campaigning, so he visited Los Angeles. On a rainy Tuesday, February 19, he answered questions at the Greater Los Angeles Press Club. Responding to a question about the right-to-work proposition, he stressed that this was a state matter, not a federal affair. He expected to campaign for both Knowland and Knight because California was crucial for Republicans to win. As "a minority party," he said, the GOP had to unite: "you can't afford the luxury of fighting members of your own party."[37]

The Democratic candidate for governor, Pat Brown, was gaining momentum. He had the advantage, as attorney general, of being the sole Democrat elected to statewide office. Brown had announced for governor in October 1957 and received the California Democratic Council's endorsement in January. Rather than run as a liberal and provide ideological ammunition for Knowland to use against him, he presented himself as a moderate and a "nice guy."[38]

The GOP primary results on June 3 were disappointing. Knowland received approximately 1.6 million votes for governor, while Brown garnered about 2.2 million from Democrats; in the Senate race, Knight received 1.2 million and Christopher 800,000, while Claire Engle, the Democrat, won 1.7 million. The two Republicans faced an almost insurmountable uphill struggle if they were to have any possibility of winning in the general election.[39]

On July 1, Harold Lutz, one of Nixon's earliest supporters in Whittier, dejectedly wrote: "I have never seen the Republicans so low since the depression or as irritable and confused as when Truman was in office, and if this continues it will be difficult to house the various candidates in a Republican Headquarters." He saw only one solution: "Obviously something drastic has to be done to shake up our own people if we are going to mount the kind of a campaign necessary to win."[40]

While the GOP faced its dismal electoral prospects, the president concentrated on troubles in the Middle East. The administration promulgated the Eisenhower Doctrine, which pledged assistance to Middle Eastern governments threatened by international communism. The pro-Western Lebanese president, Camille Chamoun, hinted in the spring of 1958 that he might invite American troops into his nation to prevent a communist revolt. He did not mention to the Eisenhower administration that this might provoke a civil war, or that he needed a martial presence to stay in power.[41]

When military leaders in Iraq staged a successful revolt on July 14 and assassinated the royal family, Chamoun asked the United States to invoke the Eisenhower Doctrine. Ike assembled an informal group of advisers to consider whether or not to dispatch American soldiers. He listened to their conflicting advice regarding possible Soviet responses, then sat back and asked Secretary Dulles: "Let us assume our intelligence is wrong. Are you prepared to take the next step?" Dulles replied that he was 90 percent certain that Moscow would not act aggressively, but even if that happened, "we should be prepared to take the next step." Nixon, in his memoirs, commented that once Eisenhower had made the decision to send Marines even if the intelligence proved inaccurate, the United States had to be victorious. To guarantee this, he employed excessive military might. The United States had to "be prepared to carry out the operation to a successful conclusion."[42]

The president, for the only time in his tenure, dispatched troops to the Middle East. He relied on Secretary Dulles for advice on the likely Soviet response and on conditions in Lebanon. Nixon, because he had visited North Africa in the spring of 1957, was asked to provide his firsthand knowledge of the region and its actors. He also gave advice on how to present the decision to send troops to

Congress, the media, and the American people. He suggested that the president brief congressional leaders after the troops landed, which he did the afternoon of July 14. The next day, the vice president also recommended that Ike release a press statement stressing the right of self-determination, and the president, after discussing the idea with Secretary Dulles, accepted that proposition. Nixon further recommended that the seasoned diplomat Robert Murphy be sent to Beirut as a special envoy to monitor conditions. The secretary called Murphy about the mission and talked it over with the president, and in a short time the diplomat was on an airplane to the Lebanese capital.[43]

The vice president spoke on July 19 about why Ike had ordered troops. He had done it, Nixon said, to strengthen the existing government and to protect the 2,500 Americans living there. In this case, the United States acted in accordance with Article 51 of the United Nations Charter, which involved the right of collective security. The move demonstrated "that when the chips were down, even though there were the risks of war, we would stand by our friends." The administration, he said, identified with movements for independence. "One objective must be to convince people everywhere that the United States and those with whom we are associated are the protagonists of the real, the true revolution, rather than the Soviet Union."[44]

Seven months after leaving the vice presidency, Nixon recorded that the Lebanon episode was "one of the most striking successes of any American political-military venture since World War II." The president was "prepared for bad luck if it came," but the United States had the benefit of good intelligence. The armed forces moved effectively; not a drop of Lebanese blood was spilled; only one American soldier died; and Robert Murphy had skillfully resolved the internal political conflict in Lebanon.[45]

While the president was focusing on the Middle East, the fall elections were approaching. Various Gallup Polls indicated that Republicans would suffer serious losses. Late in August, Ike insisted: "Knowland *must* win." California would soon become the most populous state in the nation. If the Democrats took both the governorship and the legislature, they would reapportion congressional districts to their advantage, and then try to duplicate that result in Oregon and Washington. Ike knew that many Republicans were disillusioned, but he still expected to travel to California to endorse the Republican slate. When he learned that the Hearst newspapers planned to back Brown for governor, he asked Meade Alcorn to try to dissuade them.[46]

The president knew that some considered Knowland "a bit of a bull in a china shop"; he admitted that he did not always agree with the senator. At the same time, he thought Knowland "would make an excellent Governor." He was "impeccably honest, courageous, studious and serious, and he is physically strong and tireless." Ike went so far as to ask his financial supporters to raise money if they thought Knowland had any chance of winning.[47]

But his support had limits. Before the end of September, Ike told Knowland and the press that billboards in California claiming that both he and Nixon backed the right-to-work proposition had to be taken down. The administration had consistently held that those laws applied to each state and were not federal concerns. The president and the vice president would neither endorse nor oppose the proposition.[48]

Ike and Nixon spoke about the upcoming races after Congress adjourned on August 23. Ike thought Republicans could win, but Nixon was far less sanguine. Despite his pessimism, he prepared to work energetically for GOP candidates and informed his staff on September 19 that no one would get any vacation time. "Everyone should be prepared for extra and evening work at any time next week." He refused to accept defeatist attitudes: Republicans, he said, "should be out working night and day to at least minimize the losses if they hope to salvage anything in 1960."[49]

Even with dozens of requests from many states for appearances, Nixon paid special attention to his home state. Knowland was in trouble and needed to overhaul his campaign and raise a substantial amount of money. Unions were already spending considerable sums against him and against the right-to-work initiative. To upset Brown, the vice president advised, Knowland had to push the Democrat from the center and move himself there. He had to portray Brown as a left-winger. If he did not, "he will be a dead duck." Nixon wondered "how things would have been if Knight were running for Governor and Knowland for Senator! But I guess all we can do is to work and hope for the best."[50]

From the primary election through September, the vice president received detailed information on the chaotic conditions. Reporter Carl Greenberg told Rose Mary Woods on July 22 that Knowland belonged "in an oxygen tent with day and night nurses with recovery chances just slim." Knight might win as the underdog, Greenberg thought, but many people were angry that he dropped out of the governor's race. Clint Mosher told the vice president that since early August, Brown had been climbing in the polls while Knowland slipped. Squire Behrens pointed out the obvious: "The GOP is in a hell of a mess."[51]

Adding to the misery index for the GOP was a corruption scandal in the White House. That summer a House subcommittee learned that Sherman Adams, Ike's chief of staff, had accepted such gifts as a vicuña coat, an Oriental rug, and the payment of approximately $3,000 worth of hotel bills from a New England millionaire, Bernard Goldfine. The committee accused Adams of influence peddling. The chief of staff appeared before the committee, admitted that he had accepted gifts, but adamantly denied granting any favors in return.[52]

At first, the president vigorously defended his subordinate, who he said exemplified the highest code of conduct. When Republican leaders hinted that Adams was damaging the party's chances in November, Ike rose to Adams's defense: "here was a man who was absolutely honest, who had never taken one action in government as a result of an improper influence, that there was a tremendous difference between a gift and a bribe, and that no one should be stampeded for one instant to even imply that this man was other than honest."[53]

Within days of his testimony, however, the press was publishing sensational articles about Adams's transgressions. Nixon heard from the Republican faithful, who pictured Adams as another weapon for Democrats to use against the GOP in the campaign. He had added corruption to the party's troubles and needed to resign. When the press asked about Adams, the vice president answered that any decision rested with the president. Most federal officials were honest, and he did not believe that the Goldfine-Adams linkage would damage Republicans at the polls. Adams had received gifts, but the ultimate test was whether he had granted favors in return. Nixon believed he had not.[54]

On July 7, the president met with Republican senator John Williams of Delaware to discuss Adams. The senator held that the chief of staff "went beyond the line of propriety in this instance," and if he remained at his post, the administration would be seen as condoning corruption. The president once more rose to Adams' defense: he refused to "be a party to crucifying the Governor for political reasons." He condemned Goldfine for deducting the gifts to Adams from his taxes, but that was not Adams's fault. This unwavering approval eventually began to wane. The Adams affair was affecting his ability to concentrate. No matter what pressing problems came to the president's desk, "this unfortunate matter is always in the back of his mind and it has taken a lot out of him."[55]

At breakfast on the morning of July 15, Ike talked with Nixon about whether Adams should stay or go. That afternoon the vice president met with the chief of staff, telling him that the president had not taken any position, but "that the overwhelming majority of Republicans in the House and Senate believe that he should resign." If losses occurred in the fall, Adams would be blamed whether or not he was the cause. Nixon ended by saying that he and the president wanted Adams to make the decision. Adams did not submit his resignation.[56]

On August 25, Eisenhower called Nixon at the White Sulphur Springs resort, where the Nixons were vacationing. The president had decided that Adams should resign and asked that Nixon return to the capital for another talk with the former governor. Nixon took this as an order, saw Adams the next morning, and bluntly told him that Republicans were going to lose congressional seats and lay the defeat at his office. Adams disagreed. Besides, he had discussed the subject with Ike, who had changed his mind and wanted Adams to stay.[57]

After Nixon's two conversations with Adams had failed to get the desired results, the president turned to RNC chairman Meade Alcorn on September 15 to pressure Adams. Two days later, Adams telephoned the president to say he would resign, and on the evening of September 22, he went on national television to announce his resignation, while proclaiming his innocence.[58]

Robert Cutler, the NSC adviser, wrote the president four days after the resignation. Adams had behaved admirably but was "publicly drawn-and-quartered, in the best Dark-Ages style, by little fakers not worthy to tie his shoes." Cutler could not comprehend how Adams had been forced out: "Sherm is a *good* man, if ever one lived. He is the Rock of Ages, cleft for each one of us. And I have only shame and disregard for those of our Party who were so ready to cast the first stones." In the margin, Ike underlined: *agreed*."[59]

Ike telephoned Nixon on September 26, and they agreed that Adams's nationally televised speech had gone as well as expected. The president stated that while Alcorn "was working hard," he was having trouble raising money and generating enthusiasm within the GOP. Ike believed, and Nixon concurred, that the best issue Republicans had "was fiscal irresponsibility of the Democrats"; Eisenhower vigorously opposed deficit spending because it led to inflation. Nixon would leave the capital in three days for a campaign tour, and when he returned, he would report on the audience reaction to his speeches. The president also received feedback from Alcorn regarding how to "conquer defeatism in Republican ranks." Ike saw defeatism as "complacency" and knew it had to be turned into optimism.[60]

Polls throughout October favored the opposition. A day before the voting, Democrats held a 57 to 43 percent spread nationwide in congressional races. As expected, the vice president publicly disputed these figures and privately thought that these polls damaged the GOP with swing voters, who might otherwise be persuaded to vote Republican. Still, Nixon decided to make a concerted effort to assist GOP hopefuls. Some, he felt, deserved to win.[61]

Republicans faced high hurdles. The recession had left many unemployed; farmers objected to Secretary Benson's policies, especially on parity for agricultural products; and the launching of Sputnik and doubts about the strength of United States missile program diminished the president's popularity. Even though Adams had resigned, the question of corruption in the administration lingered. And within Republican circles, the struggle between conservatives and liberals caused friction.

Adlai Stevenson answered the vice president's accusations regarding his party's "radicalism" by labeling him an "intolerable demagogue." Walter Reuther pointed out that 7 percent of the work force did not have jobs, despite the fact that Republicans correctly claimed that the recession had peaked and the nation was returning to prosperity. Truman said: "The Democrats have all the issues in the campaign. The Republicans have given them to us."[62]

Nixon took off on his first swing on the afternoon of September 29. Addressing a sympathetic audience of 3,500 in Indianapolis, he said that the pundits predicted a Democratic triumph and Republicans were struggling against the current. He refused to accept defeat because "nothing was more contemptible than running from a fight when things are tough."[63] If the "radical Democrats" controlled Congress, he said, they would try to spend excessively and bring inflation; the nation could not afford such recklessness. Hubert Hill, Governor Harold Handley's press secretary, thanked Nixon for his appearance: "Your hard-hitting efforts have thrilled Hoosier Republicans, as well as the entire nation. May the sword of the Lord and Gideon continue to be wielded by your strong arms!" Handley lost his reelection bid.[64]

From Indiana, Nixon flew to California. At his first stop, in Los Angeles on October 1, he called for unity, complimented both Knowland and Knight, and tried to rally the faithful. In San Diego, he attacked the Truman administration for creating a missile gap and praised Eisenhower for rapidly closing it. The following evening, in the San Francisco Bay Area, he became a cheerleader: "We have the fight of our lives on our hands."[65]

Ten days later, with Knowland and Knight at his side in San Francisco, the vice president conceded that the Republicans were behind in the polls, but they were gaining. He flew to the southern part of the state where he tried to energize the base to vote and to raise money. Behind the scenes, he tried to patch up the differences between Knowland and Knight, but they only grew more antagonistic. While the two Republican candidates fought each other, polls for the gubernatorial race had Brown leading Knowland, 56 percent to 34.[66]

In a press conference on October 1, the president described Republican "apathy" and "complacency" as "incomprehensible." The vice president returned on the fourth with bleak forecasts. Ike could not understand why Republicans were not going to the polls. His party should have been pleased with the "remarkably good" record of his administration over five and a half years. On Monday, the sixth, Ike chaired a luncheon for GOP leaders, after which they issued a joint statement: "More today than ever before the Democrat party is dominated by certain politico-labor bosses and left-wing extremists. . . . Any future Democrat-controlled Congress would be far to the left of the New and Fair Deals."[67]

Six days later, the president made his first campaign appearance in New York City. He met with Nelson Rockefeller, who was trying to unseat the incumbent Democratic governor, Averell Harriman, and Congressman Kenneth Keating, who was running for the Senate. The president had lunch with Republican Party officials, placed a wreath on the Christopher Columbus Monument, and posed for photographs with the candidates.[68]

Back in the White House on October 13, Ike was pleased with the enthusiastic crowds that had welcomed him in Harlem, and he commented that Rockefeller "seemed fairly enthusiastic." He had committed to an appearance in Cedar Rapids, Iowa, he said, but did not intend to give a political address. He would fly on to his boyhood home in Abilene, Kansas, and then to Denver, Colorado, where he and Mamie would visit her ailing mother. From there he would journey to Los Angeles for his first major speech of the campaign. He would not "talk too much about the state situation" because he normally did not work "too hard for a state ticket." Instead he would thank Knowland for his senatorial service and concentrate on the administration's achievements. As for the right-to-work issue, he would not list his recommendations for "labor reforms" but would focus on his opposition to "racketeers." Nixon encouraged the president to highlight the rising deficit and subsequent inflation that voters should expect if the Democrats controlled Congress. Higher expenditures translated into "cheaper money," while a balanced budget kept "the family expenditures down."[69]

Ike used the RNC celebration of his sixty-eighth birthday to campaign and "try to shame the rest into going out and do likewise." The press reported that he looked "really grim" and told his listeners that the party had to unite in order to win in November.[70] The following day, he wrote Nixon that he had read some of the material for his next campaign swing and appreciated his "strenuous and effective speeches," which he thought were "excellent." Ike had received reports on Nixon's appearances, and the president believed that Nixon had "been most successful in awakening our people to the grave issues in this political campaign and the need for supporting Republicanism enthusiastically."[71]

Nixon tested various themes such as Democratic big spenders and union corruption. He characterized Democrats as "overconfident" while the underdog Republicans were gaining momentum. The recession had ended, and recovery was accelerating. He paid special attention to fundraising and endorsed local and state GOP candidates. Republicans, Nixon believed, were not the party of the rich, nor were the Democrats the party of the working class. Indeed, the GOP favored the advancement of labor. At a campaign stop in Columbus, Ohio, he reminded voters of the corruption of the Truman years, while minimizing the Adams scandal. In Huntington, West Virginia, he assured Republicans that the party would pull out a surprising victory because voters would reject radical Democrats: "If you send to Washington a Congress composed of free-wheeling, free-spending Democrats of the northern wing of the party, you'll have an inflation such as this country had never seen."[72]

Russell Baker of the New York Times followed the vice president in the opening weeks of the campaign. He had expected to see a Red-baiter who practiced "bare-knuckles campaigning" but was surprised to learn that Nixon did not talk like a demagogue. Instead, Baker saw him as "a painfully lonesome man undergoing an ordeal. . . . No matter how artificial he looked at it [campaigning], he had to keep it up, had to keep counting."[73]

In the midst of the campaign, the conflict had resurfaced between the People's Republic of China (PRC) and Nationalist China over two islands in the channel between Taiwan and the mainland, Quemoy and Matsu. Mao Tse-tung had ordered a heavy bombardment of the islands in 1954–1955 and then stopped the shelling. On August 23, 1958, the bombing resumed. Nine days earlier, the president commented that he saw no strategic value for Chiang Kai-shek to have his soldiers stationed there, and no military benefit for the PRC if it planned an attack on Taiwan. Even with this admission, the president and secretary of state believed the islands had to be defended as a matter of principle. The United States could not afford to retreat because the PRC might see that as a sign of weakness.[74]

The vice president had spoken publicly about the situation in early February, basing his position on the belief that Mao and his followers were "seeking with all the means in their power to bring the whole of Asia under their sway." The Soviets and Chinese "are tightly linked by common ideological, strategic and politico-economic aims which would not be split by U.S. trade with Red China." The United States had imposed an embargo on the PRC because the regime would benefit from trade. Mao needed capital goods and raw materials to quicken the pace of industrialization and enhance his military power. If the United States were to soften its policy, America's allies in Asia would wonder about the administration's resolve. In September, two weeks after the shelling resumed, Nixon added: "Their ruthless bombardment of the offshore islands is another in a long series of provocative acts which demonstrates the lawless character of this Communist clique." He advocated "a strong line" and referenced the domino theory. If these islands fell to the enemy, the rest of Asia would follow.[75]

Toward the end of September, a reporter found out that state department mail was running heavily against Eisenhower's decision to defend Quemoy and Matsu. When Nixon learned about the release of this material, he claimed that some official had purposefully leaked the data to sabotage the administration's position. Secretary Dulles held a press conference, declaring that the release "was unevaluated without being accompanied by any adequate explanation of the reason."[76]

A de facto cease-fire went into effect at the beginning of October. The Democratic Advisory Council (DAC), a group of twenty-four members that included Truman, Stevenson, and Acheson, proposed on October 11 that the UN resolve the conflict. Ike had been formulating foreign policy for almost six years, and his guidance, said the DAC, ended in "leaderless vacillation." As the party out of power, Democrats acted with restraint when criticizing Ike's diplomatic actions, but with the United States not at war, there was no reason to suspend "the right of free discussion."[77]

Angered by the DAC declaration, Secretary Dulles drafted a reply and called RNC chairman Alcorn for his input. Dulles also telephoned Nixon, who asked to release the statement over his name because "it would get more play that way." The next day, he denounced the DAC critique: "the Acheson foreign policy resulted in war and the Eisenhower-Dulles policy resulted in peace." Adding welcome news, the Beijing government ordered its troops to continue the cease-fire for another two weeks.[78]

Nixon's statement prompted a reporter to ask Secretary Dulles at a press conference on October 14 whether the administration was making efforts to stop the "narrow and harmful partisan" speeches that, according to Truman, were damaging bipartisanship in foreign affairs. Without divulging that he had drafted the response, Dulles stated that he had not taken any part in electioneering and hoped "that both sides would calm down on this aspect of the debate."[79]

The following morning, at the end of the White House press conference, Marvin Arrowsmith of Associated Press inquired whether the president subscribed to Nixon's statement that Acheson's diplomacy had caused the Korean War and the administration's action had brought peace. Ike replied that he deplored having foreign policy injected into "partisan debate."[80]

Campaigning in the West, Nixon was "unhappy" with the president and secretary's statements because they seemed to repudiate his answer to the DAC. He believed that Republicans must refute Democratic charges or face "inevitable defeat." Over the past two years, the administration had permitted the opposition to criticize its policies, "and we have not stood up and answered effectively." Failing to respond was "a mistake," and during the campaign he would answer Democratic accusations. The president had a different responsibility: he had to "mobilize" the country, and thus his reluctance to respond was "proper." Nixon had to energize the GOP base, and he refused to let Democrats attack "with impunity."[81]

Later that day, Secretary Dulles issued a statement that when he objected to injecting international affairs into the campaign, he was in fact referring to the DAC. The secretary hoped to keep such matters out of partisan debate, and the vice president had answered the DAC. Ike added that Nixon and Dulles had "no real difference." Both political parties subscribed to the same basic tenets: peace, the UN Charter, and opposition to communist expansion. When Democrats attacked the "administration operation," their charges sometimes needed to be answered, and as Ike wrote to Nixon, "No one can do this more effectively than you."[82]

With those endorsements, Nixon's attitude abruptly changed. In a telephone conversation, Dulles said he did not want Nixon to think he had "let him down," and that the press had "trapped" him; Nixon interjected that reporters had tried to "trap" him, too. The Republicans' "best issues" in the campaign, he said, were foreign affairs. Democrats had raised the subject, "and we would be fools if we did not go on." Dulles wanted voters to compare both parties' diplomatic records, and Nixon said that was exactly what he was trying to accomplish.[83]

By the time the PRC resumed its shelling on October 21, the story about friction between Ike, Dulles, and Nixon had disappeared. When asked how the offshore island conflict might influence the election, the vice president said it would not have "any major political effect." The United States would maintain a "firm" commitment to defend Quemoy and Matsu because dictators would take advantage of any perceived weakness. Addressing a fundraiser, he emphasized the bipartisan spirit: "There is no war party in the United States. . . . There is no party of surrender. There is only one party of treason—the Communist party."[84]

While Nixon pursued his frantic campaign schedule, Ike entered the fray, campaigning intermittently from October 17 to 28. Starting in Cedar Rapids, where a crowd of 85,000 greeted him, he attended the National Corn Picking Contest without making a partisan speech, while praising farmers for their contribution to the American economy. He then went to California where he made appearances for Knowland and Knight. Before his arrival, Nixon had told Ike that the political climate for the GOP in California looked "very bad." Knowland and Knight were "behaving like little boys—very bad boys," and Nixon was "trying to shame them out of it." For a moment, the antipathy between the two candidates made the president consider not stopping in California, but he decided to honor "his commitment."[85]

For Eisenhower's arrival in Los Angeles on Monday, October 20, an enthusiastic crowd of 75,000 lined the sidewalks. Knowland and Knight attached themselves to Ike, each competing to appear more congenial than the other. That evening the president gave an unusually partisan speech, carried on radio and television, referring to the "self-styled liberal" Democrats and their "radical" proposals. Voters had a choice: "left-wing government or sensible forward looking government." Democrats offered two factions "hopelessly split—right down the middle." Inside this division, the majority followed an extremist agenda.[86]

The following day, the president had a televised panel discussion with a group of Republican women and held another rally in San Francisco. Referring to Democrats, he urged the GOP forward in "our common fight against radicalism in America." Union leaders, he said, had mismanaged fiscal matters, and "these conditions must be fumigated." He included "a personal salute to one hard-working dynamic Vice President, your fellow Californian, Dick Nixon. He is one of our effective leaders in this fight to produce a solid Republican representation in the State government and to give us a Republican Congress." Ike had come to California, he said, to back the Republican slate. Knowland and Knight "have proved their quality and their integrity." They were superior to their Democratic rivals: "We Republicans are flatly opposed to patronizing government, domineering government, government that panders to greed rather than to need."[87]

The president flew on to Chicago, where he delivered a nationally televised address, charging that the "dominant wing" of the Democratic Party was composed of "radicals" who had "little faith" and promoted "doubt and fear." Toward the end of the month, he went to Charleston, Pittsburgh, and New York City. Writing to RNC chairman Alcorn the day before the voting, Ike suggested that GOP apathy had "largely disappeared." Although he had received reports that various Republican groups had criticized him for not beginning earlier, he said he had agreed in August to campaign in those spots that the "'pros' felt would be best." His "four full dress political speeches, with a number of informal public appearances, before audiences of varying age and types" had exceeded expectations.[88]

Ike never intended to take a leading role in mobilizing the Republican base; that task was left to Nixon. Starting a campaign swing in Chicago on October 13, the vice president told his audience that some GOP candidates were underdogs, but the returning prosperity and the administration's having kept the nation at peace were creating a shift to the Republican Party.[89] In Salt Lake City three days later, he said that the parties should stage a partisan debate over their differences. He also denounced cabinet members, other than the secretary of state, for not fulfilling their duty to campaign for Republicans. At Brigham Young University in Provo, he deplored the recent bombing at an Atlanta synagogue and pledged to "exert all of my moral and civil influence against this un-American activity."[90]

He arrived late in the evening of October 22 in New York City, where he was scheduled to give two speeches the next day. Nelson Rockefeller, the GOP candidate for governor, had made no provision to confer with the vice president, causing the media to speculate that his advisers believed Nixon might hurt his chance for victory. These rumors did not bother Nixon. He and the president had promised to back Congressman Keating if he ran for senator. On the twenty-third, Nixon gave a statewide broadcast in which he warmly praised both Keating and Rockefeller, and then attended a late dinner where he echoed these themes. Former New York governor Thomas Dewey was there, calling the address "a *tour de force* of the first magnitude." To demonstrate solidarity, Rockefeller and Nixon had a private breakfast with photographers present the next morning.[91]

Nixon also took the opportunity to release a statement attacking what he said was Stevenson's assault on the administration's failure, and Ike's lack of leadership, on civil rights. Since Stevenson was the Democrats' "titular leader," the vice president asked, what he had done to influence southern Democratic governors to integrate their public schools? What had his party done to make southern congressmen pass civil rights legislation? Republicans, on the other hand, had taken concrete steps: "we have done more in six years of this Administration than they talked of doing in the twenty years that preceded it." The administration's goals were unequivocal: "To open the full doors of opportunity to all and to assure good schooling, job opportunities and rising standards of living for all our citizens."[92]

From New York City, Nixon flew on October 24 to Madison, Wisconsin, where for the first time, hecklers badgered him from the state house steps. Nixon was unperturbed and attacked the Democrats' "radical bloc," warning if they won the election, they would be beholden to the unions and would not vote for legislation to limit their power.[93]

Nixon continued his hectic pace through Sioux Falls, South Dakota, and Lincoln, Nebraska, urging his party to turn out on Election Day. By the time he reached Minneapolis, he was fatigued, and his hay fever was bothering him. Gallup Poll predictions of a Democratic sweep and Republican disunity caused further irritation. Before he left the Twin Cities the next morning, Philip Potter of the *Baltimore Sun*, who disliked Nixon and enjoyed needling him, asked for the vice president's views on civil rights. Visibly angry, lips trembling, Nixon "blew his stack," replying that his position was well known. That evening, Nixon apologized to Potter, telling him that he had misconstrued the question "as a slight."[94]

The vice president returned to the capital where, on October 29, he and Pat voted a straight Republican ticket on an absentee ballot. Afterward, he set off on his final swing through Iowa and Kansas and then on to Montana. He ended in Seattle on Friday, October 31, where he was met by Pat and their two daughters. This was Tricia and Julie's first campaign tour, and they were permitted to skip school because their father was heading to Alaska and the children were studying the soon-to-be forty-ninth state, so this was an "educational trip."[95]

The Nixons arrived in the territorial capital of Juneau on November 1. Alaska's statehood would formally begin in January, and these were its first senatorial and congressional elections. Even though a Democratic sweep was anticipated in Alaska, the last appointed Republican governor, Mike Stepovich, had a slim chance to win a Senate seat. After Nixon spoke at the University of Alaska in Fairbanks, the family toured a museum. The vice president stood "beside a massive stuffed Alaska brown bear, upon its hind feet towering over Nixon." As photographers set up to take pictures, Pat laughed loudly: "Ha, ha, ha. Two of a kind." Angered by the remark, her husband left without a word.[96]

The Nixons landed back in Washington as voters were casting their ballots. The results were the worst possible for the GOP. Not since FDR's landslide in 1936 had Republicans elected fewer congressmen, governors, and state legislatures. Of the roughly 104,000,000 eligible citizens, 45.7 percent voted, the second-highest turnout in an off-year election since the advent of women's suffrage. The Democrats had emerged from the 1956 election with a two-vote majority in the Senate, forty-nine to forty-seven; two years later, their advantage was sixty-four to thirty-four. The races for the House in 1956 had elected 235 Democrats and 200 Republicans; in 1958, the Democratic majority jumped to 283 to 153. In 1956, Democrats elected twenty-nine governors, the GOP nineteen; the Democrats increased that number to thirty-four, and the GOP dropped to fourteen. In state legislatures, Republicans suffered a net loss of 686 seats.[97]

The Republican political disaster extended to African American voters. Even though Ike had sent troops into Little Rock, signed the Civil Rights Act of 1957, and accomplished other civil rights breakthroughs, the Gallup Poll found that only 27 percent of blacks outside of the South were registered Republicans, while a staggering 73 percent were Democrats. In the South, just 36 percent claimed to be Republicans, and 64 percent were Democrats.[98]

The returns in California lived up to expectations. Pat Brown crushed Bill Knowland by over a million votes; Engle's victory over Knight was almost as humiliating. Aylett Cotton, a Nixon supporter since his first congressional contest, wrote that the results "were pretty grim," but without Nixon's campaign effort, they would have been worse: "Knight and Knowland both asked for what they got, and it is unfortunate that the whole Republican Party had to suffer for their stupidity."[99]

The president held a press conference on November 5. At his preconference briefing, he saw the Democratic "sweep" in "devastating proportions" and noted "there are scarcely enough Republican votes to sustain a veto." He could have added that he had the distinction of being the first president to lose three successive Congresses to the opposition party. In the press conference, he did not appear to see any need to change his policies, nor did he seem to learn any lessons from the election setback. He did not expect to modify his farm program or his foreign policies, and he would fight the "radical wing of the Democratic Party" if it proposed what he considered unnecessary federal spending.[100]

Ike realized that to maintain any control he had to mobilize the GOP, but he did not envision himself leading this effort. That job belonged to Alcorn, who would report to the White House on his progress toward that objective at least every other week. Alcorn, in turn, blamed the loss largely on the recession. Labor increased its spending in response to the right-to-work issue, and the GOP had not counterattacked. Alcorn wanted the party to present a more positive image and stress the contrast between its principles and the Democrats': "We need to get across to the voting public that there is a virtue in Party regularity."[101]

Nixon, who had watched the election results from home, talked with Secretary Dulles by telephone the next day. The vice president said that local, not national, concerns had dominated the elections. In a press interview that day, he pointed out that while Democrats had been preparing for the elections for two years, Republicans had worked for two months. This proved that campaigning was a year-round enterprise. Democrats deserved the victory: "the result was inevitable."[102]

In his memoirs, Nixon reflected that maybe he should not have taken such an active part in the campaign, because he had received "little thanks or credit." His recollection was faulty. By campaigning across the country, he helped raise $2,000,000 for candidates and put dozens of party leaders in his debt. He made sure to send letters consoling losing candidates who had run competitive races, instructing his staff "to pick out the ones we can use around the country." He also saw a fundamental change in the American public: it "no longer put the stress on initiative that was once so basic to life in the United States." Unions offered security to their members, while businesses were viewed "as a necessary evil." Republicans had to highlight their successes and minimize their antilabor propaganda. Americans disapproved of negatives, and since a large segment of the population "must earn its living it is not going to react in a friendly manner to an attack on labor."[103]

While the vice president understood his role in the elections, the president did not comprehend his. He did not see the significance of the struggle to increase party registration. When Lebanon, the Adams scandal, and the Quemoy-Matsu conflict arose during the election year, the president resolved these issues without considering their impact on his party's electoral chances. Ever focused on governing rather than politics, he did not realize, or perhaps did not accept, that one of his responsibilities as the leader of his party was to translate his enormous personal popularity into a Republican majority.

THE STEEL SOLUTION

With the exception of a sharp but brief recession in 1953 and 1954, prosperity reigned throughout Eisenhower's first term. When he first took office, in January 1953, inflation was almost nonexistent at 0.4 percent, and it remained low throughout the first term. Ike proposed, and Congress passed, balanced budgets for 1956 and 1957, only the second time since the 1920s that consecutive federal budgets were balanced. Prosperity helped him win a landslide election in 1956.

Ike remained committed, in his second term, to the economic principles that had guided him in his first: limiting inflation and balancing the budget. In many ways, he would be remarkably successful. He managed to slow increases in expenditures while passing the largest public works projects in United States history, the Interstate Highway Act and the St. Lawrence Seaway Act. His administration also extended Social Security benefits to 10.5 million wage earners, including public school teachers.[1]

The second term saw two important changes in the administration's economic leadership. Before the second inauguration, Arthur Burns resigned as chairman of the Council of Economic Advisors, to be replaced by Raymond Saulnier, who was more dogged about fighting inflation than his predecessor.[2] Treasury Secretary George Humphrey also resigned toward the end of July 1957, and Robert Anderson replaced him. In addition to mirroring the president's economic views, Anderson was a Texas Democrat who had cordial relations with two congressional power brokers from his home state: Speaker of the House Rayburn and Senate majority leader Johnson. Anderson became a liaison between the White House and those powerful Democrats.[3]

For 1958, Eisenhower proposed his third consecutive budget without a deficit, with federal expenditures fewer than $70 billion. Nearly half of this amount went to defense. But another recession began at the start of August and would last eight months. After the Soviet Union launched Sputnik, the first man-made orbiting satellite, in October, Democrats successfully applied pressure to the administration for greater spending on missiles with which to match Moscow's success. Although the president still tried to limit spending, he knew that the recession and spectacular launch of Sputnik made a balanced budget impossible.[4]

Nixon defended the administration's positions in private correspondence as well as in speeches. He believed "that the most productive source of people's wealth is individual rather than government enterprise" and that the federal government's role was "to engage in those activities which will stimulate and encourage the creative genius of individual Americans." He favored reducing taxes where possible; he supported foreign aid for national security reasons in the face of vehement congressional opposition; and he hoped to lower government costs without damaging defense and domestic programs: "this Administration believes that the principle of living within income applies to the management of our federal budget just as it does to a family budget." In his speeches, he reminded audiences that the administration had followed sound fiscal policies since 1953.[5]

The battle with the Democratic Congress over the budget had already reached an impasse by May. Many advised Nixon to stay out of the conflict, "but I am convinced that if the Administration and the President are discredited on this issue, it will hurt all of us in 1958 and 1960. I would rather take a little heat now than a whole lot later." Toward the end of the month, he spoke at the annual meeting of the American Iron and Steel Institute on the budget battle. The country prospered, he said, because of the vitality of private enterprise, not government interference. "We should spend for government only what we need to spend even if this may be less than we are able to spend." The United States was winning the Cold War, and to continue this success it had to fund defense, including the foreign aid that many congressmen deplored.[6]

That summer, as the nation was sliding toward recession, the vice president pushed for a vigorous economy and supported the Federal Reserve Bank's tight monetary policy. He was concerned that high interest rates damaged small business and homebuilders but felt that these problems were preferable to "runaway inflation." Restrictions on borrowing through high interest rates were the only sensible way to keep inflation at bay: "The alternative of direct price, wage and profit controls would move us far in the direction of socialism." The treasury department under Truman had used its influence on the Federal Reserve to maintain artificially low interest rates and high inflation. Eisenhower gave the Federal Reserve more latitude to prevent "a rubber dollar." Since 1946 the Consumer Price Index had jumped 47 percent, of which 37 points came during Truman's presidency.[7]

During a cabinet meeting on October 11, shortly after Sputnik's launch, Nixon reviewed the political pressure for a tax cut and cautioned that any encouragement of a reduction might be unwise. Technological competition with the Soviet Union had suddenly become a front-page issue that threatened to throw the budget out of balance. This meant that providing the necessary funding for national security would be more difficult. The president applauded these comments.[8]

As the weak economy dragged into November, the president vented his frustration. Even a mild recession raised fears of a depression, and he warned the cabinet that if his administration did not have a plan to prevent one, the GOP would lose the next election. Voters, Ike fretted, would say, "Here is that old Republican Administration of 1928—not doing anything." The administration might have to demand new powers from Congress: "The big question is: whether we should wait until the emergency to get this authority."[9]

As the recession worsened in the first quarter of 1958, Gallup conducted a series of polls on economic conditions. Sixty-four percent of respondents in mid-April believed the country was in a recession, while 36 percent called it a depression. By then the downturn had technically ended. Even as the economy rebounded robustly through the summer, the polls did not reflect optimism. Many saw no change or any appreciable improvement.[10]

Nixon knew that the recession spelled trouble for the 1958 elections. At the beginning of the year, he urged cabinet members to highlight the administration's accomplishments. If the GOP did not act positively and aggressively and the downturn did not reverse itself by summer, Republicans would have "a hard year" winning elections in November. During a Lincoln Day address in Phoenix, he pledged the president would not "stand by and allow a recession to continue or unemployment to rise." The government had requested an additional $5 billion for defense spending; the post office had $2 billion funded for modernization, and $2 billion went into the interstate highway program. If Congress acted promptly on the president's request, housing starts would increase.[11]

In March, the vice president publicly advocated an across-the-board tax cut instead of large public works projects "as an ultimate alternative to combat recession." He advocated legislation to provide "incentives to job creators as well as more money in the hands of consumers." The president, he knew, was in a delicate position. If he acted too quickly to stimulate the economy, it might cause inflation. The New Deal's massive public works had "proved inadequate" and would "inevitably result in government taking an even larger percentage of the national product than it does at the present time." Yet Nixon wanted Congress to enact the administration's proposals for "highways, housing, public works, etc."

The president rejected Nixon's suggestion for a tax cut, thinking it ineffective: what matters, he said, "is the holding down of expenditures."[12]

During the first week of September 1958, Nixon had an opportunity to talk about the economy at the fiftieth anniversary conference of the Harvard Business School Association. He had considered attending Harvard as an undergraduate but could not afford it,[13] and he gave his speech much thought. In a memorandum shortly beforehand, the vice president explored the idea of breaking with the president over national defense, declaring that the United States "should do considerably more." He might stress his ideas regarding the dangerous effects of wage increases without rises in productivity; he wondered about discussing tax reform and about reducing the tax rate for the highest brackets, then at 90 percent; and he hoped to present his economic philosophy and not the "stand-pat conservative economics that [Secretary] Anderson and his crowd are constantly parroting." Referring to himself in the third person, he said he did not intend to be "too conservative . . . here is a place where Nixon differs again from the [Robert] Anderson- [George] Humphrey stand-pat, hold-the-line, balance-the-budget, line." Arthur Burns supported him on tax reduction, while many fiscal conservatives resented this position because the GOP was supposedly against that kind of stimulus. Nixon expected to "go out and look for new ideas. We talk all about finding the way to the moon and the exploration of outer space—let's do a little exploration in the economic field."[14]

Nixon spent the first half of his Harvard address discussing American exceptionalism. Capitalism gave "everyone an opportunity to share in a constantly increasing pool of wealth," and while materialism was important, the national mood was dominated by idealism created by democratic values. The American system was far superior to communist totalitarianism, and the United States, not the Soviet Union, "should be the natural champion of legitimate nationalist movements."

The rest of the speech focused on economics. If the United States were judged solely on results, he said, "we can point to a record of economic progress unsurpassed in world history." Even with such a remarkable achievement, the nation needed to move forward: "Standpat, defensive thinking is not adequate for the challenge we face either at home or abroad." He recommended that 12 million workers not originally covered under the unemployment compensation system be included and that the minimum standards for the level of benefits be raised. Some concession for the common good had to be made. Business had to hold down costs by accepting low unit profits, and labor had to realize that "wage increases which force price increases are not in the best interests of union members." He also suggested tax reforms in the next session of Congress: larger depreciation allowances for business purposes to stimulate investment in new plants and equipment, lower corporate rates, overhaul of excise taxes, and lower rates in the highest income brackets. "Our goal," he said, "should be to fashion a tax structure which will create more jobs, more income and more genuine security."[15]

Nixon was pleased with his address but disappointed at the "limited play" it received in the press. Even though he and publisher Henry Luce had "talked about the need for more Republicans getting out in public with an affirmative approach to our national problems," the speech got no coverage in Luce's magazines. "If we cannot reach through to the consciousness of magazines like TIME and LIFE," Nixon wrote to Luce on September 23, 1958: "we might as well wander lost in the wilderness."[16]

Despite his misgivings, Nixon publicly supported the administration's insistence on a balanced budget at the beginning of 1959, and Ike thanked him for his loyalty. During the congressional debate over the budget, Nixon issued a statement supporting the president for holding the line against inflation, while blaming Democrats for unacceptable spending proposals. The president's opposition to the spenders checkmated Democrats. On May 25, Nixon foresaw "a rising sentiment against high taxes, inflation, and extravagance. Although the Democrats have interpreted the [1958] election results as a mandate to increase spending, I think they are mistaken."[17]

At legislative leadership and cabinet meetings, Nixon and others argued that Republicans needed more information from the White House to counter the Democratic assault on the budget. He anticipated the opposition's demand for more funding on space projects after the Sputnik launches. In regard to a bill on school construction, most Americans wanted more classrooms and did not differentiate between state and federal funding. The administration had to respond favorably to both initiatives: "We say either 'We are going to lick them [Democrats]' or 'We are going to have a program of our own.' From the standpoint of 'licking them,' I do not think we are going to get very far."

The president remained closely involved in economic policy throughout 1959. After the Democratic landslide the preceding November, Ike told Republicans at a legislative leadership meeting on January 13 that the GOP had to unite to halt "foolish" Democratic spending schemes, and he expected the party to support his call for a balanced budget. At a cabinet session three days later, he welcomed debate over a bill to provide federal funding for school construction, saying he opposed the concept philosophically even though his administration had proposed it. Democrats applauded new social programs, and once money had been allocated for school construction, the president feared that the spending would be impossible to stop. Yet poorer states, he said, needed assistance: "we have to be human and paternalistic . . . I do not know of anything I *hate* as much, but I guess we must."[18]

The president continued to call for a balanced budget throughout the year; he even suggested that the country start to reduce the enormous national debt. When reporter Rowland Evans Jr. asked Ike at a press conference on January 21 to respond to Democratic charges that the president had submitted a "propaganda budget" to Congress, he replied: "If we get down to this business of who is using the budget as a political football, I assure you it is not I." He attacked Democrats for proposing new domestic programs with large expenditures and used every available vehicle to halt these unwelcomed projects. Besides opposing excessive congressional spending, Ike fought for wage increases that were not inflationary. The Kremlin, he believed, was trying to force the United States into bankruptcy by creating international crises to push the administration to increase military spending and thus the deficit.[19]

Throughout the spring and the fall, the president tried to unite his party against Democratic spending proposals. Preaching austerity, he used his veto power 181 times to counteract legislation he considered inflationary. Congress overrode his vetoes just twice. He resisted demands for additional defense funding; pouring more money into the military, he insisted, would not provide greater security.[20]

If vetoes did not inhibit spending, the president also employed political threats. At a White House press conference on July 1, he said the American people had "changed their minds" on government spending and inflation since the 1958 elections. His administration had offered anti-inflationary policies to protect the dollar's value, and he would not accept "unconscionable spending." Even though he could not run for reelection again, if the Democrats did not support his budget requests he pledged to make inflation a major issue in 1960.[21]

The president devised another means to promote his economic policies. In his 1959 State of the Union Message, he announced the creation of the Cabinet Committee on Price Stability for Economic Growth. When Robert Pierpont of CBS News asked him about the economy at a press conference on January 21, Ike replied that he had established "a big Cabinet committee" to fight inflation. "Economic growth in the long run cannot be soundly brought about except with stability in your price structure."[22]

To maximize publicity, the president made Nixon the committee chairman; its members included the postmaster general; the secretaries of agriculture, treasury, commerce, and labor; and the chairman of the Council of Economic Advisors. When the vice president announced his new assignment, he touted the benefits of the administration's economic programs and the value of the president's leadership. Nixon planned to enlist business, labor, government, and other segments of society in promoting the committee's long-range objectives of ensuring economic growth and developing policies for price stability.[23]

W. Allen Wallis, the dean of the University of Chicago Business School, took a year's leave of absence to become executive vice chairman and direct daily operations. He began conferring with the vice president in early March. The closest Nixon had come to studying economics was a course in property at Duke Law School, so he began meeting with Wallis at least once a week for a half hour. Wallis brought along George Shultz, a young industrial economist on the University of Chicago faculty. Ike was present at the swearing-in ceremony for both of them, and afterward he pronounced: "Now you can start to fight inflation."[24]

Nixon was impressed with Wallis because he looked to the practical, not the theoretical. As for Wallis, he initially saw the fight against inflation as "a lost cause," but by the end of the summer, he no longer thought it was "hopeless." Although the committee had not yet produced concrete results, he predicted that it would before the end of the year. Nixon appreciated the enthusiasm of both Wallis and Shultz. He thought so highly of Shultz that, when he became president, he made Shultz his secretary of labor.[25]

The committee's first report, released on June 28, warned of increasing inflation unless the nation followed the policies for "reasonable price stability" that the president advocated. Congress needed to embrace a balanced budget and to start reducing the national debt. As expected, the president welcomed the report and reminded Congress that it must hold down spending.[26]

Many Democrats dismissed these recommendations. Congressman Chester Bowles from Connecticut called the report "the same shop-worn clichés which have led us into two recessions in five years." The committee, he said, had moved in the wrong direction and did not have "faith in the dynamics of our private-enterprise system." Nixon responded that Bowles's criticism tended "to make me believe we must be on the right track!" Senator Paul Douglas from Illinois, who had taught economics in college and whose Joint Economic Committee had been studying economic growth, employment, and price levels for two years, saw the report as administration propaganda and a "collection of bromides and obviousities [sic]."[27]

Throughout the last six months of 1959, Nixon's committee issued several informational statements that reinforced the president's viewpoints. It declared, somewhat tentatively, that the battle against inflation was being won. Nixon himself felt "a very cautious optimism regarding the possibility of holding the line on prices, we are a long way from thinking that the battle has been won." By the end of the year, he had dismissed theories that inflation was inevitable and that capitalism would collapse unless wars broke out to avert it. The public no longer was fatalistic about depressions; government had to avoid them: . . . there is a ratchet effect if we do not nip in the bud any incipient rises in the price level."[28]

The administration had more than theory to worry about. The president's concerns about rising prices and wages related to a strike looming in the steel industry. The steelworkers' union, at the pinnacle of its power, had staged a walkout in 1952. When President Truman tried to nationalize the steel industry to stop the strike, it led to a landmark Supreme Court decision, *Youngstown Sheet & Tube Co.* v. *Sawyer* that prevented him from doing so. The resulting walkout had lasted fifty-four days.

During the 1957–1958 recession, neither the union nor the industry wanted a strike. But by 1959, the nation's economic health had markedly improved, and after weeks of negotiations, the United Steelworkers struck on July 14. The companies had prepared by stockpiling inventories, and throughout the summer and into the fall, the strike had no major impact on the economy. At the end of October, the industry's unanimity broke when Kaiser Steel and two other companies signed separate agreements with the unions. In December, the unions signed a new contract with the aluminum and can companies. The major eleven steel companies would not budge.[29]

When the strike was announced, the president adopted a hands-off policy. The sides should settle the dispute through free collective bargaining. Although Ike did not publicly express his thoughts on any agreement, he privately wrote former treasury secretary Humphrey about his three-point "formula" on August 11: (1) local labor practices needed modification; (2) workers should receive about a six cents an hour pay increase; and (3) the industry, to keep inflation down, should reduce prices by approximately two dollars per ton. Not one element in Ike's formula was included in the final contract.[30]

On September 8, the strike entered its fifty-sixth day and became the longest since World War II. The president applied pressure by calling for "intense, uninterrupted, good-faith bargaining." When his suggestion was ignored, he met with both sides at the White House. Among the participants were Roger Blough, chairman of the board of U.S. Steel Corporation, and Conrad Cooper, the company's executive vice president and chief negotiator. Steel union president David McDonald and his general counsel, Arthur Goldberg, arrived a half hour later. The president told his guests that he feared Soviet productivity and the weakening of the American economy. He wanted the parties to resume talks, without government intervention.[31]

By the first of October, the eleventh week, the strike's effects were damaging the economy. On October 2, the industry made its first proposal, and the union rejected it as unacceptable. Five days later, Ike expressed his "keen disappointment" and threatened to invoke the provision in the Taft-Hartley Act calling for an eighty-day "cooling-off" period that would force the workers back to their jobs while the president assembled a board of mediators. When this warning was ignored, he ordered the justice department to seek an injunction. After a month of legal maneuvering, the Supreme Court ruled for the government, and the cooling-off period went into effect on November 7.[32]

Two days before that, McDonald spoke off the record with the president and Secretary of Labor James Mitchell for slightly more than an hour. After the union president left, Eisenhower and Mitchell agreed that whereas McDonald wished to settle, the companies refused to budge over their demand for changes in work rules. The president wanted more information on this impasse, so Mitchell promptly met with Blough and McDonald. He reported back to the president that they refused to budge.[33]

The industry next offered a thirty-cent-an-hour raise over three years with no change in work rules, which the union rejected in mid-November. Early in December the parties opened another round of unproductive talks. On the third of the month, the president delivered a television address in which he asked both sides to end the strike. Then he left the country on an eleven-nation goodwill tour.[34]

Five months before this trip, Mitchell had begun discussing the steel dispute with Nixon, with whom he had had a cordial relationship since becoming labor secretary late in 1953. Since he also sat on Nixon's Anti-Inflation Committee, Mitchell wanted the committee to "move into the situation boldly." Nixon, he said, should attempt to force the parties into meaningful negotiations and draw attention to any possible inflationary effects of a new contract.[35]

During his time in the Senate, Nixon had become friendly with McDonald, and they saw each other occasionally during his vice presidency. In May 1959, Nixon talked with McDonald and Blough, first separately and then together, over dinner in New York City. On July 2, the vice president issued a statement favoring collective bargaining and opposing government intervention. Five days later, he saw McDonald at baseball's All-Star Game in Pittsburgh, where McDonald complained that the companies were "provoking a shutdown" and preventing a settlement. Nixon later told both union and industry leaders that the administration "was not taking sides" in the strike.[36]

By the middle of November, Nixon openly warned management and labor of dire consequences unless the strike was settled promptly. Privately, he thought the work rules issue had turned into a test of wills that was standing in the way of an achievable settlement. He could not think of anything "worse for this country, for management, or for the union, than to throw this whole issue into the Congress during an election year. I shudder to think what would come out."[37]

Presiding over the cabinet on December 11, Nixon stated that the president wanted to maintain pressure on both sides to reach a "*voluntary* settlement." The vice president urged his audience to avoid any statement that either side could use "to deviate from the President's remarks." He did not inform the cabinet that he had secretly seen industry spokesmen three days earlier in New York City.[38]

When Ike returned to the White House on December 22, his fact-finding panel reentered the talks. On the 28th, the board halted negotiations because the parties were hopelessly deadlocked.[39]

Meanwhile, Nixon was holding private talks with labor and management at his home, on December 19 and 21. He and Mitchell recommended that the two sides split the difference on wages. The unions asked for fifty-two cents and the industry offered thirty. The vice president suggested forty-one cents. As for the changes in work rules, Nixon believed this issue should be postponed for later talks.[40]

On December 30, Nixon was ready to fly to California to be honorary grand marshal for the Rose Bowl game in Pasadena. Shortly before his departure, he and Mitchell took a commercial flight to New York City for more discussions with steel industry leaders. They spoke with twelve officials, warning them that if no settlement were reached, Congress, overwhelmingly supportive of labor, would demand compulsory arbitration detrimental to the companies. When they left the meeting, Nixon and Mitchell believed that the strike had been settled. The following morning, the vice president spoke to reporters before leaving for California, informing them that with the president's blessing, he was acting as a mediator in secret negotiations between management and labor.[41]

With Nixon out west, Mitchell continued around-the-clock negotiations. The president, on vacation in Augusta, Georgia, did not appear to be actively involved in the bargaining. In fact he was closely following events. On January 2, 1960, at 10:04 a.m., he had a conference call with Mitchell in the capital and Nixon on the West Coast. Nixon reported that neither side was willing to move from its hard-line public position for fear of losing face. He and Mitchell recommended a voluntary settlement, which both sides would accept if the vice president and labor secretary declared that it was their initiative. A memo would be signed in the next day or two, and the negotiators would need another week to work out the details. Nixon and Mitchell would keep the bargain secret until they made a public announcement. Ike, going along with the parties' condition that Nixon and Mitchell be seen as the federal government's "unofficial committee," concluded that "this is the best deal we can work out on a voluntary basis." But even though he accepted the outcome, he was displeased. The crisis illustrated how the nation was "blackmailed by the Unions" and the companies, and had "to have better and stronger laws" to prevent this kind of labor-management dispute in the future.[42]

Nixon returned to the capital on January 3, and he and Mitchell announced the settlement the following day. The new contract ran for two and a half years with the forty-one cent wage increase. The work rules dispute was put off for another day. The national media promptly carried the story, and Nixon was hailed for his role in the settlement. According to the *Washington Post,* if inflation did not result, the vice president "emerged as the hero." He received criticism from both business and labor, each alleging that he had not done enough to defend its side. A day after the announcement, Nixon wrote Secretary of Commerce Frederick Mueller that if he had the power, he would have imposed a different agreement. But "after some pretty exhausting meetings I am convinced that it was the best settlement we could get without compulsory government arbitration."[43]

On January 6, in what cabinet secretary Gordon Gray described as "one of the most dramatic recitations at a cabinet meeting," Mitchell pointed out that the steel companies did better in their labor negotiations than other companies. Nixon, reviewing his role, emphasized that the steel industry had pledged not to raise its prices immediately. The president repeated his concern that the long strike illustrated "to the public the very difficult situation that could develop in the future." He did not know how to prevent "a damaging strike without losing some of the freedom that ought to exist in our country." If the end of this contract led to another strike, how could the government successfully fight an inflationary spiral?[44]

A week later, reporter Robert Donovan asked the president how he felt about the settlement. Ike replied that the cooling-off period had not produced results, so he had asked Mitchell and Nixon "to act as some kind of mediators." They arrived at "a solution that was somewhere between the two positions," and labor and management voluntarily agreed to the terms. The president emphasized that this was the first time since World War II that a new contract did not lead to a price increase, and he hoped that management and labor would vigorously cooperate to "avoid any price rises as a result of this contract."[45]

For months, debate continued over whether the agreement was or was not inflationary; whether the administration had acted appropriately; and in an election year, whether Nixon deserved the praise that he had received. The vice president himself had no doubts.[46] After his experience with the anti-inflationary committee and his role in resolving the steel strike, he came to believe that the greatest differences between the two national parties were "in fiscal and monetary matters." Republicans had failed to explain their policies to the public, while Democrats had succeeded in making the GOP "look niggardly." Deficit spending caused inflation and weakened the dollar, and Republicans had "to demonstrate effectively the deep personal stake every citizen has in this issue." Nixon agreed with the president that Americans were experiencing "a rising sentiment against high taxes, inflation and extravagance." Democrats had taken the 1958 congressional elections as a mandate to increase spending. Nixon thought they were mistaken.[47]

The president went much farther. At a cabinet gathering on economic issues in November 1959, Ike argued at length that a balanced budget was essential for 1960 and 1961. It should even, he told his secretaries, "be a fight to the death without regard to the clamor of the political opposition." Expenditures had to be held down, and some of the national debt should be paid off. He did not expect to "roll back" programs, but the government was offering "too many services too fast." The Soviets were gaining prestige and influencing neutral nations with their expanding economy, and the United States needed a robust economy to maintain its global leadership.[48]

The president kept to this position during his last year in office. Budget director Maurice Stans urged his cabinet audience to hold 1961 expenditures to their current levels and forecast either a balanced budget or even a slight surplus for 1960. Raymond Saulnier, the chair of the Council of Economic Advisors, predicted that 1960 would be "a good year, though not marked by boom conditions." As for 1961 and beyond, he saw "sustained growth" greater "than at any time since World War II."[49]

He was wrong. The recession of 1960 started in April and lasted until February 1961. Despite being the shortest and least severe downturn since 1945, it gave an opening for Democrats to rekindle fears of another Republican depression.[50]

Ike openly attacked these tactics. He had warned early in the year that if the Democrats presented too many spending proposals that were likely to cause a budget deficit, he would make inflation an issue in the 1960 campaign. Within the administration, he lectured his cabinet on its duty to unite behind him. Nixon, Mitchell, and Burns argued for more spending and a tax cut, but as in the economic debate of 1958, the president's opposition, backed by Saulnier and Anderson, prevailed.[51]

The president also used regular GOP leadership gatherings to reiterate his pleas to hold down spending. If Democrats wanted to spend money on unnecessary programs, he would veto them, and he expected Republicans to follow his lead. Ike was especially worried about the legislation to build classrooms in depressed regions, and proposed to limit spending on the program to $75 million a year. This single piece of legislation, he said, was a symptom of a larger problem. Assisting children at school was popular, and there were other equally appealing proposals, such as new Social Security benefits and salary increases for federal employees. But when the costs were totaled, too much money was being spent. Ike met with Republican leaders on July 1 to seek their backing to sustain a veto on legislation raising federal employee salaries. Senators Dirksen, Kuchel, and Bridges told him that his veto would be overridden; the bill was too popular. Disappointed, Ike declared that congressional Republicans were abandoning fiscal integrity, but he would not fight a losing battle. GOP disloyalty troubled him; he felt that he was "being 'read out of the Party.'" As the senators left the White House, Ike said that "it would be better for the boys on the Hill to impeach him and he would be happy to support them in this fight."[52]

Nixon was not counted among those who had abandoned party principles. Ike believed that he and his vice president held similar economic views. Writing his sister-in-law Lucy on May 25, he claimed that he and Nixon were "basically conservatives" in that they wanted "to conserve all of the admirable traits of character in the American population, to avoid paternalism, and therefore . . . to prevent a deterioration in the fibre of the average citizen." Free spenders had grown popular "because the consequences of over-spending seem to be long-term and vague, whereas the advantages claimed are supposed to be immediate and discernible to all." Whereas the Democrats behaved irresponsibly, the Republican Party had to adhere to fiscal restraint.[53]

As chairman of the Anti-Inflation Committee, Nixon continued to promote the president's economic programs. In April, he predicted a "great expansion" of the economy in the 1960s if the country continued to follow the administration's guidelines. The nation would experience "higher levels of education and rising levels of living" with little change in prices. Small downturns might occur, but depression and severe recession were unlikely.[54]

At the same time, however, Nixon began to subtly distance himself from the president. On April 23, speaking before the American Society of Newspaper Editors, he identified himself as an "economic conservative." After his address, he added that conservatism "at its best must be progressive." Discussing this stance with columnist Arthur Krock on May 3, he said that he opposed excessive federal expenditures because they would weaken the dollar; he supported some "new" agricultural programs; he favored raising the minimum wage, but to $1.10, not $1.25; he wanted to cover another six million workers under the fair labor standards law; he opposed federal subsidies to teachers' pay but backed federal aid to school construction. Finally, he objected to "compulsory taxation for health insurance for the elderly," but he favored "federal aid to a good voluntary system."[55]

By summer, the presidential aspirants, including Nixon, were preparing for their parties' conventions. Ike's economic policies would be subject to partisan debate, and any rational discussion of fiscal matters would have to wait until the new chief executive was in place.

Nixon had entered the vice presidency without any serious understanding of economic policy. Eight years later, he had listened to the ideas of some of the best American economists and presided over a cabinet committee to ensure continued prosperity. He had also learned how closely the economy and politics were interconnected. If a downturn happened, Republicans would be blamed. When Nixon argued vehemently for tax cuts and greater spending to bring the nation out of recession in 1958 and 1960, the president ignored his counsel. In the 1958 elections, Republican candidates lost in staggering numbers, and in the 1960 presidential election, the recession was also a reason Nixon lost.

Eisenhower followed his economic principles without much regard for the political consequences. He pledged to balance the budget and succeeded three times. He maintained federal income taxes at their current high levels to have the necessary revenue, halted the dramatic rise in military expenditures, and left his successor a healthy economy. He inherited a $10 billion deficit in 1953 and routinely wished it could be reduced or paid off. Economist John Sloan thought that while most commentators saw this record as "a solid success," they wanted more. Historian Keith Olson, on History News Network on May 13, 2013, listed some of the president's economic accomplishments: "Eisenhower's achievements and his public image contributed to high public trust in government, belief in the role of government, and ability to form bipartisan coalitions to advance the national interest. Eisenhower's record is one Republican leaders should celebrate, not ignore."[56]

29

NIXON IN AFRICA

Of the fifty-one nations that signed the United Nation Charter in 1945, only three were in Africa: Ethiopia, Liberia, and the Union of South Africa. Most of the continent in the early 1950s still consisted of European colonies. As the Cold War deepened, the Truman administration usually deferred to the Western European colonial powers to keep order and prevent communist infiltration.[1]

Nor did Eisenhower make Africa a priority during his first term. In the spring of 1955, however, rumors spread that Nixon and his wife would travel to the Middle East. Toward the end of August, the White House announced that the Nixons would journey to the Near East, Egypt, and Ethiopia to get acquainted with the area's leaders and their views. Once more, the president was sending his vice president to a region critical to American interests to obtain his first-hand impressions. Nixon was optimistic, hoping "that we can do some good in that important area."[2]

While the press, as well as the administration's public statements, dismissed the friction then building over the Suez Canal, the vice president watched the worsening Arab-Israel situation through the summer. The Egyptians especially relayed their interest in having Nixon stop in Cairo. When Secretary Dulles drafted a statement on the Arab-Israeli border dispute, the vice president and the attorney general approved it as "tolerable from a political standpoint." But after the president's heart attack in September, Nixon's mission was canceled. He remained in the capital while Ike recuperated.[3]

During that winter, Nixon and Dulles agreed that the United States should reexamine its Middle East policy. If conditions deteriorated in the region, the administration would be blamed for lack of leadership. Dulles believed that the state department had tried to support Zionist wishes, creating Arab antagonism, and that the Soviets benefited by siding with the Arabs and opposing the Israelis.

If United States policy did not become more balanced, the Western nations would lose support in the Middle East and Africa. The secretary hoped to win bipartisan backing for this change in policy. Nixon agreed that impartiality was the right course, even if it alienated Jewish voters, but there were limits: the administration could not get Congress to send American troops to fight against Israel.[4]

By the beginning of 1956, Africa had become more closely associated with the Middle East crisis. The state department issued a special report on the continent suggesting that although it currently had little influence, the Kremlin might try to win African converts in the future. Nixon was sufficiently concerned that he asked state department director of policy planning Richard Bowie for more information.[5]

Toward the end of March, the United States representative to the United Nations, Henry Cabot Lodge, expressed his concern about U.S. relations with African and Asian countries. He noted that "some tactless Americans" traveling to those nations had demonstrated racist attitudes; they worked with the "natives" but did not "treat them as social equals." Lodge proposed that "high-ranking American officials" needed to alter that image and make people in these parts of the world "feel that *we* think *they* are attractive."[6]

Secretary Dulles responded that Lodge's suggestion had "merit." Asia had been saturated with prominent American visitors, he wrote, and the Near East had "special complications," but African goodwill missions were "welcome" and could "bring results." More Americans, especially "of high stature," should travel to Africa, which was "now in a state of rapid evolution." The president prompted Dulles to propose the idea at a cabinet meeting on April 27. The secretary and Lodge suggested the secretaries include Africa on their travel itineraries. Lodge emphasized that these visits would have a positive effect in countries then "emerging from colonial status."[7]

The president also had strategic concerns. In a press conference on May 9, Marguerite Higgins of the *New York Herald Tribune* asked about how the Suez crisis affected United States military bases in North Africa. Ike responded that they "would be endangered, and there is constant negotiation for the preservation and protection of them."[8]

During his first administration, Eisenhower had tried to formulate a program to improve Middle East conditions in such a way that both Arabs and Israelis saw the United States as an impartial arbiter. The president had understood the region's strategic significance ever since he commanded the North African landings in World War II, and he knew that with the end of European colonialism, the newly independent African nations would express their own brands of nationalism.

Egyptian president Gamal Abdel Nasser's seizure of Suez Canal on July 26, 1956, caused an irreparable rupture between the Egyptians and the British and French. Four days later, Dulles confided to Nixon that he thought the two allies were "really anxious to start a war and get us into it." He was trying to convince them that "they may have to do it alone." Even after Eisenhower firmly rejected intervention and tried to mediate a diplomatic settlement, the two European governments secretly plotted with the Israelis for a military invasion to seize the canal.[9]

The administration tried to keep Suez out of the presidential campaign by seeking a bipartisan consensus regarding Middle East policy. That lasted until October 29, when Israeli forces crossed into the Sinai, quickly followed by French and British paratroopers attacking the canal. Further complicating American diplomacy, in the midst of the fighting, Secretary Dulles was rushed to Walter Reed Army Hospital suffering from severe abdominal pains and had emergency surgery on November 2. The doctors did not disclose that he had cancer. Despite Dulles's absence, the president maintained his position that the British, French, and Israelis had to accept a cease-fire and withdraw their soldiers from Egypt.[10]

The day after the election, the British and French agreed. The following morning, the National Security Council (NSC) discussed the crisis for over two hours, and in the afternoon, the president conferred with Nixon and others to plan his strategy. Ike also had CIA director Allen Dulles brief legislative leaders from both parties on the current conditions.[11]

By the middle of November, with the Suez situation less menacing, the president held a press conference to reassure the nation that the British and French were withdrawing their military forces and the rumors over Soviet intervention were fading. Nixon felt comfortable enough to leave for Florida on the thirteenth to relax from his exhausting campaign schedule.[12]

The president also left, for Augusta, Georgia, and the day after Thanksgiving he met with Secretary Dulles, who was recuperating in Key West, Florida. Nixon also saw him for lunch on the twenty-seventh, returning to the capital the next day. At the end of the month, he presided over a NSC meeting where he expressed concern over the political weakness of the British Conservatives under Prime Minister Anthony Eden, for whom the failure in the Suez was politically devastating. (Eden would resign, citing health concerns, in early January.) Nixon wanted to offer the Conservatives financial assistance.[13]

Even before the New Year, Henry Cabot Lodge, a civil rights proponent, had another consideration. Mason Sears, the American representative to the United Nations Trusteeship Council, had written Lodge toward the end of September about colonialism and communism in Africa. Sears, who had traveled often to that continent and was pro-African and popular with "negro leaders," argued that the Eisenhower administration had to prevent the Soviet Union from gaining a foothold there. Furthermore, as African countries gained their independence, black voters in the United States would focus their attention on American policy there. Sears argued that the administration had to move against "white supremacy" in South Africa. The president was taking a successful and moderate approach to school desegregation, he wrote, and this action would "probably go down in history as a milestone in the final breaking up of racial mistrust."[14]

Lodge wrote Secretary Dulles before the end of the year that the Gold Coast, a British colony, was gaining its independence and would restore its ancient name, Ghana. It would receive its independence on March 6, 1957; this would "be a very important political occasion from an African-Asian point of view." Lodge urged the secretary to appoint a delegation to attend the ceremony and to choose Sears to represent the president.[15]

At the beginning of 1957, Dulles decided to send a delegation, but asked Nixon if he would lead it. The vice president was reluctant. As the Senate's presiding officer, he might be required to break a tie vote on civil rights legislation, making an overseas trip "a little difficult." Dulles pressed him: Africa "was the coming continent and we were anxious to do all we could." Toward the end of January, the secretary repeated his request: "here is an instance where thanks to good will, patience, and perseverance on the part of both African and European, the political, economic, and social advancement of 4.5 million Africans has been carried out peaceably and resolutely to the point where independence has become a reality." Nixon agreed that if president asked him to go, he would, and on January 29, the president made the request.[16]

A press release was issued on February 5, announcing that the vice president and his wife would attend the Ghanaian independence celebration. At the president's press conference the next day, William Lawrence of the *New York Times* inquired about broadening Nixon's role in the second term. Would his duties be "largely ceremonial," like this trip, or would the vice president have policy-making responsibilities? Ike replied that he expected his vice president to know everything so if he died, Nixon would be prepared to assume the presidency. He also assured the reporters that Nixon's foreign missions were not "merely ceremonial": his observations provided information that the White House needed.[17]

The vice president prepared for his mission with briefings from the CIA and state department. The latter cautioned that the communist bloc was giving increasing attention to Africa. Moscow had sent a large delegation to Liberia in

1956 for the inauguration of President William Tubman, and the Soviet Union and the People's Republic of China planned to attend the celebration in Ghana.[18]

While the vice president was making his preparations, the president was threatening force and economic sanctions against the Israelis if they did not leave the Sinai Peninsula, a step that the Egyptians applauded. As the Israelis withdrew, Eisenhower assured both sides that the United States would defend the region from any communist penetration. On February 21, Nixon praised both political parties for their bipartisan backing of the Eisenhower Doctrine.[19] By the end of the month, his African trip had expanded to include Morocco, Liberia, Uganda, Sudan, Ethiopia, Libya, and Tunisia, as well as Italy. He would leave on February 28 and return on March 21, traveling more than 18,000 miles. Ike would send personal messages to the leaders of each nation.[20]

African Americans were prominently featured in the delegation. Congressman Charles Diggs Jr., elected in 1954 as a Democrat from Detroit, and Walter Gordon, who had been appointed the Virgin Islands governor in 1955, were selected. E. Frederic Morrow, who served on the White House executive staff, argued that the black press was sensitive about Nixon's having traveled "to many colored countries" with no African Americans representatives. He was appointed a vice-presidential aide. The incoming Ghanaian prime minister, Kwane Nkrumah, had spent a decade in the United States and was graduated from the historically black Lincoln University in Pennsylvania. He invited a number of African American leaders, including magazine publisher John Johnson, whom Nixon described as "one of the most influential men in the Negro community in the United States," and his wife, Eunice and an emerging leader, Martin Luther King Jr. Nkrumah also invited United Nations undersecretary Dr. Ralph Bunche. (Lodge described him as "both an outstanding American negro and an outstanding man." Ike shared Lodge's opinion of Bunche "and his contribution to his race and to our country.") Adam Clayton Powell hoped to be part of the delegation too, but Speaker of the House Rayburn, angry that Powell had openly supported Ike's reelection, blocked it. The influential black intellectual W. E. B. DuBois had been denied a United States passport because he refused to sign the state department noncommunist affidavit.[21]

On February 27, the day before departure, Nixon and Ike conferred at the White House for a half hour. Afterward, Nixon and presidential press secretary Hagerty announced that the president wanted his vice president to hold "frank discussions of mutual problems" with the African leaders. The tour was meant to improve United States prestige on the continent, particularly where America had military bases.[22]

Nixon needed two airplanes for this trip. Thirty-five correspondents and photographers documented the journey. The vice president directed that special consideration be given to black reporters; of the more than twenty who went, nine or ten were accredited to African American publications.[23]

Before takeoff on the afternoon of the twenty-eighth, the vice president, who would be plagued by a lingering flu throughout his trip, told the press that Africa was increasingly significant to the United States: "As Africa goes on the side of freedom, this can be decisive in the struggle which is taking place today between the forces of freedom and the forces of slavery." Ghana, as a free nation, would follow Great Britain's "great parliamentary traditions" and would join the British Commonwealth. This trend toward a democratic form of government would continue as other African nations gained their independence.[24]

The Nixon party took off from the capital at 2:00 p.m. in a driving rain and landed in Rabat, Morocco, on March 1, the anniversary of that country's independence from France. Before nationhood was granted, John Foster Dulles characterized the sultan as moderate, popular, and a potential "counterpoise to the influence of Nasser." Nixon later described Morocco as "one of the most strategically important countries in the world." It bordered the Straits of Gibraltar and served as a bridge between Africa and Europe as well as between Africa, the Arab world, and the Middle East. The United States during World War II had built military bases there, and before France had ended its colonial rule the French allowed the United States to expand them.[25]

A crowd estimated at 200,000 greeted the vice president, and as he did throughout the journey, he stopped his limousine, got out, and shook hands with surprised spectators. Pat Nixon routinely visited hospitals and orphanages, and for the first time the sultan granted an audience to a foreign woman. Fred Morrow was pleased at the warm reception the Nixons received. He also commented that "women in this country" had "no status at all" and that "we could not help but be appalled by the scenes of overwhelming poverty and dirt and the obvious lack of sanitation." Throughout the trip, Morrow would routinely note these abysmal conditions in his extensive diary.[26]

Nixon and Mohammed V talked for an hour. The sultan expressed his agreement with the Eisenhower Doctrine even though it applied to the Middle East and not to North Africa. He did not see communism as a major issue in his region and thought African decolonization was gaining momentum. The vice president sympathized with the need for economic assistance and linked this aid to the sultan's support for United States military bases in Morocco. He also asked for the sultan's views on the fighting between French forces and Algerian rebels, saying the United States hoped both sides would reach a peaceful solution. The sultan thought UN-supervised elections were the answer.[27]

After touring Casablanca, the vice president flew south across the Sahara Desert to be present at the birth of independent Ghana. Located in West Africa on the Gulf of Guinea, about the same size as Great Britain and with a population of just over 5,000,000, Ghana was the second sub-Saharan nation to be granted independence and the second African nation to join the British Commonwealth. Although a white minority governed the first, the Union of South Africa, Ghana was almost entirely black. Like many developing nations, it depended on agriculture: cocoa accounted for two-thirds of its exports.[28]

On his arrival in Accra, with Pat at his side, the vice president told an airport crowd that he brought greetings from Eisenhower, and as vice president he was delighted to represent Ike at the ceremony. He paid tribute to the British and Ghanaian leaders who made independence possible "in an orderly manner."[29]

The next morning, accompanied by Fred Morrow, Nixon became the first foreign official to meet privately with Prime Minister Nkrumah. They spent thirty-five minutes discussing the nation's reliance on its cocoa crop and the need to diversify. Nixon suggested that the prime minister look into loans from the International Bank for Reconstruction and Development and try to attract private capital. Nkrumah then turned to his foreign policy, describing it as "nationalist," and assured his guest that "Ghana was firmly committed to parliamentary democracy and the democratic way of life."[30]

Summarizing the meeting at a press conference, Nixon told listeners that Nkrumah had pledged that in the East-West struggle, Ghana would "never be neutral." It would develop "policies which under no circumstances will accept foreign domination from any quarter." This stance was crucial "because this could indicate the trend which will be followed in other African countries as they acquire their independence." Nixon also offered a moderate amount of United States technical assistance.[31]

The next event on the vice president's schedule was the university convocation, several miles from the capital. Martin Luther King Jr., making his first trip outside the United States, would also attend. While on campus, King held an impromptu press conference in which he complained that he had asked Nixon to come to the South to survey racial discrimination, but the vice president had not responded. King said he was "not sure the President actually knows what is happening in the South in all details and the desperation of the situation"; he hoped the vice president would see the violence and discrimination at first hand and report back to Ike. Shortly afterward, King and Nixon bumped into one another; they smiled and had a friendly chat. The minister asked Nixon to visit

Alabama "where we are seeking the same kind of freedom the Gold Coast is celebrating." Nixon, impressed by King's demeanor, answered: "When you are in Washington, let me know. I would like to see you."[32]

King's comments might be responsible for an apocryphal story with several iterations. In one version, while in Accra Nixon turned to a black guest at a dinner and asked, "How does it feel to be free?" The reply was: "I don't know, I'm from Alabama." There were no media references to this incident at the time; no diplomatic dispatches included these remarks; and nothing in the Nixon archives supports this exchange. Donald Hughes, who accompanied the vice president as an aide, never heard about or witnessed this event.[33]

The Nixon-King exchange received widespread coverage. The same day, Ralph Bunche's interview was relegated to a tiny column. Bunche was the first African American to receive a doctorate in political science at an American university (Harvard), and the first of his race to receive the Nobel Peace Prize, in 1950 for his mediation efforts with the Palestinians. He told reporters that he had turned down an assistant secretary of state position in the Truman administration because he would not subject his family to the discrimination in the capital. But now, he said, "things have changed so very much." Washington had "no color bar." Under these circumstances, even though he had not been offered a position in the Eisenhower administration, he would accept one.[34]

Ghana became formally independent at midnight on March 6. Eisenhower sent a congratulatory message welcoming it into the family of nations and included a personal letter to Nkrumah praising the cooperative spirit between Ghana and Great Britain. The president was certain that "the same spirit will characterize Ghana's relations with the free world, including . . . the British Commonwealth." Nixon, at an evening press conference, warmly praised Britain's "enlightened policy," calling it "colonial policy at its best . . . a force for good rather than evil." Ghana's leaders would establish "a new and vital government which can be a shrine dedicated to liberty." Alex Rivera Jr., reporting for the *Pittsburgh Courier*, an influential black newspaper, wrote: Nixon "went to Africa to win friends for the United States of America, [and] his mission has been completed beyond his wildest imagination."[35]

For his third stop, the vice president flew to Liberia. Founded by the American Colonization Society in the 1820s for freed slaves, Liberia had become independent in 1847 and based its constitution on the United States model. President William Tubman had ruled his nation, primarily composed of indigenous people, with an iron hand since 1944 and had visited Nixon in Washington a decade later. Before landing at Roberts Field on the afternoon of March 7, engine #3 failed on the final approach, approximately a minute and a half from touchdown. Some smoke, caused by oil dripping on a hot engine, was visible, but the landing was normal.[36]

The visitors had arrived in one of the poorest and least developed of all the African states, with inadequate health services and education. During the drive to the capital Monrovia in hundred-degree heat, the air conditioning in some of the automobiles, as Fred Morrow noted, "conked out. . . . We had to turn the windows down, and the black red dust covered us like snow. It got in our nostrils, and we looked like queer creatures from the Andes."[37]

President Tubman hailed Nixon as "the greatest personality" ever to visit his nation and called the United States Liberia's "strongest, closest and most respected friend." The vice president, saying he intended to build on these statements by improving bilateral ties, presented the Liberian Navy with two Coast Guard cutters, outfitted with everything except guns, valued at $50,000 each. At a stroke, Nixon had tripled the Navy's size. Until then, its only ship was Tubman's 460-ton yacht.[38]

During a state dinner at the American embassy, Nixon and Tubman held talks. The Liberian leader had two principal needs: military assistance and public works like roads; he did not think he could raise private capital. Nixon said he would try to get public works funding. He also asked Tubman to help get Nkrumah's cooperation to prevent the Soviets from infiltrating West Africa. Tubman, hypersensitive to Ghana's new prestige, promised to visit Accra soon and thought he could have a moderating influence on the prime minister, who came from a Marxist background. Tubman dismissed Nkrumah's call for a federation of African nations. Nixon later added at a press conference that the United States had significant bonds with Liberia since its independence, but had not paid much attention since the start of World War II. That was changing, and the Eisenhower administration was moving to assist Liberia economically.[39]

After Nixon's departure, Tubman disclosed at a press conference that the Kremlin was wooing him. Moscow had extended an invitation a year earlier for a visit and repeated the offer while Nixon was in Monrovia. Tubman added that he had rejected the offer because the United States had been Liberia's historic ally.[40]

While Tubman was trying to win America economic assistance with the prospect of Soviet interest in Liberia, the Nixon party flew east to central Africa for a brief stop in the British protectorate of Uganda. In Entebbe on March 10, the vice president complimented the English for their enlightened colonial policy. Fred Morrow, in his diary, wrote that "the British have done their usual job of making themselves comfortable and developing a splendid civilization in this unique area of the Dark Continent. Despite my extreme dislike for colonialism and everything it denotes, one cannot deny that the British really benefit any-place when they move in."[41]

That evening, the vice president told reporters that the Kremlin had "suffered a very great setback in Africa." African leaders abhorred the brutal repression in Hungary, and Nixon believed that although the communists had been un-successful in promoting their ideology in Africa, it remained "a major target of the international Communist movement because of the continent's resources and its 200,000,000 people."[42]

The Uganda stopover was primarily for relaxation, but the mission to Ethio-pia was critical. According to the state department, "This is probably the most important visit from substantive viewpoint as our fences badly need mending." Ethiopia occupied the horn of Africa opposite the Red Sea from Saudi Arabia. It was the oldest independent nation in Africa, with a majority of its population Coptic Christian and a sizeable Muslim minority. During World War II, the British had occupied the naval and air bases at Massawa that guarded the ap-proaches to the Suez Canal. These had strategic value in wartime, but by 1952 the British had decided to shut them down. When the United States military did not express any interest in occupying them, the English dismantled the facilities.[43]

When the Eisenhower administration came into office, it signed a bilateral military assistance treaty with Ethiopia. Emperor Haile Selassie met with Ike in Washington and received a pledge of economic assistance. As the first term was ending, the emperor claimed that the United States had violated the agree-ment; the state department answered that there had been a misunderstanding in providing the funds.[44]

On March 11, Nixon arrived in the capital, Addis Ababa, during an early eve-ning downpour. Morrow, on the way to the Imperial Palace, noted: "The leg-end" was that Ethiopians, who were "brown in color" with "chiseled" features "of Arab or Hamitic race," did "not want to be identified with the lowly plight of the American Negro." His reception had been "warm and sincere," and he believed the "highly educated court functionaries were . . . rather proud to see a brown man in the Vice-President's entourage."[45]

Nixon and Haile Selassie held talks the next day. The American press head-lined its reports with the emperor's disappointment over the lack of United States assistance. If the Eisenhower administration agreed to equip the Ethiopian mil-itary, the emperor would grant the United States an Air Force communication base with naval anchoring facilities at Massawa. The emperor, in fact, had asked for military aid, Export-Import Bank loans, and the development of a Nile River project. The vice president listened, pledging to improve bilateral ties.[46]

Besides the rumors concerning the private exchange, the media featured a story from the Soviet news organ *Pravda*, which charged the United States with providing the rationale for South Africa's segregationist policies. Nixon responded that the Kremlin routinely railed against American discrimination. Even though the United States had made progress, he would not be satisfied "until the problem is solved and equal opportunity becomes a reality for all Americans." He pointed out that Fred Morrow, a black White House staffer, was "one of his chief aides," and the African American press was well represented on his tour.[47]

At a White House press conference the next morning, James Reston of the *New York Times* asked the president if the United States was seeking a military base in Ethiopia. Ike answered curtly: that there were "no immediate plans for a base." The United States wanted "communications facilities largely." Later, Carleton Kent of the *Chicago Sun-Times* asked if the president was receiving special reports on Nixon's trip. Eisenhower responded: "Nothing unusual has been reported to me." He did not intend to reveal that he wanted facilities to direct missile launches.[48]

Shortly after returning to Washington, Nixon wrote Secretary of Defense Wilson that the Ethiopians had not received any commitment on the base. Despite that, the United States had to improve its bilateral ties by moderately expanding its military aid and delivering it promptly. Because of its strategic location, Ethiopia was growing more significant, and its military forces "could have an important stabilizing role in the Middle East in addition to their primary mission of internal security."[49]

After leaving Ethiopia on the morning of March 13, Nixon headed west to Sudan. Independent for fifteen months, this largely Muslim nation had a population of 9,000,000. In a meeting with the Sudanese ambassador in Washington the previous August, Eisenhower had stated that he hoped to aid the "under-developed areas of Africa."[50] Two days before Nixon reached Khartoum, communist agitators had passed out leaflets calling for demonstrations protesting his visit. The Sudanese rulers made certain that no anti-American display materialized. Nixon suggested that the protestors should distribute some literature in Hungary and persuade the Soviet military to leave "so the Hungarians could have independence like the Sudan."[51]

The vice president met with Prime Minister Addullah Khalil and other Sudanese leaders for an hour. They publicly announced that Sudan did not want any American aid. Sudan, they said, had good relations with its neighbor Egypt and had no need for American military assistance. The Sudanese leaders did, in private discussions, ask for economic assistance for roads and water projects; technical aid was a priority, but they wanted it "without political conditions."[52]

The vice president headed west to Libya on March 14. Ninety minutes out of Khartoum, a partial failure of engine #1 caused a loss of power, and the plane turned around for repairs at the Sudanese capital. Another airplane was dispatched to replace the one in need of repair so that Nixon did not arrive until dusk at the massive Wheeler Air Force Base, near the Libyan capital, Tripoli, on the Mediterranean Sea. Weary and still fighting a head cold, he retired and met with Prime Minister Mustafa Ben Halim at lunch the next afternoon. As part of the long-standing friction between Libya and Egypt, Libyan leaders accused Egyptian president Nasser of plotting to assassinate them. This was the prime minister's main concern. Although he did not believe that communism was a current threat to North Africa, he supported the Eisenhower Doctrine, although he disapproved of American support for Israel, and he asked the United States to pressure the French to grant independence to Algeria. Besides these crucial diplomatic issues, Libya needed economic and military assistance. American and foreign companies were exploring for oil, and if they found it, that would greatly enrich the impoverished state.[53]

That evening the prime minister informed reporters that he had asked the Eisenhower administration to resolve the "Palestinian problem" and help Algeria win its independence. These two issues were the "root of the trouble in the Middle East." Halim then endorsed Eisenhower's Middle East policies (with some reservations) and added that the president had moved "closer" to Arab objectives than the Truman government had.[54]

On March 16, Nixon flew across the Mediterranean to Italy. Landing outside of Rome, the vice president acknowledged the close bilateral bonds between America and Italy. He had first visited Italy in the fall of 1947, on the Herter Mission to evaluate economic conditions—a trip that anticipated congressional support for the upcoming debate on the Marshall Plan—and a decade later, he was pleased at how much progress had been achieved.[55]

The next day, Sunday, the vice president, his wife, and their staff went to the Vatican for a private audience with Pope Pius XII. The pope urged an ending of the Cold War and prayed for President Eisenhower's well being. He saw Pat Nixon alone for fifteen or twenty minutes, then gave a similar amount of time to her husband, who was impressed with the pope's extensive knowledge of foreign affairs. Nixon later described this meeting as "an experience I shall never forget."[56]

Later that day, the vice president held a press conference regarding his African journey, saying that American race relations could "have a very serious effect on the success or failure of the free nations in helping Africa develop toward independence and freedom rather than toward Communist totalitarianism." Far less serious, but significant to Pat, her husband had promised a decade earlier to take her to Italy. The stop in Rome happened to coincide with her forty-fourth birthday, and Dick took her on an open carriage ride to Trevi Fountain, made famous in the 1954 hit movie *Three Coins in the Fountain*. Following the legend, the Nixons tossed coins into the fountain over their left shoulders, thus ensuring their return to Rome.[57]

The following day, March 18, the Nixon party flew across the Mediterranean for their last stop, in Tunisia, a small and very poor desert nation of about 3,800,000 people that was preparing to celebrate the first anniversary of its independence from France. Prime Minister Habib Bourguiba, who had returned from exile in 1953, led a pro-Western government. During the flight, Nixon referred to him as "one of the real top-notch figures in this area of the world." A quarter century later, the former president described Bourguiba as "very charismatic, very warm and friendly." A huge crowd, perhaps a quarter of million spectators, cheered the prime minister and the vice president as they rode standing in an open limousine on their way in to Tunis.[58]

The two men held private talks that day. Later, the prime minister told reporters that his nation opposed communist ideology and was "fully committed to the West." Bourguiba, like the Libyan and Moroccan leaders, endorsed the Eisenhower Doctrine, but he opposed Nasser's Pan-Arabism. He and Nixon agreed that Israel should not be liquidated, and that the Arab-Israeli conflict had to be resolved. The French, he felt, had poisoned the region, and he called for free elections in Algeria under international supervision. Approximately 200,000 Algerian refugees had sought asylum in Tunisia, causing its current need for economic aid. The next day, to highlight the Algerian revolt even more, Bourguiba held an evening press conference urging France to grant Algerian independence. Tunisia and Morocco offered to assist in the negotiations, and he asked the United States to work on a solution with France and the Algerian rebels.[59]

The friction between France and Tunisia increased when the French representative to the independence celebration, justice minister François Mitterrand, was seated near the Algerian rebel leader, Ferhat Abbas, at a stadium ceremony. Mitterrand and his party left, and the next day, before he and Nixon boarded their planes, they talked for twenty minutes or so in the airport lounge. The vice president said that the discussion was "friendly," and he hoped Algerian situation could be settled "by peaceful rather than violent methods." The United States had no intention of supplanting French influence in North Africa and wanted good relations among Tunisia, France, and "all free countries." He concluded by emphasizing that he had found United States prestige higher than he had anticipated in the countries he had visited.[60]

He also echoed many of Eisenhower's views on Tunisia. The president had acted to provide economic aid before Nixon's trip, and it was vastly increased afterward. When France delayed its sale of military equipment that winter and Bourguiba warned that he might have to turn to the Soviet Union, Ike quickly sent 8000 M-1 rifles to Tunisia. Writing privately on November 18, the president called the prime minister "a very fine friend of the West and the most intelligent man that I know of in the Arab world."[61]

Nixon, having been sick throughout the trip, returned to Washington on the afternoon of March 21 and the next day entered Walter Reed Army Center with a 102-degree fever. The following day, against doctor's advice, he went home to finish writing his report on the trip for the president.[62] He had already started to draw attention to some topics he considered important. While in Rome, for instance, his criticism of poorly qualified American embassy and consular officials in Africa made front-page news: "How can we expect to get things done with corn balls like that?"[63] He also called out the United States Information Agency (USIA) for its failures. Their employees were not adequately trained for their jobs and paid far too little attention to social programs such as libraries and radio shows. A year and a half after his journey, he complained that the USIA in the Middle East was "woefully inadequate and ever since I returned from Africa last year I have been doing everything I can to work for its expansion." He could never persuade Congress to authorize the necessary funds.[64]

Besides these concerns over propaganda warfare, Nixon dealt with potentially explosive diplomatic issues. During his stops in Morocco and Tunisia, both former French protectorates, he listened to Arab rulers attack the French for not granting Algeria independence. He agreed with them: he saw statehood as the only solution and thought that the longer the French resisted, the worse the situation would become. On July 2, he commented that French intransigence "would probably bring on a terrible revolution with one million European against 8 million Algerians." Two months later, he added: "We must always weigh our public statements and our actions in terms of whether they will incite additional violence, or will encourage the moderate elements to reach agreement."[65]

Ike had mixed views on the Algerian question. He had championed European unity, and granting Algeria independence would move in the opposite direction. The Algerians did not have the education or management skills to run an efficient government. But at the same time, he recognized that the United States had won its "freedom—independence—liberty" and that these could not be denied to others.[66]

Nixon had avoided any mention of Nasser during his travels, but he regarded the Egyptian leader with suspicion. North African nations, Nixon believed, should maintain their independence and not align with "slavish blocs" as Nasser had done with the Soviet Union. He thought Nasser's prestige was waning with other regional leaders, even though his popularity with the masses remained high. A quarter century later, as a former president, Nixon recalled hearing that Nasser's "voice hypnotized people." He was a charismatic symbol of decolonization whose photograph was on public display throughout Tunisia, Morocco, Libya, and Sudan.[67]

Nixon hoped to counteract Egyptian Pan-Arabism by strengthening pro-Western Arab radio stations in the wake of Eisenhower's response to Suez, which delighted African leaders: "Our stand in the Suez crisis was uniformly praised in virtually every conversation I had. If we had taken the other direction, . . . we would . . . have written off Africa for at least a generation."[68] But although Nixon had expected Arab leaders to raise Algeria and Suez as major issues, he did not anticipate that they would feel so strongly about the exodus of Palestinians from Israel after the 1948 Arab-Israeli War. To the vice president, this was "the concern right in the heart of the difficulty." African leaders who applauded American willingness to assist Hungarian refugees could not comprehend why the same nation showed so little interest in the half-million to a million Arab refugees fleeing Israel. Nixon believed the Arabs understood that "Israel is here to stay." But the exiled Palestinians were a fundamental roadblock to peace.[69]

Without fanfare, Nixon met with the president in the Oval Office on the morning of March 24 to present a confidential report on his mission. He began by urging Ike to give Africa a higher priority—partly because, with French prestige declining due to the Algerian revolt, it was important to keep North Africa pro-Western by assisting Tunisia and Morocco, where America had military bases. Even though some North Africans feared Nasser, he was still popular; the United States should encourage his enemies without appearing to do so.

The United States also had to work with the sub-Saharan countries. Ghana required aid. Conditions in Liberia under Tubman were abysmal, and he had to be prodded to move toward democratic reforms. Sudan and Libya were pro-Western and needed technical and economic assistance. Embassy staffs were unprepared to address these issues; career officers had to be upgraded based on merit and not on skin color. Blacks should not be appointed simply because of their heritage; people who were well qualified, regardless of their color, needed to be assigned to Africa even though these emerging nations were not prestigious posts.[70]

At a White House press conference three days later, Edward Morgan of the American Broadcasting Company asked Ike if Nixon had called for an expansion of "financial and technical participation in Africa" and how this would be accomplished with a Democratically controlled Congress that was cutting foreign aid. Though he attacked Congress for its refusal to allocate the necessary funding, Ike never directly answered the question. Peter Lisagor of the *Chicago Daily News*, at another press conference on July 3, raised another issue regarding Nixon's trip. Did the vice president report on the Algerian rebellion? Ike equivocated. Legally, he said, Algeria was part of metropolitan France. The vice president's written report did not mention Algeria. He had also "made a verbal report" in which he recommended that the United States try to be fair to both sides, "and just turning the whole thing loose could well result in a very great disaster."[71]

The president did not mention that he had told Britain's new prime minister, Harold Macmillan, that Nixon's mission "proved to be very informative." Nixon thought the French government had to improve its North African relations, and Ike believed this could be accomplished through careful diplomacy. The vice president, in addition, had "found a great reservoir of good will toward the West, but he concluded that a modest amount of technical and economic aid was badly needed in each of the countries visited." If the West did not supply the assistance, these nations would turn to the Soviet Union; "That would be tragic." Several other African countries feared Nasser's Pan-Arabist ideology, which they saw as Kremlin-inspired, and were searching for ways to limit his influence.[72]

Besides briefing the president, Nixon met with the Dulles brothers. On March 19, Foster Dulles wrote to the vice president that he had done "a remarkable job of winning friends" during his travels. A few days later, he invited Nixon to the state department "to give his impressions" of the journey. Nixon asked if the assemblage could also include other agencies, such as USIA, so that he could hold a single debriefing. Allen Dulles told Nixon that the CIA was following up on his recommendations by improving the "caliber of personnel, program reviews" and assigning Africa a "higher priority."[73]

The vice president released his public report on April 5. He did not mention Algeria, the Palestinian issue, and Nasser's position in the Middle East. He did recommend that the administration give Africa a higher priority and highlighted the continent's potential. He also echoed the standard view of the monolithic Soviet menace: "The course of [Africa's] development . . . could well prove to be the decisive factor in the conflict between the forces of freedom and international communism." He did not understand that the Kremlin had no master plan for Africa, that Khrushchev had scant knowledge of African matters, or that Moscow's main objective there was simply to limit Western dominance.[74]

Nixon recommended that the United States learn more about African leaders, provide better diplomatic staffing, improve propaganda, and encourage friendly relations. The United States, the United Nations, and other agencies needed to provide technical and economic assistance to promote prosperity. He also hoped to establish a free trade movement and assist in the development of the Nile River projects, and called for the creation of a Bureau of African Affairs in the state department to oversee some of these projects.[75]

As he had done since his 1953 mission to Asia, Nixon repeated that America had to confront racism at home: "We must continue to strike at the roots of this problem. We cannot talk equality to the peoples of Africa and practice inequality in the United States. In the national interest, as well as for moral issues involved, we must support the necessary steps which will assure orderly progress toward the elimination of discrimination in the United States." He returned to this theme regularly. At a conference sponsored by the American Council on Education on November 14, he said that America must address its civil rights issues: "We can not talk one way abroad and, in the long run, act another way at home. It's just as simple as that."[76]

The Nixon trip had highlighted the role of African Americans. Fred Morrow devoted an entire chapter of this book *Black Man in the White House* to the tour. One unpublished diary entry, from February 14, 1957, discussed the administration's role in civil rights. Morrow "always" got "very angry" when anyone questioned Ike's honesty "on any problem dealing with human beings," but he would remain calm and answer every inquiry "forthrightly and without any reservations." He unequivocally supported "the sincerity of the President and the Administration on all minority problems—with special emphasis on civil rights."[77]

The most influential African American media personality who accompanied the Nixons was thirty-nine year-old John Johnson, who had started the monthly magazine *Ebony* at the end of World War II and *Jet*, a weekly journal, at the beginning of the 1950s. Both publications covered the tour extensively, including numerous photographs of the vice president with African leaders. By the end of the trip, Johnson and his wife Eunice had a "new respect for Nixon." He and the publisher became "old friends," and Johnson believed that Nixon "seemed to be more relaxed and personable at Black-oriented affairs."[78]

The vice president was delighted how the black press reacted to his mission: the coverage, he said, "was outstanding and the congenial and helpful attitude of the members of the press corps meant a great deal to us as we went through our rather arduous schedule." Claude Barnett, director of the Associated Negro Press in Chicago, wrote the vice president that he had done a "magnificent job." Africa had lain dormant for too long, but the continent had "possibilities and they can be developed." Two years later, Barnett stated that Nixon enjoyed "quite wonderful raaport [*sic*] with colored people," and he wanted "to help deepen this appreciation."[79]

Alex Rivera, who had spent two decades reporting from the South, represented the *Pittsburgh Courier*. Rivera wrote afterward to thank the Nixons for the "gracious hospitality and friendship" they had shown him and his wife. If he could help the vice president in the future, he should ask.[80]

To acknowledge the positive role of the African American reporters on the journey, on May 19 the Nixons invited the Johnsons, the Riveras, and the others over to their house for a reunion. Three days later, the Capital Press Club, composed of black reporters, held its fourteenth annual awards dinner with an audience of about 500. The group made Martin Luther King Jr. its "Man of the Year," and Pat Nixon won the International Goodwill Award for her role in the African mission. Her husband told the crowd that one of the United States' worst mistakes in dealing with people of color from other countries was not treating them as equals.[81]

Almost a year since the African mission, Simeon Booker, capital bureau chief for the Johnson Publishing Company, and Ethel Payne, *Chicago Defender* reporter, both of whom had been on the trip, decided to hold a reunion. They sent out invitations on Tuesday to about thirty-five guests for that Saturday evening, March 1, 1958, including several African ambassadors, some American politicians, and the Nixons. The vice president's office promptly replied that he and Pat would attend. Congressman Diggs and Senator Theodore Green, Democrat from Rhode Island and chairman of the foreign relations committee, were among the attendees. The Nixons arrived early and left late. His contribution to the gathering was a bottle of 119 proof whiskey.[82] Val Washington, director of RNC minority affairs, wrote in a memo the next day that this was "the first time any Vice President had ever visited in the home of a Negro to his [Washington's] knowledge, and that this fact had made a most profound impression on everyone there."[83]

As a consequence of the tour and Nixon's recommendations on his return, the state department announced that it was creating a new Bureau of African Affairs and expected to establish new diplomatic consulates in the French Cameroons, the French Ivory Coast, Somalia, and Uganda. National Security Advisor Robert Cutler described Nixon as the "father" of the new African policy.[84]

Secretary Dulles called the vice president in mid-April 1958 to get his suggestions for the assistant secretary who would manage the new bureau. Nixon thought the bureau would address a major shortcoming: as he wrote deputy undersecretary for administration Loy Henderson later than month, "we have not been putting our first team on the field in Africa and . . . we consequently find ourselves at a competitive disadvantage with the Soviets, Egyptians and others who are sending top-flight officials." The state department should stop restricting black American diplomats to Africa, nor should political appointees be assigned there. Only the best-qualified professionals should serve. Henderson thanked the vice president for his advice and pointed out that the state department was making progress in selecting African Americans to the Foreign Service, and they would not automatically be sent to African stations.[85]

Enthusiasm for these new priorities was dampened when the overwhelmingly Democratic House reduced the state department's budget proposal. Joseph Palmer II, a career foreign service officer who had accompanied Nixon on his journey, wrote the vice president on May 3 to say that the House had approved an African division, but without allotting any additional funds. It established consular posts in French Equatorial Africa, Nigeria, and Madagascar but provided lower-than-normal budgets for staffing, supplies, and travel allowances. Hardship post allotments were eliminated. Critical areas like the Near East and South Asia maintained their funding, but the overall budget for consulates and embassies in Africa were cut by about 3 percent. Those in some other regions were cut by up to 6 percent.[86]

Nixon had served in Congress for six years and understood the economics of new programs. On May 17, he wrote that "the budget is really a reflection of the world in which we live today and its size is directly attributable to the fight to maintain our way of life in the face of determined attack by those who would impose a totalitarian regime upon the world." Despite feeling that Congress was underestimating the menace from the Soviet Union in Africa, the vice president hoped to demonstrate to the Africans "that we have a real interest in their future progress, and I am convinced that our diplomatic and educational programs in this region must be concentrated to that end."[87]

No historian has written any detailed account of Nixon's trip to Africa and its consequences. Recent writers have faulted the Eisenhower administration for paying too little attention to African decolonization and have linked this supposed failure to the president's alleged unconcern with domestic civil rights. In her 2013 book *In Search of Power: African Americans in the Era of Decolonization, 1956–1974*, Brenda Plummer writes: "The Eisenhower administration half-heartedly reached out to the black electorate by supporting minor civil rights laws and appointing a handful of African-American officeholders." The president "had little prior knowledge of Africa, and awkward mistakes compromised his administration's efforts to conduct normal relations with the new states." These sweeping generalizations are inaccurate: the administration accomplished far more on civil rights than Plummer postulated, and while Eisenhower had not lived in sub-Saharan Africa, he was stationed in North Africa during World War II for over a year.[88]

George White Jr.'s 2005 book *Holding the Line: Race, Racism, and American Foreign Policy toward Africa, 1953–1961* asserts that the president failed to shape a successful African policy because of his administration's racist policies. White argues that the Eisenhower administration managed its African policy to maintain "the larger power configuration of White Supremacy." Africa was subordinated "to White Supremacist needs."[89]

Five years later, White described the vice president as a bigot and said of his African journey that "Nixon's advocacy of a greater focus on African affairs did not stem from a belief in racial equality." Instead, according to White, he "used his privileged status to reinforce the assumption and prejudices of the predominantly white bureaucratic corps regarding blacks." The evidence shows that White's thesis is without merit. The vice president, as the administration's most influential civil rights spokesman, championed ending domestic segregation and promoting this effort abroad.[90]

Historian Michael Hunt's *Ideology and U.S. Foreign Policy* offers a more nuanced perspective. Hunt, looking at the hierarchy of race in American diplomacy, found that during the Eisenhower years, whites in the state department believed Caucasians were the best people to govern. Secretary Dulles and United Nations representative Lodge used the term "non-white" in a condescending manner when referring to the Third World. The president, his secretary of state, and the overwhelming majority of diplomats saw the West as superior to the Third World, which was populated by inferior races. Segregation demonstrated African American inequality in the United States as well as abroad. Racism in America was an embarrassing fact that prevailed, and rather than fading away, it was rising to a boiling point.[91]

In fact, racism was not the single factor shaping United States diplomacy toward Africa. Eisenhower realized that that European colonial possessions were moving toward decolonization; concurrently, he recognized that the European nations with colonies were trusted allies, and their positions had to be respected. Decolonization had to be carefully managed to avoid violent revolutions that gave the Soviet Union an opening to present itself as an ally of the people, but also to prevent independence from occurring so quickly that the emerging nations were left unprepared for self-governance. He hoped to persuade both European powers and their colonies to walk a fine line.[92]

The vice president's mission gave Eisenhower firsthand observations of eight African countries. Nixon visited states bordering Egypt and solicited their leaders' viewpoints on Nasser. He stopped at United States military bases in North Africa and extended discussions in Ethiopia on a communications installation. He brought details regarding the French troubles in Algeria and the Israeli-Arab conflict over Palestinian refugees. Once again, the president needed answers regarding African decolonization, and the headlines depicting Nixon's trip as a goodwill mission masked the deeper purposes that mattered to the president.

30

IKE'S COLD WAR

By the beginning of Ike's second term, the line of authority shaping American foreign policy was clearly delineated. The president made the decisions based on his extensive diplomatic knowledge, assisted by his principal adviser, Secretary Dulles. At another level, the president employed his brother Milton, Vice President Nixon, and others as forward observers who traveled and reported back to their commander on conditions outside of the United States. Eisenhower relied upon individuals with a variety of opinions in order to give himself the breadth and depth he needed to make intelligent judgments.

After Ike's heart attack in September 1955, the bond between Dulles and Nixon grew, causing a major change in the formulation of foreign policy. The two men worked closely together to present a united front. A year later, on November 2, 1956, Dulles was rushed to Walter Reed Hospital complaining of severe abdominal pain. When the doctors operated, they found incurable cancer; their findings were not released to the public. For the next two and a half years, Dulles remained in charge of the state department despite living in constant pain.[1]

Ike routinely defended his secretary. In a letter to Republican Congressman Walter Judd from Minnesota on January 4, 1958, he wrote: "Foster has now, as always before, my total support and confidence. . . . His traits of character—as well as his intellectual honesty and diplomatic knowledge—all make him as nearly indispensable as a human ever becomes."[2]

Shortly after the second term commenced, Nixon and Dulles began discussing the idea of giving the vice president more involvement in foreign affairs. Congress had drastically reduced the administration's foreign aid request before the 1956 presidential election, and Dulles wanted to map out more successful tactics for 1957. With Attorney General Brownell's approval, Dulles proposed an expanded role for Nixon, especially in dealing with Congress. Ike met with

Dulles on September 2, 1957, and told him that the proposal might conflict with the White House congressional liaison team, headed by Jerry Persons. But he agreed that the team needed to get a more positive congressional response to the administration's foreign policy initiatives—a constant struggle throughout his presidency—and he promised to talk to Nixon.[3]

The very next day Congress again slashed his request for money for foreign assistance. Perhaps in response to this news, Ike wrote to Nixon that he "might find it possible—and intriguing—to be of even more help in our whole governmental program dealing with affairs abroad than you have been in the past." The vice president's previous foreign assignments had been of "inestimable assistance" to the administration, and he had "an understanding of our foreign problems that is both unusual and comprehensive." The president asked Nixon to help guide the state and defense departments' budget through Congress, in coordination with chief of staff Adams and his deputy Persons. After Dulles talked to the vice president, the secretary informed Brownell that the vice president was "very happy about" the proposal.[4]

Historian Daun van Ee, who edited the Eisenhower papers for more than a quarter of a century, states that Ike seldom wrote this kind of correspondence and that it shows his remarkable approval of the vice president. As for the substance, during World War II, the general would send out such instructions to prevent misunderstandings and to clear obstacles. As president, he expected Adams and Persons to acquiesce and cooperate.[5]

Foreign aid was a chronic problem, carried over from the start of the Eisenhower presidency. As the Suez crisis escalated in the fall of 1956, Eisenhower saw that the British and French had lost their military supremacy in the Middle East, and he feared that the Soviet Union might fill the vacuum. To prevent this, he began to formulate a proposal whereby the United States would defend pro-Western Middle Eastern governments against communist penetration. In mid-November he told reporters at a White House press conference that his administration would assist Middle Eastern regimes against communist aggression, labeling this policy the Eisenhower Doctrine.

Early the next year, the president sent the Eisenhower Doctrine to Congress for approval. Under his plan, the United States would provide military and economic assistance to prop up Middle Eastern governments that confronted Nasser and communist infiltration. Nixon had closely followed the events in the Suez— despite spending most of the crisis on the campaign trail—and in the middle of January he wrote a memo to Republican leaders backing the president's position. If the United States prevented the Kremlin from achieving "any significant victory" over "the next few months, the deterioration of the Communist empire . . . will be greatly accelerated." When Nixon traveled to Africa that March, he visited countries that bordered Egypt and reported back to the president on Nasser and the Kremlin's influence in the Middle East.[6]

Even though Eisenhower's Middle East policy received overwhelming congressional support, his foreign assistance programs still faced roadblocks. He saw these projects as fostering economic growth in the developing countries and helping to halt communist penetration, and from the start of his presidency, he tried to increase trade and allocate aid through what he called mutual security legislation. Each year, Congress reduced his requests, calling the programs ineffective and wasteful.

Nixon worked energetically to help pass the mutual security legislation each time it was proposed. He told the National Security Council (NSC) on March 28, 1957, that the worst part of the congressional program was its "insistence on cutting the budget for foreign assistance and for informational and cultural exchanges." A month later, speaking before the American Iron and Steel Institute, he described foreign aid as "necessary to our survival." If Congress seriously reduced the administration's aid budget, it would "jeopardize not only our safety, but our chance for victory in the world struggles."

Late in 1957, Nikita Khrushchev unwittingly helped promote the American foreign aid program by calling for economic warfare against the West. On January 10, 1958, Secretary Dulles told the cabinet that the United States had to counteract the Soviet initiative. The economic battle for the allegiance of developing nations had to be taken seriously, he said, and had to be won. Ike ordered countermeasures drawn up.[7]

Nixon, who was already speaking in similar terms to Khrushchev's, was asked to lead the charge against the Soviet drive. Throughout 1958, he wrote a letters to constituents "that the current Soviet 'peace' propaganda will not make us forget the ruthless enslavement of millions of people by the rulers of the Kremlin." Toward the end of September, he stated that the Soviet economic threat was "fully as dangerous as their more obvious militarism." At NSC gatherings, the vice president said that since the Kremlin was placing more emphasis on economic aid and less on military, the United States, whenever possible, should do the same. The communists, said Nixon, argued that they wanted to improve the lot of the common man while capitalists thought only of themselves, and even though these claims were invalid, the theme "fostered sympathy toward Communist promises of change."[8]

After appointing Nixon to lead the effort for greater foreign assistance funding, Ike met with elected officials throughout 1958 to garner support for his bills. He was disheartened and could not understand how either Democrats or

Republicans, especially those on the House appropriations committee, could object to his proposals. The communists were trying to infiltrate developing countries' economies, and he was trying to stop them. The appropriation committee threatened "to wreck the effort." In late 1958, Nixon proposed linking political and military assistance because Congress was more generous with the latter and "niggardly in providing funds for assistance for political purposes." In 1960 he again called for Congress to fund mutual security assistance at adequate levels to help United States allies.[9]

During his last year in office, Eisenhower continued to put forward his mutual security bills while congressional opponents continued to cut their funding. He often pointed out that military aid had been cut from $8 billion in 1953 to $2 billion in 1960. He demanded from his cabinet and Republican congressional leaders "an intensive effort to make a factual showing of the good accomplished through the program."[10] But he never succeeded in raising foreign aid funding to the levels he thought necessary.

The Cold War rivalry shifted to a higher level on Friday, October 4, 1957, when the Soviet Union surprised the world by announcing that it had launched the first man-made satellite to orbit the earth. The satellite, named Sputnik, was a stunning scientific achievement and a propaganda triumph, and Khrushchev added to the excitement by exaggerating its military importance. Many people, of all political persuasions, thought the Kremlin had forged ahead while the United States had lost prestige.

Ike, correctly understanding that Sputnik did not threaten American security and in fact had not altered the military balance, refused to panic in the face of public hysteria. But at a White House press conference, he failed to convince his countrymen that America's military superiority remained intact. Congress, especially Democrats vying for their party's presidential nomination in 1960, seized upon the Soviet success to attack the administration and demand large increases in the defense budget to meet the Kremlin's challenge. The national mood forced Eisenhower to initiate what he considered an imprudent crash program to launch a satellite.[11] It also provoked an unprecedented increase in funding for science education and scientific research, two developments that would have profound effects on the American economy and on American life in the coming decades. Eisenhower saw these funding increases as an attack on the balanced budget that could severely disturb economic growth.

The administration was already planning a more deliberate effort toward a space program. Two months before the Sputnik launch, Nixon told reporter Chalmers Roberts of the *Washington Post* that while the "New Look [the military commitment to more nuclear dependence over ground troops] accounted for current weapons," the United States had to begin to expand its missile program. He did not intend to project "a sense of urgency." But after the Soviet launch, he immediately recognized its political implications in a way the president did not. He told Secretary Dulles that Congress would insist upon an investigation of American missile development and would want to know how the Soviet Union had surpassed the United States. Both men agreed that any congressional inquiry would be "rough." The American missile program had been plagued by spectacular failures: the rockets kept exploding on the launch pad or shortly after liftoff. If the Democrats blamed the administration, Nixon would point out that Truman had treated satellite projects "as a 5th cousin," and if they tried to belittle Eisenhower, "we can tear them to pieces."[12]

In the middle of October, without clearing his speech with either the White House or the state department (a rare omission for him), the vice president spoke out about Sputnik's significance. At the start of the second term, he said, the administration had considered proposing a tax reduction, but it had to be canceled in favor of maintaining military security. The Soviet accomplishment was a "grim and timely reminder . . . that the Soviet Union has developed a scientific and industrial capacity of great magnitude." The United States had to postpone any tax reduction and concentrate on meeting the challenge of international communism. Still, Nixon opposed the demand for a special session of Congress to increase defense spending. The president had assured American citizens that the United States would maintain its military superiority, and the "calm, thorough approach he has taken should help restore our confidence and will-to-win, and also dispel panic, confusion and hasty ill-conceived action."[13]

On December 3, the president brought together political leaders from both parties to discuss Sputnik. Democratic senator J. William Fulbright from Arkansas, who specialized in foreign affairs, recommended that the administration "ought to use the new sense of urgency in the country" to bolster military and foreign assistance spending. John Foster Dulles disagreed, and Nixon took middle ground, saying that while the administration "did not want to show panic" and the military situation had not changed, Sputnik had profoundly altered public perceptions. The vice president hoped that Ike would "use this change in the public mind to advantage and get the maximum mileage out of it in additional support for his program which had been so severely chopped down by the Congress last session."[14]

The attempted launch of the Vanguard satellite at Cape Canaveral failed three days later—the rocket rose just four feet, fell back, ruptured, and blew up—causing great worry within the administration. At the end of January 1958,

Explorer successfully lifted off. The nation expected the government to make satellite production a priority, and Congress responded. The space race was on. In the winter of 1959, Nixon told a news conference that he rejected a "massive crash program" to match the Soviet Union. The United States was "moving along at a reasonable good pace" and would eventually catch up to the Soviets.[15]

Eisenhower faced another unexpected event that called for a dramatic increase in spending—this one of his own making. Early in 1957, he had appointed a group of private citizens, chaired by H. Roman Gaither Jr., board chairman of the Ford Foundation and the RAND Corporation, to investigate the need and feasibility of building nuclear fallout shelters throughout the country. Such a program, if pursued, would cost billions of dollars. Because of the complexity of the question, the group broadened its charge and decided to tackle a wide range of national security issues. On November 7, the Gaither Report was presented to the NSC; it recommended massive increases in military spending and expansion of the second strike force. Blast shelters were not a major concern.

Ike listened, thanked the group for its effort, and later commented that while he agreed with some of its suggestions, he could not endorse such a massive increase in military spending. The report was not made public. By the end of the year, however, most of its contents had been leaked to the press, hardening the arguments of those who championed greater spending as well as those who opposed it. The president, disgusted with the leaks, concluded that he had been foolish to appoint an "outside group," and this one had exceeded its assignment.[16]

The damage, however, was done: critics charged the administration with creating a "Missile Gap." Ike knew better. At that point, having led the Allied Forces in Europe during World War II, commanded NATO forces in Western Europe in the early 1950s, and then governed as commander-in-chief as president, he had been closely monitoring the Soviet military for a decade and a half, and he knew its capabilities. He responded cautiously to those who demanded expanded military funding because he was firmly convinced that any monumental increases would damage the nation economically. Ike, through the defense department, had developed a three-pronged system to deter attack: hardened missile silos in the United States, bombers carrying nuclear warheads, and submarines with Polaris missiles—essentially the nuclear defense system the United States retains today. Peter Roman, in *Eisenhower and the Missile Gap*, writes that the president's "larger, secure, and redundant strategic and nuclear triad may be his most enduring legacy."[17]

Stuart Symington, a Democratic senator from Missouri who had been secretary of the Air Force under Truman, thought Ike was being disingenuous. Now serving on the Senate armed services committee, Symington maintained that the Soviet Union was ahead of the United States in missile delivery systems, and he relentlessly hammered the administration for its failure to acknowledge the missile gap and rapidly increase spending. He was far more than an advocate on the subject: he also had presidential aspirations and expected to use his experience in defense policy to defeat his rivals for the Democratic nomination.[18]

Nixon fiercely defended the administration against Symington and others' accusations. After he held an informal meeting with reporters on January 12, 1959, an erroneous AP story reported that he said the United States had forged ahead of the USSR in military ballistic missiles. He had actually said that the United States had the advantage in some areas and the Soviet Union in others, resulting in a stalemate. Without waiting for verification, Symington rose on the Senate floor and challenged Nixon to release the statistics to prove his point, saying "I do not know a single impartial expert in the missile field who would support it."[19]

Symington was relying on incorrect assessments. At the beginning of 1959, American missiles were more accurate than Soviet ones, and American ICBM delivery systems were superior. By the end of 1960, it was the Kremlin that faced a missile gap, and it was growing. Despite this, many charged that the United States was lagging behind.[20]

One reason the administration did not defend against this charge more strongly may have been the fear that if the Russians thought they were behind the Americans, they would redouble their efforts, accelerating the arms race and forcing the United States to further militarize its economy. If there was any benefit from Soviet complacency, it was lost early in the next administration when Secretary of Defense Robert McNamara declared that the missile gap had mysteriously disappeared. Kennedy had campaigned energetically on this failure of the Eisenhower administration and had difficulty believing his own defense secretary, and so, he ordered his own investigation to confirm McNamara's statement.

Eisenhower devoted a significant portion of his presidency to the NATO alliance. After the end of World War II, he had helped to develop the defense of Western Europe, and as president at Columbia University, he had watched with approval when Konrad Adenauer was elected chancellor of West Germany in 1949. In Paris as commander of NATO, Ike was actively involved in formulating military plans to repel a possible Soviet attack on the Western alliance.[21]

Shortly after Ike's 1953 inauguration, Chancellor Adenauer visited him and Secretary Dulles, and the three men formed a cordial bond. Once Ike started to rely on the New Look's emphasis on nuclear weapons rather than ground troops, Adenauer worried that the United States would withdraw its troops from Europe. He was reassured when the president strengthened West Germany by having it join NATO in 1955 and rearming it, and the chancellor looked for support in bolstering NATO.[22]

Disagreements between the United States and West Germany temporarily vanished on November 10, 1958, when Khrushchev unilaterally proclaimed that the East and West had to commence talks to end the Four Power occupation of Germany that had lasted since 1945. If the West refused, the USSR would sign a peace treaty with East Germany in six months, canceling the postwar agreements and turning control of Berlin over to the German Democratic Republic.[23]

Ike reacted to the ultimatum calmly but firmly. The president maintained NATO unity against the threat, and Khrushchev gracefully relented when the president gave him the opportunity. That ended the Berlin crisis during the Eisenhower presidency. Nothing changed, but the tension remained.[24]

On February 17, 1959, Khrushchev warned against any effort by the West to enter West Berlin. David Sentner of the Hearst Newspapers put the issue in graphic terms at the next day's White House press conference: how did Eisenhower respond to Khrushchev's threat that if the United States tried to "shoot our way into West Berlin," it would start a war? Ike replied that the United States would "continue carrying out our responsibilities to those people," and if Americans were prevented from entering West Berlin, "it will be somebody else using force."[25]

Nixon helped to mobilize congressional support for a "firm" but not "provocative" stand, keeping legislative leaders informed so that they could present a united front. Ike, meeting privately with the majority and minority leaders of both parties, Lyndon Johnson, Sam Rayburn, Everett Dirksen, and Charles Halleck, on March 6, pledged not to desert the 2.2 million Germans living in West Berlin. He would abide by the existing agreements and was prepared to negotiate a new peace treaty, but not under the threat of an ultimatum. Describing Khrushchev as "stupid" and yet "exceedingly shrewd and most certainly ruthless," Ike said he expected to act decisively since "any appeasement meant disaster." A week later, during a cabinet meeting, he predicted no immediate cause for concern. The Cold War forced Americans to live with tension, and Khrushchev did not want to begin a war any more than the West did.

In the end, the threat turned out to be a bluff. When the six months ended on May 26 and the chairman did not sign a separate peace treaty, the crisis was postponed. It remained in a state of limbo.[26]

Secretary Dulles steadfastly followed the president's lead, insisting on the status quo unless another peace treaty was negotiated. Ike depended on Dulles as his chief foreign policy adviser, but by late 1958, the president knew that the secretary would have to resign because of his deteriorating health. Nixon also saw that Dulles's condition was worsening. The secretary assured the vice president at the start of the second term that if his policies harmed the president, he would resign; he reiterated this during the controversies over Quemoy-Matsu and West Berlin.[27]

On April 4, 1959, the vice president visited Dulles for an hour, while he was convalescing at a Florida retreat. Dulles's cancer had progressed. He performed his duties only with great difficulty. Nixon hoped his friend would improve, but the secretary returned to Washington on the twelfth for further treatment at Walter Reed Hospital. Nixon greeted him at the airport and learned that Dulles and the president had discussed his resignation but would not make any decision until the secretary underwent "new treatment." Ike visited Dulles the next day, and the two men decided to wait a few more days before making any decision. After Dulles spoke to Nixon about that visit, the vice president thought the secretary's voice did "not sound the same as usual." When they finished, Nixon "had tears in his eyes." On the twenty-second, the president announced that Dulles had resigned. Nixon released his own statement, calling Dulles "one of the truly heroic figures of this generation."[28]

The secretary grew increasingly tired. Nixon visited when Dulles was well enough, but never saw Dulles in his hospital bed; he always was wheeled out in his wheelchair and never referred to the severity of his pain. On April 23, the president, vice president, and Dulles posed for a photograph, printed on the front page of the *New York Times*, accompanying the news that Ike had appointed Dulles as a special consultant.[29]

This picture shows that Dulles had lost a great deal of weight. On May 15, the president told his cabinet that the former secretary was in "very poor" condition. Three days later, only family members were allowed in his hospital room. A few days before his death, on a beautiful spring day, Nixon saw him for the last time. Janet Dulles later told the vice president that these visits had given her husband "an enormous boost because they lifted him out of his of desperate troubles." Nixon thought his friend had shrunk to about eighty pounds. He had trouble eating and drinking so he "just sucked on a piece of ice." After they discussed foreign policy for a bit, Dulles said: "It's too fine a day for you to be in here. . . . You should be out golfing." That was their last meeting.[30]

Dulles died early on the morning of May 24. That afternoon the president ordered that flags be lowered to half-staff until burial services were completed.

On May 27, Dulles was accorded an official funeral with full military honors.[31] The first and second families were present throughout the day's events. Although the family requested that there be no speakers at the funeral, Nixon eulogized the secretary in *Life* magazine. Dulles had been a loyal friend and a great secretary of state without "unreasoned pride and conceit" who stood fast against the communist menace. The vice president wrote that he knew the United States would win the struggle, and "while American greatness and American hope endure, John Foster Dulles will be remembered as one of their most effective and eloquent champions."[32]

Dulles was succeeded by undersecretary of state Christian Herter. Herter had served for many years in the House of Representatives and had been elected the governor of Massachusetts. Herter decided not to run for reelection because he was tired of elective office. Instead, he asked to be appointed undersecretary of state in the second Eisenhower administration, and Nixon had vigorously lobbied for him. When asked to compare the two men for an oral history, assistant secretary of state Roy Rubottom described them as "completely different." Dulles had a legal background with decades of diplomatic experience. Herter "was a softer man, a sweeter man."[33]

While Dulles was alive, Nixon had relied on the secretary. That relationship ended when Herter replaced Dulles. Throughout his vice presidency, Nixon "always followed the policy of not relying solely on the State Department for my information in the foreign area." In January 1959, he told Ike over dinner that while he had met many "very fine foreign service officers," he had also found that "an astonishing number of them" were not dedicated to their country and the diplomatic service. Both he and Pat had encountered some who were "far more vocal in their criticism of our country than many of the foreigners." He thought that some had gone into the Foreign Service during the New Deal and opposed Republican policies; others maintained "an expatriate attitude toward" the United States and planned never to return. Ike noted in his diary that Pat, who was at the dinner, was "very sensitive to those things" and "was more emphatic than her husband about these beliefs that career officials expressed." Ike said, in response to their observations, "I don't know what to do about it."[34]

Ike, too, did not have the same intimate tie with Herter as he had with his predecessor. The president treated his new secretary of state as the manager of the state department's bureaucracy who followed his commander's orders. Herter met regularly with the president, but foreign policy came out of the Oval Office.

Dulles's influence did not die with his passing. During Nixon's visits with him, they had often talked about the vice president's upcoming mission to see Khrushchev, planned for the summer of 1959. Dulles had years of experience negotiating with the Kremlin to settle problems and reduce tensions, and he knew that Khrushchev did not rise to the position of party chairman by being a weakling. If Nixon wished for peace, he had to convince Khrushchev that negotiations would give him a better result than warfare.[35]

31

A Near-Death Experience

During his first term, Eisenhower had sent Richard Nixon on assignment to Mexico, Central America, the Caribbean, and Brazil, and in the summer of 1956 the vice president wrote: "My interest in strengthening our friendship and relations with our Sister Republics in the Western Hemisphere is a deep and continuing one." The Monroe Doctrine, which declared United States supremacy in the Western Hemisphere, was for Nixon a cornerstone of American foreign policy. Communists advancing the interests of foreign governments contributed to the unsettled hemispheric conditions. The United States could not forget, Nixon wrote in a private letter to a constituent, about "the significance of the Guatemalan revolution. Communist colonialism is more subtle than the colonialism of the eighteenth and nineteenth centuries. But, nevertheless, it is just as real."[1]

On the last day of 1957, the president wrote Foster Dulles that the assistant secretary of state for inter-American Affairs, Roy Rubottom Jr., had suggested that Secretary Dulles visit South America. The changes in government and deteriorating economic conditions, Rubottom thought, needed closer attention. Ike wrote: "I urgently believe something should be done! Could we use Dick?"[2]

Critics had accused Dulles of neglecting hemispheric issues, and in March he asked the vice president to take on the assignment, adding that the trip "would be of great benefit in the conduct of our relations with all countries of the area." He wanted Nixon to meet Arturo Frondizi, the president-elect of Argentina, encourage social reform programs in Bolivia, and improve the strained relations with Uruguay. The secretary especially suggested a stop in Venezuela "because of the recent revolution and change of government in that country and also because of the special economic and strategic interests that we have there."[3]

Since Dulles was going to Brazil and the Chilean president was scheduled to come to Washington, Nixon would bypass those nations. He would visit eight states: Uruguay, Argentina, Paraguay, Bolivia, Peru, Ecuador, Colombia, and Venezuela. The schedule would be demanding, with each stop limited to two days.

Nixon had criticized the diplomatic corps during the first term. In 1961, he recalled that although he applauded career diplomats who made tough decisions, he had a low opinion of those who got ahead by keeping a low profile: "most of our poorest Ambassadors were career men who had gotten to the top by avoiding and sluffing off tough decisions rather than making them and whose sole interest in life seemed to be to finish their careers in foreign service without doing anything which would risk their getting a black mark on their fitness reports." Rubottom, however, was not like that. The vice president's aides knew him as "a fellow who pushes—he is a very eager fellow and he will try to cover everyone and fill up the schedules."[4]

The American ambassador to Colombia, John Cabot, read the plans for the vice president's visit and reacted sharply. Cabot wanted substantive meetings, but Nixon wanted a media event—"something so supercolossal that it will even wow the yokels back home in the election year." The state department's instructions, he wrote, were outrageous: "the only thing they haven't asked for is an officer to see that the V.P.'s fly isn't unbuttoned."[5]

By March 19, Nixon was committed and asked Secretary of the Interior Fred Seaton, at the appropriate moment, to "tell the people that these trips were worth the time and money spent since they did a tremendous amount of good." Three days later, the vice president wrote that "it will probably be another whirlwind tour, but we are looking forward to it."[6]

The state department announced the mission with its itinerary on March 21. The Nixons would leave on April 27 and return May 15. Before his departure, the vice president got intelligence briefings from diplomats and the CIA, who reported that labor groups, university students, and intellectuals "were most fertile spots for development of Communism." Rose Mary Woods gave Nixon's mother, Hannah, a progress report. Pat, who had limited her public appearances because of back trouble, was feeling better: "she is such a big part of each trip and it would only be a lot harder for all of us if she had been unable to accompany the Boss."[7]

At the airport shortly before takeoff, Nixon told reporters that he expected to strengthen hemispheric solidarity by meeting with a wide variety of people. He intended to hold "full and frank discussions" and wanted Latin Americans to know that the United States had not taken them "for granted." At the top of his list was the recession that had swept most of South America, primarily because most of the region's economies depended on exports of a single agricultural commodity such as coffee or wool. "Everybody should realize," he emphasized, "that these countries are not only our neighbors but our best friends."[8]

Assistant secretary Rubottom included Maurice Bernbaum, his chief aide and the director of the Office of South American Affairs. Nixon had surrounded himself with half a dozen aides to keep the professional diplomats at arm's length. In addition to Woods and his wife, the vice president brought his executive assistant, William Key; his military aides, Robert Cushman and Donald Hughes; and Samuel Waugh, president of the Export-Import Bank, who would consider loan applications. Everything Rubottom wanted to arrange had to go through the vice president's "coterie of advisers" and "that made our relationships rather tough." Jack Sherwood headed the Secret Service detail, and twenty-five reporters and photographers accompanied the party. The defense department added an intercontinental radiotelephone to the aircraft for communicating with Washington.[9]

They first stopped in Port-of-Spain, Trinidad, where Nixon met for several hours with Prime Minister Sir Grantley Adams of the West Indies Federation. With that accomplished and the airplane refueled, they arrived at Montevideo, Uruguay, on the morning of April 28, greeted by a cheering crowd shouting, "Long Live Nixon" as well as a few yelling "Go Home Nixon." As the motorcade drove into the capital, a small group of protestors tossed anti-American leaflets at Nixon's limousine. The government had recently concluded a barter agreement with the Soviet minister and top Kremlin official in Latin America, Seguel Migailov: Uruguayan wool for Soviet oil.[10]

Lieutenant Colonel Vernon Walters joined the vice president in the capital as an aide and interpreter. Ike had regularly used him and had ordered him to South America to translate for the vice president. Walters remained at the vice president's side, with few exceptions, during the rest of the journey.[11]

One reason for Uruguay's severe recession was that the United States had raised its tariffs on wool and meat imports, exports that Uruguay heavily depended upon. The government also had expropriated the Swift and Armour meat packing plants, fearing that these American companies were planning to close them. President Luis Batlle Berres promised fair compensation, and the vice president privately pledged that the United States would not intervene and that he was sympathetic to lowering trade barriers.[12]

On the morning after his arrival, Nixon ignored the state department's advice by accepting an invitation from the National University Law School. In front of a packed hall, he sat down next to Ricardo Yelpo, the twenty-six-year-old leftist leader of the Student Federation. When asked why the United States supported Latin American dictators Nixon answered: "The United States does not want to dominate other nations or impose its system on them. If the United States attempted to discriminate between governments it would be said that the Colossus of the North is seeking to impose its will on little countries." After the debate and as he left the hall, some students chanted: "Neekson, Neekson." Some asked for his autograph; others booed.[13]

Louis Nolan, counselor for economic affairs at the American embassy, declared the vice president's visit "an outstanding success." He had gone to the law school in defiance of the warnings from American diplomats, listened to attacks on the United States for half an hour, and replied skillfully. Nolan called the appearance "a masterful political stroke."[14]

At a press conference later that day, Nixon answered questions, mostly from Uruguayan reporters, and pledged to help lower trade barriers. The newsmen applauded him when he said: "Communism and the temper and principles of the Uruguayan people are completely incompatible. The tradition of freedom and independence here is so strong that any ideology dedicated to dictatorship will never find Uruguay a healthy place to grow."[15]

The ostensible reason for the mission was that Nixon was leading the United States delegation to Arturo Frondizi's inaugural ceremony in Buenos Aires, Argentina. Frondizi was Argentina's first democratically elected president since Juan Perón seized power in 1943 and was ousted in September 1955 by a coup d'état, and he had told the American embassy that he expected to improve bilateral relations with the United States.[16]

The vice president landed in Buenos Aires, proclaimed "a new era" in United States–Argentine "cooperation and friendship," and laid a wreath at the statue of the Argentine national hero José de San Martín. Even though Frondizi had severe flu, he met privately with Nixon in the afternoon. The Argentine leader stressed his country's need for economic assistance and asked how it could attract private investors to develop its petroleum industry.[17]

The vice president missed the inaugural ceremony the following morning because of large crowds and heavy traffic. Frondizi told his listeners that Perón had bankrupted the nation, and as president he would work to restore prosperity. Peronists marred the festivities by calling for their leader's return from exile. The Communist Party, although outlawed, held a May Day rally denouncing United States imperialism and Nixon's presence. Among the many dignitaries in attendance, Mikhail Tarasov, vice chairman of the Presidium of the Supreme Soviet, headed an impressive delegation.[18]

The new president warned Nixon against attending a barbecue sponsored by the vocally leftist Municipal Workers Union, but Nixon went, along with Serafino Romualdi, the AFL-CIO representative for Latin America and a member of the United States delegation. Frondizi's trepidation proved unfounded. The union leaders welcomed the vice president warmly and asked him to address the assemblage. Nixon obliged them by pointing out that unions could have both freedom and bread: "Men can have more material progress when free than when slaves."[19]

The vice president also held a roundtable discussion with Argentine business leaders, at which he emphasized that the recession in the United States would end soon and that the Eisenhower administration would not make government loans to the oil industry because funds were available through private capital. President Waugh of the Export-Import Bank pledged that if the regime requested it, he would send a mission within sixty days to study loan possibilities.[20]

Nixon then met with professors and students at the University of Buenos Aires. In response to a tirade by two communist students against United States imperialism, especially its intervention in Guatemala, he stated that his country had made mistakes in the past and would in the future, but "dictators are repugnant to our people." To solve hemispheric problems, the Americas needed "less diplomacy in the traditional sense and greater frankness." As he left, a small group of students booed, hissed, and shouted: "Argentina is free—go away Nixon."[21]

From Buenos Aires, Nixon continued to Paraguay, where Alfredo Stroessner had been dictator since 1948. He cordially welcomed the vice president and publicly called for a $17,000,000 loan. While praising Stroessner for his anticommunist commitment, Nixon also met with some opposition leaders. No one dared mount an organized protest. After returning to Washington, Nixon wrote that Stroessner's efforts toward achieving "stability and democracy should be encouraged and portrayed in a sympathetic light." He hoped that Paraguay would establish democratic institutions peacefully "rather than by the violence and bloodshed of revolution."[22]

Nixon spent the next two days in Bolivia, a poverty-stricken Andean nation to which the United States had been providing aid since 1953. The country was largely dependent on tin exports, and in 1957, when the Soviet Union unexpectedly dumped 10,000 tons of tin on world markets, the sharp drop in price that resulted had severely strained the Bolivian economy.[23] Nixon met with President Hernán Siles Zuazo, who asked that the United States stockpile Bolivian tin; Nixon refused. Zuazo then asked for loans through the International Bank for Reconstruction and Development (IBRD) and the Export-Import Bank. He needed the United States to provide $200 million over four years. The vice president listened as Siles warned that if these funds were not allocated, his government might collapse and be replaced by a communist or fascist dictatorship.[24]

Again ignoring advice, Nixon insisted on going to San Andrés University the following morning, where students and labor leaders attacked the United States for not supplying sufficient help to stabilize Latin American economies. Later, at a press conference, he commented on the "woeful lack of understanding" among South Americans regarding how American foreign aid was dispensed. Nixon thought that Latin American governments understood the Eisenhower administration's programs and their limitations, but the average person did not. He wanted, he said, to increase United States information and exchange programs to refute the misinformation distributed by communists.[25]

During the first week of his tour, Nixon followed a set pattern. On landing in each country, he made a statement at the airport and then rode an open convertible into the capital, occasionally stopping the car to get out and shake hands with surprised spectators. Photographers were encouraged to take pictures of the vice president with the crowds, and reporters were on hand to record his interactions. Small groups of agitators booed him and threw leaflets at his limousine. He laid wreaths at national monuments, spoke with the leaders about the recession and foreign aid, and attacked communist influence. He debated leftist and communist leaders at local universities in defiance of warnings from the local American embassy. Before leaving each country, he held a press conference to answer hostile inquiries.

Nixon believed his mission had been successful. He had demonstrated that the United States was not taking Latin America for granted. He walked into universities where opponents verbally attacked him and his government's policies, but left thinking that he had effectively presented his government's case. Some members of the embassy staffs applauded his efforts.

The second week was different.

Before leaving the United States, Nixon had written that he and Pat were "looking forward to our stay in Lima" as "one of the highlights of the trip." The Peruvian government planned "an interesting and active schedule for us."[26]

The United States ambassador to Peru, career diplomat Theodore Achilles, had called on Nixon in Washington, and they agreed that the vice president should do "something unusual which would please the Peruvians." No visiting dignitary had ever walked the four blocks from the statue of San Martín to the University of San Marcos, the oldest university in the Americas, founded in 1551. Shortly before reaching the campus, he would pass the Panteón de los Proceres, the shrine to Peru's national heroes, and would go inside to make a few remarks. Achilles added: "To make it appear impromptu we have deliberately left it off the schedule but have allowed time for it."[27]

On the afternoon of May 7, at the Lima airport, Nixon received the coolest reception of his trip. Along the route to the capital, Peruvians whistled, the equivalent of hissing, as his car passed. The nation was in a severe recession that many Peruvians attributed to increased United States tariffs on zinc and lead, two of the country's chief exports. President Manuel Prado, after two years in office, had granted political parties, unions, and newspapers unprecedented freedoms, and they used these to heap criticism on the United States.[28]

The vice president traveled to the center of the capital and laid a wreath at the statue of Mariscal Ramón Castillo, an early Peruvian hero. He then had lunch with Prado, who took the opportunity to ask for economic aid. That evening the Nixons left their hotel for a state dinner. Although illegal, the Communist Party was tolerated, and as they exited, about 1,000 leftist and communist students, in the largest and best organized demonstration they had yet seen, hissed and booed: "Peru, yes, Nixon, no!"[29]

Nixon was aware that he faced trouble the next morning as well. Weeks before the mission, the rector of San Marcos University had invited the vice president to come to the campus. Since he had already debated students several times, Nixon expected to keep this appointment even though the CIA had reported that he would face communist agitators, and a group of university students had declared him persona non grata. Diplomats at the American embassy talked with the rector about canceling, but he refused to withdraw his invitation.[30]

Nixon consulted various advisers. His staff and the Secret Service detail urged him against going. Ambassador Achilles said that if he canceled, it would be seen as a victory for communist intimidation and a loss of prestige for the United States. The visit might be unpleasant but would present no physical danger. According to Vernon Walters's recollection, the vice president turned to him at the end of the meeting, knowing that he had lived in South America for many years, and asked his opinion. Walters responded that to Latin Americans, the greatest virtue was "personal courage" and the worse vice was cowardice. He would be in the car with the vice president if he decided to go. If he did not, Nixon should find an excuse to cancel the remainder of the mission and return to the United States.[31]

As a precaution, Pat Nixon stayed at the hotel the next morning while her husband went to the monument of the revolutionary hero, José de San Martín, and placed a floral decoration of United States and Peruvian flags joined together. He stepped back, stood erect for a moment of silence, and returned to his open convertible. He ordered his driver to go to the university, arriving earlier than expected with the hope of catching the demonstrators off guard.[32]

He failed to surprise anyone. Accompanied by his interpreter and two Secret Service agents, he confronted 2,000 Peruvians blocking his entrance to the university and shouting for him to leave. During the four-minute confrontation, Nixon challenged the protestors: "Are you afraid to talk to me? Are you afraid of the truth?" The crowd responded by hurling oranges, bottles, and eggs. A stone nicked the vice president's neck, and another chipped the front tooth of Jack Sherwood. While the missiles flew by, the vice president jumped on the trunk of his limousine and shouted: "Cowards, you are cowards, you are afraid of the truth!" With the mob growing more violent, Nixon left, and the crowd dispersed with no further injuries. At a press conference later that day, Nixon said that he would not permit "a minority element to appear to have power, to deny freedom of expression in a great university." He described the rioters as "very old students" and "real pros" who were clearly communist agitators, adding: "This day will live in infamy in the history of San Marcos University."[33]

After leaving the university, the Nixon entourage stopped at Catholic University. He entered unannounced and arrived during balloting for student body president. After it was over, he answered questions for almost an hour. The audience was generally respectful, if not entirely cordial. Some attempted to drown him out with a loudspeaker; some questions were hostile; some applauded his appearance; some sought autographs. Nixon thanked the students for permitting him to exercise a fundamental liberty: "the overbearing ones were those of the minority who close the doors of San Marcos and denied me the opportunity of speaking."[34]

When Nixon tried to return to his hotel, he found several hundred protestors from San Marcos University waiting for him; they halted his limousine about a block away. Nixon and Achilles got out and quickly walked toward the hotel. The demonstrators recognized the vice president and rushed toward him, only partially restrained by Peruvian police and Secret Service agents. Nixon walked through the mob smiling. As he was about to enter the hotel, a man approached him and spat on his cheek. Pat Nixon watched the melee from her fourth-story window and later remarked: "I've never been so proud of Dick."[35]

President Eisenhower sent him a radiotelephone message: "Your courage, patience and calmness in the demonstration directed against you by radical agitators have brought you new respect and admiration in our country." Ike was certain that the majorities in Peru and the United States deplored the disturbances "caused by a few." The Peruvian government had expressed its regrets, and Ike felt "that every participant in the mob will finally come to feel a sense of guilt and embarrassment because of his failure to show toward a friendly visitor the ordinary measure of courtesy and hospitality." Press secretary Hagerty wrote Nixon to say he had "handled the Peru situation magnificently and I was very proud of the way you did it."[36]

Nixon moved on to Ecuador, where the five major newspapers in Quito had agreed not to report on the chaos in Lima. The Ecuadorans had developed a century-old hatred for Peruvians over a border dispute that periodically erupted into warfare. The Communist Party was legal. Some members passed out leaflets saying, "Nixon Go Home," and for the first time, there was graffiti on walls: "Death to Nixon."[37]

Nixon had canceled a roundtable discussion with labor leaders and students because these groups were mainly composed of communist sympathizers. He made a brief appearance at the University of Quito, where he debated twenty-three students. Later that afternoon, while a local barber trimmed his hair, he discussed the previous day's events with reporters. He said that he had been invited to Catholic University but had not decided to go until he faced the mob at San Marcos, which he had left because he did not want the police "around swinging clubs." He had been through other difficult situations and did not have any "fear." Indeed, he was "pretty much of a fatalist as far as accidents are concerned." While he grew tense during the turmoil, he never lost his temper.

Later, during a formal press conference, Nixon blamed the Kremlin for the events in Lima. He warned Latin America that Moscow "would impose a dictatorial system worse than any that has ever existed in South America because it would be imposed by a foreign power." The Soviet Union had already made the South American recession worse by dumping commodities on the world market, and it could easily do it again. The United States had to respond to the increase in Soviet–Latin American commerce, which alerted the Eisenhower administration to the challenges it faced in the Western Hemisphere. In addition, Soviet first deputy foreign minister Vasily Koznetsov had visited Argentina and Uruguay; he also planned to stop in Chile in the coming week.[38]

Colombia, a nation that had undergone a violent political upheaval, was next. General Gustavo Rojas Pinilla had come to power through a military coup in 1953 but had permitted Colombia's two major political parties to hold national elections on May 4, 1958. Two days before the balloting, Rojas's supporters failed in an attempt to return him to the presidency. Dr. Alberto Lleras Camargo was overwhelmingly elected president and came into office as the price of coffee, his country's primary export, plummeted.[39]

Shortly before Nixon flew to Bogotá, the Colombian government announced that it had uncovered a communist plot to foment "discourteous acts" against the vice president. He landed to a cordial reception with a visible military presence and some minor left-wing protest. He again rode into the capital in an open convertible and talked with Lleras Camargo "at some length" privately and at official functions about halting the falling price of coffee. The vice president noted that "in too many countries . . . there was opportunity only for a relatively few people, with dire poverty for the many." Communist propaganda, he said, fed on this disparity, and this vast gap between the rich and poor had to change. "If people have nothing to lose, they are just as willing to listen to the Communists as they are to ourselves." The president-elect agreed.[40]

With relatively positive receptions in Ecuador and Colombia, the party headed for its final stop, in Venezuela. General Marcos Jiménez Peréz had overthrown the regime in December 1952 and led a corrupt and brutal government with Pedro Estrada heading the dreaded national security police. At the beginning of 1958, the Eisenhower administration knew that Venezuela faced "a very uneasy situation." Rioting on January 21 had led to 1,000 arrests, leaving 20 dead and many others injured. When Jiménez Peréz and Pedro Estrada fled the country two days later, the United States granted them asylum, greatly exacerbating anti-American feelings. A five-man junta led by Admiral Wolfgang Larrazabal pledged to hold national elections as soon as reasonably possible. This unstable political situation was further complicated by the United States recession, which caused a reduction of oil imports from Venezuela and weakened its economy.[41]

Assistant secretary Rubottom later recalled that, given the unrest, he had suggested Nixon bypass Venezuela, but Nixon refused. After Mexico, Venezuela had the largest population of American expatriates and received the most United States investment of any country in Latin America. The state department recommended that the vice president stop at Caracas first because any anti-American demonstrators would not have time to plan a well-coordinated attack. Nixon rejected this option too. Venezuela would be a "good take-off place to come back to the United States."[42]

Before the start of the mission, the United States embassy in Caracas had sent mixed signals about the visit. On April 9, Henry Casler, the public affairs officer, looked upon the trip as "welcome news." The embassy was making efforts toward improved bilateral relations, he wrote, and "we feel that your visit to Caracas will be the most important of all!" Russ Olson, who had arrived in Venezuela in the summer of 1957 for his first tour as a career diplomat, wrote his brother Keith on May 2, 1958, that the embassy did not know what Nixon would confront: "The Commies are very active. We have alternative programs set up in case we get leads on demonstrations but it's impossible to anticipate everything."[43]

American diplomats were aware by the second week of May that communist cadres had passed out thousands of leaflets at the university protesting the vice president's visit. This notice of impending demonstrations led the embassy to cancel his appearance there. Despite this, most Caracas newspapers did not foresee any trouble. The junta demanded that the vice president be treated with dignity.[44]

Far more ominous, before leaving Bogotá, the CIA and the Secret Service warned that a communist group had hired a triggerman to assassinate the vice president. The Nixons, seemingly unruffled, discounted this threat, but the Secret Service, which had either three or four men guarding the vice president elsewhere on the trip, assigned him twelve in Caracas—every agent they had in South America. On the evening of May 12, as the party was preparing to leave for Venezuela, Rose Mary Woods wrote that there was "reason to put more credence in this report of violence than in some of the previous ones. However, every precaution is being taken, and no one . . . [in] the party is scared. Spirits of everyone good, although almost dead . . . [on] their feet. This trip is the worst one yet!!"[45]

Nixon landed at 10:58 a.m. at Maiquetía Airport with about five hundred agitators in their late teens and early twenties directed by older leaders prepared to create havoc. At the top of the ramp, Colonel Walters warned him that the "crowd is entirely against us." As the band played both nations' national anthems, United States ambassador Edward Sparks and Venezuelan foreign minister Oscar García Velutini welcomed the vice president. Because of the loud booing and catcalls, Nixon canceled his opening remarks. Usually the motorcade lined up near the airplane, but here the nine limousines were waiting on the other side of the main terminal. The party walked on a red carpet toward the terminal, and as the Nixons approached it, the band again played the Venezuelan national anthem. They stopped and stood at attention. From the observation deck above them, some in the crowd threw garbage and a "rain of spittle" on the Nixons. The Venezuelan honor guard, with bayonets fixed, did not intervene. The Nixons walked through the terminal covered with spit and entered their cars as police and Secret Service agents shoved protesters aside.[46]

Secret Service detail chief Jack Sherwood had demanded that the vice president ride to Caracas in a closed Cadillac. With the vice president inside, Sherwood locked the doors and shut the windows. Besides the two of them and the driver, the passengers included Walters, Secret Service agent Wade Rodham, and the Venezuelan foreign minister. The crowd hurled trash at the windows, and the driver used his windshield wipers and automatic spraying device to see. Some tried to tear the United States and Venezuelan flags off the hood. Nixon turned to the foreign minister, and in a calm voice, said: "If you don't learn to control these mobs you are going to have a dictatorship that will make Peréz Jiménez seem like an afternoon tea party."[47]

On the thirteen-mile ride to the capital, a press truck with reporters and photographers preceded the motorcade to capture the vice president's entrance into the city. Nixon's car was immediately behind. During the first part of the trip, on a four-lane highway, protesters in cars broke into line in an effort to disrupt the motorcade. As it approached a working-class suburb during the midday siesta that often caused congestion, the caravan faced its first traffic jam: two cars were parked across the highway. A mob with lead pipes and baseball bats attacked the convoy for several minutes, followed by a similar mob a few minutes later. Donald Hughes, who was in the second limousine, called them ambushes; others thought the mobs were just taking advantage of normal traffic tie-ups.[48]

The third assault, lasting about twelve minutes, came when a large stalled truck stopped traffic. Several hundred rioters surrounded the convoy and concentrated on Nixon's Cadillac. Attackers started to rock the car and tried to turn it over. Secret Service agents rushed to protect the vice president without drawing their weapons. Emery Roberts was hit by a rock, recovered, and continued at his post defending Nixon. The foreign minister got shattered glass in his eyes from individuals trying to break through the windows, and Walters bled from glass that entered his mouth. Nixon said to his interpreter, "Spit the glass out—you are going to have a lot more talking to do in Spanish for me today." The two Secret Service agents with the vice president were prepared to draw their guns. Jack Sherwood said: "Let's kill some of these sons of bitches and get out of here." Nixon answered, "You don't shoot unless I tell you to do so."[49]

Nixon admitted later that he knew his life was in danger. Sherwood knew it, too. Ambassador Achilles spoke with Nixon in Washington shortly after his return and said he agreed, "the agitators wanted to kill him."[50]

The driver maneuvered around the truck and sped away. Pat Nixon sat in the second limousine, consoling the foreign minister's hysterical wife while watching the mob attack her husband's car. The vice president's military aide, Donald Hughes, was also riding with Pat and recalled that she "never showed signs of fear."[51]

After escaping with his life, the vice president was scheduled to lay a wreath at the tomb of Simon Bolívar, Venezuela's liberator, in the heart of the city. From the limousine, Walters could see that the plaza where the ceremony was to take place was filled with protestors. He recommended that the vice president cancel the wreath laying and go directly to the embassy. Nixon agreed. As the motorcade started down a quiet residential street, he told the driver to stop and asked Walters to go back to Pat's car, ask how she was, and tell her he was unharmed. Walters relayed her husband's message and said that they were heading directly to the embassy. Even though every window in her car was shattered, Pat was composed and uninjured; she replied that "it was quite a sight to watch from back here."[52]

Nixon had no idea what was occurring at the plaza. When several American diplomats tried to deliver the wreath to the statue, the crowd destroyed it while the police stood by passively. Later, when Venezuelan troops searched the crowd, they found over 200 Molotov cocktails. The streets leading up to the tomb in the old city were very narrow, and if the Cadillacs had tried to reach the wreath-laying ceremony, they could have been fire bombed. The occupants might have been burned alive.[53]

While Nixon, the state department, and the CIA blamed communists for the riots, the mobs also included others who resented United States policy. Rubottom described the incident as "Communist-directed and *well*-directed effort." The vice president's national security advisor, Robert Cushman, believed that "all demonstrations were Communist led and inspired, although exploiting a variety of social and economic grievances."[54]

The embassy sat on the top of a hill that was not easily accessible to crowds, and the Nixons reached it without further incident. The vice president canceled all activities outside the compound; anyone wishing to see him had to come there. The vice president's damaged limousine was parked in front of the embassy. Seeing it there, the young Foreign Service officer Russ Olson wrote, "The rear windows were shattered, sputum was all over it and the windshield was just a white smear as the driver had tried to remove the spit with the wipers. It was difficult at that moment not to hate Venezuelans." While an embassy official offered to remove the car, Nixon insisted that it remain so that when the junta visited that afternoon, it would be in plain sight.[55]

Safe at the embassy and exhausted from his ordeal, the vice president showered, took a brief nap, and changed clothes. He said that the worst part of the ordeal "was watching these pigs spit in his wife's face." The junta led by Admiral Larrazabal arrived at 4:00 p.m.; Nixon let his guests wait for an hour. When they met, the admiral profusely apologized. Nixon told them he understood that communists had orchestrated the melee and the vast majority of Venezuelans sought cordial relations with the United States.[56]

Shortly after that exchange, the vice president held a press conference with ninety reporters. First, he announced that he would not leave the embassy until the junta guaranteed his safety. He was not personally affronted: "These incidents are against Venezuela. No patriotic Venezuelan would have torn down his country's flag as the mob did from the crossed flags on cars. I don't feel it at all as a personal offense and hereafter relations between the United States and Venezuela if anything should be better."[57]

Sherwood sent a message to Secret Service headquarters in Washington, reporting that the vice president had been attacked but was not injured and that no other Americans had sustained any serious injuries. But "the situation was untenable and dependent upon local authorities."[58]

When Tricia Nixon came home for lunch, turned on her television, and saw news flashes about the riots in Caracas, she asked the vice president's staff if her parents were safe. With regular communication between the two nations disrupted—possibly because the overseas circuits were tied up with correspondents wiring stories back to the United States—the children and staff had cause to worry. The vice president's Air Force pilot, Colonel Thomas Collins Jr., happened to have a ham radio, and around 3:00 he sent a message that reached the vice president's office: "Arrival very unpleasant, but everyone OK."[59]

Back at the White House, Ike had his own problems. Mobs in Lebanon had set two American libraries on fire; a military coup led by discontented French soldiers in Algeria had replaced the civilian government; and the Burmese were holding anti-American demonstrations. As for the events in Caracas, the president was furious. He could not find out what had happened or whether the Nixons were safe. Ike's private secretary Ann Whitman wrote: "Another of the worst days of our lives." In mid-afternoon, the president remarked: "This is bad enough, but by next week I think we'll be in even greater danger. . . . I am about ready to go put my uniform on."[60]

Not knowing what was happening, Ike prepared to evacuate the vice president's party using military force. The Air Force put an "actual and alert-standby" order in effect and placed B-47s on alert "for show-of-force demonstration flyover, or whatever the need required." Troops were flown from North Carolina to Guantánamo Bay, Cuba, and military equipment was placed "on stand-by alert for immediate combat deployment." Ramey Air Force Base in Puerto Rico would be "the staging and control base for the emergency."[61]

Secretary Dulles had spoken with the Venezuelan chargé d'affaires in Washington, Eduardo Acosta, who could not supply any information. Dulles urged caution and notified the defense department that it could not land troops in Venezuela without state department approval. Ike considered sending marines and a helicopter. If the Venezuelan junta could not protect the vice president, it should request United States assistance.[62]

By 4:30 p.m., the state department heard from Nixon and Rubottom that they were safe, but that conditions were unstable. The state department rejected the use of American force without Venezuelan permission. Although Dulles believed the danger might have passed, at 6:00 the defense department announced the troop mobilization as a precautionary measure. It did not mention that the Navy was stationing six destroyers, a missile cruiser, and an aircraft carrier out of sight off the Venezuelan coastline.[63]

Nixon learned of the defense department's announcement at 9:00 p.m. through AP and UP dispatches and was upset. Any troop movement would embarrass the junta and revive the specter of Yankee military intervention in the Caribbean. It had taken control, and his party was secure. He hoped that the administration would minimize the mobilization and the possible troop deployment to Caracas.[64]

At 11:15 p.m., deputy assistant secretary of state for inter-American affairs William Snow talked with Rear Admiral William Miller, who told him that technically no ships had been sent to Venezuela. The admiral, according to Snow, said that "this was merely routine—a precautionary movement placing the ships closer to Venezuela should evacuation be necessary but that their orders were not to go within the sight of land." The state department could say that no naval vessel had been dispatched, and none would be unless an evacuation plan went into effect. No ship would go without the concurrence of the state department and the junta, "or lacking that the highest level clearance in Washington would be necessary."[65]

The following morning, the White House insisted upon updates. The president telephoned Nixon, who said that he was carrying out his commitments and planned to leave Caracas "earlier than scheduled for the element of surprise." Eisenhower praised his vice president but asked him to prolong his Caracas stay so that Ike could prepare a reception in Washington. Nixon would not stay in Venezuela but instead telephoned Governor Luis Muñoz Marin of Puerto Rico from the ambassador's living room: "Luis, this is Dick Nixon. I wonder if Pat and I could spend tomorrow night with you?" After a long pause, Nixon repeated: "Luis?" The governor agreed, even though he "was a liberal with little love for Richard Nixon."[66]

Ike held a press conference. Before it started, he and Dulles discussed Nixon's earlier-than-expected return and agreed that the president would minimize the "precautionary troop movements." Ike later answered reporters' questions about economic issues in Latin America, downplayed the military precautions, and spoke about the riots in Caracas. Nixon would return the next morning, he added, and "while it would create a precedent, because of my admiration for his calmness and fortitude and his courage in very trying circumstances, I would like to make some special gesture."[67]

That afternoon the junta begged Nixon to attend a luncheon, after which his party would be escorted to the airport. The vice president was driven back to the airport by the same route he had come in on. This time, however, a military escort guarded his party. The streets were virtually deserted, with a whiff of tear gas in the air warning away potential troublemakers. The terminal, too, was almost empty. As the plane cleared the runway, "a loud cheer" of relief erupted inside.[68]

Nixon and others praised the Secret Service agents. Robert Hartmann, the *Los Angeles Times* reporter, had watched the attack from the press truck: "In the most magnificent display of courage and restraint . . . a handful of U.S. Secret Service guards . . . shooed the surging savage crowd away with open hands, never once using fists or drawing guns." One agent, Dale Grubb, exactly a year after the attack, wrote Nixon to say: "never have I been more proud of an American than all of us were of you nor have I ever been more proud to be an American than on that occasion." Every agent who guarded the vice president received an Exceptional Civilian Service Award (Gold Medal) for heroism.[69]

The vice president applauded the valor and "tremendous contribution" of Vernon Walters. He was, Nixon said, the best translator he had ever had, with vast knowledge about South America. He also displayed great courage on several occasions "when physical violence was encountered. He was at all times calm, dependable, and completely devoted to my personal safety." The vice president recommended that he be considered for promotion to full colonel. The day after returning to Washington, someone asked Walters: How did Nixon "really behave when they were trying to get at him in the car?" Walters angrily replied: "All I can tell you is that as an American, I was proud of the Vice-President of the United States." He "showed intelligence, courage and judgment."[70]

Nixon also wrote Norman Chandler, publisher of the *Los Angeles Times*, about Robert Hartmann and the other reporters who covered the journey. "Newsmen had their bodies between Pat and me and the rioters," he wrote, "just as deliberately as the Secret Service personnel."[71]

The vice president's airplane touched down on United States soil in San Juan at 7:45 p.m. He opened the doors to a crowd of 700 cheering: "Long Live Nixon, Long Live the United States, and Welcome Home." The party walked part of the way to the governor's palace while 1,000 spectators shouted a warm welcome.[72]

The Nixons took off for the United States early the next morning and arrived at noon in Washington, where Republican National Committee (RNC) campaign director Robert Humphreys had been planning a reception since the Lima incidents. A great deal of preparation had been completed before the Venezuelan riots: "what had started as a reasonably good bonfire was turned overnight into a roaring conflagration by the reports from Caracas." The GOP wanted to demonstrate its admiration for the Nixons and "open . . . the eyes of many sleeping Americans as to the quality of leadership they elected in 1952 and re-elected in 1956."[73]

The president, several cabinet members, congressmen, Latin American diplomats, and a crowd estimated at 15,000 welcomed the Nixons at the airport. Ike praised his vice president for conducting "himself effectively, efficiently, and with great dignity." The president stressed that the riots had "in no way impaired the friendship . . . between the United States and any other single one of our sister republics to the south." He then turned over the microphone to Nixon. Overwhelmed by the outpouring, Nixon seconded the president's position on hemispheric solidarity. While the Americas had many disagreements, the United States and Latin America could resolve them.[74]

The Eisenhowers and Nixons took an open convertible to the White House with 85,000 lining the route and applauding. Over lunch with the president and Secretary Dulles, Nixon talked about fundamental hemispheric problems and the basic causes of inter-American friction. The riots in Lima and Caracas, he thought, were only symbols. The Soviet Union exaggerated differences within the Western Hemisphere and encouraged its sympathizers to blame the United States for the South American recession. Nixon believed the Eisenhower administration could address the problems by an "effective program of consultation, action and information."[75]

At a stag dinner that evening, Ike pointed to the significance of the "Sino-Soviet economic offensive" against the United States. Nixon emphasized that the developing world, including Latin America, heard communist propaganda that the United States during periods of economic growth exploited the masses. The Kremlin argued that "capitalist" commerce between the United States and other nations "did nothing more than to make the rich richer, without improving the lot of the poor." The communist promise to bring something better was received sympathetically.[76]

The next day, Friday morning, Nixon explained at the cabinet meeting what he had learned from the mission. Latin Americans wanted friendship with the United States more than friendship with the Soviet Union. "The United States must not . . . do anything that would support an impression that it is helping to protect the privileges of a few; instead, we must be dedicated to raising the standard of living of the masses." The communists had inspired the riots by handing out similar signs and by having leaders incite their followers. Even though the recession added to the strain, the main Latin American complaint was that the United States harbored refugee dictators. American diplomats who dealt mainly with oligarchs had lost touch with students, intellectuals, labor, and military leaders. Communist propaganda was achieving its objective, and the United States must at least double its exchange programs. Ike agreed, while Secretary Dulles said the "lower classes" would not institute democratic government when they rose to power; "rather they will bring in more of a dictatorship of the masses."[77]

On Sunday, Ike and Dulles talked about Nixon's views on "dictatorships." The secretary agreed with some points but felt Nixon did not have a universal formula. Two days later, at his press conference, Dulles said that he had approved of sending the vice president to South America. The secretary routinely received threats and protests in many nations. He added: "If you allow yourself to be deterred by threats of that kind the result is that the communists will imprison you at home." He added that the "organized outbursts of rowdyism" in Caracas did not reflect the Venezuelan majority's views. The oversupply of oil damaged its economy, and an inadequate police force permitted the riots.[78]

The next afternoon, the vice president appeared at a packed National Press Club luncheon. When he entered, he received a standing ovation. He praised the reporters who accompanied him and Walters. He mentioned how important Pat's contributions were at the institutions she had visited. As for himself, he "would not have missed this trip for anything." After Europe, he argued, the Western Hemisphere was the most important market for American goods, and his audience had to stop thinking in terms of stereotypes like siestas and Latin dances and instead focus on "the wave of the future" like radical students and labor leaders. Communists had instigated the riots and had shown the menace they posed: "If we allowed what I would call a bunch of blackmailing bullies to keep the officials of the Government of the United States from doing what we think needs to be done to carry out our foreign policy, then we better get off the face of the earth."[79]

Speaking about the trip to the National Security Council on Thursday, May 22, Nixon warned: "the threat of Communism in Latin America was greater today than ever before in history." These nations lacked "political maturity" and with leaders and opinion makers already leaning toward Marxism, the Soviet Union used South American universities to train converts, especially in Uruguay and Venezuela. The United States Information Agency did a creditable job but was insufficient, and the United States had to develop better propaganda programs. Latin Americans needed to understand that the United States was assisting them. The administration "could combine and exploit the hemisphere's two chief hatreds in Latin America—namely, dictatorship and foreign control." Secretary Dulles agreed with the vice president that the United States had to offer more exchange programs. Ike said that the United States should stress how the Kremlin had crushed the 1956 Hungarian rebellion; they also, he said, needed to find a new name for capitalism.[80]

The photographs of Nixon defending himself while being pelted with rocks and with his limousine's windows being smashed drew enormous attention. He was universally applauded for his courage and his calm. After he left the presidency, Nixon reminisced that when he met Latin Americans, they would say, "whether we agree with you or not, we like you, because you have *cojones*." At first he had to ask what *cojones* meant. The answer was "Balls."[81]

That was personal. From the policy side, the president and others saw the need to change how the United States viewed Latin America. Congress reacted with alarm and opened hearings on improving inter-American solidarity.[82]

For the rest of his vice presidency, Nixon closely monitored hemispheric developments. He hoped his trip had "increased awareness" throughout the hemisphere "of the determination and ruthlessness of those who instigated the riots." He approved of any policy that would reduce Moscow's influence. A few days after returning to Washington, he had lunch with FBI director Hoover, who said that "one very positive result of the South American trip was that it made anti-Communism respectable again in the United States!"[83]

The vice president also understood that the United States had to change the way it associated with Latin American rulers. The Eisenhower administration needed to adopt policies that were friendlier to democratic regimes and less friendly to autocratic ones. Elites governed in the Americas, but intellectuals, students, labor leaders, the media, military personnel, and others had to be included in the political equation. The Americas had to remove communists where they "secured a foothold" in labor unions and universities and "work together to raise the living standards of the people."[84]

To achieve these results, the United States had to change USIA policies because they were not succeeding in influencing "opinion makers classes." Nixon particularly lobbied for expanded exchange programs that would bring more Latin Americans to the United States. Even though he did not think Nixon accomplished much in this regard, Roy Rubottom praised the vice president's efforts. In his oral history, the assistant secretary was asked if Nixon's trip led to any changes. He replied that the USIA budget "had a very, very low priority for Latin America" until the vice president's mission. Afterward, "this priority was moved from about the lowest category up to first or second."[85]

Finally, the vice president worked to reduce Soviet trade and to increase hemispheric prosperity based on a regional foundation. He wanted to stabilize Latin American economies by encouraging private investment, avoiding wide price fluctuations on basic commodities like coffee and tin on world markets, assisting with Eximbank loans, and sponsoring the creation of an inter-American development bank.[86]

Milton Eisenhower also had a significant stake in his brother's hemispheric policies. During an oral history interview, Milton proclaimed that the genesis for President Kennedy's Alliance for Progress came during the Eisenhower presidency: "there were more changes in policy toward Latin America by the United States during the Eisenhower Administration than in any Administration before or since." Ike advocated common markets, created an inter-American bank, and established study groups to stabilize the prices of Latin American commodities exported to the United States.[87]

Ike's younger brother and Nixon agreed on the administration's inter-American initiatives. In *The President Is Calling*, Milton noted that he "did not share . . . [Ike's] high opinion of the Vice-President." Still, the president often had him and Nixon discuss hemispheric issues, and according to Milton, they agreed "with no difficulty." About a month after the vice president returned from South America, Milton went to Central America and Puerto Rico and declared, on his return, that he and Nixon agreed "on all vital issues between the United States and Latin America."[88]

INSIDE AND OUTSIDE THE KITCHEN

Nixon's journey to the Soviet Union and Poland was his last and most critical foreign mission as vice president. Before Secretary of State Dulles died at the end of May, Ike had already decided to explore a meeting with Nikita Khrushchev. The president wanted to evaluate the chairman, and once again he used Nixon as a forward observer to meet with Khrushchev and make a preliminary assessment of him.[1]

Rumors that Nixon might travel to the Soviet Union began as early as 1955. That summer, Secretary Dulles convinced him that the visit was not "desirable" and "there was danger of overdoing the sentimental side of our relations." After this conversation, Nixon publicly denied any travel plans but added that the possibility had been raised in some low-level discussions.[2]

Any thought of a mission to Moscow collapsed when Ike had his heart attack that September, and rumors were further squelched with his ileitis operation in 1956 and a mild stroke in 1957. The Soviet ambassador to the United States, Georgi Zaroubin, sparked gossip in early 1958 when he met with Nixon and asked if the vice president would consider an exchange of delegations between Congress and the Supreme Soviet. Within two weeks, Nixon put a journey to the Soviet Union back on his agenda. But before it could happen, "there would be a thorough study of all the angles involved."[3]

The gossip resurfaced when the new Soviet ambassador to the United States, Mikhail Menshikov, presented his credentials to the president on February 11, 1958. Both men agreed that rising tensions between the two superpowers were harmful and that if there was an extended summit, Ike might send his vice president. The next day, Menshikov paid a forty-minute courtesy call on the vice president without mentioning any visit. The press still speculated that one was in the offing.[4]

Early that summer Menshikov announced that the vice president would be welcome in his country and encouraged him to make the journey. By the end of the year, Nixon felt that the United States and the Soviet Union needed to reduce tensions because Moscow was taking positions "very belligerent to the American people." To defuse the situation, he wanted to initiate disarmament talks based on verifiable inspections. Yuri Zhukov, chairman of the Soviet State Committee for Cultural Relations, came to the United States early in December and personally invited Nixon to come to Moscow for the opening of the 1959 United States Exhibition. Nixon did not directly reply but noted that he had been the first administration official to champion broader cultural exchanges.[5]

At the beginning of 1959, Anastas Mikoyan, co–first deputy premier of the Soviet Union, made an informal two-week visit to the United States. Khrushchev, according to his son Sergei, "had an extremely high opinion of Mikoyan's intellect, more precisely his wisdom and ability to negotiate." Mikoyan met with American leaders, including Nixon, and left with the impression that the vice president would travel to his country. Nixon, speaking to reporters about their interchange on January 27, concluded that Mikoyan was a committed communist who realized that the American people were united behind Eisenhower. Only through increased commerce, cultural exchanges, and other measures, Nixon said, would the Cold War become less threatening.[6]

A day later, Charles Shutt of Telenews asked the president at a press conference if he had "any plans to send Vice President Nixon to Russia." Ike responded that he had "no plans" at that moment.[7] In mid February, Nixon stated that because of the impasse over negotiations regarding the occupation of Berlin, "any plans for a trip to the Soviet Union by myself would be out of the question." Toward the end of March, he said that any trip to Moscow was "somewhat remote."[8]

In early April, the president reversed himself. On advice from outgoing Secretary Dulles and his successor, Christian Herter, the president announced on the seventeenth that the vice president would open the American National Exhibition in Moscow that July. The exchange of exhibitions between the two countries, he said, was "the kind of mutual understanding upon which our peaceful future depends."[9]

On April 20, Nixon discussed with mission with Dulles, who, at that moment, had a little more than a month to live. Dulles told his friend to "task Khrushchev" for creating an artificial crisis over West Berlin by demanding the Allies leave the city. Nixon, he advised, should maintain that by holding to this rigid position, Khrushchev was suggesting that the Kremlin did not want "peaceful coexistence and peaceful competition."[10]

In May, the vice president wrote James Bassett, a Los Angeles reporter and former Republican National Committee (RNC) public relations specialist, and said that he expected the trip to be "a tough one" because of "the buildup in the U.S. press and the fact that the Summit conference will follow." Reporters would want to hear about his talks with Khrushchev, "exactly the one subject I could not and should not discuss if the trip is to serve any useful purpose. I only hope we can find enough things to do which will keep them busy writing on other subjects." Five days before departure, Nixon reminded his staff that he did not intend to have the press always present. "There will be times when we will slip out without anyone from the press at all."[11]

Even though the vice president did not know whether he would discuss West Berlin with the Soviet leader, he believed the decision to go "was a wise one." He hoped to talk directly to the Soviet people to demonstrate the American resolve for peace. Although he doubted he could change the perceptions of the Kremlin's leaders, "I do believe that talking frankly and directly to them can substantially reduce any miscalculation they may have made as to the determination of our government and our people to stand firm against aggression of any type throughout the world."[12]

Nixon's invitation was related to a 1958 United States–Soviet exchange agreement. Frol Kozlov, the co–first deputy premier of the Soviet Union, opened a Soviet Exhibition of Science, Technology, and Culture at the Coliseum in New York City on June 29. Eisenhower previewed it as the first guest, mentioning that he had visited Moscow in 1945 to receive a decoration from Stalin. He toured the entire three floors and viewed three models of Sputnik satellites, but was most drawn to the works of Soviet painters. Nixon, on this occasion, represented the administration at the premiere, where he said he hoped the exchanges would improve bilateral relations, in contrast to the "disappointing lack of progress" on German issues at the foreign ministers' gathering then taking place in Geneva. "There is no magic formula which will settle the differences between us," he said; "no conference at the summit which will dramatically end world tension."[13]

Kozlov, who like other senior Kremlin leaders had risen to prominence during the Stalinist era, was liked and respected by Khrushchev. Kozlov agreed with Nixon that the vast differences between the two nations were regrettable but might be bridged by increased trade and other contacts. "The Soviet people want a genuine, stable peace which can be insured only in their interrelationship by the principle of peaceful coexistence."[14]

The president, meanwhile, was searching for solutions to the stalemate over Germany. Ike thought the Kremlin opposed German reunification and wanted to draw West Berlin into the Soviet orbit. When Khrushchev met with seven American governors on July 7, he indicated that he wanted an invitation to visit the United States.

The president was already considering an exchange: Khrushchev would come to the United States, and then Ike would travel to the Soviet Union. The visits would do no "harm and might do some good." The two leaders would hold informal talks in which Ike would stress that the United States would "not abandon two million West Berliners or the West Germans."[15]

Nixon prepared for his mission with extensive briefings. He later said that he had never been better prepared for a foreign visit. Undersecretary of State Douglas Dillon coached him on general policy; Foy Kohler, deputy assistant secretary of state for European affairs, summarized the Eastern and Western positions and presented topical papers, and Richard Service helped with advance planning.[16]

For the second time, the vice president worked with Tommy Thompson, who had been transferred from Austria after the Hungarian rebellion and made ambassador to the Soviet Union in 1957. He had served in Moscow during World War II and spoke Russian. Thompson and others had strongly recommended that the vice president travel to Sverdlovsk in the Ural Mountains and Novosibirsk in Siberia "to give us a chance to get into some closed areas." The ambassador hoped to persuade the Kremlin to let Nixon address the Soviet people over radio and television, as Mikoyan and Kozlov were permitted to do when they visited the United States.[17]

The CIA was also heavily involved. DCI Allen Dulles, Raymond Garthoff, and others briefed the vice president for two hours on July 13. Garthoff who spoke fluent Russian and had been a Soviet analyst at the CIA since 1957, was designated to accompany the vice president as an adviser and to seize any appropriate opportunity to gather intelligence. Three Air Force intelligence officers went as well. They were cautioned against "any illegal or risky activities."[18]

Nixon especially valued "eyewitness" accounts. On July 10, he met with Averell Harriman, who had spoken with Khrushchev for several hours in late June and described him as ignorant of the West and prone to "Hitler-like" outbursts. If the United States and its Allies threatened war over West Berlin, Khrushchev warned, and then fighting erupted, the West would be blamed. Besides, the Soviet Union was constructing missile systems that would paralyze centers in the United States and Europe.[19]

During these preparations, Nixon saw the president regularly. On July 17, he wrote to fervent anticommunist and former congressman Charles Kersten that he realized the Soviet leaders would remain staunch communists. Four days

later, he wrote a constituent "that talking frankly and directly to them [the Soviet leaders] can substantially reduce any miscalculation they may have as to the
determination of our government and our people to stand firm against aggression of any type throughout the world." He also intended to correct some misconceptions that the Soviet people had about the United States.[20]

The vice president asked the state department for fresh ideas. "You have anything we can say—anything to toss up let's don't miss this opportunity to do so."
American diplomats could not mention "co-existence" because that was former
secretary of state Dean Acheson's phrase. Anyone who used it on the trip would
"be shipped back from Russia on the next plane."[21]

As usual, the vice president brought his wife. She customarily visited hospitals, orphanages, and similar institutions, but this time Nixon had other ideas:
"women in Russia have a different status and it will be very good to have
Mrs. Nixon have a schedule which shows lots of activity." She would follow a
hectic pace, mingling with crowds, going to a worker's apartment, dancing the
polka in Siberia, and handing out candy to children. Women would stare at her
"fashionable pointed shoes, her smart suit, her attractive hairdo and modish
hat." Some in the crowds heckled her, but she generally received a pleasant
reception.[22]

Nixon also asked Milton Eisenhower to be part of the delegation. Milton was
excited and asked for his brother's consent; Ike gladly gave his blessings. When
several reporters wrote that the president was sending his brother to "spy" on or
"chaperone" Nixon, the president roared with laughter.[23]

Vice Admiral Hyman Rickover, father of the nuclear submarine, went along
as a scientific and technical adviser. He had accompanied Kozlov to visit the
atomic power station at Shippingport, Pennsylvania, and the Kremlin leader publicly pledged to reciprocate if Rickover came to the Soviet Union.[24]

Nixon brought the largest staff, twenty-two people that he had ever taken on
a foreign mission. Donald Hughes handled his appointments while Robert Cushman served as a counselor. In an oral history, Cushman recalled that he carried
"five briefcases of classified documents," which he had to carry with him whenever he went to the bathroom, because he could not let them out of his sight.[25]

Herbert Klein, a Southern California reporter and a Nixon ally since his first
congressional race in 1946, had recently joined the vice president's staff in June
as press secretary. His primary objective on the journey would be to minimize
censorship. He would find himself complaining two to five times a day about
press restrictions and usually managed to get them lifted. When Soviet officials,
for instance, sought to impose a limit of twenty-three reporters to accompany
Nixon to Siberia, Klein had the number increased to a hundred.[26] After return-

ing to the capital, he would write in a press release that his staff was "alternately harassed and toasted as it dealt with the various Soviet ministries." Hughes and Cushman negotiated the vice president's itinerary by the hour and only twice did they have a schedule twenty-four hours in advance. The Soviet officials "respected our requests only when they knew we would be tough and standing up to them."[27]

Before this battle began, Ike held his morning press conference on July 22, reminding reporters that this was an exchange of visits between Nixon and Kozlov: "It's a good will gesture and we wanted to have a prominent American to officiate at the opening of our exhibit."[28] Nixon would have no authority to bargain with Khrushchev on any issue. He might talk with Soviet leaders about the existing stalemate and then report back to the White House, but he understood, the president emphasized, that he was "going to Moscow as a prominent American. He will be able to give a clear picture of American thinking and government thinking."[29]

Afterward, Milton Eisenhower telephoned his brother to say good-bye, emphasizing he had telephoned rather than come to the White House to avoid taking attention away from Nixon. He expected to spend most of his time with the vice president and would make an attempt to study education and agriculture in the Soviet Union.[30]

At 11:45 a.m., the president conferred with Nixon. He was "not a normal part of the negotiating machinery" of the administration, and Ike suggested that he project "a cordial, almost light atmosphere." Contradicting what he had told the press, the president expanded Nixon's options. He should not be afraid to discuss "substantive matters" and take a positive approach. If Khrushchev brought up the bargaining at Geneva over West Berlin or a possible summit, the vice president needed to connect the two subjects. Ike expected to defend the Allied position in Berlin but was willing to hear new information and views on the issue. Nixon said that he would probably debate Khrushchev to uncover his "real feelings" and wished to dispel the misconception that while the American people yearned for peace, their leaders did not. He intended to emphasize that Americans supported their president.[31]

Khrushchev had gone to Poland on July 14 for a nine-day visit to strengthen Soviet-Polish bonds. He flew into Warsaw to mark the fifteenth anniversary of the founding of the Polish People's Republic. Wladyslaw Gomulka, the communist leader, embraced his guest, and the government turned out 75,000 people to greet him despite centuries of animosity between the two nations. Khrushchev ignored that pent up feeling and instead embarked on a "friendship tour." He traveled to the coal town of Katowice on July 15 and told the miners that he,

too, had a mining background. He urged them to look to their leaders for prosperity instead of the Roman Catholic Church, to which the vast majority of Poles
belonged. The next day in the mining town, he predicted that communism
would triumph over capitalism. Upon leaving Warsaw, Khrushchev described
Gomulka as a trusted ally; a joint Polish-Soviet declaration supported East Germany in its effort to force the West out of Berlin. Khrushchev called for a summit meeting to ease international tensions on the matter.[32]

The chairman occasionally referred to the United States and its missile capa-
bility. While solemnly pledging that the Soviet Union would "never, never, never,
never" begin a war, he commented that United States missiles could "send up
oranges" while the Soviet Union could "send up tons."[33] As for Nixon's visit, even
though Khrushchev did not doubt Nixon's "good intentions," his aims puzzled
the chairman. On the seventeenth, almost on the eve of Nixon's visit, Congress
declared the third week of July Captive Nations Week, a resolution that began
in 1950 and was passed annually since then, offering prayers to liberate the people
in Eastern Europe. For some unexplained reason, Khrushchev took offense at
the resolution, claiming "the only enslaved peoples are in the capitalist countries." *Pravda* blasted the resolution, saying the United States was trying "to foist
capitalist 'freedom' on the peoples of the Socialist countries."[34]

At the July 22 press conference, Marion Arrowsmith asked the president about
Khrushchev's linkage of Nixon's mission to the Captive Nations Resolution. Ike
did not see any connection. Nixon and Kozlov were making an exchange: "It's
a good will gesture." As for the Captive Nations Resolution, Congress had asked
him to issue the declaration, and he had agreed. The United States should "conduct ceremonies in memory of the plight of such peoples." The Kremlin refused
to concede that any captive nations existed, but that was communist propaganda: "distorted and untrue."[35]

Although Eisenhower had discounted Khrushchev's outrage over Captive Nations Week, Nixon realized that it might prompt a cool reception in Moscow.
He told the press he anticipated a "frank give and take" with the chairman on
fundamental differences between the superpowers. As for pushing an agreement
forward at Geneva, he hoped to "make some yardage." He also knew from the 1956
Hungarian rebellion that the United States "should not encourage people to undertake violent revolution unless we are prepared to help them and it isn't likely
that we will because of the risk of a world war." The United States still should
encourage the satellites "to assert some independence of the Soviet Union."[36]

Nixon and his party went to Friendship International Airport, south of Baltimore, on the evening of July 22 and took off at 9:06 p.m. The airplane refueled
in Keflavik, Iceland, and flew on to Moscow. Since Mikoyan and Kozlov had

flown to the United States by jet, the vice president insisted that he do the same. Ike, believing that this might have a positive effect on the Soviet leadership and world opinion, agreed, allocating a military version of a Boeing 707 to carry the vice president and twenty-four others. Clarence Francis, who flew with Nixon, wrote that "comfort and service were of the highest class."[37] The press airplane, a Boeing 707-321, left Idlewild Airport in New York at 10:30 for a 4,800-mile flight directly to Moscow, carrying seventy-three reporters and photographers.[38]

Khrushchev returned from Warsaw slightly ahead of the press airplane. A large crowd at the Moscow airport greeted him warmly, and he left for the Luzhniki Sports Palace, where he routinely spoke after traveling abroad. The first half of his address concentrated on Polish-Soviet friendship, and the second half was a bitter denunciation of the Captive Nations Resolution. "Would that the Vice President who has just landed come and see these captive people who are present here." The *New York Times* reported that this taunt drew "extensive laughter and prolonged applause."[39]

Kozlov and other Kremlin leaders met Nixon's jet that afternoon. No large crowds welcomed him. After deplaning, Nixon spoke to the press, saying, "In view of the destructive power of modern weapons, we know that if there is another war there will be no victors, only losers." He wanted to bring forth a better climate of understanding and peace. Kozlov replied: "Your visit will help to overcome the suspicion and distrust that has built up between us in recent years."[40]

On the eighteen-mile ride into Moscow, Nixon stopped his limousine several times to shake hands with bystanders. He had learned a few Russian words, like *druzhba* (friendship), and wanted "to communicate in some small way with the Russian people." Ambassador Thompson accompanied him to Spaso House, the United States embassy, where he informed the vice president that Khrushchev was furious over the Captive Nations Resolution because the strained relations with their satellites made Kremlin leaders sensitive to such criticism.[41]

While the vice president and ambassador were talking, Secret Service agents were testing the Nixons' bedroom for radiation. Both Mikoyan and Kozlov had demanded Geiger counters, dosimeters, and badges to determine nearby radiation levels when they were in the United States. Nixon's physician Dr. Walter Tkach also took a Geiger counter and authorized dosimeters and badges. The agents found no sign of radiation on the first floor at the embassy, but there were high readings in the Nixons' bedroom. The agents knew the room was bugged and loudly complained about the radiation. The next day it had disappeared. Nixon was never informed.[42]

The vice president hardly slept on his first night in Moscow. He awoke early Thursday morning and decided to visit an open-air market. There were many, and the one he went to was the Danilovsky market in the center of the city where he achieved one of his stated goals: meeting ordinary people. He talked to random individuals for about an hour. Pyote Smakhtin, a worker who checked weight at the market, complained to Nixon that he could not "find" a ticket for the exhibition; the interpreter changed it to "buy" a ticket. Although the United States opposed charging an admission fee, the Soviet government had imposed one. Nixon offered the man a hundred-ruble note to buy a hundred tickets, but he refused it. The problem was not cost but availability. The first tickets went to the party faithful. The following morning, Moscow's three major newspapers accused the vice president of trying to bribe citizens.[43]

Unaware of this spin, Nixon prepared for his first appointments at the Kremlin. At 9:15 a.m., Klimenti Voroshilov, chairman of the Supreme Soviet, warmly welcomed him and said he hoped for rapprochement between the two superpowers. The Soviet Union, he stated, was dedicated to peace, adding: "if the USSR and the United States decided that there should be no war, then there would be no more wars." Nixon agreed. President Eisenhower knew the horrors of war and was dedicated to peace. The vice president continued with a reference to Khrushchev's demand over Germany: "the policy of ultimatum is completely outdated." Both sides had to accept that "arguing must be done with words rather than fists."[44]

The vice president next met with Khrushchev. The chairman was pleasant with reporters and photographers present, but once they left, he exploded. The Captive Nations Resolution was interference in the domestic affairs of his nation; he could not comprehend how Congress could pass it and simultaneously expect to improve bilateral relations. It was provocative and did not move toward rapprochement. Nixon replied that the resolution reflected the opinion of many Americans who had relatives behind the Iron Curtain and prayed for their independence. Khrushchev's belligerent posture toward the vice president was set from that moment. In *Khrushchev Remembers*, he labeled Nixon a "son-of-a-bitch" and a "puppet" of Joe McCarthy until he fell from power, at which point the vice president abandoned him: "So he was an unprincipled puppet, which is the most dangerous kind." In the midst of his tirade toward Nixon, Khrushchev mentioned that he and the other Kremlin leaders held Eisenhower "in very high esteem" because he had "extremely high moral standards" and was "a very frank and sincere human being."[45]

After this confrontation, Khrushchev, Nixon, and other dignitaries went to preview the American National Exhibition at Sokolniki Park, a 1,500-acre wooded recreational area fifteen miles by subway ride from downtown Moscow. The exhibition was housed in three buildings, totaling 400,000 square feet or more than two square city blocks. The theme, "Image of America," showcased farming, labor, education, science, transportation, art, photographs, music, and film. The United States especially highlighted its consumer products, but the Soviet press expressed doubt that the exhibition mirrored the real lifestyle in the United States. More than 50,000 spectators entered on the first day, and thereafter, an average of 55,000 to 77,000 per day came to the park, for a total of more than three million visitors over the six weeks the exhibit was open.[46]

A little before noon, walking through the first floor, Nixon and Khrushchev stopped at a brightly lit model television studio with a new type of color videotape. An RCA technician invited the chairman to see himself on color television and to say a few words into the microphone to demonstrate instant replay.[47]

In front of the camera, Khrushchev and Nixon started an unrehearsed give-and-take that lasted for sixteen minutes. At first, the vice president was uncomfortable with the chairman's assault on capitalism. He tried to be a gracious host while Khrushchev played to the audience. Nixon asked for "a free exchange of ideas" between the two superpowers. The chairman responded that the videotape provided the answer. The conversation would be recorded in English and Russian, and the citizens of both nations could watch it. They agreed that the broadcast would be shown simultaneously in both nations and shook hands to seal the deal.

Khrushchev said that the United States and his nation were the "most powerful countries" in the world and should live in friendship. The United States had been a republic for 150 years, and the Soviet Union had existed for nearly 42 years. In another seven years, communism would surge past capitalism. Nixon replied that while the Soviet Union would move ahead of the United States in some ways, such as its space program, the United States was advanced in other ways: for instance, color television. Khrushchev refused to concede this point. Nixon responded: "You must not be afraid of ideas." The chairman shot back: "we have no reason to be afraid. We have already broken free from such a situation." The vice president then challenged him to have more exchanges.[48]

The two men, surrounded by reporters, moved to other exhibits. When they reached the model home, split down the middle so that visitors could see inside, they walked up to the barrier and stood next to the General Electric kitchen with its many electric appliances. For almost an hour, Khrushchev and Nixon argued over the merits of their two systems. The chairman said that Russian apartments had modern appliances too, lacking only useless American gadgets like a lemon squeezer. The vice president replied that thousands of these homes were built in America at a cost of $14,000—well within reach of ordinary workers.

Nixon switched tactics: he would like to speak not of "superior or inferior people, but in terms of mutual respect." It was better to debate "the comparative merits of washing machines, than to be arguing over the comparative merits of rockets."

Khrushchev raised his voice: American generals thought they would destroy his country, but they did not account for the spirit of his people. Both nations, Nixon granted, were powerful. Referring to the stalled talks at Geneva, he said that the chairman had issued an ultimatum that the Western allies had to leave Berlin. If war erupted, both sides would lose: "I believe it would be a great mistake and a blow to peace if it [the Geneva conference] were allowed to fail." Khrushchev replied that Nixon was issuing his own ultimatum and trying to frighten him. He poked his finger at Nixon, saying that the Soviet Union had the more powerful weapons, but he wanted peace, especially with the United States. He conceded that the German crisis needed to be resolved.[49]

That evening, at the gala opening the exhibition before more than 5,000 American and Soviet guests, Khrushchev announced that he would be pleased if Eisenhower would visit his country. Nixon read a message from the president: "Our nations have such a great common interest in world peace that every effort must be made to bring us closer together."

That ended the day's surprising events. Neither leader was aware that Ampex Corporation had smuggled the videotape from Moscow to New York City. When the United States embassy learned that all three commercial television networks planned to broadcast the videotape on Saturday's evening news, the diplomats implored the stations to delay it, fearing that a premature release might harm Nixon's mission. The network executives decided that this news could not be postponed and aired the videotape at 11:00 p.m. as a news special. They rebroadcast it on Sunday. Frank Stanton, president of CBS, wrote Nixon that 15 million families, or 41.7 percent of all those with television sets, tuned in for the special. Nixon had beaten *Gunsmoke*, the nation's No. 1 television program, which drew 31.0 percent. On July 27, Moscow television played the debate at 11:45 p.m. *Pravda* and *Izvestia* edited most of Nixon's comments out of their transcripts, making him look helpless in the face of Khrushchev's onslaught.[50]

On July 25, Nixon returned to the Kremlin for a one-hour meeting with Mikoyan, who expressed his dismay at the Captive Nations Resolution; the vice president repeated that the president had no control over this type of congressional action. The two then argued over who was responsible for the Cold War: was it capitalism exploiting the masses, or communist subjection of Eastern Europe? They next turned to trade issues. Mikoyan claimed that the United States had refused to lower its tariffs with the Soviet Union, and Nixon responded that these were complex issues compounded by the Soviet Union's still-outstanding lend-lease debt from World War II. He assured Mikoyan that the president wanted to increase trade, but that he would proceed cautiously. Congress needed to be convinced that greater trade with the Soviet Union would benefit the United States. Easing Cold War tensions, Nixon optimistically predicted, would enhance the possibility of economic agreements. Trade talks would proceed slowly at first, he said, and quicken if political talks moved forward. Trade negotiations did not necessarily have to precede political settlements.[51]

Nixon arrived twenty-five minutes late for his meeting with Kozlov, who also complained about the Captive Nations Resolution. This time Nixon was annoyed, saying that the topic had been thoroughly discussed. He moved on to Admiral Rickover's proposed inspection of the nuclear reactor on the recently constructed Soviet icebreaker *Lenin*. The admiral had shown Kozlov through the nuclear facility at Shippingport and expected the Kremlin leader to reciprocate. Examining the icebreaker's reactor fit into this exchange of information.[52]

While the vice president was at the Kremlin, Pat Nixon was on her "mingle-with-the-Russians" tour, visiting a hospital, sightseeing, and shopping at the large G.U.M. department store. Her husband also did some sightseeing and interacting with people. Although he usually was greeted enthusiastically, hecklers were always stationed nearby to ask loaded questions. One shouted: "Why did the United States oppose a solution to Berlin?" Two others demanded: "Why do you say that we are enslaved people?" Nixon generally responded that he had listened to them and one of the virtues of free speech was that they should allow him to answer.[53]

That evening Khrushchev and Nixon dined at the United States embassy. This time the chairman behaved pleasantly. He had admired Ike since World War II for "his sincerity and gentlemanliness." Nixon replied that he felt warmly welcomed by the Soviet people. As the dinner was ending, the chairman insisted that the Nixons, Ambassador Thompson, and his wife sleep at his *dacha* in the suburbs. At 10:00, they were chauffeured twenty miles outside the capital to their destination as Khrushchev's first Western overnight guests.[54]

The *dacha*, near the town of Osovo, had been finished in 1956. A twelve-foot concrete wall protected it, and a pier on the Moskva River stood a hundred yards from the house. Shortly before 1:00 p.m. the next day, Khrushchev took Nixon and his party to the pier, where they boarded a motorboat and cruised down the waterway where thousands of party members were swimming, picnicking, and sunbathing on the beaches. Khrushchev periodically stopped and talked to the bathers, needling Nixon: "Are these captive people? Do they look like slaves?" The swimmers laughingly answered: "Nyet, nyet [No, no]." The vice president responded: "Peace and friendship to all." He realized that this event had been staged for his benefit: "You never miss a chance to make propaganda." Khrushchev replied that he only spoke the truth.[55]

After several hours on the river, the group returned to the estate. Lunch began at 3:30 under a plastic canopy with the American and Soviet wives present. For the first half-hour, Khrushchev and Nixon exchanged pleasantries. Then the vice president expected that he and the chairman would retire for a private talk. Instead, Khrushchev held the discussion in front of everyone. Soviet ICBMs, he announced, were far superior to those in the United States. He admitted that one had malfunctioned and might have landed in Alaska; but fortunately for both nations, it crashed in the Pacific Ocean. No country, including the Peoples Republic of China, had received any of these weapons, but if the United States attacked, he would supply Mao. He called on Ike to liquidate foreign bases, especially those close to Soviet territory. He also understood that the United States might place missiles in Italy and Greece; if that happened, he would deploy similar weapons in Albania and Bulgaria. To the chairman, bombers had limited use, and the Navy, except for submarines, had no use at all. Neither side could survive a nuclear holocaust, he said, and he hoped for peace.

Nixon agreed that both sides were powerful, and neither could win a nuclear war. The United States desired peace but would protect its interests. Neither side would be intimidated. He encouraged as many bilateral exchanges as possible so that the superpowers would learn about their capabilities.[56]

The conversation continued for more than five hours, concluding at 8:45. The wives never said a word. Khrushchev walked alone with Nixon discussing the approaching announcement that the chairman was coming to the United States to meet with the president. This was the last time Nixon would see Khrushchev in the Soviet Union. The most depressing aspect of the meeting, he later reflected, was the chairman's rigidity; he refused to deviate from "doctrinaire fanatical adherence to the traditional Communist line."[57]

The next morning, Nixon took off for Leningrad, the old czarist capital, using three Soviet TU-104B jets: one for his party, the other two for correspondents and photographers. Kozlov, who had been the Communist Party leader in Leningrad, unexpectedly accompanied the vice president. Upon their arrival, officials and hundreds of American tourists greeted Nixon enthusiastically. He behaved like a candidate during an election, shaking hands and smiling at bystanders.

That afternoon, he visited the Admiralty Shipyard, where the 16,000-ton atomic-powered icebreaker *Lenin* was going through its final tests before sea trials. Admiral Rickover was present and expected to see the reactors. For an hour, the admiral met with a "runaround," but eventually he was given permission to examine the engine room. After spending several hours there and taking copious notes, he determined that the atomic power design served the icebreaker well, but there were no innovations.[58]

According to unnamed press sources, Nixon, while in Leningrad, hinted that he was considering recommending to the president that he invite Khrushchev to the United States. At a luncheon three days later, the vice president stated that he strongly favored an Eisenhower-Khrushchev exchange: "this may be one of the first steps, which will be followed by others, increasing the contacts between the leaders and people of our two countries." Several hours later, he casually added that the exchange would be "a chance for our leaders to talk seriously in a climate in which something can be done without resort to force."[59]

Ike sent Nixon a secret message on July 27 praising his efforts. He had faced many obstacles, the president wrote, and had handled them well. The state department was keeping the White House informed about the mission, and he had nothing to add. His vice president had earned "the respect and admiration of almost all Americans."[60]

While Western tourists routinely traveled to Moscow and Leningrad, the rest of the Soviet Union had been mostly off-limits since the Bolshevik Revolution. World War II brought further restrictions, and after it ended Stalin still refused to expand access. The Truman administration responded in 1952 by restricting Soviet officials to a twenty-five mile radius of New York City and Washington. Three years later, the United States adopted an "off-limits" policy as restrictive as the Soviet Union's. The Eisenhower administration had relaxed this policy so that Mikoyan and Kozlov could travel throughout America. Nixon expected that, in return, he would be permitted to travel in Siberia and the Ural Mountains, where Americans had been barred. This would permit the CIA to gather valuable intelligence.

On July 28, Nixon and his party took off from Leningrad and headed 2,000 miles to the east for the western Siberian city Novosibirsk. The vice president touched down in the evening to a friendly reception. Local officials escorted him to a factory that produced heavy machinery and hydraulic presses. The next day, he toured the hydroelectric plant and dam being constructed on the Ob River. He then went on to a scientific research center near the city that was being built to become a major research facility. Here as elsewhere, he found that planted hecklers confronted him at each stop, loudly shouting out their accusations—generally about the Captive Nations Resolution—and preventing the audience from hearing the vice president's answers. Milton Eisenhower called them "goons."

Throughout this trip, Nixon sent classified telegrams describing his observations to the state department for transmission to the president. Everywhere he went, he reported, ordinary people welcomed him warmly, provocateurs tried to unnerve him, and factory managers repeated the party line.[61]

From Siberia, the vice president flew back toward Moscow and landed in Sverdlovsk, a city in the Ural Mountains with a population of 775,000. Four decades earlier, the Bolsheviks had murdered Czar Nicholas II and family there. As the airplane was landing, CIA analyst Garthoff saw two SA-2 air defense missiles launch complexes being built, one of which shot down the U-2 on May Day 1960![62]

The next morning, Nixon went to Pervourarlsk, a city that separated Europe from Asia, and toured one of the USSR's largest steel tube and pipe factories. Next he journeyed to a copper mine in Degtyarsk, put on miner's clothes, descended 800 feet and walked a quarter mile underground. He visited the Beloyarskoye Nuclear Power Plant, set to be completed in two years. Since this was an example of the peaceful use of nuclear power, Rickover was allowed to examine the reactors.[63]

Back on the plane by the late afternoon, Nixon started making notes for his television and radio address to be delivered to the Soviet people on the evening of August 1. By 6:00 p.m., he had returned to the American embassy, and two hours later he started to write his speech. The first draft was finished early Saturday morning.

Ambassador Thompson insisted that the vice president include a reference to the alleged bribery incident in the Danilovsky market, because the Soviets made "absurd charges in the expectation that at least some of the mud will stick." Harvard government professor William Elliot, having accompanied Nixon on the journey at his request, helped write the address. Elliot was a Nixon supporter who on May 10, 1960, wrote that the vice president had "the best mind of any figure I know in public life today, bar none."[64]

With the speech written and the time approaching for the broadcast, Nixon drove to a primitive television studio, where veteran telecaster John Daly handled the technical aspects. Three cameras had been provided, but two broke down. The vice president began his one-hour address at 8:00 p.m.: half of the time was spent on translation. The broadcast potentially reached eleven million watchers; millions more heard it on the radio, and the Soviet press printed it in its entirety.[65]

Nixon began by pointing out that Mikoyan and Kozlov had spoken on United States radio and television when they visited America, and after his travels in the Soviet Union, he had been granted a similar opportunity. He had met thousands of people, and was impressed by their peaceful intentions and work ethic. He hoped that Khrushchev would lead his nation toward peace because any nuclear war would devastate both countries. As for his market visit, the Soviet press had fabricated an incident: "There was not a shred of truth to this story." While the United States wished to end atomic testing, it would do so only with verifiable inspections. He conceded that the United States had military bases near the Soviet Union, but the Soviet Union had bases in its Eastern European satellites and spent a quarter of its gross domestic product on weaponry; this would not lead to peace. Both nations had to settle their differences without resorting to fists, and they needed to expand exchanges of information and people; that meant that the Kremlin had to stop jamming broadcasts. He concluded by promising to "devote my best efforts to the cause of peace with justice for all peoples of the world."[66]

One negative note crept into the aftermath of the speech. In the early 1980s, shortly before he died, Milton Eisenhower recollected that after the vice president went back to the embassy, he had five or six martinis at a stag party for fifteen or so guests. The vice president was drunk, uncouth, and abusive. Milton never mentioned this event in his memoirs and oral histories. The second secretary of the United States embassy Vladimir Toumanoff, in the early 1980s, offered a slightly different version. The diplomat was not bothered that Nixon had "a couple of extra drinks," but he was disturbed that Nixon "was vicious," "foul-mouthed," and "coarse."[67]

Donald Hughes and another aide, both of whom accompanied Nixon throughout the trip, doubted that such a scene ever occurred. They did not recall it, and Hughes contended that the vice president "was always sober" during the trip. In addition, Nixon did not handle liquor well, and five or six martinis would probably have made him incoherent.[68]

No matter which account is accurate, Michael Beschloss in *Mayday* (1986) took the Milton Eisenhower and Vladimir Toumanoff's accounts and added a detail that has no basis in evidence. Milton, Beschloss alleged, wrote to his brother that "Nixon handled the public part of his trip with 'distinction and loyalty'" but also included the drinking episode in his report. The president, as a commanding general, had been appalled at having to put an inebriated FDR to bed. Beschloss speculated that "Milton's report may have provided Eisenhower with an additional reason for his ambivalence toward his Vice President and putative successor." Beschloss cited no document showing that Milton ever spoke with his brother about the incident, and he did not mention Milton's letter to Nixon two days after he met with his brother: "You [Nixon] did a wonderful job for our country."[69]

Many in the United States applauded Nixon's address—FBI director Hoover pronounced it "one of the most outstanding contributions to international relations in this period of unrest"—but Moscow radio voiced a different opinion. While praising the vice president's remarks concerning Soviet strength, the commentators said he had distorted the Kremlin's foreign policy, and they questioned the need for American bases abroad. Yukov Viktorov questioned the vice president's logic: "Does Mr. Nixon really think that the Soviet people are so naïve as to believe that the American military bases, which are placed thousands of kilometers from the U.S.A. and very close to the Soviet Union's frontiers, are intended to defend America's frontiers—on whom no one ever has made or will make attack?"[70]

Nixon sent three letters to Khrushchev. The first thanked the chairman for his hospitality; another dealt with the crash of a C-130 United States Air Force reconnaissance aircraft with eleven crew members, shot down by Soviet jets over Armenia in September 1958. Even though six bodies were returned, the remains of the other five were unaccounted for. The administration never received an answer. The third letter asked that relatives of United States citizens who desired to leave the Soviet Union to rejoin their families in America be allowed to do so. In return, the administration would permit the repatriation of any of its citizens who wished to return to the Soviet Union.[71]

By August 2, Nixon recalled, he was "very fatigued and had had very little sleep for days." Shortly before noon he held a press conference with more than a hundred journalists in the Spaso House ballroom. Correspondents from both nations asked pointed questions for forty-seven minutes. Nixon answered those concerning the elimination of American foreign military bases as well as Soviet bases in Eastern Europe, halting nuclear testing, expanding peaceful trade, and the Geneva deadlock over Germany. He made headlines by suggesting that Khrushchev visit the United States. Nixon believed that the chairman had to see for himself the lifestyle and unity of the American people.[72]

When the press conference adjourned, the vice president proceeded to the airport, where Kozlov showed up unexpectedly to say goodbye and to offer a twenty-minute rebuttal to Nixon's speech. While he was speaking, the departing press airplane roared overhead at full throttle, drowning out Kozlov's remarks while the crowd watched. As Nixon headed for his jet, Kozlov gave him a jovial pat on the back. The pilots rolled out the Boeing 707 and decided to give the spectators a show by lifting off quickly and climbing at a maximum forty-five degree angle. The Tupelov 114 used most of the runway and climbed slowly. This parting message was meant to show the superiority of United States aircraft.[73]

Throughout this mission, Nixon felt he "was walking on a tight rope virtually every minute I was there." He was depressed that he had not produced any concrete results. James Reston of the *New York Times*, not known as a Nixon admirer, disagreed. Surveying reporters on the trip, he found them in "almost unanimous agreement" that the vice president's mission had been "a success." Television journalist Edward Morgan broadcast at the end of July, "With the exception of obviously studied heckling and primed party-line questions, the curiosity and friendliness of these people were moving and striking." Ralph McGill of the *Atlanta Constitution* wrote that the visit enhanced America's image in the Soviet Union. People welcomed the Nixon party hospitably and heard the vice president "advance a policy of friendship and reconciliation" instead of confrontation.[74]

The vice president flew west, to Warsaw, because the Kremlin refused him permission to fly over eastern Siberia to Alaska. Until he learned of this decision, in mid-July, he had no plans to visit any other country. But during his second day in Moscow, he announced that he expected to spend two days in the Polish capital to exchange views with government officials. Nixon, Donald Hughes wrote, was "most anxious to avoid incidents on the Polish visit. . . . [He did not] want to stimulate the crowds and, possibly, incite a riot." Adam Rapacki, the Polish foreign minister, criticized the Captive Nations Resolution and called Nixon's visit "useless."[75]

This trip to Poland had been contemplated for years. After the Polish uprising in October 1956, when Eisenhower considered giving economic aid to Poland, the vice president heartily concurred. In a commencement speech at Michigan State University on June 9, 1957, Nixon called economic assistance to Poland a "gamble worth taking." The administration had already agreed to lend $95 million for agricultural products and mining equipment. Nixon believed that "the Polish people have been displaying determination to follow a course independent of the Soviet Union." If the United States provided aid, it might lead to a democratic way of life; if no aid were sent, it would drive the Poles closer to the Kremlin. In 1958 and again in 1959, the Polish government had asked the vice president to visit.[76]

During the two-hour flight to the Polish capital on the afternoon of Sunday, August 2, two members of the United States embassy in Warsaw briefed the vice president. Even though the Voice of America and Radio Free Europe broadcasts announced that he was coming, his arrival time and his route into the city were not released. The vice president's plane bypassed the commercial airport that was the closest to the capital and instead touched down at the Babice military facility, about ten miles from Warsaw. Polish officials prevented any crowd from coming to the terminal. As his jet was preparing to land, the Polish militia took its position, thus revealing the route Nixon would take into the city. After deplaning, the vice president remarked that he had arrived on the fifteenth anniversary of the Warsaw uprising and noted the significance of the Polish-American heritage and his hope for peace. He also mentioned that Admiral Rickover had been born in a nearby village.[77]

The vice president sat in an open convertible, the first limousine in the procession. As it started to leave the airport, the honor guard spontaneously and surprisingly began to cheer. As many as 400,000 spectators lined the route to the capital, tossing flowers and chanting "Hurrah America" and "Long Live Nixon." The car had to stop eight times to clear off flowers so the driver could see. Rioters had hurled rocks and bottles at him in South America; in Poland, they threw bouquets of roses. Reporter Daniel Schorr, in his memoirs, recalled opening a news bureau in Warsaw earlier that year and said he had never seen anything like the vice president's greeting in an Eastern European satellite. Neither had Nixon. The vice president was "deeply moved by the tremendously warm and friendly welcome."[78]

On Monday morning, after meeting with President Aleksander Zawadzki and Czeslaw Wycech, marshal of the Sejm (parliament) and laying a wreath at the Tomb of the Unknown Soldier, Nixon spent the afternoon with Gomulka, First Secretary of the Polish United Workers Party, who had cut short his vacation for the meeting. Seeing Gomulka was Nixon's primary reason for stopping in Warsaw, and Ike underlined that his vice president was "not negotiating there." The United States ambassador to Poland, Jacob Beam, had presented his credentials two years earlier and had never been given a meeting with Gomulka. In fact, this was the first time any high Western official had been granted an interview.[79]

Gomulka and Nixon talked for over five hours. The Polish leader described the negative effects of the Captive Nations Resolutions on his nation, and the vice president responded that the American Congress was expressing its opposition to Soviet control of its Eastern satellites. Gomulka said he realized that Polish Americans might resent what they perceived as Soviet domination, but he dismissed these worries and encouraged them to come home and see the situation for themselves. His primary concerns were Polish security and friendly relations with the Soviet Union. Khrushchev, he believed, was sincerely against war and for peace.

Gomulka feared West German rearmament and a possible invasion from the west. Nixon assured him that Poland had nothing to fear from the Adenauer government. Gomulka also desired a settlement of the common border between

Poland and Germany. If German reunification hurt his country, he opposed it, just as he objected to West Germany joining NATO. He next turned to trade, saying he wanted increased commerce with the United States and American foreign aid. Nixon responded that the two nations had to resolve past claims and foreign debts. The Pole complained that Radio Free Europe propaganda needed to be halted, and he was irritated that the *New York Times* had described the welcome accorded Nixon as a protest against the Polish government.[80]

While Nixon and Gomulka were meeting, Ike stood in front of a special press conference announcing an exchange of visits between himself and Khrushchev. Ike had told Nixon about the coming invitation before he left for Russia. He had also informed Prime Minister Harold Macmillan of Britain and other Western allies. When nine governors returned from a three-week tour of the Soviet Union, they met with the president at the White House and told him that Khrushchev said that Ike would receive a "tremendous welcome" if he came to Moscow. Ike made no comment. The next day the chairman responded to rumors of a visit: "when the time is ripe."[81]

With leaks of a possible Khrushchev visit gaining intensity, the president decided to announce the trip and give its background. He had suggested the idea to the state department early in July, and the United States and the Soviet Union had negotiated an agreement. While Ike had consulted the Western European allies, he would only speak for his government; the visit was not connected with any future summit. It was meant to "melt a little bit of the ice that seems to freeze our relationship with the Soviets" and to promote "better understanding" and "peace" between the superpowers.[82]

While the president's announcement was making headlines, early Tuesday morning, the vice president traveled to the Warsaw Ghetto where he laid a gladiola on the proposed site of the holocaust memorial. Earl Mazo, a Jew who was reporting on Nixon's trip, had been born in the capital, and his family had moved to the United States when he was two. After returning to his devastated neighborhood, he told Nixon that uncrated boxes for the memorial were rusting. After inspecting the ruins, Nixon declared that the death and destruction there should be a grim reminder of the power of prejudice. Standing near the last bunker held by Jewish fighters in the Warsaw uprising before the Nazis massacred them—where the unfinished monument was meant to be built—he stated: "All men should unite against such prejudice because here we see again what happens when such passions which are allowed to be nourished are unleashed." Mazo thought this was the best speech he ever heard against anti-Semitism. Returning to the ghetto several years later, he saw that the monument had been built.[83]

Nixon then unexpectedly went to the Warsaw Steel Mill, then under construction. The plant manager proudly showed him the machinery while ignoring the workers whom Nixon wanted to meet. Coming back to Warsaw, his Polish guide commented: "One thing about these plant managers is that they know everything about factories and nothing about people." Nixon felt that illustrated the fundamental flaw of dictatorships.[84]

That afternoon, Nixon confronted a potentially explosive situation between the two most powerful institutions in Poland, the government and the church. He stopped at the Cathedral of St. John, where Stefan Cardinal Wyszynski, the Roman Catholic Primate of Poland, prayed and preached. To avoid any friction, the cardinal had left on vacation. A priest gave the Nixons a ten-minute tour, and that evening, another one quietly gave Nixon a card from the cardinal thanking the United States for what it had done for Poland.[85]

Wednesday morning, 60,000 people lined Warsaw streets to see him off. At the airport, reflecting on the moving experience, the vice president said: "We came to Poland as friends. . . . We are leaving as better friends." The Soviet press reported that Nixon had sent Khrushchev a personal letter expressing hope for improved bilateral relations for "a peaceful settlement of the important differences between them."[86]

A crowd of more than 3,000 greeted Nixon in Washington on August 5. He told his audience that he sought to convey the peaceful intentions and friendship of the United States to the Soviets and the Poles. When he mentioned the president's name and pointed to his brother Milton, they received enthusiastic applause. Khrushchev had told Nixon that American grandchildren would live under communism. Nixon responded: "everybody should have the freedom of choice." His, he said, was democracy. Recognizing that many Americans found communism despicable, he said he expected Khrushchev to be treated with courtesy when he came to the United States. "The best part of going away from the United States," he concluded, "is to come home again."[87]

Ike, not wanting to upstage Nixon, watched the arrival on television. After leaving the airport, the vice president and Milton Eisenhower drove directly to the White House for a seventy-minute debriefing in which they advised the president how to manage the exchange with Khrushchev. Nixon recommended that Ike make it a short trip, avoid Siberia, and spend two or three days in Moscow. He gave his assessment of the chairman's personality and suggested that the Polish people were the "true Achilles Heel of the Soviet system." Khrushchev, Milton continued, never deviated from communist doctrine. He would try to distract the president, but Ike should concentrate on business.[88]

The next morning, Republican Congressman Robert Wilson from San Diego had breakfast with the president and wrote Nixon that Ike "was very much impressed with the manner in which you handled Khrushchev. He particularly mentioned the televised 'kitchen argument' as an example of your effective handling of the situation." The journey had permitted Americans "to see you in action other than during a political campaign."[89]

In the next several days, Nixon gave talks about his mission. At the NSC meeting, he reported that the Kremlin cooperated better than expected, but their media exaggerated Khrushchev's victory in the debates. Despite that spin, Soviet officials were concerned that Nixon's widely disseminated statements had a "considerable effect in the USSR." At the cabinet, he gave his impressions of Khrushchev, the Soviet people, and the political situation in Poland. On Sunday, he described his journey for a television audience, pointing out that the Soviet chairman liked to do the unexpected "and you always had to be on your guard."[90]

Even as Nixon received accolades from officials as well as the press, only the president knew how significant the mission was for his diplomatic initiatives. Nixon's trip to the Soviet Union and Poland was the most complex and rigorous one that he would ever take as vice president. The president briefed him before the journey and debriefed him immediately upon his return. Ike assimilated information that he would need in his conversations with Khrushchev, but did not disclose his hidden imperatives. He kept his enemies guessing, never revealing the cards in his hand; that was his modus operandi. What he wished for was results.

33

IKE'S HOPES COLLAPSE

Almost as soon as Nixon returned to Washington from Poland, the Soviet media's negativity over the American exhibition vanished; instead, the Kremlin expressed its elation over Khrushchev's trip to America. In Moscow on August 5, the chairman held his third press conference in the sixteen months since he had assumed the premiership, telling approximately 300 reporters that he would arrive in Washington in mid-September and that his government would work for a better understanding with the United States. The chairman spoke highly of the president but stressed that their meeting would not be a substitute for a summit. He still demanded a new peace treaty with Germany that would end the agreement that had kept occupation forces stationed there since the collapse of the Third Reich and turned Berlin into a divided city inside East Germany. He would go to America, he said, "with a pure heart and an open soul," hoping to halt the Cold War and "achieve mutual understanding in order to help insure peace throughout the world."[1]

Most in the American press welcomed the visit as an opportunity to ameliorate friction between the superpowers. Vocal opposition came from Eastern European refugees who had fled Soviet control of their countries, as well as from politicians and religious and union leaders.[2] Ike listened to these dissidents and sought the opinions of people who had visited the Soviet Union. Norman Cousins, a disarmament advocate and the editor of the *Saturday Review,* who had recently spent a month there, talked to the president in the Oval Office for a half hour. They chatted about the improved living standards in the Soviet Union, the high morale of its citizens, and the impasse over Berlin. The president also talked to his brother Milton, who was impressed with Khrushchev's abilities but added that he was poorly educated and did not understand conditions in the United States.[3]

Ike actively participated in arranging Khrushchev's itinerary. During two press conferences in August, the president emphasized that he wished to create "a bettering of the atmosphere between the East and the West." He expected to discuss disarmament and Germany in a private meeting in the White House, but he also wanted the chairman to see America at first hand and judge it for himself. Writing confidentially to a friend, Cola Parker, on August 22, Ike clarified why he had sent the invitation to Khrushchev. The world was "headed toward an arms race of such magnitude as can culminate in unbearable burdens on our peoples at best, or general war at worst," and he wanted to prevent this. He did not expect any great breakthrough, but direct talks with Khrushchev represented "nearly the only course left now to this end."[4]

To reassure the Western alliance of his commitment, Ike spent twelve days in late August and early September visiting the leaders of the Federal Republic of Germany, Great Britain, and France. When he returned to the capital on September 7, he had sharpened his views for his meetings with Khrushchev and hoped to soften "up the Russian leader even a little bit." Until then, the only thaw between the two powers had been the treaty that neutralized Austria. The talks with Khrushchev would probably be his administration's last effort at cooperation with the Soviets. He would tell the chairman that his position on Berlin was "unacceptable." If no progress were made, Ike would cancel his trip to Moscow.[5]

While the president planned for Khrushchev's arrival, Nixon concentrated on selling the visit's benefits to the American people through speeches and interviews. As vice president, he said, he had been treated courteously in Moscow; Khrushchev should be accorded the same reception. According to Nixon, Khrushchev believed that a few wealthy Americans kept down millions of discontented poor ones, many of whom objected to the president's anticommunist stance. As a consequence, said Nixon, Khrushchev reasoned that "America has strength but may lack the will to defend her vital interests." The chairman's visit, however, should not lull Americans into a false sense of security. There would be no breakthroughs, and Americans needed to support the president's defense budget: "while understanding alone will not bring peace, misunderstanding could provoke war."[6]

On the afternoon of September 15, Khrushchev arrived in a good mood. Ike usually did not welcome foreign dignitaries at the airport, preferring to wait for them at the White House, but this time he personally greeted the chairman as he stepped off his plane. They had not seen each other since the Geneva conference in the summer of 1955. The concern over vocal protests on the drive to 1600 Pennsylvania Avenue evaporated when the spectators along the route generally behaved without hostile demonstrations. Khrushchev and Ike talked in the Oval Office for about two hours and decided not to hold further substantive talks until after the chairman had traveled across the United States and returned to the capital. The following day, Ike wrote Prime Minister Nehru of India that he wanted Khrushchev "to show a more conciliatory spirit" that would move him away from potential conflict.[7]

At first, Khrushchev tried to single out Nixon as a villain who opposed peace while the president supported it. The chairman criticized the vice president for his role in the kitchen debate and for his recent supposedly anticommunist addresses. The vice president answered that Khrushchev had attacked the United States before his arrival in Moscow and that he, Nixon, was not the adversary. The next afternoon at a National Press Club luncheon, the Soviet premier complained that the vice president misperceived him and his countrymen.[8]

Khrushchev traveled across America over the next eight days. He faced hecklers at the Economic Club in New York City and visited a movie set in Hollywood, where he was visibly upset when scantily clad dancers performed the Can Can. He was furious at being prevented, for security reasons, from touring Disneyland in Anaheim, but a warm reception in San Francisco, a hybrid corn farm in Iowa, and an enthusiastic welcome in Pittsburgh improved his mood.[9]

During the chairman's journey, Nixon continued to defend the visit. At a speech before the Key Man Club in Hartford, Connecticut, on September 19, he said that "It is better to have a man with this power to know the United States . . . than to have him sitting in the Kremlin not knowing the strength and the will of our people." The next day, before the Polish National Alliance convention, he said the invitation was "justified and wise, and will serve the best interests of the people," adding that he hoped for a relaxation of tensions between the superpowers. Whatever happened in future negotiations, "we will have the Soviet man know and feel the strength of this nation."[10]

Ike wrote C.D. Jackson, his former counselor on psychological warfare, on September 23 that he was pessimistic that the chairman would "miraculously . . . make any real concessions in some of his more rigid positions." Two days later, Henry Cabot Lodge, who had accompanied Khrushchev across America as the president's personal representative, reported to Ike on his observations. The chairman, according to Lodge, "was a remarkable, although very difficult man." He wanted peace and looked forward to disarmament talks, book exchanges, expanded trade, and fewer restrictions on travel within the Soviet Union. He was especially interested in a peace treaty with the United States. Ike reacted to Lodge's description by hoping to bring Khrushchev to his Gettysburg farm, to talk with him alone and try to determine whether the chairman sincerely hoped for peace. If he put off his ultimatum on Germany for three years, that might provide time to negotiate an agreement.[11]

The president took Khrushchev to Camp David in Maryland's Catoctin Mountains on the evening of Friday, September 25, for substantive discussions. Saturday morning, the two leaders met alone for several hours without reaching any agreement. Nixon and others then joined them for lunch. During the meal, Khrushchev suddenly launched into a violent attack on the vice president for his role in the kitchen debates. Nixon defended his actions and reminded the chairman that he had attacked American policy before Nixon reached Moscow. Khrushchev ignored that criticism and went on to insult the president, who was visibly upset and barely maintained his composure.[12]

Afterward, the president took the chairman for a twenty-mile helicopter ride to visit his Gettysburg farm. When Khrushchev returned, he seemed more relaxed and congenial. A joint United States–Soviet communiqué on Sunday stated that the president would visit the Soviet Union during the following spring. Improving bilateral relations would lead "to a better understanding" and "to the achievement of a just and lasting peace." Disputes should be resolved through peaceful negotiations.[13]

As for the Berlin question, the communiqué nebulously stated that negotiations would be reopened. Earlier that morning, the president had told Khrushchev that he would never attend a summit meeting under the threat of the Berlin ultimatum. Khrushchev had responded by agreeing to lift the time limit on a Soviet–East German treaty, averting a crisis over Berlin. This was not mentioned in the communiqué. At a press conference the day after Khrushchev left the United States, Ike said that the German negotiations had "no fixed time limit on them." Ike was pleased when Khrushchev, back in Moscow, confirmed this statement.[14]

Khrushchev returned to the Kremlin elated with the success of his American journey and speaking of the "Spirit of Camp David." The American media generally agreed.[15]

The president was skeptical over the widespread euphoria. The only achievement of the mission had been the agreement on Berlin, and other than that the Soviet Union had not budged. At a press conference on October 28, Laurence Burd of the *Chicago Tribune* asked Ike to comment on the chairman's claim that the communist system was superior to the American one. Ike replied that the Kremlin took the position that the United States was slightly ahead in industrial development but the Soviets would catch up and pass America. This, he said, was propaganda and "so the best answer is a smile." Nothing had changed.[16]

Nixon echoed Eisenhower's concerns. While applauding the president for bringing Khrushchev to America, he did not see any long-term advances. The chairman had traveled across the country and probably learned "that Communist dogma of a divided and decadent America is hopelessly outmoded." Nixon and Ambassador Lodge agreed that the United States had to keep the initiative and persuade the developing world to follow the free world's leadership. Lodge worried that Khrushchev's trip might "create a sense of false security in this country and will act as a sort of soporific to the American people and Congress as regards maintaining our national defense." Nixon wanted to be certain that this did not happen. He thought that the chairman's pronouncements of his system's superiority would not fool most Americans. Even with that, the United States should not underestimate the Soviet challenge.[17]

FBI director J. Edgar Hoover added to the president and vice president's fears. At the beginning of 1960, he reported that prior to Khrushchev's mission, "the Soviet Union was directing a massive offensive of subversion at this country," and this espionage activity had not abated. Moscow had given the CPUSA $275,500 for operations and had increased its spying efforts in the federal bureaucracy and the military, and with young people. He claimed that the United States continued "to be a major target for espionage and subversive operation on a grand scale." It is not clear how trustworthy Hoover in fact was; but Eisenhower and Nixon both took his warnings seriously.[18]

Despite the FBI director's analysis, the United States planned for the summit. On April 26, the White House announced that Nixon would head the delegation if the president had to return to the capital for "domestic requirements." At a press conference the next day, Ike explained that with Congress in session, he might have to attend to pending legislation. If the summit ran longer than expected, he might want to use his vice president as an option. As for the summit agenda, he hoped to ease world tensions but would not give up America's rights in Germany. That did not mean that the Four Powers could not negotiate an acceptable solution. It did mean that he would not attend any gathering under the threat of an ultimatum.[19]

Throughout these preparations, the president continued to receive regular updates on Soviet military strength. Beginning in 1956, America's U-2 spy planes, flying at 70,000 feet, had done photographic reconnaissance of troop movements, military installations, and other critical data. The CIA, which had charge of this clandestine operation, believed that Soviet tracking radar would not detect the flights at that altitude, but its assessment was wrong. Shortly after the missions commenced, the Kremlin quietly sent out a diplomatic protest over the invasion of its air space. Ike approved each mission, and he sanctioned one two weeks before the summit was to start. On May 1, a Soviet surface-to-air missile (SAM) forced a U-2 down. Four days later, Khrushchev spoke before the Supreme Soviet in the Great Hall at the Kremlin. Without disclosing his purpose, he had invited United States ambassador Thompson to attend, and toward the end of the address, he looked at Thompson and announced that a U-2 had been shot down. He then denounced the United States; the Spirit of Camp David was gone.[20]

At first, Ike denied any knowledge of a spy plane: the administration claimed the U-2 was doing weather research for National Aeronautic and Space Administration (NASA) and the pilot had apparently passed out from lack of oxygen while flying "north of Turkey." This ploy collapsed on May 7 when Khrushchev announced that the pilot, Francis Gary Powers, had been captured alive. He exhibited the remains of the crashed U-2 as well as photographs of Soviet bases recovered from its cabin. Two days later, Nixon telephoned Secretary Herter and vigorously argued that Ike had to acknowledge that he knew about the flights. If he did not, that would "imply that war could start without the president's knowledge." The administration had to make carefully considered statements and "must not be apologetic": the United States was gathering intelligence that it needed against the possibility of a Soviet surprise attack. Ike took responsibility for the U-2 on May 11, asserting that the United States was acting in self-defense.[21]

In the midst of the U-2 debacle, Ike and his counselors worked on the summit's agenda. Khrushchev would try to dominate the meeting, Eisenhower said, by forcing his priorities on the allies. Ike would try to laugh off the U-2 incident. He would permit the chairman to talk about it as much as he wished, "and then quietly suggest that he should come around and talk privately to the President about it." For his answer, Ike said, he was having a memo prepared on the extent of Soviet spying in the United States, including detailed examples.[22]

The summit opened in Paris on May 15, and Khrushchev immediately attacked the United States and Ike, demanding an apology for the U-2 spying and effectively ending any chance for an agreement. On May 16, the conference adjourned. Ten days later at a cabinet meeting, Ike speculated about why the chairman had wrecked the gathering. It could not be that he had suddenly learned of the U-2 flights, since he had known about them for several years. Prime Minister Macmillan and French president Charles de Gaulle believed Khrushchev was looking for an excuse to cancel Ike's visit to the Soviet Union; Ike thought they were probably right because of domestic opposition inside the Kremlin over any agreement with the United States.[23]

From the middle of May onward, Nixon defended the use of the U-2. On the fifteenth, he suggested that the parties should address their mutual concern over surprise attacks. The success of a high altitude, unarmed aerial reconnaissance airplane proved that Ike's Open Skies proposal at the 1955 Geneva conference was feasible. The president had prevented any "intelligence gap." He was now prepared to halt the U-2 flights and recommend that the Four Powers turn over their aerial intelligence capabilities to the United Nations. As for Khrushchev's outrage over American espionage, Nixon announced on May 18 that on September 18, 1959, while Khrushchev was visiting America, two Soviet spies had been arrested for trying to obtain information from an American citizen. The episode had not been publicized because the United States did not want it to disrupt the chairman's visit.[24]

In Nixon's telling, Khrushchev was the reason for the summit's collapse. He wanted to destroy it and used the U-2 incident as his lever—because, Nixon speculated, he had backed down from his Berlin ultimatum. That month he wrote a constituent that he wanted to "take adequate measures to protect us against surprise attack from a nation which has openly declared its objective of world domination." World opinion, he said, supported the president's "firm stand against appeasement in Paris," and he was "convinced the consistent resolute stand we have always taken, regardless of the shifting tactical zig-zags of the Communist offensive, is the proper course of action."[25]

On the last day of May, the vice president spoke before the sixth SEATO council of ministers meeting in Washington. He began by stating that Khrushchev had made a "major propaganda blunder" by shattering any hope for peace. The president had developed to U-2 to prevent a communist surprise attack, while the Kremlin employed espionage as standard practice. Khrushchev's threats would not intimidate the United States. It would not retreat or appease Moscow. The president would continue to support adequate military strength and follow a policy of "firmness without belligerency."[26]

Although Nixon's advocacy had a positive effect at home, the failure of the summit conference ended any hope of progress on a test ban treaty or on disarmament during the Eisenhower administration. Until a new president entered the White House, United States–Soviet bargaining was stalemated. Rather than being remembered for the collapse of these negotiations at the end of his presidency, Ike's warning regarding the "military-industrial complex" is spotlighted.

IKE, NIXON, KENNEDY, AND CASTRO

No aspect of inter-American relations consumed more time during Eisenhower's second term than the 1959 Cuban revolution. The island lay only ninety miles from Florida, and United States interests there dated to colonial times. These interests grew stronger after the Spanish-American War, when the United States assumed the role of military arbiter in the island's domestic affairs and the American ambassador was often seen as the second most powerful person on the island.

During the Great Depression, the United States decided to lessen its hold under Franklin Roosevelt's "good neighbor" policy. This diplomatic slogan and the noninterference it represented were praised throughout the Western Hemisphere. In Cuba, it helped precipitate the removal of President Gerardo Machado, who ruled as a dictator into 1933, and his replacement by Fulgencio Batista, who had participated in the "revolt of the sergeants" and emerged as a charismatic leader. Batista was elected president of Cuba in 1940 and served until 1944, when he moved to the United States.[1]

In 1952, he decided to regain the presidency, but when it appeared he would lose the election, he staged a coup d'état and installed himself as dictator. The Truman administration granted prompt recognition. Batista's return to power repelled many Cubans, and one in particular, Fidel Castro, took to the mountains with an irregular army and began a guerrilla campaign known as the 26 of July Movement.[2]

As the Castro forces grew more formidable, the dictator's rule began to crumble. The United States disapproved of Batista's authoritarianism but was unsure of Castro's political leanings. In November 1958, William Pawley, a friend of Eisenhower's with extensive knowledge of Latin American affairs, went to the island on a CIA-sponsored mission to ask Batista to relinquish power; he refused, and the United States did not force him to resign. Toward the end of December, CIA director Allen Dulles predicted that Batista would fall, that Castro would assume control, and that he would bring communists into his regime. The American media had embraced Castro as a liberator, but Cuba had one of the largest communist parties in Latin America, and the Eisenhower administration hoped to prevent communists from gaining power.[3]

The state department responded ambivalently to Castro's rise but was keenly aware that Latin American liberals and the press, opposed to "right-wing dictatorships," favored him. The diplomatic consensus was that Castro was not a threat and communists would not infiltrate his government. Still, American diplomats specializing in hemispheric affairs found themselves in an impossible position. As Roy Rubottom, assistant secretary of state for inter-American affairs, put it, the administration had a choice between the known Batista tyranny and the unknown Castro. He concluded that United States was "damned if we did, and we were damned if we didn't."[4]

Batista eased the state department's dilemma by fleeing Cuba on New Year's Day, 1959. A temporary council took control, and the United States granted recognition to the Cuban provisional government on January 7. Castro marched triumphantly into Havana the next day, gradually assumed overall command, and appointed himself prime minister.[5]

Eisenhower initially responded to the regime change with restraint and conciliation. Secretary of State Dulles entered the year with terminal cancer and by spring handed over his duties to Undersecretary of State Christian Herter. Ike had relied on Dulles's counsel for six years but did not have the same high regard for Herter and instead turned to Foster's brother, DCI Allen Dulles, for guidance. Allen had grown convinced that Castro had communist sympathies and his regime would be adversarial to United States interests.[6]

While the administration was struggling to define its Cuba policy, the American Society of Newspaper Editors invited Castro to address its gathering on April 17 in Washington. Eleven days before that appearance, Assistant Secretary Rubottom wrote United Nations representative Lodge concerning the troubling situation in Cuban concerning bilateral relations and American investments. Even though the administration hoped to work with Castro, according to the inter-American expert, the Cuban revolutionary appeared "to have a basic, deep-seated anti-American prejudice which promises to make it very difficult for us to work with the new Cuban Government." Castro would be coming to the United States shortly, and this would "afford us an opportunity of sizing him up in person."[7]

Since this was an unofficial visit, the president decided not to receive the Cuban prime minister; others would talk with him and provide their assessments.

Castro especially wished to see Nixon, and after receiving state department approval, Nixon agreed to meet him in his formal office in the Capitol Building. Herter and Rubottom met with him separately. Rubottom believed these visits "might be our last opportunities to influence favorably his current thinking and deter him from leading Cuba into a position of nationalistic neutralism, which the communists will exploit to the fullest."[8]

Castro arrived in the capital on Wednesday, April 15, and had a luncheon with acting Secretary Herter the next day. They had an animated conversation throughout the meal. The prime minister spoke before the newspaper editors on Friday and held an elaborate night-time reception on Saturday at the Cuban embassy.[9]

The next day, he appeared on *Meet the Press.* Moderator Lawrence Spivak spent an hour with the prime minister before his appearance and later described him as "extraordinarily able, unbelievably naive and extremely dangerous." He thought "that in this naiveté lies Cuba's greatest danger." Castro was "a perfect set-up for communist manipulation"; he repeatedly asked his host "why we Americans were so concerned with the danger of communism in Cuba."[10]

Once the program ended, Castro drove to the vice president's office for the scheduled 7:15 p.m. meeting. Nixon had nothing else on his calendar and arrived a few minutes before his guest. Vernon Walters was there to translate, but Castro's English was good enough that Walters left five minutes into the two-and-a-half-hour conversation. Nixon greeted his guest, who seemed "somewhat nervous and tense." Castro did not believe he had done well on television and bitterly complained about his treatment by the American press. The vice president reassured him that he had done well.

After these preliminaries, Nixon suggested that Castro needed to lead and not succumb to mob rule. Cuba should be a democracy and not a dictatorship. Communist penetration should be avoided, but, from Nixon's perspective, Castro seemed naïve about a communist threat. In order to govern effectively, Nixon told him, Castro had to find officials to whom he could delegate specific administrative duties. He thought Cuba might consider the model that Luis Muñoz Marin had followed in Puerto Rico, but Castro rejected anything that smacked of American colonialism.

Nixon also urged the prime minister to hold early elections, within four years at most, but Castro countered that the island's past elections had been corrupt and led to "bad government." Nixon also hoped that Cuba would halt the executions of Batista's followers; at least 550 *batistianos* had been killed as war criminals. The prime minister replied that they were enemies of the state and had to be terminated. Nixon cautioned his guest that if he were unwilling to institute these changes, American public opinion would turn against his regime.

Nixon was surprised that Castro did not mention economic assistance or the island's sugar exports to the United States, which were regulated by an import quota. Except for subsistence farming and local markets, the Cuban agricultural sector was reliant on sugar cane as its overwhelming cash crop. Instead, the prime minister inquired about government loans, which Nixon told him were not forthcoming. The Cubans, he suggested, should employ the free enterprise system and try to attract private investors. One item they agreed upon was that the United States should stop selling military equipment to Latin America, because those sales helped keep Caribbean dictators in power.

Castro seemed sincere in his efforts to convince Nixon that he was not a communist and had the support of the majority of Cubans. Nixon conceded that Castro had leadership capabilities, but "he is either incredibly naïve about Communism or under Communist discipline." The vice president chose to think he was naïve. He also thought the prime minister had no idea how to manage a government or direct the island's economy.[11]

After the Cuban departed, Nixon asked three Americans into his office who had been waiting in the Senate lobby, Wylie Buchanan, chief of protocol; Vernon Walters; and Robert Stevenson, the state department officer in charge of Cuban affairs. The vice president, Stevenson observed, "looked very tired", but gave "the old college try" and wanted to unwind. Nixon told the three men that the prime minister lacked "a sense of humor" and was "clearly a very naïve and unsophisticated man in many ways but at the same time a real leader."

Nixon had tried to chat with his guest "just like a father" but doubted he had made "any lasting impression." Just as Stevenson was rising to leave, Nixon asked him for his evaluation of the meeting. The diplomat said the United States should not underestimate Castro. Nixon interrupted. Did he do "any good?" Stevenson thought for a moment and replied: probably not. Nixon half-rose, "clapped his hands to his thighs and said, 'That's what I think, too.'"[12]

William Baggs, editor of the Miami News and a Nixon friend, spoke with Castro at 11:00 that evening. The journalist wrote the vice president that Castro respected Nixon's "head" and "heart" but worried about "a lack of organized executive leadership in our country today." Nixon answered that Castro had the "unique qualities" of a leader and would "be a man to reckon with in the Americas in the years to come." He was also "extremely sensitive to public opinion" and might alter his position if he thought his actions produced "an unfavorable reaction either at home or abroad."[13]

Nixon also wrote a long memorandum on the interview and sent it to the president, the secretary of state, former governor Dewey, Democratic senator Mike Mansfield, and others. Milton Eisenhower received a copy and concluded that it "confirmed my deepest worries about [Castro]. He seems to be egocentric, frighteningly naive, and completely unpredictable."[14]

Senator Barry Goldwater did not get a copy, but he had already told the vice president that he had seen Cuban exiles in Miami. These refugees agreed with the original intent of the revolution but had changed their allegiance. Castro had killed too many prisoners and made too many anti-American threats to retain the backing of the island's middle class and businessmen. Many, fearing an eventual communist government, urged the United States to force Castro to modify his behavior. Some of the disenchanted were already plotting another revolution if he did not. Goldwater warned Nixon that the island was "in great danger of being turned into a Blood-Bath and the U.S.A. can do something about bringing peace if it will help now. Quick action is needed." Nixon replied on April 27: "This kind of observation is much more reliable than the opinions of the armchair intelligence expert!"[15]

Over the next few months, the administration's watchful waiting gravitated toward open skepticism. Even the state department was beginning to consider Castro either a communist or a party dupe. The United States objected to Castro's accusation that it was responsible for a bombing in Havana harbor. In mid October, the American embassy protested against allegations that it was aligning with anti-Castro groups. Congress and the media became more critical of Castro as he continued the execution of *batistianos* and refused to hold national elections.[16]

Nixon received ominous predictions that summer. Robert Kleberg Jr., president of the massive King Ranch in Texas, considered the Cuban predicament "very serious. Unless Castro is stopped in some way he will certainly succeed in communizing [*sic*] Cuba." By the end of October, Nixon was refusing to comment on Cuban affairs because they were "so inflammatory." He was a part of the administration and "could not discuss it without raising possible difficulties."[17]

In the National Security Council (NSC) meetings on December 10 and 16, he did not mince words. He saw the island's regime "being driven toward Communism more and more" and predicted that the Democrats in the next Congress "would make a massive assault on our Latin American policy" if the administration paid insufficient attention to Cuba. The United States had not canceled the Cuban sugar quota, he said, and the state department was trying to develop some kind of authority to adjust the quota to keep Cuban leaders in line. The administration could not let the Cubans act like bullies but also did not want to precipitate a crisis.[18]

The president was already considering much harsher measures. During the final months of 1959, Ike directed the CIA to devise methods for ousting

Castro, and in January 1960 a Special Group was assembled to study this objective. The prospect that the president might move forward was reinforced later that month when he met with Philip Bonsal, United States ambassador to Cuba, who was widely respected as an expert in hemispheric matters. Eisenhower began the conversation by saying that Castro was beginning "to look like a mad man."

Bonsal replied that the Cuban was "a very conspiratorial individual" who wanted to give "the impression that he and Cuba are beleaguered." He emphasized that Castro was "an extreme Leftist and is strongly anti-American." Ike asked whether communists were active in politics and how the islanders would make a living if they could not sell their sugar crop. The diplomat answered that communists operated a major newspaper and held influential government jobs. As for the economics of sugar, the regime had not addressed it. The president, Bonsal counseled, should ask Congress to change the sugar legislation so that he could raise or lower the Cuban quota as a bargaining chip in bilateral negotiations.[19]

While pondering the advantages of such economic leverage, Eisenhower proceeded with covert activities. On March 17, DCI Dulles presented his agency's recommendations to the president and his advisers. Dulles thought the proposals would take six to eight months to implement, and the agency would provide cover for their projects. The CIA would establish a unified council or junta without either *batistianos* or communists, and a successor would be identified to lead the opposition forces. Anti-Castro propaganda would be spread via mass communications and through exiles speaking against the regime throughout Latin America. A powerful radio station located on Swan Island in the Caribbean would broadcast information hostile to the regime. The agency would mount covert intelligence activities inside of Cuba for information, infiltration, defection, and propaganda, and would set up a paramilitary force outside the island that would train refugees for infiltration and exfiltration as well as provide air capabilities for supplying guerrillas in the mountains. The DCI submitted a $4,400,000 budget for this initial phase.

Ike gave his oral approval. When Dulles left, he took all written documents with him. The president, to retain plausible deniability, kept nothing.[20] The CIA initiated plans for broadcasts from Swan Island and began training approximately 300 exiles in a remote region of Guatemala for covert parachute drops in the mountains and amphibious raids on the coast.

Castro, meanwhile, was justifying United States concern. He invited Anastas Mikoyan, the Soviet deputy premier, to visit Cuba early in February on a trade mission. Two months later, Havana established diplomatic ties with Moscow.

Relations between the United States and Cuba deteriorated still further that summer, when Ike cut Cuba's sugar imports and fixed its future quota at zero. Castro reacted by expropriating American properties, and that winter the United States began an economic boycott.[21]

These events made newspaper headlines, but far from the spotlight covert CIA planning was moving forward. Ike anticipated that the Soviets would sell Cuba some of their weaponry, but he did not envision Khrushchev signing a mutual security treaty with Castro. The president also realized that the United States had to take measures to protect its prestige after the Cuban seizures of Americans' property. In mid-July, he told his advisers he had not made a final decision on any action. Some thirty days later, Ike informed a legislative conference that the United States would not accept communist rule in Cuba. The question was what to do and when. He did not tell his listeners that he had already approved a $13,000,000 budget for covert activities in Cuba.[22]

Ike shared some of his plans with British prime minister Macmillan throughout 1960. They discussed the worsening political conditions on the island and the confiscation of foreign-owned properties. Ike worried that the Soviets were trying to find a foothold in the Western Hemisphere, and Macmillan wondered if a counterrevolution was conceivable. At the end of the second week in August, the president informed the prime minister that the United States was taking economic actions against Castro. That was the last correspondence between the two leaders on Cuban matters.[23]

In mid-October, a military complication entered the mix. The United States military wanted to know how its airplanes should respond to an unprovoked attack by Cuban aircraft over international waters. The president employed the "immediate pursuit" doctrine, but the Joint Chiefs of Staff (JCS) asked for further clarification. Within this possible explosive scenario, Ike insisted that only the best American pilots be deployed and that they have photographic equipment installed on their planes to document any assault. The president also extended this order to naval vessels.[24]

Less than two months before Ike was to leave the White House, he met with his advisers on the state of Cuban affairs. Before that gathering, he had conferred with William Pawley, who complained that the training of 500 exiles in Guatemala had been proceeding too slowly. Due to security breaches, rumors were circulating that the United States was supervising the operation. Some suggested that another secret base had to be found, but Pawley argued against this. He thought the training needed to be better and the number of soldiers increased to 2,000. Also, the United States had to support an effective alternative to Castro; at present no leader had emerged. Pawley understood that Ike had a committee to handle Cuban operations, but its members had other duties. Some strong executive should be appointed to guide the effort. Pawley volunteered for that post, and the president gave some thought to the idea.

Ike let his advisers know he was displeased with the conclusions he drew from his conversation with Pawley. The president opened the meeting with two questions: "(1) Are we being sufficiently imaginative and bold, subject to not letting our hand appear; and (2) are we doing the things we are doing effectively." He did not wish to transfer "a developing emergency" to the incoming administration.

Dulles defended his agency's efforts. The leaders that the United States had assembled were unified only in their opposition to Castro, and getting unanimity from them would be "impossible." While the secrecy of the Guatemalan base had been compromised, the training of 500 guerrillas and a separate air force had been "very effective." The CIA could add another hundred trainees, but if more were necessary, another site would be required. Undersecretary of State Douglas Dillon complained about the lack of secrecy, but Ike was unconcerned. Even if the operation were publicly known, he said, "the main thing was not to let the U.S. hand show." The United States "should be prepared to take more chances and [be] more aggressive."[25]

Nixon, who was concentrating on securing the Republican nomination and then winning the general election, did not participate in most of these discussions. As a candidate, however, he occasionally referred to Cuba. In Miami Beach in January 1960, for example, he said he wished that Castro and his associates would "respect the rights and property not only of Cuban citizens, but of Americans and citizens from other parts of the world who are investing there." On January 18, Fidel described this comment as an "insolent declaration" that was part of an "international plot" against his regime.[26]

In February, in answer to another inquiry, Nixon said that the Cuban revolution was the result of past corrupt rulers and that the people could select whatever government they desired. Castro, however, had chosen an anti-American posture and seemed overly friendly toward communists, and the United States would defend American businesses against confiscation.[27] He wrote to various individuals that he was keeping a close watch on bilateral relations, supported activism to present a positive American image, and strongly favored "a dynamic and expanded program to get the truth across to our friends, the Cuban people." If the administration could not find ways to counter the "hate United States" campaign on the island, the United States would "watch the sympathy of our supporters there be eroded and lost."[28]

Nixon also received reports from FBI director Hoover on the deteriorating political conditions on the island.[29] When communist influence had clearly infiltrated the island's government, Nixon wrote Dan Gainey, an influential Republican activist, on June 22 that the United States was trying "to select a course of action which will preserve our interests without alienating the Cuban people and the rest of Latin America—and to do it before international Communism takes complete control."[30]

At NSC meetings, Nixon said he thought that the United States was better prepared to confront communism in Cuba than it had been in Guatemala in 1954. He worried that the Organization of American States (OAS) was not responding aggressively enough and hoped that Ike would declare any Soviet-Cuban agreement an "intrusion in the western hemisphere." Cuba must not become a Soviet satellite, and the United States must defend against pro-Castro elements extending their influence throughout the Americas. Nixon insisted the United States take a firm, positive stand so that the administration would not be labeled "Uncle Sucker."[31]

He also took other measures. He learned that Cuba received an annual sugar subsidy of $180,000,000 and urged that the administration use that as a lever in bilateral negotiations. He also asked the USIA why it did not answer Castro's attacks, such as when he called the vice president a "representative of United States monopolies." Nixon did not wish to appear to be "raising hell," he told the agency, and he understood it hoped to avoid confronting Fidel publicly, but he did want to know what it was doing to defend him and American citizens from unwarranted assaults. If the agency did not answer these charges, it looked "rather silly."[32]

The vice president also consulted with state department officers. Charles Davis, agriculture attaché at the Havana embassy, reported that the Castro regime was "indoctrinated with extreme socialist or communist philosophy" and was leading the country away from the United States and toward the Soviet Union. On April 10, Nixon wrote an internal memorandum where he called on American diplomats "to get off their tails." Publicly, he defended the state department's policy of forbearance, but privately he disagreed with it. Diplomats had "to show some backbone" despite their fear of the *New York Times* "and other Left wingers who have been dictating American policy toward Latin America for too long a period."[33]

Nixon's opponent in the presidential campaign, John F. Kennedy, was meanwhile attacking Eisenhower's foreign policies in general and specifically Cuba. On July 23, DCI Dulles briefed the Democratic nominee for more than two hours at his summer residence in Hyannis Port, Massachusetts. They discussed many trouble spots, especially the civil war in the Congo, and also reviewed conditions in Cuba.[34]

On October 6, campaigning in Cincinnati, JFK fired his first salvo at Eisenhower's Cuba policy, calling it "a glaring failure of American foreign policy. . . . It was our own policies, not Castro's that first began to turn our former good neighbors against us." Several days later, in Johnston, Pennsylvania, he mocked Nixon for never mentioning "standing firm on Cuba. . . . If you can't stand up to Castro, how can you be expected to stand up to Khrushchev?" On the twentieth, the candidate repeated that Ike had done nothing about the Cuban situation since the start of his presidency, and contended that since Castro came to power, there had been "two years of inaction" from the administration. That, Kennedy said, had to change; he called for assistance for the Cuban "fighters for freedom" to overthrow Castro. The United States should mobilize the OAS and its European allies to prevent the spread of communism in the Caribbean.[35]

On November 19, after his election victory, Kennedy conferred in Palm Beach, Florida, with Allen Dulles, who briefed him on the Cuban operations. The DCI may not have explained how drastically the plans had changed since his initial presentation on March 17. Instead of small guerrilla incursions, the CIA effort, without consulting the president, now leaned toward an amphibious landing.[36]

Ike greeted John F. Kennedy at the north portico of the White House mansion on December 6 with a military parade. The two men went into the Oval Office, where they briefly discussed the crises in Berlin, Laos, and Cuba. The senator asked about how the NSC operated. Ike explained its functions and suggested that he have his NSC staff assistant, Gordon Gray, brief his replacement; Kennedy should study the current structure, he advised, before making any radical changes. The incoming president asked for Ike's thoughts on Macmillan, de Gaulle, and Adenauer. Ike explained some of this trio's policies but thought that JFK would form his own opinions. The only item that troubled the president was that Kennedy asked that Andrew Goodpaster, presidential staff secretary and defense liaison, remain at the White House for a two-month transition. Ike deeply resented Republicans within his administration accepting positions in the Democratic White House. As the outgoing and incoming presidents finished their conversation, Kennedy asked Ike whether he would, if asked, serve on an appropriate occasion. The president wished to be consulted on topics where he "had some experience."[37]

By the New Year, 500 Cuban exiles still were in Guatemala, and recruitment efforts were expanded. Castro had already warned that the United States was preparing to invade the island, and on January 2, 1961, he ordered the United States to reduce its embassy staff to just eleven. The very next morning, Ike met with his advisers on Cuban affairs to discuss Castro's demand. Ike contemplated breaking off diplomatic relations, but that was a matter of timing.

Secretary of State Herter added that doing so would not affect the treaty allowing the United States to keep its naval base at Guantánamo Bay. He also asked what the state department should share with the incoming administration. The United States still had 2,000 to 3,000 citizens on the island that could be in danger. Ike dismissed this, feeling that any citizen who wanted to leave would have done so already. If it severed bilateral ties, the United States would have to find another nation, possibly Switzerland, to represent American interests. Six Latin American countries had broken relations with Cuba, and the United States was searching for more hemispheric support. Cuba was trying to prevent this by having an item placed on the UN Security Council agenda to embarrass the United States. The administration did not want hemispheric affairs openly attacked in that international forum by Cuba and its allies.

Treasury Secretary Robert Anderson, addressing the unstable economic conditions in the hemisphere, wondered how long Castro "would remain in power." If he lasted another year, the United States faced "the prospect of all of Latin America going down the drain." Venezuela was "broke," and Argentina was "just holding on." If investment to Latin America were interrupted, the United States government would have to provide support. Anderson thought the United States should "get rid of Castro."

Severing relations might jeopardize the CIA's plans, but DCI Dulles minimized that possibility. Dulles's second-in-command, Richard Bissell, believed the agency would still receive intelligence from ten Cuban agents operating clandestinely, but the information would not be "highly reliable." The United States, Bissell argued, needed to recognize an exile leader who would travel clandestinely to the island and go to the Escambray Mountains in the middle of the country, or possibly to Pinar del Rio at the island's western end.

Dulles pronounced the exile army "the best Army in Latin America" but thought the trainees would not be ready for action before March. He urged the use of some American territory "for training as well as staging." He was also working with Nicaragua. Bissell agreed: the unit needed "at least a month before their use." Up to 650 were being trained in Guatemala, 80 were being deployed for infiltration in a secluded section of Panama, and 300 or 400 more refugees could be instructed. If the United States added another battalion, a new base with buildings would be essential. Ike added that the exiles should be equipped with recoilless rifles as soon as possible. Even with the CIA's optimistic projections, United States forces would have to support the trainees.

The Guatemalan government, embarrassed by news leaks about the clandestine base, wanted the trainees out of its country at the beginning of March. All of this activity had brought "political liabilities." Bissell conceded "that there is wide recognition that there is a Cuban opposition receiving covert support from the United States." Secretary of Defense Thomas Gates wanted to "decentralize trainees throughout American bases." The United States could draw less attention by training more men in Panama and Nicaragua, or at Fort Benning and other Army units.

The CIA thought that Castro's public approval had slipped from 90 percent to 25 or 33 percent. "White collar" islanders opposed him, "but the peasants and workers were still largely for him." The trend, however, was against him. The Cuban militia and army totaled about 200,000; in a popular uprising, perhaps 20,000 would fight for Castro. Dulles was also trying to weaken the regime through propaganda and "more local sabotage."

From a military perspective, Ike thought he could move against Cuba before the end of his presidency, if Castro "provided a really good excuse." If he did not, possibly the United States could manufacture "something that would be generally acceptable." He also speculated what would happen if Cubans murdered Americans: how would the United States learn about this kind of atrocity? If that were discovered, he said, the United States could then send troops because "the United States should not tolerate being kicked around." Absent any provocation, the United States might create one: it could "stage an attack," requiring it to defend the base.

Ike also wanted to tie Castro with the brutal Trujillo dictatorship in the Dominican Republic. If he could link them and move against both simultaneously, this would be advantageous. Eisenhower thought the USIA should explore that concept, because it would encourage Latin American support for the United States position. The president insisted that Dulles brief designate secretary of state Dean Rusk about the covert activities.

In the final analysis, Ike saw two possibilities: the trainees could return to Cuba in March, or the United States could "abandon the operation." He favored the first option. After he left the White House, he hoped the new administration would continue the training and assist in the organization of the new junta. The president thought it should "mobilize a stronger invasion force so that a failure in the first effort would not wipe out the whole project." Too many candidates to replace Castro had come forward, and Ike had not decided which one to favor. He "was prepared to recognize in a great hurry the man whenever we do to find him." Whoever landed first should be the leader. Later that day, the president severed diplomatic relations with Cuba.[38]

On January 10, a front-page story in the New York Times read: "U.S. Helps Train an Anti-Castro Force at Secret Guatemalan Air-Ground Base." Bissell was correct: being seen to train Cuban exiles carried political liabilities. Even so, six days after the *Times* story appeared, the Special Group outlined its military options regarding Cuba.[39]

At 9:00 a.m. on January 19, president-elect Kennedy went to the White House and saw the president in the Oval Office. Forty-five minutes later, they entered the cabinet room and met with Secretaries Herter, Anderson, and Gates; Dean Rusk, Douglas Dillon, and Robert McNamara represented the incoming administration. The president-elect asked for Ike's judgment on the American backing of guerrilla operations inside Cuba, even if the United States was openly involved. Ike answered: "Yes as we cannot let the present government there go on." In public, Latin American nations proclaimed their opposition to United States interference; privately, they wanted the United States to "do something." The president described the training in Guatemala and said ironically that he hoped secrecy would prevail. The only alternative to United States intervention was the dubious possibility of action by the OAS.

Kennedy thanked the president and his staff for the smooth transition. Ike closed the gathering by offering his and his associates' assistance "if it were desired." The visit ended at 11:00.[40]

Kennedy took the oath of office on January 20 and, as president, received his first official briefing on the Cuban operations eight days later. From the moment he took charge until the debacle at the Bay of Pigs, he never consulted his predecessor, the general who had mounted the largest amphibious invasion in world history. As demanded, Andrew Goodpaster remained at the White House. He had been present at many of the discussions relating to Cuban covert activities during the Eisenhower years but was excluded from the Kennedy meetings.[41]

Goodpaster left his post in mid-March, about a month before the invasion, with Kennedy's personal thanks. In a letter to Ike about his transitional duties, Goodpaster commented that "all my help was on preparedness and organization, and I took very little part in the substance of matters being dealt with." He made suggestions and thought the new staff was "competent" and worked "hard." The organization was not as well defined as Eisenhower's had been, and Goodpaster wondered whether Kennedy would "achieve sufficient coordination to assure orderly government."[42]

Less than three months after taking office, JFK ordered the Bay of Pigs assault. It was, as one author entitled it, *The Perfect Failure*. There was no popular uprising. The landings were held in a swampy region. Most significantly, the exile force had several World War II fighters, while Castro had jets. The Cuban air force easily destroyed the rebel planes and sank the boats that contained supplies for the invaders.

The morning after the landing, Senator Gore met with Kennedy; he later recalled he had never seen him looking "like that." "His hair was disheveled, his tie askew, and his eyes sleepy." He complained, using vulgar language, that he had relied on DCI Dulles and JCS chairman General Lyman Lemnitzer; both had assured him that the operation would be successful and the United States did not need to provide air cover for the landings. The day of the landing, the generals advised him that he must provide air cover or the invasion would fail. Kennedy told Gore he had refused, adding that he would never trust Lemnitzer again.[43]

That same day, JFK asked his speechwriter, Theodore Sorensen, "How could I have been so stupid to let them go ahead?"[44]

Sorensen did not give an answer, other than to assure Kennedy that he could never be considered stupid. Despite that assertion, the Bay of Pigs invasion was a debacle. The novice president, in office for just three months, had tried to command a complex military operation. His most recognized military accomplishment was in the Pacific during World War II where a Japanese destroyer sliced his PT boat in half with the loss of two crewmembers. Other than that experience, he had little knowledge of military tactics and strategy or of amphibious landings.

Two days before the invasion, the CIA-sponsored exiles had used several B-26 bombers to attack some Cuban airfields, but their mission failed to eliminate the Soviet jets that American intelligence had failed to reveal. Since the World War II–era B-26s could not compete with jets, the exiles' planes were shot down, and Castro's planes sank the boats that carried the brigade's ordinance and communication equipment.

The CIA managed the entire operation, even though the agency did not specialize in amphibious invasions. The defense department handled armed conflict, but surprisingly did not play an active part in the landing. The CIA-trained troops were not acquainted with the topography and the swampy nature of the region. The brigade had 1,453 men; Castro had an army of 25,000 and a militia of 100,000 to 200,000. Somehow the CIA postulated that, once the exiles landed, the Cuban people would rise up against the regime. The refugees were confined to the beach without any plan for retreat. A number of the 2506 Brigade was killed; many more surrendered; only a few escaped.[45]

The day after the failure, a devastated President Kennedy called Nixon to the White House, where the former vice president offered his full support. Nixon said that JFK had acted courageously in approving the Bay of Pigs to assist Cuban exiles. Within a week, Nixon told the press that he had been in the minority advocating military action until March 1960, when Ike concluded that Castro intended to ally Cuba with the Soviet Union; at that point he ordered the CIA to plan for a military option. Nixon advised him that the CIA's mission was gathering data; the agency should not run military operations.[46]

Another Republican, Senator Bush, commended JFK for having taken "the blame completely on himself for the failure at the Bay of Pigs and moved on, and in doing so won back some respect."[47]

That momentarily changed on April 24 when Secretary of the Interior Stewart Udall appeared on ABC's Sunday morning talk show *Issues and Answers*. Asked about the Bay of Pigs, Udall responded that Eisenhower had conceived the idea a year earlier and JFK carried it out. The GOP reacted immediately. Republicans had rallied around the president in a spirit of bipartisanship, and they heard Udall's comment as placing the blame on Eisenhower. *Battle Line*, a Republican National Committee publication, described the secretary's comment as "a sneak attack on G.O.P. bipartisanship." Nixon joined the chorus; this was "cheap and vicious partisanship." When he and JFK had spoken earlier, the president accepted "full responsibility for mistakes resulting from decisions he" made.

Pierre Salinger, the president's press secretary, promptly reaffirmed that JFK took full responsibility. In addition, a high administration official admitted that JFK had never consulted Eisenhower on the plans and they had never discussed the landing. Secretary Udall was contrite, saying that if anyone had gained the wrong impression of Ike's involvement, he apologized.[48]

On May 3, former secretary of state Dean Acheson wrote Harry Truman: "Why were we ever engaged in this asinine Cuban adventure, I cannot imagine." Acheson told his informants inside the state department that he and Truman had rejected "similar suggestions for Iran and Guatemala." He understood that the Cuban invasion "had been put aside, or it should have been," and called Kennedy's leadership "surprisingly weak." The president, Acheson surmised, assembled "the mere inertia of the Eisenhower plan [and] carried it to execution," selecting "those elements of strength essential to its success." The former secretary portrayed the capital as "a depressed town" where state department morale had "about struck bottom." Summarizing the failure, Acheson concluded: "Brains are no substitute for judgment. Kennedy has, abroad at least, lost a very large part of the almost fanatical admiration which his youth and good looks had inspired."[49]

Truman refused to compound the new president's misery. He did not refer directly to the Bay of Pigs in his correspondence or public comments, but to Acheson, he repeated: "Brains are no substitute for judgment."[50]

Former president Eisenhower held a conference with some advisers, including Nixon, in the second week of May at his Gettysburg farm. He informed them that JFK had purposefully sought out prominent Republicans like General

Douglas MacArthur, former president Hoover, Nixon, and himself in the aftermath of the failed invasion. Ike had no intention of sharing the "blame for the fiasco by being consulted after the fact." He thought Kennedy was trying "to diffuse responsibility." Secretary Udall's remark concerning Ike's involvement had boomeranged. The former president had set up a Cuban council and had based his plans on an internal uprising. Many faulted the CIA, but Ike saw more-vexing complications: the swampy region, having all the communication equipment on a single ship (which the Cubans sank), lack of military aggressiveness by the invaders, and the surprising appearance of Cuban jets. He also asked whether the state and defense departments had approved of the military tactics. Ike applauded Kennedy's attempt to oust Castro. "However," the former president cautioned, "once a nation resorts to force it should ensure that venture is a success." When he and JFK met at Camp David after the failed assault, Kennedy had wondered what was next. Ike answered that communists should not be allowed to establish "a strongpoint" in the Western Hemisphere.[51]

That fall, Goodpaster wrote Ike about the "Cuban business." Once the United States committed to the operation, Goodpaster said, echoing his former boss, the administration had to pursue it "to a successful conclusion certainly to provide necessary air cover for the landing operation." The general hoped that the Kennedy administration had come to realize that its criticism of Ike's policy toward Cuba was unwarranted. The United States, despite its enormous power, had limitations. Castro might remain in power for a long period, a leader "that we will have to watch, worry about, influence as we can, and live with." Without powerful opposition on the island, "change" was "unlikely." The Cuban people themselves would have to decide "to be free, to govern themselves, and to bring better conditions of living to their families."[52]

A year and a half before Kennedy's assassination, Nixon released *Six Crises*. At the height of the 1960 presidential campaign, he wrote, Kennedy called upon the United States to assist Cuban exiles in their attempt to remove Castro. Nixon believed that Allen Dulles had privately briefed him, and that Kennedy had violated the secrecy of the CIA operation by openly demanding American assistance to the Cuban exiles—exactly what the Eisenhower administration was already doing. During the fourth presidential debate, Kennedy took the aggressive position on American involvement that Nixon had taken with the NSC; the vice president argued the opposite that the United States should not intervene. Nixon appeared soft and Kennedy seemed tough. The former vice president thought JFK presented a better image on Cuba.[53]

Nixon wrote an article for the November 1964 issue of *Reader's Digest* entitled "Cuba, Castro and John F. Kennedy." On the evening of April 19, in the aftermath of the disaster, he had seen Allen Dulles, who proclaimed: "This is the worst day of my life!" He admitted that the Bay of Pigs had failed dismally. The next afternoon, Nixon saw JFK. After the president cursed his advisers, he asked his former rival what he should do. Nixon responded that the president needed to find a pretext for a United States invasion. Kennedy rejected that option; he was worried about the Soviet reaction.[54]

Nixon did not absolve Eisenhower from responsibility, feeling that both Ike and Kennedy bore blame: "the Eisenhower Administration for not acting sooner and the Kennedy Administration for not acting decisively."[55]

Kennedy never had the chance to defend his decisions. But in early 1964, his brother Robert granted a series of interviews in which he touched on the Eisenhower presidency. Bobby did not think his brother respected Ike because Ike disapproved of Jack's youth. According to Bobby, JFK retained key Eisenhower appointees like Allen Dulles and the JCS, and even though he did not solicit Eisenhower's counsel when questions of policy arose, the president informed his predecessor so that he could not criticize the administration. Bobby, who had not participated in planning the invasion believed that his brother had to appear to be a more macho and passionate cold warrior than Nixon: "If he [JFK] hadn't gone ahead with it, everybody would have said it showed that he had no courage. Eisenhower trained these people, it was Eisenhower's plan; Eisenhower's people all said it would succeed—and we turned it down."[56]

A year before President Kennedy died, he read a letter that left-wing historian Gabriel Kolko had published in the *New York Times* on November 9, 1962, arguing that Unites States policy in 1959 and 1960 had pushed Cuba into the Soviet camp. Kennedy asked presidential adviser Arthur Schlesinger Jr. for his comments. Before replying, Schlesinger discussed the subject with former ambassador to Cuba Philip Bonsal and with Theodore Draper, who had written on the rise of Castro's revolution. Both men agreed, according to Schlesinger, that United States policy toward the island "was unimaginative and sterile." Bonsal asserted that the Eisenhower administration had aided Castro by its policy of restraint, and Draper thought the administration was oblivious to the infighting between the anticommunist and procommunist groups struggling for dominance within the revolutionary movement. The two experts suggested "that a more flexible policy might have kept a wider range of alternatives open to the United States."

Schlesinger included his own opinion for Kennedy's review. First, Castro had been "a romantic revolutionary nationalist with strong Marxist leanings," but from 1953 through 1958, he had not collaborated with the Cuban Communist Party. Once he achieved power, he quickly realized that the communists "could help him most both in ruling Cuba and in advancing his leadership in the hemi-sphere." The United States did not oppose Castro's regime but instead was pre-pared to provide economic assistance during his April 1959 trip to Washington. After that visit, the Eisenhower administration still behaved cautiously until the anticommunists were driven from the government and the communists took control.

Despite these attempts to accommodate Castro, Schlesinger held that American diplomacy was "comparatively unimaginative," and it grew obsessed with the compensation of owners for expropriated property. If the United States had developed "a more imaginative" program, Castro might have been less inclined to join "the Soviet bloc," and this would have helped the anticommunist fac-tion, enhancing its strength inside Cuba and ultimately leading to Castro's down-fall. But these, Schlesinger concluded, were only possibilities: "probably no United States policy could have prevented Castro's movement into the Soviet orbit."[57]

In his bestselling 1965 biography A Thousand Days, Schlesinger, by then a JFK court apologist, dismissed his earlier analysis and claimed that Ike was the responsible party for the Bay of Pigs. He summarized the events leading up to the operation: "The Eisenhower administration thus bequeathed the new pres-ident a force of Cuban exiles under American training in Guatemala, a com-mittee of Cuban politicians under American control in Florida and a plan to employ exiles in an invasion of their homeland and to install the committee on Cuban soil as the provisional government of a free Cuba."[58]

In the same year, Theodore Sorensen, who had nothing to do with the covert operation, published Kennedy, in which he conceded that the CIA had never informed Eisenhower of its changed plan, from guerrilla bands to a conventional armed force. Even with this admission, in Sorensen's telling Eisenhower re-mained the culprit. When Kennedy entered the White House, he "inherited the plan, the planners, and most troubling of all, the Cuban exile brigade. . . . Unlike an inherited policy statement or executive order, this inheritance could not be simply disposed of by presidential rescission or withdrawal."[59]

Eisenhower had completed the second volume of his memoirs, The White House Years: Waging Peace before Schlesinger's and Sorenson's books were re-leased. He largely confined his recollections to events during his tenure and said he had left Kennedy the refugee-training program, "hopefully for a return to their native land." These patriotic refugees hated what Castro had done "and were willing to die for a free Cuba." When he left the White House, the exiles had not identified a leader with broad support, and without that person, Eisen-hower asserted, "it was impossible to make specific plans for a military invasion."

In his sole reference to the Bay of Pigs, the former president noted that JFK had carried out the invasion. "Inefficient functions of governmental organization, bringing about indecision and untimely counter orders, was apparently part of the cause for the 1961 Bay of Pigs fiasco."[60]

After the Schlesinger and Sorenson books condemned Eisenhower for the disaster, Ike and several advisers reacted with hostility. Former congressional legislative assistant Bryce Harlow telephoned Ike on August 6, 1965, saying that the JFK loyalists were "deliberately trying to blame" the former president for the failure, and he had to reply to those "ridiculous articles and books."[61]

Harlow said that Harry Guggenheim, editor and publisher of the Long Island, New York, daily *Newsday*, would be willing to publish Eisenhower's Bay of Pigs reminiscences. Harlow thought the well-respected reporter Earl Mazo, who had worked for the *New York Herald Tribune* as a reporter and then moved to *The Reader's Digest* as a staff writer, should conduct the interview. On Wednesday, August 11, Mazo, Guggenheim, and Harlow met with Ike at his farm for a ninety-minute background interview. Mazo was pleased to find Ike "in such ruddy good health." The reporter had taken the information that Ike had related and was drafting an article clarifying what the Kennedy administration "inherited" from its predecessor regarding "training Cuban refugees." He wanted to incorporate some quotes from the former president, who had "no objection to using a very few, short quotations."[62]

On Monday, August 23, Mazo returned for an hour-long follow-up to the previous interview. He had taped it, but wanted Ike to confirm three quotations regarding covert planning. First, Eisenhower never discussed any "tactical or operational plan." When Kennedy took office, no Cuban exile leader had been identified, and the training force was so small that the United States had not made any commitment to using it; it could have easily been disbanded. Second, referring to the 1954 CIA action in Guatemala, as Eisenhower recounted it in his memoir *Mandate for Change*, some had urged its cancellation. Ike's response was: "If our hand had been discovered then it was more important than ever that we win." Third, Sorensen and Schlesinger had condemned Allen Dulles and the JCS for their part in the Bay of Pigs fiasco; Eisenhower's reply was that there was "no more expert group in their profession than these men . . . I had the greatest confidence in them."

The former president reviewed these passages, counseled the reporter about the statements that should be quoted, and even made suggestions on how to condense the material. Ike wanted readers to understand that he and Mazo had had probing discussions. His instructions show how carefully he orchestrated the two interviews and how he scrutinized what was included and excluded. On receiving a copy of the published article, he wrote Guggenheim that it was "accurate" and he hoped it would "help settle some misapprehensions."[63]

Just after Mazo left, Ike talked with Allen Dulles about the "falsity" of the Kennedy books. The two men agreed that Ike had begun training troops but had never discussed any invasion plan during his presidency. When Dulles briefed president-elect Kennedy in Palm Beach, he told him there was "no operational planning." Kennedy later told Ike that Cuba would not be a menace and that Castro had the traits of a "Bolivar," the South American colonial liberator. Eisenhower explained to his successor that the Cuban covert activities were his decision and that he could disband the training camp in ten minutes.

Dulles was disturbed at how JFK had behaved during the Bay of Pigs. He said the president and his staff had no "stomach for the plan." Kennedy "was very uncertain and he was surrounded by pessimists and kept watering down the plan." Dulles added that some of "these people," whom he did not identify, admired Castro.[64]

On September 10, *Newsday* released "Ike Speaks Out: Bay of Pigs Was All JFK's." Other leading newspapers also ran the story. Without mentioning Schlesinger and Sorensen, Ike answered their charges. The former president emphasized that he had nothing to do with the failure. The JCS and CIA had been unfairly attacked, and this distortion was "a perversion of history" and a disservice to the late President Kennedy, "who accepted responsibility for the fiasco." Ike had not made any decision on the use of the Cuban exiles, and the new administration could have easily disbanded them. As he and JFK were riding to the inaugural, Ike declared: "You people will have to decide what to do."[65]

Without any doubt, President Eisenhower initiated planning for the overthrow of Fidel Castro and entertained many different options for carrying it out, from guerilla assaults to OAS pressure. At no time did Ike consider an amphibious invasion. He earnestly wished that his successor would continue training the Cuban exiles and would consider the various possibilities that were being pursued. At the time he left the presidency, Ike had offered no concrete plan for removing Castro from power.

This corrective was of no concern to Salinger, an ultimate Kennedy loyalist. Even though he was not involved in the invasion discussions, he published *P.S. A Memoir* in 1995 blaming Eisenhower for drawing up the plans. According to JFK's former press secretary, Kennedy accepted "a covert operation handed to him by the previous administration to try to overcome Fidel Castro."[66]

No matter how JFK's acolytes have tried to spin the events to deflect blame, the evidence is overwhelming. Kennedy had ordered the Bay of Pigs invasion, and it had turned into a nightmare. He alone was responsible for the fiasco.

CONCLUSION: IKE AND DICK

Unless you were an extreme Richard Nixon loyalist, Ike came before Dick. Eisenhower led the Republican national ticket twice, and he governed from the top. Although he listened intently to political advice, he never had political partners. He ran his team and made the vice president his major utility player. When the president needed someone to take on a difficult assignment, Nixon was often selected. The two men never shared equal billing and were never buddies. Ike was old enough to be Nixon's father. Despite their age difference, however, they developed a close and cordial relationship and worked well together throughout Ike's tenure in office.

Ike's style of governance had not changed since his decades in the military: he was the commander, and his lieutenants followed orders. On occasion, these subordinates were disappointed that their counsel had not prevailed; other times, they were deeply wounded by some perceived slight. Dick did not understand the president's acceptance of casualties as part of his management style and sometimes was deeply hurt, as in the fund crisis and the uncertainty over his place on the ticket in 1956. The president was not troubled by this collateral damage, but Dick thought Ike had deliberately abandoned him and worried that he was losing the president's support. Sometimes Ike purposely instilled doubt to demonstrate that he alone was the supreme authority, but in the end whether he kept his vice president guessing is inconsequential.

The assumption that Eisenhower was a passive, ineffective president has been almost universally rejected. Now he is considered a great or near-great president. The partisans, who for decades pictured Ike as a golf-playing, grandfatherly incompetent, cavalierly dismissed the obvious: Ike was a brilliant general, and he brought that managerial acumen to the Oval Office. He emphasized the code that he had learned at West Point—duty, honor, country—and gave his lieutenants a great deal of discretion and authority. But at day's end, he made the decisions.

Eisenhower himself was responsible for some of the negative descriptions—the image of "pied syntax and platitudinous conviction." He sometimes concealed his objectives, especially from the press, behind a curtain of fractured sentences, disingenuous half-truths, and occasional outright lies. At other times, he gave incisive presentations when they worked to his benefit.

He behaved differently in his three major weekly meetings at the White House. Behind closed doors with his cabinet, his legislative leaders, and the National Security Council (NSC), he both taught and listened. He told his cabinet secretaries what he was considering; he tried to influence the party leadership's political direction; and he briefed the NSC on his foreign policy goals. When John Foster Dulles, Milton Eisenhower, and others were sent abroad, he briefed them before they left, debriefed them on their return, and incorporated their observations when making decisions.

Ike was an exceptional bureaucrat who knew how to cooperate with those who held opposing opinions. The president depended on Henry Cabot Lodge during the draft-Ike movement and the general election campaign. The president liked Lodge and frequently sought out his political counsel. Still the president appointed him to preside over the United States delegation to the United Nations headquartered in New York City. Even with this posting, Lodge often came to the capital to advise Ike on domestic and foreign affairs.

At the beginning of his presidency, Ike and Senate majority leader Robert Taft heatedly argued over Republican positions, but they quickly learned how to work together. Before the senator passed away in the summer of 1953, the former rivals had developed a cordial relationship. As president, Ike had congressional majorities only during his first two years. For the next six, he needed to—and often did—find common ground, especially on foreign policy, with Senator Johnson and Speaker Rayburn.

His greatest failure came as party leader. The GOP was a minority party when he entered office, and a minority party when he left. He was not the traditional politician who reached the White House by rising through the ranks. As the Republican standard bearer, he lent stature to the party, not the other way around. He brought his citizen groups into the campaign without realizing that they supported him and not necessarily the party, and he distanced himself from the party by showing his disapproval of those he labeled professional politicians and especially expressing his disdain for the old guard. After the 1956 election, he championed "modern Republicanism" without understanding that the party faithful might hear this as a call to change the GOP's traditional values.

Eisenhower separated these political considerations from other Oval Office duties. He wanted to balance the budget and did so three times. He hoped to eliminate the national debt but did not succeed. He was passionate about keeping inflation low and kept to that commitment. Despite this, he was responsible for passing the largest public works project in United States history: the interstate highway system, a project that is still ongoing.

Eisenhower is attacked on his civil rights record, and some have intimated that he was a racist; yet he did more for civil rights than any other president between Abraham Lincoln and Lyndon Johnson. He desegregated the capital as well as the armed forces. He appointed, with few exceptions, federal judges who upheld the *Brown* decision, and his Supreme Court appointments moved the cause of civil rights forward with other landmark cases. He proposed and energetically fought for the 1957 and 1960 civil rights acts. He sent, albeit reluctantly, American soldiers to Little Rock to enforce the desegregation order. He disapproved of interracial marriage, as did the vast majority of his countrymen, but he spoke out and worked for equal rights where the federal government was involved. In his personal life, Sergeant Moaney and his wife Dolores became integral members of his extended family. The Eisenhowers were not racists.

He took office at the height of the Cold War, leading a party seriously divided over America's global interests. The Fortress America wing of the GOP expected the administration to protect and defend the Western Hemisphere. As a committed internationalist, Ike found this stance unacceptable. He staunchly opposed and narrowly defeated the Bricker amendment, which would have limited the executive's ability to negotiate treaties. He knew the Republican Party's stand on the liberation of Eastern Europe was unrealistic and quietly abandoned it. Despite widespread criticism, he supported the New Look doctrine as the most effective and most economical way to uphold the American way of life.

He ended the Korean conflict; he kept American troops out of Indochina; and he forced the British, French, and Israelis to leave Suez. Under his watch, with the exception of sending troops into Lebanon, the United States did not fight in any foreign wars.

Although he respected and depended heavily on Secretary Dulles and others for diplomatic advice, Ike determined policy. He employed the CIA for operations in Iran, Guatemala, and elsewhere when he thought covert action was the best option to protect American interests. He made the NSC a forum for debate and for formulating objectives.

The Sputnik satellite launch frightened Americans, but Ike did not understand their anxiety. From U-2 photographs and other secret information, he knew that the Soviet scientific achievement did not expose the United States to missile attack. He did not grasp how unsophisticated most Americans were about missile technology, or why they rejected his assurances. The same applied to the "missile gap." He knew that none existed, but the perception of a gap became its own reality. Americans feared for their lives, and Democrats fanned the flames.

Nikita Khrushchev's visit to the United States in the fall of 1959 temporarily lessened tensions, but when a U-2 spy plane was shot down in Soviet airspace before the May 1960 summit, the president's dreams of a nuclear test ban and disarmament negotiations evaporated. He left office worried about nuclear proliferation and—in one of the few memorable phrases from any of his presidential speeches—a growing "military-industrial complex."

Although many of the policy issues during the Eisenhower administration have been studied minutely, his association with Richard Nixon has been misrepresented or ignored. He was deeply troubled by the circumstances surrounding President Roosevelt's death. Harry Truman, having been vice president for less than three months, inherited the presidency ignorant of FDR's important programs and strategies—including most notably the atomic bomb project. Ike therefore insisted that Nixon be kept thoroughly informed so that if he died in office (he was the oldest man to run for president at that time), the vice president was prepared to assume command. This explains why Nixon was included in so many top-level meetings. Ike made sure he was well informed about the issues and understood the president's direction. This treatment cannot be reconciled with the idea that Ike considered Nixon a lightweight or viewed him with contempt: he carefully and deliberately prepared his vice president to assume grave responsibilities.

Because of this commitment, Ike fundamentally changed the role of the vice presidency. Many authors reject the basic fact that Ike and Nixon worked well together. They cooperated throughout their political campaigns, and the vice president followed the president's initiative with the ruination of Joe McCarthy. On civil rights, the president moved forward, and the vice president became the administration's principal spokesman. In the shaping of American foreign policy, Eisenhower sent Nixon abroad with specific objectives; the vice president served the president well, and in the process Nixon became the most knowledgeable vice president in foreign affairs who ever reached the White House.

Yet instead of concentrating on what Ike and Dick accomplished, authors have invented stories about Eisenhower's ambivalence, dislike, or even hatred of Nixon, and repeated these fables for so long that they have morphed into fact. The stories of Eisenhower's disgusted pencil jab as he watched the Checkers/fund speech, of his nonexistent effort to dump Nixon from the 1956 Republican ticket, and of his boorish reply to a question regarding Nixon's contribution during a 1960 press conference have been passed down from decade to decade because they seemed to confirm what many people wanted to believe. But the impressions bear no resemblance to truth.

These incidents usually happened around elections. When it comes to Nixon the political operator, historians forget that they are supposed to think critically about their sources and that Democrats as well as Republicans spin stories to sway voters. In 1952, Ike did not understand the motivation of Democrats to attack Nixon's fund so vehemently, and rather than support his running mate, he made him prove his innocence before a national audience. In 1956, Harold Stassen told reporters that the president had given him a leave of absence so that he could pursue replacing Nixon with Christian Herter as the president's running mate. The press failed to report that Ike did not give Stassen any encouragement for this enterprise. In August 1960, after Ike made his thoughtless comment at a press conference, he apologized to Nixon but never comprehended how that offhand remark might have damaged his vice president's campaign.

Nixon did. He understood the political implications of Ike's refusal to come to his immediate defense in 1952. The same applied to the 1956 "dump Nixon" movement and to Ike's seemingly casual dismissal in 1960, at a moment when Nixon was trying to become his successor. These three incidents lent credence to the claim by Nixon's opponents that a breach existed between the two men.

Many authors thereafter have trivialized the linkage between Ike and Dick. Histories of the Eisenhower era offer brief glimpses of Nixon during the 1958 riots in South America and the 1959 kitchen debates in Moscow, with no analysis of why the president sent him or the results. Otherwise Nixon is barely present. But if these minimalist histories are accurate, why did President Eisenhower see Nixon for frequent private breakfasts and lunches, send him private letters of praise, and tell friends how much he respected him? Why did he give Nixon more domestic, diplomatic and political responsibilities than any of his predecessors? Why, during presidential absences, did Ike have the vice president preside over meetings when earlier presidents did not do the same? The answer is that the accepted interpretations are wrong, and by clinging to them historians have left a vital part of the Eisenhower presidency untold.

Throughout Eisenhower's tenure, Nixon welcomed the president's new assignments and built on them. Since he had more experience in elective office than any of his cabinet and NSC colleagues, he served as a political counselor, advising the president and his secretaries on how their proposals would be received by the public as well as how to get them through Congress. After Taft's death, Eisenhower tried to work with Bill Knowland, first as Senate majority leader and then as minority leader, but found him incapable of speaking for the administration. Ike called him stupid, and Nixon prevented a confrontation by becoming their liaison. As a member of the Chowder & Marching Club, Nixon also served as a conduit for the concerns of Republican House members.

At the start of the first term, Nixon volunteered to mediate between Joe McCarthy and the White House. Democratic adversaries tried to portray Nixon as a McCarthy clone, but this was a political tactic to excite the Democratic base; it was never an accurate portrayal. The vice president tried to accommodate the senator in order to maintain the slim Republican majority in the Senate. Once McCarthy attacked the president's beloved Army, conciliation was finished. When the president decided to counterattack, Nixon played a vital role in McCarthy's demise.

Most significantly, when Eisenhower selected his principal civil rights advocate, he chose Nixon. No one in the government lobbied more energetically to end segregation or speak on the national and international stage. Nixon chaired the President's Committee on Government Contracts during the entire presidency and worked closely with black leaders, especially Martin Luther King Jr., Jackie Robinson, and E. Frederic Morrow. He was the first vice president to visit sub-Saharan Africa, and he made certain that the black press had a significant presence on that journey. When the 1957 civil rights bill came before the Senate, the vice president played a major role in keeping Republican senators steadfast in favor of the legislation.

In foreign affairs, the president relied on Nixon's internationalism to support his own. Nixon had voted for the Marshall Plan and the Truman Doctrine while in Congress. As vice president, he took major trips to Asia, the Indian subcontinent, Latin America, Europe, and Africa. In all, he visited fifty-four countries on six continents. These journeys were much more than cute photographic opportunities. Ike had specific assignments that he expected Nixon to complete, and he usually succeeded.

Nixon's strengths and weaknesses were magnified in the heat of political campaigning. He rallied the GOP faithful from apathy to activism and came to represent their soul. Unlike Eisenhower, he had risen as a regular party member and worked his way from the House to the Senate and then to the vice presidency. More than any other national Republican, he tirelessly campaigned repeatedly for his party's candidates, not only during his vice presidency but afterward as well, especially in support of Barry Goldwater's run for the presidency in 1964. The many debts of gratitude he piled up eventually helped bring him into the Oval Office.

These relentless efforts to replace Democrats with Republicans turned Nixon into the Democrats' chief adversary and their worst nightmare; they characterized him as a liar, a cheat, and a manipulator of partisan bitterness. To his opponents, Nixon became the symbol of the most extreme GOP partisanship. Their loud complaints demonstrated how effective Nixon was as a campaigner. Ike followed Nixon's speeches closely and privately encouraged some of his attacks. He did not attack opponents himself because he wanted to avoid damaging his national popularity. Besides, Ike was not a charismatic public speaker, nor was he a lightning rod to ignite a partisan firestorm. Though he was a popular leader, he did not meet the GOP's need for a national spokesman; Nixon filled this space. He received the brunt of the Democrats' attacks but did so willingly.

Ike matured into an exceptional bureaucratic manager who brought peace and prosperity to the United States. Nixon evolved into one of the president's chief advisers and popularized for public consumption the president's domestic policies and foreign affairs initiatives. As a result of this long and profitable relationship, the Eisenhower presidency gained stature. Ike was pleased, and Nixon hoped to expand on that record by moving into 1600 Pennsylvania Avenue in 1961. That was the beauty of their relationship.

APPENDIX: EISENHOWER'S NOTES ON THE "CHECKERS SPEECH"

The fund crisis that Richard Nixon encountered in September 1952 was a pivotal moment in his career. Under pressure to resign his place on the presidential ticket due to the accusations of wrongdoing, he was forced to go on national TV in an effort to clear his name. It was the first nationally televised political speech in American history. General Eisenhower, campaigning in Ohio while Nixon spoke from Los Angeles, watched the address on television in the manager's office at Cleveland's Public Hall. He too was under intense pressure: he had to decide whether to stand by his running mate or ask him to resign from the ticket. As he watched Nixon speak, Eisenhower took seven pages of notes in preparation for a speech he would give in response to Nixon's address that same evening. Afterward, the manager of the Hotel Carter, Allen James Lowe, accompanied Ike to the train station; Ike gave Lowe his notes as a souvenir as they parted, and four years later Lowe mailed a copy to Nixon. These documents are the best evidence we have of Eisenhower's thoughts during the minutes that decided his and Nixon's political future. (Document images are courtesy of the Richard Nixon Presidential Library and Museum.)

EXECUTIVE OFFICE

November 28, 1956

Honorable Richard M. Nixon
Vice President of the United States
United States Senate Building
Washington, D.C.

Dear Mr. Vice President:

On September 24, 1952, you delivered a nationwide television address from California at a crucial time in your illustrious career.

On that evening I sat in the manager's office of Cleveland's Public Hall with President Dwight D. Eisenhower, Mrs. Eisenhower and a party of about fifteen persons. Mr. Eisenhower, who was then a candidate for the Presidency, watched you intently and made notes on a legal note pad.

After your address to the nation, Mr. Dwight D. Eisenhower proceeded to the rostrum in Public Hall to address a crowd of some 10,000 persons. He used notes only, for his address.

It was my privilege to accompany Mr. Eisenhower to his special train. As he was about to board the train he turned to me and said, "Here's my speech from tonite. I will give it to you." I have the original notes and treasure them highly.

I am pleased to send you this off-set copy of the notes he made that night. It is perfectly clear that he made up his mind about your immediate future as he watched you deliver your telecast from California.

You have my best wishes in all your future endeavors, which are sure to fire the imagination of the American people during the years that lie ahead.

Cordially yours,

ALLEN JAMES LOWE

AJL/n

[Page 1]
I've
have seen brave men in tough situations—

None ever came through better—

Man bares his soul to you.

I've been talking

[Page 2]
About evidence of
corruption—

~~About~~ About men who
sold their birthright
(in the words of a judge
for a dirty mess of
dollars -)

Here is

[Page 3]
Something different

Technically no
decision rests
with me -

But am not
trying to duck

[Page 4]
Any issue—
       If Chairman
calls on me—
and he wants—
I'll give ~~m~~
him my
considered
judgment.

[Page 5]
None of advantage
or dis-advantage
in getting votes
will count.

Just
~~Do~~ Is he the kind
of American of whom
you could be proud
as VP.

[Page 6]
I'll ask ~~him~~
Nixon
to see me.

My mind
will be made
up on one
~~thing~~ conclusion
only—

[Page 7]
Is this
man one
you'd like to
see [as] you[r]
Vice-President.
No consideration
of convenience.

ABBREVIATIONS

AWF	Ann Whitman File
Cabinet DDE	Kesaris and Gibson eds., *Minutes and Documents of the Cabinet Meetings of President Eisenhower 1953–61*
CCOH	Columbia Oral History Collection
CSUF	California State University, Fullerton
DDE	Eisenhower Microfilm, Dwight Eisenhower Presidential Library
DDEL	Dwight Eisenhower Presidential Library, Abilene, Kansas
DE	Dwight Eisenhower
Diary DDE	*The Diaries of Dwight D. Eisenhower, 1953–1961*
DuHe	Dulles and Herter, *Papers, 1953–1961*
DUla	Drew University Library Archives
FDRL	Franklin Delano Roosevelt Presidential Library
FR	U.S. Department of State, *Foreign Relations of the United States, 1953–1961*
Gallup Poll	Gallup ed., *The Gallup Poll*
GCMF	George C. Marshall Foundation
Hagerty Diary	Ferrell ed., *The Diary of James C. Hagerty*
HHL	Herbert Hoover Presidential Library
HML	Henry Mudd Library
HSTL	Harry S Truman Presidential Library
Ike's Letters	Griffith ed., *Ike's Letters to a Friend*
JFD	John Foster Dulles
JFD OH	John Foster Dulles Oral History Collection
JFKL	John F. Kennedy Presidential Library
LBJL	Lyndon B. Johnson Presidential Library

Legislative DDE	Lester ed., *President Eisenhower's Meetings with Legislative Leaders, 1953–1961*
LLC	Lyman Lemnitzer Center
LOC	Library of Congress
MCSL	Margaret Chase Smith Library
MHS	Massachusetts Historical Society
MLGC	Musselman Library, Gettysburg College
MLsc	Marquette University, Memorial Library, Special Collections
mss	archival manuscripts
NA II	National Archives II
NHS	New Hampshire State Archives
OF DDE	*President Dwight D. Eisenhower's Office Files, 1953–1961*
OH	Oral History
PAES	Johnson ed., *The Papers of Adlai E. Stevenson*
PDDE	Galambos and van Ee eds., *The Papers of Dwight David Eisenhower*
Pearson Diaries	Abell ed., *Drew Pearson Diaries 1949–1959*
PMLK	Carson ed., *The Papers of Martin Luther King, Jr.*
PN	Pat Nixon
PN	Eisenhower, Julie, *Pat Nixon*
PPA	Eisenhower, Dwight, *Public Papers of the President of the United States*
PRAT	Wunderlin ed., *The Papers of Robert A. Taft*
PRP	Kesaris ed., *Papers of the Republican Party*
PUsc	Pepperdine University, Special Collections
RN	Richard Nixon
RNln	Richard Nixon Pre-Presidential Papers, Laguna Nigel, California
RNyl	Richard Nixon Library, Yorba Linda, California
SDSU	San Diego State University
UCt	Thomas J. Dodd Research Center, University of Connecticut
UVa	University of Virginia
WC	Whittier College
WH	White House
WJBma	Walter J. Brown Media Archives & Peabody Awards Collection

NOTES

All interviews are by the author unless otherwise noted.

INTRODUCTION

1. Jacobs, *Eisenhower at Columbia*, 310–311; telephone call with Travis Jacobs, Aug 12, 2013.
2. *New York Times*, Oct 2, 16, and 23, 1952; email, Jacobs to Gellman, Jan 15, 2013, Gellman mss, DDEL; Jacobs, *Eisenhower at Columbia*, 267–330; Jumonville, *Commager*, 139–140.
3. Hofstadter, *Anti-Intellectualism*, 3–4 and 21–22; Leuchtenburg, *In the Shadow*, 54–55.
4. *New York Times*, Oct 2, 11, and 12, 1952; Schlesinger, "Ike Age Revisited," 2.
5. Morison, *Oxford History*, 1079–1106; note card, Virginia and Holmes Tuttle to DE re Morison book, May 4, 1965, B 5, F GI- 2T, 1965 Principal File, Post-Presidency, DDEL.
6. Morison et al., *Growth of the American Republic*, 2:695.
7. Graebner, *New Isolationism*; Albertson ed., *Eisenhower as President*, ix and 158.
8. Childs, *Eisenhower*; Reston, *Sketches*, 420–422; Rovere, *Final Reports*, 151.
9. Barber, *Presidential Character*, 134–148; Neustadt, *Presidential Power*, 3–163.
10. DE, *Mandate* and *Waging Peace*; RN, *Six Crises*; Adams, *Firsthand Report*; Benson, *Cross Fire*; Brownell, *Advising Ike*, 297.
11. Parmet, *Eisenhower*; Kempton, "Underestimation of Eisenhower."
12. Greenstein, *Hidden-Hand Presidency*, 191.
13. Schlesinger and Schlesinger eds., *Journals*, 514.
14. Ambrose, *Eisenhower*, vol. 2, and *To America*, 164.
15. Ambrose to DE, Sept 10 and Oct 15, 1964, B 24, F Am(1), Principal File, Post-Presidency, DDEL; Rives, "Ambrose and Eisenhower."
16. Rayner, "Channeling Ike," 21–22; interview with chief archivist at the Eisenhower library, Timothy Rives, 2013.
17. Ambrose, *Eisenhower*, vol. 2, p. 387.
18. Meeting, Apr 17, 1956, B 2, F legislative meetings 1956 (2), legislative meeting series, AWF, DDEL.

19. Branch, *Parting the Waters*, 213. Kraft, "Ike vs. Nixon," 83; Chafe and Sitkoff eds., *History of Our Time*, 97; Hamilton, *American Caesars*, 113 and 224.
20. See description in Ann Whitman papers at www.eisenhower.archives.gov.
21. Simon and Schuster website for Stephen Ambrose, authors.simonandschuster.com /Stephen-E-Ambrose/1063454; Eisenhower Presidential Library bookstore.
22. Nichols, *Matter of Justice* and *Eisenhower 1956*; Newton, *Eisenhower*; Smith, *Eisenhower*, xii; Thomas, *Ike's Bluff*.
23. Ricks, *Generals*, 40–58.
24. Kraft, "Ike vs. Nixon," 83; Chafe and Sitkoff eds., *History of Our Time*, 97; Hamilton, *American Caesars*, 113 and 224.
25. *San Francisco Chronicle*, Dec 2, 1962; Ike to Gross, Apr 27, 1963, B 4, F "Hu," post-presidential papers, DDEL; M. Eisenhower to Roorda, July 19, 1983, Gellman mss, DDEL; Hughes, *Ordeal*, 173 and 183; Matteson, *Stassen*, Appendix D; Smith, *Eisenhower*, 680.
26. Mazo, *Nixon*; Kornitzer, *Real Nixon*; RN, *Six Crises*; Costello, *Facts About Nixon*, 133–134.
27. Brodie, *Nixon*, book jacket, 27 and 272.
28. Ibid., 412–413.
29. Summers, *Arrogance*.
30. Gibbs and Duffy, *Presidents Club*, 105–107; C-SPAN interview with Nancy Gibbs and Michael Duffy, May 8, 2012, Reagan Presidential Library, C-SPAN2, www.c-span.org /video/?305478-1/qa-nancy-gibbs-michael-duffy.
31. Frank, *Ike and Dick*, 15.
32. Malsberger, *General and the Politician*.
33. Malsberger, "Dwight Eisenhower, Richard Nixon," 526–532, 540, and 542–545; Smith, *Eisenhower*, 521–522 and 542; Frank, *Ike and Dick*, 204 and 221; *PPA 1960–1961*, p. 658; starting in late July and until the Nixon nomination, the national newspapers like the *Los Angeles Times*, *New York Times*, *Washington Post*, and *Chicago Tribune* carried stories on Stassen's efforts to replace Nixon with Herter.
34. Robert Cushman OH, 40, DDEL; Donald Hughes interview, May 19, 2011, Gellman mss, DDEL.
35. RN to Berghoefer, Apr 21, 1961, B 237, Eisenhower ½, Series 320, RNln.
36. Oval Office tape, July 21, 1971, conv. no. 541–2, 8:04 minutes, RN WH tapes, RNln.

CHAPTER 1. THE NOMINEES

1. Sherwood, *Roosevelt and Hopkins*, 915; Adams, *Firsthand Report*, 19; for background on Eisenhower, see Parmet, *Eisenhower*; Brendon, *Ike*; Lyon, *Eisenhower*. According to Perret, *Eisenhower*, Dewey was going to use Nixon to undermine Warren's control of the California delegation at the 1952 Republican convention because Nixon was "as ambitious as he was unscrupulous" (407). That is false. Nixon never tried to stage an uprising against Warren at the convention. In addition, Perret states that Ike had never met Nixon until the convention (408). That is incorrect. Ike met Nixon at his

Paris headquarters in May 1951, and they corresponded afterward. See Gellman, *Contender*, 393–394, 396, and 422–449.

2. See *PRAT*, V. 3 and 4; Patterson, *Mr. Republican*.

3. Biographical Sketch, July 15, 1952, R 30, Lodge to General, June 14 and 20, 1961, R 29, Lodge Career, Mar 11, 1964, R 31AP Biographical Service, May 1, 1964, Globe, Aug 16, 1976, R 31, Henry Cabot Lodge, May 19, 1977, R 31, Lodge mss, MHS.

4. DE to Lodge, Mar 18, Lodge to DE, Apr 11, DE to Cabot, June 20, 1952, Globe, Nov 20, 1951, Mar 19 and Apr 9, 1952, R 30, DE to Bobby, May 24, DE to Cabot, June 9, 1961, Lodge to John, Dec 26, 1962, R 29, Lodge mss.

5. Eisenhower, *Mandate*, 44–45; Thomas Dewey OH, 13–15, CCOH; Gellman, *Contender*, 439–440; Members, *Influence of Television*, 4–8.

6. *PPA* 1955, pp. 556–567; Herbert Brownell OH, 16, DDEL.

7. James Hagerty OH 91, p. 36 and Thomas Dewey OH, 13–15, CCOH; Eisenhower, *Mandate*, 46; Gellman, *Contender*, 440–444.

8. Day 3, Tape 2, 00:02:16 [Voice] and 00:07: 23 [RN]. Gannon mss, WJBma. For background on Nixon's congressional career, see Gellman, *Contender*, 422–449. Several books cover the 1952 presidential campaign: Bernstein, "Election of 1952," in Schlesinger and Israel eds., *History of American Presidential Elections*, vol. 4, pp. 3215–3265, presents an overview; Divine, *Foreign Policy and U.S. Presidential Elections*, 42–85, concentrates on the diplomatic aspects; Greene, *Crusade*, provides an overview of the campaign; none of the above are seriously concerned with Nixon's role. Morris, *Nixon*, 737–756, details the period from July to September 1952 and should be read with skepticism. He, for example, erroneously claims that Nixon was closely tied to McCarthy. Ambrose in *Nixon*, 264–625, covers the period from Nixon's vice-presidential nomination through the end of his tenure in that office in 1961 using a chronological approach and based primarily on flawed secondary sources.

9. Film of acceptance speeches at the Republican National Convention, July 11, 1952, EL-MP16-93, Eisenhower mss, DDEL; film clips of 1952 Republican National Convention, RNLB: 57:10, RNyl; Day 3,Tape 2, 00:10:15 [RN], 00:11:15 [RN] and 00:13:01 [RN], Gannon mss, WJBma.

10. Day 3, Tape 2, 00:08:49 [RN] and 00:09:13 [RN]; Gannon mss; Pickett, *Eisenhower Decides*.

11. *San Francisco News*, July 14, 1952, PPS6.S3, RNyl; Leary, "Smith of NJ," 205; Slater, *Ike I Knew*, 22, 55 and 275; *PDDE*, XIII, pp. 1307–1308; *PPA* 1955, pp. 556–557; Pinkley, *Eisenhower*, 257–379.

12. Eisenhower, *Mandate*, 49–55.

13. *Times-Herald* (DC), July 14, PPS5.SA.116, Sign, July 14, PPS266.201.2, *News* (Whittier), July 28, 1952, PPS5.SA162, RNyl.

14. Appointment record, July 26–27, 1952, R 1, Diary DDE; memo, July 24, PPS10.139, *Washington Star* (DC), July 26, PPS5.SA134, RN itinerary, July 26–27, PPS8.2, *Rocky Mountain News*, July 27, PPS5.SA143, *Sunday Star* (DC), July 27, PPS5.SA139, *Los Angeles Times*, July 27, PPS5.SA139, *San Francisco Examiner*, July 27, 1952, PPS5.SA142,

RN to Ike, Jan 13, 1965, PPS324.243B, RNyl; *Columbus Dispatch,* July 22, 1952, B 7, F 19, Series 207, RNln; J. Eisenhower, *Strictly Personal,* 392–393.

15. *Rocky Mountain News,* July 28, PPS5.SA154, *San Francisco Examiner,* July 28, 1952, PPS5.SA140, RN to Smallwood, Aug 17, 1956, PPS320.17.129, memoirs, Mar 15, 1976, RNyl; Day 3, Tape 2, 00:17:37 [RN], Gannon mss, WJBma; Eisenhower, *Mandate,* 50.

16. Press release, July 30, PPS10.393.2, *Sacramento Bee,* Aug 1, PPS6.9, press release, Aug 3, PPS10.393.4, *New York Times,* Aug 3, PPS6.16, *News* (Whittier), Aug 6, PPS6.24, press release, Aug 9, PPS10.393.9, press release, Aug 11, PPS10.393.11, *Los Angeles Times,* Sept 9, PPS6.70, *New York Times,* Sept 11, PPS6.71, Weekly Report, Sept 3, PPS12.15.3.3, Sept 10, 1952, PPS12.15.4.1, memoirs, Mar 15, 1976, RNyl; RN to Javits, Sept 1, 1952, B 381, Javits [3/3], Series 320, RNln; Appointment Record, Aug 1, 9 and 11, Luncheon, Aug 8, press release, Aug 9, memo, Aug 11, 1952, Diaries, R 1, P 1, DDE; Summary of Minutes, Oct 19, 1952, R 13, *PRP,* P II; Adams, *Firsthand Report,* 19 and 34; *Gallup Poll,* Two, 1082, 1085–1087, 1090–1091, and 1949–1958; Lavine ed., *Smoked-Filled Rooms,* vii–ix, 1–3, 15–21 and 31; Mazo, *Nixon,* 98; J. Eisenhower, *Strictly Personal,* 392–395; Dailey, "Eisenhower-Nixon Campaign Organization," 181–203.

17. *Los Angeles Times,* July 27, PPS5.SA157, July 29, PPS5S.o.s.91, July 30, PPS5.So.s.92, *Los Angeles Mirror,* July 28, PPS5.SA155, *Los Angeles Herald Express,* July 28, 1952, PPS5.SA161, RNyl.

18. *Los Angeles Times,* July 29, PPS5.SA177 and PPS5.So.s.91, *Christian Science Monitor,* July 29, 1952, PPS5.SA167, RNyl; *La Puente Valley Journal,* July 31, 1952, B 40, Andersen, RB, Series 320 and "Whittier Homecoming," undated B 1, Audio Recordings, RNln.

19. Sanders to RN, July 12, PPS10.63, *News* (Whittier), July 29, 1952, PPS5.SA165, RNyl; "Whittier Homecoming," B 1, audio recording, RNln.

20. *Denver Post,* July 27, PPS5.SA138, *Times Herald* (DC), July 27, PPS266.S49, *San Francisco Examiner,* July 29, PPS266.S49, *Washington Daily News* (DC), Aug 2, 1952, PPS266.S57, memoirs, Mar 14, 1976, RNyl; Hillings, *Irrepressible Irishman,* 192; *PN,* 117–129; Interview with Jack Golden, July 2, 2001, Patricia Nixon disliked campaigning; interview with Donald Hughes, July 3, 2001; PN was "a very private person."

21. Irwin to RN, Nov 6, 1952, Series 320, B 372, Irwin (3 of 4), RNln; memoirs, Mar 15, 1976, RNyl; memo by S. Alsop, May 23, 1958, p. 9, B 47, Alsop mss, LOC; *PRAT,* V. 4, pp. 407–408.

22. Bullitt to RN, July 11, RN to Bullitt, Aug 11, 1952, Series 320, B 111, Bullitt, Wm, RN to Inskeep, June 15, 1961, Series 320, B 743, Taft, R Jr., RNln; Jenkins to RN, July 17, PPS10.121.1, Cotton to Anderson, Sept 18, 1952, CO, RNyl; *Lewiston Sun,* July 21, 1952, W & Y, V. 453, p. 195, Margaret Smith mss, MCSL; for background on Taft, see Patterson, *Mr. Republican.*

23. *Washington Daily News* (DC), July 18, Series 207, B 7, F 19, Taft to Inskeep, Aug 6, 1952, B 743, Taft, R Jr., Series 320, RNln; speech, July 31, PPS208(1952)28A.4, *Washington Post,* Aug 1, PPS6.13, *Sacramento Bee,* Aug 1, PPS6.9, *New York Herald Tribune,* Aug 3, PPS6.19, *Ohio Republican News,* Aug 4, PPS60.s.3.1, Lipscomb to Hurt, Sept 3, 1952, PPS11.87, RNyl; Hillings, *Irrepressible Irishman,* 57.

24. *New York Times,* Aug 4, PPS6.20, *San Francisco Examiner,* Aug 4, 1952, PPS6.20, RNyl.

25. RN itinerary, Aug 12–13, PPS8.5.2(1), *Chicago Daily News*, Aug 13, PPS6.33, *Los Angeles Times*, Aug 13, PPS6.30, *Chicago Herald-American*, Aug 13, PPS6.34, speech, Aug 13, 1952, PPS208(1952).29*1, RNyl; speech, Aug 13, 1952, B 7, F 21, Series 207, RNln.

26. *U.S. News & World Report*, Aug 29, 1952.

27. *Los Angeles Examiner*, July 23, "Washington Report," Aug 3, B 344, Hiss 1 of 3, RN to Link, Aug 20, 1952, B 454, Link, T, Series 320, RNln; Wilson to Chotiner, Aug 20, PPS205.2900.1(1), *Boston Post*, Aug 21, PPS6.51, memo, Aug 30, PP10.385, memo, Aug 30, PPS10.387, *Los Angeles Times*, Sept 1, PPS6.59, memo, Sept 15, 1952, PPS10.460, RNyl; *PAES*, Vol. IV, pp. 64–65; Gellman, *Contender*, 196–242.

28. Memoirs, Mar 15 and 16, 1976, RNyl; O'Neil, *American High*, 180; for background on Truman, see Ferrell, *Truman*; Hamby, *Man of the People*; and McCullough, *Truman*.

29. RN to Javits, Sept 1, 1952, B 381, Javits [3/3], Series 320, RNln; Press release, Sept 6, 1952, PPS208(1952).40.1, RNyl.

30. RN to Green, Sept 1, PPS5.532, RNyl; Lowenthal to Truman, Sept 17, 1952, PSF, General File, Lowenthal, Max (folder 2), Truman mss, HSTL; *Independent Review*, Aug 22, 1952, B G 281 [1 of 3], Pearson mss, LBJL; Smith ed., *Hostage*, 660; Gellman, *Contender*, 388.

31. Martin, *Adlai Stevenson of Illinois*, 605–683.

32. Ball, *Past Has Another Pattern*, 127.

33. *News* (Whittier), Aug 14, PPS6.36, clipping, Aug 15, PPS6.41, *Los Angeles Times*, Aug 24, PPS6.54, press release, Aug 25, 1952, PPS208(1952).31(1), RNyl.

34. *PAES*, Vol. IV, p.34–35.

35. Lash, *Eleanor*, 206–214; *Washington Post*, Aug 18, 1952, PPS6.44, RNyl; Gellman, *Contender*, 170–180.

36. *New York Post*, Aug 10, PPS6.28 and Aug 12, PPS6.29, *St. Louis Post Dispatch*, Sept 16, 1952, PPS6.75, RNyl; RN to Lasky, Aug 15, 1952, B 439, Lasky (2 of 3), Series 320, RNln; Schlesinger and Schlesinger eds., *Journals*, 3–12.

37. *American Weekly*, Aug 24, 1952, PPS296(1952).4.1.(1), RNyl; P. Nixon, "I Say," Sept 6, 1952, *Saturday Evening Post*.

38. Speech, Sept 4, PPS208(1952).38(6), *New York Times*, Sept 5, 1952, PPS6.68, RN address, 1952, RNLB14:18, RNyl; "Crusade," undated, B 1, Audio Recording, RNln; Hillings, *Irrepressible Irishman*, 57.

39. Scrapbook, V. 116, p.65–72, 77–79, 82–84, 90, Margaret Smith mss; *Boston Post*, Sept 2, PPS6.59, speech, Sept 2, PPS208(1952).36(1), speech, Sept 2, PPS208(1952).37.3, *Bangor Daily News*, Sept 3, PPS60.s.6A, *New York Times*, Sept 4, PPS6.62, speech, Sept 5, PPS208(1952).39.1, Cronin to Cox, Sept 5, PPS10.428.1, speech, Sept 6, PPS208(1952).41(5), speech, Sept 7, 1952, PPS208(1952).42(1), RNyl.

40. Lodge to General, Oct 3, 1952, R 28, Lodge mss, MHS; *PRAT*, V. 4, pp. 181–184 and 416–419; Patterson, *Mr. Republican*, 569–578; Reinhard, *Republican Right*, 92–93; Donovan, *Eisenhower*, 102–105; White, *Taft Story*, 184–194; Jacobs, *Eisenhower at Columbia*, 283–285 and 315; Brown, *Hofstadter*, 83–85; Eisenhower, *Mandate*, 55–64; Donovan, *Eisenhower*, 10–105; Dailey, "Eisenhower-Nixon Campaign Organization," 204–215.

41. *Meet the Press*, Sept 14, 1952, RNyl; RN to Edson, June 10, 1953, B 236, Edson, Series 320, RNln; Ball and NBC News eds., *Meet the Press*, 28–30.
42. *Riverside Enterprise*, Sept 17, PPS6.75, RN to Creel, Aug 30, PPS10.384, *Los Angeles Times*, Aug 28, 1952, PPS6.55 and memoirs, Mar 16, 1976, RNyl.

CHAPTER 2. THE FUND CRISIS

1. Alsop, *Nixon & Rockefeller*, 64–66; Frank, *Ike and Dick*, 39–62; there are many others: Foner, *Give Me Liberty!*, 931; Hamilton, *American Caesars*, 222–224; Miller, *Two Americans*, 253; Hart, *When the Going Was Good!*, 158–159; Malsberger, "Dwight Eisenhower, RN, and the Fund Crisis," 526–532 and "An Ailing Ike," 28; Huebner, "Checkers Speech After 60 Years," theatlantic.com/politics/archive/2012/09/the-checkers -speech-after 60years/26217. For Eisenhower's notes on the "Checkers Speech," see the appendix in this volume.
2. Lowe to RN, Nov 28, 1956 with Ike's notes, B 463, Lowe (1 of 2), Series 320, RNln.
3. No issue in Nixon's vice presidency has received as much attention as the fund crisis. Nixon's *RN*, 92–110, and Nixon, *Six Crises*, 73–129, provide his recollections; Parmet, *Nixon and His America*, 239–251, gives the best balanced account in a short space; Kornitzer, *Real Nixon*, 188–208, gives his mother's impressions; Mazo, *Nixon*, 101–137, has a pro-Nixon bent as does de Toledano, *Nixon*, 132–144, and *One Man Alone*, 141–154; O'Brien and Jones, *Night Nixon Spoke*, analyzes documents known at Whittier College; many anti-Nixon books are untrustworthy because of their attempt to prove his venality at any price: Costello, *Facts About Nixon*, 97–114, was a hatchet job without merit for Democratic use in the 1960 campaign; Brodie, *Nixon*, 271–289, is probably the best example of awful research to prove her conclusion that Nixon was a liar before he was ever born; Summers, *Arrogance*, 118–122, is another example of finding data to prove his point; Morris, *Nixon*, 757–850, is overwhelmingly based on newspaper accounts and memoirs; Wicker, *One of Us*, 80–108, argued that Nixon did not do well during the crisis; for Eisenhower, see his defense, *Mandate*, 65–69; for White House chief of staff Adams's recollections, see *Firsthand Report*, 37–40; Ewald, *Eisenhower*, 48–57, helped write Eisenhower's recollections and includes more information; Lyon, *Eisenhower*, 452–462, supplies a critical view; Ambrose, *Eisenhower*, vol. 1, 554–561, offers a lofty assessment of Eisenhower, and Parmet, *Eisenhower*, 134–141, uses a more balanced approach; Perret, *Eisenhower*, 413–416, is unreliable; Greene, *Crusade*, 188–198, assumes the worst about Nixon based on secondary sources. Wills, "Nixon's Dog," 91, 92, 94, 95, is riddled with embarrassing errors; Cathcart and Schwarz, "New Nixon or Poor Richard," 8–12, is cluttered with mistakes; Frier, *Conflict of Interest*, 26–41, looks at the corruption issue; Oakley, *God's Country*, 135–143, accepts just about all of the erroneous information. Although an undergraduate honors thesis, Roorda, "The President and His Boy," 7–26, is a thoughtful discussion of the material then available of the Eisenhower-Nixon relations during the fund episode, Gellman mss, DDEL; Dailey, "Eisenhower-Nixon Campaign Organization," 216–278; Mattson, *Just Plain Dick*, is a poorly researched and argued book; Mattson, "Just Plain Dick," Nov 5, 2012, C-SPAN2.

4. Day to RN, Aug 5, PPS10.181.1, *Los Angeles Times*, Aug 29, PPS6.56, RN to Smith, Sept 13, PPS10.458, press release, Sept 15, PPS10.461A(1), *San Francisco Examiner*, Sept 14, PPS6.72, *Whittier Star Reporter*, Sept 18, 1952, PPS6.76, RNyl; Dorn to Arnold, Sept 18, 1952, B 221, Dorn, E, Series 320, RNln; Louis Jones OH, 7, CSUF; Hillings, *Irrepressible Irishman*, 57.

5. RN statement, Sept 17, PPS208(1952).47(1), RN address, Sept 17, PPS208(1952).46.(1), *San Francisco Examiner*, PPS6.81, *Los Angeles Times*, Sept 18, 1952, PPS6.78, memoirs, Mar 18, 1976, RNyl; RN to O'Callaghan, May 4, 1953, RN to Hamilton, May 8, 1956, B 315, Hamilton, R, Series 320, RNln; *PN*, 117–118.

6. *Los Angeles Times*, Sept 18, PPS6.78, *New York Times*, Sept 18, PPS6.76, Peterson to RN, Sept 30, PPS8.209, Service Guide, Sept 17–Nov 4, 1952, DR, B 5, F 7 Don Phillips, "Richard M. Nixon: Rail and Romantic," *Trains*, Nov 1971, DR, B 12, F 4, RNyl; Anderson to Pearson, Sept 23, 1952, B G281 [2 of 3], Pearson mss; Lavine ed., *Smoke-Filled Rooms*, 78; Herbert Klein OH, 37, CCOH; interview with Klein, Nov 12, 2002, discussed the difficulty with communications; Lungren and Lungren, *Healing Nixon*, 45–46.

7. Cowles to RN, Sept 18, PPS296(1952).8A.4, RN remarks, Sept 18, 1952, PPS208(1952).51, memoirs, Mar 20, 1976, RNyl.

8. RN remarks, Sept 18, PPS208(1952).50, RN statement, Sept 18, PPS208(1952).49.2, *Los Angeles Mirror*, Sept 18, PPS6.81, RN remarks, Sept 19, PPS208(1952).53.(1), *New York Times*, Sept 19, PPS6.83, *Los Angeles Times*, Sept 19, PPS6.83, *San Francisco Examiner*, Sept 19, 1952, PPS60.s.10, RNyl.

9. Edson to Richard (RN), July 27, 1952, B 236, Edson, Series 320, RNln; *St. Louis Post Dispatch*, Sept 21, 1952, PPS6.100, RNyl; Earl Behrens OH, 24–25, CCOH.

10. *Meet the Press*, Sept 14, PPS208(1952).45.1, Edson to RN, Sept 17, 1952, PPS10.474.1, RNyl; Smith to Alsop, Apr 11, 1958, B 704, Smith, Dana, Series 320, RNln and B 47, R. Nixon: The Mystery, Alsop mss; Gellman, *Contender*, 346–347; Hillings, *Irrepressible Irishman*, 57–59.

11. *Washington Daily News* (DC), Sept 18, 1952, PPS6.78, RNyl; Crail to Editor, June 8, 1959, B 187, Crail, Series 320, RNln; memo, after July 1952, N G-281 [1 of 3], Pearson mss; Herbert Klein OH, 198, pp. 28–30, CCOH.

12. *New York Post*, Sept 18, PPS6.80, *St. Louis Post Dispatch*, 21, PPS6.100, memo, Sept 22, 1952, PPS10.551.2, RNyl; Rowse, *Slanted News*, 45, 47 and 48; *Time*, Oct 6, 1952, p. 19; Nissenson, *Lady Upstairs*, 145–147; Day 3, Tape 2, 00:19:06 [RN], Gannon mss, WJBma.

13. *New York Post*, Sept 18, 1952, PPS6.80, RNyl; Smith to Alsop, Apr 11, 1958, B 704, Smith, Dana, Series 320, RNln and B 47, R. Nixon: The Mystery, Alsop mss; Summers's discussion of the fund borders on the bizarre. The author claims, among other unsubstantiated accusations, that Nixon used the fund to help as a down payment for his house. That was impossible; Nixon was not allowed to write checks from the fund.

14. *Press Democrat* (Santa Rosa, Calif), Sept 18, PPS6.78, *St. Louis Post Dispatch*, Sept 24, 1952, PPS6.o.s.31; Wilson, "Is Nixon Fit?," PPS296(1953).4, platter, June 14, 1954, and memoirs, Mar 15, 1976, RNyl; diaries, III, The Eisenhower Campaign (1), B 1, p. 510, Shanley mss, DDEL; Scott to Heuges, Sept 29, Scott to Rudman, Sept 29, B 8, 1952 May–Sept, Gulick to McIlvaine, Oct 11, 1952, B 8, 1952 Oct-1953, Scott mss, UVa; James Hagerty OH, 13 and 73 and Milton Eisenhower OH, 15–17, CCOH;

Herbert Brownell OH, 20, DDEL; Ambrose's view on the fund cannot be sustained by the facts in *Eisenhower,* vol. 1, 554–561; Scott, *Come to the Party,* 110–112.

15. Phone interview with Marje Peterson Acker, Aug 18, 2001; Dorothy Cox Donnelly, Aug 18, 2001; Hughes, *Ordeal,* 38–40.

16. *Washington Post,* Sept 19, 1952, PPS6.83, RNyl; Day 3, Tape 2, 00:25:15 [RN], Gannon mss, WJBma; Mitchell, *Elm Street Politics.*

17. Lowenthal to Truman, Sept 18, memo by Lowenthal, Sept 18, Lowenthal to Truman, Sept 19, Truman to Lowenthal, Sept 22, 1952, PSF, General File, Lowenthal, Max (F 2), Truman mss, HSTL; memo by Ladd, Nov 13, 1950, Cronin FBI file Part 2, p. 94-35404, FBI mss; de Toledano ed., *Notes,* 156.

18. *San Francisco Examiner* Sept 20, PPS6.91, *Philadelphia Inquirer,* Sept 20, PPS10.514, clipping, Sept 21, 1952 PPS6.99, memo, Feb 13, 1953, PPS325(1953).194, memoirs, Mar 15, 1976, RNyl; Klein to RN, Saturday after 1960 Republican convention, B 417, Klein 1960 (2 of 2), Series 320, RNln; Lavine ed., *Smoke-Filled Rooms,* 79–80; Patterson, *Mr. Republican,* 578; Longley, *Gore,* 99–100.

19. RN address, Sept 19, PPS208(1952).52(1), clipping, Sept 19, PPS6.81, *Community Press* (NJ), Sept 26, 1952, PPS6.234, RNyl.

20. *Washington Post,* Sept 20, PPS6.93, *San Francisco Examiner,* Sept 20, 1952, PPS6.89, RNyl; memo to Pearson, Sept 23, 1952, B G 281 [2 of 3], Pearson mss; Cutler, *No Time for Rest,* 284–285; for Milton Eisenhower's assessment who was traveling with his brother, see *President Is Calling,* 251–252.

21. News bulletin, Sept 19, PPS12.45.14, *Chicago Daily News,* Sept 19, PPS6.84, *Paris Beacon-News,* Sept 20, 1952, PPS10.616.2, RNyl; Herbert Brownell OH, 20–22, DDEL.

22. *PDDE,* XIII, p. 1358.

23. *San Francisco Examiner,* Sept 20, 1952, PPS6.88, RNyl.

24. Radio reports, Sept 19, 20 and 21, PPS10.669.2, *New York Times,* Sept 20, PPS6.96, *Washington Post,* Sept 20, PPS6.92 and Sept 26, 1952, PPS13.17.8, RNyl.

25. *New York Herald Tribune,* Sept 20, PPS6.98, Stassen to RN, Sept 20, 1952, PPS10.525. (1)(2), RNyl; Barkin, "Eisenhower and Robinson," in Krieg ed., *Eisenhower,* 12 and 17; Clifford Roberts OH, 291–293, DDEL.

26. *New York Times,* Sept 20, 1952, PPS6.95, RNyl.

27. *San Francisco Examiner,* Sept 20, 1952, PPS6.88, RNyl; *PAES,* IV, p. 103; Day 3, Tape 3, 00:21:03 [RN], Gannon mss, WJBma.

28. MacKinnon to RN, Sept 19, 1952, PPS10.487.1, RNyl.

29. *Washington Post,* Sept 20, PPS6.92, *New York Times,* Sept 20, PPS6.93 and Sept 21, 1952, PPS6.98, RNyl.

30. News bulletin, Sept 20, PPS12.45.19(1), *New York Times,* Sept 21, 1952, PPS6.101, RNyl; Berthelot claimed: "Every one knew that Richard Nixon, a lawyer and a member of Congress, could well afford a fur coat for Pat," Berthelot, *Win Some,* 115.

31. Memo, Sept 20, PPS10.512A, *Evening Star* (DC), Sept 21, 1952, PPS6.84, RNyl; RN to Moran, Aug 21, 1961, B 227, Duffy, B, Series 320, RNln; Herbert Brownell OH, 21–22, DDEL; Hughes, *Ordeal,* 38–39; Smith, *Clay,* 603–604; Thompson ed., *Eisenhower,* 183.

32. *PDDE,* XIII, p. 1360.

33. Bewley to RN, Sept 20, PPS10.498, Hannah to RN, Sept 20, 1952, PPS10.512, RNyl; for Hannah's views of her son see Kornitzer, *Real Nixon;* Hillings, *Irrepressible Irishman,* 60; Martin, *Stevenson of Illinois,* 684–693, for Stevenson's reaction to the fund.

34. Arnold to RN, Sept 20, PPS10.497, news bulletin, Sept 20, PPS12.12.45.20, memo, Sept 20, PPS10.503, clipping, Sept 21, PPS6.109, *Los Angeles Times,* Sept 21, PPS6.106, *New York Times,* Sept 21, PPS6.98, Mozley scripts, Sept 21, LBM18.1, *San Francisco Examiner,* Sept 22, 1952, PPS6.114, Wilson, "Is Nixon Fit," PPS 296 (1953).4, RNyl; Smith to Mazo, June 3, B 704, Smith, Dana and Crail to Editor, June 8, 1959, B 187, Crail, Series 320, RNln.

35. *Baltimore Sun,* Sept 21, PPS6.100, *Washington Times Herald* (DC), Sept 21, 1952, PPS6.108, RNyl; interview, Day 3, Tape 2, 00:25:15 [RN], Gannon mss, WJBma.

36. News bulletin, Sept 20, PPS12.45.15, PPS12.45.17 and PPS12.45.18, *Baltimore Sun,* Sept 21, 1952, PPS6.110, RNyl.

37. *Washington Evening Star* (DC), Sept 20, PPS6.94, *Chicago Tribune,* Sept 21, 1952, PPS6.103, RNyl.

38. Eisenhower-Nixon research, Sept 21, 1952, PPS10.517, RNyl.

39. Stassen to RN, Sept 21, 1952, Series 320, B 724, Stassen, RNln and PPS10.525(1)(2), RNyl.

40. McKinnon to Chotiner, Sept 21, PPS10.520, news bulletin, Sept 21, PPS12.45.21, memo, Sept 22, 1952, PPS10.570, RNyl.

41. *Meet the Press,* Sept 21, PPS10.516, *Washington Times-Herald* (DC), Sept 21, PPS6.99, *Washington Star* (DC), Sept 22, 1952, PPS6.120, RNyl; Gorman, *Kefauver,* 163.

42. Radio reports, Sept 21, 1952, B 583, Pearson [3/13], Series 320, RNln; *Youngstown Vindicator* (Ohio), Sept 23, PPS6.140, *Los Angeles Daily News,* Sept 23, PPS12.17.3, *Washington Post,* Sept 26, 1952, PPS13.17.8, RNyl, Feldstein, "Fighting Quakers," 76–90.

43. Eisenhower-Nixon research, Sept 21, 1952, PPS10.518(1)(2), RNyl.

44. *Christian Science Monitor,* Sept 22, 1952, PPS6.o.s.21.1, RNyl.

45. Memo, Mar 5, 1960, B 322, Harris, Ele, Series 320, RNln; memoirs, Mar 15, 1976, RNyl; *PN,* 118–126.

46. Memo, Sept 20, PPS10.512B, *San Francisco Examiner,* Sept 23, 1952, PPS6.135, RNyl; Day 3, Tape 2, 00:26:52 [RN], Gannon mss, WJBma; Anderson to Pearson, Sept 23, 1952, B G281 [2 of 3], Pearson mss; A.C. Newsom OH, 12–13, CSUF; Earl Behrens OH, 25–25, CCOH; Hillings, *Irrepressible Irishman,* 60; Smith, *Dewey,* 600; Lavine ed., *Smoke-Filled Rooms,* 82–85; Milton Eisenhower OH, 15–20, CCOH; Day 3, Tape 2, 00:26:52 [RN], Gannon mss, WJBma.

47. *Whittier News,* Sept 22, PPS6.118, Kuest story, Sept 22, PPS10.565, Mozley script, Sept 22, LBM18.3, *New York Journal American,* Sept 22, 1952, PPS6.111, RNyl.

48. Arnold to Babbitt, Oct 2, 1952, B 58, Babbitt and Co, Series 320, RNln; *Chicago Daily News,* Sept 22, PPS6.132, *Washington Post,* Sept 23, PPS6.146, *Los Angeles Times,* Sept 23, 1952, PPS6.133, RNyl; O'Brien and Jones, *Night Nixon Spoke,* 5–13.

49. *Chicago Daily News,* Sept 22, PPS6.132, *Los Angeles Daily Mirror,* Sept 24, 1952, PPS6.162, RNyl.

50. *Washington Star* (DC), Sept 22, 1952, PPS6.123, RNyl; Day 3, Tape 2, 00:33:52 [RN], Gannon mss, WJBma.

51. Quotes, Sept 22, 1952, PPS10.*557, RNyl; Day 3, Tape 1, 00:25:01 [RN] and Day 3, Tape 3, 00:05:55 [RN], Gannon mss, WJBma.
52. _Illinois State Journal_, Sept 23, 1952, PPS6.o.s.28, RNyl.
53. _Chicago Daily News_, Sept 22, PPS6.114, _Minneapolis Morning Tribune_, Sept 23, 1952, PPS.o.s.29, RNyl; Anderson to Pearson, Sept 23, 1952, B G281 [2 of 3], Pearson mss, LBJL; _PRAT_, V. 4, pp. 430–431; Scott, _Come to the Party_, 114; Lavine ed., _Smoke-Filled Rooms_, 86–89.
54. News bulletin, Sept 22, PPS12.45.22, _New York Herald Tribune_, Sept 22, PPS6.122 and Sept 23, PPS6.144, _Milwaukee Journal_, Sept 23, 1952, PPS6.138, RNyl; Smith, _Iron Man_, 135–137.
55. _Chicago Sun-Times_, Sept 22, PPS6.121, _New York Herald Tribune_, Sept 23, 1952, PPS6.136, RNyl.
56. News bulletin, Sept 22, PPS12.45.23, _Washington Star_ (DC), Sept 22, PPS.125, _Chicago Daily News_, Sept 22, PPS6.114, _New York Herald Tribune_, Sept 23, 1952, PPS6.139, RNyl.
57. _Los Angeles Times_, Sept 23, 1952; RN to Chandler, Oct 2, 1952, PPS10.694, RNyl.
58. Hoffman to Blaine, Sept 29, Chronological File 1952 - September, Hoffman to Mazo, Apr 20, 1958, Eminent Personages File, Nixon, Richard M. 1952–1960, Hoffman mss, HSTL; Gibson, Dunn & Crutcher to Adams, Sept 23, PPS208(1952).62.13.1(1), Price Waterhouse & Co to Adams, Sept 23, PPS208(1952)62.13.2(1), RN statement, Sept 23, PPS208(1952).62.5, MacKinnon to New, Oct 2, 1952, PPS11.309, RNyl; RN to Conley, May 24, 1962, B 175, Conley, E, Series 320, RNln; RN to Hoffman, Apr 21, 1953, Eminent Personages File, Nixon, Richard M. 1952–1960, Hoffman mss; Rauscher, _Hoffman_, 94–95; Brownell, _Advising Ike_, 126.
59. _New York World Telegram_, Sept 23, PPS6.147, _St. Louis Post Dispatch_, Sept 24, 1952, PPS6.o.s.58, autograph, Jan 8, 1954, PPS269.7, RNyl.
60. Mozley script, Sept 23, LBM18.6, _Chicago Daily News_, Sept 24, 1952, PPS6o.s.54, RNyl; memo, early Sept 1961, B 652, Rogers (2 of 4), Series 320, RNln; _Los Angeles Times_, Mar 26, 2003, p. B-10.
61. Barnouw, _Tube of Plenty_, 137; many, including Nixon, claim that 58,000,000 saw the fund address, but this seems inflated; millions did watch, but I found no credible number for the exact number of viewers; memo from the Nielson Media Research, Sept 5, 2001, Gellman mss, DDEL.
62. Memo, early Sept 1961, B 652, Rogers (2 of 4), Series 320, RNln.
63. Smith, _Dewey_, 601; Nixon, _Six Crises_, 109–111; Ewald, _Eisenhower_, 54; interview with William Price, Aug 10, 2001; Day 3, Tape 2, 00:29:48 [RN], Gannon mss, WJBma; Herbert Klein OH, 24, 30–31 and 37, CCOH.
64. _Los Angeles Times_, Sept 23, PPS6.133 and Sept 24, PPS6o.s.43, Mozley script, Sept 23, LBM18.6 and LBM18.7, _St. Louis Post Dispatch_, Sept 24, PPS6o.s.58, _Chicago Daily Tribune_, Oct 1, PPS266.465(2), Lipscomb to Falknor, Oct 6, 1952, PPS11.326, RNyl; memo, early Sept 1961, B 652, Rogers (2 of 4), Series 320, RNln.
65. Memo, early Sept 1961, B 652, Rogers (2 of 4), Series 320, RNln; _Los Angeles Times_, Sept 24, 1954, PPS6o.s.43, Wilson, "Is Nixon Fit," PPS296(1952).12, RNyl. One claim was: "everyone knew that Richard Nixon, a lawyer and a member of Congress, could well afford a fur coat for Pat." Berthelot, _Win Some_, 115.

66. RN to Helene, Sept 24, 1952, DR 30, Mother Mary Elizabeth to RN, Mar 21, 1953, DR 55, RNyl; telephone interview with Mareen Drown Nunn, Aug 10, 2001.

67. Memo, early Sept 1961, Series 320, B 652, Rogers (2 of 4), RNln; speech, Sept 23, film, *Los Angeles Times*, Sept 24, 1952, PPS60.s.43, RNyl.

68. Speech, Sept 23, 1952, film, RN appearance, 13:11, RNyl; Perlstein ed., "Nixon," 64–79; in Perlstein, *Nixonland*, chap. 2, the author's account of Nixon's early career is riddled with factual errors; O'Brien and Jones, *Night Nixon Spoke*, 14–31 and 95–104; Day 3, Tape 2, 00:33:52 [RN] and 00:38:01 [RN], Gannon mss, WJBma.

69. *Los Angeles Times*, Sept 24, 1952, PPS60.s.43, Wilson, "Is Nixon Fit?," PPS296(1952).12, RNyl; memo, early Sept 1961, B 652, Rogers (2 of 4), Series 320, RNln; Day 3, Tape 2, 00:38:01 [RN], Gannon mss, WJBma.

70. Day 3, Tape 2, 00:38:01 [RN], Gannon mss, WJBma; almost a half century later, Ted Rogers still had a vivid recollection of that telecast, telephone interview with Edward Rogers, Oct 22, 2001.

71. *Chicago Daily News*, Sept 24, 1952, PPS6.154, memo, Aug 26, 1933, B 1, F1, Betty Lewis mss, RNyl; phone interview with Marje Peterson Acker, Aug 15, 2001; Hillings, *Irrepressible Irishman*, 61.

72. *New York Herald Tribune*, Sept 23, 1952, PPS6.142, RNyl; William Knowland OH, 6–8 and 83, CCOH; Frank Carlson OH, DDEL.

73. Diaries, Sept 23, 1952, R 1, Eisenhower mss, DDEL; *Times Herald* (DC), Sept 23, 1952, PPS6.149, RNyl; Lowe to RN, Nov 28, 1956 with enclosure of Eisenhower's notes, B 463, Lowe (1 of 2), Series 320, RNln; Cutler, *No Time for Rest*, 285–286; Snyder, *My Friend Ike*, 170.

74. Smith, *Clay*, 606.

75. Diaries, Sept 23, 1952, R 1, Eisenhower mss; *Minneapolis Star*, Sept 24, 1952, PPS6.165, RNyl; Hook to RN, Nov 11, 1952, B 350, Hook, C, Series 320, RNln; James Hagerty OH, 74, CCOH.

76. *Chicago Daily News*, Sept 24, PPS6.o.s.55, *Washington Post*, Sept 24, PPS6.181, *New York Journal American*, Sept 24, PPS6.167, *Balt Sun*, Sept 24, 1952, PPS6.167, RNyl; Wilton Persons OH, 17–20 and James Hagerty OH, 75, CCOH; *Time*, Oct 6, 1952, p. 21; S. Eisenhower, *Mrs. Ike*, 271–274; Lavine ed., *Smoke-Filled Rooms*, 91–92. Ewald, *Eisenhower*, 55–57; Morris, *Nixon*, 833; Ambrose, *Eisenhower*, vol. 1, 559–560; Parmet, *Eisenhower*, 138; Hart, *When the Going Was Good!* 158–162; Lee, *Eisenhower*, 164.

77. Ike to RN, Sept 23, 1952, PPS10.596, RNyl; *PDDE*, XIII, pp. 1361–1363; James Hagerty, pp. 73–74 and Sherman Adams OH, CCOH; Hollitz, "Eisenhower and the Admen," 29–30; Hughes, *Ordeal*, 40–41; Smith, *Clay*, 604–606.

78. *PDDE*, XIII, pp. 1365–1366.

79. RN to Ike, Sept 23, PPS10.599, Don Mozley script, Sept 24, 1952, LBM18.8, RNyl; Day 3, Tape 2, 00:40:34 and 43 [RN], Gannon mss, WJBma; Earl Behrens OH, 27–29, Prescott Bush OH, 29 and 330–331 and Herbert Klein OH, 31–34, CCOH.

80. *Jersey Shore Herald*, Sept 24, PPS6.169, *New York Times*, Sept 24, PP6.159, MacKinnon to Chotiner, Sept 24, PPS10.618.1–2, *Chicago Daily News*, Sept 24, PPS6.154, *Washington Post*, Sept 27, 1952, PPS6.242, RNyl; Rowse, *Slanted News*, 7–8; *PAES*, IV, p. 121.

81. *PAES*, IV, p. 121; *Baltimore Sun*, Sept 23, 1952, PPS6.168, RNyl; Broadwater, *Adlai Stevenson*, 123; Lavine ed., *Smoke-Filled Rooms*, 74–75; Galbraith, *Life in Our Times*, 300–302.

82. News bulletin, Sept 24, PPS12.45.24 and Sept 28, 1952, PPS12.67(1), RNyl; Woods to Smith, Nov 28, 1952, B 11, F 4, Series 207, RN to Booker, Feb 23, 1953, B 93, Booker, H, Series 320, RNln; Lavine ed., *Smoke-Filled Rooms*, 93; O'Brien and Jones, *Night Nixon Spoke*, 32–80.

83. Weis to Gentlemen, Sept 23, PPS9(FL).731, Simcox to Eisenhower, after Sept 23, PPS9(IL).58, Loring to Sirs, Sept 24, PPS9(MA).5473, Mohr to Sirs, Sept 24, 1952, PPS9(CA).60, RNyl; O'Brien and Jones, *Night Nixon Spoke*, 39–48.

84. Smith to RN, Sept 24, PPS10.628, Poulson to RNC, Sept 24, PPS16.1140.2, Stassen to RN, Sept 24, PPS10.630, Ford to RN, Sept 29, 1952, PPS10.665, RNyl.

85. Irwin to RN, Sept 24, B 371, Irwin (2 of 4), Irwin to RN, Irwin to Ike, Sept 24, Irwin (3 of 4), Warner to RN, Sept 24, RN to Warner, Nov 3, 1952, B 798, Warner, H, Series 320, RNln; interview with Beverly Lindy who sorted the California correspondence, Aug 7, 2001, Gellman mss, DDEL; without any supporting data, Ambrose concluded that Nixon failed to win new supporters and indeed made enemies: "a majority in the audience found the speech objectionable if not nauseating. Republicans never discussed it, and Democrats mocked it." Ambrose, *Nixon*, 294.

86. Lindy notes, Aug 7, 2001 and interview with Lindy, Aug 7, 2001, Gellman mss, DDEL; Members, *Influence of Television*, 25–26.

87. Cottege to AES, Sept 26, B 222, F 5, Dopp to Mitchell, Sept 26, B 222, F 6, Shelton to AES, Sept 26, Schwartz to AES, Sept 27, 1952, B 223, F 1, Stevenson mss, HML.

88. Diaries, Eisenhower schedule, Sept 24, 1952, R 1, Eisenhower mss, DDEL; Heidepriem, *Fair Chance*, 206–207.

89. Mozley script, Sept 24, LBM18.9, *Evening Star* (DC), Sept 24, 1952, PPS6.176, RNyl; Lavine ed., *Smoke-Filled*, 7 and 75; Klein, *Making It*, 138; Herbert Klein OH 198, pp. 31–34, CCOH; Herbert Klein interview, Nov 12, 2002; Klein never thought that Nixon was going to resign.

90. *Ashland Daily Press* (Wis), Sept 24, PPS6.174, *Los Angeles Times*, Sept 24, 1952, PPS6.153, RNyl.

91. Memo, Sept 23, 1952, PPS10.586.2, RN to Hoover, Jan 14, 1957, PPS320.102.38.1, RNyl; Hoover statement, Sept 24, RN to Hoover, Sept 25, 1952, Individual File Series, Hoover mss, HHL; Best, *Hoover*, Vol. 2, 362.

92. *Chicago Daily News*, Sept 24, PPS6.154, *New York Times*, Sept 25, 1952, PPS6.204, RNyl.

93. *Chico Enterprise-Record* (Calif), Sept 24, PPS60.s.40, *Jersey Shore Herald* (Pa), Sept 24, PPS6.169, *New York Daily Mirror*, Sept 25, PPS6.209, *Life*, Oct 6, 1952, PPS296(1952).12, RNyl; Diaries, Appointment Record, Sept 24, 1952, R 1, Eisenhower mss, DDEL; Lavine ed., *Smoke-Filled Rooms*, 94–95.

94. *New York Times*, Sept 25, 1952, PPS6.204, RNyl.

95. *San Francisco Examiner*, Sept 25, 1952, PPS0.s.70, RNyl; *Wall Street Journal*, Sept 25, 1952, B G281 [1 of 3], Pearson mss, LBJL.

96. Memo by Mozley, Sept 24, LBM18.12, *San Francisco Examiner*, Sept 25, 1952, PPS6.o.s.*68, RNyl; *Time*, Oct 6, 1952, p. 2; Scott, *Come to the Party*, 118.

97. Memo by Mozley, Sept 24, LBM18.12, *San Francisco Examiner*, Sept 25, 1952, PPS60.s.70, RNyl; James Hagerty OH, 75, Sherman Adams OH and Earl Behrens OH, 24–29, CCOH.

98. Thompson ed., *Eisenhower*, 182; 82-1-IV-657, Sept 24, 1952, audio-visual, Eisenhower mss, DDEL.

99. H. Nixon to Ike, Sept 23, 1952, B 237, Eisenhower statements, Series 320, RNln; closing remarks, Sept 24, PPS208(1952).63.1(3), *Los Angeles Examiner*, Sept 25, PPS60.s.*68, *New York Times*, Sept 25, PPS6.205, *Baltimore Sun*, Sept 25, PPS6.212 and PPS6.213, Mozley script, Sept 25, LBM18.10, *Times Herald* (DC), Sept 25, PPS6.219, *Life*, Oct 6, 1952, PPS296(1952).12, RNyl; Winifred Winget OH, 8–9, CSUF; *Time*, Oct 6, 1952, p. 22; Scott, *Come to the Party*, 118; Holt, *Mamie*, 57; Day 3, Tape 3, 00:03:22 [RN], Gannon mss, WJBma.

100. Day 3, Tape 3, 00:03:22 [RN], Gannon mss, WJBma; *San Francisco Examiner*, Sept 25, 1952, PPS60.s.68, RNyl; Knowland OH, 131–132, CCOH; Montgomery and Johnson, *One Step from the WH*, 122; Day 3, Tape 3, 00:04:38 [RN], Gannon mss, WJBma.

101. Memo, Sept 24, LBM18.12, "Worth Reporting," Oct 1952, LBM18.13, RNyl; Ambrose states that Ike's "response was therefore, patient, calculated, clear-headed, and in the end he turned apparent disaster into stunning triumph." That cannot be sustained because Eisenhower bore a large share of the responsibility for the crisis; he did not act forcefully, quickly, or decisively. Ambrose, *Eisenhower*, vol. 1, 555.

102. *Los Angeles Times*, Sept 26, 1952, PPS6.151, RNyl; Day 3, Tape 3, 00:02:25 [RN], Gannon mss, WJBma.

103. Nixon, *Six Crises*, 73–129 and quote on 128.

104. *PPA* 1955, p. 333.

105. Eisenhower, *Mandate*, 65–69 and quote on 69.

CHAPTER 3. TO VICTORY

1. *Times-Herald* (DC), Sept 26, PPS6.238, *Chicago Daily Tribune*, Sept 26, PPS6.231, RNyl; Ike to Friend, Sept 30, 1952,B 237, Eisenhower statements, Series 320, RNln.

2. Ike to RN, Oct 1, 1952, B 189, Creel, Series 320, RNln and PPS10.686, RNyl; *PDDE*, XIII, pp. 1366–1372; J. Eisenhower, *Strictly Personal*, 396–401; Doenecke, *Not to the Swift*, 211–216.

3. Griffith, "General and the Senator," 23–29; Broadwater, *Eisenhower and the Anti-Communist*, 51–53; Unger, *Marshall*, 476–479.

4. DE to Stassen, Oct 5, 1952, OF, Part I, Stassen, R 27, DDE; *PDDE*, XIII, pp. 1372–1374; for background on Ike's activities see Eisenhower, *Mandate*, 69–71; Parmet, *Eisenhower*, 141–142; Ambrose, *Eisenhower*, vol. 1, 561–567; Reeves, *Distinguished*, 276–289.

5. Bernstein, "Election of 1952," pp. 3250–3552.

6. Mozley script, Sept 26, 1952, LBM18.11, RNyl.

7. RN remarks, Sept 26, PPS208(1952).64A, *San Francisco Examiner*, Sept 27, PPS6.24, *New York Times*, Sept 27, 1952, PPS12.S57, RNyl; Woods to Guill, Nov 28, B 308, Guill, RN to Fletcher, Dec 23, 1952, B 264, Fletcher, E, RN to Porter, Jan 13, 1953, B 605, Porter, HJ, Series 320, RNln.

8. RN speech, Oct 1, PPS208(1952).68.2, RN speech, Oct 2, PPS208(1952).69, *New York Times*, Oct 2, PPS6.275, *Los Angeles Times*, Oct 2, 1952, PPS6.273, RNyl.

9. *St. Louis Post Dispatch*, Oct 4, 1952, PPS6.287, RNyl; Hamby, *Man of the People*, 621.

10. RN speech, Oct 6, PPS208(1952).73, *Boston Globe*, Oct 6, PPS6.289, *Boston Evening American*, Oct 6, PPS6.293, RN speech, Oct 7, 1952, PPS208(1952).74, McLaughlin to Wilson, early Feb 1953, LBN128.3, RNyl. Years later, after Nixon and Acheson had reconciled, the former president reflected in his memoirs about his attacks on the secretary of state during the 1952 race and apologized for his fierce venomous statements relating to Acheson, concluding that the intensity of the race contributed to the shrillness. The record needed that corrective: Acheson had become a valued unofficial foreign-policy adviser and a personal friend. Toward the end of his life, Nixon went further, describing Acheson as one of the three greatest secretaries of state since World War II along with John Foster Dulles and Henry Kissinger.

11. *Columbus Dispatch*, Oct 7, PPS6.301, *New York Herald Tribune*, Oct 7, PPS6.300, *St. Louis Post Dispatch*, Oct 7, PPS6.302, RN remarks, Oct 8, PPS208(1952).75, *Sidney Daily News*, Oct 8, PPS6.304, RN remarks, Oct 9, PPS208(1952).77.1, *New York Herald Tribune*, Oct 10, PPS6.314, *New York Times*, Oct 10, PPS6.310, *Sunday Star*, Oct 12, 1952, PPS6.317, RNyl.

12. RN speech, Oct 8, PPS208(1952).76, Nixon to RN, Oct 8, PPS208(1952).76.6, *New York Times*, Oct 9, 1952, PPS6.308, RNyl.

13. *New York Post*, Oct 9, 1952, PPS6.308, RNyl.

14. *New York Times*, Oct 14, 1952; Lipscomb to Summerfield, Oct 7, PPS14.260.1, Chotiner to Smith, Oct 7, PPS14.72, *New York Times*, Oct 8, PPS6.303, Rogers to RN, Oct 8, PPS208(1952).82.3A, RN to Rogers, Oct 8, PPS205.2094, Rogers to RN, Oct 8, 1952, PPS205.2905, RNyl.

15. *New York Times*, Oct 14, 1952; RN speech, Oct 13, 1952, PPS208(1952).81.2(1), RNyl; *Detroit News*, Oct 14, 1952, B 344, Hiss (1 of 3), Series 320, RNln; Kutler ed., *Abuse*, 261.

16. Washburn to Chotiner, Oct 7, 1952, PPS299.82A.50.1, RNyl; *New York Times*, Oct 20, 1952.

17. RN statement, Oct 19, PPS208(1952).92 and .93, *New York Herald Tribune*, Oct 20, PPS13.S29, *Washington Post*, Oct 20, 1952, PPS6.343, RNyl; *PDDE*, XIII, pp. 1388–1390; Wagner, "Lingering Death of the National Origins," 134–135.

18. RN remarks, Oct 15, 1952, PPS208(1952).86.6, RNyl.

19. RN remarks, Oct 16, PPS208(1952).87.2, *Post*, Oct 17, PPS6.337, *Los Angeles Times*, Oct 17, 1952, PPS6.338, RNyl.

20. Clipping, Oct 8, 1952, PPS208(1952).77.3, RNyl; Nixon, *RN*, 110–111.

21. *St. Louis Post Dispatch*, Oct 16, PPS6.333, *Freeport Journal Standard* (Calif), Oct 16, 1952, PPS6.336, RNyl; Martin, *Stevenson of Illinois*, 722–723, 725, and 741.

22. *PAES*, IV, pp. 164–170; Martin, *Stevenson of Illinois*, 737; Galbraith, *Life in Our Times*, 302–303; Schlesinger and Schlesinger eds., *Journals*, 13–22; Martin, *It Seems Like*, 140–148 and 155.

23. Memoirs, Mar 16, 1976, RNyl; DE, *Mandate*, 72; Neal ed., *Eleanor and Harry*, 219; Foot, *Wrong War*, 189–194; Caridi, *Korean War*, 209–245; Dailey, "Eisenhower-Nixon Campaign," 338–339; Millet, "Eisenhower and the Korean War," 41–54; Members, *Influence of Television*, 27–29.

24. *Washington Post*, Oct 27, PPS6.359, RN remarks, Oct 27, PPS208(1952).102, *New York Times*, Oct 28, 1952, PPS6.365, RNyl; Weeks, *Texas Presidential Politics*, 93.

25. *New York Post*, Oct 23, PPS6.354 and Oct 28, PPS6.365, *St. Louis Post Dispatch*, Nov 1, 1952, PPS6.374, RNyl.

26. *New York Herald Tribune*, Sept 9, 1956, PPS299.81S.4, RNyl; Campaigning, undated (1956?), B 700, Smears, Truman, Series 320, RNln.

27. RN remarks, Oct 28, PPS208(1952).103, memo, before Oct 29, PPS208(1952).104.1, *Los Angeles Examiner*, Oct 30, 1952, PPS60.s.124A, RNyl; RN to Bennett, Dec 23, 1952, B 75, Bennett, V, Series 320, RNln; Klein, *Making It*, 133–134.

28. *PAES*, IV, pp. 181–186.

29. Ibid.; diary, Nov 3, 1952, III, The Eisenhower Campaign (2), pp. 585–586, Shanley mss; Rogers to RN, Dec 15, 1952, B 652, Rogers (4 of 4), Series 320, RNln; *PDDE*, XIII, pp.1412–1413; DE to Hoving, Oct 11, 1956, R 10, DDE.

30. *Whittier News*, Nov 4, PPS60.s.128A, *Los Angeles Examiner*, Nov 5, PPS60.s.129, *St. Louis Post Dispatch*, Nov 6, 1952, PPS6.382, RNyl; Herbert Klein OH, 35–37, CCOH.

31. *Los Angeles Examiner*, Nov 5, PPS60.s.129, *St. Louis Post Dispatch*, Nov 6, PPS6.382, RNyl; Cotton to RN, Sept 5, 1956, B 183, Cotton, A, Series 320, RNln.

32. *New York Times*, Nov 5, 1952; Martin, *Stevenson of Illinois*, 764; Berle and Jacobs eds., *Navigating the Rapids*, 61; Martin, *It Seems Like*, 158–160.

33. Reinhard, *Republican*, 94–96; *Gallup Poll*, Two, 1101; Stanley, *Vital Statistics*, 124; Ambrose claims that Nixon cost Ike "some votes" and the general "was ambivalent about Nixon." There is no credible evidence to support either assertion. Ambrose, *Nixon*, 300.

34. The 1952 Elections, Oct 1953, PPS15.3, RNyl; The 1952 Elections: A Statistical Analysis, 1–2, 8–9, R 2, Part II, *PRP*; Martin, *Stevenson of Illinois*, 760; Parmet, *Eisenhower*, 144–148; Hamby, *Man of the People*, 615–617; Scammon, *America Votes* 3, p. 3; Scammon, *America at the Polls*, 17; Olien, *From Token*, Table 1 and 136–138; Campbell et al., *Elections*, 69–73; Campbell et al., *American Voter*, 89; Campbell et al., *Voter*, 26–27 and 184; Shade and Campbell eds., *American Presidential Campaigns*, V. 3, pp. 814–815; Members, *Influence of Television*, 31–34.

35. Harvard ed., *Changing Politics*, 46–54, 82, 111, 125, 213–214, 601, 681, 711, and 720; Bartley and Graham, *Southern Politics*, 9, 82, 86, and 90; Seagull, *Southern Republicanism*, 33–34 and 59–60; Lamis, *Two-Party*, 10–11, 46 and 85; Olien, *From Token*, 197–205; Strong, *1952 Presidential Election*, 343–389; Weeks, *Texas Presidential Politics*, 97–107; Anderson, *Eyes Off*, 212–215 and 241–248; Black and Black, *Rise of Southern*, 24, 61–67 and 69–71.

36. While many have written on the 1952 campaign, no one has seriously examined Nixon's role after the fund speech. The best overview is Bernstein, "Election of 1952," in Schlesinger and Israel eds., *Presidential Elections*, V. 4, pp. 3245–3266; Greene, *Crusade*, 199–232; Roger Morris provides a collection of newspaper stories and memoirs, *Nixon*, 851–866; Ambrose breezes through the general election *Nixon*, 295–300.

37. Jack to RN, Nov 27, 1952, DR 34, RNyl; *New York Times*, Nov 6 and 7, 1952.

38. Clipping, Nov, PPS336(1953).*6, *Herald*, Nov 11, PPS6.384, PN to Helene, Nov 13, DR 33, Arnold to Alt, Nov 19, 1952, PPS205.2940, RNyl; *New York Times*, Nov 12, 1952.

39. Memoirs, Mar 15, 1976, RNyl; *New York Times*, Nov 24 and 25, 1952; Chapman OH, p. 15 and Gaudio OH, 27, CSUF.

40. Diary 1953, PPS212(1953).1, Ike to RN, Jan 7, PPS324.4, diary, Jan 10, PPS267.3, *Evening Star* (DC), Jan 14, PPS336(1953).5, diary, Jan 15 and 17, PPS267.3, *Los Angeles Times*, Jan 17, 1953, PPS336(1953).12, RNyl.

41. Diary 1953, Jan 11–13, 1953, PPS212(1953).1, RNyl; New York trip, Jan 11–13, B 8, F 7, Series 207, RNln; RN to Creel, Nov 28, 1952, B 4, General Correspondence, Creel mss, LOC; persons attending, Jan 12, 1953, R1, Diary DDE; Parmet, *Eisenhower*, 167–173; Ambrose, *Eisenhower*, vol. 2, 36–37; Donovan, *Eisenhower*, 1–11.

42. RN remarks, Jan 17, 1953, B 8, F 8 [1 of 2], Series 207, RNln.

43. General Capsule, Jan 1953, F 8 [2 of 2], Series 207, RNln; *Los Angeles Times*, Jan 18, 1953, PPS336(1953).13, RNyl.

44. Itinerary for the Nixon family, Jan 20, 1953, B 8, F 8 [1 of 2], Series 207, RNln; *San Francisco Examiner*, Jan 21, 1953, PPS336(1953).27, RNyl; Clifford, *Counsel*, 286–287.

45. *Los Angeles Times*, Jan 21, PPS336(1953).23, *San Francisco Examiner*, Jan 21, 1953, PPS336(1953).27, RNyl; newsreel, Jan 20, 1953, EL-MP16-36, DDEL; Nixon, *RN*, 117.

46. *Los Angeles Times*, Jan 21, 1953, PPS336(1953).23, RNyl; Bewley to RN, Feb 2, 1953, B 80, Bewley ['½'], Series 320, RNln; *New York Times*, Jan 21 and 22, 1953; Keller, "Intellectuals and Eisenhower," 251–254; Ambrose, *Eisenhower*, vol. 2, 41–43.

47. Itinerary for the Nixons, Jan 20, 1953, B 8, F 8 [1 of 2], Series 207, RNln; *Washington Post*, Jan 21, PPS336(1953).30, Woods to Lang, Feb 19, 1953, PPS267.42.1, RNyl.

48. RN to St. Johns, Nov 28, B 667, St. Johns [3/3], RN to Knoop, Nov 28, B 421, Knoop, RN to Murphy, Nov 28, B 540, Murphy, G, RN to Matthews, Nov 28, 1952, B 483, Matthews, JB, RN to Hale, Mar 2, B 311, Hale, Wilma, RN to Johnson, Mar 7, 1953, Series 320, Johnson, Hi, RNln.

49. RN to Creel, Nov 28, 1952, Series 320, B 189, Creel, RNln.

50. *New York Times*, Jan 21, 1953, PPS336(1953).23, RNyl.

CHAPTER 4. THE GENERAL AS A MANAGER

1. Lodge to Jerry, July 21, 1952, R 13, press release, Nov 9, R 28, *Boston Globe*, Nov 10, *New York Herald Tribune*, Dec 1, 1952, R 30, J. Eisenhower to Lodge, Aug 24 and Sept 11, and Lodge to John, Sept 5, 1961, Lodge mss; Lodge, *As It Was*, 19–59; Whalen, *Kennedy versus Lodge*.

2. Memoirs, Mar 15, 1976, RNyl; memo, Feb 9, 1968, Anderson mss, MLGC; Eisenhower, *Mandate*, 107–13; Wills, *Nixon Agonistes*, 118–123; Kinnard, *President Eisenhower*, 136; Trohan, *Political Animals*, 291; Fishman et al. eds., *Washington*, 75–90; Henderson, *Managing the Presidency*, 1; Harlow, "White House Watch," 13; phone interview with Andrew Goodpaster, Jan 8, 2002.

3. Adams, *Firsthand Report*, 1–11; Warshaw ed., *Powersharing*, 28–30; Sennick, "Expertise in the WH," 40–42.

4. PDDE, XV, pp. 831–832; Jerry to Cabot, Mar 3, 1953 and Lodge to Jerry, Aug 26, 1954, R 13, Lodge mss; Reichard, *Reaffirmation of Republicanism*, 222–225; Burke and Thompson, *Harlow*, 45–96; George Reedy OH, V, pp. 6–7, LBJL.

5. Rabb to Cabot, Apr 29, 1957, R 29 and undated [1957], R 13, Lodge mss, MHS.

6. Donovan, *Whitman*, 169; Nixon, "Nixon's Own Story," 103.

7. Memoirs, Feb 16, 1976, RNyl; *Hagerty Diary*; Allen, *Eisenhower and Mass Media*, 51; Thompson ed., *Eisenhower Presidency*, 25; Stacks, *Scotty*, 129–186; Steel, *Lippmann*, 480–490; Anderson, *Confessions of a Muckraker*, 274–275; Pierpont, *At the WH*, 123–126.

8. *Gallup Poll*, Two, 1123, 1129, 1137, 1142, 1157, 1171 and 1181; Miller, *Piety*, 3–9; J. Eisenhower, *Strictly Personal*, 290.

9. Chernus, *General Eisenhower*, 46–47; Eisenhower meeting with Dulles, belt 1, EL-T-IBM-256-1, DDEL.

10. Eisenhower meeting with Dulles, belt 1, EL-TIBM-256-1, DDEL.

11. Nixon, "Nixon on the Vice Presidency," *Detroit Free Press*, Mar 26, 1964.

12. *PDDE*, XIV, pp. 265–266; Lodge to General, Nov 4, 1952, R 28, Lodge mss; Patterson, *Mr. Republican*, 585–593 and 592–593; White, *Taft*, 218–229; Reichard, *Reaffirmation of Republicanism*, 97–114; Donovan, *Eisenhower*, 103–108; Saltonstall, *Salty*, 156 and 173–174; Trohan, *Political Animals*, 274–282 and 292; Bowen, "Fight for the Right," 357–366.

13. RN to Terry, Aug 3, 1953, B 13, F 5, Series 207, RNln; Wilton Persons OH, 26–27, CCOH; *PDDE*, XVII, p. 2563; Patterson, *Mr. Republican*, 599–612; Donovan, *Eisenhower*, 108–113; Bowen, "Fight for the Right," 366–370; Sevareid, *Small Sounds*, 110–112.

14. Engelbourg, "Council of Economic Advisers," 193–195; McClenahan and Becker, *Eisenhower and the Cold War*, 1–20; Mieczkowski, *Eisenhower's Sputnik*, 86–89; Raymond Saulnier interview, May 26, 2006, Gellman mss, DDEL.

15. Meeting, Nov 11, 1957, R 6, Cabinet DDE; Raymond Saulnier interview, May 26, 2006, Gellman mss, DDEL.

16. Griffith, "Dwight Eisenhower and the Corporate," 87–122; McClenahan and Becker, *Eisenhower and the Cold War*, 23–42.

17. Engelbourg, "Council of Economic Advisers," 192–214; Jacoby, "President, the Constitution," 404–408; Donovan, *Eisenhower*, 165; Labor Force Statistics, 1953–1954, Bureau of Labor Statistics, www.BLS.gov.

18. Herberg, *Protestant*, 59–60 and 138–139; Whitfield, *Culture of Cold War*, 77–100; Ahlstrom, *Religious History*, 950–958; Martin, *With God*, 1–56; Gregory, *Southern Diaspora*, 197–235; Finke and Stark, *Churching*, 281–283; Marty, *Righteous*, 250–260; Hudnut-Beumler, *Looking*, 32–78; Miller, "Popular Religion," 66–74; Vinz, "Politics of Protestant," 235–260.

19. Keller, "Intellectuals," 368; Pinkley, *Eisenhower*, 270; D'Este, *Eisenhower*, 9–48; Chernus, *Eisenhower's Atoms*, 7–10; Chernus, *General Eisenhower*, 58–62.

20. Memoirs, Mar 15, 1976, RNyl; Pinkley, *Eisenhower*, 270; Pierard and Linder, *Civil Religion*, 194–205; Keller, "Intellectuals," 230–233; Miller, *Piety*, 32–35; *PDDE*, XIII, p. 1469; Eisenhower speech, Dec 22, 1952, B 2, F Oct 23, 1952 to Nov 3, 1952 and Dec 1952 (2), Whitman File, Speech Series, DDEL.

21. Eisenhower, *Mandate*, 100–101; Elson, *Wide Was*, 115–116; Lyon, *Eisenhower*, 476–478; Ahlstrom, *Religious*, 959–952; Pinkley, *Eisenhower*, 378; Pierard and Linder, *Civil Religion*, 194–205; Bergman, "Steeped in Religion," 148–165; Keller, "Intellectuals,"

235–242; Boller, "Religion and the U.S. Presidency," 11–12; Holt, "Eisenhower," paper presented on May 9, 2002, Gellman mss, DDEL.

22. Meeting, Feb 6, 1953, R 1, Cabinet DDE; Miller, *Piety*, 41; Herberg, *Protestant*, 59–60 and 138–139; Hudnut-Beumler, *Looking*, 32–78; Imboden, "Soul of," 374; Keller, "Intellectuals," 255–262; Miller, "Popular Religion," 66–74; Day 1, Tape 1, 00:44:25 [RN], Gannon mss; Miller, "Politics of Decency," 173–174; Gibbs and Duffy, *Preacher and the Presidents*, 41–53; Graham, *Just As*, 200.

23. Whitman to Whit, undated [had to be July 2 or 3, 1953], B 1, Correspondence—Whitman, E.S., Whitman, Ann C: Papers, 1949–90, DDEL.

24. *PDDE*, XIX, p. 1325; *Gallup Poll*, Two, 1222, 1252–1253, 1293–1294 and 1389; *Los Angeles Times*, Feb 21, 1955; Imboden, *Religion and American Foreign*, 1945–1960, 257–309; Marty, *Righteous*, 250–251; Hudnut-Beumler, *Looking*, 32–33, 41, 44–47 and 51–78; Silk, *Spiritual*, 96–99; Smith, *Faith and the Presidency*, 239–240; Ahlstrom, *Religious*, 954–955; Keller, "Intellectuals," 299–310 and 317–327; Fairbanks, "Religious Dimensions of Presidential," 260–266.

25. Day 8, Tape 1, 00:26:23 [RN] and 00:26:51 [RN], Gannon mss; Eisenhower, *Mandate*, 223–225.

26. Transcript, Apr 16, 1954, PPS208(1954).5, RNyl; also see, transcript, Apr 16, 1954, B 20, F 2, Series 207, RNln; *Newsweek*, Apr 26, p. 28 and June 14, 1954, p. 29; Donovan, *Eisenhower*, 294–297; Eisenhower, *Mandate*, 310–314; Pfau, *No Sacrifice*, 141–181; Sherwin and Bird, *American*, 462–550.

27. *Gallup Poll*, Two, 1189, 1213–1214 and 1248.

28. Platter, Mar 1, 1954, RNyl.

29. Memo, Mar 5, PPS325(1954).32 and platters, June 21 and 28, 1954, RNyl.

30. Bischof, "Before the Break," 94–97 and 221–222; Baxter, "Eradicating This Menace"; Theoharis, *Spying*, 54–56 and 209–211; Dean, *Imperial Brotherhood*, 66; Johnson, *Lavender Scare*, 119–146.

31. Burns et al., *Government by the People*, 410; Goldstein, *Modern American VP*, 249.

32. Johnson and Malone ed., *Dictionary*, II, pp. 7–10.

33. U.S. Constitution, Article I, Section 3, Clause 4 and Article II, Section 1, Clause 6; Tie votes, Series 320, B 792, VP votes, RNln; Natoli, *American Prince*, 8 and 16–17; Witcover, *Crapshoot*, 12–51; Nixon, "Nixon's Own Story," 106; Maravillas, "Nixon," 93–95; Ellis, *Presidential Lightning Rods*, 55.

34. Clipping, Nov 1952, PPS336(1953).*6, and memoirs, Mar 15, 1976, RNyl.

35. RN to Smith, Feb 27, 1953, B 704, Smith, DP, Series 320, RNln.

36. RN to Bewley, Mar 9, 1953, B 80, Bewley ['½], Series 320, RNln.

37. Memo, June 16, 1953, PPS325(1953).273/1, RNyl.

38. Platter, Mar 19, 1954, RNyl.

39. RN to McDermott, Dec 26, 1955, PPS325(1955).259 and RN to Ellis, Mar 10, 1956, PPS27.Economics R, RNyl.

40. *Pittsburgh Press*, Apr 10, 1955, PPS208(1955).5.1, RNyl; Day 1, Tape 1, 00:44:25 [RN], Gannon mss; Kornitzer, *Real Nixon*, 236–239.

41. Hibbs ed., *WH Sermons*, vi–vii; Pierard and Linder, *Civil Religion*, 207 and 212–216; Henderson, *Nixon*, 8–12 and 47–66; Graham, *Just As*, 440–442; East Whittier Friends

Church, "Friendly Visitor," and Edstrom, "I Remember," Gellman mss, DDEL; Kornitzer, *Real Nixon*, 235–242.

42. Woods to Shuler, Mar 27, 1953, Series 320, B 693, Shuler, B, RNln; Gregory, *Southern Diaspora*, 225–226.

43. RN to Hoey, Mar 20, 1952, B 345, Hoey, Series 320, RNln; Graham, *Just As*, 440; Martin, *A Prophet*, 146; Martin, *With God*, 30–31; Frady, *Graham*, 269; Kornitzer, *Real Nixon*, 235–238; Paddon, "Modern Mordecai," 150–161; Miller, "Politics of Decency," 173–174.

44. RN speech, Feb 1, B 9, F 2, Brotherhood Week, Feb 5, B 9, F 5, Cook to RN, June 12, 1953, B 10, F 7, Series 207, RNln; calendar, Feb 19, 1953, PPS212(1953).3.46, RNyl; Kornitzer, *Real Nixon*, 238–241; Henderson, *Nixon*, 103–106.

45. Two memos, undated, McLeod mss, NHS, with copies in Gellman mss, DDEL; Ambrose, *Nixon*, 310; no copy of this memo that Ambrose cited could be found in the Eisenhower presidential library using information from his footnote; email Abraham to Gellman, Jan 5, 2010, Gellman mss, DDEL; I believe the documents exist.

46. RN, "Lessons of the Alger Hiss Case," *New York Times*, Jan 21, 1986; Day 1, Tape 6, 00:53:01 [RN], Gannon mss; Prescott Bush OH, CCOH; George Reedy III OH, p. 55, LBJL; Gaylon Babcock OH, 110, HSTL; Miller, *Plain Speaking*, 416.

47. Cronin to RN, Feb 29, B 191, Cronin, Rev ½ and RN to Sparling, Mar 29, 1956, B 715, Sparling, Series 320, RNln; de Toledano ed., *Notes*, 207–208.

48. Haynes et al., *Spies*, 1–31; also see Mark, "In Re Alger Hiss," 26–67.

49. Diary, Aug 28, 1953, B 2, Vol. V, WH Years (3), Shanley mss; Bischof, "Before the Break," 104–106; Donovan, *Eisenhower*, 175.

50. Day 1, Tape 6, 00:46:47 [RN], Gannon mss, WJBma.

51. Memo, June 16, 1953, PPS325(1953).272.1, RNyl; Thomas to RN, July 15, 1952, B 754, Thomas, JP, RN to McDonald, Dec 3, 1960, B 771, Unamerican, Series 320, RNln; congressional conference, Feb 28 Mar 2, 1953, R 1, Legislative DDE; Donovan, *Eisenhower*, 85–87; Silk, *Spiritual*, 88.

52. Memo, June 16, 1953, PPS325(1953).271.3, RNyl.

53. Memoirs, Mar 15, 1976, RNyl; minutes, Jan 30 and Feb 12, 1953, R 1, Cabinet DDE; Hughes, *Ordeal*, 134.

54. *PDDE*, XVII, p. 2538; minutes, Apr 10 and 17, 1953, R 1, Cabinet DDE; Gray, *Eighteen Acres*, 281; Benson, *Cross Fire*, 135; Hughes, *Ordeal*, 102–103 and 117–118.

55. Henderson, *Managing the Presidency*, 52; Gray, *Eighteen Acres*, 280.

56. RN to Helene, Dec 31, 1952, DR 42, RNyl.

57. Platter, June 19, 1954, RNyl; *PDDE*, XVII, pp. 2592, 2649, 2671, 2689, and 2696.

58. Saltonstall, *Salty*, 155–157.

59. Diary, July 7, 1953, Vol. V, WH Years, B 2, Shanley mss; meetings, Jan 26, May 12 and Dec 17–19, 1953, R 1, Legislative DDE; *New York Times*, Mar 31, 1953; Saltonstall, *Salty*, 212; Olson, *Symington*, 297–304.

60. Platter, June 21, 1954, RNyl; *PDDE*, XV, pp. 828–829 and 832.

61. Calendar, Jan 21, 1953, PPS212(1953).3.17, RNyl; *PDDE*, XIV, pp. 452–453 and 799–780; Charles Halleck OH 489, pp. 12–13, 26 and 39–40, DDEL; Albert, *Little Giant*, 227; Smith, *Iron Man*, 104–108 and 168–169; Wilson, *Confessions*, 33; Gellman, *Contender*, 268.

62. *PDDE*, XVII, pp. 2593, 2683, and 2688; Erskine, "Dick and Pat Nixon," 36; *Newsweek*, Jan 23, 1956, p. 50; James Hagerty OH (1982), p. 94, CCOH.

63. James Hagerty OH (1982), p. 94, CCOH.

64. RN to Chotiner, Jan 28, PPS300.239 and Woods to Walker, Mar 27, 1953, PPS267.68, RNyl; RN to Ramsay, undated, B 43, F 1 and Woods to Horowitz, June 13, 1961, B 155, F 12, Series 207, RNln; interview with Loie Gaunt, Sept 11, 2000.

65. *Los Angeles Times*, Oct 5, 1953, PPS336(1953).163, RNyl; *Washington Post*, Oct 5, 1953, B 2, Far East Trip, *Washington Post*, Series 375, RNln; *Gallup Poll*, Two, 1175.

66. PN to Helene, Apr 1, 1953, DR 54, RNyl; Gould ed., *American First Ladies*, 374–375 and 391–392; Holt, *Mamie*, 101.

67. Diary, Feb 3, PPS267.3 and Apr 4, PPS267.3, Woods to Fleisher, Mar 3, PPS267.47.1, *Washington Evening Star* (DC), Mar 6, PPS336(1953).55, Fleisher to Woods, Mar 9, PPS267.52 and *Washington Post*, Oct 1, PPS336(1953).159, *Los Angeles Times*, Dec 27, PPS336(1953).209, PN to Drown, Mar 4, DR 50 and diary, July 14, 1953, PPS267.141, RNyl; *Herald*, Oct 1, 1953, B 2, Far East Trip, *Herald*, Series 375, RNln.

68. PN to Helene, Feb 3, 1953, DR 46, RNyl; for the definitive study see Holt, *Mamie*.

69. Mamie to PN, Apr 6, PPS268.*4 and *Washington Post*, Apr 30, 1953, PPS336(1953).73, RNyl; White House Reception, Apr 24, 1953, B 5, DAR file (2), WH social office, A.B. Tolley Records, 1952–1961, Diary DDE.

70. PN to Helene, Aug 31, 1953, DR 61, RNyl.

71. Mamie to PN, Nov 16, PPS324.45, Mamie to Julie, Nov 17, PPS324.47, Mamie to Tricia, Nov 17, 1954, PPS324.46, Mamie to PN, Mar 8, PPS268.1B.3, *Washington Post*, Mar 10, PPS336(1955).62, Burleson to PN, before Apr 18, PPS270.197, Mamie to PN, Apr 27, PPS258.2, *Washington Post*, May 6, PPS336(1955).0s.20, appointment book, May 17, PPS270.1, Mamie to PN, Nov 21, 1955, PPS324.75, Mamie to PN, June 1, PPS268.4, Ike to RN, July 31, PPS324.88 and Mamie to RN, Aug 1, 1956, PPS324.89, RNyl; PN to Mamie, Nov and Mamie to PN, Christmas, 1955, B 32, Nixon, personal file of Mamie, DDEL; Slater, *Ike I Knew*, 66–67; Holt, *Mamie*; Anthony, *First Ladies*, 551–571; Gordon and Gordon, *American Chronicle*, 345.

72. Ike to RN, Jan 7, PPS324.4, diary, Jan 10, PPS267.3, *Evening Star* (DC), Jan 14, PPS336(1953).5, diary, Jan 15 and 17, PPS267.3, *Los Angeles Times*, Jan 17, 1953, PPS336(1953).12 and PN to Helene, Jan 21, 1954, DR 71, RNyl.

73. Dinner, Jan 19, 1954, B 24, Vice President Nixon - Dinner file (1), WH Social Office, A.B. Talley Records, 1952–61, DDEL; *PDDE*, XVII, p. 2592; Ike to RN, Jan 9, PPS324.20, *Wash Star* (DC), Jan 20, 1954, PPS336(1954).S38, Ike to RN, Jan 7, PPS324.57, diary, Jan 18, PPS212(1955).1, *Evening Star* (DC), Jan 19, PPS336(1955).24, *Washington Post*, Jan 19, 1955, PPS 336(2955).0s3, Ike to RN, Jan 6, 1956, PPS324.80 and PN to Helene, Jan 21, 1954, DR 71, RNyl; *Newsweek*, Jan 31, 1955, p. 54.

74. *Evening Star* (DC), Sept 12, 1953, PPS336(1953).141, RNyl; Whitman to Woods, Apr 16, 1956, B 316, Hancock (1 of 3), Series 320, RNln; Whitman to Woods, July 25, 1956, PPS324.87A, RNyl; Erskine, "Dick and Pat Nixon," 32; Hoffer, *True Believer*.

75. Memo, Nov 12, 1954, PPS324.38, Ike to RN, Jan 7, PPS324.57, memo, Jan 12, 1955, PPS325(1955).1, RNyl; *PDDE*, XVII, pp. 2568, 2596, 2612, 2624, 2635, 2643, 2657, 2661,

2675, 2676, and 2697; Smith, *Meet Mister*, 166 and 201; *New York Times*, Sept 12 and 13, 1953.

76. Platter, June 19, 1954, pp. 6–7, RNyl; *New York Times Magazine*, Feb 27, 1955, pp. 9, 26, 28, and 30.

77. Ike to RN, Mar 11, PPS324.25, Sept 20, PPS324.35, Dec 29, 1954, PPS324.56, Dec 29, 1955, PPS324.79 and Jan 20, 1956, PPS324.82, RNyl; Pageant of Peace, Dec 18, 1955, B 44, F 14, Series 207, RNln.

78. Platter, Apr 5, Ike to RN, Mar 1, PPS324.24, Ike to RN, Dec 6, PPS324.53 and calendar, Dec 20, 1954, PPS212(1954).3.353, RNyl; RN to Stephens, Mar 4, B 216, DiGiorgio, R, Damon to RN, Apr 6, 1954, B 200, Damon and Reynolds to RN, Mar 18, 1955, B 638, Reynolds [2/2], Series 320, RNln; stag dinner, Apr 5 R 4 and additional list, Apr 27, 1954, R 3, Diary DDE; Chandler to Dick, June 20, 1955, B 34, F 10 [1 of 2], Series 207, RNln.

79. Slater, *Ike I Knew*, 55.

80. *PDDE*, XV, pp. 1470–1471.

81. Memo, June 16, PPS325(1953).273.1 and Ike to RN, Dec 30, 1953, PPS324.19, RNyl; *PDDE*, XIV, pp. 224–230, 266, and 792–793, and XV, pp. 793, 857, and 859; Project X, May to July 1954, DDEL; Leyerzapf to Gellman, Mar 10, 2005, Gellman mss, DDEL; Joyce to Buch, July 15, 2010, Gellman mss, DDEL; diary, Dec 30, 1953, R 2, Diary DDE.

82. Memo, June 16, 1953 PPS325(1953).273.1 and memoirs, Mar 5, 19765, RNyl; Nixon, *Six Crises*, 161; Crowley, *Nixon Off*, 14.

83. Day 1, Tape 2, 00:28:20 [RN] and Day 5, Tape 2, 00:11:49 [RN], Gannon mss; For example, see Jan 20, Feb 16, Apr 30, R 1, Dec 3, 1954, R 2, July 25, Aug 5, 1955, R 3, Feb 13, 1956, R 4, Cabinet DDE; RN OH, 23, Russell mss, WJBma.

84. Memoirs, Mar 15, 19766, RNyl; Clifford Roberts OH, 248, DDEL, and Wilton Persons OH, CCOH; RN, "Second Office," 89; Kornitzer, *Real Nixon*, 224.

85. Platter Mar 1, 1954, memo, Jan 14, PPS325(1954).3, memo, Apr 17, 1954, PPS325(1954).51 and RN remarks, June 16, 1955, PPS208(1955).12, RNyl.

86. Platter, June 19, 1954, RNyl.

87. Ibid., 5–6.

88. Platter, Aug 16, 1961, RNyl.

89. Day 3, Tape 1, 00:42:29 [RN], Day 5, Tape 3, 00:16:55 [RN] and 00:17:53 [RN], Gannon mss, WJBma.

CHAPTER 5. THE WORST KIND OF POLITICIAN

1. James Hagerty OH, I, pp. 10–11, LBJL; Kempton, "Underestimation of Eisenhower," 108, 109, and 156; Ambrose, *Eisenhower*, vol. 2, 57–58; Donovan, *Eisenhower*, 244–245.

2. Diary, Mar 13, 1953, Hughes mss, HML.

3. *Christian Science Monitor*, Aug 22, PPS6.53 and *Evening Star* (DC), Aug 22, 1952, PPS6.o.s.5A, RNyl; Cronin to de Antonio, Sept 10, 1974, CCRO 2/25, Cronin mss, FBI; Day 1, Tape 6, 00:44:54 [RN], Day 3, Tape 3, 00:16:46 [RN], 00:18:27 [RN], 00:35:00 [RN] and Day 9, Tape 1, 00:57:38 [RN], Gannon mss; Kornitzer, *Real Nixon*, 220–221; Garment, *Crazy Rhythm*, 75–76.

4. "Quizzing Nixon," Aug 29, 1952, *U.S. News & World Report*, 38–40.
5. *Whittier News*, Sept 9, 1952, PPS6.68, RNyl; de Toledano ed., *Notes*, 89.
6. News bulletin, Sept 21, PPS12.45.21, *Chicago Daily News*, Sept 22, PPS6.114 and *Ashland Daily Press* (Wis), Sept 24, 1952, PPS6.174, RNyl; *New York Times*, Apr 17, 1954.
7. Memo, Aug 30, PPS10.392A, *St. Louis Post-Dispatch*, Oct 13, PPS6.321 and Oct 24, PPS6.358, *New York Post*, Oct 24, PPS6.357 and PPS6.356 and *New York Times*, Oct 25, 1952, PPS6.359, RNyl.
8. Reeves, *Life and Times*, 459–460.
9. Memo, June 16, 1953, PPS325(1953).273.1 and memoirs, Mar 16, 1976, RNyl.
10. Chronology of McCarthy, undated, PPS325(1954).43, RNyl; Roorda, "President and His Boy," 46, Gellman mss, DDEL; Nixon, *RN*, 139.
11. Chronology of McCarthy, undated, PPS325(1954).43, appointment calendar, Mar 20, PPS212(1953).2.107, Apr 16, PPS212(1953).2.173, Apr 17, PPS212(1953).2.175, May 22, PPS212(1953).2.273, diary, Mar 8, PPS212(1953).1 and PPS212(1953).3.63, June 18 and 24, PPS212(1953).1 and PPS212(1953).3.166, diary and July 13, PPS212(1953).1, RNyl; Ewald, *Who Killed*, 168–169.
12. Eisenhower, *Mandate*, 212–213; Nixon, *RN*, 139; Dean, *Imperial Brotherhood*, 119–140; Ruddy, *Cautious Diplomat*, 109–124; Patterson, *Mr. Republican*, 595–596; Hughes, *Ordeal*, 83; Theoharis, *Seeds of Repression*, 184; Ybarra, *Washington*, 704–709; White, *Taft*, 230–241; Reeves, *Life and Times*, 468–476; Donovan, *Eisenhower*, 87–89; Bischof, "Before the Break," 107–124.
13. *PRAT*, V. 4, p. 470.
14. *PDDE*, XIV, pp. 265–266.
15. Minutes, Mar 27, 1952, R 1, Cabinet DDE; memo, June 16, 1953, PPS325(1953), 273.1, RNyl; Bischof, "Before the Break," 142–146 and 173–174.
16. Slater, *Ike I Knew*, 53.
17. Lewis Summary, Oct 26, 1955, McCarthy, J., Smith mss; *New York Times*, Apr 1, 1953; Stassen OH, 30–33, JFD OH; Barrett, *CIA & Congress*, 192–193; Ewald, *Who Killed*, 59–60; Stueck, *Korean War*, 318–319 and 321; Bischof, "Before the Break," 128–137; Bryan, "Joseph McCarthy," 94–102.
18. *Los Angeles Times*, Apr 6, PPS336(1953).63 and *Washington Post*, Apr 13, 1953, PPS13.17.32, RNyl; John Sparkman OH, 24–26, JFD OH; *PRAT*, V. 4, 470; Reeves, *Life and Times*, 487.
19. McCarthy to Ike, May 20, 1953, B 108, Brownell ½, Series 320, RNln; *Louisville Times*, May 26, 1953, PPS336(1953).80, RNyl; Donovan, *Eisenhower*, 245; *New York Times*, July 26, 1953; Olson, *Symington*, 279–280; Bryan, "McCarthy, RFK, and Greek," 94–102.
20. Diary, Feb 19, 1953, Hughes mss, HML; Schwenk-Borrell, "Selling Democracy," 31–34; Reeves, *Life and Times*, 477–485; Hixson, *Parting the Curtain*, 52; Bischof, "Before the Break," 102–104; Osgood, *Total Cold War*, 88–93; Cull, *Cold War and USIA*, 82–115.
21. Calendar, May 5, 1953, PPS212(1953).2.227, RNyl; diary, May 12, 1953, Hughes mss, HML; Merson, *Private Diary*, vi, 1–4, 11–19, and 36–86; Eisenhower, *Mandate*, 320–321; Reeves, *Life and Times*, 488–491; Hixson, *Parting the Curtain*, 53–54; Bischof, "Before the Break,"137–141 and 147–152.
22. Johnson to RN, May 20, 1953 and June 21, 1955, B 386, Johnson, RL, Series 320, RNln.

23. Diary, Apr 29, 1953, Hughes mss, HML.

24. Chronology of McCarthy, undated, PPS325(1954).43, RNyl; diary, June 22, 1953, Hughes mss, HML; Merson, *Private Diary,* 87–97, 105–115, and 132–134; Sevareid, *Small Sounds,* 102–104.

25. Chronology of McCarthy, undated, PPS325(1954).43, RNyl; USIA talk, Aug 17, 1954, B 26, F 2, Series 207, RNln; Merson, *Private Diary,* 116–127 and 135–170; *PDDE,* XVI, pp. 1754–1755.

26. *Newsweek,* July 20, 1953, V. 42, p. 29; *New York Times,* July 9, 1953; Merson, *Private Diary,* 128–132; Bischof, "Before the Break," 152–154; Silk, *Spiritual,* 89–91; Keller, "Intellectuals," 272–276.

27. Chronology of McCarthy, undated, PPS325(1954).43, RNyl; diary, July 8–9, Hughes mss, HML; *Newsweek,* July 20, 1953, V. 42, pp. 29–30; *New York Times,* July 11, 1953; Brownell, *Advising Ike,* 256; Heinemann, *Byrd,* 359; Hughes, *Ordeal,* 94–96.

28. Diary, July 15, 1953, Hughes mss, HML.

29. Calendar, Jan 8, 1953, PPS212(1953).2, RNyl; Reeves, *Life and Times,* 502.

30. Memoirs, Feb 17, 1976, RNyl; Bird, *Color of Truth,* 162–166; Nixon, *RN,* 139–140; Bischof, "Before the Break," 154–157.

31. Memo, July 9, 1953, PPS325(1953).284C and memoirs, Feb 17, 1976, RNyl; Day 3, Tape 3, 00:32:02 [RN], Gannon mss; Bird, *Color of Truth,* 166–168; Nixon, *RN,* 140; Barrett, *CIA & Congress,* 181–188.

32. Diary, July 16, 1953, Hughes mss, HML.

33. *New York Times,* July 11 and 26, 1953; Reeves, *Life and Times,* 502–503.

34. Diary, July 16, 1953, Hughes mss, HML.

35. RN to Caraway, Oct 18, 1953, B 1, Nixon Notes, Series 378, RNln.

36. *PDDE,* XIV, pp. 640–642; *Christian Science Monitor,* Nov 12, PPS299.85, *New York Times,* Nov 17, PPS299.85, *Washington Post,* Nov 17, PPS299.85 and *Newsweek,* Nov 23, 1953, PPS299.85.2(1), RNyl; *U.S. News & World Report,* Nov 27, 1953, p. 124; *Time,* Nov 23, 1953, pp. 24 and 26; DE, *Mandate,* 314–315; Gentry, *Hoover,* 428–430; Craig, *Treasonable,* 219–237; Donovan, *Eisenhower,* 177–181; Ambrose, *Eisenhower,* vol. 2, 136–139.

37. Memo, early Jan 1954, RNyl; Gentry, *Hoover,* 408–409; Dean, *Imperial Brotherhood,* 114–118; Baxter, "Eradicating This Menace," 544–548; for a positive view, Mollenhoff, *Investigative Reporting,* 207–208.

38. Memo, Jan 9, 1954, B 641, Richards, RW, Series 320, RNln; Nixon, *RN,* 140–141.

39. *New York Times,* Dec 31, 1953.

40. Theoharis ed., *Secret Files,* 262–263.

41. *Gallup Poll,* 1953, pp. 1135, 1154, 1164, and 1203–1204.

42. *San Francisco Examiner,* Sept 13 and *New York Herald Tribune,* Dec 20, 1953, Series 375, RNln; *Washington Daily News* (DC), Dec 16, 1953, PPS336(1953).192, RNyl; Adams, *Firsthand Report,* 139.

CHAPTER 6. THE COLLISION

1. Day 3, Tape 3, 00:22:41 [RN], Gannon mss, WJBma; RN OH 111, p. 26, Russell mss, WJBma.

2. Rogers call to Stevens, Sept 9 and Stevens call to Seaton, Sept 17, Transcripts, Lucas (1) and memo, Dec 10, 1953, Concurrent Memoranda, B 4, Eyes Only Series, Seaton mss, DDEL.
3. Lodge, *As It Was*, 131–137; Adams, *Firsthand Report*, 143; chronology McCarthy, undated, PPS325(1954).43, RNyl.
4. *Evening Star* (D.C.), Jan 6, 1954, PPS336(1954).S9, and chronology of McCarthy, undated, PPS325(1954).43, RNyl.
5. *Gallup Poll*, 1953, pp. 1220–1221; Rogin, *Intellectuals*, 232–233; Reeves, *Life and Times*, 534–535; Crandell, "Party Divided," 264–266; for the most sympathetic view of McCarthy, see Evans, *Blacklisted by History*, 443–598.
6. Brownell to Lodge, July 9 and Dec 4, Lodge to Brownell, July 12 and Dec 2, 1974, R 2, Lodge mss, MHS.
7. *Time*, Mar 8, 1954, p. 26.
8. *Time*, Mar 1, 1954, pp. 14–15; Adams, *Firsthand Report*, 145–146; Reeves, *Life and Times*, 542–544.
9. *Time*, Mar 1, 1954, p. 21; Adams, *Firsthand Report*, 143–145.
10. Memo, Feb 9, 1954, PPS325(1954).19, RNyl.
11. Reeves, *Life and Times*, 546–547; Clifford, *Counsel*, 289–292.
12. Platter, Feb 28 and Mar 3 and *San Diego Union*, June 4, 1954, PPS336(1954).S225, RNyl; interview with Nixon, Feb 26, 1954, B 1, Book II, pp. 277–278, Krock mss, HML; *Time*, Mar 8, 1954, p. 23; Nixon, *RN*, 141–142; Hulsey, *Dirksen*, 65–66; Ewald, *Who Killed*, 204 and 208; Adams, *Without Precedent*, 131–133.
13. Diary, Feb 25, 1954, B 2, IV, WH Years (4), Shanley mss, DDEL; chronology of McCarthy, undated, PPS325(1954).43, diary, Feb 24, PPS212(1954).1, platter, Feb 28, Mar 5 and 29, 1954, RNyl; RN to Laws, Mar 1, 1954, B 17, F 10, Series 207, RNyl; interview with Nixon, Feb 26, 1954, B1, Book II, pp. 278–279, Krock mss, HML; *Time*, Mar 8, 1954, pp. 23–24; *Newsweek*, Mar 8, 1954, pp. 20–22; Nixon, *RN*, 142; Eisenhower, *Mandate*, 322; Adams, *Firsthand Report*, 146; Reeves, *Life and Times*, 551–552; Ewald, *Who Killed*, 211 and 217; Adams, *Without Precedent*, 139; Hulsey, *Dirksen*, 67–68; Heidepriem, *Fair Chance*, 172.
14. Seaton call to Stevens, Feb 24, 1954, B 4, Eyes Only Series, Seaton mss, DDEL; Clark Clifford, Interview I, p. 10, LBJL.
15. Platter, Feb 28 and Mar 5, 1954, RNyl.
16. Telephone logs, Feb 25, PPS212(1954).4.70, memo, Feb 26, PPS325(1954).22 and platter, Mar 5, 1954, RNyl; *Hagerty Diary*, 20.
17. Diary, Feb 25, 1954, PPS212(1954).1, RNyl; diary, Feb 25, 1954, B 2, IV, WH Years (4), Shanley mss, DDEL; *Time*, Mar 8, 1954, p. 24; *Hagerty Diary*, 20; *PDDE*, XVII, p. 2599; Nixon, *RN*, 142–143; Eisenhower, *Mandate*, 324; Adams, *Firsthand Report*, 146–147; Ewald, *Who Killed*, 221–223; Reeves, *Life and Times*, 552–556.
18. *Time*, Mar 8, 1954, p. 24–25; *Evening Star* (D.C.), Feb 26, 1954, PPS336(1954).S94, RNyl.
19. Interview with Nixon, Feb 26, 1954, B 1, Book II, pp. 278–279, Krock mss, HML; Hagerty diary quoted in Ewald, *Who Killed*, 127.
20. Interview with Nixon, Feb 26, 1954, B 1, Book II, pp. 278–279, Krock mss, HML.
21. *New York Times*, Mar 1, 1954.

22. Meeting, Mar 1, 1954 R 1, Legislative DDE; diary, Mar 1, 1954, B 2, VI, WH Years (4), Shanley mss, DDEL; Adams, *Firsthand Report*, 147.

23. Memo, Mar 1, 1954, PPS325(1954).25 and memoirs, Feb 16, 1976, RNyl.

24. Platter, Mar 1, 1954, RNyl; Nixon, *RN*, 143.

25. Nixon, *RN*, 143, and Mar 2 and 29, 1954 and calendar, Mar 1, 1954, PPS212(1954).60; *New York Times*, Mar 2, 1954.

26. Platter, Mar 1, 1954, RNyl; Knowland OH, I, pp. 21–22, LBJL.

27. Calendar, Mar 2, PPS212(1954).3.61 and platter, Apr 3 [really Mar 2], 1954, RNyl; *Hagerty Diary*, 23; Nixon, *RN*, 149.

28. Platter, Mar 2, 1954, RNyl.

29. Ibid.; Ewald, *Who Killed*, 238.

30. *New York Times*, Mar 4 and 7, 1954.

31. Ibid., Mar 7, 1954.

32. *PAES*, IV, p. 317; *Time*, Mar 15, 1954, p. 20; *New York Times*, Mar 7 and 8, 1954; Broadwater, *Stevenson*, 140–142.

33. *PAES*, IV, pp. 327–333 and 335; *Time*, Mar 15, 1954, p. 20; *New York Times*, Mar 7, 1954; Nixon, *RN*, 144.

34. *PPA* 1954, pp. 300–301.

35. *New York Times*, Mar 8, 1954; Reeves, *Life and Times*, 562.

36. Platter, Mar 8, 1954, RNyl; *Time*, Mar 22, 1954; Ewald, *Who Killed*, 246–247.

37. Memo, Mar 8, 1954, PPS325(1954).34, RNyl.

38. Telephone logs, Mar 8, 1954, R 3, Diary DDE; platter, Mar 8, 1954, RNyl; Nixon, *RN*, 144–145.

39. Platter, Mar 8, 1954, RNyl.

40. Platter, Mar 8 and *San Diego Evening Tribune*, Mar 9, 1954, PPS336(1954).S106, RNyl; *Evening Bulletin* (Phila), Mar 9, 1954, B 18, F 7, Series 207, RNln; Day 3, Tape 3, 00:24:49 [RN], Gannon mss, WJBma.

41. RN to Jackson to RN, Mar 9, 1954, B 373, Jackson, CD, Series 320, RNln.

42. *PDDE*, XV, pp. 937–940.

43. *PPA* 1954, pp. 299–300.

44. Platter, Mar 11, 1954, RNyl.

45. *PDDE*, XV, pp. 948–949.

46. Memo, Mar 11, B 18, F 10, Series 207 and Klein to RN, Mar 11, 1954, B 418, Klein (3 of 3), Series 320, RNln.

47. Reeves, *Life and Times*, 566–577 and 592–593; *Time*, Mar 22, 1954, pp. 23–27.

48. Platter, Mar 12, 1954, RNyl; Ewald, *Who Killed*, 260–261; Nixon, *RN*, 145.

49. Platter, Mar 12, 1954, RNyl; meeting, Mar 12, 1954 R 1, Cabinet DDE.

50. Platter, Mar 12, 1954, RNyl; Nixon, *RN*, 145–146.

51. *Evening Star* (DC), Mar 16, 1954, PPS336(1954).S138, RNyl; *New York Times*, Mar 14, 1954; Friel, "Influence of Television," 179.

52. *New York Times*, Mar 14, 1954; *Time*, Mar 22, 1954, pp. 28; Friel, "Influence of Television," 180–181; Nixon, *RN*, 146; Ewald, *Who Killed*, 269–271.

53. Platter, Mar 13, 1954 and *Los Angeles Examiner*, Mar 14, 1954, PPS336(1954).o.s.16, RNyl; Nixon, *RN*, 146–147.

54. *New York Herald Tribune,* Mar 14, PPS336(1954).o.s.20, *New York Journal American,* Mar 15, PPS336(1954).S128, *Los Angeles Times,* Mar 15, PPS336(1954).S129, and *New York Post,* Mar 15, 1954, PPS336(1954).S133, RNyl; Bewley to RN, Mar 17, B 18, F 11, Series 207 and RN to Murph, Apr 7, 1954, B 546, Murphy, Ge, Series 320, RNln; Martin, *Stevenson and the World,* 108–109.

55. *New York Times,* Mar 14, 1954; Reeves, *Life and Times,* 578; Stone, *Haunted Fifties,* 65–67.

56. Diary, Mar 15, 25 and 29 and platter Mar 13, 1954, RNyl; Reeves, *Life and Times,* 578–586; Nixon, *RN,* 147.

57. Platter, Mar 22, 1954, RNyl; Nixon, *RN,* 147; Ewald, *Who Killed,* 290; Reeves, *Life and Times,* 586.

58. Platter, Mar 22, 1954, RNyl; Persons to RN, Aug 24, 1954, B 590, Persons, Series 320, RNln.

59. Platter, Mar 22, 1954, RNyl.

60. Memo, Mar 24, 1954, PPS325(1954).234, RNyl.

61. Platter, Mar 22 and 25, 1954, RNyl.

62. Ibid., Mar 26, 1954.

63. RN to McDowell, Mar 23, B 496, McDowell, Jo and RN to Hamilton, Mar 23, 1954, B 315, Hamilton, R, Series 320, RNln.

64. *PDDE,* XV, p. 1014.

65. *Gallup Poll,* 1954, pp. 1225, 1229, 1231–1232, 1234–1235, 1241–1242, 1246–1247, 1254–1255, 1263, 1271–1272, 1278–1280, and 1289–1290; *Sunday Register,* June 27, 1954, B 186, Cowles, G., Series 320, RNln; Nixon, *RN,* 147; Fried, *Men,* 279–290; Crosby, *God, Church, and Flag,* 174–192.

66. Platter, Apr 2, 1954, RNyl; Potter, *Days of Shame,* 13–23.

67. Platter, Apr 30, 1954, RNyl; *Ike's Letters,* 126; Nixon, *RN,* 147–148.

68. Platter, June 10, 1954, RNyl; *PDDE,* XV, pp. 1064–1065; Schlesinger, *Imperial Presidency,* 156.

69. Nichols to Tolson, May 21, 1954, R 4, Nichols, *Official and Confidential File.*

70. Diary, Apr 1, 5, 12 and 27, PPS212(1954).1, *Los Angeles Times,* May 2, PPS336(1954).S196, diary, May 4, 7, 10, 18, 24, *Evening Star* (D.C.), PPS336(1954).S229 and platter, June 10, 1954, RNyl; Smith to RN, May 3, 1954, B 705, Smith, H, Series 320, RNln; Ewald, *Who Killed,* 361.

71. *Los Angeles Herald Express,* May 24, PPS336(1954).S218, *Los Angeles Times,* May 27, PPS336(1954).S218 and platter, June 10, 1954, RNyl.

72. Reeves, *Life and Times,* 588–589 and 628–631; Sevareid, *Small Sounds,* 215–218 and see 218–220; Olson, *Symington,* 289–294.

73. *PPA* 1954, p. 301; *Time,* Mar 22, 1954, p. 22; Reeves, *Life and Times,* 562–564.

74. Lewis summary, Oct 26, 1955, McCarthy, J, M. Smith mss, MCSL; chronology of McCarthy, undated, PPS325(1954).43, RNyl; Nixon, *RN,* 145; Reeves, *Life and Times,* 633–634 and 642–644.

75. *San Diego Union,* Aug 2, PPS336(1954).S292 and *Evening Star* (DC), Aug 5, 1954, PPS336(1954).S301, RNyl; RN to MacDuff, Aug 2, 1954, B 469, MacDuff, G, Series 320, RNln; *New York Times,* Aug 6, 1954; Nixon, *RN,* 145.

76. *Newsweek*, Aug 16, 1954, pp. 20–21; *Tucson Daily Citizen*, Sept 9, 1954, PPS336(1954). S333, RNyl; Reeves, *Life and Times*, 652.

77. Chronology of McCarthy, undated, PPS325(1954).43, *New York Herald Tribune*, Sept 29, 1954, PPS336(1954).S400, RNyl; *New York Times*, Sept 28 and 29, 1954; Nixon, *RN*, 146; Fried, *Men*, 291–309; Reeves, *Life and Times*, 652–657.

78. Palmer to RN, Nov 9, B 577, Palmer (2 of 2) and RN to Dinkelspiel, Nov 19, 1954, B 216, Dinkelspiel 2/2, Series 320, RNln; Tipton to RN, Nov 11, 1954, PPS19.227.1, RNyl; *Newsweek*, Nov 8, 1954; Reeves, *Life and Times*, 657–658.

79. Nixon, *RN*, 146; Hulsey, *Dirksen*, 73–80; Saltonstall, *Salty*, 171–173; Goldberg, *Goldwater*, 105–108; Sevareid, *Small Sounds*, 252–257; Crosby, *God, Church, and Flag*, 216; Fried, *Men*, 309; Eisenhower, *Mandate*, 329–331; Reeves, *Life and Times*, 658–663.

80. *PDDE*, XV, pp. 1428–1430.

81. *Hagerty Diary*, 127–129.

82. Slater, *Ike I Knew*, 88; Ewald, *Who Killed*, 382–384.

83. RN to McCarthy, Dec 8, 1954, B 490, McCarthy, NS, Series 320, RNln.

84. RN to Longworth, Dec 28, 1954, B 460, Longworth, A, Series 320, RNln; *Los Angeles Times*, Dec 9, 1954; also see Fried, *Men*, 312–315.

85. RN to Binkley, Dec 7, 1954, B 82, Binkley, Series 320, RNln.

86. RN press conf, Sept 5, 1955, B 36, F 3, Series 207, RNln.

87. *Whittier News*, Nov 16, 1955, PPS336(1955).581 and *Chicago American*, Aug 22, 1956, PPS336(1956).347, RNyl; ticker, Nov 15, 1955, radio reports, Aug 5, RN to McCarthy, Aug 6, B 490, McCarthy, J and Jacobs to Woods, Aug 7, 1956, B 376, Jacobs 1957 [2/3], Series 320, RNln.

88. *Minneapolis Star*, Oct 2, King to Mahon, Oct 22, B 490, McCarthy, J and King to Efnor, Oct 17, 1956, B 236, Efnor, Series 320, RNln.

89. Interview with Herbert Klein, Oct 5, 2007.

90. Reeves, *Life and Times*, 673–674.

91. *New York Times*, May 3, 1957; RN statement, May 2, 1957, B 490, McCarthy, J, Series 320, RNyl; *Human Events*, May 11, 1957, p. 1.

92. Schedule, May 6, 1957, PPS212(1957).3.52, RNyl; Raffalovich to RN, May 6, RN to Raffalovich, June 10, B 618, Raffalovich, Mrs. McCarthy to RN, June 21, B 490, McCarthy, J. and Murphy to RN, May 7, B 541, Murphy, TJ, Series 320, RNln; Reeves, *Life and Times*, 671–674.

93. RN OH 111, Russell mss, WJBma.

94. *Washington Post*, Nov 6, 1954, PPS336(1954).S636, RNyl; memo, Nov 10, 1958, B 474, Mandel, Series 320, RNyl; Donaldson, *First Modern Campaign*, 8; Brodie, *Richard Nixon*, 290–305; Loewenberg, "Nixon, Hitler, and Power," 27–46.

CHAPTER 7. TRUMAN, EISENHOWER, NIXON, AND CIVIL RIGHTS

1. Gardner, *Harry Truman*, 17 and 218–219; Hechler, "Truman Laid the Foundation," 52; Shogun, *Los Angeles Times*, Feb 13, 2013, and *Harry Truman and the Struggle*, 145–178; Berman, *Politics of Civil Rights*; McCoy and Ruetten, *Quest and Response*; Geselbracht

ed., *Civil Rights Legacy*; Hamby, "Clash of Perspectives," 136–139; Littlejohn and Ford, "Truman and Civil Rights," 287–302.

2. Geselbracht ed., *Civil Rights Legacy*.

3. Ibid.; Berman, *Politics of Civil Rights*; McCoy and Ruetten, *Quest and Response*; Gardner, *Harry Truman*, 14–64 and 198–209.

4. Geselbracht ed., *Civil Rights Legacy*, 201; Yon and Lansford, "Political Pragmatism," 103–114.

5. Thurber, *Republicans and Race*, 5–33; Berman, *Politics of Civil Rights*; McCoy and Ruetten, *Quest and Response*.

6. Anderson, "Clutching at Civil Rights Straws," 31 and 46; Bernstein, "Ambiguous Legacy," 270–304; Sitkoff, "Years of the Locust," 100–104.

7. Mayer, "Eisenhower's Conditional Crusade," 200–202; Ferrell ed., *Truman in the White House*, 89.

8. White to Niles, Dec 15, 1948, David Niles, B 27, F Civil Rights/Negro Affairs, July 1947–48, Truman mss, HSTL; Dalfiume, "Forgotten Years," 104–105; Berg, "The Ticket," 130 and 191; Frymer, *Uneasy Alliances*, 93–96; Weiss, *Farewell to the Party*, 120–135; Ashmore, *Civil Rights*, 94–96.

9. Roberts and Klibanoff, *Race Beat*, 76 and 12–155; *Los Angeles Sentinel*, Nov 6, 1952.

10. U.S. Dept of Commerce, *Census of Population: 1960*, V. 1, P 1, pp. 1 and,150–153; Moon to White, Aug 20, 1952, B 3338, F NACCP, 1952, Anna Eleanor Roosevelt Correspondence, E. Roosevelt mss, FDRL; Wallace, "Residential," Table 2, p. 6, Table 3, p. 17; Vickery, *Economics*, 18,41 and 135–136; Danielson, *Politics*, 1–26; Campbell et al., *American Voter*, 451–452; Groh, *Black*, 60, 113–114 and 249; Johnson and Campbell, *Black Migration*, 124–151; Bartley, *Rise of Massive Resistance*, 7–8; Gregory, *Southern Diaspora*, 280 and 283; Gosnell and Martin, "Negro," 415; *Cleveland Call and Post*, Nov 22, 1952, p. 4.

11. Hamilton, *Powell*, 1; Clay, *Just Permanent*, 77–78; Lemann, *Promised Land*, 74.

12. Berg, "The Ticket," 168–172; Meier, *CORE*, 63–71.

13. Moon, *Balance of Power*, 218; Berg, "The Ticket," 191.

14. Black and Black, *Rise of Southern*, 42–57 and 207.

15. *Jet*, July 10, pp. 3–4, July 17, pp. 3–4 and July 24, 1952, pp. 3–5.

16. Ibid., July 24, p. 6, July 31, pp. 3–4, Aug 7, pp. 3–4 and Aug 14, 1952, pp. 3–4; Reichard, "Democrats, Civil Rights," 59–60.

17. U.S. Senate, *Universal Military Training*, 996; Mershon and Schlossman, *Foxholes & Color Lines*, 266–267; Nichols, *Matter of Justice*, 8–13; Mayer, "Kansan Looks at Brown," 57–58.

18. Moaney to Stephens, Oct 10, 1960, attachment, B 986, F 1940 Moaney, John W, Personnel File, Central File, Eisenhower mss, DDEL; *PDDE*, II, pp. 719 and 996–997; Eisenhower, *Mandate*, 265–266; John Eisenhower OH, 35–38, Eisenhower National Historic Site, Gettysburg, Pa; "Eisenhower Home Guide," National Park Service, Gellman mss, DDEL.

19. Hegeman to Gellman, email, June 24, 2014, Gellman mss, DDEL; Eisenhower, *Mandate*, 265–266, 268 and 570; S. Eisenhower, *Mrs. Ike*, 248.

20. S. Eisenhower, *Mrs. Ike*, 268; Eisenhower, *Waging Peace*, 255, 419–420, and 489; *PDDE*, XXI, pp. 2226–2227; Susan Eisenhower interview, Jan 4, 2008.

21. Eisenhower, *At Ease*, 69, 323, and 345; S. Eisenhower, *Mrs. Ike*, 315.

22. Dolores Moaney OH (1996), pp. 8, 18, and 32–33 and OH supplement (2013), Eisenhower National Historic Site, Gettysburg, Pa.

23. Mayer, *Eisenhower Years*; Nichols, *Matter of Justice*; Thurber, *Republicans and Race*; Beschloss, "Gang That Always Liked Ike," *New York Times*, Nov 16, 2014.

24. Email, Nichter to Gellman, Jan 17, 2013, Gellman mss, DDEL.

25. Text of interview, May 1958, B 47, Alsop mss, LOC; Newsom OH 919, p. 17 and Nichols OH 923, pp. 20–21, CSUF; Day 1, Tape 2, 00:50:36 [RN], Feb 9, 1983, Gannon mss, WJBma; Alsop, *Nixon and Rockefeller*, 199; Kornitzer, *Real Nixon*, 239 and 243.

26. Whittier College Graduates, 1931–1937, Gellman mss, DDEL; *Acropolis* 1932 (Whittier College yearbook), pp. 31, 64–65, and 74; Kotlowski, *Nixon's Civil Rights*, 9.

27. Memo, Sept 17, 1956 B 285, George, Na and memo, June 16, 1958, B 259, Finch 1958, Series 320, RNln; Nathaniel George OH 862, pp. 14–16, and Dean Triggs and Robert Gibbs OH 971, p. 93, CSUF.

28. *Pigskin Review*, Sept 23, 1933, PPC4, RNyl; Day 1, Tape 2, 01:15:34 and 01:15:34 [RN], Feb 9, 1983, Gannon mss, WJBma; Triggs and Gibbs OH 971, pp. 45 and 92 and Warner OH 978, pp. 13 and 23, CSUF; Hubert Perry interview, Feb 23, 2000; Clint Harris interview, Dec 7, 1999.

29. Brock to RN, Aug 1, 1952, B 104, Brock, Wm, Series 320, RNln.

30. Ibid., Dec 5, 1952, RN to Brock, Mar 9, 1953, memo, Feb 2, Wheeler to RN, Apr 22, 1954, McCarthy to King, July 31, 1957, Wheeler to RN, Mar 3, 1958, B 108, Brock, Wm, Series 320, RNln.

31. *Jet*, Aug 21, pp. 3–4, Aug 28, pp. 3–4 and 6–7, Sept 4, pp. 3–4, Sept 11, pp. 3–6, Sept 18, pp. 3–5, Sept 25, p. 5, Oct 2, pp. 4–5, Oct 16, pp. 4–5, Oct 23, pp. 4–5, Oct 30, pp. 3–4 and Nov 6, 1952, p. 4; *Chicago Defender*, Nov 1, 1952, p. 1.

32. *Jet*, Aug 21, pp. 3–4, Aug 28, pp. 3–4, Aug 28, pp. 6–7, Sept 4, pp. 4–5, Sept 11, pp. 3–5 and 8–9, Sept 18, pp. 3–4, Sept 25, pp. 4 and 6–7, Oct 2, pp. 3–4, Oct 16, pp. 3–4, Oct 23, pp. 3–4 and 6–7, Oct 30, pp. 4–5 and Nov 6, 1952, pp. 3–5; *Journal and Guide* (Va), Nov 1, 1952, pp. 1–2; *Washington Post*, PPS6.80, Sept 18, 1952, RNyl.

33. Hoffman to RN, Aug 20, 1952, Chronological File 1952–Aug, Hoffman mss, HSTL; *U.S. News & World Report*, Aug 29, 1952, p. 40.

34. McWhorter to Lane, Sept 14, 1960, B 435, Lane, JI, Series 320, RNln; RN to Edelsberg, Oct 11, 1956, B 50, F 5, William Rogers mss, DDEL; *Jet*, Sept 25, pp. 3 and Oct 9, 1952, p. 4–5.

35. Bartley and Graham, *Southern Politics*, 82; Harvard ed., *Changing Politics*, 681 and 711; Seagull, *Southern Republicanism*, 59–60; Bartley, *Rise of Massive Resistance*, 47; Thurber, *Republicans and Race*, 36–47.

36. *Cleveland Call and Post*, Nov 8, 1952; *Chicago Defender*, Nov 15, 1952; *Washington Afro-American*, Nov 15, 1952.

37. Howard to RN, Nov 17, 1952, B 762, Tremaine, Series 320, RNln.

38. *Chicago Defender*, Nov 22, 1952; *New York Times*, Dec 23, 1952; *Jet*, Nov 27 and Dec 11, 1952, Jan 1, 8 and Feb 5, 1953.

39. *Jet*, Jan 15, 22, pp. 5, 29, pp. 3–5 and Feb 5, 1953; *PRAT*, V. 4, p. 455; Bowen, "Fight for the Right," 362; Reichard, "Democrats, Civil Rights," 61.
40. Negro Vote, Aug 1957, B 554, F Negro V, Series 320, RNln; 1960 Elections, Apr 1961, B 9 and the 1952 Elections, Oct 1953, PPS15.3, RNyl; the same is found in Moon to Friend, Dec 29, 1952, B 3499, F Walter White, 1953–1956, E. Roosevelt mss, FDRL; Lubell, "Future of the Negro Voter," 408–417; e-mail, Re: Presidential elections from 1952–1960, June 19 and July 10, 2002, Gellman mss, DDEL.
41. Moon to Friend, Nov 15, 1954, Group III, B A246, General Office File, Presidential Campaign of 1960, Gen 1960, Sept–Dec, NAACP.
42. Bracey and Meier, Summer 1957 Yearbook, R 1, NAACP; Lamis, *Two-Party*, 10–11, 44, and 85; Bartley and Graham, *Southern Elections*, 3, 6, 24–26, 29, 31, 59, 62, 86, 90, 93, 112, 121, 141, 169, 201, 217, 241, 244, 327, 363, and 396; Harvard ed., *Changing Politics*, 46–54, 82, 111, 125, 213–214, 269, 430, 432, 549, 551, 553–554, 601, 607, and 720; Horton and Smith eds., *Statistical*, 479; Scammon compiler, *American at the Polls*, 450; Reichley, *States in Crisis*, 114–115; Lieberson, *A Piece*, 53; Berg, "The Ticket," 149–152; Banitch, "Ultraconservative," 24; Lawson, *Running for Freedom*, 47 and 81; Matthews and Prothro, "Political Factors," 355 and 367; Dobbs, *Yellow Dogs*, 91–96; Hamilton, *Powell*, 275; Glaser, *Race, Campaign*, 5–10; Moon, "Negro Vote in the Presidential Election," 219–224 and 226–228; Moon, "Election Post–Mortem," 616; *Pittsburgh Press*, Nov 15, 1952; *Chicago Defender*, Nov 15, 1952; *New York Amsterdam News*, Nov 15, 1952; *Jet*, Nov 20, 1952, pp. 6–7.
43. Caro, *Master of the Senate*, 775–776, erroneously stated that Stevenson received 68 percent of the black vote.

CHAPTER 8. EISENHOWER AND CIVIL RIGHTS

1. PBS, *Eyes on the Prize*, 1986; Huggins, "Eisenhower and Civil Rights," 114–116; Garrow, *Bearing*, 11–82; Whitfield, *Death in the Delta*, 15–69; Bartley, *Rise of Massive Resistance*, 82.
2. Duram, *A Moderate Among Extremists*; Burk, *Eisenhower Administration*; Ambrose, *Eisenhower*, vol. 2, 190.
3. Shogan, *Harry Truman*, 1–182.
4. Ibid., 183 and 189.
5. Mayer, "With Much Deliberation," 46; Johnson, "Vinson Court," 220–227.
6. Mayer, *Eisenhower Years*; Nichols, *Matter of Justice*; Thurber, *Republicans and Race*.
7. *Gallup Poll*, Two, 1118–1119.
8. Candee ed., *Current Biography 1954*, pp. 648–649; *Time*, Mar 14, 1954, p. 21.
9. *Chicago Defender*, Sept 26, 1953, Mar 20, Apr 3, and June 19, Aug 28, 1954; Nichols, *Matter of Justice*, 25–26; Donovan, *Eisenhower*, 160.
10. *Chicago Defender*, Dec 27, 1958 and Jan 20, 1959.
11. *Journal and Guide* (Va), Nov 15, 1952, *Jet*, Jan 1, 1953, pp. 8–9; Schlundt, "Civil Rights," 83; Huggins, "Eisenhower and Civil Rights," 28–32; Laird ed., *Republican*, 234; Nichols, *Matter of Justice*, 39–40.
12. *Jet*, Feb 26, 1953, p. 4 and July 16, 1959, p. 6.

13. *Jet*, May 14, 1959, p. 16; Morrow, *40 Years*, 69–111 and 210–213; Morrow, *Way Down*, 121; Katz, "Morrow and Civil Rights," 133–136.

14. *Los Angeles Sentinel*, Nov 20, 1952; *Chicago Defender*, Jan 30, 1968; Salzman et al. eds., *Encyclopedia of African-American Culture*, V. 5, p. 2784; Washington, "Freedom's Fight," 359–366; Sloane to Nichols, Nov 18, 2006 e-mail, Gellman mss, DDEL.

15. Rabb speech, Oct 12, 1955, PPS324(1955)278, RNyl; *Evening Star* (DC), May 2, 1958; *PDDE*, XVI, p. 1690; J. Eisenhower, *Strictly Personal*, 172; Donovan, *Eisenhower*, 156–159; Maxwell Rabb interview, Jan 8, 2002.

16. Meeting, Jan 26, 1953, R 1, Legislative DDE; *Jet*, Feb 5, 12, 19 and Mar 26, 1953; Bowen, "Fight for the Right," 362; Green, *Secret City*, 337; Lewis, *District*, 80; Nichols, *Matter of Justice*, 26–34; Nichols, "Showpiece of Our Nation," 47–53; Huggins, "Eisenhower and Civil Rights," 5–18; Derthick, *City Politics*, 120.

17. *Jet*, Apr 2, pp. 3–4, Apr 9, pp. 3–4, and May 7, 1953, pp. 3; Huggins, "Eisenhower and Civil Rights," 19–24; Mayer, "Eisenhower's," 40–57; Mershon and Schlossman, *Foxholes & Color Lines*, 267–272; Nichols, *Matter of Justice*, 42–50; MacGregor, *Integration of Armed Forces*, 473–500 and 609–623; Dalfiume, *Desegregation of U.S. Armed Forces*, 219.

18. Lodge to DE, Dec 4, 1952 and Lodge to DE, Aug 21, 1953, R 28, Lodge mss, MHS.

19. Lodge to DE, Dec 4, Mitchell to Palmer, Dec 4, 1952, Mitchell to Lodge, Aug 18 and Lodge to DE, Aug 21, 1953, R 28, Lodge mss, MHS.

20. *PPA* 1953, p. 205; memo for Whitman, Aug 12, 1953, B 28, RN (5), Administrative Series, DDEL; Huggins, "Eisenhower and Civil Rights," 77; Laird ed., *Republican*, 234.

21. Diary, Mar 30, 1953, B 1, WH Days (3), Shanley mss, DDEL; *Gettysburg Times*, July 6, 1953, B 11, F 14, Series 207, RNyl; Maxwell Rabb interview, Jan 8, 2002.; memo, Aug 15, 1953, PPS307.5, RNyl; Ike to RN, Aug 13, 1953, B 13, F 7, Series 207 and B 237, Eisenhower 2/2, Series 320, RNln; Ike to RN, Aug 15, 1953, diary, R 2, DDE; *PDDE*, XVI, pp. 476; *Chicago Defender*, Sept 24, 1953.

22. *PDDE*, XIV, pp. 477; *Chicago Defender*, Sept 5, 1953; Kornitzer, *Real Nixon*, 217; Donovan, *Eisenhower*, 159–160; Thurber, "Racial Liberalism, Affirmative Action," 446–450; Lawrence Walsh interview, Dec 1, 2005.

23. *Cincinnati Enquirer*, Aug 16, PPS307.18.6 and *Washington Post*, PPS336(1953),122, RNyl; *PDDE*, XVII, p. 2566; *New York Times*, Aug 16 and 20, 1953; minutes, Sept 14, 1953, PPS307.4.2, RNyl.

24. Ike to Byrnes, Aug 14, PPS307.11, Byrnes to Ike, Aug 27, PPS307.14 and diary, Sept 14, 1953, PPS212 (1953). 1, RNyl; Byrnes to Ike, Aug 27, R 2 and memo of telephone calls, Sept 3, 1953, R 3, Diary DDE; *PDDE*, XIV, pp. 498–499; *New York Times*, Sept 14, 1953; *Chicago Defender*, Sept 26, 1953; Robertson, *Sly and Able*, 492–512; Maravillas, "Nixon," 58–71.

25. Ladd to May, Nov 10, 1953, B 484, May, E, Series 320, RNln; memoirs, Mar 18 and 19, 1976, RNyl; Kotlowski, "Richard Nixon and the Origins," 524–526; Marable, *Race, Reform*, 50–55; Frymer, *Black and Blue*.

26. *Chicago Defender*, Sept 12, 1953.

27. Washington to Chotiner, Nov 12, 1952, PPS300.217, calendar, Mar 20, 1954, PPS212(1954).2.83, RNyl; Washington, "Freedom's Fight," 359–366; calendar, Jan 13,

1954, PPS212(1954).2.19, RNyl; memo, Feb 11, B 801, Washington, V, Series 320, memo, Nov 3 and 4, *Washington Post*, Nov 12, 1955, B 42, F 15, B 58, F 5, Series 207, RNln.

28. Rabb to Herter, Dec 23, 1953, Rabb to Granger, Jan 2 and 7 and Granger to Woods, Jan 12, 1954, B 29 (2) #1 and memo, July 26, Jernagin to RN, Aug 13, Jernagin to Rabb, Aug 14, memo to Rabb, Aug 24, 1954, B 14 (2), DDE; memo, Aug 6, 1954, B 25, F 8, Series 207, RNln; Kornitzer, *Real Nixon*, 216 and 225–225.

29. RN speech, Jan 31, 1954, P 18, Nixon, Richard M 1952–55, p. 18, R 19, NAACP mss, LOC.

30. Andrew Goodpaster interview, Jan 8, 2002; the best study on Eisenhower and civil rights is Nichols, *Matter of Justice*; Lawson, *Running for Freedom*, 39; Huggins, "Eisenhower and Civil Rights," 47–58; Mayer, "Eisenhower's Conditional Crusade," 189–225.

31. King, *Why We Can't*, 82–83.

32. Quoted in Nichols, *Matter of Justice*, 50.

33. Kluger, *Simple Justice*, 983–991; Nichols, *Matter of Justice*, 51–55 and 58–74.

34. Diary, May 26, 1954, V. II, H-198, R IV, Koo mss, LOC.

35. Kluger, *Simple Justice*, 943–952 and 976–977; Thurber, *Republicans and Race*, 51–64; Mayer, "A Kansan Looks at Brown," 58–61.

36. *Chicago Defender*, Nov 7, 1953, PPS307.18.27 and *New York Times*, Sept 3, 1955, PPS336(1955).263, RNyl; *PDDE*, XIV, pp. 571 and XVI, pp. 1752–1753; Huggins, "Eisenhower and Civil Rights," 123; Stern, "Presidential Strategies," 778–779; Peltason, 58 *Lonely Men*, 5–9 and 28–29; Kutler, "Eisenhower, the Judiciary," 100; Hamilton, *Powell*, 199–225; Stebenne, *Modern Republican*, 169.

37. *New York Times*, Sept 12 and 30, 1956.

38. Emanuel, *Tuttle*, 94–99, 109–114, and 153–167; Mayer, "Kansan Looks at Brown," 65–66.

39. Memoirs, Mar 16, 1976, *New York Times*, Oct 1, 1954, PPS18.1278(1), RNyl; *Evening Star* (DC), May 11, 1955, B 30, F 3, Series 207, Moon to RN, Oct 1, B 546, NAACP (5 of 5) and RN to Kihss, Nov 13, 1954, B 410, Kihss, Series 320, RNln; Kee, "Brown Decision," 205–243.

40. Memo, Feb 2 and 3, B 508, Memo BK, Series 320, King to RN, Feb 3, 1955, B 27, F 5, Series 207, RNln; *Evening Star* (DC), Feb 4, 1955, PPS336(1955).40, RNyl.

41. Schedule, June 24, B 33, F 8 and Woods to Adams, July 22, 1955, B 33, F 7 (1 of 2), Series 207, RNln; *Negro Statesman*, Feb 1, 1956, B 909, 124–A 1956, General File, DDEL; *New York Times*, June 25, 1955, *New York Herald Tribune*, June 25, 1955, PPS307.76A, RNyl; RN excerpts, June 25 and *New Jersey Herald News*, July 2, 1955, B 33, F 7 (2 of 2), Series 207, RNln.

42. RN speech, June 26, 1955, P 18, Nixon, Richard M, pp. 18, R. 19, NAACP; schedule, June 26, 1955, and RN excerpts, B 34, F 1, RNln; excerpts, June 26, 1955, PPS29.31, RNyl; *New York Times*, June 27, 1955.

43. *New York Times*, June 27, 1955; Wilkins, *Standing Fast*, 332–333.

44. *New York Amsterdam News*, July 2, 1955, PPS307.76A, RNyl; *St. Louis American*, July 7, B 34, F 1, Series 207 and *Afro-American*, July 9, 1955, B 338, Hicks, JL, RNln.

45. *White Sentinel*, June, *Richmond News Leader* (Va), July 1, B 34, F 1 and Petty to RN, July 2, 1955, B 34, F 2 [1 of 2], Series 207, RNln.

46. Mann to RN, Jan 1, 1954, B 475, Mann, E, Series 320 and RN to Freudenheim, Nov 13, 1955, B 40, F 7 [1 of 2], Series 207, RNln; *Business Week,* Jan 30, PPS296(1954).3, PCGC, Sept, PPS307.19(1), *New York Herald Tribune,* Sept 7, PPS336(1954).S332, press release, Sept 7, PPS307.26, *U.S. News & World Report,* Dec 17, 1954, PPS307.29, press release, Jan 25, PPS307.55 and *Afro-American,* Oct 1, PPS307.76A, PCGC, Dec 1955, PPS307.54, RNyl; Thurber, "Racial Liberalism, Affirmative Action," 450–458; Thurber, *Republicans and Race,* 49–54.

47. Schedule, Mar 15, 1955, B 27, F 11, Series 207, RNln; summary, Mar 15, 1955, PPS307.56, RNyl; Lichtenstein, *Most Dangerous,* 370–380.

48. RN remarks, May 28, *Sunday Star* (DC), May 29, 1955, B 30, F 15, Series 207, RNln; also RN remarks, May 28, 1955, PPS208(1955).8, RNyl.

49. Minutes, Sept 14, RN to Lodge, Oct 1, memo by RN, Oct 24, B 40, F 7 [2 of 2], press release, Oct 23, B 40, F 7 [1 of 2], Series 207, memo, Oct 24, 1955, B 508, Memo BK, Series 320, RNln; *New York Times,* Aug 28, PPS307.76A, *Evening Star* (DC), Oct 3, PPS307.76A, Ike to RN, Oct 21, PPS324.72, Ike to RN, Oct 25, 1955, PPS324.73, RNyl; press conf, Oct 25, *New York Journal American,* Oct 29, 1955, B 40, F 7 [2 of 2], Series 207, RNln; transcript, Oct 25, PPS307.70, clipping, Oct 25, PPS307.75C, *Chicago Daily News,* Oct 26, PPS307.75A and PPS307.93A, *New York Herald Tribune,* Oct 26, 1955, PPS307.75B, RNyl.

50. Mitchell to RN, Dec 14, 1955, PPS307.71, King to J. Roosevelt, Jan 4, PPS307.77, J. Roosevelt to King, Jan 6, PPS307.78, Mitchell to RN, PPS307.82 and third annual report 1956, PPS307.76.1, RNyl; *Jet,* Aug 16, 1956, p. 4.

51. Memo, Feb 3, 1955, B 508, Memo BK, memo, Nov 4, 1957, B 521, Mitchell, CD, Series 320 and King to RN, Feb 3, 1955, B 27, F 5, Series 207, RNln; *Jet,* June 4, 1959, p. 6; *Chicago Defender,* Sept 26, 1953; Mitchell, "Moods and Changes," 53–63; Watson, *Lion in the Lobby,* 229–231.

52. *PDDE,* XVI, pp. 2086–2088; Martin, *With God,* 43; Martin, *Prophet,* 201–202; Chappell, *A Stone,* 140–144; Gibbs and Duffy, *Preacher and the Presidents,* 68–69; Nichols, *Matter of Justice,* 129; Huggins, "Eisenhower's," 59–67; Paddon, "Modern Mordecai," 131–136; Hopkins, "Billy Graham," 157–163.

53. *Washington Post,* July 13, 1956, PPS336(1956).218, RNyl; Lawson and Payne, *Debating the Civil Rights,* 59–62; Longley, *Gore,* 1–2 and 123–124; Badger, "Southerners Who Refused," 517–34 and "Southern Manifesto," 77–94.

54. Graham to RN, June 4, B 299, Graham (3 of 3), Series 320, RN to Broyhill, Aug 2, Schedule, Aug 4 and *Asheville Citizen* (N.C.), Aug 6, 1956, B 56, F 16, Series 207, RNln; Martin, *With God,* 41–42.

55. Schedule, RN speech and *Times-Union* (Fla), Aug 5, 1956, B 56, F 16, Series 207, RNln; *Pacific Stars & Stripes,* Aug 6, 1956, PPS336(1956).257, RNyl; *New York Times,* Aug 6, 1956; Paddon, "Modern Mordecai," 159–164; Martin, *Prophet,* 208–209; *Charlotte Observer* (N.C.), Aug 6, *Asheville Citizen* (N.C.), Aug 6, RN to Graham, Aug 16, 1956, B 56, F 16, Series 207, RNln.

56. Breard to RN, Aug 7 and Armstrong to RN, Aug 9, 1956, B 56, F 16, Series 207, RNln.

57. *New York Times,* Feb 7, 1956; Wilkins to Stevenson, Feb 9, B 3461, F NAACP, 1954–56 and ER to Wilkins, Feb 15, 1956, B 3497, F Wilkins, Roy, general correspondence, 1953–56, E. Roosevelt mss, FDRL; Martin, *Civil Rights and the Crisis,* 117–154; Ashmore,

Civil Rights, 118–123; Pipes, *Ike's Final Battle,* 193–198; Schlesinger and Schlesinger eds., *Journals,* 41–42; Emanuel, *Tuttle,* 171; Manning, *Dawson,* 173–175.

58. *Christian Science Monitor,* July 21, 1956, PPS336(1956)230, RNyl; *New York Times,* July 2 and 24, 1956; Thurber, *Republicans and Race,* 97–99.

59. *Gallup Poll,* Two, 1438–1439.

60. RN to Williams, Mar 24, 1956, B 821, Williams, PR, Series 320, RNln; *Jet,* Aug 2, 1956, p. 3, Vol X, No 13; Horton and Smith eds., *Statistical Record,* 477; Gillon, *Politics and Vision,* 93–101; Black, *Casting Her Own,* 109–116.

61. *PPA* 1956, p. 633.

62. Larson, *President Nobody Knew,* 126–129.

63. Telephone calls, Aug 19, 1956, B 8, Aug 1956 (1), ACW diary, DDEL; Thomson and Shattuck, *1956 Presidential Campaign,* 202; *Los Angeles Times,* July 31, 1956.

64. *Chicago Defender,* Aug 23, pp. 2 and Sept 1, 1956, pp. 2; *Jet,* Sept 6, 1956, p. 3, Vol. X, No 18.

65. *PPA* 1956, p. 710.

66. *Chicago Defender,* Sept 1, 1956, p. 1.

67. *Washington Post,* Oct 5, 1956, PPS336, RNyl; Lazarowitz, *Years in Exile,* 51–72 and 99–106; Thomson and Shattuck, *1956 Presidential Campaign,* 258; Moos, "Election of 1956," p. 3352.

68. *Minneapolis Morning Tribune,* Sept 22, 1956, B 5 (5), Rabb interview; *Washington Post,* Oct 5, 1956, PPS336, RNyl; Lazarowitz, *Years in Exile,* 51–72 and 99–106; Thomson and Shattuck, *1956 Presidential Campaign,* 258; Moos, "Election of 1956," p. 3352; *New York Times,* Sept 16, 1956.

69. *New York Times,* Sept 12 and 21, 1956.

70. Notes, Aug 31, PPS22.Schedule and memo, Sept 13, 1956, PPS23.Florida, RNyl; Memo, Sept 17, 1956, B 285, George, Na and memo, June 16, 1958, B 259, Finch 1958, Series 320, RNln; Nathaniel George OH 862, pp. 14–16 and Dean Triggs and Robert Gibbs OH 971, CSUF.

71. Memo, Sept 24, 1956, PPS29.B2, RNyl.

72. *Evening Star* (DC), Sept 27, PPS336(1956).S547 and Sept 28, PPS336(1956).554 and itinerary, Sept 27, 1956, PPS23.1:1, RNyl; *New York Times,* Sept 28, 1956.

73. *PPA* 1956, pp. 850–851.

74. Mayer, "Eisenhower's Conditional Crusade," 352–388; Powell, *Adam by Adam,* 129; Hamilton, *Powell,* 268–274; Haygood, *King of the Cats,* 218–221; Lewinson, *Black Politics,* 120–122.

75. *Chicago Daily News,* Oct 11, 1956, PPS336, RNyl; *Chicago Daily Tribune,* Oct 22, 1956.

76. *PPA* 1956, pp. 912–913.

77. Ibid., 975–976.

78. *Ithaca Journal* (NY), Oct 17, 1956, PPS336, RNyl; *New York Times,* Oct 15 and 18, 1956.

79. *New York Times,* Oct 19, 1956.

80. *Chicago Daily News,* Oct 25, PPS336 and *Evening Star* (DC), Oct 26, 1956, PPS336, RNyl; *Chicago Daily Tribune,* Oct 24–26, 1956.

81. Morrow, *Black Man,* 104–105; *New York Herald Tribune,* Nov 1, 1956; *New York Times,* Nov 1, 1956.

82. *New York Herald Tribune*, Sept 24, 1956, PPS336(1956).S512, RNyl; *New York Times*, Oct 26, 1956.

83. *Evening Star* (DC), Nov 1, PPS336, RNyl; Morrow, *Black Man*, 105; *Journal and Guide* (Va), Nov 3, 1956; *New York Times*, Nov 1, 1956.

84. Lubell, "Future of the Negro Voter," 408–417; Wilkins, "Future of the Negro Voter," 424–431; Gosnell and Martin, "Negro as Voter," 415–425; Lawson, *Running for Freedom*, 52; Moon, "What Chance for Civil Rights?" 42; Sitkoff, "Harry Truman and the Election," 613; 1960 Elections, Apr 1961, PPS77, B 9, RNyl; *Atlanta Daily World*, Nov 6, 7, and 8, *Los Angeles Sentinel*, Nov 1, 8, 15, and 22, *New York Amsterdam*, Nov 10, *Chicago Defender*, Nov 10 and 17, *Call and Post* (Cleveland), Nov 10, *Journal and Guide* (Va), Nov 10 and 17, *Afro-American* (Baltimore), Nov 17 and *Jet*, Nov 22, 1956.

85. Wilkins to Peters, Feb 8, 1957, Group III, B A246, General Office File, Presidential Campaign of 1956, General 1956, Oct 1957, NAACP mss, LOC.

86. Moon, "Negro Break-Away," p. 17; Moon, "Negro Vote," 219–230; Moon, "Election Post-Mortem," 661.

87. Wilkins, "Future of the Negro Voter," 424–431; Gosnell and Martin, "Negro as Voter," 415–425; Lawson, *Running for Freedom*, 52; Branch, *Parting the Waters*, stated Negroes voted "roughly 60-40" for Ike, 374–375; O'Reilly, *Nixon's Piano*, 177 and "Racial Integration," 115 asserts that Ike received 60 percent of the black vote in 1956. These figures are incorrect. After 1936, Republican presidential candidates never received more than a third of the black vote. Moon, "What Chance for Civil Rights?" 42; Sitkoff, "Harry Truman and the Election," 613.

88. Negro Vote, Aug 1957, B 554, Negro Vote, Series 320, RNln; Rabb to Prendergast, Aug 20, 1957, B 909, 1957 (2), GF 124-A, DDEL; Caro, *Master of the Senate*, presents the position offered by many that the Democrats had suffered serious losses, 842–844.

89. Smith, "Redistribution of the Negro," 155–172; Glantz, "Negro Voter," 999–1010; Polenberg, *One Nation*, 150–153; McAdam, *Political Process*, 96; Taeuber and Taeuber, *Negroes*, 1–8; Thurber, *Republicans and Race*, 73–77.

90. Booker, *Black Man's America*, 206.

CHAPTER 9. IKE, NIXON, AND DULLES

1. Melanson and Mayers eds., *Reevaluating Ike*, 31–61; Chernus, *General Eisenhower*, 67–80.

2. Ike to Dulles, June 20, 1952, B 36, Pre-Presidential, 1916–52, Principal File, DDEL; Reichard, *Reaffirmation*, 69.

3. Meeting, Jan 26, 1953, R 1, Legislative DDE; Foot, "Making Known," 422–431; Buhite and Hamel, "War for Peace," 379–381; Caridi, *Korean War*, 246–279; Chang and Halliday, *Mao*, 365–378; Soman, *Double-Edged*, 85–100; Zhai, *Dragon*, 132; Zhang, *Deterrence*, 149–151; Pruden, *Conditional Partners*, 96.

4. Interview with Nixon, about 1955, B 47, R. Nixon 1958, Alsop mss, LOC; Jian, *Mao's China*, 38–60; Mayers, *Cracking*, 10; Melanson and Mayers eds., *Reevaluating Eisenhower*, 67–70.

5. Pruessen, *Dulles*, is definitive on Dulles's life up to his appointment as secretary of state; there are several biographies of Dulles, including his years as secretary of state. The most current is Kinzer, *Brothers*, that continues the theme of other biographers that Allen and Foster Dulles were not well acquainted with Nixon.

6. Miller, *Piety*, 166–167.

7. Gellman, *Contender*, 155, 163–164, and 186–187.

8. Telephone call from A. Dulles, Apr 8, 1958, R 7, DuHe; Nixon, "Unforgettable JFD," 99; Nixon OH, PPS208(1965).March 5, pp. 99–100; Gellman, *Contender*, 207–208, 216, and 255; White, *Alger Hiss's*, 81–102.

9. Dulles to Nixon, Feb 10, 1950, PPS205.1613A, RNyl; Gellman, *Contender*, 345, 360, and 413.

10. Dulles to Nixon, Aug 13, PPS10.256.A.1 and memo regarding Alger Hiss, Aug 13, 1952, PPS10.256A.2, RNyl.

11. Memo to Nixon, Aug 13, 1952, PPS10.256b, RNyl.

12. Nixon to Dulles, Aug 16, PPS10.A*260A, MacKinnon to Loie, undated (Aug ?), PPS208(1952).82.10.1, *Stevenson and Hiss*, undated (Aug ?), PPS208(1952).82.10.2, memo to Nixon, undated (Aug ?), 1952, PPS10.256C, RNyl.

13. Dulles to Nixon, Aug 18, 1952, PPS10.275A, RNyl.

14. Nixon OH, 6–8, 12–17, 21–27, and 42–43, PPS208(1965).March 5, RNyl; Nixon, "Unforgettable JFD," 100–102.

15. Falk, "The National Security Council," 403–417; Prados, *Keepers of the Keys*, 29–56.

16. *New York Times Magazine*, Jan 20, 1955, PPS299.65.4, RNyl.

17. Meeting, Jan 26, 1953, R 1, Legislative DDE; *PPA 1953*, pp. 120–121; Nelson, "Top of the Hill," 307–326; Falk, "NSC," 417–428; Donovan, *Eisenhower*, 64–66; Bose, *Shaping and Signaling*, 19–39; Bischof and Ambrose eds., *Eisenhower*, 111–116; Prados, *Keepers of the Keys*, 57–91.

18. Meeting, Jan 26, 1953, R 1, Legislative DDE; diary, Aug 12 and 13, 1953, B 2, WH Years (3), pp. 1147–1148, Shanley mss, DDEL; RN q and a, Feb, PPS208(1953).4A, *Washington Post*, June 21, PPS300.258.2, *Evening Star* (DC), Aug 13, 1953, PPS336(1953).120, NSC, Mar 1960, PPS299.65.5, RNyl; *Chicago Daily News*, Mar 28, 1953, B 785, Vice Presidency, Series 320, RNln; *New York Times*, Mar 31, July 13 and 26, 1953; Henderson, *Managing the Presidency*, 81.

19. Osgood, "Form Before Substance,"405–433; Osgood and Larres eds., *Total Cold War*, 46–75; Saunders, "Military Force," 114–116; Theoharis, *Spying*, 234.

20. Brands, *Cold Warriors*, 117–137.

21. Memo, Oct 19, 1954, OF, Dulles, A, R 11, Diary DDE; Barrett, *CIA & Congress*, 9–137 and 141–143; Dulles, *Craft of Intelligence*; Grose, *Gentleman Spy*, 1–296; Bird, *Color of Truth*, 154–184.

22. Nixon OH, 4, PPS208(1965).March 5, RNyl; Gellman, *Contender*, 128 and 207; Grose, *Gentleman Spy*, 297–298; Beschloss, *Mayday*, 108.

23. RN address, Feb 10, 1953, B 9, F 7, Series 207, RNln; Barrett, *CIA & Congress*, 149–150.

24. Although there are many books on Eisenhower and foreign policy, as yet there is no single, definitive study. Rabe, "Eisenhower Revisionism," 97–115. Ike left his memoirs, *Mandate*, 137–170, and so did Nixon, *RN*, 118–119; many others discuss foreign

affairs: Parmet, *Eisenhower*, 161–173; Ambrose and Brinkley, *Rise to Globalism*, 132–179; Hogan, *Cross of Iron*, 481–482; Ruane, *Rise and Fall*, 192–197; Offner, *Another Such*, 455; Bowie and Immerman, *Waging Peace*, 251–259.

25. Appleby, "Eisenhower and Arms Control," 1–2; Bundy, *Danger and Survival*, 236–238, 287–305, and 328–334; Bowie and Immerman, *Waging Peace*, 247; Donovan, *Eisenhower*, 183–193; Melanson and Mayers eds., *Reevaluating Eisenhower*, 241–248; Chernus, *Eisenhower's Atoms*, 127–129; Brands, "Age of Vulnerability," 963–989.

26. McMahon, "Eisenhower and Third World," 453–473; Kaufman, *Trade and Aid*, 12–33; Krieg ed., *Eisenhower*, 219–232; Føkand, "Selling Firearms," 221–244.

27. Most contend that Nixon did not play any serious role in foreign affairs during the Eisenhower presidency. For example, Brands, *US in the World*, 222–261, never mentions Nixon; Beschloss, *Crisis Years*, 23, declared that Ike seldom consulted Nixon. *PDDE*, XIV, pp. 403; *FR, 1952–1954*, Vol. I, P 2, p. 1467.

28. Journal, Mar 5, 1953, R 17, Lodge mss, MHS; *FR, 1952–1954*, Vol. II, P 1, p. 453, P 2, p. 1108 and Vol. X, p. 698; Osgood and Larres eds., *Cold War*, 3–92.

29. Burns, *Economic Aid*, 48–49; Holloway, *Stalin*, 368; Donovan, *Eisenhower*, 36–42; Mitrovich, *Undermining Kremlin*, 122–176 and 185–189; Zubok and Pleshakov, *Inside the Kremlin*, 280–281; Garthoff, *Assessing the Adversary*, 1–29; Kolodzieg, *Uncommon*, 166–179 and 181–252; Preble, *JFK*, 50–51; Hunt, *Ideology*, 179–180; Fish, "After Stalin's Death," 333–355; Larres, "Eisenhower and the First Forty Days," 431–469; Andrew Goodpaster interview, Jan 8, 2002.

30. Meeting, Apr 30, 1953, R 1, Legislative DDE; *FR, 1952–1954*, Vol. I, P 1, p. 594, Vol. II, P 1, pp. 296 and 300, Vol. XIII, pp. 780 and 783–784.

31. Meeting, Feb 20 and Mar 20, 1953, R 1, Cabinet DDE; memo, May 28, 1953, PPS325(1953).266A and memoirs, Feb 16 and Mar 22, 1976, RNyl; Tananbaum, "Bricker Amendment," 73–93; Tananbaum, *Bricker Amendment*, 31, 74, 87, 96–97, and 108.

32. RN to Maggs, Sept 4, 1953, B 471, Maggs, Series 320, RNln; *New York Times*, June 28, 1953; Hughes, *Ordeal*, 126 and 144.

33. Meeting, Jan 11, 1954, R 3, Legislative DDE; meeting, Jan 29, 1954, R 1, Cabinet DDE; *Hagerty Diary*, 6 and 10; *PDDE*, XV, pp. 848–849, 861, and 912–914 and Vol. XVI, p. 1511; Tananbaum, *Bricker Amendment*, 157–160; Maddox, *Senatorial Career*, 317.

34. See Pruden, *Conditional Partners*.

35. *FR, 1952–1954*, Vol. III, p. 350; *PDDE*, XIV, pp. 267–269; Pruden, *Conditional Partners*, 123–125.

36. *Whittier News*, Sept 22, PPS336(1953).150 and *Tucson Daily Star*, Sept 24, 1953, PPS336(1953).152, RNyl; *New York Times*, Sept 22 and 23, 1953.

37. Nixon OH, 7, 8 and 25, PPS208(1965), RNyl; *PDDE*, XIV, p. 224; Wilton Persons OH 161, p. 70, CCOH; Immerman, "Eisenhower and Dulles," 21–38; Tudda, *Truth*, 16–47; E. Dulles, *Dulles*, vii; Frey, Pruessen, and Yong eds., *Transformation*, 226–240.

38. Lodge to Pinkley, May 7, 1971, R 13, Lodge mss, MHS; Pinkley, *Eisenhower Declassified*.

39. Telephone calls, June 5 and Aug 13 and memo by JFD, Sept 8, 1953, R 1, DuHe; *New York Times*, Jan 3, 1953, *Current Biography* 1954, pp. 227–229; Jefferson, *JFD Book*, 2–3.

40. Telephone calls, June 8 and 10, 1953, R 1, DuHe; Nelson, "JDF and Bipartisan Congress," 43–64.

41. Telephone calls, June 17, Aug 27 and 28 and Sept 11, 1953, R 1, DuHe; diary, July 7, 1953, PPS212(1953).1, RNyl; Dulles to RN, July 17, 1953, B 1, Schedule, Series 365, RNln.
42. Diary, Feb 28, PPS212(1953).1 and May 21, PPS212(1953).3.137, memo, June 16, 1953, PPS325(1953).273.1, RNyl; *New York Times,* Mar 26 and 31, 1953; Gray, *Eighteen Acres,* 288.
43. Kitchen to Woods, Apr 3, PPS320.33A.1(1), *Hollywood Citizen News,* Apr 7, PPS336(1953).65, calendar, Apr 7, PPS212(1953).3.92 and RN remarks, Apr 7, 1953, PPS208(1953).4, RNyl; May, "American Commitment," 453–459; Melanson and Mayers eds., *Reevaluating Eisenhower,* 220–224; Ninkovich, *Germany and US,* 101–106; Jonas, *US and Germany,* 291–298; Nixon, *Leaders,* 133–168; Adenauer, *Memoirs,* 428–437 and 440–442; Ulanoff, *MATS.*
44. Memo, Sept 24, 1953, R 1, DuHe.
45. Memo, June 26, 1953, PPS325(1953).279 and memoirs, Feb 16, 1976, RNyl; *New York Times,* July 11, 1953.
46. Goldberg, "VP of Nixon," 46.
47. Ibid., 46–53 and 68; Nixon OH, 13–17 and 19, PPS208(1965).March 5 and memoirs, Mar 16 and 23, 1976, RNyl; Mosley, *Dulles,* 343–344.

CHAPTER 10. NIXON IN ASIA

1. *Christian Science Monitor,* June 30, 1953, PPS336(1953).95, RNyl; "Report by Stevenson," May 19, "Ballots and Bullets," June 2, "Fight for Freedom," June 16 and "Will India Turn Communist?" July 14, 1953, *Look,* B 1, Stevenson, Series 365, RNln; *Gallup Poll,* One, 1169; *PAES,* IV, p. 265; Martin, *Stevenson and the World,* 20.
2. Pope, "Foundations of," 94–107; Nixon, *RN,* 119; M. Eisenhower, *Wine Is Bitter.*
3. Dorn to Woods, June 9, 1953, B 12, F 10, Series 207, RNln; PN to Helene, Apr 1, DR 54 and June 9, 1953, DR 56, RNyl; meeting, June 2, 1953, R 1, Legislative DDE; RN OH, 21, JFD OH; RN, "VP Reports," 83.
4. Press release, July 7, B1, Trip to Far East, Series 366, Morton to Dulles, July 14, 1953, B 1, Schedule, Series 365, memo, July 14, 1953 and Herter to Rab, B 509, Herter, Series 320, RNln; *New York Times,* July 8, 1953.
5. *New York Herald Tribune,* Oct 4, 1953, B 1, Far East Trip, Series 375, RNln; RN speech, Dec 14–15, 1953, PPS208 (1953).10, RNyl.
6. Schedule briefings, Sept 21, Herter to RN, Sept 25, B 1, Briefings, Series 378, Woods to Jacobs, Oct 3, B 14, F 9, Series 207, notes for RN and press release, Oct 6, B 1, San Francisco, Series 365, *Washington Post,* Oct 6, 1953, B 1, Far East Trip [½], Series 375, RNln; deputies' meeting, Sept 28, CIA-RDP0167R002300130003-2, Sept 29, CIA-RDP80B0167R002300120002-3, Oct 2, CIA-80B01676R002300140015-8, and assistant directors' meeting, Oct 5, 1953, CIA- RDP80B01676R002400010027-8, CREST; *PDDE,* XVII, p. 2573; Cannon, *Politics USA,* 72; *New York Times,* Oct 6 and 11, 1953; Goodpaster phone interview, Jan 8, 2002; Smith, *Unknown CIA,* 105. See Pope, "Foundations of," 107–162, and Nixon, *RN,* 120–133, for background.
7. Report from the WH, Sept 30, 1953, B 15, F 4, Series 207, RNln.

8. *Los Angeles Times*, Oct 4, PPS336(1953).161, and *San Francisco Chronicle*, Oct 7, 1953, PPS336(1953).168, RNyl; *PN*, 135.

9. Woods to Ladd, Oct 28, 1953, B 1, General (1 of 2), Series 378, *Washington Post*, Feb 21, 1954, B 18, F 1, Series 207, RNln.

10. Notes, Sept 15 and 17, B 1, Trip to Far East—Press Conf and Herter to Johnson, Sept 29, B 1, Trip to Far East Offers, Series 366, *Washington Post*, Sept 29, B 2, Far East Trip, *Washington Post*, Series 375, Murphy to Herter, Oct 1, 1953, B 1, Financial, Series 378, RNln; *New York Times*, Oct 6, 1953.

11. Oct 12, *Evening Star* (DC), B 2, Far East Trip, *Washington Evening Star*, Series 375, Oct 15, *New Zealand Herald*, B 5, Trip—New Zealand (1 of 3), Series 376, report on visit, Oct 20, 1953, B 3, New Zealand I, Series 366, RNln; PN diary, Oct 15, 1953, PPS267.424, RNyl; *New York Times*, Oct 13, 1953.

12. McIntyre, *Background to the Anzus*, 368–394; Barclay, *Very Small*, 1–21; Reese, *Australia*, 126–149, 161–167, and 251–276; Waite, "Contesting 'the Right Decision,'" 893–917.

13. Memo, Oct 12 and report on visit, Oct 20, B 3, New Zealand I, Herter to RN, Oct 12, 1953, B 3, New Zealand IV, Series 366, RNln; memo by Herter, early Jan 1954, RNyl.

14. Report on visit, Oct 20, 1953, B 3, New Zealand I, Series 366, RNln; *New York Times*, Oct 14, 1953.

15. *New Zealand Herald*, Oct 15 and Habib to Woods, Oct 28, B 5 Trip—New Zealand (1 of 3), *Manawatu Evening Standard*, Oct 16, 1953, B 5, Trip—New Zealand (2 of 3), Series 376, report on visit, Oct 20, 1953, B 3, New Zealand I, Series 366, RNln; Holland to Eisenhower, Oct 20, 1953, New Zealand, R 24, Diary DDE.

16. PN diary, Oct 12–13, 1953, PPS267.424, RNyl; *PN*, 136.

17. PN diary, Oct 14, 1953, PPS267.424, RNyl.

18. PN diary, Oct 15, 1953, PPS267.424, RNyl; report on visit, Oct 20, 1953, B 3, New Zealand I, Series 366, RNln; *New York Times*, Oct 15, 1953.

19. *Daily Mirror*, Oct 15, B 1, Trip—Australia (1 of 4), Series 376 and Herter to RN, Dec 23, 1953, B 1, Briefings, Series 378, RNln; memo, Herter to RN, early Jan 1954, RNyl.

20. Australia, July 29, B 1, Australia [2 of 4], RN address, Oct 18, RN to (?), Oct 20, B 1, Australia [1 of 4], Series 364, RN radio talk, Oct 17, B 1, Australia, Series 366, RNln; *New York Times*, Oct 19, 1953; Reese, *Australia*, 233.

21. RN to Caraway, Oct 18, 1953, B 1, RN notes, Series 378, RNln; *New York Times*, Oct 20, 1953.

22. RN to Menzies, Oct 26, 1953, B 1, Australia [2 of 4], Series 364, RNln; Memo, Jan 8, 1954, RNyl; Nixon, *Leaders*, 312–318; Menzies, *Measure*, 52–60; Edwards, *Crises and Commitments*, 103–228; Watt, *Evolution of*, 246, 339 and 351–352.

23. PN diary, Oct 15 and 16, 1953, PPS267.424, RNyl; *Sunday Telegraph*, Oct 18, *Melbourne Sun*, Oct 20, *News-Review*, Oct 23, 1953, B 1, Trip—Australia (1 of 4), Series 376, RNln.

24. PN diary, Oct 17, 1953, PPS267.424, RNyl; *Daily Mirror*, Oct 17, B 1, Australia (1 of 4), Series 376, clipping, undated, B 1, Australia (1 of 2), Series 379, RNln; *New York Times*, Oct 18, 1953.

25. *New York Times*, Oct 18, 1953.

26. Cumming to RN, Jan 11, 1954, B 2, Indonesia III, Series 366, RNln; Gardner, *Shared Hopes*, 114–117.

27. Trip, 1953, RN notes, Series 378, RNln.

28. Memo, Jan 8, 1954, RNyl; Roadnight, *US Policy Toward Indonesia*, 103–105; McMahon, *Limits of Empire*, 48.

29. Memo, Jan 8, 1954, B 1, Trip to Far East, Series 378, RNln; Herter to RN, early Jan and memo, Jan 8, 1954, RNyl.

30. *Sunday Times*, Oct 23, B 5, Trip—Malaya (3 of 3) and *Singapore Standard*, Oct 25, B 4, Trip—Malaya-Singapore, Series 376 and Nixon's visit, Nov 10, B 3, Malaya III, Series 366 and Herter to RN, Dec 23, 1953, B 1, Briefings, Series 378, RNln; *New York Times*, Oct 25, 1953; Clutterbuck, *Conflict and Violence*, 81–82.

31. *New York Herald Tribune*, Oct 26, B 1, Far East Trip, Series 375, RN press conf, Oct 26 and Nixon visit, Nov 10, 1953, B 3, Malaya III, Series 366, RNln; *New York Times*, Oct 26, 1953.

32. MacDonald to RN, Oct 31, 1953, PPS320.84.1, RNyl; Makins to RN, Sept 30, MacDonald to Eisenhower, Nov 10, B 3, Malaya III, RN to MacDonald, Nov 13, 1953, RN to MacDonald, Mar 2 and MacDonald to RN, Apr 1, 1954, B 3, Malaya II, Series 366 and Johnson to Cox, Nov 1 and Culley to Lewis, Nov 27, 1953, B 4, Trip, Malaya-Singapore, Series 376, RNln.

33. *Malay Mail*, Oct 26, B 4, Trip—Malaya, Series 376, *New York Herald Tribune*, Oct 27, B 1, Far East Trip, Series 375, Nixon's visit, Nov 3, B 3, Malaya IV, salient facts, B 3, Malaya II, Series 366 and Herter to RN, Dec 23, 1953, B 1, Briefings, Series 378, RNln; *New York Times*, Oct 27, 1953; Carruthers, *Winning Hearts*, 72–117.

34. RN to Khanh, Apr 17, 1961, PPS320.99.66 and memo, Jan 8, 1954, RNyl; clipping, Oct 28, 1953, B 5, Trip—Malaya (3 of 3), Series 376, RNln; Brooke, "Matter of Will," 93–127; Cloake, *Templer*, 297.

35. Rose to Bob, Oct 26, 1953, B 1, Australia [3 of 4], Series 364, RNln.

36. *Malay Mail*, Oct 27, 1953, B 4, Trip—Malaya, Series 376, RNln; *New York Times*, Oct 28 and Nov 2, 1953; Cloake, *Templer*, 297.

37. *Malay Mail*, Oct 28, B 4, Trip—Malaya clipping, Oct 28, 1953, B 5, Trip—Malaya (3 of 3), Series 376 and memo, Jan 8, 1954, B 1, Trip—Far East, Series 378, RNln; *FR*, 1955–1957, Vol. XII, p. 214; *New York Times*, Oct 28, 1953; Cloake, *Templer*, 296–297; RN, *Leaders*, 9.

38. *Bangkok Post*, Oct 30, 1953, Trip—Thailand (1 of 2), Series 376 and memo, Jan 8, 1954, B 1, Trip to Far East, Series 378, Herter to RN, early Jan and memo, Jan 8, 1954, RNyl; *New York Times*, Oct 29, 1953.

39. *Life*, Sept 21, B 3, Indo-China [1 of 3], Series 364 and Heath to Dulles, Nov 7, 1953, B 2, Indo-China, Series 366, RNln; McMahon, *Limits of Empire*, 62–63; Schulzinger, *Time*, 54–56.

40. Tentative itinerary, Oct 28, 1953, B 3, Indo-China [2 of 3], Series 364, RNln; *FR*, 1952–1954, Vol. XIII, P 1, pp. 475 and 548.

41. RN speech, Oct 30, B 3, Indo-China [1 of 3], Series 364 and memo, Nov 16, 1953, B 2, Indo-China, Series 366, RNln; Nixon trip, Oct 30, 1953, RNLB 127:4, RNyl; *New York*

Times, Oct 31 and Nov 1, 1953; Smith, *Cambodia's Foreign Policy,* 52–179; Chandler, *Tragedy of,* 65–118.

42. *New York Times,* Oct 30 and Nov 1, 1953; Day 2, Tape 1, 00:09:19 [RN] and 00:10:01 [RN], Gannon mss, WJBma.

43. RN and Bao Dai toasts, Nov 1 and RN conversation, Nov 2, B 2, Indo-China, Series 366, RN to Bao Dai, Nov 9 and 13, Heath to RN, Nov 14, and Bao Dai to RN, Dec 11, 1953, B 3, Indo-China [1 of 3], Series 364, RNln; *FR,* 1952–1954, Vol. XIII, P 1, pp. 855–856; *New York Times,* Nov 2 and 3, 1953; Nixon, *RN,* 122.

44. RN to Navarre, Nov 5, 1953, PPS325(1953).19, RNyl; *New York Herald Tribune,* Nov 3, B 1, Far East Trip, Series 375, Heath to Dulles, Nov 7, B 2, Indo-China, Series 366 and RN to Navarre and RN to Nguyen Van Hinh, Nov 9, 1953, B 3, Indo-China [1 of 3], Series 364, RNln; *FR,* 1952–1954, Vol. XIII, P 1, pp. 856–857 and 875.

45. Tentative itinerary, Nov 3, B 3, Indo-China [2 of 3], Series 364 and memo by Rives, Nov 6, 1953, B 2, Indo-China, Series 366, RNln.

46. Tentative itinerary, Nov 3, B 3, Indo-China [2 of 3], RN speech, Nov 3, B 3, Indo-China [3 of 3] Series 364, *New York Herald Tribune,* Nov 4, B 1, Far East Trip, Series 375 and RN statement, undated, B 2, Indo-China, Series 366, RNln.

47. "News in Brief," Oct [sic] 1953, RNLB 127.3, RNyl; tentative itinerary, Nov 3, B 3, Indo-China [2 of 3], Series 364 and Heath to Dulles, Nov 7, 1953, B 2, Indo-China, Series 366, RNln; *FR,* 1952–1953, Vol. XIII, P 1, pp. 856 and 858; *New York Times,* Nov 5, 1953; Day 2, Tape 1, 00:11:25 [RN], Gannon mss, WJBma.

48. RN speech, Nov 4, B 2, Indo-China, Series 366, *New York Herald Tribune,* Nov 5, B 1, Far East Trip, Series 375, Dejean dinner, 1953, B 1, RN notes, Series 378, RNln; *New York Times,* Nov 5, 1953.

49. Schedule, Nov 5, 1953, PPS267.237, RNyl; Schedule, Nov 5–8, B 3, Hong Kong [1 of 2], Series 364, *New York Herald Tribune,* Nov 6, B 1, Far East Trip, Series 375, Herter to RN, Dec 23, 1953, B 1, Briefings and memo, Jan 8, 1954, B 1, Trip to Far East, Series 378, RNln; *FR,* 1952–1954, Vol. XIV, P 1, p. 347; *New York Times,* Nov 4, 1953; Tucker, *Taiwan,* 200–216.

50. Schedule, Nov 6, 1953, PPS267.237, RNyl; *Hongkong Standard,* Nov 7, 1953, B 4, Trip—Hong Kong, Series 376 and Herter to Harrington, Mar 27, 1954, B 3, Hong Kong [2 of 2], Series 364, RNln; *New York Times,* Nov 7, 1953.

51. *South China Post-Herald,* Nov 8, 1953, B 4, Trip—Hong Kong, Series 376 and Hancock to Rose, Jan 13, 1954, B 3, Hong Kong [1 of 2], Series 364, RNln; *New York Times,* Nov 8, 1953.

52. Chang, *Friends and Enemies,* 26; Xia, *Negotiating with the Enemy,* 12–42.

53. Tucker, *Taiwan,* 36–38; Accinelli, *Crisis and Commitment,* 112–113; Taylor, *Generalissimo,* 467–468.

54. Diary, July 14, F-362, Sept 25, G-122, Oct 2, G-153 and Oct, 1953, G-203, VII, R IV, Koo mss, LOC; memo by Watts, Jan 8, 1954, B 1, Trip to Far East, Series 378, RNln.

55. Madame to RN, Sept 29, B 2, Formosa [4/4] and schedule, Nov 7, B 2, Formosa [1 of 4], Series 364 and visit, Dec 9, 1953, B 4, Taiwan, Series 366, RNln; *New York Times,* Nov 8, 1953.

56. Schedule, Nov 7, B 2, Formosa [1 of 4], Series 364, RN speech, Nov 11 and visit, Dec 9, B 4, Taiwan, Series 366 and *China Post*, Nov 12, 1953, B 1, Trip—Formosa, Series 376, RNln; *New York Times*, Nov 10 and 11, 1953; Rankin, *China*, 186–187.

57. Tucker, *Taiwan*, 52–62 and 78.

58. RN to President, Dec 3, 1953, B 2, Formosa [2/4], Series 364, RNln; Fenby, *Chiang*; RN, *Leaders*, 218 and 242–246.

59. Embassy to State Dept, Nov 30, 1953, B 2, F Formosa, Series 364, RNln.

60. Interview, Nov 9–11, 1953, PPS325(1953).23, RNyl; embassy to state dept, Nov 30, 1953, B 2, F Formosa, Series 364, RNln; *New York Times*, Nov 10 and 11, 1953.

61. Interview, Nov 9–11, 1953, PPS325(1953).23, RNyl; *FR*, 1952–1954, Vol. XIV, P 1, p. 331.

62. Dulles statement, Nov 9 and foreign service dispatch, Nov 19, 1953, B 2, Formosa [1 of 4], Series 364, RNln; *FR*, 1952–1954, Vol. XIV, P I, pp. 330–331; Tucker, *Taiwan*, 37–38; Rankin, *China*, 187–188; Mayers, *Cracking the Monolith*, 128–129.

63. RN to Dulles, Nov 12, 1953, PPS325(1953).28, RNyl; RN statement, Nov 12 and visit, Dec 9, 1953, B 4, Taiwan, Series 366, RNln; *New York Times*, Nov 12, 1953; Rankin, *China*, 187.

64. Diary, Nov 12, G-30-31 and Nov 24, 1953, G-38-39, VII, R IV, Koo mss, LOC.

65. Eisenhower, *Mandate*, 171–191; Xia, *Negotiating with the Enemy*, 43–75; Donovan, *Eisenhower*, 114–129; Kaufman, *Korean War*, 304–346; Offner, *Another Such Victory*, 417–423; Foot, *Wrong War*, 204–231; Stueck, *Korean War*, 236–347; Keefer, "Ike and End of Korea," 268–289; Dingman, "Atomic Diplomacy," 89–91; Foot, "Nuclear Coercion," 107–111.

66. Dulles to RN, Nov 13, 1953, PPS325(1953).34, RNyl; *FR*, 1952–1954, Vol. XV, P 2, pp. 1543 and 1545.

67. Diaries, Dec 15, 1953, Vol. VI, WH Years (2), B 2, Shanley mss, DDEL; *PDDE*, XIV, pp. 596–597.

68. RN to Williams, July 6, F Williams, Le, B 821, Series 320, RN remarks, arrival, B 2, Korea I, Series 366, *The Korean Republic*, Nov 12, 1953 B 4, *The Korean Republic*, Series 376, RNln; Nixon's trip, Nov 12, 1953, RNLB 127:7, 128.1 and 128.2, RNyl; *New York Times*, Nov 13, 1953.

69. *PDDE*, XIV, pp. 638–639; draft letter, Nov 3, 1953, B 2, Dulles, Nov 1953, Dulles–Herter series, Eisenhower mss, DDEL; RN to Dewey, Dec 1, 1950, B 214, Dewey 2/2, Series 320, RNln.

70. RN to Dulles, Nov 19, 1953, PPS325(1953).37.1, RNyl; RN speech, Feb 24, 1954, B 17, F 9, Series 207, RNln; *FR*, 1952–1954, Vol. XV, P 2, pp. 1607–1610 and 1660–1662.

71. RN to Dulles, Nov 19, 1953, PPS325(1953).37.1, Herter to RN, early Jan, and memo, Jan 8, 1954, RNyl.

72. Rhee to RN, Nov 17, 1953, PPS325(1953).40, RNyl; *FR*, 1952–1954, Vol. XV, P 2, p. 1615; Showalter ed., *Forging*, 47–54.

73. Schedule, Nov 15–20, B 5, Japan [1 of 5], Series 364 and memo, Dec 8, 1953, B 2, Japan, Series 366, RNln; Dower, *Empire and Aftermath*, 464; Allison, *Ambassador*, 251–254.

74. Schedule, Nov 15–20, B 5, Japan [1 of 5] and RN to Yoshida, Nov 26, 1953, B 5, Japan [3 of 5], Series 364, RNln; Allison, *Ambassador*, 254–255; RN, *Leaders*, 81–132; *New York Times*, Oct 17, 1953.

75. Schedule, Nov 15–20, B 5, Japan [1 of 5], Series 364 and *New York Herald*, Nov 17, 1953, B 1, Far East Trip, Series 375, RNln; Nixon's trip, Nov 15–20, 1953, RNLB, 127:5, RNyl; *New York Times*, Nov 17, 1953; Allison, *Ambassador*, 255.

76. Schedule, Nov 15–20, 1953, B 5, Japan [1 of 5], Series 364, RNln; *New York Times*, Nov 17 and 19, *Gallup Poll*, 1953, p. 1178; Day 9, Tape 3, 00:29:24 [RN], Gannon mss, WJBma; Nixon, *Leaders*, 119–120; Dower, *Empire and Aftermath*, 449–463.

77. "American Policy," Nov 19, B 5, Japan [1 of 5], *New York Herald Tribune*, Nov 20 and 27, B 1, Far East Trip, *Daily Worker*, Nov 20, B 1, Far East Trip, Critical, Series 375 and *Nippon Times*, Nov 20, 1953, B 1, 1953 Japan, Series 379, RNln; *New York Times*, Nov 19 and 20, 1953; Allison, *Ambassador*, 255–256; Dower, *Empire and Aftermath*, 464–465; Schaller, *Altered States*, 63–69; Buckley, *US-Japanese Alliance*, 50–57; Nixon, *RN*, 129–130; JCS2101/113, Dec 10, 1953, File 381US (1-31-50 Section 32), RG 218 CCS, NA II.

78. *Washington Post*, Nov 23, 1953, B 1, Far East Trip, Critical, Series 375, RNln; Dulles to RN, Nov 23, 1953, PPS325(1953).43A.1, RNyl; Press release, Nov 24, 1953, R 27, DuHe; *New York Times*, Nov 25, 1953.

79. Memo, Jan 8, 1954, B 1, Trip to Far East, Series 378, RNln; Herter to RN, early in Jan and memo, Jan 8, 1954, RNyl.

80. RN to Odgen and RN to Bassett, Dec 18, 1953, B 4, Okinawa, Series 366, RNln; Herter to RN, early Jan 1954, RNyl; *FR*, 1952–1954, Vol. XIV, P 2, pp. 1569–1570.

81. Schedule, Nov 20, 1953, PPS267.329.1, RNyl; Lacy to RN, Dec 15, 1953, B 4, Philippines III, Series 366, RNln; *New York Times*, Nov 22 and 24, 1953; Kim, "US-Philippines," 19–63; Cullather, "America's Boy?" 320–331; Cullather, *Illusions*, 107–116.

82. *New York Herald Tribune*, Nov 23, 1953, B 1, Far East Trip, Series 375 and memo, Jan 8, 1954, B 1, Trip to Far East, Series 378, RNln; Herter to RN, early in Jan and memo, Jan 8, 1954, RNyl; *FR*, 1952–1954, Vol. XII, P 2, pp. 565–566; *New York Times*, Nov 23, 1953; Cullather, *Illusions*, 117; McMahon, *Limits of Empire*, 59; Nixon, *Leaders*, 274–279.

83. RN radio address, Nov 26, B 1, Burma IV, *Burma Weekly Bulletin*, Dec 2, B 1, Burma II, RN to Acly, Dec 8, 1953, B 1, Burma IV, Series 366 and memo by Watts, Jan 8, 1954, B 1, Trip to Far East, Series 378, RNln; *FR*, 1952–1954, Vol. XII, P 2, pp. 174–175; *New York Times*, Nov 25 and 26, 1953.

84. Sebald to Dulles, Nov 28, PPS325(1953).52, Allen to Dulles, Nov 30, PPS325(1953).54, Dulles to RN, Dec 2, 1953, PPS325(1953).58, Herter to RN, early Jan and memo, Jan 8, 1954, RNyl; RN remarks, Nov 27, 1953, B1, Burma, Ba U to RN, Jan 26, 1954, Series 366 and *Burman*, Nov 27, 1953, Nov 27, 1953, B 1, Australia (2 of 2), Series 379, RNln; *New York Times*, Nov 27, 1953.

85. PN notes, Nov 24–27, 1953 Trip, Marje Acker, 2002, programme, Nov 26, PPS267.344.1 and *Los Angeles Times*, Nov 27, 1953, PPS336(1953).181, RNyl; *New York Herald Tribune*, Nov 27, 1953, B 1, Far East Trip, Series 375, RN address, Jan 31, B 16, F 5 and *Washington Post*, Feb 21, 1954, B 18, F 1, Series 207, RNln; *New York Times*, Nov 27, 1953; Baughman, *Secret Service*, 251.

86. Memo, Dec 17, 1953, B 3, Libya and *American Weekly*, 1954, B 1, Trip to Far East—Personnel, Series 366, RNln; programme, Nov 24, 1953, PPS267.344.1 and *Washington Star* (DC), Feb 21, 1954, PPS336(1954).S89, RNyl; *PN*, 139–141; Scouten said that the Nixons were never in any danger, Rex Scouten, Apr 22, 2010.

87. RN address, Nov 28 and RN to prime minister, Dec 8, 1953, B 1, Ceylon, Series 364, RNln; *FR*, 1952–1954, Vol. XI, P 2, pp. 1127, 1129, 1137 and 1147; *New York Times*, Nov 27, 28 and Dec 13, 1953.

88. Woods to Hillings, Mar 6, 1954, B 342, Hillings [2/2], Series 320, RNln; *PDDE*, XIV, pp. 675–676; McMahon, *Cold War*, 80–122; Merrill, *Bread*, 102–136; Rotter, *Comrades at Odds*, 67; Wolpert, *Nehru*, 466; Brands, *India and US*, 75–76; Brands, *Specter*, 89–90; Gopal, *Nehru*, 184–188.

89. Memo, Dec 1(?), PPS325(1953).145 and Allen to Dulles, Dec 1, 1953, PPS325(1953).57, RNyl; *Times of India*, Dec 1, 1953, B 2, Trip—India (1 of 7), Series 376, RNln; Eisenhower to Nehru, Oct 5, 1953, OF India, R 16, Diary DDE; Gopal ed., *Selected Works*, Vol. 24, pp. 643–644: RN, *Leaders*, 269–274.

90. Allen to Dulles, Dec 3, 1953, PPS325(1953).60, RNyl; Herter to Parkash, Dec 3, B 4, India [4 of 4], RN to Nehru, Dec 10, 1953, B 4, India [2 of 4], Herter to Singh, Jan 30, 1954, B 4, India [1 of 4], Series 364, *Times of India*, Dec 3, B 2, Trip- India (2 of 7) and *Hindustan Times*, Dec 8, 1953, B2, Trip—India (1 of 7), Series 376, RN speech, Feb 24, 1954, B 17, F9, Series 207, RNln; *FR*, 1952–1954, Vol. XI, P 2, pp. 1730–1731; Kumar and Prasad eds., *Selected Works*, Vol. 24, pp. 439 and 643.

91. *Indian Express*, Dec 4, Trip -India (2 of 7), Series 376, Matthen to RN, Dec 4, 1953, RN speech, undated, B 4, India [4 of 4], Series 364, RNln; *New York Times*, Dec 4 and 8, 1953.

92. Herter to RN, early Jan 1954, RN to Schier, Apr 6, 1966, PPS320.7.58, RNyl; agenda, Dec 4–6, clippings, Dec 6, RN to Your Majesty, Dec 12, visit of VP, Dec 15, Sauer to RN, Dec 29, *Orange Girl*, Dec undated, 1953 and Ward to RN, Feb 27, 1954, B 1, Afghanistan, Series 364 and *Morning News*, Dec 5, 1953, B 5, Karachi press coverage, Series 376, RNln; *FR*, 1952–1954, Vol. XI, P 2, pp. 1403–1405 and 1407.

93. Hildreth to Dulles, Dec 1, PPS325(1953).55 and Dulles to Hildreth, Dec 2, 1953, PPS325(1953).64, RNyl; *FR*, 1952–1954, Vol. XI, Part 2, pp. 1830–1831; McMahon, "US Cold War Strategy," 831–834; Tahir-Kheli, *US and Pakistan*, 2–6; McMahon, *Cold War*, 152–153 and 167.

94. Schedule, Dec 4, B 5, Pakistan [1 of 3] and RN to Emmerson, Dec 12, 1953, B 5, Pakistan [2 of 3], Series 364, RNln; Deibel and Gaddis eds., *Containment*, 459; Gopal ed., *Selected Works*, Vol. 25, p. 439.

95. Schedule, Dec 4, B 5, Pakistan [1 of 3], Series 364 and RN statement, Dec 6, B 4, Pakistan, Series 366 and Withers to Dulles, Dec 14, 1953, B 4, Karachi, misc, Series 367, RNln.

96. Memos, Dec 7, 1953, PPS325(1953).71.2 and PPS325(1953).71.4, RNyl; *FR*, 1952–1954, Vol. XI, P 2, 1831–1834; McMahon, "US Cold War Strategy," 834–836.

97. *New York Herald Tribune*, Dec 7, B 1, Far East Trip, Series 375 and *Times of India*, Dec 8, 1953, B 2, Trip—India (1 of 7), Series 376, memo, Jan 8, 1954, B 1, Trip to Far East, 378, RNln; Hildreth to Dulles, Dec 8, 1953, PPS325(1953).70 and memo, Jan 8, 1954, RNyl; *New York Times*, Dec 9, 1953; Venkataramani, *American Role in Pakistan*, 233–234; Barrett, *Greater Middle East*, 24–25; Kux, *US and Pakistan*, 51–70.

98. Ambrose, *Ike's Spies*, 189–214; Ramazani, *Iran's Foreign*, 247–260; Prados, *Presidents' Secret*, 91–98; Bill, "America, Iran," 261–288; Bill, *Eagle*, 89–91; Gasiorowski, *US Foreign Policy*, 82–83; Brands, *Inside Cold War*, 270–272.

99. Diary, Oct 2, 1953, VII, G-124, R IV, Koo mss, LOC; schedule, Dec 4, 1953, B 5, Pakistan [1 of 3], Series 364 and RN to Henderson, Jan 15, 1954, B 2, Iran I, Series 366, RNln; Scott to Carroll, Nov 10, 1953, OF Iran, R 18, OF DDE; *PDDE*, XIV, pp. 669–670; *New York Times*, Nov 16 and Dec 9, 1953.

100. Oct 8, 1953, Eisenhower diary, www.eisenhower.archives.gov; RN to Mohamadian, Dec 10, B 2, Iran I, Series 366 and *New York Herald Tribune*, Dec 10, 1953, B 1, Far East Trip, Series 375, RNln; memo, Dec 13, 1953, PPS325(1953).78.2, RNyl; *New York Times*, Dec 10, 1953; Bill, *Eagle*, 116; Gasiorowski, *US Foreign Policy*, 90.

101. Memo, Dec 1953, PPS325(1953),160 and RN to Zahedi, Sept 4, 1963, PPS320.45.50, RNyl; *New York Times*, Dec 12 and 13, 1953; *FR*, 1952–1954, Vol. X, pp. 850–851 and 854–855; Nixon, *Leaders*, 299–302; Pahlavi, *Answer to History*, 16–17.

102. Henderson to RN, Dec 13, PPS325(1953).78.1 and Dec 17, 1953, PPS325(1953).79, Herter to RN, early Jan, and memo, Jan 8, 1954, RNyl; RN speech and memo by Melbourne, Dec 11, B 2, I, Series 366, memo, Jan 8, B 1, Trip to Far East, Series 378, RNln; *New York Times*, Dec 11, 1953.

103. Itinerary, Dec 12–13, B 3, memo, Dec 17, 1953 and memo undated, B 3, Libya, Series 366, RNln; *New York Times*, Dec 12, 1953.

104. Memo, Dec 13, memo, Dec 17, memo, Dec 18, RN to Your Majesty, Dec 18, B 3, Libya, Series 366 and *New York Herald Tribune*, Dec 14, 1953, B 1, Far East Trip, RNln; *New York Times*, Dec 14, 1953.

CHAPTER 11. THE BATTLES OVER ASIA

1. Chotiner to RN, Nov 16, 1953, B 1, General (2 of 3), Series 378, RNln; diary, Dec 14, 1953, VII, G-221, R. IV, Koo mss, LOC; *New York Herald Tribune*, Dec 15, 1953, B 1, Far East Trip, Series 375, RNln; *New York Times*, Dec 15, 1953; Nixon, *RN*, 133.

2. *New York Herald Tribune*, Dec 15, 1953, B 1, Far East Trip, Series 375 and memo, Mar 5, 1960, B 322, Harris, Ele, Series 320, RNln; *Christian Science Monitor*, Dec 15, PPS336(1953).189 and *Los Angeles Daily News*, Dec 15, 1953, PPS336(1953).188, "Nixon's Homecoming," Dec 14, 1953, RNLB, 128:3, RNyl; *New York Times*, Dec 15, 1953.

3. *PDDE*, XV, p. 761.

4. *PPA* 1953, pp. 800–801 and 831–832.

5. Report for the White House Conference of Mayors, Dec 14–15, 1953, B 15, F 5, Series 207, RNln.

6. Diary, Dec 1953, PPS212(1953).1, RNyl; diary, Dec 23, 1953, B 2, VI, WH Years (2), p. 1362, Shanley mss, DDEL; Ladd to Herter, Dec 5, B 1, General (1 of 2), Series 378 and Herter to RN, Dec 21, 1953, B 1, Trip, Series 369, RNln; *PDDE*, XV, pp. 761–762; *FR*, 1952–1954, Vol. XI, P 1, p. 577.

7. Calendar, Dec 23, 1953, PPS212(1953).3.318, RNyl; RN speech, Dec 23, 1953, B 1, Trip, Series 369 and B 15, F 6, Series 207, RNln.

8. Memo, Jan 8, 1954, PPS325(1954).4 and platter, Mar 5, 1954, RNyl; *PDDE*, XV, pp. 743–744; Mayers, *Cracking the Monolith*, 129.

9. Rhee to Eisenhower, Mar 11, 1954, R 3, Diary DDE; *PDDE*, XV, pp. 970–971.

10. *PDDE*, XV, 968–971 and 1161.

11. RN to Bratten, June 10, 1957, PPS320.53.47, RN to Mattuci, Apr 3, PPS320.53.58 and RN to Wiggin, Apr 3, 1958, PPS320.53.59, RNyl; *FR*, 1955–1957, Vol. XXIII, P 2, p. 452.

12. Platter, Mar 11, 1954, RNyl.

13. *FR*, 1955–1957, Vol. X, p. 67.

14. RN to Baxter, Jan 16, 1954, B 1, Cities [2/3], Series 363, RN speech, Mar 17, B 28, F 2, Series 207, and Cowles to RN, Dec 6, 1955, B 186, Cowles, J, Series 320, RNln; *PDDE*, XVI, p. 1551.

15. *FR*, 1952–1954, Vol. XIII, P 1, pp. 947–954, 963–964, 1014–1016, 1137–1138, and 1250–1263; platters, Mar 5 and May 22, 1954, RNyl; Dean Rusk OH, Interview III, Tape 1, p. 24, LBJL; Pope, "Foundations of," 184–188; Nixon, *RN*, 150–152; Anderson, *Trapped by Success*, 33–35; Statler, *Replacing France*, 51–84.

16. *PPA* 1954, p. 382; Clark Clifford OH, Interview II, p. 10, LBJL; Donovan, *Eisenhower*, 259–261; Helms, *Look Over*, 313–314; McFarland, *Cold War Strategist*, 62–63.

17. Transcript, Apr 16, 1954, PPS208(1954).5, memoirs, Mar 18, 1976, RNyl; transcript, Apr 16, 1954, B 20, F 2, Series 207, RNln; Branyan and Larsen eds., *Eisenhower Administration*, Vol. I, pp. 332–334; Nixon, *RN*, 152–153; Logevall, *Embers of War*, 491–495.

18. Logevall, *Embers of War*, 491–495, and Patrick to RN, May 11, 1954, PPS208(1954).5.4.2, RNyl.

19. *Times* (London), Apr 17, 1954; *New York Times*, Apr 18, 1954.

20. *Gallup Poll*, Two, 1243; Mann, *Grand Delusion*, 157–162; Longley, *Gore*, 111; Graebner, *New Isolationism*, 164–165; A.S. Monroney OH, 28, LBJL.

21. Memo, Apr 19, 1954, B 2, Mar to Apr 30, 1954(1), DuHe.

22. Memo, Apr 19, 1954, R 2, DuHe; memo, Apr 16, 1954, Koo, Vol. VII, H-65, R IV, Koo mss, LOC; Nixon OH, 44–46, JFD OH; *FR*, 1952–1954, Vol. XIII, P 1, pp. 1346–1348.

23. Memo, Apr 16, 1954, B 20, F 2, Series 207, RNln; platter, Apr 19, 1954 and memoirs, Mar 18, 1976, RNyl; telephone calls, Apr 19, 1954, R 3, Diary DDE; Adams, *Firsthand Report*, 122.

24. *Colliers*, May 6, B 162, Colliers Magazine and RN to Merwin, May 13, 1954, B 515, Merwin [2/2], Series 320, RNln.

25. RN to Patrick, July 17, 1954, PPS208(1954).5, RNyl and B 20, F 2, Series 207, RNln.

26. There are a number of books and articles already cited on Vietnam. Several are: Immerman, "Between the Unattainable," 120–146; Herring, "Good Stout Effort," 213–216; Herring and Immerman, "Eisenhower, Dulles," 343–363; Marks, "Real Hawk," 297–322; Pope, "Foundations of," 189–193, 204–209, and 213–217.

27. Statler, *Replacing France*, 88–95.

28. Platter, Mar 26, 1954, RNyl; Reedy, VI, pp. 44–46 and 48, LBJL; Billings-Yun, *Decision Against War*, 73.

29. Platter, Apr 29, 1954, RNyl.

30. *FR*, 1952–1954, Vol. XIII, P 2, pp. 1431 and 1433; Thruston Morton OH, 26–27, LBJL; Nixon, *RN*, 153–154; Billings-Yun, *Decision Against War*, 148–154; Doyle, *Inside the Oval Office*, 86; Adams, *Firsthand Report*, 122–123.

31. Platter, Apr 30, 1954, RNyl.

32. Platter, May 3, 1954, RNyl.
33. Ike meeting, Apr 2, 1967, PPS324.247 and memoirs, Mar 16, 1976, RNyl; Zhai, *China and the Vietnam*, 10–49; Donovan, *Eisenhower*, 264–165.
34. Platter, May 20, 1954, RNyl; Herter to RN, May 25, 1954, B 21, F 20, Series 207, RNln; *FR*, 1952–1954, Vol. XIII, P 2, pp. 1505, 1507–1509, and 1589–1590; calls to Hagerty, May 12, 1954, R 8, DuHe; *PDDE*, XV, p. 1051; *Gallup Poll*, Two, 1233–1234; *Pearson Diaries*, 315.
35. Platter, June 23, 1954, RNyl.
36. Telephone to RN, July 9, 1954, B 2, July 1–Aug 31, 1954 (5), DuHe.
37. *FR*, 1952–1954, Vol. XII, P 1, pp. 746 and 753; Cable, *Geneva Conference*, 1–128; Immerman, "US and the Geneva Conference," 43–66; for different scholarly opinions on the settlement, see McMahon, *Limits of Empire*, 103–104; Jian, *Mao's China*, 118–144; Zhai, *China and the Vietnam*, 49–91; Gaiduk, *Confronting Vietnam*, 12–53.
38. Minutes, Aug 6, 1954, R 2, Cabinet DDE; *PDDE*, XV, pp. 1109–1110.
39. RN OH, 49, JFD OH; Rusk OH, I, p. 33, LBJL; Dingman, "JFD and the Creation," 457–477; Brands, "From ANZUS to SEATO," 250–270; McMahon, *Limits of Empire*, 63–68; Watt, *Evolution of Australian Foreign Policy*, 152–153.
40. See Chapter 10.
41. There is an extraordinary amount of writing on Quemoy-Matsu; some are Donovan, *Eisenhower*, 300–310; Ambrose, *Eisenhower*, vol. 2, 212–255; Zhai, *Dragon*, 151–152, 175–177, and 222–224; Soman, *Double-Edged Sword*, 115–153; Chang and Halliday, *Mao*, 396–397; Ross and Changbin eds., *Re-examining*, especially, Pruessen, "Over the Volcano," 77–105; Xia, *Negotiating with the Enemy*, 81–89; Mayers, *Cracking the Monolith*, 135–142; Chang, *Friends*, 121–142; Accinelli, *Crisis and Commitment*, 158–163, 214, and 231; Gordon, "United States Opposition," 637–641; Chang, "To the Nuclear Brink," 97–123; Brands, "Testing Massive Retaliation," 124–151; Xiaolu, "China's Policy toward the US," 192–196; Sheng, "Mao and China's Relations," 477–495.
42. *FR*, 1952–1954, Vol. XIV, P 1, p. 411; platters, Apr 13 and June 10, 1954, RNyl; Tucker, "Cold War Contacts," 238–257; Tucker, "Taiwan Expendable?" 112–114; Taylor, *Generalissimo*, 583–488.
43. Pope, "Foundation of," 238–239.
44. Telephone, Jan 20, 1955, R 3, DuHe; *FR*, 1955–1957, Vol. II, p. 93; George Reedy OH, XIII, p. 19 and Karl Mundt OH, LBJL; *Hagerty Diary*, 173; Tucker, *Taiwan*, 36–43; Johnson, *Congress and the Cold War*, 64–67; Flynn, "Reconsidering the China Lobby," Vol. II, pp. 60–95, 249–252, 256–261, and 268–270.
45. Memo, Mar 2, 1955, PPS325(1955),47, RNyl; memo, Mar 11, 1955, R 6, Diary DDE.
46. *Los Angeles Examiner*, Mar 15, 1955, B 27, F 9, Series 207, RNln.
47. Telephone, Mar 16, 1955, R 3, DuHe; James Hagerty OH, 104, CCOH; Flynn, "Reconsidering the China Lobby," Vol. II, p. 257; Williamson, *Separate Agendas*, 107–128; Jones, *After Hiroshima*, 240–273; *New York Times*, Mar 15, 1955.
48. RN remarks, Mar 17, 1955, PPS208(1955).2, RNyl; *Chicago Daily Tribune*, Mar 18, 1955, B 28. F 1, Series 207, RNln.
49. *New York Times*, Mar 17, 1955.
50. *Cleveland Plain Dealer*, Apr 4, 1955, B 28, F 12, Series 207, RNln; Drukman, *Morse*, 406.

51. Telephone, Apr 27, 1955, R 3, DuHe.
52. Ibid.
53. Ibid.; William Knowland OH, I, pp. 19–20, LBJL; "Knowland Story," 37–48.
54. *Los Angeles Times*, June 8, 1955, B 31, F 4 [2 of 3], Series 207, RNln; RN OH, 11–12, JFD OH; *New York Times*, Jan 15, 1956.
55. Telephone, Apr 27, 1955, R 3, DuHe; Parker, "Cold War II," 888–892; Fraser, "American Dilemma," 115–137; Jones, "'Segregated' Asia?," 852–868; Tarling, "'Ah-Ah,'" 74–111; Di, "Most Respected Enemy," 39–40; Roadnight, *US Policy Toward Indonesia*, 125–128.

CHAPTER 12. TROUBLE WITH GOOD NEIGHBORS

1. For a recent example of U.S.–Central American and Caribbean diplomatic history with a generalist viewpoint, see Paterson, Clifford et al., *American Foreign Relations*, Vol. 2, pp. 34–53 and 157–172; for U.S.–Latin America perspective, see Longley, *In the Eagle's Shadow*, 109–164.
2. Ike, *Mandate*, 237–238; Brendon, *Ike*, 50–54.
3. Diary, July 3, 1953, Hughes mss, HML.
4. *FR*, 1952–1954, Vol. IV, pp. 304–305; telephone calls with RN, Feb 20 and Apr 7, 1954, R 2, DuHe.
5. Cabot, *First Line*, 90; Streeter, "Campaigning Against Latin American Nationalism," 194–198.
6. RN OH, 48 and 50, JFD OH; *New York Times*, Mar 6, 1954; Longley, *In the Eagle's Shadow*, 219–220.
7. PDDE, XV, pp. 807–808; diary, July 10, 1954, R 4, Diary DDE; JFD to Ike, Aug 19, 1955, R 2, DuHe.
8. Milton Eisenhower OH, 8, DDEL; Milton Eisenhower OH, 9–10 and Dean Rusk OH, Interview III, Tape 1, p. 28, LBJL; Eisenhower, *Mandate*, 420–421.
9. M. Eisenhower to RN, Mar 21, PPS422(1955).11 and RN to M. Eisenhower, Apr 6, 1955, PPS422(1955).18.12, RNyl; RN to M. Eisenhower, Apr 6, 1955, B 238, Eisenhower 2/2, Series 320, RNln; M. Eisenhower, *President Is Calling*, 236.
10. JFD to RN, Aug 24, 1954, R 33 and telephone call from Ike, R 9, DuHe; *New York Herald Tribune*, Dec 31, 1954, B 1, Trip—Previous to Departure, Series 357, RNln; clipping, Dec 31, 1954, PPS336(1954).S682, RNyl; *FR*, 1952–1954, Vol. IV, pp. 67–68; Day 3, Tape 4, 00:01:03 [RN], Gannon mss, WJBma.
11. Itinerary, undated, Trip—Previous to Departure, Series 357, RNln; Chotiner to RN, Nov 8, 1954, PPS300.353, RNyl; see Rabe, "Dulles, Latin America, and Cold War," 159–178, for his views of Ike's Latin American policy during his first term; the author allocates a paragraph on Nixon's trip; LaFeber, *Inevitable Revolutions*, 128–130, asserts that Nixon went on his trip in March and mischaracterizes the vice president's report as complimenting Batista, Castillo Armas, and other dictators.
12. Notes, Feb 1, B 2, Guatemala [1 of 4], Series 362 and RN to Holden, Aug 8, 1955, B 347, Holden, W, Series 320, RNln; RN to Gunawardene, Feb 5, 1955, P[S320.18.6, RNyl; Day 3, Tape 4, 00:01:03 [RN], Gannon mss, WJBma.

13. Memo, Feb, before trip, PPS325(1955).3, *Washington Daily News* (DC), Feb 2, 1955, PPS336(1955).40, RNyl; Ike statement, Feb 6, 1955, B 1, Misc (1 of 2), Series 361, RNln.
14. Memo, Jan 18, 1955, B 1, Misc, Series 367, RNln.
15. RN to Pendleton, Aug 8, 1955, B 586, Pendleton, M, Series 320, RNln.
16. *Los Angeles Times*, Feb 7, 1955.
17. Notes, Jan 31, B 5, Central American Trip [1 of 2], Series 358 and *Havana Post*, Feb 8, 1955, B 2, Cuba [3 of 4], Series 356, RNln; notes, early 1955, PPS325(1955).8–12, RNyl; *Los Angeles Times*, Feb 7, 1955.
18. *Havana Post*, Feb 8, 1955, PPS336(1955).0s7, RNyl; clipping, Feb 9, B 1, Trip—Feb 9, Series 357, RNln; memo, Oct 3, 1960, R 12, Paterson mss, UCt; Pérez, *Cuba and the US*, 333; Bonsal, *Cuba, Castro*, 13; Rabe, "Dulles, Latin American, and Cold War," 172; the author states: "Before cameras he gleefully embraced Trujillo and Batista." Secret Service agent Scouten, who traveled with RN never saw him embrace either ruler; Rex Scouten interview, Apr 22, 2010; I found no such pictures in my research.
19. PDDE, XVI, p. 1553; *Los Angeles Times* Feb 8, 1955; *El Mundo*, Feb 8, 1955, PPS336(1955).0s9, *Havana Post*, Feb 9, 1955, PPS299.1151, PPS336(1955).0s11 and PPS360.1, RNyl; *Daily News*, Feb 8, Trip—Feb 8, Series 357 and *Havana Post*, Feb 10, 1955, B 2, Cuba [3 of 4], Series 356, RNln; supplementary notes, June 8, 1955, R 1, Legislative DDE; memo from McCaffrey, Oct 3, 1960, R 12, Paterson mss, UCt; *New York Times*, Feb 8 and 9, 1955.
20. Goldwater to RN, Dec 13, 1956, B 293, Goldwater [2/2], Series 320, RNln; *New York Times* and *Los Angeles Times*, Feb 10–12, 1955.
21. PDDE, XV, pp. 1100–1102; *Ike's Letters*, 129; Eisenhower, *Mandate*, 239.
22. Notes, early 1955, PPS325(1955).14–20 and clipping, Feb 1955, PPS336(1955).43, RNyl; *New York Times*, Feb 10, 1955.
23. *The News*, Feb 11, 1955, B 1, Trip—Feb 11, Series 357, RNln; *Los Angeles Times*, Feb 11, 1955; *New York Times*, Feb 11, 1955.
24. White to RN, Feb 14, 1955, B 3, Mexico [1 of 3], Series 362, RNln; Niblo, *War, Diplomacy*, 277–278.
25. Notes, early 1955, PPS325(1955).22–23, RNyl; Immerman, *CIA in Guatemala*, began the discussion on this topic; Cullather, *Operation PBSUCCESS*, 2–91; Cullather, *Secret History*, passim; Leonard, "US and CA," 58–59; Barrett, *CIA & Congress*, 161–170; Longley, *In the Eagle's Shadow*, 219–226; Schlesinger and Kinzer, *Bitter Fruit*, 99–204; Cull, *Cold War and the USIA*, 121–122; Meers, "British Connection," 409–428; Holland, "Operation PBHISTORY," 300–323 and "Private Sources of U.S.," 36–73.
26. Bernays to Redmond, Mar 13, 1952, B 378, United Fruit Co, Mar 1952, Whitman to Redmond, Jan 14 and outline of discussion, Jan 14, 1953, B 380, United Fruit Co, Jan–Feb 1953, Bernays mss, LOC; Bernays, *Biography of an Idea*, 764–773.
27. PDDE, XV, pp. 1168–1169 and XVI, pp. 1540–1541; Cabot, *First Line*, 90–91.
28. FR, 1952–1954, Vol. II, P 1, pp. 438–439; Barrett, *CIA & Congress*, 163; Cullather, *Operation PBSUCCESS*, 84.
29. Telephone call from Hagerty, June 30, 1954, R 8, DuHe; Keating interview, July 2, 1954, B 24, F 6, Series 207, RNln; conversation No 587-7, 11:00 a.m., Oval Office, RN tapes; Barrett, *CIA & Congress*, 165.

30. RN speech, Aug 2, 1954, B 25, F 9 [1 of 2], Series 207, RNln; *New York Times*, Aug 3, 1954.

31. Clipping, Feb 12, 1955, B 1, Trip—Feb 12, Series 357, RNln; *Los Angeles Times*, Feb 13, 1955; *New York Times*, Feb 13, 1955.

32. Clipping, Feb 14, 1955, B 1, Trip—Feb 14, Series 357, RNln; *Los Angeles Times*, Feb 15, 1955; *New York Times*, Feb 15, 1955; Streeter, *Managing the Counterrevolution*, 123–124.

33. *FR*, 1955–1957, Vol. VII, pp. 66–67.

34. RN to Roser, Aug 12, PPS320.37.42.1 and Cushman to Costello, Dec 16, 1957, PPS320.37.51, RNyl.

35. Hill to JFD, Feb 23, 1955, R 37, DuHe; *FR*, 1955–1957, Vol. VII, p. 33; *PDDE*, XVI, p. 1600–1601.

36. Braggiotti to RN, Apr 12, 1955, B 2, El Salvador, Series 362, RNln; *New York Times*, Feb 27, 1955; Day 3, Tape 1, 00:34:29 [RN], Gannon mss, WJBma.

37. Clipping, Feb 17, B 1, Trip—Feb 17 and clipping, Feb 18, 1955, B 1, Trip—Feb 18, Series 357, RNln; *PDDE*, XV, p. 1066; *New York Times*, Feb 18–20, 1955; *Los Angeles Times*, Feb 18 and 19, 1955; Leonard, "US and CA," 61–63.

38. *FR*, 1955–1957, Vol. VI, pp. 586–588 and 611–612; Leonard, "US and CA," 63–65.

39. Clipping, Feb 19, B 1, Trip—Feb 19 and clipping, Feb 21, 1955, Trip—Feb 21. Series 357, RNln; *New York Times*, Feb 20, 1955; *Los Angeles Times*, Feb 20, 1955; Tomasek, "Defense of the Western Hemisphere," 382–383 and 385–386.

40. *New York Times*, Feb 21, 22, and 24, 1955; Clark, *US and Somoza*, 190; Longley, *In the Eagle's Shadow*, 227–229; Longley, *Sparrow and the Hawk*, 128–152; Ameringer, *Don Pepe*, 103–130; Atwood, "US and Costa Rica," 150–189; Leonard, "US and CA," 65–69 and 142–145; LaFeber stated: "Only in Somoza's Nicaragua had Nixon's reception been all the vice president could have desired, and he ever after felt a special warmth toward the dictator," *Inevitable Revolutions*, 136 (1983) and 138 (1993); I found nothing to support this statement.

41. Bernays to Lever, Feb 22, 1955, B 376, United Fruit Co 1954–59, Bernays mss, LOC; clipping, Feb 22, B 1, Trip—Feb 22, Series 357 and *Diario Nacional*, Feb 24, 1955, B 1, Costa Rica, Series 356, RNln; *FR*, 1955–1957, Vol. VII, p. 2.

42. *PDDE*, XVI, pp. 1517–1518; Conniff, *Panama and the US*, 105–110.

43. *New York Times*, Feb 26 and 27, 1955.

44. Clipping, Feb 25, 1955, B 1, Trip—Feb 25, Series 357, RNln; Hurwitz to PN, Apr 21, 1955, PPS270.205, RNyl; *Los Angeles Times*, Feb 25, 1955; Day 3, Tape 3, 00:49:29 [RN], Gannon mss, WJBma.

45. Whitman to Woods, Mar 2, 1955, B 814, Whitman, Ann, Series 320, RNln.

46. Clippings, Feb 26 and 27, B 1, Trip—Feb 26 and 27, Feb 28, B 1, Trip—Feb 28 and Mar 1, 1955, Trip—Mar 1, Series 357, RNln; Nixon Calypso, Feb 27, 1955, PPS270.102, RNyl; *New York Times*, Feb 28 and Mar 1, 1955; *Los Angeles Times*, Feb 27 and 28, 1955.

47. Clippings, Mar 2, B 1, Trip—Mar 2 and Mar 3, 1955, B 1, Trip—Mar 3, Series 357, RNln; *Dominican Republic*, Mar 1955, PPS270.114, RNyl; *New York Times*, Mar 2 and 3, 1955; *Los Angeles Times*, Mar 2, 1955; Atkins and Wilson, *Dominican Republic*, 87.

48. Clipping, Mar 3, 1955, B 1, Trip—Mar 3, Series 357, RNln; *New York Times*, Mar 4, 1955.

49. *Chicago Defender*, Mar 19 and Apr 2, 1955; Cannon, *Gentle Knight*, 266–267.
50. *Sunday Star* (DC), Mar 6, 1955, B 1, Trip—Mar 6, Series 357, RNln; *Los Angeles Times*, Mar 9, 1955, PPS336(1955).60, RNyl; telephone call to Ike, Mar 10, 1955, R 9, DuHe; *New York Times*, Mar 6, 1955.
51. *Evening Tribune*, Mar 2, B 1, Trip—Mar 2 and *San Diego Evening Tribune*, Mar 4, 1955, B 1, Trip—Mar 4, Series 357, RNln.
52. *Christian Science Monitor*, Feb 17, *Baptist Message*, Mar 17, RN to Alter, Apr 18, Kay to RN, Apr 14 and Beall to Kay, Apr 20, B 2, Statements on Catholic Church and King to Carver, June 20, 1955, B 626, Religious [2/2], Series 320, RNln; RN to Badamo, Aug 19, 1955, LBM201, RNyl.
53. *The Mirror*, Feb 28, B 1, Trip—Feb 28, clipping, Mar 4, B 1, Trip—Mar 4, clipping, Mar 5, Trip—Mar 5, *New York Herald Tribune*, Mar 5, B 1, Trip—Mar 5, Series 357, press release, Mar 8, B 2, Series 361, *New York Herald Tribune*, Mar 6, 1955, B 5, Central American Trip [1 of 2], Series 358, RNln; *New York Times*, Mar 4 and 5, 1955.
54. Clipping, Mar 5, 1955, B 1, Trip—Mar 5, Series 357, RNln.
55. Meeting, Mar 11, 1955, R 3, Cabinet DDE; cabinet meeting, Mar 11, 1955, B 1a, Mar 1955, Hagerty mss, DDEL; diary, Mar 11, 1955, B 3, VII, WH Years, Shanley mss, DDEL; King to Krupnick, Mar 14, 1955, B 429, Krupnick 1954 to 58 (3 of 3), Series 320 and RN to Ike (draft), Apr 19, 1955, B 5, Central American Trip [1 of 2], Series 358, RNln; *FR*, 1955–1957, Vol. VI, pp. 614–618.
56. *PPA* 1955, pp. 361–362; telephone call, Mar 22, 1955, R 3, DuHe; diary, Mar 29, 1955, B 1a, Mar 1955, Hagerty mss, DDEL; minutes, Mar 25, 1955, R 3, Cabinet DDE; memo, Mar 29, 1955, R 1, Legislative DDE; *FR*, 1955–1957, Vol. VI, p. 6; Edgerton to RN, Mar 25, B 1, Loans, press release, Apr 1, B 1, Central American Trip, Inter-American Highway (1 of 2) and Ike to RN, Apr 1, 1955 B 1, Central American Trip Inter-American Highway (2 of 2), Series 361, RNln; Notes from Holland, Oct 7, 1960, R 12, Paterson mss, UCt; RN, "Nixon's Own Story," 101.
57. ER, Mar 11(?), 1954, B 18. F 1, Series 207, RN statement, pr 24, King to Houghton, May 2, B 248, Exchange Program, M. Eisenhower to RN, June 3, 1955, B 238, M. Eisenhower 2/2, Series 320, RNln; *New York Herald Tribune*, Apr 27, 1955, PPS336(1955).S189, RNyl; Kersten to JFD, Apr 25, 1955, Kersten mss, MLsc.
58. Platter, Mar 11, 1954, RNyl; RN OH, 28, JFD OH; *PDDE*, XV, p. 810 and XVI, pp. 1572–1573; Kaufman, *Trade and Aid*, 34–46 and 49–57.
59. RN address, Mar 14, B 5, Central American Trip [1 of 2], Series 358, *Los Angeles Times*, Mar 13 and 15, B 27, F 9, RN to McCone, Mar 21, B 27. F 13 and RN speech, Mar 14, 1955, B 28, F 2, Series 207, RNln; RN speech, Mar 14, 1955, PPS208(1955).1.5(5), RNyl.
60. Hilton, "US, Brazil, and the Cold War," 612–617; Weis, *Cold Warriors*, 57–84; Eisenhower, *Mandate*, 135–136.
61. *San Francisco Chronicle*, Feb 15, B 1, Trip—Feb 15, Series 357, memo, Dec 15, 1955, B 48, F 1, Series 207, RNln; *FR*, 1955–1957, Vol. VI, pp. 14–15; telephone call, Dec 23, 1955, R 4, DuHe; *New York Times*, Dec 12, 1955, PPS336(1955), Supplement A.88 and Kubitschek to RN, Jan 9, 1956, PPS320.1.11, RNyl; diary, Feb 7, 1956, R 5, Diary DDE; Cobbs, *Rich Neighbor*, 218–219; Alexander, *Kubitschek*, 145; Weis, *Cold Warriors*, 84–86; Hilton, "US, Brazil and the Cold War," 617–618.

62. Telephone calls, Dec 13, 1955, DuHe; Lyons to JFD, Dec 20, 1955, memo, Jan 13, B 48, F 1, RN to Baughman, Feb 16, B 47, F 8, Series 207, Smith to RN, Feb 16, B 704, Smith, EE and press conf, Jan 25, 1956, B 237, Eisenhower Statements, Series 320, RNln.
63. Schedule, Feb 1 and 2, B 47, F 1, clipping Feb 29 or 31, B 47, F, clipping, Feb 1, RN remarks, Feb 1 and 2, 1956, B 48, F 1, Series 207, RNln; *New York Times*, Jan 31, 1956; *FR*, 1955–1957, Vol. VI, p. 382.
64. Schedule, Feb 3, B 47, F 10, RN speech, Feb 3, B 47, F 9, Series 207 and RN speech, Feb 1953, B 38, The American Daily, Series 320, RNln; *FR*, 1955–1957, Vol. VII, p. 692.
65. Diary, Feb 7, 1956, R 5, Diary DDE; *Washington Daily News* (DC), Feb 9 and *New York Herald Tribune*, Feb 9, B 48, F 1, Series 207. RN to May, Mar 29, B 485, May [2/2] and Dunn to RN, Apr 5, 1956, B 230. Dunn, J, Series 320, RNln; *Newsweek*, Feb 13, 1956, p. 50; Weis, *Cold Warriors*, 97–112; Hilton, "US, Brazil," 618–619; Tomasek, "Defense of the Western Hemisphere," 387–389.
66. Eisenhower, *Mandate*, 237–238.
67. Holland to Ike, Aug 27, 1956, R 3, DuHe; Holland, "U.S. Relations with the American Republics," Mar 2, 1955, B 1, Central American Trip Inter-American Highway (2 of 2), Series 361, RNln; notes from Holland, Oct 7, 1960, R 12, Paterson mss, UCt.
68. Milton Eisenhower OH, 11–12 and 19, LBJL.

CHAPTER 13. THE U.S. RESPONSE TO NEUTRALISM

1. *New York Times*, June 7, 1956; Department of State *Bulletin*, June 7, 1956, p. 1004.
2. Memoirs, Mar 16, 1976, RNyl; *PPA* 1955, pp. 433–434; *New York Times*, June 8, 1956.
3. Memo by Washburn, Mar 31, 1956, B 2, Manila Briefings, Series 367, RNln; Department of State *Bulletin*, June 8, 1956, pp. 999–1004.
4. Memo, Mar 31, 1956, B 2 Manila—Briefings, Series 367, RNln.
5. *FR*, 1955–1957, Vol. XXII, pp. 648–649; Telephone, May 14, B 5, May 1–June 29, 1956 (4) and memo, May 14, R 3, memo and conversation, and telephone, May 24, 1956, R 4, DuHe.
6. Telephone, June 13 and 14, R 9 and memo, June 18, 1956, R 3, memo and conversation, DuHe; Day 3, Tape 4, 00:01:03 [RN], Gannon mss, WJBma; *FR*, 1955–1957, Vol. XXII, p. 652; *New York Times*, June 19, 1956.
7. Diary, June 29, 1956, PPS212(1956).3, RNyl; schedule, July 1, B 1, Philippines - Vietnam, RN to Kauffman, July 7, B 1, Los Alamitos, Series 367, and RN to Marshall, July 12, 1956, B 477, Marshall, JP, Series 320, RNln; *New York Times*, July 1, 1956; *Los Angeles Times*, July 13, 1956.
8. Everts to Reynolds, July 2, B 53, F 20, Series 207, *Guam Daily News*, July 3, B 1, Guam, Series 374, clipping, July 2, B 2, Honolulu, RN to King and RN to Stump, July 13, 1956, B 1, General, Series 367, RNln; *Los Angeles Times*, July 2, 1956.
9. *Manila Times*, July 4, B 2, Manila [4 of 5] and Burrows to Dulles, July 13, 1956, B 2, Manila [1 of 5], Series 367, RNln; *FR*, 1955–1957, Vol. XXII, pp. 655–659; *Newsweek*, July 16, 1956, p. 38; *New York Times*, July 4, 1956; Kim, "US-Philippines," 19–107, 128–148, and 287–290; Cullather, *Illusions of Influence*, 150–153 and 189–190; McMahon, *Limits of Empire*, 90–95.

10. *FR*, 1955–1957, Vol. XXII, pp. 657–658; Burrows to Dulles, July 13, 1956. B 2, Manila [1 of 5], Series 367, RNln.

11. Schedule, July 4, B 1, Philippines–Vietnam, Burrows to JFD, July 7, B 1, Cables and July 13, B 2, Manila[1 of 5], unsent to *New York Times*, July 1956, B 2, Manila, Philippines, Series 367, RNln; RN to Webster, July 26, 1956, PPS320.77.31, RNyl; Day 3, Tape 1, 00:28:34 [RN], Gannon mss, WJBma.

12. *New York Times* and *Los Angeles Times*, July 4, 1956; some of these themes were anticipated in an earlier speech, *New York Times*, June 13, 1954.

13. *New York Daily Mirror*, July 6 and *San Diego Union*, July 7, B 1, Clippings, Series 367, memo, July 5 and Washburn to King, July 11, B 2, The Philippines (1 of 2), Series 374 and Rhyne to RN, Aug 7, 1956, B 640, Rhyne (2 of 3), Series 320, RNln.

14. Memo, July 14, 1956, B 1, Trip Reaction, Series 367, RNln; Pope, "Foundations of," 288–289; *Los Angeles Times*, July 9, 1956.

15. Wilkins to RN, July 6, 1956, PPS320.77.27, RNyl; *Los Angeles Times*, July 6, 1956.

16. *Los Angeles Times*, July 7, 1956; *New York Times*, July 8, 1956.

17. Radio reports, July 9, 1956, B 165, Combs, Series 320, RNln; *New York Times* and *Los Angeles Times*, July 10, 1956; Sharada Prasad et al. eds., *Selected Works*, Vol. 34, pp. 275 and 310–311.

18. *US Congressional Record*, July 11, 1956, p. 11132, B 1, Clippings, Series 367, RNln; *Los Angeles Times*, July 12, 1956.

19. Hoffman to Mehta, Aug 2, 1956, B 346, Hoffman, 2 of 2, Series 320, RNln and Eminent Personages File, Nixon, Richard M.—1952–1960, Hoffman mss, HSTL; RN to Hoffman, Aug 7, 1956, Eminent Personages File, Nixon, Richard M.—1952–1960, Hoffman mss, HSTL; Sharada Prasad et al. eds., *Selected Works*, Vol. 34, p. 317.

20. Day 2, Tape 1, 00:32:40 [RN], Gannon mss, WJBma; the debate over Eisenhower sending troops, see Milton Eisenhower OH, 28–29, Charles Halleck OH, Karl Mundt OH, and Wilbur Mills OH, II, p. 19, LBJL; Logevall, *Embers of War*, 669.

21. Heath to RN, Aug 23, 1954, B 330, Heath, D, Series 320, RNln.

22. RN to Reinhardt, July 20, 1956, B 3, Saigon, Series 367, RNln; *FR*, 1955–1957, Vol. I, p. 718; Anderson, "J. Lawton Collins, JFD," 127–147; Statler, *Replacing France*, 117–216; Jian, *Mao's China*, 205–207.

23. Schedule, July 6, B 1, Philippines–Viet Nam, Ngo Dinh Diem to RN, July 6, B 3, Saigon, and Reinhardt to JFD, July 9, B 1, Cables series 367, RNln; Day 2, Tape 1, 00:34:11 [RN] and 00:32:40 [RN], Gannon mss, WJBma; *Los Angeles Times*, July 7, 1956; *FR*, 1955–1957, Vol. I, p. 718; Anderson ed., *Trapped by Success*, 153.

24. Record of conversation, July 8, PPS325.1956, RN to Diem, July 19, 1956, PPS320.99.13 and Diem to RN, Feb 28, 1961, PPS320.99.64, RNyl; Part 1, 11:36, Apr 7, 1983, Gannon mss, WJBma.

25. *Los Angeles Times*, July 3 and 8, 1956; *New York Times*, July 8, 1956.

26. Memo, July 7, B 3, Taipei and Rankin to JFD, July 10, 1956, B 1, Cables, Series 367, RNln; memo, July 8, PPS325(1956).80.2, record of conversation, July 8, PPS325.1956, report, Sept 24, PPS325(1956).151.2 and Hoover to RN, Oct 9, 1956, PPS325.1956, RNyl.

27. Press conf, July 8, B 1, Foreign Press 91 of 20, Series 374 and Bishop to JFD, July 12, 1956, B 1, Cables, Series 367, RNln; RN to Pibulsonggram, July 19, 1956, PPS320.91.22.1,

RNyl; *FR,* 1955–1957, Vol. XXII, pp. 895–896; *Los Angeles Times,* July 4 and July 9, 1956.

28. Press conf, July 9, B 4, Karachi, Briefings, press conf, July 10 and Gardiner to JFD, July 11, B 1, Cables and RN to Mirza, July 20, 1956, B 4, Karachi, Thank, Series 367, RNln; *FR,* 1955–1957, Vol. VIII, pp. 463–469; *Los Angeles Times,* July 10, 1956.

29. Memo, Aug 22, 1955, B 12, Aug 1955 (3), chronological series, DuHe; *FR,* 1955–1957, Vol. XXIV, pp. 656–657.

30. *Evening Star* (DC), July 10, B 1, Ankara, Series 374, Warren to JFD, July 10 and 13, B 1, Cables, RN to Bayar, July 26 and RN to Warren, July 27, 1956, B 4, Ankara, Thank, Series 367, RNln; *FR,* 1955–1957, Vol. XXIV, p. 379; *Los Angeles Times* and *New York Times,* July 10, 1956.

31. Memo, Mar 23, B 49, F 21, Series 207, memo, July 10, B 1, Mallorca, Lodge to JFD, July 12 and 17, B 1, General and RN to Lodge, July 20, 1956, B 1, Mallorca, Series 367, RNln; *FR,* 1952–1954, Vol. VI, p. 1944–1945; *Los Angeles Times,* July 11, 1956.

32. *New York Times* and *Los Angeles Times,* July 12, 1956.

33. Telephone, July 12, 1956, R 9, DuHe.

34. *FR,* 1955–1957, Vol. X, pp. 79–82.

35. Graebner, *New Isolationism,* 239–263, declared the Ike-Dulles diplomacy failed because there was no room for Democratic participation and Nixon had no role.

CHAPTER 14. INCUMBENT POLITICS

1. Charles Halleck OH 489, p. 12, DDEL; Charles Halleck OH, LBJL.

2. RN to Creel, Apr 14, 1953, B 4, General Correspondence, Creel mss, LOC, and also see Creel correspondence in 320 Series, RNln; The 1953 Elections, Dec 1953, PPS12A.10, RNyl; Eisenhower, *Mandate,* 428–442; Nixon, *RN,* 159–163; Donovan, *Eisenhower,* 271.

3. Major political polls, Apr 1954 and Jan 1956, R 2, *PRP; Gallup Poll,* Two, 1211, 1221, 1236 and 1265.

4. *PDDE,* XIV, pp. 663–664; Moser, *Watershed and Ratifying,* 17–18; Harris, *Is There a Republican?,* 201–208.

5. Gellman, *Contender.*

6. *Los Angeles Times,* June 21, PPS336(1953).25, Chotiner to Browning, Aug 6, PPS300.280, and Woods to Chotiner, Sept 14, 1953, PPS300.306, RNyl.

7. Williams, to RN, Nov 30, B 17, F 3, Schramm to Hall Dec, B 20, F 4 and Howard to RN, Dec 8, 1953, B 17, F 2 (1 of 2), Series 207, RNln.

8. Calendar, Jan 19, 1954, PPS212(1954).2.35, *Washington Post,* Apr 6, PPS336(1955).85, diary, Apr 27, 1955, PPS212(1955).2, RNyl; RN to Jameson, Apr 19, 1955, B 378, Jameson, F, Series 320, RNln; Day 8, Tape 1, 00:02:36 [RN], Gannon mss, WJBma; Winget OH, 985, p. 7, CSUF; *Washington Post,* Aug 19, 1965.

9. RN remarks, Feb 5, 1954, B 16, F 13, Series 207, RNln; proceedings of the RNC, Feb 5, 1954, R 14, *PRP.*

10. RN speech, Feb 11 and *Bridgeport Post* (Conn), Feb 12, 1954, B 17, F 1(2 of 2), Series 207, RNln.

11. RN speech, Apr 3, B 19, F 7, Barrett to RN, Apr 26 and Button to RN, Apr 29, Box 20, F 6 (1 of 2), *Fortnight*, May 5, B 22, F 10 (1) and RN remarks, May 26, 1954, B 21, F 20, Series 207, RNln.

12. Platter, June 10, 1954, RNyl.

13. *PPA* 1954, pp. 722–723; platter, June 18, 1954, RNyl.

14. Platter, June 19, 1954, RNyl.

15. Platter, June 18, 1954, pp. 3–4, RNyl.

16. "Change in Washington," June 26, 1954, R 2, *PRP*; VP schedule, June 26–27, B 24, F 10 [1 of 2] and RN speech, June 26, 1954, F 10 [2 of 2] and *Press Gazette* (Wis), June 28, 1954, F 1 [2 of 2], Series 207, RNln; *Los Angeles Times*, June 27, PPS336(1954).S248 and *Washington Post*, July 3, 1954, PPS336(1954).S257, RNyl; *Newsweek*, July 5, 1954, p. 17.

17. Byrnes to Ike, July 6, Kohler to RN, July 8, B 24, F 11 [1 of 2] and Gainey to Siney, Aug 30, 1954, F 11 [2 of 2] Series 207, RNln.

18. *New York Times*, June 28, 1954.

19. Memo of conversation, June 28, 1954, R 1, DuHe.

20. Ike to RN, June 28 draft and Ike to RN, June 28, 1954, R 4, Diary DDE.

21. Memo, June 29, 1954, B 28, Richard Nixon (5), administrative series, DDEL; *PDDE*, XV, p. 1155.

22. Platter, June 29, 1954, RNyl.

23. Platter, June 29, 1954, *New York Herald Tribune*, July 1, 1954, PPS336(1954).S252, RNyl; *Illinois State Journal*, July 1, 1954, B 23, F 10 [1 of 2], Series 207, RNln; *PPA* 1954, pp. 610–612; *Hagerty Diary*, 81.

24. *PPA* 1954, pp. 613–614; *Washington Post*, July 4, 1954, PPS336(1954).S259, RNyl; Dulaney and Phillips eds., *"Speak, Mister Speaker,"* 253–254.

25. RN to Kohler, July 9, B 424, Kohler, WJ, Series 320 and RN to Nagle, July 16, 1954, B 23, F 9 [1 of 2], Series 207, RNln.

26. *Tucson Daily Citizen* (Az), Aug 16, 1954, PPS325(1954).108, RNyl.

CHAPTER 15. THE ILL-WILL TOUR VERSUS THE BIG LIE

1. Woods to Hannah and Frank, Sept 20, 1954, PPS18.621, RNyl. For background on the election see Donovan, *Eisenhower*, 264–284; Nixon, *RN*, 159–163; Eisenhower, *Mandate*, 428–442.

2. Hall to RN, Sept 4, PPS17.33.1, memo, Sept 16, PPS22.Advance Men 1956, memo, Sept 17, PPS18.811, Everts to Scribner, Sept 30, PPS19.24A, Chotiner to Wiggins, Dec 6, 1954, PPS300.356 and notes for memoirs, 1977–1978, PPS208(1954).53.1, RNyl; Phillips, "One-Man Task Force," 17.

3. Memo, Sept 16, PPS22.Advance Men 1956, Woods to Whitman, Sept 22, PPS18.711 and RN address, Oct 27, 1954, PPS208(1954).88.5, RNyl; Woods to Whitman, Sept 14, B 814, Whitman, An, Series 320 and Woods to Prichard, Nov 15, 1954, B 29, F 7, Series 207, RNln.

4. RN to Bliss, May 28, PPS18.2, Bow to RN, Aug 7, PPS18.5, RN to Bow, Aug 25, PPS18.10, RN speech, Sept 16, PPS208(1954).19.5(1), *Tucson Daily Citizen*, Sept 16, PPS336(1954). S342 and Pierce to RN, Oct 5, 1954, PPS18.214, RNyl.

5. Memo, Sept 29, PPS18.2032, Nagle to RN, Oct 6, PPS18.1945, *Toledo Blade*, Oct 5, PPS18.2050.3 and RN to Lowe, Nov 10, 1954, PPS18.2108.1, RNyl; Boeschenstein to RN, Oct 5, 1954, B 91, Boeschenstein, Series 320, RNln.

6. RN to Cox, Sept 13, PPS18.241, RN remarks, Sept 16, PPS208(1954).21.1(1), *Kansas City Star*, Sept 16, PPS336(1954).S346, *Wichita Eagle*, Sept 17, PPS336(1954).o.s.63, *Topeka Daily Capital*, Sept 17, PPS336(1954)o.s.62 and Manka to Woods, Nov 12, 1954, PPS18.354 and RN to Landon, Nov 12, 1955, PPS325(1955).223, RNyl.

7. Hillelson to RN, Sept 4, PPS18.368, Haggans to RN, Sept 18, PPS18.398, *St. Louis Globe Democrat*, Sept 18, PPS336(1954).S358 and Hobbs to RN, Sept 22, 1954, PPS18.407.1, RNyl.

8. Beck to RN, Aug 25, PPS18.489, RN remarks, Sept 18, PPS208(1954).23.2(1), Lovre to RN, Sept 19, PPS18.515, *Los Angeles Times*, Sept 19, PPS336(1954).S360, *Evening Star* (DC), Sept 30, PPS336(1954).S404, RN remarks, Sept 18, 1954, PPS208(1954).22.2, RNyl and B 1, F 1, Lewis mss, RNyl; Heidepriem, *Fair Chance*, 192.

9. Chotiner to Spear, Sept 13, PPS18.599, memo, Sept 19, PPS18.610, *World Herald* (Neb), Sept 20, PPS336(1954).S364 and Sept 21, PPS18.622, *St. Louis Post-Dispatch*, Sept 21, PPS336(1954).S372 and Higgins to Woods, Nov 8, 1954, PPS18.676, RNyl; Curtis to RN, Nov 24, 1954, B 197, Curtis, C, Series 320, RNln.

10. *Los Angeles Times*, Sept 20, PPS336(1954).S364, RN remarks, Sept 22, 1954, PPS208(1954).29.2 and *Detroit Free Press*, PPS18.825.2, RNyl; RN speech, Sept 21, 1954, B 28, RN (4), Administrative Series, DDEL; *Newsweek*, Oct 4, 1954, p. 21; Sevareid, "Demon A.D.A.," 17; Gillon, *Politics and Vision*, 110.

11. Woods to Bixby, Sept 25, PPS18.715, RN to Stassen, PPS8.717, Kendall to RN, Sept 15, PPS18.715, Sept 25, PPS18.714 and Oct 18, 1954, PPS18.749.1, RNyl.

12. Diary, Sept 24, 1954, B 32, Vol. VI, WH Years (7), Shanley mss, DDEL.

13. Press release, Sept 28, PPS208(1954).32.2(1), *Hampshire Gazette* (Mass), Sept 28, PPS336(1954).S391, *Boston Post*, Sept 29, PPS336(1954).S393, *Christian Science Monitor*, Sept 29, PPS336(1954).o.s.81, Treat to RN, Nov 8, PPS18.1151.1 and Celia to Woods, Dec 13, 1954, PPS18.1107, RNyl.

14. *PDDE*, XV, pp. 1302–1303.

15. *PPA* 1954, pp. 865–874; *Newsweek*, Oct 4, 1954, p. 21.

16. *PDDE*, XV, pp. 1313–1314.

17. Ibid., 1319; Woods to Ann, Sept 22 and RN speech, Sept 21, 1954, B 28, Richard Nixon (4), Administrative Series, DDEL.

18. *Newsweek*, Oct 4, 1954, pp. 21–22.

19. *Washington Daily News* (DC), Sept 23, PPS336(1954).S381, *New York Times*, Sept 27, PPS336(1954).S386, and *Washington Evening Star* (DC), Oct 1, 1954, PPS336(1954).S410, RNyl.

20. Press release, Sept 30, PPS208(1954).34.2, *Troy Record* (New York), Sept 30, PPS336(1954).S403, *Journal-Every Evening* (Del), Oct 1, PPS336(1954).S411, Weis to RN, Oct 4, PPS18.1168 and Carperter to RN, Oct 14, 1954, PPS18.1281, RNyl; diary, Sept 30, 1954, p. 1666, Vol. VI, B 2, WH Years (7), Shanley mss, DDEL.

21. Diary, Sept 30, 1954, p. 1666, Vol. VI. B 2, WH Years (7), Shanley mss, DDEL; *PDDE*, XV, pp. 1288–1290; Case to RN, Aug 6, PPS18.1310 and Aug 24, PPS18.1313 and *Journal-Every Evening* (Del), Oct 1, 1954, PPS336(1954).S411, RNyl.

22. Miele to RN, Oct 19, PPS18.1371, Kron to RN, Nov 8, PPS18.1373 and RN to Kron, Dec 6, 1954, PPS18.1376, RNyl; diary, Sept 30–Oct 1, 1954, pp. 1666–1668, Vol. VI, B 2, WH Years (7), Shanley mss, DDEL.; *New York Times*, Oct 1, 1954.

23. Chandler to RN, Oct 2, PPS18.1387, *Washington Evening Star* (DC), Oct 2, PPS336(1954). S416, RN to Atkinson, Oct 2, PPS18.429, *Louisville Courier-Journal*, Oct 3, PPS336(1954).S425, *Los Angeles Times*, Oct 4, PPS336(1954).S418 and Watkins to RN, Oct 19, 1954, PPS18.1412, RNyl; Schulman, *Cooper*, 56–66.

24. *Fortnight*, Mar 12, PPS336(1954).S141, Everts to Westrom, Oct 2, PPS18.1940, memo, Oct 4, PPS19.28 and *Washington Post*, Oct 5, 1954, PPS336(1954).S426, RNyl.

25. Woods to Sanford, Sept 1, 1954, B 26, F 1, Series 207, RNln; Goodwin to RN, Sept 29, PPS18.1936, Nagle to RN, Oct 6, PPS18.1945 and *Globe-Gazette* (Iowa) Oct 5, 1954, PPS336(1954).S427, RNyl.

26. Woods to Rogers, Oct 7, 1954, B 50, F 2, Rogers mss, DDEL.

27. *Rocky Mountain News* (Colo), Oct 9, PPS336(1954).S453 and Woods to Haskell, Nov 8, 1954, PPS18.2126, RNyl; Rogers to RN, Oct 11, 1954, B 652, Rogers (4 of 4), Series 320, RNln; *PDDE*, XV, pp. 1307–1309 and 1319; *Newsweek*, Oct 4, 1954, pp. 20–21.

28. *PDDE*, XV, pp. 1337–1338, 1345 and 1352; memoirs, Mar 15, 1976, RNyl.

29. *Washington Evening Star* (DC), Oct 13, 1954, PPS336(1954) and memoirs, Mar 16, 1976, RNyl; Geelhoed, *Wilson*, 195; Donovan, *Eisenhower*, 276–277; Adams, *Firsthand Report*, 165.

30. Mecham to RN, Aug 18, PPS18.2129 and Oct 11, PPS18.2151 and RN speech, Oct 9, 1954, PPS208(1954).47.2.1, RNyl.

31. RN to Smith, Aug 16, PPS18.2284, Mosher to RN, Sept 24, PPS18.224, RN to Knowland, Sept 27, PPS18.2235, Kuchel to RN, Oct 5, PPS18.2242, *Los Angeles Times*, Oct 10, PPS336(1954).S457, Oct 11, PPS18.2272.13, Oct 14, PPS336(1954).S490, *Fresno Bee* (Calif), Oct 12, PPS336(1954).S469, RN statement, Oct 13, PPS208(1954).59.2, RN speech, Oct 13, PPS208(1954).57 and RN address, Oct 13, 1954, PPS208(1954).60, RNyl; Bewley to RN, Aug 27, B 80, Bewley [½] and RN to McCone, Sept 8, 1954, B 493, McCone [2/2], Series 320, RNln; Spooner, "Revitalization of the Right," 112–113, in Schiesl ed., *California Politics*; Gillon, *Politics and Vision*, 110.

32. Baldwin Workers Guide, 1954, PPS18.2300, memo, Oct 10, PPS19.47, RN address, Oct 11, PPS208(1954).48.2, *San Francisco Examiner*, Oct 12, PPS336(1954).o.s.100 and *San Diego Union*, Oct 12, 1954, PPPS336(1954).S458 and fundamentals of campaign organization, Sept 7–10, 1955, PPS300.422A, RNyl; Fried, *Men Against McCarthy*, 304.

33. RN statement, Oct 24, PPS208(1954).79.2 and Oct 27, 1954, PPS208(1954).87.3, RNyl.

34. RN statement, Oct 29, PPS208(1954).97.2, RNyl; Baldwin to RN, Nov 5, 1954, B 61, Baldwin, J, Series 320, RNln; Barclay, "1954 Election in California," 598.

35. Summary, Oct 29, PPS19A.24.2, RN address, Oct 29, PPS208(1954).98.3, *Palo Alto Times* (Calif), Oct 30, PPS336(1954).S589, *San Mateo Times* (Calif), Oct 30, PPS336 (1954).o.s.138, Woods to Hancock, Nov 13, PPS19A.6.1, RN to Moore, Nov 20, PPS19A.7, *Los Angeles Times*, Nov 27, PPS19A.10, Cotton to RN, Nov 29, PPS19A.13.1, memo, Dec 2, PPS19A.16, RN to Kaiser, Dec 14, 1954, PPS19.A20 and Paterni to Baughman, Feb 23,

1955, PPS19A.25, RNyl; Hamilton to RN, May 13, 1955, B 315, Hamilton, R, Series 320, RNln; Rex Scouten interview, Apr 22, 2010.

36. Barclay, "1954 Elections in California," 597–604; Lee, *California Votes*, Table 1–2; Bell, *Ca. Crucible*, 106–114; interview with Rex Scouten, Apr 22, 2010.

37. RN to Thorton and RN to Shivers, July 17, 1954, B 692, Shivers, Series 320, RNln; RN to Black, Oct 4, PPS18.2524 and EN speech, Oct 14, 1954, PPS208(1954).61.3, RNyl; Dobbs, *Yellow Dogs*, 113–114.

38. *Washington Star* (DC), Oct 2, PPS336(1954).S417, *Los Angeles Mirror*, Oct 11, PPS18.2275.12, *Washington Post*, Oct 11, PPS336(1954).S464 and *San Diego Union*, Oct 17, 1954, PPS 336(1954).S501, RNyl; Stevenson speech, Oct 2, 1954, B 380, F 7, Stevenson mss, HML.

39. *PAES*, IV, pp. 407–417.

40. *New York Herald Tribune*, Oct 2, PPS336(1954).S417 and *Cleveland Plain Dealer* (Ohio), Oct 6, 1954, PPS336(1954).S433, RNyl; memo, Oct 8, 1954, B 508, memo before 1955, Series 320, RNln; *Gallup Poll*, Two, 1273.

41. *Washington Star* (DC), Oct 2, 1954, PPS336(1954).S417, RNyl.

42. Memo, Oct 3, PPS17.41, memo, Oct 3, PPS18.999, news release, Oct 19, PPS208(1954).172.18. *U.S. News & World Report*, Oct 22, PPS336(1954).S531 and Chotiner to Sundlun, Oct 22, 1954, PPS17.44C, RNyl; diary, Oct 18, 1954, Vol. VI, B 2, WH Years (7), Shanley mss, DDEL.

43. RN statement, Oct 18, PPS208(1954).63 and *New York Herald Tribune*, Oct 19, 1954, PPS336(1954).S508, RNyl.

44. *Pittsburgh Press*, Oct 19, PPS336(1954).S514, RN address, Oct 19, PPS208(1954).65A(1), RN address, Oct 20, PPS208(1954).66.7.2, Hodge to RN, Oct 20, PPS18.2621, *Los Angeles Times*, Oct 20, PPS336(1954).S517, Kroeger to RN, Nov 2, PPS18.2706 and PN to Helene, Oct 23, 1954, DR 95, RNyl; Fulton to RN, Dec 9, 1954, B 277, Fulton, James, Series 320, RNln.

45. *Chicago Daily Tribune*, Oct 21, PPS336(1954).S521, RN address, Oct 21, PPS208(1954).69.2, *Rock Island Argus* (Ill), Oct 22, PPS336(1954).S532 and Chotiner to Faveluke, Oct 23, 1954, PPS18.3081, RNyl; *New York Times*, Oct 22, 1954.

46. Aronson to RN, Sept 18, PPS18.2731, Denny to Woods, Oct 25, 1954, PPS18.2757, RNyl; *PDDE*, XV, pp. 1351–1352.

47. RN address, Oct 22, PPS208(1954).70.5, *Billings Gazette* (Mont), Oct 23, 1954, PPS336(1954).S541 and RN to Cullen, Oct 23, 1956, PPS18.2546, RNyl; radio reports, July 20, 1956, B 475, Mansfield, Mik, Series 320, RNln.

48. RN statement, Oct 24, PPS208(1954).768.2, *Arizona Republic*, Oct 15, PPS18.2910.2, *San Diego Union*, Oct 25, PPS336(1954).S555 and *Los Angeles Times*, Oct 25, PPS336(1954).S548, RNyl; Lodge to RN, Oct 26, 1954, B 457, Lodge (2 of 2), Series 320, RNln.

49. Temple Men's Club to member, Oct 9, PPS18.3073, RN speech, Oct 25, PPS208(1954).83.3 and PPS208(1954).81.2, *Las Vegas Sun*, Oct 25, PPS336(9154).S555, Smith to RN, Oct 26, PPS18.2847, RN speech, Oct 26, PPS208(1954).84.2 and PPS208(1954).86.3, *Daily Barometer* (Ore), Oct 27, PPS336(1954).S557, RN address, Oct 30, PPS208(1954).101.1, Gard to RN, Nov 2, PPS18.3098, Burns to RN, Nov 5, 1954, PPS18.3024, RNyl.

50. Memo, Oct 30 and RN to Morishima, Dec 27, 1954, B 530, Morishima, Series 320, RNln; *Seattle Post-Intelligencer*, Oct 31, PPS336(1954).S598, *Washington Post*, Nov 1, PPS336(1954).S605, RN to Khan, Nov 16, 1954, RNyl; *New York Times*, Oct 31 and Nov 1, 1954.

51. *San Diego Union*, Oct 28, PPS336(1954).S572 and *U.S. News & World Report*, Oct 29, 1954, PPS336(1954).S588, RNyl; *PPA* 1954, pp. 975–976; Eisenhower, *Mandate*, 437–438.

52. Gruber to RN, Nov 5, 1954, B 306, Gruber, Series 320, RNln; *PDDE*, IV, p. 2495 and XVI, pp. 1894–1895; Holt, *Mamie*, 20–21.

53. Schlesinger to RN, Oct 22, PPS19.82, *New York Herald Tribune*, Oct 23, PPS336(1954). S539 and Chotiner to Pearson, Oct 31, PPS300.352 and *New York Post*, Oct 31, 1954, PPS336(1954).S420, RNyl; *Oregonian*, Oct 21, 1954, B G281 [281 [1 of 4], Pearson mss, LBJL; *Pearson Diaries*, 334; *Reporter*, Nov 4, 1954, p. 17.

54. *Gazette* (Mont), Oct 23, PPS336(1954).S537, *Los Angeles Times*, Oct 27, PPS336(1954). S562, *Washington Evening Star* (DC), Oct 29, 1954, PPS336(1954).S568, RNyl; Martin, *Adlai Stevenson and the World*, 142–145; *PAES*, IV, pp. 392–393 and 421.

55. *Washington Post*, Nov 2, 1954, PPS336(1954).S616, RNyl; *PAES*, IV, pp. 421–428; *New York Times*, Nov 2, 1954; Eisenhower, *Mandate*, 437.

56. *PDDE*, XV, p. 1353.

57. Schedule, Nov 1, 1954, R 4, Diary DDE; *New York Times*, Nov 2, 1954; RN to Howard, Dec 28, 1954, B 357, Howard, R, Series 320, RNln.

58. *New York Times*, Nov 2, 1954.

59. RN speech, Nov 1, PPS208(1954).106.4, RN address, Nov 1, PPS208(1954).103.4, *Washington Post*, Nov 2, 1954, PPS336(1954).S613, RNyl; RN to Howard, Dec 28, 1954, B 357, Howard, R, Series 320, RNln; *New York Times*, Nov 2, 1954.

60. Day 3, Tape 3, 00:57:35 and 00:59:28 [RN], Apr 8, 1953, Gannon mss, WJBma; Adams, *Firsthand Report*, 167.

61. RN statement, Oct 28, 1954, PPS208(1954).92 (1), RNyl; major political polls, Oct 4–31 and Nov 1, 1954 and June 15–Dec 31, 1955, R 2, *PRP*; *Gallup Poll*, Two, 1276–1277; *Newsweek*, Nov 1, 1954, p. 21.

62. *New York Times*, Nov 7, PPS336(1954).S638 and Nov 11, 1954, PPS336(1954).S629, RNyl; RN speech, May 10, 1955, B 29, F 22, Series 207, RNln; *Los Angeles Times*, Nov 4, 1954; Reichard, *Reaffirmation of Republicanism*, 214–217; Busch, *Horses in Midstream*, 157; Stanley ed., *Vital Statistics*, 124; Donovan, *Eisenhower*, 282.

63. Ike to Davies, Dec 1, 1954, B 204, Davies, P, Series 320, RNln; Person OH 161, p. 96, CCOH; *Newsweek*, Nov 15, 1954, p. 37; Eisenhower, *Mandate*, 438–442; Crandell, "A Party Divided," 323–331; Adams, *Firsthand Report*, 165–166; Harris, *Is There a Republican?*, 208–214; Reichard, *Reaffirmation of Republicanism*, 213–214.

64. Telephone call, Nov 3, 1954, R 3, DuHe; Cowles to RN, Nov 4, B 186, Cowles Pub and Hall to RN, Dec 13, 1954, B 313, Hall [3/3], Series 320, RNln; *New York Journal American*, Nov 4, 1954, PPS19.177.4, RNyl.

65. RN statement, Nov 2, 1954, PPS208(1954).105.2, RNyl; *Newsweek*, Nov 15, 1954, p. 34; Day 3, Tape 3, 00:59:17 [RN], Apr 8, 1983, Gannon mss, WJBma.

66. *U.S. News & World Report*, Nov 12, 1954, pp. 46–47; *Newsweek*, Nov 15, 1954, p. 34; Saulnier, *Constructive Years*, 63–75; Sundquist, *Politics and Policy*, 430–441; Parthenakis,

"George M. Humphrey," 282–283; Morgan, *Ike versus "the Spenders,"* 69–70; Bean, *Influence in the 1954*, pp. 1–3 and 35; Lubell, *Revolt of the Moderates*, 107.

67. *Los Angeles Examiner*, Oct 29, PPS336(1954).o.s.135 and *San Diego Union*, Nov 9, 1954, PPS336(1954).S646, RNyl; RN to Lodge, Nov 19, 1954, B 458, Lodge (1 of 2), Series 320, RNln; *U.S. News & World Report*, Nov 12, 1954, p. 47.

68. Bancroft to RN, Nov 7, B 62, Bancroft, Hearst to RN, Nov 18, B 329, Hearst, WR (3 of 3), Binkley to RN, Dec 1, 1954, B 82, Binkley, Series 320, RNln; Campbell et al., *American Voter*, 51; Bean, *Influence in the 1954*, pp. 7–8 and 36; Manchester, *Glory and Dream*, 880–883; Moser, *Watershed and Ratifying*, 18–19 and 24.

69. Diary, Nov 3, 1954, B 2, Vol. IV, WH Years (7), Shanley mss, DDEL; *U.S. News & World Report*, pp. 46–48; *Newsweek*, Nov 15, 1954, p. 34; remarks, June 6, 1957, B 65, F 7, Series 207, RNln; *Reporter*, Nov 4, 1954, pp. 15–16 and 18.

70. Meeting, Nov 5, 1954, R 2, Cabinet DDE; *U.S. News & World Report*, Nov 12, 1954, pp. 47–48; *Newsweek*, Nov 15, 1954, p. 36; Bowen, *Roots of Modern Conservatism*, 185–188.

71. Meeting, Nov 5, 1954, R 2, Cabinet DDE; Adams, *Firsthand Report*, 168; Donovan, *Eisenhower*, 283–284.

72. *Los Angeles Times*, Nov 5, PPS336(1954).S628 and Nov 7, PPS336(1954).S639 and RN to Ducommon, Nov 19, 1954, PPS18.3269, RNyl; RN to Palmer, Nov 19, B 577, Palmer (2 of 2), Arbuthnot to RN, Nov 19, B 48, Arbuthnot, Chandler to RN, Dec 15, 1954, B 142, Chandler ½ and Woods to Crocker, Feb 21, 1955, B 190, Crocker, D, Series 320, RNln; *U.S. News & World Report*, Nov 4, 1954, p. 48; Tuttle, "California Democrats," 44–77.

73. RN to Krehbiel, Nov 17, 1954, PPS19.310A.1 and memoirs, Mar 16, 1976, RNyl; Day 1, Tape 6, 01:00:21 [RN], Feb 8, 1983, Gannon mss, WJBma; Nixon, *RN*, 163.

74. Press release, Nov 1954, PPS19.180, RNyl; Lubell, *Revolt of the Moderates*, 27.

75. *Los Angeles Times*, Nov 7, PPS336(1954).S640, *Press Telegram* (Ca), Nov 9, PPS336 (1954).S650, *New York Times*, Nov 15, PPS336(1954).S650 and clipping, Nov 18, 1954, PPS336(1954).S656, RNyl; Dallek, *Lone Star*, 459–461; Woods, *LBJ*, 280.

76. Dulaney and Phillips eds., *"Speak, Mister Speaker,"* 258, 264, and 343; George Reedy OH, III, p. 57, LBJL.

77. *Evening Star* (DC), Jan 14, PPS336(1955).17 and *Time*, Jan 24, 1955, PPS296(1955).5, RNyl; radio report, July 16, 1956, B 620, Raub, J, Series 320, RNln.

78. News release, Nov 8, 1954, B 313, Hall [3/3], Series 320, RNln.

79. Diary, Nov 4, 1954, B 3, Nov 1954 (5), ACW, DDEL; *U.S. News & World Report*, Jan 18, 1955, PPS296 (1955).6, RNyl.

80. Meeting, Jan 11, 1955, p. 2, R 2, Legislative DDE.

81. *PPA* 1955, pp. 55–56.

82. Homer Ferguson OH, HHL.

83. Memo, Nov 9, B 557, *New York Herald Tribune*, RN to Gough, Dec 7, B 297, Gough {2 of }, RN to Hancock, Dec 28, 1954, B 316, Hancock (2 of 3), RN to Irwin, Aug 27, B 371, Irwin (2 of 4), Curtis to King, Apr 11, 1955, B 197, Curtis, E and McWhorter to Walpin, Jan 25, 1958, B 796, Walpin, Series 320, RNln.

84. Memo, Nov 9, B 226, Drummond 2/2, RN to Carter, Dec 7, B 136, Carter, JF, RN to Robinson, Dec 8, 1954, B 649, Robinson, WE and King to Curtis, Mar 31, 1955, B 197,

Curtis, E, Series 320, RNln; *U.S. News & World Report*, Nov 12, 1954, p. 49; *Newsweek*, Jan 17, 1955, p. 25.

85. *Evening Star* (DC), Jan 11, B 701, Smear and King to Curtis, Mar 31, 1955, B 197, Curtis, E, Series 320, RNln; *U.S. News & World Report*, Nov 12, 1954, p. 49.
86. M. Eisenhower to Roorda, July 19, 1983, Gellman mss, DDEL.

CHAPTER 16. THE INCAPACITATED PRESIDENT

1. *New York Herald Tribune*, Jan 20, 1955, PPS336(1955).23, RNyl; diary, Mar 10, 1955, B3, WH Years, VII, Shanley mss, DDEL; Shanley to RN, Aug 22, 1955, B 39, F 9, Series 207, RNln; *Ike's Letters*, 148; Smith, *Meet Mister Eisenhower*, 75; S. Eisenhower, *Mrs. Ike*, 297.
2. Memo, Aug 23, F Harper's, Series 320, *Washington Post*, Sept 5, B 36, F 4 and RN to Cutler, Sept 6, 1955, B 34, F 7, Series 207, RNln; *PDDE*, XVII, p. 2702.
3. Diary, Sept 29, 1955, R 5, Diary DDE; Knebel, "Crisis," 22; Eisenhower, *Mandate*, 535–537; Donovan, *Eisenhower*, 358–361.
4. Knebel, "Crisis," 21–23; Ferrell, *Ill-Advised*, 142–143.
5. Knebel, "Crisis," 22–23; Donovan, *Confidential Secretary*, 93.
6. Diary, Sept 29, 1955, R 5, Diary DDE; *Hagerty Diary*, 233; Knebel, "Crisis," 23; Donovan, *Confidential Secretary*, 93; J. Eisenhower, *Strictly Personal*, 180–181.
7. Diary, Sept 24, PPS212(1955).1 and schedule, Sept 24, 1955, PPS325(1955).79, RNyl; Day 3, Tape 4, 00:05:58 [RN], Apr 8, 1983, Gannon mss, WJBma; Nixon, *Six Crises*, 131.
8. *Hagerty Diary*, 234; Day 3, Tape 4, 00:05:58 [RN], Gannon mss, WJBma; Knebel, "Crisis," 24; Nixon, *Six Crises*, 132; Nixon, *RN*, 164; Donovan, *Eisenhower*, 362–367.
9. *Hagerty Diary*, 234; Diary, Sept 29, 1955, R 5, Diary DDE; Knebel, "Crisis," 24.
10. Diary, Sept 29, 1955, R 5, Diary DDE; *Hagerty Diary*, 234–235.
11. Diary, Sept 29, 1955, R 5, Diary DDE; Knebel, "Crisis," 24.
12. Woods, "Nixon's My Boss," 78; Nixon, *Six Crises*, 133.
13. Memo, Sept 25, PPS325(1955).82.2, *New York Times* and *Sunday Star* (DC), Sept 25, PPS336(1955).o.s.52 and *San Francisco Examiner*, Sept 25, 1955, PPS336(1955).297, RNyl; *Los Angeles Times*, Dec 2, 1957, B 26, Alexander, H and Rogers interview, Mar 27, 1959, B 653, Rogers 1960 (1 of 2), Series 320, RNln; Knebel, "Crisis," 24; Kornitzer, *Real Nixon*, 332–333; Nixon, *Six Crises*, 134–135.
14. Knebel, "Crisis," 25; Rogers interview, Mar 27, 1959, B 653, Rogers 1960 (1 of 2), Series 320, RNln; Persons 161, pp. 71–73 and 75–76, CCOH; Kornitzer, *Real Nixon*, 333–334; Nixon, *Six Crises*, 141–142; Nixon, *RN*, 164–165; Donovan, *Eisenhower*, 367–370.
15. Saturday night, Sept 24, PPS325(1955).79 and Guylay to Woods, Sept 25, 1955, PPS325(1955).80, RNyl.
16. *New York Herald Tribune*, Sept 26, 1955, PPS336(1955).os.63, RNyl; Nixon, *Six Crises*, 144.
17. Memo, Sept 25, 1955, R 4, DuHe; Ferrell, *Ill-Advised*, 11–20.
18. *San Francisco Chronicle*, Sept 26, 1955, PPS336(1955).303, RNyl; *Hagerty Diary*, 236–237; Nixon saw Dulles as a team player; Nixon, *Six Crises*, 145.

19. Memo, Sept 26, 1955, PPS325(1955).86.2, RNyl; also see diary, Sept 29, 1955, R 5, Diary DDE.

20. Nixon phone call, Sept 26, 1955, B 1, II, p. 296, Krock mss, HML; *Los Angeles Times*, Sept 27, 1955, PPS336(1955)o.s.75, RNyl; Nixon, *Six Crises*, 146–147.

21. Memo, Sept 26, 1955, R 4, DuHe.

22. Diary, Sept 26, 1955, PPS212(1955).1, RNyl; Nixon, *RN*, 165–166; *Sunday Monitor* (Concord, NH), Sept 21, 2008, D1 and 3; Nixon, *Six Crises*, 147; Ambrose exaggerates the infighting during Ike's recovery; *Eisenhower*, vol. 2, 270–286; Adams, *Firsthand Report*, 165.

23. Memo, Sept 26, PPS325(1955).86.2, Chotiner to Woods, Sept 27, PPS325(1955).91 and RN to Woods, Sept 27(?), 1955, PPS325(1955).90.2, RNyl; Alsop to RN, Sept 26, B 29, Alsop, J, Payne to RN, Sept 26, B 582, Payne, FG, Gainey to RN, Sept 26, B 279, Gainey [½] and Cousins to RN, Sept 26, 1955, B 185, Cousins, N, Series 320, RNln.

24. Diary, Sept 28, PPS212(1955).1, *San Francisco News*, Sept 28, PPS336(1955).364, *Evening Star* (DC), Sept 28, PPS336(1955).353 and *Los Angeles Examiner*, Sept 29, 1955, PPS336(1955).381, RNyl; *New York Times*, Sept 28, 1955; Nixon, *Six Crises*, 147–148.

25. Diary, Sept 29, PPS212(1955).1, *Outline*, Sept 29, PPS325(1955).103.1 and *Washington Post*, Sept 30, 1955, PPS336(1955).390, RNyl; memos, Sept 29, 1955, R 4, DuHe; *New York Times*, Sept 30, 1955; Kornitzer, *Real Nixon*, 216.

26. Diary, Sept 30, PPS212(1955).1 and *Daily News* (DC), Sept 30, 1955, PPS336(1955).390, RNyl; meeting, Sept 30, 1955, R 3, Cabinet DDE; Nixon, *Six Crises*, 148–149; Benson, *Cross Fire*, 270–272; Donovan, *Eisenhower*, 370–376.

27. Donovan, *Eisenhower*, 370–376; Persons OH, 161, p. 74, CCOH.

28. Memoirs, Feb 16, 1976, RNyl; Adams, *Firsthand Report*, 186–187.

29. Memo, Sept 30, PPS325(1953).*107A.1 and *San Diego Union*, Oct 1, 1955, PPS336(1955).403, RNyl; memo by Dulles, Oct 7, 1955, B 229, Dulles ½, Series 320, RNln; meeting, Sept 30, 1955, R 3, Cabinet DDE; memo, Sept 30, 1955, R 4, DuHe; Wicker, *Ike*, 84; Scott, *Come to the Party*, 145; Kornitzer, *Real Nixon*, 218.

30. *New York Times*, Sept 27 and 29, 1955.

31. Memo, Sept 29, 1955, R 4, DuHe.

32. Ibid.

33. *New York Journal American*, Sept 30, 1955, PPS336(1955)).391, RNyl.

34. RN to Jackson, Sept 29, 1955, B 373, Jackson, CD, Series 320, RNln; "Nixon," P 1 (1993) declared Nixon was "a substitute president."

35. RN to Kersten, Oct 1, 1955, Kersten mss, MLsc.

36. *Los Angeles Times*, Oct 4, PPS336(1955).438 and *Denver Post*, Oct 11, 1955, PPS336(1955).507, RNyl; Hoyt to RN, Oct 3, B 358, Hoyt, Adams to RN, Oct 12, B 20, Adams, Sh (2 of 2), Goldwater to RN, Oct 18, B 293, Goldwater [½] and Smith to RN, Oct 28, B 709, Smith, WB, Series 320 and memo, Oct 15, 1955, B 44, F 1, Series 207, RNln.

37. PN to Drown, Oct 1, 1955, DR 117, RNyl; Woods to Esberg, Oct 10, 1955, B 38, F 7, Series 207, RNln.

38. Diary, Oct 1, 1955, PPS212(1955).4 (V.12), RNyl; *New York Times*, Oct 2, IV, and Oct 4, 1955.

39. Wilton Persons OH 161, p. 72, CCOH.
40. Calendar 1955, Oct 1, PPS270.2, diary, Oct 1, 1955, PPS212(1955).1 and memoirs, Mar 16, 1976, RNyl.
41. Meetings, Oct 7, 14, 21 and 28, 1955, R 3, Cabinet DDE; Donovan, *Eisenhower*, 376–383.
42. *New York Times*, Oct 2 and 28, 1955; schedule, Oct 20, 1955, B 39, F 5, Series 207, RNln; Dillon Anderson OH, 49–50, CCOH.
43. Memo, Oct 11, R 2, Dulles memos and memos, Oct 17, 1955, R 4, DuHe; *New York Herald Tribune*, Oct 13, 1955, PPS336(1955).517, RNyl.
44. Memo, Oct 21, 1955, R 2, DuHe; *PDDE*, XVI, pp. 1873–1874 and 1877.
45. *Evening Star* (DC), Oct 3, B 38, F 5 [1 of 2] and clipping, Oct 11, 1955, B 41, F 5, B 41, F 5, Series 207, RNln; *San Diego Union*, Oct 4, PPS336(1955).447 and Oct 11, 1955, PPS336(1955).508, RNyl.
46. Cronin to RN, Oct 14, 1955, B 39, F 5, Series 207, RNln.
47. Memo, Oct 16, B 39, F 1, Hancock to Woods, Oct 5, *New York Herald Tribune*, Oct 18, Hildred to RN, Oct 26, F 2 and schedule, Oct 17, 1955, F 16, Series 207, RNln.
48. Memo, Oct 1, B 38, F 16, Reid to RN, Oct 21 and RN to Reid, Oct 29, 1955, B 39, F 1, Series 207, RNln.
49. *New York Herald Tribune*, Oct 18, 1955, B 39, F 17, Series 207, RNln; *New York Herald Tribune*, Oct 19, 1955, PPS3360s(1955).102, RNyl; *New York Times*, Oct 18, 1955.
50. CBS Radio News, Oct 18, B 191, Cronin 1956 2/2 and memo, Oct 18, 1955, B 508, Memo BK, Series 320, RNln.
51. RN to Dague, Sept 30, B 198, Dague, Series 320 and RN to Derre, B 38, F 7, Series 207, RNln; *Evening Star* (DC), Oct 8, 1955, PPS336(1955).487, RNyl; memo, Oct 17, 1955, R 9, DuHe; *New York Times*, Oct 11, 1955; *Ike's Letters*, 152; *PDDE*, XVI, pp. 1864 and 1964; Donovan, *Confidential Secretary*, 97.
52. *Oakland Tribune*, Oct 6, PPS3360s(1955).94, diary, Oct 8 and 9, PPS212(1955).2, *San Francisco Chronicle*, Oct 9, PPS336(1955).485 and *Minneapolis Star*, Oct 10, 1955, PPS336(1955).505, RNyl; *PDDE*, XVII, p. 2706; *New York Times*, Oct 9, 1955; Nixon, *RN*, 166; Lasby, *Eisenhower's Heart Attack*, 124–126; Nixon, *Six Crises*, 151; J. Eisenhower, *Strictly Personal*, 182.
53. Diary, Oct 10, 1955, B 7, Oct 1955 (6), ACW diary, DDEL; Donovan, *Confidential Secretary*, 96.
54. Ike to RN, Oct 18, 1955, PPS324.69, RNyl; M. Eisenhower to RN, Oct 18 and 21, B 238, M. Eisenhower, 2/2, Series 320, RNln.
55. Memo, Oct 10, 1955, PPS325(1955).146A.2, RNyl; RN to Garland, Oct 13, B 282, Garland [½] and RN to Stewart, Oct 28, 1955, B 730, Stewart, J (New York), Series 320, RNln.
56. PN to Mrs. Eisenhower, mid Oct 1955, Personal Files of Mamie, B 32, Nixon, DDEL.
57. Mamie to PN, Oct 18, 1955, PPS324.70, RNyl.
58. Minutes, Nov 4, 1955, R 3, Cabinet DDE.
59. RN statement, Nov 11, 1955, B 42, F 16, Series 207, RNln; *Los Angeles Times*, Nov 12, 1955, PPS336(1955).576, RNyl; *PPA* 1955, pp. 840–841; Morrow, *Black Man in the WH*, 2;

New York Times, Nov 12, 1955; *PDDE*, XVI, p. 1894; Nixon, *Six Crises*, 151; J. Eisen-hower, *Strictly Personal*, 183.

60. *Daily News* (DC), Nov 14, 1955, PPS336(1955).580, RNyl; *PDDE*, XVI, pp. 1894–1895.

61. *San Diego Union*, Nov 22, 1955, PPS336(1955).586, RNyl; RN to Cutler, Nov 22, 1955, B 198, Cutler, R, Series 320, RNln; meeting, Nov 22, 1955, R 3, Cabinet DDE; *PDDE*, XVI, p. 2709; *New York Times*, Nov 22, 1955; Nixon, *Six Crises*, 151.

62. *San Diego Union*, Dec 13, 1955, PPS336os(1955).115, RNyl; *PDDE*, XVI, pp. 1921–1923; meeting, Dec 9, R 4, Cabinet DDE and meeting, Dec 12, 1955, Legislative DDE.

63. Meetings, Dec 2 and 16, 1955, R 4, Cabinet DDE.

64. Platter, Dec 1955, RNyl; Nixon, *Six Crises*, 156–158.

65. *PDDE*, XVI, pp. 1939 and 2713.

66. *Ike's Letters*, 156–158.

67. Ibid., 158; Ferrell, *Ill-Advised*, 105–111; *New York Times*, Nov 27, 1955.

CHAPTER 17. THE HUTSCHNECKER FICTION

1. *New York Times*, Jan 3, 2001; confidential sources on Hutschnecker's mental health; Summers, *Arrogance*, xiv; Herbert Klein declares that Nixon only saw Hutschnecker as an internist, *Making It*, 412.

2. U.S. Senate, hearings before the committee on rules and administration, *Nomination of Gerald R. Ford*, 189, 191, 194 and 196; U.S. House, hearings before the committee on the judiciary, *Nomination of Gerald R. Ford*, 333.

3. Hutschnecker to RN, June 21, 1954, PPS238, RNyl; Hutschnecker, *Drive for Power*, 4 and 23–24.

4. Summers, *Arrogance*, 89.

5. Hutschnecker, *Will to Live*.

6. Notes, Jan 15, prescription, Jan 16, record, Jan 25, notes, Mar 21, 1952, Erskine, "Dick and Pat Nixon," *Collier's* (July 9, 1954), PPS296(1954).25(1), RNyl; Hutschnecker, *Will to Live*; Summers, *Arrogance*, 89.

7. Notes, July 18, memo, July 22, 1952, PPS238. F 884, RNyl; Summers, *Arrogance*, xiv–xv, 7–9, 13, 40, 82, 88–94, and 100.

8. Summers, *Arrogance*, xiv, 8 and 89; Hutschnecker to RN, Sept 26, 1952, RNyl; Klein, *Making It*, 412.

9. Hutschnecker to RN, July 8, Sept 20 and 30 and RN to Hutschnecker, Sept 30, 1953, Hutschnecker, RNyl.

10. Hutschnecker to RN, Nov 5, 1952, PPS16.585, diary, Feb 1, PPS212(1953).1, Hutschnecker notes, Feb 1 and Atwater Medical Laboratory, Feb 3, 1953, Hutschnecker, Hutschnecker notes, Feb 1, 1953, RNyl; American Legion, Feb 1, B 9, F 2 and schedule, Feb 1, 1953, B 16, F 5 and B 16, F 8, Series 207, RNln; Summers asserts that Nixon visited Hutsch-necker whenever the vice president visited New York City, and the doctor "made a number of trips to see Nixon in his Washington office;" Summers, *Arrogance*, 89–90; according to Hutschnecker's notes, he never saw Vice President Nixon at his office in New York City, but saw Nixon three times at the Waldorf Astoria and twice at Nixon's office in Washington during the entire vice-presidential tenure. Even worse than

Summers is Brodie. Her wild accusations regarding Hutschnecker and Nixon in *Nixon*, 331–335, are, at the very best, unprofessional.

11. Hutschnecker notes, Aug 19, diary, Aug 19, PPS212(1954).1, calendar, Aug 19, PPS212(1954).3.231, and Hutschnecker to Woods, Nov 17, 1954, RNyl.

12. Erksine, "Dick and Pat Nixon," 35–36.

13. Jamieson to Baughman, Apr 10, 1956, PPS325A.9, RNyl; PN to Heath, Mar 20, B 283, Garber, WA, Woods to Bewley, Apr 5, B 80, Bewley (1957–1958), Series 320 and *Miami Herald*, Apr 2, 1956, B 49, F 16, Series 207, RNln; *New York Times*, Mar 24, 1956.

14. Woods call to H, Mar 29–30, 1956, RNyl; Day 8, Tape 2, 00:56:17 [RN], Gannon mss, WJBma.

15. Dr. Hutschnecker, Mar–Apr 1956(?), RNyl.

16. Telephone conversation with Zervanos, Sept 20, 2010; email, Zervanos to Gellman, Sept 17, 2010, Gellman mss, DDEL. I have also depended on a pharmacist who practiced in the 1950s for his opinion; he did not want to be identified.

17. Email, Zervanos to Gellman, Sept 17, 2010.

18. Memo, May 28, 1956, PPS238, RNyl.

19. Memo, June 4, 1956, PPS238, RNyl.

20. Schedule, Feb 13, 1956, B 48, F 5 [1 of 2], Series 207, RNln; Hutschnecker notes, Jan 16, Feb 13 and June 15 and Memo, May 26 and 28 and June 21, PPS238, and diary, June 15, PPS212(1956).2 and June 15, 1956, PPS212(1956).167, RNyl.

21. Hutschnecker to Woods, Sept 28, 1955 and memo, June 15, 1956, PPS238, RNyl; memo, June 15, 1956, B 346, Hutschnecker, Series 320, RNln.

22. Hutschnecker, *Drive for Power*, 4 and 23–24.

23. Hutschnecker to Woods, Nov 17, 1954, PPS238 and undated note, Hutschnecker to Woods, RNyl; Woods to Bewley, May 22, 1954, B 80, Bewley ['½] and Hutschnecker to Woods, Oct 15, 1956, B 346, Hutschnecker, Series 320, RNln.

24. Woods to Hutschnecker, Nov 27, 1954 and Apr 28 and Oct 6, 1955, PPS238, RNyl.

25. Hutschnecker to RN, Nov 17, 1954 and Mar 23, 1955, PPS238, RNyl; Hutschnecker, *Love and Hate*, v–vi.

26. Hutschnecker to RN, Apr 12, 1955, B 346, Hutschnecker, Series 320, RNln.

27. Hutschnecker to RN, Mar 1, 1956, RNyl; *New York Times*, Mar 1, 1956.

28. Nixon, *Six Crises*, 161.

29. Cotton to Hillings, July 30 and Cotton to MJ, Aug 24, CO, Hillings to Perry, Aug 30, 1952, PE, RNyl.

30. Tom to Rose, July 15, PPS5.414, RN to McKenna, July 19, 1952, PPS5.418, RNyl.

31. *New York Times*, Nov 4, 1955 and Feb 20, 1956; interview with Scouten, Apr 22, 2010.

32. PN to Folks, mid Nov, PPC 1952, clipping, Nov 15, PPS6.384, clipping, Nov 15, PPS16.2258.2, RNyl; RN to Kearns, Nov 28, B 398, Kearns, RN to Rebozo, Nov 28, 1952, B 622, Rebozo [1/3], RN to Garland, Feb 5, 1953, B 282, Garland ['½], Series 320, RN to Boughton, Dec 10, RN to Reverend Mother Superior, Dec 15, 1952, B 7, F 26, Series 207, RNln; Ike to RN, Nov 15, 1952, Personal Files of Mamie Eisenhower, B 32, Nixon, DDEL; *New York Times*, Nov 16, 1952.

33. Woods to Lambie, Nov 8, 1955, B 44, F 1 and RN to Peace, Jan 3, 1956, B 41, F 7 [2 of 2], Series 207 and Chase to RN, Dec 20, 1955, B 143, Chase, Wm and RN to Reid, Mar

18, 1960, B 625, Reid (1 of 2) Series 320, RNln; *Newsweek*, Dec 12, 1955, p. 48; Summers claims that Hutschnecker saw Nixon about McCarthy, but Nixon did not see Hutschnecker in 1955; Summers, *Arrogance*, 82.

34. Telephone call to RN, Jan 13, 1956, Telephone, B 5, Jan 3–Apr 30, 1956, DuHe; RN to Auchincloss, Jan 17, B 44, F 19, *San Diego Union*, Jan 17, B 44, F 20, Hobbs to Woods, Jan 25, B 46, F 7, Series 207 and RN to Fishbein, Jan 21, B 260, Fishbein and Spindell to RN, Jan 27, 1956, B 718, Spindell 5 of 5, Series 320, RNln; *New York Times*, Sept 28, 1976.

35. Dottie to Evlyn, Jan 25, N 426, Korsemier and Woods to Irwin, Jan 27, B 371, Irwin (2 of 4) and *Miami Herald*, Jan 23, B 339, Hill, MD, Series 320 and clipping, Jan 30, B 47, F 7, schedule, Feb 1, B 47, F 10, Ostermeier to Woods, Mar 5, RN to Londres, Mar 9, 1956, B 47, F 8, Series 207, RNln; Jamieson to Baughman, Feb 1, 1956, PPS325A.7, RNyl.

36. Clinical records, Feb 11 and May 10, 1956, PPS421, RNyl.

37. Jamieson to Baughman, Feb 28, 1956, PPS325A.8, RNyl; RN to Macris, Feb 28, 1956, B 622, Rebozo [1/3], Series 320, RNln.

38. Keiser to whom it may concern, Apr 10, 1956, PPS421, RNyl; Rebozo to Woods, Apr 13, B 622, Rebozo [2/3], Series 320 and RN to Keiser, May 5, 1956, B 49, F 16, Series 207, Rebozo to RN, Nov 22, B 622, Rebozo [2/3] and RN to Marshall, Nov 26, 1957, B 477, Marshall, JP, Series 320, RNln; *Miami Herald*, Dec 9, 1988, p. 6C; email, Kallina to Gellman, June 8, 2010, Gellman mss, DDEL; I would like to thank Edmund Kallina Jr., Ann McDonald, and Cheryl Klenner for finding material on Dr. Keiser.

39. Kennan to RN, May 19, 1954, B 21, F 15 and RN to Morhous, May 10, 1956, B 52, F 16, Series 207, RNln; *New York Times*, Aug 29, 1958; interview with Greenbrier historian, Robert Conte, Aug 21, 2010.

40. Woods to Hallauer, Aug 9 and RN to Hallauer, Aug 30, 1957, B 313, Hallauer, RN to Bodlaender, Feb 13, 1959, B 90, Bobst 2/2, RNln; Klein to Winter, Mar 23, PPS421 and schedule, Apr 25, 1960, PPS212(1960).196, RNyl; *Newsweek*, Dec 23, 1957, p. 18.

41. RN to McIlnay, Nov 5, B 500, McIlnay, memo, Nov 6, B 720, Squeak and Leaks, RN to Stambaugh, Nov 13, B 722, Stambaugh, C, RN to Smathers, Nov 13, B 700, Small, T, RN to Pellissier, B 586, Pellissier, clipping, Dec 9, 1957, B 313, Hallauer, memo, Nov 14, 1958, B 721, Stahlman [4/4], memo, Feb 5, B 641, Ribs, RN to Luce, Feb 13, B 464, Luce [2/2], RN to Cunningham, Apr 6, B 196, Cunningham, A, RN to Heffelfinger, Sept 8, 1959, B 330, Heffelfinger [½] and RN to Janis, May 31, 1960, B 249, Eyeglasses, Series 320 and *Miami Herald*, Nov 13, 1958, B 95, F 8 and RN to Alcorn, Oct 5, 1959, B 115, F 11, Series 207, RNln; schedule, Nov 1, 1957, PPS212(1957).174, *Washington Post*, Feb 5, PPS274, Hoover to RN, Feb 6, PPS320.102.71.1 and RN to Hoover, Feb 18, 1959, PPS320.102.72, RNyl; *New York Times*, Mar 24 and 25, Oct 31, 1957, Feb 6, Oct 2 and 3, 1959.

42. RN to Hutschnecker, July 24, 1958, Hutschnecker to RN, Mar 3, calendar, May 1, PPS212(1959).4 and Dec 8, 1959, PPS212(1959), RNyl; Hutschnecker to RN, Mar 3, RN to Hutschnecker, Mar 16, Hutschnecker to Woods, May 11 and memo, Oct 6, 1959, B 346, Hutschnecker, Series 320, RNln.

43. Hutschnecker to RN, Thanksgiving, memo, Dec 11, RN to Hutschnecker, Dec 14, 1957, Hutschnecker to Woods, July 17, RN to Hutschnecker, July 24, 1958 and Feb 3, 1960, B 346, Hutschnecker, Series 320, RNln.

44. Hutschnecker to RN, May 11, June 17 and Dec 16, 1959, B 346, Hutschnecker, Series 320, RNln.

CHAPTER 18. IKE'S DECISION TO RUN

1. RNC, Jan 1956, R 2, *PRP*; *Gallup Poll*, Two, 1228, 1266, 1291–1292, 1295–1297, 1392, and 1394.

2. *New York Herald Tribune*, June 1, 1955, PPS336(1955).130, RNyl; *PPA* 1955, pp. 311–312; *New York Times*, Mar 17 and May 24, 1955; Uebelhor, "Ticket Will Be Ike and Dick," 11–47.

3. *Los Angeles Examiner*, Aug 4, 1955, PPS336(1955).187, RNyl; *Ike's Letters*, 117; Thomson and Shattuck, *1956 Presidential Campaign*, 13–14.

4. Thomson and Shattuck, *1956 Presidential Campaign*, 117–118; *PDDE*, XV, pp. 1402–1405, and 1434–1438 and XVI, pp. 1516 and 1549–1552.

5. Ibid., 1729–1731; *Ike's Letters*, 148–149.

6. *PDDE*, XVI, pp. 1850–1851; *St. Petersburg Times* (Fla), Sept 12 and 15, 1955, Gellman mss, DDEL.

7. Milton to Ike, Sept 15, Ike to Milton, Sept 17, Milton to Ike, Sept 20 and Milton to Walter, Sept 20, 1955, Whitman File, Name Series, B 13, F Eisenhower, Milton 1956 (1), DDEL; Bowen, *Roots of Modern Conservatism*, 161.

8. *Los Angeles Examiner*, Mar 15, B 27, F 9, Series 207 and press conf, May 31, B 237, Eisenhower statements, Series 320, RNln; Ike to Krehbiel, Mar 14, PPS324.59 and *Los Angeles Examiner*, June 21, 1955, PPS336(1955).140, RNyl; diary, Apr 4, 1955, B 3, VII, WH Years, Shanley mss, DDEL; *PDDE*, XV, p. 1471; *New York Times*, Sept 4, 1955.

9. *U.S News & World Report*, Nov 12, 1954; press interview, Feb 21, B 3, Nicaragua [2 of 3], Series 362 and clipping, Mar 1, 1955, B 1, Trip, Mar 1, Series 357, RNln.

10. *Tucson Daily Citizen*, Mar 15, 1955, PPS336(1955).68, RNyl; RN to Allen, Mar 24, 1955, B 27, Allen, Le, Series 320, RNln; *Newsweek*, Mar 28, 1955, pp. 21–22; *New York Times*, Mar 15, 1955; Nixon, *RN*, 166–173.

11. Gurley to Ike, Mar 17, B 308, Gurley, F, Series 320 and speech, Mar 17, 1955, B 28, F 2, Series 207, RNln.

12. RN press conf, Sept 5, 1955, B 36, F 3, Series 207, RNln; *New York Times*, Sept 6, 1955.

13. Memo, Feb 3, PPS325(1955).3A and memo, Mar 10, 1955, PPD325(1955).52A, RNyl.

14. *Los Angeles Times*, Jan 21, 1953, PPS336(1953).25 and *Washington Post*, May 19, 1954, PPS336(1954).S209, RNyl; clipping, Feb 16, B 1, Trip Wed, Feb 16, Series 357 and press conf, Sept 5, 1955, B 36, F 3, Series 207, RNln; Roorda, "President and His Boy," 76–88, Gellman mss, DDEL.

15. RN to MacAlphine, July 1, B 467, MacAlphine, RN to Pinkley, Sept 23, B 599, Pinkley 1951 (1 of 2), Series 320 and RN to Williams, July 12, 1955, B 31, F 4 [3 of 3], Series 207, RNln; *New York Times*, Sept 18, 1955.

16. RN to Hall, Nov 19, 1954, B 313, Hall [3/3], Series 320, RNln; RN to Younger, Dec 7, 1954, LBM 115, RNyl; Erskine, "Dick and Pat Nixon," 32.

17. Hall to Kinnear, May 12, B 37, F 7, *New York Herald Tribune*, May 22, B 30, F 7 and *Evening Star* (DC), Sept 7, 1955, B 36, F 8, Series 207, RNln; *New York Herald Tribune*, Feb 27, PPS336(1955).SupplementA.6, *San Diego Evening Tribune*, June 10, PPS336(1955).135, *Los Angeles Times*, June 29, PPS336(1955).145, *Washington Post*, July 9, PPS336(1955).148, *San Diego Union*, Sept 16, PPS336(1955).284, and *Los Angeles Examiner*, Sept 20, 1955, PPS300.426.5, RNyl; Scott, "Langlie," 427; *New York Times*, Sept 6, 1955.

18. *Deep River News* (Ct), Aug 11, PPS336(1955).206 and *Greenwich Times* (Ct), Aug 18, 1955, PPS336(1955).221, RNyl; Prescott Bush OH 31, p. 327, CCOH; Herskowitz, *Duty, Honor, Country*, 178–179; *Philadelphia Daily News*, Apr 1, PPS336(1955).80, *New York Post*, Aug 21, PPS336(1955).237, and *New York Daily News*, Sept 9, 1955, PPS336(1955).274, RNyl; *Evening World-Herald* (Neb), Sept 21, 1955, B 37, F 7 [1 of 2], Series 207, RNln.

19. *Nassau Republican* (New York), June 1954, PPS296(1954).23 and memoirs, Mar 14, 1976, RNyl; RN to Dewey, Apr 28, B 214, Dewey 2/2, Series 320, RN to Dewey, Aug 28 and Dewey to RN, Aug 31, 1953, B 14, F 3 and RN to Hart, June 9, 1954, B 21, F 20, Series 207, RNln; Thomas Dewey OH, 26, CCOH; memo, Apr 10, 1953, PPS325(1953).242 and memoirs, Mar 15, 1976, RNyl; Graham to RN, Sept 13 and Oct 8, 1955, B 299, Graham {3 of}, Series 320, RNln; interview with RN, About 1955, B 47, R. Nixon 1958, Alsop mss, LOC; *New York Times*, Mar 17, 1955.

20. RN to Chandler, Aug 6, B 142, Chandler ½, Series 320, schedule, Aug 9–17, B 34, F 9 [2 of 2], RN to Buff, Aug 23 and RN to Lipscomb, Aug 24, 1955, B 34, F 10 [1 of 2], Series 207, RNln; *Los Angeles Times*, Aug 16, PPS336(1955).222 and 17, PPS336(1955).227, *Los Angeles Mirror News*, Aug 17, PPS336(1955).227 and *Los Angeles Herald & Express*, Aug 17, 1955, PPS336(1955).223, RNyl.

21. *PDDE*, XVI, p. 1493.

22. RN to Moley, Dec 8, 1954, B 524, Moley-Corres 2 of 2, Series 320, RNln.

23. Ibid., Jan 10, PPS336(1955).10, *Los Angeles Times*, Apr 15, PPS336(1955).90, and *Los Angeles Examiner*, Apr 21, 1955, PPS336(1955).92, RNyl; clipping, Apr undated, B 29, F 2, Series 207, RN to Gittings, Aug 26, B 289, Gittings and RN to Palmer, Sept 3, 1955, B 577, Palmer (2 of 2), Series 320, RNln.

24. *Los Angeles Times*, Apr 27, 1954, PPS336(1954).S189, RNyl; Barrett OH, 3–12, Knight/Brown Era, Government History Documentation Project; Pitney, "Nixon, California, and American Politics," 219–232; Clark, "1958 California Gubernatorial Election," 23–26; Thompson ed., *White at Large*, 365–366; Schuparra, *Triumph*, 24.

25. Memo, May 25, 1955, PPS325(1955).63.A.2, RNyl.

26. Memo, Apr 26, PPS325(1955).61B.2 and *Los Angeles Times*, May 1, 1955, PPS336(1955).104, RNyl; *Time*, Mar 28, 1955, p 19, Vol. LXV, No 13.

27. *Los Angeles Times*, Dec 6, PPS336(1954).S664, *San Francisco Examiner*, Dec 31, 1954, PPS336(1954).S683, *New York Times*, Jan 22, PPS336(1955).28, *Los Angeles Times*, June 4, PPS300.394, and *Los Angeles Herald-Express*, Aug 17, 1955, PPS300.416.2, RNyl; *Weekend*, Jan 30, B 52, Arnow, and *Los Angeles Times*, June 4, 1955, B 420, Knight [½], Series 320, RNln.

28. Diary, Mar 25, 1955, B 3, VII, WH Years, Shanley mss, DDEL.

29. Memo, Apr 27, PPS325(1955).61A.2, notes, May 3, PPS325(1955).63, *Los Angeles Times*, May 4, PPS336(1955).110, and *San Diego Union*, May 11, 1955, PPS336(1955).119, RNyl; memo, May 10, B 534, Mosher and Knight to RN, May 19, 1955, B 420, Knight [½] Series 320, RNln.

30. Diary, May 3 and 4, 1955, pp. 1919–1920 and 1923, VII, B 3, WH Years (3), Shanley mss, DDEL; diary, May 3, 1955, R 5, Diary DDE.

31. RN to Knight, June 3, 1955, B 420, Knight [½], Series 320, RNln.

32. *PAES*, IV, p. 266; *Newsweek*, Nov 15, 1954, pp. 36–37; Thomson and Shattuck, *1956 Presidential Campaign*, 23–29.

33. *PAES*, IV, pp. 468–476 and 539; Martin, *Stevenson and the World*, 172–174.

34. Day 3, Tape 3, 00:07:37 [RN], Gannon mss, WJBma.

35. *PDDE*, XVI, p. 2138.

36. Memo, Oct 10, 1955, PPS325(1955).146A.2, RNyl.

37. Diary, Oct 10, 1955, R 5, DDE; Adams, *Firsthand Report*, 220–234.

38. *Ike's Letters*, 153–154.

39. *Hagerty Diary*, 241–246.

40. Memo, Jan 1956, R 29, Lodge mss, MHS.

41. Platter, Dec 26, 1955, RNyl; RN to Nelson, Dec 27, 1955, B 43, F 2, Series 207, RNln.

42. Platter, Dec undated and Dec 26, 1955, RNyl.

43. RN to Landon, Nov 12, 1955, B 435, Landon, A, Series 320, RNln.

44. Smith to RN, Oct 4, B 707, Smith, LH, Landon to Allen, Nov 3, B 435, Landon, A and memo, Nov 21, 1955, B 312, Hall, Fre, Series 320, RNln; *Charlotte Observer* (NC), Oct 11, 1955, PPS336(1955).507, RNyl.

45. Luce to RN, Oct 8, 1955, B 464, Luce [2/2], Series 320, RNln.

46. *Washington Post*, Apr 14, PPS320.109.S1, *Minneapolis Morning Tribune*, Apr 16, PPS336(1955).90, and *U.S. News & World Report*, Apr 22, 1955, PPS336(1955).SupplementA.14, RNyl; *Newsweek*, Apr 25, 1955, pp. 34–35; Newton, *Justice for All*, 333–334.

47. *Washington Post*, Oct 9, PPS336(1955).491 and Nov 6, PPS336(1955).566, and *Newsweek*, Dec 12, 1955, p. 33, PPS300.447, RNyl; Patton to Sweet, Oct 13, B 775, *U.S. News & World Report*, Arnold to Newsweek, Dec 17, B 50, Arnold, R and Norris to Arnold, Dec 29, 1955, B 559, *Newsweek* [2/2], Series 320, RNln; *Newsweek*, Oct 17, p. 30 and Nov 14, 1955, p. 31; *New York Times*, Sept 26, 1955.

48. Agronsky to Dave, Dec 10, 1956, B 68, F 9, "US Supreme Court," Agronsky mss, LOC.

49. *PPA 1956*, pp. 194–195; *PDDE*, XVI, pp. 1995–1996; *Newsweek*, Feb 6, 1956, p. 23.

50. Memo, Oct 5(?), PPS325(1955).122.2, *Los Angeles Times*, Oct 7, PPS336(1955).485, *San Diego Evening Tribune*, Oct 31, PPS336(1955).554, *San Francisco Chronicle*, Nov 5, PPS336(1955).564, *Evening Star* (DC), Dec 9, PPS336(1955).SupplementA.77, and *Washington Post*, Dec 19, 1955, PPS336(1955).620, RNyl; Clark, "1958 California Gubernatorial Election," 30–32; Montgomery and Johnson, *One Step from the WH*, 190–194.

51. Memo, Sept, PPS325(1955).89A.2 and memo, Sept 28, 1955, PPS325(1955).102.2, RNyl; Worthen, *Young Nixon*, 153–157.

52. Memo, Oct 2, PPS325(1955).110, *New York Herald Tribune*, Oct 2, PPS325(1955).117.2, *Los Angeles Times*, Oct 2, PPS336(1955).414, memo, Oct 3, PPS325(1955).112, and memo, Oct 3, 1955, PPS325(1955).113, RNyl.

53. Memo, Oct 5, 1955, PPS325(1955).129, RNyl.
54. Memo, Oct 5, PPS325(1955).123, memo, Oct, PPS325(1955).127, Hancock to Woods, Oct 5, PPS325(1955).130, *Los Angeles Times*, Oct 5, PPS336(1955).456, and *Los Angeles Mirror News*, Oct 6, 1955, PPS336(1955).462, RNyl.
55. Memo, Oct 10, 1955, PPS325(1955).146A.2, RNyl; Pattee to RN, Oct 11, 1955, B 581, Pattee ['½], Series 320, RNln.
56. *San Francisco Chronicle*, Oct 14, PPS336os(1955).99, and *Los Angeles Times*, Oct 14, 1955, PPS336(1955).518, RNyl; Poulson to RN, Oct 17 and RN to Poulson, Oct 26, B 607, Poulson and Knezevick to RN, Oct 22, 1955, B 419, Knezevick, Series 320, RNln.
57. *Gallup Poll*, Two, 1395–98 and 1402; Runyon et al., *Source Book of American Presidential Campaign*, 274; Sloan, *Eisenhower and the Management*, 54–56.
58. Memo, Jun 13, 1956, R 29, Lodge mss, MHS.
59. Ibid.; diary, Jan 11, 1956, B 8, Jan 1956, Whitman File, DDEL; Wilton Persons OH 161, pp. 97–98, CCOH; *PDDE*, XVI, pp. 1962–1965; J. Eisenhower, *Strictly Personal*, 183–185 and 384–388.
60. Diary, Feb 9, 1956, B 8, Feb 1956, Whitman File, DDEL; Friel, "Influence of Television," 97–101; Ewald, *Eisenhower the President*, chap XI.
61. Bittner, *Lausche*, 39–40 and 43–45; Odenkirk, *Frank J. Lausche*, 238–241, 242–244, and 250–251; Gobetz ed., *Ohio's Lausche*, 58.
62. Pre–press confs, Jan 25 and Feb 7, 1956, R 7, DDEL; *PPA 1956*, pp. 182 and 195–196.
63. RN speech, Jan 20, B 46, F 8 [3 of 3] and *Chicago American*, Jan 21, 1956, B 46, F 5 [2 of 2], Series 207, RNln; *PPA 1956*, 173–176.
64. Memo, Feb 14, B 48, F 5 [1 of 2], Series 207 and Lipscomb to RN, Feb 14, 1956, B 455, Lipscomb, G, Series 320, RNln; *New York Times*, Jan 25 and Feb 14, 1956.
65. *Daily News*, Jan 11, RN to Keating and RN to Allen, Jan 12 B 44, F 18, Series 207, RN to Byrnes, Jan 12, 1956, B 119, Byrnes, Jo, Series 320, RNln; RN to Drowns, Jan 18, DR 120, Drown mss, RNyl; diary, May 9, 1956, PPS212(1956).3, calendar, Jan 21, 1959, PPS212(1959).2, schedule, Apr 27, 1960, PPS212(1960).200, and calendar, Jan 18, 1961, PPS212(1961).24, RNyl; *New York Times*, Jan 8 and Jan 22, 1956, Part IV; *Newsweek*, Jan 23, 1956, p. 50; Harris, "Dark Hours of the Richard Nixons," Mar 4, 1956, p. 11; I would like to thank Craig Ellefson at the Richard Nixon Library for providing me with this article; Smith, *Iron Man*, 170–171; Van Atta, *With Honor*, 31–33.
66. *Los Angeles Times*, Jan 8, PPS336(1956)5, Jan 15, PPS336(1956)10, Jan 25, PPS336(1956)14 and Feb 18, 1956, PPS336(1956)34, RNyl; Chandler to Palmer, Feb 27, 1956, B 142, Chandler ½, Series 320, RNln.
67. Memo, Feb 6, 1956, R 29, Lodge mss, MHS.
68. Memo with Ike, Feb 27 and memo with Hagerty, Feb 29, 1956, B 8, very private memos, DuHe.
69. Diary, Feb 29, 1956, VII, B 3, WH Years (6), Shanley mss, DDEL; Memo on *Time*, Feb 28 and pre–press conf, Feb 29, 1956, R 7, DDE; *PPA 1956*, p. 263; *PDDE*, XVI, pp. 2041–2042; *Washington Post*, Oct 13, 1961; Donovan, *Eisenhower*, 402–403 and 406–407.
70. Pre–press conf, Feb 29, 1956, R 7, Diary DDE.

CHAPTER 19. NIXON'S AGONY

1. *PPA* 1956, pp. 266–267; *New York Times,* Mar 1, 1956.
2. RN statement, Feb 29, 1956, B 28, administrative series, RN (2), DDEL; Ike to RN, Mar 6, 1956, PPS324.83, RNyl.
3. Cederberg to RN, Feb 29, B 139, Cederberg, Cronin to RN, Feb 29, B 191, Cronin 1956 ½ and memo, Mar 1, 1956, B 162, Coleman, To, Series 320, RNln.
4. *Daily News* (DC), Dec 22, 1955, PPS336(1955).618, RNyl; Lash, *Eleanor: Years Alone,* 243.
5. *Los Angeles Times,* Nov 27, 1955, PPS299.81S.4, RNyl; *Washington Post,* Nov 29, 1955, B 43, F 4 [2 of 2], Series 207, RNln; *New York Times,* Nov 29 and 30, 1955; *Newsweek,* Dec 12, 1955, p. 96; *Time,* Dec 12, 1955, p. 23.
6. *New York Times,* Feb 4, 1956.
7. Memo, Feb 4, PPS325(1956).21B, memo, Feb 16, PPS325(1956).30 and memo, Feb 22, 1956, PPS325(1956).36, RNyl; Knight to Ike, Feb 16, 1956, B 124, Ca Delegation 1956, Series 320, RNln.
8. Memo, Feb 16, PPS325(1956).29, memo, Feb 22, PPS325(1956).35, memo, Feb 23, PPS325(1956).37, and *LA Examiner,* Feb 24, 1956, PPS336(1956)41, RNyl; Knowland to Knight, Feb 23, Knight to RN, Feb 29, Knight to RN, Mar 7, B 124, Ca Delegation 1956, RN to Knight, Feb 23, B 420, Knight [½] and RN to Brennan, Mar 1, 1956. B 100, Brennan (2), Series 320, RNln.
9. RNC, R 2, *PRP; Gallup Poll,* Two, 1403–1404, 1411–1412, 1414, 1422, and 1424.
10. Memoirs, Mar 22, 1976, RNyl; *PRP,* R 2; *PAES,* VI, 45–48; *Gallup Poll,* Two, 1397; Childs, *Witness to Power,* 101–103; *New York Times,* Sept 26 and Feb 18, 1956; *Newsweek,* Feb 13, 1956, p. 28.
11. Pre–press conf, Mar 7, 1956, R 8, Diary DDE.
12. *PPA* 1956, pp. 286–287 and 289.
13. Ibid., 287–288, 291–292, and 295; *New York Times,* Mar 8, 1956.
14. Memo, Mar 8, 1956, R 8, Diary DDE.
15. *PDDE,* XVI, p. 2061.
16. Ibid., 2063–2065.
17. Diary, Mar 13, 1956, R 5, Diary DDE.
18. RN to Arnold, Mar 2, B 50, Arnold, R, Series 320 and RN to Peale, Mar 5, B 48, F 5 [1 of 2] and *San Francisco Examiner,* Mar 8, 1956, B 49, F 8, Series 207, RNln.
19. Memo, Mar 7, B 364, Hutchinson, W, memo, Mar 10, B 824, Wilson [3/3], Church to RN, Mar 13, B 150, Church, M, Dague to RN, Mar 12, B 198, Dague and Jenkins to RN, Mar 14, 1956, B 382, Jenkins, TA, Series 320, RNln.
20. *New York Herald Tribune,* Mar 15, PPS336(1956)107 and *Manchester Union Leader,* Mar 15, 1956, PPS336(1956)102, RNyl; Jackson to RN, Mar 16, 1956, B 373, Jackson, HE, Series 320, RNln; RNC, R 2, *PRP;* Treat OH, 15–19 and 21; Michael Birkner in the history department at Gettysburg College conducted the oral history with William Treat and has a copy; *Naples Daily News,* May 1, 1994; *New York Times,* Mar 14, 15, and 18, 1956; Drown, *In the Arena,* 168–169 and 172–174.

21. RN to Milloy, Mar 30, B 520, Milloy, RN to MacKinnon, Mar 31, B 470, MacKinnon, GE, RN to Allen, Apr 4, B 27, Allen, C and RN to Bewley, Apr 5, B 80, Bewley ['½], Series 320, RNln; memoirs, Mar 16, 1956, RNyl.

22. Loeb to RN, Mar 16, 1956, B 458, Loeb (2 of 2), Series 320, RNln.

23. *Capital Journal* (Ore), Mar 22, B 329, Healy, W, Gainey to Dear, July 21, B 279, Gainey ['½] and Ellsworth to Friend, July 25, 1956, B 564, Norblad, Series 320, RNln; Day 3, Tape 4, 00:09:57 [RN], Gannon mss, WJBma; *New York Times*, May 19 and 20, 1956.

24. Diary, Mar 13, 1956, R 5, Diary DDE.

25. *PPA* 1956, p. 302; Morrow, *Black Man in the WH*, 54.

26. *PDDE* , XVI, pp. 2074–2075.

27. *Life*, Mar 19, 1956, V 40, P 2, p. 42; *Newsweek*, Mar 26, p. 108 and Apr 23, 1956, p. 27; *New York Times*, Mar 18, 1956.

28. Diary, Mar 20 and Apr 9, 1956, Whitman File, B 8, Mar 1956 (2) and Apr 1956 (2), DDEL.

29. RN remarks, Apr 17 and *Washington Post*, Apr 18, 1956, B 51, F 2, Series 207, RNln; *Newsweek*, Apr 30, 1956, pp. 29–30; *New York Times*, Apr 18, 1956.

30. *PPA* 1956, pp. 431–432 and 438.

31. RN press conf, Apr 26, 1956, B 237, Eisenhower statements, Series 320, RNln; diary, Apr 26, 1956, R 8, Diary DDE; James Hagerty OH 639, pp. 75–76, CCOH; *New York Times*, Apr 27, 1956; Thomson and Shattuck, *1956 Presidential Campaign*, 73–81.

32. Meeting, Apr 27, 1956, R 8, Cabinet DDE; telephone call, Apr 27, 1956, B 4, Jan 3–Apr 30, 1956, DuHe.

33. *New York Times*, June 8, 1956; Persons, 161, p. 150, CCOH; Ferrell, *Ill-Advised*, 118–120; Gilbert, *Mortal Presidency*, 99–104.

34. *New York Times*, June 9, 1956; J. Eisenhower, *Strictly Personal*, 185–186; Gray, *Eighteen Acres*, 193–195.

35. *New York Times*, June 9, 1956; Lasby, *Eisenhower's Heart Attack*, 208–226; Gray, *Eighteen Acres*, 195.

36. *Washington Post*, June 9, *Evening Star*, June 9, 1956, B 54, F 1, Series 207, RNln; *New York Times*, June 10 and 11, 1956; Ferrell, *Ill-Advised*, 122–123.

37. *New York Times*, June 9, 11, 12, and 13, 1956; J. Eisenhower, *Strictly Personal*, 187; Gray, *Eighteen Acres*, 196; Nixon, *Six Crises*, 167–169; Adams, *Firsthand Report*, 193–195.

38. RN to Jack, June 15, 1956, DR 125, RNyl; *Washington Post*, June 19, 1956, B 54, F 12, Series 207, RNln; *PDDE*, XVII, pp. 2747–2748.

39. Radio reports, June 17, 1956, B 310, Hagerty, J, Series 320, RNln; Thomas Dewey OH, 31–32, CCOH.

40. Memo, June 18, 1956, PPS325(1956).77A, RNyl.

41. *Gallup Poll*, Two, 1430–1431; *Newsweek*, June 25, 1956, pp. 25–26; *New York Times*, June 19, 1956.

42. *Minneapolis Morning Tribune*, May 31, B 330, Heffelfinger [2/2], radio reports, June 24, B 437, Langlie, A, press conf, June 24 and July 18, B 102, Bridges (2), radio reports, B 293, July 2, Goldwater [2/2], *Minneapolis Star*, July 11, B 279, Gainey ['½], clipping, July 18, B 181, Corbett, R, Series 320 and *Manila Times*, July 9, 1956, B 2, Manila [3 of 5],

Series 367, RNln; *New York Times*, June 26, PPS336(1956)197 and *Washington Sunday Star* (DC), July 8, 1956, PPS336(1956)209, RNyl.

43. Hoffman to RN, May 31, B 346, Hoffman, 2 of 2, Pearson letter, June 30, McCloy to Humphrey, July 3 and Humphrey to RN, July 9, B 361, Humphrey, G and radio reports, July 8, 1956, B 492, McCloy, Series 320, RNln; *U.S. News & World Report*, July 20, 1956, PPS336(1956)228, RNyl.

44. *Los Angeles Times*, July 7, 1956.

45. *New York Herald Tribune*, July 13, 1956, PPS336(1956)218, RNyl; radio reports, July 15, 1956, B 177, Considine, B, Series 320, RNln; *Los Angeles Times*, July 11, 1956.

46. *San Diego Union*, July 16, 1956, PPS336(1956)226, RNyl; *Los Angeles Times* and *New York Times*, July 15, 1956.

47. *Newsweek*, July 23, 1956, p. 19.

48. *PAES*, VI, pp. 81–82; *New York Times*, Mar 15, 1956; Martin, *It Seems Like*, 164–170; Thomson and Shattuck, *1956 Presidential Campaign*, 30–71.

49. Smith ed., *Hostage*, 673–675.

50. Memo, Apr 7, 1960, B I, Book II, Krock mss, HML.

51. Robert Anderson OH 521, pp. 26–27, DDEL.

52. Anderson notes, Feb 9, 1968, D. Anderson mss, MLGC; Bernard Shanley OH 348, p. 58, DDEL; Brownell, *Advising Ike*, 296; Thompson ed., *Eisenhower Presidency*, 178.

53. Milton Eisenhower OH 292, 46–49 and OH (1969), 31–33, CCOH; M. Eisenhower, *President Is Calling*, 325–326; M. Eisenhower to Roorda, July 19, 1983, Gellman mss, DDEL.

CHAPTER 20. STASSEN'S FOLLY

1. Drew, *Nixon*, 16.

2. Baker to Hall, July 6 and Baker to RN, July 14, 1956, B 60, Baker, H, Series 320, RNln; Baker to Ike, July 13, 1956, R 9, Diary DDE.

3. Stassen to RN, June 30, 1955, B 725, Stassen [3/4], Series 320, RNln; memoirs, Mar 16, 1976, RNyl; Kirby, "Childe Harold's Pilgrimage," 344–398; see Kirby et al., *Harold E. Stassen*.

4. Clipping, Jan 17, PPS336(1955).18, *Whittier News*, Feb 1, PPS336(1955).40, *San Diego Union*, Sept 3, PPS336(1955).263 and Oct 10, PPS336(1955).502 and *New York Times*, Dec 13, 1955, PPS336(1955).SupplementA.81, RNyl; PRP, R 2; *PDDE*, XVI, p. 1621; Kirby, "Childe Harold's Pilgrimage," 403–405; *Los Angeles Times*, July 11, 1956; Slater, *Ike I Knew*, 104.

5. Stassen to Whitman, after July 23, 1956, B 34, Stassen 1956(2), Administrative Series, DDEL; Uebelhor, "Ticket Will Be Ike And Dick," 210–212.

6. Stassen to Ike, July 19, 1956, B 34, Stassen 1956 (2), Administrative Series, DDEL.

7. *New York Times*, July 24, 1956; Stassen to Whitman, after July 23, 1956, B 34, Stassen 1956(2), Administrative Series, DDEL; Stassen on Booknotes, C-SPAN, Sept 7, 1990.

8. *New York Times*, July 24, 1956; Uebelhor, "Ticket Will Be Ike and Dick," 212–213.

9. Stassen to Ike, July 19, 1956. Stassen 1956 (2), Administrative Series, DDEL; Ferrel ed., *American Secretaries of State*, Vol. 18, 14–18.
10. *Gallup Poll*, Two, 1410–1411; Prescott Bush OH 31, p. 327, CCOH; Herskowitz, *Duty, Honor, Country*, 180–181.
11. Diary, Mar 13, 1956, R 5, Diary DDE.
12. Herter to RN, Aug 25, 1954, PPS18.973, RNyl; Gellman, *Contender*, 125–138.
13. Herter to RN, Sept 21, 1955, B 334, Herter 102, Series 320, RNln.
14. Woods call, Sept 10, 1955, B 28, RN (4), AS, DDE; RN to Robinson, Nov 15, 1955, PPS325(1955).254, RNyl; RN to Arnold, Sept 6, 1955, B 34, F 7, Series 207 and RN statement, July 23, B 334, Herter 102, news release, July 23, B 313, Hall [2/3] and RN to Gainey, undated [July 23, 1956], B 279, Gainey [2/2], Series 320, RNln; Nixon, *RN*, 173–174.
15. RN to Hiestand, July 26, B 338, Hiestand, RN to St. George, July 26, B 667, St. George and RN to Byrnes, July 26, 1956, B 119, Byrnes, Jo, Series 320, RNln; *Los Angeles Times*, July 24, 1956.
16. *Los Angeles Times* and *New York Times*, July 25 and 26, 1956.
17. Diary, July 23, 1956, Vol. VII, p. 2218, B 3, WH Years (6), Shanley mss, DDEL.
18. Stassen to St. George, July 26, 1956, B 677, St. George, Series 320, RNln; *Los Angeles Times* and *New York Times*, July 26, 1956.
19. Radio reports, July 27, 1956, B 686, Sevareid, Series 320, RNln; *Los Angeles Times* and *New York Times*, July 27, 1956.
20. Diary, July 26, 27 and 31, 1956, Vol. VII, pp. 2220–2223, B 3, WH Years (7), Shanley mss, DDEL.
21. *Los Angeles Times* and *New York Times*, July 29, 1956; Hillings, *Irrepressible Irishman*, 75.
22. *Los Angeles Times*, July 30, 1956.
23. Ibid., July 31, 1956.
24. Stassen to Ike, July 30, 1956, B 34, Stassen 1956 (2), Administrative Series, DDEL; Uebelhor, "Ticket Will Be Ike and Dick," 221.
25. *Los Angeles Times*, July 24, 1956; see Starr, *Golden Dreams*, 191–212, for the background of this period.
26. Senators, July 24 and ticket, Aug 13, B 421, Knott, W, RN to Baer, Aug 10, B 59, Baer, Knowland to Hancock, July 16, *Call-Bulletin* and Hancock to Woods, Aug 7, 1956, B 316, Hancock (1 of 3), Series 320, RNln; *New York Times*, Aug 14, 1956; Montgomery and Johnson, *One Step from the WH*, 195–199.
27. Pre–press conf briefing, Aug 1, 1956, B 8, Aug 1956 (2), ACW diary, DDEL; Morrow, *Black Man in the WH*, 85.
28. Ike to Unger, Aug 2, 1956, B 717, 138-C-11, Nixon—pro, OF, Diary DDE; *PPA* 1956, pp. 622–636; *PDDE*, XVII, p. 2227; Trohan to Woods, Aug 2, 1956, PPS325(1956).127, RNyl; *Newsweek*, Aug 13, 1956, pp. 33–34; *U.S. News & World Report*, Aug 10, 1956, p. 25.
29. Clipping, Aug 3, 1956, B 334, Herter 107, Series 320, RNln; *Boston Sunday Herald*, Aug 5, 1956, File 43, Bridges mss, NHS; Nixon, *RN*, 174–175.
30. Robinson to RN, Aug 3, 1956, B 646, Robinson 1956, Series 320, RNln; Robinson to Johnston, Aug 3, 1956, PPS325(1956).129, RNyl.

31. Chandler to Stassen, Aug 10, B 142, Chandler ½ and memo, Aug 10, 1956, B 237, Eisenhower 2/2, Series 320, RNln; diary, Aug 10, 1956, Vol. VII, p. 2231, B 3, WH Years (7), Shanley mss, DDEL; memo, Aug 10, 1956, B 717, 138-C-11 Nixon-Stassen, OF DDEL; *PDDE*, XVII, p. 2755; Young, "Stassen Incident," 113–116.
32. *Boston Herald*, Aug 4, 1956, File 43, Bridges mss, NHS.
33. Radio reports, Aug 5, 1956, B 313, Hall [2/3], Series 320, RNln; *Washington Post*, Oct 6, 1955, PPS336(1955).459 and Hall to Woods, Aug 9, 1956, PPS325(1956).134, RNyl.
34. Runyon et al., *Source Book of American Presidential Campaign*, 65–70; Thomson and Shattuck, *1956 Presidential Campaign*, 113, 138, 152, 161, and 165–167; Schlesinger and Schlesinger eds., *Journals*, 43–44; Moos, "Election of 1956," pp. 3345–3346 and 3348–3349; *New York Times*, Aug 17, 1956.
35. Memo, Aug 15, 1956, B 420, Knight [½], Series 320, RNln; *Christian Science Monitor*, Aug 16, 1956, PPS336(1956)279, RNyl; Barrett OH, 48–50, 52, and 54–55, Knight/Brown Sr. Era, Regional OH Office.
36. Knight to RN, Aug 7 and schedule, Aug 18, 1956, B 57, F 6, Series 207, RNln; *San Francisco Examiner*, Aug 19, PPS336os(1956).44 and *San Francisco Chronicle*, Aug 22, 1956, PPS336(1956).358, RNyl; Earl Behrens OH, 31–32, CCOH; Robert Finch OH, 71, CSUF; William Knowland OH 333, pp. 75–79, CCOH; Knowland OH, I, pp. 27–28, LBJL; *New York Times*, Aug 19, 1956; Montgomery and Johnson, *One Step from the WH*, 198–201.
37. Poulson, *Genealogy*, 187–188 and 310, Gellman mss, DDEL; Worthen, *Young Nixon*, 164–166.
38. *New York Times*, Aug 22, 1956; *Newsweek*, Aug 27, 1956, p. 20.
39. Stassen to RN, Aug 16, 1956, B 725, Stassen [2/4], Series 320, RNln; *New York Times*, Aug 10, 1956.
40. Comments, Aug 16, 1956, B 34, Stassen 1956 (2), Administrative Series, DDEL.
41. Stassen to Ike, Aug 17, 1956, B 34, Stassen 1956 (2), Administrative Series, DDEL; diary, Aug 17, 1956, p. 2231, Vol. VII, B 3, WH Years (7), Shanley mss, DDEL; *New York Times*, Aug 18, 1956.
42. *New York Times*, Aug 18, 1956.
43. *Chicago Sun Times*, Aug 20, 1956, PPS336(1956)299, RNyl; *Newsweek*, Aug 27, 1956, p. 21.
44. Memo, Aug 20, 1956, B 34, Stassen 1956 (2), Administrative Series, DDEL.
45. Memo, Aug 13, 1956, B 534, Mosher, Series 320, RNln; *San Diego Union*, Aug 15, 1956, PPS336(1956)273, RNyl; *Gallup Poll*, Two, 1440.
46. Hancock to Woods, July 30, 1956, B 316, Hancock (1 of 3), Series 320, RNln; *Los Angeles Herald & Express*, Aug 17, PPS336(1956)278, *Whittier News*, Aug 18, PPS336(1956)280 and *San Francisco Examiner*, Aug 19, 1956, PPS336os(1956).44, RNyl.
47. RN to M. Eisenhower, Aug 17, 1956, B 238, Eisenhower 2/2, Series 320, RNln; *New York Times*, Aug 20, 1956.
48. Schedule, Aug 20, 1956, B 57, F 6, Series 207, RNln; *New York Times*, Aug 20 and 21, 1956.
49. Allen, *Eisenhower and the Mass Media*, 113–123; Cannon, *Politics USA*, 277–279; Reinhard, *Republican*, 132–135.
50. *New York Herald Tribune*, Aug 22, 1956, PPS336(1956).354, RNyl; *Ike's Letters*, 169.

51. *Washington Post*, Aug 22, 1956, PPS336(1956).364, RNyl; *Newsweek*, Aug 20, 1956, p. 31; Holt, *Mamie*, 118–119.

52. *New York Times*, Aug 22, 1956.

53. Ibid.

54. Hannah to Everts, July 14, LBM13, *Whittier News*, July 17, PPS336(1956)226 and Aug 17, PPS336(1956)281 and *Washington Post*, Aug 23, 1956, PPS336(1956).367 and memoirs, Mar 19, 1976, RNyl; I. Kraushaar OH 994, p. 4, CSUF; I. Kraushaar OH, 3–5, WC; *New York Times*, Jul 17, Aug 21 and 22, 1956; Nixon, *RN*, 175–177; Nixon and Olson, *Nixons*, 185–186.

55. *Chicago American*, Aug 22, 1956, PPS336os(1956).123, RNyl.

56. Leonard Hall OH 478, pp. 52–54, DDEL; Brownell, *Advising Ike*, 298–299.

57. *New York Times*, Aug 23, 1956; Hall OH 478, pp. 55 and 59; *Newsweek*, Sept 3, 1956, pp. 21–22; Slater, *Ike I Knew*, 133; Adams, *Firsthand Report*, 243; Martin, *My First Fifty Years*, 172; Nixon, *RN*, 175.

58. *PPA* 1956, pp. 693–701; diary, Aug 22, 1956, p. 2233, Vol. VII, B 3, WH Years (7), Shanley mss, DDEL; Thomson and Shattuck, *1956 Presidential Campaign*, 205–207.

59. *San Francisco Examiner*, Aug 22, PPS336OS(1956).157, *Call-Bulletin*, Aug 23, PPSos(1956).147, and *Los Angeles Times*, Aug 24, 1956, PPS336os(1956).134, RNyl; *Newsweek*, Sept 3, 1956, p. 22; *New York Times*, Sept 20, 1956.

60. Reed to Lodge, Aug 7, 1973, R 13, Lodge mss, MHS.

61. *New York Times*, Aug 23, 1956; Thomson and Shattuck, *1956 Presidential Campaign*, 208–209.

62. *New York Times*, Aug 23, 1956; RN to Herter, Aug 27, 1956, B 334, Herter 102, Series 320, RNln; Thomson and Shattuck, *1956 Presidential Campaign*, 211–212.

63. *New York Times*, Aug 23, 1956.

64. *San Francisco News*, Aug 23, 1956, PPS336(1956).372, RNyl; RN to Johnston, Sept 11, 1956, B 388, Johnston, HA, Series 320, RNln.

65. Memo, Feb 13, B 48, F 5[1 of 2], memo, Mar 21, B 51, F 8 and draft, Aug 5, 1956, B 56, F 16, Series 207, RNln; memoirs, Mar 22, 1976 and RN to Parmet, Dec 10, 1986, RNyl; Cronin to Reuben, June 24, 1974, CCRO 2/25, Cronin mss, FBI; Wills, *Nixon Agonistes*, 28; Donovan, *Crusader in the Cold War*, iii–v and 1–107. Cronin claimed that during this period, he was Nixon's only speechwriter; this is incorrect. RN to Reid, Aug 29 and Reid to RN, Sept 11, 1956, B 625, Reid (2 of 2), Series 320, RNln.

66. Klein to RN, Aug 28, B 416, Klein (1 of 2), Gruenther to RN, Aug 28, B 306, Gruenther, H and RN to Perlman, Sept 17, B 589, Perlman, Series 320 and Atkinson to RN, Oct 8, 1956, B 58, F 11, Series 207; *New York Times*, Aug 24, 1956; Slater, *Ike*, 135; Thomson and Shattuck, *1956 Presidential Campaign*, 214–215.

67. Meeting, July 25, 1956, R 9, Diary DDE; *PPA* 1956, pp. 702–715; diary, Aug 24, 1956, pp. 2234–2235, Vol. VII, B 3, WH Years (7), Shanley mss, DDEL; *New York Times*, Aug 24, 1956; Thomson and Shattuck, *1956 Presidential Campaign*, 217–219.

68. RN to Morhouse, Sept 15, 1956, B 530, Morhouse, Series 320, RNln; *New York Times*, Aug 28, 29 and Sept 5, 1956; Nixon, *RN*, 176.

69. Memoirs, Mar 16, 1976, RNyl; interview, Day 3, Tape 4, 00:03:36 [RN], Gannon mss, WJBma; Klein, *Making It*, 166.

70. Diary, Oct 13, 1956, p. 2249, Vol. VII, B 3, WH Years (7), Shanley mss, DDEL; memo, Dec 3, 1956, R 3, DuHe.
71. Scherer to Alcorn, Jan 29, B 674, Scherer, G and Kearns to RN, Jan 29, 1957, B 398, Kearns, C, Series 320, RNln; diary, Jan 1957, B 8, Jan 1957 (1), ACW, DDEL; *New York Times*, Jan 29, 1957; Gwinn, "Why the Republicans," *Human Events*, Jan 26, 1957, pp. 1–2; "Did Nixon Hurt the Ticket?" *U.S. News & World Report*, Feb 8, 1957, pp. 40–47, V. 42, P 1; Stanley ed., *Vital Statistics*, 124.
72. M. Eisenhower to RN, Aug 6, B 238, Eisenhower 2/2 and Knebel to RN, Sept 6, 1956, B 419, Knebel, Series 320, RNln; M. Eisenhower to Roorda, July 19, 1983, Gellman mss, DDEL.
73. Adams to Shaw, Sept 10, 1956 and memo, Nov 13, 1957, B 20, Adams, Sh (2 of 2), Series 320, RNln; Herskowitz, *Duty, Honor, Country*, 179; Adams, *Firsthand Report*, 232 and 240–241.
74. Eisenhower, *Waging Peace*, 9.
75. RN to Hall, Aug 22, B 313, Hall [2/3], RN to Adkins, Aug 22, B 21, Adkins, B, RN to Morhouse, Aug 22, B 530, Morhouse and RN to Dewey, Aug 22, 1957, B 214, Dewey 2/2, Series 320, RNln; Nixon, *RN*, 167; Day 3, Tape 4, 00:03:18 [RN], Gannon mss, WJBma; Uebelhor, "Ticket Will Be Ike and Dick," 214–215; Aitken, *Nixon*, 239 and 242.

CHAPTER 21. THE LAND OF SMEAR AND GRAB

1. *PPA* 1956, p. 818; Answer desk, 1956, PPS29.B2, RNyl; phone calls, Sept 4, 1956, R 9, Diary DDE; *New York Times*, Sept 4, 1956.
2. *PAES*, VI, pp. 439–440; Birkner, "Election of 1956," pp. 839–842; Thomson and Shattuck, *1956 Presidential Campaign*, 233–237; Ball, *The Past Has*, 145–147; Greene, *Eisenhower, Science Advice*, 87–111; Maddock, *Nuclear Apartheid*, 111–114.
3. Memo, Sept and RN address, Sept 6, 1956. B 58, F 9, Series 207, RNln; *New York Times*, Sept 7, 1956.
4. Thomson and Shattuck, *1956 Presidential Campaign*, 223–232.
5. *New York Times*, Sept 11 and 12, 1956.
6. Telephone calls, Sept 12, 1956, R 9, Diary DDE; diary, Sept 12, 1956, Hughes mss, HML; Nixon, *RN*, 176–177.
7. Memo, Sept 12, 1956, B 360, Hughes, Em, Series 320, RNln.
8. RN address, Sept 12 and *Evening Star* (DC), Sept 13, 1956, B 59, F 7, Series 207, RNln; *Newsweek*, Sept 24, 1956, p. 32; Adams, *Firsthand Report*, 297–298.
9. *PPA* 1956, pp. 767–772; diary, Sept 3–11, 1956, Hughes mss, HML.
10. Friel, "Influence of Television," 98–105; Gilbert, *Television and Presidential Politics*, 148–161.
11. *PAES*, VI, pp. 215–218; *New York Times*, Sept 14, 1956; diary, Sept 14, 1956, Hughes mss, HML.
12. *New York Herald Tribune*, Sept 20, PPS336(1956).467, *Washington Post*, Sept 21, PPS336(1956).481 and Oct 18, PPS336, *San Diego Union*, Sept 25, PPS336(1956).S518, *Los Angeles Times*, Oct 5, PPS336, and *San Diego Tribune*, Oct 15, 1956, PPS336, RNyl; Gorman, *Kefauver*, 272–273; Fontenay, *Kefauver*, 283.

13. *Los Angeles Times*, Sept 19, 1956, PPS336(1956).455, RNyl; ER to Verbeck, Sept 26, B 784, Verbeck, ER to Singmaster, Oct 6, ER to Cleveland, Oct 9 and Nov 6, 1956, B 654, Roosevelt, E (FDR), King to Jordon, Oct 19, 1956, B 654, Roosevelt, E (FDR) and RN to J. Roosevelt, Jan 14, 1957, B 656, Roosevelt, J, Series 320, RNln; Black, *Casting Her Own*, 232.

14. Recent remarks, 1956 campaign, PPS27.Harry Truman, RNyl; *New York Times*, Oct 3 and 9, 1956.

15. *New York Times*, Sept 11, 1956; PPA 1956, p. 814.

16. PDDE, XVII, p. 2764; *New York Times*, Sept 19, 1956.

17. PN to Cooper, Sept 14, 1956, B 179, Cooper, John [2/2], Series 320, RNln; *New York Herald Tribune*, Sept 23, PPS336(1956).S502, *Whittier News*, Sept 24, PPS336(1956)S519 and *Salt Lake Tribune*, Sept 25, 1956, PPS336(1956).S519, RNyl; Sheldon Beeson OH 809, pp. 11–12, CSUF; A. Koch OH, 2nd interview, 8, WC.

18. Hearst to RN, Sept 12, B 329, Hearst, WR (2 of 3), RN to Murphy, Sept 17, B 541, Murphy, TJ and Bassett to Adams, Sept 19, 1956, B 19, Adams, Ju, Series 320, RNln; *Indianapolis News*, Sept 18, PPS336(1956).453, *Whittier News*, Sept 19, PPS336os(1956).186, memo, Sept 19, PPS23.1:27, RN to Knight, Sept 19, PPS23.1.27 and *Reno Evening Gazette*, Sept 19, 1956, PPS336os(1956).189, RNyl; A.C. Newsom OH 919, p. 10, CSUF.

19. Speech suggestions, Sept 19, PPS29.B.1, *Daily Statesman* (Ind), Sept 21, PPS336 (1956).477, *Evening Star* (DC), Sept 24, PPS336(1956).S513 Sept 29, 1956, PPS336 (1956).566, RNyl; Prescott Bush OH 31, pp. 201–202, CCOH; *New York Times*, Sept 21, 1956; *Newsweek*, Oct 8, 1956, p. 24; Ashby and Gramer, *Fighting the Odds*, 47–68.

20. *Houston Post*, Sept 26, 1956; *Philadelphia Inquirer*, Sept 28, PPS336(1956).550 and *Cincinnati Enquirer*, Sept 29, 1956, PPS336(1956).217, RNyl.

21. Diary, Sept 29, 1956, Hughes mss, HML; *New York Times*, Sept 21 and 30, 1956; Martin, *Stevenson and the World*, 368–369.

22. Press release, Aug 29, B 34, AFL, Hoyt to RN, Sept 26, B 358, Hoyt and King to Miller, Oct 1956, B 432, Labor, Series 320, RNln; *Rocky Mountain News* (Colo), Sept 23, PPS336(1956)S500, *Denver Post*, PPS336(1956).S511, speech suggestions, Sept 25, PPS29. B1, *San Diego Tribune*, Sept 28, PPS336(1956).562 and *Philadelphia Inquirer*, Sept 29, 1956, PPS336(1956).567, RNyl; PPA 1956, p. 813.

23. Memo, Sept 29, 1956, B 313, Hall [2/3], Series 320, RNln; *New York Times*, Sept 24, 1956; Benson, *Cross Fire*, 333.

24. *New York Times*, Sept 30, 1956; Schlesinger and Schlesinger eds., *Journals*, 44–46; Galbraith, *A Life*, 343.

25. Martin, *Stevenson and the World*, 358; RNC, R 2, PRP; *Gallup Poll*, Two, 1441, 1443–1444, and 1446–1453; McClenahan and Becker, *Eisenhower and the Cold War*, 53–80; Lasby, *Eisenhower's Heart Attack*, 226–229.

26. Memo, Oct 2, 1956, PPS29.B2, RNyl; diary, first week in Oct, 1956, Hughes mss, HML.

27. *Springfield Union* (Mass), Oct 4, PPS336, *Evening Bulletin* (Pa), Oct 4, PPS336 and *New York Herald Tribune*, Oct 5, 1956, PPS336, RNyl; *New York Times*, Oct 4, 1956.

28. *New York Times*, Oct 5, 1956.

29. Press briefing, Oct 5, 1956, R 10, DDE; *PDDE*, XVII, p. 2768; *PPA* 1956, p. 853; *New York Times*, Oct 5, 1956.

30. *PPA* 1956, p. 859; *New York Times*, Oct 9, 1956; Maddock, *Nuclear Apartheid*, 81–114.

31. Diary, Oct 8–10, 1956, Hughes mss, HML; *Gallup Poll*, Two, 1448; *New York Herald Tribune*, Oct 7, 1956, PPS336, RNyl.

32. *PAES*, VI, pp. 258–259; *New York Times*, Oct 6, 1956.

33. *PPA* 1956, p. 855; *PDDE*, XVII, p. 2410; *New York Times*, Oct 5, 1956.

34. *New York Times*, Oct 1 and 8, 1956.

35. Memo and Richard Nixon, Oct 10, 1956, R 42, DuHe.

36. *PPA* 1956, pp. 903–921; *PDDE*, XVII, pp. 2324–2325; diary, Oct 15–20, 1956, Hughes mss, HML.

37. *New York Times*, Oct 17 and 18, 1956; *Newsweek*, Oct 29, 1956, p. 29.

38. *San Diego Tribune*, Oct 13, 1956, PPS336, RNyl; *New York Times*, Oct 14, 1956.

39. *New York Times* and *Chicago Tribune*, Oct 18, 1956; Nixon, *RN*, 178.

40. *Whittier News*, Oct 9, PPS336 and *San Antonio Light*, Oct 10, 1956, PPS336, RNyl; *New York Times*, Oct 10, 1956.

41. *San Diego Union*, Oct 14, 1956, PPS336, RNyl; Gainey to RN, Oct 19, 1956, B 279, Gainey [½], Series 320, RNln.

42. *Evansville Courier* (Ind), Oct 17, PPS336 and *Washington Post*, Oct 20, 1956, PPS336, RNyl; Van Sickle to RN, Oct 21, 1956, B 781, Van Sickle, Series 320, RNln; *New York Times*, Oct 17, 1956.

43. *New York Times*, Oct 24, 26, 27, and 28, 1956.

44. Ibid., Oct 28 and 29, 1956.

45. Diary, Oct 22–26; Hughes mss, HML; *New York Times*, Oct 30, 1956; *Chicago Tribune*, Oct 30, 1956.

46. *New York Times*, Oct 23, 24, and 27, 1956; *Newsweek*, Oct 29, 1956, p. 28.

47. *Los Angeles Times*, Oct 29, 1956, PPS336, RNyl; *Gallup Poll*, Two, 1452.

48. *PAES*, VI, p. 307; Martin, *It Seems Like*, 169.

49. *PAES*, VI, pp. 302–307; *New York Times*, Oct 28, 1956; Martin, *Stevenson and the World*, 382–383; Galbraith, *A Life*, 345–346.

50. *PAES*, VI, pp. 308–309.

51. *Chicago Daily Tribune*, Oct 23, 1956.

52. *New York Times*, Oct 24, 1956; Lungren and Lungren, *Healing RN*, 157–158.

53. *Chicago Daily Tribune*, Oct 25, 1956.

54. Nixon, *RN*, 179.

55. Nichols, *Eisenhower 1956*, pp. 199–232.

56. Diary, Oct 28, 1956, Hughes mss, HML.

57. *PAES*, VI, 313–316; *New York Times*, Oct 29–31, 1956; *Philadelphia Inquirer*, Nov 1, 1956; Helgerson, *Getting to Know*, 43–45.

58. Diary, Oct 29–31, 1956, Hughes mss, HML.

59. Diary, Oct 31, 1956, Hughes mss, HML; *New York Times*, Oct 30 to Nov 2, 1956.

60. *PDDE*, XVII, pp. 2353–2360.

61. Telephone call, Oct 29, 1956, R 5, DuHe; *Evening Star* (DC), Oct 30, 1956, PPS336, RNyl; Ike to Simpson, Nov 2, 1956, Simpson, RM, Series 320, RNln; Klein, *Making It*, 233; Hughes, *Ordeal*, 182–183.

62. Hagerty to Woods, Oct 31, 1956, PPS29.B1, RNyl; *FR*, 1955–1957, Vol. XV, pp. 884–885.

63. *San Diego Union*, Oct 31, 1956, PPS336, RNyl; Day 4, Tape 2, 00:46:44 [RN], Gannon mss, WJBma.

64. *Evening Star* (DC), Oct 31, 1956, PPS336, RNyl.

65. *Times Leader* (Pa), Nov 1, PPS336 and *Post-Gazette* (Pa), Nov 2, PPS336, speech suggestions, Nov 2, PPS29.B1 and memo, Nov 2, PPS29, B1 and *Evening Star* (DC), Nov 3, 1956, PPS336, RNyl; memo, Feb 29, 1960, B 213, de Toledano, Series 320, RNln; *New York Times*, Nov 2 and 3, 1956.

66. Memoirs, Mar 18, 1976, RNyl; *Chicago Tribune*, Nov 4, 1956; *New York Times*, Nov 4, 1956.

67. *New York Herald Tribune*, Nov 5, 1956, PPS336, RNyl.

68. PPA 1956, pp. 1085–1089; diary, Nov 5, 1956, Hughes mss, HML; *New York Times*, Nov 6, 1956; Allen, *Eisenhower and the Mass Media*, 148.

69. Schlesinger and Schlesinger eds., *Journals*, 44–46; Goldman, *Crucial Decade—And After*, 296.

70. Thomson and Shattuck, *1956 Presidential Campaign*, 310–312.

71. *PAES*, VI, pp. 322–325; McClure to AES, Nov 6, 1956, B 492, McClure, J, Series 320, RNln; Martin, *Stevenson and the World*, 389–390; Thomson and Shattuck, *1956 Presidential Campaign*, 312–313; *Gallup Poll*, Two, 1458.

72. Day 3, Tape 4, 00:05:12 [RN], Gannon mss, WJBma; *Washington Post*, Nov 6, 1956, PPS336, RNyl; *Washington Post*, Oct 31, 1961; Lasby, *Eisenhower's Heart Attack*, 238–239; Allen, *Eisenhower and the Mass Media*, 147; Martin, *It Seems Like*, 171; Donovan, *Confidential Secretary*, 110.

73. Memo, Nov 3, 1956, B 59, F 11, Series 207, RNln; *PPA 1956*, pp. 1089–1091; diary, Nov 6, 1956, Hughes mss, HML; *New York Times*, Nov 7, 1956; Thomson and Shattuck, *1956 Presidential Campaign*, 317–318; Klein, *Making It*, 50.

74. Stanley ed., *Vital Statistics*, 124; Day 9, Tape 4, 00:17:17 [RN], Gannon mss, WJBma; memoirs, Feb 16 and Mar 22, 1976, RNyl; Moos, "Election of 1956," p. 3353.

75. *New York Times*, Nov 7 and 8, 1956.

76. Nixon, *RN*, 180–181; Adams, *Firsthand Report*, 298–299.

77. *New York Herald Tribune*, Nov 7, 1956, PPS336, and Elections, May 1957, PPS31.B1, RNyl; Thomson and Shattuck, *1956 Presidential Election*, 346–350; Scammon ed., *America at the Polls*, 19; Martin, *Stevenson and the World*, 391.

78. Nixon, *RN*, 181.

79. RN to Milbank, Jan 15, 1957, B 515, Milbank, Sr., Series 320, RNln.

80. *PAES*, VI, p. 399–400.

81. Ball, *Past Has Another*, 145–148.

CHAPTER 22. THE HUNGARIAN REVOLUTION AND
THE FREEDOM FIGHTERS

1. Ostermann ed., *Uprising in East Germany.*
2. RN to Irwin, Aug 26, 1955, B 34, F 1 [1 of 2], Series 207, RNln; Békés et al. eds., *1956 Hungarian Revolution,* 130–135.
3. Tudda, *Truth Is Our Weapon,* 101; Kovrig, *Myth of Liberation,* 126–172, 236–237, and 290–291; Lendavi, *One Day That Shook,* 189–192; Krebs, *Dueling Visions,* 16–24, 28–68, and 124; Dockrill, *Eisenhower's New-Look,* 153–167; Murphy, *Diplomat,* 428–432; Ailinger, "Cold War," 1–66; Marchio, "Rhetoric and Reality," 199–330 and 407–502; Bischof, "Collapse of Liberation Rhetoric," 51–62; Borhi, "Rollback, Containment," 67–110.
4. *PDDE,* XVII, pp. 2334–2335; Granville, *First Domino,* 3–35; Kramer, "New Evidence on Soviet," 369–370 and "Soviet Union and the 1956 Crises," 182–195; Kramer, "Soviet Union and the 1956 Crises," 175–208; Puhan, *Cardinal in the Chancery,* 102–103.
5. Kenez, *Varieties of Fear,* 188; Bursten, *Escape from Fear,* 69–81; email, Kramer to Gellman, Oct 21, 2011, Gellman mss, DDEL; telephone call with Kenez, Oct 19, 2011.
6. RN to Streibert, Jan 14, 1957, B 735, Streibert and memo, Feb 3, 1958, B 194, Crusade, Series 320, RNln; *FR,* 1958–1960, Vol. X, pp. 218–219; *New York Times,* July 4, 1956; Nixon, *RN,* 183; Kornitzer, *Real Nixon,* 254–255; Gati, *Failed Illusions,* 99–100 and 108; Belmonte, *Selling the American Way,* 72–74; Cull, *Cold War and the USIA,* 131–133, 140, and 161; Johnson, *Radio Free Europe,* 91–118; Granville, "Caught with Jam," 811–839.
7. Bipartisan legislative meeting, Nov 9, 1956, R 10, Diary DDE; Machcewicz, *Rebellious Satellite,* 87–213; Granville, "Hungarian and Polish Reactions," 1054–1058; Granville, "Poland and Hungary," 383–389.
8. *PDDE,* XVII, pp. 2377, 2380, and 2382–2383.
9. *PPA* 1956, pp. 1100–1101; Ike meeting, Apr 2, 1967, PPS324.247, RNyl.
10. Ibid.
11. *FR,* 1955–1957, Vol. XV, p. 1085 and XXV, pp. 418–421.
12. Phone calls, Nov 27 and NSC meeting, Nov 30, 1956, R 10, Diary DDE. telephone calls, Dec 6 and Dec 7, R 5 and Dec 7, 1956, R 9, DuHe.
13. *New York Times,* Oct 17, 1945.
14. *PDDE,* XIV, p. 101; Davis, "Cold War, Refugees, and U.S.," 26–43; Bon Tempo, "Americans at the Gate," 60–93.
15. *PDDE,* XIV, pp. 101 and 327; Eisenhower, *Mandate,* 216 and 547; Davis, "Cold War, Refugees, and U.S.," 223; Bon Tempo, "Americans at the Gate," 96–153; "Campaign Statements of Eisenhower," A Reference Index, REF E816 E421, c.2, Book Collection, DDEL.
16. Background papers, Dec 1956, PPS325(1956).166.4–5, RNyl; Markowitz, "Humanitarianism Versus Restrictionism," 46–48; Davis, "Cold War, Refugees, and U.S.," 104–105 and 122–127; Wagner, "Lingering Death," 303–339; Bon Tempo, "Americans at the Gate," 156–169.

17. *PDDE*, XVII, p. 2411.
18. *New York Times*, Dec 7, 1956; Kovrig, *Myth of Liberation*, 215.
19. Clipping, Dec 12, B 362, Hungarian (2 of 4), Series 320, RNln; PN to Helene, Dec 11, DR 134 and calendar, Dec 12–14, 1956, PPS212(1956).267a, RNyl; *New York Times*, Dec 13, 1956; I have relied on "VP Nixon's Trip to Austria," in Glant, *Remember Hungary 1956*.
20. *PDDE*, XVII, p. 2411; *New York Times*, Dec 14, 1956; *Newsweek*, Dec 24, 1956, p. 15; Nixon, *RN*, 182.
21. For examples, see *New York Times*, Dec 7 and 17, 1956.
22. Gelher, "From Non-alignment to Neutrality," 104–116; Cronin, *Great Power Politics and the Struggle*, 120–171; Bischof, *Austria in the First Cold War*, 142–149; Rosenberg, *Soviet-American Relations*, 40–70.
23. Granville, "Neutral Encounters of the Paranoid Kind," 144–151; Gelher, "From Non-alignment to Neutrality," 117–121.
24. *Newsweek*, Dec 24, 1956, p. 14.
25. Barrett, *CIA & Congress*, 253–254; Colby and Forbath, *Honorable Men*, 7–179; Helms, *Look Over My Shoulder*, 378.
26. *New York Times*, Dec 17, 1956.
27. RN to Langston, Dec 17, 1956, B 653, Rogers 1953 (3 of 3), Series 320, RNln; *Washington Post*, Dec 20, 1956, PPS336, RNyl; *New York Times*, Dec 19, 1956.
28. *PDDE*, XVII, p. 2785 and Doc #2139; *New York Times*, Dec 19, 1956.
29. Chronological record, Dec 18, 1956, Gellman mss, DDEL; memo, Dec 28, 1956, B 824, Wilson [3/3], Series 320, RNln; Wilson, *Confessions*, 73; Morrow, *Black Man in the WH*, 111; chronological record, Dec 19, 1956, Gellman mss, DDEL; *New York Times*, Dec 20, 1956.
30. Interview with Rex Scouten, May 20, 2012.
31. Chronological record, Dec 19, 1956, Gellman mss, DDEL; *New York Times*, Dec 20, 1956; Nixon, *RN*, 182; Kornitzer, *Real Nixon*, 227, 261, and 263–264; Frankel, *Times of My Life*, 139.
32. Chronological record, Dec 20, 1956, Gellman mss, DDEL; *New York Times*, Dec 21, 1956; Granville, "Neutral Encounters of the Paranoid," 151–152 and 155; Granville, "Of Spies, Refugees and Hostile Propaganda," 75–76; Kornitzer, *Real Nixon*, 263.
33. Chronological record, Dec 20, 1956, Gellman mss, DDEL; *New York Times*, Dec 21, 1956; Nixon, *RN*, 182.
34. Chronological record, Dec 20, 1956, Gellman mss, DDEL; *New York Times*, Dec 23, 1956; Kornitzer, *Real Nixon*, 255–258; Bursten, *Escape from Fear*, 120–121; Wilson, *Confessions*, 73–75.
35. Chronological record, Dec 20, 1956, Gellman mss, DDEL; Nixon, *RN*, 182; interview with Rex Scouten, Apr 22, 2010.
36. Chronological record, Dec 21, 1956, Gellman mss, DDEL; interviews with Schaerf, Raab, and Pammer, undated (probably early Jan 1957), B 425, Kornitzer (1 of 4), Series 320, RNln; RN to Kornitzer, Jan 28, 1957, B 8, F 4, Kornitzer mss, DUla; *New York Times*, Dec 22, 1956; Wilson, *Confessions*, 73; Kornitzer, *Real Nixon*, 252 and 265–267; *Newsweek*, Dec 31, 1956, p. 17; Nixon, *RN*, 183; interview with Scouten, Apr 22, 2010.

37. Chronological record, Dec 21 and 22, 1956, Gellman mss, DDEL; memo, Dec 28, 1956, B 508, Memo BK, Series 320, RNln and RN to Klaus, Jan 3, 1957, PPS320.7.7, RNyl; *New York Times*, Dec 22 and 23, 1956; Kornitzer, *Real Nixon*, 253 and 260; Puhan, *Cardinal in the Chancery*, 104–105; Nixon, *RN*, 260.

38. Chronological record, Dec 22, 1956, Gellman mss, DDEL; RN to Hoegner, Jan 3, 1956 [*sic* 1957], PPS320.33.7 and RN to Turner, Jan 3, 1957, PPS320.33.24, RNyl; re: Hungarian Refugee trip, Mar 1957, Gellman mss, DDEL; Kornitzer, *Real Nixon*, 260 and 262; interview with Rex Scouten, May 20, 2012.

39. Chronological record, Dec 23, 1956, Gellman mss, DDEL; *New York Times*, Dec 25, 1956.

40. Kornitzer to RN, Dec 20, 1957, B 8, F 4, Kornitzer mss, DUla; Kornitzer, *Real Nixon*, 14.

41. Interview with Figl, Jan 4 [1957], B 425, Kornitzer (1 of 4), Series 320, RNln; Kornitzer to RN, Jan 4, 1957, B 8, F 4, Kornitzer mss, DUla; Kornitzer, *Real Nixon*, 264–265.

42. *New York Times*, Dec 26, 1956.

43. *FR*, 1955–1957, Vol. XXV, pp. 535–539; *PDDE*, XVII, p. 2786; "Result of Nixon's Visit," *U.S. News & World Report*, Dec 28, 1956, pp. 48 and 51–52.

44. Notes, Dec 26, 1956, B 8, Dec 1956, ACW diary, DDEL.

45. Mattei to RN, July 13, 1954, B 26, F 1, Series 207, RNln; RN to Weise, July 24, 1954, PPS320.102.19, memo, Oct 18, 1955, PPS320.102.23, RN to Hoover, Aug 9, PPS320.102.29.1 and Dec 15, 1956, PPS320.102.35, RNyl; Dulles to RN, Dec 20, 1956, R 42, DuHe; *New York Times*, Dec 28, 1956; Glant, *Remember Hungary 1956*, pp. 164 and 166.

46. Hoover to Perry, Apr 5, 1954, B 589. Perry, Series 320 and *New York Herald Tribune*, Oct 28, 1955, B 41, F 1, Series 207, RNln; memo, Dec 9, 1955, Individual File Series, Nixon and Knowland OH, HHL; Hoover to RN, Aug 21, 1954, PPS320.102.20, Hoover to RN, Nov 9, 1956, PPS320.102.34 and RN to Hoover, Jan 14, 1957, PPS320.102.38.1, RNyl; Day 1, Tape 2, 00:28:13 [Frank Gannon], Gannon mss, WJBma.

47. Hoover to RN, Dec 14, 1956, Individual File Series, Nixon, HHL; Hoover to RN, Dec 26, 1956, PPS320.102.36 and RN to Hoover, Jan 14, 1957, PPS320.102.38.1, RNyl.

48. RN to Folger, Jan 18, 1957, B 266, Folger, M, Series 320, RNln; *New York Times*, Dec 28, 1956; *Newsweek*, Jan 7, 1957, pp. 18–19 and 32–33; Bursten, *Escape from Fear*, 155–190; Glant, *Remember Hungary 1956*, p. 166.

49. *New York Times*, Jan 2, 1957.

50. Notes on meeting, Jan 1, 1957, R 2, Legislative DDE; *PPA* 1957, pp. 1–2; *New York Times*, Jan 2, 1957; Bon Tempo, "Americans at the Gate," 193–195.

51. *New York Times*, Dec 23, 1956 and Jan 2, 1957; *PPA* 1957, pp. 3–4; Granville, *First Domino*, 196–200; Glant, *Remember Hungary 1956*, pp. 168–173; Bursten, *Escape from Fear*, 113–135 and 193–209; Lendavi, *One Day That Shook*, 207–208; Nixon, *RN*, 183.

52. *New York Times*, Dec 20, 22, and 27, 1956; *Newsweek*, Dec 31, 1956, p. 18; Bon Tempo, "Americans at the Gate," 170–220.

53. Thompson to King, Jan 31, 1957, B 755, Thompson, LE, Series 320, RNln; Bon Tempo, "Americans at the Gate," 221–278.

54. *PPA* 1957, pp. 84–85, 110–113, and 340–341; Markowitz, "Humanitarianism Versus Restrictionism," 49–59; Davis, "Cold War, Refugees, and U.S.," 129–164.

55. RN to Ernst, Jan 24, B 245, Ernst, M, RN to Dressler, Apr 24, B 362, Hungarian (1 of 4), RN to Kovacs, May 9, 1957, B 426, Kovacs, J, memo, Mar 6, 1959, B 844, Zellerbach (1 of 2) and RN to Tollas, Sept 20, 1962, B 362, Hungarian (3 of 4), Series 320, RNln; *New York Times*, May 1, 1957; RN, *Challenges We Face*, 188–192.
56. Frick, *Reinventing Nixon*, 187–188; Glant, *Remember Hungary 1956*, pp. 176–181.
57. Nixon, *RN*, 183–184.

CHAPTER 23. IKE AND DICK RETURN

1. *New York Times*, Jan 21, 1957.
2. *Gallup Poll*, Two, 1471, 1476, 1486, 1492, 1500, 1522, 1536, 1541, 1545, 1566, 1570, and 1579, and Three, 1589, 1609, 1611, 1615, 1625, 1629, 1632, 1639,1651, 1660, 1690, and 1959; Edwards, *On Deaf Ears*, 87 and 224.
3. *Gallup Poll*, Two, 1535 and Vol. Three, 1650.
4. Ike to RN, Jan 8, PPS324.104 and Dec 30, 1957, PPS324.114, Aug 6, PPS324.130 and Dec 29, 1959, PPS324.133 and Jan 28, 1960, PPS324.136, RNyl; *PDDE*, XVIII, pp. 646–647.
5. Telephone calls, July 14, 1958, R 17, Aug 4 and 15, 1958, R 18, Jan 7, R 20, Aug 28, R 23, Dec 24, 1959, Jan 24, R 24, Apr 14, May 4, June 23 and July 14, 1960, R 26 R 25, diary, May 21, 1959, R 21, Diary DDE; *PDDE*, XXI, pp. 2296, 2337, 2351, 2364, 2366, 2372, 2374–2375, 2382, 2385, 2387, 2407, 2417, 2438, 2440, 2442–2443, 2458, 2460, 2463, 2466, 2468, 2470, 2478, 2483, 2501–2508, 2513, 2520, 2522, 2525, 2528, 2532, 2537, 2544–2545, 2551–2552, and 2560.
6. Appointments, Dec 3, 1957, R 15, Diary DDE.
7. *PPA 1957*, pp. 338–339; *Ike's Letters*, 194–195; schedule, Nov 25, 1957, R 15, Diary DDE; memo, Nov 25, 1957, R 10, DuHe; Gray, *Eighteen Acres*, 196–198; Morrow, *Black Man in the WH*, 188; *New York Times*, Nov 27, 1955 and Nov 29, 1957; Ferrell, *Ill-Advised*, 128–130; RN, *Six Crises*, 171–173.
8. Schedule, Nov 25, 1957, PPS212(1957).3.195, RNyl; schedule, Nov 25, 1957, R 15, Diary DDE; *New York Times*, Nov 27, 1957; J. Eisenhower, *Strictly Personal*, 196; Nixon, *RN*, 184; Adams, *Firsthand Report*, 195–198; Nixon, *Six Crises*, 170–174.
9. *New York Times*, Nov 27, 1955.
10. Ibid., Nov 28, 1955; memo, Nov 27, 1927, R 10, DuHe; RN, *Six Crises*, 172–173; Adams, *Firsthand Report*, 198.
11. *New York Times*, Nov 27, 28, and 29, 1957.
12. Ibid., Nov 27, 28, and 29, 1957; memo, Nov 27, 1957, R 7, DuHe; Larson, *Eisenhower*, 175–176; J. Eisenhower, *Strictly Personal*, 195–196; RN, *Six Crises*, 173–175.
13. *New York Times*, Nov 30, 1957.
14. Ibid., Nov 27 and 30, 1957; memo, Dec 3, 1957, RNyl; B 50, Eyes Only memorandum, Nixon—Vice President (Corres) (6), William Rogers mss; platter, Dec 3, 1957, RNyl; Day 5, Tape 1, 00:22:17 and 00:25:07 [RN], Gannon mss; Persons OH 161, p. 150, CCOH; Nixon, *RN*, 184–185: Morrow, *Black Man in the WH*, 189; Nixon, *RN*, 165.
15. *PDDE*, XXI, pp. 2317–2318, 2322, 2344, 2358, 2372–2373, 2375, 2379, 2410, 2445, 2473, 2483, 2506, 2527, 2539, 2541, 2543, 2548, 2554, 2557, and 2562.

16. Memo, Oct 6, 1954, PPS324.39 and Ike to RN, Oct 2, 1957, PPS324.110, RNyl; appointments, Oct 2, 1957, R 14, Diary DDE; *PDDE*, XXI, p. 2420.
17. Gruenther to RN, Dec 8, 1957, B 306, Gruenther, A, Series 320, RNln; Slater, *Ike I Knew*, 155.
18. *PPA* 1958, p. 830.
19. Larson, *Eisenhower*, 10.
20. RN to Gleeson, Mar 17, B 290, Gleeson, WL and memo, Apr 4, 1958, B 310, Hagerty, J, Series 320, RNln.
21. Slater, *Ike I Knew*, 205; *Newsweek*, Oct 19, 1959, pp. 27–28.
22. Ike to Lucy Eisenhower, May 6, 1960, R 25, Diary DDE.
23. Gruenther to RN, Dec 6, 1957, B 306, Gruenther, H, Series 320, RNyl; *Gallup Poll*, Two, 1508–1509, 1535–1536 and 1584.
24. RN to Reeves, June 5, 1956, B 624, Reeves, AB, Clarvoe to RN, Nov 27, 1957, B 156, Clarvoe, *San Francisco Chronicle* late June or July, Aug 23, and Sept 4, 1959, B 121, Caen, Series 320, RNln; Buckley ed., *Odyssey of a Friend*, 200.
25. Stacks, *Scotty*, 295.
26. Weekly schedule, Oct 30, 1955, PPS270.2, RNyl; Reston to RN, May 23, 1957, B 637, Reston [2/2], Series 320, RNln; memo, Jan 21, 1957, B 50, Confidential Memoranda, Jan 1953–Aug 1959, Record Series 26/20/120, Reston mss; I would like to thank Chris Prom, assistant university archivist at the University of Illinois for providing this document; Stacks, *Scotty*, 295–296.
27. Schedule, Feb 12, 1957, PPS212(1957).3.13, RNyl; *Pasadena Star-News*, Jan 3, B 667, St. Johns [3/3] and Childs to RN, Jan 13, 1958, B 144, Childs, Series 320, RNln.
28. St. Johns to RN, Jan 27, B 667, St. Johns [3/3], Series 320 and RN to St. Johns, Jan 31, B 79, F 11 and press conf, Feb 18, 1958, B 80, F 3, Series 207, RNln.
29. Alsop to RN, Mar 12, B 337, Hibbs, B, Series 320, RNln; Yoder, *Joe Alsop's Cold War*, 118–163.
30. *New York Herald Tribune*, Mar 14, B 1, Articles Good, Series 389 and Key to Crabtree, Apr 7, 1958, B 186, Crabtree, N, Series 320, RNln.
31. J. Alsop to Lippmann, Apr 10, 1958, B 14, F Apr 1956, Alsop mss; Alsop to RN, Apr 26, 1958, B 29, Alsop, S, Series 320, RNln; Barbara Mashburn OH, 5, WC; Merry, *Taking on the World*, 328.
32. RN to Hunter, July 25, B 91, F 6, Series 207 and memo, Aug 4, B 213, de Toledano 2/3 and RN to Moley, Aug 19, 1958, B 29, Alsop, S, Series 320, RNln; Alsop, "The Mystery of Richard Nixon," 28–29+; *Newsweek*, July 14, 1958, p. 62; Merry, *Taking on the World*, 315 and 328–329.
33. PN to Mamie, early Sept and mid Nov 1957, Personal Files of Mamie, B 32, Nixon, DDE.
34. Memo, Dec 4, 1956, PPS324.102, diary, Jan 9, PPS212(1958).1, Mamie to PN, Feb 7, 1958, PPS268.7, Feb 3, PPS268.9a and May 18, 1959, PPS268.13, RNyl; *New York Times*, Mar 14 and Nov 13, 1959; J. Eisenhower, *Special People*, 187–217; S. Eisenhower, *Mrs. Ike*, passim.
35. *Star-Bulletin* (Hi), Dec 26, 1956, PPS336, RNyl; *Pasadena Star News* (Calif), May 7, B 427, Krehbiel 1957–1959, RN to Drown, June 28, 1957, B 225, Drown ½, Guill to PN, May 27, 1958, B 308, Guill, memo, memo, B 322, Harris, Ele, and Kahn to Jacobs, Mar

15, 1960, B 757, Time, Series 320 and memo, Oct 6, 1959, B 118, F 4, Series 207, RNln; A.C. Newsom OH 919, p. 11, CSUF; *Newsweek*, Dec 23, 1957, p. 59; Taves, "Pat Nixon," 30, 32–33, and 90–92.

36. Memo, Dec 5, 1956 and schedule, Jan 9, 1957, B 61, F 11, Series 207, RNln; PN to Helene, Dec 28, 1956, DR 135 and *Washington Post*, Jan 11, 1957, B 2, PPS272, RNyl.

37. PN to Helene, Dec 28, 1956, DR 135, RNyl.

38. Diary, Apr 2, 1958, PPS212(1958).1 and PN to Helene, Mar 20, 1959, DR 186.1, RNyl; PN to Brown, Sept 14, B 106, Brown, Do, King to Davis, Dec 6, 1956, B 617, Racial 1957, RN to Townsley, Aug 1, B 112, Bunker, E, RN to Culmer, Dec 17, 1957, B 289, Girl, memo, Jan 7, B 719, Sports I, Sherman, May 26, PN to Cree, June 30, 1958, B 691, Sherman, R and Klein to Bond, Feb 1, 1960, B 221, Dodd, Mead, Series 320 and *Charlotte Observer*, June 23, 1958, B 89, F 2, Series 207, RNln.

39. RN to Drury, Aug 27, 1957, B 226, Drury and RN to Edwards, Sept 23, 1958, B 236, Edwards, W, Series 320, RNln; "Nixon Children," Sept 1957, B 3, Nixon Girls, PPS272 and *Chicago Tribune*, Sept 21, 1958, B 4, Sept, PPS273, RNyl.

40. McWhorter to Reuter, Apr 30, B 3, Bolivia, Series 401 and clipping, fall 1958, B 727, Steele, Ja, Series 320, RNln; Roberts, *First Rough Draft*, 275.

41. RN to Fleming, May 1, B 264, Fleming, RV and *San Diego Union*, Nov 8, 1957, B 180, Copley [2/2], Series 320 and *Washington Post*, Dec 19, 1958, B 96, F 3, Series 207, RNln; *Newsweek*, Feb 9, 1957, *New York Times*, Jan 27, 1957.

42. PN to Helene, Dec 29, 1955, DR 119, RNyl; RN to Gross, Apr 5, 1955, B 306, Gross, J, Series 320, RNln; Harris, "Dark Hours of the Richard Nixons," 8.

43. RN to Helen, Apr 17, 1957, DR 162, PN to Helene, Feb 24, DR 169 and mid Dec 1958, DR 181 and diary, Feb 22, 1958, PPS212(1958).1, RNyl; *Los Angeles Times*, Dec 20, 1958, B 96, F 3, Series 207, RNln; Ike to PN, Dec 20, 1958, PPF 794, DDEL; *PDDE*, XXI, p. 2443.

44. *PPA* 1957, p. 434; *New York Times*, Jan 27, 1957; Residence Office, www.whitehouse.gov /about/vp-residence.

CHAPTER 24. PRELUDE TO THE STRUGGLE

1. See Chapters 7 and 8 of this volume.

2. Telephone logs, Feb 2, 1954, PPS212(1954).4.40, RNyl; Robinson to RN, Mar 19, 1957, B 649, Robinson (1 of 2), Series 320, RNln; Long ed., *First Class Citizenship*, 30–31 and 33–34; Morrow, *Black Man in the WH*, 110; Robinson, *I Never Had It Made*, 137–148; Allen, *Robinson*, 206–215; Falkner, *Great Time Coming*, 249–266; Rampersad, *Robinson*, 261 and 324; Clark, "Civil Rights Movement," 239–266.

3. *Jet*, June 6, 1957, pp. 6–7; Taylor, *Randolph*, 216–217; D'Emilio, *Lost Prophet*, 265–266; Farmer, *Lay Bare the Heart*, 185–191.

4. *PMLK*, IV, pp. 101, 135 and 202–203; *Jet*, Nov 22, 1956, p. 16; Reddick, *Crusader Without Violence*, 184–186.

5. Streitmatter, "No Taste for Fluff," 532; Booker, *Black Man's America*, 208–209; Dunnigan, *Black Woman's Experience*, 308–309 and 374–380; Ritchie, *Reporting from Washington*, 28–46.

6. *Jet*, Sept 12, 1957, p. 3.
7. Minutes, Jan 8, B 62, F 14 and RN to Embry, Feb 15, B 62, F 12, Series 207 and RN to Summerfield, Feb 28 and July 8, B 739, Summerfield (3 of 3), memo, May 22, B 546, NAACP (5 of 5) and RN to Chamberlain, Oct 8, 1957, B 141, Chamberlain, D, Series 320, RNln; press release, Jan 6, PPS307.106, Youth Training–Incentives Conf, Feb 4, PPS307.105 and Fourth Annual Report, 1956–1957, PPS307.95.1 (1), RNyl; *Jet*, May 16, p. 4 and Aug 1, 1957, p. 3; Robert Cushman OH, 13–14, DDEL.
8. Nichols, *Matter of Justice*, 51–90.
9. Morrow, *Black Man in the WH*, 114–119; Morrow, *Forty Years*, 108–109 and 134–136.
10. *Los Angeles Sentinel*, Nov 22, 1956.
11. Telephone interview with Lawrence Walsh, Dec 1, 2005; Brownell, "Eisenhower's Civil Rights Program," 235–242; Brownell, *Advising Ike*, 202–221; Anderson, *Eisenhower, Brownell and Congress*, 22–23 and 42–43; Edelsberg, "New Civil Rights Law," 2; Thompson ed., *Eisenhower Presidency*, 169–170; Mayer, "Eisenhower Administration and the Civil Rights Act," 137–145.
12. The 1960 Elections, Apr 1961, PPS77.B 9, RNyl.
13. *Atlanta Daily World*, Nov 6, 7, and 8, *Los Angeles Sentinel*, Nov 1, 8, 15, and 22, *New York Amsterdam*, Nov 10, *Chicago Defender*, Nov 10 and 17, *Call and Post* (Cleveland), Nov 10, *Journal and Guide* (Va), Nov 10 and 17, *The Afro-American* (Baltimore), Nov 17 and *Jet*, Nov 22, 1956.
14. Moon, "Negro Break-Away from the Democrats," 17; Moon, "Negro Vote in the Presidential Election of 1956," 219–230.
15. Wilkins to Peters, Feb 8, 1957, Group III, B A246, General Office File, Presidential Campaign of 1956, General 1956, -Oct- 1957, NAACP mss, LOC.
16. Lubell, "Future of the Negro Voter in the United States," 408–417; Sitkoff, "Harry Truman and the Election of 1948," 613; Wilkins, "Future of the Negro Voter in the US," 424–431; Gosnell and Martin, "Negro as Voter and Officeholder," Americans voted "roughly 60-40" for Ike, 374–375; O'Reilly, *Nixon's Piano*, 177, and "Racial Integration," 115, asserts that Ike received 60 percent of the black vote in 1956. These figures are incorrect. After 1936, Republican presidential candidates never received more than a third of the black vote. Caro, *Master of the Senate*, presents even more outlandish and erroneous figures, 775–776. He presents confusing and erroneous data. FDR and Truman did receive between 80 percent to 90 percent in some black wards, but Stevenson did not poll 68 percent of the black vote nationally in 1952. FDR did not receive half of the black vote in 1932, and he and Truman never reached 80 percent nationally. Stevenson received about 79 percent in 1952 and 64 percent or 61 percent in 1956; Moon, "What Chance for Civil Rights?" 42; *New Republic*, Nov 19, 1956, p. 6.
17. The Negro Vote, Aug 1957, B 554, Negro Vote, Series 320, RNln; Rabb to Prendergast, Aug 20, 1957, B 909, 1957 (2), GF 124-A, DDEL; Caro, *Master of the Senate*, presents the position, offered by many, that the Democrats had suffered serious losses, 842–844.
18. Smith, "The Redistribution of the Negro Population of the US," 155–172; Glantz, "Negro Voter in Northern Industrial Cities," 999–1010; Polenberg, *One Nation Divisible*, 150–153; McAdam, *Political Process and the Development of Black Insurgency*, 96; Taeuber and Taeuber, *Negroes in Cities*, 1–8.

19. *Atlanta Constitution,* Nov 17, PPS32.B 2 and *Whittier News,* Nov 29, 1956, PPS366, RNyl; RN to Hill, Jan 25, B 547, NAACP—Monrovia and Apr 15, 1957, B 339, Hill, B, Series 320, RNln.
20. Schulyer to RN, Nov 5, 1956, B 677, Schuyler, G, Series 320, RNln.
21. Nichols, *Matter of Justice,* 120–123; Adams, *Firsthand Report,* 336–338; Abramowitz, *Polarized Public,* 33–34.
22. Wilkins to RN, Nov 23, B 546, NAACP (5 of 5) and Washington to RN, Dec 21, 1956, B 801, Washington, V, Series 320, RNln; *Christian Science Monitor,* Dec 28, 1956, PPS336, RNyl.
23. Book I, Dec 11, 1956, B II, p. 307, Krock mss, HML; *New York Times,* Dec 30, 1956.
24. Anderson to RN, Aug 1, 1953, B 40, Anderson, CP, Series 320, RNln; *Clovis News-Journal* (NM), Oct 10, 1954, PPS336(1954).o.s.95, RNyl; Floyd Riddick OH, Interview #4, pp. 122–133 and Howard Shuman, Interview #3, pp. 134–143, U.S. Senate Historical Office; Anderson, *Outsider in the Senate,* 124–125 and 144.

CHAPTER 25. THE CIVIL RIGHTS ACT OF 1957

1. Rovere, *Final Reports,* 152; Kearns, *Lyndon Johnson,* 146–151; Reedy, *U.S. Senate,* 36; Galbraith, *A Life,* 379; Evans and Novak, *Johnson,* 140; Mooney, *Politicians,* 271.
2. Ambrose, *Eisenhower,* vol. 2, 406–410. Caro, *Master of the Senate,* accepts Ambrose's thesis, 695 and also 696 and 777–781.
3. *Newsweek,* July 1, 1957, p. 17; Dyer, "LBJ," 120; Ashby and Gramer, *Fighting the Odds,* 79–82; Oberdorfer, *Mansfield,* 148; Scates, *Magnuson,* 186–187; Caro, *Master of the Senate,* 895–909; the best published article on the act is Mayer, "Eisenhower Administration and the Civil Rights Act," and the best overall is Johnson's unpublished "Southern Response to Civil Rights," 70–141. Also see Howard Shuman OH, Interview 3, pp. 134–138 and 144; Caro does not cite either in his book, and neither author mentions Hells Canyon as a subject. The Johnson thesis is in the Lyndon Baines Johnson reading room and is also listed on the library's electronic catalogue.
4. Email, Anderson to Gellman, Aug 9, 2013, Gellman mss, DDEL. The three most knowledgeable historians on Eisenhower and civil rights are Mayer, *Eisenhower Years;* Nichols, *Matter of Justice;* and Thurber, *Republicans and Race.* Not one of these three scholars found anything on Hells Canyon and the civil rights debate.
5. Caro, *Master of the Senate,* 1130–1131; Wicker, *One of Us,* xi.
6. George Aiken OH, Interview I, p. 13, Jacob Javits OH, Interview I, p. 6 and Hubert Humphrey OH, Interview II, p. 3, LBJL; email Hadad to Gellman, Oct 6, 2014, Gellman mss, DDEL.
7. Russell Long OH, Interview II, pp. 4–5 and Interview III, p. 5, Henry Jackson OH, Interview I, p. 12 and Frank Church OH, Interview I, pp. 4, 6, and 11, LBJL.
8. Robert Oliver OH, Interview II, pp. 20–22, George Siegel, Interview IV, pp. 1–2, and George Reedy OH, Interview I (a), p. 20, LBJL; Robert Baker OH, 73, Senate Historical Office.
9. Clarence Mitchell OH, Interview I, Tape No. One, 1, 7, 14, and 25–26, LBJL.

10. Caro, *Master of the Senate*, 1001–1005; for the extent of the adulation, see McGrath, "Robert Caro's Big Dig," *New York Times*, Apr 12, 2012.

11. Bartley, *New South*, 176–199; Nichols, *Matter of Justice*, 83–127.

12. *Jet*, Sept 12, 1957, p. 3.

13. Minutes, Jan 8, B 62, F 14 and RN to Embry, Feb 15, B 62, F 12, Series 207 and RN to Summerfield, Feb 28 and July 8, B 739, Summerfield (3 of 3), memo, May 22, B 546, NAACP (5 of 5) and RN to Chamberlain, Oct 8, 1957, B 141, Chamberlain, D, Series 320, RNln; press release, Jan 6, PPS307.106, Youth Training-Incentives Conf, Feb 4, PPS307.105 and Fourth Annual Report, 1956–1957, PPS307.95.1 (1), RNyl; *Jet*, May 16, p. 4 and Aug 1, 1957, p. 3; Robert Cushman OH, 13–14, DDEL.

14. Nichols, *Matter of Justice*, 51–90.

15. Anderson to RN, Aug 1, 1953, B 40, Anderson, CP, Series 320, RNln; *Clovis News-Journal* (NM), Oct 10, 1954, PPS336(1954).o.s.95, RNyl; Floyd Riddick OH, Interview #4, pp. 122–133 and Howard Shuman, Interview #3, pp. 134–143, U.S. Senate Historical Office; Anderson, *Outsider in the Senate*, 124–125 and 144.

16. Telephone call from RN, Jan 2, 1957, R 5, DuHe.

17. Telephone calls to RN, Jan 2 and 3, 1957, R 5, DuHe; *Washington Post*, Jan 2, 1957, PPS337.B3, RNyl.

18. Telephone call from Hill, Jan 3, 1957, R 5, DuHe; *Gallup Poll*, Two, 1463.

19. *New York Times*, Jan 5, 1957; in an unpublished biography of Humphrey, "Liberal Without Apology," Arnold Offner discusses Humphrey's role in the 1957 civil rights debate; Offner makes no mention of any deal over Hells Canyon; Chapter Nine, 17–27, Gellman mss, DDEL.

20. *Los Angeles Times*, Jan 5, 1957, PPS337.B 3, RNyl; Edelsberg to RN, Jan 4, 1957, B 235, Edelsberg, Cushman to Rudeebock, Apr 6, 1960, B 685, Senate Rule (2 of 4), Series 320, RNln; RN opinion, Jan 4, 1957, R 47, DuHe; RN OH 111, p. 14, Russell mss, WJBma; *New York Times*, Jan 5, 1957; Saltonstall, *Salty*, 146; Douglas, *In the Fullness*, 284–285.

21. Memoirs, Mar 22, 1976, RNyl; memo by BeLieu, May 18, 1969, Hoff-Wilson ed., *Papers of the Nixon WH*, P 2; Wilkins to Peters, Feb 8, 1957, Group III, B A246, General Office File, Presidential Campaign of 1956, General 1956, Oct 1957, NAACP mss, LOC; Howard Shuman OH, Interview 3, pp. 147–149; Reedy to Gillette, June 2, 1982, George Reedy OH, Interview XI, LBJL; Anderson, *Outsider in the Senate*, 144–145; Javits, *Ordeal of Battle*, 215.

22. Washington to RN, Jan 8, B 801, Washington, V and memo, Jan 11, 1957, B 687, Shaffer, S, Series 320, RNln; *Jet*, Jan 10, 1957, Vol. XI, No. 10, p. 3.

23. Frank Church OH, 1–2 and 6–8, LBJL; Ashby and Gramer, *Fighting the Odds*, 75–78.

24. *Gallup Poll*, Two, 1465, 1487, 1493, 1507, and 1515; Erskine, "Polls," 137–138.

25. Nichols, *Matter of Justice*, 141–145.

26. Adams, *Firsthand Report*, 339–341.

27. Wilton Persons OH 161, pp. 120–124, CCOH.

28. Ross to RN, Feb 16 and RN to Ross, Feb 25, B 658, Ross, E and RN to Ryan, Feb 25, 1957, B 831, World Pe, Series 320, RNln; telephone call to RN, Jan 8, 1957, B 6, Jan–Feb 28, 1957 (5), DuHe.

29. Jackson to RN, Apr 11, 1957, Group III, O.F. Nixon, B 239, NAACP mss, LOC; memo, Feb 28, 1958, B 374, Jackson, LK, Series 320, RNln.

30. RN to Jackson, May 18, 1957, B 374, Jackson, LK, Series 320, RNln.

31. Wilkins to RN, Mar 19, 1957, Group III, A, B 239, NAACP mss, LOC.

32. Wilkins to RN, May 2, 1957, Group III, A, B 239, NAACP mss, LOC; B 820, Wilkins, R, Series 320, RNln.

33. RN to Wilkins, May 10, 1957, B 820, Wilkins, R, Series 320, RNln; Group III, A, B 239, NAACP mss, LOC.

34. *New York Post*, Mar 6, 1957, B 2, Africa Trip Clippings [1/3], Series 349, RNln; MLK to RN, May 28, 1957, PPS320.107.9, RNyl; *New York Herald Tribune*, Mar 6, 1957; Morrow, *Forty Years*, 117; *PMLK*, IV, pp. 193 and 204.

35. Prentice to Reddick, June 29, 1959, PPS320.107.21, RNyl; *PMLK*, IV, pp. 205–206; Lewis, *King*, 88–93; Branch, *Parting the Waters*, 216–218.

36. Schedule, June 13, PPS320.107.69.1, memo, June 13, PPS320.107.69-1-8 and memo, June 27, 1957. PPS320.107.11A, RNyl; memo, June 24, 1957, O.F. 142-A, F (2), B 731, Central File, DDEL; *PMLK*, IV, pp. 8, 15–16, 23 and 222–223; Kempton, *America Comes*, 165–166; Reddick, *Crusader Without Violence*, 198–200.

37. *Jet*, June 27, 1957, pp. 4–6; *PMLK*, IV, pp. 14–15, 17 and 222–224; Reddick, *Crusader Without Violence*, 201–202.

38. Memo, June 24, 1957, O.F. 142-A, F (2), B 731, Central File, DDEL.

39. Afro-American (Baltimore), Dec 1, 1956; *New York Herald Tribune*, Feb 19, 20, and 28 and Mar 31, 1957; *Los Angeles Times*, Feb 28 and Mar 31, 1957; *New York Times*, June 14, 1957.

40. *U.S. Congressional Record*, V. 103, P 7, pp. 9516–9517; Day, *Southern Manifesto*; Hasenfus, "Managing Partner," 325–393.

41. George Reedy OH, III, pp. 47–48 and VIII, pp. 98–102 and Harry McPherson OH, Interview I, Tape 1, pp. 12 and 15, LBJL; Parker, *Capitol Hill in Black and White*, 16.

42. Carl Albert OH, Interview I, pp. 13–14, LBJL; Dulaney and Phillips eds., *"Speak, Mister Speaker,"* 324.

43. William Knowland OH, I, pp. 37–38 and 40, Everett Dirksen OH, Interview III, Tape 2, pp. 1–2, Thomas Kuchel OH, I, pp. 12–14 and Clifford Case OH, I, pp. 10–11, LBJL; Cater, "Knowland," 34; Montgomery and Johnson, *One Step from the WH*, 213–216.

44. Paul Douglas OH, 2–5 and 10–11, LBJL; Howard Shuman OH, Interview #3, pp. 156–159, U.S. Senate Historical Office.

45. Howard Shuman OH, Interview 3, pp. 134–138 and 144; U.S. Senate Historical Office.

46. *Chicago Defender*, Nov 24, 1956; Frank Church OH, Paul Douglas OH, pp. 2–5 and 11, William Proxmire OH, I, p. 13; Neuberger, "Democratic Dilemma," 14–15 and 17; Scates, *Magnuson*, 226–238; Lazarowitz, *Years in Exile*, 152–153.

47. Cox, *Yarborough*, 148–150; Davidson, *Race and Class in Texas*, 30; Green, *Establishment in Texas Politics*, 190; Gore, *Let the Glory Out*, 110–111; Longley, *Gore*, 139–141; Gorman, *Kefauver*, 314–321; Fontenay, *Kefauver*, 336.

48. RN OH 111, pp. 2–3, 13, and 16–17, Russell mss, WJBma; James Rowe OH, I, p. 35 and William Jordon Jr. OH, I, pp. 1, 9–11, and 13, LBJL; Howard Shuman OH, In-

terview 3, p. 147, U.S. Senate Historical Office; Stern, "Johnson and Russell," 693–695; Fite, *Russell*, 329–336.

49. Memoirs, Mar 22, 1956, RNyl; Strom Thurmond OH, I, p. 8, LBJL; Fite, *Russell*, 271–295, 301–302, and 309–310; Fite, "Russell and Johnson," 125–132; Stern, "Johnson and Russell," 687–695.

50. Nichols, *Matter of Justice*, 141–168; Billington, "Johnson and Blacks," 2642; Lerner, "'To be Shot by the Whites,'" 245–273. I have also depended on Mayer, "Eisenhower Administration and the Civil Rights Act," pp. 137–150, and Thurber, *Republicans and Race.*

51. Gaskin, "Johnson and U.S. Foreign Policy," 91–93; Martin, "Senator Long of Louisiana," 54–56.

52. Johnson, "Southern Response to Civil Rights," 1–79 and 176–179; Reedy to Gillette, June 2, 1982, George Reedy OH, Interview XI, LBJL; Dyer, "LBJ," 52–109 and 210–211; Mayer, "Eisenhower's," 399–401; Schulman, *Johnson and American Liberalism*, 51–53; Dallek, *Lone Star Rising*, 445 and 496–498; Kearns, *Johnson and the American Dream*, 146–149; Caro, *Passage of Power*, 8–9; Baker, *Johnson Eclipse*, 198–208. I would like to thank Donald Ritchie for sharing his views on LBJ with me.

53. Telephone call with Ronnie Dugger, sometime in 2010; Lister Hill OH, 10–11, James Eastland OH, I, p. 9, John Sparkman OH, II, pp. 11–12, Allen Ellender OH, 4, 6–8, and 12, Herman Talmadge OH, I, p. 6, Edwin Weisl Jr. OH, 15–19, W. Jordan OH, I, p.12 and George Reedy OH, IV, p. 39, LBJL; Howard Shuman OH, Interview 3, p. 146, U.S. Senate Historical Office; Frantz, "Opening a Curtain," 2–26; Hamilton, *Hill*, 218 and 220–221; Heinemann, *Byrd*, 374–375; Becnel, *Ellender*, 210–211; Talmadge, *Talmadge*, 170 and 177–180.

54. George Reedy OH, III, pp. 29–27 and VII, pp. 11–13 and Harry McPherson OH, Interview, I, Tape 1, pp. 10–12, LBJL; McPherson, *Political Education*, 135–155; Reedy, *U.S. Senate*, 178–179.

55. Bryce Harlow, I, p. 52 and II, pp. 24, 37, and 39 and see Helen Gahagan Douglas OH, pp. 1–26, LBJL; RN OH 111, pp. 15–16 and 20, Russell mss, WJBma.

56. Ike to Howard, June 12, 1957, R 13, Diary DDE; *New York Times*, June 20, 1957; Nichols, *Matter of Justice*, 151–155; Flynn, "Reconsidering the China Lobby," Vol. II, pp. 235–297.

57. RN address, June 5, B 65, F 6 and RN remarks, June 21, 1957, B 66, F 12, Series 207, RNln; *New York Herald Tribune*, June 6, 1957, PPS337.B5, RNyl.

58. LBJ to RN, Feb 4, PPS320.105.26 and autograph, Feb 12, 1957, PPS320.105.27, RNyl; telephone call with Donald Hughes, July 8, 2003; Mazo, *Richard Nixon*, 292; Beschloss ed., *Taking Charge*, 137, claimed that LBJ never forgave RN for implying Helen Gahagan Douglas was a communist in the 1950 California senatorial election. I found nothing that supports this accusation. Caro, in *Master of the Senate*, 145, asserts that RN published a pamphlet printed on pink paper to illustrate Douglas was "soft on Communism," and RN's staff "launched a whispering campaign harping on the fact that her husband was Jewish." It was not a pamphlet; indeed it was one piece of page called "the pink sheet." Second, RN's campaign manager was Murray Chotiner. He was Jewish, and I found no evidence that he conducted an anti-Semitic campaign against Melvyn Douglas.

59. *U.S. Congressional Record*, June 20, 1957, V. 103, P 8, 9827–9828; RN to Champion, June 17, 1957 B 141 and RN record, 1960, B 649, Robinson (1 of 2), Series 320 and Champion, G, *Milwaukee Journal*, June 26, 1957, B 66, F 16, Series 207, RNln; William Knowland, I, pp. 38–39, George Reedy OH, III, p. 22, LBJL; Howard Shuman OH, Interview 3, p. 151 and 154, U.S. Senate Historical Office; *New York Times*, June 19, 1957; Edelsberg, "New Civil Rights Law," 2; Shuman, "Senate Rules and the Civil Rights," 963–970; Mayer, "Eisenhower's Conditional Crusade," 418–419; Lawson, *Black Ballots*, 177; Montgomery and Johnson, *One Step from the WH*, 215–216.

60. Memo, July 2, 1957, B 306, Gross, J, Series 320, RNln.

61. Campbell, *Ervin*, 116–120.

62. *Newsweek*, July 15, p. 23 and July 22, 1957, pp. 22–23; Shuman, "Senate Rules and the Civil Rights," 974–975.

63. George Reedy OH, III, pp. 15–16; George Reedy OH, XI, p. 28, LBJL; Nichols, *Matter of Justice*, 155.

64. Nichols, *Matter of Justice*, 156–158; Potenziani, "Look to the Past," 150–158.

65. *U.S. Congressional Record*, July 18, 1957, p. 11832; Montgomery and Johnson, *One Step from the WH*, 216–217.

66. *Ike's Letters*, 186–187.

67. *U.S. Congressional Record*, V. 103, P 9, p. 12565; supplementary notes, July 23, 1957, R 2, legislative meeting, DDEL; Howard Shuman OH, Interview 3, pp. 166–167, U.S. Senate Historical Office; *Newsweek*, July 29, pp. 23–24 and Aug 5, 1957, p. 24; Shuman, "Senate Rules and the Civil Rights," 970–972 and 974; Coffin, "How Lyndon Johnson Engineered Compromise," 3–4; Ashby and Gramer, *Fighting the Odds*, 83–84; Brownell, *Advising Ike*, 221–226.

68. George Reedy OH, III, p. 16, LBJL; Reedy, *U.S. Senate*, 41.

69. *Newsweek*, July 29, 1957, p. 31; *Time*, Aug 12, 1957, p12; Dyer, "LBJ," 127–138; Blum ed., *Public Philosopher*, 589.

70. RN to Middlebrook, July 31, 1957, B 514, Middlebrook, Series 320, RNln.

71. RN to Abbell, Aug 12, 1957, B 18, Abbell, Series 320, RNln; Kenneth Keating OH 197, p. 34, CCOH; *Newsweek*, Aug 5, 1957, p. 25.

72. Cater, "How the Senate Passed the Civil Rights," 12–13.

73. *U.S. Congressional Record*, Aug 1, 1957, V. 103, P 10, p. 13356; George Reedy OH, VII, pp. 31–32 and XI, pp. 45, Frank Church OH, 8–11 and Hubert Humphrey OH, Interview I, pp. 15–16, LBJL; *Newsweek*, Aug 12, 1957, pp. 25–26; *Time*, Aug 12, 1957, pp. 11–16; Shuman, "Senate Rules and the Civil Rights," 972–974; Auerbach, "Jury Trials and Civil Rights," 16–18; Eliff, *United States Department of Justice*, 495–510; Ashby and Gramer, *Fighting the Odds*, 84–90.

74. RN record, 1960, B 649, Robinson (1 of 2), Series 320, RNln; Evans and Novak, *Johnson*, 138–140.

75. *Time*, Aug 12, 1957, p. 11.

76. Minutes, Aug 2, 1957 R 6, Cabinet DDE; supplementary notes, Aug 6, 1957, R 2, Legislative DDE.

77. *Washington Post* and RN to Childs, Aug 2, 1957, B 144, Childs, Series 320, RNln.

78. Washington to RN and Washington to LBJ, Aug 6, B 801, Washington, V and Barnett to LBJ, Aug 8, B 63, Barnett and *Chicago Defender*, Aug 17, 1957, B 144, Chicago De, Series 320, RNln; *New York Times*, Aug 6 and 7, 1957; "GOPer Val Washington," *Jet*, May 15, 1995.

79. Schedule, Aug 7, 1957, PPS212(1957).3.108, RNyl.

80. Edelsberg, "New Civil Rights Law," 8; memo from Reedy, Aug 21, 1957, B 5, memo file, pre-presidential, LBJL.

81. Supplementary notes, Aug 13, 1957, R 2, Legislative DDE; Taylor, *Randolph*, 217.

82. RN to Whigham, Aug 14, B 811, Whigham, J, RN to Murphy, Aug 20, B 153, Civil Rights and RN to Anderson, Sept 7, 1957, B 559, Newsweek, [2/2], Series 320, RNln; *New York Times*, Aug 15 and 18, 1957; *Newsweek*, Aug 19, p. 23 and Aug 26, 1957, p. 26; Rovere, "Letter from Washington," Aug 31, 1957, 72, 75–78, and 81–82; Edelsberg, "New Civil Rights Law," 8; Nichols, *Matter of Justice*, 161–167.

83. Strom Thurmond OH, I, pp. 9–10, George Reedy OH, XI, p. 24, W. Jordan OH, I, pp. 7–8, William Proxmire OH, I, p. 11 and Herman Talmadge OH, I, pp. 6–7, LBJL; *Newsweek*, Sept 2, p. 17 and Sept 9, 1957, p. 32; Cohodas, *Strom Thurmond*, 294–297; Bass and Thompson, *Ol' Strom*, 178–180.

84. *New York Times*, Aug 31, 1957; Caro, *Master of the Senate*, constantly talks about the filibuster as a real option.

85. *Jet*, Sept 5, 1957, pp. 4–5.

86. Hill to RN, Aug 30, B 339, Hill, B, Mitchell to RN, Aug 30 and RN to Mitchell, Sept 19, B 521, Mitchell, CD, RN to Mansfield, Aug 31, 1957, B 475, Mansfield, W, Series 320, RNln.

87. Robert Baker OH, 9, Senate Historical Office.

88. Adams to King, June 13, Adams to RN, May 13, July 26, Aug 19 and 23 and RN to Adams, Aug 2 and 31, 1957, B 19, Adams, Ju Series 320, RNln; *New York Times*, Aug 4, 1989.

89. Long ed., *First Class Citizenship*, 35–38 and 48; Rampersad, *Robinson*, 327.

90. *PMLK*, IV, pp. 263–264 and 277.

91. Roy Wilkins OH, Interview I, pp. 1–2, Clarence Mitchell OH, Interview I, pp. 1–5 and Thurgood Marshall OH, Interview I, pp. 2–3, LBJL; Louis Martin OH, Interview I, p. 7, JFKL.

92. *San Diego Union*, Aug 9, 1957, PPS337. B3, RNyl; Howard Shuman OH, Interview 3, pp. 151 and 167; Clarence Mitchell OH, Interview I, p. 7 and Hubert Humphrey OH, Interview III, p. 11, LBJL; Montgomery and Johnson, *One Step from the WH*, 216–219; Ashby and Gramer, *Fighting the Odds*, 91–95.

93. *Los Angeles Examiner*, June 24, 1957, PPS337, B 3, RNyl; RN to Mann, Aug 30, B 475, Mann, E and RN to Shishkin, B 692, Shishkin, Series 320, RNln; Howard Shuman OH, Interview 3, p. 169, U.S. Senate Historical Office.

94. Vann to RN, June 26, B 780, Vann, Case to RN, Aug 15, B 137, Case 2/2, White to RN, Aug 28, 1957, B 813, White, Wa and Kuchel to RN, Dec 12, 1962, B 430, Kuchel [½] and memo, Mar 13, 1958. B 82, F 7. Series 207, RNln; *Chicago Defender*, Aug 17, 1957, PPS337, B 3, RNyl.

95. Howard Shuman OH, Interview 3, p. 166, U.S. Senate Historical Office; Larson, *Eisenhower*, 129–130.
96. Booker, "What 'Ike' Thinks," 83–84 and 86; Nichols, *Matter of Justice*, 167–168.
97. Pierpont, *At the WH*, 232–233; telephone call from Moyers, Aug 5, 1965, Box 13, Memorando (1) Principal File, and diary, Oct 12, 1966, B 1, F 1966 (Aug 11 to Dec 8, 1966), post-presidency, DDEL; Dwight Eisenhower OH, July 13, 1967, pp. 28–29 and 31, HHL.
98. U.S. Congressional Record, Apr 29, pp. 6130–6133, p. D105, D109, D407, D413, D446, D463, D467, and D470 and 1958, D49 and D325; *New York Times*, July 25 and 27, 1957; Bessey, "Political Issues of the Hells Canyon," 676–690; Brooks, *Public Power, Private Dams*, 176–225.

CHAPTER 26. LITTLE ROCK AND ITS CONSEQUENCES

1. There are many studies of the Little Rock crisis. Unless otherwise cited, I have used Nichols, *Matter of Justice*, 169–213; Thurber, *Republicans and Race*; and Ellis, *Presidential Lightning Rods*, 130–133.
2. Brownell, *Advising Ike*, Appendix D, pp. 365–384.
3. Graham, *Just As I*, 201; Miller, *Billy Graham and the Rise*, 13–74.
4. Meeting with DDE, Oct 1, 1957, B 22, F memo book, Oct 1957 #1, Larson mss, DDEL.
5. *Ike's Letters*, 193; Booker, "What 'Ike' Thinks," 90.
6. Notes and typescript, Larson meeting with Dulles, Rogers, Adams, and Persons, "Black Day at the WH," Nov 26, 1957, B 22, F memo book Nov 1957, #2, Larson mss, DDEL.
7. *New York Times*, Sept 24, 1957; Strout, *TRB*, 176.
8. *PDDE*, XVIII, pp. 474–475.
9. Editor and Publisher, Oct 19, B 69, F 15 and RN to Ewing, Nov 5, 1957, B 69, F 16, Series 207, RNln.
10. Erskine, "Polls," 137–142.
11. Memo, Aug 20, 1958, B 276, Fulbright, Series 320, RNln; Stern, "Johnson and Russell," 695–696; Sampson, "Rise of the 'New' Republican," 291–296; Hamilton, *Hill*, 222–223; Campbell, *Ervin*, 125–126; Finley, *Delaying the Dream*, 191–195.
12. *Jackson Daily News*, Oct 1 and 2, 1957; Land, "Presidential Republicans and the Growth," 98–101.
13. Interviews with Coleman, Nov 14, Griffin, Dec 2, 1957, and Faubus, June 17, 1958, Log of Trip II - 1957, Herschensohn mss, PUSc; also see Wallace and Gates, *Close Encounters*, 54–58; Wallace, *Between You and Me*, 74.
14. *Chicago Defender*, Jan 11, 1958, p. 12.
15. *Gallup Poll*, Two, 1523, 1539, 1546, 1570, 1596, 1610–1611, and 1632–1633.
16. *PDDE*, XVIII, pp. 597–598; *New York Herald Tribune*, Sept 19, 1957; Ellis, *Presidential Lightning Rods*, 122–123.
17. Memo, Feb 9, 1959, B 606, F Potter, I, Series 320, RNln; *New York Times*, Dec 9 and 10, 1957; *New York Times Magazine*, Apr 6, 1958, pp. 22, 36, and 39; Morrow, *Black Man in the WH*, 198.
18. Greene interview, dcchs.org/HaroldHGreene/HaroldHGreene.pdf; memo, Jan 20, 1959, black notebooks, Krock mss, HML.

19. Lichtman, "Federal Assault Against Voting," 346–356; Winquist, "Comments," 625–630; Eliff, *U.S. Department of Justice*, 340–400 and 546–554; McMahon, *Reconsidering Roosevelt*, 144–150.

20. Harold Tyler interview, May 27, 2003; Lawrence Walsh interview, Dec 1, 2005; civil rights division history, www.justice.gov/crt/; Lewis and *New York Times, Portrait of a Decade*, 112–113; Nichols, *Matter of Justice*, 223.

21. Meeting, Mar 2, 1959, R 8, Cabinet DDE; *Chicago Defender*, Mar 5, 1958; Nashville *Banner* (Tn), Nov 17, 1959, PPS336(1960).25, RNyl; Dulles, *Civil Rights Commission*, 1–131; Johnson, "Southern Response to Civil Rights," 157–160.

22. *Chicago Defender*, Mar 8, 1958; U.S. Commission on Civil Rights, *Report of the U.S. Commission 1959*, pp. x–xiv.

23. U.S. Commission on Civil Rights, *Report of the U.S. Commission 1959*, pp. x–xiv, 134–142, 324–330, 534–540, and 545–540; Potenziani, "Look to the Past," 184–185; Campbell, *Ervin*, 127.

24. *Evening Star* (DC), May 2, 1958; Robert Cushman OH, 31, DDEL; Morrow, *Forty Years*, 160–162; Morrow, *Black Man in the WH*, 223 and 240; Nichols, *Matter of Justice*, 216.

25. Harold Tyler interview, May 27, 2003; Persons OH 161, p. 119, CCOH; Siciliano, *Walking on Sand*, 171; Morrow, *Black Man in the WH*, 287; Morrow, *Forty Years*, 190; Nichols, *Matter of Justice*, 236 and 260; Clark, *Schoolhouse Door*, 20, 30–31, 33, and 38–40.

26. PPA 1958, p. 213; Morrow, *Black Man in the WH*, 238–239; Nichols, *Matter of Justice*, 222.

27. Nichols, *Matter of Justice*, 144; Morrow, *Black Man in the WH*, 179.

28. *Washington Post*, Oct 9, 10 and 12, 1957; Nwaubani, *U.S. and Decolonization*, 124–125 and 234.

29. PPA 1958, p. 391; Long ed., *First Class Citizenship*, 56–58; Morrow, *Black Man in the WH*, 218–219; Morrow, *Forty Years*, 163–164; Booker, *Black Man's America*, 208–209; Nichols, *Matter of Justice*, 217–218; Booker, "What 'Ike' Thinks," 86.

30. Roberts and Siciliano, *Eisenhower and Civil Rights*, 25–44; Huggins, "Eisenhower and Civil Rights," 180–194; Siciliano, *Walking on Sand*, 130–134 and 156–170; Morrow, *Forty Years*, 165–178; Nichols, *Matter of Justice*, 218–221.

31. A. Philip Randolph OH, Interview I, p. 15, LBJL; *PMLK*, IV, pp. 28–29.

32. Morrow, *Black Man in the WH*, 243.

33. Memo, Oct 22, 1957, B 1, B II, 308A, Krock mss, HML.

34. Mazo, *Nixon*, 292 and 298–299.

35. RN appearance, Nov 14, 1957, B 72, F 2, Series 207, RNyl.

36. *New York Times*, Dec 16, 1957.

37. *Washington Post*, Apr 17, B 103, F 11, Series 207 and Oxnam to RN, Apr 20, 1959, B 575, Oxnam, Series 320, RNln.

38. RN to Morris, Dec 2, 1957, B 530, Morris, A, RN to Malin, Jan 20, B 473, Malin, RN to Bishop, Jan 29, B 153, Civil Rights and RN to Wright, Aug 15, 1958, B 832, Wright, C, Series 320, RNln.

39. RN to Klein, Oct 11, 1958, B 144, Chicago Daily, Series 320, RNln; RN to Dawson, Nov 18, 1958, B 239, III, NAACP mss, LOC.

40. RN to Hays, Nov 18, *Face the Nation*, Nov 30 and Hays to RN, Dec 1, 1958, B 327, Hays, B, Series 320, RNln; Reed, *Faubus*, 246–251; Hays, *Politics Is My Parish*, 179–193.

41. Memo, Apr 1, 1959, B 102, F 4, Series 207, RNln; interview with Lawrence Walsh, Dec 1, 2005; interview with Harold Tyler, May 27, 2003; Walsh, *Gift*, 161.

42. RN to Wofford, Jan 13, B 166, Commission on Civil Rights (2), RN to Wilkins, Jan 21, 1958, B 546, NAACP (5 of 5), memo, Mar 31, B 52, Arth, memo, early Oct, B 235, Edelsberg, RN to Wilkins, Oct 5, B 820, Wilkins, R and Hesburgh to RN, Dec 1, RN to Hesburgh, Dec 7, B 335, Hesburgh, Series 320, RNln.

43. Memo, May 18 and Wilkins to RN, Sept 3, B 820, Wilkins, R, memo, July 2 and RN to Morsell, July 8, B 546, NAACP (3 of 5) and memo, Aug 13, 1959, B 153, Civil Rights, Series 320, RNln.

44. Robinson to Morrow, Apr 15, 1959, B 649, Robinson (1 of 2), Series 320, RNln; Long ed., *First Class Citizenship*, 43, 49–50, and 63; Falkner, *Great Time Coming*, 267–272.

45. Long ed., *First Class Citizenship*, 48 and 51–52.

46. Wofford to RN, Dec 30, 1957, B 828, Wofford and Hill to RN, Aug 19, 1958, B 340, Hill, RC, Series 320, RNln; RN to King, Dec 5, 1958, PPS320.107.19, RNyl; *PMLK*, IV, pp. 490–491 and 536.

47. *PMLK*, IV, pp. 481–483.

48. *PMLK*, IV, p. 500; *Washington Post*, Sept 24, 1958, PPS320.107.700s, RNyl; *New York Times*, Sept 22, 1958.

49. Morrow, *Black Man in the WH*, 192–193.

50. Ibid., 239–240; Morrow, *Forty Years*, 185–187.

51. McWhorter to Revercomb, Apr 9, 1958. B 637, Revercomb, Series 320, RNln; Seidenberg to Reid, Jan 30, 1959, PPS307.130.1, RNyl.

52. *U.S. News & World Report*, Dec 6, 1957, PPS307.95.2(1), RNyl; Zieger, *For Jobs and Freedom*, 140–142, 148–154, and 164–174; Delton, *Racial Integration in Corporate America*, 33; Marable, *Race, Reform, and Rebellion*, 54.

53. Hoover to Ferman, June 29, FE35, press release, June 29, 1959 FE29.1 and Foster to Ferman, Jan 4, 1960, Ferman mss, RNyl; Mitchell to RN, July 6, B 521, Mitchell, CD, RN to Mitchell, July 9, 1959, B 549, NAACP (3 of 5), Series 320, RNln; Gentry, *Hoover*, 439–440.

54. Ferman to Hess, Feb 25, 1968, FE458, Ferman mss, RNyl.

55. Report, Jan 15, PPS307.120, *Tampa Times* (Fl), Feb 20, PPS307.122, memo, Sept 18, 1958, PPS307.118, Five Years of Progress 1953–1958, PPS3307.123, memo, Jan 5, 1959, PPS307.127 and Pattern for Progress, 1961, PPS307.178, RNyl; RN to Mitchell, Oct 13, B 523, Mitchell [3/4], RN to Freudenheim, Nov 13, 1958, B 275, Freudenheim and RN to Burns, July 2, 1959, B 18, Abrams, M, Series 320, RNln.

56. *PMLK*, V, pp. 197–202; Reid to RN, May 13, B 624, Series 320 and *New York Herald Tribune*, May 12 and *Presbyterian Outlook*, June 1, 1959, B 105, F 7, Series 207, RNln; memo, Jan 29, PPS307.128 and transcript, May 11, 1959, PPS307.142, RNyl; Garrow, *Bearing the Cross*, 117–118.

57. *Los Angeles Sentinel*, Oct 8, 1959, PPS307.146 and memo, Mar 28, FE383.2 and memo, May 19, 1960, FE405(1), Ferman mss, RNyl; Roper to RN, May 2 and RN to Roper, May 6, B 656, Roper, E and RN to Mitchell, June 29, 1960, B 523, Mitchell [½], Series 320, RNln; *New York Times*, Aug 28, 1957.

58. Memo, Jan 18, 1960, B 637, Reuther, W, Series 320, RNln; McLaughlin to RN, Jan 22, PPS307.149, press conf, Feb 16, PPS307.151.3(1), *Evening Star* (DC), Feb 17, PPS307.S17, *New York Post*, Feb 25, PPS307.S20, *Amsterdam News* (NY), Feb 27, PPS307.S22 and Reuther to Ferman, June 20, 1960, FE432, Ferman mss, RNyl; Moreno, *From Direct Action*, 184–188.

59. Meeting, Dec 18, 1959, R 10, Cabinet DDE; Ferman to Ike, May 16, 1960, FE403.1 and memo, May 25, 1962, FE446.s, RNyl.

60. Press release, Jan 11, PPS307.176B(1), press release, Jan 11, PPS324.150 and Ike to RN, Jan 12, 1961, PPS324.150, RNyl.

61. Nichols, *Matter of Justice*, 217 and 222–232.

62. *PPA* 1958, p. 722.

63. *Christian Science Monitor*, PPS336(1959).19, *New York Herald Tribune*, PPS336(1959).19, Jan 13, 1959, RNyl; *New York Times*, Jan 13, 1959.

64. Legislative meeting, Feb 3, 1959, R 20, Diary DDE; Nichols, *Matter of Justice*, 235–246; Laird ed., *Republican Papers*, 235–236.

65. Nichols, *Matter of Justice*, 241–242.

66. RN to Jones, May 28, 1959, B 546, NAACP (3 of 5), Series 320, RNln.

67. Memo, Sept 6 and RN to Fuller, Sept 13, 1958, B 93, F 1, Series 207, RNln; Lon Fuller OH, 10, WC; *Newsweek*, Sept 15, 1958, pp. 92 and 94.

68. *New York Times*, July 9, 1959; *Jet*, July 23, 1959, p. 7.

69. Morris, "Black Southern Student Sit-In," 744–766; Sewell, "'Not-Buying Power' of the Black Community," 139–144; Chafe, *Civilities and Civil Rights*, 99–141; Morris, *Origins of the Civil Rights*, 196–223; Marable, *Race, Reform, and Rebellion*, 61–62.

70. *Jet*, Mar 3, 1960, p. 5; *New York Times*, Mar 17, Apr 18–19 and June 20, 1960; Reston, *Sketches*, 121–123.

71. Memo, Jan 13, B 454, Lindsay and memo, Jan 6 and Wilkins to RN, Jan 22, 1960, B 820, Wilkins, R, Series 320, RNln; *Washington Post*, Jan 9, 1960; *Jet*, Jan 21, 1960, pp. 6–7; Nichols, *Matter of Justice*, 246–247.

72. Excerpts, Jan 15, 1960, B 123, F 2, Series 207, RNln; conversation, May 3, 1960, B 1, Krock mss, HML.

73. Meeting, Feb 2, 1960, R 2, Legislative DDE; RN excerpts, Feb 15, 1960, R 2, PRP; Nichols, *Matter of Justice*, 247–249.

74. Meeting, Mar 15 and Apr 5 and 26, R 2, Legislative DDE, meeting, Apr 5, R 25, Diary DDE and meeting, Apr 29, 1960, R10, Cabinet DDE; *Newsweek*, Feb 22, p. 28 and Mar 7, 1960, p. 28; Howard Shuman OH, 169–171, U.S. Senate Historical Office; Harry McPherson OH, Interview I, Tape 1, pp. 3–7 and George Reedy OH, XVI, pp. 19, 23–24, 28–35, and 46, LBJL; Stern, "Johnson and Russell," 697–698; Johnson, "Southern Response to Civil Rights," 142–175; Potenziani, "Look to the Past," 162–163 and 187–191; Martin, "Senator Russell B. Long," 96–104; Douglas, "1960 Voting Rights Bill," 82–86; Talmadge, *Talmadge*, 185–187; Campbell, *Ervin*, 127–129; Ellis, *Freedom's Pragmatist*, 102–106.

75. *PPA* 1960, pp. 300–301; *Texas Observer*, Apr 22, 1960, p. 3; Peltason, *Fifty-Eight Lonely Men*, 252–253; Cohodas, *Thurmond*, 308–311; Finley, *Delaying the Dream*, 227–232; Nichols, *Matter of Justice*, 254–256.

76. Berg, "The Ticket," 199–200; Nichols, Matter of Justice, 257; Sundquist, Politics and Policy, 238–250; Thurber, Politics of Equality, 109; Biles, Crusading Liberal, 143–144.

77. PPA 1961, p. 927.

78. Memo, May 3, 1960, B 1, Krock mss, HML; Cronin to Reuben, June 24, 1974, CCRO 2/25, Cronin mss, FBI; Crowley, Nixon in Winter, 142; also see Nixon, Challenges We Face, 181–186.

79. Shogun, Harry Truman, book jacket; Geselbracht ed., Civil Rights Legacy, 17–29 with quote on 17.

80. Kansas City Times, Nov 14, speech file, 1957, Nov. 13 and statement, Dec 7, 1957, secretary's office file, "Civil Rights," post-presidency files, Truman mss, HSTL; New York Times, Dec 8, 1957, p. 132; Independent Examiner (Mo.) Sept 9, 1963, p. 12; Geselbracht ed, Civil Rights Legacy, 88–89; Gardner, Truman and Civil Rights, 225–230.

81. Email, Sowell to Gellman, Oct 10 and 16, and Geselbracht to Gellman, Nov 7 and Dec 6, 2012, Gellman mss, DDEL; New York Times, Mar 23, 1965, p. 28; Geselbracht ed., Civil Rights Legacy, 90 and 144–147.

82. Booker, Black Man's America, 208; Rovere, Final Reports, 152.

83. PDDE, XX, p. 1937; Stebenne, Modern Republican, 213–216.

84. Edwards, Strategic President, 9–10.

85. Reston, Sketches, 121–123.

86. San Francisco Chronicle, Dec 2, 1962.

87. DE to Young, June 17 and Aug 18, 1964, B 16, F IN-2 invitations declined X,Y,Z, 1964 Principal File, DDEL; D. Eisenhower, Going Home, 138–140.

CHAPTER 27. THE IMPLOSION

1. Duff to RN, Nov 9, B 227, Duff, Ja, Young to RN, Nov 12, B 837 and Young, C, Carrigg to RN, Nov 19, 1956, B 135, Carrigg, Series 320, RNln; New York Herald Tribune, Dec 12, 1956, PPS336, RNyl.

2. Morrow, Black Man in the WH, 111 and 122–123.

3. Gallup Poll, Two, 1477; PDDE, XVIII, pp. 396–399; Ike to Little, Sept 12, 1957, R 14, Diary DDE.

4. RN to Wernicke, July 1, B 808, Wernicke and RN to Cramer, B 187, Cramer, Wm, Series 320, RNln; Lowndes, From the New Deal to New Right, 47–48; Green, Establishment in Texas, 197–198.

5. RN to Bermingham, Jan 14, B 78, Bermingham, RN to Thorton, Jan 18, B 756, Thorton, D, RN to MacCabe, B 468, MacCabe, RN to Houghton, May 31, B 356, Houghton, DD, RN to Hillings, June 3, B 342, Hillings ['½] and RN to Clarke, Aug 19, 1957, B 156, Clark, 1 of 2, Series 320 and RN speech, Apr 2, 1957, B 63, F 16, Series 207, RNln.

6. RN speech, June 6, 1957, R 15, PRP; New York Herald Tribune, May 25, 1957.

7. RN to Chotiner, Sept 17, B 147, Chotiner (1957–1958), RN to Moley, Sept 19, B 259, Finch ['½] and RN to Kuehn, Sept 19, 1957, B 430, Kuehn, Series 320, RNln; RNC, 1957 elections, R 2, PRP; PDDE, XVIII, p. 398.

8. PDDE, XVIII, p. 399.

9. *Jackson Daily News* (Miss), Oct 2, 1957; Wilkins, "Development of the Miss.," 43–47; Kalk, *Origins of the Southern Strategy*, 35–36.
10. Shanley to RN, Feb 14, Passaic New Jersey *Herald-News*, Feb 14, B 62, F 17 and *New York Herald Tribune*, Feb 13, B 62, F 18 and Heckman to RN, Oct 27 and *Newark Evening News*, Oct 24, B 71, F 1, Series 207 and RN to Ryepanjian, Aug 2, B 269, Forbes, M, RN to Reid, Oct 28, B 625, Reid (2 of 2) and Guylay to RN, Nov 14, 1957, B 309, Guylay (2 of 2), RNln; *PDDE*, XVIII, p. 399; *New York Herald Tribune*, Mar 27, 1957; *New York Times*, Oct 24, 1957.
11. *New York Times*, Nov 7, 1957.
12. RN to Stringfellow, Nov 21, 1957, B 736, Stringfellow, G, Series 320, RNln.
13. Tuttle, "California Democrats," 82–103.
14. Clipping, June 25, 1957, B 292, Goldman [2/2], Series 320, RNln; JFD to Knowland, Jan 8, 1957, R 5, DuHe; William Knowland OH, I, p. 46, LBJL; *New York Times*, Jan 22, 1957; *Los Angeles Times*, Mar 5 and 25, 1957; Faries, *Rememb'ring*, 188; Teiser ed., *Remembering Knowland*, 3–6; Worthen, *Young Nixon*, 169–170; Bell, *Ca. Crucible*, 125–154.
15. *Los Angeles Times*, Feb 24 and Mar 20 and 27, 1957; *Newsweek*, June 10, 1957, p. 120; Clark, "1958 Ca. Gubernatorial Election," 23–29; Worthen, *Young Nixon*, 170–171.
16. RN to Bassett, Jan 14, B 79, F 10, Series 207 and RN to Smith, Jan 28, B 704, Smith, Dana, memo, Aug 1, B 508, Memo, CMcW, RN to Krehbiel, Aug 10, 1957, B 427, Krehbiel 1957–1959 and Key to Drummond, June 25, 1958, B 420, Knight [2/2] and B 226, Drummond ½, Series 320, RNln.
17. Hancock to RN, Mar 8, Hancock to Woods, May 3 and 12, B 316, Hancock (2 of 2) and June 26, 1957, B 316, Hancock (1 of 2), Series 320, RNln.
18. RN to May, Aug 30, B 104, Broder and memo, Sept 17, 1957, B 534, Mosher, Series 320, RNln; Earl Behrens OH, 35–38, CCOH; *Human Events*, Sept 14, 1957, p. 1; *Gallup Poll*, Two, 1505–1506 and 1516; Teiser ed., *Remembering Knowland*, 7–8; Schuparra, "Freedom vs. Tyranny," 542 and *Triumph of the Right*.
19. RN to Eaton, Aug 30, B 234, Eaton, R and RN to Mudd, Aug 30, 1957, B 536, Mudd, H, Series 320, RNln.
20. Memo, Sept 9, 1957, B 421, Knott, W, Series 320, RNln.
21. Memo, Sept 30, 1957, B 534, Mosher, Series 320, RNln.
22. Memoirs, Mar 19, 1976, RNyl; memo, Aug 21, 1957, B 534, Mosher, Series 320, RNln; William Knowland OH, I, p. 46, LBJL; *Human Events*, Nov 16, 1957, p. 1; *Pearson Diaries*, 404–405; Clark, "1958 Ca. Gubernatorial Election," 54–60; Worthen, *Young Nixon*, 172–177.
23. Memoirs, Mar 19, 1976, RNyl; RN to Bassett, Oct 29, 1957, B 66, Bassett, J (1), Series 320, RNln; *New York Times*, Nov 1, 1958; Rarick, *Ca. Rising*, 7–86; Melendy and Gilbert, *Governors of Ca.*, 439–457; Anderson, "1958 Election in Ca.," 283–284.
24. Memo, Nov 1, 1957, B 534, Mosher, Series 320, RNln; telephone calls, Nov 1, 1957, R 15, Diary DDE; *Pearson Diaries*, 403.
25. Memo, Nov 5, 1957, R 15, Diary DDE.
26. Memos, Nov 4 and 5, 1957, B 420, Knight [½], Series 320, RNln; *Newsweek*, Nov 11, 1957, p. 36; *New York Times*, Nov 6, 1957.

27. RN to Polzin, Nov 13, B 69, F 18, Series 207 and RN to Lapham, Nov 23, B 420, Knight [½] and memo, Dec 6, 1957, B 421, Knott, W, Series 320, RNln; Douglas Barrett OH, 60–68, and Tom Bright OH, 29, Goodwin Knight/Edmund Brown, Sr. Era, Government History Documentation Project; Clark, "1958 Ca. Gubernatorial Election," 63–64.

28. Halsey, "Beware the Tender Trap," 7–9; PAES, VII, pp. 154–156, 165, and 170.

29. Memo, May 8, 1958, B 557, New Republic [2/2], Series 320, RNln.

30. RN to Metzer, Mar 13 and Washington Post, Apr 15, 1958, B 764, Truman, H, Series 320, RNln.

31. Diary, Feb 25, 1958, R 16, Diary DDE; Ike's Letters, 197–200.

32. Memo, Jan 22, 1958, R 15 and Diary DDE; memo, June 5, 1958, R 2, Legislative DDE; PPA 1958, p. 357; Newsweek, Feb 10, p. 37 and May 5, 1958, p. 31.

33. Memo, Nov 13, 1957, B 753, Thomas, CS, Series 320, RNln.

34. Murph to RN, Dec 11, 1957, B 540, Murphy, Ge, Series 320, RNln.

35. Telephone call, Dec 23, 1957, R 7, DuHe; Earl Behrens OH, 35–38; Clark, "1958 Ca. Gubernatorial Election," 18–22 and 68–92.

36. RN to Earle, Aug 7, B 232, Earle, G, RN to Romney, Oct 9, B 654, Romney and RN to Reuther, Nov 5, 1957, B 637, Reuther, W, Series 320, RNln.

37. Memo, Feb 6, 1958, B 28, RN 1958 (3), Administrative Series, DDEL; transcript, Feb 18, B 80, F 3, Series 207 and RN to Irwin, Feb 26, 1958, B 371, Irwin (4 of 4), Series 320, RNln.

38. RN to Acker, Mar 9, B 78, F 6, Series 207, RN to Dart, Mar 12, B 202, Dart 2/3, RN to Knight, Mar 12, B 420, Knight [2/2], RN to Hamilton, Apr 1, B 315, Hamilton, R and RN to Irwin, Apr 7, 1958, B 371, Irwin (1 of 4), Series 320, RNln.

39. Woods to HR, June 7, 1958, B 311, Haldeman, HR 2 of 2, Series 320, RNln; Anderson, "1958 Election in Ca.," 278; Clark, "1958 Ca. Gubernatorial Election," 68–92; Newsweek, June 16, 1958, p. 31.

40. Lutz to Hillings, July 1, 1958, B 341, Hillings [½], Series 320, RNln.

41. There are many works on the Lebanon crisis; I have relied on the following: Alin, The United States and the 1958 Lebanon Crisis, 90–91, 105–134, and 141–149; Gendzier, Notes from the Minefield, 295–337; Hahn, Caught in the Middle East, 240–242; Karabell, Architects of Intervention, 136–172; and Yaqub, Containing Arab Nationalism, 205–236.

42. Time table, July 14–19, 1958, R 23, OF Middle East, Diary DDE; draft, after July 18, 1958, B 447, Letters (1958–59, Series 320, RNln; platter, Aug 16, 1961, RNyl; Day 6, Tape 2, 00:39:42 [RN], Gannon mss, WJBma; RN interview 1991, Eisenhower Legacy Collection, C-SPAN3, Oct 18, 2012.

43. Telephones calls, July 15, 1958, R 7, DuHe; platter, Aug 16, 1961 and memoirs, Mar 16, 18 and 19, 1976, RNyl; staff notes, July 15, memo of conference, July 16, cabinet meeting, July 18, R 18, telephone call, July 15, 1958, R 17, Diary DDE.

44. RN to Beebe, July 12, B 71, Beebe, D, Series 320 and RN speech, July 19, 1958, B 91, F 5, Series 207, RNln.

45. Platter, Aug 16, 1961 and memoirs, Feb 15 and Mar 17, 1976, RNyl; Murphy, Diplomat Among Warriors, 394–418.

46. Ike to Knowland, Aug 23, Ike to Roberts, Aug 23, and Sept 4, 1958, R 18, Diary DDE.; Ike to Alcorn, Aug 30, 1958, R 1, OF DDE; *PDDE*, XIX, pp. 1064–1068; *Gallup Poll*, Two, 1556 and 1568.

47. *Gallup Poll*, Two, 1556 and 1568.

48. Memo, Sept 23, 1958, B 338, Hiestand, Series 320, RNln; Ike to Knowland, Sept 23, 1958, R 18, Diary DDE; *PDDE*, XIX, p. 1123.

49. Memoirs, Feb 15, 1976, RNyl; memo, Sept 19, B 508, Memo [2/2] and RN to Chotiner, Sept 22, 1958, B 147, Chotiner 1957–58, Series 320, RNln.

50. RN to Graham, Aug 7, B 299, Graham, Pa, RN to Moley, Aug 19, B 524, Moley – Corres 2 of 2, RN to Kemper, Aug 23, B 403, Kemper, J, RN to Behrens, Aug 23, B 72, Behrens and memo, Sept 17, 1958, B 409, Key, W, Series 320, RNln.

51. Memo, July 22, B 302, Greenberg, C, memo, Aug 5, B 534, Mosher, Chotiner to RN, Sept 18, B 147, Chotiner (1957–1958) and Corey to Finch, Sept 29, 1958, B 125, Ca. Polls, Series 320, RNln.

52. Frier, *Conflict of Interest*, 11–25; Birkner, "Sherman Adams' Fall," 1–11, Gellman mss, DDEL.

53. Ike to Adams, Jan 8, 1958, R 1, OF, DDE; notes, June 17, 1958, R 2, Legislative DDE.

54. Memo, June 21, B 20, Adams, Sh (1 of 2), memo, June 24, B 509, Memo, K, Series 320, *Washington Post*, June 30 and July 2, B 89, F 8, RN press conf, June 26, 1958, B 90, Series 207, RNln; *Newsweek*, June 30, p. 18, July 14, p. 78 and July 28, 1958, p. 43; Krock, *In the Nation*, 235–238; Nixon, *RN*, 193–199.

55. Memo, July 7, 1958, R 18, Diary DDE; *PDDE*, XIX, p. 1089; Hoffecker, *Williams*, 131–132.

56. Notes, July 15, 1958, B 28, RN 1958 (3), Administrative Series, DDEL; *PDDE*, XXI, p. 2408.

57. Telephone call, Aug 25 and diary, Sept 1, 1958, B 28, RN 1958 (3), Administrative Series, DDEL.

58. Memo, Sept 11, 1958, B 25, Alcorn, Series 320, RNln; diary, Sept 17, Adams statement, Sept 22, 1958, R 1, OF DDE; Wilton Person OH 161, CCOH; Adams, *Firsthand Report*, 447–451.

59. RN statement, Sept 22, 1958, B 20, Adams, Sh (1 of 2), Series 320, RNln; and Ike to Adams, Sept 22 and Cutler to Ike, Sept 26, 1958, R 1, OF DDE.

60. Telephone calls, Sept 26 and 27 and memo, Sept 29, 1958, R 18, Diary DDE; Wilder, *Alcorn and the 1958 Election*, 1–16.

61. Moley to RN, Nov 7, 1958, B 524, Moley – Corres 2 of 2, Series 320, RNln; *New York Times*, Oct 13 and 27, 1958; *Newsweek*, Oct 20, p. 35 and Oct 27, 1958, p. 21; Erskine, "Polls," 128–130; *Gallup Poll*, Two, 1571–1574 and 1577; Edwards, *On Deaf Ears*, 224–225; Mazo, *Richard Nixon*, 299.

62. *Daily News* (DC), Oct 20, PPS42.B 3, Labor and *San Jose Mercury* (Calif), Oct 23, 1958, PPS42. B 1, 1958 Campaign, RNyl; *Newsweek*, Oct 20, 1958, p. 35.

63. RN to Royster, Sept 29, 1958, B 661, Royster, Series 320, RNln; *New York Times*, Sept 30, 1958, PPS42.B 1, 1958 Campaign, RNyl; Friel, "Influence of Television," 207; Nixon, *RN*, 199.

64. Alcorn to RN, Oct 1, B 25, Alcorn and Hill to RN, Oct 10, 1958, B 317, Handley (2 of 2), Series 320, RNln.

65. *San Francisco Examiner*, Oct 3, 1958, PPS42, B 6, Campaign, RNyl; memo, Oct 7, B 323, Hartman (3 of 3) and Steele to RN, Oct 26, 1958, B 727, Steele, R, Series 320, RNln.

66. Wilson to RN, Oct 14, B 824, Wilson [3/3] and Kruse to RN, Oct 27, 1958, B 430, Kruse, A, Series 320, RNln; Alsop, "Great Ca. Drama," 34–35 and 102–104; *New York Times*, Oct 15–17, 1958, Anderson, "1958 Election in Ca.," 285–292; Reston, *Sketches*, 29–30.

67. Appointments, Oct 6, 1958, R 18 and 19, Diary DDE; *PPA* 1958, pp. 712–713; *New York Times*, Oct 6 and 7, 1958.

68. *New York Times*, Oct 13 and 15, 1958.

69. Telephone calls, Oct 13 and Ike to RN, Oct 15, 1958, R 19, Diary DDE.

70. Telephone call, Oct 13, 1958, R 19, Diary DDE; *New York Times*, Oct 15, 1958.

71. Ike to RN, Oct 15, 1958, R 19, Diary DDE.

72. *Philadelphia Inquirer*, Oct 9 and 11, PPS42.B 4, Pennsylvania and *Charleston Daily Mail* (WV), Oct 11, 1958, PPS42.B 7, West Virginia, RNyl; *New York Times*, Oct 10, 11 and 12; Kotlowski, "Unhappily Yoked?" 238.

73. Baker, *Good Times*, 313–315.

74. FR, 1958–1960, Vol. XIX, pp. 52–55.

75. RN to Gold, Feb 4, B 292, Goldman [2/2] and RN to Wong, Sept 8, 1958, B 145, China ½, Series 320, RNln.

76. Press release, Sept 27, memo, Sept 28 and Dulles press conf, Sept 30, 1958, PPS325.1958, RNyl; telephone calls, Sept 25 and 29 and memo, Oct 2, 1958, R 8, DuHe; *New York Times*, Sept 14 and Oct 3, 1958; *New Yorker*, Oct 11, 1958, p. 108 and 110–116; *Newsweek*, Oct 6, 1958, p. 17–18; E. Dulles, *Dulles*, 179.

77. *New York Times*, Oct 12, 1958; *PAES*, VII, p. 296.

78. Telephone calls, Oct 12, 1958, R 8, DuHe; *New York Times*, Oct 13 and 14, 1958.

79. *New York Times*, Oct 15, 1958.

80. *PPA* 1958, pp. 740–741.

81. Telephone calls, Oct 15, R 7 and Oct 15, 1958, R 10, DuHe; *New York Times*, Oct 16, 1958.

82. Telephone calls, Oct 15, R 10 and Dulles statement, Oct 15, 1958, R 66, DuHe; *PDDE*, XIX, pp. 1150–1152; *New York Times*, Oct 17, 1958.

83. Telephone calls, Oct 16, 1958, R 7 and 10, DuHe; Roberts, *First Rough Draft*, 272–273.

84. *New York Times*, Oct 22 and 23, 1958.

85. *PPA* 1958, pp. 752–756; Dart call, Oct 1, R 9 and Woods call, Oct 3, R 1, OF DDE and telephone calls, Oct 6, 1958, R 19, Diary DDE; *PPA* 1958, pp. 744–745.

86. *PPA* 1958, pp. 757–765; Appointments, Oct 20, 1958, R 18, Diary DDE; *New York Times*, Oct 21, 1958.

87. *PPA* 1958, p. 765; Appointments, Oct 21, 1958, R 18, Diary DDE; *PPA* 1958, pp. 774–777.

88. Ike to Alcorn, Nov 3, 1958, R 19, Diary DDE; *New York Times*, IV, Oct 19 and 26, 1958.

89. *Chicago Sun-Times*, Oct 15, 1958, PPS42.B 2, RNyl.

90. RN to Prinz, Oct 24, 1958, B 35, Amer. Jewish Congress, Series 320, RNln; *Desert News* (Utah), Oct 17, 1958, PPS42.B 6, 1958 Campaign, RNyl; *New York Times*, Nov 17, 1958.

91. Dewey to RN, Oct 24, B 214, Dewey 2/2 and Hall to RN, Oct 28, 1958, B 313, Hall [2/3], Series 320, RNln; *New York Times*, Oct 23–25, 1958; Kenneth Keating OH 197, pp. 30–31, CCOH; Friel, "Influence of Television," 208–209; Klein, *Making It*, 236.

92. *New York Times*, Oct 24, 1958.

93. *Eau Claire Leader*, Oct 25, PPS42, B7, Wisconsin and *St. Paul Pioneer Press*, Oct 25, 1958, PPS42, B 4, Minnesota, RNyl; *New York Times*, Oct 25, 1958.

94. Woods to Potter, Oct 19, 1958, B 606, Potter, P, Series 320, RNln; *St. Paul Pioneer Press*, Oct 27, PPS42, B 4, Minnesota, *Washington Post*, Oct 27 and 28, PPS42, B 6, *Washington Post* and *Garretson News*, Oct 30, 1958, PPS42, B 6, South Dakota, RNyl; *New York Times*, Oct 26 and 28, 1958; Friel, "Influence of Television," 210; Potter, "Political Pitchman," 80–81; Roberts, *First Rough Draft*, 271 and 273; Klein, *Making It*, 234; Baker, *Good Times*, 325.

95. *New York Times*, Oct 30 and 31 and Nov 2, 1958.

96. *Daily Alaska Empire*, Oct 31, PPS42, B 2, Alaska, and *Daily News-Miner* (Alaska), Nov 3, 1958, PPS273, B 4, F PN 1958, RNyl; *New York Times*, Nov 3 and 4, 1958; Roberts, *First Rough Draft*, 274; Klein, *Making It*, 233–236; Johnson, *Gruening and the American Dissenting Tradition*, 198.

97. "Summary of the Results of the 1958 Elections," R 2, *PRP*; *New York Times*, IV, Nov 9, 1958; Harry McPherson OH, Interview I, Tape 1, pp. 18–19 and 27–28 and George Reedy OH, Interview XIII, pp. 25–26, LBJL.

98. Memo, Nov 10, 1958, B 532, Morrow, F, Series 320, RNln; *Gallup Poll*, Two, 1554 and 1572; *Ebony*, Sept 1958, p. 98; Beito and Beito, *Black Maverick*, 182–187.

99. Cotton to RN, Nov 7, 1958, B 183, Cotton, A, Series 320, RNln; Clark, "1958 Ca. Gubernatorial Election," 125; Anderson, "1958 Election in Ca.," 277–280.

100. Notes, Nov 5, 1958, R 19, Diary DDE; *PPA* 1958, pp. 827–830 and 832–833.

101. Alcorn to Ike, Dec 15, 1960, B 25, Alcorn, Series 320, RNln; Ike to Alcorn, Nov 17, 1958, R 19, Diary DDE; *PDDE*, XIX, pp. 1195–1196; *Newsweek*, Nov 17, 1958, p. 29.

102. Memoirs, Feb 16, 1976, RNyl; telephone call, Nov 5, 1958, R 8, DuHe; *New York Times*, Nov 5, 1958.

103. RN to Abele, Nov 7, B 18, Abele, memo, Nov 10, B 508, Memo CMcW, and RN to Dart, Nov 24, B 202, Dart, Series 320 and RN to Parker, Nov 22, 1958, B 94, F 8, Series 207, RNln; Nixon, *RN*, 200.

CHAPTER 28. THE STEEL SOLUTION

1. Vatter, *U.S. Economy*, 98–115; Morgan, *Eisenhower v. "the Spenders,"* 72–73; Lewis, *Divided Highways*, 86–153.

2. Saulnier interview, May 26, 2006, Gellman mss, DDEL; Sloan, *Eisenhower and the Management*, 39–42.

3. *New York Times Magazine*, July 7, 1957, pp. 12–13; Pinkley, *Ike*, 358–359; McClenahan and Becker, *Eisenhower and the Cold War*, 83–84.

4. Meeting, Jan 10, 1958, R 6, Cabinet DDE; Wilbur Mills OH, II, pp. 34–35, LBJL; Murphy, "Budget and Eisenhower," 96, 98–99, 228, and 231; Morgan, *Ike v. "the Spenders,"* 74–98; Sloan, *Eisenhower and the Management,* 47, 69–104 and 143–151; McClenahan and Becker, *Eisenhower and the Cold War,* 96–103; Mieczkowski, *Eisenhower's Sputnik,* 82–92; Saulnier, *Constructive Years,* 97–116; Vatter, *U.S. Economy,* 115–120; Bremner, *Chairman of the Fed,* 120–136; Morgan, *Eisenhower v. "the Spenders,"* 14; Labor Force Statistics, 1953–1954 and 1957–1958, Bureau of Labor Statistics Website.

5. RN to Bolen, Feb 27, B 91 and RN to Armstrong, Apr 19, B 50, Series 320 and remarks, Apr 29, 1957, B 63, F 32, Series 207, RNln; *New York Times,* Dec 7, 1957.

6. RN to Hancock, May 7, B 316, Hancock (2 of 2) and address, May 24, 1957, B 64, F 17, Series 207, RNln.

7. RN to Snodgrass, July 9, 1957, B 711, Snodgrass, W, Series 320, RNln.

8. Meeting, Oct 11, 1957, R 6, Cabinet DDE.

9. Important points, Nov 15, 1957, R 6, Cabinet DDE.

10. *Gallup Poll,* Two, 1534, 1549–1550 and 1558–1559.

11. Meeting, Jan 3, 1958, R 6, Cabinet DDE; RN to Unander, Feb 6, B 771, Unander [2 of 2], Series 320 and *Cleveland Plain Dealer,* Feb 28, B 80, F 15, Series 207and RN to Burns, June 17, 1958, B 115, Burns 2/3 and RN to Gengler, May 16, 1961, B 285, Gengler, Series 320, RNln; Murphy, "WH and the Recession," 106–109 and 242, 244, and 246; Morgan, *Eisenhower v. "the Spenders,"* 99–119; *New York Times,* Feb 15, 1958.

12. RN to Harris, Mar 5, B 80, F 11, press conf, Mar 10, B 81, F 21, RN to Hoover, Mar 17, B 85, F 13 and speech, Apr 24, B 84, F 16, Series 207 and RN to MacArthur, Mar 18, B 468, MacArthur, DA, memo, Mar 25, B 230, Dunn 2/2, RN to Moley, Mar 31, B 24, Moley–Corres 2 of 2and RN to Witwer, Apr 9, 1958, Series 320, RNln; meeting, Mar 11, R16 and meeting, Oct 1, 1958, R 19, Diary DDE; *New York Times,* Mar 11, 1958; *Newsweek,* Mar 24, 1958, p. 32; Murphy, "WH and the Recession," 250 and 252; Morgan, *Eisenhower v. "the Spenders,"* 119–123; Mazo, *Nixon,* 294.

13. Meeting, Jan 24 and Feb 28, R 6, Cabinet DDE and meeting, Mar 11, 1958, R 2, Legislative DDE; RN to Birkel, Feb 19, 1954, B 83, Birkel, Series 320, RNln.

14. Memo, Apr 21, B 93, F 2, Series 207, and Burns to RN, Aug 25, 1956, B 115, Burns 3/3, Series 320, RNln.

15. Speech, Sept 6, 1958, B 93, F 2, Series 207, RNln.

16. RN to Wood, Sept 10, 1958, Corres File, Wood mss, HHL; Burger to RN, Sept 10, B 113, Burger, W, Gainey to RN, Sept 15, B 279, Gainey [1/2], memo, Sept 19, B 727, Steele, Ja and RN to Luce, Sept 23, B 464, Luce [2/2], Series 320, memo, Sept 8, B 94, F 7, RN to Bell, Sept 15, B 94, F 8 and RN to Henry, B 94, F 1, Series 207 and RN to Robinson, Sept 15, 1958, B 1, Nov 26 Dedication, Series 380, RNln; *Newsweek,* Sept 15, 1958, pp. 92 and 94; *New Republic,* Sept 23, 1958, V. 138, p. 6; *New York Times,* Sept 27, 1958.

17. Ike to RN, Jan 16, 1959, PPS324.126, RNyl; *Washington Post,* Jan 12, B 96, F 14, Series 207 and RN to Bassett, Mar 28, B 66, Bassett, J (1), RN to Cullison, May 1, B 196, Cullison, RN to Manfredi, May 25, B 474, Manfredi, RN to Dunn, June 24, B 230, Dunn ½ and statement, June 25, 1959, B 121, Cabinet, Series 320, RNln.

18. Meeting, Jan 13, R 2, Legislative DDE and meeting, Jan 16, 1959, R 8, Cabinet DDE; Morgan, *Eisenhower v. "the Spenders,"* 124–151.

19. Meeting, Jan 20, R 19, meeting, Mar 10, R 20 and June 6, Diaries, meeting, Feb 3 and June 2 and 22, R 2, Legislative DDE, meeting, May 1 and June 22, 1959, R 8, Cabinet DDE; *PDDE*, XIX, pp. 1369–1370; *New York Times*, Jan 22, 1959.
20. Sloan, *Eisenhower and the Management*, 63–68.
21. *New York Times*, July 2, 1959.
22. *PPA* 1959, p. 125; *New York Times*, Jan 18, 1959; *Washington Post*, Feb 3, 1959, B 120, Cabinet 1/3, Series 320, RNln.
23. *New York Times*, Jan 18, 1959; statement, Feb 1, 1959, B 121, Cabinet, June 29, Series 320, RNln.
24. Memo, Mar 7, press conf, Mar 18, B 795, Wallis [2 of 3] and memo, May 6, 1959, B 796, Wallis [2 of 2], Series 320, RNln; *PDDE*, XXI, p. 2462; *New York Times*, Mar 19, Apr 29 and May 10, 1959; Klein, *Making It*, 134; Rung, "RN, State, and Party," 421–431.
25. RN to Smith, June 5 and Wallis to Kimpton, Aug 25, B 796, Wallis [2 of 2], Wallis to Flynn, Aug 20, 1959, B 795, Wallis [2 of 3] and RN to Shultz, undated, Shultz, B 693, Shultz, G, Series 320, RNln; memoirs, Mar 18 and 19, 1976, RNyl; George Shultz interview, Jan 31, 2002.
26. RN to Boggs, May 21, B 91, Boggs, C, press release, June 29, B 121, Cabinet and RN to Howard, July 2, 1959, B 357, Howard, R, Series 320, RNln; meeting, June 2, 12, and 22, 1959, R 9, Cabinet DDE; *New York Times*, June 29, 1959.
27. RN to Humphrey, July 1, B 361, Humphrey, G and *Wall Street Journal*, Sept 23, 1959, B 120, Cabinet 2/3, Series 320, RNln; *New York Times*, June 29, July 5, Aug 22 and 31, 1959.
28. RN to Hoyt, Sept 28, B 358, Hoyt and RN to May, Dec 3, 1959, B 484, May, AW, Series 320, RNln; *New York Times*, Aug 17, Sept 7 and Nov 19, 1959.
29. *New York Times*, Jan 5, 1960 for chronology; Stebenne, *Goldberg*, 197–211.
30. *PPA* 1959, pp. 520–522; DDE to Humphrey, Aug 11, 1959, R 22, Diary DDE.
31. Meetings, Sept 30, 1959, R 23, Diary DDE; *PDDE*, XVI, pp. 2089–2091.
32. Memo, Nov 5, R 23, Diary and memo, Nov 10 and meeting, Nov 11, 1959, R 9, Cabinet DDE; Saulnier interview, May 26, 2006, Gellman mss, DDEL; Eisenhower, *Waging Peace*, 453–457.
33. *PDDE*, XX, p. 1727.
34. *New York Times*, Jan 5, 1960; Eisenhower, *Waging Peace*, 490.
35. Mitchell to RN, Apr 1 and memo, Dec 18, B 523, Mitchell [2/4], Wallace to Finch, June 21 and Mitchell to RN, Aug 19, B 522, Mitchell [1/4] and RN to Bolich, May 11, B 91, Bolich, RN to Hitt, June 22, 1959, B 344, Hitt, P, Series 320, RNln; calendar, Dec 19, 1959, PPS212(1959).2, RNyl; meeting, Apr 24, 1959, R 8, Cabinet DDE.
36. *The Progress* (Pa), July 8, B 496, McDonald [1/2] and McDonald to RN, Apr 4, RN to McDonald, July 16, 1956 and RN to McDonald, Jan 6, 1958, B 496, McDonald [2/2], memo, May 19, B 643, Riesel [2/2], statement, July 2, B 121, Cabinet, memo, Aug 31, B 432, Labor and memo, Oct 26, 1959, B 753, Thomas, CS, Series 320, RNln; meeting, July 8, 1959, R 22, Diary DDE; McDonald, *Union Man*, 258; Herling, *Right to Challenge*, 32.
37. Sigma Delta Chi q and a, Nov 13, B 121, F 4, Series 207 and RN to Gould, Dec 8, B 105, Broomfield and RN to Chait, Nov 19, 1959, B 140, Chait, Series 320, RNln.

38. Meeting, Dec 11, 1959, R 10, Cabinet DDE; memo, Feb 12, 1960, B 425, Kornitzer (3 of 4), Series 320, RNln; Nixon, *Challenges We Face*, 175–176.

39. *New York Times*, Jan 5, 1960.

40. Memo, Feb 12, 1960, B 425, F Kornitzer (3 of 4), Series 320, RNln; *Newsweek*, Jan 18, 1960, p. 66; P. Nixon, "Crises of a Candidate's Wife," 118; Nixon, *Challenges We Face*, 176–177; McDonald, *Union Man*, 264–279; Stebenne, *Goldberg*, 212–213.

41. Memo, Feb 12, 1960, B 425, Kornitzer (3 of 4), Series 320, RNln; *New York Times, Washington Post*, and *New York Herald Tribune*, Jan 1, 1960.

42. Telephone call, Jan 2, 1960, R 24, Diary DDE; Eisenhower, *Waging Peace*, 458 and Appendix I, pp. 705–706.

43. *New York Times, Washington Post*, and *New York Herald Tribune*, Jan 4 and 5, 1960; RN to Mueller, Jan 5, B 536, Mueller, F, Series 320 and transcript, Feb 15, 1960, B 127, F 4, Series 207, RNln; RN called Mitchell's contribution "indispensible," memoirs, Mar 22, 1976, RNyl.

44. Meeting, Jan 6, 1960, R 24, Diary DDE; transcript, Feb 15, 1960, B 127, F 4, Series 207, RNln; RN, "Nixon's Own Story," 102; Kistiakowsky, *Scientist at the WH*, 216–217; Gray, *Eighteen Acres*, 291–292.

45. *PPA* 1960, pp. 24–25.

46. White to Directors, Jan 11, B 812, White, Ch, RN to Graham, Jan 22, 1960, B 299, Graham {2 of 2}, Series 320, RNln; Mitchell to RN, Jan 13, 1960, B 95, Jan 13 and Mitchell to Editor, Jan 14, 1960, B 95, Jan 14, Mitchell mss, LBJL; Nixon, *Challenges We Face*, 177–181; McDonald, *Union Man*, 280; Herling, *Right to Challenge*, 68–69.

47. RN to Anthes, Mar 12, B 45, Anthes and RN to Hall, Dec 30, B 313, Hall, Ro, Series 320, RNln.

48. Meeting, Nov 27, 1959, R 9, Cabinet DDE.

49. Meeting, Jan 22, Mar 4 and 25, R 10, Cabinet DDE and meeting, Feb 26, R 24, Apr 29, May 12, R 25 and July 1, 1960, R 26, Diary DDE.

50. Bridges, "A Year End Review," 9; McClenahan and Becker, *Eisenhower and the Cold War*, 103–109; Bremner, *Chairman of the Fed*, 136–148.

51. Memoirs, Mar 31, 1976, RNyl; *Newsweek*, Feb 1, 1960, p. 62; Saulnier, *Constructive Years*, 116–129.

52. Meeting, Feb 16, R 24, Mar 8, Apr 5 and 26, May 10, R 25, June 2, 9 and 28, and memo, July 1, 1960, R 26, Diary DDE.

53. *PDDE*, XX, pp. 1961–1962.

54. *New York Times*, Jan 11 and 16, Feb 15 and Apr 17, 1960.

55. Conversation, May 3, 1960, B 1, Krock mss, HML; *New York Times*, Apr 24 and June 22, 1960.

56. HNN, May 13, 2013; Sloan, *Eisenhower and the Management*, 154 and 162; HNN, May 13 and interview with Keith Olson, Sept 15, 2013.

CHAPTER 29. NIXON IN AFRICA

1. Noer, *Cold War and Black Liberation*, 15–33; Noer, "Truman, Eisenhower, and South Africa," 75–86; Kitchen, "Still on Safari in Africa," 172; Farzanegan, "U.S. Response

and Reaction to the Emergence of Arab and African States in International Politics," 239–244; Nwaubani, *US and Decolonization in West Africa*, 54–55 and 86–118; Schraeder, *U.S. Foreign Policy*, 1–59; Lauren, *Power and Prejudice*, 197–207; Birmingham, *Decolonization of Africa*, 1–84.

2. Memo, Apr 27 and Aug 11, 1955, R 2, DuHe; RN to de Toledano, Aug 8, B 213, de Toledano 3/3, Series 320 and RN to Coleman, Aug 25, B 34, F 10 [1 of 2] and RN to Thornburg, Sept 22, 1955, B 42, F 8, Series 207, RNln; *Newsweek*, Aug 22, p. 30, Sept 5, p. 16 and Sept 26, 1955, p. 42; *New York Times*, Aug 24, 1955.

3. Memo, July 30, 1955, B 12, chronological series, B 12, July 1955 (1), memo, Aug 10, R 3, JFD to DE, Aug 19, 1955, R 2, DuHe; *FR*, 1955–1957, Vol. XIV, pp. 368–369 and Vol. XII, pp. 163–164.

4. *FR*, 1955–1957, Vol. XIV, pp. 612–613, 624, 664, 667, 697, and 826–827.

5. Africa, Jan 3, PPS325(1956).13.2 and Bowie to RN, Feb 14, 1956, PPS325(1956).13.1, RNyl.

6. Lodge to DE, Mar 28, 1956, memo and conversation, R 3, DuHe.

7. Memos, Apr 12 and 16, 1956, memo and conversation, R 2, DuHe; cabinet, Apr 27, 1956, R 8, Diary DDE.

8. *PPA* 1956, p. 479.

9. Telephone call, July 30, 1956, R 5, DuHe; Bartlett, *Special Relationship*, 77–87; Dimbleby and Reynolds, *Ocean Apart*, 224–228; Stivers, "Eisenhower and the Middle East," 195–197; Fry, "Eisenhower and the Suez Crisis," 160–161.

10. *FR*, 1955–1957, XV, pp. 169–170; meeting, Aug 12, 1956, R 2, Legislative DDE; *PPA* 1956, pp. 687–689; I have depended on Nichols, *Eisenhower 1956* for his analysis of the crisis.

11. Nichols, *Eisenhower 1956*, 233–265.

12. Woods to Drowns, Nov 21, DR 132 and Jamieson to Baughman, Dec 7, 1956, PPS325A.12, RNyl; Rebozo to Neal, Nov 28, 1956, B 59, F 12, Series 207, RNln.

13. *Los Angeles Times* and *Daily News* (Wash., D.C.), Nov 28, 1956, PPS, RNyl; *FR*, 1955–1957, XV, pp. 1223 and 1227; Nichols, *Eisenhower 1956*, 271–273.

14. Sears to Lodge, Sept 24, Lodge to Stephens, Sept 25, 1956, Lodge to Washington, Mar 20, Washington to Lodge, Mar 24, Schuyler to Lodge, Apr 16, 1959, R 14, Lodge mss, MHS.

15. Lodge to Dulles, Sept 19 and Dec 17, 1956, R 5, Lodge mss, MHS.

16. Telephone calls, Jan 8 and 28–29, R 5 and memo, Jan 30, 1957, R 4, DuHe; Dulles to RN, Jan 24, 1957, B 1, schedule, Series 351, RNln; *PDDE*, XVIII, pp. 17–18.

17. Telephone call, Feb 4, 1957, R 5, DuHe; press release, Feb 5, 1957, B 1, schedule, Series 351, RNln; *PPA* 1957, pp. 132–133.

18. Calendar, Feb 25 and 26, 1957, PPS212(1957).2, RNyl; memo, Feb 14, 1957, CIA-RDP80B01676R003200160030-9, CREST; *FR*, 1955–1957, Vol. XVIII, pp. 367 and 372–374; Robert and Gretchen King OH, 16, WC; Mazov, *Distant Frontier in the Cold War*, 43–46.

19. *Los Angeles Times*, Feb 22 and 26, 1957.

20. *New York Herald Tribune* and *Los Angeles Times*, Feb 21, 1957.

21. Diary, Feb 14, 1957, Morrow mss, DDEL; RN to Burgess, Aug 28, 1957, B 385, Johnson, JH, Series 320, RNln; Lodge to DE, Sept 28 and DE to Lodge, Oct 2, 1958, R 29,

Lodge mss, MHS; *Jet*, Feb 21, p. 3 and Apr 4, 1957, p. 3, Morrow, *Black Man in the WH*, 125–126 and the entries for the African trip run to 154; Hamilton, *Powell*, 281–282; Haygood, *King of the Cats*, 224–225; Lewis, *Du Bois*, 565; Horne, *Black and Red*, 214–217; Meriwether, *Proudly We*, 150–180.

22. *Los Angeles Times*, Feb 28, 1957.

23. Morgan broadcast, Apr 1, 1957, B 529, Morgan [2/2], Series 320 and *Washington Star* (DC), Apr 14, 1957, B 1, Africa, Series 349, RNln; diary, Feb 28, 1957, Morrow mss, DDEL; Ethel Payne OH, 126, Women in Journalism; Wolseley, *Black Press, U.S.A.*, 206.

24. RN to Bassett, Apr 15, 1957, B 79, F 10, Series 207, RNln; *New York Times*, Mar 1, 1957.

25. Calendar, Feb 28, 1957, PPS212(1957).2, RNyl; country background, Feb 1957, B 1, African trip, Series 351 and RN to Dewey, Mar 25, 1957, B 214, Dewey 2/2, Series 320, RNln; memo, Sept 28, 1956, B 40, Morocco (5), International Series, DDEL; diary, Feb 28, 1957, Morrow mss, DDEL; Day 6, Tape 3, 00:36:24 [RN], Gannon mss, WJBma; Robert Cushman OH, 21–23, DDEL; Donald Hughes lecture, May 19, 2011; Zingg, "Cold War in North Africa," 41–42; Zartman, "Moroccan-American Base Negotiations," 27–40; Nwaubani, *US and the Decolonization in West Africa*, 115.

26. Program for Morocco, Mar 1, B 1, African trip [6/6], Series 350 and Morgan broadcast, Mar 1, 1957, B 529, Morgan [2/2], Series 320, RNln; Morrow, *Black Man in the WH*, 127–129; *Los Angeles Times*, Mar 2, 1957; *New York Herald Tribune*, Mar 2 and 3 and Apr 12, 1957.

27. Howe memo, Mar 27, 1957, R 23, OF, Morocco, DDE; *FR*, 1955–1957, Vol. XVIII, pp. 561–564; *PPA* 1957, p. 84; Morrow, *Black Man in the WH*, 130–131; *Los Angeles Times*, Mar 3, 1957.

28. Ghana, 1957, B 1, African trip, administration, Series 351, RNln; *New York Herald Tribune*, Mar 3, 1957; *Jet*, Mar 21, 1957, pp. 16–19; *Newsweek*, Mar 11, 1957, pp. 44 and 47–49; *Ebony*, Mar 17–19 and June 1957, pp. 32–33; *New York Times*, July 20, 1958, p. SM14; Milne, *Nkrumah*, vi; I have relied on Montgomery, "Eyes of the World Were Watching," 13–113, for information on Ghana-U.S. relations.

29. Schedule, Mar 3–7, 1957, B 1, African trip [6/6], Series 350, RNln; *Los Angeles Times* and *New York Herald Tribune*, Mar 4, 1957.

30. *FR*, 1955–1957, Vol. XVIII, pp. 377–378; Morrow, *Black Man in the WH*, 131–132.

31. Morgan broadcast, Mar 4, 1957, B 529, Morgan [2/2], Series 320, RNln; *Los Angeles Times* and *New York Herald Tribune*, Mar 5, 1957.

32. Memo, Apr 11, 1957, PPS320.107.4, RNyl; *New York Herald Tribune*, Mar 6, 1957; *Pittsburgh Courier*, Mar 16, p. 2 and Mar 23, 1957, p. 6; *Jet*, Mar 21, 1957, p. 12; Day 9, Tape 3, 00:13:57 [RN], Gannon mss, WJBma; Earl Mazo interview, July 17, 2001; Smith, *Events Leading*, 231; C. King, *My Life*, 154–155; Morrow, *Black Man in the WH*, 133–134; Lewis, *King*, 90–91.

33. Campbell, *Middle Passages*, 318–319; Lauren, "Seen from the Outside," 32; Tinker, *Race*, 84; Rooney, *Nkrumah*, 133.

34. *New York Herald Tribune*, Mar 6, 1957; Urquhart, *Bunche*, 277.

35. *PPA* 1957, pp. 170–171; *Los Angeles Times* and *New York Herald Tribune*, Mar 7, 1957; *Pittsburgh Courier*, Mar 16, 1957, p. 4.

36. *Washington Daily News* (DC), Oct 19, 1954, PPS336(1954).S515, schedule, Mar 7–9, B 1, African trip [6/6], Series 350 and Liberia, Mar 1957, B 1, African trip – administration and Scouten to Baughman, June 12, 1957, B 1, Secret Service, Series 351, RNln; *New York Herald Tribune*, Mar 8, 1957.

37. Diary, Mar 7, 1957, Morrow mss, DDEL; Morgan broadcast, Mar 8, 1957, B 529, Morgan [2/2], Series 320, RNln.

38. *Los Angeles Times* and *New York Herald Tribune*, Mar 10, 1957.

39. FR, 1955–1957, Vol. XVIII, pp. 397–401; *Los Angeles Times* and *New York Herald Tribune*, Mar 10, 1957; Morrow, *Black Man in the WH*, 135.

40. Tubman to DE, Mar 9 and memo June 25, 1957, B 38, Liberia (1), International Series, DDEL; *Los Angeles Times*, Mar 10 and 13, 1957; *New York Herald Tribune*, Mar 10, 1957; *Pittsburgh Courier*, Mar 16, p. 3 and Mar 30, 1957, p. 6; *Jet*, Mar 28, 1957, p. 20; Mazov, *Distant Frontier in the Cold War*, 32–42.

41. Uganda, 1957, B 1, African trip – Administration, Series 351, RNln; Morrow, *Black Man in the WH*, 136–137; *New York Times*, Mar 11, 1957.

42. *New York Times, Los Angeles Times* and *New York Herald Tribune*, Mar 11, 1957.

43. Ethiopia, B a, African trip, administration, Series 351 and schedule, Mar 11–13, 1957, B 1, Ethiopia, Series 352, RNln; *Newsweek*, Mar 25, 1957, p. 52.

44. Memo, May 29, 1954, B 9, Ethiopia (4) and memo Nov 15, 1956, B 9, Ethiopia (3), International Series, DDEL; Lefebvre, *Arms for the Horn*, 67–93 and 107–108; Marcus, *Ethiopia*, 89–114.

45. Morrow, *Black Man in the WH*, 137–138.

46. Morgan broadcast, Mar 11 and 12, 1957, B 359, Morgan [2/2], Series 320, RNln; FR, 1955–1957, Vol. XVIII, pp. 339–348; *Jet*, Mar 28, 1957, p. 21; *Los Angeles Times*, Mar 12, 1957; *New York Herald Tribune*, Mar 12 and 13, 1957.

47. *New York Herald Tribune*, Mar 13, 1957.

48. PPA 1957, pp. 197–198 and 202; Lefebvre, *Arms for the Horn*, 102–103.

49. RN to Dulles, Mar 25, 1957, B 229, Dulles 2/2, Series 320, RNln; RN to Selassi, Apr 5, 1957, PPS320.31.1, RNyl; FR, 1955–1957, Vol. XVIII, pp. 339–360.

50. Memo, Aug 29, 1956, B 47, Sudan, International Series, DDEL.

51. Ahmed to Powell, Mar 26, 1957, B 3, Sudan – Misc, Series 352, RNln; *Los Angeles Times* and *New York Herald Tribune*, Mar 14, 1957; *Pittsburgh Courier*, Mar 23, 1957, p. 6; Morrow, *Black Man in the WH*, 142.

52. FR, 1955–1957, Vol. XVIII, pp. 633–639; Salih to DE, Apr 1, 1957, B 47, Sudan, International Series, DDEL.

53. Libya, B 1, African trip – administrative, Series 351 and Morgan broadcast, Mar 15, 1957, B 529, Morgan [2/2], Series 320 and Scouten to Baughman, June 12, 1957, B 1, Secret Service, Series 351, RNln; FR, 1955–1957, Vol. XVIII, pp. 467–472 and 484 and FR, 1958–1960, Vol. XIII, p. 730; *New York Herald Tribune*, Mar 15, 1957; Morrow, *Black Man in the WH*, 144–146.

54. *New York Herald Tribune*, Mar 16, 1957.

55. Schedule, Mar 16–18, B 1, Schedule, Series 351 and RN to Gronchi, Apr 15, 1957, B 1, Thank You, Series 352, RNln; RN to Gronchi, Apr 5, 1957, PPS320.49.53, RNyl; FR,

1955–1957, Vol. XXVII, pp. 405–407; *Los Angeles Times* and *New York Herald Tribune*, Mar 17, 1957; Morrow, *Black Man in the WH*, 148–149.

56. Diary, Mar 17, 1957, Morrow mss, DDEL; RN to Casariego, undated, African trip, Series 351, RN to Pope, Apr 5, B 1, Thank You, Series 352, Woods to Hillings, July 23, B 3, African trip – Rome, Series 349, and RN to Holiness, Apr 5, B 605, Pope, P and O'Connor to RN, June 19, 1957, B 567, O'Connor, M, Series 320, RNln; RN to Helene, Apr 14, 1957, DR, Drown mss, RNyl; *New York Times* and *New York Herald Tribune*, Mar 18, 1957.

57. RN to Sadlak, Apr 1, 1957, B 666, Sadlak, Series 320, RNln; RN to Brioni, Apr 2, 1957, PPS320.49.51, RNyl; *New York Herald Tribune*, Mar 18, 1957.

58. Tunisia 1957, B 1, African trip – Administration, Series 351 and Jones to Dulles, Mar 28, B 3, Tunisia – Schedules, Series 352 and Morgan broadcast, Mar 18, 1957, B 529, Morgan [2/2], Series 320, RNln; Day 6, Tape 3, 00:40:02 [RN], Gannon mss, WJBma; *New York Times*, Mar 2 and 19, *New York Herald Tribune* and *Los Angeles Times*, Mar 19, 1957; Morrow, *Black Man in the WH*, 149–152.

59. *FR*, 1955–1957, Vol. XVIII, pp. 660–664.

60. Morgan broadcast, Mar 19 and 20, 1957, B 529, Morgan [2/2], Series 320, RNln; *New York Herald Tribune* and *Los Angeles Times*, Mar 20 and 21, 1957; Connelly, *Diplomatic Revolution*, 119–137.

61. Memo, Nov 11, 1956, B 48, Tunisia (2), International Series and diary, Nov 14, 1957, DDEL; *PPA* 1957, 423–424; *Ike's Letters*, 190–192; *Newsweek*, Nov 25, 1957, p. 50; Sangmuah, "Eisenhower and Containment," 78 and 81–86.

62. Schedule, Mar 21, 1957, PPS212(1957).2, RNyl; *New York Herald Tribune*, Mar 21, 1957; *Los Angeles Times*, Mar 24, 1957; *Newsweek*, Mar 18, 1957, p. 58; Morrow, *Black Man in the WH*, 153–154.

63. *New York Herald Tribune*, Mar 17, 1957.

64. Fulbright to RN, Apr 17, 1957, B 276, Fulbright, J and RN to Woodward, Sept 4, 1958, B 830, Woodward, T, Series 320 and RN to Njoku, June 14, 1957, B 2, African trip (4 of 6), Series 351, RNln.

65. Dulles to RN, May 28, 1957, B 229, Dulles /2, Series 320, RNln; Dulles to RN, after May 28, PPS320.4.5 and RN to Emery, Aug 26, 1957, PPS320.4.1, RNyl; leadership meeting, July 2, R 13, Diary DDE; *FR*, 1955–1957, Vol. XXVII, p. 118 and Vol. XVIII, pp. 291–294; Zoubir, "U.S. and Soviet Policies Towards France's Struggle," 439–466; Cogan, *Oldest Allies*, 106–108; Horne, *Savage War*, 247; Pruden, *Conditional Partners*, 178–185.

66. Legislative leadership meeting, July 2, 1957, R 13, Diary DDE.

67. Morgan broadcast, Mar 21, 1957, B 529, Morgan [2/2], Series 320, RNln; Day 6, Tape 2, 00:17:54 [RN], Gannon mss, WJBma; *New York Herald Tribune*, Mar 22, 1957; Nixon, *Leaders*, 290–296 and 307–308.

68. Memo, Apr 5, B 577, Palmer, Jo and RN to Lodge, Apr 29, B 457, Lodge (1 of 2), Series 320, RNln; RN to Tappin, Jan 31, 1958, PPS320.59.16, RNyl.

69. RN to Klein, June 29, 1957, B 144, Chicago Daily, Series 320, RNln; *Newsweek*, Apr 1, 1957, p. 26; *Los Angeles Times*, *New York Times* and *New York Herald Tribune*, Mar 22, 1957.

70. Report to the President, Mar 24, 1957, B 1, Report on African Trip, Series 351, RNln; Lodge to Thompson, Mar 9, 1960, R 15, Lodge mss; *PDDE*, XXI, p. 2303.
71. *PPA* 1957, pp. 218–220 and 525–526.
72. *PDDE*, XVIII, pp. 166–168.
73. Dulles to RN, Apr 18, 1957, B 228, Dulles, A, Series 320, RNln; Dulles to RN, Mar 19, R 47 and telephone call, Mar 27, 1957, R 6, DuHe.
74. RN to Hoffman, Apr 3, 1957, Eminent Personages File, Nixon, Richard, Hoffman mss, HSTL; RN to McCone, Apr 18, 1957, B 493, McCone [2/2], Series 320, RNln; *New York Times*, Apr 7, 1957; *Pittsburgh Courier*, Mar 30, 1957, p. 9; Mazov, *Distant Frontier in the Cold War*, 13–28.
75. RN to Owen, Apr 3, B 574, Owen, L and RN to Miller, Apr 26, 1957, B 517, Miller, P (Gannett), Series 320, RNln; *New York Times*, Apr 7, 1957.
76. *New York Times*, Apr 7, 1957; RN speech, Nov 14, 1957, B 72, F 2, Series 207 and RN to Olive, Dec 16, 1958, B 569, Olive, L, Series 320, RNln; Nixon, *Challenges We Face*, 186–187.
77. Diary, Feb 14, 1957, Morrow mss, DDEL.
78. *Ebony*, Mar and June and *Jet*, Mar 21, pp. 3–4 and 20–21, Mar 28, pp. 4 and 20–21, and Apr 4, 1957, pp. 8–9; *Philadelphia Inquirer Magazine*, Aug 10, 2005; Johnson, *Succeeding Against the Odds*, 258–261 and 302.
79. Barnett to RN, Apr 1, RN to Barnett, Apr 25, 1957 and Barnett to Klein, Nov 28, 1959, B 63, Barnett, Series 320, RNln.
80. RN to Vann, Apr 24, B 780, Vann and Rivera to RN, July 13, 1957, B 644, Rivera, AM, Series 320, RNln.
81. Johnson to RN, May 23, 1957, B 385, Johnson, JH, Series 320, RNln; *New York Herald Tribune*, May 25, 1957; *Jet*, June 13, 1957, p. 10; Booker, *Black Man's America*, 207–208.
82. *Chicago Defender*, Mar 1, p. 11 and Mar 8, 1958; Ethel Payne OH, interview #6, pp. 123–124, Women in Journalism; Streitmatter, "No Taste for Fluff," 528–540,
83. Washington to RN, Mar 3 and memo, Mar 4, 1958, B 801, Washington, V, Series 320, RNln.
84. *New York Herald Tribune*, Mar 24, 1957; *FR*, 1955–1957, Vol. XVIII, p. 72; Namikis, "Battleground," Vol. I, pp. 57–58; Meriwether, "Torrent Overrunning Everything," 182–185.
85. Telephone call, Apr 18, 1957, R 6, DuHe; RN to Henderson, Apr 25, 1957, PPS325, RNyl; Henderson to RN, May 8, 1957, B 332, Henderson, L, Series 320, RNln; Nixon, "Nixon's Own Story," 100–101; Namikis, "Battleground," Vol. I, pp. 59–60; Noer, *Cold War and Black Liberation*, 49; without ever examining a single document from Nixon's vice-presidential manuscripts that this chapter draws upon, historian George White wrongly concluded that "the vice president played no direct role in the formation of the State Department's African Bureau"; White, "Big Ballin'!?," 8.
86. Memo, May 3, 1957, PPS320.2.2, RNyl.
87. RN to Bullis, May 17, 1957, B 63, F 32, Series 207, RNln; *FR*, 1955–1957, Vol. XVIII, pp. 72–73; RN, "Nixon's Own Story," 100.
88. Plummer, *In Search of Power*, 2 and 52–53; Plummer makes factual mistakes: for example, she said Nixon belonged to the Los Angeles chapter of the NAACP, 53; he did

not; she declared that Truman's legacy was the integration of the armed forces; Truman issued the order to desegregate, but this was not completed until 1954, p. 60. Email, Rives to Gellman, Dec 23, 2013, Gellman mss, DDEL. Others who follow these themes are Muehlenbeck, *Betting on the Africans*, xix, 3–33, and 197; Layton, *International Politics*, 104–105 and 138; Fraser, "Crossing the Color Line in Little Rock," 264; Von Eschen, *Race Against*, 134 and *Satchmo Blows*, 1–91; Krenn, *Black Diplomacy*, 87; Borstelmann, *Cold War*, 85–93, 111–126, and 133–134, offers a more balanced view, but is still influenced by earlier works on Ike and civil rights.

89. White, *Holding the Line*, 5, 39, and 133–146.
90. White, "Big Ballin'!?" 9.
91. Hunt, *Ideology and U.S. Foreign Policy*, 46–91 and 163–165; Osgood, *Total Cold War*, 275–280; Borstelmann, *Cold War*, 133–134.
92. Noer, "Truman, Eisenhower and South Africa," 86–92 and "New Frontiers and Old Priorities in Africa," 253–255; Meriwether, "A Torrent Overrunning Everything," 176–182; Pruden, *Conditional Partners*, 217–222; Noer, *Cold War and Black Liberation*, 34–48.

CHAPTER 30. IKE'S COLD WAR

1. Drummond to RN, Jan 11, 1960, B 266, Drummond ½, Series 320, RNln; memoirs, Feb 15, 1976, RNyl; Nixon, "VP Nixon Writes," 36.
2. DE to Judd, Jan 4, 1958, R 4, DuHe.
3. *PDDE*, XVIII, pp. 410–412; memo, Sept 2, 1957, B 5, meeting with DE – 1957 (3), DuHe.
4. *PDDE*, XVIII, pp. 410–412; memo, Sept 3, 1957, B 5, meeting with DE – 1957 (3), DuHe.
5. van Ee to Gellman, Mar 6, 2007, email, Gellman mss, DDEL.
6. RN to Donovan, Jan 14, 1957, B 221, Donovan, H, Series 320 and press question, Mar 4, 1958, B 81, F 9, Series 207, RNln; RN to Poulson, Apr 22, 1957, PPS320.72.5, RNyl; memo, Dec 23, 1958, R 19, Diary DDE; Little, "Gideon's Band," 529–530; Walker, "Lyndon B. Johnson's Senate," 1000–1005; Takeyh, *Origins of the Eisenhower Doctrine*, 152–153 and 157–158; Yaqub, *Containing*, 269–217.
7. Meeting, Jan 10, 1958, R 15, Diary DDE.
8. SD Bulletin, Nov 4, B 69, F 18, Series 207 and RN to Oviatt, Dec 26, 1957 B 574, Oviatt, memo, Jan 10, B 229, Dulles ½ and RN to Krehbiel, Apr 18, 1958, B 427, Krehbiel 1957–1959, Series 320, RNln; RN to Randolph, Mar 31, PPS320.82.26 and RN to Gregory, Sept 22, 1958, PPS320.82.47, RNyl; meeting, Feb 28, 1958, R 16, Diary DDE; *FR*, 1955–1957, Vol. X, p. 200 and Vol. X, pp. 706–708 and *FR*, 1958–1960, Vol. IV, pp. 4–5 and 22–23.
9. RN to Barstow, Jan 18, 1957, Barstow, R and RN to Andersen, May 19, 1960, B 40, Andersen, HC, Series 320, RNln; memo, Oct 30, 1957, B 28, Nixon (1), Administrative Series, DDEL; telephone call to RN, Jan 21, 1958, R 7, DuHe; *FR*, 1955–1957, Vol. XIX, p. 453 and *FR*, 1958–1960, Vol. IV, pp. 424, 436, and 440; *New York Times*, May 24, 1957.

10. Meeting, July 25, R 7, cabinet and meeting, July 1, 1958, R 2, legislative and memo, Jan 30, 1958, and R 15, DE to Dodge, Oct 16, 1959, R 23 and legislative meeting, May 10, 1960, R 25, Diary DDE; RN interview, Oct 18, 2012, "Eisenhower Legacy Collection," C-SPAN3; *FR*, 1958–1960, Vol. IV, p. 409; Barry Goldwater OH, I, p. 15, LBJL; Kaufman, *Trade and Aid.*

11. Mieczkowski, *Eisenhower's Sputnik Moment*, 11–70 and 95–111; Dickson, *Sputnik*, 110–122, and 145–164; Divine, *Sputnik*, vii–viii; Zaloga, *Kremlin's Nuclear Sword*, 54–57; Kolodzieg, *Uncommon*, 253–324.

12. Telephone call to RN, Oct 15, 1957, R 6, DuHe; *FR*, 1955–1957, Vol. XXIV, p. 165; RN interview, Oct 18, 2012, "Eisenhower Legacy Collection," C-SPAN3; Roberts, *First Rough Draft*, 270–271; Divine, *Sputnik*, 20; Mieczkowski, *Eisenhower's Sputnik Moment*, 187–188.

13. *New York Times*, Oct 15–16, 1957; *Newsweek*, Oct 28, 1957, p. 26.

14. Platter, Dec 3, 1957, RNyl.

15. RN to McMahon, Nov 21, B 773, United Pub, RN to Stout, Dec 4, B 732, Stout, G and RN statement, Dec 7, 1957, B 780, Vanguard, Series 320 and RN remarks, Feb 17, 1958, B 79, F 13, Series 207, RNln; RN to Wertz, Feb 11, 1958, PPS320.35.82, RNyl; RN excerpt, Jan 16, 1960, R 2, RNC; telephone call to RN, Dec 6, 1957, R 8, DuHe; meeting, Feb 7, 1958, R 6, Cabinet DDE; *New York Times*, Dec 7, 1957 and Oct 7 and 10, 1959; *FR*, 1955–1957, Vol. XIX, p. 693; *FR*, 1958–1960, Vol. III, pp. 348 and 373–374; Haines and Leggett eds., *CIA's Analysis*, 122–124; *Newsweek*, Feb 10, 1958, p. 31; Dickson, *Sputnik*, 172–176; Mieczkowski, *Eisenhower's Sputnik Moment*, 127–130.

16. Memo, Dec 26, 1957, R 4, DuHe; memo, July 16, 1958, B 91, F 3, Series 207, RNln; Halperin, "Gaither Committee," 360–384; Snead, *Gaither*; Adams, *Eisenhower's Fine Group of Fellows*, 171–192; Kaplan, *Wizards of Armageddon*, 125–143.

17. Garthoff, *Assessing the Adversary*, 41–42; Bundy, *Danger and Survival*, 334–350; Roman, *Eisenhower and the Missile Gap*, 60–62, 109–111, 146–149, 192–193 (quote on 193), and 200.

18. Memo, Oct 21, 1957, B 742, Symington, S, Series 320, RNln; McFarland, *Cold War*, 77–96; Barrett, *CIA & Congress*, 301–313; Olson, *Symington*, 326–337; Roman, *Ike and Missiles*, 140.

19. AP, Jan 12, B 742, Symington, S, Harkness radio, Jan 12 and memo, Jan 17, 1959, B 320, Harkness, R, Series 320, RNln; telephone call to RN, Aug 22, 1958, R 8, DuHe; *PPA* 1959, pp. 25–26; *Newsweek*, Jan 26, 1959, p. 26; Olson, *Symington*, 330–331; McFarland, *Cold War*, 87; Wenger, *Living with Peril*, 160; Bottome, *Missile Gap*, 50, 60, and 83.

20. *FR*, 1958–1960, Vol. III, pp. 356–357; Bose, *Shaping and Signaling*, 85–89; Garthoff, *Journey through the Cold War*, 47–48; Zaloga, *Kremlin's Nuclear Sword*, 60–62, 64–66, and 99–100; Bundy, *Danger and Survival*, 350–351.

21. Brady, *Eisenhower and Adenauer*, 8–15.

22. Ibid., 57–87 and 149–191; Kastner, "Ambivalent Ally," 43 and 49–148.

23. Brady, *Eisenhower and Adenauer*, 197–224 and 232–250; Bundy, *Danger and Survival*, 358–361 and 371–378; Haslam, *Russia's Cold War*, 176–180; Schick, *Berlin Crisis*, 3–133; Taubman, *Khrushchev*, 396–408; Kastner, "Ambivalent Ally," 192–209 and 229–342; Burr, "Avoiding the Slippery Slope," 177–205.

24. Brady, *Eisenhower and Adenauer*, 232–250; Smyser, *Kennedy and the Berlin Wall*, 6–21.
25. J. Eisenhower, *Strictly Personal*, 213; *PPA* 1959, p. 196.
26. Memo, Mar 6, 1959, B 727, Steele, Ja, Series 320, RNln; RN to Adenauer, Sept 23, 1959, PPS320.33a.24, RNyl; memos, Mar 6 and 26, R 20, staff notes, Aug 13, 1959, R 22 and telephone calls, Apr 26, 1960, R 25, Diary DDE; meeting, Mar 13, 1959, R 8, Cabinet DDE; Taubman, *Khrushchev*, 408–412; Trachtenberg, *Constructed Peace*, 251–282; Erdmann, "War No Longer Has," 112.
27. Memo, Jan 15, 1960, B 226, Drummond ½, Series 320, RNln; RN, unpublished memoirs, RNyl.
28. *Washington Post*, Apr 5, B 102, F 2, Series 207, RN to Bales, Apr 6, B 61, Bales, J and press release, Apr 15, 1959, B 229, Dulles ½, Series 320, RNln; memo, Apr 12–15, 1959, PPS325(1959), RNyl; telephone call to RN, Apr 13 and 16, 1959, R 8, DuHe.
29. Nixon, "Unforgettable JFD," 103–104; *New York Times*, Apr 24, 1959.
30. Meeting, May 15, 1959, R 9, Cabinet DDE; memo, May 18, 1959, B 833, Wright, Co, Series 320, RNln; RN OH 111, p. 42, Russell mss, WJBma; Nixon, *RN*, 204; RN, *Leaders*, 36.
31. Mossman and Stark, *Last Salute*, 132–142.
32. Roy Rubottom OH, 86, JFD OH; Nixon, "VP Writes About Dulles," *Life*, June 8, 1959, pp. 34–37; *Newsweek*, June 1, 1959, p. 32. Gray, *Eighteen Acres*, 287–288.
33. Roy Rubottom OH, 84–85, JFD OH.
34. *PDDE*, XIX, pp. 1315–1316.
35. Memo, Apr 12–15, 1959, PPS325, RNyl; RN OH 111, pp. 37–40, JFD OH; Day 4, Tape 1, 00:37:25 [RN], Gannon mss, WJBma; Colburn, "RN Interview," The Eisenhower Legacy Collection, C-SPAN 3, Oct 18, 2012.

CHAPTER 31. A NEAR-DEATH EXPERIENCE

1. RN to Suarez, July 14, 1956, B 738, Suarez and N to Hoes, Mar 25, 1957, B 346, Hoes, Series 320, RNln; Earl Mazo wrote the chapter in *Six Crises* on Nixon's South American trip, and a shorter version is found in Nixon, *RN*. RN to McCormick, Aug 8, B 494, McCormick, K and RN to St. Johns, Aug 16, 1961, B 667, St. Johns [2/3], Series 320, RNln. Zahniser and Weis, "A Diplomatic Pearl Harbor?," do not use Nixon's vice-presidential manuscripts; I have relied on them and the following for background: Pope, "Foundations of," 314–344, uses Nixon's vice-presidential papers; Wellman, "VP Nixon's Trip to South America, 1958," and McCann, "V-P Nixon's Trip to South America, 1958" are two useful master's theses.
2. *PDDE*, XVIII, p. 631.
3. JDF to DE, Jan 7, R 4, telephone calls to Rubottom, Jan 22, R 7 and press conf, Apr 1, 1958, R 4, DuHe; *FR*, 1958–1960, Vol. V, pp. 222–223.
4. Don – Bill, Mar 15, 1958, B 10, RN memos, Series 401, RNln; Platter, Aug 16, 1961, RNyl.
5. Diary, Apr 16, 1958, R 2, Cabot mss, DDEL; Cabot, *First Line*, 104–105.
6. Memo, Mar 19, B 82, F 7, Series 207 and RN to Bates, Apr 9, 1958, B 66, Bates, C, Series 320, RNln.

7. Calendar, Mar 24, PPS212(1958).3 and diary, Apr 27, 1958, PPS212(1958).1, RNyl; press release, Mar 21, B 84, F 17, Series 207, intelligence briefing, Apr 25, B 10, Series 401, Woods to Hannah, Apr 26, B 451, Lightfoot, E and Gaunt to Cotton, May 1, 1958, B 183, Cotton, A, Series 320, RNln; Dick to Mother, Mar 21, 1958, B 8, F 3, Kornitzer mss, DUla.

8. *Los Angeles Times*, Apr 27, 1958.

9. Press release, Apr 25, B 10, Latin America—Programs, Series 401, RNln; special staff note, Apr 24, 1958, R 16, Diary DDE; Roy Rubottom OH, 38–39, JFD OH.

10. Memo, Apr 28, 1958, B 1, Montevideo, Series 397, RNln; *New York Times* and *Los Angeles Times*, Apr 28 and 29, 1958; *Newsweek*, Apr 28, p. 48 and May 12, 1958, p. 57; Roy Rubottom OH, 40, JFD OH.

11. Hagerty to McElroy, Mar 2, 1959, R 3, Diary DDE; Walters, *Silent Missions*, 315–316.

12. Memo, Nov 3, 1955, PPS422(1955).49.8 and *Diplomat*, Jan 1956, PPS336(1955).Supplement A.91, RNyl; memo on Batlle, Apr 28 and 29, 1958, B 1, Montevideo, Series 397, RNln; *FR*, 1958–1960, Vol. V, p. 915.

13. Woodward to RN, May 10, 1958, B 1, Montevideo, Series 397, RNln; *New York Times* and *Evening Star* (DC), Apr 30, 1958; Roy Rubottom OH, 40–41, JFD OH.

14. Nolan memo, May 2, 1958, B 1, Montevideo, Series 397, RNln.

15. *Los Angeles Times*, Apr 30, 1958.

16. Staff notes, Mar 3, 1958, R 16, Diary DDE; press release, Mar 13, B 3, South American Trip, Series 390, Herter to RN, Mar 13, B 1, South American trip, Series 397 and DE to Embassy, Apr 19, 1958, B 1, Argentina, Series 401, RNln; *PDDE*, XIX, pp. 841–842; *New York Times* and *Los Angeles Times*, May 1, 1958; Sheinin, *Argentina and US*, 113–115.

17. Summary report, June 19, 1958, B 1, Buenos Aires, Series 397, RNln; *FR*, 1958–1960, Vol. V, pp. 477–478; *New York Times* and *Los Angeles Times*, May 1, 1958; Gonzalez, "U.S.-Argentine Relations in the 1950s," 346.

18. *New York Times* and *Los Angeles Times*, May 2, 1958; *Newsweek*, May 12, 1958, p. 57; Tulchin, *Argentina and US*, 119–120; Walters, *Silent Missions*, 316.

19. Romualdi to RN, May 16 and RN to Romualdi, June 16, 1958, B 654, Romualdi [2/2], Series 320, RNln; *FR*, 1958–1960, Vol. V, p. 479; *Los Angeles Times*, May 2, 1958.

20. Supplemental to staff notes, May 10, 1958, R 17, Diary DDE; *FR*, 1958–1960, Vol. V, pp. 482–483; *Los Angeles Times* and *New York Times*, May 3, 1958.

21. *Sunday Star* (DC), *Los Angeles Times*, and *New York Times*, May 4, 1958; Walters, *Silent Missions*, 317.

22. RN statement, May 4, B 6, Paraguay, Series 401, Hilton to state dept, May 6, B 2, South American trip—misc (1 of 2), Series 390 and Carter to state dept, May 16, 1958, B 1, Asuncion, Series 397, RNln; RN to Amberg, Oct 6, 1958, PPS320.75.13, RNyl; *Los Angeles Times* and *New York Times*, May 5, 1958; Walters, *Silent Missions*, 317–318.

23. Schedule, May 5 and 6, B 1, Schedule, Series 392 and Bonsal to Rubottom, May 2, 1958, B 1, South American trip, Series 397, RNln; *Los Angeles Times* and *New York Times*, May 6, 1958; McCann, "VP Nixon's," 53–56; Wellman, "VP Nixon," 58–59; Walters, *Silent Missions*, 318–319.

24. Memos and Bonsal to state dept, May 5, B 1, La Paz, Series 397 and RN remarks and memo, May 5, 1958, B 2, Bolivia, Series 401, RNln; *FR*, 1958–1960, Vol. V, p. 654; *Evening Star* (DC), May 7, 1958; Lehman, *Bolivia and US*, 131–133.
25. RN to Rector, May 6, 1958, B 3, Bolivia, Series 401, RNln; *Evening Star* (DC), *Los Angeles Times*, and *New York Times*, May 7, 1958.
26. RN to Coon, Apr 9, 1958, B 179, Coon, S, Series 320, RNln.
27. Achilles to Bernbaum, Apr 29, 1958, B 7, Peru—misc., Series 401, RNln; Achilles memoirs tell a different story, 619–620, Achilles mss, LLC.
28. Macomber to RN, May 13, 1959, PPS320.76.136, RNyl; Patch, "Nixon in Peru," 8–9; *Newsweek*, May 19, 1958, p. 59; Carey, *Peru and US*, 11–12, 186–198, and 222.
29. Patch, "Nixon in Peru," 1; *New York Times* and *Los Angeles Times*, May 8, 1958.
30. Memos, May 4 and 7, B 7, Peru—maps, Achilles to state dept, May 9, 1958, B 7, Peru—background, Series 401, RNln; Achilles memoirs, 621–623, Achilles mss, LLC; *Los Angeles Times* and *New York Times*, May 8, 1958.
31. Achilles to RN, June 2 and RN to Achilles, June 20, 1958, B 18, Achilles, Series 320, RNln; Achilles memoirs, 623–624, Achilles mss, LLC; Walters, *Silent Missions*, 320–321.
32. Telephone call to Snow, May 14, 1958, R 7, DuHe; Achilles memoirs, 624, Achilles mss, LLC; *New York Times*, May 9, 1958.
33. Achilles to state dept, May 12, B 2, loose material (1 of 3), Series 390, schedule, May 7 and 8, B 1, schedule, Series 392, memo, May 8, Salvatierra to state dept, May 20 and Achilles to state department, May 27, B 1, Lima, Series 397 and memos, May 4 and 7, Peru—maps and Achilles to state dept, May 9, 1958, B 7, Peru—background, Series 401, RNln; Patch, "Nixon in Peru," 1–7 and 10; RN interview, May 1958, B 47, p. 3, Alsop mss, LOC; Achilles memoirs, 624–625; *New York Times*, May 8 and 9, *Los Angeles Times*, May 9 and *Evening Star* (DC), May 9, 1958; Don Hughes lecture, Jan 10, 2011, RNyl; Walters, *Silent Missions*, 321–323.
34. Key to McGill, June 3, 1958, B 3, South American trip—press, Series 390, RNln; *Los Angeles Times*, May 9, 1958; Achilles memoirs, 626; Patch, "Nixon in Peru," 2; Walters, *Silent Missions*, 324.
35. Achilles to state dept, May 14, B 1, Lima, Series 397 and memo, May 16, 1958, B 3, South American trip, Series 390, RNln; Achilles memoirs, 626–627, Achilles mss, LLC; *Los Angeles Times*, May 9, 1958; Walters, *Silent Missions*, 323–324.
36. PPA 1958, pp. 390–391; Hagerty to RN, May 9, 1958, B 310, Hagerty, J, Series 320, RNln.
37. *Los Angeles Times*, *Evening Star* (DC) and *New York Times*, May 10, 1958; Walters, *Silent Missions*, 325.
38. *Los Angeles Times* and *New York Times*, May 11, 1958.
39. *New York Times*, May 5, *Evening Star* (DC), May 5 and 12 and *Los Angeles Times*, May 12, 1958; Achilles memoirs, 105, Achilles mss, LLC; Hartlyn, "Military Governments and the Transition," 248–272; Randall, *Colombia and US*, 204–207; Coleman, *Colombia and US*, 138–171.
40. Cabot to JFD, Apr 25, 1958, R 2, Cabot mss, DDEL; schedule, May 11, B 1, Schedule, Series 392, memo, May 11, B 1, State Docs, Wells to state dept, May 21, B 1, Bogota,

memo, May 11, 1958 B 3, Colombia—thank you (2 of 2), Series 401, RNln; RN to Lleras Camargo, May 13, 1958, PPS320,21.14, RNyl; *Los Angeles Times*, May 10, 1958; platter, Aug 16, 1961, RNyl; *PPA* 1958, pp. 473–474.

41. Pre-press conf notes, Jan 15, 1958, R 15, Diary DDE; telephone memo, Jan 21, 1958, R 7, DuHe; McCann, "VP Nixon's," 70–73; Liss, *Diplomacy & Dependency*, 154–159; Rabe, *Road to OPEC*, 117–134; McPherson, in *Yankee No!*, stated: "The [Caracas] incident brought a climax to protests that marred every stop on Nixon's itinerary" (p. 9); this statement is false and is regularly repeated; a few examples are Jones, *Crucible of Power*, 316; Kolko, *Confronting the Third World*, 108; and Sheinin, *Argentina and US*, 91.

42. Roy Rubottom OH, 39, JFD OH; Manny Chavez, "Just Why Did Nixon Go to Venezuela in 1958 Anyway?," HNN, May 3, 2015.

43. Casler to RN, Apr 8, 1958, B 9, Venezuela—misc #2, Series 401, RNln; Olson, "You Can't Spit," 29 and 31.

44. Memo, Apr 22 and Sparks to state dept, B 9, Venezuela—Maps #2, memo, undated, B 10, int. briefing, B Series 401, Sparks to state dept, May 21, 1958, B 1, Caracas— Report, Series 397, RNln; *New York Times*, May 5 and 12, 1958.

45. Memo, May 13, B 3, South American trip—USA, Series 390, Cates memo, after May 15, 1958, B 1, Caracas—Report, Series 397 and Sherwood to Agnes, Aug 25, 1961, B 1, South American trip, Series 388, RNln; *Los Angeles Times* and *Evening Star* (DC), May 13, 1958; telephone call, May 15, 1958, R 7, DuHe; Day 9, Tape 3, 00:16:28 [RN], Gannon mss, WJBma; Roy Rubottom OH, 42, JFD OH; Walters, *Silent Missions*, 328.

46. Schedule, May 13 and 14, B 1, Schedule, Series 392 and Moskowitz memo, May 21, 1958, B 1, Caracas—Report, Series 397, RNln; Olson, "You Can't Spit," 33; Day 9, Tape 3, 00:16:28 [RN], Gannon mss, WJBma; *Evening Star* (DC), *New York Times* and *Los Angeles Times*, May 13, 1958; Walters, *Silent Missions*, 328–329.

47. Memo, May 12 and Moskowitz memo, May 21, 1958, B 1, Caracas—Report, Series 397 and Sherwood memo, July 6, 1960, B 691, Sherwood, J, Series 320, RNln; Olson, "You Can't Spit," 32–33; Walters, *Silent Missions*, 329–330.

48. Moskowitz memo, May 21, B 1, Caracas—Report, Series 397 and Editorial, May 25, 1958, B 1, Series 389, RNln; Olson, "You Can't Spit," 33–34 and 36; Walters, *Silent Missions*, 330; Donald Hughes lecture, Jan 10, 2011, at the Nixon library.

49. *New York Herald Tribune*, May 14, B 2, S.A., South American trip—Caracas, Series 340, Annex No. 1, 2, and 3, May 21 and Burrows to state dept, June 9, B 1, Caracas— Report, Series 397 and Woods to Ports, June 23, 1958, B 605, Ports, memo, Mar 5, B 322, Harris, Ele and memo, July 6, 1960, B 691, Sherwood, J, Series 320, RNln; *FR*, 1958–1960, Vol. V, pp. 226–227; *Los Angeles Times* and *New York Times*, May 13–15, 1958; Robert Cushman OH, 23–27, DDEL; Donald Hughes lecture, Jan 10, 2011, at the Nixon library; Day 9, Tape 3, 00:16:28 [RN] and 00:23: 53 [RN], Gannon mss, WJBma; Walters, *Silent Missions*, 330–332; Baughman, *Secret Service Chief*, 246–248.

50. Rex Scouten said that Sherwood told him that Nixon was in mortal danger. Rex Scouten telephone interview, Apr 22, 2010; Achilles memoirs, 629, Achilles mss, LLC; Day 9, Tape 3, 00:24:26 [RN] and 00:24:27 [RN], Gannon mss, WJBma; RN OH 111, pp. 23–24, Russell mss, WJBma.

51. Los Angeles Times, May 14, 1958; Olson, "You Can't Spit," 37; interview with Donald Hughes, Jan 20, 2011, at the Nixon library; Day 9, Tape 4, 00:24:48 [RN] and 00:43:35 [RN], Gannon mss, WJBma; Walters, *Silent Missions*, 332–333.

52. Editorial, May 25, B 1, Series 389 and Baker memo, June 18, 1958, B 2, South American Trip—Misc (1 of 2), Series 390, RNln; Olson, "You Can't Spit," 34; Day 9, Tape 3, 00:16:28 [RN] and 00:25:34 [RN], Gannon mss, WJBma; telephone interview with Donald Hughes, July 8, 2003; Walters, *Silent Missions*, 332–333.

53. Baker memo, June 18, 1958, B 2, South American Trip—Misc (1of 2), Series 390, RNln; Olson, "You Can't Spit," 34; *New York Times* and *Los Angeles Times*, May 14, 1958.

54. Memo, May 13, B 1, Caracas—Report and memo, May 19, 1958, B 1, South American Trip, Series 397 and RN to Buchanan, Apr 25, 1961, B 302, Great D, Series 320, RNln; memo, July 9, 1959, RNyl; *FR*, 1958–1960, Vol. V, p. 237; 00:16:28 [RN], Gannon mss, WJBma.

55. Olson, "You Can't Spit," 34; platter, Aug 16, 1961, RNyl.

56. Walters, *Silent Missions*, 334–335; Olson, "You Can't Spit,"39.

57. *Los Angeles Times*, May 14, 1958; platter, Aug 16, 1961, RNyl.

58. Sherwood to Agnes, Aug 25, 1961, B 1, South American Trip, Series 388, RNln.

59. Memo, May, B 84, F 17, Series 207, RN to White, May 23, B 3, South American Trip—Staff, Series 390 and memo, Aug 23, 1961, B 10, RN memos, Series 401, RNln; Olson, "You Can't Spit," 35–36; telephone interview with Donald Hughes, May 19, 2011.

60. Donovan, *Confidential Secretary*, 122; Olson, "You Can't Spit," 38; Connelly, *Diplomatic Revolution*, 168–169.

61. Clark to Hughes, Sept 15, 1958, RNyl; M. Eisenhower to Roorda, July 19, 1983, Gellman mss, DDEL.

62. Telephone call from Knowland, May 13, 1958, R 7, DuHe; *FR*, 1958–1960, Vol. V, pp. 228–230; Cabot to Wells, May 20, 1958, R 2, Cabot mss, DDEL.

63. *FR*, 1958–1960, Vol. V, pp. 229–232; *Los Angeles Times* and *New York Times*, May 14, 1958.

64. *FR*, 1958–1960, Vol. V, pp. 232–235; memo, May 21, 1958, B 1, Caracas—Report, Series 397, RNln.

65. Memo, May 13, 1958, B 1, Caracas—Report, Series 397, RNln; I would like to thank Jeffrey Barlow of the Naval History and Museums Command at the Navy Yard for identifying Rear Admiral Miller's first name and job description, Mar 4, 2014.

66. Telephone call to Snow, May 14, R 7 and telephone call from DE and telephone call from Hagerty, May 14, 1958, DuHe; telephone calls, May 14, 1958, R 17, Diary DDE; *FR*, 1958–1960, Vol. V, pp. 235–236; Olson, "You Can't Spit," 36.

67. *PPA* 1958, pp. 395–400; telephone call from Knowland, R 7 and telephone calls from Adams and telephone call to Hagerty, May 14, 1958, R 10, DuHe; Morrow, *Black Man in the WH*, 219–220.

68. *Evening Star* (DC), *New York Times*, and *Los Angeles Times*, May 14–15, 158; Olson, "You Can't Spit," 36–38; Donald Hughes lecture, Jan 10, 2011, Nixon library; Walters, *Silent Missions*, 336–337.

69. Grubb to RN, May 14 and RN to Grubb, May 29, 1959, B 306, Grubb, D, Series 320 and Woods to Key, June 20, 1958, B 1 South American Trip, Series 388, RNln; *PDDE*, XIX, pp. 899–900.

70. RN to Taylor, May 21, 1958, B 746, Taylor, MD, Series 320, RNln; Olson, "You Can't Spit," 35; Walters, *Silent Missions*, 337.

71. RN to Chandler, June 20, 1958, B 142, Chandler ½, Series 320, RNln.

72. RN to Munoz, June 17, 1958, B 613, Puerto Rico (2 of), Series 320, RNln; *New York Times* and *Evening Star* (DC), May 15, 1958; LaFeber, in *Inevitable Revolutions*, stated after the demonstrations in South America: "Only in Somoza's Nicaragua had Nixon's reception been all the vice-president could have desired, and he ever after felt a special warmth toward the dictator" (p. 136); when LaFeber published a revised edition, the same material was repeated. Nixon never stopped in Nicaragua; he went directly to Puerto Rico.

73. Lavine ed., *Smoke-Filled Rooms*, 174–178.

74. Diary, May 15, 1958, B 10, Ann Whitman diary, DDE; *PDDE*, XXI, p. 2393; *PPA* 1958, pp. 411–412; *Evening Star* (DC), May 14–16, *Los Angeles Times*, May 15 and *New York Times*, May 16, 1958; memoirs, Feb 16, 1976, RNyl; Prescott Bush OH 31, pp. 335–336, CCOH; Horace Busy OH, VIII, pp. 2–4, LBJL; Baker, *Good Times*, 289; Kornitzer, *Real Nixon*, 87.

75. Schedule, May 15, 1958, R 17, Diary DDE; *New York Times*, *Los Angeles Times*, and *Evening Star* (DC), May 16, 1958.

76. Memo of May 15, May 19, 1958, R 17, Diary DDE.

77. Memo on agenda, May 14, minute, May 16 and record of action, May 17, 1958, R 7, Cabinet DDE; *FR*, 1958–1960, Vol. V, pp. 238–239; platter, Aug 16, 1961, RNyl; RN to Kersten, May 19, 1958, Kersten mss; *Los Angeles Times* and *Evening Star* (DC), May 18, 1958; Larson, *President Nobody Knew*, 100–101.

78. Memo with DE, May 18, memos and conversations, R 4, telephone call with Herter, May 18, R 7, press conf, May 20, 1958, R 66, DuHe.

79. RN address, May 21, B 86, F 3 and Rubottom to RN, May 22, 158, B 661, Rubottom, Series 320, RNln; RN to Kornitzer, May 29 and RN to Senora, Sept 15, 1958, B 8, F 5, Kornitzer mss, DUla.

80. *FR*, 1958–1960, Vol. V, pp. 239–245 and Vol. X, Part 1, pp. 15–16; Cutler to RN, May 9, 1958, PPS320.55.6A and platter, Aug 16, 1961, RNyl; A. Dulles to RN, May 28, 1958, B 228, Dulles, A, Series 320, RNln; Cull, *Cold War and the USIA*, 157.

81. Day 9, Tape 3, 00:16:28, Gannon mss, WJBma.

82. *FR*, 1958–1960, Vol. V, p. 238; *New York Times*, May 11 and June 22, *Los Angeles Times*, May 11 and 18, *Evening Star* (DC), May 18, 1958.

83. RN to Hoover, June 10, 1958, PPS320.103.134, RNyl; RN to Mervar, June 12, B 2, Argentina—Misc, Series 401 and RN to Chotiner, June 23, 1958, B 147, Chotiner (1957–1958), Series 320, RNln; *FR*, 1958–1960, Vol. V, pp. 81–82.

84. RN to Rojas, July 21, 1958, PPS320.5.100(1), RNyl; RN address, July 9, B 90, Series 207 and RN to North, Aug 19, 1958, B 565, North, R, Series 320, RNln; *FR*, 1958–1960, Vol. XVI, p. 101.

85. Memo, Sept 18, B 10, memoirs, Series 401, RN to North, Aug 19, B 565, North, R and RN to Burger, Dec 15, 1958, B 113, Burger, G, Series 320, RNln; Roy Rubottom OH, 36–37, JFD OH.
86. Rubottom to Cushman, B 661, Rubottom, RN to Roberts, July 7, B 645, Roberts, Cl, memo, Sept 18, B 409, Key, W, RN to Hartmann, Dec 31, 1958, B 323, Hartmann (3 of 3) and memo, May 25, 1959, B 649, Rock and Roll, Series 320, RNln; *FR*, 1958–1960, Vol. IV, p. 421 and Vol. V, p. 28.
87. M. Eisenhower OH, 10–11, LBJL; Stroder ed., *"Let Us Begin Anew,"* 222.
88. M. Eisenhower, *President Is Calling*, 326.

CHAPTER 32. INSIDE AND OUTSIDE THE KITCHEN

1. Alexander, *Holding the Line*, 249, claimed that Ike "placed little importance on the trip and certainly did not see it as a prelude to Khrushchev's visit." Wills, *Nixon Agonistes*, 125, stated that RN wanted to make this trip to help his presidential bid; Ike "gave him no help at all." These erroneous views are widely held.
2. *Daily News* (DC), May 13, PPS336(1955).120, *Chicago American*, July 28, PPS336(1955).175, and *U.S. News & World Report*, Aug 19, 1955, PPS336(1955).232, RNyl; memo, Aug 22, 1955, B 12, chronological series, Aug 1955 (3), DuHe; *New York Times*, Aug 20, 1955; *FR*, 1955–1957, Vol. XXIV, p. 33.
3. Memo, Jan 24, 1958, PPS320.82.6.1, RNyl; RN to Irwin, Feb 5, 1958, B 79, F 9, Series 207, RNyl; *New York Times*, Jan 25 and 26, 1958, *Newsweek*, Feb 3, 1958, pp. 19–20.
4. Memo, Feb 11, 1958, PPS320.82.11.2, RNyl; *Washington Post*, Feb 13, 1958, B 79, F 7, Series 207, RNln; *New York Times*, Feb 2, 1958.
5. *San Diego Union*, June 3, PPS320.82.51A and memo, Nov 20, 1958, PPS320.82.51A, RNyl; *FR*, 1958–1960, Vol. X, P 2, pp. 19–22. Wills, *Nixon Agonistes*, 124, stated that RN was not asked to make the trip; he volunteered.
6. Lodge to DE, Feb 9, 1959, R 4, Lodge mss, MHS; RN to Kersten, Mar 6, 1959, Kersten mss, MLsc; *PPA* 1959, pp. 26–27; *New York Times*, Jan 28, 1959; *FR*, 1958–1960, Vol. X, P 1, p. 326; Vladimir Toumanoff OH, 83–84, Association for Diplomatic Studies; S. Khrushchev, *Nikita Khrushchev and the Creation*, 196.
7. *PPA* 1959, pp. 141–142.
8. ABC program, Feb 17, B 100, F 3, Series 207 and RN to McClellan, Mar 26, 1959, B 534, Moscow T, Series 320, RNln.
9. RN to Nippe, Apr 27, 1959, PPS320.82.86, RNyl; *PPA* 1959, pp. 330–331.
10. *FR*, 1958–1960, Vol. X, P 1, p. 327; RN, "VP Writes," 36; Krock, *In the Nation*, 302–303.
11. RN to Bassett, May 11, B 66, Bassett, J (1), Series 320 and Memo, July 17, 1959, B 1, Instructions, Series 407, RNln.
12. RN to Allard, June 10, 1959, B 26, Allard, J, Series 320, RNln.
13. *New York Times*, June 30 and July 5, 1959; *Newsweek*, July 13, 1959, pp. 18–19; Haddow, *Pavilions of Plenty*, 207–208.
14. *New York Times*, June 30 and July 14, 1959; Haddow, *Pavilions of Plenty*, 207–208; S. Khrushchev, *Khrushchev and the Creation*, 677–679.

15. Telephone calls, July 8, memo, July 13 and 20, R 22 and DE to Voroshilov, July 20, 1959, OF, P 2, R 29, Diary DDE; *PPA* 1959, pp. 506–509 and 515; Tocchet, "September Thaw," 76–80.

16. Calendar, July 20–22, 1959, PPS212(1959).4, RNyl; RN to Nelsen, July 2, B 1, F Outside US, Series 317 and memo, July 11, B 226, Drummond ½ and RN to Herter, Aug 28, 1959, B 334, Herter 102, Series 320, RNln.

17. Thompson to Merchant, Apr 20, 1959, PPS325, RNyl; *FR*, 1958–1960, Vol. X, P 1, pp. 326–328; Thompson "was wonderful" during the visit according to Donald Hughes, interview on May 19, 2011; Salisbury, *Journey for Our Times*, 474.

18. RN briefing, July 13, CIA-RDP62/S00545A000100080011-7, briefing RN and M. Eisenhower, July 15, CIA-RDP62S00545A000100080012-5 and monthly report, Aug 4, 1959, CIA-RDP62S00231A000100210041-6, CREST; telephone interview with Raymond Garthoff, Mar 9, 2011; Garthoff, "Intelligence Aspects," 1–5; Garthoff, *Journey through the Cold War*, 1–23 and 39–86.

19. Memos, May 8 and July 8, *Evening Star* (DC), July 11, B 321, Harriman and RN to Eaton, July 1, 1959, B 233, Eaton, C Series 320, RNln; military power gains, Aug 18, 1959, OF, R 11, Dulles, A, OF DDE; *FR*, 1958–1960, Vol. III, p. 318; *PPA* 1959, p. 507; *New York Times*, July 11, 1959; Time, July 13, 1959, p. 18; Abramson, *Spanning Century*, 573.

20. RN to Kersten, July 17, 1959, Kersten mss, MLsc; RN to Bukota, July 21, 1959, B 1, Letter Copies, Series 408, RNln; *PDDE*, XXI, p. 2492; Day 4, Tape 1, 00:34:31 [RN], Gannon mss, WJBma.

21. Memos, July 17 and 19, 1959, B 1, Ideas and Suggestions, Series 407, RNln; Garthoff notes on mss, Gellman mss, DDEL.

22. Memos, May 6 and July 19, B 1, RN instructions, Series 407, *Evening Star* (DC), July 31, *San Jose Mercury*, Aug 4 and *Albany Times-Union*, Aug 8, B 4, USSR trip, Series 413, *Pittsburgh Sun-Telegram*, B 1, Hearst, Series 402 and memo, Dec 7, 1959, B 425, Kornitzer (4 of 4), Series 320, RNln; *New York Times*, July 27 and 31 and Aug 1, 1959; Haddow, *Pavilions of Plenty*, 211–212.

23. Washburn to M. Eisenhower, May 25, B 1, Quito, Peru, Series 397 and M. Eisenhower to RN, May 26, 1959, B 238, Eisenhower 2/2, Series 320, RNln; pre-press briefing, June 17, 1959, R 22, Diary DDE; *PPA* 1959, p. 493; M. Eisenhower OH, 9, LBJL; *Times-Picayune* (La), Aug 22, 1959; *New York Times Magazine*, Aug 22, 1959; Vladimir Toumanoff OH, 85–87, Association for Diplomatic Studies; M. Eisenhower, *President Is Calling*, 326–327.

24. Memo, Aug 22, Prentice to Wilson, Sept 23, 1959, Rickover to RN, Aug 18, 1961 and Barcelia to RN, Dec 4, 1962, B 642, Rickover, Series 320, RNln; Day 1, Tape 4, 00:14:54 [RN], Gannon mss, WJBma; Vladimir Toumanoff OH, 87, Association for Diplomatic Studies; *New York Times*, July 25, 1959; Rockwell, *Rickover Effect*, 265–267; Polar and Allen, *Rickover*, 222 and 553.

25. Woods to McLaughlin, June 1, B 505, McWhorter, Woods to Chotiner, July 13, B 147, Chotiner 1957–58, RN to Pate, Sept 15, B 197, Cushman, Bob and memo, Sept 23, 1959, Series 320, RNln; Robert Cushman OH, 36, DDEL.

26. RN to Bassett, May 11, B 66, Bassett, J (1), Klein to Brown, Aug 10, B 235, Editor & Pub, Emory to RN, Aug 11, B 243, Emory, Barcella to RN, Aug 15, B 62, Barcella, RN

to Gross, Sept 3, B 306, Gross, R, Klein to Eastabrook, Sept 4, B 246, Eastabrook and RN to Copley, Sept 7, 1959, B 180, Copley [1/2], Series 320, Finch to Goodman, June 1, B 1, Russian Trip—Misc, Series 411, RNln; Herbert Klein OH 198, pp. 38–39, CCOH.

27. Press release, Sept 12, 1959, B 416, Klein 1958–59 (1 of 3), Series 320, RNln.

28. *PPA* 1959, p. 536.

29. Memo, July 21 and pre-press briefing, July 22, 1959, R 22, Diary DDE; *PDDE*, XX, p. 1586; *New York Times*, July 23, 1959.

30. Telephone calls, July 22, 1959, R 22, Diary DDE.

31. Memo, July 22, 1959, R 22, Diary DDE; *FR*, 1958–1960, Vol. X, P 1, pp. 332–333.

32. *New York Times*, July 15–24, 1959; *New York Times Magazine*, Sept 13, 1959, pp. 24, 96, 99, 101, 103, 106, and 108; *Time*, July 27, 1959; Khrushchev ed., *Memoirs of Khrushchev*, Vol. 3, pp. 637–638 and 1027.

33. *New York Times*, July 17, 1959.

34. Ibid., July 22, 1959; *New York Herald Tribune*, July 22–23, 1959.

35. Pre-press briefing, July 22 and memo, Aug 6, 1959, R 22, Diary DDE; *PPA* 1959, pp. 536–537 and 541; *FR*, 195–1960, Vol. X, P 1, pp. 99–100 and 338; Nixon, *RN*, 205–206; Kovrig, *Myth of Liberation*, 229–231.

36. *Newsweek*, July 27, 1959, pp. 39–42; Mazo, *Nixon*, 294–295.

37. Hill to RN, Apr 24 and RN to Hill, May 21, 1959, B 340, Hill, RC, RNln; calendar, July 22, PPS212(1959).2 and RN to Muccio, Aug 17, 1959, PPS30.41.14, RNyl; Trip to Russia (4), pp. 1–4; *PDDE*, XX, pp. 1466–1467 and 1589–1590; *New York Times*, July 23, 1959.

38. RN to Cutler, July 20, B 198, Cutler, R, Morgan broadcast, July 23, B 529, Morgan [1/2] and *Evening Star* (DC), July 24, 1959, B 498, McGill [2/3], Series 320, RNln; *New York Times*, July 24, 1959; *Times-Picayune*, Aug 8 and 9, 1959; Hearst, *Ask Me*, 188–189.

39. *Des Moines Register* (Io), July 24, 1959, USSR Trip, Series 414, RNln; *New York Times*, July 24, 1959; Khrushchev ed., *Memoirs of Khrushchev*, Vol. 3, p. 1027.

40. *New York Times*, July 24, 1959; *New York Herald Tribune*, July 24, 1959; *Atlanta Constitution*, July 25, 1959; Hearst, *Ask Me*, 189.

41. Memo, Apr 21, B 1, Ideas and Suggestions, Series 407 and RN to Shattuck, June 1, 1959, B 688, Shattuck 1959, Series 320, RNln; Vladimir Toumanoff OH, 74 and 80–81, Association for Diplomatic Studies; Nixon, *RN*, 206.

42. Memo, June 17, PPS325A.3.1, report, July 23 to Aug 5, 1959, PPS325A.20.3.2, memo, Apr 28, 1976, PPS325A.20.6 and memo, Mar 22, 1978, PPS325A.1, RNyl; *PPA* 1959, pp. 750–751; telephone calls with Jack Golden, July 2 and Donald Hughes July 3, 2001; Garthoff, "Intelligence Aspects," 5; Garthoff notes on mss, Gellman mss, DDEL.

43. Morgan broadcast, July 24, 1959, B 529, Morgan [1/2], Series 320, RNln; Day 1, Tape 5, 01:08:21 [RN], Gannon mss, WJBma; *FR*, 1958–1960, Vol. X, P 1, pp. 334 and 337; Khrushchev ed., *Memoirs of Khrushchev*, Vol. 3, pp. 125 and 184–185; S. Khrushchev, *Khrushchev and the Creation*, 321–323; Nixon, *RN*, 206; M. Eisenhower, *President Is Calling*, 331.

44. *FR*, 1958–1960, Vol. X, P 1, pp. 333–336.

45. *FR*, 1958–1960, Vol. X, P 1, pp. 336–445; Day 4, Tape 1, 00:39:20 [RN] and 00:40:13 [RN] and Day 5, Tape 1, 00:19:30 [RN], Gannon mss, WJBma; RN, *RN*, 206–208; M. Eisenhower, *President Is Calling*, 327–328; Talbott, *Khrushchev Remembers* (1970),

388–367 and 458; S. Khrushchev ed., *Memoirs of Khrushchev*, Vol. 3, pp. 106–107; Salisbury, *Journey for Our Times*, 481.

46. Facts about, July 25–Sept 4, 1959, B 1, Facts, Series 404, RNln; *New York Times*, July 23–26, 29, 31, and Aug 2, 1959; *New York Herald Tribune*, July 23 and 25, 1959; cabinet agenda, May 18, R 9, Cabinet DDE; cabinet, May 22 and legislative meeting, June 30, R 21, staff notes, July 16 and 24 and memo, Sept 10, 1959, Diary DDE; *FR*, 1958–1960, Vol. X, P 2, pp. 26–28; *PPA* 1959, pp. 490–491; Tuttle, *Official Training Book*; Cull, *Cold War and the USIA*, 161–166; Reid, "Our Kitchen Is Just As Good," 154–161; Richmond, *U.S.-Soviet Cultural Exchanges*, 2–9 and 26; Belmonte, *Selling the American Way*, 87–93; J. Eisenhower, *Strictly Personal*, 234–235.

47. *New York Times*, July 25, 1959; Roorda, "President and His Boy," 64; George Allen OH 280, pp. 72–74, CCOH; Hearst, *Ask Me*, 191–193; Nixon, *RN*, 208; Frankel, *Times of My Life*, 172; Salisbury, *Journey for Our Times*, 482.

48. Conversation, July 24, B 1, Russian Trip, Series 411, RNln; *New York Times*, July 25, 1959; Day 4, Tape 1, 00:45:32 [RN] and 00:35:36 [RN] and Day 4, Tape 2, 00:02:31 [RN]. Gannon mss, WJBma; M. Eisenhower, *President Is Calling*, 328; Nixon, *RN*, 208.

49. *New York Times*, July 25 and 26, 1959; William Safire OH, 2008, Nixon presidential library; "1959 Kitchen Debate," on C-SPAN3, June 29, 2011; Day 4, Tape 1, 00:49:06 [RN], Day 4, Tape 2, 00:08:01 [RN] and 00:10:24 [RN], Gannon mss, WJBma; M. Eisenhower, *President Is Calling*, 328–331 and 333–334; Nixon, *RN*, 208–209; Khrushchev ed., *Memoirs of Khrushchev*, Vol. 3, pp. 182–184; Beam, *Multiple Exposure*, 270; Hearst, *Ask Me*, 195–197; Salisbury, *Journey for Our Times*, 482–483; Talbott, *Khrushchev Remembers* (1970), 364–366; Taubman, *Khrushchev*, 416–418; May, *Homeward Bound*, 162–164; Marling, *As Seen*, 243–283.

50. Stanton to RN, Aug 19, 1959, B 723, Stanton [2/2], Series 320, RNln; *FR*, 1958–1960, Vol. X, P 1, p. 329; *New York Times*, July 26–28 and 31, 1959; George Allen OH 280, pp. 78–86, DDEL; Carlson, *K Blows Top*, 28–31.

51. *FR*, 1958–1960, Vol. X, P 1, pp. 346–353; *New York Times*, July 28, 1959.

52. *FR*, 1958–1960, Vol. X, P 1, pp. 353–358.

53. *New York Times*, July 26, 1959.

54. Memo, Dec 7, 1959; B 425, Kornitzer (4 of 4), Series 320, RNln; *New York Times*, July 26, 1959; Day 4, Tape 1, 00:51:38 [RN], Gannon mss, WJBma; Hearst, *Ask Me*, 198–199; RN, *RN*, 209.

55. Memo, Dec 7, 1959, B 425, Kornitzer (4 of 4), Series 320, RNln; *New York Times*, July 27, 1959; Day 4, Tape 1, 00:54:17 [RN], Day 4, Tape 3, 00:38:59 [RN] and Day 5, Tape 1, 00:01:59 [RN], Gannon mss, WJBma; S. Khrushchev ed., *Memoirs of Khrushchev*, Vol. 3, pp. 1027–1028; Dobrynin, *In Confidence*, 197; S. Khrushchev, *Khrushchev and the Creation*, 324–325; Nixon, *Leaders*, 178–189; Thompson ed., *Eisenhower Presidency*, 11; Hearst, *Ask Me*, 198–200; Kornitzer, *Real Nixon*, 312–361.

56. RN remarks, Oct 5, 1959, B 117, F 4, Series 207, RNln; *FR*, 1958–1960, Vol. X, P 1, pp. 359–373 and Vol. XIX, p. 568; *New York Herald Tribune*, July 27–28, 1959; *New York Times*, July 27 and Aug 2, 1959; Day 4, Tape 2, 00:11:45 [RN], Gannon mss, WJBma; RN, *RN*, 209–212; Thompson ed., *Eisenhower Presidency*, 11; M. Eisenhower, *President Is Calling*, 327; S. Khrushchev, *Khrushchev and the Creation*, 325–326.

57. Nixon, *Leaders*, 193.

58. *New York Times*, July 27–29, 1959; *New York Herald Tribune*, July 28, 1959; *Atlanta Constitution*, July 29, 1959; *Times-Picayune* (La), Aug 14, 1959; Vladimir Toumanoff OH, 73–74, Association of Diplomatic Studies; Polar and Allen, *Rickover*, 553–554; Rockwell, *Rickover Effect*, 265–270.

59. *New York Times* and *New York Herald Tribune*, July 28 and 31, 1959.

60. *PPDE*, XX, p. 1594.

61. Novosibirsk mayor, July 28, B1, Greetings, Series 410 and Morgan broadcast, July 29, B 529, Morgan [2/2] and memo, Dec 7, 1959, B 425, Kornitzer (4 of 4), Series 320, RNln; *FR*, 1958–1960, Vol. 1, P 1, pp. 337–339; *New York Times*, July 29–30, 1959; *Atlanta Constitution*, July 31, 1959; *Times-Picayune* (La), Aug 15, 1959; Hearst, *Ask Me*, 202–204; Reston, *Sketches*, 116 and 237–239.

62. Garthoff notes on mss, Gellman mss, DDEL.

63. Memo, July 1959, B 213, De Toledano and Morgan broadcast, July 30, 1959, Series 320, RNln; Day 6, Tape 1, 00:34:40 [RN], Gannon mss, WJBma; *New York Times*, July 30–31 and Aug 1, 1959; *New York Herald Tribune*, July 30–31, 1959; *Times-Picayune* (La), Aug 11, 1959; *Atlanta Constitution*, Aug 1, 1959; Reston, *Sketches*, 116–118; Garthoff, *Assessing the Adversary*, 40–42; M. Eisenhower, *President Is Calling*, 332–333.

64. Memoirs, Mar 22, 1976, RNyl; RN to Bassett, Aug 10, B 66, Bassett, J (1), memo, Dec 7, 1959, B 425, Kornitzer (4 of 4), Elliott to Crick, May 10, B 239, Elliott, Wm 1960, Thompson to RN Aug 13 and RN to Thompson, Sept 8, 1960, B 755, Thompson, LE, Series 320 and Klein to Rhine, Aug 27, 1959, B 1, TV address, Series 408, RNln; *FR*, 1958–1960, Vol. X, P 1, p. 330; *New York Times* and *New York Herald Tribune*, Aug 1, 1959; Kornitzer, *Real Nixon*, 320; Nixon, *RN*, 212.

65. Klein to Daly, Sept 3, 1959, B 200, Daly, J, Series 320, RNln; *New York Herald Tribune*, Aug 3, 1959; Klein, *Making It*, 256–258; Hearst, *Ask Me*, 206; Kornitzer, *Real Nixon*, 320.

66. For copies of the speech, *New York Times*, Aug 2, 1959; Nixon, *Six Crises*, 435–442; Nixon, *Challenges We Face*, 235–246.

67. Beschloss, *Mayday*, 183; Vladimir Toumanoff OH, 85–87, Association of Diplomatic Studies; Roorda, "President and His Boy," 65, Gellman mss, DDEL; M. Eisenhower, *President Is Calling*, 332.

68. Confidential source did not recall that Nixon was intoxicated; Donald Hughes telephone interviews, July 3, 2001 and May 19, 2011.

69. Beschloss, *Mayday*, 183–184; M. Eisenhower to RN, Aug 7, 1959, B 12, Russian Trip, PPS325, RNyl; Garthoff does not have any recollection of this incident, Garthoff notes on mss, Gellman mss, DDEL; I have not found any documents that suggest Milton ever spoke to anyone about this incident.

70. *New York Times*, Aug 2, 1959.

71. Memo, Dec 7, B 425, Kornitzer (4 of 4), Series 320, RN to Khrushchev, Aug 1, 1959, B 1, Soviet Union Trip, Series 404 and RN to Murphy, Mar 11, 1960, B 1, Letter Copies, Series 408, RNln; *FR*, 1958–1960, Vol. X, P 1, pp. 377–380 and Vol. XI, P 1, pp. 187–189; *PPA* 1959, p. 361.

72. Memo, July 17, 1959, B 1, Soviet Union—Misc, Series 411, RNln; platter, Aug 16, 1961, RNyl; copies of the press conf, Nixon, *Six Crises*, 443–449 and *New York Times*, Aug 3, 1959.
73. Memo, Dec 7, 1959, B 425, Kornitzer (4 of 4), Series 320, RNln; *New York Herald Tribune*, Aug 3, 1959; Kornitzer, *Real Nixon*, 320; Hearst, *Ask Me*, 209–210.
74. Morgan broadcast, July 31, 1959, B 529, Morgan [1/2], Series 320, RNln; *New York Times*, Aug 1, 1959; *Atlanta Constitution*, Aug 3, 1959.
75. RN to Dewicki, July 15, B 214, Dewicki, Series 320, memo, May 5, B 1, Russian Trip, Series 407 and memo, undated July 1959, B 1, Trip to Poland, Series 411, RNln; *FR*, 1958–1960, Vol. X, P 1, pp. 328–329; *Los Angeles Times* and *New York Times*, July 4, 1959; *New York Herald Tribune*, July 26, 1959; Garthoff, *Journey through the Cold War*, 88; Beam, *Multiple Exposure*, 101.
76. RN to Niemo, May 9, PPS320.78.6.2, *Chicago Daily News*, June 10, Appearances, PPS337.B1, RN to Brasol, June 20, 1957, PPS320.78.8, memo, Aug 1, 1959, PPS325 and RN to Fraser, Nov 2, 1959, PPS320.78.33, RNyl; RN to Davis, Mar 28, 1958, B 204, Davis, D, Series 320, RNln; *FR*, 1958–1960, Vol. X, P 2, p. 190.
77. Memo, July 31, B 1, Trip to Poland, Series 411, RNln; *New York Times*, Aug 3, 1959; Day 4, Tape 2, 00:16:47 [RN], Day 7, Tape 1, 00:01:55 [RN], Gannon mss, WJBma; Beam, *Multiple Exposure*, 101–102; Klein, *Making It*, 259; Nixon, *Leaders*, 191.
78. RN to Hill, Aug 3, 1959, B 340, Hill, RC, Series 320 and Polish-Amer celebration, May 1, 1960, B 122, F 7, Series 207, RNln; *FR*, 1958–1960, Vol. X, P 2, p. 190; *Atlanta Constitution*, Aug 3–5, 1959; *New York Times*, Aug 3–4, 1959; *Times-Picayune* (La), Aug 4, 11 and 18–19, 1959; *New York Herald Tribune*, Aug 3, 1959; *San Francisco Chronicle*, May 7, 1962; Day 4, Tape 2, 00:16: 47 [RN] and Day 7, Tape 1, 00:01: 55 [RN], Gannon mss, WJBma; Donald Hughes telephone interview, May 19, 2011; Nixon, *RN*, 213; Nixon, *Leaders*, 192; Klein, *Making It*, 259; Bean, *Multiple Exposure*, 102–103; Schorr, *Staying Tuned*, 112 and 140–141.
79. Memo, July 20, 1959, R 22, Diary DDE; briefing book, Aug 1959, B 11, PPS325, RNyl; 1959, *FR*, 1958–1960, Vol. X, P 2, pp. 190–191; Beam, *Multiple Exposure*, 80–81, 83, and 103.
80. Morgan broadcast, Aug 3, 1959, B 529, Morgan [1/2], Series 320, RNln; *FR*, 1958–1960, Vol. X, P 2, pp. 192–218, 256–269, and 276; *New York Times* and *Atlanta Constitution*, Aug 4, 1959; Beam, *Multiple Exposure*, 103–106.
81. Ike to RN, July 30, 1959, B 1, TV Address, Series 408, RNln; memos, July 28, Aug 1, pre-press briefing, July 29, telephone call, July 30, R 22, telephone call, Aug 1, R 23, Diary DDE and meeting, July 29, 1959, R 2, Legislative DDE; *PDDE*, XX, pp. 1601–1602 and 1604; *PPA* 1959, pp. 550–551 and 556–559; *FR*, 1958–1960, Vol. X, P 1, pp. 374–376; *New York Times*, Aug 1–2, 1959; *New York Herald Tribune*, Aug 1, 1959.
82. Telephone call, Aug 3, 1959, R 23, Diary DDE; *PPA* 1959, pp. 560–565; *New York Times*, Aug 2–4, 1959; *New York Herald Tribune*, Aug 4, 1959; Tocchet, "September Thaw," 76–85.
83. *New York Journal American*, Aug 4, B 1, USSR Trip and *New York Herald Tribune*, Aug 9, B 4, USSR Trip, Series 414, *Los Angeles Times*, Sept 5, 1959, B 3, USSR Trip, Series 413, Reid to RN, Aug 18, 1959, B 625, Reid (1 of 2) and RN to Katz, June 7, 1960, B 89,

B'Nai B'Rith, Series 320, RNln; memo, Aug 26, 1959, FE 179, RNyl; Earl Mazo telephone interview, July 17, 2001; Kornitzer, *Real Nixon*, 321–323.

84. Morgan broadcast, Aug 4, 1959, B 529, Morgan [1/2], Series 320, RNln; *FR*, 1958–1960, Vol. X, P 2, p. 191; Day 5, Tape 1, 00:06:32 [RN], Gannon mss, WJBma; *Atlanta Constitution*, Aug 6, 1959; RN conf on occup safety, Mar 1, 1960, Gellman mss, DDEL.

85. Memo by Cronin, before trip 1959, B 1, Trip to Poland, Series 411 and *Washington Post*, Aug 5, 1959, B 4, USSR Trip, Series 414 and memo, Dec 7, 1959, B 425, Kornitzer (4 of 4), Series 320, RNln; *New York Herald Tribune*, July 28 and Aug 5–6, 1959; *New York Times*, Aug 5, 1959; Schorr, *Staying Tuned*, 141; Kornitzer, *Real Nixon*, 322–324.

86. RN to Gomulka, Aug 6, 1959, B 1, TV Address, Series 408, RNln; *FR*, 1958–1960, Vol. X, P 2, p. 191; *New York Times*, Aug 5 and 6, 1959; *New York Herald Tribune*, Aug 6, 1959.

87. *New York Times* and *New York Herald Tribune*, Aug 6, 1959; Gray, *Eighteen Acres*, 281.

88. *FR*, 1958–1960, Vol. X, P 2, pp. 218–219 and 381–386; *PDDE*, XXI, p. 2498; *New York Times*, Aug 5 and 6, 1969; Tocchet, "September Thaw," 136–137; J. Eisenhower, *Strictly Personal*, 238–239.

89. Wilson to RN, Aug 6, 1959, B 824, Wilson [2/3], Series 320, RNln and B 71, Political Affairs II, Robert Wilson mss, SDSU; Ike to RN, Aug 6, 1959, PPS324.130, RNyl.

90. Meeting, Aug 7, 1959, R 9, Cabinet DDE; *FR*, 1958–1960, Vol. X, P 1, pp. 386–387; *New York Times*, *Times-Picayune* (La) and *New York Herald Tribune*, Aug 10, 1959.

CHAPTER 33. IKE'S HOPES COLLAPSE

1. *New York Times*, Aug 5 and 6, 1959; *New York Herald Tribune*, Aug 6, 1959.

2. Tocchet, "September Thaw," 90–107; Berkowitz, "Khrushchev Goes to Washington," 73 and 138–149; Schoenwald, *Time for Choosing*, 40–44; Allitt, *Catholic*, 67–70.

3. Memo, Aug 6, 1959, R 22, Diary DDE; comments, Aug 7, 1959, B 12, F Russian Trip, PPS325, RNyl.

4. Memo, Aug 10, DE to Parker, Aug 22, memos, Aug 24 and 25, 1959, R 22, Diary DDE; *PPA* 1959, pp. 573–574, 576, 580–581, and 592–593; J. Eisenhower, *Strictly Personal*, 254–256; Berkowitz, "Khrushchev Goes to Washington," 149–153.

5. Meeting, Sept 8 and memo, Sept 14, 1959, R 23, Diary DDE; meeting, Sept 8, 1959, R 2, Legislative DDE; assessment, Nov 3, 1959, R 9, Cabinet DDE; *PPA* 1959, pp. 590–591; *New York Times*, Aug 26 and Sept 8, 1959; J. Eisenhower, *Strictly Personal*, 237.

6. Interview with Keating, Aug 14, B 112, F 9 and interview with Scott, Aug 18, B 112, F 10, Series 207 and transcript, Sept 3, 1959, B 141, Chamberlain, C, Series 320, RNln; meeting, Aug 25, 1959, R 22, Diary DDE; *New York Times*, Aug 14 and 15, Sept 1 and 15, 1959; Schulman, *Cooper*, 91–92.

7. Memo, Sept 15, DE to Nehru, Sept 16 and DE to Jackson, Sept 23, 1959, R 23, Diary DDE; *PPA* 1959, pp. 656–658; James Hagerty OH 91, pp. 133–138, CCOH; Tocchet, "September Thaw," 157–175; J. Eisenhower, *Strictly Personal*, 256–257.

8. *FR*, 1958–1960, Vol. X, P 1, pp. 392 and 489; memoirs, Mar 22, 1976, RNyl; Day 4, Tape 2, 00:21:16 [RN], Gannon mss, WJBma; Tocchet, "September Thaw," 175; Nixon, *Leaders*, 193–196; Carlson, *K Blows Top*, 78–79; J. Eisenhower, *Strictly Personal*, 257–258.

9. Memo, Sept 28, 1959, R 23, Diary DDE; *New York Times*, Sept 13, 1959; Talbott, *Khrushchev: Last Testament*, 368–416; Tocchet, "September Thaw," 199–259.

10. Speech, Sept 19, B 115, F 8, Series 207 and RN to Merwin, Sept 16, B 511, Merwin [1/2] and RN to Fuller, Sept 23, 1959, B 277, Fuller, S, Series 320, RNln; *New York Times*, Sept 20–21, 1959.

11. DE to Jackson, Sept 23 and memo Sept 28, 1959, R 23, Diary DDE.

12. Activities, Sept 29, 1959, R 23, Diary DDE; *PDDE*, XXI, p. 2509; Kistiakowsky, *Scientist at the WH*, 89–91; Tocchet, "September Thaw," 278–279.

13. *New York Times*, Sept 27 and 28, 1959; Wilton Persons OH #161, p. 156, CCOH; Berkowitz, "Khrushchev Goes to Washington," 42; Tocchet, "September Thaw," 274–281 and 292–297; Kistiakowsky, *Scientist at the WH*, 92–93.

14. *New York Times*, Sept 28, 1959; Day 4, Tape 2, 00;24:54 [RN]. Gannon mss, WJBma; J. Eisenhower, *Strictly Personal*, 262–264; Kistiakowsky, *Scientist at the WH*, 93–94.

15. *New York Times*, Sept 28, 1959.

16. Cabinet assessment, Nov 3, 1959, R 9, Cabinet DDE; *PPA 1959*, p. 271.

17. RN speech, Oct 5, B 117, F 2, Series 207 and RN to Powers, Oct 8, B 608, Powers, C, RN to Lodge, Nov 16, Lodge to RN, Nov 24, B 457, Lodge (2 of 2) and RN to Lodge, Dec 15, 1959, B 457, Lodge (1 of 2), Series 320, RNln; RN speech, Mar 1, 1960, Gellman mss, DDEL.

18. Edgar to Dick, Jan 5, 1960, PPS320.103.209A, RNyl.

19. Telephone call with Goodpaster, Apr 20, 1960, R 10, DuHe; telephone call with RN, Apr 21, 1960, R 25, Diary DDE; *New York Times*, Apr 27, 1960; *PPA 1960*, pp. 361–366.

20. Vladimir Toumanoff OH, 89–91, Association for Diplomatic Studies; Ambrose, *Spies*, 265–278; Beschloss, *Mayday*, pp. 183–184; M. Eisenhower, *President Is Calling*, 335–336.

21. Telephone call from RN, May 9, 1960, B 12, 3/28/60-6/30/60 (2), Herter mss, DuHe; Bryce Harlow OH, II, p. 12 and 25–27; Beschloss, *Mayday*, 216–304; Ambrose, *Spies*, 279–287.

22. Memo, May 12, 1960, R 25, Diary DDE; *FR*, 1958–1960, Vol. IX, p. 388, memoirs, Mar 23, 1978, RNyl.

23. Cabinet, May 26, 1960, R 25, Diary DDE; Haslam, *Russia's Cold War*, 180–183; Taubman, *Khrushchev*, 442–468.

24. RN to McCloy, May 24, B 492, McCloy and Rogers to Celler, May 27, 1960, B 653m Rogers 1960 (2 of 2), Series 320, RNln; *New York Times*, May 16 and 18, 1960; *Washington Post*, May 19, 1960.

25. RN to McGill, May 16, B 498, McGill [2/3], RN to Sheppard, B 691, Sheppard, J, RN to Goodfellow, May 24, B 295, Goodfellow, Series 320 and RN speech, May 17, B 134, F 9 and press conf, May 27, 1960, B 135, F 10, Series 207, RNln; RN to Kersten, May 24, 1960, B 1, Series 9, Kersten mss, MLsc; *FR*, 1958–1960, Vol. IX, p. 512.

26. RN speech, May 31, 1960, R 2, PRP.

CHAPTER 34. IKE, NIXON, KENNEDY, AND CASTRO

1. Gellman, *Roosevelt and Batista.*
2. Paterson, *Contesting Castro*, 3–254; also see Thomas Paterson microfilm collection on Cuba, UCt.
3. *FR*, 1958–1960, Vol. VI, pp. 302–303; special staff note, Jan 13, 1959, R 20, Diary DDE; Eisenhower, *Waging Peace*, 520–521.
4. Telephone memo, Jan 6, 1959, R 11, Roy Rubottom OH, 82–83, JFD OH.
5. Jenkins, "Initial American Responses to Castro," 160.
6. Ibid., passim.
7. Rubottom to Cabot, Apr 6, 1960, R 10, Loeb, J, Cabot mss, DDEL.
8. *Washington Daily News* (DC), Mar 30, PPS320.23.130 and Prentice to Conroy, Apr 10, 1959, PPS320.23.135, RNyl; *FR*, 1958–1960, Vol. VI, pp. 446 and 449; telephone memo, Apr 8, 1959, R 11, DuHe; *New York Times*, Apr 11, 1959; Falcoff ed., *Cuban Revolution and US*, 106.
9. Staff notes, Apr 10, synopsis of state and intelligence material, Apr 14, memo of conference, Apr 22, 1959, R 21, Diary DDE; unofficial visit, Apr 20, 1959, Dulles-Herter Series, B 11, Herter, Apr 1959 (2), AWF, DDEL.
10. Spivak to RN, May 12, 1959, B 719, Spivak, L, Series 320, RNln.
11. Calendar, Apr 19, 1959, PPS212(1959).2 and PPS212(199).4, RNyl; Safford, "Nixon-Castro Meeting," 425–431; Jenkins, "Initial American Responses to Castro," 167–186; Nixon, *RN*, 201–202; Day 4, Tape 2, 00:56:41 [RN], Gannon mss, WJBma.
12. Stevenson to Bonsal, Apr 22 and Bonsal to Stevenson, May 8, 1959, B 1, F 7, Cuba 1959, Jan–July, Bonsal mss, LOC; Bonsal, *Cuba, Castro*, 62–66; Stevenson OH, Association for Diplomatic Studies, www.adst.org/OH%20TOCs/Stevenson%Robert%20A .toc.pdf; I would like to thank Daun van Ee for supplying me with these documents.
13. *Miami Daily News*, July 15, 1952, PPS266.S57, RNyl; Baggs to RN, Apr 21 and RN to Baggs, May 18, 1959, B 59, Baggs, Series 320, RNln.
14. M. Eisenhower to RN, May 12, 1959, B 238, Eisenhower 2/2, Series 320, RNln; M. Eisenhower, *Wine Is Bitter*, 259; also see RN to JFD, Apr 24, B 229, Dulles ½ and Finch to Dewey, May 8, 1959, B 214, Dewey ½, RNln.
15. Memo from Goldwater, Apr 17 and RN to Goldwater, Apr 27, 1959, B 293, Goldwater [1/2], Series 320, RNln.
16. Jenkins, "Initial American Responses to Castro," 189–193 and 227–251.
17. Kleberg to Krupnick, July 14, B 429, Krupnick 1959 (1 of 3) and RN to Stewart, Oct 31, 1959, B 730, Stewart, J (NY), Series 320, RNln.
18. *FR*, 1958–1960, Vol. VI, pp. 699–700 and 704–706.
19. Memo of conference, Jan 26, 1960, R 24, Diary DDE; memo of telephone conversation, Feb 18, 1960, R 10; DuHe; memo of meeting, Mar 15, 1960, Osansa, B 4, Special Assistant, DDE; I would like to thank David Nichols for providing the documents from Osansa and the Gray mss, DDEL; Eisenhower, *Waging Peace*, 522–525; Bissell and Lewis, *Reflections of a Cold Warrior*, 152; Kornbluh ed., *Bay of Pigs*, 268.

20. CIA policy paper, Mar 17, B 4, White House office staff secretary, and Ike to Gray, Sept 22 and Gray to Ike, Sept 26, 1966, B 2, Gray mss, DDEL; *FR, 1958–1960*, Vol. VI, pp. 861–863; Eisenhower, *Waging Peace*, 534; Bissell and Lewis, *Reflections of a Cold Warrior*, 153; Kornbluh ed., *Bay of Pigs*, 268–269; Vandenbroucke, *Perilous Options*, 9–18; Salisbury, *Without Fear or Favor*, 137–138; Nixon, *RN*, 202.

21. Kornbluh ed., *Bay of Pigs*, 270–272; Fursenko and Naftali, *"One Hell of a Gamble,"* 36–40 and 56–73; Quirk, *Castro*, 244–343; Pérez, *Cuba and US*, 238–242; Roy Rubottom OH, 74–75, JFD OH.

22. Memo of meeting, July 6, B 4 and July 14, 26 and Aug 22, 1960, Osana, B 5, special assistant, DDEL; *FR, 1958–1960*, Vol. VI, p. 518; Kornbluh ed., *Bay of Pigs* 274–275.

23. Horne, *Macmillan*, Vol. II, pp. 297–299.

24. Memo, Oct 17 and memo of meeting, Nov 14, 1960, Osansa, B 5, special assistant, DDEL.

25. Memo of meeting, Dec 5, 1960, Osansa, B 5, special assistant, DDEL; RN to Pawley, May 8, 1963, B 582, Pawley, Series 320, RNln; Kornbluh ed., *Bay of Pigs*, 278.

26. *Miami Herald*, Jan 16, B 277, Fuller, GG, Series 320 and *Tampa Tribune*, Jan 19, B 123, F 1(2 of 2) and news conf, Jan 20, 1960, B 123, F 4, Series 207, RNln; news conf, Jan 16, 1960, R 2, *PRP*; *New York Times*, Jan 17, 1960.

27. News conf, Feb 6, 1960, B 125, F 1, Series 207, RNln.

28. RN to Garcia, Jan 6, PPS320.23.174 and RN to O'Rourke, Mar 11, 1960, PPS320.23.182, RNyl; memo, Jan 29, B 298, Grace, W, RN to Ehrlich, Feb 11, B 236, Ehrlich, G, RN to Gardner, Mar 2, Gardner, AR and RN to O'Rourke, Mar 11, 1960, B 572, O'Rourke, J, Series 320, RNln.

29. RN to Hoover, Jan 6, PPS320.103.210.2, Edgar to Dick, Feb 12, PPS320.103.219A.2 and July 5, 1960, PPS320.103.234F.1, RNyl.

30. RN to Gainey, June 22, B 279, Gainey 1960, RN to Dresser, July 15, B 223, Dresser and RN to Price, Aug 16, 1960, B 611, Price, EC, Series 320, RNln; RN to Diggs, Sept 3, 1960, PPS320.23.194, RNyl.

31. *FR, 1958–1960*, Vol. V, p. 807 and Vol. VI, pp. 744, 895–897, 950–951, 984, and 989; Falcoff ed., *Cuban Revolution and US*, 323–324, 340, 343, and 385.

32. Memo, Jan 21, 1960, PPS320.23.178, RNyl.

33. Davis to RN, Mar 17, B 204, Davis, C and memo, Apr 10, 1960, B 654, Romualdi [1/2], Series 320, RNln; *FR, 1958–1960*, Vol. IV, p. 629 and Vol. VI, p. 968.

34. Kornbluh ed., *Bay of Pigs*, 273–274.

35. *New York Times*, Oct 6, 16 and 21, 1960; Quirk, *Castro*, 347–350; for Nixon's complaints about JFK, Cuba, and the election, see Nixon, *Six Crises*, 353–357.

36. Kornbluh ed., *Bay of Pigs*, 277–279.

37. Memo, Dec 6, 1960, B 1, presidential transition series, F memos – staff-re change of administration (6), AWF, DDEL.

38. Memo, Jan 9, 1961, B 5, special assistant's series, presidential subseries, F meeting with the president 1960, V. 2 (2), DDEL; for Trujillo and Castro, see Rabe, "Caribbean Triangle," 55–78.

39. *New York Times*, Jan 10, 1960; Cabot, *First Line*, 118–119.

40. Memo, Jan 19, 1961, B 2, Augusta Walter Reed Series, F Kennedy, John F. 1960–61 (2), DDEL.
41. Gleijeses, "CIA and the Bay of Pigs," 26–27.
42. Goodpaster to DE, middle of Mar 1961, B 9, 1961, Principal File, F Goodpaster, Andrew J, Post-Presidency, DDEL; department of the Army, special orders, No. 45 – 21, Feb 1961 and department of defense, news release No. 142-61 – Feb 23, 1961, Goodpaster mss, GCMF; I would like to thank Jeffrey Kozak, archivist and assistant librarian at the George C. Marshall Foundation for locating these documents.
43. Higgins, *Perfect Failure*; Gore, *Let the Glory Out*, 148.
44. Sorensen, *Kennedy*, 294; Roy Rubottom OH, 78, JFD OH; Bissell and Lewis, *Reflections of a Cold Warrior*, 152–159; Vandenbroucke, *Perilous Options*, 188; Bohning, *Castro Obsession*, 12.
45. There are many accounts of the failed invasion. See Bissell and Lewis, *Reflections of a Cold Warrior*, for Bissell's perspective; see Kornbluh ed., *Bay of Pigs*, for CIA documents; for Maxwell Taylor's assessment, see Taylor, *Swords and Plowshares*, 178–194; for earlier studies, see Wyden, *Bay of Pigs* and Higgins, *Perfect Failure*; see Gleijeses, "Ships in the Night," for the interaction between the WH and the CIA; see Bohning, *Castro Obsession*, for how the CIA continued covert operations. Dallek, *An Unfinished Life*, 356–370, continues the spin that Eisenhower was responsible for the invasion; Howard Jones used the Kennedy presidential library to write *Bay of Pigs*, but never examined any documents from the Eisenhower presidential library; for a defense of the military see, Landa and Drea, *History of the Office of the Secretary of Defense*, Vol. 5, pp. 172–194.
46. *Evening Star* (DC), Apr 25, 1961, B 151, F 15, Series 207, RNln; Nixon, "Cuba, Castro, and Kennedy," 289–295.
47. Herskowitz, *Duty, Honor, Country*, 168.
48. *New York Times*, Apr 25, 1961.
49. Geselbracht and Acheson eds., *Affection and Trust*, 259–260.
50. Ibid., 260.
51. Memo of conf, May 12, 1961, B 2, Augusta Walter Reed Series, F memo of conf, 1961–63 (1), Post-Presidency, DDEL.
52. Goodpaster to DE, Sept 13, 1961, B 9, 1961, Principal File, F Goodpaster, Andrew J., Post-Presidency, DDEL.
53. Nixon, *Six Crises*, 353–357.
54. Nixon, "Cuba, Castro, and Kennedy," 289–295.
55. RN to Pawley, May 8, 1963m B 582, Pawley, Series 320, RNln.
56. Guthman and Shulman eds., *Robert Kennedy in His Own Words*, 55, 246–247, and 346.
57. *New York Times*, Nov 9 and 16, 1962. Memo, Nov 17, 1962, B WH5, Subject File, 1961–1965, Cuba 11/1/62-12/29/62, Schlesinger mss, JFKL; I would like to thank Marika Cifor and the reference staff at the Kennedy presidential library for supplying me with this document.
58. Schlesinger, *Thousand Days*, 238.
59. Sorensen, *Kennedy*, 295.
60. Eisenhower, *Waging Peace*, 520–525, 612–614, and 631.

61. Telephone call with Harlow, Aug 6, 1965, B 2, appointment books series, F calls and appointments 1965 (5), Post-Presidency, DDEL.

62. Appointment book entry, Aug 11, appointment book series, B 2, F 1965 (5), Mazo to Ike, Aug 15 and Ike to Mazo, Aug 18, 1965, B 38, 1965 Principal File, F May (2), Post-Presidency, DDEL.

63. Appointment book entry, Aug 23, B 2, appointment book series, F calls and appointments 1965 (5), Mazo to Ike, Aug 25 and Ike to Mazo, Aug 27, B 38, 1965, Principal File, F May (2) and Ike to Guggenheim, Sept 13 and Oct 23, 1965, B 30, 1965 Principal File, F GU (1), Post-Presidency, DDEL.

64. Appointment book entry, Aug 23, 1965, B 2, appointment book series, F calls and appointments 1965 (5), Post-Presidency, DDEL; Vandenbroucke, "'Confessions' of Allen Dulles," 365–375.

65. Telephone call with Harlow, Aug 6, B 2, appointment books series, F calls and appointments 1965 (5) and Guggenheim to Ike, Sept 10, 1965, B 30, 1965, Principal File, F GU (1), Post-Presidency, DDEL; Mazo, "Ike Speaks Out," 50–51.

66. Salinger, P.S., 107–108 and 288–289.

Bibliography

MANUSCRIPT COLLECTIONS AND UNPUBLISHED ORAL HISTORIES

AIR FORCE, HISTORICAL RESEARCH PROGRAM, MAXWELL
AIR FORCE BASE, MONTGOMERY, ALABAMA

Hughes, Donald, K 239.0512-1349 (OH)

CALIFORNIA STATE UNIVERSITY, FULLERTON ORAL
HISTORY, FULLERTON, CALIFORNIA

Beeson, Sheldon
Chapman, Irvin
Finch, Robert
Gaudio, Joe
George, Nathaniel
Jones, Louis
Kraushaar, I.N.
Newsom, A.C.
Nichols, Ray
Triggs, Dean and Robert Gibbs
Warner, Edward
Winget, Winifred

COLUMBIA ORAL HISTORY COLLECTION, COLUMBIA CENTER FOR ORAL HISTORY,
COLUMBIA UNIVERSITY, NEW YORK CITY, NEW YORK

Adams, Sherman
Allen, George
Anderson, Dillon

Behrens, Earl
Bush, Prescott
Dewey, Thomas
Dillon, Douglas
Eisenhower, Milton
Hagerty, James
Keating, Kenneth
Klein, Herbert
Knowland, William
Persons, Wilton, #161 and #334

DREW UNIVERSITY LIBRARY ARCHIVES, MADISON, NEW JERSEY

Kornitzer, Bela

DWIGHT D. EISENHOWER PRESIDENTIAL LIBRARY, ABILENE, KANSAS .

Allen, George (OH)
Anderson, Robert (OH)
Brownell, Herbert (OH)
Carlson, Frank (OH)
Cabot, John C.
Cushman, Robert (OH)
Eisenhower, Milton, #13 (OH)
Fox, Frederic, and James Lambie Jr., "Staff Book 1953–61"
Francis, Clarence
Gellman, Gloria Gae
Gray, Gordon
Hagerty, James, diary
Hall, Leonard, #478 (OH)
Halleck, Charles (OH)
Larson, Arthur
Morrow, E. Frederic
Motion pictures, audiovisual division
Post-Presidency
    Principal File
Roberts, Clifford (OH)
Rogers, William
Scott, Hugh (OH)
Seaton, Fred
Shanley, Bernard
Whitman, Ann Series
Young, Howard

EISENHOWER NATIONAL HISTORIC SITE, GETTYSBURG, PENNSYLVANIA

Eisenhower, John (OH)
Moaney, Dolores (OH)

FEDERAL BUREAU OF INVESTIGATION, WASHINGTON, DC

Cronin, John

FOREIGN AFFAIRS ORAL HISTORY COLLECTIONS, THE ASSOCIATION
FOR DIPLOMATIC STUDIES AND TRAINING, ARLINGTON, VIRGINIA

Stevenson, Robert
Toumanoff, Vladimir

FRANKLIN DELANO ROOSEVELT PRESIDENTIAL LIBRARY, HYDE PARK, NEW YORK

Douglas, Helen (OH), Eleanor Roosevelt collection
Roosevelt, Eleanor

GEORGE C. MARSHALL FOUNDATION, LEXINGTON, VIRGINIA

Goodpaster, Andrew

GOODWIN KNIGHT/EDMUND BROWN SR. ERA,
GOVERNMENT HISTORY DOCUMENTATION PROJECT,
REGIONAL ORAL HISTORY PROJECT,
BANCROFT LIBRARY, UNIVERSITY OF CALIFORNIA, BERKELEY

Barrett, Douglas (OH)
Bright, Tom (OH)

HARRY S TRUMAN PRESIDENTIAL LIBRARY, INDEPENDENCE, MISSOURI

Babcock, Gaylon (OH)
Hoffman, Paul
Lloyd, David
Lowenthal, Max

HENRY MUDD LIBRARY, MANUSCRIPT COLLECTIONS, PRINCETON UNIVERSITY,
PRINCETON, NEW JERSEY

Hughes, Emmet Diary
Krock, Arthur
Stevenson, Adlai

HERBERT HOOVER PRESIDENTIAL LIBRARY, WEST BRANCH, IOWA

Eisenhower, Dwight (OH)
Ferguson, Homer (OH)
Knowland, William (OH)
Wood, Robert

JOHN F. KENNEDY PRESIDENTIAL LIBRARY,
COLUMBUS POINT, MASSACHUSETTS

Martin, Louis (OH)
Schlesinger Jr., Arthur

JOHN FOSTER DULLES ORAL HISTORY COLLECTION, PRINCETON UNIVERSITY,
PRINCETON, NEW JERSEY

Nixon, Richard
Rubottom, Roy
Sparkman, John
Stassen, Harold

LIBRARY OF CONGRESS, MANUSCRIPT DIVISION, WASHINGTON, DC

Agronsky, Martin
Alsop, Stewart and Joseph
Bernays, Edward
Bonsal, Philip
Creel, George
Koo Jr., Wellington

LYMAN LEMNITZER CENTER FOR NATO AND EUROPEAN UNION STUDIES,
KENT STATE UNIVERSITY, KENT, OHIO

Achilles, Theodore, "How Little Wisdom: Memoirs of an Irresponsible Memory"

LYNDON B. JOHNSON PRESIDENTIAL LIBRARY, ORAL
HISTORY, AUSTIN, TEXAS

Aiken, George
Albert, Carl
Busy, Horace
Case, Clifford
Church, Frank
Clifford, Clark

Dirksen, Everett
Douglas, Helen
Douglas, Paul
Eastland, James
Eisenhower, Milton
Ellender, Allen
Goldwater, Barry
Hagerty, James
Halleck, Charles
Harlow, Bryce
Hill, Lister
Humphrey, Hubert
Jackson, Henry
Javits, Jacob
Jordon, William
Knowland, William
Kuchel, Thomas
Long, Russell
McPherson, Harry
Marshall, Thurgood
Mills, Wilbur
Mitchell, Clarence
Monroney, A.S.
Morton, Thruston
Mundt, Karl
Oliver, Robert
Pearson, Drew
Proxmire, William
Randolph, A. Philip
Reedy, George
Rowe, James
Rusk, Dean
Siegel, George
Sparkman, John
Talmadge, Herman
Thurmond, Strom
Weisl, Edwin
Wilkins, Roy

MARGARET CHASE SMITH LIBRARY, NORTHWOOD UNIVERSITY,
SKOWHEGAN, MAINE

Smith, Margaret

MARQUETTE UNIVERSITY, MEMORIAL LIBRARY, SPECIAL COLLECTIONS, MILWAUKEE, WISCONSIN

Kersten, Charles

MASSACHUSETTS HISTORICAL SOCIETY, BOSTON, MASSACHUSETTS

Henry Cabot Lodge II

MUSSELMAN LIBRARY, SPECIAL COLLECTIONS, GETTYSBURG COLLEGE, GETTYSBURG, PENNSYLVANIA

Anderson, Dillon

NATIONAL ARCHIVES II, COLLEGE PARK, MARYLAND

CREST, CIA Records Search Tool, third floor library

NATIONAL ASSOCIATION FOR THE ADVANCEMENT OF COLORED PEOPLE (NAACP), LIBRARY OF CONGRESS, WASHINGTON, DC

NEW HAMPSHIRE STATE ARCHIVES, CONCORD, NEW HAMPSHIRE

Bridges, Henry Styles
McLeod, Scott

PEPPERDINE UNIVERSITY, SPECIAL COLLECTIONS AND UNIVERSITY ARCHIVES, MALIBU, CALIFORNIA

Bruce Herschensohn, Collection No. 0006

RICHARD NIXON PRE-PRESIDENTIAL PAPERS, NATIONAL ARCHIVES AND RECORDS ADMINISTRATION, PACIFIC REGION, LAGUNA NIGUEL, CALIFORNIA—NOW HOUSED AT THE RICHARD NIXON PRESIDENTIAL LIBRARY AND MUSEUM

RICHARD NIXON PRESIDENTIAL LIBRARY AND MUSEUM, YORBA LINDA, CALIFORNIA

Cotton, Aylett
Drown, Helene (DR)
Ferman, Irving
Finch, Robert
Lewis, Betty
Library Birthplace Manuscripts (LBM)
Mozley, Don

Nixon White House Tapes—Online
Perry, Herman
Safire, William (OH)

SENATE HISTORICAL OFFICE, WASHINGTON, DC

Baker, Robert
Riddick, Floyd, Interview #4
Shuman, Howard, Interview #3

SAN DIEGO STATE UNIVERSITY, SPECIAL COLLECTIONS AND UNIVERSITY ARCHIVES,
SAN DIEGO, CALIFORNIA

Wilson, Robert

THOMAS J. DODD RESEARCH CENTER, UNIVERSITY OF CONNECTICUT,
STORRS, CONNECTICUT

Paterson, Thomas

UNIVERSITY OF CALIFORNIA AT LOS ANGELES (UCLA), SPECIAL COLLECTIONS
DEPARTMENT, UNIVERSITY RESEARCH LIBRARY

Bergholz, Richard
Cray, Ed

UNIVERSITY OF ILLINOIS ARCHIVES, URBANA, ILLINOIS

Reston, James

UNIVERSITY OF VIRGINIA, ALDERMAN LIBRARY, SPECIAL COLLECTIONS,
CHARLOTTESVILLE, VIRGINIA

Scott, Hugh

WALTER J. BROWN MEDIA ARCHIVES & PEABODY AWARDS COLLECTION,
UNIVERSITY OF GEORGIA, ATHENS, GEORGIA

Gannon, Frank, Interviews
Russell, Richard
Nixon, Richard (OH)

WASHINGTON PRESS CLUB, FOUNDATION, WASHINGTON, DC

WHITTIER COLLEGE ORAL HISTORY, WHITTIER, CALIFORNIA

Brock, William
Fuller, Lon
George, Nathaniel
King, Gretchen and Robert
Koch, A.
Kraushaar, I.N.
Mashburn, Barbara

WOMEN IN JOURNALISM, WASHINGTON PRESS CLUB FOUNDATION,
WASHINGTON, DC

Payne, Ethel (OH)

YALE UNIVERSITY LIBRARY, MANUSCRIPT DIVISION,
NEW HAVEN, CONNECTICUT

Bullitt, William

BOOKS, ARTICLES, FILMS, AND OTHER SOURCES

Abell, Tyler, ed., *Drew Pearson Diaries 1949–1959*. New York: Holt, Rinehart and Winston, 1974.
Abernathy, Ralph, *And the Walls Came Tumbling Down*. New York: Harper & Row, 1989.
Abramowitz, Alan, *The Polarized Public? Why American Government Is So Dysfunctional*. Boston: Pearson, 2013.
Abramson, Rudy, *Spanning the Century: Averell Harriman 1891–1986*. New York: Morrow, 1992.
Accinelli, Robert, *Crisis and Commitment: United States Policy toward Taiwan, 1950–1955*. Chapel Hill: University of North Carolina Press, 1996.
———, "Eisenhower, Congress, and the 1954–55 Offshore Island Crisis," *Presidential Studies Quarterly*, Vol. 20, Spring 1990.
Adams, John, *Without Precedent: The Story of the Death of McCarthyism*. New York: Norton, 1983.
Adams, Sherman, *Firsthand Report: The Story of the Eisenhower Administration*. New York: Harper, 1961.
Adams, Valerie, *Eisenhower's Fine Group of Fellows: Crafting a National Security Policy to Uphold the Great Equation*. Lanham, Md: Lexington Books, 2006.
Adenauer, Konrad, *Memoirs 1950–53*, trans. Beate Rujm von Oppen. Chicago: Regnery, 1966.
Agung, Ide Anak Agung Gde, *Twenty Years: Indonesian Foreign Policy 1945–1965*. The Hague: Mouton, 1973.

Ahlstrom, Sydney, *A Religious History of the American People*. New Haven: Yale University Press, 1972.

Ailinger Jr., Joseph, "Cold War Policy Under Fire: The United States Response to Revolution in Hungary," MA thesis, Boston College, Boston, Mass, 1990.

Aitken, Jonathan, *Nixon: A Life*. Washington, DC: Regnery, 1993.

Albert, Carl, *Little Giant: The Life and Times of Speaker Carl Albert*. Norman: University of Oklahoma Press, 1990.

Albertson, Dean, ed., *Eisenhower as President*. New York: Hill and Wang, 1963.

Alexander, Charles, *Holding the Line: The Eisenhower Era 1952–1961*. Bloomington: Indiana University Press, 1975.

Alexander, Robert, *Juscelino Kubitschek and the Development of Brazil*. Athens, Ohio: Ohio University Center for International Studies, 1991.

Aliano, Richard, *American Defense Policy from Eisenhower to Kennedy: The Politics of Changing Military Requirements, 1957–1961*. Athens: Ohio University Press, 1975.

Alin, Erika, *The United States and the 1958 Lebanon Crisis: American Intervention in the Middle East*. Lanham, Md: University Press of America, 1994.

Allen, Craig, *Eisenhower and the Mass Media: Peace, Prosperity, & Prime-Time TV*. Chapel Hill: University of North Carolina Press, 1993.

Allen, Maury, *Jackie Robinson: A Life Remembered*. New York: Franklin Watts, 1987.

Allison, John, *Ambassador from the Prairie or Allison Wonderland*. Boston: Houghton Mifflin, 1973.

Allitt, Patrick, *Catholic Intellectuals and Conservative Politics in America, 1950–1985*. Ithaca, NY: Cornell University Press, 1993.

Alsop, Stewart, "The Great California Drama," *Saturday Evening Post*, Oct 18, 1958.

——, "The Mystery of Richard Nixon," *Saturday Evening Post*, Vol. 231, July 12, 1958.

——, *Nixon & Rockefeller: A Double Portrait*. New York: Doubleday, 1960.

——, *Stay of Execution: A Sort of Memoir*. Philadelphia: Lippincott, 1973.

Altman, Nancy, *The Battle for Social Security: From FDR's Vision to Bush's Gamble*. New York: Wiley, 2005.

Ambrose, Stephen, *Eisenhower: Soldier General of the Army President-Elect 1890–1952*. Vol. 1. New York: Simon and Schuster, 1983.

——, *Eisenhower: The President*. Vol. 2. New York: Simon and Schuster, 1984.

——, *Ike's Spies: Eisenhower and the Espionage Establishment*. New York: Doubleday, 1981.

——, *Nixon: The Education of a Politician 1913–1962*. New York: Simon and Schuster, 1987.

——, *To America: Personal Reflections of an Historian*. New York: Simon & Schuster, 2002.

——, and Douglas Brinkley, *Rise to Globalism: American Foreign Policy since 1938*. 8th rev. ed. New York: Penguin, 1997.

Ambrose, Stephen, and Richard Immerman, *Milton S. Eisenhower: Educational Statesman*. Baltimore: Johns Hopkins, 1983.

Ameringer, Charles, *Don Pepe: Political Biography of José Figueres of Costa Rica*. Albuquerque: University of New Mexico Press, 1978.

Anderson, Carol, "Clutching at Civil Rights Straws: A Reappraisal of the Truman Years and the Struggle for African American Citizenship," in Geselbracht, ed., *The Civil Rights Legacy*.

———, *Eyes Off the Prize: The United Nations and the African American Struggle for Human Rights, 1944–1955.* Cambridge: Cambridge University Press, 2003.

Anderson, Clinton, *Outsider in the Senate: Senator Clinton Anderson's Memoirs.* New York: New World Publishing, 1970.

Anderson, David, "J. Lawson Collins, John Foster Dulles, and the Eisenhower Administration's 'Point of No Return' in Vietnam," *Diplomatic History,* Vol. 12, Spring 1988.

———, ed., *Trapped by Success: The Eisenhower Administration and Vietnam, 1953–1961.* New York: Columbia University Press, 1991.

Anderson, J.W., *Eisenhower, Brownell, and the Congress: The Tangled Origins of the Civil Rights Bill of 1956–1957.* Tuscaloosa: University of Alabama Press, 1964.

Anderson, Jack, *Confessions of a Muckraker: The Inside Story of Life in Washington during the Truman, Eisenhower, Kennedy and Johnson Years.* New York: Random House, 1979.

Anderson, Jervis, A. *Philip Randolph: A Biographical Portrait.* New York: Harcourt Brace Jovanovich, 1972, 1973.

Anderson, Totton, "Extremism in California Politics: The Brown-Knowland and Brown-Nixon Campaigns Compared," *Western Political Quarterly,* Vol. 16, No. 2, June 1963.

———, "The 1958 Election in California," *Western Political Quarterly,* Vol. 12, 1959.

Anthony, Carl, *First Ladies: The Saga of the Presidents' Wives and Their Power.* New York: Morrow, 1990.

Appleby Jr., Charles, "Eisenhower and Arms Control, 1953–1961." PhD dissertation, Johns Hopkins University, Baltimore, Md, 1987.

Ashby, LeRoy, and Rod Gramer, *Fighting the Odds: The Life of Senator Frank Church.* Seattle: Washington State University Press, 1994.

Ashmore, Harry, *Civil Rights and Wrongs: A Memoir of Race and Politics 1944–1994.* New York: Pantheon, 1994.

Atkins, G. Pope, and Larman Wilson, *The Dominican Republic and the United States: From Imperialism to Transnationalism.* Athens: University of Georgia Press, 1998.

Atkinson, Frank, *The Dynamic Dominion: Realignment and the Rise of Virginia's Republican Party Since 1945.* Fairfax, Va: George Mason, 1992.

Atwood, Paul, "The United States and Costa Rica, 1945–1960: The Containment of Liberal Nationalism," PhD dissertation, Boston University, Boston, Mass,1991.

Auerbach, Carl, "Jury Trials and Civil Rights," *New Leader,* Vol. 40, No. 17, Apr 29, 1957.

Badger, Anthony, "Southerners Who Refused to Sign the Southern Manifesto," *Historical Journal,* Vol. 42, No. 2, 1999.

———, "The Southern Manifesto: White Southerners and Civil Rights, 1956," in Kroes and van de Bilt, eds., *The US Constitution.*

Bailey Jr., Harry, ed., *Negro Politics in America.* Columbus, Ohio: Charles E. Merrill Books, 1967.

Baker, Bobby, *Wheeling and Dealing: Confessions of a Capitol Hill Operator.* New York: Norton, 1978.

Baker, Leonard, *The Johnson Eclipse: A President's Vice Presidency.* New York: Macmillan, 1966.

Baker, Russell, *The Good Times.* New York: Morrow, 1989.

Ball, George, *The Past Has Another Pattern: Memoirs*. New York: Norton, 1982.

Ball, Rick, and NBC News, eds., *Meet The Press: 50 Years of History in the Making*. New York: McGraw-Hill, 1998.

Banitch, George, "The Ultraconservative Congressman from Dallas: The Rise and Fall of Bruce Alger, 1954–1964," MA thesis, University of Texas at Arlington, 2001.

Barber, James, *The Presidential Character: Predicting Performance in the White House*. 3rd ed. Englewood Cliffs, NJ: Prentice-Hall, 1985.

Barclay, Glen, *Friends In High Places: Australian-American Diplomatic Relations since 1945*. Melbourne: Oxford University Press, 1985.

——, *A Very Small Insurance Policy: The Politics of Australian Involvement in Vietnam, 1954–1967*. Indooroopilly: University of Queensland Press, 1988.

Barclay, Thomas, "The 1954 Election in California," *Western Political Quarterly*, Vol. 7, 1954.

Barnouw, Erik, *Tube of Plenty: The Evolution of American Television*. 2nd rev. ed., New York: Oxford, 1990.

Barrett, David, *The CIA & Congress: The Untold Story from Truman to Kennedy*. Lawrence: University Press of Kansas, 2005.

Barrett, Roby, *The Greater Middle East and the Cold War: US Foreign Policy under Eisenhower and Kennedy*. London: I.B. Tauris, 2007.

Bartlett, C. J., *"The Special Relationship": A Political History of Anglo-American Relations since 1945*. London: Longman, 1992.

Bartley, Numan, *The New South 1945–1980*. Baton Rouge: Louisiana State University Press, 1995.

——, *The Rise of Massive Resistance: Race and Politics in the South during the 1950s*. Baton Rouge: Louisiana State University Press, 1969.

——, and Hugh Graham, compilers, *Southern Elections: County and Precinct Data, 1950–1972*. Baton Rouge: Louisiana State University Press, 1978.

——, and Hugh Graham, *Southern Politics and the Second Reconstruction*. Baltimore: Johns Hopkins University Press, 1975.

Bass, Jack, and Marilyn Thompson, *Ol' Strom: An Unauthorized Biography of Strom Thurmond*. Atlanta: Longstreet, 1998.

Baughman, Urbanus, *Secret Service Chief*. New York: Harper & Row, 1962.

Baxter, Randolph, "'Eradicating This Menace': Homophobia and Anti-Communism in Congress, 1947–1954." PhD dissertation, University of California, Irvine, 1999.

Beam, Jacob, *Multiple Exposure: An American Ambassador's Unique Perspective on East-West Issues*. New York: Norton, 1978.

Bean, Louis, *Influence in the 1954 Mid-Term Elections*. Washington, DC: Public Affairs Institute, 1954.

Becnel, Thomas, *Senator Allen Ellender of Louisiana: A Biography*: Baton Rouge: Louisiana State University Press, 1995.

Beers, Paul, compiler, *The Pennsylvania Sampler*. Mechanicsburg, Pa: Stackpole Books, 1970.

Behrens, Earl, "California: The New Men," in Reichley, ed., *States in Crisis*.

Beito, David, and Linda Beito, *Black Maverick: T.R.M. Howard's Fight for Civil Rights and Economic Power.* Urbana: University of Illinois Press, 2009.

Békés, Csaba, Malcolm Byrne, and Janos Rainer, eds., *The 1956 Hungarian Revolution: A History in Documents.* Budapest and New York: Central European University Press, 2002.

Bell, Jonathan, *California Crucible: The Forging of Modern American Liberalism.* Philadelphia: University of Pennsylvania Press, 2012.

Belmonte, Laura, *Selling the American Way: U.S. Propaganda and the Cold War.* Philadelphia: University of Pennsylvania Press, 2008.

Bensel, Richard, *Sectionalism and American Political Development, 1880–1980.* Madison: University of Wisconsin Press, 1984.

Benson, Ezra, *Cross Fire: The Eight Years with Eisenhower.* New York: Doubleday, 1962.

Berg, Manfred, *"The Ticket to Freedom": The NAACP and the Struggle for Black Political Integration.* Gainesville: University Press of Florida, 2005.

Bergman, Jerry, "Steeped in Religion: President Eisenhower and the Influence of the Jehovah's Witnesses," *Kansas History,* Vol. 21, No. 3, Autumn 1998.

Berkowitz, Aaron, "Mr. Khrushchev Goes to Washington: Domestic Opposition to Nikita Khrushchev's 1959 Visit to America," PhD dissertation, University of Illinois at Chicago, 2010.

Berle, Beatrice, and Travis Jacobs, eds., *Navigating the Rapids, 1918–1971: From the Papers of Adolf A. Berle.* New York: Harcourt Brace Jovanovich, 1973.

Berman, Daniel, *A BILL becomes LAW: The Civil Rights Act of 1960.* New York: Macmillan, 1962.

Berman, William, *The Politics of Civil Rights in the Truman Administration.* Columbus: Ohio State University Press, 1970.

Bernays, Edward, *Biography of an Idea: Memoirs of Public Relations Counsel.* New York: Simon and Schuster, 1965.

Bernstein, Barton, "The Ambiguous Legacy: The Truman Administration and Civil Rights," in Bernstein, ed., *Politics and Policies.*

——, "Election of 1952," in Schlesinger and Israel, eds., *History of American Presidential Elections.*

——, *Politics and Policies of the Truman Administration.* Chicago: Quadrangle Books, 1970.

Berthelot, Helen, *Win Some Lose Some: G. Mennen Williams and the New Democrats.* Detroit: Wayne State University Press, 1955.

Beschloss, Michael, *The Crisis Years: Kennedy and Khrushchev 1960–1963.* New York: HarperCollins, 1991.

——, *Mayday: Eisenhower, Khrushchev and the U-2 Affair.* New York: Harper & Row, 1986.

——, *Taking Charge: The Johnson White House Tapes, 1963–1964.* New York: Simon & Schuster, 1997.

——, ed., *Reaching for Glory: Lyndon Johnson's Secret White House Tapes, 1964–1965.* New York: Simon & Schuster, 2001.

Bessey, Roy, "The Political Issues of the Hells Canyon Controversy," *Western Political Quarterly*, Vol. 9, No. 3, Sept 1956.

Best, Gary, *Herbert Hoover: The Postpresidential Years 1933–1964*. Vol. 2. Stanford: Hoover Institution, 1983.

Biles, Roger, *Crusading Liberal: Paul H. Douglas of Illinois*. Dekalb: Northern Illinois University Press, 2002.

Bill, James, "America, Iran, and the Politics of Intervention," in Bill and Louis, eds., *Musaddig, Iranian Nationalism, and Oil*.

——, *The Eagle and the Lion: The Tragedy of American-Iranian Relations*. New Haven: Yale University Press, 1988.

——, and Wm. Roger Louis, eds., *Musaddiq, Iranian Nationalism and Oil*. Austin: University of Texas Press, 1988.

Billings-Yun, Melanie, *Decision Against War: Eisenhower and Dien Bien Phu, 1954*. New York: Columbia University Press, 1988.

Billington, Monroe, "Lyndon B. Johnson and Blacks: The Early Years," *Journal of Negro History*, Vol. 62, No. 1, Jan 1977.

Bird, Kai, *The Color of Truth: McGeorge and William Bundy: Brothers in Arms: A Biography*. New York: Simon & Schuster, 1998.

——, and Martin Sherwin, *American Prometheus: The Triumph and Tragedy of J. Robert Oppenheimer*. New York: Knopf, 2005.

Birkner, Michael, "Eisenhower and the Red Menace," *Prologue*, Vol. 33, No. 1, Fall 2001.

——, "The Eisenhowers at Twilight: A Visit to the Eisenhower Far 1967," *Adams County History*, Vol. 13, 2007.

——, "The Election of 1956," in Shade and Campbell, eds., *American Presidential Campaigns and Elections*.

——, "Sherman Adams' Fall, and the Scandal Behind the Scandal," Political Science Conference, Shippensburg University, June 21–22, 2012.

Birmingham, David, *The Decolonization of Africa*. Athens: Ohio University Press, 1995.

Bischof, Günter, *Austria in the First Cold War, 1945–55: The Leverage of the Weak*. New York: St. Martin's, 1999.

——, "Before the Break, The Relationship between Eisenhower and McCarthy, 1952–1953," MA thesis, University of New Orleans, 1980.

——, "The Collapse of Liberation Rhetoric: The Eisenhower Administration and the 1956 Hungarian Crisis," *Hungarian Studies Review*, Vol. 20, Issue 1, Spring 2006.

Bischof, Günter, and Saki Dockrill, eds., *Cold War Respite: The Geneva Summit of July 1955*. Baton Rouge: Louisiana State University Press, 2000.

——, and Stephen Ambrose, eds., *Eisenhower: A Centenary Assessment*. Baton Rouge: Louisiana State University Press, 1995.

Bischof, Günter, Anton Pelinka, and Michael Gehler, eds., *Austrian Foreign Policy in Historical Context*. Piscataway, NJ: Transaction Publishers, 2005.

Bissell, Richard, and Jonathan Lewis, *Reflections of a Cold Warrior: From Yalta to the Bay of Pigs*. New Haven: Yale University Press, 1996.

Bittner, William, *Frank J. Lausche: A Political Biography*. New York: Studia Slovenica, 1975.

Black, Allida, *Casting Her Own Shadow: Eleanor Roosevelt and the Shaping of Postwar Liberation*. New York: Columbia University Press, 1996.

———, ed., *What I Hope to Leave Behind: The Essential Essays of Eleanor Roosevelt*. New York: Carlson Publishing, 1995.

Black, Conrad, *The Invincible Quest: The Life of Richard Milhous Nixon*. Toronto: McClelland & Stewart, 2007.

Black, Earl, and Merle Black, *Politics and Society in the South*. Cambridge: Harvard University Press, 1987.

———, *The Rise of Southern Republicans*. Cambridge: Harvard University Press, 2002.

Bliss Jr., Edward, ed., *In Search of Light: The Broadcasts of Edward R. Murrow 1938–1961*. New York: Knopf, 1967.

Blum, John, ed., *Public Philosopher: Selected Letters of Walter Lippmann*. New York: Ticknor & Fields, 1985.

Blumberg, Nathan, *One-Party Press? Coverage of the 1952 Presidential Campaign in 35 Daily Newspapers*. Norman: University of Nebraska Press, 1954.

Bohlen, Charles, *Witness to History 1929–1969*. New York: Norton, 1973.

Bohning, Don, *The Castro Obsession: Covert Operations against Cuba 1959–1965*. Washington, DC: Potomac, 2005.

Boller Jr., Paul, "Religion and the U.S. Presidency," *Journal of Church and State*, Vol. 21, Winter 1979.

Bon Tempo, Carl, "Americans at the Gate: The Politics of American Refugee Policy, 1952–1989," PhD dissertation, University of Virginia, Charlottesville, Va, 2004.

Bonsal, Philip, *Cuba, Castro and the United States*. Pittsburgh: University of Pittsburgh Press, 1971.

Booker, Simeon, *Black Man's America*. Englewood Cliffs, NJ: Prentice-Hall, 1964.

———, "What 'Ike' Thinks About Negroes," *Ebony*, Vol. 18, Dec 1962.

Borhi, László, "Liberation or Inaction? The United States and Hungary in 1956," in Schmidl, ed., *Die Ungarnkrise 1956 und Österreich*.

———, "Rollback, Containment, or Inaction? U.S. Policy and Eastern Europe in the 1950s," *Journal of Cold War Studies*, Vol. 1, No. 3, Fall 1999.

Borstelmann, Thomas, *The Cold War and the Color Line: American Race Relations in the Global Arena*. Cambridge: Harvard University Press, 2001.

Bose, Meena, *Shaping and Signaling Presidential Policy: The National Security Decision Making of Eisenhower and Kennedy*. College Station: Texas A&M Press, 1998.

Bottome, Edgar, *The Missile Gap: A Study of the Formulation of Military and Political Policy*. Madison, NJ: Farleigh Dickinson University Press, 1971.

Bowen, Michael, "Fight for the Right: The Quest for Republican Identity in the Postwar Period," PhD dissertation, University of Florida, Gainesville, Fla, 2006.

———, *The Roots of Modern Conservatism: Dewey, Taft and the Battle for the Soul of the Republican Party*. Chapel Hill: University of North Carolina Press, 2011.

Bowie, Robert and Richard Immerman, *Waging Peace: How Eisenhower Shaped an Enduring Cold War Strategy*. New York: Oxford University Press, 1998.

Bowles, Chester, *Africa's Challenge to America*. Berkeley: University of California Press, 1956.

——, *Promises to Keep: My Years in Public Life 1941–1969.* New York: Harper Colophon, 1972.

Bracey Jr., John H., and August Meier, eds., *Papers of the NAACP*, Supplement to P 4, Voting Rights, General Office Files, 1956–1965. Lanham, Md: University Publications of America, 1995. Microfilm.

Brady, Steven, *Eisenhower and Adenauer: Alliance Maintenance under Pressure, 1953–1960.* Lanham, Md: Lexington, 2010.

Branch, Taylor, *Parting the Waters: America in the King Years 1954–63.* New York: Simon and Schuster, 1988.

Brandon, Henry, *Special Relationships: A Foreign Correspondent's Memoirs from Roosevelt to Reagan.* New York: Atheneum, 1988.

Brands Jr., H.W., "The Age of Vulnerability: Eisenhower and the National Insecurity State," *American Historical Review*, Vol. 94, Oct 1989.

——, *Cold Warriors: Eisenhower's Generation and American Foreign Policy.* New York: Columbia University Press, 1988.

——, "From ANZUS to SEATO: United States Strategic Policy towards Australia and New Zealand, 1952–1954," *International History Review*, Vol. 9, May 2, 1987.

——, *India and the United States: The Cold Peace.* Boston: Twayne, 1990.

——, *Inside the Cold War: Loy Henderson and the Rise of the American Empire 1918–1961.* New York: Oxford University Press, 1991.

——, *The Specter of Neutralism: The United States and the Emergence of the Third World, 1947–1960.* New York: Columbia University Press, 1989.

——, "Testing Massive Retaliation: Credibility and Crisis Management in the Taiwan Straits," *International Security*, Vol. 12, Spring 1988.

——, *The United States in the World: A History of American Foreign Policy.* Vol. 2. Boston: Houghton Mifflin, 1994.

Branyan, Robert, and Lawrence Larsen, eds., *The Eisenhower Administration 1953–1961: A Documentary History.* Vols. 1–2. New York: Random House, 1971.

Bremner, Robert, *Chairman of the Fed: William McChesney Martin Jr. and the Creation of the Modern American Financial System.* New Haven: Yale University Press, 2004.

Brendon, Piers, *Ike: His Life and Times.* New York: Harper, 1986.

Bridges, Edson, "A Year End Review of the 1961 Economy," *Financial Analysts Journal*, Vol. 17, No. 6, Nov–Dec 1961.

Briggs, Ellis, *Farewell to Foggy Bottom: The Recollections of A Career Diplomat.* New York: David McKay, 1964.

——, *Proud Servant: The Memoirs of a Career Ambassador.* Kent, Ohio: Kent State University Press, 1998.

Brinkley, Douglas, *Dean Acheson: The Cold War Years, 1953–71.* New Haven: Yale University Press, 1992.

Broadwater, Jeff, *Adlai Stevenson and American Politics: The Odyssey of a Cold War Liberal.* New York: Twayne, 1994.

——, *Eisenhower and the Anti-Communist Crusade.* Chapel Hill: University of North Carolina Press, 1992.

Brodie, Fawn, *Richard Nixon: The Shaping of His Character.* New York: Norton, 1981.

Brooke III, George, "A Matter of Will: Sir Robert Thompson, Malaya, and the Failure of American Strategy in Vietnam," PhD dissertation, Georgetown University, Washington, DC, 2004.

Brooks, Karl, *Public Power, Private Dams: The Hells Canyon High Dam Controversy.* Seattle: University of Washington Press, 2006.

Brown, David, *Richard Hofstadter: An Intellectual Biography.* Chicago: University of Chicago Press, 2006.

Brown, Judith, *Nehru: A Political Life.* New Haven: Yale University Press, 2003.

Brown, L. Carl, ed., *Centerstage: American Diplomacy since World War II.* New York: Holmes & Meier, 1990.

Brownell Jr., Herbert, *Advising Ike: The Memoirs of Attorney General Herbert Brownell.* Lawrence: University of Kansas Press, 1993.

———, "Eisenhower's Civil Rights Program: A Personal Assessment," *Presidential Studies Quarterly,* Vol. 21, No. 2, Spring 1991.

———, "Presidential Disability: The Need for a Constitutional Amendment," *Yale Law Journal,* Vol. 68, No. 1, 1958–1959.

Bryan, Gerald, "Joseph McCarthy, Robert Kennedy, and the Greek Shipping Crisis: A Study of Foreign Policy Rhetoric," *Presidential Studies Quarterly,* Vol. 24, No. 1, Winter 1994.

Buckley, Roger, *U.S.-Japanese Alliance Diplomacy 1945–1990.* Cambridge: Cambridge University Press, 1992.

Buckley, William, ed., *Odyssey of a Friend: Whittaker Chambers' Letters to William F. Buckley, Jr. 1954–1961.* New York: Putnam, 1969.

Buhite, Russell, and Christopher Hamel, "War for Peace: The Question of an American Preventive War against the Soviet Union, 1945–1955," *Diplomatic History,* Vol. 14, Summer 1990.

Bundy, McGeorge, *Danger and Survival: Choices about the Bomb in the First Fifty Years.* New York: Random House, 1988.

Buni, Andrew, *The Negro in Virginia Politics 1902–1965.* Charlottesville: University of Virginia Press, 1967.

———, *Robert L. Vann of the Pittsburgh Courier: Politics and Black Journalism.* Pittsburgh: University of Pittsburgh Press, 1974.

Burk, Robert, *The Eisenhower Administration and Black Civil Rights, 1953–1961.* Knoxville: University of Tennessee Press, 1984.

Burke, Bob, and Ralph Thompson, *Bryce Harlow: Mr. Integrity.* Oklahoma City: Oklahoma Heritage Foundation, 2000.

Burns, James, et al., *Government by the People.* Texas Version, 2nd ed. Upper Saddle River, NJ: Prentice Hall, 1998.

Burns, William, *Economic Aid and the American Foreign Policy toward Egypt, 1955–1981.* Albany: State University of New York Press, 1985.

Burr, William, "Avoiding the Slippery Slope: The Eisenhower Administration and the Berlin Crisis, November 1958–January 1959," *Diplomatic History,* Vol. 18, No. 2, Spring 1994.

Bursten, Martin, *Escape from Fear.* New York: Syracuse University Press, 1958.

Busch, Andrew, *Horses in Midstream: U.S. Midterm Elections and Their Consequences*. Pittsburgh: University of Pittsburgh, 1991.

Butcher, Harry, *My Three Years with Eisenhower. The Personal Diary of Captain Harry C. Butcher, USNR, Naval Aide to General Eisenhower, 1942 to 1945*. New York: Simon and Schuster, 1946.

Cable, James, *The Geneva Conference of 1954 on Indochina*. New York: St. Martin's, 2000.

Cabot, John, *First Line of Defense: Forty Years' Experience of a Career Diplomat*. Washington, DC: School of Foreign Service, Georgetown, 1979.

Campbell, Angus, et al., *The American Voter*. New York: Wiley, 1960.

———, *Elections and the Political Order*. New York: Wiley, 1966.

———, *The Voter Decides*. Westport, Conn: Greenwood, 1954.

Campbell, James, *Middle Passages: American Journeys to Africa, 1787–2005*. New York: Penguin, 2006.

Campbell, Karl, *Senator Sam Ervin, Last of the Founding Fathers*. Chapel Hill: University of North Carolina Press, 2007.

Candee, Marjorie, ed., *Current Biography Yearbook 1954*. New York: Wilson, 1954.

———, *Current Biography Yearbook 1958*. New York: Wilson, 1958.

Cannon, James, ed., *Politics U.S.A.: A Political Guide to the Winning of Public Office*. New York: Doubleday, 1960.

Cannon, Poppy, *A Gentle Knight: My Husband, Walter White*. New York: Rinehart, 1956.

Carey, James, *Peru and the United States, 1900–1962*. Notre Dame: Notre Dame University Press, 1964.

Caridi, Ronald, *The Korean War and American Politics: The Republican Party as a Case Study*. Philadelphia: University of Pennsylvania Press, 1968.

Carlson, Peter, *K Blows Top: A Cold War Comic Interlude, Starring Nikita Khrushchev, America's Most Unlikely Tourist*. New York: Public Affairs, 2009.

Caro, Robert, *The Years of Lyndon Johnson: Master of the Senate*. New York: Knopf, 2002.

———, *The Years of Lyndon Johnson: The Passage of Power*. New York: Knopf, 2002.

Carruthers, Susan, *Winning Hearts and Minds: British Governments, the Media and Colonial Counter-Insurgency 1944–1960*. London: Leicester, 1995.

Carson, Claybourne, ed., *The Papers of Martin Luther King, Jr.*, Vol. 4: *Symbol of the Movement January 1957–December 1958*. Berkeley: University of California Press, 2000.

———, ed., *The Papers of Martin Luther King, Jr.*, Vol. 5: *Threshold of a New Decade January 1959–December 1960*. Berkeley: University of California Press, 2000.

Cater, Douglas, "How the Senate Passed the Civil Rights Bill," *The Reporter* Vol. 17, No. 3, Sept 5, 1957.

———, "Knowland: The Man Who Wants to Be Taft," *The Reporter*, Vol. 14, Mar 8, 1956.

Cathcart, R.S., and E.A. Schwarz, "New Nixon or Poor Richard," *North American Review*, New Series, Vol. 5, No. 5, Sept 1968.

Catledge, Turner, *My Life and The Times*. New York: Harper & Row, 1971.

Chafe, William, *Civilities and Civil Rights: Greensboro, North Carolina, and the Black Struggle for Freedom*. New York: Oxford University Press, 1980.

——, and Harvard Sitkoff, eds., *A History of Our Time: Readings on Postwar America*. 5th ed. New York: Oxford University Press, 1999.

Chandler, David, *The Tragedy of Cambodian History: Politics, War, and Revolution since 1945*. New Haven: Yale University Press, 1991.

Chang, Gordon, *Friends and Enemies: The United States, China, and the Soviet Union, 1948–1972*. Stanford: Stanford University Press, 1990.

——, "To the Nuclear Brink: Eisenhower, Dulles and the Quemoy-Matsu Crisis," *International Security*, Vol. 12, Spring 1988.

——, and He Di, "The Absence of War in the U.S.-China Confrontation over Quemoy and Matsu in 1954–1955: Contingency, Luck, Deference," *American Historical Review*, Vol. 98, No. 5, Dec 1993.

Chang, Jung, and John Halliday, *Mao: The Unknown Story*. New York: Knopf, 2005.

Chappell, David, *A Stone of Hope: Prophetic Religion and the Death of Jim Crow*. Chapel Hill: University of North Carolina Press, 2004.

Chernus, Ira, *Apocalypse Management: Eisenhower and the Discourse of National Insecurity*. Stanford: Stanford University Press, 2008.

——, *Eisenhower's Atoms for Peace*. College Station: Texas A&M Press, 2002.

——, *General Eisenhower: Ideology and Discourse*. East Lansing: Michigan State University Press, 2002.

Childs, Marquis, *Eisenhower: Captive Hero*. New York: Harcourt, Brace, 1958.

——, *Witness to Power*. New York: McGraw-Hill, 1975.

Christensen, Thomas, *Useful Adversaries: Grand Strategy, Domestic Mobilization, and Sino American Conflict, 1947–1958*. Princeton: Princeton University Press, 1996.

Chu, Pao-chin, V.K. *Wellington Koo: A Case Study of China's Diplomat and Diplomacy of Nationalism, 1912–1966*. Hong Kong: Chinese, 1981.

Clancy, Paul, *Just a County Lawyer: A Biography of Sam Ervin*. Bloomington: Indiana University Press, 1974.

Clark, E. Culpepper, *The Schoolhouse Door: Segregation's Last Stand at the University of Alabama*. New York: Oxford University Press, 1993.

Clark, Kenneth, "The Civil Rights Movement: Momentum and Organization," *Daedaulus*, Vol. 95, No. 1, Winter 1966.

Clark Jr., Paul, *The United States and Somoza, 1933–1956: A Revisionist Look*. Westport, Conn: Praeger, 1992.

Clark, Roy, "The 1958 California Gubernatorial Election: How Republican Party Infighting Affected the Outcome," MA thesis, California State University, Long Beach, 1999.

Clay, William, *Just Permanent Interests: Black Americans in Congress, 1870–1991*. New York: Amistad, 1992.

Clifford, Clark, *Counsel to the President: A Memoir*. New York: Random House, 1991.

Clifford, J. Garry, "McCarthyism," In Jentleson, Paterson, and Rizopoulos, eds., *Encyclopedia of U.S. Foreign Relations*.

Cloake, John, *Templer: Tiger of Malaya: The Life of Field Marshal Sir Gerald Templer*. London: Harrap, 1985.

Clowse, Barbara, *Brainpower for the Cold War: The Sputnik Crisis and the National Defense Education Act of 1958*. Westport, Conn: Greenwood, 1981.

Clutterbuck, Richard, *Conflict and Violence in Singapore and Malaysia 1945–1983*. Boulder: Westview, 1985.

Cobbs, Elizabeth, *The Rich Neighbor Policy: Rockefeller and Kaiser in Brazil*. New Haven: Yale University Press, 1992.

Coffin, Tris, "How Lyndon Johnson Engineered Compromise on the Civil Rights Bill," *New Leader*, Vol. 40, No. 31, Aug 5, 1957.

Cogan, Charles, *Oldest Allies, Guarded Friends: The United States and France since 1940*. Westport, Conn: Praeger, 1994.

Cohen, Warren, *The Cambridge History of American Foreign Relations: America in the Age of Soviet Power, 1945–1991*. Vol. 4. Cambridge: Cambridge University Press, 1993.

———, and Akire Iriye, eds., *The Great Powers in East Asia, 1953–1906*. New York: Columbia University Press, 1990.

Cohodas, Nadine, *Strom Thurmond & the Politics of Southern Change*. New York: Simon & Schuster, 1993.

Colburn, George, "Richard Nixon Interview," The Eisenhower Legacy Collection, Oct 18, 2012, C-SPAN3.

Colby, William, and Peter Forbath, *Honorable Men: My Life in the CIA*. New York: Simon and Schuster, 1978.

Coleman, Bradley, *Colombia and the United States: The Making of an Inter-American Alliance, 1939–1960*. Kent, Ohio: Kent State University Press, 2008.

Conant, James, *My Several Lives: Memoirs of a Social Inventor*. New York: Harper & Row, 1970.

Connelly, Matthew, *A Diplomatic Revolution: Algeria's Fight for Independence and the Origins of the Post-Cold War Era*. New York: Oxford University Press, 2002.

Conniff, Michael, *Panama and the United States: The Forced Alliance*. Athens: University of Georgia Press, 1992.

Cook, Blanche, *The Declassified Eisenhower: A Divided Legacy*. New York: Doubleday, 1981.

Costello, William, *The Facts About Nixon: An Unauthorized Biography*. New York: Viking, 1960.

Cotham, Perry, ed., *Christian Social Ethics*. Grand Rapids, Mich: Baker Book House, 1979.

Cotton, Norris, *In the Senate: Amidst the Conflict and the Turmoil*. New York: Dodd, Mead, 1978.

Cox, Patrick, *Ralph Yarborough, The People's Senator*. Austin: University of Texas Press, 2001.

Craig, Campbell, *Destroying the Villages: Eisenhower and Thermonuclear War*. New York: Columbia University Press, 1998.

Craig, R. Bruce, *Treasonable Doubt: The Harry Dexter White Spy Case*. Lawrence: University of Kansas Press, 2004.

Crandell, William, "A Party Divided Against Itself: Anticommunism and the Transformation of the Republican Right, 1945–1956," PhD dissertation, Ohio State University, Columbus, 1983.

Cray, Ed, *Chief Justice: A Biography of Earl Warren*. New York: Simon & Schuster, 1997.

Crispell, Brian, *George Amistad Smathers and Cold War America*. Athens: University of North Georgia Press, 1999.

Critchlow, Donald, *The Conservative Ascendancy: How the GOP Right Made Political History*. Cambridge: Harvard University Press, 2007.

Cronin, Audrey, *Great Power Politics and the Struggle over Austria*. Ithaca, NY: Cornell University Press, 1986.

Cronkite, Walter, *A Reporter's Life*. New York: Knopf, 1996.

Crosby, S.J., Donald, *God, Church, and Flag: Senator Joseph R. McCarthy and the Catholic Church 1950–1957*. Chapel Hill: University of North Carolina Press, 1978.

Crowley, David, and Jane Pavitt, eds., *Cold War Modern: Design 1945–1970*. London: V&A, 2008.

Crowley, Monica, *Nixon in Winter*. New York: Random House, 1998.

——, *Nixon Off the Record: His Candid Commentary on People and Politics*. New York: Random House, 1996.

Cull, Nicholas, *The Cold War and the United States Information Agency: American Propaganda and Public Diplomacy, 1945–1989*. Cambridge: Cambridge University Press, 2008.

Cullather, Nick, "America's Boy? Ramon Magsaysay and the Illusion of Influence," *Pacific Historical Review*, Vol. 63, No. 3, Aug 1993.

——, *Illusions of Influence: The Political Economy of United States-Philippine Relations, 1942–1960*. Stanford: Stanford University Press, 1994.

——, *Operation PBSUCCESS: The United States and Guatemala 1952–1954*. Washington, DC: CIA, 1994.

——, *Secret History: The CIA's Classified Account of Its Operations in Guatemala, 1952–1954*. Stanford: Stanford University Press, 1999.

Cutler, Robert, *No Time for Rest*. Boston: Little, Brown, 1966.

Dailey, Joseph, "The Eisenhower-Nixon Campaign Organization of 1952," PhD dissertation, University of Illinois at Urbana-Champaign, 1975.

Dalfiume, Richard, *Desegregation of the U.S. Armed Forces: Fighting on Two Fronts 1939–1953*. Columbia: University of Missouri Press, 1969.

——, "The 'Forgotten Years' of the Negro Revolution," *Journal of American History*, Vol. 55, No. 1, June 1968.

Dallek, Robert, *Lone Star Rising: Lyndon Johnson and His Times, 1908–1960*. New York: Oxford University Press, 1991.

——, *An Unfinished Life: John F. Kennedy 1917–1963*. Boston: Little, Brown, 2003.

Danielson, Michael, *The Politics of Exclusion*. New York: Columbia University Press, 1976.

Davidson, Chandler, *Race and Class in Texas Politics*. Princeton: Princeton University Press, 1990.

Davies, Richard, *America's Obsession: Sports and Society Since 1945*. Fort Worth: Harcourt Brace, 1994.

Davis, Michael, "The Cold War, Refugees, and U.S. Immigration Policy, 1952–1965," PhD dissertation, Vanderbilt University, Nashville, Tenn, 1996.

Day, John, *The Southern Manifesto: Mass Resistance and the Fight to Preserve Segregation*. Jackson: University Press of Mississippi, 2014.

De Roche, Andrew, *Black, White, and Chrome: The United States and Zimbabwe, 1953–1998*. Trenton, NJ: African World, 2001.

——, "Francis Bolton, Margaret Tibbitts and the U.S. Relations with the Rhodesian Federation, 1950–1960," in Gewald and Macola, *Living the End of Empire*.

de Toledano, Ralph, *Lament for a Generation*. New York: Farrar, Straus, and Cudahy, 1960.

——, *Nixon*. New York: Holt, 1956.

——, *One Man Alone: Richard Nixon*. New York: Viking, 1960.

——, ed., *Notes from the Underground: The Whittaker Chambers–Ralph de Toledano Letters 1949–1960*. Washington, DC: Regnery, 1997.

Dean, Robert, *Imperial Brotherhood: Gender and the Making of Cold War Foreign Policy*. Amherst: University of Massachusetts Press, 2001.

Deibel, Terry, and John Gaddis, eds., *Containment: Concept and Policy*. Vol. 2. Washington, DC: National Defense University Press, 1986.

Delton, Jennifer, *Racial Integration in Corporate America, 1940–1990*. Cambridge: Cambridge University Press, 2009.

D'Emilio, John, *Lost Prophet: The Life and Times of Bayard Rustin*. New York: Free Press, 2003.

Derthick, Martha, *City Politics in Washington, DC*. Cambridge: Harvard University Press, 1962.

D'Este, Carlo, *Eisenhower: A Soldier's Life*. New York: Holt, 2002.

Di, He, "The Most Respected Enemy: Mao Zedong's Perception of the United States," *China Quarterly*, No. 137, Mar 1994.

Diamond, Robert, ed., *A Guide to U.S. Elections*. Washington, DC: Congressional Quarterly, 1975.

The Diaries of Dwight D. Eisenhower, 1953–1961. Lanham, Md: University Publications of America, 1986.

Dickerson, Nancy, *Among Those Present: A Reporter's Twenty-five Years in Washington*. New York: Random House, 1976.

Dickson, Paul, *Sputnik: The Shock of the Century*. New York: Walker & Co, 2001.

Dimbleby, David, and David Reynolds, *An Ocean Apart: The Relationship between Britain and America in the Twentieth Century*. New York: Random House, 1988.

Dingman, Roger, "Atomic Diplomacy During the Korean War," *International Security*, Vol. 13, Winter 1988/1989.

——, "John Foster Dulles and the Creation of the South-East Asia Treaty Organization in 1954," *International History Review*, Vol. 11, Aug 1989.

Divine, Robert, *Foreign Policy and U.S. Presidential Elections 1952–1960*. New York: New Viewpoints, 1974.

——, *The Sputnik Challenge*. New York: Oxford University Press, 1993.

Dmohowski, Joseph, "From a Common Ground: The Quaker Heritage of Jessamyn West and Richard Nixon," *California History*, Vol. 73, No. 3, 1994.

Dobbs, Ricky, *Yellow Dogs and Republicans: Allan Shivers and Two-Party Politics*. College Station: Texas A&M Press, 2008.-

Dobrynin, Anatoly, *In Confidence: Moscow's Ambassador to America's Six Cold War Presidents*. New York: Random House, 1995.

Dockrill, Saki, *Eisenhower's New-Look National Security Policy, 1953–61.* New York: St. Martin's, 1996.

——, ed., *Controversy and Compromise: Alliance Politics between Great Britain, the Federal Republic of Germany, and the United States of America, 1945–1967.* Germany: Philo, 1998.

Doenecke, Justus, *Not to the Swift: The Old Isolationists in the Cold War Era.* Lewisburg, Penn: Bucknell, 1979.

Donaldson, Gary, *The First Modern Campaign: Kennedy, Nixon, and the Election of 1960.* Lanham, Md: Rowman & Littlefield, 2007.

Donovan, John, *Crusader in the Cold War: A Biography of Fr. John S. Cronin, S.J. (1908– 1994).* New York: Peter Lang, 2005.

Donovan, Robert, *Boxing the Kangaroo: A Reporter's Memoir.* Columbia: University of Missouri Press, 2002.

——, *Confidential Secretary: Ann Whitman's Twenty Years with Eisenhower and Rockefeller.* New York: Dutton, 1988.

——, *Eisenhower: The Inside Story.* New York: Harpers & Brothers, 1956.

Douglas, Helen, *A Full Life,* New York: Doubleday, 1982.

Douglas, Paul, *In the Fullness of Time: The Memoirs of Paul H. Douglas.* New York: Harcourt Brace Jovanovich, 1971, 1972.

——, "The 1960 Voting Rights Bill: The Struggle, the Final Results, and the Reasons," *Journal of Intergroup Relations,* Vol. 1, Summer 1960.

Dower, John, *Empire and Aftermath: Yoshida Shigeru and the Japanese Experience 1878– 1954.* Cambridge: Harvard University Press, 1979.

Doyle, William, *Inside the Oval Office: The White House Tapes from FDR to Clinton.* New York: Kodansha International, 1999.

Drew, Elizabeth, *Richard M. Nixon.* New York: Times Books, 2007.

Drown, Merle, *In the Arena: Life and Times of William W. Treat.* Brookline, NH: Hobblebush Bush, 2009.

Drukman, Mason, *Wayne Morse: A Political Biography.* Portland: Oregon Historical Society Press, 1997.

Dudziak, Mary, *Cold War Civil Rights: Race and the Image of American Diplomacy.* Princeton: Princeton University Press, 2000.

Dugger, Ronnie, *The Politician: The Life and Times of Lyndon Johnson—The Drive for Power, from the Frontier to Master of the Senate.* New York: Norton, 1982.

Dulaney, H.G., and Edward Phillips, eds., *"Speak, Mister Speaker."* Bonham, Texas: Sam Rayburn Foundation, 1978.

Dulles, Allen, *The Craft of Intelligence.* New York: Harper & Row, 1963.

Dulles, Eleanor, *John Foster Dulles: The Last Year.* New York: Harcourt, Brace & World, 1963.

Dulles, Foster, *The Civil Rights Commission: 1957–1965.* East Lansing: Michigan State University Press, 1968.

Dulles, John Foster, and Christian A. Herter, *Papers, 1953–1961: The White House Correspondence and Memoranda Series.* Lanham, Md: University Publications of America, 1986. Microfilm.

Dunnigan, Alice, *A Black Woman's Experience: From Schoolhouse to White House*. Philadelphia: Dorrance, 1974.

Duram, James, *A Moderate Among Extremists: Dwight D. Eisenhower and the School Desegregation Crisis*. Chicago: Nelson-Hall, 1981.

Dyer, Stanford, "Lyndon B. Johnson and the Politics of Civil Rights, 1935–1960: The Art of 'Moderate Leadership'," PhD dissertation, Texas A&M University, College Station, 1978.

Edelsberg, Herman, "The New Civil Rights Law: How It Happened," *ADL Bulletin*, Vol. 14, Oct 1957.

Edwards III, George, *On Deaf Ears: The Limits of the Bully Pulpit*. New Haven: Yale University Press, 2003.

———, *The Strategic President: Persuasion and Opportunity in Presidential Leadership*. Princeton: Princeton University Press, 2009.

Edwards, Lee, *The Conservative Revolution: The Movement that Remade America*. New York: Free Press, 1999.

Edwards, Peter, *Crises and Commitments: The Politics and Diplomacy of Australia's Involvement in Southeast Asian Conflicts, 1948–1965*. North Sydney, Australia: Allen and Unwin, 1992.

Ehrlichman, John, "In the Eye of the Storm," Vol. I, Studio American International Television, 1997.

"Eisenhower: The President," *American Experience*, transcript, WGBH/PBS.

Eisenhower, David, *Going Home to Glory: A Memoir of Life with Dwight D. Eisenhower, 1961–1969*. New York: Simon and Schuster, 2010.

Eisenhower, Dwight, *At Ease: Stories I Tell to Friends*. New York: Doubleday, 1967.

———, "The Central Role of the President in the Conduct of Security Affairs," in Jordon, ed., *Issues of National Security in the 1970's*.

———, *Public Papers of the President of the United States: Dwight D. Eisenhower 1953–1961*. Washington, DC: GPO, 1960.

———, "Some Thoughts on the Presidency," *Reader's Digest*, Nov 1968.

———, "What I Have Learned," *Saturday Review*, Vol. 49, Sept 10, 1966.

———, *The White House Years: Mandate for Change 1953–1956*. New York: Doubleday, 1963.

———, *The White House Years: Waging Peace*. New York: Doubleday, 1965.

Eisenhower, John, *Strictly Personal*. New York: Doubleday, 1974.

Eisenhower, Julie, *Pat Nixon: The Untold Story*. New York: Simon and Schuster, 1986.

———, *Special People*. New York: Simon and Schuster, 1977.

Eisenhower, Milton, *The President Is Calling*. New York: Doubleday, 1974.

———, *The Wine Is Bitter: The United States and Latin America*. New York: Doubleday, 1963.

Eisenhower, Susan, *Mrs. Ike: Memoirs and Reflections in the Life of Mamie Eisenhower*. New York: Farrar, Straus and Giroux, 1996.

Eliff, John, *The United States Department of Justice and Individual Rights 1937–1962*. New York: Garland, 1987.

Ellis, Richard, *Presidential Lightning Rods: The Politics of Blame Avoidance*. Lawrence: University of Kansas Press, 1994.

Ellis, Sylvia, *Freedom's Pragmatist: Lyndon Johnson and Civil Rights*. Gainesville: University Press of Florida, 2013.

Elman, Philip, and Norman Silber, "The Solicitor General's Office, Justice Frankfurter, and Civil Rights Litigation, 1946–1960," *Harvard Law Review*, Vol. 100, No. 4, Feb 1987.

Elson, Edward, *Wide Was His Parish*. Wheaton, Ill: Tyndale House, 1986.

Emanuel, Anne, *Elbert Parr Tuttle: Chief Jurist of the Civil Rights Revolution*. Athens: University of North Georgia Press, 2011.

Emblidge, David, ed., *My Day: The Best of Eleanor Roosevelt's Acclaimed Newspaper Columns, 1936–1962*. New York: De Capo, 2001.

Engelbourg, Saul, "The Council of Economic Advisers and the Recession of 1953–54," *Business History Review*, Vol. 54, No. 2, Summer 1980.

Erdmann, Andrew, "'War No Longer Has Any Logic Whatever': Dwight D. Eisenhower and the Thermonuclear Revolution," in Gaddis and Gordon, *Cold War Statesmen Confront the Bomb*.

Erskine, Helen, "Dick and Pat Nixon: The Team on Ike's Team," *Collier's*, Vol. 134, July 9, 1954.

——, "The Poll: Race Relations," *Public Opinion Quarterly*, Vol. 27, No. 1, Spring 1962.

——, ed., "Revival: Reports from the Polls," *Public Opinion Quarterly*, Vol. 25, No. 1, Spring 1961.

Evans, M. Stanton, *Blacklisted By History: The Untold Story of Joseph McCarthy and His Fight Against America's Enemies*. New York: Crown, 2007.

Evans, Rowland, and Robert Novak, *Lyndon B. Johnson: Exercise of Power*. New York: New American Library, 1966.

Ewald Jr., William, *Eisenhower the President: Crucial Days, 1951–1960*. Upper Saddle River, NJ: Prentice Hall, 1981.

——, *Who Killed Joe McCarthy?* New York: Simon and Schuster, 1984.

Eyes on the Prize: America's Civil Rights Years: Episode I: "Awakenings (1954–1956)" and Episode 2: "Fighting Back (1957–1962)". PBS, 1986.

Fairbanks, James, "Religious Dimensions of Presidential Leadership: The Case of Dwight Eisenhower," *Presidential Studies Quarterly*, Vol. 12, No. 2, Spring 1982.

Falcoff, Mark, ed., *The Cuban Revolution and the United States: A History in Documents 1958–1960*. Washington, DC: U.S. Cuba Press, 2001.

Falk, Stanley, "The National Security Council Under Truman, Eisenhower, and Kennedy," *Political Science Quarterly*, Vol. 79, No. 3, Sept 1964.

Falkner, David, *Great Time Coming: The Life of Jackie Robinson, from Baseball to Birmingham*. New York: Simon & Schuster, 1995.

Faries, McIntyre, *Rememb'ring*. Glendale, Ca: Griffin Publishing, 1993.

Farmer, James, *Lay Bare the Heart: An Autobiography of the Civil Rights Movement*. New York: Plume, 1985.

Farzanegan, Bahram, "United States Response and Reaction to the Emergence of Arab and African States in International Politics," PhD dissertation, American University, Washington, DC, 1966.

Feerick, John, "The Twenty-Fifth Amendment: Its Origins and History," in Gilbert, ed., *Managing Crisis*.

Feldman, Glenn, ed., *Painting Dixie Red: When, Where, Why, and How the South Became Republican*. Gainesville: University Press of Florida, 2011.

Feldstein, Mark, "Fighting Quakers: The 1950s Battle Between Richard Nixon and Columnist Drew Pearson," *Journalism History*, Vol. 30, No. 2, Summer 2004.

Fenby, Jonathan, *Chiang Kai-Shek: China's Generalissimo and the Nation He Lost*. New York: Carroll & Graf, 2003.

Ferrell, Robert, *Harry S. Truman: A Life*. Columbia: University of Missouri Press, 1994.

——, *Ill-Advised: Presidential Health and Public Trust*. Columbia: University of Missouri Press, 1992.

——, ed., *The American Secretaries of State and Their Diplomacy*, Vol. 17: Louis Gerson, "John Foster Dulles." New York: Copper Square, 1967.

——, ed., *The American Secretaries of State and Their Diplomacy*, Vol. 18: G. Bernard Noble, "Christian A. Herter." New York: Copper Square, 1970.

——, ed., *The Diary of James C. Hagerty: Eisenhower in Mid Course, 1954–1955*. Bloomington: Indiana University Press, 1983.

——, ed., *Truman in the White House: The Diary of Eben A. Ayers*. Columbia: University of Missouri Press, 1991.

Finke, Roger, and Rodney Stark, *The Churching of America, 1776–1990: Winners and Losers in Our Religious Economy*. 2nd ed. New Brunswick, NJ: Rutgers University Press, 2005.

Finley, Keith, *Delaying the Dream: Southern Senators and the Fight against Civil Rights, 1938–1965*. Baton Rouge: Louisiana State University Press, 2008.

Fish, Steven, "After Stalin's Death: The Anglo-American Debate Over a New Cold War," *Diplomatic History*, Vol. 10, No. 4, Fall 1986.

Fishman, Ethan, William Pederson, and Mark Rozell, eds., *George Washington: Foundation of Presidential Leadership and Character*. Westport, Conn: Praeger, 2001.

Fite, Gilbert, *Richard B. Russell, Jr., Senator from Georgia*. Chapel Hill: University of North Carolina Press, 1991.

——, "Richard B. Russell and Lyndon B. Johnson: The Story of a Strange Friendship," *Missouri Historical Review*, Vol. 83, Jan 1989.

Flournoy, Houston, "The 1958 Knowland Campaign in California—Design for Defeat," *Western Political Quarterly*, Vol. 12, June 1959.

Flynn, Matthew, "Reconsidering the China Lobby: Senator William F. Knowland and US-China Policy, 1945–1958," Vols. 1 and 2, PhD dissertation, Ohio University, Athens, 2004.

Førland, Tor Egil, "'Selling Firearms to the Indians': Eisenhower's Export Control Policy, 1953–54," *Diplomatic History*, Vol. 15, Issue 2, Apr 1991.

Foner, Eric, *Give Me Liberty!* New York: Norton, 2013.

Fontenay, Charles, *Estes Kefauver: A Biography*. Knoxville: University of Tennessee Press, 1980.

Foot, Rosemary, "Making Known the Unknown War: Policy Analysis of the Korean Conflict in the Last Decade," *Diplomatic History*, Vol. 15, No. 3, 1991.

——, "Nuclear Coercion and the Ending of the Korean Conflict," *International Security*, Vol. 13, Winter 1988/1989.

——, *The Wrong War: American Policy and the Dimensions of the Korean Conflict, 1950–1953*. Ithaca, NY: Cornell University Press, 1985.

Frady, Marshall, *Billy Graham: A Parable of American Righteousness*. Boston: Little, Brown, 1979.

Frank, Jeffrey, *Ike and Dick: Portrait of a Strange Political Marriage*. New York: Simon and Schuster, 2013.

Frankel, Max, *The Times of My Life and My Life with The [the] Times*. New York: Random House, 1999.

Franklin, John, and Alfred Moss, Jr., *From Slavery to Freedom: A History of African Americans*. New York: Knopf, 1994.

Frantz, Joe, "Opening a Curtain: The Metamorphosis of Lyndon B. Johnson," *Journal of Southern History*, Vol. 45, No. 1, Feb 1979.

Fraser, Cary, "An American Dilemma: Race and Realpolitik in the American Response to the Bandung Conference, 1955," in Plummer, ed., *Window on Freedom*.

——, "Crossing the Color Line in Little Rock: The Eisenhower Administration and the Dilemma of Race for U.S. Foreign Policy," *Diplomatic History*, Vol. 24, No. 2, Spring 2000.

Frey, Marc, Ronald Pruessen, and Tan Tai Young, eds., *The Transformation of Southeast Asia: International Perspectives on Decolonialization*. New York: Sharpe, 2003.

Frick, Daniel, *Reinventing Richard Nixon: A Cultural History of an American Obsession*. Lawrence: University of Kansas Press, 2008.

Fried, Richard, *Men Against McCarthy*. New York: Columbia University Press, 1976.

——, *Nightmare in Red: The McCarthy Era in Perspective*. New York: Oxford University Press, 1990.

Friedman, Joel, *Champion of Civil Rights: Judge John Minor Wisdom*. Baton Rouge: Louisiana State University Press, 2009.

Friel, Charlotte, "The Influence of Television in the Political Career of Richard M. Nixon, 1946–1962," PhD dissertation, New York University, New York, 1968.

Frier, David, *Conflict of Interest in the Eisenhower Administration*. Ames: Iowa State University Press, 1969.

Fry, Michael, "Eisenhower and the Suez Crisis of 1956," in Warshaw, ed., *Reexamining the Eisenhower Presidency*.

Frymer, Paul, *Black and Blue: African Americans, the Labor Movement and the Decline of the Democratic Party*. Princeton: Princeton University Press, 2008.

——, *Uneasy Alliances: Race and Party Competition in America*. Princeton: Princeton University Press, 1999.

Fursenko, Alekansandr, and Timothy Naftali, *Khrushchev's Cold War: The Inside Story of an American Adversary*. New York: Norton, 2006.

——, *"One Hell of a Gamble": Khrushchev, Castro, and Kennedy, 1958–1964*. New York: Norton, 1997.

Gaddis, John Lewis, and Philip H. Gordon, *Cold War Statesmen Confront the Bomb: Nuclear Diplomacy since 1945*. New York: Oxford University Press, 1999.

Gaiduk, Ilya, *Confronting Vietnam: Soviet Policy toward the Indochina Conflict, 1954–1963*. Stanford: Stanford University Press, 2003.

Galambos, Louis, and Daun van Ee, eds., *The Papers of Dwight David Eisenhower*. Vols. 10–21. Baltimore: Johns Hopkins, 1984–2001.

Galbraith, John, *A Life in Our Times: Memoirs*. Boston: Houghton, Mifflin, 1981.

Gallup, George, ed., *The Gallup Poll: Public Opinion 1935–1971*. Vols. 2 and 3, New York: Random House, 1972.

Gardner, Michael, *Harry Truman and Civil Rights: Moral Courage and Political Risks*. Carbondale: Southern Illinois University Press, 2002.

———, "A President Who Regarded Civil Rights as a Moral Imperative," in Geselbracht, ed., *The Civil Rights Legacy*.

Gardner, Paul, *Shared Hopes, Separate Fears: Fifty Years of U.S.–Indonesian Relations*. Boulder: Westview, 1997.

Garment, Leonard, *Crazy Rhythm: My Journey from Brooklyn, Jazz, and Wall Street to Nixon's White House, Watergate, and Beyond*. New York: Times Books, 1997.

Garrow, David, *Bearing the Cross: Martin Luther King, Jr. and the Southern Christian Leadership Conference*. New York: Morrow, 1986.

Garthoff, Raymond, *Assessing the Adversary: Estimates by the Eisenhower Administration of Soviet Intentions and Capabilities*. Washington, DC: Brookings Institution, 1991.

———, "Intelligence Aspects of Early Cold War Summitry (1959–60)," *Intelligence and National Security*, Vol. 14, No. 3, Fall 1999.

———, *A Journey through the Cold War: A Memoir of Containment and Coexistence*. Washington, DC: Brookings Institution, 2001.

Gasiorowski, Mark, *U.S. Foreign Policy and the Shah: Building a Client State in Iran*. Ithaca, NY: Cornell University Press, 1991.

Gaskin, Thomas, "Senator Lyndon B. Johnson and U.S. Foreign Policy," PhD dissertation, University of Washington, Seattle, 1989.

Gati, Charles, *Failed Illusions: Moscow, Washington, Budapest, and the 1956 Hungarian Revolt*. Stanford: Stanford University Press, 2006.

Geelhoed, E. Bruce, *Charles E. Wilson and Controversy of the Pentagon, 1953–1957*. Detroit: Wayne State University Press, 1979.

Gelher, Michael, "From Non-alignment to Neutrality: Austria's Transformation during the First East-West Détente, 1953–1958," *Journal of Cold War Studies*, Vol. 7, No. 4, Fall 2005.

Gellman, Irwin, *The Contender: Richard Nixon: The Congress Years, 1946–1952*. New York: Free Press, 1999.

———, "The Richard Nixon Vice Presidency: Research Without the Nixon Manuscripts," in Small, ed., *A Companion to Richard M. Nixon*.

———, *Roosevelt and Batista: Good Neighbor Diplomacy in Cuba, 1933–1945*. Albuquerque: University of New Mexico Press, 1973.

Gendzier, Irene, *Notes from the Minefield: United States Intervention in Lebanon and the Middle East, 1945–1958*. New York: Columbia University Press, 1997.

Gentry, Curt, *J. Edgar Hoover: The Man and His Secrets*. New York: Norton, 1991.

Geselbracht, Raymond, "The Truman Library and Truman's Civil Rights Legacy," in Geselbracht, ed., *The Civil Rights Legacy*.

——, ed., *The Civil Rights Legacy of Harry S. Truman*. Kirksville, Mo: Truman State University Press, 2007.

Geselbracht, Ray, and David Acheson, eds., *Affection and Trust: The Personal Correspondence of Harry S. Truman and Dean Acheson, 1953–1971*. New York: Knopf, 2010.

Gewald, Jan-Bart, Marja Hinfelaar, and Giacomo Macola, eds., *Living the End of Empire*. Boston: Brill, 2011.

Giannattasio, Gerald and Linda, "Eisenhower, Constitutional Practice, and the Twenty-fifth Amendment," in Krieg, ed., *Dwight D. Eisenhower*.

Gibbs, Nancy, and Michael Duffy, *The Preacher and the Presidents: Billy Graham in the White House*. New York: Center Street, 2007.

——, *The Presidents Club: Inside the World's Most Exclusive Fraternity*. New York: Simon & Schuster, 2012.

——, "The Presidents Club," May 8, 2012, C-SPAN2, www.c-span.org/video/?305478-1/qa-nancy-gibbs-michael-duffy.

Gilbert, Robert, "Eisenhower's 1955 Heart Attack: Medical Treatment, Political Effects and the 'Behind the Scenes' Leadership Style," *Politics and The Life Sciences*, Vol. 27, No. 1, 2007.

——, ed., *Managing Crisis: Presidential Disability and the Twenty-Fifth Amendment*. New York: Fordham University Press, 2000.

——, *The Mortal Presidency: Illness and Anguish in the White House*. New York: Basic Books, 1992.

——, *Television and Presidential Politics*. Hanover, Mass: Christopher Publishing House, 1972.

Gillon, Steven, *Politics and Vision: The ADA and American Liberalism, 1947–1985*. New York: Oxford University Press, 1987.

Glant, Tibor, *Remember Hungary 1956: Essays on the Hungarian Revolution and War of Independence in American Memory*. Montclair, NJ: Center for Hungarian Studies and Publications, 2007.

Glantz, Oscar, "The Negro Voter in Northern Industrial Cities," *Western Political Quarterly*, Vol. 13, Dec 1960.

Glaser, James, *Race, Campaign Politics and the Realignment in the South*. New Haven: Yale University Press, 1996.

Gleijeses, Piero, "Ships in the Night: The CIA, the White House and the Bay of Pigs," *Journal of Latin American Studies*, Vol. 27, No. 1, Feb 1995.

Gobetz. Edward, ed., *Ohio's Lincoln Frank J. Lausche: A Tribute and Festschrift for His 90th Birthday*. Willoughby Hills, Ohio: Slovenian Research Center of America, 1985.

Goldberg, Benjamin, "The Vice Presidency of Richard M. Nixon: One Man's Quest for National Respect, an International Reputation, and the Presidency." PhD dissertation, College of William and Mary, Williamsburg, Va, 1998.

Goldberg, Robert, *Barry Goldwater*. New Haven: Yale University Press, 1995.

Goldfield, David, "Border Men: Truman, Eisenhower, Johnson, and Civil Rights, *Journal of Southern History*, Vol. 80, No. 1, Feb 2014.

Goldman, Eric, *The Crucial Decade—And After: America, 1945–1960*. New York: Knopf, 1966.

Goldsmith, John, *Colleagues: Richard B. Russell and His Apprentice, Lyndon B. Johnson*. Macon, Ga: Mercer, 1998.

Goldstein, Joel, *The Modern American Vice Presidency: The Transformation of a Political Institution*. Princeton: Princeton University Press, 1982.

———, "The Vice Presidency and the Twenty-Fifth Amendment: The Powers of Reciprocal Relationships," in Gilbert, ed., *Managing Crisis*.

Goldwater, Barry, *Goldwater*. New York: Doubleday, 1988.

———, *With No Apologies: The Personal and Political Memoirs of United States Senator Barry M. Goldwater*. New York: Morrow, 1979.

Gonzalez, Norma, "U.S.-Argentine Relations in the 1950s." PhD dissertation, University of Massachusetts, Amherst, 1992.

Gopal, Sarvepalli, *Jawaharlal Nehru: A Biography*. Vol. 2: 1947–1956. London: Jonathan Cape, 1979.

———, ed., *Selected Works of Jawaharlal Nehru*. Second Series. Vol. 24 (1 October 1953–31 January 1954). New Delhi: Jawaharlal Nehru Memorial Fund, 1999.

Gordon, Leonard, "United States Opposition to Use of Force in the Taiwan Strait, 1954–1962," *Journal of American History*, Vol. 72, Dec 1985.

Gordon, Lois, and Alan Gordon, *American Chronicle: Six Decades in American Life, 1920–1980*. New York: Atheneum, 1987.

Gore, Albert, *Let the Glory Out: My South and Its Politics*. New York: Viking, 1972.

Gorman, Joseph, *Kefauver: A Political Biography*. New York: Oxford University Press, 1971.

Gosnell, Harold, and Robert Martin, "The Negro as Voter and Officeholder," *Journal of Negro Education*, Vol. 32, No. 4, Autumn 1963.

Gould, Lewis, ed., *American First Ladies: Their Lives and Their Legacy*. New York: Routledge, 2001.

Graebner, Norman, *The New Isolationism: A Study in Politics and Foreign Policy Since 1950*. New York: Ronald, 1956.

Graham, Billy, *Just As I Am: The Autobiography of Bill Graham*. San Francisco: Harper Collins, 1997.

Granville, Johanna, "'Caught with Jam on Our Fingers': Radio Free Europe and the Hungarian Uprising of 1956," *Diplomatic History*, Vol. 29, No. 5, Nov 2005.

———, *The First Domino: International Decision Making during the Hungarian Crisis of 1956*. College Station: Texas A&M Press, 2004.

———, "Hungarian and Polish Reactions to the Events of 1956: New Archival Evidence," *Europe-Asia Studies*, Vol. 53, No. 7, Nov 2001.

———, "Imre Nagy, Hesitant Revolutionary," *Cold War International History Project Bulletin*, Issue 5, Spring 1995.

———, "Neutral Encounters of the Paranoid Kind: Austria's Reactions to the Hungarian Crisis of 1956," in Bischof et al., *Austrian Foreign Policy in Historical Context*.

———, "Of Spies, Refugees and Hostile Propaganda: How Austria Dealt with the Hungarian Crisis of 1956," *History*, Vol. 91, No. 301, Jan 2006.

———, "Poland and Hungary, 1956: A Comparative Essay Based on New Archival Findings," *Australian Journal of Politics and History*, Vol. 48, No. 3, 2002.

Gray, Charles, "Coalition, Consensus, and Conflict in the United States Senate (1957–1960)," PhD dissertation, University of Colorado, Boulder, 1962.

Gray, Gordon, *Eighteen Acres Under Glass*. New York: Doubleday, 1962.

Green, Constance, *The Secret City: A History of Race Relations in the Nation's Capital*. Princeton: Princeton University Press, 1967.

Green, George, *The Establishment in Texas Politics: The Primitive Years, 1938–1957*. Westport, Conn: Greenwood, 1979.

Greene, Benjamin, *Eisenhower, Science Advice, and the Nuclear Test-Ban Debate, 1945–1963*. Stanford: Stanford University Press, 2007.

Greene, Robert, *The Crusade: The Presidential Election of 1952*. Lanham, Md: University Press of America, 1985.

Greenstein, Fred, ed., *The Hidden-Hand Presidency: Eisenhower as Leader*. New York: Basic, 1982.

Gregory, James, *The Southern Diaspora: How the Great Migrations of Black and White Southerners Transformed America*. Chapel Hill: University of North Carolina Press, 2005.

Griffith, Robert, "Dwight D. Eisenhower and the Corporate Commonwealth," *American Historical Review*, Vol. 87, No. 1, Feb 1982.

———, "The General and the Senator: Republican Politics and the 1952 Campaign in Wisconsin," *Wisconsin Magazine of History*, Vol. 54, Autumn 1970.

———, ed., *Ike's Letters to a Friend*. Lawrence: University Press of Kansas, 1984.

Groh, George, *The Black Migration: The Journey to Urban America*. New York: Weybright and Talley, 1972.

Gromyko, Andrei, *Memoirs*. New York: Doubleday, 1989.

Grose, Peter, *Gentleman Spy: The Life of Allen Dulles*. Boston: Houghton Mifflin, 1994.

———, *Operation Rollback: America's Secret War Behind the Iron Curtain*. Boston: Houghton Mifflin, 2000.

Gunther, John, *Inside Africa*. New York: Harper & Brothers, 1955.

Guthman, Edwin, and Jeffrey Shulman, eds., *Robert Kennedy in His Own Words: The Unpublished Recollections of the Kennedy Years*. New York: Bantam, 1988.

Haddow, Robert, *Pavilions of Plenty: Exhibiting American Culture Abroad in the 1950s*. Washington, DC: Smithsonian Institution, 1997.

Hahn, Peter, *Caught in the Middle East: U.S. Policy toward the Arab-Israeli Conflict, 1945–1961*. Chapel Hill: University of North Carolina Press, 2004.

Haines, Gerald, and Robert Leggett, eds., *CIA's Analysis of the Soviet Union, 1947–1991: A Documentary Collection*. Washington, DC: GPO, 2001.

Halperin, Morton, "The Gaither Committee and the Policy Process," *World Politics*, Vol. 13, No. 3, Apr 1961.

Halsey, Margaret, "Beware the Tender Trap," *New Republic*, Jan 13, 1958.

Hamby, Alonzo, "Clash of Perspectives," in Geselbracht, ed., *The Civil Rights Legacy*.

———, *Man of the People: A Life of Harry S. Truman*. New York: Oxford University Press, 1995.

Hamilton, Charles, *Adam Clayton Powell, Jr.: The Political Biography of an American Dilemma*. New York: Atheneum, 1991.

Hamilton, Nigel, *American Caesars: Lives of the Presidents from Franklin D. Roosevelt to George W. Bush*. New Haven: Yale University Press, 2010.

Hamilton, Virginia, *Lister Hill: Statesman from the South*. Chapel Hill: University of North Carolina Press, 1987.

Hardeman, D.B., and Donald Bacon, *Rayburn: A Biography*. Austin: Texas Monthly Press, 1987.

Harding, Harry, and Yuan Ming, eds., *Sino-American Relations, 1945–1955: A Joint Reassessment of a Critical Decade*. Wilmington, Del: SR Books, 1989.

Harlow, Bryce, "White House Watch," *New Republic*, May 13, 1978.

Harris, Eleanor, "The Dark Hours of the Richard Nixons," *American Weekly*, Mar 4, 1956.

Harris, Louis, *Is There a Republican Majority?* New York: Harper, 1954.

Hart, Jeffrey, *When the Going Was Good! American Life in the Fifties*. New York: Crown, 1982.

Hartlyn, Jonathan, "Military Governments and the Transition to Civilian Rule: The Colombian Experience of 1957–1958," *Journal of Interamerican Studies and World Affairs*. Vol. 26, No. 2, May 1984.

Harvard, William, ed., *The Changing Politics of the South*. Baton Rouge: Louisiana State University Press, 1972.

Hasenfus, William, "Managing Partner: Joseph W. Martin Jr., Republican Leader of the United States House of Representatives, 1939–1959," PhD dissertation, Boston College, Chestnut Hill, Mass, 1986.

Haslam, Jonathan, *Russia's Cold War: From the October Revolution to the Fall of the Wall*. New Haven: Yale University Press, 2011.

Hatfield, Mark, *Vice Presidents of the United States 1789–1993*. Washington, DC: GPO, 1997.

Haygood, Will, *King of the Cats: The Life and Times of Adam Clayton Powell, Jr*. Boston: Houghton Mifflin, 1993.

Haynes, John, and Harvey Klehr, *In Denial: Historians, Communism, & Espionage*. San Francisco: Encounter, 2003.

——, and Alexander Vassiliev, *Spies: The Rise and Fall of the KGB in America*. New Haven: Yale University Press, 2009.

Hays, Brooks, *Politics Is My Parish*. Baton Rouge: Louisiana State University Press, 1981.

Hearst Jr., William, et al., *Ask Me Anything: Our Adventures with Khrushchev*. New York: McGraw-Hill, 1960.

Hébert, Edward, *"Last of the Titans": The Life and Times of Congressman F. Edward Hébert*. Lafayette: Center for Louisiana Studies, University of Southwestern Louisiana, 1976.

Hechler, Ken, "Truman Laid the Foundation for the Civil Rights Movement," in Geselbracht, ed., *The Civil Rights Legacy*.

——, *Working with Truman: A Personal Memoir of the White House Years*. Columbia: University of Missouri Press, 1986.

Heidepriem, Scott, *A Fair Chance for a Free People: Biography of Karl E. Mundt, United States Senator*. Madison, SD: Leader Printing, 1988.

Heinemann, Ronald, *Harry Byrd of Virginia*. Charlottesville: University of Virginia Press, 1996.

Helgerson, John, *Getting to Know the President: CIA Briefings of Presidential Candidates 1952–1992*. Washington, DC: Center for the Study of Intelligence, 1996.

Helms, Richard, *A Look Over My Shoulder: A Life in the Central Intelligence Agency*. New York: Random House, 2003.

Henderson Jr., Charles, *The Nixon Theology*. New York: Harper & Row, 1972.

Henderson, Phillip, "Duty, Honor, Country: Parallels in the Leadership of George Washington and Dwight David Eisenhower," in Fishman, Pederson, and Rozell, eds., *George Washington: Foundation of Presidential Leadership and Character*.

——, *Managing the Presidency: The Eisenhower Legacy—From Kennedy to Reagan*. Boulder: Westview, 1988.

Herberg, Will, *Protestant—Catholic—Jew: An Essay in American Religious Sociology*. New York: Doubleday, 1955.

Herling, John, *Right to Challenge: People and Power in the Steelworkers Union*. New York: Harper & Row, 1972.

Herring, George, *From Colony to Superpower: U.S. Foreign Relations since 1776*. New York: Oxford University Press, 2008.

——, "'A Good Stout Effort': John Foster Dulles and the Indochina Crisis, 1954–1955," in Immerman, ed., *John Foster Dulles and the Diplomacy of the Cold War*.

——, and Richard Immerman, "Eisenhower, Dulles, and Dienbienphu: The Day We Didn't Go to War Revisited," *Journal of American History*, Vol. 71, No. 2, Sept 1984.

Hershberg, James, *James B. Conant: Harvard to Hiroshima and the Making of the Nuclear Age*. New York: Knopf, 1993.

Herskowitz, Mickey, *Duty, Honor, Country*. Nashville: Rutledge Hill, 2003.

Hibbs, Ben, ed., *White House Sermons*. New York: Harper & Row, 1972.

Higgins, Trumbull, *The Perfect Failure: Kennedy, Eisenhower, and the C.I.A. at the Bay of Pigs*. New York: Norton, 1987.

Higham, Charles, *American Swastika*. New York: Doubleday, 1985.

Hill, Ruth, ed., *The Black Women Oral History Project*. Vol. 3, Westport, Conn: Meckler, 1991.

Hillings, Pat, *The Irrepressible Irishman: A Republican Insider*. Harold D. Dean, 1993.

Hilton, Stanley, "The United States, Brazil and the Cold War, 1945–1960: End of the Special Relationship," *Journal of American History*, Vol. 68, Dec 1981.

Hinderaker, Ivan, "Harold Stassen and Developments in the Republican Party in Minnesota, 1937–1943," PhD dissertation, University of Minnesota, Minneapolis, 1949.

Hiss, Alger, *In the Court of Public Opinion*. New York: Knopf, 1957.

——, *Recollections of a Life*. New York: Seaver Books, 1988.

Hixson, Walter, *Parting the Curtain: Propaganda, Culture, and the Cold War, 1945–1961*. New York: St. Martin's, 1997.

Hoff-Wilson, Joan, ed., *Papers of the Nixon White House*. Lanham, Md: University Publications of America, 1987. Microfilm.

Hoffecker, Carol, *Honest John Williams: U.S. Senator from Delaware*. Newark: University of Delaware Press, 2000.

Hoffer, Eric, *The True Believer: Thoughts on the Nature of Mass Movements*. New York: Harper & Row, 1951.

Hofstadter, Richard, *Anti-Intellectualism in American Life*. New York: Knopf, 1963.

Hogan, Michael, *A Cross of Iron: Harry S. Truman and the Origins of the National Security State, 1945–1954*. New York: Cambridge University Press, 1998.

Holland, Max, "Operation PSHISTORY: The Aftermath of Success," *International Journal of Intelligence and Counterintelligence*, Vol. 17, No. 2, Summer 2004.

———, "Private Sources of U.S. Foreign Policy: William Pawley and the 1954 Coup d'État in Guatemala, "*Journal of Cold War Studies*, Vol. 7, No. 4, Fall, 2005.

Hollitz, "Eisenhower and the Admen: The Television 'Spot' Campaign of 1952," *Wisconsin Magazine of History* Vol. 66, No. 1, Autumn, 1982.

Holloway, David, *Stalin and the Bomb: The Soviet Union and Atomic Energy 1939–1956*. New Haven: Yale University Press, 1994.

Holt, Marilyn, *Mamie Doud Eisenhower: The General's First Lady*. Lawrence: University of Kansas Press, 2007.

Hopkins, Jerry, "Billy Graham and the Race Problem," PhD dissertation, University of Kentucky, Lexington, 1986.

Horne, Alistair, *Harold Macmillan*, Vol. 2, 1957–1986. London: Macmillan, 1989.

———, *A Savage War of Peace: Algeria 1954–1962*. London: Macmillan, 1977.

Horne, Gerald, *Black and Red: W.E.B. Du Bois and the Afro-American Response to the Cold War, 1944–1963*. Albany: State University of New York Press, 1986.

Horton, Carrell, and Jessie Smith, eds., *Statistical Record of Black America*. Detroit: Gale Research, 1990.

Hudnut-Beumler, James, *Looking for God in the Suburbs: The Religion of the American Dream and Its Critics, 1945–1965*. New Brunswick: Rutgers University Press, 1994.

Huebner, Lee, "The Checkers Speech After 60 Years," *Atlantic*, Sept 2012.

Huggins, Ronald, "Eisenhower and Civil Rights," PhD dissertation: University of California at Los Angeles, 1985.

Hugh, John, "The Negro's New Economic Life," *Fortune*, Vol. 54, No. 3, Sept 1956.

Hughes, Donald, Annual Nixon Legacy Lecture, Jan 10, 2011.

Hughes, Emmet, *The Ordeal of Power: A Political Memoir of the Eisenhower Years*. New York: Atheneum, 1963.

Hulsey, Byron, *Everett Dirksen and His Presidents: How a Senate Giant Shaped American Politics*. Lawrence: University of Kansas Press, 2000.

Humphrey, Hubert, *The Education of a Public Man: My Life and Politics*: Minneapolis: University of Minnesota Press, 1991.

Hunt, Michael, *Ideology and U.S. Foreign Policy*. New Haven: Yale University Press, 1987.

———, and Niu Jun, eds., *Toward a History of Chinese Communist Foreign Relations 1920s–1960s: Personalities and Interpretive Approaches*. Washington, DC: Woodrow Wilson International Center for Scholars, 1992.

Hutschnecker, Arnold, *The Drive for Power*. New York: M. Evans, 1974.

———, *Love and Hate in Human Nature*. New York: Thomas Crowell, 1955

———, "The Mental Health of Our Leaders," *Look*, July 15, 1969.

———, *The Will to Live*. New York: Permabooks, 1951

Imboden, William, *Religion and American Foreign Policy, 1945–1960: The Soul of Containment*. Cambridge: Cambridge University Press, 2008.

———, "The Soul of American Diplomacy: Religion and Foreign Policy, 1945–1960," PhD dissertation, Yale University, New Haven, Conn, 2003.

Immerman, Richard, "Between the Unattainable and the Unacceptable: Eisenhower and Dienbienphu," in Melanson and Mayers, eds., *Reevaluating Eisenhower.*

———, *The CIA in Guatemala: The Foreign Policy of Intervention*. Austin: University of Texas Press, 1982.

———, "Eisenhower and Dulles: Who Made the Decisions?" *Political Psychology,* Vol. 1, Autumn 1979.

———, "The United States and the Geneva Conference of 1954: A New Look," *Diplomatic History*, Vol. 14, Winter 1990.

———, ed., *John Foster Dulles and the Diplomacy of the Cold War*. Princeton: Princeton University Press, 1990.

———, *John Foster Dulles: Piety, Pragmatism, and Power in U.S. Foreign Policy*. Wilmington, Del: Scholarly Resources, 1999.

Inderfurth, Karl, and Loch Johnson, eds., *Fateful; Decisions: Inside the National Security Council*. New York: Oxford University Press, 2004.

Ingimundarson, Valur, "The Eisenhower Administration, the Adenauer Government, and the Political Uses of the East German Uprising in 1953," *Diplomatic History*, Vol. 20, No. 3, Summer 1996.

Jacobs, Seth, "'Sink or Swim with Ngo Dinh Diem': Religion, Orientalism, and United States Intervention in Vietnam 1950–1957," PhD dissertation, Northwestern University, Evanston, Ill, 2000.

Jacobs, Travis, *Eisenhower at Columbia*. Piscataway, NJ: Transaction Publishers, 2001.

Jacoby, Neil, "The President, the Constitution, and the Economist in Economic Stabilization," *History of Political Economy*. Vol. 3, No. 2, Fall 1971.

James, D. Clayton, ed., *The Years of MacArthur*. Vol. 3, *Triumph and Disaster 1945–1964*. Boston: Houghton Mifflin, 1985.

Jamieson, Kathleen, *Packaging the Presidency: A History and Criticism of Presidential Campaign Advertising*. 2nd ed. New York: Oxford University Press, 1992.

Janken, Kenneth, *White: The Biography of Walter White, Mr. NAACP*. New York: New Press, 2003.

Javits, Jacob, *Javits: The Autobiography of a Public Man*. Boston: Houghton Mifflin, 1981.

———, *Ordeal of Battle: A Republican's Call to Reason*. New York: Atheneum, 1964.

Jefferson, Louis, *The John Foster Dulles Book of Humor*. New York: St. Martin's, 1986.

Jenkins, David, "Initial American Responses to Fidel Castro, 1957–1959," PhD dissertation, University of Texas, Austin, 1992.

Jentleson, Bruce W., Thomas G. Paterson, and Nicholas X. Rizopoulos, eds. *Encyclopedia of U.S. Foreign Relations*. 4 vols. New York: Oxford University Press, 1997.

Jian, Chen, *Mao's China and the Cold War*. Chapel Hill: University of North Carolina Press, 2001.

Johnson, A. Ross, *Radio Free Europe and Radio Liberty: The CIA Years and Beyond*. Stanford: Stanford University Press, 2010.

Johnson, Allen, and Dumas Malone, eds., *Dictionary of American Biography*, Vol. 2, New York: Scribner's, 1957, 1958.

Johnson, Carolyn, "A Southern Response to Civil Rights: Lyndon Baines Johnson and Civil Rights Legislation 1956–1960," MA thesis, University of Houston, 1975.

Johnson, Daniel, and Rex Campbell, *Black Migration in America: A Social Demographic History*. Durham, NC: Duke University Press, 1981.

Johnson, David, *The Lavender Scare: The Cold War Persecution of Gays and Lesbians in the Federal Government*. Chicago: University of Chicago Press, 2004.

Johnson, John, *Succeeding Against the Odds*. New York: Warner, 1989.

Johnson, Lyndon, *The Vantage Point: Perspectives of the Presidency 1963–1969*. New York: Holt, Rinehart and Winston, 1971.

Johnson, Paul, *Eisenhower*. New York: Viking, 2014.

Johnson, Robert, *Congress and the Cold War*. New York: Cambridge University Press, 2006.

——, *Ernest Gruening and the American Dissenting Tradition*. Cambridge: Harvard University Press, 1998.

Johnson, Walter, ed., *The Papers of Adlai E. Stevenson*. Vols. 4–8. Boston: Little, Brown, 1974–1979.

Johnson, Whittington, "The Vinson Court and Racial Segregation, 1946–1953," *Journal of Negro History*, Vol. 63, No. 3, July 1978.

Jonas, Manfred, *The United States and Germany: A Diplomacy History*. Ithaca, NY: Cornell University Press, 1984.

Jones, Howard, *The Bay of Pigs*. New York: Oxford University Press, 2008.

——, *Crucible of Power: A History of U.S. Foreign Relations Since 1897*. Wilmington, Del: Scholarly Resources, 2001.

Jones, Matthew, *After Hiroshima: The United States, Race and Nuclear Weapons in Asia, 1945–1965*. Cambridge: Cambridge University Press, 2010.

——, "A 'Segregated' Asia? Race, the Bandung Conference and Pan Asianist Fears in American Thought and Policy, 1954–1955," *Diplomatic History*, Vol. 29, No. 5, Nov 2005.

Jordan, A.A., ed., *Issues of National Security in the 1970's*. New York: Praeger, 1967.

Jumonville, Neil, *Henry Steele Commager: Midcentury Liberalism and the History of the Present*. Chapel Hill: University of North Carolina Press, 1999.

Jurika Jr., Stephen, *From Pearl Harbor to Vietnam: The Memoirs of Admiral Arthur W. Radford*. Stanford: Hoover Institution, 1980.

Kaenel, André, ed., *Anti-Communism and McCarthyism in the United States (1946–1954): Essays in the Politics and Culture of the Cold War*. Paris: Editions Messene, 1995.

Kalk, Bruce, *The Origins of the Southern Strategy: Two Party Competition in South Carolina, 1950–1972*. Lanham, Md: Lexington, 2001.

Kaplan, Fred, *The Wizards of Armageddon*. New York: Simon & Schuster, 1983.

Karabell, Zachary, *Architects of Intervention: The United States, the Third World, and the Cold War, 1946–1962*. Baton Rouge: Louisiana State University Press, 1999.

Kastner, Jill, "The Ambivalent Ally: Adenauer, Eisenhower and the Dilemmas of the Cold War, 1953–1960," PhD dissertation, Harvard University, Cambridge, Mass, 1999.

Katz, Milton, "E. Frederic Morrow and Civil Rights in the Eisenhower Administration," *Phylon*, Vol. 42, June 1981.

Kaufman, Burton, *The Korean War: Challenges in Crises, Credibility, and Command*. Philadelphia: Temple, 1986.

——, *Trade and Aid: Eisenhower's Foreign Economic Policy, 1953–1961*. Baltimore: Johns Hopkins University Press, 1982.

Kearns, Doris, *Lyndon Johnson and the American Dream*. New York: Harper & Row, 1976.

Kee, Ed, "The Brown Decision and Milford, Delaware, 1954–1965," *Delaware History*, Vol. 27, Fall–Winter 1997.

Keefer, Edward, "President Dwight D. Eisenhower and the End of the Korean War," *Diplomatic History*, Vol. 10, Summer 1986.

Keller, Craig, "The Intellectuals and Eisenhower: Civil Religion, Religious Publicity and the Search the Morale and Religious Communities," PhD dissertation, George Washington University, Washington, DC, 2002.

Kempton, Murray, *America Comes of Middle Age: Columns 1950–1962*. Boston: Little, Brown, 1963.

——, "The Underestimation of Dwight D. Eisenhower," *Esquire*, Vol. 68, No. 3, September 1967.

Kenez, Peter, *Varieties of Fear: Growing Up Jewish under Nazism and Communism*. Washington, DC: American University Press, 1995.

Kenneally, James, *A Compassionate Conservative: A Political Biography of Joseph W. Martin Jr., Speaker of the U.S. House of Representatives*. Lanham, Md: Lexington, 2003.

Keogh, James, *This Is Nixon*. New York: Putnam, 1956.

Kesaris, Paul, ed., *Papers of the Republican Party*, Part 2. Lanham, Md: University Publications of America, 1986.

——, and Jean Gibson, eds., *Minutes and Documents of the Cabinet Meetings of President Eisenhower 1953–61*. Washington, DC: University Publications of America, 1980.

Khrushchev, Sergei, *Nikita Khrushchev and the Creation of the Superpower*. University Park: Pennsylvania State University Press, 2000.

——, ed., trans. George Shriver, *Memoirs of Nikita Khrushchev*, Vol. 3: *Statesman [1953–1964]*. University Park: Pennsylvania State University Press, 2007.

Killian Jr., James, *Sputnik, Scientists, and Eisenhower: A Memoir of the First Special Assistant to the President for Science and Technology*. Cambridge: MIT Press, 1982.

Kim, Sung Yong, *United States–Philippine Relations, 1946–1956*. Washington, DC: Public Affairs, 1968.

King, Coretta, *My Life with Martin Luther King, Jr.* New York: Holt, Rinehart and Winston, 1969.

King Sr., Martin, *Daddy King: An Autobiography*. New York: Morrow, 1980.

King Jr., Martin, *The Papers of Martin Luther King, Jr.*, Vol. 4: *Symbol of the Movement January 1957–December 1958*. Ed. Claybourne Carson. Berkeley: University of California Press, 2000.

———, *The Papers of Martin Luther King, Jr.*, Vol. 5: *Threshold of a New Decade January 1959–December 1960.* Ed. Claybourne Carson. Berkeley: University of California Press, 2000.

———, *Why We Can't Wait.* New York: Harper & Row, 1963, 1964.

Kinnard, Douglas, *President Eisenhower and Strategy Management: A Study in Defense Politics.* Lexington: University Press of Kentucky, 1977.

Kinzer, Stephen, *The Brothers: John Foster Dulles, Allen Dulles, and Their Secret World War.* New York: Times Books, 2013.

Kirby, Alec, "Childe Harold's Pilgrimage: A Political Biography of Harold Stassen," PhD dissertation, George Washington University, Washington, DC, 1992.

———, et al., *Harold E. Stassen: The Life and Perennial Candidacy of the Progressive Republican.* Jefferson, NC: McFarland, 2012.

Kirkendall, Richard, ed., *The Truman Period as a Research Field, a Reappraisal, 1972.* Columbia: University of Missouri Press, 1974.

Kistiakowsky, George, *A Scientist at the White House: The Private Diary of President Eisenhower's Special Assistant for Science and Technology.* Cambridge: Harvard University Press, 1976.

Kitchen, Helen, "Still on Safari in Africa," in Brown, ed., *Centerstage.*

Klarman, Michael, *From Jim Crow to Civil Rights: The Supreme Court and the Struggle for Racial Equality.* New York: Oxford University Press, 2004.

Klein, Herbert, *Making It Perfectly Clear: An Inside Account of Nixon's Love/Hate Relationship with the Media.* New York: Doubleday, 1980.

Kluger, Richard, *Simple Justice: The History of Brown. Board of Education and Black America's Struggle for Equality.* Vol. 2. New York: Knopf, 1975.

Knebel, Fletcher, "Crisis," *Look*, Vol. 19, No. 26, Dec 27, 1955.

———, "Did Ike Really Want Nixon?" *Look*, Vol. 20, No. 22, Oct 30, 1956.

"The Knowland Story," *U.S. News & World Report*, Vol. 37, Dec 24, 1954.

Kolko, Gabriel, *Confronting the Third World: United States Foreign Policy, 1945–1960.* New York: Pantheon, 1988.

Kolodzieg, Edward, *The Uncommon Defense and Congress, 1945–1963.* Columbus: Ohio State University Press, 1966.

Koo, Wellington, *Memoirs*, Vol. 7, Reel 4. New York: Microfilming Corp of America, 1978. Microfilm.

Korda, Michael, *Journey to a Revolution: A Personal Memoir and History of the Hungarian Revolution of 1956.* New York: HarperCollins, 2006.

Kornbluh, Peter, ed., *Bay of Pigs Declassified: The Secret CIA Report on the Invasion of Cuba.* New York: New Press, 1998.

Kornitzer, Bela, *The Real Nixon: An Intimate Biography.* New York: Rand McNally, 1960.

Kotlowski, Dean, *Nixon's Civil Rights: Politics, Principle, and Policy.* Cambridge: Harvard University Press, 2001.

———, "Richard Nixon and the Origins of Affirmative Action," *The Historian*, Vol. 60, No. 3, 1998.

———, "Unhappily Yoked? Hugh Scott and Richard Nixon," *Pennsylvania Magazine of History and Biography*, Vol. 125, No. 3, July 2001.

Kovrig, Bennett, *The Myth of Liberation: East-Central Europe in U.S. Diplomacy and Politics since 1941*. Baltimore: Johns Hopkins University Press, 1973.

Kraft, Joseph, "Ike vs. Nixon," *Esquire*, Apr 1960.

Kramer, Mark, "New Evidence on Soviet Decision-Making and the 1956 Polish and Hungarian Crises," *Cold War International History Project Bulletin*, Nos. 8–9, Winter 1996–1997.

———, "The Soviet Union and the 1956 Crisis in Hungary and Poland: Reassessments and New Findings," *Journal of Contemporary History*, Vol. 33, No. 2, Apr 1998.

Krebs, Ronald, *Dueling Visions: U.S. Strategy toward Eastern Europe under Eisenhower*. College Station: Texas A&M Press, 2001.

Krenn, Michael, *Black Diplomacy: African Americans and the State Department 1945–1969*. New York: Sharpe, 1999.

Krieg, Joann, ed., *Dwight D. Eisenhower: Soldier, President, Statesman*. New York: Greenwood, 1987.

Krock, Arthur, *In the Nation: 1932–1966*. New York: McGraw-Hill, 1966.

Kroes, Rob, and Eduard van de Bilt, eds., *The US Constitution: after 200 Years*. Amsterdam: Free University Press, 1988.

Kumar, Ravinder, and Sharada Prasad, eds., *Selected works of Jawaharlal Nehru*, Vol. 24. London: Oxford University Press, 2000.

Kutler, Stanley, "Eisenhower, the Judiciary, and Desegregation: Some Reflections," in Bischof and Ambrose, eds., *Eisenhower*.

———, ed., *Abuse of Power: The New Nixon Tapes*. New York: Free Press, 1997.

Kux, Dennis, *India and the United States: Estranged Democracies 1941–1991*. Washington, DC: National Defense University Press, 1993.

———, *The United States and Pakistan, 1947–2000: Disenchanted Allies*. Baltimore: Johns Hopkins, 2001.

LaFeber, Walter, *Inevitable Revolutions: The United States in Central America*. 2nd ed. New York: Norton, 1993.

Laird, Melvin, ed., *Republican Papers*. New York: Praeger, 1968.

Lamis, Alexander, *The Two-Party South*. New York: Oxford University Press, 1988.

Land, Guy, "Presidential Republicans and the Growth of the Mississippi Republican Party, 1952–1960," MA thesis, University of Georgia, Athens, Ga, 1974.

Landa, Ronald, and Edward Drea, *History of the Office of the Secretary of Defense: The McNamara Ascendency 1961–1965*. Vol. 5. Washington, DC: GPO, 1984.

Larres, Klaus, "Eisenhower and the First Forty Days After Stalin's Death: The Incompatibility of Détente and Political Warfare," *Diplomacy and Statecraft*, Vol. 6, 1995.

Larson, Arthur, *Eisenhower: The President Nobody Knew*. New York: Charles Scribner's Sons, 1968.

Lasby, Clarence, *Eisenhower's Heart Attack: How Ike Beat Heart Disease and Held on to the Presidency*. Lawrence: University Press of Kansas, 1997.

"Las Vegas: The Money and the Power," A & E, May 13, 2002.

Lash, Joseph, *Eleanor: The Years Alone*. New York: Norton, 1972.

Lauren, Paul, *Power and Prejudice: The Politics and Diplomacy of Racial Discrimination.* Boulder: Westview, 1988.

——, "Seen from the Outside: The International Perspective on the American Dilemma," in Plummer, ed., *Window on Freedom.*

Lavine, Harold, ed., *Smoke-Filled Rooms.* Englewood Cliffs, NJ: Prentice-Hall, 1970.

Lawrence, Bill, *Six Presidents, Too Many Wars.* New York: Saturday Review, 1972.

Lawson, Steven, *Black Ballots: Voting Rights in the South, 1944–1969.* New York: Columbia University Press, 1976.

——, *Running for Freedom: Civil Rights and Black Politics in America since 1941.* 2nd ed. New York: McGraw-Hill, 1997.

——, and Charles Payne, *Debating the Civil Rights Movement, 1945–1968.* Lanham, Md: Rowman & Littlefield, 2006.

Layton, Azze Salama, *International Politics and Civil Rights Policies in the United States, 1941–1960.* Cambridge: Cambridge University Press, 2000.

Lazarowitz, Arlene, *Years in Exile: The Liberal Democrats, 1950–1959.* New York: Garland, 1988.

Leak, Jeffrey, ed., *Rac[e]ing to the Right: Selected Essays of George S. Schuyler.* Knoxville: Tenn., 2001.

Leary Jr., William, "Smith of New Jersey: A Biography of H. Alexander Smith, United States Senator from New Jersey, 1944–1959," PhD dissertation, Princeton University, Princeton, NJ, 1966.

Lee, Eugene, *California Votes, 1928–1960.* Berkeley: Institute of Government Studies, 1963.

Lee, R. Alton, *Dwight D. Eisenhower: Soldier and Statesman.* Chicago: Nelson-Hall, 1981.

——, *Eisenhower & Landrum-Griffin: A Study in Labor-Management Politics.* Lexington: University Press of Kentucky, 1990.

Lefebvre, Jeffrey, *Arms for the Horn: U.S. Security Policy in Ethiopia and Somalia 1953–1991.* Pittsburgh: University of Pittsburgh Press, 1991.

Lehman, Christopher, "Strategic Policy and Process: An Assessment of the Evolution of American Nuclear Strategy, Its Determinants, and Its Implications," PhD dissertation, Fletcher School of Law and Diplomacy, Medford, Mass, 1993.

Lehman, Kenneth, *Bolivia and the United States: A Limited Partnership.* Athens: University of Georgia Press, 1999.

Lemann, Nicholas, *The Promised Land: The Great Black Migration and How It Changed America.* New York: Knopf, 1991.

Lendavi, Paul, *One Day That Shook the Communist World: The 1956 Hungarian Uprising and Its Legacy.* Trans. Ann Major. Princeton: Princeton University Press, 2008.

Lenezowski, George, *American Presidents and the Middle East.* Durham, NC: Duke University Press, 1990.

Leonard, Thomas, *Central America and the United States: The Search for Stability.* Athens: University of Georgia Press, 1991.

——, "The United States and Central America 1955–1960," *Valley Forge Journal,* Vol. 3, June 1986.

Lerner, Mitchell, "'To be Shot at by the Whites and Dodged by the Negroes': Lyndon Johnson and the Texas NYA," *Presidential Studies Quarterly*, Vol. 39, No. 2, June 2009.

Lester, John, ed., *John Moors Cabot Papers 1929–1978*. Medford, Mass: Fletcher School of Law, Tufts University, 1985. Microfilm.

Lester, Robert, ed., *President Eisenhower's Meetings with Legislative Leaders, 1953–1961*. Lanham, Md: University Publications of America, 1986.

Leuchtenburg, William, *In the Shadow of FDR: From Harry Truman to George W. Bush*. 3rd ed. Ithaca, NY: Cornell University Press, 2001.

Lewinson, Edwin, *Black Politics in New York City*. New York: Twayne, 1974.

Lewis, Anthony, and *The New York Times, Portrait of a Decade: The Second American Revolution*. New York: Random House, 1964.

Lewis, David, *District of Columbia: A Bicentennial History*. New York: Norton, 1976.

———, *King: A Biography*. 2nd ed. Urbana: University of Illinois Press, 1978.

———, *W.E.B. Du Bois: The Fight for Equality and the American Century 1913–1963*. New York: Holt, 2000.

Lewis, Tom, *Divided Highways: Building the Interstate Highways, Transforming American Life*. New York: Viking, 1997.

Lichtenstein, Nelson, *The Most Dangerous Man in Detroit: Walter Reuther and the Fate of American Labor*. New York: Basic, 1995.

Lichtman, Allan, "The Federal Assault Against Voting Discrimination in the Deep South 1957–67," *Journal of Negro History*, Vol. 53, 1969.

Lieberson, Stanley, *A Piece of the Pie: Black and White Immigrants since 1880*. Berkeley: University of California Press, 1980.

Liss, Sheldon, *Diplomacy & Dependency: Venezuela, the United States, and the Americas*. Chapol Hill, NC: Documentary Publications, 1978.

Little, Douglas, "Gideon's Band: America and the Middle East since 1945," *Diplomatic History*, Vol. 18, No. 4, Oct 1994.

———, "His Finest Hour? Eisenhower, Lebanon, and the 1958 Middle East Crisis," *Diplomatic History*, Vol. 20, No. 1, Winter 1996.

Littlejohn, Jeffrey, and Charles Ford, "Truman and Civil Rights," in Margolies, *A Companion to Harry S. Truman*.

Lodge Jr., Henry, *As It Was: An Inside View of Politics and Power in the Sixties*. New York: Norton, 1976.

———, *The Storm Has Many Eyes: A Personal Narrative*. New York: Norton, 1973.

Loewenberg, Peter, "Nixon, Hitler and Power: An Ego Psychological Study," *Psychoanalytic Inquiry*, Vol. 6, 1986.

Logevall, Fredrik, *Embers of War: The Fall of an Empire and the Making of America's Vietnam*. New York: Random House, 2012.

Long, Michael, ed., *First Class Citizenship: The Civil Rights Letters of Jackie Robinson*. New York: Times, 2007.

Longley, Kyle, *In the Eagle's Shadow: The United States and Latin America*. 2nd ed. Wheeling, Ill: Harlan Davidson, 2009.

———, *Senator Albert Gore, Sr.: Tennessee Maverick*. Baton Rouge: Louisiana State University Press, 2004.

——, *The Sparrow and the Hawk: Costa Rica and the United States during the Rise of José Figueres*. Tuscaloosa: University of Alabama Press, 1997.

Lowndes, Joseph, *From the New Deal to New Right: Race and the Southern Origins of Modern Conservatism*. New Haven: Yale University Press, 2008.

Lubell, Samuel, "The Future of the Negro Voter in the United States," *Journal of Negro Education*. Vol. 26, No. 3, Summer 1957.

——, *Revolt of the Moderates*. New York: Harper & Brothers, 1956.

Lungren, John, and John Lungren Jr., *Healing Richard Nixon: A Doctor's Memoir*. Lexington: University Press of Kentucky, 2003.

Lyon, Peter, *Eisenhower: Portrait of a Hero*. Boston: Little, Brown, 1974.

MacGregor Jr., Morris, *Integration of the Armed Forces 1940–1965*. Washington DC: Center for Military History, 1981.

Machcewicz, Pawel, *Rebellious Satellite: Poland 1956*. Stanford: Stanford University Press, 2009.

Maddock, Shane, *Nuclear Apartheid: The Quest for American Atomic Supremacy from World War II to the Present*. Chapel Hill: University of North Carolina Press, 2010.

Maddox, Robert, *The Senatorial Career of Harley Martin Kilgore*. New York: Garland, 1981.

Malsberger, John, "An Ailing Ike," *Prologue*, Vol. 44, No. 3, Fall 2012.

——, "Dwight Eisenhower, Richard Nixon, and the Fund Crisis of 1952," *The Historian*, Vol. 73, Issue 3, Fall 2011.

——, *The General and the Politician: Dwight Eisenhower, Richard Nixon, and American Politics*. Lanham, Md: Rowman & Littlefield, 2014.

Manchester, William, *The Glory and the Dream: A Narrative History of America 1932–1972*. Vol. 2. Boston: Little, Brown, 1973, 1974.

Mann, Robert, *A Grand Delusion: America's Descent into Vietnam*. New York: Basic, 2001.

——, *Legacy to Power: Senator Russell Long of Louisiana*. New York: Paragon House, 1992.

——, *The Walls of Jericho: Lyndon Johnson, Hubert Humphrey, Richard Russell, and the Struggle for Civil Rights*. New York: Harcourt Brace, 1996.

Manning, Christopher, *William L. Dawson and the Limits of Black Electoral Leadership*. Dekalb: Northern Illinois University Press, 2009.

Marable, Manning, *Race, Reform, and Rebellion: The Second Reconstruction in Black America, 1945–1990*. Jackson: University Press of Mississippi, 1991.

Maravillas, Anthony, "Nixon in the Fifties," PhD dissertation, University of Illinois at Chicago, 2001.

Marchio, James, "Rhetoric and Reality: The Eisenhower Administration and Unrest in Eastern Europe, 1953–1959," PhD dissertation, American University, Washington, DC, 1990.

Marcus, Harold, *Ethiopia, Great Britain, and the United States, 1941–1974: The Politics of Empire*. Berkeley: University of California Press, 1983.

Margolies, Daniel S., ed., *A Companion to Harry S. Truman*. Malden, Mass: Wiley-Blackwell, 2012.

Mark, Eduard, "In Re Alger Hiss: A Final Verdict from the Archives of the KGB," *Journal of Cold War Studies*, Vol. 11, No. 3, Summer 2009.

Markowitz, Arthur, "Humanitarianism Versus Restrictionism: The United States and the Hungarian Refugees," *International Migration Review*, Vol. 7, No. 1, Spring 1973.

Marks III, Frederick, "The Real Hawk at Dienbienphu: Dulles or Eisenhower?" *Pacific Historical Review*, Vol. 59, Aug 1990.

Marling, Karal, *As Seen on TV: The Visual Culture of Everyday Life in the 1950s*. Cambridge: Harvard University Press, 1994.

Martin, Joe, *My First Fifty Years in Politics*. New York: McGraw-Hill, 1960.

Martin, John, *It Seems Like Only Yesterday: Memoirs of Writing, Presidential Politics, and Diplomatic Life*. New York: Morrow, 1986.

Martin, John B., *Adlai Stevenson of Illinois: The Life of Adlai E. Stevenson*. New York: Doubleday, 1976.

——, *Adlai Stevenson and the World: The Life of Adlai E. Stevenson*. New York: Book World Promotions, 1977.

Martin, John. F., *Civil Rights and the Crisis of Liberalism: The Democratic Party 1945–1976*. Boulder: Westview, 1979.

Martin, Michael, "Senator Russell B. Long of Louisiana: A Political Biography, 1948–1987," PhD dissertation, University of Arkansas, Fayetteville, 2003.

Martin, Thomas, "Defending a Lost Cause? France and the United States Vision of French North Africa, 1945–1956," *Diplomatic History*, Vol. 26, No. 2, Spring 2002.

Martin, William, *A Prophet with Honor: The Billy Graham Story*. New York: Morrow, 1991.

——, *With God on Our Side: The Rise of the Religious Right in America*. New York: Broadway, 1996.

Marty, Martin, *Modern American Religion: Under God, Indivisible, 1941–1960*. Vol. 3. Chicago: University of Chicago Press, 1996.

——, *Righteous Empire: The Protestant Experience in America*. New York: Dial, 1970.

Marvillas, Anthony, "Nixon in Nixonland," *Southern California Quarterly* Vol. 84, No. 2, Summer 2002.

Matteson, Robert, *Harold Stassen, His Career, the Man, and the 1957 London Arms Control Negotiations*. Inver Grove Heights, Mn: Desk Top Ink, 1993.

Matthews, Donald, and James Prothro, "Political Factors and Negro Voter Registration in the South," *American Political Science Review*, Vol. 57, No. 2, June 1963.

Mattson, Kevin, *Just Plain Dick: Richard Nixon's Checkers Speech and the "Rocking, Socking" Election of 1952*. New York: Bloomsbury, 2012.

May, Ann, "President Eisenhower, Economic Policy, and the 1960 Presidential Election," *Journal of Economic History*, Vol. 50, No. 2, June 1990.

May, Elaine, *Homeward Bound: American Families in the Cold War Era*. New York: Basic, 1988.

May, Ernest, "The American Commitment to Germany, 1949–1955," *Diplomatic History*, Vol. 13, Fall 1989.

Mayer, Michael, "The Eisenhower Administration and the Civil Rights Act of 1957," *Congress and the Presidency*, Vol. 16, No. 2, Autumn 1989.

——, "The Eisenhower Administration and the Desegregation of Washington, DC," *Journal of Policy History*, Vol. 3, No. 1, 1991.

——, "Eisenhower's Conditional Crusade: The Eisenhower Administration and Civil Rights, 1953–1957," PhD dissertation, Princeton University, Princeton, NJ, 1984.

——, "A Kansan Looks at Brown," in Wunder, ed., *Law and the Great Plains.*

——, "Regardless of Station, Race, or Calling: Eisenhower and Race," in Krieg, ed., *Dwight D. Eisenhower.*

——, "With Much Deliberation and Some Speed: Eisenhower and the Brown Decision," *Journal of Southern History*, Vol. 52, Feb 1986.

——, ed., *The Eisenhower Years*. New York: Facts on File, 2010.

Mayers, David, "After Stalin: The Ambassadors and America's Soviet Policy, 1953–1962," *Diplomacy & Statecraft*, Vol. 5, No. 2, July 1994.

——, *Cracking the Monolith: U.S. Policy Against the Sino-Soviet Alliance, 1949–1955*. Baton Rouge: Louisiana State University Press, 1986.

Mazo, Earl, "Ike Speaks Out: Bay of Pigs was all JFK's," *Newsday*, Vol. 26, No. 6, Sept 10, 1965.

——, *Richard Nixon: A Political and Personal Portrait*. New York: Harpers, 1959.

Mazov, Sergey, *A Distant Frontier in the Cold War: The USSR in West Africa and the Congo, 1956–1964*. Washington, DC: Woodrow Wilson Center Press with Stanford University Press, 2010.

McAdam, Doug, *Political Process and the Development of Black Insurgency 1930–1970*. Chicago: University of Chicago Press, 1982.

McCann Jr., Francis, "Vice–President Nixon's Trip to South America, 1958," MA thesis, Kent State University, Kent, Ohio, 1961.

McClenahan Jr., William, and William Becker, *Eisenhower and the Cold War Economy*. Baltimore: Johns Hopkins University Press, 2011.

McCoy, Donald, and Richard Ruetten, *Quest and Response: Minority Rights and the Truman Administration*. Lawrence: University Press of Kansas, 1973.

——, and J.R. Fuchs, eds., *Conference of Scholars on the Truman Administration and Civil Rights, April 5–6, 1968 of the Henry S. Truman Library*. Independence, Mo: Institute for National and International Affairs, 1968.

McCullough, David, *Truman*. New York: Simon and Schuster, 1992.

——, ed., *Affection and Trust: The Personal Correspondence of Harry S. Truman and Dean Acheson*. New York: Knopf, 2010.

McDonald, David, *Union Man*. New York: Dutton, 1969.

McFarland, Linda, *Cold War Strategist: Stuart Symington and the Search for National Security*. Westport, Conn: Praeger, 2001.

McIntyre, W. David, *Background to the Anzus Pact: Policy-Makers, Strategy and Diplomacy, 1945–55*. London: Macmillan, 1994.

McLellan, David, and David Acheson, eds., *Among Friends: Personal Letters of Dean Acheson*. New York: Dodd, Mead, 1980.

McMahon, Kevin, *Reconsidering Roosevelt on Race: How the President Paved the Road to Brown*. Chicago: University of Chicago Press, 2004.

McMahon, Robert, *The Cold War on the Periphery: The United States, India, and Pakistan*. New York: Columbia University Press, 1994.

———, "Eisenhower and Third World Nationalism: A Critique of the Revisionists," *Political Science Quarterly*, Vol. 101, 1986.

———, *The Limits of Empire: The United States and Southeast Asia since World War II*. New York: Columbia University Press, 1999.

———, "United States Cold War Strategy in South Asia: Making a Military Commitment to Pakistan, 1947–1954," *Journal of American History*, Vol. 75, No. 3, Dec 1988.

McPherson, Alan, *Intimate Ties, Bitter Struggles: The United States and Latin American Since 1945*. Washington, DC: Potomac, 2006.

———, *Yankee No! Anti-Americanism in U.S.-Latin American Relations*. Cambridge: Harvard University Press, 2003.

McPherson, Harry, *A Political Education: A Washington Memoir*. Boston: Atlantic Monthly, 1988.

McQuaid, Kim, *Uneasy Partners: Big Business in American Politics, 1945–1990*. Baltimore: Johns Hopkins University Press, 1994.

Meers, Sharon, "The British Connection: How the United States Covered Its Tracks in the 1954 Coup in Guatemala," *Diplomatic History*, Vol. 16, No. 3, Summer 1992.

Meier, August, and Elliot Rudwick, *CORE: A Study in the Civil Rights Movement, 1942–1068*. New York: Oxford University Press, 1973.

Melanson, Richard, and David Mayers, eds., *Reevaluating Eisenhower: American Foreign Policy in the 1950s*. Urbana: University of Illinois Press, 1987.

Melendy, H. Brett, and Benjamin Gilbert, *The Governors of California: Peter H. Burnett to Edmund G. Brown*. Georgetown, Ca: Talisman, 1965.

Members of the Department of Marketing Miami University, Oxford, Ohio, *The Influence of Television on the Election of 1952*. Oxford, Ohio: Oxford Research Associates, 1954.

Menzies, Robert, *The Measure of the Years*. London: Cassell, 1970.

Meriwether, James, *Proudly We Can Be Africans: Black Americans and Africa*. Chapel Hill: University of North Carolina Press, 2002.

———, "Torrent Overrunning Everything: Africa and the Eisenhower Administration," in Statler and Johns, eds., *Eisenhower Administration*.

———, "'Worth a Lot of Negro Votes': Black Voters, Africa, and the 1960 Presidential Campaign," *Journal of American History*, Vol. 95, No. 3, Dec 2008.

Merrill, Dennis, *Bread and the Ballot: The United States and India's Economic Development, 1947–1963*. Chapel Hill: University of North Carolina Press, 1990.

Merry, Robert, *Taking on the World: Joseph and Stewart Alsop—Guardians of the American Century*. New York: Viking, 1996.

Mershon, Sherie, and Steven Schlossman, *Foxholes & Color Lines: Desegregating the U.S. Armed Forces*. Baltimore: Johns Hopkins University Press, 1998.

Merson, Martin, *The Private Diary of a Public Servant*. New York: Macmillan, 1955.

Metz, Stephen, "Eisenhower and the Planning of American Grand Strategy," *Journal of Strategic Studies*, Vol. 14, No. 1, Mar 1991.

Michener, James, *The Bridge at Andau*. New York: Random House, 1957.

Mieczkowski, Yanek, *Eisenhower's Sputnik Moment: The Race for Space and World Prestige*. Ithaca, NY: Cornell University Press, 2013.

Millar, T.B., ed., *Australian Foreign Minister: The Diaries of R.G. Casey 1951–60*. London: Collins, 1972.

Miller, Douglas, "Popular Religion of the 1950's: Norman Vincent Peale and Billy Graham," *Journal of Popular Culture*, Vol. 9, Summer 1975.

Miller, Merle, *Plain Speaking: An Oral Biography of Harry S. Truman*. New York: Berkeley, 1973, 1974.

Miller, Steven, *Billy Graham and the Rise of the Republican South*. Philadelphia: University of Pennsylvania Press, 2009.

———, "The Politics of Decency: Billy Graham, Evangelicalism, and the End of the Solid South, 1950–1980," PhD dissertation, Vanderbilt University, Nashville, Tenn, 2005.

Miller, William, *Piety along the Potomac: Notes on Politics and Morals in the Fifties*. Boston: Houghton, Mifflin, 1964.

———, *Two Americans: Truman, Eisenhower and a Dangerous World*. New York: Knopf, 2012.

Millett, Alan, "Eisenhower and the Korean War: Cautionary Tale and Hopeful Precedent," in Showalter, ed., *Forging the Shield*.

Milne, June, ed., *Kwame Nkrumah, the Conakry Years: His Life and Letters*. London: Panaf, 1990.

Mitchell, Clarence, "Moods and Changes: The Civil Rights Record of the Nixon Administration," *Notre Dame Lawyer*, Vol. 49, 1973–74.

Mitchell, Stephen, *Elm Street Politics*. New York: Oceana, 1959.

Mitrovich, Gregory, *Undermining the Kremlin: America's Strategy to Subvert the Soviet Bloc, 1947–1956*. Ithaca, NY: Cornell University Press, 2000.

Mollenhoff, Clark, *Investigative Reporting: From Courthouse to White House*. New York: Macmillan, 1981.

Montgomery, Gayle, and James Johnson, *One Step from the White House: The Rise and Fall of Senator William F. Knowland*. Berkeley: University of California Press, 1998.

Montgomery, Mary, "The Eyes of the World Were Watching: Ghana, Great Britain, and the United States 1957–1966," PhD dissertation, University of Maryland at College Park, 2004.

Moon, Henry, *Balance of Power: The Negro Vote*. New York: Doubleday, 1948.

———, "Election Post-Mortem," *Crisis*, Vol. 59, Dec 1952.

———, "The Negro Break-Away from the Democrats," *The New Republic*, Vol. 135, Dec 3, 1956.

———, "The Negro Vote in the Presidential Election of 1956," *Journal of Negro Education*, Vol. 26, No. 3, Summer 1957.

———, "What Chance for Civil Rights?" *The Crisis*, Feb 1949.

Mooney, Booth, *The Politicians, 1945–1960*. Philadelphia: Lippincott, 1970.

Moos, Malcolm, "Election of 1956," in Schlesinger and Israel, eds., Vol. 4, *History of American Presidential Elections*.

Moreno, Paul, *From Direct Action to Affirmative Action: Fair Employment Law and Policy in America, 1933–1972*. Baton Rouge: Louisiana State University Press, 1997.

Morgan, Iwan, *Eisenhower versus "the Spenders": The Eisenhower Administration, the Democrats and the Budget, 1953–1960*. London: Pinter, 1990.

———, *Nixon*. London: Arnold, 2002.

Morison, Samuel, *The Oxford History of the American People*. New York: Oxford University Press, 1965.

——, et al., *Growth of the American Republic*, Vol. 2. New York: Oxford University Press, 1962.

Morris, Aldon, "Black Southern Student Sit-In Movement: An Analysis of Internal Organization," *American Sociological Review*, Vol. 46, No. 6, Dec 1981.

——, *The Origins of the Civil Rights Movement: Black Communities Organizing for Change*. New York: Free Press, 1984.

Morris, Roger, *Richard Milhous Nixon: The Rise of an American Politician*. New York: Holt, 1990.

Morrow, E. Frederic, *Black Man in the White House: A Diary of the Eisenhower Years by the Administrative Officer for Special Projects, the White House, 1955–1961*. New York: Coward-McCann, 1963.

——, *Forty Years a Guinea Pig*. New York: Pilgrim Press, 1980.

——, *Way Down South Up North*. Philadelphia: United Church, 1973.

Moser, Charles, *Watershed and Ratifying Elections: A Historical View of the 1934 and 1954 Midterm Congressional Elections*. Washington, DC: Free Congress Research & Educational Foundation, 1982.

Mosley, Leonard, *Dulles: A Biography of Eleanor, Allen, and John Foster Dulles and Their Family Network*. New York: Dial, 1978.

Mossman, B.C., and M.W. Stark, *The Last Salute: Civil and Military Funerals 1921–1969*. Washington, DC: GPO, 1991.

Muehlenbeck, Philip, *Betting on the Africans: John F. Kennedy's Courting of African Nationalist Leaders*. New York: Oxford University Press, 2012.

Mundt, Karl, Karl E., Mundt Historical and Educational Foundation, Dakota State University, Madison, South Dakota. Microfilm.

Murphy, Charles, "The Budget and Eisenhower," *Fortune*, Vol. 56, No. 1, July 1957.

——, "The White House and the Recession," *Fortune*, Vol. 57, No 5, May 1958.

Murphy, Robert, *Diplomat Among Warriors*. New York: Doubleday, 1964.

NAACP, *Administrative File, General Office File* [Richard M. Nixon] 1956–1960. Lanham, Md: University Publications of America, 1997. Microfilm.

NAACP, *NAACP 1940–55: General Office File*. Lanham, Md: University Publications of America, 1994. Microfilm.

Namikis, Lise, "Battleground Africa: The Cold War and the Congo Crisis, 1960–1965," Vol. 1, PhD dissertation, University of Southern California, Los Angeles, 2002.

Natoli, Marie, *American Prince, American Pauper: The Contemporary Vice Presidency in Perspective*. Westport, Conn: Greenwood, 1985.

Neal, Steve, ed., *Eleanor and Harry: The Correspondence of Eleanor Roosevelt and Harry S. Truman*. New York: Scribner, 2002.

Nelson, Anna, "John Foster Dulles and the Bipartisan Congress," *Political Science Quarterly*, Vol. 102, No. 1, Spring 1987.

——, "The 'Top of the Hill': President Eisenhower and the National Security Council," *Diplomatic History*, Vol. 7, Fall 1983.

Neuberger, Richard, "Democratic Dilemma: Civil Rights. A Senator Proposes a Way to Resolve Party Differences over the Burning Issue," *New York Times Magazine*, July 7, 1957.

Neustadt, Richard, *Presidential Power and the Modern Presidents: The Politics of Leadership from Roosevelt to Reagan*. New York: Free Press, 1990.

Newton, Jim, *Eisenhower: The White House Years*. New York: Doubleday, 2011.

——, *Justice for All: Earl Warren and the Nation He Made*. New York: Riverhead, 2006.

Niblo, Stephen, *War, Diplomacy, and Development: The United States and Mexico 1938–1954*. Wilmington, Del: Scholarly Resources, 1995.

Nichols, David, *Eisenhower 1956: The President's Year of Crisis: Suez and the Brink of War*. New York: Simon & Schuster, 2011.

——, *A Matter of Justice: Eisenhower and the Beginning of the Civil Rights Revolution*. New York: Simon & Schuster, 2007.

——, "'The Showpiece of Our Nation': Dwight D. Eisenhower and the Desegregation of the District of Columbia," *Washington History*, Vol. 16, No. 2, Fall/Winter 2004–2005.

Nichols, Louis, *Official and Confidential File and the Clyde Tolson Personal File*. Lanham, Md: University Publications of America, 1990. Microfilm.

Ninkovich, Frank, *Germany and the United States: The Transformation of the German Question since 1945*. Boston: Twayne, 1988.

Nissenson, Marilyn, *The Lady Upstairs: Dorothy Schiff and the New York Post*. New York: St. Martin's, 2007.

Nixon, Edward, and Karen Olson, *The Nixons: A Family Portrait*. Washington, DC: Book Publishers Network, 2009.

Nixon, Hannah, "Nixon: A Mother's Story," *Good Housekeeping*, Vol. 150, June 1960.

Nixon, Pat, "Crises of a Candidate's Wife," *Ladies Home Journal*, Nov 1962.

——, "I Say He's A Wonderful Guy," *Saturday Evening Post*, Sept 6, 1952.

Nixon, Richard, "Cuba, Castro and John F. Kennedy," *Reader's Digest*, Nov 1964.

——, *Leaders*. New York: Warner, 1982.

——, "Nixon's Own Story of 7 Years in the Vice Presidency," *U.S. News & World Report* Vol. 48, No. 20, May 16, 1960.

——, *RN: The Memoirs of Richard Nixon*. New York: Grosset & Dunlap, 1978.

——, "Russia as I Saw It," *National Geographic Magazine*, Vol. 116, No. 6, Dec 1959.

——, "The Second Office," in *The 1964 World Book Year Book*. Chicago: Enterprises Educational Corp, 1964.

——, *Six Crises*. New York: Doubleday, 1962.

——, "Unforgettable John Foster Dulles," *Reader's Digest*, July 1967.

——, "Vice President Nixon Writes About Dulles," *Life*, Vol. 46, No. 23, June 8, 1959.

——, "The Vice President Reports," *Reader's Digest*, Vol. 67, Sept 1955.

——, compiler, *The Challenges We Face*. New York: McGraw-Hill, 1960.

"Nixon," Part One, PBS, David Esper producer, 1993.

Noer, Thomas, *Cold War and Black Liberation: The United States and White Rule in Africa, 1948–1968*. Columbia: University of Missouri Press, 1985.

——, "New Frontiers and Old Priorities in Africa," in Paterson, ed., *Kennedy's Quest for Victory.*

——, "Truman, Eisenhower, and South Africa: The 'Middle Road' and Apartheid," *Journal of Ethnic Studies,* Vol. 11, No. 1, Spring 1983.

Nwaubani, Ebere, *The United States and Decolonization in West Africa, 1950–1960.* Rochester, NY: University of Rochester Press, 2001.

Oakley, J. Ronald, *God's Country.* New York: Dembner, 1986.

Oberdorfer, Don, *Senator Mansfield: The Extraordinary Life of a Great American Statesman and Diplomat.* Washington, DC: Smithsonian, 2003.

O'Brien, Robert, and Elizabeth Jones, *The Night Nixon Spoke: A Study of Political Effectiveness.* Los Alamitos, Ca: Hwong Publishing Co., 1976.

Odenkirk, James, *Frank J. Lausche: Ohio's Great Political Maverick.* Wilmington, Ohio: Orange Frazer Press, 2005.

Offner, Arnold, *Another Such Victory: President Truman and the Cold War, 1945–1953.* Stanford: Stanford University Press, 2002.

Olien, Roger, *From Token to Triumph: The Texas Republicans Since 1920.* Dallas: Southern Methodist University Press, 1982.

Olson, James, *Stuart Symington: A Life.* Columbia: University of Missouri Press, 2003.

Olson, Russ, "You Can't Spit on a Foreign Policy," *Society of Historians of American Foreign Relations Newsletter,* Sept 2000.

O'Neill, William, *American High: The Years of Confidence, 1945–1960.* New York: Free Press, 1986.

O'Reilly, Kenneth, *Nixon's Piano: Presidents and Racial Politics from Washington to Clinton.* New York: Free Press, 1995.

——, "Racial Integration: The Battle General Eisenhower Chose Not to Fight," *Journal of Blacks in Higher Education,* No. 18, Winter 1997–1998.

Osgood, Kenneth, "Form Before Substance: Eisenhower's Commitment to Psychological Warfare and Negotiations with the Enemy," *Diplomatic History,* Vol. 24, No. 3, Summer 2000.

——, and Klaus Larres, eds., *The Cold War After Stalin's Death: A Missed Opportunity for Peace?* Lanham, Md: Rowman & Littlefield, 2006.

——, *Total Cold War: Eisenhower's Secret Propaganda Battle at Home and Abroad.* Lawrence: University of Kansas Press, 2006.

Ostermann, Christian, ed., *Uprising in East Germany 1953: The Cold War, the German Question, and the First Major Upheaval Behind the Iron Curtain.* New York: Central European University Press, 2001.

Pach Jr., Chester, and Elmo Richardson, *The Presidency of Dwight D. Eisenhower.* Rev. ed. Lawrence: University of Kansas Press, 1991.

Paddon, Eric, "Modern Mordecai: Billy Graham in the Political Arena, 1948–1990," PhD dissertation, Ohio University, Athens, 1999.

Pahlavi, Mohammed Reza, *Answer to History.* New York: Stein and Day, 1980.

Pais, Abraham, *J. Robert Oppenheimer: A Life.* New York: Oxford University Press, 2006.

Pankratz, Herbert, compiler, *Eisenhower and Religion: A Guide to Historical Holdings in the Dwight D. Eisenhower Library*. Abilene: United States Archives, 2001.

Parker, Jason, "Cold War II: The Eisenhower Administration, the Bandung Conference, and the Reperiodization of the Postwar Era," *Diplomatic History*, Vol. 30, No. 5, Nov 2006.

Parker, Robert, *Capitol Hill in Black and White*. New York: Dodd, Mead, 1986.

Parmet, Herbert, *Eisenhower and the American Crusades*. New York: Macmillan, 1972.

———, *Richard Nixon and His America*. New York: Konecky & Konecky, 1990.

Parthenakis, Thomas, "George M. Humphrey, Secretary of Treasury 1953–1957: A Political Biography," PhD dissertation: Kent State University, 1985.

Patch, Richard, "Nixon in Bolivia," *American Universities Field Staff, West Coast South American Series, Reports*, Vol. 5, 1958.

———, "Nixon in Peru," *American Universities Field Staff, West Coast South American Series, Reports*, Vol. 5, 1958.

Paterson, Thomas, ed., *Contesting Castro: The United States and the Triumph of the Cuban Revolution*. New York: Oxford University Press, 1994.

———, *Kennedy's Quest for Victory: American Foreign Policy, 1961–1963*. New York: Oxford, 1989.

Paterson, Thomas, J. Garry Clifford et al., *American Foreign Relations*. Vol. 2. 7th ed. Independence, Ky: Cangage Learning, 2010.

Patterson, James, *Mr. Republican: A Biography of Robert A. Taft*. Boston: Houghton Mifflin, 1972.

Peltason, Jack, *Fifty-Eight Lonely Men: Southern Federal Judges and School Desegregation*. 2nd ed. Urbana: University of Illinois Press, 1971.

Pérez, Louis, *Cuba and the United States: Ties of Singular Intimacy*. 2nd ed. Athens: University of Georgia Press, 1997.

Perlstein, Rick, *Nixonland: The Rise of a President and the Fracturing of America*. New York: Scribner, 2008.

Perret, Geoffrey, *Eisenhower*. New York: Random House, 1999.

Pfau, Richard, *No Sacrifice too Great: The Life of Lewis L. Strauss*. Charlottesville: University of Virginia Press, 1984.

Phillips, Cabell, "One-Man Task Force of the G.O.P.," *New York Times Magazine*, Oct 24, 1954, Sec VI.

Pickett, William, *Dwight David Eisenhower and American Power*. Wheeling, Ill: Harlan Davidson, 1995.

———, *Eisenhower Decides to Run: Presidential Politics and Cold War Strategy*. Chicago: Ivan Dee, 2000.

Pierard, Richard, "One Nation Under God: Judgment or Jingoism?" in Cotham, ed., *Christian Social Ethics*.

———, and Robert Linder, *Civil Religion & the Presidency*. Grand Rapids, Mich: Academie Books, 1988.

Pierpont, Robert, *At the White House: Assignment to Six Presidents*. New York: Putnam's Sons, 1981.

Pinkley, Virgil, *Eisenhower Declassified*. Old Tappan, NJ: Fleming H. Revell, 1979.

Pipes, Kasey, *Ike's Final Battle: The Road to Little Rock and the Challenge to Equality*. Los Angeles: World Ahead Media, 2007.

Pitney Jr., John, "Nixon, California, and American Politics," *Nexus: A Journal of Opinion*, Vol. 6, Spring 2001.

Plummer, Brenda, *In Search of Power: African Americans in the Era of Decolonization, 1956–1974*. New York: Cambridge University Press, 2013.

———, ed., *Window on Freedom: Race, Civil Rights, and Foreign Affairs, 1945–1958*. Chapel Hill: University of North Carolina Press, 2003.

Poen, Monte, ed., *Strictly Personal and Confidential: The Letters Harry Truman Never Mailed*. Boston: Little, Brown, 1982.

Polar, Norman, and Thomas Allen, *Rickover*. New York: Simon and Schuster, 1982.

Polenberg, Richard, *One Nation Divisible: Class, Race, and Ethnicity in the United States since 1938*. New York: Viking, 1980.

Pope, Philip, "Foundations of Nixonian Foreign Policy: The Pre-Presidential Years of Richard M. Nixon, 1946–1968, "Vols. 1 and 2. PhD dissertation, University of Southern California, Los Angeles, 1988.

Potenziani, David, "Look to the Past: Richard B. Russell and the Defense of Southern White Supremacy," PhD dissertation, University of Georgia, Athens, 1981.

Potter, Charles, *Days of Shame*. New York: Coward-McCann, 1965.

Potter, Philip, "Political Pitchman," in Sevareid, *Candidates 1960*.

Poulson, Norris, *The Genealogy and Life Story of Erna and Norris Poulson*. Self-published, 1975.

Powell Jr., Adam, *Adam by Adam, The Autobiography of Adam Clayton Powell, Jr*. New York: Dial, 1971.

Prados, John, *Keepers of the Keys: A History of the National Security Council from Truman to Bush*. New York: Morrow, 1991.

———, *Presidents' Secret Wars: CIA and Pentagon Covert Operations Since World War II*. New York: Morrow, 1986.

Preble, Christopher, *John F. Kennedy and the Missile Gap*. DeKalb: Northern Illinois University Press, 2004.

President Dwight D. Eisenhower's Office Files, 1953–1961, P 1, Eisenhower Administration Series. Lanham, Md: University Publications of America, 1990.

Price, Hugh, "The Negro and Florida Politics, 1944–1954," *Journal of Politics*, Vol. 27, No. 2, May 1955.

Pruden, Caroline, *Conditional Partners: Eisenhower, the United Nations, and the Search for a Permanent Peace*. Baton Rouge: Louisiana State University Press, 1998.

Pruessen, Ronald, "Beyond the Cold War—Again: 1955 and the 1990s," *Political Science Quarterly*, Vol. 108, No. 1, Spring 1993.

———, "Cold War Threats and America's Commitment to the European Defense Community: One Corner of the Triangle," *Journal of European Integration History*, Vol. 2, No. 1, Spring 1996.

———, "From Good Breakfast to Bad Supper: John Foster Dulles and the Geneva Foreign Ministers Meeting, 1955," in Bischof and Dockrill, eds., *Cold War Respite: The Geneva Summit of July 1955*.

——, "John Foster Dulles and Decolonization in Southeast Asia," in Frey, Pruessen, and Yong, eds., *The Transformation of Southeast Asia: International Perspectives on Decolonization.*

——, *John Foster Dulles: The Road to Power.* New York: Free Press, 1982.

——, "Over the Volcano: The United States and the Taiwan Strait Crisis," in Ross and Changbin, eds., *Re-examining the Cold War: U.S.-China Diplomacy.*

Puhan, Alfred, *The Cardinal in the Chancery and Other Recollections.* New York: Vantage, 1990.

Pulliam, Russell, *Publisher: Gene Pulliam, Last of the Newspaper Titans.* Ottawa, Ill: Jameson Books, 1984.

Quester, George, "Was Eisenhower a Genius?" *International Security*, Vol. 4, No. 2, Autumn 1979.

Quirk, Robert, *Fidel Castro.* New York: Norton, 1991.

Raat, W. Dirk, *Mexico and the United States: Ambivalent Vistas.* Athens: University of Georgia Press, 1992.

Rabe, Stephen, "The Caribbean Triangle: Betancourt, Castro, and Trujillo and U.S. Foreign Policy, 1958–1963," *Diplomatic History*, Vol. 20, No. 1, Winter 1996.

——, "Dulles, Latin America, and Cold War Anticommunism," in Immerman, ed., *John Foster Dulles and the Diplomacy of the Cold War.*

——, "Eisenhower Revisionism: A Decade of Scholarship," *Diplomatic History*, Vol. 17, No. 1, Jan 1983.

——, *The Road to OPEC: United States Relations With Venezuela.* Austin: University of Texas Press, 1982.

Ramazani, Rouhollah, *Iran's Foreign Policy 1941–1973: A Study of Foreign Policy in Modernizing Nations.* Charlottesville: University of Virginia Press, 1975.

Rampersad, Arnold, *Jackie Robinson: A Biography.* New York: Knopf, 1997.

Randall, Stephen, *Colombia and the United States: Hegemony and Interdependence.* Athens: University of Georgia Press, 1992.

Rankin, Karl, *China Assignment.* Seattle: University of Washington Press, 1964.

Rarick, Ethan, *California Rising: The Life and Times of Pat Brown.* Berkeley: University of California Press, 2005.

Rasenberger, Jim, *The Brilliant Disaster: JFK, Castro, and America's Doomed Invasion of Cuba's Bay of Pigs.* New York: Scribner, 2011.

Rauscher, Alan, *Paul G. Hoffman: Architect of Foreign Aid.* Lexington: University Press of Kentucky, 1985.

Rayner, Richard, "Channeling Ike," *New Yorker*, Apr 26, 2010.

Reddick, L.D., *Crusader Without Violence: A Biography of Martin Luther King, Jr.* New York: Harper & Brothers, 1959.

Reed, Christopher, *The Chicago NAACP and the Rise of Black Professional Leadership, 1910–1966.* Bloomington: Indiana University Press, 1997.

Reed, Roy, *Faubus: The Life and Times of an American Prodigal.* Fayetteville: Arkansas University Press, 1997.

Reedy, George, *The U.S. Senate: Paralysis or a Search for Consensus?* New York: Crown, 1986.

Reese, Trevor, *Australia, New Zealand, and the United States: A Survey of International Relations 1941–1968*. London: Oxford University Press, 1969.

Reeves, Thomas, *The Life and Times of Joe McCarthy: A Biography*. New York: Stein and Day, 1982.

Reich, Cary, *The Life of Nelson A. Rockefeller: Worlds to Conquer 1908–1958*. New York: Doubleday, 1996.

Reichard, Gary, "Democrats, Civil Rights, and Electoral Strategies in the 1950s," *Congress & the Presidency*, Vol. 13, No. 1, Spring 1986.

———, *Politics as Usual: The Age of Truman and Eisenhower*. Wheeling, Ill: Harlan Davidson, 1988.

———, *The Reaffirmation of Republicanism: Eisenhower and the Eighty-Third Congress*. Knoxville: University of Tennessee Press, 1975.

Reichley, James, ed., *States in Crisis: Politics in Ten American States, 1950–1962*. Chapel Hill: University of North Carolina Press, 1964.

Reid, Susan, " 'Our Kitchen Is Just as Good': Soviet Responses to the American National Exhibition in Moscow, 1959," in Crowley and Pavitt, eds., *Cold War Modern*.

Reinhard, David, *The Republican Right Since 1945*. Lexington: University Press of Kentucky, 1983.

Reston, James, *Sketches in the Sand*. New York: Knopf, 1967.

Reuther, Victor, *The Brothers Reuther: and the Story of the UAW*. Boston: Houghton Mifflin, 1976.

Richmond, Yale, *U.S.-Soviet Cultural Exchanges, 1958–1986: Who Wins?* Boulder: Westview, 1987.

Ricks, Thomas, *The Generals: American Military Command from World War II to Today*. New York: Penguin, 2012.

Ritchie, Donald, *Reporting from Washington: The History of the Washington Press Corps*. New York: Oxford, 2005.

Rives, Timothy, "Ambrose and Eisenhower: A View from the Stacks in Abilene," *History News Network*, May 17, 2010.

Roadnight, Andrew, *United States Policy Toward Indonesia in the Truman and Eisenhower Years*. New York: Palgrave, 2002.

Roberts, Chalmers, *First Rough Draft: A Journalist's Journal of Our Times*. New York: Praeger, 1973.

Roberts, Gene, and Hank Klibanoff, *The Race Beat: The Press, the Civil Rights Struggle, and the Awakening of a Nation*. New York: Knopf, 2006.

Roberts, George, *Paul M. Butler: Hoosier Politician and National Political Leader*. Lanham, Md: University Press of America, 1987.

Roberts, Terrence, and Rocco Siciliano, *President Dwight D. Eisenhower and Civil Rights*. Washington, DC: Eisenhower World Affairs Institute, 2000.

Robertson, David, *Sly and Able: A Political Biography of James F. Byrnes*. New York: Norton, 1994.

Robinson, Jackie, *I Never Had It Made*. New York: Putnam, 1972.

Rockwell, Theodore, *The Rickover Effect: How One Man Made a Difference*. Annapolis: Naval Institute, 1992.

Rogin, Michael, *The Intellectuals and McCarthy: The Radical Specter*. Cambridge: MIT Press, 1967.

Roman, Peter, *Eisenhower and the Missile Gap*. Ithaca, NY: Cornell University Press, 1995.

Rooney, David, *Kwane Nkrumah: The Political Kingdom in the Third World*. New York: St. Martin's 1988.

Roorda, Eric, "The President and His Boy: The Relationship Between Dwight D. Eisenhower and Richard M. Nixon," Honors thesis, College of William and Mary, Williamsburg, Va, 1983.

Rose, Mark, *Interstate: Express Highway Politics 1941–1956*. Lawrence: University of Kansas Press, 1979.

Rosenberg, Victor, *Soviet-American Relations, 1953–1960: Diplomacy and Cultural Exchange During the Eisenhower Presidency*. Jefferson, NC: McFarland, 2005.

Ross, Robert, and Jiang Changbin, eds., *Re-examining the Cold War: U.S.-China Diplomacy, 1954–1973*. Cambridge: Harvard University Press, 2001.

Rotter, Andrew, *Comrades at Odds: The United States and India, 1947–1964*. Ithaca, NY: Cornell University Press, 2000.

Rovere, Richard, *Final Reports: Personal Reflections in Politics and History in Our Time*. New York: Doubleday, 1984.

———, "Letter From Washington," *New Yorker*, Vol. 33, No. 28, Aug 31, 1957.

Rowan, Carl, *Breaking Barriers: A Memoir*. Boston: Little, Brown, 1991.

———, "Harry Truman and the Negro," *Ebony*, Vol. 15, No. 1, Nov 1959.

Rowse, Arthur, *Slanted News: A Case Study of the Nixon and Stevenson Fund Stories*. Westport, Conn: Greenwood, 1973.

Ruane, Kevin, *The Rise and Fall of the European Defense Community*. New York: St. Martin's, 2000.

Ruddy, T. Michael, *The Cautious Diplomat: Charles E. Bohlen and the Soviet Union, 1929–1969*. Kent, Ohio: Kent State University Press, 1986.

Rung, Margaret, "Richard Nixon, State, and Party: Democracy and Bureaucracy in the Postwar Era," *Presidential Studies Quarterly*, Vol. 29, No. 2, June 1999.

Runyon, John, et al., compilers, *Source Book of American Presidential Campaign and Election Statistics, 1948–1968*. New York: Frederick Unger, 1971.

Safford, Jeffrey, "The Nixon-Castro Meeting of 19 April 1959," *Diplomatic History*, Vol. 4, No. 4, Oct 1980.

Salinger, Pierre, *P.S.: A Memoir*. New York: St. Martin's, 1995.

Salisbury, Harris, *A Journey for Our Times: A Memoir*. New York: Harper & Row, 1983.

———, *Without Fear or Favor: The New York Times and Its Times*. New York: Times, 1980.

Saltonstall, Leverett, *Salty: Recollections of a Yankee in Politics*. Boston: Boston Globe, 1976.

Salzman, Jack, et. al, eds., *Encyclopedia of African-American Culture and History*. New York: Macmillan, 2001.

Sampson, Gregory. "The Rise of the 'New' Republican Party in South Carolina, 1948–1974: A Case Study of Political Change in a Deep South State," PhD dissertation, University of North Carolina, Chapel Hill, 1984.

Sangmuah, E.N., "Eisenhower and Containment in North Africa, 1956–1960," *Middle East Journal*, Vol. 44, No. 1, Winter 1990.

Saulnier, Raymond, *Constructive Years: The U.S. Economy Under Eisenhower*. Lanham, Md: University Press of America, 1991.

Saunders, Richard, "Military Force in the Foreign Policy of the Eisenhower Presidency," *Political Science Quarterly*, Vol. 100, Spring 1985.

Scammon, Richard, compiler and ed., *America at the Polls: A Handbook of American Presidential Election Statistics 1920–1964*. New York: Arno, 1976.

———, *America Votes 3: A Handbook of Contemporary American Election Statistics*. Pittsburgh: University of Pittsburgh Press, 1959.

———, *America Votes 4: A Handbook of Contemporary American Election Studies*. Pittsburgh: University of Pittsburgh Press, 1962.

Scates, Shelby, *Warren G. Magnuson and the Shaping of Twentieth-Century America*. Seattle: University of Washington Press, 1997.

Schaller, Michael, *Altered States: The United States and Japan Since the Occupation*. New York: Oxford, 1997.

Schelle, Henry, *Charlie Halleck: A Political Biography*. New York: Exposition, 1966.

Schick, Jack, *The Berlin Crisis 1958–1962*. Philadelphia: University of Pennsylvania Press, 1971.

Schiesl, Martin, ed., *California Politics & Party*. Los Angeles: Edmund G. "Pat" Brown Institute of Public Affairs, 1997.

Schlesinger, Andrew, and Stephen Schlesinger, eds., *Journals 1952–2000: Arthur M. Schlesinger, Jr.* New York: Penguin, 2007.

Schlesinger Jr., Arthur, "The Ike Age Revisited," *Reviews in American History*, Vol. 11, Mar 1983.

———, *The Imperial Presidency*. Boston: Houghton Mifflin, 1973.

———, *A Thousand Days: John F. Kennedy in the White House*. Boston: Houghton Mifflin, 1965.

———, and Fred Israel, eds., *History of American Presidential Elections*. Vol. 4. New York: Chelsea House, 1971.

Schlesinger, Stephen, and Stephen Kinzer, *Bitter Fruit: The Story of the American Coup in Guatemala*. Cambridge: Harvard University Press, 1999.

Schlundt, Ronald, "Civil Rights Policies in the Eisenhower Years," PhD dissertation, Rice University, Houston, Tex, 1973.

Schmidl, Erwin, ed., *Die Ungarnkrise 1956 und Österreich*. Vienna: Böhlau, 2003.

Schoenwald, Jonathan, *A Time for Choosing: The Rise of Modern American Conservatism*. New York: Oxford University Press, 2001.

Schorr, Daniel, *Staying Tuned: A Life in Journalism*. New York: Pocket Books, 2001.

Schraeder, Paul, *United States Foreign Policy Toward Africa: Incrementalism, Crisis and Change*. Cambridge: Cambridge University Press, 1994.

Schulman, Bruce, *Lyndon B. Johnson and American Liberalism*. Boston: Bedford, 1995.

Schulman, Robert, *John Sherman Cooper: The Global Kentuckian*. Lexington: University Press of Kentucky, 2004.

Schulte, Reneé, ed., *The Young Nixon: An Oral Inquiry*. Fullerton: California State University, Oral History Program, Richard M. Nixon Project, 1978.

Schulzinger, Robert, *A Time for War: The United States and Vietnam, 1941–1975*. New York: Oxford University Press, 1997.

Schuparra, Kurt, "Freedom vs. Tyranny: The 1958 California Election and the Origins of the State's Conservative Movement," *Pacific Historical Review*, Vol. 63, 1994.

——, *Triumph of the Right: The Rise of the California Conservative Movement, 1945–1966*. New York: Sharpe, 1998.

Schwenk-Borrell, Melinda, "Selling Democracy: The U.S. Information Agency's Portrayal of American Race Relations 1953–1976," PhD dissertation, University of Pennsylvania, Philadelphia, 2004.

Scott, George, "Arthur Langlie: Republican Governor in a Democratic State," PhD dissertation, University of Washington, Seattle, 1971.

Scott, Hugh, *Come to the Party*. Englewood Cliffs, NJ: Prentice-Hall, 1968.

Seagull, Louis, *Southern Republicanism*. Cambridge, Mass: Schenkman, 1972.

Sennick, Marianne, "Expertise in the White House: A Topology of Six White House Staffs," PhD thesis, Rutgers University, New Brunswick, NJ, 1999.

Sevareid, Eric, *Candidates 1960: Behind the Headlines in the Presidential Race*. New York: Basic Books, 1959.

——, "The Demon A.D.A.," *The Reporter*, Nov 4, 1954.

——, *Small Sounds in the Night: A Collection of Capsule Commentaries on the American Scene*. Westport, Conn: Greenwood, 1977.

——, *This Is Eric Sevareid*. New York: McGraw-Hill, 1964.

Sewell, Stacy, "Contracting Racial Equality: Affirmative Action Policy and Practice in the United States, 1945–1970," PhD dissertation, Rutgers University, New Brunswick, NJ, 1999.

——, "The 'Not-Buying Power' of the Black Community: Urban Boycotts and Equal Employment Opportunity, 1960–1964," *Journal of African American History*, Vol. 89, No. 2, Spring 2004.

Shade, William G., and Barrard C. Campbell, eds., *American Presidential Campaigns and Elections*. Armonk, NY: M.E. Sharpe Inc., 2003.

Sharada Prasad, H.Y., A.K. Damodaran, and Mushirul Hasan, eds., *Selected Works of Jawaharlal Nehru*. Vol. 34. New York: Oxford University Press, 2006.

Sheinin, David, *Argentina and the United States: An Alliance Contained*. Athens: University of Georgia Press, 2006.

——, ed., *Beyond the Ideal: Pan Americanism in Inter-American Affairs*. Santa Barbara, Ca: Praeger, 2000.

Sheng, Michael, "Mao and China's Relations with the Superpowers in the 1950s," *Modern China*, Vol. 34, No. 4, Oct 2008.

Sherman, Janann, *No Place for a Woman: A Life of Senator Margaret Chase Smith*. New Brunswick, NJ: Rutgers University Press, 2000.

Sherwin, Martin and Kai Bird, *American Prometheus: The Triumph and Tragedy of J. Robert Oppenheimer*. New York: Knopf, 2005.

Sherwood, Robert, *Roosevelt and Hopkins: A Biography*. New York: Harper, 1948, 1949.

Shogun, Robert, "Harry Truman—Lincoln's Heir," *Los Angeles Times*, Op-Ed, Feb 17, 2013.

——, *Harry Truman and the Struggle for Racial Justice*. Lawrence: University Press of Kansas, 2013.

Showalter, Dennis, ed., *Forging the Shield: Eisenhower and National Security for the 21st Century*. Chicago: Imprint, 2005.

Shuman, Howard, "Senate Rules and the Civil Rights Bill: A Case Study," *American Political Science Review*, Vol. 51, No. 4, Dec 1957.

Siciliano, Rocco, *Walking on Sand: The Story of an Immigrant Son and the Forgotten Act of Public Service*. Salt Lake City: University of Utah Press, 2004.

Silber, Norman, ed., *With All Deliberate Speed: The Life of Philip Elman: An Oral History Memoir*. Ann Arbor: University of Michigan Press, 2004.

Silk, Mark, *Spiritual Politics: Religion and America Since World War II*. New York: Simon and Schuster, 1988.

Sitkoff, Harvard, "Harry Truman and the Election of 1948: The Coming of Age of Civil Rights in American Politics," *Journal of Southern History*, Vol. 37, No. 4. Nov 1971.

——, "Years of the Locust: Interpretations of Truman's Presidency Since 1965," in Kirkendall, ed., *The Truman Period*.

Slater, Ellis, *The Ike I Knew*. Ellis D. Slater Trust, 1980.

Sloan, John, *Eisenhower and the Management of Prosperity*. Lawrence: University Press of Kansas, 1991.

Small, Melvin, ed., *A Companion to Richard M. Nixon*. Malden, Mass: Wiley-Blackwell, 2011.

Smiley, Sara, "The Political Career of Thruston B. Morton: The Senate Years, 1956–1968," PhD dissertation, University of Kentucky, Lexington, 1975.

Smith, Amanda, ed., *Hostage to Fortune: The Letters of Joseph P. Kennedy*. New York: Viking, 2001.

Smith, Gary, *Faith and the Presidency: From George Washington to George W. Bush*. New York: Oxford, 2006.

Smith, Howard, *Events Leading Up to My Death: The Life of a Twentieth-Century Reporter*. New York: St. Martin's, 1996.

Smith, Jean, *Eisenhower: In War and Peace*. New York: Random House, 2012.

——, *Lucius D. Clay: An American Life*. New York: Holt, 1990.

Smith, Kevin, *The Iron Man: The Life and Times of Congressman Glenn R. Davis*. Lanham, Md: University Press of America, 1994.

Smith, Merriman, *Meet Mister Eisenhower*. New York: Harper & Row, 1955.

Smith, Richard, *Thomas E. Dewey and His Times*. New York: Simon and Schuster, 1982.

Smith, Roger, *Cambodia's Foreign Policy*. Ithaca, NY: Cornell University Press, 1965.

Smith, Russell, *The Unknown CIA: My Three Decades with the Agency*. New York: Brassey's, 1989.

Smith, T. Lynn, "The Redistribution of the Negro Population of the United States, 1910–1960," *Journal of Negro History*, Vol. 51, No. 3, July 1966.

Smith, Timothy, ed., *Merriman Smith's Book of Presidents: A White House Memoir*. New York: Norton, 1972.

Smyser, W.R., *Kennedy and the Berlin Wall: "A Hell of a Lot Better Than a War."* Lanham, Md: Rowman & Littlefield, 2009.

Snead, David, *The Gaither Committee, Eisenhower, and the Cold War.* Columbus: Ohio State University Press, 1999.

Snyder, Marty, *My Friend Ike.* New York: Frederick Fell, 1956.

Solomon, Daniel, *Breaking Up with Cuba: The Dissolution of Friendly Relations Between Washington and Havana, 1956–1961.* Jefferson, NC: McFarland, 2011.

Soman, Appu, *Double-Edged Sword: Nuclear Diplomacy in Unequal Conflicts: The United States and China, 1950–1958.* Westport, Conn: Praeger, 2000.

Sorensen, Theodore, *Kennedy.* New York: Harper & Row, 1965.

Spector, Ronald, *Advice and Support: The Early Years of the U.S. Army in Vietnam, 1941–1960.* New York: Free Press, 1985.

Spooner, Denise, "The Revitalization of the Right: The GOP in California During the Brown Years," in Schiesl, ed., *California Politics & Policy.*

Stacks, John, *Scotty: James B. Reston and the Rise and Fall of American Journalism.* Boston: Little, Brown, 2003.

Stanley, Harold, ed., *Vital Statistics on American Politics.* 4th ed. Washington, DC: Congressional Quarterly, 1994.

Starr, Kevin, *Golden Dreams: California in an Age of Abundance, 1950–1963.* New York: Oxford University Press, 2009.

Stassen, Harold, and Marshall Houts, *Eisenhower: Turning the World Toward Peace.* St. Paul: Merrill/Magnus, 1990.

Stathis, Stephen, "Presidential Disability Agreements Prior to the 25th Amendment," *Presidential Studies Quarterly,* Vol. 12, No. 2, Spring 1982.

Statler, Kathryn, *Replacing France: The Origins of American Intervention in Vietnam.* Lexington: University Press of Kentucky, 2007.

——, and Andrew Johns, eds., *The Eisenhower Administration, the Third World and the Globalization of the Cold War.* Lanham, Md: Rowman & Littlefield, 2006.

Stebenne, David, *Arthur J. Goldberg, New Deal Liberal.* New York: Oxford University Press, 1996.

——, *Modern Republican: Arthur Larson and the Eisenhower Years.* Bloomington: Indiana University Press, 2006.

Steel, Ronald, *Walter Lippmann and the American Century.* Boston: Little, Brown, 1980.

Steinberg, Alfred, *Sam Rayburn: A Biography.* New York: Hawthorn, 1975.

Stephenson, Shirley, ed., *Oral History Collection.* Fullerton, Ca: Oral History Program, 1985.

Stern, Mark, "Lyndon Johnson and Richard Russell: Institutions, Ambitions and Civil Rights," *Presidential Studies Quarterly,* Vol. 21, No. 4, Fall 1991.

——, "Presidential Strategies and Civil Rights: Eisenhower, the Early Years, 1952–54," *Presidential Studies Quarterly,* Vol. 19, No. 4, Fall 1989.

Stivers, William, "Eisenhower and the Middle East," in Melanson and Mayers, eds., *Reevaluating Eisenhower.*

Stone, I.F., *The Haunted Fifties, 1953–1963*. Boston: Little, Brown, 1969.

Streeter, Stephen, "Campaigning Against Latin American Nationalism: U.S. Ambassador John Moors Cabot in Brazil, 1959–1961," *The Americas*, Vol. 51, Oct 1994.

——, *Managing the Counterrevolution: The United States and Guatemala, 1954–1961*. Athens: Ohio University Press, 2000.

——, "The Myth of Pan Americanism: U.S. Policy toward Latin America during the Cold War, 1954–1963," in Sheinin, ed., *Beyond the Ideal*.

Streitmatter, Roger, "No Taste for Fluff: Ethel L. Payne, African-American Journalist," *Journalism Quarterly*, Vol. 68, No. 3, Fall 1991.

Stroder, Gerald, ed., *"Let Us Begin Anew": An Oral History of the Kennedy Presidency*. New York: HarperCollins, 1993.

Strong, Donald, *The Presidential Election in the South, 1952*. Tuscaloosa: University of Alabama Press, 1955.

Strout, Richard, *TRB: Views and Perspectives on the Presidency*. New York: Macmillan, 1979.

Stueck, William, *The Korean War: An International History*. Princeton: Princeton University Press, 1995.

Suggs, Henry, ed., *The Black Press in the Middle West, 1865–1985*. Westport, Conn: Greenwood, 1996.

——, *The Black Press in the South, 1865–1979*. Westport, Conn: Greenwood, 1983.

Sulzberger, C.L., *The Last of the Giants*. New York: Macmillan, 1970.

——, *A Long Row of Candles: Memoirs and Diaries [1934–1954]*. New York: Macmillan, 1969.

Summers, Anthony, *The Arrogance of Power: The Secret World of Richard Nixon*. New York: Viking, 2000.

Sundquist, James, *Politics and Policy: The Eisenhower, Kennedy and Johnson Years*. Washington, DC: Brookings Institution, 1968.

Swift, Will. *Pat and Dick: The Nixons, an Intimate Portrait of a Marriage*. New York: Threshold Editions, 2014.

Taeuber, Karl, and Alma Taeuber, *Negroes in Cities: Residential Segregation and Neighborhood Change*. Chicago: Aldine Publishing, 1965.

Tahir-Kheli, Shirin, *The United States and Pakistan*. New York: Praeger, 1982.

Takeyh, Ray, *The Origins of the Eisenhower Doctrine: The U.S., Britain and Nasser's Egypt, 1953–1957*. New York: St. Martin's, 2000.

Talbott, Strobe, trans., *Khrushchev Remembers*. Boston: Little, Brown, 1970.

——, *Khrushchev Remembers: The Last Testament*. Boston: Little, Brown, 1974.

Talmadge, Herman, *Talmadge: A Political Legacy, A Politician's Life*. Lawrenceville, Ga: Peachtree Press, 1987.

Tananbaum, Duane, *The Bricker Amendment Controversy: A Test of Eisenhower's Political Leadership*. Ithaca, NY: Cornell University Press, 1988.

——, "The Bricker Amendment Controversy: Its Origins and Eisenhower's Role," *Diplomatic History*, Vol. 9, Winter 1985.

Tarling, Nicholas, "'Ah-Ah': Britain and the Bandung Conference of 1955," *Journal of Southeast Asian Studies*, Vol. 23, No. 1, Mar 1992.

Taubman, Philip, *Secret Empire: Eisenhower, the CIA, and the Hidden Story of America's Space Espionage*. New York: Simon & Schuster, 2003.

Taubman, William, *Khrushchev: The Man and His Era*. New York: Norton, 2003.

Taves, Isabella, "Pat Nixon: Problems of a Perfect Wife," *Redbook*, May 1956.

Taylor, Cynthia, *A. Philip Randolph: The Religious Journey of an African American Labor Leader*. New York: New York University Press, 2006.

Taylor, Jay, *The Generalissimo: Chiang Kai-shek and the Struggle for Modern China*. Cambridge, Mass: Belknap, 2009.

Taylor, Maxwell, *Swords and Plowshares*. New York: Norton, 1972.

Teachout, Terry, ed., *Ghosts on the Roof: Selected Journalism of Whittaker Chambers, 1931–1959*. Washington, DC: Regnery, 1989.

Teiser, Ruth, ed., *Remembering William Knowland*. Berkeley: University of California Press, 1981.

Theoharis, Athan, ed., *From the Secret Files of J. Edgar Hoover*. Chicago: Ivan Dee, 1991.

———, *Seeds of Repression: Harry S. Truman and the Origins of McCarthyism*. Chicago: Quadrangle, 1971.

———, *Spying on Americans: Political Surveillance from Hoover to the Huston Plan*. Philadelphia: Temple, 1978.

Thomas, Evan, *Ike's Bluff: President Eisenhower's Secret Battle to Save the World*. New York: Little, Brown, 2012.

Thompson, Edward, ed., *Theodore H. White at Large: The Best of His Magazine Writing, 1939–1986*. New York: Pantheon, 1992.

Thompson, Kenneth, ed., *The Eisenhower Presidency: Eleven Intimate Perspectives of Dwight D. Eisenhower, Portraits of American Presidents*. Vol. 3. Lanham, Md: University Press of America, 1984.

Thomson, Charles, and Frances Shattuck, *The 1956 Presidential Campaign*. Washington, DC: Brookings Institution, 1960.

Thurber, Timothy, *The Politics of Equality: Hubert H. Humphrey and the African America Freedom Struggle*. New York: Columbia University Press, 1999.

———, "Racial Liberalism, Affirmative Action, and the Troubled History of the President's Committee on Government Contracts," *Journal of Policy History*, Vol. 18, No. 4, 2006.

———, *Republicans and Race: The GOP's Frayed Relationship with African Americans, 1945–1974*. Lawrence: University Press of Kansas, 2013.

Tinker, Hugh, *Race, Conflict, and the International Order: From Empire to United Nations*. London: Macmillan, 1977.

Tocchet, Gary, "September Thaw: Khrushchev's Visit to America, 1959," PhD dissertation, Stanford University, Stanford, Ca, 1995.

Tomasek, Robert, "Defense of the Western Hemisphere: A Need for Reexamination of United States Policy," *Midwest Journal of Political Science*, Vol. 3, No. 4, Nov 1959.

Trachtenberg, Marc, *A Constructed Peace: The Making of the European Settlement, 1945–1963*. Princeton: Princeton University Press, 1999.

Trohan, Walter, *Political Animals: Memoirs of a Sentimental Cynic*. New York: Doubleday, 1975.

Tucker, Nancy, *The China Threat: Memoirs, Myths, and Realities in the 1950s*. New York: Columbia University Press, 2012.

———, "Cold War Contacts: America and China, 1952–956," in Harding and Ming, eds., *Sino-American Relations*.

———, "Taiwan Expendable? Nixon and Kissinger Go to China," *Journal of American History*, Vol. 92, No. 1, June 2005.

———, *Taiwan, Hong Kong, and the United States, 1945–1992: Uncertain Friendships*. New York: Twayne, 1994.

Tudda, Christopher, "'Reenacting the Story of Tantalus': Eisenhower, Dulles, and the Failed Rhetoric of Liberation," *Journal of Cold War Studies*, Vol. 7, No. 4, Fall 2005.

———, *The Truth Is Our Weapon: The Rhetorical Diplomacy of Dwight D. Eisenhower and John Foster Dulles*. Baton Rouge: Louisiana State University Press, 2006.

Tulchin, Joseph, *Argentina and the United States: A Conflicted Relationship*. Boston: Twayne, 1990.

Tuttle, Dorothy, *Official Training Book for Guides at the American National Exhibition in Moscow 1959* [undated].

Tuttle Jr., Frederick, "The California Democrats: 1953–1966," PhD dissertation, University of California at Los Angeles, 1975.

Uebelhor, Tracy, "'The Ticket Will Be Ike and Dick': Eisenhower, Nixon, and the Republican Nomination of 1956," PhD dissertation, Indiana University, Bloomington, 2000.

Ulanoff, Stanley, *MATS; The Story of the Military Air Transport Service*. New York: Franklin Watts, 1964.

Unger, Debi, and Irwin Unger, *George Marshall*. New York: Harper, 2014.

Unger, Irwin, and Debi Unger, *LBJ: A Life*. New York: Wiley, 1999.

Unruh, Gail, "Eternal Liberal: Wayne L. Morse and the Politics of Liberalism," PhD dissertation, University of Oregon, Eugene, 1987.

Urofsky, Melvin, ed., *The Douglas Letters: Selections from the Private Papers of Justice William O. Douglas*. New York: Adler & Adler, 1987.

Urquhart, Brian, *Ralph Bunche: An American Life*. New York: Norton, 1993.

U.S. Commission on Civil Rights, *Report of the U.S. Commission 1959*.

U.S. *Congressional Record*, 1953–1961.

U.S. Department of Commerce, *Census of Population: 1960*, Vol. 1, P. 1. Washington, DC: GPO, 1964.

———, Vol. 1, P. 15. Washington, DC: GPO, 1963.

U.S. Department of State, *Foreign Relations of the United States, 1953–1961*. Washington, DC: GPO, 1991–1996.

U.S. House of Representatives, Committee on the Judiciary, *Nomination of Gerald R. Ford*, 1973.

U.S. Senate, Committee on Rules and Administration, *Nomination of Gerald R. Ford*, 1973.

U.S. Senate, *Universal Military Training*, Hearings before the Committee on Armed Services, 1948.

Van Atta, Dale, *With Honor: Melvin Laird in War, Peace, and Politics.* Madison: University of Wisconsin Press, 2008.

Van Dusen, George, "Politics of 'Partnership': The Eisenhower Administration and Conservation, 1952–60," PhD dissertation, Loyola University, Chicago, 1974.

Vandenbroucke, Lucien, "The 'Confessions' of Allen Dulles: New Evidence on the Bay of Pigs," *Diplomatic History,* Vol. 8, Fall 1984.

———, *Perilous Options: Special Operations as an Instrument of U.S. Foreign Policy.* New York: Oxford University Press, 1993.

Vatter, Harold, *The U.S. Economy in the 1950's: An Economic History.* New York: Norton, 1963.

Venkataramani, M.S., *The American Role in Pakistan, 1947–1958.* New Delhi: Radiant Publishers, 1982.

Vickery, William, *The Economics of the Negro Migration 1900–1960.* New York: Arno, 1977.

Vinz, Warren, "The Politics of Protestant Fundamentalism in the 1950s and 1960s," *Journal of Church and State,* Vol. 14, No. 2, Spring 1972.

Von Eschen, Peggy, *Race Against Empire: Black Americans and Anticolonialism 1937–1957.* Ithaca, NY: Cornell University Press, 1997.

———, *Satchmo Blows Up the World: Jazz Ambassadors Play the Cold War.* Cambridge: Harvard University Press, 2004.

Vose, Clement, *Caucasians Only: The Supreme Court, the NAACP, and the Restrictive Covenant Cases.* Berkeley: University of California Press, 1959.

Wagner, Steven, *Eisenhower Republicanism: Pursuing the Middle Way.* DeKalb: Northern Illinois University Press, 2006.

———, "The Lingering Death of the National Origins Quota System: A Political History of United States Immigration Policy, 1952–1965," PhD dissertation, Harvard University, Cambridge, Mass, 1986.

Waite, James, "Contesting 'the Right Decision': New Zealand, the Commonwealth, and the New Look," *Diplomatic History,* Vol. 30, No. 5, Nov 2006.

Walker Jr., Philip, "Lyndon B. Johnson's Senate Foreign Policy Activism: The Suez Canal Crisis, Reappraisal," *Presidential Studies Quarterly,* Vol. 26, No. 4, Fall 1996.

Wallace, David, "Residential Concentration of Negroes in Chicago," PhD dissertation, Harvard University, Cambridge, Mass, 1953.

Wallace, Mike, *Between You and Me: A Memoir.* New York: Hyperion, 2005.

———, and Gary Gates, *Close Encounters.* New York: Morrow, 1984.

Walsh, Lawrence, *The Gift of Insecurity: A Lawyer's Life.* Chicago: American Bar Association, 2003.

Walters, Vernon, *Silent Missions.* New York: Doubleday, 1978.

Wang, Jessica, "Science, Security, and the Cold War: The Case of E.U. Condon," *Isis,* Vol. 83, No. 2, June 1992.

Ware, Gilbert, "The National Association for the Advancement of Colored People and the Civil Rights Act of 1957," PhD dissertation, Princeton University, Princeton, NJ, 1962.

Warren, Earl, *Memoirs.* New York: Doubleday, 1977.

Warshaw, Shirley, *Powersharing: White House Cabinet Reflections in the Modern Presidency.* New York: State University of New York Press, 1996.

——, ed., *Reexamining the Eisenhower Presidency.* Westport, Conn: Greenwood, 1993.

Washington, Val, "Freedom's Fight from Abe to Ike," *Phylon,* Vol. 16, No. 4, 4th Quarter 1955.

Waters, Enoch, *American Diary: A Personal History of the Black Press.* Chicago: Path, 1987.

Watson, Denton, *Lion in the Lobby: Clarence Mitchell, Jr.'s Struggle for the Passage of the Civil Rights Law.* New York: Morrow, 1990.

Watt, Alan, *The Evolution of Australian Foreign Policy 1938–1965.* Cambridge: Cambridge University Press, 1967.

Wechsler, James, *Reflections of an Angry Middle-Aged Editor.* New York: Random House, 1960.

Weeks, O. Douglas, *Texas Presidential Politics in 1952.* Austin: University of Texas Press, 1953.

Weis, W. Michael, *Cold Warriors & Coup d'État: Brazilian-American Relations, 1945–1964.* Albuquerque: University of New Mexico Press, 1993.

Weiss, Nancy, *Farewell to the Party of Lincoln: Black Politics in the Age of FDR.* Princeton: Princeton University Press, 1983.

Welles Jr., Samuel, "The Origins of Massive Retaliation," *Political Science Quarterly,* Vol. 96, 1981.

Wellman, Francesa, "Vice President Nixon's Trip to South America, 1958," MA thesis, University of California at Davis, 1969.

Wenger, Andreas, *Living with Peril: Eisenhower, Kennedy, and Nuclear Weapons.* Lanham, Md: Rowman & Littlefield, 1997.

Whalen, Thomas, *Kennedy versus Lodge: The 1952 Massachusetts Senate Race.* Boston: Northeastern University Press, 2000.

White, G. Edward, *Alger Hiss's Looking-Glass Wars: The Covert Life of a Soviet Spy.* New York: Oxford, 2004.

White Jr., George, " 'Big Ballin'!?: Vice President Nixon and the Creation of the Bureau of African Affairs in the U.S. Department of State." *Passport,* Vol. 3, Aug 2010.

——, *Holding the Line: Race, Racism, and American Foreign Policy toward Africa, 1953–1961.* Lanham, Md: Rowman & Littlefield, 2005.

White, William, *The Taft Story.* New York: Harper & Bros., 1954.

Whitfield, Stephen, *The Culture of the Cold War.* 2nd ed. Baltimore: Johns Hopkins University Press, 1996.

——, *A Death in the Delta: The Story of Emmet Till.* New York: Free Press, 1988.

Wicker, Tom, *Dwight D. Eisenhower.* New York: Times Books, 2002.

——, *One of Us: Richard Nixon and the American Dream.* New York: Random House, 1991.

Wilder, Philip, *Meade Alcorn and the 1958 Election.* New York: Holt, 1959.

Wilkins, Martha, "The Development of the Mississippi Republican Party," Master's thesis, Mississippi College, 1965.

Wilkins, Roy, "The Future of the Negro Voter in the United States," *Journal of Negro Education*, Vol. 26, Issue 3, Summer 1957.

———, *Standing Fast: The Autobiography of Roy Wilkins*. New York: Viking, 1982.

Williamson, Daniel, *Separate Agendas: Churchill, Eisenhower and Anglo-American Relations, 1953–1955*. Lanham, Md: Lexington, 2006.

Wills, Garry, *Nixon Agonistes: The Crisis of the Self-Made Man*. Boston: Houghton Mifflin, 1969, 1970.

———, "Nixon's Dog: How the 37th President of the United States Brilliantly Outwitted the 34th President of the United States," *Esquire*, Vol. 72, No. 2, Aug 1969.

Wilson, Bob, *Confessions of a Kinetic Congressman*. San Diego: San Diego State Foundation, 1996.

Winquist, Thomas, "Comments," *Michigan Law Review*, Vol. 56, No. 4, Feb 1958.

Witcover, Jules, *Crapshoot: Rolling the Dice on the Vice Presidency*. New York: Crown, 1992.

Wolpert, Stanley, *Nehru: A Tryst with Destiny*. New York: Oxford University Press, 1996.

Wolseley, Roland, *The Black Press, U.S.A.*. Ames: Iowa State University Press, 1971.

Woods, Randall, *LBJ: Architect of American Ambition*. New York: Free Press, 2006.

Woods, Rose Mary, "Nixon's My Boss, "*Saturday Evening Post*, Vol. 230, No. 26, Dec 28, 1957.

Worthen, James, *The Young Nixon and His Rivals: Four California Republicans Eye the White House, 1946–1958*. Jefferson, NC: McFarland, 2010.

Wunder, J.R., ed., *Law and the Great Plains: Essays on the Legal History of the Heartland*. New York: Praeger, 1996.

Wunderlin, Clarence, *Robert A. Taft: Ideas, Tradition, and Party in U.S. Foreign Policy*. Lanham, Md: Rowman & Littlefield, 2005.

Wunderlin Jr., Clarence, ed., *The Papers of Robert A. Taft*. Vol. 4. Kent, Ohio: Kent State University Press, 2006.

Wyden, Peter, *Bay of Pigs: The Untold Story*. New York: Simon and Schuster, 1979.

Xia, Yafeng, *Negotiating with the Enemy: U.S.-China Talks during the Cold War, 1949–1972*. Bloomington: Indiana University Press, 2006.

Xiaolu, Chen, "China's Policy toward the United States, 1949–1955," in Harding and Ming, eds., *Sino-American Relations*.

Yaqub, Salim, *Containing Arab Nationalism: The Eisenhower Doctrine and the Middle East*. Chapel Hill: University of North Carolina Press, 2004.

Ybarra, Michael, *Washington Gone Crazy: Senator Pat McCarran and the Great American Communist Hunt*. Hanover, NH: Steerforth Press, 2004.

Yoder, Edwin, *Joe Alsop's Cold War: A Study of Journalistic Influence and Intrigue*. Chapel Hill: University of North Carolina Press, 1995.

Yon, Richard, and Tom Lansford, "Political Pragmatism and Civil Rights Policy: Truman and Integration of the Military," in Geselbracht, ed., *The Civil Rights Legacy*.

Young, Robert, "The Stassen Incident of the 1956 Campaign: A Case Study in Newspaper Political Tactics," MA thesis, University of California at Los Angeles, 1958.

Zahniser, Marvin, and W. Michael Weis, "A Diplomatic Pearl Harbor? Richard Nixon's Goodwill Mission to Latin America in 1958," *Diplomatic History*, Vol. 13, Spring 1989.

Zaloga, Stephen, *The Kremlin's Nuclear Sword: The Rise and Fall of Russia's Strategic Nuclear Forces, 1945–2000*. Washington, DC: Smithsonian Institution, 2002.

Zartman, William, "The Moroccan-American Base Negotiations," *Middle East Journal*, Vol. XVIII, Winter 1964.

Zhai, Qiang, *China and the Vietnam Wars, 1950–1975*. Chapel Hill: University of North Carolina Press, 2000.

——, *The Dragon, the Lion, & the Eagle: Chinese-British-American Relations, 1949–1958*. Kent, Ohio: Kent State University Press, 1994.

Zhang, Shu Guang, *Deterrence and Strategic Culture: Chinese-American Confrontations, 1949–1958*. Ithaca, NY: Cornell University Press, 1992.

Zieger, Robert, *For Jobs and Freedom: Race and Labor in America since 1865*. Lexington: University Press of Kentucky, 2007.

Zingg, Paul, "The Cold War in North Africa: American Foreign Policy and Postwar Muslim Nationalism, 1945–1962," *The Historian*, Vol. 39, No. 1, Nov 1976.

Zoubir, Yahia, "U.S. and Soviet Policies Towards France's Struggle with Anticolonial Nationalism in North Africa," *Canadian Journal of History*, Vol. 30, No. 3, Dec 1995.

Zubok, Vladislav, and Constantine Pleshakov, *Inside the Kremlin's Cold War: From Stalin to Khrushchev*. Cambridge: Harvard University Press, 1996.

INTERVIEWS BY THE AUTHOR

Acker, Marje Peterson, Aug 15 and 18, 2001.

Conte, Robert, Aug 21, 2010.

Donnelly, Dorothy Cox, Aug 18, 2001.

Flanigan, Peter, July 17, 2003.

Gaunt, Loie, Sept 11, 2000

Gleason, James, Jan 4, 2002.

Golden, William, July 2, 2001.

Goodpaster, Andrew, Jan 8, 2002.

Hechler, Ken, Sept 14, 2006.

Hughes, Donald, numerous dates

Kenez, Peter, Oct 19, 2011.

Khrushchev, Sergei, Sept 27–29, 2009.

Klein, Herbert, Nov 12, 2002.

Lindy, Beverly, Aug 7, 2001.

Mazo, Earl, July 17, 2001.

Nixon, Clara Jane, Sept 7, 2001.

Nunn, Mareen Drown, Aug 10, 2001.

Perry, Hubert, Feb 23, 2000

Price, William, Aug 10, 2001.

Rabb, Maxwell, Jan 8, 2002.

Rives, Timothy, 2013
Rogers, Edward "Ted," Oct 22, 2001.
Schultz, George, Jan 31, 2002.
Scouten, Rex, Apr 22, 2010.
Tyler, Harold, May 27, 2003.

INDEX